W9-CWL-794

History of Programming Languages–II

Edited by

THOMAS J. BERGIN, JR.

and

RICHARD G. GIBSON, JR.

The American University
Washington, D.C.

ACM Press

New York, New York

Addison-Wesley Publishing Company

Reading, Massachusetts • Menlo Park, California • New York
Don Mill, Ontario • Wokingham, England • Amsterdam • Bonn
Sydney • Singapore • Tokyo • Madrid • San Juan • Milan • Paris

3-24-2003
WW
$ 59.99

This book is published as part of ACM Press Books—a collaboration between the Association for Computing (ACM) and Addison-Wesley Publishing Company. ACM is the oldest and largest educational and scientific society in the information technology field. Through its high-quality publications and services, ACM is a major force in advancing the skills and knowledge of IT professionals throughout the world. For further information about ACM, contact:

ACM Member Services
1515 Broadway, 17th Floor
New York, NY 10036-5701
Phone: 1-212-626-0500
Fax: 1-212-944-1318
E-mail: ACMHELP@ACM.org

ACM European Service Center
108 Cowley Road
Oxford OX41JF
United Kingdom
Phone: +44-1865-382338
Fax: +44-1865-381338
E-mail: acm_europe@acm.org
URL: http://www.acm.org

Library of Congress Cataloging-in-Publication Data

History of programming languages / edited by Thomas J. Bergin, Richard G. Gibson.
p. cm.
Includes bibliographical references and index.
ISBN 0-201-89502-1
1. Programming languages (Electronic computers)--History.
I. Bergin, Thomas J. II. Gibson, Richard G.
QA76.7.H558 1996 95-33539
005.13'09--dc20 CIP

Copyright © 1996 by ACM Press, A Division of the Association for Computing Machinery, Inc. (ACM).

All rights reserved. No part of this publication may be reproduced, stored in a retrieval system, or transmitted, in any form or by any means, electronic, mechanical, photocopying, recording, or otherwise, without the prior permission of the publisher. Printed in the United States of America.

3 4 5 6 7 8 9 10–MA–009989796

CONTENTS

EDITORS' INTRODUCTION

In 1978, the ACM Special Interest Group on Programming Languages (SIGPLAN) sponsored a Conference on the History of Programming Languages (HOPL). Papers were prepared and presentations made at a Conference in Los Angeles, California. The Program Committee selected thirteen languages that met the criteria of having been in use for at least 10 years, had significant influence, and were still in use. The languages were: ALGOL, APL, APT, BASIC, COBOL, FORTRAN,GPSS, JOSS, JOVIAL, LISP, PL/I,SIMULA, and SNOBOL. The results of that conference were recorded in *History of Programming Languages*, edited by Richard L. Wexelblat [New York: Academic Press, 1981].

The Second ACM SIGPLAN History of Programming Languages Conference (HOPL-II) took place on April 20-23, 1993 in Cambridge, Massachusetts. The papers prepared for that conference form the basis of this present volume, along with the transcripts of the presentations, a keynote address "Language Design as Design" by Fred Brooks, a discussion of the period between HOPL and HOPL-II by Jean Sammet, and a talk on "What Makes History" by Mike Mahoney (the conference historian). There was also a banquet, hosted by Bernie Galler, and a closing panel of six language developers, chaired by Mike Mahoney. Unfortunately due to page limitations, the transcripts of the banquet, Forum, and the closing panel are not included in this volume. It is our hope that they can be published elsewhere. The Conference was preceeded by a Forum on the History of Computing, chaired by Bob Rosin, and the papers presented at the Forum complete this volume.

The Program Committee for HOPL-II decided to have both invited and submitted papers, and we believe that the range of languages and the quality of presentation will make this volume a classic in the history of programming literature. The languages at HOPL-II were: **Ada, ALGOL 68, C, C++, CLU, Discrete Simulation Languages, FORMAC, Forth, Icon, Lisp, Monitors and Concurrent Pascal, Pascal, Prolog, and Smalltalk.**

The majority of this volume is the material on the individual languages, with a chapter devoted to each language, as follows:

- a paper by each author;
- a transcript of the author's presentation;
- a transcript of a discussant's remarks (not all languages);
- a transcript of the question and answer session;
- biographies of the authors.

It should be noted that some authors' presentations closely followed their papers, and since the book is oversized, the transcripts of these presentations were omitted, with the kind permission of the authors.

All papers were published as preprints in *ACM SIGPLAN Notices*, Vol. 28, No. 3 (March 1993). The papers are reprinted here with the permission of ACM and of the authors. In some cases changes have been made by the authors to correct typographical or factual errors. In some cases additional material has been added, with an appropriate notation by an author or editor.

Jan Lee, Jean Sammet, and Bob Rosin, in their various capacities, have identified the numerous people who worked so long and hard on the Conference; however, we would like to identify the people who assisted us in the production of this volume:

Betty Henderson patiently transcribed 24 hours of difficult computer jargon, and put it on diskettes so Rick and I could begin editing;

We are especially grateful for the support of the National Science Foundation for providing partial funding for the conference and for the preparation of this book, under grant CCR -9208568 and to Nora Cortes-Comerer of ACM Press who secured the additional funding necessary for the completion of the project. In addition to sponsoring the conference, SIGPLAN and its current Chair, Barbara Ryder, provided additional funding for the preparation of photographs for this volume;

Alan Rose of Multiscience Press, Inc. (New York, NY) served as our producer, and Lauralee B. Reinke of Context Publishing Services (Sausalito, CA) formatted all of the material; without their expertise, the technical details of preparing a book of this size would have overwhelmed us;

Special thanks go to Anita LaSalle, Chair of the Computer Science and Information Systems Department at The American University for casettes, diskettes, thousands of pages of photocopies, and FedEx charges to send materials around the globe; and to Sandy Linden, Mark Davidson, and Maureen O'Connell who provided us with administrative support;

And last, but not least, a special thanks to Dick Wexelblat who started this book project; he was always there to share his experience and to give advice when asked.

We are especially indebted to those individuals whose presentations were deleted from this volume due to page limitations, colleagues who gave of their time and talent without the reward of seeing their efforts in print.

Our families deserve our sincere appreciation, since efforts of this magnitude naturally intrude on family life:

Diane, John and Jeannine, Michael and Kathleen Bergin, and a special thanks to Karen and *baby* Gibson.

Finally, we would be remiss if we did not thank Jean Sammet, who has spent much of her professional life preserving the history of programming languages. There is no way to thank her adequately for inspiring the conference or for almost two years of campus visits, telephone conversations, telephone reminders, e-mail messages, and other support that she willingly gave us during the preparation of this book. Without her single-minded devotion to her profession, our discipline would be missing the incredibly rich history captured in this volume.

Tim Bergin
Rick Gibson

GENERAL INTRODUCTION

We are indeed pleased to provide this introductory material for this book. The book is the culmination of work on a 1993 conference (HOPL-II) whose development started in 1990; HOPL-II in turn was a follow-on to the first HOPL, held 15 years earlier (1978).

First HOPL Conference

In order to put this conference in perspective, it is useful to provide some information about the first conference of this type that was held. In 1978 ACM SIGPLAN sponsored a History of Programming Languages Conference (HOPL) with Jean E. Sammet as General Chair and Program Chair, and John A. N. Lee as the Administrative Chair. That conference was composed of invited papers for the 13 languages that met the following criteria:

> "(1) were created and in use by 1967;
>
> (2) remain in use in 1977; and
>
> (3) have had considerable influence on the field of computing."
>
> [*History of Programming Languages*, Richard L. Wexelblat, ed., Academic Press, ACM Monograph Series, 1981), page xviii.]

(The cutoff date of 1967 was chosen to provide perspective from a distance of at least ten years.)

The languages chosen by the Program Committee as meeting those criteria were: ALGOL, APL, APT, BASIC, COBOL, FORTRAN, GPSS, JOSS, JOVIAL, LISP, PL/I, SIMULA, and SNOBOL. A key person involved in the early development of each of those languages was invited to write a paper according to very strict guidelines and with numerous rewrites expected. That conference was deemed a great success by its attendees. The final proceedings, edited by R. L. Wexelblat, is now the definitive work on the early history of those particular languages.

Several people asked at that time why a conference was held rather than simply having people prepare the papers and publish them in a book. We felt initially—and this was confirmed by the actual occurrence—that the audience discussion after each presentation would provide greater insight into the history of the events and decisions that led to the definition of the languages in their early forms. Some of the "cross talk" publicly and privately among the attendees—many of whom participated in the creation of several languages—provided significant insights into the early developments.

Second HOPL Conference

The first HOPL conference was intended to be only the beginning, and not the end of any consideration of programming language history. As a result, not long after the end of that conference, we began thinking about a second HOPL Conference, with the intent of building on what we learned from the first conference, and expanding its scope and coverage. Due to the pressure of other activities, it took many years before we were able to focus on a second conference. During that time period, a cadre of our colleagues was developed that also strongly promulgated the need to study the history of computing. In fact, the establishment of the journal *Annals of the History of Computing*, to be published by AFIPS, was announced at the end of the first HOPL Conference with Bernard A. Galler as Editor-in-Chief. Since 1987, John A. N. Lee has been the Editor-in-Chief, and in 1992 the IEEE Computer Society became the publisher. In January 1996, Michael R. Williams took over as the third *Annals* Editor-in-Chief. ACM has also sponsored several other history conferences, covering the fields of scientific computing, medical informatics, and personal workstations.

Finally, we developed a proposal in 1990, and the ACM SIGPLAN Executive Committee authorized us to proceed with this Second History of Programming Languages Conference (HOPL-II). We then called back to voluntary duty several members of the original conference-organizing committees and many of them were happy to join us in this new endeavor. In addition, we made a conscious effort to bring in newer/younger people who also have an interest in examining the past. But organizing a history conference is by no means as simple as organizing a technical conference dealing with current or recent research in which all the papers are to be contributed and for which there is tremendous competition to participate. This is primarily because most professionals in the computer field prefer to concentrate on current and future work rather than looking backward to what they have accomplished. A detailed description of how the final program was created is given in the next section of this introduction.

The study of various aspects of computing history is not merely an intellectual exercise; it shows us how we reached our current condition, indicates effective approaches as well as past errors, and provides perspective and insight for the future, and a surer sense of how to get there.

The conference itself was held April 20 to 23, 1993, in Cambridge, Massachusetts with preprints issued as the March 1993 issue of *ACM SIGPLAN Notices* (Volume 28, Number 3). This book contains an enormous amount of material not included in the preprints, including some revised papers as well as transcripts of the talks, the Forum papers, the keynote address, and other material that provide a record of what occurred during the conference. We regret that space limitations prevented the inclusion of the transcripts of the banquet, the closing panel and the Forum. We hope that they can be published elsewhere.

We appreciate the hard work done by all the people who helped organize and run the conference. We are particularly grateful to Tim Bergin and Rick Gibson who unexpectedly took on the enormous task of preparing this book for publication.

John A. N. Lee (Conference Chair)
Virginia Polytechnic Institute and State University

Jean E. Sammet (Program Chair)
Programming Language Consultant
(IBM, Retired)

DEVELOPMENT OF THE HOPL-II PROGRAM

The success we tried to achieve in this conference is due to an extremely hard-working and dedicated Program Committee and equally hard-working authors and numerous other volunteers. This section explains how—and to some extent why—the program was developed.

MEMBERS OF PROGRAM COMMITTEE

The Program Committee consisted of the following people, and almost all of them carried out a major task in addition to his/her standard role on a program committee. The affiliations shown are those at the time the conference was held.

Chair:	Jean E. Sammet	(Programming Language Consultant)
Secretary:	Thomas J. Bergin	(American University)
Conference Historian:	Michael S. Mahoney*	(Princeton University)
Forum Chair:	Robert F. Rosin	(Enhanced Service Providers, Inc.)
Other members:	Jacques Cohen	(Brandeis University)
	Michael Feldman	(The George Washington University)
	Bernard A. Galler*	(University of Michigan)
	Helen M. Gigley	(Naval Research Laboratory)
	Brent Hailpern*	(IBM)
	Randy Hudson	(Intermetrics)
	Barbara Ryder*	(Rutgers University)
	Richard L. Wexelblat	(Institute for Defense Analyses)

*Chair of a Program Review Committee (as described below)

APPROACH TO CREATING THE PROGRAM

In order to appreciate the papers presented at this conference and the accompanying Forum on the History of Computing, it is important to understand how the program was developed.

Three fundamental decisions were made at the beginning:

1. there would be invited *and* contributed papers,
2. the scope of the conference would include papers on the early history of specific languages—as in the first HOPL conference—and papers on (a) evolution of a language, (b) history of language features and concepts, and (c) classes of languages for application-oriented languages and paradigm-oriented languages,
3. the conference was not intended to honor anyone.

Invited Speakers

For the invited speakers, the Program Committee used the same types of criteria used for the first HOPL conference, as indicated in the preceding section, but changed the cutoff date to require that "preliminary ideas about the language were documented by 1982 and the language was in use or being taught by 1985." We issued six invitations for people to prepare papers because these languages met the three indicated criteria, that is, compliance with the date, were still in use, and had influence on the computing field):

Alain Colmerauer	Prolog
Jean Ichbiah	Ada (technical development)
Alan Kay	Smalltalk
Dennis Ritchie	C
William Whitaker	Ada (project management)
Niklaus Wirth	Pascal

Each of these people was deemed a key person in the early development of the language; all of them accepted the invitation/request to prepare detailed papers, but subsequently Jean Ichbiah was unable to prepare a paper within the specified conference schedule due to the pressure of other responsibilities and withdrew his participation.

Guidance to Authors and Paper Submission

The Program Committee followed the earlier successful plan from the first HOPL Conference by providing authors with detailed questions to guide them in writing their papers. We used the original questions for early history from the first HOPL Conference, and then developed three new sets of questions to deal with the three new types of papers we expected. Randy Hudson coordinated and edited those four sets of questions; they appear in this book as Appendix B.

A call for papers was issued in December of 1990 (Appendix B) with notification to potential authors that their papers would go through two rounds of refereeing with a major rewrite probably needed between them. Dick Wexelblat served as submissions coordinator, and provided administrative support for the Call for Papers, the distribution of manuscripts (twice), and hosting two Program Committee meetings. In his role as editor of the preprints (Volume 28, Number 3, March 1993 issue of *ACM SIGPLAN Notices*), he also developed the format guidelines used by the authors.

Program Review Committees

Because of the complexity of the paper processing and refereeing, we established four Program Review Committees (PRCs), each serving essentially as a subcommittee of the Program Committee but with additional people serving on each PRC. The PRC scopes corresponded approximately to the types of papers we expected. The chairs of those PRCs were responsible for most of the interaction with the authors and referees on each specific paper. The PRC chairs were:

Early History	Brent Hailpern
Evolution	Bernard A. Galler
Features & Classes	Barbara Ryder
Invited Papers	Michael S. Mahoney and Brent Hailpern

Each of the PRC Chairs also recruited additional people to help with the refereeing and selection. While I would like to list their names, as is often done for conferences, it is not appropriate to do so here because almost all of them were selected because of knowledge of specific language(s) so it would be too easy for the authors to identify their referees!

Paper Selection

In September 1991 the Program Committee gave "conditional acceptance" to some of the contributed papers. The authors were given referees' comments and told that if they complied with a reasonable number of those suggestions the paper would be accepted (i.e., they would not be in competition with one another).

In August 1992 the Program Committee decided which contributed papers met the standards for the conference, and those are printed here, along with the invited papers, which also underwent a similar process of rewrites.

Guidance to Authors on Historiography

In addition to other steps taken to try to achieve high quality, we asked Michael S. Mahoney, a professor with significant expertise and experience in historiography—and specifically the history of computing—to provide guidance to the Program Committee and the authors. He reviewed *all* the papers and provided specific assistance to any author who requested it. His paper "Making History" appears in Chapter 1; another paper, "What Makes History?", was sent to prospective authors and is included as Appendix A.

Language Experts

To assist the authors, each PRC chair assigned a technical expert in the subject to help each author with the paper by reviewing the various drafts. In some sense, these experts are the unsung heroes of the conference, and so it is appropriate to list and thank them.

Language/Topic	*Expert*	*Language Summary*
Ada	Anthony Gargaro	Anthony Gargaro
ALGOL 68	Henry Bowlden	Henry Bowlden
C	William McKeeman	William McKeeman
C++	Jerry Schwarz	Jerry Schwarz
Clu	John Guttag	John Guttag
Concurrent Pascal	Narain Gehani	Charles Hayden
FORMAC	James Griesmer	James Griesmer
Forth	Phil Koopman	Phil Koopman
Icon	David Hanson	David Hanson
Lisp	Gerald Jay Sussman	Gerald Jay Sussman, Guy L. Steele, Jr., and Richard P. Gabriel
Pascal	C. A. R. Hoare	Peter Lee
Prolog	Fernando Pereira	Fernando Pereira
Simulation languages	Philip Kiviat	Philip Kiviat
Smalltalk	Adele Goldberg	Tim Budd

Language Descriptions

We wanted the authors to concentrate on writing a history paper and not on describing the language. Therefore we asked knowledgeable individuals to provide a very short introduction to each language and these "language summaries" appeared in the preprints. Unfortunately, space limitations prevented our including them here. The authors of these language summaries are listed above; the preparation and editing of these language descriptions was coordinated by Michael Feldman.

Reasons for Some Language Absences

In examining the list of papers accepted for this conference, the reader might well wonder about the absence of some obvious subjects. For example, since FORTRAN and COBOL were included in the first HOPL Conference—and remain as major languages—one might have expected papers on their evolution to appear in this conference. The Program Committee decided to invite only papers dealing with the early history of the major languages developed since the first HOPL conference. Therefore, the omission of these subjects, and numerous others, is due to the policy of having contributed as well as invited papers; if people did not submit acceptable papers on an important topic it could not be included in this conference.

FORUM ON THE HISTORY OF COMPUTING

Many SIGPLAN Conferences precede the main paper sessions with a day of tutorials. The Program Committee adapted that practice to provide an afternoon and evening devoted to a Forum on the History of Computing. The intent of the Forum was to sensitize computer scientists to issues and challenges in the history of computing, and to entice some of them to become involved in this work. The Forum activity was chaired by Robert F. Rosin, who assembled a committee to help organize the topics and sessions, invite the participants, and review written material. An introduction by Robert Rosin, the written papers prepared for the Forum, and a transcript of the closing panel are included in this book. Unfortunately, there was not enough room in this volume to include transcripts of the presentations.

The Forum Committee operated under the general guidance and approval of the Program Committee, and consisted of the following people, whose affiliations at the time of the conference are shown:

Chair:	Robert F. Rosin	(Enhanced Service Providers, Inc.)
Members:	Thomas J. Bergin	(American University)
	Michael S. Mahoney	(Princeton University)
	Michael Marcotty	(General Motors; now a consultant)
	Tom Marlowe	(Seton Hall University)
	Jean E. Sammet	(Programming Language Consultant)

PERSONAL COMMENT

It is not common for the Program Chair of a conference to have a paper included in that conference. The Program Committee decided initially that it was reasonable for me to submit a paper, but in order to maintain objectivity and fairness I was kept completely separated from any refereeing or decision process on my paper, and I don't know any more than any other author as to who the referees were or what general evaluation comments were turned in.

CONCLUSION

The entire Program Committee and its supporting subcommittees have spent literally hundreds—and in some cases thousands—of hours preparing this conference. I am personally very grateful to Tim Bergin and Rick Gibson for the hundreds of hours they have spent in preparing this book. We hope you will find it valuable initially and in the future.

Jean E. Sammet
Program Chair

ACKNOWLEDGMENTS

My special thanks go to Jean Sammet, Program Chair, who coincidentally moved from full-time work to consultancy just about the time the intense effort on the development of the program started. Over the past five years she has spent an immense amount of time on this task, and without her drive, enthusiasm, and high standards, we would not have the high quality of historiography represented by the papers in this volume.

Michael Mahoney, Conference Historian, led the program committee in learning and applying the techniques and methods of historical research. At least one program committee member was heard to say that he or she never realized before how difficult historical research was. In fact, the whole program committee deserves our thanks for developing an outstanding, high quality program.

The preparation of the preprints was more complicated than usual due to the size and variety of material. The efforts by Dick Wexelblat and Janice Hirst in preparing the preprints are greatly appreciated. The work to prepare this book was enormous, and the willingness of Tim Bergin and Rick Gibson to unexpectedly assume this task is greatly appreciated.

The organizing committee worked for approximately one year before the conference. A very visible aspect reflects the work of Dan Halbert, Publicity Chairman. Many of the attendees would not have known of the conference without his efforts; his patience in providing numerous drafts of publicity items satisfied our demands for high standards of presentation even in the ancillary materials.

The results of the efforts of many members of the organizing committee was best seen during the conference itself, though some, like Richard Eckhouse, Conference Treasurer, remained unseen to participants. Our thanks to them all.

Members, Organizing Committee:

Program Chair:	Jean E. Sammet	(Programming Language Consultant)
Treasurer:	Richard Eckhouse	(University of Massachusetts, Boston)
Local arrangements:	Peter S. Mager	(Perception Technology Corporation)
Publications:	Richard L. Wexelblat	(Institute for Defense Analyses)
Recordings:	Mary van Deusen	(IBM)
Registration:	Karen Lemone	(Worcester Polytechnic Institute)
Book exhibits:	James P. Bouhana	(Performance International)
Publicity:	Dan Halbert	(Diqital Equipment Corporation)

Our thanks also go to the National Science Foundation which provided support for speakers, students, and this final book under grant #CCR-9208568.

John A. N. Lee
General Chair

I

The Opening Session

CONFERENCE CHAIRMAN'S OPENING REMARKS, ***John A. N. Lee***
"LANGUAGE DESIGN AS DESIGN," ***Frederick P. Brooks, Jr.***
"FROM HOPL TO HOPL-II," ***Jean E. Sammet***
"MAKING HISTORY," ***Michael S. Mahoney***

CONFERENCE CHAIRMAN'S OPENING REMARKS

J.A.N. LEE: Welcome to the Second History of Programming Languages Conference. My name is Jan Lee; I'm the general chairman of this conference. We started thinking about this conference in 1978; that was the year of the first History of Programming Languages Conference (HOPL-I), chaired by Jean Sammet. It had been enormously successful and we were enthused enough at that time to begin thinking about our next history conference. We had many suggestions, perhaps the most serious of which was to consider the history of operating systems. In fact, we even had a name for it, HOOS. But it was obvious that the history of programming languages was continuing to happen, even in 1978 as we held that meeting. Pascal had begun to replace FORTRAN as the language of choice in computer science education, and the Department of Defense was talking about an all-purpose new language. There were programming developments that we left out of that meeting simply because there was not enough time to cover them. There were already things happening that would clearly be on the agenda of the next meeting.

In the history of computing we generally choose to observe past events from a viewpoint of fifteen years; thus, 1993 was the obvious date not only to hold a second conference, but to regard that original meeting itself as a historical event. Jean Sammet and I have always known there would be another meeting. And in 1990 we convinced ACM and SIGPLAN to support that next meeting. Jean then recruited an impressive program committee who have worked very hard, as have the authors they selected, for almost three years. Most recently, we recruited a team of organizers to arrange the physical arrangements for you. Jean will introduce her committee to you at a later time and I will introduce the administrative volunteers. Similarly, Jean will relate to you the history of programming languages between the two conferences.

My colleagues in academia believe there are three signs of senility in a professor—when his dreams turn lightly to thoughts of education, or to ethical considerations, or to history. However, in our profession I feel it's a sign of maturity when we have concerns for these aspects of the science. ACM started in about 1968 to concern itself with education and curricula. Prior to that it had introduced one of the first codes of professional conduct. In the mid-1970s we were concerned about the preservation of our history as, regrettably, we began to lose some of our pioneers. We are still concerned with curricula. We've recently updated the code of professional conduct. And we continue to have concerns about preserving our heritage.

ACM and SIGPLAN agreed to support this conference three years ago and the National Science Foundation agreed to provide additional support to our invited speakers. NSF also provided funding for scholarships for students, and was joined by SHL System House Inc., the employer of one of our 1978 scholarship winners, for support of a fifth student. Of course the major sponsors of our conference are the employers of our volunteers, who provide the time and funding for their participation. You will meet all of our speakers later in the meeting, but let me now introduce and congratulate our student scholarship holders and ask them to stand. From the United Kingdom, Ross Hamilton, University of Warwick. From Norway, Jan Rune Holmevik, University of Trondheim. Close to home, Stephen P. Masticola, Rutgers University; Rajeev Pandey, from Oregon State University; and Patricia A. Summers from Virginia Polytechnic Institute and State University.

In 1978, the time of HOPL-I, there had been two earlier major history projects. The AFIPS/Smithsonian projects on history and the National Science Foundation sponsorship of a great reunion of pioneers of Los Alamos National Laboratory. In 1978, we knew about two proposals, one to establish a computer history institute, which would be sponsored by a then anonymous donor, and the anticipated publication of an AFIPS journal to be called *Annals of the History of Computing*. In that year also, Ken Olsen approached Gwen Bell to ask whether the TX-0 could be faithfully recreated at Marlboro. That gave her the impetus to establish a collection of artifacts and set her on the road to establishing a museum. That was 1978.

In the past 15 years, the awareness of computing as a historical event has grown. Part of that awareness is due to The Computer Museum, which we will visit tonight; the transmogrification of that original digital museum at Marlboro is now a museum of international standing. It's not just a collection of musty artifacts. It has become, under Gwen Bell's leadership, a learning place about the past, the present, and the future of computing. In the 1960s, the Smithsonian had created a gallery in the National Museum of American History which included artifacts from the ENIAC and the Whirlwind. But more recently, the Institution has opened galleries in both the National Air and Space Museum and the Museum of American History, which emphasize computers and information technology. The Charles Babbage Institute was established at the University of Minnesota by Erwin Tomash. CBI has become our primary document archive and research institute. Recently, the IEEE center for the history of electrical engineering has also become a new center for the study of the history of computing at Rutgers University.

In Great Britain, the Science Museum at Kensington recently completed the great work of Charles Babbage, on the bicentenary of his birth, by building his Difference Engine. Dorin Swade, the curator, accomplished what Babbage and Clemment had been unable to do in the 19th century and proved that Babbage's design was both correct and constructable still using 19th century tooling techniques. Apart from a couple of obvious oversights in the drawings that any professional engineer would have found, Babbage's Engine—different from most of our software—worked the first time. Building on the work of Konrad Zuse, The Deutsches Museum in Munich has created a gallery that includes not only a construction of his Z-3 machine, but also Fritz Bauer's Stanishlaus machine.

Next year, Europe will commemorate the D-Day landing in Normandy, which led to the end of World War II. One of the contributions of that success has got to be the work of the code breakers at Bletchley Park. Recently the Bletchley Park Trust has been created and has raised £1,000,000 to preserve the park and its significant buildings, and to create a museum to memorize COLOSSUS, Alan Turing, Telecommunication, and Air Traffic Control. We wish them luck.

In the aftermath of HOPL-I, ACM organized three history conferences on workstations, medical informatics, and scientific computation. There have been conferences in Europe, including, in 1991, a magnificent bicentennial conference on Babbage and Farraday at St John's College, Cambridge. The French conference will have its third instance this year. During this period, we've also seen the development of a number of organizations. The IFIP working group on history will have its first meeting later this year and is attempting its first pioneer day, following the concept of the AFIPS pioneer days, which will be held in Hamburg next year.

We've seen many things happen; the history of computing has come a long way in 15 years. It involves many more interested and interesting people, several archival institutions, textbooks, and publications, one electronic bulletin board, an annual computer trivia game—The Computer Bowl—and a TV series which won the 1992 Peabody Award for Journalism. It is also changing; we are finally beyond the phase of merely collecting and preserving our heritage. We have to work seriously on analysis, evaluation, and application. We have come a long way since 1978.

Let's get on with it; let's have a conference.

Editor's Note: Due to space limitations, welcoming remarks by Gwen Bell, President of ACM, and Stuart Feldman, Chair of SIGPLAN were deleted, as were the remarks of the Program Chair, Jean E. Sammet.

INTRODUCTION OF FREDERICK P. BROOKS, JR.

PROGRAM CHAIR, JEAN E. SAMMET: The Program Committee thought long and hard about selecting a keynote speaker. We wanted someone who had been around for quite a while [audience laughter]—you may interpret that phrase any way you want; but since most of us on this platform have been around for quite a while it seems allright to say that. We also wanted somebody who had a very broad background in the general field of computing (not necessarily limited to programming languages), but we did want somebody with significant work in software. Fred Brooks has had a very distinguished career and I can only indicate some of the highlights.

He received a Ph.D in 1956 in Applied Mathematics from Harvard University, and his advisor was the legendary Howard Aiken. (If there are any of you in the audience who are young enough not to know who Howard Aiken is, then perhaps that is a good reason for you to go and study something about the history of the hardware.) Dr. Brooks founded the Computer Science Department at the University of North Carolina at Chapel Hill in 1964, and served as its chair for 20 years. He remains on the faculty there.

He worked at IBM from 1956 to 1964. While he was there, he served in two major capacities. One was as the manager of the IBM System/360 hardware development and the corporate processor manager for the System/360. So he was largely the technical guiding light behind the S/360. His second major capacity at IBM was as manager of the OS/360 development. So he really handled the 360 from both the hardware and software sides. Prior to his work on the 360, he participated in the development of STRETCH and HARVEST at IBM; they were pioneering computers to push the state of the art in several directions.

Dr. Brooks has received numerous honors—far too many to list all of them. Among others, he received the National Medal of Technology, the AFIPS Harry Goode Memorial Award, the IEEE Computer Society McDowell Award, the ACM Distinguished Service Award, the DPMA Computer Sciences Man-of-the-Year award, election to the National Academy of Engineering, and just recently, the John von Neumann medal from the IEEE.

Dr. Brooks has served on numerous advisory boards and boards of directors. He has authored or co-authored over 70 papers or book chapters. Probably his best known publication is his book *The Mythical Man-Month: Essays on Software Engineering*. He is going to talk here on "Language Design as Design."

KEYNOTE ADDRESS: LANGUAGE DESIGN AS DESIGN

Frederick P. Brooks, Jr.

When Jean called and said what she wanted me to talk about, I said I had not done any thinking about that and didn't see any opportunity to do any. I considered that an impediment to talking about it. But I had done some thinking about another subject that I would be glad to talk about. She said, "All right." Hence today's topic.

(SLIDE 1) I have been especially interested in the process of design. So I welcomed the opportunity to speak to a room full of experienced designers and to share some of my thinking to date. Because this is in very early stages of formulation, I should like to ask you at the breaks, at lunch, and at the reception, to share with me your thoughts on the design process.

Here are the subtopics:

- What is the design process?
- Why should anyone do language design now?
- Some principles for how to do design
- The role of esthetics in technical design
- An assertion about the nature of design, namely, that great designs come from great designers, not committees.

(SLIDE 2) The *Oxford English Dictionary* defines design as "To form a plan or scheme of, to arrange or conceive in the mind for later execution." That's a sufficiently general definition.

(SLIDE 3) I have had the opportunity in my life to work on five machine languages, three high level languages, a half a dozen molecular graphics tools, some application systems in virtual reality, and four buildings.

Language Design as Design

1. **What is the design process?**
2. **Why do language design now?**
3. **Some design principles**
4. **Esthetics in technical design**
5. **Great designs come from great designers**

SLIDE 1

Design

"To form a plan or scheme of,

to arrange or conceive in the mind...

for later execution."

OED

SLIDE 2

Why Study Design?

My design experiences:

As a Principal	As a Participant
5 computer architectures	S/360 Macroassembler
APL	PL/I
GRIP, GRINCH, GROPE	VIEW, SCULPT
Walkthrough	Several VR systems
Beach house	Computer Science bldg
Home wing	Church fellowship hall

SLIDE 3

Why Study Design?

- These experiences are more alike than different!
- Can we design *better* by studying design as a process?

SLIDE 4

(SLIDE 4) The conclusion I reach is that the experiences across these fields—hardware, programming languages, computer application systems, and buildings—are more alike than different. So the intellectual question is "Can we design better by studying design as a process?"

(SLIDE 5) Engineers think of design in a very simple-minded way. You have a goal; you have some desiderata; the desiderata combine in a non-linear utility function. You have a slue of constraints that form budgets, and one of these is critical. It is not always dollars, but there is always a critical constraint. You have a design tree of possible decisions. You make the various decisions, working your way down the tree by a very straightforward process.

(SLIDE 6) Until the design is good enough or you don't have any more time, you keep trying to improve the utility function. And until the design is complete, you make another design decision, as long as you have a feasible design. When you don't, you backtrack, and you explore a new path. When you have to quit, you take the best design that you have so far. That is a rational design process.

(SLIDE 7) Now what is wrong with this simple-minded model? The first difficulty is that we rarely really know the goal. I will assert that the hardest part in any design is deciding what it is you want to design. I have found that to be true across the spectrum of different kinds of designs. Second, the place where experts go wrong is that the vision is either not high enough or not fresh enough. The mini and micro revolutions are good examples of where the experts were plowing on in conventional courses while an entirely fresh vision was waiting in the wings. The third difficulty is that we usually don't know the design tree until we get into it.

How Engineers Think of Design

- Goal
- Desiderata
- Non-linear utility function
- Constraints, especially budget (not necessarily $ cost)
- Design tree of decisions

SLIDE 5

Engineers' Design Model

```
UNTIL ( "good enough") or (no more time)
  DO another design (to improve utility function)
    UNTIL design complete
      WHILE design feasible,
        make another design decision
      END WHILE
      Backtrack up design tree
      Explore a new path
    END UNTIL
  END DO
  Take best design
END UNTIL
```

SLIDE 6

SLIDE 7

SLIDE 8

(SLIDE 8) Fourth, and most important, the desiderata keep changing. In the design of a house wing that we completed two years ago, we found that the breakthrough on the design came when we finally realized that a critical function that we had not at all taken into account was where to put the coats of guests when they came to large functions. That warped the whole design. I added a room at one end and took another away at the other end of the house. But that is the kind of thing that happens in the middle of the design process. As Donald Schön, Professor of Architecture at MIT and one of the people who has written important books on the theory of the design process, says, "One wrestles with the problem." As one, in fact, makes the trade-offs, the weights change. I have found that to be uniformly true. I would be interested in whether you find that true. As you get into it, things that you thought were important seem to become less important; things you thought unimportant become more important. Sometimes, one hits new opportunities. The things that you have already designed make it possible to put in at very low cost things that you have not thought about as desiderata, and yet you are able to realize those opportunities.

Then the constraints keep changing—sometimes by inspiration. I have worked many years with Gerrit Blaauw. Gerry Blaauw is one of the very best machine designers in the world. He has an uncanny gift for taking cases that look like one has an unfortunate choice on this side versus an unfortunate choice on that side, and finding a third way where no one could see there was one at all. I think that is part of the genius of design.

In the house wing experience, we wrestled with one problem: how to make the music room work. It had to hold two pianos, an electronic organ, a string octet, and a one-foot working strip for a teacher. The constraint was a set-back requirement. *Nothing* would work. Finally, the answer was to buy a five-foot strip of land from the neighbor. It unlocked the design; it made the whole design possible. I have seen the same thing happen in machines. Sometimes the right answer is to change the constraints by a process completely orthogonal to the design process itself. How do we know when to even try to do that?

The other thing that happens is that the ever-changing world around us keeps changing the constraints for us. And these changes are not always advantageous.

(SLIDE 9) Why should anybody today undertake to do computer language design? This is probably a question that never crossed your mind. The first possibility: Do we want to just redo the old ones better? Well, I am the person who tried to displace FORTRAN with PL/1. That was not a winning undertaking. Part of the reason is that as the field evolves, the marginal utility of the next step goes down, down, down. Also there is the principle that Gerry Blaauw has called *the persistence of established technology.* That was the one we ran up against with FORTRAN. As a competitive threat

Why Do Language Design Now?

- To redo old ones better?
- Need new ones?
  For new algorithms — especially parallel
  To embody new concepts
- To get published?
- Because it is fun?
- As a discipline for thought?

SLIDE 9

Programming Languages and Software Building

- Software productivity
  5 x for Fortran
  Much more for Excel, LISP, Smalltalk
- Software reliability
  If you can't say it, you can't say it wrong.
- Concepts for communication
- Concepts for algorithms

SLIDE 10

appears, the established technology starts evolving and moving to accommodate the same needs within the old framework.

(SLIDE 10) What have the existing high level languages contributed to software? The first step, the FORTRAN step, has been measured at giving about a five-to-one productivity improvement. It gives perhaps a ten-to-one improvement in the number of statements. But the statements are longer and a little complicated, and it cooks down to about five times over assembly language. If one looks at special-purpose application domains, and looks at the power of languages such as the Excel spreadsheet, or LISP, or Smalltalk, each in its own domain, the productivity improvements of today's high level languages are much higher than that original step function. Well, what idea do you have that is going to give anything like another five-times productivity improvement? This is the low marginal utility point.

The second, and maybe most important, step that high level languages have already contributed to programming is software reliability, because of the elementary principle that if you cannot say it, you cannot say it wrong. The details that are suppressed, or abstracted, or implied are a whole host of ways that you used to go wrong. Either conceptually, or just syntax, or even typos, you cannot go wrong there anymore.

The most important contribution, I think, is that high level languages by their abstraction have given us ways of thinking and ways of talking to each other. So we routinely talk about concepts such as *binding time*. One thinking in assembler just doesn't think about binding time. We routinely talk about *recursive-descent parsing*. A whole new concept, not only useful for communication, but one that leads to other ideas. The whole technology of high level languages, including their compilation, has contributed ideas for doing other algorithms.

(SLIDE 11) So I think that the notion of redoing old programming languages to make marginal improvements in them is not a motive that would drive one to do language design. Well, why do we? Is it because we have a desperate need for new high level languages? In fact, I think we do. In the first place, we need new languages to express new algorithms. The place where we are feeling that crunch most keenly today is in concurrency, parallel algorithms, and massively parallel data types. I consider an SIMD machine to be one that has special data types and is not really a multiprocessor. The most important reason is to embody new higher level concepts. Let me come back to that in a moment.

One reason for designing new languages that seems to be very common is to get published. The national president of the Humane Society pointed out that this country is about a million puppies and kittens over what would be a normal population. The Society has called for a one-year moratorium on the breeding of any more dogs or cats in the United States. I am tempted to call for a similar

Why Do Language Design Now?

- To redo old ones better?
- Need new ones?
  For new algorithms — especially parallel
  To embody new concepts
- To get published?
- Because it is fun?
- As a discipline for thought?

SLIDE 11

Language as Concept Carrier

- Detailed enough for execution.
- Maximize (Shannon information = surprise).
- Abstract out redundant detail.
- Carry most required detail by implication.
- Define classes, each with shared properties.
- Class usefulness depends upon frequency.
- Same program as Mathematics.

SLIDE 12

moratorium on new computing languages, because much of our literature has the same property as kittens—it has a negative price; you have to pay people page charges to take it away. (A new language that embodies new concepts should be designed and should get published.)

Maybe the best reason to design new languages is because it is fun. Designing anything is fun. But it is also an important discipline for thought. J.R.R. Tolkien, the author of *The Lord of the Rings*, in his professional youth as a philologist undertook to design a language he called "High Elvish." He designed the whole language, the lexicon, the syntax, the semantics, the whole bit. Somebody asked him, "Why go through a really vacuous kind of exercise of making up a natural language, High Elvish?" He said, "One doesn't really understand the bones of language until one has tried to design one." I think he is quite right. Of course you see the richness of that exercise in his writings. It colors and illuminates and glorifies various parts of his writing. But I think the important thing it did for him professionally was to help him understand all language.

(SLIDE 12) The same thing is true as a reason for undertaking to design a programming language. This slide I want to discuss quickly because you can do it better than I could. If we look on language design as a discipline for the mind in understanding languages, we see that the design program looks like this. We have to make the language detailed enough for execution. That gets rid of much arm waving about algorithmic and data concepts.

Next, we want to maximize the Shannon information, that is, the *surprise*. This means we want to abstract out the redundant detail. There is required detail if one is going to make a language detailed enough for real execution. The technique that has developed through the decades is to carry most of the required details by implication so that you don't have to state it but once in the whole process. Today that means defining classes, each one of which has shared properties, and then determining what you can do with the class as a logical consequence of the properties that have been defined for it. I will observe in passing that the usefulness of different classes depends on their frequency of use.

If you look back over this research program, it is exactly the same program as has characterized mathematics through the years. What we do is define a class of things, a set, or a group, or a ring. Define its properties exactly, and then see what corollaries follow from that set of properties and no other properties. I would assert that the undertaking of defining a programming language intellectually is essentially the same program as the classical program for mathematics. That is the reason why language design is a good exercise. Language design is a discipline.

Let me turn to the second part of the talk, and talk about some design principles. Here I am treading boldly on dangerous ground, because I am talking about design principles in your field, when I am not a language designer. Therefore I am more subject to correction and would appreciate it.

(SLIDE 13) The first principle: Design a language; don't just hack one up.

Design Principle 1

Design a language;

don't just hack one up.

SLIDE 13

The Worst Language—
OS/360 JCL

- One job language for all programming languages
- Like Assembler language, rather than PL/I, etc.
- But not exactly like Assembler
- Card-column dependent
- Too few verbs
- Declaration parameters do verbish things
- Awkward branching
- No clean iteration
- No clean subroutine call

SLIDE 14

(SLIDE 14) People will debate forever about what is the best programming language ever designed. But I expect no challenges when I offer a candidate for the worst programming language ever designed, OS/360 Job Control Language. You are familiar with its faults, so I won't dwell at length. The biggest mistake was making one job language for a system that was intended to run many different programming languages instead of one per programming language. What is worse, at the same time that we were shifting to high level language usage, we made the job control language at the assembler level. But not exactly like the assembler, just incompatible enough to make a nice little mess of rules. It is card-column dependent, so really awkward on a teletype and worse on a terminal. Too few verbs; the boast of the designers is that it had only six verbs. Yes, but you cannot say what you have to say with only six verbs. So guess what? The declaration parameters do verbish things all over the place. There was a discipline that said, "No verbs," but there was no discipline saying, "No more declaration parameters," and they multiplied. The branching is extremely awkward. There is no clean iteration, and there is no clean subroutine call. And you can add favorites of your own to this list.

(SLIDE 15) I was not a designer of the Job Control Language, but it was done under my management. Like the Attorney General and the Branch Davidian fiasco, I have to take responsibility for it. It is instructive to look at major mistakes so let's see what lessons we can learn from this one. The basic problem was pedestrian vision. We did not see it as a *programming language* at all. Those words never came anywhere near the JCL project. There were programming languages in the same overall, OS/360 project, but the concepts and the people familiar with those ideas never came near the Job Control Language team. Instead, it was seen as, "We will provide a few control cards to let people tell the Scheduler what to do with the jobs." Then it was not *designed*, even as a few control cards; it just grew as needs appeared during the definition of the operating system scheduler.

(SLIDE 16) I think JCL is typical of the fact that programming languages appear in many different guises. We have machine languages. I have spent the last twenty years thinking about machine languages. You probably called them assembler languages. But for the computer architect this language design is a major concern. Machine languages are a specialized set of programming languages in which high level is not in fact possible.

In machine languages, utterances are costly. The static bit budget is one of the two principal criteria for excellence. The utilization of the memory bandwidth, that is, the dynamic bit budget, is the other criterion for excellence. So, many of the things I say come from these experiences of working with languages in which every bit counts.

Job control languages are languages in disguise. Shell scripts are languages in disguise. Spreadsheet languages are languages in disguise. I will be teaching the computer literacy course next year, "Power Tools for the Mind," a course in which students become acquainted with applications. How

The Worst Language— OS/360 JCL

- **Done under my management.**
- **Basic problem was pedestrian vision.**
  - **We did not see it as a schedule-time programming *language* at all, but as a "few control cards."**
  - **It was not *designed*, it just grew as needs appeared.**

SLIDE 15

Languages in Disguise

- **Machine languages — utterances are costly**
- **Job control languages**
- **Shell scripts**
- **Spreadsheet languages**
- **Interaction motion languages**

SLIDE 16

are we going to sneak up on programming and spreadsheets? The things you put in the cell are, in fact, utterances in a programming language. As soon as you get away from constants, it becomes obvious that those expressions are languages.

Then in working with interactive systems of all kinds, whether 2-D or, in my field, 3-D interactive systems, we have motion languages for which we do not even know the lexicons or the grammar. But we do know that it is useful to think in terms of sentences and utterances and responses. We are at the primitive stage of understanding the linguistic content of interactive protocols. So I would assert that one of the reasons to think about language design today is not that there are so many undone jobs with the old procedural languages, but that there are so many areas in which we do programming language design without bringing to bear what we have learned about language design.

(SLIDE 17) The second design principle: Study other people's designs. I would assert that the characteristic of an amateur in any design field is that he brings to the task his own experience, period. And the trained professional brings to the task the whole craft's experience. Bach walked 60 miles to copy Buxtehude's music and Buxtehude's collection. Bach was a much greater composer than Buxtehude, but not at the time he did that. He was stronger because he undertook the mastery of the arts of his predecessors. The Bach biographies identify perhaps ten musicians whose works he especially studied in detail to see what they did and to try to figure out why they did it. I think that is still a valid and fruitful undertaking.

Design Principle 2

Study and use other people's designs.

Amateur — draws on own experience

Professional — draws on craft's experience

SLIDE 17

Study Matrix for Languages

	APL	Oberon	C	Fortran	LISP
Data					
Ops					
Naming					
Control					
Syntax					

SLIDE 18

(SLIDE 18) I have found this kind of matrix to be useful for looking at machine languages. That is, to identify in many lines what we call the *design decisions.* What the data types and data structures will be, for example. What the operations proper to those data types will be. For example, the whole system of naming and binding, the whole system of sequence control and the syntax. I think it is fruitful to study across this direction. Take a design decision and look and see how the different languages have done it. We have been doing that for machine languages.

It is essential, however, to also study down the column direction, because the principle of consistency means that if you are going to have any conceptual integrity for the language at all, everything in the column has to work together. But I think much of the surprise comes in looking along the rows.

(SLIDE 19) One of the things we, and many people, have observed is that in any kind of design process, designs that are all-new are relatively rare. And most designs start with go-bys. That is, you have an example in front of you to use as a conceptual base on which to make major or minor structural modifications in the design process. I will remark in passing that the opportunity to do an all-new design is really wonderful. They are very exciting to do—to go into a new area where there are not any go-bys—but you do not get many such chances in a lifetime.

Since go-bys are important, it is important to do the collection of specimens. This is why the HOPL documentation is important. This is why Jean Sammet's language book is very important. The collection must capture the artifacts of previous designers in enough detail that you can understand and see the whole design, not just a casual description. Even a technical paper does not usually capture all the details necessary. Moreover, collecting rationales behind the designs is important for the serious student of the design. I will maintain that as a design discipline matures, it grows from first *collection,* to then *criticism* (I use that in the normal sense of looking at the virtues as well as the flaws), to *analysis,* and then finally to *synthesis rules* for how one should do a new design.

(SLIDE 20) The third design principle applies to all the areas of design that I am familiar with: Design top-down. You may have to build bottom-up, but it is important to design top-down.

(SLIDE 21) If we ask ourselves what it means to design top-down in the language area, I find that, at least for machine languages, these are the principal elements of design. The data types and data structures are crucial, and yet the designer has not a lot of freedom here, because the data types follow from the application domain. If you have carefully specified the application domain, then imagination can show you powerful and natural data types and data structures. But they do grow out of the application itself. Likewise, the operations follow from the data types one has chosen. The whole notion of an operation set as being proper to a data type is, I think, very powerful. Where the designers

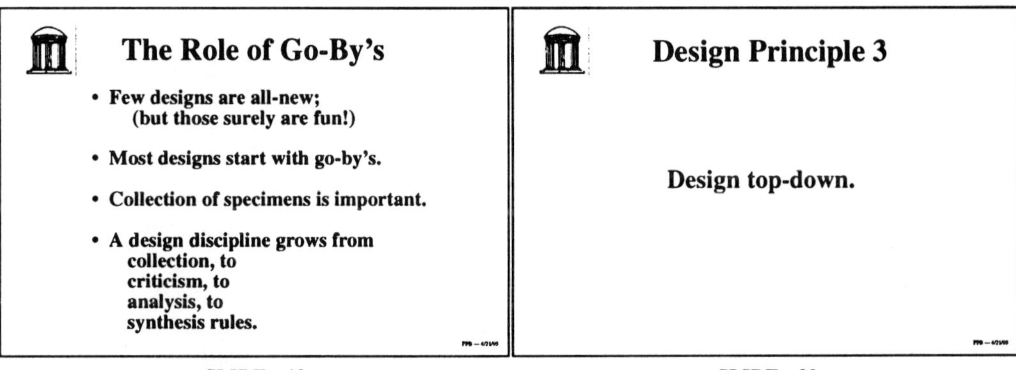

SLIDE 19 SLIDE 20

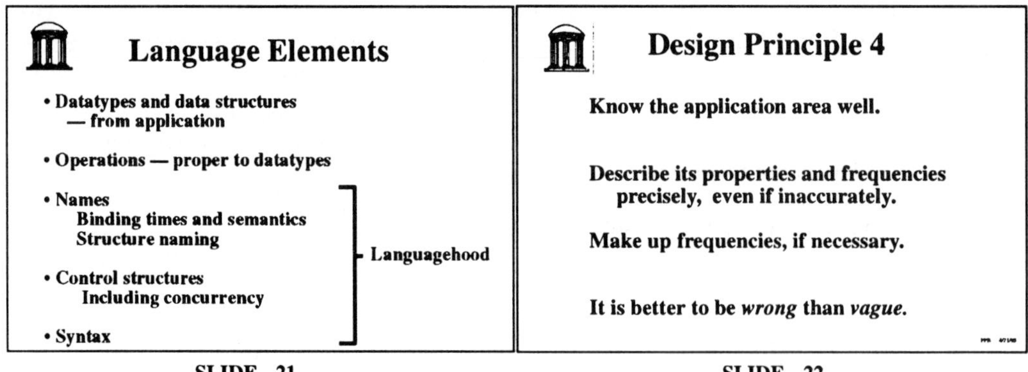

SLIDE 21

SLIDE 22

really cut loose are in names, binding times, and naming semantics. The whole question, once I have picked a data structure, of how I do sub-structure naming, leaves great room for bringing new ideas to bear. Then we come to control structures, because in any computer there are indeed sequences. Today the important issues are: How do I specify the opportunities for concurrency and the mandates for synchronization?

Finally, what is a natural syntax? That which makes it easy to say what one means is a crucial part of language design. I call these components *languagehood*. In a machine language I called them *machinehood*. These are things that are essentially independent of the application, although which direction you may choose to go on some of these designs may be influenced by application characteristics, especially frequencies. But they have more to do with what Tolkien calls "the bones of a language," whereas the earlier design decisions follow more from the careful definition of the application domain. As we look over high level languages, it seems to me that we see more powerful concepts and more exciting concepts in these languagehood areas as the languages have evolved.

(SLIDE 22) Design principle four: Know the application area well. One of the paradoxes of design is it is more difficult to design a general purpose object than a special purpose object. One of the exciting things that has happened in high level language design is the proliferation of specialized languages. The spreadsheet language is an example, but not the only example. Simulation languages, logical languages, functional languages, the whole set goes on and on. Therefore the first thing that the designer has to do is to describe the intended scope of use of the language, its domain. I tell my students when they are setting out to do this to describe the properties and frequencies of the application precisely, even if inaccurately. Notice that the frequencies are as important as the properties; if we approach design from a mathematical point of view, we are apt to overlook that. But if we approach it from an information-theory point of view, we cannot ignore the frequencies. I assert that it is useful to fabricate or postulate frequencies if necessary. In stating and defining precisely the domain of a language's application, *it is better to be wrong than to be vague.*

Why would anybody with reasonably good sense assert a fool thing like that? Because, if you write down the assumptions about frequencies and say, "This is the set of frequencies I believe exists out there," then it is public and open to criticism by other members of the design team and the potential users. Furthermore, you might get illuminated by people offering facts you didn't know about as to what the real frequencies are. So, (A) you might get different opinions to help you modify your view of what the frequencies are, and (B) you might learn the true facts. Consequently, this kind of anti-intellectual approach says, by all means, *make up* missing frequency data, don't be vague.

(SLIDE 23) Design principle five: Iterate the design with independent test problems. As any experiment designer knows, you can pilot with one set of test problems as your driving problems

Design Principle 5

Iterate

- **with independent test problems**
- **with real users other than yourself**

SLIDE 23

Rationalism vs. Empiricism in Design

- **Aristotle vs. Galileo;**
  France vs. Britain;
  Descartes vs. Hume;
  Napoleonic law vs. Anglo-Saxon law
- **Wegner: Prolog vs. Lisp;**
  Algol vs. Pascal;
  Dijkstra vs. Knuth;
  Proving programs vs. testing programs
- **I am a died-in-the-wool empiricist.**

SLIDE 24

during a design of an experiment. Then you must run a different set to see how it came out. Each of us, in doing a design, first programs some things ourselves in our language; these examples become the driving problems of our design. It is not a sufficient test to then see how well we can write them in our own language.

(SLIDE 24) Now from this whole notion of trial and error to a much more fundamental issue, and one that Peter Wegner has described. I saw it first in a brochure from the Brown University department, but he has now put it in a paper. He says there is a long-running tension between rationalism and empiricism in design. You can see it in Aristotle versus Galileo; in French intellectual thinking versus British, as epitomized by Descartes versus Hume; in Napoleonic law about how things ought to work versus the Anglo-Saxon law that says we won't know until we've seen some cases. Then Wegner goes on to talk about some examples of Prolog versus LISP, ALGOL versus Pascal, Dijkstra's approach to life versus Donald Knuth's, and (I threw in, gratuitously and debatably) proving programs versus testing programs. My position is very clear. I am a dyed-in-the-wool empiricist on this black/white map.

(SLIDE 25) I would assert there is no hope of getting our complex designs right the first time. The things we programmers make now are as complex as anything the human race has ever made. A major airplane is nowhere near as complex as a major operating system in terms of the number of different elements and different relationships among them. There is no hope of getting them right the first time by pure thought. To expect to do so is arrogant; a little bit of professional humility goes a long way here.

That means we have to adopt design and building processes that provide for evolutionary growth. That is, versus the classical waterfall: specify, design, build. It is also evolutionary growth in many stages versus the simplistic notion I put in *The Mythical Man-Month*: plan to build one, then throw it away and start over. Instead, we may not have to throw designs away, but we certainly have to plan to grow them bit by bit.

I remember how shocked I was the first time I ever heard a person talk about *building* a program as opposed to *writing* a program. It was a whole new idea for me. Well, it is equally shocking and equally important to think about *growing* programs as opposed to *building* programs. I think Harlan Mills first put that clearly in my mind; it is a really important idea. This means that we also have to be prepared to throw away, if necessary, and we have to iterate. If iterating means making working prototypes of some kind and testing with real users, that is less difficult in language design because we can fake the compilation with hand compiles.

(SLIDE 26) Let me say a few words about esthetics. Even invisible designs have an esthetic, and it shows in the way we talk about them. We talk about a *clean machine.* What is a clean machine? We

Rationalism vs. Empiricism

No hope of getting our complex designs right first time by pure thought.

To expect to is arrogant.

So, we must adopt design-build processes with
- evolutionary growth
  vs. waterfall specify-design-build,
  vs. "Plan to throw one away."
- iteration, and restart if necessary
- early prototyping and testing with *real users*

SLIDE 25

Esthetics in Technical Design

- Even invisible designs have an esthetic:
  - A "clean" machine
  - An "elegant" language
- Elegance: "Accomplishing many things with few elements."
- Not enough. Need *straightforwardness*, too.
  - van der Poel's one-instruction computer
  - APL one-liner, idiomatic style

SLIDE 26

have an implicit set of esthetic principles about what a clean computer is. We talk about an elegant language. What is elegance? One dictionary definition says "accomplishing many things with few elements." Ken Iverson said what they tried to do with APL was make it so that if you knew a construct and you wanted to know another construct, you could figure it out without knowing, and *"It does what you expect it to do."* This assumes that everybody would expect it to do the same thing.

Elegance is not enough. This, I think, has often been overlooked. One needs straightforwardness, too. Van der Poel built a magnificent little computer that had only one operation code. It is a marvel of ingenuity. Van der Poel's coding for it is a marvel of ingenuity. No one else has ever coded for it, as far as I can tell. Van der Poel is a great designer, and he also carves intricate little Chinese puzzles for a hobby. I am a fan of APL, but I am not a fan of the one-liner idiomatic style in which the purpose of the designer is to make the program as obscure as possible under the guise of calling it elegance, or to see what can be done by idiomatic, that is, weird, uses of operators for purposes that were far from their original intention and definition. This means we have counter-balancing forces between elegance and straightforwardness in a language design.

(SLIDE 27) Here are a few principles that certainly apply to machine languages. The consistency principle can be elaborated into *orthogonality, propriety* (that is, make sure you don't have anything there that doesn't belong), and *generality* (making sure you don't leave out anything that does belong). Leave plenty of room to put more function in as evolution occurs. And if you notice a certain tension between those—yes, any such design is a tight-rope act between countervailing forces. The skill of the designer is a balancing skill, a judgment skill. It is not a mathematical evaluation skill of measures of propriety and of generality.

Now I will assert but not debate today, for lack of time, the thesis that "Good esthetics yields good economics," even in computer language design, where economics is severe. This has to do with an argument that one wants to minimize long-run overall cost, and that the cost of what you save by doing things dirtily will be more than paid for by instruction and maintenance over the lifetime of the artifact, if your artifact has any lifetime.

(SLIDE 28) Some years ago I wrote down a little thought experiment, and I set a different criterion from one you usually assess with. And that is, what languages or software entities have fan clubs? By *fan clubs*, I mean fanatics, people who think the language is really great. Well, here is my list: FORTRAN, Pascal, C, IBM VM System, Unix, Macintosh, and APL. What are successful, widely used, effective, valuable contributing products that I never saw any sign of a fan club for? COBOL, ALGOL, PL/1, OS/360 and today's descendant MVS/360, DEC's VMS, and PC DOS. What is the difference? I think the difference is that the things on the left were originally designed to satisfy a

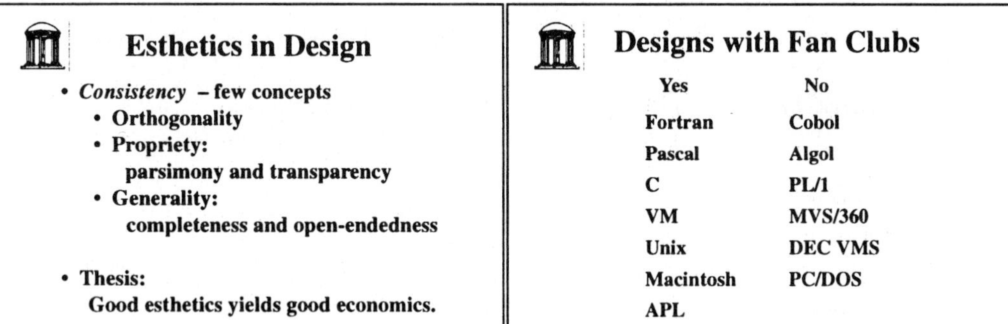

SLIDE 27

SLIDE 28

designer or a very small group of designers. And the things on the right were designed to satisfy a large set of requirements.

(SLIDE 29) Great designs come from great designers, not from great processes. The issue is conceptual integrity of the design. A solo design is much likelier to have conceptual integrity than committee design. If we go back and look at that list, the ones on the left were done outside of product processes. All the ones on the right were done inside of product processes. What does that tell us about software product processes? They produce serviceable things but not great things.

I was on a review team with another reviewer who was a Marine general (retired) who spent his entire life building military aircraft. We were reviewing the design for the LHX helicopter. The colonel who was briefing us went through how the LHX would jump up and sail over the woods in the dark rainy night, and pop up, and shoot, and jump back down. Then without batting an eyelash, he said, "It has to ferry itself across the Atlantic." No one who had ever designed anything could be insensitive to the damage that putting that requirement on is going to do to all the operational characteristics. This ferrying is a one-in-a-plane's-lifetime task. Twice, if you are lucky.

"Why does it have to do that?"

"Oh, there are not enough C5's to carry them."

"Why don't you take some of the money from the LHX budget and buy some more C5's ?"

"We can't do that."

But the problem was that this was a unified set of requirements laid on by a committee from various services. The committee included, when the smoke cleared, military bureaucrats and civilian bureaucrats, but neither helicopter pilots nor aircraft engineers. Have you ever heard such a story before, closer to home?

This raises three important issues that we have to face:

- What are product procedures for? I think they are for making follow-on products.
- How does one do great designs within a product process? That's hard.
- How does one make a product process that encourages rather than inhibits great designs?

(SLIDE 30) Well, where do great designers come from? We have to grow them deliberately, and that means we recruit them for design brilliance and not just meeting skills. One of the very best language designers I have ever known was totally incapable of holding his own in any meeting. We

SLIDE 29

SLIDE 30

have to make the dual ladder real and honorable. We have to plan their careers and the rotation of training experiences just as we do for managers. We have to furnish them with design mentors. We have to manage them imaginatively. Two great case histories I commend to you are those of Steinmetz, who invented alternating current theory as applied to iron, and John Cocke, inventor of pipelining and RISC. We have to protect them fiercely, from both managers and management.

FROM HOPL TO HOPL-II (1978–1993): 15 Years of Programming Language Development

Jean E. Sammet

JEAN E. SAMMET: The Program Committee felt that it might be of some interest to you to get two pieces of information. One was some perception of what has happened in the programming language area in the last fifteen years, and then a little bit of introduction to making history, particularly for those of you who were not at the Forum yesterday.

(SLIDE 1) I am about to give you Sammet's insight into what has happened in the last 15 years of programming language development. As I am sure all of you recognize, that is a major undertaking and each one of you might choose to do it completely differently than I did, but I have control of the microphone so you are out of luck!

(SLIDE 2) In 1978, according to the data that I had—and some of you may recall that for about ten years I tried to publish what I called the Roster of Programming Languages to keep track of what was available and in use in the United States. The only reason for restricting it to the United States was that I had enough trouble trying to get my hands on that data without worrying about what was in Europe as well. You see the numbers that are in Slide 2. Please note, in particular, the languages for specialized application areas, which I will say more about later because they represent a little over half of them, and that has been a fairly consistent pattern even though many of my computer science and programming language guru friends don't like these, don't care about them, and don't think they belong. I do.

(SLIDE 3) The HOPL criteria for the selection of invited languages are shown here. The criteria were simply that they were ten years old, still in use, and had a major impact.

(SLIDE 4) Just for the sake of the record, I am showing the 13 languages that were considered to meet those three criteria in 1978. Of these, I think it is fair to say (and certainly quite accurate) that both ALGOL and JOSS are relatively dead by now. JOVIAL is maybe not quite dead but certainly

"From HOPL to HOPL-II: (1978–1993)

15 Years of Programming Language Development"

Jean E. Sammet

Programming Language Consultant

(Program Chair, ACM SIGPLAN HOPL-II)

SLIDE 1

WHERE WE WERE IN PROGRAMMING LANGUAGES IN 1978

Approximately 170 languages used in US

Numerical scientific	**20**
Business data processing	**4**
String & list processing	**11**
Formula manipulation	**10**
Multipurpose	**34**
Specialized application	**90**

SLIDE 2

dormant, having been essentially replaced in the military area by Ada. SIMULA 67 has essentially been overtaken by Smalltalk and some of its derivatives.

(SLIDE 5) Here is a personal view of what I consider major languages *in 1978*. The criteria I used for major was either use, or lots of publications, or lots of implementations, or any combinations thereof. I think the only one that you might question would be APT and that turns out to be one of the major specialized application area languages implemented on almost all computers.

(SLIDE 6) Here is a list of some more languages and again this is simply an arbitrary decision on my part. These are just some things that I thought would be interesting and of value to put on the foil.

(SLIDE 7) This shows a few of the ninety specialized languages. These are for application areas that are sort of outside of the normal computer science-oriented mainstream. For those of you who are not familiar with these, let me point out that ATLAS is for writing programs to test equipment. COGO is for civil engineers, particularly doing surveying. COURSEWRITER is a CAI type language. GPSS and SIMSCRIPT are simulation languages. Pilot is another CAI language. SCEPTRE is for electrical design.

(SLIDE 8) This is perhaps the most interesting. Please realize that 15 years ago, these languages were on the horizon. They essentially didn't exist. Ada was still (in at least early 1978) being called DoD-1, but certainly was in the phase of competitive design. At that stage, Smalltalk 80 was obviously not in existence.

PROGRAMMING LANGUAGES in 1978

HOPL Criteria

- **over 10 years old**
- **still in use**
- **major impact**

SLIDE 3

PROGRAMMING LANGUAGES in 1978

HOPL Languages

ALGOL	**JOSS**
APT	**JOVIAL**
APL	**LISP**
BASIC	**SIMULA 67**
COBOL	**PL/I**
FORTRAN	**SNOBOL**
GPSS	

SLIDE 4

PROGRAMMING LANGUAGES in 1978

Major Languages
(based on use and/or publications and/or many implementations)

APT	FORTRAN
BASIC	LISP 1.5
COBOL	

SLIDE 5

PROGRAMMING LANGUAGES in 1978

Some Other Languages

ALGOL 60	MACSYMA
APL	MAD
ALGOL 68	MADCAP
C	MUMPS
FORMAC	Pascal
FORTH	PL/I
JOVIAL	Simula 67
JOSS	SNOBOL4

SLIDE 6

(SLIDE 9) I am a great believer in standards and the importance thereof. So note that in 1978, we had standards for the languages listed. Note that APT and ATLAS, which were two of the specialized application areas, had standards, and in fact APT had two standards.

(SLIDE 10) There were some other things going on besides languages *per se*. Among the buzz words and the related topics at that point were structured programming, software engineering, and systems programming languages, because people were still very worried about whether you could really write systems programs effectively in high level languages.

(SLIDE 11) In the 1980s, in my opinion, there were only two significant pure language developments. I am not talking about peripheral concepts and peripheral ideas. But in the 1980s, there were the standardization, implementation, and use of Ada (which did not even exist in 1978), and the significant use of C for systems programming and its beginning use for other areas.

(SLIDE 12) But, there were other things going on in the programming language field in the 1980s. This involved an emphasis in areas other than pure language development. These are the ones that I put on the chart. *Language bindings* is the attempt to develop some frameworks and subroutines in topics that are of importance in and across many languages; graphics is the prime example with GKS. Then later, is the database SEQUEL stuff. *Fourth generation languages* is a term I hate and despise, but I felt to be fair and complete I ought to put it on there. The *application packages*—as distinguished

PROGRAMMING LANGUAGES in 1978

Some Specialized Languages

ATLAS	PILOT
COGO	SCEPTRE
COURSEWRITER	SIMSCRIPT I.5
GPSS	SIMSCRIPT II.5

SLIDE 7

PROGRAMMING LANGUAGES in 1978

On the Horizon

Ada
Prolog
Smalltalk-80

SLIDE 8

PROGRAMMING LANGUAGES in 1978

Existing ANSI Standards

APT	(1974, 1977)
ATLAS	(1978)
BASIC (Minimal)	(1978)
COBOL	(1968, 1974)
FORTRAN	(1966, 1978)
MUMPS	(1977)
PL/I	(1976)

SLIDE 9

PROGRAMMING LANGUAGES in 1978

Some related issues or topics

structured programming
software engineering
systems programming languages

SLIDE 10

from languages—and here, as much as I regret to, I must disagree slightly with the eminent Fred Brooks—I don't consider spreadsheets a language. But that is a debate for another time. The *functional languages*, starting with the FP work of John Backus, was starting. And of course, the *object-oriented programming* and *object-oriented languages* were coming into fruition in that time period.

(SLIDE 13) In 1993, as best as I can estimate, there were approximately 1000 languages that had been implemented since the beginning of the computer field, and probably 400 to 500 that had been dreamed about and even had lots of publications but which were never implemented. There are a couple of famous languages that had so many papers published that I kept trying to find out what machines these were implemented on. Finally, I got some shame-faced responses from the developers who were busy publishing all these papers, that they had never been implemented. I would estimate there are not more than about 300 in use today. I really don't have any data to back that up—it is just an estimate. And you will see most of this list tonight at the Computer Museum as part of the exhibit.

(SLIDE 14a) It turns out that in the past fifteen years we have lost a number of people who were prominent in the computer field and who died in that time period. The Program Committee felt it was appropriate to point these out and to acknowledge them for the sake of the record. They are all alphabetically listed on the next four slides, except for Grace Hopper, who obviously belongs at the top of any such list.

PROGRAMMING LANGUAGES in the 1980s

[Only major language developments]

Ada	standardization implementation use
C	significant use for systems programming

SLIDE 11

PROGRAMMING LANGUAGES in the 1980s

Emphasis in areas other than pure language development

Language bindings (e.g., graphics)
"Fourth generation"
Application packages
Functional languages
Object-oriented programming and languages

SLIDE 12

WHERE WE ARE in PROGRAMMING LANGUAGES in 1993

Approximately 1000 languages implemented since beginning of computer field

(estimate 700 are dead in 1993)

SLIDE 13

"PROGRAMMING LANGUAGE PEOPLE" WHO HAVE DIED SINCE 1978 [1 of 4]

- **Grace Hopper**
  (first compiler)
  (leader of FLOW-MATIC, MATH-MATIC)
  (persuaded early managers of the value of programming languages)
- **Saul Gorn**
  (theoretician)
  (computer science education pioneer)
- **John Kemeny**
  (co-developer of BASIC)

SLIDE 14a

Special Note: A few of the people listed in these slides were added after the conference because their death was unknown to me at that time, and the appropriate remarks have been inserted into this text. The speaker and editor felt it was better to do this than to omit them, even though the latter would have maintained strict accuracy with the original presentation.

Among Grace Hopper's credits are the first compiler, the leader of the FLOW-MATIC and MATH-MATIC developments, and a major role she played (which is almost forgotten by now) in persuading the early managers to acknowledge the value of programming languages. For those of you who have not read the appropriate documents and wonder about the absence of COBOL there, I regret to inform you that Grace was not a developer or co-developer of COBOL. If you want to see what the facts are, go back to the COBOL paper I put into the first HOPL Conference, or in fact, look at the much briefer description that was in the biography of Grace that I published in the *ACM Communications* last year.

Saul Gorn was a theoretician and one of the early pioneers in computer science education. John Kemeny was the co-developer of BASIC along with Tom Kurtz. BASIC was one of the languages in the first HOPL conference.

(SLIDE 14b) Barry Mailloux was one of the co-developers and co-editors of the ALGOL 68 report. Al Newell was best known for artificial intelligence work but also as the co-developer of the list concept. From a language point of view, he was the co-developer of IPL-V and the earlier versions of the IPLs. Roy Nutt, while working for United Technologies (or some similar name but not IBM), helped implement the first FORTRAN.

(SLIDE 14c) Al Perlis was a speaker at the first HOPL Conference. He was the primary developer of IT, which was an early language on the 650. He was on the ALGOL 58 and ALGOL 60 committees and another computer science education pioneer. Klaus Samelson from Germany was on the ALGOL 58 and ALGOL 60 committees, and made major contributions to early compiler scanning techniques. J. Cliff Shaw (who is different from C. J. Shaw) was the developer of JOSS, which was one of the languages in the first HOPL conference, although Cliff Shaw did not develop the paper personally; he declined to do so and we had somebody else who had worked on JOSS write the paper. Shaw was a co-developer (with Al Newell and Herb Simon) of the list concept and a co-developer of the IPL languages.

(SLIDE 14d) Peter Sheridan, who was at IBM, helped implement the first FORTRAN. Aad van Wijngaarden was the lead developer of ALGOL 68, the lead editor of the ALGOL 68 reports, and the

"PROGRAMMING LANGUAGE PEOPLE" WHO HAVE DIED SINCE 1978 [2 of 4]

- **Barry Mailloux**
  (co-developer of ALGOL 68)
  (co-editor of ALGOL 68 Report)
- **Alan Newell**
  (co-developer of IPL-V)
  (co-developer of list concept)
  (artificial intelligence)
- **Roy Nutt**
  (helped implement 1st FORTRAN)

SLIDE 14b

"PROGRAMMING LANGUAGE PEOPLE" WHO HAVE DIED SINCE 1978 [3 of 4]

- **Alan Perlis**
  (co-developer of IT)
  (on ALGOL 58 and 60 committees)
  (computer science education pioneer)
- **Klaus Samelson**
  (on ALGOL 58 and 60 committees)
  (co-developer of scanning technique)
- **J. Cliff Shaw**
  (developer of JOSS)
  (co-developer of the list concept)
  (co-developer of IPL languages)

SLIDE 14c

developer of a complex metalanguage used to define ALGOL 68. He was also one of the major figures in Dutch and European computing.

Now, even though fortunately they are not deceased, I want to acknowledge two people who in this time period received significant honors—namely Nobel prizes! Herb Simon, who is primarily in the artificial intelligence area but is also involved in the list concept and IPL-V, and Howard Markowitz, who was involved in the early SIMSCRIPT, both received Nobel Prizes in economics. And I must tell you that when I heard about the Nobel Prize for Herb Simon, I thought, "interesting—another person with the same name as *our* Herb Simon." Then later, I heard mention of Professor Herb Simon of Carnegie Mellon; I thought, "isn't that amazing, two people with the same name at the same university." Finally, I saw a TV picture and I finally got the message! Those are two of our shining stars who had some involvement with languages, albeit there are no Nobel Prizes for languages.

(SLIDE 15) This list shows what, in my opinion, are the major languages in 1993. You are entitled to dispute this, but that is my judgement using the same criteria as for the 1978 list—either major use and/or lots of publications and/or lots of implementations.

(SLIDE 16) This bears some resemblance to Fred Brooks' comments about "fan clubs." The APL, FORTH, and MUMPS languages, in my opinion, have significant "fan clubs" or "cults." Some of the

"PROGRAMMING LANGUAGE PEOPLE" WHO HAVE DIED SINCE 1978 [4 of 4]

- **Peter Sheridan**
  (helped implement 1st FORTRAN)
- **Aad van Wijngaarden**
  (lead developer of ALGOL 68)
  (lead editor of ALGOL 68 Report)
  (developer of complex metalanguage)

SLIDE 14d

PROGRAMMING LANGUAGES in 1993

Major Languages
(based on use and/or publications and/or many implementations)

Ada	Common LISP
APT	FORTRAN
C	Pascal
C++	Prolog
COBOL	Smalltalk

SLIDE 15

SLIDE 16

SLIDE 17

other programming languages that I think are of some significance that are in use today are the ones I have listed there.

(SLIDE 17) Back to the specialized application languages. And in case you haven't gotten the message yet, that is an area that I happen to be very strongly interested in personally, even though I know many of the computer science and many of the computer language people are not. I think these are under-played, under-appreciated, misunderstood and so forth. I listed half a dozen of them that are in use today in the areas that I have indicated.

(SLIDE 18) Standards: These are brand new, relative to 1978. These are languages which were not standardized in any way whatsoever in 1978 and do have standards in 1993. C-ATLAS is some version of ATLAS, which is the testing language. CHILL is a European language, a very large, powerful language in the genre of ALGOL 68 or PL/I or Ada. DIBOL is some kind of a business data processing language; it doesn't look like very much. PANCM has been standardized. PILOT is a CAI language. And SCHEME is an offshoot or dialect with regard to LISP.

(SLIDE 19) This shows the standards that have been revised relative to 1978. In other words, those seven languages all had standards in 1978 and there are now newer versions of those standards.

(SLIDE 20) What is going on today? Here is my personal view of what seems to be happening today. Certainly, object-oriented programming as a separate intellectual discipline; that is, somewhat separate from the languages *per se*, is a major area of interest and concern in the programming

SLIDE 18

SLIDE 19

SLIDE 20

SLIDE 21

community in general, and as this is often manifested by programming languages, it tends to be very relevant. User interface—again, that is not a major language issue, but certainly an important issue for the people who are using the computers. Software engineering is always with us, and certainly that is a major area. Parallelism—Fred Brooks also made an allusion to that this morning, and it is certainly an area of importance; people are concerned with languages that enable you to exploit parallelism of computers and also with parallelism as a general topic. Finally, functional programming is a new way of looking at programming languages.

(SLIDE 21) HOPL XXX, as one of my colleagues on the Program Committee said, "I don't know when it will be but I know I won't be on the Program Committee." We don't know when 20XX will be. I certainly hope it is less than 15 years and I would be very happy if there were another HOPL in 1998, or something of that kind. I don't know what the number of languages will be. I think it will not increase that much. As best as I can tell from the data I have and the examinations I've made, the number of new languages is certainly increasing at a very much smaller slope. I think to a large extent that the curve has pretty much leveled off; there are not as many new ones coming along. Most of the new ones that come along are not really justified, just as most of the thousands that existed are not justified. Some of the reasons you saw on Fred's chart, and it is interesting because we had no collaboration on any of this. You will see tonight a series of panels at the Computer Museum—something I insisted on—which attempts to list some of the reasons that there are so many programming languages and certainly the fact that it is fun is one of them. There are going to be some major other specialized languages, but I don't know what they are going to be because I think there the increase is moving somewhat faster. I don't know what the standards will be, but certainly the standards committees continue on forever, and I think they serve a very useful purpose. I don't want any remark I made to be misinterpreted against standards; I am very much in favor of the standards. Finally, I don't know what the general or major issues in programming languages will be. This talk is a look backwards not a look forwards.

INTRODUCTION OF MICHAEL S. MAHONEY

SESSION CHAIR, JEAN E. SAMMET: Michael Mahoney is a Professor of History at Princeton University and a member of its Program in the History of Science. According to him, he met his first computer, which was a Datatron 204, as a part time programmer for Melpar Electronics while he was a senior at Harvard in 1959 to 1960. He was apparently unimpressed. So after graduation he turned to the History of Science and Medieval Science—first at the University of Munich and then at Princeton, where he earned his Ph.D. in 1967. I can't help interspersing this more formal biography with the fact that frequently over the past couple of years when I had occasion to either call him on the phone or communicate with him by e-mail he told me he was worrying about his course in Medieval History or leading a tour for some group looking at history that goes back a thousand years. I keep thinking this must be two people, but it isn't; it is really all one person.

After Mike Mahoney got his Ph.D., he spent a decade or so teaching and doing research in the history of science and mathematics in the early modern era, which included writing a book on the mathematician Pierre Fermat. At this point he looked again to see what computers had been doing. Apparently he found that they had acquired a history. After writing several exploratory articles, including one in the *Annals of the History of Computing* entitled "The History of Computing in the History of Technology," he is now nearing completion of a book tentatively entitled *The Structures of Computation: Mathematics and Theoretical Computer Science, 1950–1970*. Heaven forbid we should bring that any closer to today than 1970; that is *my* comment, *not* his. After he finishes that, he plans to return to the project that started him on much of this—namely, the origins and early development of software engineering. He has served as the HOPL-II historian, for which I am eternally grateful, is a member of the HOPL-II Program Committee, and a member of the Forum Committee.

MAKING HISTORY

MICHAEL S. MAHONEY: What we are doing here this morning is making history. We are making history in what would seem an obvious way. That is, we are here over the next few days to hear from the people who have made history through their creative work. We are here to hear how they did it. But we are also making history ourselves by being here. We are here in essence doing what the software development people call "validation and verification."

We are here to help the authors to make sure that we have the history right, and more importantly, to think about whether we have the right history. That is the function of questions, comments, and conversations, the interactive activities that make it seem worthwhile for all of us in fact to get together here in one place and sit down and talk with one another, instead of just reading the papers in their published form. We think about Gwen Bell's remark about establishing the history that people like the producers of "The Machines That Changed the World" will use to tell our story. In essence, what we are here for today in this conference is to establish what that story of programming languages is, the story that we think best fits our experience. That is making history, and we are all a part of it.

So what to listen for and what ought we be talking about? Let me briefly review what I said to the authors about "What Makes History?" in a piece I sent to them after the first drafts had been reviewed. I think we can help the authors and ourselves by thinking through the issues.

First of all, the obvious, are the facts right and are they in the right chronological order? We want to make sure that is the case, that is the *sine qua non*. But actually that is a subtle question. Are the facts right? But, we may also ask, are we getting the right facts? Is this the story we want to be telling? Are the facts chronologically appropriate? Are they the right facts for the time? Are there other facts that we ought to be thinking about? What we want to aim for is to meet Dick Hamming's charge, made at the pioneer's historical conference back in 1976 in the title of his keynote talk: "We Would Know What They Thought When They Did It." By which he meant, to get through the explicit documentation and back to the undocumented practice to recreate the frame of mind and the body of practice at another time. Fred Brooks talks about great design as reflecting craft experience, experience of the craft is necessary to understand design at any time.

It is necessary, then, for us to be sure that we know what the experience of the craft was at that time. It is a tricky problem. It is not a problem of memory alone. It is not only that our memories fail. Indeed, as Alan Kay reminds us in the second of the leitmotifs for his paper on Smalltalk, quoting Thomas Hobbes, "Part of the problem is that we remember the past by reconstructing it," that memory and imagination tend to mix. I think the artificial intelligence people actually have something to say about the way we remember things, in part by reconstruction. And there, the mind can play tricks. If you look at the published version of this, the piece that was sent around to the authors, I tell a story there. It is probably apocryphal, but then again, apocryphal stories have their purposes, too.

What it comes down to is the following: once you know the answer to a question, it is very hard to imagine what it was like not to know it, to recreate the frame of mind you were in before you knew what the answer was, or indeed, before you were sure what the question was. Because in the act of answering, the problem gets reshaped. Having an answer, in many ways, makes clear what questions one should have been asking. And here comes the reconstruction. What question was I answering? Why, the obvious question. Maybe it is obvious, maybe it is not. Fred Brooks said the hardest thing in the world is knowing what to design. I submit that quite often we find out what we are designing in the process of designing. And when we are finished it is hard for us to imagine that we were ever looking for anything else. Indeed, it is important, as he points out, to know sometimes that you are just wrong. But even that is not clear; we usually start out with confusion.

That leads to an interesting paradox of pioneers—people who were there—because the very act of creativity makes it harder to recreate the circumstances that the people involved should be best able to tell us about. That is, they are on the one hand our best witnesses and, in another very real sense, our worst, simply because of the way the mind plays tricks.

Here is where others less directly involved can help out. If they are less directly involved in the creative act but were around at the time, informed about the time, they can help by recalling what the problem was. Maybe for some people it is still a problem. They don't have the enlightenment of the answer.

This is tied up with the problem of language, which is a matter that historians are very conscious of. This is what I mean about getting the right facts. Fred Brooks reminded us of something we do know, but it was important to bring it out. Language enables us to think about certain things in certain ways. There is a corollary to that. Before we had that language, we were not thinking that way. Now, quite often one sees people, scientists and engineers who make history, talk about work they were doing, or they will look back and say, "So and so was really doing X," where X is some modern concept. In many ways, to use modern terms that way is simply to make our problem, the problem I have just been describing, opaque. It does not clarify things to say, "What he was really doing was . . ." "Now this is really object-oriented programming thirty years ago," because the emergence of that concept out of the earlier concepts is what we are interested in. That is, ideas grow roughly as trees do; Fred talked about the decision tree. It is important to get back to the root but not identify the root with the branch. Because the branch may actually have emerged in quite different ways than that assumption, that single backtrack, might reveal. Again, here, I think we can help. We can say, "Wait a second. We weren't talking that way back then. We didn't call it that. We called it something else. Now that we use that other language, maybe we are not quite sure what *it* is."

A major point you want to bear in mind, and this is something historians must insist on: being right is not an explanation. Right answers require as much explanation as wrong answers because in many cases at the time there was no way of knowing that you were right. You made choices or people involved made choices. What we have to do is to recreate the choices. What were the options open? How did decisions foreclose certain options and open other options? We need to know what the reasons were for making those choices, and actually what we would like to know is what the standards were at the time for being judged to be right? What constituted a right answer by what standards?

What makes history? It is a matter of going back to the sources, of reading them in their own language and thinking one's way back to the problems and solutions as they looked then. It involves the imaginative exercise of suspending one's knowledge of how things turned out, so as to recreate the possibilities that were still open at the time. It is to imagine an alternative present.

In *The Go-Between*, Leslie Hartley remarked (and I quote), "The past is a foreign country. They do things differently there." The historian must learn to be an observant tourist alert to the differences that lie behind what seems to be familiar. Now I wrote that before I went on the trip that Jean referred to. A colleague and I took a group of Princeton alumni to Spain last October to follow Columbus across Spain. We gave lectures but we also visited various sites in Spain. Again and again we would take people to a site because Columbus had visited there, or talked to the Queen there, and in one place Queen Isabella had died. Time and time again, we would arrive at the site to have the tour guide tell us, "Well no, actually Columbus never was here. No, Queen Isabella did not die here." We discovered a whole new Columbian Spain, quite different from the one we have read about in the books.

Well, folks, we are a mixture of tourists and former residents. We are trying to recreate a land that is no more, but a land that can be deceptively familiar. That is what we are up to, and I think it is going to be a good deal of fun to see if we can do that.

ALGOL 68 Session

Chair: *Jacques Cohen*

A HISTORY OF ALGOL 68

C. H. Lindsey

5, Clerewood Avenue, Heald Green,
Cheadle, Cheshire SK8 3JU, U.K.

ABSTRACT

ALGOL 68 is a language with a lot of "history." The reader will hear of discord, resignations, unreadable documents, a minority report, and all manner of politicking. But although ALGOL 68 was produced by a committee (and an unruly one at that), the language itself is no camel. Indeed, the rigorous application of the principle of "orthogonality" makes it one of the cleanest languages around, as I hope to show. Moreover, when the language came to be revised, the atmosphere was quite different, enabling a much more robust and readable defining document to be produced in a spirit of true cooperation. There are some lessons here for future language design efforts, but I am not optimistic that they have been learned.

CONTENTS

2.1 INTRODUCTION

The world seems to have a rather negative perception of ALGOL 68. The language has been said to be "too big," to be defined by an "unreadable Report" produced by a committee which "broke up in disarray," to have no implementations, and to have no users. The only phrase that *everybody* can quote from the Report is the one that says, "It is recognized, however, that this method may be difficult for the uninitiated reader" [R 0.1.1]. While these stories do have some basis in fact, which it will be the purpose of this paper to explore, they are at the least a considerable oversimplification of what really took place. In fact most of the people who pass on these things have never read the Report, or tried to use the language, and the observed fact is that those who have used the language have become totally addicted to it.

I should point out that my own involvement with the project came after the basic design of the language, and of its original Report, were complete. I was an onlooker at the fracas, as confused as any outsider as to what was going on. It is only now, in the course of studying the minutes and other documents from that time, that I have come to see what the real fuss was about, and I hope that all this has enabled me to take a dispassionate view of the events. The reader of this paper will certainly see discord, but I believe he will see also how good design can win through in the end.

ALGOL 68 clearly grew out of ALGOL 60, but many other language developments were taking place at that time—Lisp, COBOL, PL/1, Simula—all of them aimed at wider markets than the numerical computations for which ALGOL 60 was so well suited. The territory into which ALGOL 68 was now pushing was largely unmapped. Individual research languages had probed far ahead; ALGOL 68 was to advance into this landscape on a broad front. We indeed discovered what was there, but it seems to have been left to other, later languages to complete the colonization.

2.1.1 The Political Background

ALGOL 60 [Naur *et al.* 1960] was produced by a group of persons, half nominated by ACM and half by various European institutions. Apart from that initial sponsorship, the group had no official standing or authority. Meanwhile, the International Federation for Information Processing (IFIP, founded in 1960), through the auspices of its Technical Committee 2 on Programming Languages (TC2), had founded a Working Group on ALGOL (WG 2.1). At their meeting in Rome in April of 1962, upon completion of the Revised ALGOL 60 Report, the authors

> accepted that any collective responsibility which they might have with respect to the development, specification and refinement of the ALGOL language will from now on be transferred [to WG 2.1].

Thus, it will be seen that IFIP is a hierarchical organization with a General Assembly and a Council, a layer of Technical Committees, and a layer of Working Groups below that. There is a procedure for promulgating an "IFIP Document," the product of some Working Group, with some variant of the following wording:

> This Report has been accepted by Working Group 2.1, reviewed by Technical Committee 2 on Programming Languages and approved for publication by the General Assembly of the International Federation for Information Processing. Reproduction of the Report, for any purpose, but only of the whole text, is explicitly permitted without formality.

Over the last thirty years, some eight IFIP Documents have been produced by WG 2.1 under this procedure, as shown in Table 2.1.

IFIP does not have any significant funds at its disposal. The costs of bringing members together at a Working Group meeting falls on those members' employers or funding agencies, and on the organization hosting the meeting. If it were possible to add up the total cost of bringing ALGOL 68 before the world, it would come to a tidy sum. Whether the world has now the benefit of this investment is an interesting question.

TABLE 2.1

IFIP Documents produced by WG 2.1.

Revised report on the algorithmic language ALGOL 60	Naur *et al.* 1962]
Report on SUBSET ALGOL 60 (IFIP)	[WG 2.1 1964a]
Report on input-output procedures for ALGOL 60	[WG 2.1 1964b]
Report on the algorithmic language ALGOL 68	[Van Wijngaarden 1969]
Revised report on the algorithmic language ALGOL 68	[Van Wijngaarden 1975]
A supplement to the ALGOL 60 revised report	[De Morgan 1976]
A sublanguage of ALGOL 68	[Hibbard 1977]
The report on the standard hardware representation for ALGOL 68	[Hansen 1977]

2.1.2 Historical Outline

As will be seen from Table 2.1, The early years of WG 2.1 were spent in various activities arising out of ALGOL 60. But even as early as March 1964 there was mention of a language, ALGOL X, to be a "short-term solution to existing difficulties," and a "radically reconstructed" ALGOL Y [Duncan 1964].

Table 2.2 shows the milestones in the life of ALGOL 68, which can be divided into three phases.

- 1965 through 1969, culminating, in spite of much dissention, in the original Report [Van Wijngaarden 1969].
- 1970 through 1974, leading to the Revised Report [Van Wijngaarden 1975].
- 1975 onwards—the maintenance phase, resulting in various supplementary documents.

The milestones themselves are most conveniently remembered by the names of the meeting places at which the events took place.

2.1.3 Some Conventions

ALGOL 68 and the documentation that surrounds it adopt by convention various usages that I shall follow in this paper. In particular, I shall refer to [Van Wijngaarden 1969] as [R], often followed by a section number, and to [Van Wijngaarden 1975] as [RR]. Also, the long series of draft Reports leading up to [R] will be known by the numbers given them by the Mathematisch Centrum, of the form [MR*nn*]. References of the form (*n.m*) are to sections within this paper.

[R] is noted for its number of arcane technical terms used with a very precise meaning. Some were introduced purely to facilitate the syntax and semantics, but others denote concepts of definite interest to the user, and of these many are now in common parlance (for example, 'dereference', 'coercion', 'elaborate', 'defining/applied occurrence', 'environment enquiry'). Often, however, the authors chose terms for existing (or only marginally altered) concepts that have failed to come into common usage, such as the following:

mode	instead of	type
multiple value	" "	array
name	" "	variable
scope	" "	extent (a dynamic concept)

reach	"	"	scope (a static concept)
routine	"	"	procedure
range	"	"	**block**
identity-declaration		"	**constant-declaration**

To avoid confusion, I shall be using the terms in the right hand column in the rest of this paper.

TABLE 2.2

Summary of the main events in the history of ALGOL 68.

The ORIGINAL REPORT

Date	Meeting Place	Document	Events
May 1965	Princeton		Start of ALGOL X. Draft proposals for a full language solicited.
Oct 1965	St. Pierre de Chartreuse	[MR 76]	Drafts presented by Wirth/Hoare, Seegmüller and Van Wijngaarden. Commission given to these four to produce an agreed draft.
Apr 1966	Kootwijk		Meeting of the commissioned authors.
Oct 1966	Warsaw	[W-2]	Van Wijngaarden commissioned to produce and circulate a draft ALGOL X Report.
May 1967	Zandvoort	[MR 88]	Progress meeting.
Feb 1968		[MR 93]	Draft Report [MR 93] circulated as a supplement to the ALGOL Bulletin.
Jun 1968	Tirrenia		Intense discussion of [MR 93].
Aug 1968	North Berwick	[MR 95]	A week of political wrangling.
Dec 1968	Munich	[MR 100]	ALGOL 68 Report accepted by WG 2.1.3
Sep 1969	Banff	[MR 101]	Final cleanup before publication.

The REVISED REPORT

Date	Meeting Place	Events
Jul 1970	Habay-la-Neuve	Discussion of "Improvements." Subcommittee on "Data processing."
Apr 1971	Manchester	Subcommittee on "Maintenance and Improvements to ALGOL 68".
Aug 1971	Novosibirsk	Decision to produce a Revised Report by the end of 1973.
Apr 1972	Fontainebleau	Editors for the Revised Report appointed.
Sep 1972	Vienna	Progress meeting. Hibbard's Sublanguage proposal.
Apr 1973	Dresden	Progress meeting.
Sep 1973	Los Angeles	Revised Report accepted, subject to "polishing". Subcommittee on ALGOL 68 Support.
Apr 1974	Cambridge	Meeting of Support Subcommittee to discuss transput.

See Table 2.5 (Section 2.6) for events after 1974 (the Maintenance Phase).

[R] is writing about language, and this always causes problems when one needs to distinguish clearly between a word and the thing it denotes. Distinguish, for example, between the following: "*John* has four daughters", "*John* has four letters", "*John* is in italic." In these the word "*John*" stands for, respectively, the object denoted by the word, the syntactic structure of the word, and the appearance of the word.

To ease this sort of problem, it has long been traditional to print fragments of program text in italic, but [R] goes further by introducing a special font for constructs produced by the grammar (*foo* is an **identifier**). Moreover, when talking about the grammar symbols themselves (or fragments thereof) single quotes are used as well (the mode of the **identifier** *foo* is '**integral**'). To express the text of an ALGOL 68 program, two alphabets are necessary, and in the days when computers did not support two cases of characters a variety of 'stropping' conventions (this term comes from [Baecker 1968]) were used (for example, *'REAL' X* or *.REAL X*, or *REAL x* once two cases did become available). However, it has always been traditional to use a bold font for the stropped words in printed documents (***real*** *x*). When preparing [RR] we took special care in choosing suitable fonts. The stropping font, although still slanted like italic, is also sans serif, and the font for constructs and grammar symbols is bold roman (as opposed to the insufficiently distinctive sans serif used in [R]).

I follow the same conventions in this paper, but I also adopt a practice not used in the Report, which is to use a type (usually written as a stropped word) to indicate some value of that type (*foo* is an ***int***). Thus I will talk about ***string***s and ***struct***s and ***proc***s, and by analogy, about ***array***s, even though the word "***array***" is not an official part of the language. And I take the liberty of applying these conventions to other languages where appropriate. Finally, to avoid confusion with an ever changing language, the examples in this paper are generally written using the syntactic sugar of the final language, even when discussing features of earlier versions.

2.1.4 Layout of the Rest of This Paper

- 2.2 The history of the original Report, up to 1969. This is the period during which all the controversies arose.
- 2.3 The concepts of ALGOL 68. This traces the sources of the various ideas, including some that fell by the wayside, and a few that only appeared in the revision.
- 2.4 The history of the Revised Report, from 1970 to 1975.
- 2.5 The method of description. This changed substantially during the revision, which is why it is considered here.
- 2.6 The maintenance phase: enhancements and problems.
- 2.7 Implementations.
- 2.8 Conclusions, including "Whatever happened to ALGOL 68?" and "Whatever have we learned from ALGOL 68?"

I have included in this paper those incidents in the history of ALGOL 68 that I considered to be significant. Space did not permit me to tell all the stories that could have been told; for a different subset and an alternative perspective, especially of the early days, the reader is referred to [Van der Poel 1986].

2.2 HISTORY OF THE ORIGINAL ALGOL 68 REPORT

2.2.1 Dramatis Personae

Table 2.3 lists those members of WG 2.1 who were active in the development, in the order in which they became full members of the Group.

Most members of the Group were there on account of their involvement with, or experience of, ALGOL 60. Those belonging to academic institutions would have teaching duties and research interests not necessarily connected directly with ALGOL 68. Only the team at Amsterdam (Van Wijngaarden, Mailloux, Peck, and Koster) together with Goos, who was preparing an implementation, worked full-time on the project. McCarthy had been responsible for LISP, regarded as a tool for his work on artificial intelligence; Wirth, after initially working on ALGOL X, devoted his energy to his own ALGOL W; Ross was working on his own languages, AED-0 and AED-1; and Yoneda was working on the Japanese ALGOL N.

The nonacademics were subject to the bidding of their employers, although those in large research establishments would have much opportunity to do their own thing. Thus Woodger and Duncan at NPL and Sintzoff at MBLE could devote their time to programming language research. Randell had been responsible for a major ALGOL 60 implementation at English Electric, but at IBM he was into system architecture; and Hoare had implemented ALGOL 60 for Elliot and was now trying to provide operating systems to match; Bekic was part of the group that developed the Vienna Definition Language.

2.2.2 Princeton (May 1965)

The first public mention of ALGOL X (which eventually became ALGOL 68) and of the mythical ALGOL Y (originally conceived as a language that could manipulate its own programs, but in fact degenerating into a collection of features rejected for ALGOL X) was in a paper entitled "Cleaning up ALGOL 60" [Duncan 1964]. Although it had been discussed at Tutzing (March 1964) and Baden (September 1964), work started in earnest at the Princeton meeting in May 1965.

The chairman's Activity Report to TC2 for that meeting [Van der Poel 1965] shows a wide ranging discussion on basic aspects of the language. There was much interest in the language EULER [Wirth 1966a] and particularly in its 'trees' or 'lists'. There was a strong feeling towards what now we should call 'strong typing', and even a firm decision to have coercion from integer to real to complex. Draft proposals for a full language were solicited for the next meeting.

2.2.3 St. Pierre de Chartreuse (October 1965)

There were three drafts on the table: [Wirth 1965], [Seegmüller 1965b], and [MR 76], which was Aad van Wijngaarden's famous "Orthogonal design and description of a formal language."

[Wirth 1965] had been written while the author was on sabbatical at the Mathematisch Centrum over the summer, and was available sufficiently in advance of the meeting that a substantial set of comments on it was also available. It was a straightforward compilation of features as discussed at Princeton, including the trees from EULER. In the meantime, however, Record Handling [Hoare 1965b] had been proposed and Wirth much preferred this to his trees. Henceforth, the Wirth/Hoare proposal must be regarded as one.

[Seegmüller 1965b] was really an extension of [Wirth 1965] and never a serious contender. Its main feature was a system of References, also described in [Seegmüller 1965a] (see also Section 2.3.4).

TABLE 2.3

WG 2.1 members active in the original design of ALGOL 68.

Fritz Bauer	Techn. Hochschule, Munich
Edsger Dijkstra†	Tech. University, Eindhoven
Fraser Duncan†	National Physical Lab., UK
Tony Hoare†	Elliot Automation, UK
P. Z. Ingerman	RCA, Camden, NJ
John McCarthy	Stanford University, Palo Alto, CA
J. N. Merner	General Electric, Phoenix, AZ
Peter Naur‡	A/S Regnecentralen, Copenhagen
Manfred Paul	Techn. Hochschule, Munich
Willem van der Poel	Techn. Hogeschool Delft, Chairman of WG 2.1
Klaus Samelson	Techn. Hochschule, Munich
Gerhard Seegmüller†	Techn. Hochschule, Munich
Aad van Wijngaarden	Mathematisch Centrum, Amsterdam
Mike Woodger†	National Physical Lab., UK
Jan Garwick†	Oak Ridge National Lab., Oak Ridge, TN
Brian Randell†	IBM, Yorktown Heights, NY
Niklaus Wirth‡	Stanford University, Palo Alto, CA
Peter Landin	Univac, New York, NY
Hans Bekic	IBM Lab., Vienna
Doug Ross	M.I.T., Cambridge, MA
W. M. Turski†	Academy of Sciences, Warsaw, Secretary of WG 2.1
Barry Mailloux	Mathematisch Centrum, Amsterdam
John Peck	University of Calgary
Nobuo Yoneda	University of Tokyo
Gerhard Goos	Techn. Hochschule, Munich
Kees Koster	Mathematisch Centrum, Amsterdam
Charles Lindsey	University of Manchester, UK
Michel Sintzoff	MBLE, Brussels

† Signatories to the Minority Report.

‡ Resigned after [MR 93].

[MR 76], distributed only the week before the meeting, introduced three basic ideas:

1. The two-level grammar notation we now know as a W-Grammar (2.5.1.1).
2. The combination of a minimal number of language concepts in an orthogonal way (2.3.4.3), thus providing the power of the language. (This process is much facilitated by using a W-Grammar.)
3. An expression-oriented language, that is, no distinction between statements and expressions.

Apart from these, the language described by [MR 76] was nothing special, and the document itself was exceedingly hard to read (no examples, no pragmatics, and only 26 one-letter metanotions of not much mnemonic significance). Nevertheless, WG 2.1 was sufficiently impressed to resolve formally (but with misgivings from Hoare) that "whatever language is finally decided upon by WG 2.1, it will be described by Van Wijngaarden's metalinguistic techniques as specified in MR 76." Whether they had bought just the notation, or whether it included (2) and (3) as well, is not clear.

The meeting spent most of its time discussing language issues, mainly in terms of the Wirth/ Hoare proposal (which was not expression-oriented, be it noted), and by the end of the week the participants felt that they had a fair idea what ALGOL X was going to look like. Meanwhile, it had established a subcommittee consisting of Hoare, Seegmüller, Van Wijngaarden, and Wirth with instructions to prepare a Draft Report along the lines agreed upon. A second subcommittee, set up to consider I/O, consisted of Ingerman, Merner, and (in their absence) Garwick and Paul; it was charged with producing facilities somewhat between [Knuth *et al.* 1964] and [Garwick 1965].

Nevertheless, all was not plain sailing. A bad attack of cold feet occurred on the Thursday morning (a traditional time for cold feet in WG meetings), and serious suggestions were made by Naur and Randell that ALGOL X should be dropped and ALGOL Y proceeded with.

At the end of the meeting, the Subcommittee announced that Van Wijngaarden would write a draft report for the other three to consider, and that it would be circulated well in advance of the next meeting (with the proviso that members wishing to change anything would have to rewrite those parts of the report affected). The next meeting was fixed for six months hence, and it was well understood that the time for radically new concepts was already passed.

Throughout the whole project, the WG in general, and Van Wijngaarden in particular, consistently underestimated the time it would take by substantial factors. Recall that ALGOL 60 was put together in six days, albeit after various preliminary meetings over the previous six months. Naur's draft for [Naur *et al.*, 1960] was written in two months, and the final version was circulated within two months after the meeting [Naur 1981]. But the art of language design and definition had advanced since 1960 and things could not be done at that pace anymore. In the event, Van Wijngaarden's draft was nowhere near complete, and the next meeting had to be postponed for a further six months. However, the Subcommittee members themselves did get together on the date originally proposed at Kootwijk.

2.2.4 Kootwijk (April 1966)

In addition to the four members of the Subcommittee, this meeting was attended by Barry Mailloux, Van Wijngaarden's doctoral student from Canada, and W. L. van der Poel, chairman of WG 2.1. Contrary to the arrangement made at St. Pierre, there were two drafts available: Van Wijngaarden's incomplete one, written in the agreed formalism, and a Wirth/Hoare "Contribution to the development of ALGOL" [Wirth 1966b], which had been prepared from [Wirth 1965] and [Hoare 1965b] for publication in *Communications of the ACM* after the adoption of [MR 76] at St. Pierre. It was generally agreed that the Contribution described more or less the right language, but in the wrong formalism.

Due to the incompleteness of Van Wijngaarden's document, the meeting worked initially by amending the Contribution (although still with the intent that Van Wijngaarden's version should be brought into line and become the official definition, as agreed by the WG). However, there arose a complete disagreement between Seegmüller and Van Wijngaarden on the one hand, and Hoare and Wirth on the other, concerning the parameter mechanism (2.3.4.3), and as Van Wijngaarden's parameter mechanism could not easily be incorporated into the Contribution, it was clear that the two documents must now diverge. Certainly, there was little prospect that the Van Wijngaarden approach would produce a document within 1966, whereas Hoare and Wirth were especially concerned about achieving a short timescale.

The Subcommittee made a long list of points that the Van Wijngaarden version should attend to, and he continued to work on it, assisted by Mailloux, a further incomplete draft being sent to WG 2.1 members during July, and a more-or-less complete draft just ten days before the next meeting.

The language defined in the Contribution was subsequently implemented by Wirth as ALGOL W (see also [Wirth 1966c]).

2.2.5 Warsaw (October 1966)

The draft submitted to this meeting was [W-2] (which apparently never did get an MR number). There was fierce debate as to whether this document by one member could be accepted as the report of the Subcommittee: Hoare was willing to accept it as such if time were allowed for missing parts to be completed; Wirth, who had had grave misgivings about the formalism at Kootwijk, had resigned from the Subcommittee and declined to attend this meeting, complaining of insufficient time to study the document, and insisting that it could no longer be regarded as a Subcommittee product.

There was also a report [Merner 1966] from the I/O subcommittee, which had held meetings at Oak Ridge and at the University of Illinois. However, this was not yet incorporated into [W-2].

At the start of the week there was some expectation that the two documents could be put together and submitted to TC2. However, there was strong debate on the subject of references. Orthogonality dictated that references could exist to any object, whether a record or not and whether that object were declared locally or on the heap, and this also considerably simplified the parameter-passing mechanism. Hoare and some others wanted to restrict references to records only (as in [Hoare 1965b] and [Wirth 1966b])—the so-called "diagonal" approach (2.3.4.3). Moreover, McCarthy had introduced fresh proposals for operator overloading (2.3.6), and had also been demanding serial elaboration of ***and*** and ***or*** (2.3.3.6), and Samelson had asked for anonymous routines (2.3.5). So by Thursday afternoon the customary depression had set in, to the extent that they even considered abandoning it altogether, and certainly the most to be expected was publication as a Working Document, while further editing and implementation studies continued.

Finally, the following were formally agreed:

1. [W-2] to be amended, incorporating at least [Merner 1966], together with proper pragmatics. (A 'pragmatic remark' is to the Report as a **comment** is to a **program**.)
2. The amended document to be published in the ALGOL Bulletin, and possibly other informal, non-refereed journals.
3. The results of implementation studies to be incorporated.
4. Van Wijngaarden to be charged with the editing, alone without any subcommittee (provided he was not pressed for any specific time schedule, although he could foresee mailing it the following February).
5. The next meeting in May would be too soon to consider the revised draft, and would be devoted to ALGOL Y. The following meeting in September would take the final decision.
6. McCarthy's overloading could be incorporated if the editor found it feasible.

It will be seen that the content of the language was growing steadily (and more was to come). It should be stressed that Hoare made several attempts to limit the content to something like [Wirth 1966b], or at least to "within the intersection of the agreement of WG 2.1," but to no avail. It is also noteworthy that Van Wijngaarden was beginning to realize just how long the revision might take, although he was still out by a factor of two.

2.2.6 Zandvoort (May 1967)

This meeting was supposed to discuss ALGOL Y: it spent nearly all its time on ALGOL X. The document available (in spite of there being no obligation to produce one at all) was [MR 88], which was now beginning to look substantially like the eventual [R]. John Peck, on sabbatical from the University of Calgary, had now joined the editorial team. It had been mailed four weeks in advance of the meeting. McCarthy's overloading was there "in all its glory", as were Samelson's anonymous routines.

There was pressure to get the process finalized before a TC2 meeting in October (which could lead to final acceptance as an IFIP document at the forthcoming General Assembly meeting in Mexico), but the timing was very tight. So the motions passed were

1. The report published in the ALGOL Bulletin (as agreed in Warsaw) should also be submitted to TC2, who would accept it subject to subsequent adoption by WG 2.1 "without substantive changes."
2. The next meeting was to be held not less than three and a half months after the circulation of the report.

On this basis, the earliest date for the next meeting would be October 22 (but, by application of the formula, it did not actually happen until the following June 3).

The meeting spent much time in constructive discussion of language issues (and also of the description method) without (so far as I can tell from the minutes) threats of resignation or rebellion, apart from a considerable disgust expressed by Wirth. They even spent an afternoon on ALGOL Y, from which it emerged that no one had very concrete ideas of what it was about, and that the only role model was LISP, on account of the fact that that language could construct its own programs and then *eval* them.

2.2.7 MR 93

The draft Report commissioned at Warsaw was eventually circulated to the readership of the ALGOL Bulletin as [MR 93] in February 1968, and was the cause of much shock, horror, and dissent, even (perhaps especially) among the membership of WG 2.1. It was said that the new notation for the grammar and the excessive size of the document made it unreadable (but they had said the same about ALGOL 60 and, although it may have been the longest defining document at that time, it is rather shorter than most of its successors). Moreover, it was not all gloom—there was also a substantial number of positive reactions and constructive comments. Another of Van Wijngaarden's students, Kees Koster, had now joined the team, with special responsibility for "transput," as I/O was now to be known.

This is where I entered the picture myself. Everything described up to now has been gleaned from the minutes and other documents. However, a copy of [MR 88] happened to come into my possession, and I set out to discover what language was hidden inside it. Halfway through this process, I switched to [MR 93]. The task occupied me for fully six man-weeks (the elapsed time was much more, of course), and as it progressed I incorporated my knowledge into an ALGOL 68 program illustrating all the features, embedded within comments so as to read like a paper. At that time, the ALGOL

Specialist Group of the British Computer Society announced a meeting to discuss the new language, so I circulated my document in advance under the title "ALGOL 68 with fewer tears" (non-native English speakers need to be aware of an English school textbook entitled "French without Tears"). On arrival at the meeting, at which three members of WG 2.1 (Duncan, Hoare, and Woodger) were present, I found that I was the only person there who knew the language well enough to present it, and I was hauled out in front to do just that. "Fewer tears" went through several revisions, appearing in the *ALGOL Bulletin* [Lindsey 1968], and finally in the *Computer Journal* [Lindsey 1972].

Of course my report contained errors, but the only important feature of the language I failed to spot was the significance of what could be done with records (or ***struct***s as they had now become), and the necessity for garbage collection arising therefrom. Nevertheless, it served as an existence proof of the language, and when Duncan took a copy to the next WG meeting it helped to redeem some of the damage. In addition to myself, several people (notably G. S. Tseytin of Leningrad) succeeded in interpreting the Report "from cold."

In May 1968, the tenth anniversary of ALGOL 58, a colloquium was held in Zürich, where the recently distributed [MR 93] came in for much discussion, being "attacked for its alleged obscurity, complexity, inadequacy, and length, and defended by its authors for its alleged clarity, simplicity, generality, and conciseness" [AB 28.1.1]. Papers given at the colloquium included "Implementing ALGOL 68" by Gerhard Goos, "Successes and failures of the ALGOL effort" [Naur 1968], and a "Closing word" [Wirth 1968]. Naur's paper contained criticism of [MR 93], as providing "the ultimate in formality of description, a point where ALGOL 60 was strong enough," and because "nothing seems to have been learned from the outstanding failure of the ALGOL 60 report, its lack of informal introduction and justification." IFIP seemed to be calling for immediate acceptance or rejection, and thus IFIP was the "true villain of this unreasonable situation," being "totally authoritarian" with a committee structure and communication channels entirely without feedback and with important decisions being taken in closed meetings. "By seizing the name of ALGOL, IFIP has used the effort . . . for its own glorification." Strong words indeed! Wirth's contribution was also critical of [MR 93], and of the method whereby the WG, after a week of "disarray and dispute," and then "discouragement and despair" would accept the offer of any "saviour" to work on the problems until next time. Eventually the saviours "worked themselves so deeply into subject matter, that the rest couldn't understand their thoughts and terminology any longer." Both Naur and Wirth resigned from the Group at this time.

However, Naur's point about "lack of informal introduction and justification" was correct. Starting from [W-2], which contained no informal material whatsoever, the amount of pragmatics in the successive drafts had been steadily increasing, particularly under pressure from Woodger, but it still had far to go. And Wirth's caricature of the meetings was not far off the truth.

2.2.8 Tirrenia (June 1968)

Three and a half months after the distribution of [MR 93] (four days less, to be exact), WG 2.1 met to consider it. Van Wijngaarden had had a considerable response from readers of the ALGOL Bulletin, and came armed with pages of errata, including some modest language changes. There was concern that the use of the name "ALGOL 68" might turn out to be premature. Van Wijngaarden had been invited to talk on "ALGOL 68" at the forthcoming IFIP Congress, but there might be no ALGOL 68 by then. Randell questioned the need for the "mystical IFIP stamp," and others wanted publication delayed until implementations existed. But without the stamp, manufacturers would not implement it, so maybe it should be stamped, but with a proviso that it would be revised in the light of experience.

Seegmüller produced a list of demands:

1. An expanded syntax in an Appendix.
2. A formal semantics (perhaps using VDL [Lucas 1969]). But the WG had rejected that as far back as Princeton in order to avoid "unreadability." However, competitive descriptions ought to be invited.
3. There should exist implementations.
4. There should be an informal introduction to the language (and to its method of description), preferably within the final Report.
5. The final vote on the report should be delayed until all these requirements were met.

In a series of straw votes, the WG showed itself in broad agreement with these requirements.

But the meeting was not all like this. The bulk of the time was spent considering technical points of the language. Members would ask about some particular situation, and Van Wijngaarden would explain how the Report covered it. There seems to have been a consensus for approval of the language itself. It was the Report that was the sticking point.

Came the last day, and what were they to do? First, two decisions were made:

1. Changes already made to [MR 93] were too "substantive" for the Zandvoort mechanism to be applied (see 2.2.6 (1)).
2. The Warsaw resolutions (see 2.2.5 (2)) had been fulfilled.

This put the whole project into limbo, with nobody charged to do anything anymore.

At this point Van Wijngaarden presented a Statement (some saw it rather as a threat) in which the authors offered to make just one more edition of the document, which would be submitted at some agreed moment to WG 2.1 which would then either accept it or reject it. If it was rejected, then the authors would have the right to publish it as their own. And he pointed out that the WG had worn out its first editor (Peter Naur), and then two authors (Wirth and Hoare), and now it might have worn out four more.

After the tea break, this statement was turned into a formal resolution, and the authors were asked to produce their final draft by October 1 for consideration by a full WG meeting on December 16.

2.2.9 North Berwick (August 1968)

This meeting, held just before the IFIP Congress, had been fixed before the decision quoted above. Hence it was not clear what this meeting should do, except talk—which is just what it did. It was the first meeting that I attended myself, and it was five days of continuous politics. For example, a poll was taken concerning the future work of the group, and the best part of a whole day, both before and after the poll, was taken up with its form, and how its results were to be interpreted. Mutual trust among the parties had been entirely lost, and jockeying for position was the order of the day, and of every day. Much time was devoted to discussion of whether and how minority reports might be attached to the final Report. Barely half a day was spent in technical discussion.

The document before the meeting was [MR 95], a half way stage to the document requested in Tirrenia, and containing much improved pragmatics and also extensive cross referencing of the syntax. But at the end of the meeting it was clear that the future of ALGOL 68 was still very finely balanced.

On a personal note, it was here that I met Sietse van der Meulen who had been asked by Van Wijngaarden to write the Informal Introduction requested by Seegmüller at Tirrenia. He asked me to join him in this task, and together we worked out the plan of our book during the IFIP Congress the following week.

2.2.10 Munich (December 1968)

By October, Van Wijngaarden had circulated his report [MR 99] to the Working Group as promised. In the meantime, Ross had been trying to organize a Minority Report that would be constructive and well thought out [Ross 1969]. Also, Dijkstra, Hoare, and Randell each circulated drafts of brief minority reports, which they invited others to join in signing.

At Munich, another draft was available [MR 100] whereas, some said, the meeting should have been considering only [MR 99]. To resolve this, three of us had to be dispatched to a side room to list all the differences between the two (not that I think anybody actually read our list). A draft of the first chapters of the Informal Introduction was also presented to the meeting by Van der Meulen and myself.

Although this meeting had much political content, there was more willingness than at North Berwick to reach a compromise, and there was also more technical discussion. Nevertheless, there were clearly some who would wish to move on from ALGOL 68 and who were already considering (following discussion at a NATO software engineering conference two months earlier) the possibility of a group devoted to Programming Methodology. It was therefore proposed that TC2 should be asked to form a new Working Group in this area (WG 2.3, as it later became).

To try to preserve the unanimity of the Group, a covering letter to be issued with the Report was drafted. This "did not imply that every member of the Group, including the authors, agreed with every aspect of the undertaking" but affirmed that "the design had reached the stage to be submitted to the test of implementation and use by the computing community." Then a motion to transmit the report with its Covering Letter to TC2 was proposed by Hoare and Woodger. There was heated discussion of the wording of the Covering Letter, but both it and the motion were accepted by substantial majorities, and we thought we were done.

However, in the last hour of the meeting some who were unhappy with the final form of the Covering Letter, and with interpretations which were being put upon it, produced a minority report. It had been constructed at the last moment, based upon the draft circulated by Dijkstra, and could clearly have been improved if its authors had had more time. Following the agreements at North Berwick the meeting had to accept it, and the point was clearly made that TC2 should be asked to publish it alongside the main Report.

In January of 1969, TC2 duly forwarded the Report and a mauled version of the Covering Letter to the IFIP General Assembly, which in a postal vote in March authorized publication. But TC2 refused to forward the Minority Report. The texts of the original Covering Letter and of the Minority Report are reproduced in Appendix A and Appendix B.

2.2.11 Banff (September 1969)

This was a very peaceful meeting by comparison with its predecessors. The agreed Report had been printed [MR 101], plus copious sheets of errata. Arrangements were in hand to have it published in *Numerische Mathematik* and *Kybernetika.* The decision of TC2 not to publish the Minority Report was regretted (but it had meanwhile been published in the *ALGOL Bulletin* [AB 31.1.1]).

During the meeting some small additional errata to [MR 101] were discussed (including a few extra representations to facilitate writing programs in ASCII). Thus was the final published text of [Van Wijngaarden 1969] established.

A much more substantial draft of the Informal Introduction was available, and discussions proceeded as to how it should be published. The decision was to ask TC2 to arrange for publication under IFIP copyright (which was subsequently done, and it appeared as [Lindsey 1971]).

In order to promote implementation of the language and to provide feedback from implementors, the WG empowered Mailloux to set up an Informal Implementers' Interchange as a means of getting a rapid dissemination of implementation techniques. Later, at Manchester, this responsibility was taken over by Branquart. It never did work fully as intended, but it enabled us to know who was implementing and to provide a channel for communication to them.

2.2.12 So What Had Gone Wrong?

It would be wrong to describe the seven who signed the Minority Report (or the two who resigned) as wreckers. They were all honourable men who cared about programming languages (even about ALGOL 68) and most of them had contributed substantially towards it. But their objections were diverse.

First, it should be said that Dijkstra had attended none of the crucial meetings from St. Pierre to Tirrenia, and Garwick had been entirely absent from St. Pierre to the end (although he had been active on the I/O subcommittee [Merner 1966]).

Some of them were opposed to the language. In particular, Hoare had grave misgivings about the language all along, as he has described in his Turing lecture [Hoare 1981], and he published his specific criticisms in [Hoare 1968]. He much preferred the way things had been done in SIMULA 67 [Dahl 1968]. Basically, he had hoped that more of the language definition could have made use of its own overloading facility (2.3.6), and he thought that the whole reference concept had been taken much too far (2.3.4.3). He had consistently expressed these opinions at the meetings, always in the most polite terms, always acknowledging the immense amount of work that Van Wijngaarden had put into it. It would seem that Wirth shared Hoare's views on most of these issues.

For some, notably Dijkstra, the whole agenda had changed. The true problem, as he now saw it, was the reliable *creation* of programs to perform specified tasks, rather than their *expression* in some language. I doubt if any programming language, as the term was (and still is) understood, would have satisfied him.

I think the rest were more concerned with the method of description than with the language, and with the verbosity and possible unsoundness of the semantics as much as with the W-Grammar (see [Turski 1968]). As Randell said at Tirrenia, "From our discussions . . ., it seems to follow that there is reasonable agreement on the language, but that there is the need for the investigation of alternative methods of description."

But how had the WG managed to support the description so far, only to become so upset at the last minute? After all, [MR 93] was not so different in style from [MR 88], and the discussion of [MR 88] at Zandvoort had been all about the language, not the document. It may be that having three months to read it had changed their perception. Duncan in particular did not like the W-Grammar, but he did try to do something about it by proposing an alternative syntax notation and even a complete rewrite of Chapter 1. And [MR 95] was much more readable than [MR 93], as Woodger admitted at North Berwick (but Ross, when trying to produce his own minority report [Ross 1969], still could not get to grips with [MR 99] although he dissociated himself from the Minority Report actually produced). Contrariwise, in spite of all the complaints from within the working group, I must report that I have never heard an actual implementor complain about the method of description.

The text of the Munich Covering Letter seems to have been the last straw, at least for Turski, who wanted a clearer expression of the preliminary nature of the Report and of the deep divisions within the WG. He also shared the view, often expressed by Hoare, on the necessity for simplicity in programming languages, and he has written on this [Turski 1981].

However, all the dissenters shared an exasperation with Van Wijngaarden's style, and with his obsessional behaviour in trying to get his way. He would resist change, both to the language and the document, until pressed into it. The standard reply to a colleague who wanted a new feature was first to say that it was too late to introduce such an upheaval to the document, then that the colleague should himself prepare the new syntax and semantics to go with it. But then, at the next meeting, he would show with great glee how he had restructured the entire Report to accommodate the new feature and how beautifully it now fitted in. Moreover, there were many occasions when he propagated vast changes of his own making throughout the document.

2.2.13 The Editorial Team

At Tirrenia, Van Wijngaarden described the editorial team in Amsterdam as follows:

Koster	Transputer	(from Oct. 1967)
Peck	Syntaxer	(on sabbatical from Univ. of Calgary Sep. 1966 to Jul. 1967)
Mailloux	Implementer	(doctoral student Apr. 1966 to Aug. 1968)
Van Wijngaarden	Party Ideologist	

Peck and Mailloux worked on the project full time, and all the pages of the Report were laboriously typed and retyped as changes were made. Van Wijngaarden, whose full time job was to direct the Mathematisch Centrum, would receive daily reports of progress. Mailloux was also responsible for ensuring that what was proposed could be implemented (as reported in his doctoral thesis [Mailloux, 1968]; see also 2.7.1).

The use of a distinctive font to distinguish the syntax (in addition to italic for program fragments) commenced with [MR 93], using an IBM golf-ball typewriter with much interchanging of golf balls. Each time Van Wijngaarden acquired a new golf ball, he would find some place in the Report where it could be used (spot the APL golf ball in the representations chapter). In fact, he did much of this typing himself (including the whole of [MR 101]).

From late 1967 on, intermediate drafts of parts of the document were circulated among an "inner circle" that included Yoneda, Goos' implementation team in Munich, Landin and, most importantly, the quadrumvirate of Michel Sintzoff, P. Branquart, J. Lewi, and P. Wodon from MBLE in Brussels. This latter group was particularly prolific in the number of comments that they submitted, to the extent that there were effectively two teams involved—one in Amsterdam creating the text and another in Brussels taking it apart again. Peck continued to submit comments and suggestions after returning to Calgary, and he returned to Amsterdam to resume the old routine during the hectic summer of 1968.

2.3 THE CONCEPTS OF ALGOL 68

Historically, ALGOL 68 arose out of ALGOL 60 and, although it soon became apparent that strict upwards compatibility with ALGOL 60 was not a realistic goal, there was always reluctance to adopt new syntactic sugar for familiar constructs, and there were many rearguard actions to maintain, at least the appearance of, certain cherished features (such as ***switch***es, call-by-name, and Jensen's device). All this led to some strange quirks in the final product.

From our present vantage, it is amazing to see how ill-understood in the early sixties were concepts that we now take quite for granted. It was at those early meetings of WG 2.1 that these concepts were painfully hammered out. In spite of the differences that surfaced, the membership of WG 2.1

comprised as good a collection of international programming language experts as could have been gathered together at that time. Everybody had something to contribute, especially, perhaps, those who were eventual signatories of the minority report.

2.3.1 The Easy Bits

In spite of the stormy passage of some items, many new features were proposed and went into the language with hardly any discussion.

Complex arithmetic (type ***compl***) was accepted without qualm, as were bit patterns (type ***bits***) and ***long*** versions of ***int***, ***real***, etc. (also ***short*** versions in [RR]). Naur [1964] proposed various standard **operators** (***mod***, ***abs***, ***sign***, ***odd***, and so forth) and also 'environment enquiries' such as *max int*, *max real*, *small real*, and *long* versions thereof.

It was agreed that there should be a ***string*** type, but some wanted them to be of indefinite length with a concatenation operator [Duncan 1964], and some assumed that each ***string*** variable would be declared with some maximum length [Seegmüller 1965a]. In both [MR 76] and [Wirth 1965] ***string*** was a primitive type. You could declare ***string*** variables, assign literal ***string***s to them, and concatenate ***string***s, but that was all; a delight to use, but requiring a heap for implementation. An inconclusive discussion at St. Pierre seemed to support the maximum length view, but in the event [MR 88] they turned out to be ***flex***ible ***array***s of the primitive type ***char***. This meant that sub-strings could easily be extracted and assigned to, but the ***flex*** facility itself was a mistake (2.3.2). ALGOL 68 is still the only major language not to require a maximum length with each ***string*** variable.

It was agreed that the ALGOL 60 **for-statement** was too complicated (although hankerings after **for-lists** continued to crop up). Hoare [1965a] proposed what eventually became the **loop-clause**:

for *identifier* ***from*** *first* ***by*** *increment* ***to*** *last* ***do*** *statements* ***od***

where *identifier* is an implicitly declared ***int*** constant (unassignable) for the duration of the loop only, and *first*, *increment*, and *last* are ***int*** expressions to be evaluated once only at the start. It was agreed that there should be a separate ***while*** statement, although eventually it became just another option of the **loop-clause** (defaulting to ***true***).

That ALGOL 68 is an expression-oriented language is due to [MR 76], which made no distinction between **expressions** and **statements** (this idea having been first proposed in [Wirth 1966a]). Thus, all forms of **conditional-**, **case-** and **closed-clauses** (that is, **blocks**) return values, as do (after [W-2]) **assignations**. For example,

x := (***real*** *a* = *p***q*; ***real*** *b* = *p*/*q*; ***if*** *a*>*b* ***then*** *a* ***else*** *b* ***fi***) + (*y* := 2**z*);

In addition, it is also possible to declare an **identifier** as an (unassignable) constant (as *a* and *b* above). Neither of these features was in [Wirth 1965], although **constant-declarations** were in [Seegmüller 1965b]. They are, of course, now the basis of functional languages such as SML [Milner 1990], but contemporary imperative languages seem to have fought shy of being expression-oriented, although **constant-declarations** are now well accepted (as in Ada).

The example shows another important feature that appeared without comment in [W-2], namely the matching of ***if*** by ***fi*** (likewise ***case*** by ***esac*** and, in [RR], ***do*** by ***od***). This removes the dangling else problem and, at the same time, the requirement for a **compound-statement**. Most modern languages have followed this lead except that, being without any sense of humour, they reject the easily memorable ***fi*** in favour of ***end if***, or ***endif***, or even plain ***end***. (How *do* you remember which one it is?)

2.3.2 Arrays

A 2-dimensional array can be regarded in two ways. First, it can be an ***array*** of ***array***s, and this was the view taken in both [Wirth 1965] and [MR 76]. Thus, one might expect to declare

```
loc [1:4][1:5] int a4a5;
```

and subscript it by *a4a5[i][j]*, and the type of *a4a5* would be described as **'row of row of integral'** (indeed that example is legal in [RR]). A consequence is that *a4a5[i]* is then a row-vector, but there is no way to construct a column-vector. WG 2.1 understood and approved this at St. Pierre, Bauer remarking, "It is not necessary for our two-dimensional arrays to have all the characteristics of matrices." But they did ask that "*][*" be written as "," allowing *a4a5[i, j]* after all (but titter ye not! for this is exactly the situation now in Pascal, and also in ALGOL W as implemented [Wirth 1966c]).

In [W-2], however, we find genuine 2-dimensional ***array***s:

```
loc [1:4, 1:5] int a45;
```

subscripted by *a45[i, j]* and with type **'row row of integral'** (also legal in [RR]). Semantically, this was modelled in [R] as a linear sequence of elements together with a descriptor composed of an origin c, and two each of lower bounds l_i, upper bounds u_i, and strides s_i. The element at *a45[i, j]* is then found in the sequence at $c + (i-l_1) * s_1 + (j-l_2) * s_2$. This suggests an obvious implementation. Moreover, it now allows all sorts of **slices**, such as

```
a45[2,  ]       row 2
a45[ , 3]       column 3
a45[2:3, 3]     part of column 3
a45[2:3, 2:4]   a little square in the middle.
```

This was accepted with enthusiasm; it is simple to implement and does not hurt those who do not use it; I cannot understand why other languages (excepting, in some degree, PL/1) have not done the same. It also provides the possibility to extract diagonals, transposes and the like.

The next facility added, in [MR 88], was flexible arrays. These allowed the size of an ***array*** variable to be changed dynamically.

```
loc flex [1:0] int array;      # initially empty #
array := (1, 2, 3);            # now it has bounds [1:3] #
array := (4, 5, 6, 7, 8)       # now it has bounds [1:5] #
```

That seems nice, but every student who has ever tried to use the facility has wanted to extend the *array* with bounds *[1:3]* by adding *5* extra elements at the end, leaving the existing values in *array[1:3]* untouched. But that goodie is *not* on offer, and what *is* on offer can be achieved in other ways anyway.

Van Wijngaarden has explained to me that flexible arrays were provided simply to facilitate ***string***s, which are officially declared as

```
mode string = flex [1:0] char;
```

But ***string***s *can* be extended

```
loc string s := "abc";
s +:= "defgh";     # now s = "abcdefgh" #
```

It would have been better, in my opinion, to omit the ***flex*** feature entirely and to provide ***string***s as a primitive type. In [RR] ***flex*** was made a property of the ***ref***erence to the ***array*** rather than of the ***array*** itself, thus bringing ***flex***ibility within the strong typing. This avoided a run-time check required in [R] to prevent the preservation of ***ref***s to no-longer-existent elements of ***flex array***s.

It was a fundamental principle that every value in the language should be expressible by some external denotation. Hence the **row-display** (the *(4, 5, 6, 7, 8)* in the example) has been present since [MR 76], although the corresponding **structure-display** did not appear until after Tirrenia. Unfortunately, this does not provide a convenient way to initialize the whole of an array to some same value (Ada has better facilities in this respect), and another problem, pointed out by Yoneda, is that although *()* and *(1, 2)* are valid **row-displays**, *(1)* is not (it is just a *1* with *( )* around it), and if you want to initialize your array with it you have to rely on the rowing coercion (2.3.3.5). Oddly, this bug was also present in the Preliminary Ada Reference Manual—*Plus ça change* ... .

Operators ***lwb*** and ***upb*** were provided in [MR 99] to determine the actual bounds of any given array. These replaced the less useful **flexible-bounds** used up to then in **formal-parameters** (as in *[1:**int** upper] **int** a*). However, bounds could still be specified, optionally, in **formal-parameters**. This possibility was removed in [RR] because, so it was said, there was nothing useful that implementors could do with that information. I now think this was a mistake, since to have such preconditions (even if all they trigger is a run-time check) can simplify writing the body of a routine.

2.3.3 Coercion

Although coercions had existed in previous programming languages, it was ALGOL 68 that introduced the term and endeavoured to make them a systematic feature (although it is often accused of a huge overkill in this regard). They existed in [W-2] (not by that name) but reached their full fruition in [MR 93], provoking three quarters of a day's discussion at Tirrenia. Coercion can be defined as the implicit change of the type (a priori) of an **expression** to match the type (a posteriori) required by its context.

There were eight different coercions in [R], diminishing to six in [RR]. These will now be examined, starting with the least controversial.

2.3.3.1 *Widening*

You can 'widen' from ***int*** to ***real*** and from ***real*** to ***compl***. This is quite natural, and most languages (Ada is the notable exception) allow it. Note that there is no 'narrowing' in ALGOL 68 as there is in FORTRAN and PL/1. Thus *realvariable := intvalue* is allowed, but not *intvariable := realvalue.*

2.3.3.2 *Dereferencing*

This changes a ***ref***erence into the thing ***ref***erred to. Thus, having declared *y* as a **real-variable**, so that its type is ***ref real*** (2.3.4.3), it is necessary to dereference *y* in *x := y*. The term 'dereferencing' is now used by many languages (even those that call their references 'pointers' and those that use an explicit operator for the purpose).

2.3.3.3 *Deproceduring*

This is the method whereby parameterless ***proc***s are called (the alternative used by some languages is to write *p()*). A coercion is necessary to distinguish the case requiring the value returned by the ***proc*** (as in ***loc real*** *x := random*) from that requiring the ***proc*** value itself (as in ***loc proc*** *anotherrandom := random*).

2.3.3.4 *Uniting*

Any language with ***union***s needs this coercion, which can turn, for example, an a priori ***int*** into an a posteriori ***union(int, real)***.

These four coercions are uncontroversial, either they, or some syntactic equivalent, being obviously necessary to perform their respective functions. The next four are all peculiar in one way or another.

2.3.3.5 *Rowing*

This turns a value of some type into an ***array*** of that type, but it is not, as might be expected, a means to initialize a whole ***array*** to some given value. Rather, it produces an ***array*** with just one element, and the only reason it exists is to overcome the Yoneda ambiguity described in 2.3.2. Consider

[] ***int*** *zero = (), one = (1), two = (1, 2);*

() and *(1, 2)* are **row-displays** yielding ***array***s of, respectively, 0 and 2 elements. *(1)* however is a **closed-clause** and its a priori value is an ***int***, which must be 'rowed' to make an ***array*** of 1 element to suit the context. The same thing arises with ***string***s:

string *zero = "", one = "A", two = "AB";*

since *"A"* is, a priori, a **character-denotation** whereas *"AB"* is a **string-denotation**.

The rowing coercion was clearly a mistake. There just has to be some other way (some new kind of brackets perhaps) to solve this problem.

2.3.3.6 *Proceduring*

It was agreed at St. Pierre that the elaboration of **operands** should be in parallel, to the discouragement of side effects (2.3.8). However, at Warsaw McCarthy raised the issue of ***or*** and ***and***, where it might be considered reasonable not to elaborate the second **operand** if the first had already determined the outcome (as in ***true or*** *doesitmatter*). Although McCarthy pressed strongly, it was agreed to leave matters alone in the interest of semantic consistency.

What did appear, instead, was the proceduring coercion, as in the following example taken from [R 7.5.2].

op cand = *(****bool*** *john,* ***proc bool*** *mccarthy)* ***bool:***
    if *john* ***then*** *mccarthy* ***else false fi;***

Now, in *p* ***cand*** *q*, *q* is 'procedured' from ***bool*** to ***proc bool*** and, according to the definition of ***cand***, the resulting ***proc*** will never be called unless *p* turns out to be ***true***. The proceduring coercion can also be used to make Jensen-like operations look more Jensen-like when **formal-parameters** are parameterless ***proc***s.

Now the proceduring coercion complicated the syntax considerably (it is necessary to avoid cycles of proceduring and deproceduring) and it was a pain to implement. Moreover, it did not do the job it was intended to do, for in

p ***cand*** *(a := b; q)*

it is only *q* that gets procedured, and *a* := *b* is elaborated whether *p is* ***true*** or not. For these reasons, proceduring was removed entirely from [RR].

2.3.3.7 *Hipping*

Jumps, ***skip***, and ***nil*** have no type a priori, but they can occur in some contexts where a value is (syntactically) expected (for example, *x* := ***if*** *p* ***then*** *y* ***else goto*** *error* ***fi***). In [R] they were said to be 'hipped' to the required mode. The same things are acceptable in [RR], but are not described as coercions.

2.3.3.8 *Voiding*

Voiding is a trick to satisfy the syntax when, upon encountering a ';' (as in *x* := *y*; *a* := *b*), the value of the **unit** just elaborated (*x* := *y*) is to be discarded. The user need not be aware of it.

The real complication of the coercions lay in the rules that governed how they might be cascaded. The removal of proceduring simplified things considerably, as may be seen by comparing the Coercion Chart on page 208 of [Lindsey 1971] with that on page 196 of [Lindsey 1977].

2.3.4 The Type System (or Records, References, and Orthogonality)

Orthogonality, as a guiding principle of design, had been introduced by Van Wijngaarden in [MR 76]. The idea was that if a range of features (say type constructors) exists along one axis, and another range (say types) along another, then every meaningful application of the one to the other should be present in the language. Whether WG 2.1 had accepted it as a guiding principle is another matter.

The effect of this principle on the language is nowhere more apparent than in the case of parameter passing and records—features that are superficially unrelated.

2.3.4.1 *Parameter Passing*

It is said that an Irishman, when asked how to get to some remote place, answered that if you really wanted to get to that place, then you shouldn't start from here. In trying to find an acceptable parameter-passing mechanism, WG 2.1 started from ALGOL 60 which, as is well known, has two mechanisms—call-by-value (which is well understood) and call-by-name (with which is associated Jensen's Device, and which is nowadays regarded as obsolete). Starting from ALGOL 60 was a mistake. All subsequent proposals were measured by how well they stood up to the classic *Innerproduct* and other such Jensen paradigms. ([R 11.2, 3, 4] contains no less than three *innerproduct* examples.)

Moreover, they still used the term 'name' even when discussing alternatives that might replace it. It was soon realized that there were two cases of call-by-name; where the **actual-parameter** was an **expression** and a 'thunk' had to be generated (sometimes termed 'call-by-full-name'), and where the **actual-parameter** was a **variable** to be assigned to (which was thus termed 'simple-name').

Here is the classic example of Jensen's device in ALGOL 60, the *Innerproduct* example from [Naur *et al.* 1962]:

```
procedure Innerproduct(a, b) Order: (k, p) Result: (y);
        value k;
        integer k, p; real y, a, b;
```

```
begin real s; s := 0;
    for p := 1 step 1 until k do s := s+a*b;
    y := s
end Innerproduct
```

and here is a call:

```
real array x1, y1[1:n]; integer j; real z;
Innerproduct(x1[j], y1[j], n, j, z);
```

Observe that the **formal-parameters** *a* and *b* are called-by-(full-)name, and *p* and *y* are called-by-(simple-)name. See how *j*, the **actual-parameter** for *p*, is also used within the **actual-parameters** for *a* and *b*. The semantics of call-by-name then require that the **for-statement** behave as if it had been written

```
for j := 1 step 1 until k do s := s+x1[j]*y1[j];
```

In [MR 76] **formal-parameters** could be marked as ***val***, ***loc*** or ***var***, which might nowadays be rendered as ***in***, ***out*** and ***in out***. Things declared ***loc*** or ***var*** could be used on the left of an **assignation**, and things declared ***val*** or ***var*** within **expressions** on the right.

```
proc f = (real val x, real loc y, real var z) real: . . . ;
```

In a **call** of *f*, the coercion rules allowed

- an ***int*** or ***real*** value for *x*;
- a ***real*** or ***compl*** variable for *y*;
- only a ***real*** variable for *z*.

Actual-parameters must be compatible with their **formal-parameters** as regards ***val***, ***loc***, or ***var***, so that the accident of assigning to an **expression**, which could happen (and be detected only at run-time) in ALGOL 60, is avoided. If call-by-full-name is required, it must be indicated by ***expr:*** at the point of call. Here is *innerproduct*:

```
proc innerproduct = (real val a, b, int val k, int loc p, real loc y) void:
    begin real var s := 0;
        for p := 1 step 1 until k # ALGOL 60 loop semantics #
        do s := s+a*b;
        y := s
    end;
```

and here is a **call**:

```
loc [1:n] real x1, y1; loc int j; loc real z;
innerproduct(expr: x1[j], expr: y1[j], n, j, z);
```

Seegmüller [1965b] proposed that **formal-parameters** for call-by-full-name should be explicitly declared as parameterless ***procedure***s (that is, explicit thunks), with the corresponding **actual-parameter** indicated at the point of call (as in [MR 76]). Simple-name parameters, however, would be explicitly declared ***reference*** (and ***reference*** variables were also to be allowed, but ***reference reference*** types were forbidden). An explicit ***ref*** operator was provided to indicate that a reference to some variable, rather than to its contents, was to be taken (if you like, an anti-dereferencing operator like the '&' of C).

```
int reference ii; int i;
ref ii := ref i;         # to assign a reference to i #
ii := i;                 # to assign the int in i to the place indicated by ii #
```

Here is *innerproduct*:

```
proc innerproduct =
        (proc real a, b, int k, int reference p, real reference y) void:
    begin loc real s := 0;
        for p := 1 step 1 until k # ALGOL 60 loop semantics #
        do s := s+a*b;
        y := s
    end;
```

And here is the **call**:

```
loc [1:n] real x1, y1; loc int j; loc real z;
innerproduct(expr: x1[j], expr: y1[j], n, ref j, ref z);
```

One can see how Seegmüller's proposal derived from EULER [Wirth 1966a], but EULER was a dynamically typed language so that ***reference***s could refer to values of any type. EULER was the first language, so far as I am aware, to introduce the terms 'call-by-reference' and 'call-by-procedure'.

At St. Pierre, Hoare presented a concept of 'value/anti value', which appears to have been what we now call 'copy/copy back'. At any rate, this is what appeared in [Wirth 1966b] alongside an untouched call-by-name as in ALGOL 60 and parameterless ***procedure*** parameters (to be matched by **statements** or **expressions** in the **actual-parameters**). Here is *innerproduct* in ALGOL W:

```
procedure innerproduct
        (real a, real procedure b, integer value k, integer p, real result y);
    begin y := 0; p := 1;
        while p≤k do begin y := y+a*b; p := p+1 end
    end;
```

Just to be contrary, I declared *a* by-name and *b* by-procedure. The effect is the same. Here is the **call**:

```
real array [1:n] x1, y1; integer j; real z;
innerproduct(x1[j], y1[j], n, j, z);
```

This then was the State-of-the-Art of parameter passing in October 1965, and its total confusion may be contrasted with the limited set of options to which modern programming language designers confine themselves, and with the simplicity and elegance of the system that presently emerged for ALGOL 68. At the end of the St. Pierre meeting they voted against "Seegmüller's references," but everything else was left undecided.

2.3.4.2 *Records*

A concept of 'trees' had been introduced at Princeton (they seem to have been somewhat like the 'lists' of EULER) and had consequently been included in both [Wirth 1965] and [MR 76]. Shortly before St. Pierre, however, Hoare [1965b] had proposed 'records', each being of some named 'record ***class***' and with local ***ref*** *(some class)* variables to locate them, and also ***ref*** fields within the records themselves. Records of a given class could be created, on demand, on the heap (but there were to be *no* local records on the stack). With these, one could create all manner of lists, trees, graphs, and so forth. This technique is quite familiar to us now, but it seemed like a revolution at the time, and the WG accepted it with enthusiasm.

The idea of records in fact derived from several sources. McCarthy [1964] had proposed a type constructor ***cartesian*** (also a rather elaborate ***union***), Naur [1964] had proposed similar 'structures', but without ***class***es, and of course COBOL had used records as the basic unit to be transferred to/from files. But it was AED-0 [Ross 1961] that first showed how complex structures could be built up using records and ***ref***s. The difference between AED-0 and Hoare's scheme is that the latter was strongly typed; thus if you had a ***ref*** you knew which of the fields within its record were themselves ***ref***s, and thus you could do garbage collection (although Hoare did have an explicit *destroy* operation as well). AED-1, which appeared subsequently, was also strongly typed. In the absence of garbage collection, a record would disappear when the **block** in which its ***class*** was defined was exited. (This feature is also present in Ada, but it is only appropriate in a language with a name-equivalence rule for its types (2.3.4.7).)

Hoare also proposed some optional features, including the possibility of specifing a default initialization for a ***class*** (this useful feature was resurrected for Ada) and discriminated ***union***s (with even a **conformity-clause** (2.3.4.6) such as eventually appeared in [RR]). He also wrote a further paper [Hoare 1966] which included, by way of example, Dijkstra's well-known algorithm for finding the shortest path between two nodes of a graph.

In fact, the records actually introduced into ALGOL 68 were known as 'structures', and introduced by the word ***struct***.

2.3.4.3 *Orthogonality vs Diagonality*

Seegmüller [1965b] had ***ref***s for call-by-reference (which the WG had rejected). Hoare [1965b] had ***ref***erences for accessing records (which the WG had accepted). By Kootwijk, Van Wijngaarden had brought these two concepts together, and everything fell into place (at least that was his view, which Seegmüller was happy to share at that time).

According to the principle of orthogonality

- A record ***class*** was a type (just as an ***array*** was a type).

  ∴ there should be record variables, record parameters, and record results.
- ***ref x*** was a type, for any ***x*** (whether a record or not).

  ∴ ***ref ref x*** was a type.
- ***ref***s could be used for parameters (for call-by-simple-name).

  ∴ ***ref***s should be able to refer to any variable of suitable type, even (especially) local variables. In fact, the concepts of variable and reference had become synonymous, and the type of a ***real*** **variable** *x*, as declared in ***loc real*** *x*, is actually ***ref real***.
- ***proc***s could be used for parameters (for call-by-full-name).

  ∴ there should be ***proc*** variables, ***proc*** parameters, and ***proc*** results.

  ∴ also there should be syntax for constructing anonymous ***proc***s (see 2.3.5, where the final version of *innerproduct* will also be found).
- The left hand of an **assignation** had customarily been a **variable**.

  ∴ Now it would be any ***ref*** valued **expression**.

In fact, the only major feature altered from Seegmüller's scheme was that a dereferencing **operator** ***val*** took the place of the anti-dereferencing **operator** ***ref***. And because of the automatic coercion, ***val*** was hardly ever necessary. At the last moment, in [MR 100], ***val*** was abolished in favour of the newly invented **cast**.

Hoare was horrified. In his Turing Award lecture [Hoare 1981] he describes his dismay at the "predominance of references" and other complex features being added to the language at that time. In his opinion, records had been provided for one specific purpose, and he had therefore deliberately eschewed local records and ***ref***s to local variables [Hoare, 1965b]. As he said at Warsaw:

> In the last two years I spent a tremendous amount of energy trying to persuade people not to have any indirect addressing in programming languages. There was a discussion in Princeton and Grenoble and the Committee was against indirect addresses. I wanted to have references only in connection with the records. I do not understand what all these general references are about. I think an ordinary programmer will have a tremendous scope for mistakes.

Throughout the meeting he strove to have the facilities of references limited to the things he considered safe (this being dubbed the "diagonal" approach).

> If you kept references to records and parameter-passing mechanisms apart, we could save ourselves a tremendous amount of confusion.

The discussion lasted for the best part of a day, but Van Wijngaarden was able to demonstrate that his system was self-consistent, and the only technical objection that stuck was the possibility that a ***ref*** to a local variable might still exist after exit from the **block** where it was declared, and this was fixed by a rule forbidding **assignations** that could lead to this possibility; usually this rule could be enforced at compile-time, although run-time checks would be needed in some circumstances. Hoare remained unhappy about this, although my experience of using the language with students is that violations of this rule arise very seldom in actual programming, and it is not a serious practical issue.

Thus the battle within WG 2.1 was won by Orthogonality. Moreover, most modern programming languages have tended to follow this lead, judging by the emphasis that is customarily placed upon all types of values being "first class citizens" of the language.

The type system of ALGOL 68 has been adopted, more or less faithfully, in many subsequent languages. In particular, the ***struct***s, the ***union***s, the pointer types, and the parameter passing of C were influenced by ALGOL 68 [Ritchie 1993], although the syntactic sugar is bizarre and C is not so strongly typed. Another language with a related type system is SML [Milner 1990], particularly with regard to its use of ***ref*** types as its means of realizing variables, and C++ has also benefitted from the ***ref*** types [Stroustrup 1996]. Even the Intuitionistic Theory of Types [Löf 1984] uses essentially the same type system.

2.3.4.4 *The Bend*

There was an additional feature inherent in allowing the left side of an **assignation** to be any ***ref*** **expression**, and this was that ***ref***s to individual fields within records, or elements within ***array***s, had to be permitted, for how else could you write

age ***of*** *tom := 16;* or *a[i] := 3.142;* ?

Orthogonality then demanded that such ***ref***s (to fields within records) could be passed as parameters and preserved in variables. Getting this correct in the syntax of **selections** and **slices** nearly drove the authors "round the bend"; hence, the title given to it.

Now although modern languages tend to have adopted the orthogonal approach (Pascal is more orthogonal than ALGOL W, and Ada is more orthogonal than Pascal), very few of them (except for

C) allow their ***ref***s to do this, or to point to locals, so is there any benefit to be gained apart from satisfying some philosophical principle?

Now the claim for orthogonality must be that, by providing a very clean and systematic language, serendipitous benefits, not foreseen at the time of language design, will arise during actual use. The technique, which became known as the "3-***ref*** trick," and was only discovered after the necessary features were already in place [R 10.5.1.2.b], illustrates this point.

Here is a recursive program to insert a new item at its correct place in a binary tree. This is the classic example to illustrate the benefits of recursion in programming languages.

```
mode node = struct (int val, ref node left, right);
ref node nonode = nil;
loc ref node start := nonode;

proc insert = (int v, ref ref node place) ref node:
        if place :≠: nonode
        then    if v<val of place then insert (v, left of place)
                else #v≥val of place# insert (v, right of place)
                fi
        else place := heap node := (v, nonode, nonode)
        fi;
```

Now the recursion here is tail recursion, and it is well known that tail recursion can always be changed into iteration. It would be a strange language in which this could not be done and indeed, in this case, it is straightforward and one can imagine a mechanical tool to do the transformation automatically.

```
proc insert = (int v) ref node:
        begin loc ref ref node place := start;
            while place :≠: nonode
            do  if v<val of place then place := left of place
                else #v≥val of place# place := right of place
                fi
            od;
            ref ref node(place) := heap node := (v, nonode, nonode)
        end;
```

Observe that the ***ref ref node*** **formal-parameter** *place* has become a ***loc***al ***ref ref node*** **variable**. (The type of *place* is therefore ***ref ref ref node***; hence the term "3-***ref*** trick.") Observe also that *place* is required to point at both a local variable (*start*) and at a field of a ***struct*** variable (*left* ***of*** *place*).

Now the first version of *insert* can easily be written in Pascal (*place* will be a ***var*** parameter) or in Ada, but try to write the second version in either of those languages. It just cannot be done. The only other modern language in which this works is C, and there you have to be exceedingly careful to watch the types of everything.

2.3.4.5 *Variable-declarations*

The history of how variables are created is interesting. As explained in 2.3.4.3, a **'real'** variable is the same thing as a **'reference to real'** constant. A variable is created by means of a **generator**:

loc real or ***heap real***

and a **variable-declaration** is equivalent to a **constant-declaration** containing a **generator**. Thus:

loc real *x;*	means the same as	***ref real*** *x* = ***loc real;***
heap real *x;*	means the same as	***ref real*** *x* = ***heap real;***

Indeed, in [R] the **variable-declaration** was defined by that equivalence. Now in [MR 88] ***loc*** was not a symbol writable by the user, but from [MR 93] the user could write his own **local-generators** (as well as **heap-** ones), which was a pity because they are painful to implement and not particularly useful. And in the **heap-generator** the ***heap*** was optional, which was a pity because it made it difficult to parse. Also, the explicit ***loc*** was not then permitted in the **variable-declaration** (you could only write ***real*** *x;* just as in ALGOL 60).

In [RR] we made the ***heap*** compulsory in **heap-generators** and introduced the optional ***loc*** into the **variable-declaration** (too late to make it compulsory, but it made things more or less symmetrical). An explicit ***loc*** in a **variable-declaration** has considerable advantages didactically (readers will observe its consistent inclusion in this paper), and it prevents any possible confusion between

real *e := 2.718;*	a **variable-declaration** for a variable *e*, and
real *e = 2.718;*	a **constant-declaration** for a constant *e*.

If only the ***loc*** had been present and compulsory all along, there would have been an enormous simplification of implementation (see 2.7.1 for a full discussion), but the ALGOL 60 influence was still too strong.

2.3.4.6 *Unions*

Languages with Hoare-style record handling can benefit greatly from having ***union***s as well [Hoare 1965b]. [W-2] actually had a type ***free***, effectively the union of all possible types. However, after discussions at Warsaw, Hoare's ***union***s were incorporated in [MR 88] in its place.

To determine the actual type in residence, there was the **conformity-relation**, which could test whether the actual type was suitable for assignment to a given **variable**, and even assign it if asked.

```
mode man = struct(string hisname, . . . ), woman = struct(string hername, . . . );
mode person = union(man, woman);
loc man tom; loc woman mary; loc person body;
tom ::= body;        # assigns and returns true iff body is actually a man #
```

There was also a **conformity-case-clause**

```
case tom, mary ::= body in hisname of tom, hername of mary esac
```

However, in [RR], both of these were replaced by a **conformity-clause**

```
case body in
        (man m): tom := m; hisname of tom,
        (woman w): mary := w; hername of mary
esac
```

As originally proposed, ***union(real, int, bool)***, ***union(int, real, bool)*** and ***union(real, union (int, bool))*** were different types, but at Tirrenia, Yoneda asked for ***union***s to be both commutative and accumulative, in the interests of mathematical tidiness (although it must be said that there is quite a price to be paid in the implementation). The members pounced on the idea, saying that a W-Grammar could not express it, but the next day Van Wijngaarden produced the syntax—a weird and wonderful constructive use of syntactic ambiguity which now appears in [R 7.1.1cc–jj].

2.3.4.7 *Type Equivalence*

In Hoare's record proposal, it was assumed that every record would belong to a ***class***, and that the ***class*** would be identified by its name (so two ***class***es would be distinct even if they had identical structures, and hence the possibility existed to destroy all instances of a ***class*** once the **block** where it was introduced had been exited). In ALGOL 68, however, the naming of a ***struct*** type is optional (though usually to be recommended) and a rule of structural equivalence of types applies, so that even ***a*** and ***b*** in the following are of the same type:

```
mode a = struct (int val, ref a next);
mode b = struct (int val, ref struct (int val, ref b next) next);
```

both being descriptions of the following graph:

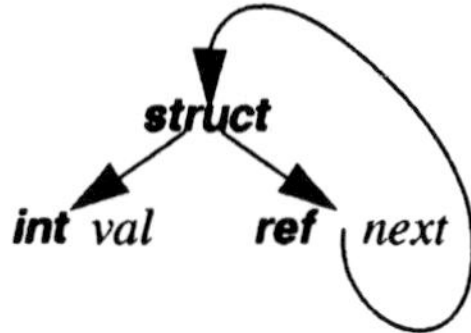

This caused much furore at Tirrenia, not because of structural equivalence as such (the existence of the distinction was never mentioned), but because of the infinite protonotion that arose in describing it. However, that is a matter of the description method, and will be discussed in (2.5.1.4).

Pascal (eventually) and Ada have a rule of name equivalence, and with hindsight maybe ALGOL 68 should have done the same. (It would have made the future introduction of abstract data types more secure, although it is awkward for generic or polymorphic type schemes, which is why recent languages such as SML have reverted to structural equivalence.)

2.3.5 Procedures

A proposal in [Naur 1966] to amalgamate the **specification** (of the type) of **formal-parameters** into the same line as the **parameters** themselves was accepted with enthusiasm (such that to modern eyes the separation of these items in ALGOL 60 seems strange). The idea of letting the value of the last thing in a **block** be the value of the whole **block** (and hence the way to show the result of a ***proc***) comes from [Naur 1964], although it also featured in EULER [Wirth 1966a].

Since in [W-2] ***proc***s could be **formal-parameters**, and hence by orthogonality could be anything else, it was natural that a means to construct anonymous values of ***proc*** types should exist (essentially a lambda-expression, but here known as a **routine-text**). The idea came from Samelson [1965] where it was conceived more as a way of cleaning up Jensen's device. Here is *innerproduct* taken from [RR 11.2]:

```
proc innerproduct1 = (int n, proc (int) real x, y) real:
        begin long real s := long 0;
            for i to n do s +:= leng x(i) * leng y(i) od;
            shorten s
        end;
```

And here is the **call**, with **routine-texts**:

```
loc [1:n] real x1, y1;  loc real z;
z := innerproduct1(n,  (int j) real: x1[j],  (int k) real: y1[k]);
```

Now that ***proc***s were first class citizens it was hoped that full functional programming would become possible, but the following example, produced by Landin at Tirrenia, shows the snag.

```
proc curryplus = (real u)proc(real)real:  (real v)real: u+v;
proc(real)real addthree = curryplus (3);
addthree (5)          # should yield 8 #
```

The **routine-text** *(**real** v)**real**: u+v* yielded by *curryplus* has built into it the **identifier** *u*, itself a **formal-parameter** of *curryplus*, and in any reasonable stack-based implementation the value of *u* is no longer around by the time *addthree* comes to be called. There is therefore an extent restriction to forbid this usage [RR 7.2.2.c].

After publication of [R], Bekic made strong pleas at Habay-la-Neuve, and subsequently, to have this restriction lifted, but it would have implied a fundamental change to the underlying philosophy (namely, that ALGOL 68 was a stack-based language). At Vienna I was able to show that the same effects could be achieved by introducing partial parametrization into the language (as was later published in [Lindsey 1976], although never implemented to my knowledge). Modern functional languages such as SML do not have this restriction, but in consequence they pay an extra run-time overhead.

2.3.6 Overloading

This was McCarthy's pet topic. Seemingly he had raised it at Baden in 1964; Naur [1964] suggested essentially the same thing, and apparently Hoare had also proposed it at a NATO Summer School. But it was not among the features agreed on at Princeton, so the next time McCarthy appeared at a meeting, at Warsaw, he raised it again. By sheer persistence, he persuaded a somewhat reluctant WG to let Van Wijngaarden put it in.

The feature allows the user to declare his own **monadic-** or **dyadic-operators**, together with a **priority-declaration** if the (**dyadic-**)**operator** has not a priority already (**monadic-operators** always have the highest priority regardless).

```
prio max = 9;
op max = (int a, b)int: if a>b then a else b fi;
op max = (real a, b)real: if a>b then a else b fi;
```

Observe that the body of ***max*** is just a **routine-text**, so it might be said that we have just a fancy new way of calling ***proc***s, but observe also that we have separate definitions of ***max*** for the cases ***int-int*** and ***real-real*** (and ***int-real*** and ***real-int*** ought to have been defined also). Thus ***max*** has been 'overloaded', and to see which version of ***max*** is intended in any particular context the compiler simply has to look at the types of its two **operands**. Contrast this with the situation in Ada (which along with C++ [Stroustrup 1996], has adopted this overloading) in which, not only the types of the **operands**, but also the type required for the result must be taken into account. This puts a hugely increased burden on the compiler, with little real practical benefit that I can see.

Now it is the coercion of the **operands** that provides the interest in overloading. Clearly, in *x* ***max*** *y* the coercion of *x* and *y* must not be allowed to include widenings, but it should include the 'firm' coercions such as dereferencing (for *x* and *y* might well be **variables** of type ***ref int***, say). We have also modified the rules of block-structure, for a **block** can now contain several definitions of the same **operator**, but not so that more than one of them can be legitimately chosen in a given **formula**. There has to be a rule forbidding the coexistence of two definitions the types of whose **operands** are 'loosely related' [R 4.4.2.c] or 'firmly related' [RR 7.1.1]. (Checking this property is quite hard work, and in the sublanguage promulgated in [Hibbard 1977] there is a less permissive 'meekly related' rule.)

Incorporating overloading into the Report was a major upheaval. Not only did the coercion rules and context conditions have to be overhauled, but all the existing "built-in" **operators** had to be taken out of the syntax and replaced in the **standard-prelude**. At Zandvoort, Yoneda asked why could not ***proc***s be overloaded also? Because we expect to be able to do widening coercions to **actual-parameters** (note that Ada can overload its ***procedure***s because it has no widening coercion). Hoare [1968] wanted subscripting, ':=' and even ';' to be defined as overloaded **operators**, but these would have needed user access to the descriptors of ***array***s (dangerous), right-associative **dyadic-operators**, and other such complications.

2.3.7 Labels and Switches

ALGOL 60 had the most horrendous collection of **labels**, **designational-expressions**, and **switch-declarations**. Trouble was that people got used to using them. (This was long before such things had been declared "harmful" [Dijkstra 1968b]), and as a result some really horrid constructs were proposed (some even made their way into the final language). Things actually started by getting worse. Duncan [1964] proposed ***label*** as a type, with ***array***s of them instead of ***switch***es, and the ability to jump *into* a **block**. Naur [1964] realized that an environment has to be a part of every ***label*** value, rendering jumps into **blocks** inappropriate.

The solution to the ***switch*** problem came with [Hoare 1964], which proposed a **case-clause** of the (eventual) form

> ***case*** *integer expression* ***in*** *first, second, third* ***esac***

but without any ***out*** (or ***otherwise*** option). Clearly, this would be implemented by a table of jumps (in contrast to the **case-clause** in more recent languages where each alternative is preceded by a possible value of the *expression*). This was well received, and was the end of the ALGOL 60 ***switch*** (but it still left the possibility of ***label*** values and ***array***s thereof).

At St. Pierre, Wirth [1965] would not allow jumps *into* a syntactic entity, nor any **designational-expressions** (these were accepted), nor ***label***s as parameters (which was not accepted). Van Wijngaarden then asked whether **declarations** might not be labelled (apparently so that one could jump back to them to change the size of ***array***s). Surprisingly, and in the face of grim warnings from Hoare, the meeting agreed to let him look into this (but fortunately the idea never came to fruition).

label variables and parameters had been a feature of [Seegmüller 1965b], but following St. Pierre the only way to pass a ***label*** around was to encapsulate it as a **jump** inside a ***proc***. So Seegmüller complained that to pass *label* to a procedure *p* he would have to write something like *p(****expr****:* ***goto*** *label)*. Van Wijngaarden promised to look into it. The result was that, in [MR 88], first a **jump** in a suitable context was automatically turned into a ***proc***, allowing *p(****goto*** *label);* and second the ***goto*** in a **jump** was made optional (to the great inconvenience of compiler writers, as it transpired), allowing *p(label)*. But worse! Van Wijngaarden was now able to exhibit his pride and joy—his pseudo-switch [R 8.2.7.2].

```
[ ] proc void switch = (e1, e2, e3); # e1, e2 and e3 are jumps to labels #
switch[i];
```

or even

***loc** [1:3] **proc void** switch := (e1, e2, e3);*
switch[2] := e1;

To my shame, I must admit that this still works in [RR], although implementations tend not to support it.

2.3.8 Parallel and Collateral

At St. Pierre there was discussion as to whether the order of elaboration of the two **operands** of a **formula**, or of the **actual-parameters** of a **call**, or of the two sides of an **assignation**, should be prescribed. In spite of some protest from Naur, it was agreed that it should be explicitly undefined (and all subsequent languages seem to share this view).

Meanwhile, [MR 76] contained a proposal for explicit parallelism in which the elementary actions in the parallel branches were to be merged in an undefined order. This was agreed (again over the protests of Naur) but with the proviso that a serial elaboration should be among the legal interpretations (hence there was no idea of fairness). Questions of synchronization and resource sharing were hardly discussed, it being supposed that interlocks could easily be programmed (that this was not so was shown by [Dijkstra 1968a], of which earlier drafts were available in 1965, but apparently not known to the WG). However, [MR 76] also suggested that elaboration of **operands** of a **formula** and so on should be implicitly in 'parallel', thus going further than merely undefining the order. Of course the reason was to allow the implementor as much leeway as possible to introduce optimizations, and it later turned out that this proposal also permits the elimination of common sub-expressions, even when they contain side effects.

Certainly there was a demand for genuine parallelism (see for example [Dahl 1966]), and by the time the issue was discussed at Zandvoort, [Dijkstra 1968a] was well known; hence [MR 88] provided for the symbol ***elem*** in front of a **closed-clause**, the whole of which was to be treated as an elementary action. Van Wijngaarden seemed to think this sufficient to enable Dijkstra's semaphores to be written (but I cannot see how he could have avoided using spin locks). Randell then proposed that semaphores should be included as an explicit feature. This led to a bad attack of cold feet concerning whether parallelism should be in at all, and if so whether it was to support multiple processes on one or more processors, or was just a device to undefine the order of elaboration. The trouble was that [MR 88] did not distinguish between these two usages.

The outcome was that in [MR 93] the term 'collateral elaboration' was used to indicate where the implementor might do his optimizations, and an explicit construction

par begin** process1, process2, process3 **end

was introduced for 'parallel elaboration', within which Dijkstra's semaphores (written as ***up*** and ***down***) could be used [R 10.4; RR 10.2.4]. The ***elem*** symbol was still present, but it had disappeared by [MR 101]. With hindsight, it is debateable whether such a low-level feature as the semaphore was a proper feature of such a high-level language. At North Berwick, even Dijkstra was expressing doubt on this point.

2.3.9 Transput

The report of the I/O subcommittee established at St. Pierre [Merner 1966] was in the form of an addition to [Wirth 1965]. It provided separate procedures for converting numerical values to/from ***string***s, as opposed to transmitting them to external media (an explicit request of the WG at St. Pierre). There was an elaborate system of formats (represented internally as ***string***s), largely derived from [Knuth *et al.* 1964]. At Zandvoort, the WG asked for an explicit ***format*** type (one benefit of which was the possibility of introducing **dynamic-replicators**). However, this was about the only action on transput taken by anybody up until October 1967, when Koster returned from his military service and serious work began.

Koster's main contribution was the 'rectangular book' model in which an external document was conceived as composed of so many pages, each of so many lines, each of so many characters, it being the responsibility of the system to keep track of the 'current position' and to institute action if the boundaries were exceeded. (ALGOL 68 is the only major language to provide this service.) Actually, the prime reason for adopting this particular model was to ensure implementability on IBM mainframes, whereon the alternative idea of a file as an undifferentiated stream of characters (with perhaps some newlines thrown in) would be quite unimaginable. (Just think—there might then be more than 80 characters between newlines.) IBM was not to be given any such excuses.

The conversion and transmission of values were now recombined so as to provide a usable system, although the explicit conversions to/from ***string***s were still present (but in a not very satisfactory form, so that in the revision new functions *whole*, *fixed*, and *float* were provided in their place). For reasons of orthogonality, the transput of ***struct***s and ***array***s had appeared (as 'straightened' sequences of their primitive components). A nice feature was the ability to gather a sequence of disparate values and layout procedures into one procedure **call**:

```
print((newpage,
        "Some Title", newline,
        "index = ", someinteger, space, somestruct, ", ", somereal, newline));
```

With the removal of the type ***free*** after Warsaw, this had to be done by a fictitious ***union*** of all transputable types, and it required some trickery to fit it into the language framework. The ***proc*** *read* was made to be, so far as possible, complementary with *print*. The ***format***s were derived from those of [Merner 1966] with the addition of **dynamic-replicators**, and **alignments** to control line and page endings. Considerable effort was devoted to making the action of ***format***s on input complement that on output.

[MR 93] was the first that anyone had seen of the detailed transput specifications, but serious discussion was lost in the general furore about other matters. Following discussions at Tirrenia, 'on' routines to handle exceptions such as line and page overflow, and facilities for *open*ing named files were added in [MR 95]. However, many detailed problems remained. If you took it too literally (and evidently you were intended to take the rest of the Report literally) you found that all sorts of strange behaviours were mandated.

The changes in the revision were mostly minor, to remove such unintended behaviours. They were concerned with the fact that the old model assumed every line to be padded with spaces to some fixed width and with a presumption that the **particular-program** was the only program running in the whole universe. Various problems with ***format***s were fixed (for example, that the effect of the **format** *$ 5z $* differed from that of *$ zzzzz $*). The only new features were the conversion routines *whole*, *fixed*, and *float*, and the facility to *associate* a ***file*** with a ***[ ]char*** in place of an external ***book***.

TABLE 2.4

WG 2.1 members active in the revision of ALGOL 68

Of the members already listed in Table 2.3, the ones who continued to be active in the revision were Bauer, Bekic, Goos, Koster, Lindsey, Mailloux, Paul, Peck, Van der Poel, Samelson, Sintzoff, Van Wijngaarden, and Yoneda.

Newcomers to the scene were:

Steve Bourne	Bell Labs, Murray Hill, NJ
Henry Bowlden	Westinghouse Research Labs, Pittsburgh, PA [Secretary of WG 2.1]
Ian Currie	RRE, Malvern, UK
Paul Branquart	MBLE, Brussels
Peter Hibbard	University of Liverpool, UK
Lambert Meertens	Mathematisch Centrum, Amsterdam
Sietse van der Meulen	Rijks Universitaet, Utrecht
Stephen Schuman	IRIA, Paris
Robert Uzgalis	UCLA, Los Angeles, CA

2.4 HISTORY OF THE REVISED ALGOL 68 REPORT

2.4.1 Dramatis Personae

Many who had earlier been prominent in WG 2.1 resigned from the group after Munich (most moving over to the newly formed WG 2.3), although Turski, Duncan, and Hoare remained in WG 2.1 for the time being. Table 2.4 lists some new members active in the revision.

The style of WG meetings, under the new chairman, Manfred Paul, was very different (and less confrontational). Much of the work was done by setting up subcommittees, each with a Convenor who could invite members from both within WG 2.1 and outside.

2.4.2 Improvements

2.4.2.1 *Habay-la-Neuve to Fontainebleau*

Habay-la-Neuve (July 1970) was the week after a TC2-sponsored conference on ALGOL 68 Implementation in Munich [Peck 1971]. Although the implementations by Goos at Munich and Branquart at MBLE had been underway since before the finalization of [R], the race had been won by an outsider, a team from the Royal Radar Establishment at Malvern in England, who had implemented a dialect they named ALGOL 68R. This had caused quite a stir at Munich. It was simple, and it worked, even though it was not quite ALGOL 68. There had also been discussion at Munich about features that had caused implementation problems, and there had been suggestions for sublanguages that would avoid them.

At the meeting, there was a wish-list, prepared by Van Wijngaarden and myself, of things we might like to change. As the meeting progressed, this list was augmented until it was three times its original size. A selection of these items for serious consideration was chosen, and an ad hoc subcommittee on "improvements" hammered them into shape. It was clearly envisaged that there was going to be a Revised Report, and there was tension between doing it later (to make it as complete as possible, an option strongly advocated by Samelson) and doing it earlier (so that fewer implementations would be affected). There was, however, a firm decision that, when the time came, there would be just one revision "once and for all."

The pattern established was for the two subcommittees established at this time to meet between and during WG meetings and to produce reports for consideration by the full WG. After each meeting, some official message from the WG to the Computing Community would be published in the *ALGOL Bulletin*, together with edited versions of the subcommittee reports. So after the Manchester meeting (April 1971), a letter to the readership of the *ALGOL Bulletin*, quoting from the Covering Letter (Appendix A) the remark about having subjected ALGOL 68 "to the test of implementation and use," announced that there would presently be a single Revision but that, in the meantime, the changes under consideration were being published "for their critical appraisal [WG 2.1, 1971c].

By the time of Novosibirsk (August 1971) it was felt possible to fix a definite timetable, and a formal resolution [WG 2.1, 1972a] laid down that the definitive list of changes would be published in the *ALGOL Bulletin* after the next meeting, at which time editors would be commissioned to prepare the Revised Report, which was to be approved and published before the end of 1973. This schedule was known to be extremely tight, and Sintzoff pointed out that two further meetings of the Maintenance subcommittee would be required before the next full meeting.

Fraser Duncan, who had edited the *ALGOL Bulletin* since shortly after the beginning of WG 2.1, had announced his intention to resign, and at a moment when I was absent from the meeting attending to some business or other I was elected to take his place, a post I held until the *ALGOL Bulletin* finally expired in 1988.

At Fontainebleau (April 1972), the Editors commissioned were Van Wijngaarden, Mailloux, and Koster, together with Sintzoff and Lindsey (the convenors of the two sub committees). Peck, who was now Professor at Vancouver, did not become an editor officially until the following meeting. Our brief, as expressed in the formal resolution, was to "consider, and to incorporate as far as practicable" the points from the two subcommittee reports and, having corrected all known errors in the Report, "also to endeavour to make its study easier for the uninitiated reader" [WG 2.1 1972d].

2.4.2.2 *Maintenance and Improvements*

This subcommittee, successor to the ad hoc improvements subcommittee at Habay, was officially constituted at Manchester with Sintzoff as convenor (although I acted as the "scribe," keeping the texts of the reports on paper tape and editing them on a Flexowriter). It met at Amsterdam (August 1971), Malvern (November 1971), and Brussels (February 1972), as well as during WG meetings, and each time it passed over the accumulated proposals together with comments received, and everything that was deemed "safe" by the full WG was published [WG 2.1 1971b, 1972b, and 1972e].

The report presented at Fontainebleau contained 53 specific suggestions for change, which were discussed, re-examined, and voted upon every which way. Many points that had seemingly been decided at earlier meetings were reopened and revoted, not always with the same result. By the time [WG 2.1 1972e] was published in the *ALGOL Bulletin*, implementors of the language had a pretty good idea of what was going to happen, and could bend their implementations accordingly.

After that the responsibility for improvements effectively passed to the Editors, who brought further items to the Vienna meeting, resulting in [WG 2.1 1973a], and to Dresden and Los Angeles, resulting in [WG 2.1 1973b].

In the event, the agreed changes amounted to a thorough tidying up of minor ambiguities, oversights, and inorthogonalities in the original language. Various redundancies, most notably proceduring (2.3.3.6) and formal bounds (2.3.2), were removed. ("The language is too fat," as Bauer remarked at Novosibirsk.) ***void*** became a type, ***flex*** became part of the type (2.3.2), a new **confor-**

mity-clause replaced the old **conformity-relation** (2.3.4.6), and various matters of representation were tidied up (for example, you could no longer write ***if*** *c* | *a* | *b* ***esac***). The only major language change that might have happened, the lifting of the extent restriction on ***proc***s advocated by Bekic (2.3.5), was left to a possible future extension.

2.4.2.3 *Data processing and Transput*

This subcommittee was established at Habay with myself as convenor. It met the week before Manchester and considered many small changes to tidy up the transput. However, its main consideration was a concept of 'record transfer' in which complex structures could be sent to backing store and later retrieved exactly as they had been written. There was a concept of a 'masskey', which was to backing store what a ***ref*** was to ordinary store, and there was a proposal for 'modals'—a facility for generic/polymorphic procedures. These things continued to be discussed for some considerable time, but never did make it into the revision.

A further meeting was held in Amsterdam (August 1971), after which transput discussions tended to happen at the same time as the Maintenance subcommittee. The reports of this subcommittee were [WG 2.1 1971a, 1972c, and 1972f]. At Fontainebleau, we presented 32 specific suggestions for change but we ran out of time before these could be discussed. (It has always been a problem within the WG to get people who have a strong understanding and concern for language issues to discuss transput seriously.) The transput proposals were therefore all left for decision until Vienna, where they were mostly accepted and included in [WG 2.1 1973a]. The changes were mostly minor, and have already been described in (2.3.9).

2.4.3 Revision

Of the Editors appointed, Van Wijngaarden immediately announced that he would leave all the hard work to the rest of us, and in the event, Koster, who was in the process of becoming Professor at Berlin, did not play an active role either. The rest of us were geographically well separated: myself in Manchester, Mailloux in Edmonton, Peck in Vancouver, and Sintzoff in Brussels.

For keeping the text, machine assistance was needed, and we decided to keep it on the MTS system at Edmonton using a line editor called *ed* and a formatting program known as *fmt*. Edmonton had an AM typesetter for which we had a special disc made. It was the craziest mixture of fonts and symbols ever found on a typesetter disc, which may explain why it took them over two years to produce it. Mailloux was in charge of the text, and wrote a typesetting program compatible with *fmt*.

2.4.3.1 *Vancouver (July 1972)*

John Peck invited us all to spend three weeks in Vancouver during July. There we all became familiar with MTS, *ed*, and *fmt*, and agreed how to divide the task. I was to be responsible for Chapters 1 and 2, which introduced the syntax notation and the semantic model (2.5.2). Peck was to be responsible for the syntax, and Sintzoff for the semantics. Mailloux was to be Keeper of the Text. We invented (or discovered) production trees, predicates (2.5.1.2), '**NEST**'s (2.5.1.3), and environs (2.5.2), and established a new 'structured' style for the semantics (2.5.3).

Sintzoff returned home via Edmonton, and as he sat in Mailloux's office the telephone rang. There was a temporary nine-months teaching post available, and did he (Mailloux) know anyone who could fill it? Well of course he did! Thus it came about that the centre of gravity of the whole operation moved to Canada. It was particularly fortunate that Vancouver and Edmonton ran the same MTS operating system.

2.4.3.2 *Vienna (September 1972)*

The next WG meeting was in Vienna. (The Editors had a private meeting beforehand.) We had available samples of what we had written, in particular the **'NEST'** syntax (2.5.1.3), and also a large number of detailed issues to raise on the improvements. The meeting gave first priority to transput, whose discussion had been curtailed at Fontainebleau, and then proceeded to discuss and vote on the various improvements.

But then started the biggest attack of cold feet I have ever witnessed (brought about, perhaps, by the extent of the changes we were proposing to the method of description, and by the **'NEST'** syntax in particular). A "Petition for the Status Quo of ALGOL 68," signed by five members and five observers, claimed that the Revised Report had become a pointless undertaking (beyond a few corrections to ambiguities or inconsistencies) and that the idea should be abandoned. This was debated on the very last day of the meeting. The motion was that the revision should consist of [R] plus an addendum, and the petitioners produced a small list of the changes they conceded should be allowed (and clearly there was no time left at that meeting to re-vote all the detailed decisions already made).

We pointed out that some errors (for example, the infinite mode problem (2.5.1.4)) were almost impossible to correct in the old framework; we pointed out that implementors seemed content with the intentions as published and that only three implementations were anything like complete (and Malvern already incorporated many of the changes); we pointed out that, to remove troublesome points so as to have a basis for upwards-compatible future extensions, we would need at least twice the list proposed by the petitioners; we pointed out that it would then require an addendum half the size of the Report, and that it was crazy to define the changes to be made by the length of an addendum—we were getting nowhere, and now it was time for the vote.

It had long been a Working Group tradition to phrase straw votes in the form "Who could live with . . .?" rather than "Who prefers . . .?" Therefore, to let everybody see the full consequences before taking the formal vote, I proposed the questions, "Who could live with the state if the resolution was passed?" and "Who could live with the opposite state?" The results were 12-5-1 (for-against-abstain) and 12-1-5.

Now Van Wijngaarden was always a superb politician. Having observed who had actually voted, he now pointed out that passing the resolution "would cause the death of five of the six editors. That seems a most unproductive situation." And when the formal motion was put the vote was 6-6-6, and we were through.

2.4.3.3 *Revision by Mail*

For the next nine months we worked separately on our pieces. Each circulated his texts to the others, and we all checked each other's work. The text of the syntax was maintained in Vancouver and the rest in Edmonton. (Periodically, I sent long *ed* scripts to Edmonton on paper tape—and surprisingly they usually worked without error.) This method of collaboration proved to be exceedingly fruitful. You don't launch a text over such distances until you are quite sure it is really what you intend to say. We survived together, accepting and appreciating each other's strengths and weaknesses, because that was the only way that could work.

It became apparent, right from Vancouver, that a major rewrite of the Report was necessary if it was to be made more accessible to the uninitiated reader. From time to time we were shocked and surprised by some outrageous consequence of the original definition, and each time, rather than patching it up, we stood back, identified *why* the misunderstanding had arisen, and modified the method of description so that it was no longer possible to express problems of that class. (Examples are the removal of extensions (2.5.4.1) and of infinite modes (2.5.1.4).) We treated the Report as a large programming project, and consciously applied the principles of structured programming and good system design. The syntax and semantics are now written so that it is generally easy to check that all possible cases have been accounted for, and wherever there was any doubt about this we generated a proof of the doubtful property, even incorporating the proof in the pragmatics [RR 7.3.1]. That we succeeded in our aims is evidenced by the fact that, disregarding the transput section (which is another story), the total number of bugs now known in [RR] can be counted on the fingers of one hand (2.6.2.1).

During August of 1972 I had met Koster in Manchester, where we worked over the transput. However, there was no obvious person available actually to do the work. Transput, as usual, was receiving less attention than it should. Eventually, in February 1973, Richard Fisker, a student at Manchester, came to me looking for a project for his Masters thesis. He embarked upon it and had a small sample to show at Dresden, but the work was barely complete by the deadline in Los Angeles.

We circulated a draft two months before the next WG meeting in Dresden (April 1973), and I wrote an explanation of how the descriptive method had changed. This time there were no significant calls for abandonment, and many people gave their opinion that the new document was clearer to read, especially Sintzoff's semantics. A few further improvements were discussed and voted on.

2.4.3.4 *Edmonton (July 1973)*

We had obtained funding from the NATO Science Committee that enabled the Editors to meet in Edmonton. Lambert Meertens, who had been playing an increasingly active role in monitoring the progress of the revision, was sent by Van Wijngaarden as his representative; Fisker was also present, and thus we had now reached our final complement of eight editors. The texts of the various parts were now merged into one document, and a hectic three weeks ensued.

As before, we discussed, argued, and compromised, but always retaining our mutual respect. The technique used if one of us thought his opinion was being shouted down was to say to the others, "Eat!" (these arguments often took place at mealtimes); by established convention the others then kept silent while the point was made; the paradigm is specified formally in [RR 3.3]. Finally, we produced a text for circulation to the WG in advance of the next meeting that was complete except for the pragmatics in the transput section (and much of these were included in a further edition provided at the meeting itself).

The Los Angeles meeting (September 1973) considered the Report, proposed some minor changes, and authorized its submission to TC2 subject only to "editorial polishing and explanatory material which make no additional substantive changes." The Editors were instructed to make it available to the subscribers of the *ALGOL Bulletin* and to submit it for publication in appropriate journals. WG 2.1 also established a standing subcommittee on ALGOL 68 Support (convened by Robert Uzgalis, and then by Van der Meulen from 1978) "to act as a point of contact with users and implementors of the language, and to serve their needs by preparing complementary specifications and enhancements."

2.4.4 The Aftermath

The Editors met once again in Manchester to discuss the polishing, and Fisker and I continued to tidy up the transput and complete the missing pragmatics. Since the typesetting disc still had not arrived, the Report was eventually issued to the *ALGOL Bulletin* readership reproduced from a lineprinter listing [TR 74-3].

2.4.4.1 *Cambridge (April 1974)*

The newly formed Support subcommittee held its first meeting in Cambridge. A close study of the transput section, mainly in Amsterdam, had revealed a number of bugs and inconsistencies, and these formed the main topic of discussion. Now this meeting was, in my experience, the first time that any group of people sufficiently concerned with transput and competent to discuss it had ever assembled in one place, and the result was a very thorough review leading to a considerable cleanup (2.3.9). Whether we were entitled to make such changes as were shortly to be published in AB 37 as errata to [TR 74-3] is a legal nicety, but we certainly did, and the language is all the better for it. For a report of this meeting see [King 1974].

2.4.4.2 *Typesetting*

The WG met in Breukelen in August 1974, but our special typesetting disc still had not been delivered. A further set of errata to [TR 74-3] appeared in AB 38.

The disc finally appeared early in 1975, so that at the Munich meeting of WG 2.1 (August 1975) the Editors spent all of their free time reading through the galleys, spotting all the things that were not quite right. [Van Wijngaarden 1975] just made it by the year's end, and a final set of errata in AB 39 brought [TR 74-3] into line.

2.4.5 Postscript

What have we learned about designing programming languages? First, a small group of people (four or five) must do the actual work, and geographical separation (as between Amsterdam/Brussels in [R] or Manchester/Edmonton/Vancouver in [RR]) is a great encouragement to careful work. (The advent of e-mail may undo this in the future.) The editors need to have very tidy and pernickety minds (which does not necessarily qualify them as good designers of language features); moreover, constructing the formal definition at the same time as the language is being designed is a sure way to avoid obscure corners—a simultaneous *prototype* implementation would be even better.

A large committee is a good place for brainstorming to get initial ideas, but it must recognize its limitations, the most important of which is that it is incapable of attending to detail. A large committee is also necessary to give democratic approval to the work of the editors. (In spite of the fact that this arrangement was observed to be unstable, I still do not know how to dampen it.) Moreover, the large committee will often take decisions which the editors *know* to be technically flawed—but that is in the nature of democracy.

Finally, there is much to be said for doing the whole job twice, but in any event it always takes twice as long as you think (even when you think you have allowed for this factor). Any attempt to rush it is doomed to failure (although it must be admitted that our revision did, bar a few items, meet its deadline—but it was hard work). My opinion is that in this Revision we did get it just about right, and what I have observed of other language design efforts since that time only serves to confirm this view.

2.5 THE METHOD OF DESCRIPTION

The word "on the street" is that ALGOL 68 is defined by an "unreadable" document. Certainly [MR 93], when it first came out, was a tough nut to crack (I should know!), but [R] was already a big improvement and we tried strenuously to attack this problem for [RR]. But unfortunately, much of the mud slung at [MR 93] is probably still sticking.

The language is defined by its Report in four parts: the Syntax, the Semantic Model, the Semantics proper, and the **Standard-prelude**. These will now be examined in turn.

2.5.1 Syntax

2.5.1.1 *W-Grammars*

The notation now known as a W-Grammar seems to be the main stumbling block to people approaching the Report for the first time. When this completely new notation first appeared, its readers had no previous model on which to build. Today there are several similar notations (for example, Attribute Grammars and Prolog) with which people are familiar. So a good way to explain it to a modern audience is to start from Prolog. This will also help to illuminate both the power and the limitations of W-Grammars.

That a W-Grammar can be explained in terms of Prolog is not surprising when it is realized that Prolog actually stems from some attempts at natural language processing by Colmerauer. His first system [Chastellier 1969] actually used W-Grammars. This developed into the more structured Q-Systems, and finally into Prolog [Colmerauer 1996].

Here is a rule written in Prolog:

***assignation**(ref(MODE)) :-*
        ***destination**(ref(MODE)), **becomes_symbol**, **source**(MODE).*

This is Prolog, so *MODE* is a variable (it begins with an upper case letter) and *ref* is a functor (with no inherent meaning). The meaning is that we have a goal "do we see an ***assignation*** here?", and to answer this we must test the subgoals "do we see a ***destination*** here?", followed by "do we see a ***becomes_symbol*** here?", etc. (I have cheated slightly by regarding the source text as an implicit variable). Prolog will keep backtracking if it fails, and if it gets into a loop, one just says, "Ah! but that was just the procedural meaning—the declarative meaning clearly expressed the right intention." The nice thing about Prolog is that the values of variables such as *MODE* may be deduced from the subgoals or imposed with the question; and again, from the declarative point of view, the distinction does not matter—the value of the variable just has to be consistent throughout.

Here now is the corresponding rule in a W-Grammar [R 8.3.1.1.a].

reference to MODE assignation :
        reference to MODE destination, becomes symbol, MODE source.

The difference is that in Prolog the parameters of goals are well-formed expressions built out of functors, atoms and variables, whereas in a W-Grammar they are just free strings of characters, or 'protonotions', and the variables, or 'metanotions', stand for other strings of characters as produced by a context-free 'metagrammar'. Some possible 'metaproductions' of the metanotion **'MODE'** are

'real', **'integral'**, **'reference to integral'**, **'row of reference to integral'**

and so on. So if you substitute **'integral'** for **'MODE'** you get

reference to integral assignation :
        reference to integral destination, becomes symbol, integral source.

(observe the consistent substitution for **'MODE'** throughout), which will eventually produce familiar things like *i := 99*. But observe how we have insisted that the type (or mode) of the **destination** *i* must be ***ref int*** because the type of the **source** *99* is ***int*** (or *99* must be ***int*** because *i* is ***ref int***—you can argue both ways round, just as in Prolog).

The unstructured and potentially ambiguous strings of characters that form the rules of a W-Grammar give it great power; indeed, Sintzoff [1967] shows that it can produce any recursively enumerable set, and hence is equivalent to a Chomsky Type-0 Grammar. One can say things that simply cannot be expressed using the well-formed expressions of Prolog. The Bad News is that it is quite impossible to write a parser based on unrestricted W-Grammars. If you want to do that, you must introduce some more structure, as in Prolog, or as in the Affix Grammars described in Koster 1971.

Here is an example that cannot be written in Prolog (although it was possible in Q-Systems). First, some metagrammar:

MOOD :: real ; integral ; boolean ; etc.
LMOODSETY :: MOOD and LMOODSETY ; EMPTY.
RMOODSETY :: RMOODSETY and MOOD ; EMPTY.

Hence, in the rule [R 8.2.4.1.b],

one out of LMOODSETY MOOD RMOODSETY mode FORM :
MOOD FORM; . . . .

'LMOODSETY MOOD RMOODSETY' can metaproduce a sequence such as **'real and integral and boolean'** in such varying ways that the **'MOOD'** can be chosen as any of the three (for example, choose **'real and integral'** for **'LMOODSETY'**, **'EMPTY'** for **'RMOODSETY'**, and thus **'boolean'** for **'MOOD'**).

Thus a W-Grammar is a much more powerful notation than Prolog; but this power must be used by report editors with the utmost discretion, if the result is to be intelligible.

Here is another rule [R 8.3.0.1.a]:

MODE confrontation : MODE assignation ; MODE conformity relation ;
MODE identity relation ; MODE cast.

With this you can try to produce a **confrontation** for any **'MODE'**—so how about a **real-confrontation**? But the rule already given for **'assignation'** will produce only a **reference-to-MODE-assignation**. Likewise, the only rule for **'conformity relation'** is for a **boolean-conformity-relation**. In fact, the only alternative on the right side of the rule that has productions for every possible **'MODE'** is **'MODE cast'**. All the other attempts at a **real-confrontation** lead to 'blind alleys'. Duncan was much concerned about blind alleys, especially as to how the reader could recognize one without an exhaustive search through the whole syntax, and he was not satisfied by their indication by a '–' in the cross references. Nevertheless, blind alleys turn out to be a very powerful tool in the hands of the grammar writer. Blind alleys occur also in Prolog.

In [RR] we made three major changes to the syntax, as will now be described.

2.5.1.2 *Predicates*

In the Revision we discovered new and helpful ways to use a W-Grammar. Consider the following: First the metagrammar

NOTION :: ALPHA ; NOTION ALPHA.
ALPHA ::
a ; b ; c ; d ; e ; f ; g ; h ; i ; j ; k ; l ; m ; n ; o ; p ; q ; r ; s ; t ; u ; v ; w ; x ; y ; z.
NOTETY :: NOTION ; EMPTY.

and now the ordinary rules

where true : EMPTY.
where (NOTETY) is (NOTETY) : where true.

So if I ask for productions of **'where (abc) is (abc)'** I will get the terminal production **'EMPTY'**, but if I ask for productions of **'where (abc) is (def)'** I am forced into a blind alley, and I get no terminal production at all.

There is also a rule of the form

unless (NOTETY1) is (NOTETY2) : . . .

which produces **'EMPTY'** if **'NOTETY1'** and **'NOTETY2'** are different, and a blind alley if they are the same. This is quite a bit harder to write than the **'where'** case; for the full story see [RR 1.3.1].

Rules that can produce only **'EMPTY'** or a blind alley are known as 'predicates', and their use greatly simplifies the number and complexity of rules required in the Report. Here is an example of their use [RR 6.1.1.a]. The intention is to forbid deproceduring for a certain subclass of **FORMs**.

strong MOID FORM coercee :
  where (FORM) is (MORF), STRONG MOID MORF ;
  where (FORM) is (COMORF), STRONG MOID COMORF,
    unless (STRONG MOID) is (deprocedured to void).

2.5.1.3 *Context Conditions vs NESTs*

In [R] a whole chapter is devoted to 'context conditions', which seek to ensure, for example, that each applied occurrence of an **identifier** 'identifies' its correct defining occurrence. In other languages these conditions are often referred to as 'static semantics'. So in [R 4.1.2.a], for example, there is a fairly straightforward set of Steps for starting at an applied occurrence and searching in ever wider **blocks** for its defining occurrence. But this is deceptively straightforward; people will quote it at you to show you how simple it all is. What they do not show you is the corresponding rule [R 4.3.2.b] for identifying **operators**, with this alternative form for the Step 3 of [R 4.1.2.a].

> Step 3: If the home contains an operator-defining occurrence **O** {, in an **operation-declaration** (7.5.1.a,b),} of a terminal production **T** of **'PRAM ADIC operator'** which is the same terminal production of **'ADIC indication'** as the given occurrence, and which {, the identification of all descendent **identifiers**, **indications** and **operators** of the **operand**(s) of **F** having been made,} is such that some **formula** exists which is the same sequence of symbols as **F**, whose **operator** is an occurrence of **T** and which is such that the original of each descendent **identifier**, **indication** and **operator** of its **operand**(s) is the same notion as the original of the corresponding **identifier**, **indication** and **operator** contained in **F** {, which, if the **program** is a proper **program**, is uniquely determined by virtue of 4.4.1.a}, then the given occurrence identifies **O**; otherwise, Step 2 is taken.

Every word of that (except for the pragmatic remarks between {. . .}) is essential for its correct interpretation. I know that it is correct because I have, in my time, studied it carefully, and I have seen all the half dozen incorrect versions that preceded it. But how can one have confidence with mechanisms requiring such turgidity?

In the Revision, therefore, we removed all the context conditions and brought the whole identification process into the syntax. The tools required to do this are still complex, but once one has understood them they hardly intrude. And their formality ensures that it is always possible to work through any particular case and to see whether and why it is or is not allowed.

Briefly [RR 1.2.3], there is a metanotion **'NEST'** that metaproduces a sequence of **'LAYER'**s (each corresponding to a **block**). Each **'LAYER'** metaproduces a sequence of **'DEC'**s (each corresponding to a **declaration** in the **program**). The **'NEST'** of each **block** contains one more **'LAYER'** than its parent **block**, and the syntax of **declarations** enforces that the **'DEC'**s of that extra **'LAYER'** correspond to the things declared, and moreover that they are 'independent' of each other (for example, that the same **identifier** is not declared twice) [RR 7.1.1]. Each syntax rule carries a **'NEST'**, so that the new rule for **assignation** [RR 5.2.1.1.a] is

REF to MODE NEST assignation :
REF to MODE NEST destination, becomes token, MODE NEST source.

Now, if the **source** is, or contains, an **applied-identifier**, the syntax fishes its **'DEC'** out of the **'NEST'** [RR 7.2.1] (it is required to be there) and checks its **'MODE'**. Of course, all of this machinery makes heavy use of predicates.

2.5.1.4 *Infinite Modes*

Consider the following:

mode language = struct (int *age,* ***ref language*** *father);*
loc language *algol;*

In [R] the mode of *algol* is **'reference to [language]'**, where **'[language]'** stands for **'structured with integral field [age] and reference to [language] field [father]'**. In other words, the string of characters describing this mode is infinite. Why did this need to be so? Consider:

algol := father ***of*** *algol .*

If the mode of *algol* had been represented finitely, by some such notation as **'reference to structured with integral field [age] and reference to *language* field [father]'**, then the mode of *father* ***of*** *algol* (after coercion) would be ***'language'***. Substituting these in the right side of the syntax rule for **'assignation'** gives

reference to structured with integral field [age] and
reference to *language* field [father] destination,
becomes symbol, *language* source.

And this is not allowed, since the **'MODE'** in the rule has not been substituted consistently. With an infinite string the substitution is consistent, provided only that you believe that, if $\mathbf{X}^{\infty}$ stands for **. . . XXXX**, then $\mathbf{X}^{\infty}\,\mathbf{X}$ is no different from $\mathbf{X}^{\infty}$.

Infinite modes caused much discussion at Tirrenia and after. The strange thing is that the fuss had not started earlier, as infinite modes had been present since [MR 88]. Maybe the one obscure pragmatic remark in [MR 88] had been overlooked, whereas a second more obvious remark in [MR 93] had invited attention.

Duncan was particularly concerned (he claimed he could not read the Report beyond a certain point because he was still unfolding some infinite production). The question asked was "how could an infinite sequence be written on a finite piece of paper?", to which Van Wijngaarden's famous reply was that you wrote the first character on the first half of the sheet, the second character on half of the remaining part of the sheet, the third on half of what remained after that, and so on. More seriously, he claimed that (from the viewpoint of a constructivist mathematician) it was the mechanism that produced the infinite sequences that was important, not the sequences themselves. However, [R] did not discuss these mathematical niceties, and it was not at all clear that the procedure was mathematically sound.

Meertens [1969] (quoting a letter from Tseytin) and Pair [1970] were the first to suggest that there might be flaws, but these doubts were expressed so vaguely, or so abstractly, that they went unnoticed. It was not until Boom [1972] exhibited an actual ambiguity that we were forced to take note. Here is Boom's example:

```
mode n = struct(ref n a, c);
mode hendrik = struct(ref struct(ref n a, b, c) c);  # 1 field #
mode boom = struct(ref n b, c);                      # 2 fields #
```

Now if you write out (in imagination) the full modes for ***hendrik*** and ***boom***, you will find that they cannot be distinguished under any reasonable understanding of infinity, certainly not one that regards $\mathbf{X}^{\infty}\,\mathbf{X}$ as equivalent to $\mathbf{X}^{\infty}$, yet their modes are clearly supposed to be different.

For [RR], therefore, we resolved that any **program** should be producible in only a finite number of moves. The mode of *algol* is now **'reference to mui definition of structured with integral field [age] reference to mui application field [father] mode'** (read **'mui'** as a kind of label). However, there are many other ways of 'spelling' that same mode, just by expanding the **'mui application'** a few more times, but all these spellings are equivalent (in fact, a mode is now an equivalence class). The equivalence is defined by means of a predicate [RR 7.3.1] that systematically compares two (possibly infinite) trees, essentially following the algorithm of [Koster 1969]. Writing the syntax for this predicate was hard work. We all had a go at it, first to get a version that worked, and then to get a version tidy enough to present. It is, admittedly, also hard work to read (in spite of copious pragmatics), but the Report is written so that it does not obtrude, and the naive reader need hardly be aware of it.

2.5.2 The Semantic Model

Any definition of a programming language needs to define very carefully the "domain of discourse," or model, in terms of which everything is to be explained. Even today, many language definitions do not do this (they suppose that the reader can infer the meaning "obviously" intended), or they scatter this important information throughout the text. But McCarthy had explained this need to the WG as early as 1963, leading to its adoption by the Vienna school [Lucas 1969]. Following an explicit request from the Subcommittee at Kootwijk, [R2] was therefore devoted to describing the rules of the 'hypothetical computer'.

This particular hypothetical computer is well removed from "reality," giving little comfort to the man who wants to relate it to concepts with which he is already familiar (variables, addresses, and the like). Essentially, it is a graph of 'objects' (including 'external' constructs as produced by the syntax, and 'internal' values). Objects may have attributes (for example, values have types and scopes). The arcs of the graph are 'relationships' (both static and dynamic) between objects (for example, 'to access', 'to refer to', 'to be newer than', and 'to be a subname of').

The terminology used is often arcane and different from common usage, as already pointed out in Section 2.1.3. For example, the attribute 'scope' would nowadays be termed 'extent'. (It will be noted that I have been using such present-day terminology throughout this paper.) The worst example was the term 'name'. Names are allowed 'to refer to' values, and from time to time (during **assignations**) they may be made to refer to other values. If you read 'name' as 'variable', and 'to refer' as 'to contain', then you might suddenly begin to understand things a whole lot better. And you must not confuse (internal) names with (external) **identifiers**, although the latter may, in appropriate circumstances, 'access' the former.

The 'actions' available to the hypothetical computer are the creation of new objects and the changing of dynamic relationships. The semantics for the various constructs of the language prescribe the actions that comprise their 'elaboration'.

One of the actions provided by the original Report was to take a copy of some construct, to replace some of its identifiers systematically by other identifiers, and then to elaborate it. This technique was in the tradition of the semantics of ALGOL 60, although other language definitions, such as [Lucas 1969], had already abandoned it. If carefully applied, it does give the expected and well-known semantics of block-structured languages, but its operation is counter intuitive as regards the way programmers normally think of a running program, and it is exceedingly difficult to ensure that it has indeed been "carefully applied" throughout. Having been caught out several times, therefore, we abandoned this concept and introduced a system of 'environs' and 'locales'.

An 'environ' comprises a 'locale' (which models the objects accessible locally within some **block**) together with an older environ (whose locales model objects that were declared outside of that **block**). Every elaboration is deemed to take place within some identifiable environ, and the chain of locales comprising that environ corresponds to the 'dynamic stack' familiar to implementors. (A separate chain of locales is defined for the 'static stack'.)

2.5.3 The Semantics

The semantics of ALGOL 68 is an operational semantics. In [R] the semantics were described in sequences of Steps, with frequent jumps to other Steps (a program full of ***goto***s, in effect). Also, there was some very turgid phraseology that we were able to remove by defining terminology in the semantic model more carefully.

In [RR], Sintzoff set out to adhere to the principles of structured programming, with 'If's, 'Case's, and nice indentation. The new semantics is therefore much shorter (only 12 pages total, which for 12 months work might not seem much). Here is the semantics of assigning a value to a name in both the old and the new styles.

First, from [R 8.3.1.2.c]:

An instance of a value is assigned to a name in the following steps:

Step 1: If the given value does not refer to a component of a multiple value having one or more states equal to **0** {2.2.3.3.b}, if the scope of the given name is not larger than the scope of the given value {2.2.4.2} and if the given name is not **nil**, then Step 2 is taken; otherwise, the further elaboration is undefined;

Step 2: The instance of the value referred to by the given name is considered; if the mode of the given name begins with **'reference to structured with'** or with **'reference to row of'**, then Step 3 is taken; otherwise, the considered instance is superseded {a} by a copy of the given instance and the assignment has been accomplished;

Step 3: If the considered value is a structured value, then Step 5 is taken; otherwise, applying the notation of 2.2.3.3.b to its descriptor, if for some **i**, **i=1**, . . ., **n**, $\mathbf{s_i}$**=1** ($\mathbf{t_i}$**=1**) and $\mathbf{l_i}$ ($\mathbf{u_i}$) is not equal to the corresponding bound in the descriptor of the given value, then the further elaboration is undefined;

Step 4: If some $\mathbf{s_i}$**=0** or $\mathbf{t_i}$**=0**, then, first, a new instance of a multiple value **M** is created whose descriptor is a copy of the descriptor of the given value modified by setting its states to the corresponding states in the descriptor of the considered value, and whose elements are copies of elements, if any, of the considered value, and, otherwise, are new instances of values whose mode is, or a mode from which is united, the mode obtained by deleting all initial **'row of'**s from the mode of the considered value; next **M** is made to be referred to by the given name and is considered instead;

Step 5: Each field (element, if any,) of the given value is assigned {in an order which is left undefined} to the name referring to the corresponding field (element, if any,) of the considered value and the assignment has been accomplished.

And now from [RR 5.2.1.2.b]:

A value **W** is "assigned to" a name **N**, whose mode is some **'REF to MODE'**, as follows:

It is required that

- **N** be not nil, and that
- **W** be not newer in scope than **N**;

Case A: **'MODE'** is some **'structured with FIELDS mode'**:

- For each **'TAG'** selecting a field in **W**,
- that field is assigned to the subname selected by **'TAG'** in **N**;

Case B: **'MODE'** is some **'ROWS of MODE1'**:

- let **V** be the {old} value referred to by **N**;
- it is required that the descriptors of **W** and **V** be identical;
- For each index **I** selecting an element in **W**,
- that element is assigned to the subname selected by **I** in **N**;

Case C: **'MODE'** is some **'flexible ROWS of MODE1'**:

- let **V** be the {old} value referred to by **N**;
- **N** is made to refer to a multiple value composed of

  (i) the descriptor of **W**,

  (ii) variants {4.4.2.c} of some element {possibly a ghost element} of **V**;
- **N** is endowed with subnames {2.1.3.4.g};
- For each index **I** selecting an element in **W**,
- that element is assigned to the subname selected by **I** in **N**;

Other Cases {e.g., where **'MODE'** is some **'PLAIN'** or some **'UNITED'**}:

- **N** is made to refer {2.1.3.2.a} to **W**.

On the face of it that looks straightforward enough, but if you peer closely you will observe that no less than 20 apparently ordinary words are being used with a very precise meaning, as defined in the semantic model. Here they are:

> value; name; mode; is; require; nil; newer than; scope; select; field; subname; refer to; descriptor; index; element; make to refer to; multiple value; variant; ghost element; endow with subnames.

Thus much of the improved readability of [RR] came from a careful choice of new technical terms and abbreviations—the art of choosing such abbreviations lay in making them "suggest" to the reader the same "obvious" meaning that he found when he actually looked them up. But the price paid was the piling of more and more concepts and definitions into the semantic model, their purpose and necessity not always being immediately apparent. It is probably fair to say that the model is too big. (It certainly occupied more space than the semantics proper.)

Although the semantics is ostensibly written in English, it is in effect a formal notation ("syntax-directed English," as Mailloux described it). It is therefore proper to ask why we did not, in the revision, go the whole way and make it entirely formal. This would clearly have been possible, but the growth of our understanding of the new semantics and its model did not happen overnight, but indeed occupied all the time available to us, so the possibility could not be considered seriously. Moreover, it would have, in my opinion, added nothing to the rigour achieved, and the formalization of the large semantic model itself would have been a major task, not necessarily resulting in a clearer product.

2.5.4 Standard-prelude

It is always tempting to define parts of a language in terms of other parts already defined, but there are dangers, as I shall explain. This was done in two places in [R], in the 'extensions' and in the **standard-prelude**, especially in the transput.

2.5.4.1 *Extensions*

Having defined a core language (which was actually about 90% of the total), [R 9] purported to define the rest by providing replacements for certain sequences of symbols. For example, according to [R 9.2.c] you could replace

struct **s** = (***int*** *a, b*), ***struct*** **t** = (***real*** *x, y*); by ***struct*** **s** = (***int*** *a, b*), **t** = (***real*** *x, y*);

and you could replace

*[1:n]****real*** *a1*, *[1:n]****real*** *a2;* by *[1:n]****real*** *a1, a2;* .

Effectively, these extensions were defining both syntax and semantics at the same time. So it turned out that the first example also allowed you to produce, by extension,

struct **s** = (***int*** *a, b*), **t** = ***real***;

which is nonsense (this is a syntactic problem), and the second example mandates that, given *[1:n]****real*** *a1, a2;* it is quite in order for the side effects of *n* to happen twice (this is a semantic problem).

WG members had expressed doubts about the safety of this mechanism as far back as Zandvoort. We now found so many further shocks and surprises that our confidence in the mechanism entirely evaporated and we abandoned it, incorporating these features (where they were retained at all) into the main syntax. Extensions seemed like a good idea at the time, but they are only really appropriate for a language where the core really is small (say 30 percent), and even then some separate method of specifying the syntax should be used.

2.5.4.2 *Transput*

Defining the built-in **operators** in the **standard-prelude** by means of **operation-declarations** turned out to be quite satisfactory, but doing the same thing for the transput routines was a grave mistake.

The underlying model of the transput system has already been described (2.3.9). To write this model and the ***proc***s using it in ALGOL 68 was a substantial programming task, running to 68 pages in [RR 10.3]. This was akin to writing an actual implementation, insofar as we had to add numerous

declarations and so forth with which to 'implement' the model. But it still was not (and was not intended as) an implementation that you could run (you were simply meant to read it in order to see what requirements were being defined), and care was taken to leave many things undefined.

The net result was that you could not see the forest (the model) for the trees (the details of its implementation), and it was difficult to show that it was free of bugs and inconsistencies (which it was not). Most of the problems we had in the maintenance phase (2.6.2.2) lay in sorting out the resultant mess. If I were doing this job over again, I would certainly define the meaning of the transput ***proc***s in a more axiomatic style—by providing the preconditions and postconditions on the state of the model that each was supposed to satisfy, for example.

2.5.5 Style

[R] was written in a very pedantic style. This was necessary because the more formal your document is seen to be, the more people will actually believe what you actually wrote, as opposed to what you intended. Van Wijngaarden's English followed a very set style, with punctilious punctuation (as may be seen from the examples already quoted). In the revision, we tried to adhere to the same high standards (I believe I learned to write a good pastiche of Van Wijngaarden's style), and we often spent much time discussing what was and what was not correct English. For example, we had great arguments as to the proper form of the negative subjunctive ("It is required that the value *be not* nil") and I remember a full 15 minutes devoted to whether *well-formedness* should be hyphenated.

The successive drafts of [R] gradually established the style. In [MR 76] the metanotions consisted of just one upper-case letter. (Hence there were just 26 of them.) There was no explanatory material and no examples, and that document really was unreadable (in addition to being buggy), so that I find it hard to imagine why WG 2.1 agreed to go with it. The meeting at Kootwijk agreed that the metanotions should be English words with suggestive meanings. By [MR 88] 'pragmatic remarks' (comments enclosed within {...}) had appeared and by [MR 101] had been elevated to an art form. The choice of words used for metanotions and nonterminals was initially too arbitrary. (One can recognize the overzealous use of Roget's Thesaurus in the sequence **'adapted'**, **'adjusted'**, **'fitted'**, **'peeled'** which preceded the now familiar **'strong'**, **'firm'**, **'weak'**, **'soft'**.) It took much pressure from the WG, in Zandvoort and Tirrenia, to persuade Van Wijngaarden to include more motivations, more cross references, different fonts for syntactic objects, and so on. In the revision, we tried to take this policy even further. The additions to the syntactic tools enabled us to use fewer nonterminals, and we systematically introduced each section with pragmatics that set out the goods to be described (indeed, you can almost discover the language from the pragmatics alone).

If a reader approaches some piece of mathematical formalism with the wrong preconceived idea of what is to be presented, he can waste hours before his internal model becomes corrected. I therefore regard the principle purpose of pragmatics to be to "preload" the reader with the appropriate model. This of course introduces redundancy into the document, but this is no bad thing (as seems to have been accepted when this came up at Tirrenia), for if the formal and pragmatic descriptions are found, after close scrutiny, to disagree, this may well alert the reader to the presence of a bug in the formalism; better to recognize this (and to seek clarification from the proper authorities) than to implement the bug.

I therefore offer the following guidelines, based on our experience.

- Pragmatic remarks should be copious, but well delineated from the formal text. Their purpose is to educate the reader (in the sense of the Latin *educare*).

- Motivation should be given for *why* things are as they are. Redundancy is no bad thing, except within the strictly formal parts.
- Syntax should be fully cross referenced, both forwards and backwards; semantics likewise.
- Each syntax rule should be accompanied by examples.
- There should be copious glossaries, indices, and summaries.
- The Report should not take itself too seriously. With the best will in the world, it is not going to be perfect. Our Report contains some good jokes, many quotations from Shakespeare, Lewis Carroll, A. A. Milne and others, and even a picture of Eeyore. The various translations of it have been made in the same spirit.
- Above all, the Report should be fun to write.

Unfortunately, Standards Bodies and Government Departments do not always encourage these practices in their guidelines. I invite the reader to consider the extent to which they have been followed, or otherwise, in more recent programming language definitions, together with the perceived success of those definitions. On that basis, I will rest my case.

2.6 THE MAINTENANCE PHASE

After 1974, WG 2.1 proceeded to other things and left most ALGOL 68 activity to its Support Subcommittee. This considered enhancements to the language, together with the various bugs and problems that were reported. It met whenever there was a meeting of the full WG, but its main activities took place in independent meetings, as listed in Table 2.5.

TABLE 2.5

Meetings of the Support Subcommittee.

Date	Meeting place	Meeting	Topics discussed
Apr 1974	Cambridge	SC	Transput (2.4.4.1); Sublanguage.
Aug 1974	Breukelen	WG, SC	
Jan 1975	Boston	SC	Modules; Standard Hardware Representation; Sublanguage; Partial Parametrization.
Aug 1975	Munich	SC, WG	TUM-10 mechanism; acceptance of Sublanguage, Standard Hardware Representation, and Partial Parametrization.
Sep 1976	St. Pierre de Chartreuse	WG, SC	Sublanguage still being polished.
Aug 1977	Kingston	SC	Modules; Bugs and problems; TP task force formed.
Dec 1977	Oxford	TP, SC, WG	Implementation Model; Transput problems; 1st Commentaries released.
Aug 1978	Amsterdam	TP	Transput problems; Implementation Model.
Aug 1978	Jablonna	WG, SC	Acceptance of Modules and TORRIX; 2nd Commentaries released.
Dec 1978	Cambridge	TP	Transput problems; Implementation model.
Apr 1979	Summit	TP, SC, WG	Acceptance of Test Set and Implementation Model; 3rd Commentaries released.

WG = full Working Group; SC = Support Subcommittee; TP = Transput task force.

2.6.1 Enhancements

2.6.1.1 *The Sublanguage*

Although a Subcommittee on Sublanguages had been formed at Manchester, it never produced anything concrete, and it was an independent effort by Peter Hibbard, implementing on a minicomputer with only 16K words at Liverpool, which eventually bore fruit. Hibbard's sublanguage, first introduced to the WG at Vienna, was intended for mainly numerical applications, and the features omitted from it were intended to simplify compilation. It was discussed by the WG and the Support Subcommittee on several occasions, and finally formulated as an addendum to the Report and released for publication as an IFIP Document at Munich. However, the final polishing lasted for some time until it eventually appeared as [Hibbard 1977]. A more informal description will be found in Appendix 4 of [Lindsey 1977].

2.6.1.2 *The Standard Hardware Representation*

ALGOL 68 was conceived in the days when every computer had its own character code. Even with the advent of ASCII things were not entirely settled, since many printers still did not support lower case letters. The conclusion reached, and sold to the Support Subcommittee by Wilfred Hansen and Hendrik Boom, was that one could easily transliterate between two character sets, provided that implementations restricted themselves to a set of 60 'worthy characters', each representable by a single character in each set. This still left the problem of 'stropping' (2.1.3) and the solution adopted was for *POINT* stropping, which would always be enabled (as in *.REAL X*) with a choice of *UPPER* stropping (as in *REAL x*) or *RES*erved stropping (as in *REAL X*) under control of a **pragmat**.

The document formalizing this [Hansen 1977] was also released for publication as an IFIP Document at Munich. For an informal treatment, see Appendix 5 of [Lindsey 1977].

2.6.1.3 *TUM-10*

The hassle of getting a document approved through the IFIP hierarchy was considered too great for every small enhancement to the language, and a simpler mechanism was agreed on at Munich. The Support Subcommittee was to scrutinize proposals to ensure that they were consistent, upwards-compatible, and useful, and release them "to encourage implementors experimenting with features similar to those described ... to use the formulation here given, so as to avoid proliferation of dialects," and the full WG would then authorize publication in the *ALGOL Bulletin* with this wording. This principle was enshrined in a document numbered TUM-10 [WG 2.1 1975].

2.6.1.4 *Partial Parametrization*

After the failure of the Bekic proposal to relax the extent restriction on ***proc***s (2.3.5), it was agreed that this problem ought to be solved by partial parametrization. At Boston the Support Subcommittee appointed a task force (Bekic, Foster, Hibbard, Meertens, and myself) which brought forward a proposal to incorporate this [Lindsey 1976], and it was adopted under the newly invented TUM-10 mechanism at Munich.

Here is an example:

```
proc compose = (proc(real)real f, g, real x) real:
                    f(g(x));
proc(real)real sqex = compose(sqrt, exp,   );
```

2.6.1.5 *Modules and Separate Compilation*

The basic idea for program encapsulation using modules was first presented (so far as I am aware) by Steve Schuman at the Fontainebleau meeting of WG 2.1 (see [Schuman 1974] for a fuller account). The inclusion of such a facility within ALGOL 68 was discussed by the Support Subcommittee on various occasions, and finally agreed under the TUM-10 mechanism at Jablonna [Lindsey 1978]. The people involved at various times, in addition to myself and Hendrik Boom who wrote the final document, included Steve Bourne, Robert Dewar, Mike Guy, John Peck, and Steve Schuman.

Here is an example:

```
module stack =
        def int stacksize = 100;
            loc [1:stacksize] int st, loc int stptr := 0;
            pub proc push = (int n)int:
                ((stptr+:=1)<=stacksize | st[stptr] := n | print("stack overflow"); stop);
            pub proc pop = int:
                (stptr>0 | st[(stptr-:=1)+1] | print("stack underflow"); stop);
        postlude
            (stptr/=0 | print("stack not emptied"); stop)
        fed;
...
access stack (push(1); push(2); print(pop); pop)
```

There was provision for separate compilation of ***module***s at the global level, but there was also a second mechanism for separately compiling an ***egg*** in an environment known as a ***nest***, which could be declared at any level within a **program**. It is interesting to note that Ada also has two separate compilation mechanisms, of a similar sort.

2.6.1.6 *TORRIX*

TORRIX was an ALGOL 68 library for handling vectors and matrices, developed at the University of Utrecht [van der Meulen 1978]. At its Jablonna meeting WG 2.1 commended its use, using a variation of the TUM-10 wording.

2.6.1.7 *The MC Test Set*

This was a suite of 190 ALGOL 68 programs, developed at the Mathematisch Centrum [Grune 1979], and designed to establish confidence that an ALGOL 68 compiler was correct with respect to the Report. It therefore contained many "pathological" examples as well as some more straightforward programs. The Summit meeting of WG 2.1 authorized a statement of commendation to be attached to it.

2.6.2 Problems

It was not long before people began to report problems with [RR]. The policy for dealing with them was hammered out by the Support Subcommittee at Kingston and Oxford, the principles being that

- Clerical errors and misprints in [RR] could be corrected by publication of errata.
- [RR] would not be changed in any substantive fashion.

- Commentaries would be published stating the opinion of the Support Subcommittee on problems that had been raised, but they were "not to be construed as modifications to the text of the Revised Report." Their definitive forms can be found in [WG 2.1 1978] and [WG 2.1 1979].

2.6.2.1 *Language Problems*

Only three of the commentaries refer to the main body of the Report, that is, to the syntax and the semantics, and one of these is arguably discussing a non-problem. There are also a couple of problems with [RR 10.2] (the non-transput part of the **standard-prelude**). Allowing a margin for these uncertainties and for some problems that might be counted as two, it is still safe to say that the number of known problems in the main part of the Report can be counted on the fingers of one hand.

2.6.2.2 *Transput Problems*

Unfortunately, the same cannot be said for [RR 10.3], the transput part of the **standard-prelude**. A continuous stream of problems was reported, notably by Hans van Vliet who had been trying to construct a machine-independent implementation model of the transput. At Kingston a task force, convened by Chris Cheney, was set up with a brief to review [RR 10.3] and to provide a reasonable interpretation for it.

Over a succession of meetings the task force decided to adopt Van Vliet's implementation model, adjusting both it and the Report to ensure that they were consistent (of course, proving the equivalence of two programs is not easy, but a very intensive study of [RR 10.3] had now been taking place, resulting in some confidence that we at last understood it, warts and all). Commentaries were prepared to establish the "approved" understanding of the Report, and the final version of Van Vliet's model [Van Vliet 1979] was released with a TUM-10-like wording.

2.7 IMPLEMENTATIONS

Shortly after publication of the ALGOL 60 Report there were implementations on a large variety of machines, written in universities and research establishments and by machine manufacturers. There was a natural expectation that the same thing would happen with ALGOL 68 and, for example, it was reported at Novosibirsk that 20 implementations were underway on 15 different machines. The sad fact is that the great majority of implementations that were started were never completed.

2.7.1 The Early Implementations

The implementations by Goos at Munich on a Telefunken TR4, and by Branquart at MBLE on an Electrologica-X8 were well under way by the appearance of [R]. Moreover, Mailloux had had a particular responsibility among the authors for ensuring that the language, as it was being defined, was implementable.

In his thesis, Mailloux [1968] considered examples such as the following:

```
begin real x;
      proc p = void:
           begin proc q = begin somelongexpression + x; ... end;
                abc x;
                ...
           end;
```

```
#either#    mode abc = ... ;
#or#        op abc = ... ;
```

When **abc** *x* is encountered, we do not yet know whether it declares a new **variable** *x* of an as-yet-undeclared mode **abc**, or whether it is an application of an as-yet-undeclared **operator** **abc** to the previously declared x. So a first pass of the compiler is needed to detect all declarations of **mode**s and **op**s before it can be known what **identifiers** have been declared. But now, supposing the first pass shows **abc** to be a mode, we cannot tell on the second pass whether the *x* within **proc** *q* is of mode **real** or of mode **abc**. Therefore, we cannot tell which overloaded version of the **operator** + is meant in **proc** *q* until the third pass, by which time it is too late to compile code to coerce *somelongexpression*. Hence a fourth pass is required to generate the code. Thus Mailloux established the classical 4-pass ALGOL 68 compiler, and they all said how clever he was and gave him his degree. What they ought to have said was how clever he was to have discovered a flaw in the language that could easily be fixed by a small syntactic change, such as a compulsory **loc** in front of each **variable-declaration** (2.3.4.5), thus saving an entire pass in every compiler.

But compile-time efficiency was not regarded as important although run-time efficiency was always a prime goal. As Van Wijngaarden said at North Berwick, ". . . yes, it does some extra work for the compiler but we should not be concerned with the efficiency of compiling. You do not lose any run-time efficiency, and that is what we are most concerned with." Strangely, Goos, who was well into writing his compiler at that time, seemed quite content with this philosophy. Goos' compiler in fact had six passes.

Branquart's compiler was a piece of research into compiler methodology rather than a serious production tool, but it did establish many features necessary to all compilers, particularly the storage of values and the layout of the stack, all documented in a series of MBLE Reports that were finally collated into [Branquart 1976]. The project consumed 20 man-years of effort, spread over the years 1967 to 1973.

Being implementations of the original language, neither of these compilers ever came into use outside their home bases. The Malvern ALGOL 68R compiler, on the other hand, restricted the language so as to permit 1-pass compilation and also made numerous small language changes, for convenience of implementation. Some, but not all, of these changes were subsequently blessed by inclusion within [RR]. Thus [R], [RR], and ALGOL 68R could be regarded as three vertices of an equilateral triangle. It was available from 1970 onwards on ICL 1900 series machines, and became the most widely used implementation, especially in Great Britain.

A TC2-sponsored conference on ALGOL 68 implementation was held in Munich in July 1970, and the proceedings [Peck 1971] contain papers on all the three compilers mentioned, together with several papers discussing garbage collection, showing this problem not to be as intractable as had been feared.

2.7.2 Implementations of the Revised Language

A full list of compilers available at the time can be found in [AB 52.3.1]. It is now apparent that implementing full ALGOL 68 requires an effort beyond what a university department can usually provide, which is why so many attempts failed. But by making some quite modest restrictions to the language the effort is reduced quite significantly, as Malvern showed, and such restrictions or omissions hardly affect the functionality or the orthogonality of the language. We therefore need to distinguish between full commercial implementations and small partial ones.

2.7.2.1 *Full Implementations*

The most successful commercial implementation was by CDC Netherlands, first delivered in 1977 in response to a threat from several Dutch universities to buy only machines with ALGOL 68 available. It was an excellent compiler, but the parent company in the USA never showed any interest in it.

Next, Malvern produced their second attempt, ALGOL 68RS, for their own in-house machines and available from 1977. This was much closer to [RR] than their first product, it was written to be machine independent, and it has been ported to the ICL 2900 series, to MULTICS and to VMS Vaxen. It is still the best starting point, should anyone wish a new (almost) full implementation.

The final commercial-strength product, called FLACC and first shipped in 1978, was a checkout compiler for IBM machines. This was produced by two of Mailloux's ex-students who set up their own company. Again, this was an excellent product (not fast, being a checkout system), but it did not spread far because they completely misjudged the price the market would pay.

2.7.2.2 *Partial Implementations*

Hibbard's Liverpool implementation, around which his sublanguage (2.6.1.1) was designed, was rewritten in BLISS for a PDP-11 when he moved to Carnegie Mellon, and was rewritten again by myself in Pascal and now runs on various machines. On the way, it acquired **heap-generators** (not in the original sublanguage), giving it nearly the functionality of the full language.

ALGOL 68C was a portable implementation originated by Steve Bourne and Mike Guy at Cambridge in 1975, and now available on IBM machines, DEC-20s (anyone still have one?), VMS Vaxen, Primes, Telefunken TR440, and even a CYBER 205. Its development continued for a while, but it was never completed (for example, it still has no garbage collector, although one was "almost working" at one stage). It was quite widely used, especially on IBM machines where it is much faster than FLACC.

ALGOL 68LGU is a system for IBM 360 clones, written by Tseytin and his colleagues at Leningrad State University (as it then was). As with other university products, it lacked features such as garbage collection, but it has now been adopted by Krasnaya Zarya, a "commercial" company in Leningrad, which has produced various products around it, including cross compilers and a portable version. Indeed, the former Soviet Union is the only place where there exists an official Standard for ALGOL 68 [GOST 27974/9-88].

Finally, an interactive implementation by Peter Craven of Algol Applications Ltd, originally developed for MS-DOS systems, is now available in the form of a public-domain interpreter, written in C.

2.8 CONCLUSION

2.8.1 Whatever Happened to ALGOL 68?

Well, one could say that it is alive and well and living in Pascal, or C, or C++, or SML, or Ada; and indeed this is true in part for all of these languages (see 2.3.1, 2.3.4.3 and 2.3.6 for some specific mentions).

The real question is why it did not come into more widespread use, and the answer here is simple enough: because it was not implemented widely enough, or soon enough. And the reason for that is that implementation was too hard, and the reason for that was on account of a relatively small number of troublespots, not inherently necessary for the basic principles of the language and certainly not for its orthogonality. It was possible only to correct a few of these problems during the revision.

But it *was* in fact used in many places (and still is in some), especially in Great Britain where the ICL machines were popular. Universally, those who had once used it never wanted to use anything else, and would gleefully point out the shortcomings of any other language you might care to name. It was the orthogonality that they liked (and the troublespots were in such obscure corners that no-one beyond the implementors ever noticed them).

The most successful feature was the strong typing. It was a not at all uncommon experience for a program of significant size to work first time, once it had got past the compiler. Thus it was in actual use a very safe language. Another successful concept was orthogonality. No subsequent language has achieved it to quite the same degree, but it is now firmly fixed in every language designer's agenda.

Some features, strangely, have not made it into more recent languages. Among these are truly unlimited ***string***s (2.3.1), **slices** (2.3.2), and the transput model (2.3.9), none of which is particularly difficult to implement.

It was often used as a first teaching language. Students usually demand to be taught the language that they are most likely to use in the world outside (FORTRAN or C). This is a mistake. A well-taught student (that is, one who has been taught a *clean* language) can easily pick up the languages of the world, and he or she will be in a far better position to recognize their bad features as he or she encounters them. It still has a role in teaching because of the concepts that it can illustrate. It is still a widely talked-about language (even among those who have never used it) and no respectable book on Comparative Programming Languages can afford to ignore it.

Has it a future? The honest answer must now be "No." The world has moved on. To be accepted now, your language needs modules, exception handling, polymorphism, safe parallelism, and clean interfaces to everything else (not to mention a rich and powerful sponsor). Moreover, you need all these things *from the start*—this is certainly one place where Ada got it right.

Was it TOO BIG? It has often been so accused, but it is really quite a small language compared with PL/1, or Ada. What, for example, does it provide beyond Pascal? Dynamic ***array***s, **slices**, **formats**, overloading, full block-structure, and expression-orientedness. Put these things into Pascal, make it orthogonal where it is not, and you have ALGOL 68.

2.8.2 Whatever Have We Learned from ALGOL 68?

The chief legacy of ALGOL 68 must be what the world has learned from it. I, personally, have learned a lot, and a major purpose of writing this paper was in order that others might do the same, bearing in mind that the chief lesson of history is that we do not learn from history.

So, first I know more about the dynamics and instabilities (but also the benefits) of large committees, and against that I know what can be achieved by a small band of people dedicated to working towards a common aim (2.4.5).

Next, there is the requirement for absolute *rigour* (which is not the same as formality) in the description of programming languages. I claim that we have shown that it can be done, but examples of *real* programming languages whose official definitions match this ideal are few and far between, and I know of no others where the rigorous definition was not a retrofit. What we achieved we achieved by consciously applying principles of good program design (2.4.3.3). We also recognized that rigour must be counterbalanced by adequate motivations and commentaries (2.5.5). And we must also warn of the considerable price to be paid in time and effort in order to do the job properly.

Was the WG wrong to attempt too much innovation in what was intended as a language for widespread use? Possibly so. It may be that experimental features should be tried out in *small* experimental languages. Instead, we found ourselves with a *large* experimental language on our hands. That might have been avoided, but only at the expense of more time.

Whether the ultimate benefit was worth all the effort and argumentation and heartbreak that went into it is another matter—and whether a good product can ever be made at all without some degree of heartbreak is also debatable.

ACKNOWLEDGMENTS

I would like to acknowledge the help of several people who have read earlier versions of this paper and offered constructive comments, notably Tony Hoare, Kees Koster, John Peck, Brian Randell, Michel Sintzoff, Peter Lucas, and Henry Bowlden. I should also like to thank Wlad Turski for the excellent and almost verbatim minutes of WG meetings which he took down in longhand, and without which my task would have been impossible.

REFERENCES

The *ALGOL Bulletin*, in which many of the following references appeared, was the official publication of WG 2.1. It is kept in a few academic libraries but, as the former Editor, I still have copies of most back numbers since AB 32, and could also probably arrange for photocopying of earlier issues.

[AB 28.1.1] News item—Tenth anniversary colloquium, Zürich, May 1968, *ALGOL Bulletin* AB28.1.1, Jul. 1968.

[AB 31.1.1] News item—Minority report, *ALGOL Bulletin* AB31.1.1, Mar. 1970.

[AB 52.3.1] Survey of viable ALGOL 68 implementations, *ALGOL Bulletin* AB52.3.1, Aug. 1988.

[Baecker, 1968] Baecker, H. D., ASERC—a code for ALGOL 68 basic tokens, *ALGOL Bulletin* AB28.3.5, Jul. 1968.

[Boom, 1972] Boom, H. J., IFIP WG 2.1 Working Paper 217 (Vienna 4), Sep. 1972.

[Branquart, 1976] Branquart, P., Cardinael, J.-P., Lewi, J., Delescaille, J.-P., and Vanbegin, M., *An optimized translation process and its application to ALGOL 68*, LNCS 38. New York: Springer-Verlag, 1976.

[Chastellier, 1969] De Chastellier, G., and Colmerauer, A., W-Grammar, *Proc. 24th National Conference*. New York: ACM Publication P-69, 1969.

[Colmerauer, 1996] Colmerauer A., and Roussel, P., The birth of Prolog, in these Proceedings.

[Dahl, 1966] Dahl, O-J, A plea for multiprogramming, *ALGOL Bulletin* AB24.3.5, Sep. 1966.

[Dahl, 1968] Dahl, O-J, Myhrhaug, B., and Nygaard, K., *The Simula 67 Common Base Language*. Oslo: Norwegian Computing Centre, Oslo, 1968.

[De Morgan, 1976a] De Morgan, R. M., Hill, I. D., and Wichman, B. A., A supplement to the ALGOL 60 revised report, *Comp. Jour.* 19:3, Aug. 1976, pp. 276–288; also *SIGPLAN Notices* 12:1, January 1977, pp. 52–66.

[De Morgan, 1976b] De Morgan, R. M., Modified report on the algorithmic language ALGOL 60, *Comp. Jour.* 19:4, Nov. 1976, pp. 364–379 ([Naur *et al.* 1962] as modified by [De Morgan 1976]).

[De Morgan, 1978] De Morgan, R. M., Hill, I. D., and Wichman, B., A. Modified ALGOL 60 and the step-until element, *Comp. Jour.* 21:3, Aug. 1978, p. 282 (essential errata to [De Morgan, 1976a] and Modified report [1976b]).

[Dijkstra, 1968a] Dijkstra, E. W., Cooperating sequential processes, In *Programming Languages*, F. Genuys, Ed., New York: Academic Press, 1968.

[Dijkstra, 1968b] Dijkstra, E. W., Goto considered harmful, letter to the Editor, *Comm. ACM* 11:3, Mar. 1968.

[Duncan, 1964] Duncan, F. G., and van Wijngaarden, A., Cleaning up ALGOL 60, *ALGOL Bulletin* AB16.3.3, May 1964.

[Garwick, 1965] Garwick, J. V., The question of I/O procedures, *ALGOL Bulletin* AB19.3.8, Jan. 1965.

[GOST 27974/9-88] *Programming language ALGOL 68 and ALGOL 68 extended*, GOST 27974-88 and GOST 27975-88, USSR State Committee for Standards, Moscow, 1989.

[Grune, 1979] Grune, D., *The Revised MC ALGOL 68 test set*, IW 122/79, Amsterdam: Mathematisch Centrum, 1979.

[Hansen, 1977] Hansen, Wilfred J., and Boom, Hendrik, The report on the standard hardware representation for ALGOL 68, *SIGPLAN Notices* 12:5, May, 1977; also *Acta Informatica* 9, 1978, pp. 105–119.

[Hibbard, 1977] Hibbard, P. G., A sublanguage of ALGOL 68, *SIGPLAN Notices* 12:5, May 1977.

[Hoare, 1964] Hoare, C. A. R., Case expressions, *ALGOL Bulletin* AB18.3.7, Oct. 1964.

[Hoare, 1965a] Hoare, C. A. R., Cleaning up the for statement, *ALGOL Bulletin* AB21.3.4, Nov. 1965.

[Hoare, 1965b] Hoare, C. A. R., Record Handling, *ALGOL Bulletin* AB21.3.6, Nov. 1965.

[Hoare, 1966] Hoare, C. A. R., Further thoughts on record handling AB21.3.6, *ALGOL Bulletin* AB23.3.2, May 1966.

[Hoare, 1968] Hoare, C. A. R., Critique of ALGOL 68, *ALGOL Bulletin* AB29.3.4, Nov. 1968.

[Hoare, 1981] Hoare, C. A. R., The emperor's old clothes (the 1980 ACM Turing award lecture), *Comm. ACM* 24:2, Feb. 1981, pp. 75–83.

[King, 1974] King, P. R., WG 2.1 subcommittee on ALGOL 68 support, *ALGOL Bulletin* AB37.3.1, Jul. 1974.

[Knuth *et al.*, 1964] Knuth D. (Chairman), Bumgarner, L. L., Hamilton, D. E., Ingerman, P. Z., Lietzke, M. P., Merner, J. N., and Ross, D. T., A proposal for input-output conventions in ALGOL 60, *Comm. ACM* 7:5, May 1964, pp. 273–283.

[Koster, 1969] Koster, C. H. A., On infinite modes, *ALGOL Bulletin* AB30.3.3, Feb. 1969.

[Koster, 1971] Koster, C. H. A., Affix-grammars, in *ALGOL 68 Implementation*, J. E. L. Peck, Ed., North Holland, 1971, pp. 95–109.

[Lindsey, 1968] Lindsey, C. H., ALGOL 68 with fewer tears, *ALGOL Bulletin* AB28.3.1, Jul. 1968.

[Lindsey, 1971] Lindsey, C. H., and Van der Meulen, S. G., *Informal Introduction to ALGOL 68*, North Holland, 1971.

[Lindsey, 1972] Lindsey, C. H., ALGOL 68 with fewer tears, *Comp. Jour.* 15:2, May 1972.

[Lindsey, 1976] Lindsey, C. H., Specification of partial parametrization proposal, *ALGOL Bulletin* AB39.3.1, Feb. 1976.

[Lindsey, 1977] Lindsey, C. H., and Van der Meulen, S. G., *Informal Introduction to ALGOL 68* Revised Edition, North Holland, 1977.

[Lindsey, 1978] Lindsey, C. H., and Boom, H. J., A modules and separate compilation facility for ALGOL 68, *ALGOL Bulletin* AB43.3.2, Dec. 1978; also IW 105/78, Mathematisch Centrum, Amsterdam, 1978.

[Löf, 1984] Martin-Löf, P., Constructive mathematics and computer programming, in *Mathematical logic and programming languages*, Hoare, C. A. R., and Shepherdson, J. C., Eds. New York: Prentice-Hall, 1985.

[Lucas, 1969] Lucas, P., and Walk, K., On the formal description of PL/1, in *Annual review in automatic programming* 6:3, Pergammon, 1969, pp. 105–182.

[Mailloux, 1968] Mailloux, B. J., *On the implementation of ALGOL 68*, Mathematisch Centrum, Amsterdam, 1968.

[McCarthy, 1964] McCarthy, J., Definition of new data types in ALGOL X, *ALGOL Bulletin* AB18.3.12, Oct. 1964.

[Meertens, 1969] Meertens, L. G. L. T., On the generation of ALGOL 68 programs involving infinite modes, *ALGOL Bulletin* AB30.3.4, Feb. 1969.

[Merner, 1966] Merner, J. M., Garwick, J. V., Ingerman, P. Z., and Paul, M., Report of the ALGOL X I-O subcommittee, IFIP WG 2.1 Working Paper 48 (Warsaw 3), July 1966.

[Milner, 1990] Milner, R., Tofte, M., and Harper, R., *The definition of standard ML*, Cambridge, MA: MIT Press, 1990.

[MR 76] Van Wijngaarden, A., Orthogonal design and description of a formal language, *MR 76*, Mathematisch Centrum, Amsterdam, Oct. 1965.

[W-2] Van Wijngaarden, A., and Mailloux, B. J., A draft proposal for the algorithmic language ALGOL X, IFIP WG 2.1 Working Paper 47 (Warsaw 2), Oct. 1966.

[MR 88] Van Wijngaarden, A., Mailloux, B. J., and Peck, J. E. L., A draft proposal for the algorithmic language ALGOL 67, *MR 88*, Mathematisch Centrum, Amsterdam, May 1967.

[MR 93] Van Wijngaarden, A., Ed., Mailloux, B. J., Peck, J. E. L., and Koster, C. H. A., Draft report on the algorithmic language ALGOL 68, *MR 93*, Mathematisch Centrum, Amsterdam, Jan. 1968.

[MR 95] Van Wijngaarden, A., Ed., Mailloux, B. J., Peck, J. E. L., and Koster, C. H. A., Working document on the algorithmic language ALGOL 68, *MR 95*, Mathematisch Centrum, Amsterdam, Jul. 1968.

[MR 99] Van Wijngaarden, A., Ed., Mailloux, B. J., Peck,J. E. L., and Koster, C. H. A., Penultimate draft report on the algorithmic language ALGOL 68, *MR 99*, Mathematisch Centrum, Amsterdam, Oct. 1968.

[MR 100] Van Wijngaarden, A., Ed., Mailloux, B. J., Peck, J. E. L., and Koster, C. H. A., Final draft report on the algorithmic language ALGOL 68, *MR 100*, Mathematisch Centrum, Amsterdam, Dec. 1968.

[MR 101] The first printing of [Van Wijngaarden 1969].

[Naur *et al.*, 1960] Backus, J. W., Bauer, F. L., Green, J., Katz, C., McCarthy, J., Naur, P. Ed., Perlis, A. J., Rutishauser, H., Samelson, K., Vauquois, B., Wegstein, J. H., Van Wijngaarden, A., and Woodger, M., Report on the algorithmic language ALGOL 60, *Numerische Mathematik* 2: 1960, pp. 106–136; also *Comm. ACM* 3:5, May 1960, pp. 299–314.

[Naur *et al.*, 1962] Backus, J. W., Bauer, F. L., Green, J., Katz, C., McCarthy, J., Naur, P. Ed., Perlis, A. J., Rutishauser, H., Samelson, K., Vauquois, B., Wegstein, J. H., Van Wijngaarden, A., and Woodger, M., Revised report on the algorithmic language ALGOL 60, *Numerische Mathematik* 4: 1963, pp. 420–453; also *Comm. ACM* 6:1, Jan. 1963, pp. 1–17; also *Comp. Jour.*, 5:1, Jan. 1963, pp. 349–367.

[Naur, 1964] Naur, P., Proposals for a new language, *ALGOL Bulletin* AB18.3.9, Oct. 1964.

[Naur, 1966] ———, The form of specifications, *ALGOL Bulletin* AB22.3.7, Feb. 1966

[Naur, 1968] ———, Successes and failures of the ALGOL effort, *ALGOL Bulletin* AB28.3.3, Jul. 1968.

[Naur, 1981] ———, The European side of the last phase of the development of ALGOL 60, in *History of Programming Languages*, Richard L. Wexelblat, Ed. New York: Academic Press, 1981.

[Pair, 1970] Pair, C., Concerning the syntax of ALGOL 68, *ALGOL Bulletin* AB31.3.2, Mar. 1970.

[Peck, 1971] Peck J. E. L., ed., *ALGOL 68 Implementation*, North Holland, 1971.

[R] See [Van Wijngaarden 1969].

[RR] See [Van Wijngaarden 1975].

[Ritchie, 1993] Ritchie, D. M., The development of the C language, in these Proceedings.

[Ross, 1961] Ross, D. T., A generalized technique for symbol manipulation and numerical calculation, *Comm. ACM*, 4:3, Mar. 1961, pp. 147–50.

[Ross, 1969] Ross, D. T., Concerning a minority report on ALGOL 68, *ALGOL Bulletin* AB30.2.3, Feb. 1969.

[Samelson, 1965] Samelson, K., Functionals and functional transformations, *ALGOL Bulletin* AB20.3.3, Jul. 1965.

[Seegmüller, 1965a] Seegmüller, G., Some proposals for ALGOL X, *ALGOL Bulletin* AB21.3.1, Nov. 1965.

[Seegmüller, 1965b] Seegmüller, G., A proposal for a basis for a report on a successor to ALGOL 60, Bavarian Acad. Sci., Munich, Oct. 1965.

[Sintzoff, 1967] Sintzoff, M., Existence of a Van Wijngaarden syntax for every recursively enumerable set, *Annales Soc. Sci. Bruxelles*, II, 1967, pp. 115–118.

[Schuman, 1974] Schuman, S. A., Toward modular programming in high-level languages, *ALGOL Bulletin* AB37.4.1, Jul. 1974.

[Stroustrup, 1996] Stroustrup, B., A history of C++, in these Proceedings.

[TR 74-3] The first printing of [Van Wijngaarden 1975], published as Technical Report TR74-3, Dept. of Computing Science, University of Alberta, Mar. 1974; subject to errata published in *ALGOL Bulletin* AB37.5 Jul. 1974, AB38.5.1 Dec. 1974, and AB39.5.1 Feb. 1976.

[Turski, 1968] Turski, W. M., Some remarks on a chapter from a document, *ALGOL Bulletin* AB29.2.4, Nov. 1968.

[Turski, 1981] Turski, W. M., ALGOL 68 revisited twelve years later or from AAD to ADA, in *Algorithmic Languages*, J. W. de Bakker and J. C. van Vliet, Eds., North Holland, 1981.

[Van der Meulen, 1978] Van der Meulen, S. G. and Veldhorst, M., *TORRIX—a programming system for operations on vectors and matrices over arbitrary fields and of variable size Vol. 1*, Mathematical Centre Tracts 86, Mathematisch Centrum, Amsterdam, 1978.

[Van der Poel, 1965] Van der Poel, W. L., extract from WG 2.1 Activity Report, *ALGOL Bulletin* AB21.1.1.

[Van der Poel, 1986] Van der Poel, W. L., Some notes on the history of ALGOL, in *A quarter century of IFIP*, H. Zemanek, Ed., North Holland, 1986.

[Van Vliet, 1979] Van Vliet, J. C., *ALGOL 68 transput, Pt 1: Historical review and discussion of the implementation model, Pt 2: An implementation model*, Mathematical Centre Tracts 110 and 111, Mathematisch Centrum, 1979.

[Van Wijngaarden, 1969] Van Wijngaarden, A., Ed., Mailloux, B. J., Peck, J. E. L., and Koster, C. H. A., Report on the algorithmic language ALGOL 68, *Numerische Mathematik* 14: 1969, pp. 79–218; also A. P. Ershov and A. Bahrs, transl., *Kybernetica* 6, 1969, and 7, 1970, bilingual; also I. O. Kerner (transl.), *Bericht über die algorithmische sprache ALGOL 68*, Akademie-Verlag, Berlin, 1972, bilingual; also J. Buffet, P. Arnal and A. Quéré (transl.), *Définition du langage algorithmique ALGOL 68*, Hermann, Paris, 1972; also Lu Ru Qian (transl.), 算法语言 *ALGOL 68* 报告, Beijing, Science Press, 1977.

[Van Wijngaarden, 1975] Van Wijngaarden, A., Mailloux, B. J., Peck, J. E. L., Koster, C. H. A., Sintzoff, M., Lindsey, C. H., Meertens, L. G. L. T., and Fisker, R. G., Revised report on the algorithmic language ALGOL 68, *Acta Informatica* 5:1–3, 1975; also *Mathematical Centre Tract 50*, Mathematisch Centrum, Amsterdam; also *SIGPLAN Notices* 12:5, May 1977; also I. O. Kerner, (transl.), *Revidierter bericht über die algorithmische sprache ALGOL 68*, Akademie-Verlag, Berlin, 1978; also A. A. Bahrs (transl.) and A. P. Ershov (Ed.), *Peresmotrenoye So'obszczeniye ob ALGOLE 68*, Izdatelstvo "MIR," Moscow, 1979; also Lu Ru Qian (transl.), 算法语言 *ALGOL 68* 修改报告, Beijing, Science Press, Aug. 1982.

[W-2] Van Wijngaarden, A., and Mailloux, B. J., A draft proposal for the algorithmic language ALGOL X, IFIP WG 2.1 Working Paper 47 (Warsaw 2), Oct. 1966.

[WG 2.1, 1964a] Report on SUBSET ALGOL 60 (IFIP), *Numerische Mathematik* 6: (1964), pp. 454–458; also *Comm. ACM* 7:10, Oct. 1964, p, 626.

[WG 2.1, 1964b] Report on input-output procedures for ALGOL 60, *Numerische Mathematik* 6: pp. 459–462; also *Comm. ACM* 7:10, Oct. 1964, p 628.

[WG 2.1, 1971a] Report of the subcommittee on data processing and transput, *ALGOL Bulletin* AB32.3.3, May 1971.

[WG 2.1, 1971b] Report of the subcommittee on maintenance and improvements to ALGOL 68, *ALGOL Bulletin* AB32.3.4, May 1971.

[WG 2.1, 1971c] Letter concerning ALGOL 68 to the readers of the ALGOL Bulletin, *ALGOL Bulletin* AB32.2.8, May 1971.

[WG 2.1, 1972a] WG 2.1 formal resolution: Revised report on ALGOL 68, *ALGOL Bulletin* AB33.1.1, Mar. 1972.

[WG 2.1, 1972b] Report of the subcommittee on maintenance of and improvements to ALGOL 68, August 1971, *ALGOL Bulletin* AB33.3.3, Mar. 1972.

[WG 2.1, 1972c] Report of the subcommittee on data processing and transput, August 1971, *ALGOL Bulletin* AB33.3.4, Mar. 1972.

[WG 2.1, 1972d] Report on the meeting of working group 2.1 held at Fontainebleau, *ALGOL Bulletin* AB34.3.1, Jul. 1972.

[WG 2.1, 1972e] Report on considered improvements, *ALGOL Bulletin* AB34.3.2, Jul. 1972.

[WG 2.1, 1972f] Proposals for revision of the transput section of the report, *ALGOL Bulletin* AB34.3.3, Jul. 1972.

[WG 2.1, 1973a] Further report on improvements to ALGOL 68, *ALGOL Bulletin* AB35.3.1, Mar. 1973.

[WG 2.1, 1973b] Final report on improvements to ALGOL 68, *ALGOL Bulletin* AB36.3.1, Nov. 1973.

[WG 2.1, 1975] IFIP WG 2.1 Working Paper 287 (TUM 10), Munich, Aug. 1975.

[WG 2.1, 1978] Commentaries on the revised report, *ALGOL Bulletin* AB43.3.1, Dec. 1978.

[WG 2.1, 1979] Commentaries on the revised report, *ALGOL Bulletin* AB44.3.1, May 1979.

[Wirth, 1965] Wirth, N., A proposal for a report on a successor of ALGOL 60, *MR 75*, Mathematisch Centrum, Amsterdam, Oct. 1965.

[Wirth, 1966a] Wirth, N., and Weber, H., EULER: A generalization of ALGOL, and its formal definition: Part II, *Comm. ACM* 9:2, Feb. 1966, pp. 89–99.

[Wirth, 1966b] Wirth, N., and Hoare, C. A. R., A contribution to the development of ALGOL, *Comm. ACM* 9:6, Jun. 1966, pp. 413–431.

[Wirth, 1966c] Wirth, N., Additional notes on "A contribution to the development of ALGOL," *ALGOL Bulletin* AB24.3.3, Sep. 1966.

[Wirth, 1968] ALGOL colloquium—closing word, *ALGOL Bulletin* AB29.3.2, Nov. 1968.

APPENDIX A: THE COVERING LETTER

Working Group 2.1 on ALGOL of the International Federation for Information Processing has been concerned for many years with the design of a common programming language and realises the magnitude and difficulty of this task. It has commissioned and guided the work of the four authors of this first Report on the Algorithmic Language ALGOL 68, and acknowledges the great effort which they have devoted to this task. The Report must be regarded as more than just the work of the four authors, for much of the content has been influenced by and has resulted from discussions in the Group. Consequently, this Report is submitted as the consolidated outcome of the work of the Group. This does not imply that every member of the Group, including the authors, agrees with every aspect of the undertaking. It is however the decision of the Group that, although there is a division of opinion amongst some of its members, the design has reached the stage to be submitted to the test of implementation and use by the computing community.

The Group intends to keep continuously under review the experience thus obtained, in order that it may institute such corrections and revisions to the Report as may become desirable. To this end, it requests that all who wish to contribute to this work should do so both via the medium of the ALGOL Bulletin, and by writing to the Editor directly.

APPENDIX B: THE MINORITY REPORT

We regard the current Report on Algorithmic Language ALGOL 68 as the fruit of an effort to apply a methodology for language definition to a newly designed programming language. We regard the effort as an experiment and professional honesty compels us to state that in our considered opinion we judge the experiment to be a failure in both respects.

The failure of the description methodology is most readily demonstrated by the sheer size of the Report in which, as stated on many occasions by the authors, "every word and every symbol matters" and by the extreme difficulty of achieving correctness. The extensive new terminology and the typographical mannerisms are equally unmistakable symptoms of failure. We are aware of the tremendous amount of work that has gone into the production of the Report, but this confirms us in our opinion that adequacy is not the term that we should employ of its approach. We regard the high degree of inaccessibility of its contents as a warning that should not be ignored by dismissing the problems of "the uninitiated reader." That closer scrutiny has revealed grave deficiencies was only to be expected.

Now the language itself, which should be judged, among other things, as a language, in which to *compose* programs [*sic*]. Considered as such, a programming language implies a conception of the programmer's task. We recognize that over the last decade the processing power of commonly available machines has grown tremendously and that society has increased its ambition in their application in proportion to this growth. As a result the programmer of today and tomorrow, finding his task in the field of tension between available equipment and desired applications, finds himself faced with tasks of completely different and still growing scope and scale. More than ever it will be required from an adequate programming tool that it assists, by structure, the programmer in the most difficult aspects of his job, that is, in the *reliable creation* of sophisticated programs. In this respect we fail to see how the language proposed here is a significant step forward: on the contrary, we feel that its implicit view of the programmer's task is very much the same as, say, ten years ago. This forces upon us the conclusion that, regarded as a programming tool, the language must be regarded as obsolete.

The present minority report has been written by us because if we had not done so, we would have forsaken our professional responsibility towards the computing community. We therefore propose that this Report on the Algorithmic Language ALGOL 68 should not be published under IFIP sponsorship. If it is so published, we recommend that this "minority report" be included in the publication.

Signed by:
Dijkstra, Duncan, Garwick, Hoare, Randell, Seegmüller, Turski, Woodger.

(In a letter dated Dec. 23 1968, Jan. V. Garwick, who had not been present at the Munich meeting, requested that his name be affixed to this Minority Report.)

TRANSCRIPT OF PRESENTATION

C. H. LINDSEY: (SLIDE 1) My story starts with IFIP, which is the International Federation for Information Processing. It is a hierarchical organization, as you see, with a layer of Technical Committees (TC1, TC2 and so on), and finally a layer of Working Groups (such as Working Group 2.1, Working Group 2.2 and so on). And here we have the authors of the original ALGOL 60 Report.

And, in 1962, these authors in fact became Working Group 2.1 of IFIP.

In due course Working Group 2.1 started out to produce a new language to follow ALGOL 60. Ideas for this future language, which became known as ALGOL X, were being discussed by the Working Group from 1964 onwards, culminating in a meeting at Princeton in May 1965. There was also a language ALGOL Y—originally it was a language which could modify its own programs, but in actual fact it turned out to be a "scapegoat" for features that would not fit into ALGOL X. At any rate, at Princeton they thought they were ready, and accordingly they solicited drafts of a complete language to be presented at the next meeting.

(SLIDE 2) The next meeting, at St. Pierre de Chartreuse, there were three drafts on the table officially, but observe that a fourth document has crept in, and this was Hoare's paper on Records, which Wirth immediately accepted as an improvement on his own. Henceforth we must regard the Wirth/ Hoare proposal as one, and it was eventually published in *CACM* as "A Contribution to the development of ALGOL," and in due course it became the language ALGOL W.

Seegmüller's document was not a serious contender, but it did contain some interesting ideas for call-by-reference, of which more anon. Van Wijngaarden's document was entitled "Orthogonal design and description of a formal language." Its chief innovation was a new 2-level grammar, which so impressed the Working Group that they resolved formally, "Whatever language is finally decided upon by Working Group 2.1, it *will* be described by Van Wijngaarden's metalinguistic techniques." I find this rather surprising because Van Wijngaarden's document, in its original form, was both unreadable and buggy. These four authors were now charged to write THE Report for THE language, with the clear intention that the whole project would be completed within the next year.

The history of what followed is very much concerned with parameter passing, so I propose to follow the development of this in some detail. It is said that an Irishman, when asked how to get to some remote place, answered that if you really want to get to that place, then you shouldn't start from

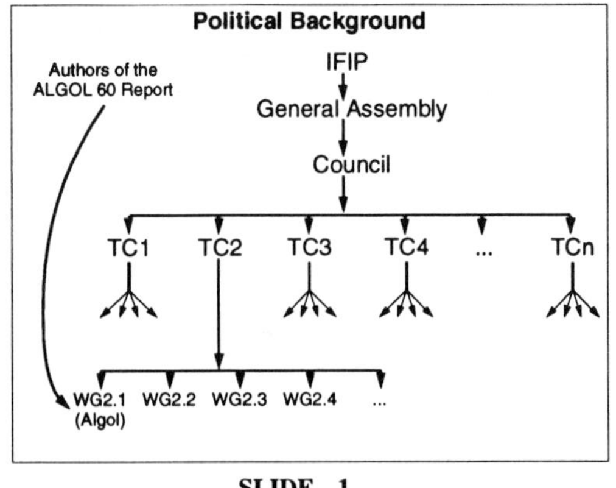

SLIDE 1

St. Pierre de Chartreuse (Oct 1965)

Three draft proposals on the table:

1) Wirth ⟶ The "Contribution" ⟶ ALGOL W
   Hoare's Records ⟶

2) Seegmüller

3) Van Wijngaarden ⟶ ALGOL 68
   "Orthogonal Design ..."

Hoare, Seegmüller, van Wijngaarden and Wirth charged to write The Report.

SLIDE 2

here. In trying to find an acceptable parameter-passing mechanism, Working Group 2.1 started from ALGOL 60 which, it is well known, has two parameter-passing mechanisms—call-by-value and call-by-name. This was a grave mistake.

(SLIDE 3) Here is call-by-name in ALGOL 60, and this example is straight out of the ALGOL 60 Report. There are two ways to use call-by-name:

- *y* must be called by name, because it is a result parameter,
- but *a* and *b* must be called by name because their corresponding actual-parameters in the call—*x1[j]* and *y1[j]*—are expressions that involve another actual-parameter, *j*,

  which corresponds to another formal-parameter *p*, also called by name,

  which is used in the loop counter of this for-statement,

  and the whole effect is then equivalent to this for-statement down at the bottom.

  And that *j* stands for "Jensen."

This technique was known as "Jensen's Device," and nowadays we should call it "Jensen's Hack." That is what it was—a Neat Hack. But Hacks, however neat, should never be applied outside of their original context, but this is just what the Working Group now tried to do.

(SLIDE 4) Well here is the Working Group's first attempt:

- the result parameter *y* is now distinguished by the reserved word **loc**,
- but the need for call-by-name is now indicated, not in the procedure heading, but *at the point of call*, here, by this word **expr**ession.

And the mysterious "*j*" for Jensen is still there, so this is just a minor tinkering with Jensen's Device.

(SLIDE 5) This is Seegmüller's proposal, and it is call-by-reference much as we now know it:

- *y* is now a **reference** parameter,
- *a* and *b* are explicitly declared as **proc**edures,
- and at the point of call we have this word **expr**ession, here, to correspond to those **proc**edure parameters.

And Jensen's mysterious *j* is still there as a parameter.

Call-by-name in ALGOL 60

```
procedure Innerproduct(a, b, k, p, y);
  value k;
  integer k, p; real y, a, b;
  begin real s; s := 0;
    for p := 1 step 1 until k do s := s+a*b;
    y := s
  end Innerproduct
```

Here is a call:

```
  real array x1, y1 [1:n]; integer j; real z;
  Innerproduct(x1[j], y1[j], n, j, z);
```

Which is equivalent to:

```
  for j := 1 step 1 until k do s := s+x1[j]*y1[j];
```

SLIDE 3

Call-by-name before St. Pierre

```
proc innerproduct =
    (real val a, b, int val k, int loc p, real loc y)
void:
    begin real var s := 0;
      for p := 1 step 1 until k
      do s := s+a*b;
      y := s
    end;
```

and here is a call:

```
loc [1:n] real x1, y1;  loc int j;  loc real z;
innerproduct(expr: x1[j],  expr: y1[j],  n,  j,  z);
```

SLIDE 4

(SLIDE 6) This is the scheme from the Hoare/Wirth proposal and the example is actually written in ALGOL W:

- here y is now what they called an "anti-value" parameter, or call-by-value-result, as we should now say,
- but this *x1[j]*, here, is just call-by-name, exactly as in ALGOL 60, so Jensen is still with us.

This then was the State-of-the-Art of parameter passing in October 1965, and its total confusion may be contrasted with the limited set of options to which modern programming language designers now confine themselves, and with the simplicity and elegance of the system that presently emerged for ALGOL 68.

(SLIDE 7) Now we need to look at Hoare's Records. The concepts here should now seem quite familiar:

- we have a **record class** with fields *val* and *next*,
- here we declare *start* as the start of an empty *link*ed list,
- and now, down here, when we say *start* := *link*, this is the *only* way to create new values of this *link* **record class**—and this means that *link*s or records always live on the heap,

Call-by-reference (Seegmüller)

```
proc innerproduct = (proc real a, b, int k,
                     int reference p, real reference y)
void:
  begin loc real s := 0;
    for p := 1 step 1 until k
    do s := s+a*b;
    y := s
  end;
```

And here is the call:

```
  loc [1:n] real x1, y1;  loc int j;  loc real z;
  innerproduct(expr: x1[j],  expr: y1[j],
                n,  ref j,  ref z);
```

SLIDE 5

Call-by-value/result (ALGOL W)

```
procedure innerproduct (real a, real b,
        integer value k, integer p, real result y);
  begin y := 0; p := 1;
    while p≤k do
      begin y := y+a*b; p := p+1 end
  end;
```

a is by-name and *b* by-procedure.

Here is the call:

```
real array [1:n] x1, y1;  integer j;  real z;
innerproduct(x1[j],  y1[j],  n,  j,  z);
```

SLIDE 6

Hoare's Records

```
record class link;
  begin
    integer val;
    reference next (link)
  end;
begin reference start, temp (link);
    start := null;

    temp := start;
    start := link;      comment creates new link;
    val(start) := 99; next(start) := temp;
end
```

SLIDE 7

Orthogonality

- A ***record class*** was a type.
  ∴ record variables, parameters, and results.
- ***ref x*** was a type, for any ***x***.
  ∴ ***ref ref x*** was a type.
- ***refs*** could be used for call-by-reference.
  ∴ ***refs*** to local variables.
- ***procs*** could be used for parameters
  ∴ ***proc*** variables, parameters, and results.
  ∴ also constructors for anonymous ***procs***.
- The left hand of an **assignation** had been a **variable**. Now it would be any ***ref*** valued **expression**.

SLIDE 8

- and these **references**, here and here, are *nothing at all* to do with Seegmüller's **references**—as they cannot point to local variables and they are certainly not to be used for call-by-reference.

Well, there should have been a full Working Group meeting in April 1966 to consider the report of the subcommittee, but the subcommittee Report was nowhere near ready. Instead, it was the subcommittee itself—Wirth, Hoare, Van Wijngaarden and Seegmüller—that met at Kootwijk.

Now, it had been agreed at St. Pierre that Van Wijngaarden should write the Draft Report for the subcommittee, using his formalism, but instead there were two documents on the table. The Wirth/Hoare one was called "A Contribution to the development of ALGOL," and indeed it bore more resemblance to the language that the Working Group intended, but it wasn't in Van Wijngaarden's formalism. Well, discussions proceeded amicably enough, many points were agreed, until they came to the parameter passing mechanism.

And at this point a complete split developed within the subcommittee. So, what was all the fuss about?

(SLIDE 8) Van Wijngaarden was pressing the parameter-passing mechanism that arose from his principle of "orthogonality." (Remember his original document "Orthogonal design and description of a formal language.") Now, according to the principle of orthogonality,

- A ***record class*** was a type; therefore we could have record variables, record parameters and record results. Nowadays we should say that a record was a "1st class citizen" of the language.
- Similarly, we have references, so ***ref x*** was a type, for any ***x***; therefore it follows that ***ref 'ref x'*** was a type.
- These ***ref***erences were values, so they could be used for call-by-reference, just as Seegmüller had proposed;
  therefore we needed to be able to have ***ref***erences to local variables, which Hoare did not allow for *his* references.
- Similarly, you could pass ***proc***edures as parameters;
  therefore a procedure was a 1st class citizen. You could have procedure variables, procedure parameters and procedure results, and also constructors for *anonymous* procedures.
- And now, you see, traditionally in the older languages, the left hand side of an **assignation** had been a **variable**. Now it would simply be any ***ref*** valued **expression**.

Everything is call-by-value

```
proc innerproduct =
      (proc (int) real a, b, int k, ref real y) void:
   begin loc real s := 0;
      for i to k do s +:= a(i) * b(i) od;
      y := s
   end;
```

And here is the call:

```
loc [1:n] real x1, y1;  loc real z;
innerproduct(
      (int j) real: x1[j], (int k) real: y1[k],
      n, z);
```

SLIDE 9

(SLIDE 9) So Hoare's records and Seegmüller's references had now been coalesced into one grandiose scheme, in which *everything* was going to be called by value.

This example is now written in true ALGOL 68:

- *y* is declared as a **ref** parameter: the *value* we pass is simply a reference,
- *a* and *b* are now ***proc***edure parameters,
- and the corresponding actual parameter is now a constructed procedure, that is, a procedure of which *j* is just an ordinary formal-parameter. So Jensen is finally dead.

It was orthogonality, and the use (or misuse) of references, that caused the split in the subcommittee, and Wirth and Hoare could not accept them at all.

Of course all this came up again at the next meeting in Warsaw. The document Warsaw-2 had Van Wijngaarden as its only author. Could this be accepted as the document that had been commissioned from a subcommittee of four? Hoare was dubious at best and Wirth had resigned from the subcommittee and didn't even attend this meeting.

Now came the great "Orthogonality" vs "Diagonality" debate. The discussion lasted the best part of a day, but Van Wijngaarden was able to demonstrate that *his* system was entirely self-consistent.

The other thing which came up at Warsaw was McCarthy's scheme for overloaded operators. This was an entirely new topic, and it was resisted by Van Wijngaarden on the grounds that it was too late for such a major change.

Clearly, the document Warsaw-2 was not going to be finalized that week, as some had initially imagined. So these are the decisions that the Working Group took at Warsaw:

- First of all, the document was to be amended, with proper pragmatics. Note that "pragmatics" are to a Report as "comments" are to a program.
- Then the document was to be published in the *Algol Bulletin* for all the world to see.
- And implementation studies were to be incorporated in it.
- Van Wijngaarden was to be the sole editor.
- And at the next meeting they would get a chance to talk about ALGOL Y, and the meeting after that would take the final decision.
- Oh! and McCarthy's overloading could be incorporated, if Van Wijngaarden found it to be feasible.

The next meeting was at Zandvoort, and it was quite a constructive meeting (relatively speaking) although it didn't actually discuss much ALGOL Y. And there was no sign of rebellion.

McCarthy's overloading was now in "in all its glory." Here I should say that those who were eventually to urge rejection of the Report all shared an exasperation with Van Wijngaarden's style, and with his obsessional behaviour in trying to get his way. He would resist change, both to the language and to the document, until pressed into it.

- The standard reply to a colleague who wanted a new feature was first to say that it was too late to introduce such an upheaval to the document.
- Then that the colleague should himself prepare the new syntax and semantics to go with it.
- But then, at the next meeting, he would show with great glee how he had restructured the entire Report to accommodate the new feature and how beautifully it now fitted in.

McCarthy's overloading, which required an enormous upheaval to the Report, provides the finest example of this behaviour.

Well, the draft Report, as commissioned at Warsaw for publication in the *Algol Bulletin*, was dropped onto an unsuspecting public in February of 1968, and was the cause of much shock, horror, and dissent, even (and perhaps especially) among the membership of Working Group 2.1. At an ALGOL 58 Anniversary meeting at Zurich in May,

- it was attacked for its alleged "obscurity, complexity, inadequacy, and length,"
- and defended by its authors for its alleged "clarity, simplicity, generality, and conciseness."

And both Naur and Wirth resigned from the Working Group at this time.

The next meeting at Tirrenia was a stormy one, and the Report was the sticking point. As Randell said at that meeting,

> "From our discussions . . ., it seems to follow that there is reasonable agreement on the language, but there is the need for an investigation of alternative methods of description."

So what to do? Well, it was decided,

- First, that the present document could not go upwards to TC2;
- But second, nevertheless, it *was* the document that had been commissioned at Warsaw, and so the author had fulfilled his obligation.

Now what? Well, in the last hours of the meeting, Van Wijngaarden offered to prepare one last edition for final acceptance or rejection in December 1968.

But there was one more meeting before that, at North Berwick, just before the IFIP Congress in Edinburgh. This was the first meeting I attended myself. It was a rude introduction into five days of continuous politics—Oh! there was one afternoon devoted to technical discussion. And the possibility of a Minority Report was being raised.

The next meeting at Munich was relatively calm. Of course we had a decision to reach. A covering letter was prepared and its tenor was that

> This Report is submitted as the consolidated outcome of the work of the Group. It is ... the decision of the Group that, although there is a division of opinion amongst some of its members, the design has reached the stage to be submitted to the test of implementation and use by the computing community.

(SLIDE 10) However, in the last hour of the meeting, some who were unhappy with the final form of the Covering Letter, and with interpretations which were being put upon it, produced a minority

The Minority Report

Signed by
Dijkstra
Duncan
Garwick
Hoare
Randell
Seegmüller
Turski
Woodger

Note that Naur and Wirth had already resigned.

TC2 declined to publish it.

SLIDE 10

The Editorial Team

Kees Koster	Transputer
John Peck	Syntaxer
Barry Mailloux	Implementer
Aad van Wijngaarden	Party Ideologist

The Brussels Brainstormers

M. Sintzoff
P. Branquart
J. Lewi
P. Wodon

SLIDE 11

report. The text of that minority report is in the paper, and as you see, it was signed by some very worthy names. It was clearly intended to be published alongside the full Report, and the decision by TC2 not to do so I can only describe as Unethical and Inexcusable.

(SLIDE 11) Well, there is the team that actually wrote the Report:

- Kees Koster (transputer) was a student at the Mathematisch Centrum under Van Wijngaarden.
- John Peck (syntaxer) was on sabbatical leave from the University of Calgary.
- Barry Mailloux (implementer) had been Van Wijngaarden's doctoral student from the time of Kootwijk.
- And, of course, Aad van Wijngaarden himself (party ideologist) kept the whole thing together.

Now, during the preparation of the Report, drafts and comments were being circulated among an "inner circle," of whom the group of Branquart, Lewi, Sintzoff, and Wodon at MBLE in Brussels is especially to be noted. Effectively, you see, there were two teams: One in Amsterdam creating the text, and another in Brussels taking it apart again, and this mechanism was actually very fruitful.

(SLIDE 12) These are some of the new language features that appeared in ALGOL 68.

- There were many new types and type constructors (references, unions, and so on), leading to the possibility of dynamic data structures.
- There were lots of new operators.
- There were environment enquiries.
- The ***if*** was matched by ***fi***, and other similar things. That solved the "dangling ***else***" problem.
- There were decent multi-dimensional arrays with nice slicing facilities.
- There was a **constant-declaration**. As an example, here you could not assign to this *pi* as declared here because it is declared as a constant with this value.
- Coercions. The three coercions shown here were known as 'widening' (***int***eger to ***real***), 'dereferencing' (***ref***erence to ***real*** to ***real***), and 'deproceduring' (***proc***edure returning ***real*** down to ***real***).
- And there was overloading of operators such as these two versions of + declared here, one for ***int***egers and one for ***real***s.

The new Features	
New types	***compl bits long... string***
Type constructors leading to dynamic data structures	***ref struct(...) union(...) proc(...)***
New operators	***mod abs sign odd ...***
Environment enquiries	*max int small real ...*
No dangling else	***if... case...esac do...od***
Slices	*aa[2:3, 4]*
Constant-declaration	***real*** *pi = 4.arctan(1);*
Coercion	*x := 2; y := x; x := random;*
Overloading	***op*** *+ = (**int** a, b)**int**: ...;* ***op*** *+ = (**real** a, b)**real**: ...;*

SLIDE 12

The Revision	
Habay-la-Neuve (July 1970)	
Manchester (Apr 1971)	
Novosibirsk (Aug 1971)	Timescale established
Fontainebleau (Apr 1972)	Editors appointed
Vancouver (July 1972)	Editors' meeting
Vienna (Sep 1972)	
Dresden (Apr 1973)	
Edmonton (July 1973)	Editors' meeting
Los Angeles (Sep 1973)	[RR] accepted
Revised Report published in *Acta Informatica* late 1975.	

SLIDE 13

(SLIDE 13) The style of Working Group meetings became much less confrontational after 1968. The first implementation of something like ALGOL 68, by the Royal Radar Establishment at Malvern, appeared early in 1970. It now became clear that there were many irksome features of the language that hindered implementation and upwards-compatible extensions, while not providing any user benefit, and thus a revision was called for.

The slide shows the timescale up to the point where Editors were appointed in 1972. The new Editors included Michel Sintzoff, from Brussels, and myself, later to be joined by Lambert Meertens and Richard Fisker. Van Wijngaarden and Koster, on the other hand, withdrew from any active role. Our brief was

> to consider, and to incorporate as far as possible" the points from various subcommittee reports and, having corrected all known errors in the Report, "also to endeavour to make its study easier for the uninitiated reader.

The new editors got together in Vancouver in July of 1972, and it soon became apparent that, to make the language definition both watertight and readable, a major rewrite was going to be necessary. I therefore intend to take a look at the method of description used in the Report, starting with the 2-level van Wijngaarden grammar.

(SLIDE 14) I am going to explain W-Grammars in terms of Prolog, since Prolog itself can be traced back to some early work by Colmerauer using W-Grammars.

- So this rule is written in Prolog. We have a goal "do we see an ***assignation*** here?", and to answer this we must test subgoals "do we see a ***destination*** here?", "do we see a ***becomes_symbol*** here?", and so on. And in Prolog, the values of variables such as *MODE* may be deduced from the subgoals, or they may be imposed with the question—in Prolog the distinction does not matter: the value of the variable just has to be consistent throughout.
- In the corresponding ALGOL 68 rule, a goal is just a free string of characters, in which variables such as **MODE** stand for strings produced by a separate context-free 'metagrammar'.
- So **MODE** can produce **real**, or **integral**, or **reference to** some other **MODE**, and so on (metagrammar is usually recursive).
- So by choosing for '**MODE**' the value '**real**' you get the following production rule: a **reference to real assignation** is a **reference to real destination**, a **becomes symbol** and a **real source**.
- Of course, this can produce things like *x := 3.142*.

W-Grammars

Here is a rule written in Prolog:

```
   assignation(ref(MODE)) :-
         destination(ref(MODE)),
                    becomes_symbol, source(MODE).
```

Corresponding W-Grammar:

```
   reference to MODE assignation :
         reference to MODE destination,
                    becomes symbol, MODE source.
```

Where

```
   MODE :: real ; integral ; reference to MODE ; ... .
```

Hence

```
   reference to real assignation :
         reference to real destination,
                    becomes symbol, real source.
```

Which can produce *x := 3.142*

SLIDE 14

Predicates

Grammar:

```
where (NOTETY) is (NOTETY) : EMPTY.
```

Example:

```
   strong MOID FORM coercee :
      where (FORM) is (MORF),
         STRONG MOID MORF ;
      where (FORM) is (COMORF),
         STRONG MOID COMORF,
      unless (STRONG MOID) is (deprocedured to void).
```

SLIDE 15

But observe how we have insisted that the **MODE** of the **destination** *x* must be ***ref**erence to **real*** because the **MODE** of the **source** *3.142* is ***real*** (or you could argue the other way round—*3.142* must be ***real*** because *x* is known to be ***ref**erence to **real***—you can argue both ways round just as in Prolog).

(SLIDE 15) In the Revision, we found newer and cleaner ways to use W-Grammars, most notably through the use of "predicates." Here we have a rule to produce a thing called a **strong-MOID-FORM-coercee**. Now it so happens that **FORMs** can be various things—some of them are called **MORFs,** some of them are called **COMORFs**.

And the whole purpose of this rule is actually to forbid deproceduring of certain **COMORFS**, so

If the particular **FORM** we are dealing with happens to be a **MORF**

- this so-called "predicate" **where (FORM) is (MORF)** produces **EMPTY**, so then we go ahead and produce what we wanted to produce.

But if the **'FORM'** is a **'COMORF'**

- then we satisfy this predicate **where (FORM) is (COMORF),**
- after which we also have to satisfy this one, which says that "**unless** the **'STRONG MOID'** happens to be **'deprocedured to void'**." And that is so arranged that *if* the **'STRONG MOID'** is *not* **'deprocedured to void'**, then it does produce **EMPTY**, but not so if the **'STRONG MOID'** *is* **'deprocedured to void'**.
- And in that case, since it doesn't produce anything at all, I am prevented from producing a **deprocedured-to-COMORF**, as intended.

Well, the point is that, with predicates, you can do the most amazing things, once you have learned how to use them.

In the original Report, a whole chapter had been devoted to what we now call "static semantics." But we found too many bugs—shocks and surprises—in this chapter to have any confidence in its correctness. We were now determined that the Report should be written in such a way that we could successfully argue the correctness of any part of it. Hence the static semantics was put into the grammar, using predicates. Here is how it was done. (SLIDE 16)

- Here again is the syntax of an **assignation**. Now you see that the **assignation** is accompanied by a **'NEST'** containing all the declarations visible at that point in the program, and the **destination** is accompanied by the same **'NEST'**, and likewise the **source**.

NESTs

Grammar:

REF to MODE NEST assignation :
REF to MODE NEST destination,
becomes token, MODE NEST source.

SLIDE 16

Step 3: If the home contains an operator-dening occurrence **O** {, in an **operation-declaration** (7.5.1.a,b),} of a terminal production **T** of **'PRAM ADIC operator'** which is the same terminal production of **'ADIC indication'** as the given occurrence, and which {, the identication of all descendent **identiers** , **indications** and **operators** of the **operand(s)** of **F** having been made,} is such that some **formula** exists which is the same sequence of symbols as **F**, whose **operator** is an occurrence of **T** and which is such that the original of each descendent **identier** , **indication** and **operator** of its **operand(s)** is the same notion as the original of the corresponding **identier** , **indication** and **operator** contained in **F** {, which, if the **program** is a proper **program**, is uniquely determined by virtue of 4.4.1.a}, then the given occurrence identies **O**; otherwise, Step 2 is taken.

SLIDE 17

And if the **destination** or the **source** contains any **identifiers**, then predicates in the grammar ensure that each **identifier** occurs properly in its **'NEST'**, and the syntax of **declarations**, of course, ensures that the **'NEST'** corresponds to the things that actually were declared. And suitable **'NEST'**s are propagated throughout the whole of the grammar, so that all the static semantics are incorporated. Well, that is the grammar, but the real problem with the original Report was *not* the W-Grammar; it was the style of the semantics, which was pedantic, verbose, and turgid.

(SLIDE 17) Here is a nice example from the Original Report, which is concerned with the static semantics of overloaded operators. Let me read it to you.

[Dramatic reading of the slide, with applause].

Now that text happens to be both necessary and sufficient for its purpose, but I hope you can see why we concluded that the static semantics would be more safely described in the Syntax.

(SLIDE 18) So we treated the Report as a large-scale programming project, consciously applying the principles of structured programming. Here, for example, is the original semantics of assignment.

- It is made up of all these Steps, and it is clearly a program full of **goto**s, and it conveys a general feeling of wall-to-wall verbosity.

(SLIDE 19) Here is the revised semantics of assignment, and I hope you will believe, from its layout alone, that you could readily set about understanding it if you had to.

- You see it has nice indentation, cases, local declarations, and for-loops.

Well, we took some examples of the new style of syntax and semantics to the next Working Group meeting in Vienna, where they were greeted with horror by some members. A "Petition for the Status Quo of ALGOL 68" was presented, claiming that the Revised Report had become a pointless undertaking and that the idea should be abandoned. This was debated on the very last day of the meeting, the motion being that the Revision should merely consist of the Old Report plus an addendum.

- Well, we pointed out that some errors were almost impossible to correct in the old framework.
- We pointed out that, to have a basis for upwards-compatible future extensions, we would need at least twice the list of changes proposed by the petitioners.
- We pointed out that it would then require an addendum half the size of the Report.
- We were getting nowhere. Now it was time for the vote.

From the Original Report:

An instance of a value is assigned to a name in the following steps:

Step 1: If the given value does not refer to a component of a multiple value having one or more states equal to **0** {2.2.3.3.b}, if the scope of the given name is not larger than the scope of the given value {2.2.4.2} and if the given name is not **nil**, then Step 2 is taken; otherwise, the further elaboration is undefined;

Step 2: The instance of the value referred to by the given name is considered; if the mode of the given name begins with **'reference to structured with'** or with **'reference to row of'**, then Step 3 is taken; otherwise, the considered instance is superseded {a} by a copy of the given instance and the assignment has been accomplished;

Step 3: If the considered value is a structured value, then Step 5 is taken; otherwise, applying the notation of 2.2.3.3.b to its descriptor, if for some **I**, **I=1, ..., n**, **sI=1** (**tI=1**) and **lI** (**uI**) is not equal to the corresponding bound in the descriptor of the given value, then the further elaboration is undefined;

Step 4: If some **sI=0** or **tI=0**, then, first, a new instance of a multiple value **M** is created whose descriptor is a copy of the descriptor of the given value modified by setting its states to the corresponding states in the descriptor of the considered value, and whose elements are copies of elements, if any, of the considered value, and, otherwise, are new instances of values whose mode is, or a mode from which is united, the mode obtained by deleting all initial **'row of'**s from the mode of the consider Step 5: Each field (element, if any,) of the given value is assigned {in an order which is left undefined} to the name referring to the corresponding field (element, if any,) of the considered value and the assignment has been accomplished.An instance of a value is assigned to a name in the following steps:ed value; next **M** is made to be referred to by the given name and is considered instead;

Step 5: Each field (element, if any,) of the given value is assigned {in an order which is left undefined} to the name referring to the corresponding field (element, if any,) of the considered value and the assignment has been accomplished.

SLIDE 18

And now from the Revised Report:

A value **W** is "assigned to" a name **N**, whose mode is some **'REF to MODE'**, as follows:

It is required that
- **N** be not nil, and that
- **W** be not newer in scope than **N**;

Case A: **'MODE'** is some **'structured with FIELDS mode'**:
For each **'TAG'** selecting a field in **W**,
- that field is assigned to the subname selected by **'TAG'** in **N**;

Case B: **'MODE'** is some **'ROWS of MODE1'**:
- let **V** be the {old} value referred to by **N**;
- it is required that the descriptors of **W** and **V** be identical;

For each index **I** selecting an element in **W**,
- that element is assigned to the subname selected by **I** in **N**;

Case C: **'MODE'** is some **'flexible ROWS of MODE1'**:
- let **V** be the {old} value referred to by **N**;
- **N** is made to refer to a multiple value composed of
  (i) the descriptor of **W**,
  (ii) variants {4.4.2.c} of some element {possibly a ghost element} of **V**;
- **N** is endowed with subnames {2.1.3.4.g};

For each index **I** selecting an element in **W**,
- that element is assigned to the subname selected by **I** in **N**;

Other Cases {e.g., where **'MODE'** is some **'PLAIN'** or some **'UNITED'**}:
- **N** is made to refer {2.1.3.2.a} to **W**.

SLIDE 19

It had long been a Working Group tradition that straw votes were phrased in the form "Who could live with . . .?" rather than "Who prefers . . .?". So to let everybody see the full consequences before taking the formal vote, I proposed these questions.

"Who could live with the state if the resolution was passed?"

- 12 could live with it, 5 could not live with it, and 1 abstained.

"Who could live with the opposite state?"

- 12 could live with the opposite state, 1 could not, and 5 abstained.

Now van Wijngaarden was always a superb politician. Having observed who had actually voted, he pointed out that passing the resolution "would cause the death of five of the six editors, which seemed a most unproductive situation." And then the formal motion was put.

[6-6-6]

And we were through.

By the next meeting in Dresden, all the fuss had subsided, and people even complimented us on the improved clarity. The editors held a second three-week get-together in Edmonton, and the Revised Report was accepted, subject to polishing, in September 1973 in Los Angeles.

So here are my recommendations to people who essay to design programming languages.

- The work should be done by a small group of people (four or five is plenty).
- There is considerable advantage in geographical separation, as between Amsterdam and Brussels the first time, or between Manchester, Vancouver, and Edmonton the second time.
- The Editors need tidy and pernickety minds and, incidentally, good editors are not necessarily good language designers, nor vice versa.
- You should construct a formal definition of the language at the *same* time. I believe ALGOL 68 is the only major language in which the Formal Definition was not a retrofit.
- There is considerable benefit in doing the whole job twice. We had that advice this morning also.
- And we most certainly observed that large committees are unstable (although they may be necessary for democratic reasons).

And here are my recommendations for writing Reports.

- There must be copious pragmatic remarks, well delineated from the formal text. The purpose of these remarks is to *educate* the reader.
- Motivation should be given for *why* things are as they are. This means that we have redundancy, but redundancy is no bad thing.
- The syntax should be fully cross referenced, forwards, backwards, and every which-way; and the semantics likewise.
- And the Report should not take itself too seriously. The Report is not going to be perfect. Our Report contained some good jokes, many quotations from Shakespeare, Lewis Carroll, A. A. Milne and others, and even a picture of Eeyore.
- So, above all, the Report should be *fun* to write.

Unfortunately, Standards Bodies and Government Departments do not always encourage these practices in their guidelines. I invite you to consider the extent to which they have been followed, or otherwise, in more recent programming language definitions, together with the perceived success of those definitions.

On that basis I will rest my case.

TRANSCRIPT OF QUESTION AND ANSWER SESSION

HERBERT KLAEREN (University of Tubingen): Could you explain the hipping coercion a bit. In your example, *x* := ***if*** *p* ***then*** *y* ***else goto*** *error* ***fi***, I would expect that *x* doesn't change if *p* is ***false***. How does the coercion come in?

LINDSEY: The hipping coercion was a dirty piece of syntax in the original Report. It is simply that, if you have got a conditional expression, one half of it ***if*** *some condition* ***then*** *some value*, then that presumably is the mode of the result. If the ***else*** part says ***goto*** *error*, what is the mode of ***goto*** *error*? So there was a fictitious coercion to make everything look tidy. It was syntactic tidiness.

STAVROS MACRAKIS (OSF Research Institute): Was the schedule of three meetings per year good or bad?

LINDSEY: It would average nearer two, except when things got hectic in 1968. The work has to be done off-line by a small group of four or five people. The function of a committee is simply to oversee. So two meetings a year is plenty. This matter might come up again with Colonel Whitaker this afternoon.

MARTIN CAMPBELL-KELLY (University of Warwick): Is ALGOL 68 completely dead, or just a dying language?

LINDSEY: It is a matter of common knowledge—it is not currently in widespread use, but, there are places that still use it. If you want a compiler, see me afterwards. Incidentally, there are some documents at the back, and one of them is a copy of the *Algol Bulletin* (AB 52, August 1988) listing all the implementations that currently exist, or did exist a few years ago.

MIKE WILLIAMS (University of Calgary): I once asked John Peck if ALGOL 68 was ever intended to be used or if it was an intellectual exercise.

LINDSEY: It was quite definitely intended as a language to be used. The reasons why languages do, or do not, get used bear little resemblance to the goodness or badness of the language. And which is the most commonly used language at the moment, and is it a good one? I won't name it, but I am sure you all have your ideas. Yes, it was definitely intended to be used, and the reasons it wasn't are as much political as technical, I think.

HERBERT KLAEREN (University of Tubingen): ALGOL 68 has been criticized as being a committee-designed language, and looking that way. From your history of the original ALGOL 68 Report, I got the impression that it was much more Van Wijngaarden's language than it was a committee language. Could you comment on that?

LINDSEY: I think it was a well-designed language in spite of being designed by a committee. You say that a camel is a horse designed by a committee. ALGOL 68 was no camel. It was Van Wijngaarden's personality, I think, which kept it clean in spite of the committee. Nevertheless, many of the odd little features which are in, are in because the committee said—voted—"we want this X in like this"; and there it is if you look. Usually, where there are unfortunate little holes in the language, they are usually small little things—nothing to do with the orthogonality. Many of those, I think, were put in because suddenly the Working Group said "I want this," and they got it. Van Wijngaarden always reserved to himself the right as to how the thing was described. I am not sure whether this was necessarily a good thing or not. It was done in spite of a rather large and somewhat unruly committee. But, in a democracy, committees are necessary.

HERBERT KLAEREN (University of Tubingen): Why is the rowing coercion "clearly" a mistake? In connection with string processing, it would seem natural to coerce a character "*A*" into a one-element string, if necessary.

LINDSEY: Because its effect is counter-intuitive (my students were always surprised when it did not produce an ***array*** of some appropriate size with all the elements initialized to the given value). It was put in to fix a hole in the syntax. Indeed, it also turns a ***char*** into a one-element ***string***, but that could have been brought about in other ways. No other language has had to do it this way.

BIOGRAPHY OF C. H. LINDSEY

Charles Lindsey was born in Manchester, UK, in 1931. He obtained his Bachelor's degree in Physics at Cambridge University in 1953, and his PhD in 1957 for a thesis exploring use of the newly invented ferrite cores for logical purposes rather than for storage. At that time, he was clearly an engineer, although he did write some programs for the EDSAC.

From 1957, he worked for Ferranti (now a part of ICL), becoming project leader for the Orion computer (that was actually the first commercial time-sharing computer, although it was never a commercial success). After that, he worked on "Design Automation" (or Computer Aided Design, as we should now say), and designed his first programming language for simulating hardware.

In 1967, he joined the staff of the recently created Department of Computer Science at the University of Manchester, where he immediately became interested in the language ALGOL 67 (as it then was) under development by IFIP Working Group 2.1. A paper "ALGOL 68 with fewer tears" written to explain the new language informally to the "uninitiated reader" brought him to the notice of WG 2.1, of which he soon became a full member. Enhancement and development of ALGOL 68 kept him fully occupied until about 1983.

This was followed by some work on extensible languages, and participation in the continuing work of WG 2.1, which was now centered around specification languages. He retired from the University in 1992, but took his computer home with him, so as to be able to continue working in Computer Science.

Pascal Session

Chairman: *Jacques Cohen*
Discussant: *Andrew B. Mikel*

RECOLLECTIONS ABOUT THE DEVELOPMENT OF PASCAL

N. Wirth

Institut für Computersysteme, ETH Zurich
CH-8092 Zurich

ABSTRACT

Pascal was defined in 1970 and, after a slow start, became one of the most widely used languages in introductory programming courses. This article first summarizes the events leading to Pascal's design and implementation, and then proceeds with a discussion of some of the language's merits and deficiencies. In the last part, developments that followed its release are recounted. Its influence chiefly derived from its being a vehicle for structured programming and a basis for further development of languages and for experiments in program verification.

CONTENTS

3.1 EARLY HISTORY

The programming language Pascal was designed in the years 1968–1969, and I named it after the French philosopher and mathematician, who in 1642 designed one of the first gadgets that might truly be called a digital calculator. The first compiler for Pascal was operational in early 1970, at which time the language definition also was published [Wirth 1970].

These facts apparently constitute the anchor points of the history of Pascal. However, its genuine beginnings date much further back. It is perhaps equally interesting to shed some light on the events and trends of the times preceding its birth, as it is to recount the steps that led to its widespread use. I shall therefore start with a more or less chronological narrative of the early history of Pascal.

In the early 1960s, there existed two principal scientific languages: FORTRAN and ALGOL 60 [Naur 1963]. The former was already in wide use and supported by large computer manufacturers. The latter—designed by an international committee of computing experts—lacked such support, but attracted attention by its systematic structure and its concise, formalized definition. It was obvious that ALGOL deserved more attention and a wider field of applications. In order to achieve it, ALGOL needed additional constructs to make it suitable for purposes other than numerical computation. To this end, IFIP established a Working Group with the charter of defining a successor to ALGOL. There was hope that the undesirable canyon between scientific and commercial programming, by the mid-1960s epitomized as the FORTRAN and COBOL worlds, could be bridged. I had the privilege of joining Working Group 2.1 in 1964. Several meetings with seemingly endless discussions about general philosophies of language design, about formal definition methods, about syntactic details, character sets, and the whole spectrum of topics connected with programming revealed a discouraging lack of consensus about the approach to be taken. However, the wealth of ideas and experience presented also provided encouragement to coalesce them into a powerful ensemble.

As the number of meetings grew, it became evident that two main factions emerged from the roughly two dozen members of the Working Group. One party consisted of the ambitious members, unwilling to build upon the framework of ALGOL 60 and unafraid of constructing features that were largely untried and whose consequences for implementors remained a matter of speculation, who were eager to erect another milestone similar to the one set by ALGOL 60. The opponents were more pragmatic. They were anxious to retain the body of ALGOL 60 and to extend it with well-understood features, widening the area of applications for the envisaged successor language, but retaining the orderly structure of its ancestor. In this spirit, the addition of basic data types for double precision real numbers and for complex numbers was proposed, as well as the record structure known from COBOL, the replacement of ALGOL's *call-by-name* with a *call-by-reference* parameter, and the replacement of ALGOL's overly general **for-statement** by a restricted but more efficient version. They hesitated to incorporate novel, untested ideas into an official language, well aware that otherwise a milestone might easily turn into a millstone.

In 1965, I was commissioned to submit a proposal to the WG, which reflected the views of the pragmatists. In a meeting in October of the same year, however, a majority of the members favored a competing proposal submitted by A. van Wijngaarden, former member of the ALGOL 60 team, and decided to select it as the basis for ALGOL X in a meeting in Warsaw in the fall of 1966 [van Wijngaarden, 1969]. Unfortunately, but as foreseen by many, the complexity of ALGOL 68 caused many delays, with the consequence that, at the time of its implementation in the early 1970s, many users of ALGOL 60 had already adopted other languages [Hoare 1980].

I proceeded to implement my own proposal in spite of its rejection, and to incorporate the concept of dynamic data structures and pointer binding suggested by C. A. R. Hoare. The implementation was made at Stanford University for the new IBM 360 computer. The project was supported by a grant from the U.S. National Science Foundation. The outcome was published and became known as ALGOL W [Wirth 1966]. The system was adopted at many universities for teaching programming courses, but the language remained confined to IBM 360/370 computers.

Essentially, ALGOL W had extended ALGOL 60 with new data types representing double precision floating-point and complex numbers, with bit strings and with dynamic data structures linked by pointers. In spite of pragmatic precautions, the implementation turned out to be rather complex, requiring a run-time support package. It failed to be an adequate tool for systems programming, partly because it was burdened with features unnecessary for systems programming tasks, and partly because it lacked adequately flexible data structuring facilities. I therefore decided to pursue my original goal of designing a general-purpose language without the heavy constraints imposed by the necessity of finding a consensus among two dozen experts about each and every little detail. Past experience had given me a life-long mistrust in the products of committees, where many participate in debating and decision making, and few perform the actual work—made difficult by the many. In

1968, I assumed a professorship at the Federal Institute of Technology in Zurich (ETH), where ALGOL 60 had been the language of choice among researchers in numeric computation. The acquisition of CDC computers in 1965 (and even more so in 1970), made this preference hard to justify, because ALGOL compilers for these computers were rather poorly designed and could not compete with their FORTRAN counterparts. Furthermore, the task of teaching programming—in particular, systems programming—appeared highly unattractive, given the choice between FORTRAN and assembler code as the only available tools. After all, it was high time to not only preach the virtues of structured programming, but to make them applicable in actual practice by providing a language and compilers offering appropriate constructs. The discipline of structured programming had been outlined by E. W. Dijkstra [Dijkstra 1966] and represented a major step forward in the battle against what became known as the "Software Crisis." It was felt that the discipline was to be taught at the level of introductory programming courses, rather than as an afterthought while trying to retrain old hands. This insight is still valid today. Structured programming and stepwise refinement [Wirth 1971a] marked the beginnings of a *methodology* of programming, and became a cornerstone in helping program design become a subject of intellectual respectability.

Hence, the definition of a new language and the development of its compiler were not a mere research project in language design, but rather a blunt necessity. The situation was to recur several times in the following decades, when the best advice was: Lacking adequate tools, build your own! In 1968, the goals were twofold: The language was to be suitable for expressing the fundamental constructs known at the time in a concise and logical way, and its implementation was to be efficient and competitive with existing FORTRAN compilers.

The latter requirement turned out to be rather demanding, given a computer (the CDC 6000) that was designed very much with FORTRAN in mind. In particular, dynamic arrays and recursive procedures appeared as formidable obstacles, and were therefore excluded from an initial draft of the language. The prohibition of recursion was a mistake and was soon to be rectified, in due recognition that it is unwise to be influenced severely by an inadequate tool of a transitory nature.

The task of writing the compiler was assigned to a single graduate student (E. Marmier) in 1969. As his programming experience was restricted to FORTRAN, the compiler was to be expressed in FORTRAN, with its translation into Pascal and subsequent self-compilation planned after its completion. This, as it turned out, was another grave mistake. The inadequacy of FORTRAN to express the complex data structures of a compiler caused the program to become contorted and its translation amounted to a redesign, because the structures inherent in the problem had become invisible in the FORTRAN formulation. The compiler relied on syntax analysis based on the table-driven bottom-up (LR) scheme adopted from the ALGOL W compiler. Sophistication in syntax analysis was very much in style in the 1960s, allegedly because of the power and flexibility required to process high-level languages. It occurred to me then that a much simpler and more perspicuous method could well be used, if the syntax of a language was chosen with the process of its analysis in mind.

The second attempt at building a compiler therefore began with its formulation in the source language itself, which by that time had evolved into what was published as Pascal in 1970 [Wirth 1970]. The compiler was to be a single-pass system based on the proven top-down, recursive-descent principle for syntax analysis. We note here that this method was eligible because the ban against recursion had been lifted: recursivity of procedures was to be the normal case. The team of implementors consisted of U. Ammann, E. Marmier, and R. Schild. After the program was completed—a healthy experience in programming in an unimplemented language!—Schild was banished to his home for two weeks, the time it took him to translate the program into an auxiliary, low-level language available on the CDC computer. Thereafter, the bootstrapping process could begin [Wirth 1971b].

This compiler was completed by mid-1970, and at this time the language definition was published. With the exception of some slight revisions in 1972, it remained stable thereafter. We began using Pascal in introductory programming courses in late 1971. As ETH did not offer a computer science program until ten years later, the use of Pascal for teaching programming to engineers and physicists caused a certain amount of controversy. My argument was that the request to teach the methods used in industry, combined with the fact that industry uses the methods taught at universities, constitutes a vicious circle barring progress. But it was probably my stubborn persistence rather than any reasoned argument that kept Pascal in use. Ten years later, nobody minded.

In order to assist in the teaching effort, Kathy Jensen started to write a tutorial text explaining the primary programming concepts of Pascal by means of many examples. This text was first printed as a technical report and thereafter appeared in Springer-Verlag's Lecture Notes Series [Jensen 1974].

3.2 THE LANGUAGE

The principal role of a language designer is that of a judicious collector of features or concepts. Once these concepts are selected, forms of expressing them must be found, that is, a syntax must be defined. The forms expressing individual concepts must be carefully molded into a whole. This is most important, as otherwise the language will appear as incoherent, as a skeleton onto which individual constructs were grafted, perhaps as afterthoughts. Sufficient time had elapsed that the main flaws of ALGOL were known and could be eliminated. For example, the importance of avoiding ambiguities had been recognized. In many instances, a decision had to be taken whether to solve a case in a clear-cut fashion, or to remain compatible with ALGOL. These options sometimes were mutually exclusive. In retrospect, the decisions in favor of compatibility were unfortunate, as they kept inadequacies of the past alive. The importance of compatibility was overestimated, just as the relevance and size of the ALGOL 60 community had been. Examples of such cases are the syntactic form of structured statements without closing symbol, the way in which the result of a function procedure is specified (assignment to the function identifier), and the incomplete specification of parameters of formal procedures. All these deficiencies were later corrected in Pascal's successor language, Modula-2 [Wirth 1982]. For example, ALGOL's ambiguous conditional statement was retained. Consider

```
IF p THEN IF q THEN A ELSE B
```

which can, according to the specified syntax, be interpreted in the following two ways:

```
IF p THEN [IF q THEN A ELSE B]
IF p THEN [ IF q THEN A ] ELSE B
```

Pascal retained this syntactic ambiguity, selecting, however, the interpretation that every **ELSE** be associated with the closest **THEN** at its left. The remedy, known but rejected at the time, consists of requiring an explicit closing symbol for each structured statement, resulting in the two distinct forms for the two cases as shown below:

```
IF p THEN                          IF p THEN
     IF q THEN A ELSE B END             IF q THEN A END
END                                ELSE B
                                   END
```

Pascal also retained the incomplete specification of parameter types of a formal procedure, leaving open a dangerous loophole for breaching type checks. Consider the declarations

```
PROCEDURE P (PROCEDURE q);
BEGIN q(x, y) END ;

PROCEDURE Q (x: REAL);
BEGIN ... END ;
```

and the call **P(Q)**. Then **q** is called with the wrong number of parameters, which cannot in general be detected at the time of compilation.

In contrast to such concessions to tradition stood the elimination of conditional expressions. Thereby the symbol **IF** clearly becomes a marker of the beginning of a statement, and bewildering constructs of the form

```
IF p THEN x := IF q THEN y ELSE z ELSE w
```

are banished from the language.

The baroque *for-statement* of ALGOL was replaced by a tamed version, which is efficiently implementable, restricting the control variable to be a simple variable and the limit to be evaluated only once instead of before each repetition. For more general cases of repetitions, the while statement was introduced. Thus it became impossible to formulate misleading, nonterminating statements, as, for example

```
FOR I := 0 STEP 1 UNTIL I DO S
```

and the rather obscure formulation

```
FOR I := n-1, I-1 WHILE I > 0 DO S
```

could be expressed more clearly by

```
I := n;
WHILE I > 0 DO BEGIN I := I-1; S END
```

The primary innovation of Pascal was to incorporate a variety of data types and data structures, similar to ALGOL's introduction of a variety of statement structures. ALGOL offered only three basic data types: integers, real numbers, and truth values, and the array structure; Pascal introduced additional basic types and the possibility to define new basic types (enumerations, subranges), as well as new forms of structuring: record, set, and file (sequence), several of which had been present in COBOL. Most important was of course the recursivity of structural definitions and the consequent possibility to combine and nest structures freely.

Along with programmer-defined data types came the clear distinction between type definition and variable declaration, variables being instances of a type. The concept of strong typing—already present in ALGOL—emerged as an important catalyst for secure programming. A type was to be understood as a template for variables specifying all properties that remain fixed during the time span of a variable's existence. Whereas its value changes (through assignments), its range of possible values remains fixed, as well as its structure. This explicitness of static properties allows compilers to verify whether rules governing types are respected. The binding of properties to variables in the program text is called early binding and is the hallmark of high-level languages, because it gives clear expression to the intention of the programmer, unobscured by the dynamics of program execution.

However, the strict adherence to the notion of (static) type led to some less fortunate consequences. We refer here to the absence of dynamic arrays. These can be understood as static arrays with the number of elements (or the bounding index values) as a parameter. Pascal did not include parameterized types, primarily for reasons of implementation, although the concept was well understood. Whereas the lack of dynamic array variables may perhaps not have been too serious, the lack of dynamic array parameters is clearly recognized as a defect, if not in the view of the compiler-designer, then certainly in the view of the programmer of numerical algorithms. For example, the following declarations do not permit procedure P to be called with x as its actual parameter:

```
TYPE     A0 = ARRAY [1 .. 100] OF REAL;
         A1 = ARRAY [0 .. 999] OF REAL;
VAR      x: A1;
PROCEDURE P(x: A0); BEGIN ... END
```

Another important contribution of Pascal was the clear conceptual and denotational separation of the notions of structure and access method. Whereas in ALGOL W, arrays could only be declared as static variables and hence could only be accessed directly, record structured variables could only be accessed via references (pointers), that is, indirectly. In Pascal, all structures can be either accessed directly or via pointers, indirection being specified by an explicit dereferencing operator. This separation of concerns was known as "orthogonal design," and was pursued (perhaps to extreme) in ALGOL 68. The introduction of explicit pointers, that is, variables of pointer type, was the key to a significant widening of the scope of application. Using pointers, dynamic data structures can be built, as in list-processing languages. It is remarkable that the flexibility in data structuring was made possible without sacrificing strict static type checking. This was due to the concept of pointer binding, that is, of declaring each pointer type as being bound to the type of the referenced objects, as proposed by [Hoare 1972]. Consider, for instance, the declarations

```
TYPE    Pt = ↑ Rec;
        Rec = RECORD x, y: REAL END ;
VAR     p, q: Pt;
```

Then p and q, provided they had been properly initialized, are guaranteed to hold either values referring to a record of type **Rec**, or the constant **NIL**. A statement of the form

```
p↑.x := p↑.y + q↑.x
```

turns out to be as type-safe as the simple **x := x + y.**

Indeed, pointers and dynamic structures were considerably more important than dynamic arrays in all applications except numeric computation. Intricately connected to pointers is the mechanism of storage allocation. As Pascal was to be suitable as a system-building language, it tried not to rely on a built-in run-time garbage collection mechanism, as had been necessary for ALGOL W. The solution adopted was to provide an intrinsic procedure **NEW** for allocating a variable in a storage area called "the heap," and a complementary one for deallocation (**DISPOSE**). **NEW** is easy to implement, and **DISPOSE** can be ignored, and indeed it turned out to be wise to do so, because system procedures depending on programmer's information are inherently unsafe. The idea of providing a garbage collection scheme was not considered in view of its complexity. After all, the presence of local variables and of programmer-defined data types and structures requires a rather sophisticated and complex scheme, crucially depending on system integrity. A collector must be able to rely on information about all variables and their types. This information must be generated by the compiler and, moreover, it must be impossible to invalidate it during program execution. The subject of parameter-passing methods had already been a source of endless debates and hassles in the days of the search for a successor to ALGOL 60. The impracticality of its name parameter had been clearly established, and the indispensability of the value parameter was generally accepted. Yet there were valid arguments for a reference parameter, in particular for structured operands on the one hand, and good reasons for result parameters on the other. In the former case the formal parameter constitutes a hidden pointer to the actual variable; in the latter the formal parameter is a local variable to be assigned to the actual variable upon termination of the procedure. The choice of the reference parameter (in Pascal called *VAR-parameter*) as the only alternative to the value parameter turned out to be simple, appropriate, and successful.

And last but not least, Pascal included statements for input and output, whose omission from ALGOL had been a source of continuing criticism. Particularly with regard to Pascal's role as a language for instruction, a simple form of such statements was chosen. Their first parameter designates a file and, if omitted, causes the data to be read from or written to the default medium, such as keyboard and printer. The reason for including a special statement for this purpose in the language definition, rather than postulating special, standard procedures, was the desire to allow for a variable number and different types of parameters:

```
Read(x, y); ... ; Write(x, y, z)
```

As mentioned before, a language designer collects frequently used programming constructs from his or her own experience, from the literature, or from other languages, and molds them into syntactic forms in such a way that they together form an integrated language. Whereas the basic framework of Pascal stems from ALGOL W, many of the new features emerged from suggestions made by C. A. R. Hoare, including enumeration, subrange, set, and file types. The form of COBOL-like record types was due to Hoare, as well as the idea to represent a computer's "logical words" by a well-known abstraction—namely, sets (of small integers). These "bits and pieces" were typically presented and discussed during meetings of the IFIP Working Group 2.1 (ALGOL), and thereafter appeared as communications in the *ALGOL Bulletin.* They were collected in Hoare's *Notes on Data Structuring* [Hoare 1972].

In Pascal, they were distilled into a coherent and consistent framework of syntax and semantics, such that the structures were freely combinable. Pascal permits the definitions of arrays of records, records of arrays, arrays of sets, and arrays of records with files, to name just a few possibilities. Naturally, implementations would have to impose certain limits as to the depth of nesting due to finite resources, and certain combinations, such as a file of files, might not be accepted at all. This case may serve as an example of the distinction between the general concepts defined by the language, and supplementary, restrictive rules governing specific implementations.

Although the wealth of data types and structuring forms was the principal asset of Pascal, not all of the components were equally successful. We keep in mind that success is a subjective quality, and opinions may differ widely. I therefore concentrate on an "evaluation" of a few constructs where history has given a reasonably clear verdict. The most vociferous criticism came from Habermann, who correctly pointed out that Pascal was not the last word on language design. Apart from taking issue with types and structures being merged into a single concept, and with the lack of constructs such as conditional expressions, the exponentiation operator, and local blocks, which were all present in ALGOL 60, he reproached Pascal for retaining the much-cursed **goto** statement [Habermann 1973]. In hindsight, one cannot but agree; at the time, its absence would have deterred too many people from trying to use Pascal. The bold step of proposing a **goto-less** language was taken ten years later by Pascal's successor Modula-2, which remedied many shortcomings and eliminated several remaining compatibility concessions to ALGOL 60, particularly with regard to syntax [Wirth 1982]. A detailed and well-judged reply to the critique by Habermann was written by Lecarme, who judged the merits and deficiencies on the basis of his experience with Pascal in both teaching and compiler design

[Lecarme 1975]. Another significant critique [Welsh 1977] discusses the issue of structural versus name equivalence of data types, a distinction that had unfortunately been left open in the definition of Pascal. It caused many debates until it was resolved by the standards committee.

Perhaps the single most unfortunate construct was the variant record. It was provided for the purpose of constructing nonhomogeneous data structures. Both for array and for dynamic structures in Pascal, the element types must be fixed by type declarations. The variant record allows variations of the element types. The unfortunate aspect of the variant record of Pascal stems from the fact that it provides more flexibility than required to achieve this legitimate goal. In a dynamic structure, typically every element remains of the same type as defined by its creation. The variant record, however, allows more than the construction of heterogeneous structures, that is, of structures with elements of different, although related types. It allows the type of elements themselves to change at any time. This additional flexibility has the regrettable property of requiring type checking at run-time for each access to such a variable or to one of its components. Most implementors of Pascal decided that this checking would be too expensive, enlarging code and deteriorating program efficiency. As a consequence, the variant record became a favorite feature to breach the type system by all programmers in love with tricks, which usually turn into pitfalls and calamities. Variant records also became a major hindrance to the notion of portability of programs. Consider, for example, the declaration

```
VAR R:    RECORD maxspeed: INTEGER;
             CASE v: Vehicle OF
             truck: (nofwheels: INTEGER);
             vessel: (homeport: String)
          END
```

Here, the designator **R.nofwheels** is applicable only if **R.v** has the value **truck**, and **R.homeport** only if **R.v = vessel**. No compiler checks can safeguard against erroneous use of designators, which, in the case of assignment, may be disastrous, because the variant facility is used by implementations to save storage by overlaying the fields **nofwheels** and **homeport**.

With regard to input and output operations, Pascal separated the notions of data transfer (to or from an external medium) and of representation conversion (binary to decimal and vice versa). External, legible media were to be represented as files (sequences) of characters. Representation conversion was expressed by special read and write statements that have the appearance of procedures but allowed a variable number of parameters. Whereas the latter was essentially a concession to programmers used to FORTRAN's I/O statements, the notion of sequence as a structural form was fundamental. Perhaps also in this case, providing sequences of any (even programmer-defined) element types was more than what was genuinely needed in practice. The consequence was that, in contrast to all other data types, files require a certain amount of support from built-in run-time routines, mechanisms not explicitly visible from the program text. The successors of Pascal—Modula-2 and Oberon—later retreated from the notion of the file as a structural form at the same level as array and record. This became possible, because implementations of sequencing mechanisms could be provided through modules (library packages). In Pascal, however, the notion of modules was not yet present; Pascal programs were to be regarded as single, monolithic texts. This view may be acceptable for teaching purposes where exercises are reasonably compact, but it is not tenable for the construction of large systems. Nevertheless and surprisingly, Pascal compilers could be written as single Pascal programs.

3.3 LATER DEVELOPMENTS

Even though Pascal appeared to fulfill our expectations in regard to teaching, the compiler still failed to satisfy the stated goals with regard to efficiency in two aspects: First, the compiler as a relatively large stand-alone program resulted in fairly long "turn-around times" for students. In order to alleviate the problem, I designed a subset of the language containing those features that we believed were to be covered in introductory courses, and a compiler/interpreter package that fitted into a 16K-word block of store, which fell under the most-favored program status of the computation center. The Pascal S package was published in a report, and was one of the early comprehensive systems made widely available in source form [Wirth 1981].

Comparable FORTRAN programs were still substantially faster, an undeniable argument in the hands of the Pascal adversaries. As we were of the opinion that structured programming, supported by a structured language and efficiency of compilation and of produced code were not necessarily mutually exclusive, a project for a third compiler was launched, which on the one hand was to demonstrate the advantage of structured top-down design with step-wise refinement [Ammann 1974], and on the other hand was to pay attention to generating high-quality code. This compiler was written by U. Ammann and achieved both goals quite admirably. It was completed in 1976 [Ammann 1977].

Although the result was a sophisticated compiler of high quality and reliability, in hindsight we must honestly confess that the effort invested was not commensurate with its effect. It did not win over many engineers and even fewer physicists. The argument that FORTRAN programs "ran faster" was simply replaced by "our programs are written in FORTRAN." And what authorizes us to teach structured, "better" programming to experts of ten years' standing? Also, the code was generated for the CDC 6000 computer which—with its 60-bit word and super-RISC structure—was simply not well suited for the task. Much of Ammann's efforts went into implementing the attribute packet of records. Although semantically irrelevant, it was requested by considerations of storage economy on a computer with very long words. Having had the freedom to design not only the language but also the computer would have simplified the project considerably. In any event, the spread of Pascal came from another front.

Not long after the publication of the Pascal definition, we received correspondence indicating interest in that language and requesting assistance in compiler construction, mainly from people who were not users of CDC computers. It was this stimulus that encouraged me to design a suitable computer architecture. A version of Ammann's compiler—easily derived from an early stage of the sequence of refinements—would generate code for this "ideal" architecture, which was described in the form of a Pascal program representing an interpreter. In 1973, the architecture became known as the *P-machine*, the code as *P-code*, and the compiler as the *P-compiler*. The *P-kit* consisted of the compiler in *P-code* and the interpreter as a Pascal source program [Nori 1981]. Recipients could restrict their labor to coding the interpreter in their favorite assembler code, or proceed to modify the source of the *P-compiler* and replace its code-generating routines. This *P-system* turned out to be the key to Pascal's spread onto many computers, but the reluctance of many to proceed beyond the interpretive scheme also gave rise to Pascal's classification as a "slow language," restricted to use in teaching.

Among the recipients of the *P-kit* was the team of K. Bowles at the University of California at San Diego (UCSD) around 1975. He had the foresight to see that a Pascal compiler for an interpretive system might well fit into the memory of a microcomputer, and he mustered the courage to try. Moreover, the idea of *P-code* made it easy to port Pascal to a whole family of micros and to provide a common basis on all of them for teaching. Microcomputers had just started to emerge, using early microprocessors such as Intel's 8080, DEC's LSI-11, and Rockwell's 6502; in Europe, they were hardly known at the time.

Bowles not only ported our compiler. His team built an entire system around the compiler, including a program editor, a file system, and a debugger, thereby reducing the time needed for an edit-compile-test step dramatically over any other system in educational use. Starting in 1978, this UCSD-Pascal system spread Pascal very rapidly to a growing number of users [Bowles 1980; Clark 1982]. It won more "Pascal friends" in a year than the systems used on large "mainframes" had won in the previous decade. This phenomenal success had three sources: (1) a high-level language, which would pervade educational institutions, was available on microcomputers; (2) Pascal became supported by an integrated system instead of a "stand-alone" compiler; and (3), perhaps most importantly, Pascal was offered to a large number of computer novices, that is, people who were not burdened by previous programming habits. In order to adopt Pascal, they did not have to give up a large previous investment in learning all the idiosyncracies of assembler or FORTRAN coding. The microcomputer made programming a public activity, hitherto exclusively reserved to the high priests of computing centers, and Pascal effectively beat FORTRAN on microcomputers. By 1978, there existed over 80 distinct Pascal implementations on hosts ranging from the Intel 8080 microprocessor to the Cray-1 supercomputer. But Pascal's usefulness was not restricted to educational institutions; by 1980, all four major manufacturers of workstations (Three Rivers, HP, Apollo, Tektronix) were using Pascal for system programming.

Besides being the major agent for the spread of Pascal implementations, the *P-system* was significant in demonstrating how comprehensible, portable, and reliable a compiler and system program could be made. Many programmers learned a great deal from the *P-system*, including implementors who did not base their work on the *P-system*, and others who had never before been able to study a compiler in detail. The fact that a compiler was available in source form caused the *P-system* to become an influential vehicle of extracurricular education.

Several years earlier, attempts had been made to transport the Pascal compiler to other mainframe computers. In these projects no interpreter or intermediate code was used; instead they required the design of new generators of native code. The first of these projects was also the most successful. It was undertaken by J. Welsh and C. Quinn from Queen's University, Belfast [Welsh 1972]. The target was the ICL 1900 computer. The project deserves special mention, because it should be considered as one of the earliest, genuinely successful ventures that were later to be called software engineering efforts.

As no CDC computer was available at Belfast, the goal was to employ a method that required as little work on a CDC machine as possible. What remained unavoidable would be performed during a short visit to ETH in Zurich. Welsh and Quinn modified the CDC-Pascal compiler, written in Pascal, by replacing all statements affecting code generation. In addition, they wrote a loader and an interpreter of the ICL architecture, allowing some tests to be performed on the CDC computer. All these components were programmed before the crucial visit, and were completed without any possibility of testing. In Zurich, the programs were compiled and a few minor errors were corrected within a week. Back in Belfast, the generated compiler code was executable directly by the ICL-machine after correction of a single remaining error.

This achievement was due to a very careful programming and checking effort, and it substantiated the claimed advantages to be gained by programming in a high-level language such as Pascal, which provides full, static type checking. The feat was even more remarkable, because more than half of the week had to be spent on finding a way to read the programs brought from Belfast. Aware of the incompatibilities of character sets and tape formats of the two machines (seven- versus nine-track tapes), Welsh and Quinn decided to use punched cards as the data carrier. Yet, the obstacles encountered were probably no less formidable. It turned out to be a tricky, if not downright impossible, task to read cards punched by an ICL machine with the CDC reader. Not only did the machines use different sets of characters and different encodings, but certain hole combinations were interpreted directly by the reader as end of records. The manufacturers had done their utmost best to ensure incompatibility! Apart from these perils, the travelers had failed to reckon with the thoroughness of the Swiss customs officers. The two boxes filled with some four thousand cards surely had to arouse their deep suspicion, particularly because these cards contained empty cubicles irregularly spaced by punched holes. Nevertheless, after assurances that these valuable possessions were to be reexported anyway, the two might-be smugglers were allowed to proceed to perform their mission. Upon their return, the fact that now the holes were differently positioned luckily went unnoticed.

Other efforts to port the compiler followed; among them were those for the IBM 360 computers at Grenoble, the PDP-11 at Twente [Bron 1976], and the PDP-10 at Hamburg [Grosse-Lindemann 1976].

By 1973, Pascal had started to become more widely known and was being used in classrooms as well as for smaller software projects. An essential prerequisite for such acceptance was the availability of a user manual including tutorial material in addition to the language definition. Kathy Jensen embarked on providing the tutorial part, and by 1973 the booklet was published by Springer-Verlag, first in their Lecture Notes Series, and, after selling very quickly, as an issue on its own [Jensen 1974]. It was soon to be accompanied by a growing number of introductory textbooks from authors from many countries. The *User Manual* itself was later to be translated into many different languages, and it became a bestseller.

A dedicated group of Pascal fans was located at the University of Minnesota's computer center. Under the leadership and with the enthusiasm of Andy Mickel, a Pascal Users' Group (PUG) was formed, whose vehicle of communication was the *Pascal Newsletter*, at first edited by G. H. Richmond (University of Colorado) and later by Mickel. The first issue appeared in January 1974. It served as a bulletin board for new Pascal implementations, for new experiences and—of course—for ideas of improving and extending the language. Its most important contribution consisted in tracking all the emerging implementations. This helped both consumers to find compilers for their computers and implementors to coordinate their efforts.

At ETH Zurich, we had decided to move on towards other projects and to discontinue distribution of the compiler, and the Minnesota group was ready to take over its maintenance and distribution. Maintenance here refers to adaptation to continually changing operating system versions, as well as to the advent of the Pascal standard.

Around 1977, a committee had been formed to define a standard. At the Southampton conference on Pascal, A. M. Addyman asked for help in forming a standards committee under the British Standards Institute (BSI). In 1978, representatives from industry met at a conference in San Diego hosted by K. Bowles to define a number of extensions to Pascal. This hastened the formation of a standards committee under the wings of IEEE and ANSI/X3. The formation of a Working Group within ISO followed in late 1979, and finally the IEEE and ANSI/X3 committees were merged into the single Joint Pascal Committee.

Significant conflicts arose between the U.S. committee and the British and ISO committees, particularly over the issue of conformant array parameters (dynamic arrays). The latter became the major difference between the original Pascal and the one adopted by ISO, the other being the requirement of complete parameter specifications for parametric procedures and functions. The conflict on the issue of dynamic arrays eventually led to a difference between the standards adopted by ANSI on one hand, and BSI and ISO on the other. The unextended standard was adopted by IEEE in 1981 and by ANSI in 1982 [Cooper 1983; Ledgard 1984]. The differing standard was published by BSI in 1982 and approved by ISO in 1983 [ISO 1983; Jensen 1991].

In the meantime, several companies had implemented Pascal and added their own, supposedly indispensable extensions. The standard was to bring them back under a single umbrella. If anything might have had a chance to make this dream come true, it would have been the speedy action of declaring the original language as the standard, perhaps with the addition of a few clarifications about obscure points. Instead, several members of the group had fallen prey to the devil's temptations: They extended the language with their own favorite features. Most of these features I had already contemplated in the original design, but dropped either because of difficulties in clear definition or efficient implementation, or because of questionable benefit to the programmer [Wirth 1975]. As a result, long debates started, requiring many meetings. When the committee finally submitted a document, the language had almost found its way back to the original Pascal. However, a decade had elapsed since publication of the report, during which individuals and companies had produced and distributed compilers; and they were not keen to modify them in order to comply with the late standard, and even less keen to give up their own extensions. An implementation of the standard was later published in Welsh [1986].

Even before publication of the standard, however, a validation suite of programs was established and played a significant role in promoting compatibility across various implementations [Wichmann, 1983]. Its role even increased after the adoption of the standard, and in the United States it made a Federal Information Processing Standard for Pascal possible.

The early 1970s were the time when, in the aftermath of spectacular failures of large projects, terms such as structured programming and software engineering were coined. They acted as symbols of hope for the drowning, and too often were believed to be panaceas for all the troubles of the past. This trend further raised interest in Pascal, which—after all—was exhibiting a lucid structure and had been strongly influenced by E. W. Dijkstra's teachings on structured design. The 1970s were also the years when, in the same vein, it was believed that formal development of correctness proofs for programs was the ultimate goal. C. A. R. Hoare had postulated axioms and rules of inference about programming notations (it later became known as Hoare-logic). He and I undertook the task of defining Pascal's semantics formally using this logic. However, we had to concede that a number of features had to be omitted from the formal definition (e.g., pointers) [Hoare 1973].

Pascal thereafter served as a vehicle for the realization of program validators in at least two places—namely, Stanford University and ETH Zurich. E. Marmier had augmented the compiler to accept assertions (in the form of marked comments) of relations among a program's variables holding after (or before) executable statements. The task of the assertion checker was to verify or refute the consistency of assertions and statements according to Hoare-logic [Marmier, 1975]. His was one of the earliest endeavors in this direction. Although it was able to establish correctness for various reasonably simple programs, its main contribution was to dispel the simple-minded belief that everything can be automated.

Pascal exerted a strong influence on the field of language design. It acted as a catalyst for new ideas and as a vehicle to experiment with them, and in this capacity gave rise to several successor languages. Perhaps the first was P. Brinch Hansen's Concurrent Pascal [Brinch Hansen 1975]. It embedded the concepts of concurrent processes and synchronization primitives within the sequential language Pascal. A similar goal, but with emphasis on simulation of discrete event systems based on (quasi-) concurrent processes, led to Pascal-Plus, developed by J. Welsh and J. Elder at Belfast [Welsh 1984]. A considerably larger language was the result of an ambitious project by Lampson *et al.*, whose goal was to cover all the needs of modern, large-scale software engineering. Although deviating in many details and also in syntax, this language, Mesa, had Pascal as its ancestor [Mitchell 1978]. It added the revolutionary concept of modules with import and export relationships, that is, of information hiding. Its compiler introduced the notion of separate—as distinct from independent—compilation of modules or packages. This idea was adopted later in Modula-2 [Wirth 1982], a language that in contrast to Mesa retained the principles of simplicity, economy of concepts, and compactness that had led Pascal to success.

Another derivative of Pascal is the language Euclid [London 1978]. The definition of its semantics is based on a formalism, just as the syntax of ALGOL 60 had been defined by the formalism BNF. Euclid carefully omits features that were not formally definable. Object Pascal is an extension of Pascal incorporating the notion of object-oriented programming, that is, of the abstract data type binding data and operators together [Tesler 1985]. And last but not least, the language Ada [Barnes 1980] must be mentioned. Its design was started in 1977 and was distinctly influenced by Pascal. It lacked, however, an economy of design without which definitions became cumbersome and implementations monstrous.

3.4 IN RETROSPECT

I have been encouraged to state my assessment of the merits and weaknesses of Pascal, of the mistaken decisions in its design, and of its prospects and place in the future. I prefer not to do so explicitly, and instead to refer the reader to my own successive designs, the languages Modula-2 [Wirth 1982] and Oberon [Wirth 1988]. Had I named them Pascal-2 and Pascal-3 instead, the questions might not have been asked, because the evolutionary line of these languages would have been evident.

It is also fruitless to question and debate early design decisions; better solutions are often quite obvious in hindsight. Perhaps the most important point was that someone did make decisions, in spite of uncertainties. Basically, the principle to include features that were well understood, in particular by implementors, and to leave out those that were still untried and unimplemented, proved to be the most successful single guideline. The second important principle was to publish the language definition after a complete implementation had been established. Publication of work done is always more valuable than publication of work planned.

Although Pascal had no support from industry, professional societies, or government agencies, it became widely used. The important reason for this success was that many people capable of recognizing its potential actively engaged themselves in its promotion. As crucial as the existence of good implementation is the availability of documentation. The conciseness of the original report made it attractive for many teachers to expand it into valuable textbooks. Innumerable books appeared in many languages between 1977 and 1985, effectively promoting Pascal to become the most widespread language used in introductory programming courses. Good course material and implementations are the indispensable prerequisites for such an evolution.

Pascal is still widely used in teaching at the time of this writing. It may appear that it undergoes the same fate as FORTRAN, standing in the way of progress. A more benevolent view assigns Pascal the role of paving the way for successors.

ACKNOWLEDGMENTS

I heartily thank the many contributors whose work played an indispensable role in making the Pascal effort a success, and who thereby directly or indirectly helped to advance the discipline of program design. Particular thanks go to C. A. R. Hoare for providing many enlightening ideas that flowed into Pascal's design; to U. Ammann, E. Marmier, and R. Schild for their valiant efforts to create an effective and robust compiler; to A.

Mickel and his crew for their enthusiasm and untiring engagement in making Pascal widely known by establishing a user group and a newsletter; and to K. Bowles for recognizing that our Pascal compiler was also suitable for microcomputers and for acting on this insight. I also thank the innumerable authors of textbooks, without whose introductory texts Pascal could not have received the acceptance that it did.

REFERENCES

[Ammann, 1974] Ammann, U., The Method of Structured Programming Applied to the Development of a Compiler, in *International Computing Symposium 1973*, Amsterdam: North-Holland, 1974, pp. 93–99.

[Ammann, 1977] Ammann, U., On Code Generation in a Pascal Compiler, *Software—Practice and Experience*, Vol. 7, 1977, pp. 391–423.

[Barnes, 1980] Barnes, , An Overwiew of Ada, *Software—Practice and Experience*, Vol. 10, 1980, pp. 851–887.

[Bowles, 1980] Bowles, K. L., *Problem Solving Using Pascal*. Springer-Verlag, 1977.

[Brinch Hansen, 1975] Brinch Hansen, P., The Programming Language Concurrent Pascal, *IEEE Transactions on Software Engineering*, Vol. 1, No. 2, 1975, pp. 199–207.

[Bron, 1976] Bron, C., and W. de Vries, A Pascal Compiler for the PDP-11 Minicomputers, *Software—Practice and Experience*, Vol. 6, 1976, pp. 109–116.

[Clark, 1982] Clark, R., and S. Koehler, *The UCSD Pascal Handbook*, Englewood Cliffs, NJ: Prentice-Hall, 1982.

[Cooper, 1983] Cooper, D., *Standard Pascal, User Reference Manual*, Norton, 1983.

[Dijkstra, 1966] Dijkstra, E. W., *Structured Programming*, Technical Report, University of Eindhoven, 1966. Also in Dahl, O.-J. *et al,*. *Structured Programming*, London: Academic Press, 1972.

[Grosse-Lindemann, 1976] Grosse-Lindemann, C. O., and H. H. Nagel, Postlude to a Pascal-Compiler Bootstrap on a DECSystem-10, *Software—Practice and Experience*, Vol. 6, 1976, pp. 29–42.

[Habermann, 1973] Habermann, A. N., Critical Comments on the Programming Language Pascal, *Acta Informatica* Vol. 3, 1973, pp. 47–57.

[Hoare, 1972] Hoare, C. A. R., Notes on Data Structuring, in Dahl, O.-J. *et al.*, *Structured Programming*, London: Academic Press, 1972.

[Hoare, 1973] Hoare, C. A. R. and N. Wirth, An Axiomatic Definition of the Programming Language Pascal, *Acta Informatica*, Vol. 2, 1973, pp. 335–355.

[Hoare, 1980] Hoare, C. A. R., The Emperor's Old Clothes. *Communications of the ACM*, Vol. 24, No. 2 , Feb. 1980, pp. 75–83.

[ISO, 1983] International Organization for Standardization, *Specification for Computer Programming Language Pascal*, ISO 7185, 1982.

[Jensen, 1974] Jensen, K., and N. Wirth, *Pascal—User Manual and Report*, Springer-Verlag, 1974.

[Jensen, 1991] Jensen, K., and N. Wirth, revised by A. B. Mickel and J. F. Miner, *Pascal—User Manual and Report*, ISO Pascal Standard, Springer-Verlag, 1991.

[Lecarme, 1975] Lecarme, O., and P. Desjardins, More Comments on the Programming Language Pascal, *Acta Informatica*, Vol. 4, 1975, pp. 231–243.

[Ledgard, 1984] Ledgard, H., *The American Pascal Standard*, Springer-Verlag, 1984.

[London, 1978] London, R. L., J. V. Guttag, J. J. Horning, B. W. Lampson, J. G. Mitchell, and G. J. Popek, Proof Rules for the Programming Language Euclid, *Acta Informatica*, Vol. 10, 1978, pp. 1–26.

[Marmier, 1975] Marmier, E., *Automatic Verification of Pascal Programs*, ETH Dissertation No. 5629, Zurich, 1975.

[Mitchell, 1978] Mitchell, J. G., W. Maybury, R. Sweet, *Mesa Language Manual*, Xerox PARC Report CSL-78-1, 1978.

[Naur, 1963] Naur, P., Ed., Revised Report on the Algorithmic Language ALGOL 60, *Communications of the ACM*, Vol. 3, 1960, pp. 299–316; *Communications of the ACM*, Vol. 6, 1963, pp. 1–17.

[Nori, 1981] Nori, K.V. *et al.*, The Pascal P-code Compiler: Implementation Notes, in *Pascal—The Language and Its Implementation*. D.W. Barron, ed., New York: John Wiley & Sons, 1981.

[Tesler, 1985] Tesler, L., Object Pascal Report,. *Structured Programming* (formerly *Structured Language World*), Vol. 9, No. 3, 1985, pp. 10–14.

[van Wijngaarden, 1969] van Wijngaarden, A., Ed., Report on the Algorithmic Language ALGOL 68, *Numer. Math*. Vol. 14, 1969, pp. 79–218.

[Welsh, 1972] Welsh, J., and C. Quinn, A Pascal Compiler for ICL 1900 Series Computers, *Software—Practice and Experience*, Vol. 2, 1972, pp. 73–77.

[Welsh, 1977] Welsh, J., W. J. Sneeringer, and C. A. R. Hoare, Ambiguities and Insecurities in Pascal, *Software—Practice and Experience*, Vol. 7, 1977, pp. 685–696. Also in D. W. Barron, Ed., *Pascal—The Language and its Implementation*, New York: John Wiley & Sons, 1981.

[Welsh, 1984] Welsh, J., and D. Bustard, *Sequential Program Structures*, Englewood Cliffs, NJ: Prentice-Hall, 1984.

[Welsh, 1986] Welsh, J., and A. Hay, *A Model Implementation of Standard Pascal*. Englewood Cliffs, NJ: Prentice-Hall, 1986.

[Wichmann, 1983] Wichmann, B., and Ciechanowicz, *Pascal Compiler Validation*, New York: John Wiley & Sons, 1983.

[Wirth, 1966] Wirth, N. and C. A. R. Hoare, A Contribution to the Development of ALGOL, *Communications of the ACM*, Vol. 9, No. 6, June 1966, pp. 413–432.

[Wirth, 1970] Wirth, N., *The Programming Language Pascal*, Techical Report 1, Fachgruppe Computer-Wissenschaften, ETH, Nov. 1970; *Acta Informatica*, Vol. 1,1971, pp. 35–63.

[Wirth, 1971a] Wirth, N., Program Development by Step-wise Refinement, *Commnications of the ACM*, Vol. 14, No. 4, Apr. 1977, pp. 221–227.

[Wirth, 1971b] Wirth, N., The Design of a Pascal Compiler, *Software—Practice and Experience*, Vol. 1, 1971, pp. 309–333.

[Wirth, 1975] Wirth, N. An assessment of the programming language Pascal. *IEEE Transactions on Software Engineering*, Vol. 1, No. 2, June 1975, pp. 192–198.

[Wirth, 1981] Wirth, N., Pascal-S: A Subset and its Implementation, in *Pascal—The Language and its Implementation*, D. W. Barron, Ed., New York: John Wiley & Sons, 1981.

[Wirth, 1982] Wirth, N., *Programming in Modula-2*, Springer-Verlag, 1982.

[Wirth, 1988] Wirth, N., The Programming Language Oberon, *Software—Practice and Experience*, Vol. 18, No. 7, July 1988, pp. 671–690.

TRANSCRIPT OF PRESENTATION

Editor's note: Niklaus Wirth's presentation closely followed his paper and we have omitted it with his permission.

TRANSCRIPT OF DISSCUSSANT'S REMARKS

SESSION CHAIR JACQUES COHEN: The discussant is Andy Mickel, who is the Computer Center Director at the Minneapolis College of Art and Design. Prior to his current position, he worked for ten years at the University of Minnesota Computer Center, where he managed the language processor's group supporting micros through CDC and VAX mainframes, up to the Cray-1. He cofounded the Pascal Users Group at ACM '75, and assumed editorship of the *Pascal Newsletter* in the summer of 1976. Through 1979, he coordinated the Users Group and edited the quarterly, *Pascal News*. Beginning with the Southampton Pascal Conference in 1977, he facilitated the international effort to standardize and promote the use of Pascal. After the standard was complete in 1983, he and his colleague, Jim Miner, revised the popular tutorial, *Pascal User Manual and Report*, in a third edition to conform to the standard. From 1983 to 1989, he worked at Apollo Computer, where in 1986 he led the project to develop the first commercial, two-pass Modula-2 compiler.

ANDREW B. MIKEL: My talk is on the origins of the Pascal Users Group and its effect on the use and dissemination of Pascal. I was introduced to programming languages by Daniel Friedman (who is here today), in my senior year at the University of Texas at Austin, 1971. He taught me language definition and programming language semantics. I went on to grad school at the University of Minnesota, where I got a job at the Computer Center and became interested in promoting the use of good, practical, general-purpose programming languages, but we had a Control Data machine. And that was a good thing, but along came Pascal and my efforts to promote it were met with resistance from FORTRAN users and other skeptics. So, my goal became to make the world safe for a language, that I, a nonguru, mortal programmer enjoyed using.

(SLIDE 1) I have a slide here where I have listed the sort of situation we found ourselves in 1970. Even though there were some Pascal compilers coming into use, there was a reluctance, particularly by American computer science departments, to teach Pascal. Along came George Richmond, from the University of Colorado, who started the *Pascal Newsletter* and created some momentum in our

Origins: Pascal User's Group

A. Situation, 1972, first compilers widespread.
B. 1972–1976 reluctance by CS Depts to teach Pascal.
C. Early 1975—good momentum—3 newsletters/13 months.
D. Early 1976—losing momentum.
   1. Habermann's spiteful article touted as truth.
   2. No newsletters for over a year.
   3. Pascal-P4 compiler writers duplicating efforts.

SLIDE 1

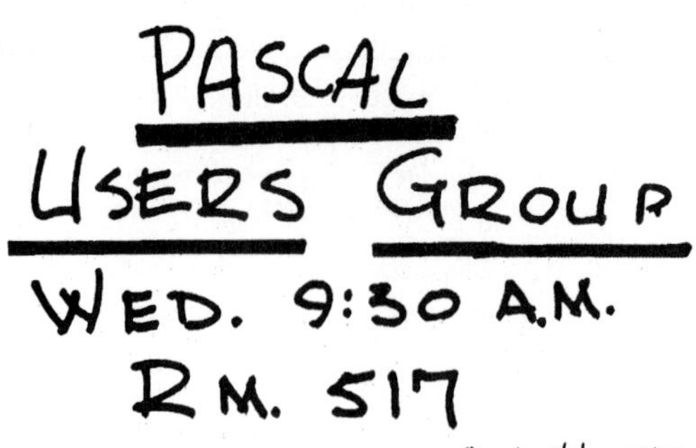

SLIDE 2

eyes by producing three newsletters in 13 months. But, then the newsletters stopped and people were quoting Habermann's article as if they had read it and had not studied Pascal. A lot of people using Pascal-P4 to build compilers were duplicating each others' efforts.

(SLIDE 2) We have a photocopy of the original sign used by Richard Cichelli at ACM '75 in Minneapolis, announcing a Pascal Users Group. I had never heard of this before. But I went. Bob Johnson, his friend from Saint Cloud State (Richard was from Lehigh University), Charles Fischer and Richard LeBlanc (who is here) from the University of Wisconsin, and 31 other people showed up in a hotel room. We talked about what to do. A lot of us were pretty angry.

(SLIDE 3) We formed a strategy. We decided to follow William Waite's advice in the *Software—Practice and Experience* article editorial about programming languages as organisms in an ecosystem. And if FORTRAN was a tough weed, we needed to grow a successful competing organism and starve FORTRAN at the roots. So we talked about forming little clubs like Society to Help Abolish FORTRAN Teaching (that's SHAFT), or the American COBOL Society "dedicated to the elimination of COBOL in our lifetime" (like the American Cancer Society). I was fresh from working at George McGovern's political campaign and you have to remember that the early seventies was the era of Watergate and the truth, integrity and full disclosure. So, in 1976, I decided to pro-actively mail directly to every college with a math department a notice that we had a Pascal Users Group. We rapidly built a large mailing list. We used the newsletter as a means to organize this whole activity. It was

Origins: Pascal User's Group

A. Solution: Follow William Waite's ecosystem analogy.
B. Found S.H.A.F.T. and A.C.S.
C. Use political-organizing skills developed in McGovern's campaign.
D. Organize and network supports via stronger Newsletter.
E. Add structure to Pascal Newsletter:
   1. Here and There with Pascal (includes roster).
   2. Open Forum/Articles/Implementation Notes.

SLIDE 3

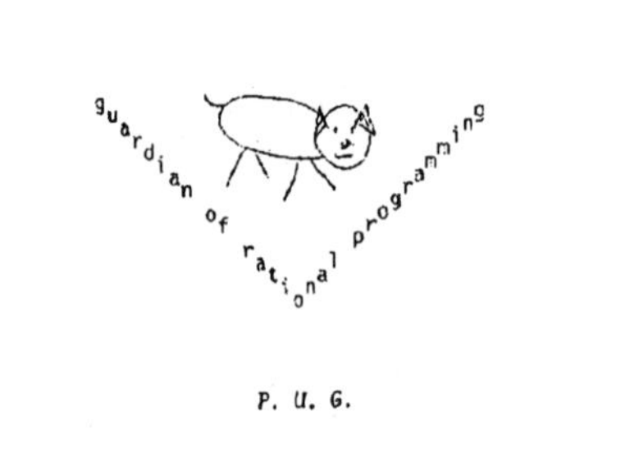

SLIDE 4

much like the language supplements to *SIGPLAN Notices*. The average size was 150 pages.

(SLIDE 4) We didn't take ourselves too seriously. Here is what the guardian of rational programming, the PUG mascot looked like. It is sort of a weakling looking dog, a pug dog.

(SLIDE 5) We started getting things back on track. We had an aggressive attitude. In the 90s we would say we were a User Group with "an attitude." We indulged in self-fulfilling prophesies. We tried to make it look like there was a lot going on around Pascal by publishing everything that we could find on it. And lo and behold, there was a lot going on with Pascal because some of the neutral bystanders became less afraid and started joining in. David Barron in Southampton scheduled the first Pascal Conference. One hundred and forty people attended. At that conference, Tony Addyman teased people with the idea of starting a formal standards effort. That was the beginning of standards, which took place in Europe, something a little different from what most American computer manufacturers were used to. Some of the early influences at that time were Wilhelm Burger at the University of Texas at Austin; John Strait, Jim Miner, and John Easton at Minnesota; Judy Bishop with David Barron at Southampton; Arthur H. J. Sale at the University of Tasmania in Australia; and Helmet Weber at the Bavarian University of Munich.

(SLIDE 6) This is an sample cover of *Pascal News*, which sort of illustrates its use of a self-organizing tool. The newsletters contain information about users, compilers, standards, vendors, applications, teaching, textbooks, and even the roster of all the members. My plan was if my Computer Center jerked the support out from under me, anybody could pick up the User Group and keep going.

(SLIDE 7) So, we were finally on a roll. The American committee starts, we get them cooperating without trying to dominate the standards process—we argued that it was a European Language being standardized by Europeans. We derailed the UCSD conference and "extensions-with-Pascal" people. The people at UCSD (the

PUG Effects

A. Newsletters: July 76, Sept 76, Nov 76.
B. a la 90's: "a user group with an Attitude!"
C. Roberto Minio at Springer: lower price of *PUM&R*.
D. Start standards effort without the powerful vendors.
E. Create self-fulfilling prophesy of explosion of activity.
F. Southhampton Conference, Feb 77, 140 people.
G. Tony Addyman, U of Manchester, UK, BSI Standards.

SLIDE 5

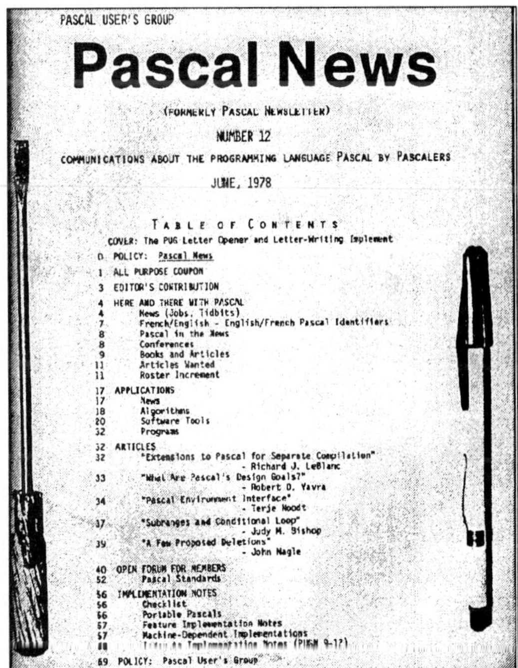

PASCAL USER'S GROUP

Pascal News

(FORMERLY PASCAL NEWSLETTER)

NUMBER 12

COMMUNICATIONS ABOUT THE PROGRAMMING LANGUAGE PASCAL BY PASCALERS

JUNE, 1978

TABLE OF CONTENTS

COVER: The PUG Letter Opener and Letter-Writing Implement

0 POLICY: Pascal News
1 ALL PURPOSE COUPON
3 EDITOR'S CONTRIBUTION
4 HERE AND THERE WITH PASCAL
4 News (Jobs, Tidbits)
7 French/English - English/French Pascal Identifiers
8 Pascal in the News
8 Conferences
9 Books and Articles
11 Articles Wanted
11 Roster Increment
17 APPLICATIONS
17 News
18 Algorithms
20 Software Tools
32 Programs
32 ARTICLES
32 "Extensions to Pascal for Separate Compilation" - Richard J. LeBlanc
33 "What Are Pascal's Design Goals?" - Robert D. Yavra
34 "Pascal Environment Interface" - Terje Noodt
37 "Subranges and Conditional Loop" - Judy M. Bishop
39 "A Few Proposed Deletions" - John Nagle
40 OPEN FORUM FOR MEMBERS
52 Pascal Standards
56 IMPLEMENTATION NOTES
56 Checklist
56 Portable Pascals
57 Feature Implementation Notes
57 Machine-Dependent Implementations
[illegible] Index to Implementation Notes (PUGN 9-12)
69 POLICY: Pascal User's Group

SLIDE 6

PUG Effects

A. U of Colorado, Boulder, ANSI/IEEE (JPC) Apr 78.
B. UCSD Conference on Extension, July 78.
C. *Pascal News* issues: Feb, May, Sep 77: circ. 1500.
D. Move to canonical compiler development
   1. Tracking 84 different implementations.
   2. From Intel 8080 to Cray-1.
E. Develop Suite of Software Tools/Validation Suite.
F. Develop Subprogram Libraries and Applications.

SLIDE 7

Growth in Use of Pascal Called Revolutionary

SLIDE 8

bad guys) were confusing the language definition with its implementation. Circulation of *Pascal News* increased. We also sorted out a lot of duplicated efforts among the PDP-11 and IBM 370 implementations: There were 20 different compiler efforts. That is not counted in the total of 84; that is just the ones that weren't canonical. There was a lot of software written in Pascal becoming available.

(SLIDE 8) Then all hell broke loose. This article appeared in *ComputerWorld* in April 1978 and down here it says, "You can join the two thousand members of the Pascal Underground by sending four dollars to the Pascal Users Group." My mail went from 15 pieces a day to 80-something pieces a day.

(SLIDE 9) This is a picture of me up against a wall pasted with copies of all the articles on Pascal out of the industry journals.

(SLIDE 10) This is sample of what kind of coverage we were starting to get in the industry press in 1978: *ComputerWorld, Byte, Electronics Magazine, IEEE Computer, and Datamation.* By the next year, our circulation was up to 4,600 in 43 countries.

(SLIDE 11) So we were riding high. Arthur Sale produced a little cartoon, "Pascal Riding on the Microwave."

(SLIDE 12) From an American point of view, industry led over academia, and here are some of the projects. A lot of them were internal to the companies over here that nobody really knew about. It was only in 1981, that the commercial versions of UCSD Pascal started to appear. I want to point out that Three Rivers PERQ, Tektronix, and the Hewlett-Packard 9000 are workstations.

(SLIDE 13) This may be controversial, too. It may be fortuitous that the first compiler was on Control Data equipment because at that time in the seventies, CDC had a disproportionately large installed base at universities. For example, the size of the student body at Minnesota was 55,000, at UT Austin it was 40,000, 45,000 at UC Berkeley, and all had Control Data equip-

SLIDE 9

PUG Effects – Press

A. Industry Press articles.
   1. *ComputerWorld*, page 24, 1 page, April, 1978.
   2. *Byte*: cover story, August, 1978.
   3. *Electronics*: cover mention, October, 1978.
   4. *IEEE Computer*: cover mention, April, 1979.
   5. *Datamation*: cover mention, July 1979.

B. *Pascal News*: Jan, Sep, Oct 79: circ 4600 in 43 countries.

SLIDE 10

SLIDE 11

PUG Effects – Industry over Academe

A. Control Data 1700, 1975.
B. Texas Instruments, ASC, 990 and 9900, 1976.
C. Control Data/NCR Joint Project, 1979.
D. Three Rivers PERQ, 1978.
E. Tektronix, 1978.
F. Apollo DOMAIN, 1980.
G. Apple Apple][, 1981.
H. Hewlett Packard 9000, 1981.

SLIDE 12

PUG Effects – Industry over Academe

A. CDC 6000/7000/Cyber sites at large universities in USA.
   1. U of Minnesota, 55,000.
   2. U of Texas at Austin, 40,000.
   3. U of California, Berkeley, 35,000.

B. Last to teach Pascal.
   1. M.I.T.
   2. Stanford U.
   3. Carnegie-Mellon U.

SLIDE 13

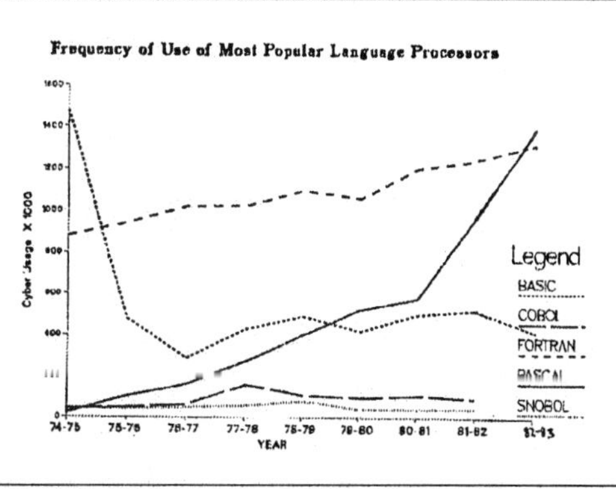

SLIDE 14

PUG Accomplishments

A. No bureaucracy, simply vast bulletin board.
B. *Pascal News* gave harmless outlet to frustrated designers.
C. Rick Shaw, Mar/May/Sep/Dec, 80; Apr/Sep, 81, Oct 82.
D. Charlie Gaffney, Jan/Apr/Jul/Nov 83.
E. Users organized before standards process began.
F. Portable Software Tools, Validation Suite.
G. In 1980's Pascal used to teach programming at U's.

SLIDE 15

Does Not Compute

I think, Brian, you'd be of greater service, at least for a while, bussing tables, eating crayfish, anything but reviewing film & people in so many words, I see the outline:

```
Procedure LambertWrite;
Begin
    Contract the Focal Point (film/person)
    vs. Industry; 'a distressingly pinstriped
    buttondown industry'
    ReadYearbook; 'Leafing through the yearbook'
    AddAdjectives; 'distressingly pinstriped'
    'fascinating trivia bits' 'deceptively unimposing'
    Generalize; 'It is my experience that most legends are an
    anticlimax in person. It is their creations which reflect greatness,'
    Print;
End; (* of Procedure LambertWrite *)
```

SLIDE 16

ment exceeding those small, more elite schools. I was chagrined that the last universities in the United States to use Pascal as a teaching language were MIT, Stanford, and Carnegie Mellon.

(SLIDE 14) This is an example of the usage at the University of Minnesota and of the number of compilations by language from 1974 to 1983. If we just take 1975 as a baseline, there were 900,000 FORTRAN compilations to 100,000 to Pascal. And by 1983, it was 1.3 million FORTRAN to 1.4 million Pascal—that is, not including all the compiles that were done on TERAK (which were LSI-11's and Apple II's running UCSD Pascal).

(SLIDE 15) So, what were our accomplishments? This is sort of a summary. The Users Group was not a bureaucracy. We could fold it up at any time. It was simply a vast bulletin board. I hope I can reassure Niklaus that the *Pascal News* articles provided a harmless outlet to frustrated language designers who wanted to extend Pascal. It dissipated their energy harmlessly. My successors were Rick Shaw (not a transportation vehicle) and Charlie Gaffney. One of the important things about the standards process is that the users were organized before the standards process began.

(SLIDE 16) This is a letter to the editor of a mainstream newspaper in the Twin Cities that is in the form of a Pascal program—so that by 1983, Pascal had even leaked out into the common culture. It's a critique of a movie or film critic.

Post-PUG—Pascal Today

A. Seamless transition to MODUS Quarterly, Jan 85.
B. Borland Turbo Pascal on DOS-PC's.
C. Think Pascal on Apple Macintosh.
D. HP/Apollo, Silicon Graphics, DEC, SUN workstations.
E. U of Minnesota Internet Gopher, 1992.
   1. Internet public server browser.
   2. Macintosh, DOS-PC, VAX, VM all in Pascal!
   3. NeXT and other UNIX, NOT!

SLIDE 17

(SLIDE 17) It turns out that *Pascal News* may have stopped publishing in 84 but there was a seamless transition to *MODUS Quarterly*, the Modula-2 Users Society. Here is the list of the current Pascal compilers, and the most famous application newly written in Pascal: the University of Minnesota Internet Gopher. And the versions for clients for Macintosh, DOS PC, VAX, and IBM VM are all in Pascal, but none of the UNIX boxes.

TRANSCRIPT OF QUESTION AND ANSWER SESSION

ANDREW BLACK (Digital Cambridge Research Laboratory): The omission of dynamic arrays from Pascal was as much a mistake as the omission of recursion. True or False?

WIRTH: In hindsight, true. You have to recall that I had not only to make language design decisions but also to implement them. Under these circumstances it is a question of whether to include more features, or to get ahead first with those needed to implement the compiler. In principle, you are right: Dynamic arrays should have been included. (Note: Recursion was excluded in a preliminary version only.)

HERBERT KLAEREN (University of Tubingen): The current ISO draft of Modula-2 contains a full formal semantics. Do you consider this useful?

WIRTH: Not really. It makes the report too voluminous for the reader. The Modula-2 report is 45 pages and the formal standardization document is about one thousand pages long. The definition of the empty statement alone takes a full page. The difference is intolerable.

MARTIN CAMPBELL-KELLY (University of Warwick): If, on a scale of excellence in programming language design, FORTRAN was awarded two, and Pascal was awarded five, what score would Modula-2 deserve?

WIRTH: Six. (In the Swiss school system, one is the worst and six is the best grade.)

BRENT HAILPERN (IBM Research): Did you foresee the type "abuse" resulting from variant records? If not, what crossed your mind when the loophole was discovered?

WIRTH: I did not foresee it, but I was told so by Tony Hoare. The reason for including the variant record was simply the need for it, and the lack of knowledge of how to do better. In the compiler itself several variants of records occur in the symbol table. For reasons of storage economy, variants are needed in order to avoid unused record fields. With memory having become available in abundance, the facility is now less important. Furthermore, better, type-safe constructs are known, such as type extensions (in Oberon).

RANDY HUDSON (Infometrics): What relationship do you see between the design of Pascal and the design of Ada?

WIRTH: I believe Ada did inherit a few ideas from Pascal, such as structures, concepts, and perhaps philosophy. I think the main differences stem from the fact that I, as an individual, could pick the primo areas of application, namely teaching and the design of systems of moderate complexity. Ada was devised according to a large document of requirements that the designers could not control. These requirements were difficult, extensive, partly inconsistent, and some were even contradictory. As a result, its complexity grew beyond what I considered acceptable.

BOB ROSIN: Was the P-code concept inspired by earlier work? For example, the Snobol-4 implementation?

WIRTH: It wasn't particularly the Snobol-4 implementation. The technique of interpreters was well known at the time.

ALLEN KAY (Apple Computers): Your thesis and Euler were going in a pretty interesting direction. Why did you go back to more static languages?

WIRTH: For a thesis topic you have to do something that is new and original, you are expected to explore new ways. Afterwards, as an engineer, I felt the need for creating something that is pragmatic and useful.

ROSS HAMILTON (University Of Warwick): Why did Pascal not allow source code to be split across multiple files (as in FORTRAN II)?

WIRTH: We didn't perceive a need to provide such a facility. It is an implementation consideration, but not one of language design.

ELLEN SPERTUS (MIT): You discussed the IEEE/ANSI standard for Pascal. There is also the *de facto* Borland Turbo Pascal definition. Could you comment on the differences, in effect and content, of standards from democratic committees and from single companies?

WIRTH: I think that would take too much time here. But the point is well taken that the actual standard for Pascal has been defined by Borland, just by producing a compiler and distributing it cheaply and widely. If you talk to anyone about Pascal today, probably Turbol Pascal from Borland is meant.

Borland extended Pascal over the years, and some of these extensions were not as well integrated into the language as I would have wished. I was less compromising with my extensions and therefore gave the new design a new name. For example, what Borland calls **Units** we call **Modules**. However, **Units** are inclusions in the form of source code, whereas **Modules** are separate units of compilation, fully type checked and linked at load time.

JEAN SAMMET (Programming Language Consultant): You mentioned COBOL twice— once in connection with control structures and once in connection with records. Please clarify whether COBOL had any influence on Pascal and if so, in what way?

WIRTH: Pascal inherited from COBOL the record structure, in fact indirectly via Tony Hoare's proposal included in Pascal's predecessor, ALGOL W.

DANIEL J. SALOMON (University of Manitoba): Although the pragmatic members of the ALGOL 68 Working Group have been shown, by time, to be correct, has not the ALGOL 68 report been valuable, flaws and all?

WIRTH: It has fostered a method of defining languages with precision and without reference to implementations. Its failure was probably due to driving certain ideas, such as "orthogonality" (mutual independence of properties) to extremes. The design was too dogmatic to be practical.

STAVROS MACRAKIS (OSF Research Institute): The original Pascal was small, limited in function, and completely defined. ISO's Pascal is large, comprehensive, and presumably well defined. What happened? Is it fair to consider ISO Pascal a diagnosis of Pascal's failings?

WIRTH: I rather consider the standard as the belated result of a long-winded effort to make the definition more precise, and at the same time, of extending the language.

HERBERT KLAEREN (University of Tubingen): I always wondered why Pascal's dynamic data structures did not turn recursive data structures into "first class citizens." Instead of having the programmer himself handle explicit pointers (and doing all kinds of mischief with them), the compiler could have detected the need of introducing implicit pointers automatically (and transparently). Did this idea ever come up and if so, why did you reject it?

WIRTH: We did not see a way to incorporate recursive structures in a way that was as flexible and as effective as explicit pointers. I could not wait until a solution appeared; time was precious and the need for an implementation language pressing.

HERBERT KLAEREN (University of Tubingen): Given your comments on the Pascal standardization, what are your feelings about the ongoing ISO standardization of Modula-2? Wouldn't it be a good idea if the creator of a programming language gave, along with its definition, a list of the features contemplated, but dropped, along with the reasons for dropping them?

WIRTH: I am sure this would be a good idea, preventing later designers from having to repeat the same considerations.

ADAM RIFKIN (California Institute of Technology): Why do you think the minority report signed in Munich (December 1968) had so many followers? Can you cite one main reason?

WIRTH: The Working Group 2.1 had been divided since the advent of A. van Wijngaarden's initial draft design in late 1965. The decision to pursue his draft rather than mine was taken in Warsaw in late 1966. The principal difference was that I had followed the goal of creating a successor to ALGOL 60 by essentially building upon ALGOL 60 and widening its range of application by adding data structures. Van Wijngaarden wanted to create an entirely new design, in fact another milestone (not millstone) in language design. The faction of "pragmatists" foresaw that it would take a long time to implement van Wijngaarden's proposal, and that by the time of its completion the majority of ALGOL users would have chosen another language already. (Note that ALGOL 68 compilers did not become available before 1972.)

Question is to ANDY MICKEL: The speaker mentioned an early anti-Pascal letter. Could you say more about that?

MIKEL: That was an article that appeared in *Acta Informatica* by A. N. Habermann, who wrote the paper called "Critical Comments on the Programming Language in Pascal" that Niklaus Wirth cited in his talk. It was countered by a reply from Oliver Lacarme and Pierre Dejardins. A lot of the self appointed experts at the University of Minnesota Computer Science Department preferred to beat us up in Computer Center about how Pascal should not have been taught, based on Habermann's paper, rather than even trying to use Pascal and see for themselves.

BIOGRAPHY OF NIKLAUS WIRTH

Niklaus Wirth received the degree of Electronics Engineer from the Swiss Federal Institute of Technology (ETH) in Zurich in 1958. Thereafter he studied at Laval University in Quebec, Canada, and received the M.Sc. degree in 1960. At the University of California at Berkeley he pursued his studies, leading to the Ph.D. degree in 1963. Until 1967, he was Assistant Professor at the newly created Computer Science Department at Stanford University, where he designed the programming languages PL360 and—in conjunction with the IFIP Working Group 2.1—ALGOL W. In 1967, he became Assistant Professor at the University of Zurich, and in 1968 he joined ETH Zurich, where he developed the languages Pascal between 1968 and 1970 and Modula-2 between 1979 and 1981.

Further projects include the design and development of the Personal Computer Lilith, a high-performance workstation, in conjunction with the programming language Modula-2 (1978–1982), and the 32-bit workstation computer Ceres (1984–1986). His most recent works produced the language Oberon, a descendant of Modula-2, which served to design the operating system with the same name (1986–1989). He was Chairman of the Division of Computer Science (Informatik) of ETH from 1982 until 1984, and again from 1988 until 1990. Since 1990, he has been head of the Institute of Computer Systems of ETH.

In 1978, Professor Wirth received Honorary Doctorates from York University, England, and the Federal Institute of Technology at Lausanne, Switzerland, in recognition of his work in the fields of programming languages and methodology. In 1983, he was awarded the Emanuel Priore prize by the IEEE, in 1984 the A. M. Turing prize by the ACM, and in 1987 the award for Outstanding Contributions to Computer Science Education by ACM. In 1987, he was awarded an Honorary Doctorate by the Universite Laval, Canada, and in 1993 by the Johannes Kepler Universitat in Linz, Austria. In 1988, he was named a Computer Pioneer by the IEEE Computer Society. In 1989, Professor Wirth was awarded the Max Petitpierre Prize for outstanding contributions made by Swiss noted abroad, and he received the Science and Technology Prize from IBM Europe. He was awarded the Marcel Benoist Prize in 1990. In 1992, he was honored as a Distinguished Alumnus of the University of California at Berkeley. He is a member of the Swiss Academy of Technical Sciences and a Foreign Associate of the U.S. Academy of Engineering.

IV

Monitors and Concurrent Pascal Session

Chair: *Michael Feldman*

MONITORS AND CONCURRENT PASCAL: A PERSONAL HISTORY

Per Brinch Hansen

School of Computer and Information Science
Syracuse University
Syracuse, NY

ABSTRACT

This is a personal history of the early development of the monitor concept and its implementation in the programming language Concurrent Pascal. The paper explains how monitors evolved from the ideas of Dahl, Dijkstra, Hoare, and the author (1971–1973). At Caltech the author and his students developed and implemented Concurrent Pascal and used it to write several model operating systems (1974–1975). A portable implementation of Concurrent Pascal was widely distributed and used for system design (1976–1990). The monitor paradigm was also disseminated in survey papers and textbooks. The author ends the story by expressing his own mixed feelings about monitors and Concurrent Pascal.

CONTENTS

4.1 A PROGRAMMING REVOLUTION

In the 1970s new programming languages were developed to express asynchronous, concurrent processes. These languages support the now familiar paradigms for process communication known as *monitors*, *remote procedure calls*, and *synchronous communication*. The most influential early idea was the monitor concept and its implementation in the programming language *Concurrent Pascal*.

This is a personal history of how monitors and Concurrent Pascal were invented. I have tried to write the history of an *idea*—how it arose and spread through the scientific community. I have also described the struggles of the creative process, how you grope your way through obscurities and blind alleys until you find an elegant way of expressing an idea.

The story of Concurrent Pascal frequently refers to my own work. However, I have let other researchers assess the merits and flaws of the language through quotations from the published literature. At the end of the paper I express my own reservations about the monitor concept and Concurrent Pascal. The appendix includes the personal comments of computer scientists who reviewed earlier drafts of this paper.

As someone who participated in these discoveries, I cannot claim to have written a complete and unbiased history of these events. In many cases my knowledge of related work is derived solely from the literature. I hope that historians will take care of these flaws by comparing my story with other sources.

From my perspective there are three distinct phases in the early history of monitors:

1971–1973. Monitors evolved from the ideas of Ole-Johan Dahl, Edsger Dijkstra, Tony Hoare, and me. In 1973 Hoare and I independently published programming notations for monitors.

1974–1975. Working with a few students and a professional programmer at Caltech, I developed and implemented the first programming language with monitors. My ambition was to do for operating systems what Pascal (and other programming languages) had done for compilers: to reduce the programming effort by an order of magnitude compared to assembly language. This was indeed achieved for small operating systems (but not for larger ones).

1976–1990. A portable implementation of Concurrent Pascal was widely distributed and used for system design. The monitor paradigm was now disseminated throughout the computer science community in survey papers and textbooks on operating systems, concurrent programming, and programming languages.

Each phase will be described in a separate section of the paper.

After 1975 the monitor concept inspired other researchers to develop verification rules, monitor variants, and more programming languages [Andrews 1983]. Originally I intended to include a broad review of these later developments, which I know only from the literature. However, after writing several earlier drafts of this paper, I realized that I can only provide meaningful historical remarks on ideas and events which I have firsthand knowledge about. The reviewers' comments confirmed this impression.

I will therefore limit the scope of this personal history to the discovery of the monitor concept and the development and use of the first monitor language Concurrent Pascal. Since I can only speak for myself, I have not imposed the same restriction on the reviewers' comments quoted in the appendix.

4.2 MONITORS

On the road toward monitors, several alternatives were considered. It may be easier to appreciate the piecemeal discovery if I briefly summarize the final idea. Monitors enable concurrent processes to share data and resources in an orderly manner. A monitor is a combination of shared variables and procedures. Processes must call these procedures to operate on the shared variables. The monitor procedures, which are executed one at a time, may delay the calling processes until resources or data become available.

Beginner's Luck

I started out in industry as a systems programmer for the Danish computer manufacturer Regnecentralen in Copenhagen. In 1967 I became responsible for the development of the RC 4000 multiprogramming system.

In the 1960s most operating systems were huge unreliable programs that were extremely difficult to understand and modify. The RC 4000 system was a radical departure from this state of affairs. It was not a complete operating system, but a small kernel upon which operating systems for different purposes could be built in an orderly manner. The kernel provided the basic mechanisms for creating a hierarchy of parallel processes that communicated by messages. The idea of designing a general kernel for operating system design was due to Jørn Jensen, Søren Lauesen, and me [Brinch Hansen 1969].

I consider myself lucky to have started in industry. The RC 4000 project convinced me that a fundamental understanding of operating systems would change computer programming radically. I was so certain of this that I decided to leave industry and become a researcher.

In November 1970 I became a Research Associate in the Department of Computer Science at Carnegie-Mellon University. My goal was to write the first comprehensive textbook on operating system principles [Brinch Hansen 1973b].

As soon as I started writing, it became clear that I needed an algorithmic language to express operating system functions concisely without unnecessary trivia. In an outline of the book I explained my choice of description language [Brinch Hansen 1971a]:

> So far nearly all operating systems have been written partly or completely in machine language. This makes them unnecessarily difficult to understand, test and modify. I believe it is desirable and possible to write efficient operating systems almost entirely in a *high-level language*. This language must permit *hierarchal structuring* of data and program, extensive *error checking* at compile time, and production of *efficient machine code.*
>
> To support this belief, I have used the programming language *Pascal* throughout the text to define operating system concepts concisely by algorithms. Pascal combines the clarity needed for teaching with the efficiency required for design. It is easily understood by programmers familiar with Algol 60 or Fortran, but is a far more natural tool than these for the description of operating systems because of the presence of data structures of type record . . . and pointer.
>
> At the moment, Pascal is designed for sequential programming only, but I extend it with a suitable notation for multiprogramming and resource sharing.

Bold words indeed from a programmer who had never designed a programming language before, who did not have access to a Pascal compiler, and who had no way of knowing whether Pascal would ever be used for teaching! Niklaus Wirth [1971] had just published the first paper on Pascal, and there were, of course, no textbooks based on this new language.

A Beautiful Idea

The key problem in concurrent programming was to invent language concepts for asynchronous processes that share data in a common memory.

Dijkstra [1965] had argued that it is essential to treat operations on shared variables as *critical regions* that must be performed strictly one at a time in arbitrary order. He had also shown how to implement critical regions using semaphores. But he had not suggested a notation for this idea.

Hoare [1971b] proposed a notation that identifies a variable as a *resource* shared by concurrent processes. A good example is a ring buffer represented by an array with input/output indices and a message counter:

```
B: record inpointer, outpointer, count: integer;
      buffer: array 0..N-1 of T end;
{resource B; Producer//Consumer}
```

The buffer is shared by two concurrent processes which produce and consume messages, respectively. (In most examples, including this one, I have used the programming notation of the original papers.)

In his paper Hoare also introduced the elegant concept of a *conditional critical region* that is delayed until a resource satisfies a particular condition (defined by a Boolean expression).

The send operation on the ring buffer is a conditional critical region that is executed when the buffer is not full:

```
with B when count < N do
     begin buffer[inpointer] := next value;
           inpointer := (inpointer + 1) mod N;
           count := count + 1
     end
```

The receive operation is similar:

```
with B when count > 0 do
     begin this value := buffer[outpointer];
           outpointer := (outpointer + 1) mod N;
           count := count - 1
     end
```

A compiler must check that the resource is accessed only within critical regions. A computer must guarantee that these regions are executed one at a time without overlapping.

In retrospect, the limitations of conditional critical regions are perhaps obvious:

- The resource concept is unreliable.

The same variable may be treated as a scheduled resource in some contexts and as an ordinary variable in other contexts. This may enable one process to refer directly to a variable while another process is within a "critical" region on the same variable.

- The scheduling mechanism is too restrictive.

When a process is delayed by a Boolean expression without side effects, it cannot indicate the urgency of its request to other processes. This complicates the programming of priority scheduling.

- The context switching is inefficient.

It did not seem possible to implement conditional critical regions efficiently. The problem was to limit the repeated reevaluation of Boolean expressions until they became true.

- There is no precise idea of data abstraction.

The declaration of a resource and the operations associated with it are not combined into a single, syntactical form, but are distributed throughout the program text.

Attempts to remove these problems eventually led to the discovery of monitors.

Readers and Writers

During the International Summer School in Marktoberdorf, Germany, July 1971, I removed the first two limitations of conditional critical regions by solving an interesting problem [Brinch Hansen 1972a].

Two kinds of processes, called *readers* and *writers*, share a single resource. Readers can use it simultaneously, but a writer can use the resource only when nobody else is using it. When a writer is ready to use the resource, it should be enabled to do so as soon as possible [Courtois 1971]. This is, of course, a priority scheduling problem.

First, I solved a slightly simpler problem that permits several writers to use the resource simultaneously. A *shared variable* was now introduced by a single declaration:

```
var v: shared record readers, writers: integer end
```

This notation makes it clear that a shared variable may be accessed *only* within critical regions.

A reader waits until writers are neither using the resource nor waiting for it:

```
region v when writers = 0 do
  readers := readers + 1;
read;
region v do readers := readers - 1
```

A writer immediately announces itself and waits until no readers are using the resource:

```
region v do writers := writers + 1
  await readers = 0;
write;
region v do writers := writers - 1
```

The scheduling condition may appear at the beginning or at the end of a critical region. The latter permits *scheduling with side effects*. It was an obvious extension to permit a scheduling condition to appear anywhere within a critical region [Brinch Hansen 1972b].

Courtois [1972] and others had strong reservations about conditional critical regions and my solution to the readers and writers problem [Brinch Hansen 1973a].

A New Paradigm

The idea of *monitors* evolved through discussions and communications among E.W. Dijkstra, C.A.R. Hoare, and me during the summer and fall of 1971. My own ideas were particularly influenced by our discussions at the International Summer School in Marktoberdorf, Germany, July 19–30, 1971. Hoare and I continued the exchange of ideas at the Symposium on Operating Systems Techniques in Belfast, August 30–September 3, 1971.

At Marktoberdorf, Dijkstra [1971] briefly outlined a paradigm of *secretaries* and *directors*:

> Instead of *N* sequential processes cooperating in critical sections via common variables, we take out the critical sections and combine them into a $N + 1^{st}$ process, called a "secretary"; the remaining *N* processes are called "directors."
>
> A secretary presents itself primarily as a bunch of non-reentrant routines with a common state space.
>
> When a director calls a secretary . . . the secretary may decide to keep him asleep, a decision that implies that she should wake him up in one of her later activities. As a result the identity of the calling program cannot remain anonymous as in the case of the normal subroutine. The secretaries must have variables of type "process identity." Whenever she is called the identity of the calling process is handed over in an implicit

input parameter; when she signals a release—analogous to the return of the normal subroutine—she will supply the identity of the process to be woken up.

In Belfast I presented an outline of a course on operating system principles that included the following remarks [Brinch Hansen 1971a]:

> The conceptual simplicity of simple and conditional critical regions is achieved by ignoring the sequence in which waiting processes enter these regions. This abstraction is unrealistic for heavily used resources. In such cases, the operating system must be able to identify competing processes and control the scheduling of resources among them. This can be done by means of a *monitor*—a set of shared procedures which can delay and activate individual processes and perform operations on shared data.

During a discussion on monitors I added the following [Discussion 1971]:

> You can imagine the (monitor) calls as a queue of messages being served one at a time. The monitor will receive a message and try to carry out the request as defined by the procedure and its input parameters. If the request can immediately be granted the monitor will return parameters . . . and allow the calling process to continue. However, if the request cannot be granted, the monitor will prevent the calling process from continuing, and enter a reference to this transaction in a queue local to itself. This enables the monitor, at a later time when it is called by another process, to inspect the queue and decide which interaction should be completed now. From the point of view of a process a monitor call will look like a procedure call. The calling process will be delayed until the monitor consults its request. The monitor then has a set of scheduling queues which are completely local to it, and therefore protected against user processes. The latter can only access the shared variables maintained by the monitor through a set of well defined operations . . . the monitor procedures.

At the Belfast Symposium, Hoare expressed his own reservations about conditional critical regions [Discussion 1971]:

> As a result of discussions with Brinch Hansen and Dijkstra, I feel that this proposal is not suitable for operating system implementation.
>
> My proposed method encourages the programmer to ignore the question of which of several outstanding requests for a resource should be granted.
>
> The scheduling decision cannot always be expressed by means of a single Boolean expression without side effects. You sometimes need the power of a general procedural program with storage in order to make scheduling decisions. So it seems reasonable to take all these protected critical regions out, and put them together and call it a secretary or monitor.

In the 1960s the resident part of an operating system was often known as a *monitor*. The kernel of the RC 4000 multiprogramming system was called the monitor and was defined as a program that "can execute a sequence of instructions as an indivisible entity" [Brinch Hansen 1969].

At Belfast we discussed the disadvantages of the classical monitor written in assembly language [Discussion 1971]:

> Brinch Hansen: The difficulty with the classical "monolithic" monitor is not the fact that while you are performing an operation of type *A* you cannot perform another operation of type *A*, but that if you implement them by a single critical section which inhibits further monitor calls then the fact that you are executing an operation *A* on one data set prevents all other operations on completely unrelated data sets. That is why I think the ability to have several monitors, each in charge of a single set of shared data, is quite important.
>
> Hoare: A monitor is a high-level language construction which has two properties which are not possessed by most monitors as actually implemented in machine code. Firstly, like all good programming ideas it can be called in at several levels: monitors can call other monitors declared in outer blocks. Secondly, the use of the high-level language feature enables you to associate with each monitor the particular variables and tables

which are relevant for that monitor in controlling the relative progress of the processes under its care. The protection, which prevents processes from corrupting this information and prevents monitors from gaining access to information which has no relevance, is established by Algol-like scope rules.

These quotations show that Dijkstra, Hoare, and I had reached an informal understanding of monitors. But it was still no more than a verbal outline of the idea. The discovery of a queuing mechanism, a notation, and an implementation was left as an exercise for the reader.

Abandoned Attempts

When a programming concept is understood informally, it would seem to be a trivial matter to invent a language notation for it. But in practice this is hard to do. The main problem is to replace an intuitive, vague idea with a precise, unambiguous definition of its meaning and restrictions.

In the search for a suitable monitor notation many ideas were considered and rejected. I will describe two proposals that were abandoned. You may find them hard to understand. In retrospect, so do I!

At the Belfast Symposium, Hoare [1971a] distributed an unpublished draft of a monitor proposal that included a single-buffer characterized as follows:

status = −1 buffer empty (consumer waiting)
status = 0 buffer empty (consumer not waiting)
status = 1 buffer full (producer not waiting)
status = 2 buffer full (producer waiting)

The send operation is defined by a monitor entry named *p*:

```
p(prod) entry
begin
  if status <= 0 then input (prod)p(buffer);
  if status = -1 then output (cons)c(buffer);
  status := status + 1
end
```

This entry is not a procedure in the usual sense; *p* is the name of a communication between a producer and the buffer. The entry defines the protocol for this communication.

A producer outputs a message *e* to the buffer by executing the statement

```
output p(e)
```

The following takes place:

1. The producer is automatically delayed and its identity is assigned to a variable named *prod*.
2. If the buffer is empty, it immediately inputs the message from the producer and assigns it to a variable named *buffer* by executing the statement

   ```
   input (prod)p(buffer)
   ```

   The input automatically enables the producer to continue its execution.
3. If a consumer is waiting to input a message, the buffer immediately outputs the last message by executing the statement

   ```
   output (cons)c(buffer)
   ```

   The details of this statement will be explained shortly.

4. If the buffer is full it cannot input the message yet. In that case, the producer will remain delayed until a consumer empties the buffer, as explained below.
5. Finally, the buffer status is updated.

The receive operation is defined by a similar monitor entry named *c*:

```
c(cons) entry
begin
  if status >= 1 then output (cons)c(buffer);
  if status = 2 then input (prod)p(buffer);
  status := status - 1
end
```

A consumer inputs a message and assigns it to a variable *x* by executing the statement

```
input c(x)
```

This has the following effect:

1. The consumer is automatically delayed and its identity is assigned to a variable named *cons*.
2. If the buffer is full, it immediately outputs the last message to the consumer by executing the statement

   ```
   output (cons)c(buffer)
   ```

3. If a producer is waiting to output a message to the buffer, the buffer now accepts that message by executing the statement

   ```
   input (prod)p(buffer)
   ```

4. If the buffer is empty, it cannot output a message yet. In that case, the consumer will remain delayed until a producer fills the buffer, as explained earlier.
5. Finally, the buffer status is updated.

The proposal offers an efficient mechanism for process scheduling. The basic idea is that one monitor entry can complete a communication that was postponed by another monitor entry. This is the programming style one naturally adopts in a monolithic monitor written in assembly language.

The description of parameter transfers as unbuffered input/output later became the basis for the concept of *communicating sequential processes* [Hoare 1978].

This early monitor proposal did not combine monitor entries and shared variables into a modular unit and did not specify parameter types. In an attempt to remedy these problems, I sent Hoare an unpublished draft of "a monitor concept which closely mirrors the way in which the RC 4000 monitor was programmed" [Brinch Hansen 1971c]. Algorithm 4.1 illustrates the use of this notation to implement a single-buffer.

A monitor is now a module that combines shared variables, procedures, and an initial statement. The latter must be executed before the monitor can be called.

When the producer calls the *send* procedure, the following happens:

1. A reference to the call is stored in a local variable named *send1*. This is called a send reference.
2. If the consumer has called the *receive* procedure and is ready to receive a message, the monitor completes the send and receive calls simultaneously by assigning the value parameter *x* in the send call to the variable parameter *y* in the receive call. The completion statement extends the

scope of the send entry with the parameters of the corresponding receive entry. It also has the side effect of resuming the two processes associated with the procedure calls.

3. If the consumer is not ready, the monitor stores the identity of the send call in a global variable named *send2* and indicates that the producer is ready to communicate.

The *receive* procedure is similar.

The use of *call references* enables a compiler to check parameter declarations in completion statements.

The most serious flaw of both proposals is the unreliable nature of process scheduling. As Hoare put it: "It would be a grave error for a monitor to specify an interaction with a process which was not waiting for that interaction to take place." I concluded that it is generally "impossible . . . to check the validity of process references."

In a collection of papers by Hoare [1989], C.B. Jones introduces Hoare's 1974 paper on monitors and writes: "The first draft of this paper was distributed to the participants of the 1971 Belfast Symposium."

However, there is very little resemblance between these two papers. The reason is quite simple. In 1971 we had some understanding of abstract data types. But a key ingredient of monitors was still missing: a secure, efficient method of context switching. We now turn to this problem.

ALGORITHM 4.1

An abandoned proposal.

```
monitor
var send2: ref send; receive2: ref receive;
  ready: Boolean;

entry send(const x: message)
call send1;
begin
  if ready then
    complete send1, receive2 do
    begin y := x; ready := false end
  else
    begin send2 := send1; ready := true end
end

entry receive(var y: message)
call receive1;
begin
  if ready then
    complete receive1, send2 do
    begin y := x; ready := false end
  else
     begin receive2 := receive1; ready := true end
end

begin ready := false end
```

The Waiting Game

On February 16, 1972, I presented a completely different solution to the problem of process scheduling at the California Institute of Technology [Brinch Hansen 1972b].

I will illustrate the idea by an exercise from Brinch Hansen [1973b]. Processes $P_1, P_2, \ldots, P_n$ share a single resource. A process requests exclusive access to the resource before using it and releases it afterwards. If the resource is free, a process may use it immediately; otherwise the process waits until another process releases the resource. If several processes are waiting for the resource, it is granted to the waiting process P_i with the lowest index i.

Algorithm 4.2 shows a priority scheduler for this problem.The resource is represented by a *shared record r*. The key idea is to associate *scheduling queues* with the shared variable. The queues are declared as variables of type *event r*. The resource scheduler can delay processes in these queues and resume them later by means of two standard procedures named *await* and *cause*.

If a process P_i calls the request procedure when the resource is not free, the Boolean *waiting[i]* is set to true and the process is entered in the event queue *grant[i]*. The await operation makes the process leave its critical region temporarily.

When a process P_j calls the *release* procedure while other processes are waiting, the most urgent process P_i is selected and enabled to resume as soon as P_j leaves its own region. At that moment P_i reenters its previous region and continues execution after the await statement.

Instead of letting one critical region complete the execution of another region, we simply switch back to the context of the previous region. Consequently, a scheduling decision can be viewed merely as a delay during the execution of a critical region.

This queuing mechanism enables the programmer to ignore the identity of a process and think of it only as "the calling process" or "the process waiting in this queue." There is no need for variables of type process reference.

The only possible operations on a queue are *cause* and *await*, performed within critical regions. The problem of dangling process references is solved by making the queues empty to begin with and preventing assignments to them.

My proposal included a feature that was never used. Suppose several processes are waiting in the same queue until a Boolean expression B is true. In that case, a *cause* operation on the queue enables *all* of them to resume their critical regions one at a time. Mutual exclusion is still maintained, and processes waiting to resume critical regions have priority over processes that are waiting to enter the beginning of critical regions. In this situation, a resumed process may find that another process has made the scheduling condition B false again. Consequently, processes must use waiting loops of the form

```
while not B do await(q)
```

My 1972 paper, which introduced scheduling queues, was an invited paper written under great time pressure. When someone later mentioned that multiple resumption might be inconvenient, I looked at the paper again and saw that it presented only one example of the use of scheduling queues. And that example used a separate queue for each process! The programming examples in my operating systems book [Brinch Hansen 1973b] did the same. In Concurrent Pascal I turned this programming style into a programming language rule [Brinch Hansen 1974d].

In spite of the unintended generality, my 1972 process queues were *not* the same as the classical event queues of the 1960s, which caused the programmer to lose control over scheduling. The crucial difference was that the new queues were associated with a shared variable, so that all scheduling operations were mutually exclusive operations. The programmer could control the scheduling of

ALGORITHM 4.2

Context switching queues.

```
var r: shared record
              free: Boolean;
              waiting: array [1..n] of Boolean;
              grant: array [1..n] of event r
            end

procedure request(i: 1..n);
region r do
begin
  if free then free := false
  else
    begin
      waiting[i] := true;
      await(grant[i]);
      waiting[i] := false
    end
  end
end

procedure release;
var i, m: 1..n;
  region r do
  begin
    i := 1; m := n;
    while i < m do
      if waiting[i] then m := i
      else i := i + 1;
    if waiting[i] then cause(grant[i])
  else free := true
end
```

processes to any degree desired by associating each queue with a *group* of processes or an *individual* process.

The idea of associating scheduling queues with a shared variable to enable processes to resume critical regions was the basis of all subsequent monitor proposals. Context switching queues have been called *events* [Brinch Hansen 1972b], *queues* [Brinch Hansen 1973b], and *conditions* [Hoare 1973a]. Some are single-process queues; others are multiprocess queues. The details vary, but they all combine process scheduling with context switching and mutual exclusion.

We now had all the pieces of the monitor puzzle. And I had adopted a programming style which combined shared variables, queues, critical regions, and procedures in a manner that closely resembled monitors (Algorithm 4.2).

A Moment of Truth

In the spring of 1972 I read papers by Dahl [1972b] and Hoare [1972b] on the *class* concept of the programming language *Simula 67*. Although Simula is not a concurrent programming language, it

ALGORITHM 4.3

A monitor with conditional waiting.

```
shared class B =
  buffer: array 0..max-1 of T;
  p, c: 0..max-1;
  full: 0..max;

  procedure send(m: T);
  begin
    await full < max;
    buffer[p] := m;
    p := (p + 1) mod max;
    full := full + 1;
  end

  procedure receive(var m: T);
  begin
    await full > 0;
    m := buffer[c];
    c := (c + 1) mod max;
    full := full - 1;
  end

 begin p := 0; c := 0; full := 0 end
```

inspired me in the following way: So far I had thought of a monitor as a program module that defines all operations on a *single* instance of a data structure. From Simula I learned to regard a program module as the definition of a *class* of data structures accessed by the same procedures.

This was a moment of truth for me. Within a few days I wrote a chapter on resource protection for my operating systems book. I proposed to represent monitors by *shared classes* and pointed out that resource protection and type checking are part of the same problem: to verify automatically that all operations on data structures maintain certain properties (called *invariants*).

My book includes the buffer monitor defined by Algorithm 4.3. The shared class defines a data structure of type *B*, two procedures which can operate on the data structure, and a statement that defines its initial state.

The class notation permits multiple instances of the same monitor type. A buffer variable *b* is declared as follows:

```
var b: B
```

Upon entry to the block in which the buffer variable is declared, storage is allocated for its data components, and the buffer is initialized by executing the statement at the end of the class definition.

Send and *receive* operations on the buffer *b* are denoted

b.send(x)   b.receive(y)

A shared class is a notation that explicitly restricts the operations on a data type and enables a compiler to check that these restrictions are obeyed. It also indicates that all operations on a particular instance must be executed as critical regions.

In May of 1972 I submitted the manuscript of my book to Prentice-Hall and sent copies to Dijkstra and Hoare. On November 3, 1972, I gave a seminar on shared classes at the University of California at Santa Barbara.

In July 1973, *Operating System Principles* was published with my monitor proposal based on Simula classes [Brinch Hansen 1973b]. My decision to use conditional waiting in this proposal was a matter of taste. I might just as well have used queues, which I had introduced in another chapter.

I also included the monitor notation in the first draft of a survey paper on concurrent programming [Brinch Hansen 1973d]. A referee, who felt that it was inappropriate to include a recent idea in a survey paper, suggested that I remove it, which I did.

I discussed monitors with queues in the first report on Concurrent Pascal, April 1974, and at the IFIP Congress in Stockholm, August 1974 [Brinch Hansen 1974a, 1974c].

Parallel Discovery

Two influential papers concluded the early development of monitors. In the first paper Hoare [1973b] used a monitor in the design of a paging system. He begins the paper by acknowledging that "The notations used . . . are based on those of Pascal . . . and Simula 67." In the second paper Hoare [1974a] illustrated the monitor concept by several examples, including a ring buffer (Algorithm 4.4). Communicating processes are delayed and resumed by means of *wait* and *signal* operations on first-in, first-out queues called *condition* variables.

ALGORITHM 4.4

A monitor with queues.

```
bounded buffer: monitor
  begin buffer: array 0..N-1 of portion;
    lastpointer: 0..N-1;
    count: 0..N;
    nonempty, nonfull: condition;
    procedure append(x: portion);
      begin if count = N then nonfull.wait;
        note 0 <= count < N;
        buffer[lastpointer] := x;
        lastpointer := lastpointer ⊕ 1;
        count := count + 1;
        nonempty.signal
      end append;
    procedure remove(result x: portion);
      begin if count = 0 then nonempty.wait;
        note 0 < count <= N;
        x := buffer[lastpoint ⊖ count];
        count := count - 1;
        nonfull.signal
      end remove;
    count := 0; lastpointer := 0
  end bounded buffer;
```

In an unpublished draft of his condition proposal Hoare [1973a] correctly pointed out that

> The synchronization primitives proposed here are very similar to Brinch Hansen's "await" and "cause," but they involve less retesting inside waiting operations, and may be slightly more efficient to implement.

According to Hoare [1989], his first monitor paper was submitted in October 1972; his second paper was submitted in February 1973 and the material presented at IRIA, Paris, France, on May 11, 1973. I received them shortly before they were published in August 1973 and October 1974, respectively.

While writing this history I discovered a working paper by McKeag [1973] submitted to an ACM meeting in Savannah, Georgia, April 9–12, 1973. This early paper includes a single example of Hoare's monitor notation.

Milestones

The classical monitor of the 1960s was not a precisely defined programming concept based on rules enforced by a compiler. It was just a vague term for the resident part of an operating system, which was programmed in assembly language. The monitor concept that emerged in the 1970s should not be regarded as a refinement of an operating systems technique. It was a new programming language concept for concurrent programs running on shared-memory computers. Operating systems were just a challenging application area for this synchronization concept.

This brings us to the end of the phase where the monitor concept was discovered. The milestones were:

1971 Conditional critical regions
Scheduling with side effects
Monitor idea
1972 Context switching queues
Class concept papers
Monitor notation
1973 *Operating System Principles*
Monitor papers

The next task was to develop a programming language with monitors.

4.3 CONCURRENT PASCAL

Concurrent Pascal extended the sequential programming language Pascal with concurrent processes, monitors, and classes. The polished presentations of the language in professional journals and textbooks fail to show the long arduous road we had to travel to understand what undergraduates now take for granted.

A Matter of Philosophy

In designing Concurrent Pascal I followed a consistent set of principles for programming languages. These principles carried structured programming into the new realm of modular concurrent programming. Let me summarize these principles and show *when* and *how* I first expressed them in writing.

- Concurrent programs can be written exclusively in high-level languages.

In the fall of 1971 I expressed this belief, which seems commonplace today, but was novel at the time (see the earlier quotation in "Beginner's Luck"). Later I will explain why I did not consider Burroughs Algol and PL/I as high-level programming languages for operating system design.

In Brinch Hansen [1974c] I repeated the same idea:

> I am convinced that in most cases operating system designers do not need to control low-level machine features (such as registers, addresses, and interrupts) directly, but can leave these problems to a compiler and its run-time environment. A consistent use of abstract programming concepts in operating system design should enable a compiler to check the access rights of concurrent processes and make enforcement of resource protection rules at run time largely unnecessary.

Hoare [1971b] and Brinch Hansen [1971b] introduced a fundamental requirement of any concurrent programming language:

- Time-dependent programming errors must be detected during compilation.

In the spring of 1972 I explained this requirement as follows [Brinch Hansen 1973b]:

> The main difficulty of multiprogramming is that concurrent activities can interact in a time-dependent manner which makes it practically impossible to locate programming errors by systematic testing. Perhaps, more than anything else, this explains the difficulty of making operating systems reliable.
>
> *If we wish to succeed in designing large, reliable multiprogramming systems, we must use programming tools which are so well-structured that most time-dependent errors can be caught at compile time.* It seems hopeless to try to solve this problem at the machine level of programming, nor can we expect to improve the situation by means of so-called "implementation languages," which retain the traditional "right" of systems programmers to manipulate addresses freely.

In 1976 I put it this way [Brinch Hansen 1977b]:

> One of the primary goals of Concurrent Pascal is to push the role of *compilation checks* to the limit and reduce the use of *execution checks* as much as possible. This is not done just to make compiled programs more efficient by reducing the overhead of execution checks. In program engineering, compilation and execution checks play the same role as preventive maintenance and flight recorders do in aviation. The latter only tell you why a system crashed; the former prevents it. This distinction seems essential to me in the design of real-time systems that will control vital functions in society. Such systems must be highly reliable *before* they are put into operation.

Time-dependent errors occur when processes refer to the same variables without proper synchronization. The key to preventing these *race conditions* turned out to be the following requirement that:

- A concurrent programming language should support a programming discipline that combines data and procedures into modules.

I realized this even *before* discovering a monitor notation. The following quotation refers to my earlier proposal of associating shared variables with critical regions and scheduling queues [Brinch Hansen 1972b]:

> The basic idea is to associate data shared by concurrent processes explicitly with operations defined on them. This clarifies the meaning of programs and permits a large class of time-dependent errors to be caught at compile-time.

In the spring of 1972 I described my own monitor notation as a natural extension of the module concept of Simula 67 [Brinch Hansen 1973b]:

> In Simula 67, the definition of a structured data type and the meaningful operations on it form a single syntactical unit called a *class*.
>
> An obvious idea is to represent critical regions by the concept *shared class*, implying that the operations . . . on a given variable *v* of type *T* exclude one another in time.
>
> My main purpose here is to show a notation which explicitly restricts operations on data and enables a compiler to check that these restrictions are obeyed. Although such restrictions are not enforced by Simula 67, this would seem to be essential for effective protection.

Concurrent Pascal was the first realization of *modular, concurrent programming*. During the 1970s researchers also introduced modularity in sequential programming languages. However, these languages were completed and implemented *after* Concurrent Pascal [Popek 1977; Liskov 1981; Shaw 1981].

In the spring of 1975, after implementing Concurrent Pascal and writing the first operating system in the language, I wrote the following [Brinch Hansen 1975c]:

> The combination of a data structure and the operations used to access it is called an *abstract data type*. It is abstract because the rest of the system only needs to know what operations one can perform on it but can ignore the details of how they are carried out. A Concurrent Pascal program is constructed from three kinds of abstract data types: processes, monitors, and classes.

Race conditions are prevented by a simple scope rule that permits a process, monitor, or class to access its own variables only. In a suitably restricted language this rule can easily be checked by a compiler. However, in a language with pointers and address arithmetic, no such guarantee can be offered.

The principles discussed so far were largely derived from my perception of concurrent programming in 1972. Intuitively I also followed a more general principle of language design, which I only formulated four years later:

- A programming language should be abstract and secure.

In the spring of 1976 I explained this requirement as follows [Brinch Hansen 1977b]:

> The main contribution of a good programming language to simplicity is to provide an abstract *readable notation* that makes the parts and structures of programs obvious to a reader. An abstract programming language *suppresses machine detail* (such as addresses, registers, bit patterns, interrupts, and sometimes even the number of processors available). Instead the language relies on *abstract concepts* (such as variables, data types, synchronizing operations, and concurrent processes). As a result, program texts written in abstract languages are often an order of magnitude shorter than those written in machine language. This *textual reduction* simplifies program engineering considerably.
>
> We shall also follow the crucial principle of language design suggested by Hoare: *The behavior of a program written in an abstract language should always be explainable in terms of the concepts of that language and should never require insight into the details of compilers and computers.* Otherwise, an abstract notation has no significant value in reducing complexity.

A programming language that satisfies this requirement is said to be *secure* [Hoare 1974b].

A programming language that permits unrestricted use of assembly language features, such as jumps, typeless machine words, and addresses is insecure. A program written in such a language may have unpredictable effects that force the programmer to go beyond the abstract concepts, which the programming language pretends to support. In order to locate obscure programming errors, the programmer may now have to consider machine-dependent details, which vary from one computer to another (or even from one execution to another on the same computer).

The Burroughs B6700 and Multics operating systems were written in programming languages that permit unrestricted address manipulation (extended Algol 60 and PL/I). These insecure programming languages and operating systems had no influence on Concurrent Pascal and the model operating systems written in the language. The Unix system, written in the insecure language C, had not yet been described when Concurrent Pascal was being developed.

The controversy over whether a programming language should give you unrestricted access to hardware features or impose restrictions that simplify programs and facilitate error detection has continued to this day.

Facing Complexity

On July 1, 1972, I became Associate Professor of Computer Science at the California Institute of Technology. During my first academic year I prepared three new courses and introduced Pascal on campus. These tasks kept me busy for a while.

I also started thinking about designing a programming language with concurrent processes and monitors. To reduce the effort, I decided to include these concepts in an existing sequential language. Pascal was an obvious choice for me, since I had used the language in my operating systems book. I liked Pascal because of its similarity to Algol 60, which I had used extensively at Regnecentralen. I named the new language *Concurrent Pascal* and did not consider any other base language. Apart from that, nothing else was obvious.

With a notation for monitors now in hand, you would think it would be easy to include it in Pascal. I had no idea of how to do this. I remember sitting in my garden in Pasadena, day after day, staring at a blank piece of paper and feeling like a complete failure.

Let me just mention some of the complicated issues I faced for the first time:

How can a programming language support

- The different scope rules of Pascal blocks and Simula classes?
- Hierarchical composition of processes and monitors?
- Multiple instances of the same process or monitor type?
- Dynamic activation and termination of processes and monitors?
- Elementary input/output from arbitrary peripherals?

How can a compiler check that

- Processes communicate by monitor procedures only?
- Monitors do not deadlock by calling themselves recursively (either directly or indirectly)?

How can a minicomputer with inadequate facilities for dynamic memory allocation

- Execute concurrent programs efficiently?

It took me almost two years to find reasonable solutions to most of these problems and make compromises that enabled me to ignore the most thorny issues.

A New Language

In September 1973 and April 1974 I distributed the first descriptions of Concurrent Pascal. A final paper and a language report were both published in June 1975 [Brinch Hansen 1973c, 1974a, 1974d, 1975a].

I now understood what I was doing. One day the Caltech president, Harold Brown, came to my office and asked me to explain my research. After listening for half an hour, he said, "That sounds easy." I agreed because that was how I felt at the time.

A Concurrent Pascal program defines a fixed number of concurrent processes that communicate by monitors only. One of the first programs I wrote in Concurrent Pascal implements a pipeline that reads and prints an endless sequence of punched cards. Figure 4.1 shows the hierarchical structure of the pipeline. It consists of three processes connected by two line buffer monitors. An arrow from a process to a monitor indicates that the process can call that monitor. I named this kind of representation an *access graph*. It became our main tool for "programming in the large."

I will use the pipeline in Figure 4.1 to illustrate the *syntax* and *semantics* of Concurrent Pascal.

Both *line buffers* in this pipeline are defined by the same *monitor type* (Algorithm 4.5). Each buffer can hold a single line at a time. A Boolean variable defines whether or not a buffer is full. Two variables of type *queue* are used to delay and continue the sender and receiver, respectively.

The pipeline program uses two line buffers, which are declared and initialized as follows:

```
var inbuffer, outbuffer: linebuffer;

init inbuffer, outbuffer
```

For each buffer, the *init* statement allocates memory space for fresh instances of the shared variables declared at the beginning of the monitor type. The initialization also causes the statement at the end of the monitor to be executed, which makes a buffer empty to begin with. Each buffer is now ready to be shared by a sender and a receiver, as shown in Figure 4.1.

The Concurrent Pascal compiler checks that processes only access a line buffer by calling the monitor procedures *send* and *receive*. This restriction is guaranteed by a scope rule that makes the shared variables inaccessible from outside the monitor.

A sender outputs a line of text through a particular buffer by calling the *send* procedure as follows:

```
var text: line;

outbuffer.send(text)
```

FIGURE 4.1
An access graph.

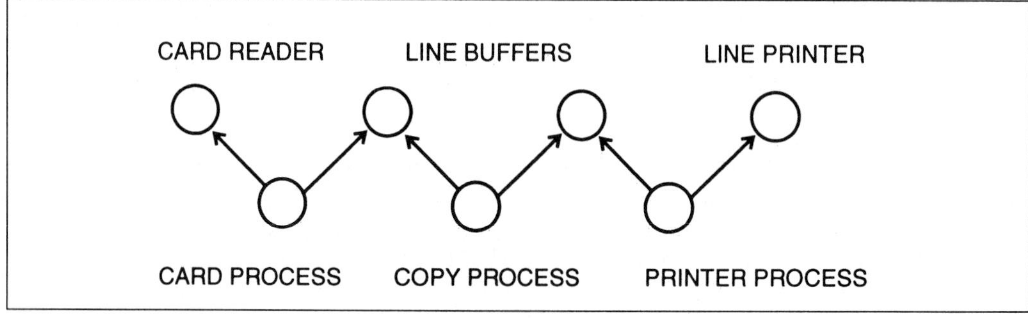

ALGORITHM 4.5

A monitor type.

```
type linebuffer =
monitor
var contents: line; full: Boolean;
  sender, receiver: queue;

procedure entry receive(var text: line);
begin
  if not full then delay(receiver);
  text := contents; full := false;
  continue(sender)
end;

procedure entry send(text: line);
begin
  if full then delay(sender);
  contents := text; full := true;
  continue(receiver)
end;

begin full := false end
```

If the buffer is full, the send procedure *delays* the calling process in the sender queue. The delay lasts until another process calls the *receive* procedure, which performs a *continue* operation on the sender queue. In any case, the sender cannot complete the *if* statement until the buffer is empty. At that point, the sender puts a message in the queue, performs a continue operation on the receiver queue, and returns from the send procedure.

The *receive* procedure is similar.

While a process executes a monitor procedure, it has exclusive access to the shared variables. If another process attempts to call the same monitor while a process has exclusive access to that monitor, the latter call will automatically be delayed until the former process has released its exclusive access.

A process releases its exclusive access to a monitor in one of three ways:

1. By reaching the end of a monitor procedure.
2. By delaying itself temporarily in a queue declared within the monitor. The process regains its exclusive access when another process performs a continue operation on the same queue.
3. By performing a continue operation on a queue. The process performing the continue operation automatically returns from its monitor procedure. If another process is waiting in the queue, that process will immediately resume the execution of the monitor procedure in which it was delayed.

A monitor queue is either empty or holds a single process. A multiprocess queue can be implemented as an array of single-process queues.

In October 1973 Ole-Johan Dahl suggested to Tony Hoare that a continue operation should terminate a monitor call [Hoare 1974a; McKeag 1991]. Hoare may have told me about this idea during his visit to Caltech in January 1974.

ALGORITHM 4.6

A process type.

```
type printerprocess =
process(buffer: linebuffer);
var param: ioparam; text: line;
begin
  param.operation := output;
  cycle
    buffer.receive(text);
    repeat io(text, param, printdevice)
    until param.status = complete
  end
end
```

In the pipeline example a *printer process* is defined by a *process type* (Algorithm 4.6). A process parameter defines the only monitor (a line buffer) that is accessible to the process.

The pipeline program initializes a printer process as follows:

```
var outbuffer: linebuffer; writer: printerprocess;

init writer(outbuffer)
```

The *init* statement allocates memory for fresh instances of the local variables declared at the beginning of the process type and starts execution of the process.

The Concurrent Pascal compiler ensures that the local variables of a process are inaccessible to other processes (and monitors). It also checks that a printer process uses its own line buffer only.

A printer process repeats the same *cycle* of operations endlessly. In each cycle the process receives a line from the buffer and prints it. The standard procedure *io* delays the process until the line has been output (or the printing has failed). In this simple example, the printing is repeated until it has been successfully completed.

All input/output are indivisible operations that hide peripheral interrupts. Consequently, a process and a peripheral device cannot access the same variable simultaneously.

The complete *pipeline program* defines a parameterless process known as the *initial process*. This process includes definitions of all the monitor and process types used by the pipeline (Algorithm 4.7).

The execution of the program activates a single initial process, which then initializes two buffer monitors and activates three concurrent processes (by means of an *init* statement).

In addition to processes and monitors, Concurrent Pascal also includes classes. A class is a module that cannot be called simultaneously by processes. It must be local to a single process, monitor, or class.

Algorithm 4.8 shows a *class type*. A module of this type has access to a single line buffer. The class procedure extends a line with a left margin of 26 spaces and terminates it with a newline character before sending the line through the buffer.

A Simula program can bypass the procedures of a class and change the class variables in ways that are incompatible with the function of the class. This loophole was removed in Concurrent Pascal. A variable declared within a class can be read (but not changed) outside the class, provided the variable is prefixed with the word *entry*. Entry variables are not permitted in monitors.

ALGORITHM 4.7

A program.

```
type linebuffer =
monitor
  ...
end;

type cardprocess =
process(buffer: linebuffer);
  ...
end;

type copyprocess =
process(inbuffer, outbuffer: linebuffer);
  ...
end;

type printerprocess =
process(buffer: linebuffer);
  ...
end;

var inbuffer, outbuffer: linebuffer;
  reader: cardprocess;
  copier: copyprocess;
  writer: printerprocess;
begin
  init inbuffer, outbuffer,
    reader(inbuffer),
    copier(inbuffer, outbuffer),
    writer(outbuffer)
end.
```

Table 4.1 shows how Concurrent Pascal differs from Pascal. It lists the features that were added to Pascal as well as those that were excluded.

I have already illustrated the major concepts of Concurrent Pascal: processes, monitors, classes, and queues, as well as init and cycle statements (Algorithms 4.5–4.8).

The programming of terminal and printer drivers is supported by a notation for *control characters*. The following example

```
const formfeed = '(:12:)'
```

defines *form feed* as ASCII character number 12.

When you program a procedure that reads a disk page, you cannot anticipate all the possible data types that users will assign to this page in the future. This is one of the few cases in which one cannot hide machine detail.

ALGORITHM 4.8

A class type.

```
type linemaker =
class(buffer: linebuffer);
var image: line; charno: integer;

procedure entry write(text: line);
begin
  for charno := 27 to 106 do
    image[charno] := text[charno-26];
  buffer.send(image)
end;

begin
  for charno := 1 to 26 do
    image[charno] := space;
  image[107] := newline
end
```

Concurrent Pascal uses *universal parameters* to relax type checking in device procedures. In the following procedure declaration

```
type diskpage = array [1..256] of integer;

procedure readdisk(pageno: integer;
  var page: univ diskpage);
begin ... end
```

the key word *univ* indicates that the procedure may be called with any argument that has the same length as an array of 256 integers. The type checking is relaxed only at the point where the procedure is called. No variable is treated as a typeless bit pattern throughout a program [Brinch Hansen 1975d].

TABLE 4.1

Concurrent Pascal versus Pascal.

Added features	Excluded features
process types	file types
monitor types	pointer types
class types	packed arrays
queues	variant records
init statements	goto statements
cycle statements	recursion
control characters	
universal parameters	
program declarations	

A *program declaration* enables a Concurrent Pascal program to call a sequential user (or system) program written in a subset of Pascal. The program declaration includes a list of procedures that the Pascal program may call. The details of this *ad hoc* mechanism are described in the Concurrent Pascal report [Brinch Hansen 1975a].

Since an operating system written in Concurrent Pascal must implement its own filing system, *file types* cannot be built into the language.

Pointer types were excluded to prevent a process from obtaining unsynchronized access to a variable of another process through a pointer transmitted through a monitor. In the absence of pointers, processes can access shared variables through monitor procedures only.

Packed arrays, *variant records*, and *goto statements* were eliminated to simplify the language.

Later I will explain my reasons for eliminating *recursive procedures and functions*.

The complete syntax and semantics of Concurrent Pascal are defined in the language report [Brinch Hansen 1975a].

Concurrent Pascal was designed according to the principles discussed earlier. It is a programming language that supports modular programming with processes, monitors, and classes. The syntax clearly shows that each module consists of a set of variables, a set of procedures, and an initial statement. Each module defines the representation and possible transformations of a data structure. A module cannot access the variables of another module. This simple scope rule enables a compiler to detect race conditions before a program is executed. The automatic synchronization of monitor calls prevents other race conditions at run time.

The programming tricks of assembly language are impossible in Concurrent Pascal: there are no typeless memory words, registers, and addresses in the language. The programmer is not even aware of the existence of physical processors and interrupts. The language is so secure that concurrent processes run without any form of memory protection!

My working habits unfortunately make it impossible for me to remember the alternative forms of syntax, scope, and type rules that I must have considered while designing the language. I evaluate language concepts by using them for program design. I develop a program by writing numerous drafts of the program text. A draft is immediately rejected if it is not in some way simpler and more elegant than the previous one. An improved draft immediately replaces the previous one, which is thrown in the wastebasket. Otherwise I would drown in paper and half-baked ideas. As I jump from one draft to another without slowing myself down, a beautiful design eventually emerges. When that happens, I write a simple description of the program and rewrite it one more time using the same terminology as in the description. By then I have already forgotten most of the alternatives. And, twenty years later, I don't remember any of them.

The Translation Problem

An early six-pass compiler was never released. Although it worked perfectly, I found it too complicated. Each pass was written by a different student who had difficulty understanding the rest of the compiler.

From June through September 1974 my student, Al Hartmann, wrote another Concurrent Pascal compiler. His goal was to be able to compile small operating systems on a PDP 11/45 minicomputer with at least 32 k bytes of memory and a slow, removable disk. The compiler was divided into seven passes to fit into a small memory. It consisted of 8300 lines written in Pascal and could be completely understood by one person. Systematic testing of the compiler took three months, from October through December 1974.

The Concurrent Pascal compiler was used from January 1975 without problems. It was described in the Ph.D. thesis [Hartmann 1975], later published as a monograph.

In another month Al Hartmann derived a compiler for a Pascal subset known as *Sequential Pascal* [Brinch Hansen 1975b]. It compiled the largest pass of the Concurrent Pascal compiler in three minutes. The compilation speed was limited mostly by the disk.

When we say that a program is concurrent, we are really talking about its behavior at run time. During compilation, a program written in any language is just a piece of text, which is checked for correct syntax, scope of declarations, and types of operands. Consequently, the compilation of processes, monitors, and classes in Concurrent Pascal is very similar to the compilation of data types and procedures in Sequential Pascal.

The Art of Compromise

The Concurrent Pascal compiler generated code for a simple machine tailored to the language. I borrowed this idea from a portable Pascal compiler [Nori 1974]. My main concern was to simplify code generation. The portability of Concurrent Pascal was just a useful byproduct of this decision.

The Concurrent Pascal machine was simulated by a kernel of 8 k bytes written in assembly language. The kernel multiplexed a PDP 11/45 processor among concurrent processes and executed them using a technique known as *threaded code* [Bell 1973]. It also performed basic input/output from a fixed set of peripherals (terminal, disk, magnetic tape, line printer, and card reader).

I wrote the kernel in Pascal extended with classes. Robert Deverill and Tom Zepko translated the kernel into assembly language. It was completed in January 1975 and described in a report [Brinch Hansen 1975e].

I made major compromises to make program execution as efficient as possible:

- All procedures must be nonrecursive. This rule imposes a strict hierarchical structure on processes and monitors that prevents monitor deadlocks.
- All processes, monitors, and classes exist forever. This is acceptable in operating systems and real-time systems that perform a fixed number of tasks forever.
- All processes and monitors must be activated by the initial process.

These compromises made memory allocation trivial. The first rule enabled the compiler to determine the memory requirements of each module. The first two rules made static memory allocation possible. The third rule made it possible to combine the kernel, the program code, and all monitor variables into a single memory segment that was included in the address space of every process. This prevented fragmentation of a limited address space and made monitor calls almost as fast as simple procedure calls.

By putting simplicity and efficiency first we undoubtedly lost generality. But the psychological effect of these compromises was phenomenal. Suddenly an overwhelming task seemed manageable.

Fifteen years later, I realized that the severe restrictions of Concurrent Pascal had made it impossible for me to discover and appreciate the powerful concept of recursive processes [Brinch Hansen 1989a, 1989b].

Learning to Program Again

After defining Concurrent Pascal, I wrote a series of model operating systems to evaluate the language. The new language had a dramatic (and unexpected) impact on my style of programming.

It was the first time I had programmed in a language that enabled me to divide programs into modules that could be programmed and tested separately. The creative part was clearly the initial selection of modules and the combination of modules into hierarchical structures. The programming of each module was often trivial. I soon adopted the rule that each module should consist of no more than one page of text. This discipline made programs far more readable and reliable than traditional programs that operate on global data structures.

The first operating system written in Concurrent Pascal (called *Deamy*) was used only to evaluate the expressive power of the language and was never built [Brinch Hansen 1974b]. The second one (called *Pilot*) was used for several months but was too slow.

In May 1975 I finished the *Solo* system, a single-user operating system for the development of Concurrent and Sequential Pascal programs on a PDP 11/45. The operating system was written in Concurrent Pascal. All other programs, including the Concurrent and Sequential Pascal compilers, were written in Sequential Pascal. The heart of Solo was a job process that compiled and ran programs stored on a disk. Two additional processes performed input and output simultaneously. System commands enabled the user to replace Solo with any other Concurrent Pascal program stored on disk, or to restart Solo again. Al Hartmann had already written the compilers. I wrote the operating system and its utility programs in three months. Wolfgang Franzen measured and improved the performance of the disk allocation algorithm.

Solo was the first major example of a concurrent program consisting of processes, monitors, and classes [Brinch Hansen 1975c].

At Regnecentralen I had been involved in the design of process control programs for a chemical plant, a power plant, and a weather bureau. These real-time applications had one thing in common: each was unique in its software requirements. Consequently, the programs were expensive to develop.

When the cost of a large program cannot be shared by many users, the only practical way of reducing cost is to give process control engineers a high-level language for concurrent programming. I illustrated this point by means of a real-time scheduler, which had been programmed in assembly language at Regnecentralen. I now reprogrammed the same scheduler in Concurrent Pascal.

The *real-time scheduler* executed a fixed number of task processes with frequencies chosen by an operator. I wrote it in three days. It took three hours of machine time to test it systematically. Writing a description took another couple of days. So the whole program was developed in less than a week [Brinch Hansen 1975f].

At the end of 1975 I wrote a *job-stream system* that compiled and executed short Pascal programs input from a card reader and output on a line printer. Input, execution, and output took place simultaneously using buffers stored on a disk. A user job was preempted if its compilation and execution time exceeded one minute. I designed, programmed, and tested the system in ten days. When the system was finished, it ran short jobs continuously at the speed of the line printer [Brinch Hansen 1976a].

It was a pleasant surprise to discover that 14 modules from Solo could be used unchanged in the job stream system. This is the earliest example I know of different operating systems using the same modules.

Each model operating system was a Concurrent Pascal program of about 1,000 lines of text divided into 15–25 modules. A module was roughly one page of text (50–60 lines) with about five procedures of 10–15 lines each (Table 4.2).

These examples showed that it was possible to build nontrivial concurrent programs from very simple modules that could be studied page by page [Brinch Hansen 1977a].

TABLE 4.2
Model operating systems.

	Solo	Job stream	Real time
Lines	1300	1400	600
Modules	23	24	13
Lines/module	57	58	46
Procedures/module	5	4	4
Lines/procedure	11	15	12

Compared to assembly language, Concurrent Pascal reduced my programming effort by an order of magnitude and made concurrent programs so simple that a journal could publish the entire text of a 1,300 line program [Brinch Hansen 1975c].

The modules of a concurrent program were tested one at a time starting with those that did not depend on other modules. In each test run, the initial process was replaced by a short test process that called the top module and made it execute all its statements at least once. When a module worked, another one was tested on top of it. Detailed examples of how this was done are described in Brinch Hansen [1977b and 1978d].

Dijkstra [1967] had used a similar procedure to test the T.H.E. multiprogramming system, which was written in assembly language. Concurrent Pascal made bottom-up testing secure. The compilation checks of access rights ensured that new (untested) modules did not make old (tested) modules fail. My experience was that a well-designed concurrent program of 1,000 lines required a couple of compilations followed by one test run per module. And then it worked [Brinch Hansen 1977a].

The End of the Beginning

In July 1976 I joined the University of Southern California as Professor and Chairman of Computer Science. I also finished a book on the new programming methodology entitled *The Architecture of Concurrent Programs* [Brinch Hansen 1977b].

My research on Concurrent Pascal was now entering its final phase. I wrote my last Concurrent Pascal program: a message router for a *ring network* of PDP 11/45 computers. I proved that it was deadlock-free and would deliver all messages within a finite time. The ideas of this program were developed in discussions with B. Heidebrecht, D. Heimbigner, F. Stepczyk, and R. Vossler at TRW Systems [Brinch Hansen 1977c].

My Ph.D. student, Jørgen Staunstrup, and I introduced *transition commands*—a formal notation for specifying process synchronization as state transitions [Brinch Hansen 1978a]. In his Ph.D. thesis, Staunstrup [1978] used this tool to specify major parts of the Solo system.

Another of my Ph.D. students, Jon Fellows, wrote one more operating system in Concurrent Pascal: the *Trio* system, which enabled users to simultaneously develop and execute programs on a PDP 11/55 minicomputer with three terminals and a memory of 160 k bytes. Jon Fellows was assisted in a few cases by Habib Maghami [Brinch Hansen 1980; Fellows 1980].

I now moved into another area that was little understood at the time: the programming of processes on a multicomputer without shared memory. I introduced the idea of a synchronized procedure that can be called by one process and executed by another process [Brinch Hansen 1978b]. This proposal combined processes and monitors into a single concept, called *distributed processes*.

This communication paradigm is also known as *remote procedure calls*. I recently discovered that it was first proposed by Jim White [1976]. However, White did not explain how to prevent race conditions between unsynchronized remote calls and local processes that are being executed by the same processor. This flaw potentially made remote procedure calls as unsafe as interrupts that cannot be disabled! Disaster was avoided by a programming convention: a process that handled a remote call immediately made a similar call to a local monitor [Lynch 1991]. In other words, insecure remote procedure calls were used only as an implementation technique for secure remote monitor calls.

My Ph.D. student, Charles Hayden [1979], implemented an experimental language with distributed processes on an LSI 11 and evaluated the new paradigm by writing small simulation programs.

According to Roubine [1980], my proposal was "a source of inspiration in the design of the Ada tasking facilities." The Ada *rendezvous* combines the remote procedure call of distributed processes with the selection of alternative interactions in communicating sequential processes [Hoare 1978].

My keynote address on concurrent programming at the IEEE Computer Software and Applications Conference in Chicago (November 1978) concluded five years of experience with the first abstract programming language for operating system development [Brinch Hansen 1978c].

The *milestones* of the project were:

1974	Concurrent Pascal defined
	Concurrent Pascal implemented
1975	Concurrent Pascal paper
	Solo operating system
	Real-time scheduler
	Job-stream system
1976	Solo papers
	System distribution
1977	*The Architecture of Concurrent Programs*
	Ring network
1978	Trio operating system
	Distributed processes

In Brinch Hansen [1980], Jon Fellows and I concluded that

> The underlying concepts of processes, monitors and classes can now be regarded as proven tools for software engineering. So it is time to do something else.

Feedback

Concurrent Pascal and Solo have been assessed by a number of computer scientists.

In a paper on programming languages for real-time control, C.A.R. Hoare [1976] summarized Concurrent Pascal:

> This is one of the few successful extensions of Pascal, and includes well structured capabilities for parallel processing, for exclusion and for synchronization. It was tested before publication in the construction of a small operating system, which promises well for its suitability for real-time programming. Although it does not claim to offer a final solution of the problem it tackles, it is an outstanding example of the best of academic research in this area.

In a detailed assessment of Concurrent Pascal, D. Coleman [1980] wrote:

> The process, monitor and class concepts work equally well for application and system programs. Therefore in that respect the language works admirably. However, because the language is meant for operating systems, all programs run on the bare Pascal machine and every application program must contain modules to provide facilities normally provided by the operating system, e.g. to access the file store.

P.W. Abrahams [1978] found that the modularity of the model operating systems definitely contributed to their readability. However,

> Since the programs are always referring to entities defined earlier, and since these entities are often quite similar, I found that a good deal of page flipping was in fact necessary.

In a review of *The Architecture of Concurrent Programs*, R.A. Maddux and H. Mills [1979] wrote: "This is, as far as we know, the first book published on concurrent programming." They were particularly pleased with the Solo system:

> Here, an entire operating system is visible, with every line of program open to scrutiny. There is no hidden mystery, and after studying such extensive examples, the reader feels that he could tackle similar jobs and that he could change the system at will. Never before have we seen an operating system shown in such detail and in a manner so amenable to modification.

In a survey paper on Concurrent Programming, R.E. Bryant and J.B. Dennis [1979] found:

> The ability to write an operating system in a high level language, including the communication and synchronization between processes, is an important advance in concurrent programming.

A final remark by D. Coleman [1980]:

> Concurrent Pascal's main achievement is that it shows how much can be achieved by a simple language that utilises compile time checking to the maximum. It will be a great pity if future language designers do not adhere to these same two principles.

The limitations of the language will be discussed below.

4.4 FURTHER DEVELOPMENT

Since 1975 many other researchers have explored the use of Concurrent Pascal on a variety of computers.

Moving a Language

At Caltech we prepared a distribution tape with the source text and portable code of the Solo system, including the Concurrent and Sequential Pascal compilers. The system reports were supplemented by implementation notes [Brinch Hansen 1976b].

By the spring of 1976 we had distributed the system to 75 companies and 100 universities in 21 countries: Australia, Austria, Belgium, Canada, Denmark, Finland, France, Germany, Great Britain, Holland, India, Ireland, Italy, Japan, Norway, South Africa, the Soviet Union, Spain, Sweden, Switzerland, and the United States.

D. Neal and V. Wallentine [1978] moved Concurrent Pascal and Solo to an Interdata 8/32 minicomputer in four months and to an NCR 8250 in another two months. The biggest stumbling block was the addressing scheme of the PDP 11. They wrote:

> It is clear that a system requiring so little effort to be moved between vastly differing architectures must have been well designed from the outset. In addition, with a single exception (sets and variants), all of the problem points were mentioned by the implementation notes accompanying the distributed system.

M.S. Powell [1979] and two students moved Concurrent Pascal to a Modular 1 in six months. Architectural differences between the source and target computers caused some portability problems. According to Powell,

> Brinch Hansen makes no claims about the portability of Solo, yet our experience shows that a system designed and documented this way can be moved fairly easily even when the target machine has a totally different architecture to that of the source machine.
>
> Since the system has been in use we have found it easy to use and simple to modify at both high and low levels.

S.E. Mattson [1980] moved Concurrent Pascal (without Solo) to an LSI 11 in four months. He found four errors in the compiler. He felt that

> The kernel is a rather complex program and although the assembly code was commented in a language that resembles Concurrent Pascal it was hard to understand in detail.
>
> The implementation is a tool of significant value for teaching, research, and engineering. It has been used with success in an undergraduate course.

J.M. Kerridge [1982] moved Concurrent Pascal to an IBM 370/145 in nine months part-time by rewriting the kernel in Fortran. He then moved it to a Honeywell system in one day! In his view

> The original software was extremely well documented and commented but there was still a large amount of 'hacking' which had to be undertaken before the system could be transported.

Concurrent Pascal was moved to many other computers [Löhr 1977; Bochmann 1979; Dunman 1982; Ravn 1982].

The Limits of Design

Several researchers described the experience of using Concurrent Pascal for system design.

A research group at TRW Systems used Concurrent Pascal for signal and image processing on a network of PDP 11/70s. Initially, the group had to extend the kernel with complicated device drivers written in assembly language. Later, D. Heimbigner [1978] redefined the *io* procedure and was able to program arbitrary device drivers in Concurrent Pascal (without extending the kernel).

N. Graef [1979] and others designed a small time-sharing system based on Solo with swapping of job processes. They described the performance as unsatisfactory compared to Unix.

After designing a multiterminal version of Solo, D. Coleman [1979] and others concluded that

> *writing minicomputer operating systems by using Concurrent Pascal to provide the framework of concurrency for Sequential Pascal utilities is only really suited to single user systems.*

G.V. Bochmann and T. Joachim [1979] implemented the X.25 communication protocol in Concurrent Pascal on a Xerox Sigma 6.

H.S.M. Kruijer [1982b] described a multiterminal system for transaction processing implemented by a Concurrent Pascal program of 2,200 lines for a PDP 11/34. He wrote:

> The work described in this paper shows that Concurrent Pascal is suitable for the construction of medium-sized multi-user systems. It has been found that the application of techniques which aim at enhancing portability,

> namely the exclusion of low-level features from the language and their implementation in the form of a kernel simulating a virtual machine, does not prevent systems written in Concurrent Pascal from being efficient. Moreover, both the properties of the language (its simplicity, high level, dependence on syntax rules) and its facilities (especially those for modularization) greatly contribute to obtaining reliable and adaptable system software. To illustrate this point it is relevant to mention that for the Multi operating system, a number of modules of Solo have been used which together amount to about 700 lines of Concurrent Pascal. The use of these modules in a different context was accomplished without interfacing problems and revealed only one error in one of the modules. These observations are in sharp contrast to our experience with commercially available operating systems.

Kruijer [1982a] also discovered a single (but subtle) error in the Concurrent Pascal kernel.

P. Møller-Nielsen and J. Staunstrup [1984] summarized four years of experience with a multiprocessor programmed in Concurrent Pascal. They discussed parallel algorithms for quicksort, mergesort, root finding, and branch-and-bound optimization.

The static memory allocation of the Concurrent Pascal implementation made the language impractical for the design of larger operating systems. In Brinch Hansen [1977b], I pointed out that the language was never intended for that purpose:

> This book describes a range of small operating systems. Each of them provides a special service in the most efficient and simple manner. They show that Concurrent Pascal is a useful programming language for minicomputer operating systems and dedicated real-time applications. I expect that the language will be useful (but not sufficient) for writing large, general-purpose operating systems. But that still remains to be seen. I have tried to make a programming tool that is very convenient for many applications rather than one which is tolerable for all purposes.

Evolution of an Idea

Concurrent Pascal was followed by more than a dozen *monitor languages* (Table 4.3). Some were inspired by Concurrent Pascal; others were developed independently, inspired by the monitor concept.

I will not attempt to discuss monitor languages that were developed after Concurrent Pascal. I hope that the designers of these languages will write personal histories of their own contributions. However, since I have not programmed in their languages, I cannot evaluate them or compare them with Concurrent Pascal.

Spreading the Word

Monitors and monitor languages have been discussed in many survey papers and textbooks. The following list of publication dates gives an idea of how rapidly the monitor paradigm spread through the computer science community.

- *Survey papers*

  Brinch Hansen [1973d], Andrews [1977], Bryant [1979], Stotts [1982], Andrews [1983], Appelbe [1985], Bal [1989].

- *Operating systems texts*

  Brinch Hansen [1973b], Tsichritzis [1974], Peterson [1983], Deitel [1984], Janson [1985], Krakowiak [1988], Pinkert [1989], Nutt [1992], Tanenbaum [1992].

TABLE 4.3

Monitor languages.

Language	Reference
Concurrent Pascal	Brinch Hansen (1974d)
Simone	Kaubisch (1976)
Modula	Wirth (1977)
CSP/k	Holt (1978)
CCNPascal	Narayana (1979)
PLY	Nehmer (1979)
Pascal Plus	Welsh (1979)
Mesa	Lampson (1980)
SB-Mod	Bernstein (1981)
Concurrent Euclid	Holt (1982)
Pascalc	Whiddett (1983)
Concurrent C	Tsujino (1984)
Emerald	Black (1986)
Real-time Euclid	Kligerman (1986)
Pascal-FC	Burns (1988)
Turing Plus	Holt (1988)
Predula	Ringström (1990)

- *Concurrent programming texts*

  Brinch Hansen [1977b], Holt [1978], Welsh [1980], Ben-Ari [1982], Holt [1983], Andre [1985], Boyle [1987], Perrott [1987], Whiddett [1987], Bustard [1988], Gehani [1988], Krishnamurthy [1989], Raynal [1990], Williams [1990], Andrews [1991].
- *Programming language texts*

  Turski [1978], Tennent [1981], Ghezzi [1982], Young [1982], Horowitz [1983a], Schneider [1984], Bishop [1986], Wilson [1988], Sebesta [1989].
- *Annotated bibliography*

  Bell [1983].

4.5 IN RETROSPECT

It seems natural to end the story by expressing my own mixed feelings about monitors and Concurrent Pascal.

The Neglected Problems

Today I have strong reservations about the monitor concept. It is a very clever combination of shared variables, procedures, process scheduling, and modularity. It enabled us to solve problems that we would not have undertaken without a commitment to this paradigm. But, like most of our programming tools, it is somewhat baroque and lacks the elegance that comes only from utter simplicity.

The monitor concept has often been criticized on two grounds: the complex details of process scheduling and the issue of nested monitor calls.

As a language designer, I have always felt that one should experiment with the simplest possible ideas before adopting more complicated ones. This led me to use single-process queues and combine process continuation with monitor exit. I felt that the merits of a signaling scheme could be established only by designing real operating systems (but not by looking at small programming exercises). Since Concurrent Pascal was the first monitor language, I was unable to benefit from the practical experience of others. After designing small operating systems, I concluded that first-in, first-out queues are indeed more convenient to use.

In 1974, when I designed the language, the papers by Howard [1976a, 1976b] and Kessels [1977] on monitor signaling had not yet been published. In any case, the virtues of different signaling mechanisms still strike me as being only mildly interesting. In most cases, any one of them will do, and all of them (including my own) are somewhat complicated. Fortunately, monitors have the marvelous property of *hiding* the details of scheduling from concurrent processes.

In my first monitor paper [Brinch Hansen 1974c] I characterized *nested monitor calls* as a natural and desirable programming feature:

> A monitor can call shared procedures implemented within other monitors. This makes it possible to build an operating system as a *hierarchy of processes and monitors*.

If a process delays itself within a nested sequence of monitor calls, it releases access to the last monitor only, but leaves the previous monitors temporarily inaccessible to other processes. Lister [1977] felt that this situation might degrade performance or cause deadlock:

> The only implementation known to the author in which the nested call problem is tackled head-on, rather than being merely avoided, is that by Brinch Hansen [1975e]. In this [Concurrent Pascal] implementation a local exclusion mechanism is used for each monitor, and a [delay] operation causes release of exclusion on only the most recently called monitor. It is not clear what measures, if any, are taken to avoid the degradation of performance and potential for deadlock mentioned earlier.

Lister [1977] offered no performance figures or program examples to prove the existence of such a problem. The hypothetical "problem" of nested monitor calls was discussed further by Haddon [1977], Keedy [1978], Wettstein [1978], and Kotulski [1987]—still without experimental evidence. In a paper on "The non-problem of nested monitor calls" Parnas [1978] finally declared that the problem was too vaguely formulated to be solvable.

Two years before this discussion started I had written three model operating systems in Concurrent Pascal. I used nested monitor calls in every one of them without any problems. These calls were a natural and inevitable consequence of the hierarchical program structures.

The Discomfort of Complexity

The monitor was undoubtedly a paradigm that for a time provided model problems and solutions to the computer science community. It may be argued that its proper role is to define a useful programming style, and that it is a mistake to include it in a programming language. To an engineer, this viewpoint has merits. To a scientist, it is less convincing.

When an idea is seen just as a programming style, programmers seldom define it precisely. They constantly bend the (unstated) rules of the game and mix it with other imprecise paradigms. This lack of rigor makes it rather difficult to explore the limits of a new idea.

I never considered Concurrent Pascal to be a final solution to anything. It was an experimental tool that imposed an intellectual discipline on me. By embedding monitors in a programming language I committed myself to defining the concept and its relationship to processes concisely. I deliberately made monitors the only communication mechanism in the language to ensure that we would discover the limitations of the concept.

Concurrent Pascal was the first programming language I designed. From my present perspective, it has all the flaws that are inevitable in a first venture.

In a later essay on language description, I wrote [Brinch Hansen 1981]:

> The task of writing a language report that explains a programming language with complete clarity to its implementors and users may look deceptively easy to someone who hasn't done it before. But in reality it is one of the most difficult intellectual tasks in the field of programming [Brinch Hansen 1981].

Well, I was someone who hadn't done it before, and the Concurrent Pascal report suffered from all the problems I mentioned in the essay.

I am particularly uncomfortable with the many *ad hoc* restrictions in the language. For example,

- Module types cannot be defined within procedures.
- Procedures cannot be defined within procedures.
- Module instances cannot be declared within procedures.
- Queues can only be declared as global variables of monitor types.
- Queues cannot be parameters of procedure entries.
- Process instances can only be declared in the initial process.
- A module type cannot refer to the variables of another module type.
- A module type cannot call its own procedure entries.
- A procedure cannot call itself.
- A continue operation can only be performed within a monitor procedure entry.
- Assignments cannot be performed on variables of type module or queue.

These rules were carefully chosen to make the language secure and enforce the compromises discussed earlier. But they all *restrict* the *generality* of the language concepts and the ways in which they may be combined.

There are about twenty rules of this kind in Concurrent Pascal [Brinch Hansen 1975a]. I will spare you the rest. They are an unmistakable symptom of complexity.

After Concurrent Pascal I developed two smaller languages. Each of them was again designed to explore a single programming concept: conditional critical regions in *Edison*, and synchronous communication in *Joyce* [Brinch Hansen 1981, 1989a].

There are exactly three *ad hoc* restrictions in Joyce:

- A process cannot access global variables.
- A message cannot include a channel reference.
- Two processes cannot communicate by polling the same channel(s).

I think only the first one is really necessary.

Inventing the Future

What am I most proud of? The answer is simple: We did something that had not been done before! We demonstrated that it is possible to write nontrivial concurrent programs exclusively in a secure programming language.

The particular paradigm we chose (monitors) was a detail only. The important thing was to discover if it was possible to add a new dimension to programming languages: *modular concurrency.*

Every revolution in programming language technology introduces abstract programming concepts for a new application domain. Fortran and Algol 60 were the first abstract languages for numerical computation. Pascal was used to implement its own compiler. Simula 67 introduced the class concept for simulation.

Before Concurrent Pascal it was not known whether operating systems could be written in secure programming languages without machine-dependent features. The discovery that this was indeed possible for small operating systems and real-time systems was far more important (I think) than the introduction of monitors.

Monitors made process communication abstract and secure. That was, of course, a breakthrough in the art of concurrent programming. However, the monitor concept was a detail in the sense that it was only one possible solution to the problem of making communication secure. Today we have three major communication paradigms: monitors, remote procedures, and message passing.

The development of secure language concepts for concurrent programming started in 1971. Fifteen years later Judy Bishop [1986] concluded:

> It is evident that the realm of concurrency is now firmly within the ambit of reliable languages and that future designs will provide for concurrent processing as a matter of course.

In the first survey paper on concurrent programming I cited 11 papers only, written by four researchers. None of them described a concurrent programming language [Brinch Hansen 1973d]. The development of monitors and Concurrent Pascal started a wave of research in concurrent programming languages that still continues. A recent survey of the field lists over 200 references to nearly 100 languages [Bal 1989].

I don't think we have found the right programming concepts for parallel computers yet. When we do, they will almost certainly be very different from anything we know today.

ACKNOWLEDGMENTS

This paper is dedicated to my former students who contributed to the Concurrent Pascal project:

Jon Fellows	Charles Hayden	Jørgen Staunstrup
Wolfgang Franzen	Habib Maghami	Tom Zepko
Al Hartmann		

I thank the following 60 colleagues for their helpful comments on earlier drafts of this paper:

Birger Andersen	Tony Hoare	Harlan Mills
Greg Andrews	Ric Holt	Peter O'Hearn
Bill Atwood	Jim Horning	Ross Overbeek
Art Bernstein	Giorgio Ingargiola	Niels Pedersen
Jean Bezivin	David Jefferson	Ron Perrott
Judy Bishop	Mathai Joseph	Malcolm Powell
Coen Bron	Eric Jul	Brian Randell
Dave Bustard	Jon Kerridge	Anders Ravn

Mani Chandy
Derek Coleman
Ole-Johan Dahl
Peter Denning
Jerry Feldman
Jon Fellows
Narain Gehani
Jonathan Greenfield
Al Hartmann
Charles Hayden
Dennis Heimbigner
John Hennessy
Don Knuth
Henk Kruijer
Andrew Lister
Bart Locanthi
Ewing Lusk
Bill Lynch
Rich McBride
Mike McKeag
Jan Madey
Roy Maddux
Mike Mahoney
Skip Mattson
Charles Reynolds
Johan Ringström
Bob Rosin
Fred Schneider
Avi Silberschatz
Jørgen Staunstrup
Wlad Turski
Virgil Wallentine
Peter Wegner
Dick Whiddett
Niklaus Wirth
Tom Zepko

I also thank the anonymous referees for their careful reviews of earlier drafts.

The Concurrent Pascal project was supported by the National Science Foundation under grant numbers DCR74-17331 and MCS77-05696, the design of Trio by the Army Research Office under contract number DAAG29-77-G-0192, and the development of Distributed Processes by the Office of Naval Research under contract numbers NR048-647 and NR049-415.

APPENDIX: REVIEWERS' COMMENTS

In 1991 I sent earlier drafts of this paper to a number of computer scientists with a letter asking for their comments "with the understanding that I may quote your letter in the final paper." Many of their suggestions are incorporated in the revised paper. Here are some of their remaining remarks.

G. ANDREWS: You claim that the particular paradigm you chose (monitors) was a . . . detail. The most important aspect of monitors is their role as a data encapsulation mechanism.

. . .

The contribution of Concurrent Pascal was indeed that it added a new dimension to programming languages: modular concurrency. Monitors (and classes) were essential to this contribution. And the modularization they introduced has greatly influenced most subsequent concurrent language proposals.

What is debatable about monitors are the details of synchronization, especially the signaling discipline.

. . .

I have not seen any radical new programming ideas emerge for several years now. Thus, I suspect that in the future the programming concepts we use for parallel computers will merely be refinements of things we know today.

D.W. BUSTARD: The statement . . . "Today I have strong reservations about the monitor concept" tends to suggest that the *concept* is flawed. I don't agree. The basic concept of a data structure allowing processes exclusive access to its data still seems very important. What has never been handled satisfactorily, however, is the explicit queuing mechanism for process suspension and activation. I tinkered with several possibilities over a period of years but now (like Parnas) I feel that it would be better to give access to lower level facilities that allow users to implement a policy of their own liking. It is a mistake for language designers to treat potential users like children!

O.-J. DAHL: I am grateful for your recognition of the role of the Simula 67 class concept; however, in the reference to it the name of my colleague Kristen Nygaard should occur along with mine . . . [Our] own historic paper, given at the ACM Conference on the "History of Programming Languages," . . . shows the extent to which either of us was dependent on the other in the discovery of the class concept.

. . .

I take issue with some of your reservations about Concurrent Pascal. Of course a language built around a small number of mechanisms used orthogonally is an ideal worth striving for. Still, when I read your 1977 book my reaction was that the art of imposing the right restrictions may be as important from an engineering point of view.

So, here for once was a language, beautiful by its orthogonal design, which at the same time was the product of a competent engineer by the restrictions imposed in order to achieve implementation and execution efficiency. The adequacy of the language as a practical tool has been amply demonstrated.

P.J. DENNING: I had a love-hate relationship with monitors since first meeting them as "critical regions" in your 1973 book and then in Hoare's 1974 paper in the *ACM Communications*. What I loved about them was the way they brought together data abstraction (as we now call it) and synchronization. Suddenly we had a simple notation that allowed the expression of correct programs for the hard problems we faced constantly in operating systems design. What I hated about them was the need to understand the details of the queuing mechanism in order to understand how to use them. My students had to study carefully Hoare's notes on using semaphores to do the queueing. In this sense monitors had not broken away from the fine-grain mechanisms of semaphores.

I was therefore much interested in the next stages that you and Hoare reached, expressed in your 1978 papers in the *ACM Communications*. You had continued the line of development of monitors into distributed processes; Hoare had proposed communicating sequential processes, an approach motivated by the constraints of microprocessor design. I was more attracted to Hoare's proposal because of my own biases in thinking about how operating systems and parallel computers are actually built and how they manage work.

. . .

Even though in the end I found the monitor concept less to my liking than communicating processes, I still think that the monitor is a good idea, and that the observer it makes one of how operating systems work is a worthy observer to learn to be.

J.A. FELDMAN: I was not personally involved with the [Concurrent Pascal] effort, but admired it and now find somewhat to my surprise that my current parallel Sather project relies on a version of monitors.

. . .

[It is] now clear that any large, scalable parallel machine will have physically distributed memory. There is a great deal of current research on hardware and software for uniform memory abstractions, but this seems to me unlikely to work. The structure of the programming language and code can provide crucial information on locality requirements so that the system doesn't need to do it all mindlessly. And that is where monitors come in.

Sather is an object-oriented language . . .The parallel constructs . . . are based on a primitive monitor type . . . [It] is remarkable that 20 years later the monitor concept is central to language developments well beyond the original conception.

J. FELLOWS: Looking back at my studies at USC from 1978 to 1981, I can separate my thoughts into three areas: the concepts that underlie monitors and classes, the language constructs that implement these concepts, and the quality of the demonstration programs that you (PBH) wrote. You have already addressed the first two in your paper. As for the third, I believe that the beauty of the structures you created using Concurrent Pascal created an aura of magical simplicity. While working with my own programs and those of other graduate students, I soon learned that ordinary, even ugly, programs could also be written in Concurrent Pascal . . . My current feeling is that the level of intellectual effort required to create a beautiful program structure cannot be reduced by programming language features, but that these features can more easily reveal a program's beauty to others who need to understand it.

. . .

The topic I chose to explore [in the Trio system] was the use of Concurrent Pascal's access restrictions to explicitly create a program access graph (or "uses" hierarchy between type instances) that achieved least privilege visibility between program components, meaning that no component has access to another component unless it is needed. For this purpose, I still believe that Concurrent Pascal's initialization-time binding of components is an improvement over the scope-based facilities of Modula, Edison, and Ada.

. . .

It is interesting to note that one of the most common complaints I heard (and made myself) was that classes should have been left in [Sequential Pascal]. This would have extended many of the benefits available to system programmers to application programmers.

. . .

As I discovered when moving the compilers from Solo to Trio, there was a point at which the Operating System/Sequential Pascal interface was unsafe. As I recall, there was no type checking across the program invocation interface, which depended on correct hand-tailoring and consistent usage of the prefix for Sequential Pascal programs. In general, program invocation was the one operating system area that was not made transparently simple in Solo and Trio.

A.C. Hartmann: There are really two histories interwoven in this paper—the history of the development of concurrent modular programming, and the history of one man's ruthless quest for simplicity in design and programming. The former topic is indifferent to whether one chooses to develop concurrency mechanisms for greater expressive power and more complex functionality, or, as you have chosen, to radically shorten and simplify the design of common concurrent systems. The Solo operating system is downright primitive in the sparseness of its features, representing a counter-cultural current against ever-increasing operating system complexity. Your style and taste in programming run almost counter to the second law of thermodynamics, that all closed systems tend towards increasing entropy and disorder.

In a world of Brinch Hansens (which may exist in some parallel dimension to ours), all systems tend towards reduced entropy over time and toward a blissful state of ultimate simplicity. Each new release of the operating system for one's personal workstation is smaller than the previous release, consumes fewer system resources, runs faster on simpler hardware, provides a reduced set of easier to use features than the last release, and carries a lower price tag. Hardware designers espousing the same philosophy produce successive single-chip microprocessors with exponentially declining transistor counts from generation to generation, dramatically shrinking die sizes, and reducing process steps by resorting to fewer, simpler device types. No one would need to "invent" RISC computing in this world, since reduced feature sets would be an inexorable law of nature.

. . .

Ironically the Concurrent Pascal compiler that I wrote was written in the language of its sister Sequential Pascal compiler, which had neither classes nor monitors. It was fifteen years later when I finally had access to a C++ system on a personal computer that I wrote my first modular program using abstract typing. To this day I have not written a concurrent program.

C.C. Hayden: What was remarkable about [Concurrent Pascal] is that one could write experimental operating systems on a virtual machine without having to resort to machine registers, assembly language, etc. The development environment provided a way to do operating systems in a controlled way, on the "bare hardware" of a much nicer machine than any real computer . . .

I think the significance of the system was . . . that one could provide a protected environment for concurrent programming—a high-level language environment which could maintain the illusion that there was no "machine" level. It was remarkable that through compile time restrictions and virtual machine error checking, that you could understand the program behavior by looking at the Pascal, not at the machine's registers and memory. It was remarkable that the machine could retain its integrity while programs were being developed, without hardware memory protection.

. . .

How has the monitor concept evolved? From my perspective, the concept of message passing between processes in disjoint address spaces was around before monitors, and has continued to dominate the monitor concept. The operating systems in most common use today have message passing paradigms. The Macintosh, Microsoft Windows, Unix running X windows: all force applications to be organized around an event loop, which receives an event message, unpacks it and dispatches to a handler, and carries out an action. These are just the "real-time" system architectures of the 1960s. The monitor concept was an advance over the earlier message passing systems because it eliminated the event loop, message packing and unpacking, dispatching, etc. Concurrent Pascal hid all that mess, and made it possible to do it more efficiently by absorbing it into machine code or microcode, and eliminated the possibility of making errors. Why did it not become better accepted?

. . .

Maybe the problem [that] monitors were meant to solve (concurrency in shared memory systems) was never really that important after all. The conventional wisdom is that concurrent systems cannot scale up if they share memory.

...

I have a deep respect for the monitor concept: in my opinion it is better than message passing, which is what we are stuck with. It is particularly powerful if used in the form of conditional critical regions. And I think the language Concurrent Pascal made a real advance in permitting easy experimentation with operating systems concepts and implementations. It allowed me to further my own education by building programs that I would not otherwise have been able to build. This taught me valuable lessons about programming styles and paradigms, about how important it is to be able to reason about programs when they cannot be reliably tested. Concurrent Pascal had to deal with such restrictive and peculiar hardware, almost unthinkably limiting by today's standards.

As your thinking evolved, the systems you built seemed to get smaller and more elegant, trying to achieve more generality and less complexity. This is a laudable goal for research languages, but I could never come to believe in it as applied to programming tools such as editors, formatters, etc. I know of few people who would want to adopt simpler tools . . . Perhaps there is no longer any call for this kind of programming . . . I am glad that I was able to educate myself before it was too late. The Concurrent Pascal system made that possible.

D. HEIMBIGNER: Concurrent Pascal is one of those languages that is very much under-appreciated. It was one of the first widely available languages to introduce both object-oriented concepts and concurrency (in the form of processes and monitors).

Concurrent Pascal is perhaps best known as one of the first languages to provide monitors as a synchronization device. Initially, I was a very strong believer in the monitor construct. After using the construct for a while, I recognized its flaws and was rather disenchanted with them. Since then, I have had some experience with Ada and its tasking model, and I am beginning to think that perhaps monitors were not such a bad concept after all.

I should also note that I am continually surprised at how long it is taking for concurrency constructs to become a standard part of every programmer's toolkit. The C and C++ communities, for example, are still arguing over a standard threads package. Most Unix kernels (except Mach) have no special provisions for handling threads, most Unix libraries are still not capable of working correctly in a parallel environment, and most Unix machines are still single processor. This seems to me to be a disgrace.

The concurrency elements of Concurrent Pascal were important, but I would also like to comment on its object-orientation. It was my first introduction to an object-oriented language. At the same time, (1976–1978), Smalltalk was mostly a rumor; it would be several years before it became available. Simula-67 was not widely available on any machine to which I had access.

So, when I encountered Concurrent Pascal, I spent a fair amount of time experimenting with its object-oriented constructs. As a result, I became a firm believer in that approach for programming and have continued to use the paradigm to this day.

It is interesting to compare Concurrent Pascal with, for example, Modula-2 and Ada. At one time, there was a discussion in the language community about the merits of objects (as represented in Smalltalk and Concurrent Pascal and Euclid) versus the merits of packages (as represented in Modula-2 and Ada). In retrospect, it seems amusing that these two concepts were considered comparable, rather than complementary. It also clear that the object point of view has prevailed (witness Modula-3 and Ada 9x).

J. HENNESSY: I had one interesting insight that I wanted to communicate to you. We have been experimenting with an object-oriented language (called Cool and based on C++) for programming parallel machines. The idea is to use the object structure as a basis for synchronization, dealing with data locality, and for implementing load balancing. Initially, we anticipated using a variety of synchronization primitives, including things such as futures, in addition to monitor-based constructs. Surprisingly, we found that the synchronization mechanisms based on monitors were adequate for most cases, and were much easier to implement (more efficient), and easier to understand. My advice is not to undersell monitors. I suspect that we will find that there are many more instances where this basic concept is useful!

C.A.R. HOARE: I read your personal history with great enjoyment: it brings back with sharp clarity the excitement of our discussions at Marktoberdorf and Belfast in 1971. Even more valuably, it describes the whole history of a remarkably successful research engineering project, conducted with utmost regard for scientific integrity and principles, which has enlarged the understanding of a whole generation of computing scientists and software engineers. That a subsequent generation has lost the understanding could be explained in another, much sadder, paper.

My only serious debate with your account is with the very last sentence. I do not believe that there is any "right" collection of programming concepts for parallel (or even sequential) computers. The design of a language is always a compromise, in which the good designer must take into account the desired level of abstraction, the target machine architecture, and the proposed range of applications. I therefore believe that the monitor concept will continue to be highly appropriate for implementation of operating systems on shared-store multiprocessors. Of course, it will improve and adapt; its successful evolution is now the responsibility of those who follow your footsteps. Your full account of the original voyage of exploration will continue to inform, guide, and inspire them.

G. Ingargiola: Your paper is faithful to what I remember.

You had this tremendous clarity about what you were doing in concurrency and languages; you made restrictive choices usually on the basis of efficiency (you list a number of such choices in your paper). You stated something like "Start with as few and simple mechanisms as possible; add later only if it becomes necessary."

At least in your discussions and lectures, you built programs from English statements, making explicit the invariants and refining these statements, usually not modifying them, until the program was done.

I was amazed at how slowly you developed code when lecturing, and, by contrast, how fast you got debugged running code for the Concurrent Pascal compiler, and for various concurrent programs and the Solo OS.

You had very little interest in computer science topics outside of the area in which you were doing research. You made polite noises, you indicated interest, but your span of attention was minimal . . .

The personnel involved in the Concurrent Pascal implementation is as small as you say . . . Deverill contributed with his knowledge of the PDP 11 architecture and of its assembly language. Hartmann and you did the work.

. . .

I remember your excitement with the notion of "threaded code"; if I remember correctly, you thought it was your own invention and found out only later that others found it before.

In 1977, on the phone, you told me that you were working on a model of distributed computing where processes could make synchronous calls across processors. When later I heard about remote procedure calls, I assumed it was a variation on what you had said.

M. Joseph: [Your paper] made very interesting reading and it took me back to the exciting days of early 1975 when you lectured on Concurrent Pascal in Bombay!

We spent quite a lot of 1975 studying Concurrent Pascal and deciding whether and how it could be used for our multiprocessor operating system project . . .

Our version of the language (which we called CCNPascal, both because of its antecedents in Concurrent Pascal and because it was the language for the Close-Coupled Network project) . . . was implemented on a DEC-10 and generated code for the DEC-10, PDP-11 and TDC-16 (and later a group produced a code generator for the Intel 8086). So perhaps it is fair to say that Concurrent Pascal had close 'cousins' on all of these machines!

I think there has been some general confusion about the role of Concurrent Pascal. On the one hand, it was used very successfully in the version that you supplied, by many people and for a variety of applications. On the other hand, the design of Concurrent Pascal also provided the springboard for people (like us) to make use of its concepts for designing larger languages which were applied to fairly ambitious tasks. So the monitor concept was fairly rugged and stood up well to the test of being used for large applications, and this is something that is not widely known.

Moreover, it was a language for which high quality code could be generated (something that implementors of Ada still aspire to). We had multi-pass cross-compiling versions of our compiler which generated extremely tight code and I later produced a one-pass version of the compiler which did a lot of on-the-fly optimization and produced PDP-11 code . . .

With interest returning to shared memory multiprocessors, it seems quite appropriate that people should be reminded of the achievements of Concurrent Pascal.

J.M. KERRIDGE: One of the reasons that I acquired Concurrent Pascal was to enable access to a Pascal system which at the time (1978) was the only way it could be made accessible on our IBM 370. It had the added benefit of introducing me to concurrent programming. This has led me to continue working in the area of parallel systems allowing me to build highly parallel database machines based around the transputer and occam.

In this respect I find your comments ... concerning the compromises that were made to effect efficient processing surprising. In the transputer/occam combination the same limitations have, to a large extent, also been imposed. This enables compile time checking of memory allocation and process interaction, which is vital for real-time embedded control systems. It is interesting that this too was the application environment from which you came originally.

If we consider the use of Ada for such safety-critical real-time systems then we have to use Safe Ada, which has exactly the same limitations. The full capability of Ada is only available with a large run-time support system about which it is impossible to reason!

Given the above points I believe that you have been somewhat hard in criticising Concurrent Pascal ... Hindsight is a valuable tool especially after nearly 20 years! Many of the restrictions were reasonable given that you were experimenting with concurrency and not constructing a sequential language. Keeping things simple is a good axiom and though it is useful to have nested procedure declarations, as an example, it was not fundamental to the needs of concurrency experimentation. If many of these restrictions had been relaxed then Concurrent Pascal may never have seen the light of day.

H.S.M. KRUIJER: I (continue to) regard the specification and implementation of Concurrent Pascal as an impressive piece of work, combining the best results of Computer Science and making them available in the area of Software Engineering. More specifically, I regard this work and the publications on it as large-scale examples of the application of sound (computer) science resulting into high-quality "real-life" (software) engineering products, which still serve as a yardstick and a source of inspiration not only for (computer) scientists but also (more importantly) for practicising (software) engineers ...

The use of Concurrent Pascal has played a major organising and professionalising role in the Computer Science & Software engineering section of our Mathematics and Systems Engineering department. My paper in "Software—Practice and Experience" [1982] described a project carried out in the period 1976–1980, but other work has been done that has not been published:

- We have extended, during 1981–1983, the prototype application system referred to in my paper (namely a multi-user system for order taking and stock updating suited to Shell's Marketing (Sales) business) so as to run on a number of PDP 11 computers coupled via one common, shared communication channel (eventually an Ethernet). Therefore the Multi operating system described was transformed systematically into a distributed version, using remote procedure calls and client-server mechanisms and using Concurrent Pascal for the implementation of the data communication software needed.

...

- A prototype data acquisition system (for Shell's process control system in refineries and chemical plants) has been developed during 1981–1985, using Concurrent Pascal as implementation language.
- A data acquisition system for our Materials Research department has been developed during 1986–1989, using Concurrent Pascal for specification and design and using DEC hardware and software for implementation.

E.L. LUSK: Our group's adoption of monitors as a central theme in our parallel programming work did not arise from an interest in elegant operating systems; it was absolutely forced on us by the task of writing application programs for real parallel processors. In 1983 Los Alamos obtained a Denelcor HEP, in many respects the first commercially available multiprocessor. Several different groups at Argonne tried it out (in 1984 Argonne got one too), and that facility evolved into Argonne's Advanced Computing Research Facility.

The HEP was programmed in a dialect of Fortran that allowed direct access to the full/empty bits in memory as a way of allowing ordinary program variables to be used for a kind of dataflow synchronization. The mechanism was efficient but dangerous. Ross Overbeek and I chose as our first project the parallel implementation of the unification algorithm from theorem proving. We found this a humbling experience, to say the least. While our colleagues proceeded smoothly with parallel versions of regular numerical algorithms, we suffered every type of bug associated with parallel algorithms. Finally we realized that we would have to retreat to intellectually higher ground. For the shared-memory computational model, monitors represented an abstraction that could be understood, reasoned about, and efficiently implemented. We used the HEP constructs to implement locks, used the locks to construct the basic monitor-building primitives, used these to build (portable, now, at this level) a library of useful monitors, and our problems disappeared for good. The macro package for the HEP has evolved through several generations, and its descendants are widely used for programming nearly all current shared-memory machines in C and Fortran.

. . .

I believe that the simple domain-composition algorithms that pay the freight for the current generation of massively-parallel machines are distracting many current users from realizing the long-term validity of the shared-memory model. Fast communication speeds do not make the shared memory irrelevant; it is the programming model that is important. Although the programming model for message passing is now relatively stable . . ., no such consensus has arisen for the shared memory model . . . In the long run monitors will be seen as the most useful paradigm for expressing algorithms for the shared-memory model. The shared-memory model, in turn, will return to greater prominence as more complex algorithms are moved to parallel computers.

Monitors shall arise again!

W.C. Lynch: I think that monitors may have achieved more contemporary success than you might believe. In one sense I think of your description as one of the birth pains of an idea that has matured and stood the test of time.

. . .

In 1977 Xerox PARC/SDD [had] to construct a real time . . . operating system (subsequently called "Pilot"). A large part of the problem was the specification of facilities for concurrent operation. The input experiences were . . . 1) my experience in the design and implementation 1970–1971 of Chios utilizing light-weight processes and Dijkstra PV operators . . ., 2) Butler Lampson's proposal to incorporate Monitors and Condition variables, as described by Hoare, into Mesa and hence into Pilot . . ., 3) the pre-disposition of management to leverage their experience with message passing paradigms in the SDS-XDS operating systems.

I was the convenor of this task force. Among others, Butler Lampson, Dave Redell, and Hugh Lauer were participants. Roger Needham was an occasional consultant.

Inputs 1) and 2) quickly converged, supported by the reality of your previous experience with Concurrent Pascal, but 3) led to a contentious stalemate, with each party claiming some inherent superiority over the other. This was finally resolved by the argument presented in [Lauer 1978] which demonstrated that the views were equivalent in the sense that each could be executed in terms of the other. Since the intention was to combine support for concurrent processing with the benefits of Mesa, it was clear that the procedural view of Monitors was most compatible with the procedural language Mesa.

The design that resulted, smoothly incorporating threads (nee light weight processes), monitors, and condition variables into Mesa as built-in types, was eventually described in [Lampson 1980].

Lampson, Redell, and others moved on to DEC SRC and continued their work there. With the work on and introduction of the object-oriented Modula-3, it was realized that a class structure allows the above threads related types to be implemented as a library without being implemented in the language . . .

Today threads libraries, a direct linear descendant of monitors, are de rigeur in the Unix world. I would say that the ideas created in the process that you describe are still a major force today.

. . .

I don't know what more one could ask in the way of ultimate triumph for an idea.

R.A. Overbeek: In the early 1980s, E. Lusk and I were offered the opportunity of developing applications for a new parallel processor, the Denelcor HEP. Our application area was automated deduction, and our background in parallel computation was quite limited. In our first experiments, we worked with the programming constructs offered by Denelcor Fortran, which were low-level synchronization constructs. It became immediately apparent that we needed to develop higher-level, portable constructs. Our central source of both ideas and implementation guidelines during that period was Concurrent Pascal and your work that gave detailed implementation information. We developed a rather primitive set of tools and began work on several applications.

A year later, we were faced with moving our applications to several other machines. To our delight, we were able to port a 50,000 line implementation of a parallel logic programming engine from the HEP to a new Sequent Balance in just four hours. We went on to port the code to a variety of other shared-memory multiprocessors, and the benefits of portable constructs were quite apparent. Indeed, the ability to develop programs on machines in which the environment was relatively stable and for which adequate performance monitoring and debugging tools existed (most notably, the Sequent machines) and then move them to a number of "production" environments was extremely useful.

Later, we shifted our programming paradigm to include message-passing constructs. It is a tenable position that there are relatively few applications that benefit substantially from parallel processing, and that a majority of these can be formulated in ways that allow effective use of parallelism with message-passing constructs; that is, they do not require the capabilities we built into our earlier tools based on monitors. Furthermore, the ability to port applications based on message-passing to platforms like multicomputers or clusters of workstations is really quite attractive. I consider this a far from settled issue, but I have tentatively adopted this position.

Our work based on developing portable tools for exploring the potential exploitation of parallelism on the wide variety of machines that appeared in the 1980s benefited directly from the pioneering work on monitors. While we were never fortunate enough to be directly involved with the individuals that drove that effort, we did gradually come to grasp some of the issues that they had clarified.

N. Holm Pedersen: It is with a feeling of nostalgia that we, at Brüel & Kjœr, read about the emerging of the ideas on which we have based most of the programming of our instruments for the last decade. We are still using the Concurrent Pascal (CP) language in full scale, i.e., just finishing two instruments, each with programs of more than 1 Mbyte code written in Concurrent Pascal.

It is remarkable that the idea of Concurrent Pascal is having a major effect on modern blockstructured languages such as Ada and C++. Excluding the monitor concept, Ada has inherited the structures of CP, and C++ has reinvented the Class-type. It caused some confusion in our company to hear C++ being named "the invention of the century" as we have created objects since 1980 in the form of Monitors and Classes. We are in the process of discovering that the freedom (nonhierarchical nature) of C++ is very nice but dangerous . . .

M.S. Powell: I read the first draft of your paper "Monitors and Concurrent Pascal: A Personal History" with great interest. The work I did with Concurrent Pascal and the Solo system took place near the beginning of my academic career and much of my subsequent work has been strongly influenced by it. Your paper fills in many gaps in my knowledge of the history of the development of the underlying ideas. A number of things I did with Concurrent Pascal and Solo which may be of interest, but have never been published, are described below.

The characteristics of Solo which made it easy to port to a machine with a very different architecture to the PDP-11, also made it very easy to change and extend for practical and experimental purposes. The final configuration supported on Modular 1 hardware at UMIST ran across three processors with the file store distributed across two 28M byte exchangeable disk drives shared between the three processors. In this form the system supported many final year project students and research projects. Many compiler and language extensions were introduced, e.g. the Concurrent Pascal compiler was modified to support generic classes and the compiler and virtual machine were modified to support message passing through inter-process channels. A system which ran up to two passes of the compiler pipelined concurrently by two processors was also implemented.

. . .

After the Modular 1 system (around 1982) we moved onto a network of DEC LSI-11s connected together by a Cambridge ring. A distributed Concurrent Pascal implementation was constructed for this environment. During execution of the initial process, extensions to the virtual machine allowed processes and monitors to be assigned interactively to selected processors on the network. Monitor entry routine calls were implemented by remote procedure calls, and distribution was transparent to the concurrent program, i.e. we were able to run programs produced on the Modular 1 without recompilation.

. . .

A spin-off of my research work has been a system called Paradox which has been used to support teaching in the Computation Department for the last four years.

. . .

Inside the implementation of Paradox, unseen by most, Concurrent Pascal is alive and well at UMIST, and helping to support nearly 250 users every year.

A.P. Ravn: I really enjoyed reading your paper on the history of monitors and Concurrent Pascal. I shall refrain from commenting on who got the ideas for the monitor first; but I am sure that Concurrent Pascal was central for the dissemination of these ideas in software engineering.

. . .

The Concurrent Pascal system and its literature made it possible to combine theoretical concepts with experimental work. Probably the only way engineering can be taught.

It was a pleasure teaching courses based on Concurrent Pascal, and the students, who are now software developers, received a thorough knowledge of good system programming concepts. In some ways too good; when I meet them now, they find it hard to break away from these paradigms, even in distributed systems.

C.W. Reynolds: There seem to me to be two central issues treated during the early period 1971–1973. First was the issue of medium term scheduling. How does a process wait for some condition to be true? . . .

It seems to me that the critical insight occurred in realizing that the responsibility for determining an awaited event has occurred must lie with the application programmer and not with the underlying run-time support. The awakening of processes awaiting events is part of the application algorithm and must be indicated by explicit announcement of the events by means of "signal" or "cause" commands present in the application algorithm.

This idea is clearly present as early as Brinch Hansen [1972b]. Of less importance, but necessary to mention, is that there and in Concurrent Pascal, at most one process can be suspended in a single queue. Although this can be efficiently implemented and although it is possible to use it to simulate a queue containing multiple processes, the history of the last twenty years has shown the multiple process condition queue of Hoare [1974a] to be more popular.

The second central issue in this early period is the class notion from Simula. And there are two aspects to this. First is the encapsulation of procedures together with their shared variables and the prohibition of access to these shared variables by any procedures other than those encapsulated procedures. This notion of encapsulation appears in the unpublished draft Brinch Hansen [1971c] and it definitely appears in the textbook Brinch Hansen [1973b].

The second important aspect of the class concept is that a class is a mechanism for type definition so that multiple distinct variables of a class can be declared . . . But, in the context of monitors, there is an important difference that appears in short-term scheduling of exclusive access to the monitor. Is this exclusion enforced for each class instance or is it enforced for the whole class at once? . . . Mutual exclusion on individual instances of a class is possible in languages such as Concurrent Pascal and Mesa which adopted the Simula class style, whereas it is not possible in languages such as Pascal Plus, SP/k, Concurrent Euclid, Modula-2, and Ada, which did not.

The treatment of monitors as Simula classes appears in the textbook Brinch Hansen [1973b] and is notably absent in Hoare [1974a].

I believe that another central issue treated but never resolved in this early period was the relationship between short-term scheduling in monitor access and medium term scheduling for awaited events. Evidence of this issue is found in the variety of signaling semantics proposed during this period. These included the Signal/Return semantics of Concurrent Pascal, the Signal/Unconditional-Wait semantics of Hoare [1974a] and the more prevalent Signal/Wait semantics of languages like SP/k and others. Multiple not-quite-satisfactory solutions to the problem indicate that it has not been resolved.

V. Wallentine: Your comments on our experience porting Concurrent Pascal were completely accurate.

However, many things cannot be included in journal articles. The thrill of porting a useful language with such a small investment of time made it possible to use Concurrent Pascal in the academic environment. Many, many students were able to learn the concepts of concurrent programming and encapsulation using Concurrent Pascal.

Having a concrete language to experiment with is essential to understanding the monitor concept. Using the concept of monitors as implemented in Concurrent C as a concrete example, they were able to better understand additional scheduling (and signaling) techniques.

I remember spending many hours with my research group discussing different signaling paradigms and hierarchical monitors. We also spent a significant amount of time implementing a distributed operating system (on top of Unix). This was a good test for the strength of the monitor concept.

T. ZEPKO: Part of the history you describe is an important part of my own history.

At the time I was involved with Concurrent Pascal, I was an undergraduate and not so much concerned with the conceptual significance of the language as with learning how to build a language system from the ground up. I got the practical experience I wanted by working on the Concurrent Pascal compiler, the threaded code interpreter, and the operating system kernel. I have continued to do this same kind of work for the last fifteen years.

The concepts behind the Concurrent Pascal, the evolution of the ideas as you describe them, are clearer to me now than they were as a student. The needs you were addressing do require some years of experience to appreciate. But even as a student, some things left a lasting impression. What I learned from you, beyond specific programming techniques, is what I can only describe as a passion for clear thinking. This was obvious in the way you approached program design, and it was obviously the driving force behind the design of the Concurrent Pascal language.

...

Some of the ideas embodied in Concurrent Pascal were radical at the time. That they seem less so now is a tribute to the trailblazing nature of your work. Your approach to programming and to language design now has many advocates. Structured programming, modular design, strong typing, data encapsulation, and so on, are all considered essential elements of modern programming and have found their way into a wide variety of languages. I'm thankful to have played a part in this work.

REFERENCES

[Abrahams, 1978] Abrahams, P.W. Review of the Architecture of Concurrent Programs. *Computing Reviews 19*, Sept. 1978.

[Andre, 1985] Andre, F., Herman, D., and Verjus, J.-P. *Synchronization of Parallel Programs*, Cambridge, MA: MIT Press, 1985.

[Andrews, 1977] Andrews, G.R. and McGraw, J.R. Language features for process interaction. *SIGPLAN Notices 12*, Mar. 1977, pp. 114–127.

[Andrews, 1983] Andrews, G.R. and Schneider, F.B. Concepts and notations for concurrent programming. *ACM Computing Surveys 15*, Jan. 1983, pp. 3–43. Reprinted in Gehani [1988], pp. 3–69.

[Andrews, 1991] Andrews, G.R. *Concurrent Programming: Principles and Practice*. Redwood City, CA: Benjamin/Cummings, 1991.

[Appelbe, 1985] Appelbe, W.F. and Hansen, K. A survey of systems programming languages: concepts and facilities. *Software—Practice and Experience 15*, Feb. 1985, pp. 169–190.

[Bal, 1989] Bal, H.E., Steiner, J.G. and Tanenbaum, A.S. Programming languages for distributed computing systems. *ACM Computing Surveys 21*, Sept. 1989, pp. 261–322.

[Bauer, 1976] Bauer, F.L. and Samelson, K. Language hierarchies and interfaces. Proceedings of an International Summer School at Marktoberdorf, Germany, July 23–August 2, 1975. *Lecture Notes in Computer Science 46*, New York: Springer-Verlag, 1976.

[Bell, 1983] Bell, D.H., Kerridge, J.M., Simpson, D., and Willis, N. *Parallel Programming—A Bibliography*. New York: Wiley Heyden, 1983.

[Bell, 1973] Bell, J.R. Threaded code. *Communications of the ACM 16*, Jun. 1973, pp. 370–372.

[Ben-Ari, 1982] Ben-Ari, M. *Principles of Concurrent Programming*. Englewood Cliffs, NJ: Prentice-Hall, 1982.

[Bergland, 1981] Bergland, G.D. and Gordon, R.D., Eds. *Software Design Strategies*. Los Angeles: IEEE Computer Society, 1981.

[Bernstein, 1981] Bernstein, A.J. and Ensor, J.R. A Modula based language supporting hierarchical development and verification. *Software—Practice and Experience 11*, Mar. 1981, pp. 237–255.

[Bishop, 1986] Bishop, J. *Data Abstraction in Programming Languages*. Reading, MA: Addison-Wesley, 1986.

[Black, 1986] Black, A., Hutchinson, N., Jul, E., and Levy, H. Object structure in the Emerald system. *SIGPLAN Notices 21*, Nov. 1986, pp. 78–86.

[Bochmann,] Bochmann, G.V. and Joachim, T. The development and structure of an X.25 implementation. *IEEE Transactions on Software Engineering 5*, May 1979, pp. 429–439.

[Boyle, 1979] Boyle, J., Butler, R., Disz, T., Glickfeld, B., Lusk, E., Overbeek, R., Patterson, J., and Stevens, R. *Portable Programs for Parallel Processors*. New York: Holt, Rinehart and Winston, 1987.

[Brinch Hansen, 1969] Brinch Hansen, P. *RC 4000 Software: Multiprogramming System*. Regnecentralen, Copenhagen, Denmark, April 1969; revised version in Brinch Hansen [1973b], pp. 237–286.

[Brinch Hansen, 1971a] Brinch Hansen, P. An outline of a course on operating system principles. *Seminar on Operating Systems Techniques*, Belfast, Northern Ireland, Aug. 1971. In Hoare [1972a], pp. 29–36. Review: *Computing Reviews*, 26738, (1973).

[Brinch Hansen, 1971b] Brinch Hansen, P. Short-term scheduling in multiprogramming systems. *ACM Symposium on Operating System Principles*, Palo, Alto, CA, Oct. 1971. Review: Bibliography 27, *Computing Reviews*, (1972).

[Brinch Hansen, 1971c] Brinch Hansen, P. Multiprogramming with monitors. Pittsburgh, PA: Carnegie-Mellon University, Nov. 1971. Privately circulated.

[Brinch Hansen, 1972a] Brinch Hansen, P. A comparison of two synchronizing concepts. *Acta Informatica 1*, 1972, pp. 190–199. Submitted November 1971. Review: *Computing Reviews*, 26837, (1974).

[Brinch Hansen, 1972b] Brinch Hansen, P. Structured multiprogramming. Invited paper, *Communications of the ACM 15*, July 1972, pp. 574–578. Also in Gries [1978], 215–223. Review: *Computing Reviews*, 24238, 1972.

[Brinch Hansen, 1973a] Brinch Hansen, P. A reply to comments on "A comparison of two synchronizing concepts." *Acta Informatica 2*, 1973, pp. 189–190.

[Brinch Hansen, 1973b] Brinch Hansen, P. *Operating System Principles*, Englewood Cliffs, NJ: Prentice-Hall, July 1973. Submitted May 1972. Translations: Kindai Kagaku Sha, Tokyo, Japan, 1976; Carl Hanser Verlag, Munich, Germany, 1977; SNTL, Prague, Czechoslovakia, 1979; Wydawnictwa Naukowo-Techniczne, Warsaw, Poland, 1979; Naučna Knjiga, Belgrade, Yugoslavia, 1982. Reviews: *Computing Reviews*, 26104, 1973, and 29801, 1976; *American Scientist, Computer, BIT*, 1975; *Embedded Systems Programming*, 1990.

[Brinch Hansen, 1973c] Brinch Hansen, P. On September 6, 1973, I sent Mike McKeag "a copy of a preliminary document that describes my suggestion for an extension of Pascal with concurrent processes and monitors" [McKeag 1991]. No longer available.

[Brinch Hansen, 1973d] Brinch Hansen, P. Concurrent programming concepts. Invited paper, *ACM Computing Surveys 5*, Dec. 1973, pp. 223–245. Review: *Computing Reviews*, 26927 (1974).

[Brinch Hansen, 1974a] Brinch Hansen, P. Concurrent Pascal: a programming language for operating system design. Information Science, Pasadena, CA: California Institute of Technology, Apr. 1974. Referenced in Silberschatz [1977]. No longer available.

[Brinch Hansen, 1974b] Brinch Hansen, P. Deamy—a structured operating system. Information Science, Pasadena, CA: California Institute of Technology, May 1974. Referenced in Brinch Hansen [1975c].

[Brinch Hansen, 1974c] Brinch Hansen, P. A programming methodology for operating system design. Invited paper, *Proceedings of the IFIP Congress 74*, Aug. 1974, pp. 394–397. Amsterdam, The Netherlands: North-Holland. Review: *Computing Reviews*, 27985, 1975.

[Brinch Hansen, 1974d] Brinch Hansen, P. The programming language Concurrent Pascal, (Part I. The purpose of Concurrent Pascal; Part II. The use of Concurrent Pascal). Information Science, Pasadena, CA: California Institute of Technology, Nov. 1974. Revised February 1975. Also in Proceedings of the International Conference on Reliable Software, Los Angeles, CA, April 1975, *SIGPLAN Notices 10*, 305–309 (Part I only); Invited paper, *IEEE Transactions on Software Engineering 1*, June 1975, 199–207; Bauer [1976], 82–110; Gries [1978], 244–261; Wasserman [1980], pp. 465–473; Kuhn [1981], 313–321; Horowitz [1983b], pp. 262–272; Gehani [1988], 73–92. Review: *Computing Reviews*, 29418, 1976.

[Brinch Hansen, 1975a] Brinch Hansen, P. Concurrent Pascal report. Information Science, Pasadena, CA: California Institute of Technology, June 1975. Also in Brinch Hansen [1977b], pp. 231–270.

[Brinch Hansen, 1975b] Brinch Hansen, P. and Hartmann, A.C. Sequential Pascal report. Information Science, Pasadena, CA: California Institute of Technology, July 1975.

[Brinch Hansen, 1975c] Brinch Hansen, P. The Solo operating system. Information Science, Pasadena, CA: California Institute of Technology, June–July 1975. Also in *Software—Practice and Experience 6*, April–June 1976, pp. 141–200; Brinch Hansen [1977b], pp. 69–142. Review: *Computing Reviews*, 31363, 1977.

[Brinch Hansen, 1975d] Brinch Hansen, P. Universal types in Concurrent Pascal. *Information Processing Letters 3*, Jul. 1975, pp. 165–166.

[Brinch Hansen, 1975e] Brinch Hansen, P. Concurrent Pascal machine. Information Science, Pasadena, CA: California Institute of Technology, Oct. 1975. Also in Brinch Hansen [1977b], pp. 271–297.

[Brinch Hansen, 1975f] Brinch Hansen, P. A real-time scheduler. Information Science, Pasadena, CA: California Institute of Technology, Nov. 1975. Also in Brinch Hansen [1977b], pp. 189–227.

[Brinch Hansen, 1976a] Brinch Hansen, P. The job stream system. Information Science, Pasadena, CA: California Institute of Technology, Jan. 1976. Also in Brinch Hansen [1977b], pp. 148–188.

[Brinch Hansen, 1976b] Brinch Hansen, P. Concurrent Pascal implementation notes. Information Science, Pasadena, CA: California Institute of Technology, 1976. Referenced in Powell [1979]. No longer available.

[Brinch Hansen, 1977a] Brinch Hansen, P. Experience with modular concurrent programming. *IEEE Transactions on Software Engineering 3*, Mar. 1977, pp. 156–159.

[Brinch Hansen, 1977b] Brinch Hansen, P. *The Architecture of Concurrent Programs*. Englewood Cliffs, NJ: Prentice-Hall, July 1977. Submitted July 1976. Translations: Kagaku-Gijyutsu, Tokyo, Japan, 1980; Oldenbourg, Munich, Germany, 1981. Reviews: *Choice, Ingeniøren*, 1978; *Computing Reviews*, 33358, *Computer*, 1979; *Embedded Systems Programming*, 1990.

[Brinch Hansen, 1977c] Brinch Hansen, P. Network—a multiprocessor program. *IEEE Computer and Software Applications Conference*, Chicago, IL, Nov. 1977, pp. 336–340. Also in *IEEE Transactions on Software Engineering 4*, May 1978, pp. 194–199. Review: *Computing Reviews*, 33840, 1978.

[Brinch Hansen, 1978a] Brinch Hansen, P. and Staunstrup, J. Specification and implementation of mutual exclusion. *IEEE Transactions on Software Engineering 4*, Sept. 1978, pp. 365–370.

[Brinch Hansen, 1978b] Brinch Hansen, P. Distributed Processes: a concurrent programming concept. *Communications of the ACM 21*, Nov. 1978, pp. 934–941. Submitted September 1977, revised December 1977. Also in Bergland [1981], pp. 289–296; Saib [1983], pp. 500–507; Gehani [1988], pp. 216–233.

[Brinch Hansen, 1978c] Brinch Hansen, P. A keynote address on concurrent programming. *IEEE Computer Software and Applications Conference*, Chicago, IL, Nov. 1978, pp. 1–6. Also in *Computer 12*, May 1979, pp. 50–56; *Selected Reprints in Software*, M.V. Zelkowitz, Ed., IEEE Computer Society, Los Angeles, CA, 1982, pp. 42–48. Review: *Computing Reviews*, 35247, 1979.

[Brinch Hansen, 1978d] Brinch Hansen, P. Reproducible testing of monitors. *Software—Practice and Experience 8*, Nov.–Dec. 1978, pp. 721–729.

[Brinch Hansen, 1980] Brinch Hansen, P. and Fellows, J.A. The Trio operating system. Computer Science Department, University of Southern California, Los Angeles, CA, June 1980. Also in *Software—Practice and Experience 10*, Nov. 1980, pp. 943–948. Review: *Computing Reviews*, 37637, 1981.

[Brinch Hansen, 1981] Brinch Hansen, P. The design of Edison. *Software—Practice and Experience 11*, Apr. 1981, pp. 363–396.

[Brinch Hansen, 1989a] Brinch Hansen, P. The Joyce language report. *Software—Practice and Experience 19*, Jun. 1989, pp. 553–578.

[Brinch Hansen, 1989b] Brinch Hansen, P. A multiprocessor implementation of Joyce. *Software—Practice and Experience 19*, Jun. 1989, pp. 579–592.

[Bryant, 1979] Bryant, R.E. and Dennis, J.B. Concurrent programming. In Wegner [1979], pp. 584–610.

[Burns, 1988] Burns, A. and Davies, G. Pascal-FC: a language for teaching concurrent programming. *SIGPLAN Notices 23*, Jan. 1988, pp. 58–66.

[Bustard, 1988] Bustard, D.W., Elder, J., and Welsh, J. *Concurrent Program Structures*. Englewood Cliffs, NJ: Prentice-Hall, 1988.

[Coleman, 1979] Coleman, D., Gallimore, R.M., Hughes, J.W., and Powell, M.S. An assessment of Concurrent Pascal. *Software—Practice and Experience 9*, Oct. 1979, pp. 827–837. Also in Gehani [1988], pp. 351–364.

[Coleman, 1980] Coleman, D. Concurrent Pascal—an appraisal. In McKeag [1980], pp. 213–227.

[Courtois, 1971] Courtois, P.J., Heymans, F., and Parnas, D.L. Concurrent control with "readers" and "writers." *Communications of the ACM 14*, Oct. 1971, pp. 667–668.

[Courtois, 1972] Courtois, P.J., Heymans, F., and Parnas, D.L. Comments on "A comparison of two synchronizing concepts." *Acta Informatica 1*, 1972, pp. 375–376.

[Dahl, 1972a] Dahl, O.-J., Dijkstra, E.W., and Hoare, C.A.R. *Structured Programming*. New York: Academic Press, 1972a.

[Dahl, 1972b] Dahl, O.-J., and Hoare, C.A.R. 1972b. Hierarchical program structures. In Dahl [1972a], pp. 175–220.

[Deitel, 1984] Deitel, H.M. *An Introduction to Operating Systems*. Revised first edition, Reading, MA: Addison-Wesley, 1984.

[Dijkstra, 1965] Dijkstra, E.W. Cooperating sequential processes. Mathematical Department, Technological University, Eindhoven, The Netherlands, Sept. 1965. Also in Genuys [1968], pp. 43–112.

[Dijkstra, 1967] Dijkstra, E.W. The structure of the "THE"-multiprogramming system. *ACM Symposium on Operating System Principles*, Gatlinburg, TN, 1967. Also in *Communications of the ACM 11*, May 1968, pp. 341–346, and *26*, Jan. 1983, pp. 49–52.

[Dijkstra, 1971] Dijkstra, E.W. Hierarchical ordering of sequential processes. *Acta Informatica 1*, 1971, pp. 115–138. Also in Hoare [1972a], pp. 72–93.

[Discussion 1971] Discussion. Discussion of conditional critical regions and monitors. *Seminar on Operating Systems Techniques*, Belfast, Northern Ireland, Aug. 1971. In Hoare (1972a), pp. 110–113.

[Dunman, 1982] Dunman, B.R., Schack, S.R., and Wood, P.T. A mainframe implementation of Concurrent Pascal. *Software—Practice and Experience 12*, Jan. 1982, pp. 85–90.

[Fellows, 1980] Fellows, J.A. Applications of abstract data types: The Trio operating system. Ph.D. thesis, Computer Science Department, University of Southern California, Los Angeles, CA, 1980.

[Gehani, 1988] Gehani, N. and McGettrick, A.D., Eds. *Concurrent Programming*. Reading, MA: Addison-Wesley, 1988.

[Genuys, 1968] Genuys, F., Ed. *Programming Languages*. New York: Academic Press, 1968.

[Ghezzi, 1982] Ghezzi, C. and Jazayeri, M. *Programming Language Concepts*. New York: John Wiley, 1982.

[Graef, 1979] Graef, N., Kretschmer, H., Löhr, K.-P., and Morawetz, B. How to design and implement small time-sharing systems using Concurrent Pascal. *Software—Practice and Experience 9*, Jan. 1979, pp. 17–24.

[Gries, 1978] Gries, D., Ed. *Programming Methodology—A Collection of Articles by Members of IFIP WG2.3*. New York: Springer-Verlag, 1978.

[Haddon, 1977] Haddon, B.K. Nested monitor calls. *Operating Systems Review 11*, Oct. 1977, pp. 18–23.

[Hartmann, 1975] Hartmann, A.C. A Concurrent Pascal compiler for minicomputers. Ph.D. thesis, Information Science, Pasadena, CA: California Institute of Technology, Sept. 1975. Also published as *Lecture Notes in Computer Science 50*, New York: Springer-Verlag, 1977.

[Hayden, 1979] Hayden, C. Distributed processes: experience and architectures. Ph.D. thesis, Computer Science Department, University of Southern California, Los Angeles, CA, 1979.

[Heimbigner, 1978] Heimbigner, D. Writing device drivers in Concurrent Pascal. *Operating Systems Review 12*, Apr. 1978, pp. 16–33.

[Hoare, 1971a] Hoare, C.A.R. Towards a theory of parallel programming. Queen's University, Belfast, Northern Ireland, Aug. 1971. Privately circulated. Not to be confused with Hoare [1971b] of the same title.

[Hoare, 1971b] Hoare, C.A.R. Towards a theory of parallel programming. *Seminar on Operating Systems Techniques*, Belfast, Northern Ireland, Aug. 1971. In Hoare [1972a], pp. 61–71. Also in Gries [1978], pp. 202–214. Not to be confused with Hoare [1971a] of the same title.

[Hoare, 1972a] Hoare, C.A.R. and Perrott, R.H., Eds. *Operating Systems Techniques*, Proceedings of a seminar at Queen's University, Belfast, Aug. 30–Sept. 3, 1971. New York: Academic Press, 1972.

[Hoare, 1972b] Hoare, C.A.R. Proof of correctness of data representations. *Acta Informatica 1*, 1972, pp. 271–281. Submitted Feb. 1972. Also in Bauer [1976], pp. 183–193; Gries [1978], pp. 269–281; Hoare [1989], pp. 103–115.

[Hoare, 1973a] Hoare, C.A.R. A pair of synchronising primitives. On January 11, 1973, Hoare gave Jim Horning a copy of this undated, unpublished draft [Horning 1991].

[Hoare, 1973b] Hoare, C.A.R. A structured paging system. *Computer Journal 16*, Aug. 1973, pp. 209–214. Submitted Oct. 1972. Also in Hoare [1989], pp. 133–151.

[Hoare, 1974a] Hoare, C.A.R. Monitors: an operating system structuring concept. *Communications of the ACM 17*, Oct. 1974, pp. 549–557. Submitted Feb. 1973, revised Apr. 1974. Also in Gries [1978], pp. 224–243; Wasserman [1980], pp. 156–164; Gehani [1988], pp. 256–277; Hoare [1989], pp. 171–191.

[Hoare, 1974b] Hoare, C.A.R. Hints on programming language design. In *Computer Systems Reliability*, C. Bunyan, Ed., Berkshire, England: Infotech International, 1974, pp. 505–534. Also in Wasserman [1980], pp. 43–52; Hoare [1989], pp. 193–216.

[Hoare, 1976] Hoare, C.A.R. Hints on the design of a programming language for real-time command and control. In *Real-time Software: International State of the Art Report*, J.P. Spencer, Ed., Berkshire, England: Infotech International, 1976, pp. 685–699.

[Hoare, 1978] Hoare, C.A.R. Communicating sequential processes. *Communications of the ACM 21*, Aug. 1978, pp. 666–677. Submitted Mar. 1977, revised Aug. 1977. Also in Wasserman [1980], pp. 170–181; Bergland [1981], pp. 277–288; Kuhn [1981], pp. 323–334; *Communications of the ACM 26*, Jan. 1983, pp. 100–106; Horowitz [1983b], pp. 306–317; Saib [1983], pp. 508–519; Gehani [1988], pp. 278–308; Hoare [1989], pp. 259–288.

[Hoare, 1989] Hoare, C.A.R. and Jones, C.B., Ed., *Essays in Computing Science*. Englewood Cliffs, NJ: Prentice-Hall, 1989.

[Holt, 1978] Holt, R.C., Graham, G.S., Lazowska, E.D., and Scott, M.A. *Structured Concurrent Programming with Operating Systems Applications*. Reading, MA: Addison-Wesley, 1978.

[Holt, 1982] Holt, R.C. A short introduction to Concurrent Euclid. *SIGPLAN Notices 17*, May 1982, pp. 60–79.

[Holt, 1983] Holt, R.C. *Concurrent Euclid, the Unix System and Tunis*. Reading, MA: Addison-Wesley, 1983.

[Holt, 1988] Holt, R.C. Device management in Turing Plus. *Operating System Review 22*, Jan. 1988, pp. 33–41.

[Horning, 1991] Horning, J.J. Personal communication, May 1991.

[Horowitz, 1983a] Horowitz, E. *Fundamentals of Programming Languages*. Rockville, MD: Computer Science Press, 1983.

[Horowitz, 1983b] Horowitz, E., Ed. *Programming Languages: A Grand Tour*. Rockville, MD: Computer Science Press, 1983.

[Howard, 1976a] Howard, J.H. Proving monitors. *Communications of the ACM 19*, May 1976, pp. 273–279.

[Howard, 1976b] Howard, J.H. Signalling in monitors. *IEEE Conference on Software Engineering*, San Francisco, CA, Oct. 1976, pp. 47–52.

[Janson, 1985] Janson, P.A. *Operating Systems: Structures and Mechanisms*. New York: Academic Press, 1985.

[Kaubisch, 1976] Kaubisch, W.H., Perrott, R.H., and Hoare, C.A.R. Quasiparallel programming. *Software—Practice and Experience 6*, July–Sept. 1976, pp. 341–356.

[Keedy, 1978] Keedy, J.L. On structuring operating systems with monitors. *Australian Computer Journal 10*, Feb. 1978, pp. 23–27.

[Kerridge, 1982] Kerridge, J.M. A Fortran implementation of Concurrent Pascal. *Software—Practice and Experience 12*, Jan. 1982, pp. 45–56.

[Kessels, 1977] Kessels, J.L.W. An alternative to event queues for synchronization in monitors. *Communications of the ACM 20*, July 1977, pp. 500–503.

[Kligerman, 1986] Kligerman, E. and Stoyenko, A.D. Real time Euclid: a language for reliable real time systems. *IEEE Transactions on Software Engineering 12*, Sept. 1986, pp. 941–949.

[Kotulski, 1987] Kotulski, L. About the semantic nested monitor calls. *SIGPLAN Notices 22*, Apr. 1987, pp. 80–82.

[Krakowiak, 1988] Krakowiak, S. *Principles of Operating Systems*. Cambridge, MA: MIT Press, 1988.

[Krishnamurthy, 1989] Krishnamurthy, E.V. *Parallel Processing: Principles and Practice*. Reading, MA: Addison-Wesley, 1989.

[Kruijer, 1982a] Kruijer, H.S.M. Processor management in a Concurrent Pascal kernel. *Operating Systems Review 16*, Apr. 1982, pp. 7–17.

[Kruijer, 1982b] Kruijer, H.S.M. A multi-user operating system for transaction processing written in Concurrent Pascal. *Software—Practice and Experience 12*, May 1982, pp. 445–454.

[Kuhn, 1981] Kuhn, R.H. and Padua, D.A., Eds. *Parallel Processing*. Los Angeles, CA: IEEE Computer Society, Aug. 1981.

[Lampson, 1980] Lampson, B.W. and Redell, D.D. Experience with processes and monitors in Mesa. *Communications of the ACM 23*, Feb. 1980, pp. 105–117. Also in Gehani [1988], pp. 392–418.

[Lauer, 1978] Lauer, H.C. and Needham, R.M. On the duality of operating system structures. *International Symposium on Operating Systems*, IRIA, France, Oct. 1978. Also in *Operating Systems Review 13*, Apr. 1979, pp. 3–19.

[Liskov, 1981] Liskov, B., Atkinson, R., Bloom, T., Moss, E., Schaffert, J.C., Scheifler, R., and Snyder, A. CLU reference manual. *Lecture Notes in Computer Science 114*, 1981. Quote: "By the summer of 1975, the first version of the language had been completed. Over the next two years, the entire language design was reviewed and two implementations were produced . . . A preliminary version of this manual appeared in July 1978" (p. III).

[Lister, 1977] Lister, A.M. The problem of nested monitor calls. *Operating Systems Review 11*, July 1977, pp. 5–7.

[Löhr, 1977] Löhr, K.-P. Beyond Concurrent Pascal. *SIGPLAN Notices 12*, Nov. 1977, pp. 128–137.

[Lynch, 1991] Lynch, W.C. Personal communication, Oct. 1991.

[McKeag, 1973] McKeag, R.M. Programming languages for operating systems. *ACM SIGPLAN/SIGOPS Interface Meeting*, Savannah, GA, Apr. 1973. In *SIGPLAN Notices 8*, Sept. 1973, pp. 109–111.

[McKeag, 1980] McKeag, R.M. and Macnaghten, A.M., Eds. *On the Construction of Programs*. New York: Cambridge University Press, 1980.

[McKeag, 1991] McKeag, R.M. Personal communication, Aug. 1991.

[Maddux, 1979] Maddux, R.A. and Mills, H.D. Review of The Architecture of Concurrent Programs. *IEEE Computer 12*, May 1979, pp. 102–103.

[Mattson, 1980] Mattson, S.E. Implementation of Concurrent Pascal on LSI-11. *Software—Practice and Experience 10*, Mar. 1980, pp. 205–218.

[Møller-Nielsen, 1984] Møller-Nielsen, P. and Staunstrup, J. Experiments with a multiprocessor. Computer Science Department, Aarhus University, Aarhus, Denmark, Nov. 1984.

[Narayana, 1979] Narayana, K.T., Prasad, V.R., and Joseph, M. Some aspects of concurrent programming in CCNPascal. *Software—Practice and Experience 9*, Sept. 1979, pp. 749–770.

[Neal, 1978] Neal, D. and Wallentine, V. Experiences with the portability of Concurrent Pascal. *Software—Practice and Experience 8*, May–June 1978, pp. 341–354.

[Nehmer, 1979] Nehmer, J. The implementation of concurrency for a PL/I-like language. *Software—Practice and Experience 9*, Dec. 1979, pp. 1043–1057.

[Nori, 1974] Nori, K.V., Ammann, U., Jensen, K., and Naegeli, H.H. The Pascal P compiler: implementation notes. Institut für Informatik, ETH, Zurich, Switzerland, Dec. 1974.

[Nutt, 1992] Nutt, G.J. *Centralized and Distributed Operating Systems*. Englewood Cliffs, NJ: Prentice-Hall, 1992.

[Parnas, 1978] Parnas, D.L. The non-problem of nested monitor calls. *Operating Systems Review 12*, Jan. 1978, pp. 12–14.

[Perrott, 1987] Perrott, R.H. *Parallel Programming*. Reading, MA: Addison-Wesley, 1987.

[Peterson, 1983] Peterson, J.L. and Silberschatz, A. *Operating Systems Concepts*. Reading, MA: Addison-Wesley, 1983.

[Pinkert, 1989] Pinkert, J.R. and Wear, L.L. *Operating Systems: Concepts, Policies and Mechanisms*. Englewood Cliffs, NJ: Prentice-Hall, 1989.

[Popek, 1977] Popek, G.J., Horning, J.J., Lampson, B.W., Mitchell, J.G., and London, R.L. Notes on the design of Euclid. *SIGPLAN Notices 12*, 1977, pp. 11–12. Quote: "The System Development Corporation is currently implementing Euclid" (p. 12).

[Powell, 1979] Powell, M.S. Experience of transporting and using the Solo operating system. *Software—Practice and Experience 9*, Jul. 1979, pp. 561–570.

[Ravn, 1982] Ravn, A.P. Use of Concurrent Pascal in systems programming teaching. *Microprocessing and Microprogramming 10*, 1982, pp. 33–35.

[Raynal, 1990] Raynal, M. and Helary, J.-M. *Synchronization and Control of Distributed Systems and Programs*. New York: John Wiley, 1990.

[Ringstöm, 1990] Ringstöm, J. Predula: a multi-paradigm parallel programming environment. Department of Computer and Information Science, Linköping University, Linköping, Sweden, Nov. 1990.

[Roubine, 1980] Roubine, O. and Heliard, J.-C. Parallel processing in Ada. In McKeag [1980], pp. 193–212. Also in Gehani [1988], pp. 142–159.

[Saib, 1983] Saib, S.H. and Fritz, R.E., Eds. *The Ada Programming Language*. Los Angeles, CA: IEEE Computer Society, 1983.

[Schneider, 1984] Schneider, H.J. *Problem Oriented Programming Languages*. New York: John Wiley, 1984.

[Sebesta, 1989] Sebesta, R.W. *Concepts of Programming Languages*. Redwood City, CA: Benjamin/Cummings, 1989.

[Shaw, 1981] Shaw, M., Ed. *Alphard: Form and Content*. New York: Springer-Verlag, 1981. Quotes: "The preliminary language report appeared as a . . . technical report [in February 1978]. No final report was issued;" . . . "We curtailed development of the compiler in 1979 when it became clear that another iteration on the language design was necessary" (pp. 191 and 315).

[Silberschatz, 1977] Silberschatz, A., Kieburtz, R.B., and Bernstein, A.J. Extending Concurrent Pascal to allow dynamic resource management. *IEEE Transactions on Software Engineering 3*, May 1977, pp. 210–217.

[Staunstrup, 1978] Staunstrup, J. Specification, verification, and implementation of concurrent programs. Ph.D. thesis, Computer Science Department, University of Southern California, Los Angeles, CA, May 1978.

[Stotts, 1982] Stotts, P.D. 1982. A comparative survey of concurrent programming languages. *SIGPLAN Notices 17*, Oct., pp. 76–87. Also in Gehani [1988], pp. 419–435.

[Tanenbaum, 1992] Tanenbaum, A.S. *Modern Operating Systems*. Englewood Cliffs, NJ: Prentice-Hall, 1992.

[Tennent, 1981] Tennent, R.D. *Principles of Programming Languages*. Englewood Cliffs, NJ: Prentice-Hall, 1981.

[Tsichritzis, 1974] Tsichritzis, D.C. and Bernstein, P.A. *Operating Systems*. New York: Academic Press, 1974.

[Tsujino, 1984] Tsujino, Y., Ando, M., Araki, T., and Tohura, N. Concurrent C: a programming language for distributed multiprocessor systems. *Software—Practice and Experience 14*, Nov. 1984, pp. 1061–1078.

[Turski, 1978] Turski, W.M. *Computer Programming Methodology*. Philadelphia, PA: Heyden, 1978.

[Wasserman, 1980] Wasserman, A.I., Ed. *Programming Language Design*. Los Angeles, CA: IEEE Computer Society, Oct. 1980.

[Wegner, 1979] Wegner, P., Ed. *Research Directions in Software Technology*. Cambridge, MA: MIT Press, 1979.

[Welsh, 1979] Welsh, J. and Bustard, D.W. Pascal-Plus—another language for modular multiprogramming. *Software—Practice and Experience 9*, Nov. 1979, pp. 947–957.

[Welsh, 1980] Welsh, J. and McKeag, R.M. *Structured System Programming*. Englewood Cliffs, NJ: Prentice-Hall, 1980.

[Wettstein, 1978] Wettstein, H. The problem of nested monitor calls revisited. *Operating Systems Review 12*, Jan. 1978, pp. 19–23.

[Whiddett, 1983] Whiddett, R.J. Dynamic distributed systems. *Software—Practice and Experience 13*, Apr. 1983, pp. 355–371.

[Whiddett, 1987] Whiddett, R.J. *Concurrent Programming for Software Engineers*. New York: Halstead Press, 1987.

[White, 1976] White, J.E. A high-level framework for network-based resource sharing. *National Computer Conference*, Montvale, NJ: AFIPS Press, Jun. 1976, pp. 561–570.

[Williams, 1990] Williams, S.A. *Programming Models for Parallel Systems*. New York: John Wiley, 1990.

[Wilson, 1988] Wilson, L.B. and Clark, R.G. *Comparative Programming Languages*. Reading, MA: Addison-Wesley, 1988.

[Wirth, 1971] Wirth, N. The programming language Pascal. *Acta Informatica 1*, 1971, pp. 35–63.

[Wirth, 1977] Wirth, N. Modula: a programming language for modular multiprogramming. *Software—Practice and Experience 7*, 1977, pp. 3–35. Also in Horowitz [1983b], pp. 273–305.

[Young, 1982] Young, S.J. *Real Time Languages: Design and Development*. New York: Halstead Press, 1982.

TRANSCRIPT OF PRESENTATION

Editor's note: Per Brinch Hansen's presentation summarized his paper and we have omitted it, with his permission, due to page limitations. Per asked that the following photographs be included.

The Architecture of Concurrent Programs (1977).

Operating System Principles (1973).

Al Hartman (1973).

Jon Fellows (1982).

Charles Hayden.

Per Brinch Hansen (1978).

TRANSCRIPT OF QUESTION AND ANSWER SESSION

BARBARA RYDER: How would you contrast a language for parallel computation through extending an existing language versus inventing a new programming language?

BRINCH HANSEN: I have designed two parallel programming languages, Concurrent Pascal and SuperPascal, as extensions of an existing language (Pascal). I have also designed two parallel languages, Edison and Joyce, from scratch. The advantage of using an existing base language is that you don't have to explain the well-known sequential concepts. The disadvantage is that you must firmly resist the temptation to "improve" the base language. If you design a completely new language, you can do exactly as you like, but you now have the burden of writing a complete language report. And there are probably only a handful of people in the world who can write a language report as concise as the ALGOL 60 report.

JAY CONNE: Are you familiar with Burroughs ESPOL (Executive System Programming Language) a less constrained version of Burroughs Extended ALGOL? It had concurrent programming constructs for their MCP OS (Master Control Program). Similar functionality was available in the application language, Extended ALGOL.

BRINCH HANSEN: Burroughs Extended ALGOL and ESPOL are mentioned in Elliott Organick's book, *Computer System Organization* (Academic Press, 1973). Both languages extended ALGOL 60 with low-level features for concurrent programming, which were as error prone as assembly language. In Extended ALGOL for the B5700/6700 computers, the termination of a parent process could cause its active decendants to lose their stack space! These languages were designed before anyone understood how to make concurrent programming languages secure.

BIOGRAPHY OF PER BRINCH HANSEN

Per Brinch Hansen was born in Copenhagen, Denmark, in 1938. After receiving the Master's degree in electrical engineering from the Technical University of Denmark in 1962, he joined Regnecentralen, Copenhagen, and participated in the programming of a COBOL compiler under the direction of Peter Naur and Jørn Jensen. From 1967 to 1970, he was responsible for the development of the *RC 4000 multiprogramming system*, one of the earliest systems based on message communication.

In 1970, Alan Perlis invited him to spend a year as a Research Associate at Carnegie-Mellon University, where he wrote the first comprehensive textbook on *Operating Systems Principles*, which appeared in 1973 and was published in six languages.

In 1972, he became Associate Professor of Computer Science at the California Institute of Technology. From then on his main contribution has been the development of programming language concepts for parallel computing. The most influential early idea was the *monitor* concept introduced in his operating systems book. At Caltech, he developed *Concurrent Pascal*, the first parallel programming language based on monitors, and wrote the *Solo* operating system in the language in 1975.

In 1976, Brinch Hansen became Professor and the first chairman of the Computer Science Department at the University of Southern California. He also wrote the first book on parallel programming, *The Architecture of Concurrent Programs*, published in 1977. In recognition of this work, he was awarded the Doctor Technices degree in 1978 by the Technical University of Denmark. In 1982, he was named the first Henry Salvatori Professor of Computer Science at USC.

From 1984 to 1986 he held a professorship in computer science at the University of Copenhagen.

Dr. Brinch Hansen returned to the United States in 1987 as Distinguished Professor of Computer Science at Syracuse University. His recent interest has been the development of programming paradigms for parallel scientific computing.

Dr. Brinch Hansen was elected an IEEE Fellow in 1985, received the Chancellor's Medal at Syracuse University in 1989, and became a citizen of the United States in 1992.

V

Ada Session

Chair: *Michael Feldman*
Discussant: *John B. Goodenough*

ADA—THE PROJECT: The DoD High Order Language Working Group

William A. Whitaker, Colonel USAF, Retired

P.O. Box 3036
McLean VA 22103

ABSTRACT

The Department of Defense (DoD) High Order Language Commonality program began in 1975, with the goal of establishing a single high order computer programming language appropriate for DoD real-time embedded computer systems. A High Order Language Working Group (HOLWG) was chartered to formulate the DoD requirements for High Order Languages, to evaluate existing languages against those requirements, and to implement the minimal set of languages required for DoD use. Other parts of the effort included administrative initiatives toward the eventual goal: specifically, DoD Directive 5000.29, which provided that new defense systems should be programmed in a DoD "approved" and centrally controlled high order language, and DoD Instruction 5000.31, which gave the interim defining list of approved languages. The HOLWG language requirements were widely distributed for comment throughout the military and civil communities worldwide. Each successive version of the requirements, from STRAWMAN through STEELMAN, produced a more refined definition of the proposed language. During the requirement development process, it was determined that the set of requirements generated was both necessary and sufficient for all major DoD applications (and the analogous large commercial applications). Formal evaluations were performed on dozens of existing languages. It was concluded that no existing language could be adopted as a single common high order language for the DoD, but that a single language, meeting essentially all the requirements, was both feasible and desirable. Four contractors were funded to produce competitive prototypes. A first-phase evaluation reduced the designs to two, which were carried to completion. In turn, a single language design was subsequently chosen. Follow-on steps included the test and evaluation of the language, control of the language, and validation of compilers. The production of compilers and a program development and tool environment were to be accomplished separately by the individual Service Components. The general requirements and expectations for the environment and the control of the language were addressed in another iterative series of documents. A language validation capability (the test code suite), and associated facilities, were established to assure compliance to the language definition of compilers using the name "Ada." The name Ada was initially protected by a DoD-owned trademark.

CONTENTS

5.1 INTRODUCTION

The computer programming language, Ada, was the outcome of one part of a rare engineering project initiated and technically managed at the level of the Office of the Secretary of Defense (OSD), specifically, by the Office of the Director of Defense Research and Engineering (DDR&E). This paper describes the early days of the project, in which the development of Ada took place. However, the purpose of the project encompassed more than just another language definition and development. This paper covers the broad project, but not the internal details of the winning language design-team effort led by Jean Ichbiah.

Because the Ada effort was an extraordinarily open project, all the concrete information about it is already a matter of public record. In addition, there have been a number of summaries [Carlson 1980], one in the front of most every Ada book, for instance. This raises the question of what this paper is going to add to this literature. My goal is to add a firsthand perspective of the details that get lost in the textbooks, to provide insight into DoD handling of a project like this, and to point out some of the transient aspects that seemed very important at the time. This will put a very personal slant on the presentation; it is as I remember it.

5.2 BACKGROUND

Because this a personal history, I will give some background about how I became involved. I spent 15 years at the Air Force Weapons Lab (AFWL) at Kirtland AFB, New Mexico, then the largest scientific computing organization in the DoD. Over this period software programs had gotten much larger and more expensive, but tools and support had not kept pace. With each new machine, operating system, or compiler it appeared that all the common, first-level tools had to be regenerated. I wrote various tools half a dozen times over the years, and finally felt like giving up. The tools never got out of the first generation because one could not build with confidence or share with others who had different machines. We did manage to greatly improve the applications codes because each was supported by several people full time. Like everyone else, we did not usually worry if that code was portable, because we initially did all the production in-house. This was fine locally, but bad for the DoD. Finally a very elaborate and successful porting system was implemented, but it was only for applications code.

In the late sixties, several manufacturers were designing the next generation of supercomputers. As a major potential customer, AFWL was involved to determine how our software would mate to their designs, if the code could be structured for their architectures, parallel, pipeline, or otherwise. As a customer, we were in a favored position and had access to the proprietary designs of each manufacturer. I discovered that each was planning a different FORTRAN-like language, extended beyond the 1966 standard. I proposed that it would be more convenient for the customers (namely, the government) and for competitive evaluations, if the language could be common, so far as was feasible. This thought was violently rejected by all parties without any discussion. I considered this attitude to be very short-sighted on the part of the manufacturers. Nevertheless, the thought stayed with me, and might be considered the genesis of the DoD common language program.

When I came to OSD in January 1973, the office to which I was assigned had recently had its name changed from Electronics and Computer Sciences (E&CS) to Electronics and Physical Sciences (E&PS), which showed that computers stood very low in the Services' research pecking order. I was responsible for the Service basic research (6.1) programs, advanced weaponry research (because I was from the Weapons Lab), and any computer activity I could find.

In 1973 I initiated the DoD "Software Initiative" to reduce the "High Cost of Software". (There have been several later "Software Initiatives" in the DoD, but this was the first and must have been well received as a talking point as the name has been reused.) While conducting "math area" research reviews in April, I was struck by the total lack of DoD research into improving the development of operational software. This seemed like a major DoD problem to me but there was no recognition of it by the Service research organizations [Army Research Office (ARO), Office of Naval Research (ONR), and Air Force Office of Scientific Research (OSR)—known collectively as the OXRs]. The Defense Advanced Research Projects Agency (DARPA) supported computer research, but none of it was directed toward operational software, and DARPA was not under my control anyway. The Service research organizations were reasonably responsive to someone who could hold up their money, so I tasked the OXRs to explore the area of software for possible research opportunities. That summer a "Symposium on the High Cost of Software" was organized at the Navy Post Graduate School in Monterey [Monterey 1973].

At the symposium, Barry Boehm of TRW gave the keynote speech. He had just completed a study sponsored by the Air Force Space and Missile Systems Office (SAMSO) on Command and Control Information Processing for the 80s (CCIP-85). Volume 4 [SAMSO 1972] of the study (originally Volume 6)—the one on software—estimated that the Air Force was spending over $1.5 billion a year on software, which was often late and unreliable, and that the costs were rising. This was a shocking conclusion at the time, and the dollar estimates, now seemingly small, were rejected out-of-hand. When the Air Force published the rest of the study, but refused to publish this volume, my boss, George Heilmeier, Director of E&PS, thought that was inappropriate and obtained its release by suggesting that he might find it necessary to copy and distribute such critical information within the Pentagon, if the Air Force did not do so.

At that point I met David A. Fisher from the Institute for Defense Analyses (IDA), a DoD funded "think tank" from which each OSD office could request some support. E&PS asked for an IDA study to validate Boehm's figures. It was not that we doubted the figures, but that we needed all the documentation we could get if we were to initiate a major effort. Further, IDA could draw on Pentagon figures and get a different perspective on software costs. Fisher did the IDA study [Fisher 1974] and substantiated the Boehm figures exactly, but by an entirely different procedure. He so impressed us that he was co-opted into the follow-on project.

We got some agreement that software cost and reliability was a problem, but the question was, what could be done—more specifically—what could be done by OSD? We got the problem passed to the Services in the annual Budget Memorandum of the Secretary of Defense, which is raising it to the "highest level" in the DoD. The question was then, "What programs should OSD enter into to solve the problem?"

We had identified the proliferation of programming languages as having a major impact on costs, or at least, this proliferation made it effectively impossible to do anything to improve the cost picture. At this time, each of the Services had programs to develop unique languages, computer architectures, and hardware. Their previous efforts certainly had not reduced the cost of software, and none of these programs was likely to do so either, but maybe a joint effort could. I figured that a common language for use throughout the DoD would be a first step to building an engineering discipline of software, to supersede the then current "black art." My initial proposal was that a common language would facilitate the development of common tools, techniques, training, and metrics, and would not coerce, but enable, the sort of cooperation and long-term development that characterizes a scientific or engineering culture. Key to the payoff from the project was the expectation that a common language would promote the production and use of common tools and reusable code. Early economic analyses concluded that half the benefit of a single powerful language would be from its technical merits, and half simply from the advantages of commonality.

This was the DoD and it took a while to get organized. During that time (1974) I was encouraged by a number of people; chief among them was Bernie Zempolich of the Naval Air Systems Command (NAVAIRSYSCOM). He had just returned from the Industrial College of the Armed Forces (ICAF), where after graduation he remained as the first civilian Research Fellow. His study was entitled "An Analysis of Computer Software Management Requirements for Operationally Deployable Systems." We interacted when he was the Command Technology Manager for the Navy All Applications Digital Computer (AADC). He became a founding member of the project. In fact, before the working group was established, his pioneering work in this area gave impetus and technical support to the entire DoD thrust. During the early years of the project, he served as secretary and spokesman. He contributed enormously to the early work of the project. These contributions—technical, administrative, and policy—established the future direction of the program. Credit also goes to him for jokingly dubbing the future HOL with the acronym "DOD-1."

5.2.1 Justification

The starting position in 1974, of the Common DoD High Order Language Program, was to produce a minimal number of common, modern, high order computer programming languages for Department of Defense embedded computer systems applications and to assure a unified, well-supported, widely available, and powerful programming support environment for these languages. This was an intuitive statement of the task. To obtain acceptance, a justification had to be made, especially to initiate an effort at the OSD level, rather than the usual Service programs. We had to make sure we were addressing the real problem, rather than just doing what was easy, in order that this be a needs-driven engineering development, not a research exercise.

The total cost of DoD software increasingly attracted the attention of the highest levels of management within the Department of Defense. Cost studies estimated that the then-annual expenditure of funds for software within the DoD was in excess of $3.0 billion dollars (small now, but impressive at the time). A large portion of these growing software costs represented increased performance requirements and the transference of efforts, previously considered a part of the hardware system design. The percentage of this amount that was susceptible to reduction through technical improvements could not be precisely determined. However, there was extensive anecdotal support visible to OSD, in frequent reports of software development troubles, indicating that the percentage would be significant, especially when the indirect costs of schedule slippage and system readiness problems attributable to software development delays and poor reliability were included.

Software costs include the design, development, acquisition, management, and operational support and maintenance of software. Only a small fraction of these tasks are involved with the functions that are defined by the Federal Government as "Automatic Data Processing," those functions that have their exact analogy in the commercial sector and share a common technology, both hardware and software. A much larger fraction, more than 80 percent, of the DoD's computer investment is in computer resources that are embedded in, and procured as part of, major weapons systems, communications systems, command and control systems, etc. In this environment, the DoD found itself spending an even larger share of its systems resources on software.

At this point, I must offer some definitions, and explain how they came about. Computers in the DoD are of two general varieties. Automatic Data Processing (ADP) covers those "stand alone" systems that do ordinary commercial computer jobs: accounting, financial management, payroll, inventory, word processing, etc. The other kind, now popularly called Embedded Computer Systems (ECS), are those "embedded" in aircraft, missiles, tanks, shipboard, etc. An ECS can be a computer-on-a-board, or a special purpose device hardened to heat, cold, gravitational pull (g's) and electromagnetic or nuclear radiation. Or, it may be an ordinary commercial machine operating in the traditional air-conditioned room, indistinguishable from the hardware in accounting.

The distinction is not hardware, but under what set of regulations the computer is procured. Historically there have been two computer hierarchies in the DoD, corresponding to two different responsible Committees of the Congress. ADP is administered under provisions of the Brooks ADP Act (Public Law 89-306) and through Comptroller organizations in the DoD. For these systems, there is a set of rules designed to eliminate duplication and promote competition in that part of the computer industry that concerns itself mainly with the private sector, and deals with roughly interchangeable products and simple economic judgments.

Weapons systems are handled and monitored (oversight), by different Congressional Committees and by different organizational elements in the DoD, responsive to those Committees. At the time of the HOLWG, this was DDR&E at the OSD, and the Service Assistant Secretaries for Research and Development. There was a "5000 Series" of regulations (DoD Directives and Instructions) to govern weapons systems, including their computers. In the early seventies these were generally called "weapons systems computers." A short time later they were called "embedded systems," to convey the message that they also included functions such as control, communications, and intelligence systems, not just bombs and guns. More correctly, the name referred to the fact that they were procured as part of an overall system, not to their being physically "embedded" in a weapon. Nevertheless, the image of "embedded" is strong and this has become the popular expression. Later an Appropriations Act invented the name "mission critical," which is certainly morale boosting anyway. Any attempt to parse these terms out of historical context is doomed.

These distinctions may seem esoteric to an outsider, but within the DoD the great religious conflicts of history pale to insignificance by comparison. The software initiative was specifically for the defense system, developed under the 5000 series of regulations, and originated by the organization (DDR&E) in charge of those systems. However, there was no intent to exclude the ADP applications or their problems. Indeed, there was an active liaison and consideration of this area during the whole process, but all the documents were very carefully worded to make sure they were within the proper administrative scope.

In determining the scope of the problem, we set out to address the "tall pole in the tent," that is, the major portion of DoD software costs associated with Embedded Computer Systems, software integral to defense or weapon systems, including target detection and tracking, weapons direction, communications, command and control, avionics, simulators, test equipment, and other such applications and their run-time support systems. In addition, software that supports the design, development, and maintenance of such systems must be included when identifying total costs. Within this systems environment, the DoD found itself spending an increasingly larger share of its financial and manpower resources on software. Although programming language commonality throughout the DoD would not, by itself, make software less expensive, it would enable a large number of technical and managerial initiatives leading to such savings. And it was something that was uniquely within the scope and power of OSD to implement.

Another consideration was the impact of software on hardware costs. We were entering a period in which there was the expectation that systems would become much more responsive and flexible because they were controlled by "easily changeable" software, rather than hardwired hardware, practically impossible to modify. This enormous advantage would be realized only if software really was modifiable. There was a growing experience that assembly language "spaghetti software" was becoming more difficult to modify and maintain. Clearly some change in the way we were doing business was necessary.

The ultimate hardware advantage from software is the potential for switching out a piece of obsolete and expensive hardware for new smaller, cheaper technology. Much of the obsolete hardware in the field was being kept because the software would run on no other machine. It may be that the contractors were not eager to change this situation, because such old hardware required a lot of expensive maintenance and, probably, only the one who made it could keep it up. But the DoD was left with systems for which the yearly maintenance cost might exceed the cost of modern hardware.

A corollary to this situation is that, when hardware was selected at the beginning of a major development, it was sure to be obsolete 10 years later when the system was in the field. Unfortunately it could not be effectively upgraded. These weapons systems implications are not unlike those for general ADP; however, the application must color the requirements. Software transportability (like reuse) was a major factor to the DoD, but not to an individual manager with a three-month horizon.

Although significant progress had been made in achieving commonality in computer hardware and software for scientific and business applications, the physical and real-time constraints imposed on embedded computer systems placed technical obstacles in the path of commonality efforts for these systems. In addition, in the case of scientific and business systems, there had been a powerful incentive for the computer industry to develop standards (FORTRAN and COBOL) as a marketing tool. This incentive had not been present in the development of embedded computer systems for the DoD. On the contrary, it could be argued that short-term management goals (contractor and government) encouraged proliferation.

Another factor in the decision was that at that time, the DoD had a greater influence on software technology than on hardware. Some years previous, the DoD was the major innovator and consumer of the most sophisticated computer hardware possible. By 1974, the DoD represented only a small fraction of the total commercial market. In software, that unique position still existed. A significant fraction of the total software industry was devoted to DoD related programs and that was true in an even larger proportion for the more advanced and demanding systems. Thus, there was both an opportunity and a responsibility in the software arena, which was long past for hardware.

To summarize, the logic of the initiative was as follows: the use of a high order language reduces programming costs, increases the readability of programs and the ease of their modification, facilitates maintenance, etc., and generally addresses many of the problems of life cycle program costs. A modern powerful high order language performs these tasks and, in addition, may be designed to serve in the specification phase and provide facilities for automatic test. A modern language is required if real-time, parallel processing, and input/output portions of the program are to be expressed in high order language rather than assembly language inserts, which destroy most of the readability and transportability advantages of using an HOL. A modern language also provides error checking, more reliable programs, and the potential for more efficient compilers.

Many of the advantages of a high order language can be realized only through computer tools. A total programming environment for the language includes not just compilers and debugging aids, but text editors and interactive programming assistance, automatic testing facilities, extensive module libraries, and even semi-automatic programming from specifications. Universal use of these tools can significantly reduce the cost of software and lead to the development of more powerful tools. The average DoD programmer's tool box was rather bare in the 1970s. Because of the difficulty of preparing these tools for each new language and machine and operating system, and the time involved, only the very largest projects had been able to assemble even a representative set. Although in many cases, development of tools can be shown to be desirable in the long run, day-to-day pressures not to perform the tool development activities usually prevailed. The use of a common high order language across many projects, controlled at some central facility, allows the sharing of resources in order to make available the powerful tools that no single project could generate. It makes those previously generated tools available at the beginning of a project, reducing start-up time.

Reducing the number of languages supported to a minimal number, therefore, should provide the greatest economic benefit. There are costs associated with supporting any particular project and general costs of supporting the language. For a sufficiently large number of users, presumably the basic cost would be proportionally less. Perhaps 200 active projects contributing to a single support facility may not be much cheaper than two facilities each supporting 100 projects. There are, however, unique advantages to having a single military computer language. For a single language, one could reasonably expect that language to be supported on new computers with a compiler (based upon the experience of the British with their common language effort, CORAL). Such support is not a reasonable expectation with five or ten common languages. Indeed, for a single common language, its use in DoD, and the provision of tools by the DoD, could make it a popular candidate for use elsewhere. The multitude of languages adopted by the military in the past (excepting FORTRAN and COBOL) did not receive this sort of acceptance. A single powerful supported high order language might even be expected to influence academic curricula, improving the training, not so much of individual programmers, but the understanding and capabilities of the general engineering community for support of DoD programs.

During 1974, elements in each of the Military Departments independently proposed the adoption of a common programming language for use in the development of major defense systems within their own Departments and undertook efforts to achieve that goal. Those efforts included the Army's Implementation Language for Real-Time Systems study, the Navy's CS-4 effort, and the Air Force's High Order Language Standardization for the Air Force study. In addition, the Defense Communications Agency had pursued the "Development of a Communications Oriented Language." The fact that each of the Military Departments independently sought a standard military language to supplement COBOL and FORTRAN illustrated the need for a DoD-wide coordinated approach, as well as its timeliness.

Nevertheless, the proposal for language commonality across DoD was extremely radical at the time, and initially met almost universal opposition. In fact, it was regarded as unrealistic to expect to use a high order language for embedded systems. It may be surprising to hear that a consensus did not mandate a common high order language for embedded systems much earlier. There are, however, a number of managerial and technical constraints that acted against this. For many DoD systems, severe timing and memory considerations were dominant, governed by real-time interaction with the exterior environment. Because of these constraints, and restrictions in developmental cost and time scale, many systems opted for assembly language programming. This decision was influenced by past experience with poor quality compilers and the fact that an assembler routinely comes with the machine, whereas the compiler and its tools usually must be developed after the project has begun. The advantages of high order languages, however, were compelling, and more systems turned to them. Because of limitations of available high order languages, the programs generated often included very large portions done in assembly code and linked to an HOL structure, negating many of the HOL advantages.

Further, many systems found it convenient to produce their own high order language or some incompatible dialect of an existing one. Because there was no general facility for control of existing languages, each systems office did the configuration control on its language and compilers, and continued this for their particular dialect through the entire maintenance phase of the system. This had the effect of reducing the contractual flexibility of the government, and restricting competition in maintenance and further development. This lack of commonality negated many advantages of high order languages including transportability, sharing of tools, the development of very powerful tools of high efficiency and, in fact, not only raised the total cost of existing tools, but in some cases essentially priced them out of the market. Development projects were very poorly supported and forced to live with technology far below what should have been state-of-the-art.

The target for a major language project was to be DoD "software in the large." This is often given a limited interpretation, namely that DoD programs are individually large, which is certainly true and drives many of the technical requirements on the language. But, the fact that the DoD has hundreds of such large programs provides an opportunity for economies of scale that are potentially much greater than the sum of individual projects. The problem is not just that of producing a subsystem of 200,000 lines of code, but of the servicing of a "system" that is all the code produced by the DoD for (by 1990) $30 billion per year ("programming in the very large"). This path drives other requirements and properties, like machine independence, which forces the validation requirement and the rejection of subsets. But these advantages can be realized only if the technology is applied with consistency over the whole of the DoD, and an even larger community if possible. So a strong position from the DoD was vital to the plan.

5.2.2 Coordinating Committees

The process of building a constituency for the Software Initiative began with the setting up of a fairly informal Weapons System Software Committee between DDR&E and OSD Installations and Logistics (I&L), the branch responsible for maintenance. I represented DDR&E and R. D. "Duke" Hensley, who made a very large contribution in this starting year of 1974, represented I&L. Meetings involved discussions of the software problem and possible actions. From this, grew the nucleus of the DoD language project and the coordination that led to the establishing memo.

In December 1974 this Committee was renamed the Weapon System Software Management Steering Committee (SMSC) in a memo "Management of Weapon System Software" by M. R. Currie, A. I. Mendolia, and T. E. McClary and added representation from the Office of the Assistant Secretary of Defense (Comptroller) (ASD (Comp)), to study the general area of software management for weapon systems. This committee was later renamed the Management Steering Committee for Embedded Computer Resources (MSC-ECR). Barry DeRoze from I&L became the first Chairman. He was the prime mover in the OSD arena for coordination of the Directives. This position was later occupied by H. Mark Grove, who shepherded the formation of the Ada Joint Program Office (AJPO) in 1980.

The enabling memo [Currie 1975a] (Figure 5.1) for a DoD High Order Language Working Group (HOLWG) was issued in January 1975, but by that time the work was fairly well under way. The technical work proceeded in the HOLWG. The SMSC drafted DoD Directive 5000.29 [DoD 1976b], which formally established the committee and renamed it as the MSC-ECR. Then the HOLWG formally became a subcommittee of the MSC-ECR, and in November 1976, a HOLWG Charter was formalized, long after the fact. It all sounds a little baroque. These dates, which are the "facts" of history that an outsider might find in the records, have nothing to do with what was actually going on. There was a studied and logical progression, but the paper trail was constructed after the fact to please those who needed boxes filled.

The MSC-ECR took care of much of the general administrative coordination. It wrote and coordinated DoD Directive 5000.29 and DoD Instruction 5000.31. On January 31, 1977, the MSC-ECR issued an Issue Paper 77-1 recommending authorization to proceed with the preliminary design phase for a common language, with $300,000 from each Service. Throughout the lifetime of the program, monies were allocated as necessary. Although prudent management was exercised, this was recognized as an important program, and there was never any funding or timing constraint imposed from above, after approval, to proceed to the next step.

The MSC-ECR also sponsored economic analyses of the benefits of language commonality. This was a necessary step in the formal process. The MITRE Corporation performed an economic analysis of language commonality [Clapp 1977] under the auspices of the MSC-ECR and ASD(I&L). An automated decision analysis sponsored by DARPA was generated by Decision and Design Incorporated [Fox 1978] to investigate introduction strategies and benefits. The HOLWG internally generated a program to quantify economic benefits [HOLWG 1977c]. These were targeted to questions of the expectation of savings to the Department of Defense resulting from the successful completion of this program. They further examined various introduction strategies and rates. Significant savings were demonstrated, and these were magnified by rapid introduction. Savings of hundreds of millions to tens of thousands of millions of dollars were independently derived.

As a result of these studies, and of general concerns, the program was exceptionally well supported at OSD. Monies were always made available once a decision was made. However, because this program was a new start and not in the five-year plan, this often meant persuading the Services to divert funds from other projects. No schedule was imposed from above, but there was a feeling that this was a fleeting moment of opportunity.

5.3 HOLWG

The intent was to have a common real-time language to replace the existing mix, while maintaining the standards of FORTRAN and COBOL, the success of which had provided impetus to this consolidation program. Further, to assure nonproliferation during this effort, all other implementations of new high order programming languages for R&D programs were halted. The January 1975 DDR&E memo (Figure 5.1) to the Military Departments directed "A working group should be formed from representatives of your Departments and chaired by ODDR&E," establishing the HOLWG, and making it the agent for this effort. This initial authorization was the first major milestone of the project; others are listed in Figure 5.14.

At this point it is necessary to explain something about the workings of OSD. Contrary to what one might expect, OSD does not rule the DoD and the Services with an iron rod. The main control is money, and the DoD has very little money of its own—most of the money is appropriated to the Services. But the Service funding passes through DoD on the way, and the distribution process could get very slow and sticky, so the Services do listen. Nevertheless, OSD actions can usually be characterized as coordination. If OSD memos, such as that setting up the HOLWG, sometimes seem to be expressed mildly, one should not misjudge their import. There are fairly few directing memos. They, like Directives and Instructions, are extensively coordinated before they are issued, not only within OSD but with the Service recipients. Characteristically, the action is agreed to by all parties,

FIGURE 5.1

DIRECTOR OF DEFENSE RESEARCH AND ENGINEERING
WASHINGTON, D. C. 20301

28 Jan 1975

MEMORANDUM FOR ASSISTANT SECRETARIES OF THE MILITARY DEPARTMENTS (R&D)

SUBJECT: DoD Higher Order Programming Language

In studying the computer software problems of the DoD, it has become clear that standardization in higher order programming languages is necessary. The advantages in training, instrumentation, module reutilization, program transportability, etc. are obvious. In business and scientific applications, COBOL and FORTRAN have evolved as standards, but in the areas of weapon systems, command and control, test equipment, etc., the DoD has supported a large number of limited use developments, many for a single project.

That each of the Military Departments has independently proposed a standard military language to supplement COBOL and FORTRAN testifies to the need. We concur that such standard language efforts should do much to reduce the high cost of software to the DoD and further suggest that the benefits would be multiplied if a single common military language were the outcome. We call upon the Military Departments to immediately formulate a program to assure maximum DoD software commonality. A working group should be formed from representatives of your Departments and chaired by ODDR&E. This group will investigate the requirements and specifications for such commonality, compare with existing DoD efforts, and recommend adoption or implementation of the necessary common language or languages.

My office has informally discussed this in some detail with various Service Offices, primarily USACSC, NAVAIR-360 and AFSC/XRF. We have been working closely with OASD(Comp) and OASD(I&L) who will also participate in the study. Until the matter is resolved, we do not intend to support any further implementation of new higher order programming languages in R&D programs. As this may impact proposed program schedules, we regard the completion of this task as a matter of urgency and request you name working group representatives within one week of the date of this letter. You may have your representatives contact Lieutenant Colonel William A. Whitaker, OX7-4197.

Malcolm R. Currie

not necessarily without some arm twisting, before a memo is signed. Everyone knows the intent and what is expected, even when the memo is worded gently and with delicate political sensitivity. So a memo may mean more than it says.

The membership of the HOLWG consisted of a chairman, myself, appointed by and representing DDR&E, plus representatives of each Military Department appointed by, and reporting to, the Departmental Assistant Secretaries (Research & Development), plus other components and agencies to be called upon to present their comments and specific expertise. (Specific membership of the HOLWG is discussed later.) Throughout the program, authority came from DDR&E and the memos were the form of communicating this authority. These memos may appear to be mild, not what one might think of as a military order, but in the DoD this is the way most things get done. Each DDR&E memo was a major milestone in the effort.

The organization and procedures of the HOLWG were up to the chairman—anything I could make work. The only reporting was to DDR&E and I made the reports. This sounds dictatorial, and to a large degree it was, but it only worked as long as I held it together. In fact, it was a consensus operation. Every formal vote that the HOLWG ever took was unanimous! That is not to say that there were not many lively discussions and opposing views, but I waited until everybody agreed on a course of action before posing a formal vote. The question was usually not "Which of these is your favorite?," but "Which should be the HOLWG choice?" Under those conditions, the HOLWG functioned smoothly.

The HOLWG was not a committee of language designers. It was a group representing the users. It eventually contracted for language designers, but design was not its only function. The exact working membership of the HOLWG was never a fixed list. I was the only name mentioned in the DDR&E memo, as Chairman. After that, the HOLWG was constituted from members nominated by the Services. There is a list in the Charter of November 1976, but it is *pro forma* and does not necessarily represent the workings of the group.

Each of the Services has its own personality and that was reflected in the personnel assigned to the HOLWG. The Army is very formal and works on orders, often from the Adjutant General (TAG). Major Brehault, from Army Computer Systems Command (USACSC), was the first representative, replaced on his reassignment by Major Ben Blood. Dr. Serafino Amoroso, from Ft. Monmouth, was brought in as a technical representative of the Electronics Command (USAECOM then CORADCOM).

For the Air Force, whoever is in the office responsible is the representative. Lt. Col. John H. Manley, from the Air Force Systems Command (AFSC), was their first representative, shortly followed by Major Thomas H. Jarrell. Samuel A. Di Nitto of Rome Air Development Center (RADC/ISIS) gave technical support. Col. Robert Ziernicki and Lt. Col. John Marciniak provided headquarters (AFSC/XR) support. Eventually Major Al Kopp represented the Air Force to Ada, and Ada to the Air Force.

The Navy is much more complex, because it is organized along the lines of major platform types (air, surface, and land). Bernard Zempolich, then with the Naval Air Systems Command (NAVAIR), was an original member, as was Robert Kahane. Lt. Col. Joseph G. Schamber represented the Marine Corps during the entire life of the HOLWG. CDR Jack D. Cooper was subsequently designated representative by the Naval Material Command (NAVMAT). LCDR David C. Rummler, from ONR-London, facilitated our early European contacts and meetings. Warren Loper, of Naval Ocean Systems Center (NOSC), was brought in as technical expert, and no one worked harder or contributed more than he.

The Agencies were represented by William Carlson (DARPA), Paul Cohen (Defense Communication Engineering Center of the Defense Communications Agency—DCA), and Steve Squires, followed by Terry Ireland (National Security Agency—NSA).

Dave Fisher (IDA) was the technical secretariat of the HOLWG and ran all aspects of the technical operation.

This project was conceived of as an effort in international cooperation and a number of Europeans were involved, in the meetings, working full-time in Washington, or coordinating and supporting from Europe:

For the United Kingdom Ministry of Defence (UK MOD), the Royal Signals and Radar Establishment (RSRE—Malvern) contributed the efforts of Nick Neve in the United Kingdom and Philip Wetherall who spent a year in the United States working within the DoD structure on the Ada effort.

For the Federal Republic of Germany (FRG), Dr. Horst Clausen (Industrieanlagen-Betriebsgesellschaft mbH—IABG) was in close contact with the project and attended HOLWG meetings. Dr. Eberhard Wegner (Gesellschaft für Mathematic und Datenverarbeitung) provided governmental coordination. Dipl. Phys. Peter Elzer (Physics Instiutut, Erlangen) spent a year in the United States working on the program. His presence was particularly gracious, as he was responsible for PEARL, the language that the Germans had proposed for an International Standard, with which the HOLWG product would be in direct competition.

For France, Nicholos Malagardis (Bureau d'Orientation de la Normalization en Informatique) and Jean Robert (CAP—Sogeti Logiciel) were especially helpful, and P. A. Parayre representing the Ministre de Marine made many trips to attend HOLWG meetings.

Each of these countries was fully consulted and a voting member of the HOLWG. (At this time there was an initiative called the "Two Way Street," which was to promote Defense acquisition cooperation between the United States and its NATO allies. The DDR&E once told me that he thought that the HOLWG program was the only example that was working.)

Other Federal organizations were kept informed of the HOLWG progress but were not involved programmatically to any significant degree. By contrast, members of the standards community for COBOL, FORTRAN, and PL/I were major contributors to the HOL investigations. The Navy COBOL Validation Facility had a major input for validation concepts.

5.3.1 Requirements

The HOLWG was established to: (a) formulate the requirements for common DoD high order languages, (b) compare those requirements with existing languages, and (c) recommend adoption or implementation of the necessary common languages. This was the original charge in the DDR&E HOLWG memo, that is, this was a direction taken before the formal organization of the HOLWG. There was work, and a number of memos to the Services, before the January, 1975, founding of the HOLWG.

The first charge to the High Order Language Working Group was to establish requirements. In terms of reference, the working group was to consider general purpose computer programming languages. This was a limited goal and did not include either generalized requirements languages or very specific applications packages, which are formulated like languages but have only limited access to the capabilities of the computer. Such applications-specific languages include simulation programs, such as SIMSCRIPT or GPSS, and ATLAS, an automatic test equipment language that is for communications between the test engineer and the technician, and is the DoD standard for maintenance tests.

There were "requirements for requirements," part of the background of any engineering project, well known by those involved, but often unappreciated by those on the outside. In discussions, we often forget to state some of these because they seem so obvious, but I will mention a few that did not seem to be understood in the academic community.

The new language project was a DoD engineering development and had to live in the DoD environment. This project did not set out to break new ground nor invent new computer science, nor was its purpose to showcase particular ideas of language design, but it did have to push some ideas into concrete form. It had to produce a powerful and complete language, or it could not satisify the requirement of being able to implement whole systems with machine independence (for portability), avoiding the extensive assembly language inserts that plagued the then current DoD HOL applications.

The character set discussion is a prime example of a misunderstanding of the basic environment. For the DoD there was never any question. From 1955 to 1975 we had progressed from IBM 026 to 029 keypunches, and there still were old ones in the field, and many machines used 6-bit characters! To be able to write programs in that environment, there was a requirement for the language to work with a limited character set. The comments from the major Computer Science Departments universally condemned this "step back." They said, "We must have 256 characters." They all had local systems with many interesting properties, each incompatible with everything else in the world, which they assumed were available to everyone. From DARPA, I had a chance to inspect a large number of such facilities and never could get much recognition for the fact that they did not represent the real world. (Note that the world never did go to APL, or even PL/I, keyboards. The ISO LATIN-1 proposal for Ada 9X has no relation to anything academically proposed for an 8-bit set in 1976. Even now, any extension beyond LATIN-1 is ambitious.) They would say that *anybody* can do it, but for a common language the requirement is that *everybody* can do it. The purpose of HOLWG was a common DoD language. (This leads to a standard language, but the converse is not necessarily true. One may need a standard even for very limited use.) In the absence of such practical considerations, the reliability goal would have demanded that there be no distinction between upper and lower case in identifiers. Jean Robert of CAP, the largest software house in Europe, and LTPL-E, vetted the final 55-character set requirement for European acceptance.

Another requirement in this area was for fixed point arithmetic. Although large scientific machines had provided floating point hardware for decades, such facilities had not reached military weapons computers. Many had difficulty understanding a fixed point requirement that was in the language, for purely practical, not mathematical, reasons, prompting a special study [Fisher 1978a] in this area. (An extraordinary situation was generated when Headquarters Air Force, contrary to recommendations from the field, adopted, in 1976, a standard language for avionics software that provided only floating point arithmetic. At that time the Air Force had no avionics computer with floating point hardware! [Whitaker 1990])

There were other common language metarequirements. For example, the language must be an applications user language. This went against certain academic concepts of a mathematically minimalistic formulation such as ALGOL 68. The language must also be "complete" in the sense of the user being able to write all usual programs without having to resort to assembly language or local extensions. It had to have real-time capability and it had to be set up to produce programs for the bare machine in a missile, without support of an operating system. It also was required to support large Command and Control systems, so it had to have a file input/output system, however messy that might be.

The applications for this language were the large, long-lived, and lethal systems of the DoD. The users were the military and contractor personnel developing and maintaining these systems. These were professionals in a professional environment, not students or hobbyists. They would have various levels of talent and experience, but would be expected to have discipline, management, and adequate hardware and software support. The environment was one of large teams. The systems were compiled, so there was no requirement for the language to be interpretable on-the-fly, although there was nothing against that. Resources should be sufficient that one could support a compiler that could do extensive checking. The cost of compilers and the computer resources they demanded would be offset by the benefits of reliable systems and reduced maintenance.

Because the developed systems were to be long-lived, maintenance and modification of the software would cost several times as much as initial development. Readability was much more important than writability, a requirement contrary to those advocating the "economy of expression" that leads to incomprehensible C and APL code. Maintainability also argued for rigid interfaces and powerful compiler checking.

There were also certain "non-negotiable" demands of the users. The Navy insisted on a "goto" being written in as a basic requirement. There were, and may be still are, those in the Navy not enthusiastic about the project, so we paid that price for coordination.

The technical goals of such a high order language that were agreed upon, at that time, were the following:

- The language should facilitate the reduction of software costs. The costs must be reckoned on the total burden of the life cycle including maintenance, not just the cost of production or program writing.
- Transportability allows the reusing of major portions of software and tools from previous projects, and the flexibility for a system to change hardware while keeping the same software.
- The maintenance of very long-lived software in an ever-changing threat situation requires responsiveness and timely flexibility.
- Reliability is an extremely severe requirement in many Defense systems and is often reflected in the high cost of extensive testing and verification procedures.
- The readability of programs produced for such long-term systems use is clearly more important than coding speed, or writability.
- The general acceptability of high order languages is often determined by the efficiency and quality of the compiled code. Although rapidly falling costs of hardware may make this difficult to substantiate in the abstract, each project manager will compare the efficiency of the object code produced against an absolute standard of the best possible machine language programming. Very little degradation is acceptable.

These goals and "ilities" can be accepted, but they do not lend themselves to a quantifiable or rational assessment of programming languages. We needed to establish criteria that were sufficiently explicit, determining the capability, but not necessarily the form, of the language. Rigorous definition of the exact level of requirement proved difficult. The method chosen for the preliminary requirements was to define this level by illustration. The HOLWG considered the problem from their experience of other developments, and found that it was going to be difficult to do justice to the task. In fact, it was hard to even get started. Finally, a group from the HOLWG just sat down and proposed a set of requirements. There was no claim that they were self-consistent or agreed to by all. But there had to be a start and this was done by February 1975, so the program was under way.

David Fisher acted as the Secretariat for the HOLWG, and so became the one who assembled, sifted, correlated, and integrated the requirements, because during the first couple of years, this was the primary action and output of the HOLWG. Fisher had designed machines at Burroughs and taught at Vanderbilt University, before joining IDA. His position was that of the technical heart of the project. It would be improper to say that he "wrote" the requirements, as this was an integration effort of Service needs with worldwide technical input. However, it was he that produced the final requirements documents; they were his offspring.

The resulting document, entitled STRAWMAN [HOLWG 1975a], was forwarded to the Military Departments, other government agencies, the academic community, and industry. In addition, a number of technical experts outside the United States were solicited for comments. The European community was especially responsive—particularly valuable as language research had been more active there than in the United States over the previous decade. ONR London paid several academics (Dijkstra, Hoare, Wirth, ...) to provide inputs, but we got more valuable aid from European industry.

A May 1975 DDR&E memo [Currie 1975b] (Figure 5.2) reaffirmed the HOLWG goals to define and implement the minimum number of HOLs to satisfy the needs of the DoD, and spelled out a program to evaluate candidates and prove the feasibility of meeting requirements, followed by implementation. The Military Departments were tasked to fund these efforts.

As a result of the widespread review of the STRAWMAN, the HOLWG received input and commentary from individuals and organizations representing many different areas of application within the DoD. There were mixed reviews. Some said it was too specific, others that it was too vague. So we knew we were on the right trail. The input and comments received by the HOLWG were codified and merged into a more complete, but still tentative, set of language requirements. This document was entitled the WOODENMAN [HOLWG 1975b], and it, in turn, was widely distributed for comment. Note that the thrust of the project, at this time, was to measure and compare language candidates. WOODENMAN was 88 typed pages, and contained considerable description of project goals, as well as the desired characteristics of languages to support these goals. The following text example from WOODENMAN shows the level of the document. Figure 5.3 illustrates a discussion of conflicts between goals and the proposed weighting and resolution. Figure 5.4 gives a few examples of the required characteristics.

A third generation set of requirements was subsequently produced, the TINMAN [HOLWG 1976] of January 1976. TINMAN was synthesized from the formally stated requirements of the Military Departments, submitted to DDR&E by the respective Service Assistant Secretaries for Research and Development and worldwide technical input. It was formally blessed by the Services. The stated characteristics provided a design philosophy, indicated general structure, and constrained certain detailed properties of the common language; but they did not identify specific language features, consider the tradeoffs among various design and implementation mechanisms, nor demonstrate the feasibility of achieving all the characteristics simultaneously. TINMAN retained some discussion of goals, and Figure 5.5 provides an example. The format for the needed characteristics is illustrated in Figure 5.6, which is closer to a requirement specification, but with discussion. At this point we had a fairly firm grip on the problem; further versions were to be refinements.

One significant point agreed to, was that the requirements for all Services and applications addressed were consistent with a single language. Up to this point, there had been an argument about "the minimum number of languages." There was a general concern that, although a single common language was a goal, it was not technically feasible. The requirements exercise addressed this as a major consideration. We had been faced with the universal, and very strongly stated, opinions of the Services that different user communities had fundamentally different requirements with insufficient overlap to permit a common language among them. Such communities included avionics, weapons guidance, command and control, communications, training simulators, etc. In addition to the embedded computer applications, even the scientific and the financial management communities were solicited for requirements for the sake of completeness. The surprising result was that the requirements so generated were identical. It was impossible to single out different sets of requirements for different communities. All users needed input/output, real-time capability, strong data typing for compiler checking, modularity, etc. Upon reflection, the reason for this was clear; the surprise was historical, stemming from the observation that previously the different communities had adopted different

FIGURE 5.2

DIRECTOR OF DEFENSE RESEARCH AND ENGINEERING
WASHINGTON, D. C. 20301

2 MAY 1975

MEMORANDUM FOR Assistant Secretary of Defense (Comptroller)
Assistant Secretary of Defense (I&L)
Assistant Secretaries of the Military Departments (R&D)
Director, Telecommunications and Command and Control Systems

SUBJECT: DoD Higher Order Programming Language Working Group

This is to update you on the progress of the DoD Working Group on Higher Order Programming Languages. This group, composed of OSD members and designated representatives of the Services, was established pursuant to my memo of 28 January 1975. Their goal is to establish a minimal number of common higher order programming languages for utilization throughout the DoD. In the past, the multitude of pertinent DoD applications has caused a proliferation of special languages and, with them, excessive and extensive software costs.

The first step in attaining the goal of the Working Group is to firmly establish the requirements for higher order languages from all possible users, even those for applications which are believed to have programming requirements not satisfied by any existing higher order language. Detailed requirements from those programs which use the existing common languages, COBOL and FORTRAN, are also desired, although there is no intent to supersede these languages.

To initiate this process, the Working Group has drawn up a requirements "strawman", i.e., a list of possible requirements which, while indicative of the thinking of the committee, are primarily illustrative of the level of information needed. This strawman provides the Service representatives on the Working Group with a definitive example to use in their subsequent inquiries with users. A number of the requirements in the strawman have been selected to be provocative in order to stimulate comment. An additional purpose of the strawman is to elucidate the differences between objectives (economy and readability), requirements (the minimum primitive operators or capabilities for parallel processing), and features (which distinguish individual languages, but are not necessarily fundamental requirements).

The Working Group intends to distribute a request to all possible users for inputs so that the eventual common language/languages resulting from this effort will be directly keyed to foreseeable programs.

I request that you give all possible assistance to the Service representatives of the Working Group when they solicit such inputs. It is expected that these inputs will be informal initially, but eventually, a consolidated and coordinated official input will be required from each Service.

Malcolm R. Currie

Attachment
DoD HOL Strawman

FIGURE 5.3

Example from WOODENMAN—conflicts in criteria.

B. PROGRAMMING EASE VS. SAFETY FROM PROGRAMMING ERRORS

There is a clear tradeoff between programming ease and safety. The more tolerant the programming language and the less it requires in specifications of the intent and assumptions of the programmer, the easier the coding task. A language which does not require declaration of variables, permits any type of structure of data to be used anywhere without specification, allows short cryptic identifiers, has large numbers of default conventions and coercion rules to permit the use of any operator with any operand, and is capable of assigning meaning to most strings of characters presented as a program will be very easy to use, but also easy to abuse. Safety from errors is enhanced by redundant specifications, by including not only what the program is to do, but what are the author's intentions. and under what assumptions. If everything is made explicit in programs with the language providing few defaults and implicit data conversions, then translator can automatically detect not only syntax errors but a wide variety of semantic and logic errors. Considering that coding is less than one sixth the total programming effort and that there are major software reliability and maintenance problems, this tradeoff should be resolved in favor of error avoidance and against programming ease.

C. OBJECT EFFICIENCY VS. PROGRAM CLARITY AND CORRECTNESS

Two apparently opposing views have been suggested. One, that a simple analysis of either development or life cycle costs shows that reliability, modifiability and maintainability are the most important factors and consequently clarity and correctness of programs must be given consideration over efficiency of the object code which only increases the cost of computer hardware (which is relatively cheap compared to software). In fact, if programs need not work correctly they can easily be implemented with zero cost. The other view points out real problems and applications within DOD software in which the machine capability is fixed and in which object code efficiency is of utmost importance and must be given preference over other considerations.

These views are not inconsistent with regard to the effort on programming language selection. In the vast majority of cases clarity and correctness is more important that is object code efficiency and the programming language should do the utmost to aid the programmer in developing correct and understandable programs within constraints of reasonable object efficiency. In most cases language features which improve clarity do not adversely affect efficiency. In many cases additional information supplied to clarify a program may permit the compiler to use optimizations not applicable in more general cases. There remain, however, special situations in which efficiency is critical. The language should not prohibit access to machine features necessary to accomplish those optimizations when the need arises. Thus, the major criteria in selecting a programming language should be clarity and correctness of programs within the constraint of allowing generation of extremely efficient object code when necessary.

FIGURE 5.4

Example from WOODENMAN—needed characteristics.

K. SYNTAX

1. The source language should be free format, should allow the use of mnemonically significant identifiers, should be based on conventional forms, should be simple uniform and probably LR(1), should not provide unique notations for special cases, and should not permit abbreviation of identifiers or key words.

Clarity and readability of programs should be the primary criteria for selecting a syntax. Each of the above points can contribute to program clarity. The use of free format, mnemonic identifiers and conventional forms allows the programmer to use notations which have their familiar meanings, to put down his ideas and intentions in order and form that humans think about them, and to transfer skills he already has to the solution of the problem at hand. A simple uniform language reduces the number of cases which must be dealt with by anyone using the language. If programs are difficult for the translator to parse, they will be difficult for people. Similar things should use the same notations with the special case processing reserved for the translator and object machine. The purpose of mnemonic identifiers and key words is to be informative and increase the distance between lexical units of programs. The use of abbreviations eliminates these advantages for a questionable increase in coding ease.

2. The user should not be able to modify the source language syntax. Specifically, he should not be able to modify operator hierarchies, introduce new precedence rules, define new word forms of define new infix operators.

If the user can change the syntax of the language then he can change the basic character and understanding of the language. The distinction between semantic extensions and syntactic extensions is similar to that between being able to coin new words in English or being able to move to another natural language. Coining words requires learning those new meanings before they can be used but at the same time increases the power of the language for some application area. Changing the grammar (e.g., using French) however, undermines the basic understanding of the language itself, changes the mode of expression, and removes the commonalities which obtain between various specializations of the language. Growth of a language through definition of new data and operations and the introduction of new words and symbols to identify them is desirable but there should be no provision for changing the structure of the language. The language should, of course, provide sufficiently general forms that they can be adopted to new possibly unforeseen situations. Neither does this preclude associating new meanings with existing infix operators.

3. The syntax of source language programs should be composable from a character set suitable for publication purposes, but no feature of the language should be inaccessible using the 64 character ASCII subset.

FIGURE 5.4

(Cont.)

```
A common language should use notations and a character set convenient
for communicating algorithms, programs, and programming techniques
among its users. On the other hand, the language should not require spe-
cial equipment (e.g., card readers and printers) for its use. The use
of the 64 character ASCII subset will make the language compatible with
the Federal information processing standard 64 character set, FIPS-1,
which has been adopted by the .S.A. Standard Code for Information Inter-
change (USASCII).

4.   The language definition should provide the formation rules for
identifiers and literals. These should include a language defined break
character for use internal to identifiers and literals.

   ...
```

language approaches. Further investigation showed that the origin of this disparity was primarily administrative, rather than technical. The Navy was organized into branches for the employment of airplanes, surface ships, and submarines. The Air Force had ground electronics systems (ESD), aircraft systems (ASD), and space systems (SAMSO). Each thought it had to have its own special language. Upon this discovery, the result that a single set of requirements would satisfy a broad set of users became less of a surprise. This did not, however, establish that a single language could meet all the stated requirements, only that a language meeting all of the requirements would satisfy the users' needs.

Also, for TINMAN, we properly began computer automation. This, and all subsequent documents, were machine processed and printed on a "laser printer" (Xerox XGP), high tech in 1975. DARPA had the hardware to handle this. Also, through DARPA, as the OSD agent, HOLWG was officially authorized mail franking privileges. The combination of these conveniences made it possible for the HOLWG to rapidly disseminate information and documents.

During 1976, the TINMAN was subjected to a thorough review for consistency and technical feasibility. The document was circulated to more than 1,000 individuals in the industrial and academic communities. An international workshop was held at Cornell University in the fall of 1976 [Williams 1977] to illuminate the current state-of-the-art of programming language design and implementation. In January 1977, a new version was issued called the IRONMAN [HOLWG 1977b]. This was much the same set of requirements as the TINMAN, modified slightly for consistency, feasibility, and clarity, but presented in an entirely different format. The TINMAN was discursive and organized around general areas of discussion. The IRONMAN, on the other hand, was very brief and organized like a language manual. It was essentially a specification with which to initiate the design of a language, still sufficiently general so as not to constrain a particular structure of the language, but rather, to define its capabilities. The IRONMAN was revised in July, 1977 [HOLWG 1977d], mainly to clarify the intent, but also to correct the few errors and inconsistencies that had been identified.

The requirements documents can be viewed as an evolving series. The early ones have a great deal of explanation about the program, motivation, and explanation. Those that were following the program, presumably followed the evolving arguments, and the versions might be considered

FIGURE 5.5

Example from TINMAN—general goals.

READABILITY/WRlTABILITY

The other major advantage initially claimed for high order languages was that they were easier to read and write, being closer to natural language than is machine code. Claims in this direction were sometimes carried to an extreme and some were promoted so highly that their advocates would have you believe that the coder need not know anything about the machine, simply write out the requirements in English. History does not always support these claims. Many such languages advocated on this basis now are the ones who have the most specialized programmers as their users. The DoD environment is sufficiently large and specialized that the allocation of personnel specifically for software is the rule anyway and there is no strong requirement to eliminate other specialists in this area. This is in contradistinction to a very small commercial firm which may have insufficient demands to justify a full-time programming staff.

Our requirement for readability and writability is therefore primarily among specialists. The desire to communicate with a computer system in natural language is an entirely different one in the DoD and involves query languages or applications programs outside the scope of this high order language effort.

Readability is clearly more important to the DoD than writability. The program is written once, but may have to be read dozens of times over over a period of years !or verification, modification, etc. This is certainly true all weapons systems applications and even most of our scientific and simulation programs are very long lived. This requirement is very much different from one which might be generated, for instance, in a university environment when a program may have a life of only a few months and a single person working on it.

Ease of writing is not an inconsiderable goal but one which may be promoted through intelligent terminals, preprocessors, interactive systems, etc. The language evaluation should favor readability where conflict arises.

cumulative, in that sense. There was a rationale for each requirement; early on the documents concentrated on the goals, whereas later the rationales were primarily technical discussions expanding on the implications of the specific requirements.

Requirements decisions made in 1975 proved essentially correct, and remained valid for more than a decade. Fixed point, **goto**, and the selected character set were requirements that were questioned outside the DoD, but supported inside. Fixed point may now be obsolescent as a result of the cheap hardware implementing the IEEE floating point standard [IEEE 1985]. The **goto** is essentially never used, but causes no harm. A more extensive standard character set is only now becoming a possibility.

FIGURE 5.6

Example from TINMAN—needed characteristics.

H. SYNTAX AND COMMENT CONVENTIONS

1. General Characteristics
2. No Syntax Extensions
3. Source Character Set
4. Identifiers and Literals
5. Lexical Units and Lines
6. Key Words
7. Comment Conventions
8. Unmatched Parentheses
9. Uniform Referent Notation
10. Consistency of Meaning

H1. The source language will be free format with an explicit statement delimiter, will allow the use of mnemonically significant identifiers, will be based on conventional forms, will have a simple uniform and easily parsed grammar, will not provide unigue notations for special cases, will not permit abbreviation of identifiers or key words, and will be syntactically unambiguous.

Clarity and readability of programs will be the primary criteria for selecting a syntax. Each of the above points can contribute to program clarity. The use of free format, mnemonic identifiers and conventional forms allows the programmer to use notations which have their familiar meanings to put down his ideas and intentions in the order and form that humans think about them, and to transfer skills he already has to the solution of the problem at hand. A simple uniform language reduces the number of cases which must be dealt with by anyone using the language. If programs are difficult for the translator to parse they will be difficult for people. Similar things should use the same notations with the special case processing reserved for the translator and object machine. The purpose of mnemonic identifiers and key words is to be informative and increase the distance between lexical units of programs. This does nat prevent the use of short identifiers and short key words.

H2. The user will not be able to modify the saurce language syntax. Specifically, he will not be able to modify operator hierarchies, introduce new precedence rules, define new key word forms or define new infix operator precedences.

FIGURE 5.6

(Cont.)

If the user can change the syntax of the language, then he can change the basic character and understanding of the language. The distinction between semantic extensions and syntactic extensions is similar to that between being able to coin new words in English or being able to move to another natural language. Coining words requires learning those new meanings before they can be used, but at the same time increases the power the language for some application areas. Changing the grammar, (e.g., Franglais, the use of French grammar with interspersed English words) however, undermines the basic understanding of the language itself, changes the mode of expression, and removes the commonalities which obtain between various specializations of the language. Growth of a language through definition af new data and operations and the introduction of new words and symbols to identify them is desirable, but there should be no provision for changing the grammatical rules of the language. This requirement does not conflict with E4 and does not preclude associating new meanings with existing infix operators.

H3. The syntax of source language programs will be camposable from a character set suitable for publication purposes, but no feature of the language will be inaccessible using the 64 character ASCll subset.

A common language should use notations and a character set convenient for communicating algorithms, programs, and programrning techniques among its users. On the other hand, the language shoufd not require special equipment (e.g., card readers and printers) for its use. The use of the 64 character ASCII subset will make the language compatible with the federal information processing standard 64 character set, FIPS-1, which has been adopted by the U.S.A. Standard code for Information Interchange (USASCll). The language definition will specify the translation from the publication language into the restricted character set.

H4. The language definition will provide the formation rules for identifiers and literals. These will include literals for nurnbers and character strings and a break character far use internal to identifiers and literals.

...

5.3.2 Foreign Relations

This project, from the beginning, was considered to be international in scope. It was recognized that Europe had much to contribute technically, and that successful outcome to the effort would be as useful to European military and industrial computing, as it would to that of the United States.

LTC Philip H. Enslow of the Army Research Office in London set up an Army Programming Conference in April 1975, attended by European computer scientists, including C. A. R. Hoare, Jacob Palme, David Parnas, Ian Pyle, John Webb, and Brian Wichmann, to provide input to the HOLWG effort.

LCDR David C. Rummler from the European branch of the Office of Naval Research facilitated our early European contacts and meetings, and eventually returned to the United States to serve on the HOLWG.

The most successful national common language effort to date was that of the British Ministry of Defence (MOD) in specifying the language CORAL 66 for all MOD real-time applications. From extensive interchanges with the MOD, the HOLWG received invaluable technical and managerial insight into a major national language standardization effort. Furthermore, the MOD assigned Philip Wetherall, a senior technical expert, to be resident in Washington providing both technical input to the HOLWG and liaison with the MOD. Wetherall's contribution was particularly important because he was there during the critical period in the evolution of the requirements.

The MOD also provided a two-week course in Washington, on the CORAL 66 language and its implementations, to members of the HOLWG and its contractors, giving valuable insight into a particularly successful program. As part of this cooperative effort, MOD made available CORAL compilers resident on a computer located at the Royal Signals and Radar Establishment (RSRE, Malvern) in the United Kingdom, but accessible through the ARPANET for the use of U.S. evaluation teams. The ARPANET connection was inaugurated during a visit to RSRE by Her Royal Highness Queen Elizabeth II. Her Majesty sent a message of greetings to the members of the HOLWG from her net account, **EIIR**, by pressing a red velvet Royal carriage return. Because the address list was long, it took about 45 seconds for the confirmation to come back, 45 seconds of dead air. Prince Philip remarked, joking respectfully, that it looked like she broke it.

The International Purdue Workshops (IPW) on Industrial Computer Systems, chaired by Professor Ted Williams, was another group that was working in the same area. It is interesting to note how many independent efforts we found, once we had established the program. I believe that the wide publicity of the DoD program enabled us to bring together the talents of those who were working in the various independent communities, to the benefit of all. We contacted Williams on the recommendation of a Navy official, who had been his roommate in college. Their subgroup, Long-Term Procedural Language, especially the European branch, LTPL-E, had as a goal the generation of a language much like the proposed DoD HOL. The Commission of the European Communities (CEC) had adopted the concept of a common international industrial language for the European Economic Community (EEC). There was an active relationship between the LTPL-E, the EEC, and the HOLWG. LTPL-E was closely analogous to the HOLWG in trying to satisfy the requirements of a number of sovereign countries with diverse application areas. It was at an EEC sponsored LTPL-E meeting that I first met Dr. Jean Ichbiah. He became interested and involved in the program, and was the eventual winner of the design competition. In October 1977, the International Purdue Workshops resolved to cooperate fully with the HOLWG program. In November 1977, Christopher Layton, Director, Science and Technology Directorate, CEC, announced, at an international conference, that the CEC would evaluate the HOLWG efforts for adoption.

The International Standards Organization (ISO) set up a Working Group (Programming Languages for Industrial Processes—TC 97/SC 5/WG 1) on real-time languages at about this time. The early thrust was to establish a standard for real-time FORTRAN, but the Group included an international group of experts in the area, who were invited to participate in the HOLWG effort. They made enormous contributions to the program. The technical body representing the American National Standards Institute (ANSI) in forming WG 1, was the US portion of IPW.

The German and French governments initiated procedures to standardize on existing high order languages, PEARL and LTR, respectively, in a move similar to DoD's establishment of approved HOLs in 5000.31. HOLWG involved the people responsible for these languages and they supported us unselfishly, in spite of the prospect of our program competing with theirs.

The Japanese government, through its Ministry of Information Technology and Industry, subsidized a consortium of the computer industry to produce a software production environment, central to which was to be a common programming language, CTL-B. The Comite Consultatif International Telegraphique et Telephonique (CCITT) developed a common high order language for international use in communications. This was done at the same time as the HOLWG effort, and I was told off-line by members of the developing committee that they made a policy not to communicate with the competition. In any case, they never answered any of my letters. CHILL was the product of that development.

Just to keep things legal, the U.S. State Department was consulted on all of the HOLWG international contacts and advised on the progress of the program. One has to proceed with due care in Washington. We made it clear that this was an open effort and responded to all correspondence. Several on our mailing list were from behind the Iron Curtain, although we did not get any official queries from the USSR at that time.

5.3.3 Administrative Action

The scope of the project went beyond the technical aspects of languages and included direction to the Services, and the follow-on of language control and implementation. To start with, we had to lay the groundwork leading to the adoption of a common language for the DoD. First we established the principle that the use of high order language was advantageous and technically feasible (not a trivial selling job in itself, because the vast majority of weapons system code was being done in assembly language, or a covering HOL with most of the code in embedded assembly language), and that standardizing on a minimum number of DoD HOLs was a reasonable goal. Given this premise and the several Service language programs, it was prudent to stop all other language work to concentrate on the one program. This is the sort of position that has an overwhelming force of logic and to which everyone must acquiesce. However, this does not mean that they will go out of their way to support it, or indeed that they will not oppose it.

The first administrative action was the issuing of DoD Directive 5000.29 (April 26, 1976) [DoD 1976b] which specified that "DoD approved high order programming languages will be used to develop Defense systems software unless it is demonstrated that none of the approved HOLs are cost effective or technically practical over the system life cycle...Each DoD approved HOL will be assigned to a designated control agent ... ." Thus, the use of high order languages was established and indeed very strongly mandated, as life cycle costs are usually dominated by maintenance where the high order languages have considerable advantage over assembly language. Only approved high order languages were to be used, thereby reducing the proliferation; and further, these languages were to be controlled by central facilities.

DoD Instruction 5000.31 (November 1976) [DoD 1976c], "Interim List of DoD Approved High Order Programming Languages," designated the "approved" languages called for by 5000.29 and assigned control responsibility. (Note that this was the "interim" list. The declared intention was to reduce to the DoD common language(s).) COBOL and FORTRAN would be controlled by the Office of the Assistant Secretary of Defense (Comptroller), acting with the National Bureau of Standards and the American National Standards Institute, TACPOL by the Army, CMS-2 and SPL/1 by the Navy, and JOVIAL J3 and J73 by the Air Force. All these languages were exactly those nominated by the Services. This is an example of how things work. We wanted to reduce the number of languages from several hundred to a handful. The only way to not argue forever and lose the moment was to let the Services have their way on their own selections unrestrained. The resulting list may have been flawed [Whitaker 1990], but you go along to get along.

Formalization of these languages was a major step forward and recognized for the first time the corporate commitment of the Department of Defense to provide support for languages in the long term. It stopped the proliferation of languages in that all new systems were to be programmed in one of these languages, but there was no intent that already existing programs be redone or that the projects change if already committed to a language. There were limitations. The languages themselves were selected from the then-present Service inventories and were not modern powerful languages. They were generally deficient in the areas of tools and in availability of compilers. Further, only the seeds of control were established here. It would be some time before we reached the goal of a well-supported and controlled language. The direction of the program was reported to the Military Departments in a 10 May, 1976, memo from DDR&E [Currie 1976] (Figure 5.7), which also authorized and requested funds for the next phase.

5.3.4 Evaluations

The next step, beginning in June 1976, was the evaluation of existing languages against the integrated set of requirements. Ideally, it was expected that the language requirements should be met through selection or modification of existing languages. A number of languages were proposed as potential candidates to meet the common language requirements as stated in the then current *Department of Defense Requirements for High Order Computer Programming Languages "TINMAN"* [HOLWG 1976]. Subsequently, each of these candidate languages was evaluated to determine the degree of compliance with the TINMAN requirements. In addition, a number of other languages, although not full candidates, were examined because they contained special features and technological innovations.

The languages chosen were:

- Widely used, standard languages such as COBOL, FORTRAN, and PL/I.
- Languages specifically designed for DoD embedded computer systems applications such as those which were later chosen for the interim standard list (example: TACPOL, CMS-2, J-73), and those widely used elsewhere for similar applications such as HAL/S and CORAL 66.
- Those languages which best represented modern computer science techniques such as Pascal, ALGOL 68, and SIMULA 67.
- Other languages were also evaluated but in a less formal fashion. They were nominated as "interest items" during the progress of this work, for example, LIS, EUCLID, and RTL-2.

The following languages received formal evaluations: ALGOL 60, ALGOL 68, CMS-2, COBOL, CORAL 66, CS-4, ECL, EUCLID, FORTRAN, HAL/S, JOVIAL J-3B, JOVIAL J-73, LIS, LTR, MORAL, RTL/2, Pascal, PDL/2, PEARL, PL/I, SIMULA 67, SPL/1, TACPOL.

Evaluations were conducted under contracts funded and administered by the Military Departments or by other interested parties such as the British MOD. All candidate languages were evaluated by more than one contractor, and each contractor evaluated several languages, thereby providing a technical crosscheck on the individual evaluations. The general statement of work for all contractors was drawn up by the HOLWG. It specified that for each language requirement, the contractor was to determine the degree of compliance of each of the candidate languages, to comment on the feasibility of modifying the language to bring it into compliance, and to identify features in excess of the requirements. In addition, the statement of work contained a provision for the contractors to comment in detail on the technical feasibility and strength of each requirement, based on their examination of the languages as well as their own corporate experience, to be input for revising the TINMAN. This led to the update of requirements to IRONMAN [HOLWG 1977b] in January 1977, but the differences

FIGURE 5.7

DIRECTOR OF DEFENSE RESEARCH AND ENGINEERING
WASHINGTON, D. C. 20301

10 MAY 1976

MEMORANDUM FOR THE ASSISTANT SECRETARIES OF THE MILITARY DEPARTMENTS (RESEARCH AND DEVELOPMENT)

SUBJECT: DoD High Order Language Program

References: a. My memos on Software and DoD Higher Order Programming Language, dated 3 December 1974, 28 January 1975, 2 May 1975

b. DoD Directive "Management of Computer Resources in Major Defense Systems"

To reduce the high and rising costs of software programs in weapon systems, the referenced memoranda (a) formed a Software Steering Committee to study the problem; (b) established a High Order Language (HOL) Working Group to provide maximum DoD software commonality; (c) stopped implementation of new high order programming languages; and (d) established a program to delineate software requirements. The following guidance is provided to clarify the present goals and status of the program, and to indicate appropriate directions for the continuation of this program.

- o The present goal is to define and implement the minimum number of high order languages that will satisfy the needs of the various DoD communities.
- o Other work in progress to improve present high order languages can continue, in contrast to work on implementing new high order languages, which is to be discontinued.
- o The first phase of this program has now been completed with the merging of Service requirements, as provided by your memoranda, into a consolidated DoD set. This document is attached.
- o The second phase of the program will consist of evaluating (1) various candidate language approaches against these requirements, and (2) the feasibility of modifying the language forms to meet these requirements.
- o The third phase of this program will consist of a six month effort of $1.8 million to present preliminary specifications for common language selection.

FIGURE 5.7

(Cont.)

- o The final phase will involve the implementation of these selections.

I request that $300,000 of FY 76/7T funds be made available by each Military Department to address the second phase of this program. This phase consists of a program of four month's duration in which at least two programs will be issued by each Military Department to perform this work. A dozen existing languages, selected by the Services, will be included, and each contractor will study several languages such that each language will be covered by at least two contractors. At the completion of this phase, I request that the Working group and technical representatives of the Military Departments evaluate and recommend, via the Management Steering Committee for Embedded Computer Resources, the minimum language approaches that will satisfy the Defense requirements.

Until a set of new high order languages are developed under this program, language proliferation should be avoided. Accordingly, a set of existing languages will be approved in the interim for new weapon systems as prescribed in DoD Directive . I request that the Military Departments nominate by 1 July 1976 existing high order computer programming languages for interim approval. Such nomination should include the detailed formal specification of the language, a list of several major current users and a suggested facility for control of the language and its tools.

I believe this project is of vital importance in alleviating the current DoD software problem and making possible the management initiatives, technology advances, and fiscal savings which we are looking for in this area. I again call upon your help in keeping this program moving.

signed

Malcolm R. Currie

Attachment:
DoD Requirements for High Order
Computer Programming Languages

cc: DARPA
DTACCS
ASD(I)
ASD(C)
ASD(I&L)

between the TINMAN and the IRONMAN were so minor as not to affect the conclusions of the evaluation.

There were also a number of separate formal evaluations made of individual languages by other organizations having unique experience with a particular language, or its designers ("fathers"). In addition, other less formal input included evaluations of requirements different from the TINMAN, examination of special features in certain languages, and briefings and exchange of reports.

Other languages were considered for formal evaluation, but were not included because preliminary examination led one to believe that they would not meet the requirements so were not viable candidates for the purposes of the DoD. One such language was C. At that time, DARPA was working with Western Electric/Bell Labs on UNIX, contractually supporting some DARPA contractors and other government facilities using UNIX. It was the evaluation policy to have the owners provide assessments of their own languages, in addition to the contracted evaluations, so HOLWG took advantage of this connection between DARPA and Bell Labs to request their cooperation. When Bell Labs were invited to evaluate C against the DoD requirements, they said that there was no chance of C meeting the requirements of readability, safety, and the like, for which we were striving, and that it should not even be on the list of evaluated languages. We recognized the truth in their observation and honored their request.

In January 1977, a report on the consolidation of evaluations was prepared by a subcommittee chaired by Serafino Amorosa, using in-house personnel, the contractors participating in the evaluation, and special consultants [HOLWG 1977a]. This publication included the complete text of each evaluation report and a resolution of any conflicting reports from contractors evaluating the same language. It provided a summary of the technical evaluations and an assessment of the applicability of each language to the requirements. There was a determination whether any existing candidate so nearly met the requirements as to have it chosen intact, or with simple modifications, and thereby forego a major design phase in the program. The results from the Evaluation Subcommittee were :

- Among all the languages considered, none was found that satisfied the requirements so well that it could be adopted as the common language.
- All evaluators felt that the development of a single language satisfying the requirements was a desirable goal.
- The consensus of the evaluators was that it would be possible to produce a language within the current state-of-the-art meeting essentially all the requirements.
- Almost all the evaluators felt that the process of designing a language to satisfy all the requirements should start from some carefully chosen base language.
- Without exception, the following languages were found by the evaluators to be inappropriate to serve as base languages for a development of the common language: FORTRAN, COBOL, TACPOL, CMS-2, JOVIAL J-73, JOVIAL J-3B, SIMULA 67, ALGOL 60, and CORAL 66.
- Proposals should be solicited from appropriate language designers for modification efforts using any of the languages, Pascal, PL/I, or ALGOL 68 as a base language from which to start. These efforts should be directed toward the production of a language that satisfied the DoD set of language requirements for embedded computer applications.
- At some appropriate time, a choice should be made among these design efforts to determine which are most worthy of being continued to completion.

The definition of a base language that evolved during this procedure called for one which was familiar to the community so that a number of contractors could use it as a starting point and provide an audit trail, which could be used by government personnel to compare between contractors. For instance, PEARL or HAL/S could be considered modifications in the PL/I family towards the desired real-time language. This definition did not imply that those deemed inappropriate as a base language were not perfectly adequate for their operational use at the time. Indeed, the presence of COBOL and FORTRAN, to which the DoD has been committed on a long-term basis, belied that implication. Nevertheless, these languages would not have been good starting points for a new language as they had basic inconsistencies with the requirements, or had been superseded by more appropriate starting points.

"Base" must be distinguished from languages influencing Ada. There was impact, not just in language design but in the requirements:

> FORTRAN was significant because that was the successful language—we are still apologizing for FORTRAN features not in Ada (intrinsic math functions (e.g., SQRT, SIN, etc.), interpretive I/O (i.e., with dynamic formatting)), no matter how proper the exclusion;
>
> COBOL pioneered validation—made sure we did not allow the subsets that in 1976 made COBOL systems difficult to validate and compare (may be right for COBOL but not for the purposes of Ada)—data handling, and readability;
>
> JOVIAL and CORAL were languages of major military users whose experiences made considerable contribution to the requirements;
>
> Pascal contributed mostly its syntactic form.

The unanimous recommendations of the evaluation committee, adopted unanimously by the HOLWG were:

- That none of the evaluated languages met the requirements to such an extent as to be selected with little or no modifications for a DoD-wide standard;
- That it appeared feasible within the state-of-the-art to construct a single language to meet essentially all the requirements;
- That the construction of such a language would most likely be done by modification (albeit substantial) of an existing language. The approaches recommended as a basis for further development were the language families of PL/I, Pascal, and ALGOL-68.

A sidelight on the evaluation was the form of the distributed report. The data consisted of 2,600 pages of individual and group reports. They were typed and handwritten; many were on metric-sized paper. I felt a responsibility to make sure that everybody involved had a complete record; that was the way the program was run. Conventional methods were impossible; we had no staff or secretarial help for a normal retyping and publication. I took what I know to be an innovative step (because I had to continue to fight for this two years later). I had the whole report put directly on microfiche. (Although this may not be the favorite medium in some homes, it is now the media used for most secondary distribution of Government technical documentation. Fiche was the only feasible medium at the time. After 1979, essentially everything was electronic.) I reproduced a sufficient number of copies for the HOLWG distribution and the masters went to the Defense Documentation Center (DDC, now DTIC) for outside requests as [HOLWG 1977a]. This was bending the system and it took some talking to bring it off, but I thought it was a real breakthrough. The later Phase I and Phase II design evaluations, up to 5,600 pages, were also produced only in fiche. There was never what one could call a hard copy document.

After formal adoption of the Program Management Plan by the Management Steering Committee for Embedded Computer Resources, the recommendations of the evaluation committee, the IRONMAN requirements, and the Statement of Work for the language design were forwarded to the MSC-ECS for coordination. This coordination was signed at an MSC-ECS meeting on 31 January, 1977.

5.4 LANGUAGE DESIGN

5.4.1 Phase I

The next phase of the program was the award of contracts for the "language modification and preliminary design." Alternatively this might be considered an elaborate feasibility proof. The design was to be informal but fairly complete, and to consider the cost and nature of implementations. Although we realized that the product was to be a new language, we got in the habit of using the term "language modification," referring to the plan to start from an existing base. This preliminary design was done from the IRONMAN revised requirements and was to draw upon the previous work done on evaluations. The syntax was to be fully specified with complete, but informal, semantics. An analysis of the feasibility and cost of implementation was to be produced.

The driving concern of the HOLWG was to assure that the design was guided by a responsible principal investigator, and to preclude "design by committee." On the other hand, picking a single contractor to do the job and trusting to luck would have been imprudent. The procurement was through multiple competitive contracts, with the best products to be selected for continuation to full rigorous definition and developmental implementation. These were contracts with three phases and options to down select (drop competitors) at each break after evaluation and public review. This procurement technique was advocated by Bill Carlson, modeled on an architectural competition.

Monies for these contracts were only from funds of the Services. It is important to make the point that this was a joint program of the Services, not a DARPA program. Although I was working at DARPA and was strongly supported by the Director, George Heilmeier, we were working for DDR&E on this project. DARPA was represented on the HOLWG as a DoD Agency, but there was no DARPA contract money involved during the time I was there. However, DARPA did provide personnel and the major support of the ARPANET. This project was run almost entirely over the net, perhaps the first independent project to have been.

DARPA served as a funnel to collect the monies provided by the Services for these contracts into one pot for administrative convenience. Service funds were transferred on Military Interagency Purchase Requests (MIPRed) to DARPA which issued ARPA Order 3341 to the Defense Supply Service-Washington (DSS-W), the procuring agent, which actually signed contracts and dispersed payments. The individual at DARPA who was actually in charge of all further HOLWG contractual activities was Bill Carlson of the Information Processing Technology Office (IPTO). He was formerly an officer in the Air Force computing center in the Pentagon, so had wide experience with military computing. At this time, he was responsible for a large DARPA university research program, giving him unequaled access to the academic computing community. He was responsible for most of the innovation in the contracting process and for the daily management of the contracts. He particularly represented the computer science and non-military communities to the HOLWG, and his public relations efforts made sure that they were welcomed in the process.

The Statement of Work (SOW) was approved in March 1977, and a Request for Proposal (RFP), Solicitation No. MDA903 77 R 0082, was released in April 1977. The DSS-W buyer was

Stephan R. Bachhuber. This effort was unusual in that foreign bidders were actively encouraged, and there were several. The quality of these bids was exceptional. I have evaluated thousands in my career, and these had the highest quality, as a group, of any that I have experienced. In fact, I was approached by several well-known firms that told me that in the normal course of business they would have bid, but that this procurement was too important and that others could do a better job. I have never, before or after, heard of such a recommendation for a government program.

The proposals were evaluated by government technical teams, and in August 1977, four contracts were awarded to produce competitive prototypes of the common high order language. There were fourteen bids (some teaming), both U.S. and foreign. The four successful contractors were CII-Honeywell Bull, Intermetrics, SofTech, and SRI-International.

Although different approaches were offered, all four winning contractors proposed to start from Pascal as a base. This restricted the products in form, but would make it easier to compare the results. Any of the three different base languages was acceptable, so the outcome was coincidental. It should be noted that the requirements against which the language was being designed were not those driving Pascal and the result was not be expected to be a superset of Pascal.

The contracts had the normal time constraints. The project had no hard deadlines, but contract administration demands certain adherence to schedules when they are laid out. The philosophy was that we had to do the job right; there was no timetable imposed from above. We did feel an urgency to get the job done while the time was right. We set our own internal schedule and this came out to be very accurate. We scheduled the date of completion of competition and selection of the winning design two years in advance, before the design contracts were let, and met it to within two days.

During this phase, an advisory committee of military users was established. This advisory committee, with experience from their particular applications areas, helped evaluate those difficult to quantify, but tangible, attributes such as readability, writability, and acceptability by the military users.

The products of Phase I, the preliminary designs, were received in February 1978. The considerable interest that this project generated in the outside community made it possible to seek technical input for the evaluation of these designs from the industrial and academic communities worldwide. Eighty volunteer analysis teams were formed and produced extensive technical analysis of the designs. These teams represented not only language expertise but also the eventual users of the language. In order to make the evaluations as fair as possible, each report was given a color designation; green for CII, red for Intermetrics, blue for SofTech, and yellow for SRI. There was no other significance to the colors. Of course, this was no guarantee of anonymity and there was no legal requirement to hide the sources, but it seemed like a good idea at the time. This technique has been used elsewhere since. If one were very familiar with the style of a design group, their work would be detectable; however, the sources were concealed from most of the evaluators.

The period available for design was short, but the designs were only preliminary and the purpose of the analyses was to determine which should be continued to completion. On the basis of these analyses, CII-Honeywell Bull, and Intermetrics were selected to continue and resume work in April 1978, and a Memo [Perry 1978] (Figure 5.8) continuing the program was issued by DDR&E. All the evaluation materials were again microfiched and distributed to all participants [HOLWG 1978a].

As a result of both the designs and the analyses, the requirements were updated in June 1978 to a STEELMAN version [HOLWG 1978b]. As this was logically expected to be the final set of requirements, some care was taken to clean it up, and particularly to remove apparent misunderstandings and discrepancies which surfaced as the result of the actual design of the four languages. The rigorous review of the languages by the analysis teams in the context of the requirements was a further exceptional test. It was the specific goal of this revision to assure that the level of the requirements was properly functional, neither too specific nor too general. Some portions of the requirements were

FIGURE 5.8

THE UNDER SECRETARY OF DEFENSE
WASHINGTON, D.C. 20301

RESEARCH AND
ENGINEERING

April 11, 1978

MEMORANDUM FOR ASSISTANT SECRETARY OF THE ARMY (RESEARCH, DEVELOPMENT AND ACQUISITION)
ASSISTANT SECRETARY OF THE NAVY (RESEARCH, ENGINEERING AND SYSTEMS)
ASSISTANT SECRETARY OF THE AIR FORCE (RESEARCH, DEVELOPMENT AND LOGISTICS)
DIRECTOR, DEFENSE ADVANCED RESEARCH PROJECTS AGENCY
DIRECTOR, DEFENSE COMMUNICATIONS AGENCY

SUBJECT: DoD High Order Language Commonality Program

The DoD program to produce a common high order computer programming language has passed a major milestone. Four competitive prototype designs were delivered to the government on February 15, 1978. Detailed analysis and comparisons of these designs were performed by 80 defense and civil organizations. On the basis of these analyses and data, and with the technical representatives of the United Kingdom, France, and the Federal Republic of Germany, the High Order Language Working Group (HOLWG) selected two designs to be continued to full language definition. While either of these could result in a successful common language design, the continued competition was regarded as a very important factor in the program. The two designs exhibit significantly different approaches and act so as to reduce the criticality of undiscovered technical risk.

In expectation of success of the final design phase, the High Order Language Working Group is preparing a detailed plan for the introduction and support of the language, the rigorous control of the language both inside and outside the DoD, and the implications of its use in the NATO environment. I commend to your attention the drafting and coordination of this plan.

Several independent economic analyses have promised large benefit from the adoption of this modern common language. I solicit your support to make this a reality.

William J. Perry

deleted or modified as a result of these reviews, and the parallel processing requirements were generalized. The document remains a set of realistic requirements for large-scale systems. As befits the maturity of the project, this version is more direct. Although much of the discussion of previous versions is still valid, it is not repeated here. STEELMAN reads much more like a specification, but it still allows significant flexibility in design decisions. It states specific criteria for a language, but does not describe a language. Figure 5.9 reproduces the section on syntax requirements.

STEELMAN criteria were not for an abstract, ideal language, but one dealing with operational realities. Restrictions on character sets reflect the distribution of input devices across all communities at that time. The **goto** remained, although restricted, to ensure acceptability in those communities where it was still widely used. (In fact, an argument could be made that there are situations in which the **goto** is the preferred solution, albeit, very few. It is powerful and it can be easily detected and controlled by management, thereby reducing the dangers of misuse. Fortunately, the user demand relieved us of having to make a decision in this one case.)

Not as part of the competition, but for general technical input, there were two other submissions around this time. A group at Carnegie-Mellon University that had long been supported by DARPA in the compiler field, submitted a conceptual design they named "TARTAN" [Shaw 1978] (another color?). A group from IBM provided a study of what would be the result of cutting and filling PL/I to meet the DoD requirements. Their approach was to reduce the base PL/I by 75 percent and supplement it by 15 percent.

5.4.2 Phase II

Two language designs, those of CII and Intermetrics (Green and Red), were continued through the second phase of the contract. A full language specification was derived from the informal specification delivered by each in Phase I. In addition to the specification, the contractor produced a "Rationale" and programs of solutions to several applications programming problems. Finally, the contractors were to produce a test translator to test and evaluate the language in actual use. In the end the translator products were insufficiently complete, amd perhaps too slow, to provide any input to the evaluation process, contrary to our early expectations.

An elaborate evaluation of the products, which the two contenders delivered on 15 March, 1979, was more exhaustive that the earlier semi-final shoot-out, as the products were more complete. Again, a number of teams representing various interests, applications, and organizations, analyzed reports from many reviewers. (This raw data was documented on microfiche produced at Eglin AFB, after I was transferred there [HOLWG 1980a].) This time there was an opportunity to question the design teams personally, in great depth, at a large evaluation meeting held in April 1979, in the Washington, DC area.

On 2 May, 1979, a meeting of the HOLWG, including the representatives of the United Kingdom, France, and Germany, selected the design of CII-Honeywell Bull, code-named "Green" during the competition. Before the last mail that afternoon I reproduced and sent 3000 green postcards announcing "Green is Ada!" The formal announcement to the world was the Duncan letter of 14 May, 1979, [Duncan 1978a] (Figure 5.10). Within a month I was reassigned to be Technical Director for Digital Applications at the Air Force Armament Laboratory, Eglin AFB, Florida. David Fisher became a government employee and took over my previous job with DDR&E, chairing the HOLWG until he and Carlson left in November 1980, and the HOLWG was superseded by the Ada Joint Program Office.

FIGURE 5.9

Example from STEELMAN—Technical Requirements.

2. General Syntax

2A. Character Set. The full set of character graphics that may be used in source problems shall be given in the language definition. Every source program shall also have a representation that uses only the following 55 character subset of the ASClI graphics:

```
%&'()*+,-./:;<=>?
0123456789
ABCDEFGHIJKLMNOPQRSTUVWXYZ
```

Each additional graphic (i.e., one in the full set but not in the 55 character set) may be replaced by a sequence of (one or more) characters fram the 55 character set without altering the semantics of the program. The replacement sequence shall be specified in the language definition.

2B. Grammar. The language should have a simple, uniform, and easily parsed grammar and lexical structure. The languake shall have free form syntax and should use familiar notations where such use does not conflict with other goals.

2C. Syntactic Extensions. The user shall not be able to modify the source language syntax. In particular the user shall not be able to introduce new precedence rules or to define new syntactic forms.

2D. Other Syntactic Issues. Multiple occurrences of a language defined symbol appearing in the same context shall not have essentially different meanings. Lexical units (i.e., identifiers, reserved words, single and multicharacter symbols, numeric and string literals, and comments) may not cross line boundaries of a source program. All key word forms that contain declarations or statements shall be bracketed (i.e., shall have a closing as well as an opening key word). Programs may not contain unmatched brackets of any kind.

2E. Mnemonic ldentifiers. Mnemonically significant identifiers shall be allowed. There shall be a break character for use within identifiers. The language and its translators shail not permit identifiers or reserved words to be abbreviated. [Note that this does not preclude reserved words that are abbreviations of natural language words.]

2F. Reserved Words. The only reserved words shall be those that introduce special syntactic forms (such as control structures and declarations) or that are otherwise used as delimiters. Words that may be replaced by identifiers, shall not be reserved (e.g., names of functions, types, constants, and variables shall not be reserved). All reserved words shall be listed in the language definition.

FIGURE 5.9
(Cont.)

```
2G.   Numeric Literals. There shall be built-in decimal literals. There
shall be no implicit truncation or rounding of integer and fixed point
literals.

2H.   String Literals. There shall be a built-in facility for fixed
length string literals. String literals shall be interpreted as one-di-
mensional character arrays.

2I.   Comments. The language shall permit comments that are introduced
by a special (one or two character) symbol and terminated by the next
line boundary of the source program.
```

The Reference Manual and the Rationale were published as the June, 1979, issue of *ACM SIGPLAN Notices* (Vol. 14, N. 6, June 1979, Parts A & B) [Ada 1979a; 1979b], in order to get wide exposure for public comment during the early months of testing. This version was known as "Preliminary Ada," to be refined as the result of comments and testing. SIGPLAN had been kept informed during the project [Whitaker 1977] and Paul Abrahams of SIGPLAN suggested that the Manual be published by SIGPLAN, as had been done for other developments. I contracted with their printer for 3,000 additional copies for the HOLWG distribution. I was fairly proud of this connection, because not only did we get very wide distribution in the computer science community, but I was able to get the additional copies from the printer at just over $1 a copy. This resulted in an enormous saving over their being printed by the government. I took the precaution of obtaining proper permission to bypass use of the Government Printing Office, as required by Congress for such actions.

5.4.3 The Name

"Ada" was chosen as the name for the common language. This honors Ada Augusta, the Countess of Lovelace, the daughter of the poet Lord Byron, and Babbage's "programmer."

In spite of rumor, DOD-1 was never a candidate for the name, and was never used by the HOLWG in any formal context. It was immediately recognized that we were looking for something that could have wide acceptance and that the name should not have a parochial flavor. However, we did sometimes jokingly refer to the whole project as DOD-1, and we used that as the password of the common HOLWG computer account, until we picked "Ada."

It has been reported that Jack Cooper suggested the name "Ada," while sitting with other members of the HOLWG in a sidewalk cafe in Paris in the summer of 1978. I cannot testify to the accuracy of the milieu, as I was not in Paris at the time. I do remember that we had long struggled with the question of an appropriate name. A number of suggestions were brought up with no result. This indecision became embarrassing because the selection of a name was a scheduled milestone in the program, and the only one that we had missed by more than a few days—we missed this one by over a year!

After the suggestion was made by Cooper at a HOLWG meeting, there was still a fair amount of divergence. Amorosa brought up the book "Faster than Thought" [Bowden 1953] from which we all learned about Lady Lovelace. (Other biographies [Moore 1977; Morrison 1961; Stein 1985] dwell

FIGURE 5.10

THE SECRETARY OF DEFENSE
WASHINGTON D. C. 20301

MAY 14 1979

The Department of Defense High Order Language Commonality program began in 1975 with the goal of establishing a single high order computer programming language appropriate for DoD embedded computer systems. This effort has been characterized by extensive cooperation with the European Community and NATO countries have been involved in every aspect of the work. The requirements have been distributed worldwide for comment through the military and civil communities, producing successively more refined versions. Formal evaluations were performed on dozens of existing languages concluding that a single language meeting these requirements was both feasible and desirable. Such a language has now been developed.

I wish to encourage your support and participation in this effort, and I submit the design of this language for your review and comment. Such comments and detailed justified change proposals should be forwarded to HOLWG, DARPA, 1400 Wilson Boulevard, Arlington, VA 22209 by 30 November 1979. The language, as amended by such response, will become a Defense standard in early 1980. Before that, changes will be made; after that, we expect that change will be minimal.

Beginning in May 1979, the effort will concentrate on the technical test and evaluation of the language, development of compilers and programming tools, and a capability for controlling the language and validating compilers. The requirements and expectations for the environment and the control of the language are being addressed in a series of documents already available to which comment is also invited. We intend that Government-funded compilers and tools will be widely and cheaply available to help promote use of the language.

Ada has been chosen as the name for the common language, honoring Ada Augusta, Lady Lovelace, the daughter of the poet, Lord Byron, and Babbage's programmer.

C W Duncan Jr
DEPUTY

more on personal aspects, and Baroness Wentworth's own words [Wentworth 1938] correct Bowden's misrepresentations of her.) Eventually there was a general consensus. Still, it seemed presumptuous to appropriate somebody's name; and even the dead should have some rights. So we took what might be a unique turn. We wrote to the heir of Lady Lovelace and asked permission to use the name "Ada." Phil Wetherall, our U.K. representative, wrote the letter and there followed this exchange that authorized use of the name [Wetherall 1978; Lytton 1978; Duncan 1978b] (Figures 5.11–5.13).

FIGURE 5.11

Procurement Executive, Ministry of Defence

ROYAL SIGNALS AND RADAR ESTABLISHMENT

St. Andrews Road GREAT MALVERN WORCS WR14 3PS
Telex 339747-8 Telephone MALVERN (06845) 2733 ext

10th October 1978

The Earl of Lytton
Lillycombe
PORLOCK
Somerset

Dear Lord Lytton

For some years now, the United States Department of Defense has been engaged in a project to define a new computer programming language for use in weapon systems, as opposed to scientific or business and commercial applications. This effort will shortly reach its climax with the publication of the language design in April 1979. Until now, the language has not had a distinctive name, and the steering committee of the project has been open to suggestions for such a name. The only serious contender, and one the committee would like to adopt, is Ada - in honour of Countess Lovelace. She had the distinction of being amongst the first to appreciate the significance of Charles Babbage's work on the Analytic Engine (ie the forerunner of modern computers) and she was a great presenter of Babbage's ideas. Indeed, she could be called the first programmer.

As the representative from the Ministry of Defence to the project, I have been tasked with seeking the concurrence of Lady Lovelace's family to this suggestion. We gather that your mother, 16th Baroness Wentworth, was extremely interested in her grandmother, and so I am writing to you in the first instance to seek your approval of this suggestion. If you believe that other members of the family, for example Lord Lovelace, should also be approached, I will do so with alacrity, but it has been suggested that your branch of the family are the "heirs" to the computing influence of Lady Lovelace as a result of Lady Wentworth's interest.

In the book "Faster than Thought" by Dr Bowden (Pitman 1953) Lady Wentworth is recorded as possessing many of Lady Lovelace's letters. This new programming language is likely to have a considerable impact on the community of those concerned with computing, and could well sponsor a revival of interest in Lady Lovelace if the name Ada is chosen. I have been asked to discover whether these letters are still in your family's possession and, if not, where they could be located.

FIGURE 5.11
(Cont.)

```
If you would like more information on the project, I shall be only too
happy to oblige. Fortunately this is not an area in which secrecy is a
matter of concern.

Yours sincerely



P R Wetherall
Principal Scientific Officer
Computer Applications Division
```

5.4.4 Test and Evaluation

The next step in the process was an evaluation of the definition with public comment and actual experience in coding with it. Languages can take many years to mature because they are exercised by different users, serially. The HOLWG attempted to speed up this process for Ada. This test and evaluation phase was intended to get many different organizations rewriting their particular applications [HOLWG 1979b], which both exercised the language and exposed it to potential users. Note that this was a test of the language, not of implementations, which is more often the case in language evaluations for project use.

This exercise was conducted in the HOLWG tradition; a wide request for coding input, a large public meeting to present results, and solicitation (by the Deputy Secretary of Defense) of public comments on the Preliminary Ada document. An interpreter was made available over the ARPANET to anyone requesting access. The goal was to let users reprogram their applications in Ada to verify that the language was sufficiently powerful and usable. (I did a missile inertial guidance program at Eglin.) Because we were serious about exercising the language knowledgeably, training was provided for the participants. In June and July 1979, five one-week courses were held at Service institutions, Georgia Tech, and at the National Physical Laboratory in England. The instructors were from the language design team, and included: Jean Ichbiah, Robert Firth, and John Barnes.

The experiences and code results were reported at a meeting, 23–26 October, 1979, in Boston at the Museum of Science [HOLWG 1979c]. This open location was arranged by Carlson to encourage people other than just DoD contractors to attend.

5.4.5 Phase III

The third scheduled phase of the language design was a polishing of the definition as a result of the test and evaluation. CII Honeywell-Bull was funded to revise "Preliminary Ada" and provide a final Language Reference Manual to be a military standard (MIL-STD). The process was supported by a group of technical experts known as the "Distinguished Reviewers," established and chaired by Carlson. Formal comments were solicited and processed electronically. Hundreds of papers were prepared on individual questions. On 24 July, 1980, CII delivered the revised design. On 25 August, the HOLWG voted to accept the product [Cohen 1981].

FIGURE 5.12

HOUSE OF LORDS - WESTMINSTER

18 October 1978

Keeper Knight's
Pound Hill
Crawley
-Sussex RH10 3PB

Dear Mr. Wetherall,

Your letter of 10 October comes to the right person and this is now my address.

Ada was Byron's daughter.

She married William King, the first Earl of Lovelace as his first wife.
William and Ada begat (Ralph - 2nd Earl
(Anne - married W. S. Blunt. (Wilfrid)

Ralph's line died out but he made a will trust in favor of his sister Anne's daughter and her descendants. He wrote a book called "Astarte" and made a collection of papers called the "Lovelace Papers". He also resuscitated the older title of Wentworth which can be taken by daughters in the absence of sons. At his death his title of Lovelace went to the son of his father out of a second wife: the title of Wentworth went to his daughter who died childless: on her death the Wentworth Barony went to his sister Anne for a few weeks before her death.

Anne & Wilfrid begat Judith who married Neville Lytton later 3rd Earl of Lytton and became 16 Baroness Wentworth on the death of her mother Anne. Neville became 3rd Earl after the dissolution of his first marriage to Judith. Judith & Neville begat Anthony (myself) and 2 girls (both childless). On the death of Neville, Anthony became 4th Earl of Lytton; On the death of Judith Anthony became 17th Baron Wentworth. Anthony married Clare Palmar and begat

John (Viscount Knebworth)
Roland (The Hon. R. Lytton) - all young
Caroline Lytton all unmarried as yet
Lucy Lytton
Sarah Lytton

From this you will see that I am directly descended from Ada and the present Earl of Lovelace is not. We have a common ancestor in William but he is out of the 2nd wife, I am out of the first.

Doris Langley Moore has written a book on Ada. Professor Bowden's book "Faster Than Thought" pays a fair tribute to Ada but suggests something like an acclaim on the part of Judith whose mathematical acumen certainly did not enable her to breed Arabian horses that won races in world record times from 1/2 mile to 300 miles. I do not think you will

FIGURE 5.12

(Cont.)

```
find an Arabian horse among the names in any Epson Derby and its equiva-
lent elsewhere.

The Science Museum gave prominence to Ada in their Babbage Exhibit -
several years ago. I inherited the Lovelace papers (including some Ada
letters) and they are now deposited at the Bodlean Oxford for students
to consult - The deposit is in the name of my son John. I think we
shall all be happy if you name your Radar Language "Ada" in honour of
Ada Lovelace. By chance the name already lies at the
heart of RADAR.

Yours Sincerely,



Lytton
```

Was it really as open a program as we said? The process seemed to be enormous and commenters sometimes felt overwhelmed. I myself submitted a number of revision comments from afar, as a simple user no longer involved in the contract. I thought to myself, as people will, that my insightful suggestions had mostly been rejected. I then did a quantitative audit and found that more than 80 percent of my suggestions had been incorporated in the final product.

In December 1980, there was an ACM SIGPLAN Conference on Ada in Boston [ACM 1980]. This was the first technical conference on Ada not organized or run by the DoD. While the meeting was taking place, Mark Grove, Chairman of the MSC-ECR, was in Washington settling final details on the MIL-STD. He managed to arrange that the MIL-STD be given the number 1815, the year of Ada's birth, and to get it approved on 10 December, the day of her birth. He could also announce the formation of the Ada Joint Program Office (AJPO) to supersede the HOLWG and maintain the language. Here ended the initial language development part of the project.

5.5 LANGUAGE CONTROL

There is a very large payoff to the DoD for being able to update hardware without having to rewrite the software. Further, there is a large payoff for being able to take modules of code generated on one project for use on another. Also, one would like to be able to use a common software base over a variety of machines and architectures within a single system. An identical functional capability may be required in a number of physical implementations of various sizes, speeds, and powers. These may require running the same code on a large scientific computer or a distributed system of microprocessors. The effort, therefore, emphasized two key factors of transportability: technical capability and control of implementations.

The technical capability for transportability and reuse requires that the source code be as machine independent as possible in items such as word length, the precision of variables, and the like, and be able to specify representations and hardware dependencies in an encapsulated form. This was the requirement and Ada satisfied it. The effort was keyed to a hard definition of the language and validation of compilers to assure that a program written for one project or machine would be

FIGURE 5.13

THE SECRETARY OF DEFENSE
WASHINGTON D. C. 20301
MAY 14, 1979

The Earl of Lytton
Keeper Knight's
Pound Hill
Crawley Sussex RH10 3PB
England

Dear Lord Lytton:

The United States Department of Defense would like to express its thanks to you and your family for permission to use the name of your ancestor in connection with a new common computer programming language for military systems. Ada Augusta Byron, Lady Lovelace, was a woman of exceptional ability and wit. Her pioneering work in describing the procedures through which a computer solves a useful problem, a discipline we now call programming, is still fresh after more than a century. We believe that she would have appreciated this new language for computer programmers designed specifically for precision and clarity.

The US DoD and the British Ministry of Defence have been cooperating in producing the language for programming military computer systems. After an extensive requirements and study phase, several candidate designs were produced and, on 2 May 1979, a selection was made between competing definitions. We now have a language which we can designate "Ada". The next few months will be a period of testing and polishing of the definition. In 1980 we will begin to use Ada in the development of large military systems.

There appears to be a pressing need for such an advanced programming language outside the Defense community, and this project has received a great deal of attention from industry. It is our expectation that Ada and the associated programming facilities will see very widespread international use. We hope that it will serve as a fitting reminder of a lady of great talent and foresight.

Sincerely,

C. W. Duncan, Jr.
DEPUTY

transportable in a realistic fashion. Control of the language was one of the most important aspects of this program and was planned for early on. Primarily, it meant maintenance of the final language specification including answering questions, making necessary decisions, distributing information as required, etc., and the certification of compilers. No compiler can be validated that does not respond appropriately to all legal programs, within our ability to test. Further, compilers must be checked to ensure that they do not exceed the scope of the language. This idea of checking for features beyond the language was radical when first proposed, but it was vital to the overall purpose of the project. In some sense, it is not a matter of the language, but use of the language. Herein lies the difference between a "standard" and a "common" language. Standards are sometimes taken as a starting point from which deviations and "enhancements" proceed. If it is to be common, transportability and reuse depend on the language being the same everywhere. Here, also, is the origin of the controversial "no subsets/no supersets" rule.

I made it a principle that there were to be no subset and no superset compilers for Ada. This was really not much of a problem in selling to the Services and the users. However, it was a continuous battle with the implementers, primarily academic. The argument was that they could make a cheap subset compiler to get started. This usually meant minor syntactic modifications to a Pascal compiler. Few of these subset advocates ever intended to go to a complete compiler. Some more serious proposals were made to define a standard subset of the language, in the manner of FORTRAN or COBOL. Those serious discussions failed to produce a proposal because everyone had a different idea of what features to suspend. Attacks on this policy continued long after I left the HOLWG and I periodically had to strengthen the resolve of my successors.

At the other end, there were those who insisted that there should be only one compiler, mandated by the government for all Ada users, or one per Service. There were those who demanded that all compilers use a common database for compiler syntax and semantics, or have a common intermediate language or internal interface. We had to confront this monolithic stance through a technical capability to ensure that compilers from different sources would not generate dialects.

In October 1979, soon after the language was selected, a contract was let to SofTech to provide a suite of validation test programs. SofTech was a Phase I contender (Blue) and, although they were unsuccessful, their work showed an attention to detail that was ideal for this effort. John Goodenough led this program, for which he was required to distance himself from any SofTech Ada compiler contracts. The testers could not be developers.

The product of the contract was the Ada Compiler Validation Capability (ACVC) [Goodenough 1980], a set of test programs, now numbering several thousand, that try the limits of the language. To validate, a compiler must not fail any applicable test. Standards facilities in the United States and abroad have been authorized to certify with this set of tests. It was recognized during the language development that testing, although never complete, was the only technically feasible method to assure compliance to the full and exact Ada standard. The test suite has grown through the years and because the purpose is to make sure a compiler is Ada, there was no leniency towards compilers that may have passed a previous version. When new tests are approved, compilers must revalidate, otherwise the validations expire. This is a significant burden on suppliers, but it is necessary to maintain the transportability and reuse goals, and is a consequence of the expectation that Ada must support high-integrity systems.

The idea of trademarking the name, as a control on implementations, was initiated while I was there, but not carried through until later. The use of the trademarked name, "Ada," was restricted to validated implementations. This gave very powerful psychological protection during the start-up when the concept of strict control was still vulnerable. In 1987, when the community had matured, AJPO relinquished the trademark protection.

Although we set out to make a DoD common language, not necessarily a civil standard, we did work closely with the ISO PLIP Working Group (WG 1) so as to prepare for standardization as a method of control. I presented the HOLWG program to ISO SC 5 at the Turin meeting in the fall of 1978, to help prepare the way. The thought was to raise the control of the language to the highest level possible, out of the DoD, out of the United States, in order to make it harder for even a very large project to undermine the stability of the definition by propagating dialects, as had been the case with previous military languages.

In this connection, we needed to assure the world that this was truly an available commercial reality, and not something that the DoD was going to keep to itself. The openness during development contributed to this, but there were other pitfalls. Coincidentally, I was the U.S. technical representative for computers in the export control arena, where I sold the policy that there could be no control on languages that were subject to International Standardization, like FORTRAN, COBOL, or Ada; this cut off one possible disastrous scenario. Of course, this did not cover programs written in those languages.

5.5.1 Ada JPO

Upon the completion of the development project in late 1980, Fisher and Carlson left, and the loose organization of the HOLWG was superseded by a DoD Ada Joint Program Office (AJPO), chartered 12 December, 1980. Mark Grove was Chairman of the MSC-ECR and shepherded this through, along with Larry Druffel, who became the initial Director of the AJPO. This office managed the standardization processes with ANSI and ISO. One consequence of the transition was that this new organization was exclusively involved in the control and support of Ada, not in the overall DoD software problem. Although initially proposed and budgeted to generate tools and applications libraries, the AJPO abandoned that role and concerned itself mainly with the control and with DoD policies.

The chief task was to continue to polish the language definition in connection with an ANSI canvass process leading to ANSI, and eventually ISO, standardization. A major challenge was to maintain close international involvement in the development and ensure that national and international standards did not differ (a real possibility in the standards world of that time, but much less likely today). Through the usual Ada open process, the definition was refined to MIL-STD 1815A, and this was endorsed by ANSI in February 1983 [Ada 1983], with updated Rationale [Ichbiah 1987]. Ada was endorsed as ISO Standard 8652 in 1987.

A vital consideration in language control is that there must be some place to address questions and resolve ambiguities. A normal ANSI committee development has the possibility of using the committee itself as the ultimate judge. A process had to be devised for Ada. Ada is the responsibility of ANSI through an Ada Board advising AJPO, and of ISO through a Working Group, now designated TC 97/SC 22/WG 9. In the initial organization, both these groups were chaired by the then Director of the AJPO, Robert F. Mathis. At the time, this was a vital necessity for smooth coordination, forestalling possible divergences between the national and international standard. (When a later Director of the AJPO abdicated as WG 9 Convener, Mathis picked it up again and preserved this vital continuity.) There were elaborate organizational minutia and formal reporting and approval, but in essence, comments and questions on the language were resolved in summary papers, called "Ada Commentaries," by the Ada Rapporteur Group (formally the Language Maintenance Committee), chaired by John Goodenough. All queries are recorded and considered. The resolution of issues are available from a number of sources and were a starting point for the language update.

Another possible path to control involved a formal definition of Ada. There are those in the computer science community who advocate a formal definition as the only way to specify a language. Although this position is contested, formal definitions have been valuable in resolving difficult questions of interpretation. During the language development, the French (INRIA) began a formal definition based on denotational semantics [Donzeau-Gouge 1979, 1980]. This effort was particularly noteworthy in that it used Ada as the metalanguage which made it much more readable than most formal definitions. In 1979, RADC redirected an effort that it had been supporting to an operational definition of Preliminary Ada based on SEMANOL [Berning 1980]. The NYU Ada/Ed interpreter was also advocated as an operational definition [Dewar 1983]. Some Europeans were particularly interested in pushing a formal definition and proposed that such be the only basis for an ISO standard. The EEC supported research efforts in this area, beginning with the Danish work [Bjorner 1980], and culminating in a large project completed in 1987 [Botta 1987; Nielsen 1987; Giovini 1987]. These efforts have illuminated a number of aspects of the language and have led to clarifications, but the authoritative definition remains the natural language text of the Language Reference Manual.

Periodic review is required by ANSI and ISO for standards. Every five years a language standard must be revised or reaffirmed. Historically, this has meant a revision every ten years. In 1988, the Ada Board reaffirmed 1815A to ANSI and began a revision process, working on an update for about 1993, prudently called Ada 9X. My only connection is that Christine Anderson, who is running the revision project, was at the Air Force Armament Lab at Eglin AFB at the time. Although she did not join the Lab until after I left, I would like to think that my being there started a chain of events that led to her selection for 9X.

5.5.2 Environment

Because the purpose of the program was the improvement of DoD software, there were things beyond the language to be done, still within the scope of the HOLWG. Aspects of the development environment were studied with procedures similar to that for the language requirements. A document was prepared addressing those features of controlled support that would be required for the optimal utilization of the language. These were requirements in a different sense from the rigorous complete set of the STEELMAN, but the iteration methodology was also used here. An initial version, SANDMAN, drafted in January 1978, turned out to be entirely unsatisfactory and was never distributed. It did serve to show us that this problem might be more difficult than the language requirements, as languages were well known and environments were essentially nonexistent.

In July 1978, a more appropriate document was issued, PEBBLEMAN [HOLWG 1978c], replaced in January 1979, by PEBBLEMAN Revised [HOLWG 1979a]. Peter Elzer did most of the work on this. Comment was solicited from the software development community, a somewhat different group than the language experts who addressed the language requirements. A meeting was held at the University of California (Irvine) in June 1978 [Standish 1978] discussing all aspects of the requirements. In September 1978, a meeting at Eglin AFB, Florida, discussed primarily the technology of retargetable compilers [AFATL 1978]. PEBBLEMAN covered such topics as the language configuration control board, whose responsibility is to maintain the definition and resolve any possible questions. A language control facility would provide validation and certification of compilers to ensure that they conformed to the official definition within the limits of the current ability to test. The bulk of the document was concerned with defining those tools that could be provided in common to the use of language, and outlining the methodology for producing and interrelating those tools.

A further iteration, STONEMAN [HOLWG 1980b], primarily the work of John Buxton from the University of Warwick, England, was concerned with the integration of a set of Ada tools. A meeting in San Diego in November 1979, reviewed the thrusts of software development technology and discussed a Draft of a STONEMAN. The STONEMAN was issued in February 1980. It formalized the layers or levels of the Ada Program Support Environment (APSE), with the supporting Kernel (KAPSE) and Minimal (MAPSE) levels.

5.5.3 Compilers

It was never the intent that the HOLWG program would implement compilers. This was the prerogative of the individual Services and of industry. It was hoped that settling on one language would make it attractive for the industry to produce compilers as commercial products, without government funding or control (as it has worked out). However, it was important that the Services show support for the standard by putting their money into some products. If no one thought the Services were interested (and money spells interest), then why should industry risk its own money? It was not actually necessary that the Service programs be successful, just that they exist. Indeed, there was a certain inhibitory factor; a company may not want to invest in a compiler for a particular machine if the government was doing the same and it might be available for free later. So we walked a fine line. I do not know how we could have proceeded differently. Tools and environments were also the province of the Services and industry.

There were several early implementations that should be noted. In connection with the language design there was an interpreter produced by Honeywell. This ran on the MULTICS system and fielded at MIT and Rome Air Development Center (RADC) for use in the Test and Evaluation phase. It let a large number of users get hands-on experience over the ARPANET very early, but it was incomplete and very slow. Because of these limitations, it was important to provide a more satisfactory support for those evaluating the language. Another interpreter was produced in 1980 by Intermetrics for the DEC-10. This was made available via the ECLB machine on the ARPANET. Although certainly limited, it was much more useful than the previous system.

A complete interpreter, called Ada/Ed, was done by New York University. Although nominally for "educational use," this evolved to a complete, validatable system, which served to explore implementability during the polishing phase. It was considered by its developers to be an operational definition of the language. It was initially implemented in the set language SETL on a CDC Cyber machine.

The U.S. Army (CORADCOM) contracted for the first large scale Service effort, the Ada Language System (ALS). This consisted of a complete environment along STONEMAN lines, including a production quality compiler. This development was contracted to SofTech in Waltham, MA. The implementation was done in a "Pascal-like" subset of Ada and was hosted and targeted for a DEC VAX. This effort was managed as a major system procurement, not a research effort. There was a competitive procurement, elaborate design documentation for every facility of the system, and a very large commitment of funds. The outcome was disappointing and the project was eventually shelved. Strangely enough, some time later the Navy chose this to be the basis of their major procurement, called ALS/N, although with another contractor. Cross-compilers hosted on the VAX from this effort, called ADA/L (targeted for the AN/UYK-43) and ADA/M (AN/UYK-14 & 44), have been validated, but have not generated much general interest.

The Air Force (RADC/IS) initiated a similar procurement in 1980, called the Ada Integrated Environment (AIE). This was also a two-step competitive procurement. A design run-off was held among the first phase contractors: Computer Sciences Corp., Intermetrics, and Texas Instruments. The winner selected for the full-scale development was Intermetrics in Boston. The AIE was coded in a large subset of Ada and hosted/targeted to IBM 370 series machines. The contract included also both a compiler and STONEMAN environment. This project also fell on difficulties and the environment portion was deferred in favor of completing the compiler. Eventually the contractor completed the compiler after the expiration of the contract. Both the ALS and the AIE were embarrassing contractual failures for the sponsoring Service; however, they were necessary for the overall effort.

While I was at AFATL at Eglin, I proselytized for Ada and converted some people. Captain Jim Bladen did an early in-house compiler (hosted on a CDC Cyber, targeted to a Zilog Z8000 microprocessor) that is notable in that it led to, what I believe was, the first "operational" military use of Ada [Whitaker 1983]. In early 1981, Jim Jones of AFATL programmed a briefcase Z8000 computer to check out missile computers upon delivery. AFATL also contracted with Florida State University for a compiler. This was validated but found no users.

The British Government sponsored an effort at the University of York, subsequently York Software Engineering, that eventually validated. The German MoD contracted with University of Karlsruhe and GPP for an Ada compiler for the Siemens 7000 series machines.

The expectation of good, validated commercial compilers was fulfilled. Validation of 1815A implementations started shortly after ANSI approval. The first 1815A validation certificate was issued for the Ada/Ed interpreter on 11 April 1983, followed quickly by compilers from ROLM and Western Digital STC. There was an initial slow growth of implementations as companies mastered the language. By 1987 there were more than 100 validated compilers, and by 1992 this number had grown to about 400.

There were two sidelights of the compiler thrust, DIANA and CAIS.

By 1980 there were a number of large Ada compiler efforts under way. They were all facing the same problems with the same level of technology. In sharing experiences, it was noted that the projects used different, but technically similar, high level intermediate languages. The two main representations were TCOL-Ada from Carnegie-Mellon University (CMU) [Newcomer 1979] and AIDA from the University of Karlsruhe [Dausmann 1980]. By August 1980, there was a general feeling in the Ada community that these were close enough that there should be some effort at reaching common ground. Unfortunately, there never seemed to be time for the busy developers to get together, so nothing was happening. It appeared to me that a great opportunity was being missed, so I approached the government sponsors of the compiler developments at the December 1980, SIGPLAN Ada conference in Boston, and convinced them to use the power of the purse to encourage the necessary coordination.

In January 1981, I hosted a two week parley in my office at Eglin AFB with representatives from Karlsruhe (G. Goos, G. Winterstein, M. Dausmann), CMU (W. Wulf, J. Nestor, D. Lamb), Softech (R. Simpson, L. Weissmann), and Intermetrics (B. Brosgol, M.Tighe). I supplied coffee, cookies, and fruit, and would not let them out until the matter was resolved. Agreement came much quicker than anyone had imagined, and DIANA (Descriptive Intermediate Attributed Notation for Ada) was born [DIANA 1981]. DIANA is a high level tree-structured intermediate language for Ada and provides communication internal to compilers and other tools. It used the abstract syntax tree of the formal specification and had many attributes based on AIDA. From TCOL-Ada it inherited the symbol table attributes and some separate computation features. The meta notation is the Interface Definition Language (IDL) of CMU. There were some differences between the formal definition and DIANA. These were all resolved in early February at a meeting in Murnau, Germany.

DIANA was never supposed to be a standard to be enforced on all implementers. The purpose was simply to avoid duplication among those who were doing approximately the same thing anyway. There was some continued maintenance of DIANA [DIANA 1983, 1986]. It is being used by a number of developers, although with some variations. Other implementers have opted for different representations.

Another Ada-related standardization initiative was the Common Ada Interface Set (CAIS). This started somewhat like DIANA. Because the ALS and the AIE were comparable Ada environments, it seemed a good idea to have a common interface definition to promote tools interoperability. In September 1982, a definition was begun by a DoD Kernel Ada Programming Support Environment

(KAPSE) Interface Team (KIT) to foster compatibility between the ALS and AIE developers. Shortly after, the goals were expanded and volunteers were solicited (through a Commerce Business Daily announcement) to form a KAPSE Interface Team, Industry and Academia (KITIA). The CAIS Version 1.0 [CAIS 1983; Oberndorf 1983] was released for comment in September 1983. Eventually it developed into MIL-STD 1838 [CAIS 1986]. This interface has not been generally adopted, having lost the impetus that might have been sustained if the ALS and AIE had been successful, but it is the U.S. contribution to a cooperative effort with Europe.

5.5.4 SIGAda

An informal group, known as the "Ada Implementors," started meeting in May 1979, led by Gerald Fisher of New York University (NYU), which was developing Ada/Ed. This was the idea of Serafino Amoroso, a HOLWG representative of the Army that was funding NYU. By August 1980, the group was issuing an Ada Implementor's Newsletter, edited by Mary Van Deusen of Prime Computer, Inc., which provided the financial backing. Wishing to establish a more formal organization, the group voted at the March 1981 meeting to seek recognition, and in a vote chose to affiliate with the ACM (vs. the IEEE). The name of the Newsletter was changed to *Ada Letters* [ACM 1981]. On May 6, 1981, this group was chartered as AdaTEC, a technical committee under ACM SIGPLAN; Gerald Fisher was appointed Chairman. In 1984 the group was rechartered as SIGAda, the ACM Special Interest Group on Ada, and elected its first Chairman, Anthony Gargaro. This organization has provided the civil forum for Ada technical discussion and publication. It holds and sponsors frequent meetings that are the voice of the Ada community. By 1980 an Ada U.K. organization was established, and more than a dozen other national organizations are now active. Ada Europe provides a European forum much like SIGAda. There is an active, organized, worldwide community outside the DoD devoted to the use of Ada, as the HOLWG had hoped, and which did not exist for previous military embedded languages.

5.6 BEYOND THE LANGUAGE

The purpose of the project was to reduce the cost of DoD software, not to build one more language. Reuse was the major thrust driving the imposition of a common language on the DoD. If only the technical features of the language were important, the DoD should have been as well served by 100 good languages. But commonality holds no profit unless it is put to advantage.

There are three aspects of the use of Ada, each important in its potential for cost reduction.

1. The first is the technical capability of the language:

   capability to express the necessary functions;
   easy to read, write, and understand;
   support for reliable programming;
   support for modularity and large program engineering.

2. The second is commonality:

   based on technical capability;
   supported by machine independence;
   promotes the spread of tools;
   sanctioned by standards bodies.

3. The third is reuse:

    a product of machine independence and commonality;
    requires facilities to reuse and a way to get to them.

Throughout the project, there was the expectation, explicitly promised and budgeted for, that the government would develop, control, and provide certain basic tools and applications packages. These included the first level of software tools: compilers, editors, program analyzers, testing aids, and such. There was never the intent that all such capabilities were to be furnished by the government; as the preceding discussion on compilers points out, one expected that commercial offerings would eventually be superior to the basic level common set. Nevertheless, we viewed it as the responsibility of the project, or of the accompanying Service programs, to get things started. Although still in the AJPO budget in late 1981, this never was accomplished. In addition, we had planned that libraries of reusable code specific for particular applications areas would be maintained by organizations knowledgeable in the area. (We use the term "library" or "toolbox" but that sends the wrong message. A library is a collection of things that are available. What we need is a concept of a bunch of parts that are necessary and sufficient, and are put together, and polished and improved over the years.)

As far as I know, there was no single decision to abandon these goals, but I have my suspicions as to how it happened. The DoD management had found that single point promises of universal capabilities were unreliable, be it the capability of a single aircraft design for all Services, or a single compiler; competition was the solution. The validity of this position had certainly been established by experience, the latest being the discouraging results of the highly touted ALS and AIE compiler/environment contracts. These had each been sold by the sponsoring Service as a complete capability efficiently produced. The results could have only reinforced the distrust of the Deputy Secretary of Defense, William Howard Taft IV, for such a solution, and his favor toward letting industry handle the situation, unfettered by government interference. I sense this as the prevailing philosophy. Although there was no explicit hindrance to the follow-on programs, indeed they were approved, it turned out that they could be accomplished only with extraordinary support at the OSD level. The language development had this support and succeeded; the tools effort did not, and languished.

I do not mean this speculation as a criticism of the OSD philosophy; in fact, I support it and agree with it in detail, as my vindicated expectations for the Ada compiler industry show. But I wanted to make a small exception in this case. The idea was that the government should sponsor a starter set of tools, which would not be exclusive, to show the way, and then stand aside and let industry refine and continue. The thought was that the government had sufficient experience to know what was immediately required, but should not expect to dictate future developments. This is a concept that one could sell at an instant, but one which did not have staying power in the face of other demands.

Nevertheless, while recognizing the predilection against this mode, I pursued the dream. I got involved with two other joint programs, in 1982 and in 1986, both run by Colonel Joseph S. Greene, with whom I had worked at Kirtland AFB. The World Wide Military Command and Control System (WWMCCS) Information System (WIS) was a joint project to modernize the nation's strategic command and control capability. Greene and I were responsible for advanced technology on this program and believed that the right software technology for the extraordinary demands of this system was Ada, a bold position in 1982. Supported by a number of investigations and demonstrations, the WIS Joint Program Management Office selected Ada as its implementation language in May 1983. In June, perhaps influenced by this commitment, Richard DeLauer, then Under Secretary of Defense for Research and Engineering, sent out a memo [DeLauer 1983] to all Services and Agencies mandating Ada for future DoD mission critical systems, directing that

> The Ada programming language shall become the single common programming language for Defense mission-critical applications. Effective 1 January 1984 for programs entering Advanced Development and 1 July 1984 for programs entering Full-Scale Engineering Development, Ada shall be the programming language.

In support of this view, WIS let 54 Ada contracts, known as the NOSC tools, because procurement was done by the Naval Ocean Systems Center. The purpose of these was to prove that the state-of-the-practice would support Ada systems developments. These contracts exercised the state-of-the-practice among DoD contractors and evaluated available compilers, training, management capabilities, all that goes into a system development. The large number of contracts meant that one could determine if Ada was ready, not just whether a single contractor was capable. It was quite permissible for some contracts to fail; they often do even with mature technologies. The success of a large number was sufficient to establish the viability of Ada. Along the way, a number of tools were developed and made publicly available, for WIS and for any other Ada development, primarily by being submitted to an Ada repository. Rick Conn, of General Electric, was chiefly responsible for promoting this pioneering component library of Ada source code set up on a machine (SIMTEL20) at White Sands Missile Range, NM, accessible over the ARPANET. WIS was also concerned with, and funded, the bindings of Ada programs to exterior standards, such as the Graphical Kernel System (GKS) and database systems, without which systems could not port, even with portable code.

We expected that the technology work would be continued by the WIS prime contractor, the tools would be refined, and a machine independent environment set of high quality components would ensue. Machine independence was to be the key to settling the hardware predicament of this system. Managerial and contractual circumstances negated this plan and little additional component work was forthcoming.

In 1986 Colonel Greene became the Director of the DoD Software Technology for Adaptable Reliable Systems (STARS). I had served my 30 years and was retired from the Air Force so could only participate as a supporter from the sidelines, but maintained a keen interest. STARS was part of a three-pronged "Software Initiative," the other two being the AJPO and the Software Engineering Institute (SEI) in Pittsburgh. Again, contractual constraints shaped the program. Initially there were a number of "STARS Foundations" contracts, in the line of the NOSC Tools, this time chiefly through the Naval Research Laboratory (NRL). The main program consisted of three prime contractors who were supposed to integrate and exercise environment technologies. The contracts specifically required 60 percent of the effort to be done by subcontractors, in order to stimulate innovation. Again, development of a repository was a major feature of the program. Once again, managerial and budgetary constraints conspired against our expectations.

Another early try was the Common Ada Missile Packages (CAMP) program at AFATL, which was the first large government effort to develop a specific applications library. This was managed by Christine Anderson, who became the director of the Ada 9X program. CAMP was contracted for in the normal government fashion, from a single contractor. It might have been more Ada-like if it were open and funded for continued polishing and extension. The moral of all these efforts is that it is vital that components be supported and polished, and subject to continual peer review.

5.7 EXPECTATIONS

5.7.1 Realized

Ada, the project and the language, was driven by the goal of encouraging good software design and programming practice. The modularity provided by packages and the separation of specifications and bodies is exceptionally useful in this regard. Properly managed, it is applicable to all levels of the design process, as well as to the programming task. Ada itself is used as a program design language [IEEE 1987], and its use has spawned general interest in design languages. Used in design, Ada allows designs to be compiled, and even mock executed, rigorously verifying critical interfaces at a point in the process where adjustments are convenient. Ada facilitates the effective direction of a development effort involving hundreds of people, even in different organizations, and the controlled maintenance and modification of software over many years. It does the technical job that was required.

Ada was designed to support and encourage "object-oriented design," and it does. Ada packages can be used to create "objects." In the seventies there were some very vocal objections that Ada did not have "abstract data types" (the buzzword of the day), as a package was not limited to someone's notion of what that meant. During the eighties the use of the "object-oriented" buzzword changed; one now implies "object-oriented programming" features such as "inheritance," which are even dangerous in high-integrity systems. Ada 9X will provide this support in order to promote programmer acceptance, but this addition neither enhances the system engineering capability of Ada nor disparages the original design.

Ada has achieved a level of acceptance beyond what was required, a level that we had hoped for. It is an ANSI and ISO standard, as well as a military standard. It is mandated, not only by the DoD, but by the Congress. It is used by many other large organizations. This was the goal of the project and it succeeded.

Ada had to satisfy a large set of requirements. One of the dangers was that a poor design would result in a language that was too large or too complicated to be useful for the DoD. There is no "agreed to" quantitative measure for computer languages, but I could argue that Ada is smaller than COBOL, and not enormously larger than FORTRAN. The text of a good Ada program is extremely readable. These properties combine to make Ada very teachable to DoD programmers.

The educational aspects of Ada are the most bewildering. It is being taught in a fairly large number of institutions, from high schools on up, but, while growing, it has certainly not become the principal language of choice. I have had excellent results teaching Ada to brand new Airmen with a high school diploma and 11 weeks in the Air Force [Whitaker 1983]. But there are institutions where it has been proclaimed too difficult to introduce below graduate Computer Science. It might be fair to say that Ada is a language for software engineering, rather than just "programming," and that discipline is very young.

5.7.2 Denied

Tools for, and in, Ada are now widely available, but it is my greatest disappointment that there are not more, and better, tools publicly available for Ada than for all other languages combined. There was much effort and many opinions on how to integrate tools but few new ideas for tools beyond those in general use. I had expected that Ada would have lots of facilities because we could now have them machine independent. I tried to do a bit, pick up the slack, prime the pump, and get people interested, but not very successfully. WIS made a start on such simple things as math packages, a copy of the UNIX tools, an I/O generalization (from simple terminal to windows), communications capabilities, graphics, and such. We could exert influence, but it was administratively impossible to actually command a bunch of programmers to do such tools. Beyond Ada programming tools, I wanted to use Ada to introduce and support other standards efforts for the DoD, such as the Standard Generalized Markup Language (SGML) and the Computer Graphics Metafile (CGM), which are now being used by the DoD Computer Aided Logistics System (CALS). Maybe I was wrong and the world would not have been better off, but I doubt it. 9X reiterates the promises to release tools into the public domain. I hope this finally takes off.

There are a lot of things that one can do differently because there is a truly common language. Ada provides a *lingua franca* for communication beyond programming. Pure Ada is used as a design language, a command language, database entry and checking, and for message format definition, resulting in enormous benefits in development time and system reliability. But much of the applications are of conventional design and have not exploited the full range of novel Ada techniques.

Educationally, Ada has been beset with two unique obstacles, neither technical. There is a feeling that Ada facilitates all those aspects of good design and management that one puts under the umbrella term of "software engineering," and it certainly does. Some managers have taken this to the extreme, and decided that there is no point in using Ada unless they can train their personnel to a total "software engineering" capability. While admirable, this is difficult, and possibly undefined, so the result is delay, intentional or not.

The other obstacle, which affects especially the academic world, is that good Ada compilers were initially expensive relative to some other languages. Although the academic price of Ada compilers is now competitive and the computer resources required are available in present desktop computers, the requirements may exceed (mostly in memory) those purchased some time ago. It is certainly true that such constraints are not limited to the academic community, but I note the example of the U.S. Air Force Academy teaching ALGOL for years to cadets because Burroughs gave them a machine effectively supporting only ALGOL, in spite of the fact that ALGOL was not used elsewhere by the Air Force. I protested this at the time. In 1992, the Military Academies still do not teach Ada as their primary language!

Both the tools and the compiler availability situations illustrate the limits on a U.S. government program, because it is a government program. The absolute amount of money that could be involved in producing all the tools one could imagine and providing a free compiler for every computer in the country is trivial compared to what the DoD spends on software every month. (In the past, large corporations have had much more freedom for such intiatives, but are facing stricter controls.) However, any such direct government program would be contrary to law and the U.S. economic system, and I would not wish it otherwise. Perhaps the question is whether the government should provide a competitive environment for its internal use.

Ada planned for training, and the expected commercial courses and books became available. A large Ada training problem was instructors that had to show off by making it seem as difficult as possible in order to snow the students. There were even groups that did not want to make the transition to Ada and used training as a delaying tactic. Some suggested that programmers have to know every feature in order to begin (but this is not the way anyone approached any other language), and that they had to have a three-month training course before they could proceed (although they had no training program for their present languages). Furthermore, they could not use Ada without lots of training in software engineering (although they were accepting the government's billions without apparently any knowledge of, and certainly no training in, software engineering). Although all these preparations are important, and they should be important for software development in any language, they have been used as disingenuous excuses not to use Ada.

5.8 WRAP UP

The development was extraordinarily open. Not only were thousands kept informed, they had a chance to participate, and did. During my chairmanship, I had a mailing list of over 3,000 who had contacted me, and many were the contacts for their lab or company. The project was extraordinarily well documented and the documentation was a fundamental working tool, not an after the fact exercise. The requirements were extensively circulated externally, certainly far more so than any other language effort, before or since. The evolution of the requirements is explicitly revealed in this series of documents. The language comparisons and contract evaluations were published in excruciating detail and are available to the public. These documents have the complete text of all designs and evaluations submitted to the HOLWG. During the polishing process, there were numerous Language Study Notes written and made available to a large community over the ARPANET. Since standardization, there have been hundreds of questions processed by a the Ada Rapporteur Group. These range from trivial questions that are answered in the Language Reference Manual (LRM) to complex issues that require a significant binding interpretation. All issues submitted have been addressed, results were available on the ARPANET, and have been published commercially.

The project was a continuous fight. The Service bureaucracies had to be reminded continuously about the program. Everyone was demanding several languages; they could not imagine Air Force and Navy F-4s being programmed in the same language. There were those who just objected to OSD doing anything technical. The project was under continuous scrutiny and pressure. It survived and prevailed.

My figures, through FY 78, for the total funds expended by the program from the beginning through final language selection (FY 76–78 funds—although selection was in FY 79, funding must be allocated at the begining of a contractual period) and the beginning of the validation effort, was $3.550 million, with another $550,000 in related Service programs. I do not offer this as an audited value, but the best number I can find in my records.

Was the project a success? It was prudently run. The language product was on time and within budget, and of very high quality. The public requirements development was a unique success, thanks to the technical leadership of David Fisher. The procurement went smoothly, thanks to Bill Carlson who averted lurking bureaucratic delays. When we started, there were more than 450 languages in use in the DoD, each with its own compiler, in almost all cases limited to one machine and weapons system. There is now a single language with more than 450 compilers. Other aspects have come about more slowly than we had hoped. When we started we were worried about a $3 billion a year DoD problem; today it is a $30 billion expense to the DoD. It is hard to make a *prima facie* case that we stemmed the "high cost of software." However, the growth of total software costs reflects the growth of hardware capabilities permitting (or demanding) more software. I believe that as a result of the HOLWG program, software productivity and quality is improving steadily. It may be taking longer than we had hoped.

I expected a certain natural conservative reluctance on the part of military System Program Offices to adopt a new language in the early days, and even some diehard opposition, to be subdued only slowly through direction. However, upon adoption of the common language, I had envisioned a rapid growth of components and tools within a cooperating community, an Ada Culture. It did not happen as quickly as I had hoped. "Repository" is now a universal buzzword, but DoD contracting limits (and the mindset that these have built up) long strangled the vision for cooperation and growth. I mistakenly thought that with the influence of the DoD we could pull it off. The thrust of cooperative development struggled and faded, several times. But there are other achievements that exceeded our original expectations. The language itself is better than we could have hoped. There is a lot more structure in the community, much of which this project injected. Reuse is happening.

FIGURE 5.14

Ada PROJECT Milestones.

Formation of HOLWG	JAN 75
STRAWMAN Issued	APR 75
WOODENMAN Issued	AUG 75
TINMAN Issued	JAN 76
DoDD 5000.29	APR 76
DDR&E Directs Service Funding	MAY 76
DoDI 5000.31	NOV 76
Languages Evaluation Completed	DEC 76
Program Management Plan	JAN 77
Report of Evaluation	JAN 77
IRONMAN Issued	JAN 77
Final SOW for Design	MAR 77
RFP Issued	APR 77
Revised IRONMAN Issued	JUL 77
Design Contracts Awarded	AUG 77
Economic Analyses	JAN 77–NOV 77
Language Design—Phase I	SEP 77–FEB 78
Language Design Evaluation	MAR 78–APR 78
Select contractors to Continue	APR 78
STEELMAN Issued	JUN 78
Program Decision Date	APR 78
Language Design—Phase II	MAY 78–FEB 79
PEBBLEMAN Issued	JUL 78
PEBBLEMAN Revised Issued	JAN 79
Final Selection	MAY 79
Test & Evaluation	MAY 79–SEP 79
Preliminary Ada published	JUN 79
MIL-STD 1815	DEC 80
STONEMAN Issued	FEB 80
ANSI/MIL-STD 1815A	FEB 83
First 1815A validation	APR 83
DeLauer mandate for Ada	JUN 83
ISO Standard 8652	JUN 87
Ada 9X Revision process initiated	SEP 88

In summary, I think we did a good job. I think the project was well run and is an example for the world. For Ada, acceptance is not what the computer science community thinks of it, or whether it is popular on home computers, the question is what does DoD, NATO, NASA, FAA, and so forth, think. Ada is a success. For evaluating a common language, the users are projects, not programmers, and such users are conservative. They will use what they have used previously because they know it, or use whatever the contractor wants. It takes time to bring the community over, even with direction from above. Most projects in DoD started with it because it was mandated; however, many commercial and foreign firms have adopted it without such influence. For large systems, there is no comparable capability. After experience with Ada, managers and programmers are enthusiastic.

Our goal was to create a common language for DoD software. On November 5, 1990, the President signed the 1991 Appropriation Bill (Public Law 101-511), which reads in Section 8092:

> Notwithstanding any other provisions of law, after June 1, 1991, where cost effective, all Department of Defense software shall be written in the programming language Ada, in the absence of special exemption by an official designated by the Secretary of Defense.

ACKNOWLEDGMENTS

This history would not have been possible without the help of John Walker of the IIT Research Institute at the AJPO. He found the source documents that were needed to assure the accuracy of the paper. I also received invaluable comments and help from Jean E. Sammet and Anthony Gargaro, and from the anonymous reviewers who made suggestions resulting in enormous improvements in the paper.

REFERENCES

Documents with AD number are available from the Defense Technical Information Center or the National Technical Information Service.

[ACM, 1980] *Proceedings–ACM SIGPLAN Symposium on the Ada Programming Language*, Boston. MA, December 9–11, 1980, ACM *SIGPLAN Notices*, Vol. 15, No. 11, Nov. 1980.

[ACM, 1981] ACM *Ada Letters*, (1981 and continuing), previously *Ada Implementor's Newsletter* (from 1979).

[Ada, 1979a] Preliminary Ada Reference Manual, *SIGPLAN Notices*, Vol. 14, No. 6A, June 1979, AD-A071 761.

[Ada, 1979b] Rationale for the Design of the Ada Programming Language, *SIGPLAN Notices*, Vol. 14, No. 6B, June 1979, AD-A073 854.

[Ada, 1983] ANSI/MIL-STD-1815A-1983, *Reference Manual for the Ada Programming Language*, 1983, AD-A131 511.

[AFATL, 1978] Report of the Eglin Workshop on Common Compiler Technology, AFTAL, 28 Sept. 1978.

[Berning, 1980] Berning, Paul. T. *Formal SEMANOL Specification of Ada*, Rome Air Development Center Report RADC-TR-80-293, Sept. 1980, AD-A091 682.

[Bjorner, 1980] Bjorner, D. and Oest, O. N., *Towards a formal definition of Ada*, Lecture Notes in Computer Science, Vol. 98, Springer-Verlag, 1980.

[Botta, 1987] Botta, N. and Pertersen, J. Storbank, *The Draft Formal Definition of Ada, The Static Semantics Definition*, Vol. 1-4 Jan. 1987, Dansk Datamatik Center, Lyngby, Denmark.

[Bowden, 1953] Bowden, B. V., *Faster Than Thought*, London: Pitman, 1953.

[CAIS, 1983] *Draft Specification of the Common APSE Interface Set (CAIS), Version 1.0*, prepared by KIT/KITIA Working Group for Ada JPO, 26 Aug. 1983.

[CAIS, 1986] DOD-STD-1838 *Common APSE Interface Set (CAIS)*, Oct. 1986.

[Carlson, 1980] Carlson, W. E., Druffel, L. E., Fisher, D. A., and Whitaker, W. A., Introducing Ada, in *Proceedings of the 1980 ACM Annual Conference*, ACM, Oct. 1980, pp. 27–29.

[Clapp, 1977] Clapp, Judy A., Loebenstein, E., and Rhymer, P., *A Cost/Benefit Analysis of High Order Language Standardization*, M78-206, The MITRE Corporation, Sept. 1977.

[Cohen, 1981] Cohen, Paul M., *From HOLWG to AJPO—Ada in Transition*, Ada Joint Program Office, (internal document), 1981.

[Currie, 1975a] Currie, Malcolm R., DoD Higher Order Programming Language, Memorandum from Director of Defense Research and Engineering, Washington, DC, 28 Jan. 1975. Figure 5.1 of this paper.

[Currie, 1975b] Currie, Malcolm R., DoD Higher Order Programming Language Working Group, Memorandum from Director of Defense Research and Engineering, Washington, DC, 2 May 1975. Figure 5.2 of this paper.

[Currie, 1976] Currie, Malcolm R., DoD High Order Language Program, Memorandum from Director of Defense Research and Engineering, Washington, DC, 10 May 1976. Figure 5.3 of this paper.

[Dausmann, 1980] Dausmann, M., Drossopoulou, S., Goos, G., Persch, G., and Winterstein, G., *AIDA Reference Manual (Preliminary Draft)*, Institut fur Informatick II, University of Karlsruhe, Report 2/80, 4 Feb. 1980.

[DeLauer, 1983] DeLauer, Richard D., Interim DoD Policy on Computer Programming Languages, Memorandum from Undersecretary of Defense (Research and Engineering), Washington, DC, 10 June 1983.

[Dewar, 1983] Dewar, R., Froelich, R. M., Fisher, G. A., and Kruchten, P., *An Executable Semantic Model for Ada, Ada/Ed Interpreter*, Ada Project, Courant Institute New York University, 1983

[DIANA, 1981] *Diana Reference Manual*, Institut fur Informatik II, Universitat Karlsruhe and Department of Computer Science, Carnegie-Mellon University; Report 1/81, Mar. 1981.

[DIANA, 1983] Evans, Jr., Arthur and Butler, Kenneth J., *DIANA (Descriptive Intermediate Attribute Notation for Ada) Reference Manual, Revision 3*, 1983, AD-A128 232.

[DIANA, 1986] McKinley, Kathryn L. and Schaefer, Carl F., *DIANA Reference Manual, Revision 4*, Intermetrics, Inc, IR-MD-078, May 1986.

[DoD, 1976b] Department of Defense Directive 5000.29, *Management of Computer Resources in Major Defense Systems*, 26 April 1976.

[DoD, 1976c] Department of Defense Instruction 5000.31, *Interim List of DoD High Order Programming Languages (HOL)*, 24 Nov. 1976.

[Donzeau-Gouge, 1979] Donzeau-Gouge, Veronoque, Kahn, G., and Lang, B., *Green Language, A Formal Definition*, Honeywell, CII Honeywell Bull, INRIA, 1979, ADA058 047.

[Donzeau-Gouge, 1980] Donzeau-Gouge, Veronoque, Kahn, G., and Lang, B., *Formal Definition of the Ada Programming Language*, Honeywell, CII Honeywell Bull, INRIA, 1980.

[Duncan, 1979a] Ducan, C. W. Jr., Letter from Deputy Secretary of Defense, Washington, DC, 14 May 1979. Figure 5.5 of this paper.

[Duncan, 1979b] Ducan, C. W. Jr., Letter from Deputy Secretary of Defense to The Earl of Lytton, Washington, DC, 14 May 1979. Figure 5.8 of this paper.

[Fisher, 1974] Fisher, David A., *Automatic Data Processing Costs in the Defense Department*, Paper P-1046, Institute for Defense Analyses, Oct. 1974, AD-A004 841.

[Fisher, 1978a] Fisher, D. A. and Wetherall, P. R., *Rationale for Fixed-Point and Floating-Point Computation Requirements for a Common Programming Language*, Institute for Defense Analyses, Report IDA-P-1305, Jan. 1978.

[Fox, 1978] Fox, Joseph M., *Benefit Model for High Order Language*, Decisions and Designs Incorporated, TR78-2-72, Mar. 1978.

[Giovini, 1987] Giovini, Alessandro, Mazzanti, Franco, Reggio, Gianna, and Zucca, Elena, *The Draft Formal Definition of Ada, The Dynamic Semantics Definition, Current Algebra*, Vol. 4, Dec. 86, Dansk Datamatik Center, Lyngby, Denmark.

[Goodenough, 1980] Goodenough, John, The Ada Compilation Validation Capability, in *Proceedings–ACM SIGPLAN Symposium on the Ada Programming Language*, Boston, MA, Dec. 9–11, 1980, ACM *SIGPLAN Notices*, Vol. 15, No. 11, Nov. 1980, pp. 1–8.

[HOLWG, 1975a] *"STRAWMAN" Requirements for a DoD High Order Programming Language*, February 1975.

[HOLWG, 1975b] *"WOODENMAN" Set of Criteria and Needed Characteristics for a Common DoD Programming Language*, David A. Fisher, IDA, 13 Aug. 1975.

[HOLWG, 1976] *Department of Defense Requirements for High Order Computer Programming Languages* "TINMAN", June 1976.

[HOLWG, 1977a] Amoroso, S., Wegner, P., Morris, D., White, D., Loper, W., Cambell, W., and Showalter, C., *Language Evaluation Coordinating Committee Report to the High Order Language Working Group (HOLWG)*, 14 Jan. 1977, AD-A037 634.

[HOLWG,1977b] *Department of Defense Requirements for High Order Computer Programming Languages "IRONMAN"*, Jan. 1977.

[HOLWG, 1977c] High Order Language Working Group, Studies of the Economic Implications of Alternatives in the DoD High Order Commonality Effort, Internal Study, 1977.

[HOLWG, 1977d] *Department of Defense Requirements for High Order Computer Programming Languages "IRONMAN" Revised*, July 1977.

[HOLWG, 1978a] *HOLWG, DoD High Order Language Commonality Effort—Design, Phase I Report and Analyses*, June 1978, AD-B950 587.

[HOLWG, 1978b] *Department of Defense Requirements for High Order Computer Programming Languages "STEELMAN"*, June 1978, AD-A059 444.

[HOLWG, 1978c] *Department of Defense Requirements for the Programming Environment for the Common High Order Language "PEBBLEMAN"*, July 1978.

[HOLWG, 1979a] *Department of Defense Requirements for the Programming Environment for the Common High Order Language "PEBBLEMAN" Revised*, Jan. 1979.

[HOLWG, 1979b] Test and Evaluation Newsletter Number 1; 25 May 1979; also in *SIGPLAN Notices*, Sept. 1979, pp.77–80.

[HOLWG, 1979c] *Ada Test and Evaluation Workshop (Proceedings)*, DARPA and MIT Laboratory for Computer Science; Oct. 1979, pp. 23–26.

[HOLWG, 1980a] *HOLWG, DoD High Order Language Commonality Effort—Ada Design, Phase II Reports and Analyses*, Jan. 1980, ADA-80-1-M or AD-A141 817 (available only from DTIC).

[HOLWG, 1980b] *DoD Requirements for Ada Programming Support Environments, "STONEMAN"*, Feb. 1980, AD-A100 404.

[Ichbiah, 1987] Ichbiah, Jean D., Barnes, John G. P., Firth, Robert J., and Woodger, Mike, *Rationale for the Design of the Ada Programming Language*, Honeywell, 1987, AD-A187 106.

[IEEE, 1985] ANSI/IEEE Std 754-1985, *IEEE Standard for Binary Floating-Point Arithmetic*, New York: IEEE, 1985 (Reaffirmed 1991).

[IEEE, 1987] ANSI/IEEE Std 990-1987, *IEEE Recommended Practice for Ada As a Program Design Language*, New York: IEEE, 1987.

[Lytton, 1978] Lytton, Letter to Phillip Wetherall from The Earl of Lytton, Keeper Knight's, Pound Hill, Crawley, Sussex, England, 18 Oct. 1978. Figure 5.7 of this paper.

[Monterey, 1973] *Proceedings of a Symposium on the High Cost of Software Held at the Naval Postgraduate School, Monterey California on September 17–19, 1973*, SRI Project 3272, Stanford Research Institute, Menlo Park, CA, Sept. 1973.

[Moore, 1977] Moore, Doris Langley-Levy, *Ada, Countess of Lovelace: Byron's Legitimate Daughter*, London: Murray, 1977.

[Morrison, 1961] Morrison, P. and E., *Charles Babbage and His Calculating Engines*, New York: Dover, 1961.

[Nielsen, 1987] Nielsen, C. Bendix and Karlsen, E. W., *The Draft Formal Definition of Ada, The Dynamic Semantics Definition*, Vol. 1-3, Jan. 87, Dansk Datamatik Center, Lyngby, Denmark.

[Newcomer, 1979] Newcomer, J. M., Lamb, D. A., Leverett, B. W., Levine, D., Reiner, A. H., Tighe, M., and Wulf, W. A., *TCOL-Ada; Revised Report on an Intermediate Representation for the DoD Standard Programming Language*, Department of Computer Science, Carnegie-Mellon University, Report CMU-CS-79-128, 20 June 1979.

[Oberndorf, 1983] Oberndorf, Patricia, *Kernel Ada Program Support Environment (KAPSE) Interface Team, Public Report*, Report NOSC/TD-552, Vol. 1, Oct. 1983, AD-A115 590, Vol. 2, AD-A123 136, Vol. 3, AD-A141 576.

[Perry, 1978] Perry, William J., DoD High Order Language Commonality Program, Memorandum from Director of Defense Research and Engineering, Washington, DC, 11 April, 1978. Figure 5.4 of this paper.

[SAMSO, 1972] *Information Processing/Data Automation Implication of Air Force Command and Control Requirements in the 1980s (CCIP-85)*, Vol. 4, *Technology Trends: Software*, SAMSO-TR-72-122-V-4, AD-919-267L.

[Shaw, 1978] Shaw, M., Hilfinger, P. and Wulf, W. A., *TARTAN—Language Design for the Ironman Requirement; Notes and Examples*, Department of Computer Science, Carnegie-Mellon University, Report CMU-CS-78-133, June 1978, AD-A062 856/0.

[Standish, 1978] Standish, Thomas, *Proceedings of the Irvine Workshop on Alternatives for the Environment, Certification, and Control of the DoD Common High Order Language, Held at University of California, Irvine on 20–22 June 1978*, Report UCI-ICS-78-83, AD-A089 090.

[Stein, 1985] Stein, Dorothy, *Ada: A Life and a Legacy*, Cambridge MA: MIT Press, 1985, ISBN 0-262-19242-X.

[Wetherall, 1978] Wetherall, Phillip R., Letter to The Earl of Lytton, Royal Signals and Radar Establishment, Great MAlvern, Worcs, England, 10 Oct. 1978. Figure 5.6 of this paper.

[Wentworth, 1938] Wentworth, Lady, *Thoroughbred Racing Stock and its Ancestors: The Authentic Origin of Pure Blood*, London: George Allen & Unwin Ltd., 1938 (editor's note: has the real story on horses that Bowen mistook).

[Whitaker, 1977] Whitaker, William A., The US Department of Defense Common High Order Language Effort, *SIGPLAN Notices*, Feb. 1977.

[Whitaker, 1983] Whitaker, William A., Three Ada Examples, in *COMPCON 83, 26th IEEE Computer Society International Conference, 1983*, pp. 355–359.

[Whitaker, 1990] Whitaker, William A., Programming Languages Overview, in *Aerospace Software Engineering*, Christine Anderson and Merlin Dorfman, eds., Washington; American Institute of Aeronautics and Astronautics, pp. 353–362, 1990.

[Williams, 1977] Williams, John H. and Fisher, David A., eds., *Design and Implementation of Programming Languages—Proceedings of a DoD Sponsored Workshop, Ithaca, Oct. 1976*, Lecture Notes in Computer Science, Vol. 54, Springer-Verlag, 1977.

Author's Note: In Feburary 1995, the International Standards Organization adopted the 9X revision of Ada as ANSI/ISO/IEC 8652:1995.

TRANSCRIPT OF DISCUSSANT'S REMARKS

Editor's note: William Whitaker's presentation closely followed his paper and we have omitted it, with his permission, due to page limitations.

SESSION CHAIR MICHAEL FELDMAN: Dr. John Goodenough, who is the discussant for this presentation. Dr. Goodenough has been continuously involved in the Ada effort from its initial emergence in public view up to the present time. In 1975, when the STRAWMAN requirements were first circulated, Dr. Goodenough was working at Softech in Waltham, Massachusetts on an effort concerned with comparing and analyzing the programming languages. Being very interested in programming language design and having recently finished the design of a JOVIAL-based language used by Boeing, Dr. Goodenough was of course very interested in this new language development and effort. He sent in comments on the WOODENMAN and was eventually the project leader for one of the four initial Ada design efforts. His design was not accepted. Subsequently, Dr. Goodenough became a consultant for the Army, helping to monitor the Ada development efforts as a distinguished Ada reviewer. His successful bid for the Ada compiler validation capability effort in September, 1979, ensured a long-term association with the CII Honeywell/Bull chosen design for Ada. Shortly after the adoption of the Standard in 1983, Dr. Goodenough was appointed chair of the group responsible for issuing recommended interpretations of the Standard. And he is still chair of that group today. In 1986, Dr. Goodenough joined the Software Engineering Institute at Carnegie Mellon University where his initial project was focused on analytical technique for engineering real-time software, namely, Rate Monotonic Analysis. This technique is increasingly used today as a basis for understanding the timing behavior of real time systems. He also maintained his involvement with Ada by serving as the principle author and editor of the Requirements Document for the Ada 9X effort, and serves currently as a distinguished reviewer for Ada 9X.

JOHN B. GOODENOUGH: First of all I'd like to say that when I heard William Whitaker's biography, I was struck by the fact that he started out his contact with computers at Kirtland AFB where the current manager of the Ada 9X project is head of a software engineering laboratory. So, it certainly makes a certain circularity, a return to history in that sense.

Secondly, I would like to emphasize that Bill Whitaker is really the reason that Ada exists today. Bill's ability to shepherd money through the DoD, to get DoD services to give up their individual languages and to support the development of a common programming language, was no mean feat. Certainly, the Navy felt that only the Navy could design a language that would meet Navy needs. Only the Air Force could design a language that would meet Air Force needs. Only the Army for Army needs. Overcoming that kind of thinking was a major bureaucratic in-fighting win of considerable talent.

The contracting approach that was used to develop the Ada language was really remarkable. The idea of designing requirements for a language before the language would be developed, was really a novel idea. Having a competitive design with a down selection process is much more common today for hardware systems, but I don't know if it was even used for hardware systems at that time. And making sure that everything was public and in the open. You can imagine making that happen within a bureaucratic environment. It was quite extraordinary. So I think that Bill deserves an enormous accolade for his work in making this happen.

I should mention one other thing about it, too. Jean Ichbiah told me, one time, that he certainly expected to be selected as one of the designers. But he expected to wind up second in the design competition, because certainly in France no one would give the contract to a foreign designer. In fact, the fact that it was done in the U.S. was pretty extraordinary, as well.

Now I would like to turn to addressing some of the myths about the Ada development effort and the Ada language, some of which have already been addressed. Not that I think that by talking about these myths and correcting them, that will make them go away. Because certain myths are just too good not to be true. Nonetheless, in an attempt to address historic accuracy, one myth already mentioned is that Ada was a committee-designed language. There was just no doubt that this was a designer-based language, and that Jean was the designer. I remember sitting at many meetings with the distinguished reviewers, at which, sometimes, votes were taken on the resolution of issues. I remember many votes that went 9 to 1, 12 to 1, 15 to 1. The proposition lost because the one vote was Jean's. Jean was very good at getting input from a large variety of people, contentious people, people who had lots of opinions. But in the end, it was always his decision as to what went into the language. So, its defects and its strong points, he can take the credit and the blame for both.

There is another aspect of the myth. There is not only the myth that it is a committee-designed language; even if people say that Jean was the designer, they say the requirements were really a committee-based requirement process. That is not true either. David Fisher was just as strong as Jean in the process of assembling these requirements, cutting them down and making sure that they were what he felt would be a minimal set of requirements to meet the diverse needs of DoD embedded systems. Embedded systems is what the language was supposed to address. But, of course, everybody hoped that it would address the need of a variety of systems. I think that in terms of the Requirements Document, which was quite a remarkable document, it is really not fair to say that it was a committee produced document, although there were certainly lots of input from lots of people. But anybody who tried to get David Fisher to change his mind on some requirement knew that this was not a committee process.

An interesting contrast is the level of requirements for the Ada effort, and for the Ada 9X effort. If you look in Bill's paper, you will see that the requirements are, I would say, at a high-level design area because they specify certain details about how the language design was to be done. The Ada 9X requirements are very different in character. They are much higher level. They specify user needs and requirements that are derived from those user needs. Personally, as the principle author of the document, I really want to recommend that you look at the 9X requirements document as well as the original requirements document to see an example of how one can write requirements to guide a language design effort.

There is another myth that is not really a myth, but relates to something that one of speakers this morning talked about. Namely, the nature of facts of history and the fact that facts are not quite as simple as they appear. It's the fact that Ada is a Pascal-based language. This is addressed in Bill's paper. But as part of the bidding process, you had to specify what language you would base your design on. And I can speak for myself in specifying Pascal as the base language. I certainly thought that I would do whatever I wanted. But I had to say Pascal because if I picked ALGOL 68 or PL/1, my credibility as a good language designer would be held in question. So, it was only defensive proposal maneuvering that, in my case, certainly led me to choose Pascal. I suspect that may have been at the heart of some of the other winners' choice of that language as well. Certainly, if you look in the language, you can see as many elements of ALGOL 68 as you can of Pascal. Look at LONG-INTEGER for example, which certainly harkens back to ALGOL 68 or the notion of elaborating declarations. The term elaboration was used for the whole program execution process in ALGOL 68.

One of the interesting parts in the design process was that Jean always felt that the Reference Manual needed to be simple, clear and immediately understandable by readers. And in large part, that was a success and was one of the reasons why Jean's design was chosen over the other design. Because the other designs were perceived to be much more complex because they didn't pay as much attention to that. Jean realized that the design effort was a proposal process from start to finish, and that only when people had actually started to use the language, would the proposal effort be over. I think the other designers didn't keep that important aspect of the effort in mind.

I would like to close with a bit of re-creation of history. There was a conference in Cornell in 1976, which was the first time that a group of people who would eventually work on the Ada effort were assembled to address the WOODENMAN requirements at the time, writing a variety of papers, and so on. At the end of the first day of the conference, there was an after-dinner speech that was given by Jim Horning, who some of you may know. At the time he resided in Canada. I think he is in the U.S. now. Here from the proceedings it said, "Just after dinner on the first evening of the workshop, a tall gaunt and bearded man rose quietly and moved toward the front of the hall. He looked tired and worn as though exhausted by his long arduous journey from the night before. As he turned to speak, a hush fell upon the room. And with a soft and solemn voice, he began. 'Four score and seven weeks ago, ARPA brought forth upon this community a new specification conceived in desperation and dedicated to the proposition that all embedded computer applications are equal. Now we are engaged in a great verbal war, testing whether that specification or any specification so conceived and so dedicated can long be endured. We are met on a great battlefield of that war. We have come to dedicate a proceedings of that battle as a final resting place for those papers that here gave their ideas that that specification might live. It is altogether fitting and proper that we should do this. And now it is for us to be here dedicated to the great task remaining before us, that from these honored papers, we make increased devotion to that cause for which they gave the last full measure of devotion, that we here highly resolve that these papers shall not have been written in vain. That this specification under DoD shall have a new birth of reason and that programming of common problems, by common programmers, in common languages shall not perish from the earth.'"

BIOGRAPHY OF WILLIAM A. WHITAKER, Col. USAF, Ret.

Born 10 January 1936, Little Rock, Arkansas, USA. Attended school in Alexandria, VA, and high school at the American Community School of Paris, France. Received B.S. 1955 and M.S. 1956 in Physics from Tulane University, New Orleans LA; taught and was a Research Assistant, MS thesis "Beta and Gamma Ray Spectroscopy of Antimony-124". Used computers at the New Orleans IBM Service Bureau using card punch calculation on the IBM 604 for data analysis of physics experiments. PhD in Physics, University of Chicago, 1963, thesis "Heating of the Solar Corona by Gravity Waves."

Entered USAF, 1956. Assigned Kirtland Air Force Base, 1957, engaged in systems analysis and nuclear weapons phenomenology, rising to the position of Chief Scientist of the Air Force Weapons Laboratory. While at Kirtland, he was Project Officer on several rocket programs for measurements at nuclear tests and directed a large computational physics organization.

In 1973, he went to the Office of the Director of Defense Research & Engineering (ODDR&E) as Military Assistant for Research, responsible for all programs of the Military Services in fundamental research as well as advanced weapons and advanced computer technology. He steered DoD Basic Research from a badly decaying program, unpopular in both the DoD and the Universities following Viet Nam and the Mansfield Amendment, to a sustained growth rate of 10 percent per year over inflation. While overseeing the computer technology program, he brought the DoD software problem to national attention. He recognized that a major obstacle to the evolution of an engineering technology for software was the multiplicy of languages throughout the DoD. He conceived and sold the notion that a small number of common languages was the prerequisite for any orderly progress in this area, furthermore, an initiative in that direction was within the scope of ODDR&E. He established and, for its five years, Chaired, the DoD High Order Language Working Group, which produced the standard computer language, Ada. This was both a technical and a political position, orchestrating a program between the Military Services and several Allied Governments, while coopting the efforts of thousands of academic and industrial experts worldwide. The philosophy of the program was his: extraordinary openness, user requirements first, funding shared among the Services, competition in design, and consensus in decisions. The day-to-day decisions and personnel responsibilities were also his. The Ada development was successfully completed on schedule, within budget.

VI

Lisp Session

Chair: *Randy Hudson*
Discussant: *John Foderaro*

THE EVOLUTION OF LISP

Guy L. Steele Jr.
Thinking Machines Corporation

Richard P. Gabriel
Lucid, Inc.

ABSTRACT

Lisp is the world's greatest programming language—or so its proponents think. The structure of Lisp makes it easy to extend the language or even to implement entirely new dialects without starting from scratch. Overall, the evolution of Lisp has been guided more by institutional rivalry, one-upsmanship, and the glee born of technical cleverness that is characteristic of the "hacker culture" than by sober assessments of technical requirements. Nevertheless, this process has eventually produced both an industrial-strength programming language, messy but powerful, and a technically pure dialect, small but powerful, that is suitable for use by programming-language theoreticians.

We pick up where McCarthy's paper in the first HOPL conference left off. We trace the development chronologically from the era of the PDP-6, through the heyday of Interlisp and MacLisp, past the ascension and decline of special purpose Lisp machines, to the present era of standardization activities. We then examine the technical evolution of a few representative language features, including some notable successes and failures that illuminate design issues that distinguish Lisp from other programming languages. We also discuss the use of Lisp as a laboratory for designing other programming languages. We conclude with some reflections on the forces that have driven the evolution of Lisp.

CONTENTS

6.1 INTRODUCTION

A great deal has happened to Lisp over the last thirty years. We have found it impossible to treat everything of interest coherently in a single linear pass through the subject, chronologically or otherwise. Projects and dialects emerge, split, join, and die in complicated ways; the careers of individual people are woven through these connections in ways that are sometimes parallel but more often orthogonal. Ideas leap from project to project, from person to person. We have chosen to present a series of slices through the subject matter. This organization inevitably leads to some redundancy in the presentation.

Moreover, we have had to omit a great deal of material for lack of space. The choice of topics presented here necessarily reflects our own experiences and biases. We apologize if your favorite corner of the sprawling Lisp community has gone unmentioned.

Section 6.2 discusses the history of Lisp in terms of projects and people, from where McCarthy left off [McCarthy 1981] up through the efforts to produce official standards for Lisp dialects within IEEE, ANSI, and ISO. Section 6.3 examines a number of technical themes and traces separately their chronological evolution; here the emphasis is on the flow of ideas for each topic. Section 6.4 traces the use of Lisp as a language laboratory and implementation tool, especially for the development of AI languages; particular attention is paid to ways in which feedback from the AI languages influenced the development of Lisp itself. Section 6.5 draws some conclusions about why Lisp evolved as it did.

6.2 IMPLEMENTATION PROJECTS CHRONOLOGY

Early thoughts about a language that eventually became Lisp started in 1956 when John McCarthy attended the Dartmouth Summer Research Project on Artificial Intelligence. Actual implementation began in the fall of 1958. In 1978 McCarthy related the early history of the language [McCarthy 1981], taking it approximately to just after Lisp 1.5. (See also McCarthy [1980].) We begin our story where McCarthy left off.

6.2.1 From Lisp 1.5 to PDP-6 Lisp: 1960–1965

During this period, Lisp spread rapidly to a variety of computers, either by bootstrapping from an existing Lisp on another computer or by a new implementation. In almost all cases, the Lisp dialect was small and simple and the implementation straightforward. There were very few changes made to the original language.

In the early 1960s, Timothy P. Hart and Thomas G. Evans implemented Lisp 1.5 on the Univac M 460, a military version of the Univac 490. It was bootstrapped from Lisp 1.5 on the IBM 7090 using a cross-compiler and a small amount of machine language code for the lowest levels of the Lisp implementation [Hart 1964].

Robert Saunders and his colleagues at System Development Corporation implemented Lisp 1.5 on the IBM-built AN/FSQ-32/V computer, often called simply the Q-32 [Saunders 1964b]. The implementation was bootstrapped from the IBM 7090 and PDP-1 computers at Stanford University. (The PDP-1 Lisp at Stanford was implemented by John McCarthy and Steve Russell.)

In 1963, L. Peter Deutsch (at that time a high school student) implemented a Lisp similar to Lisp 1.5 on the PDP-1 at Bolt Beranek and Newman (BBN) [Deutsch 1964]. This Lisp was called Basic PDP-1 Lisp.

By 1964 a version of Lisp 1.5 was running in the Electrical Engineering Department at MIT on an IBM 7094 computer, running the Compatible Time Sharing System (CTSS). This Lisp and Basic PDP-1 Lisp were the main influences on the PDP-6 Lisp [PDP-6 Lisp 1967] implemented by DEC and some members of MIT's Tech Model Railroad Club in the spring of 1964. This Lisp was the first program written on the PDP-6. Also, this Lisp was the ancestor of MacLisp, the Lisp written to run under the Incompatible Timesharing System (ITS) [Eastlake 1968, 1972] at MIT on the PDP-6 and later on the PDP-10.

At BBN, a successor to Basic PDP-1 Lisp was implemented on the PDP-1 and an upward-compatible version, patterned after Lisp 1.5 on the MIT CTSS system, was implemented on the Scientific Data Systems 940 (SDS 940) by Daniel Bobrow and D. L. Murphy. A further upward-compatible version was written for the PDP-10 by Alice Hartley and Murphy, and this Lisp was called BBN-Lisp [Teitelman 1971]. In 1973, not long after the time that SDS was acquired by Xerox and renamed Xerox Data Systems, the maintenance of BBN-Lisp was shared by BBN and Xerox Palo Alto Research Center and the name of the Lisp was changed to Interlisp [Teitelman 1974].

The PDP-6 [DEC 1964] and PDP-10 [DEC 1969] computers were, by design, especially suited for Lisp, with 36-bit words and 18-bit addresses. This allowed a **CONS** cell—a pair of pointers or addresses—to be stored efficiently in a single word. There were half-word instructions that made manipulating the **CAR** and **CDR** of **CONS** cells very fast. The PDP-6 and PDP-10 also had fast, powerful stack instructions, which enabled fast function calling for Lisp.

Almost all of these implementations had a small hand-coded (assembly) core and a compiler; the rest of the Lisp was written in Lisp and compiled.

In 1965, virtually all of the Lisps in existence were identical or differed only in trivial ways. After 1965—or more precisely, after MacLisp and BBN-Lisp diverged from each other—there came a plethora of Lisp dialects.

During this period there was little funding for language work, the groups were isolated from each other, and each group was directed primarily towards serving the needs of a local user group, which usually consisted of only a handful of researchers. The typical situation is characterized by the description "an AI lab with a Lisp wizard down the hall." During this period there was a good deal of experimentation with implementation strategies. There was little thought of consolidation, partly because of the pioneering feeling that each laboratory embodied.

An exception to all this was the Lisp 2 project [Abrahams 1966], a concerted language development effort that was funded by ARPA and represented a radical departure from Lisp 1.5. There appears to have been some hope that this design would supersede Lisp 1.5 and bring symbolic processing closer to ALGOL 60. (See Section 6.3.5 for an example of Lisp 2 code.) Lisp 2 was implemented for the Q-32 computer but never achieved wide acceptance. Jean Sammet remarked [Sammet 1969, p. 596]:

> . . . in contrast to most languages, in which the language is first designed and then implemented . . . it was facetiously said of LISP 2 that it was "an implementation in search of a language."

The first real standard Lisps were MacLisp and Interlisp; as such they deserve some attention.

6.2.2 MacLisp

MacLisp was the primary Lisp dialect at the MIT AI Lab from the late 1960s until the early 1980s. Other important Lisp work at the Lab during this period included Lisp-Machine Lisp (later named Zetalisp) and Scheme. MacLisp is usually identified with the PDP-10 computer, but MacLisp also ran on another machine, the Honeywell 6180, under the Multics operating system [Organick 1972].

6.2.2.1 *Early MacLisp*

The distinguishing feature of the MacLisp/Interlisp era is the attention to production quality or near production quality implementations. This period saw a consolidation of implementation techniques, with great attention to detail.

A key difference between MacLisp and Interlisp was the approach to syntax. MacLisp favored the pure list style, using **EVAL** as the top level. Interlisp, along with Lisp 1.5, used **EVALQUOTE**.

To concatenate the lists **(BOAT AIRPLANE SKATEBOARD)** and **(CAR TRUCK)** in MacLisp, one would type this expression to **EVAL**:

```
(APPEND (QUOTE (BOAT AIRPLANE SKATEBOARD)) (QUOTE (CAR TRUCK)))
```

or, using the syntactic abbreviation **'x** for **(quote x)**,

```
(APPEND '(BOAT AIRPLANE SKATEBOARD) '(CAR TRUCK))
```

The result would of course be **(BOAT AIRPLANE SKATEBOARD CAR TRUCK)**.

In Lisp 1.5, one would type an expression (actually two expressions) like this to **EVALQUOTE**:

```
APPEND((BOAT AIRPLANE SKATEBOARD) (CAR TRUCK))
```

The first expression denotes a function, and the second is a list of arguments. The "quote" in the name **EVALQUOTE** signifies the "implicit quoting of the arguments" to the function applied. MacLisp forked off and used **EVAL** exclusively as a top level interface. BBN-Lisp (and thus Interlisp) accommodated both: if the first input line contained a complete form and at least one character of a second form, then BBN-Lisp finished reading the second form and used the **EVALQUOTE** interface for that interaction; otherwise it read exactly one form and used the **EVAL** interface for that interaction.

The phrase "quoting arguments" actually is misleading and imprecise. It refers to the actions of a hypothetical preprocessor that transforms the input from a form like

```
APPEND((BOAT AIRPLANE SKATEBOARD) (CAR TRUCK))
```

to one like

```
(APPEND (QUOTE (BOAT AIRPLANE SKATEBOARD)) (QUOTE (CAR TRUCK)))
```

before evaluation is performed. A similar confusion carried over into the description of the so-called **FEXPR** or "special form." In some texts on Lisp one will find descriptions of special forms that speak of a special form "quoting its arguments," when in fact a special form has a special rule for determining its meaning and that rule involves not evaluating some forms [Pitman 1980].

McCarthy [McCarthy 1981] noted that the original Lisp interpreter was regarded as a universal Turing machine: It could perform any computation given a set of instructions (a function) and the initial input on its tape (arguments). Thus it was intended that

```
APPEND((BOAT AIRPLANE SKATEBOARD) (CAR TRUCK))
```

be regarded not as a syntactically mutated version of

```
(APPEND (QUOTE (BOAT AIRPLANE SKATEBOARD)) (QUOTE (CAR TRUCK)))
```

but as a function and (separately) a literal list of arguments. In hindsight we see that the **EVALQUOTE** top level might better have been called the **APPLY** top level, making it pleasantly symmetrical to the **EVAL** top level; the BBN-Lisp documentation brought out this symmetry explicitly. Indeed, **EVALQUOTE** would have been identical to the function **APPLY** in Lisp 1.5 if not for these two differences: (a) in Lisp 1.5, **APPLY** took a third argument, an environment (regarded nowadays as something of a mistake that resulted in dynamic binding rather than the lexical scoping needed for a faithful reflection of the lambda calculus); and (b) "**EVALQUOTE** is capable of handling special forms as a sort of exception" [McCarthy 1962]. Nowadays such an exception is referred to as a *kluge* [Raymond 1991]. (Note, however, that MacLisp's **APPLY** function supported this same kluge.)

MacLisp introduced the **LEXPR**, which is a type of function that takes any number of arguments and puts them on the stack; the single parameter of the function is bound to the number of arguments passed. The form of the lambda-list for this argument—a symbol and not a list—signals the **LEXPR** case. Here is an example of how to define **LIST**, a function of a variable number of arguments that returns the list of those arguments:

```
(DEFUN LIST N
  (DO ((J N (- J 1))
       (ANSWER () (CONS (ARG J) ANSWER))
      ((ZEROP J) ANSWER)))
```

Parameter **N** is bound to the number of arguments passed. The expression **(ARG J)** refers to the Jth argument passed.

The need for the **LEXPR** (and its compiled counterpart, the **LSUBR**) arose from a desire to have variable arity functions such as **+**. Though there is no semantic need for an n-ary **+**, it is convenient for programmers to be able to write **(+ A B C D)** rather than the equivalent but more cumbersome **(+ A (+ B (+ C D)))**.

The simple but powerful macro facility on which **DEFMACRO** is based was introduced in MacLisp in the mid-1960s. See Section 6.3.3.

Other major improvements over Lisp 1.5 were arrays; the modification of simple predicates—such as **MEMBER**—to be functions that return useful values; **PROG2**; and the introduction of the function **ERR**, which allowed user code to signal an error.

In Lisp 1.5, certain built-in functions might signal errors, when given incorrect arguments, for example. Signaling an error normally resulted in program termination or invocation of a debugger. Lisp 1.5 also had the function **ERRSET**, which was useful for controlled execution of code that *might* cause an error. The special form

(ERRSET *form***)**

evaluates *form* in a context in which errors do not terminate the program or enter the debugger. If *form* does not cause an error, **ERRSET** returns a singleton list of the value. If execution of *form* does cause an error, the **ERRSET** form quietly returns **NIL**.

MacLisp added the function **ERR**, which signals an error. If **ERR** is invoked within the dynamic context of an **ERRSET** form, then the argument to **ERR** is returned as the value of the **ERRSET** form.

Programmers soon began to use **ERRSET** and **ERR** not to trap and signal errors but for more general control purposes (dynamic nonlocal exits). Unfortunately, this use of **ERRSET** also quietly trapped unexpected errors, making programs harder to debug. A new pair of primitives, **CATCH** and **THROW**, was introduced into MacLisp [Lisp Archive 1972, item 2] so that **ERRSET** could be reserved for its intended use of error trapping.

The lesson of **ERRSET** and **CATCH** is important. The designers of **ERRSET** and later **ERR** had in mind a particular situation and defined a pair of primitives to address that situation. But because these facilities provided a combination of useful and powerful capabilities (error trapping plus dynamic nonlocal exits), programmers began to use these facilities in unintended ways. Then the designers had to go back and split the desired functionality into pieces with alternative interfaces. This pattern of careful design, unintended use, and later redesign is common in the evolution of Lisp.

The next phase of MacLisp development began when the developers of MacLisp started to see a large and influential user group emerge—Project MAC and the Mathlab/MACSYMA group. The emphasis turned to satisfying the needs of their user community rather than doing language design and implementation as such.

6.2.2.2 *Later MacLisp*

During the latter part of its life cycle, MacLisp adopted language features from other Lisp dialects and from other languages, and some novel things were invented.

The most significant development for MacLisp occurred in the early 1970s when the techniques in the prototype "fast arithmetic compiler" LISCOM [Golden 1970] were incorporated into the MacLisp compiler by Jon L White, who had already been the principal MacLisp maintainer and developer for several years. (John Lyle White was commonly known by his login name **JONL**, which can be pronounced as either "jónnell" (to rhyme with "O'Donnell") or "john-ell" (two equally stressed syllables). Because of this, he took to writing his name as "Jon L White" rather than "John L. White".)

Steele, who at age 17 had already hung out around MIT for several years and had implemented a Lisp system for the IBM 1130, was hired as a Lisp hacker in July 1972 by the MIT Mathlab group, which was headed by Joel Moses. Steele soon took responsibility for maintaining the MacLisp interpreter and run-time system, allowing Jon L to concentrate almost full time on compiler improvements.

The resulting new MacLisp compiler, NCOMPLR [Moon 1974; Lisp Archive; Pitman 1983], became a standard against which all other Lisp compilers were measured in terms of the speed of running code. Inspired by the needs of the MIT Artificial Intelligence Laboratory, which covered the numeric computations done in vision and robotics, several new ways of representing and compiling numeric code resulted in numeric performance of compiled MacLisp on a near par with FORTRAN compilers [Fateman 1973].

Bignums—arbitrary precision integer arithmetic—were added circa 1971 to meet the needs of MACSYMA users. The code was a more or less faithful transcription of the algorithms in Knuth [1969]. Later, Bill Gosper suggested some improvements, notably a version of **GCD** that combined the good features of the binary GCD algorithm with Lehmer's method for speeding up integer bignum division [Knuth 1981, ex. 4.5.2-34].

In 1973 and 1974, David Moon led an effort to implement MacLisp on the Honeywell 6180 under Multics. As a part of this project he wrote the first truly comprehensive reference manual for MacLisp, which became familiarly known as "the Moonual" [Moon 1974].

Richard Greenblatt started the MIT Lisp Machine project in 1974 [Greenblatt 1974]; David Moon, Richard Stallman, and many other MIT AI Lab Lisp hackers eventually joined this project. As this project progressed, language features were selectively retrofitted into PDP-10 MacLisp as the two projects cross-fertilized.

Complex lambda lists partly arose by influence from Muddle (later called MDL [Galley 1975]), which was a language for the Dynamic Modeling Group at MIT. It ran on a PDP-10 located in the same machine room as the AI and Mathlab machines. The austere syntax of Lisp 1.5 was not quite powerful enough to express clearly the different roles of arguments to a function. Complex lambda-lists appeared as a solution to this problem and became widely accepted; eventually they terribly complicated the otherwise elegant Common Lisp Object System.

MacLisp introduced the notion of *read tables*. A read table provides programmable input syntax for programs and data. When a character is input, the table is consulted to determine the syntactic characteristics of the character for use in putting together tokens. For example, the table is used to determine which characters denote whitespace. In addition, functions can be associated with characters, so that a function is invoked whenever a given character is read; the function can read further input before returning a value to be incorporated into the data structure being read. In this way the built-in parser can be reprogrammed by the user. This powerful facility made it easy to experiment with alternative input syntaxes for Lisp, ranging from such simple abbreviations as `'x` for `(quote x)` to the backquote facility and elaborate ALGOL-style parsers. See Section 6.3.5.1 for further discussion of some of these experiments.

MacLisp adopted only a small number of features from other Lisp dialects. In 1974, about a dozen persons attended a meeting at MIT between the MacLisp and Interlisp implementors, including Warren Teitelman, Alice Hartley, Jon L White, Jeff Golden, and Steele. There was some hope of finding substantial common ground, but the meeting actually served to illustrate the great chasm separating the two groups, in everything from implementation details to overall design philosophy. (Much of the unwillingness of each side to depart from its chosen strategy probably stemmed from the already severe resource constraints on the PDP-10, a one-megabyte, one-MIPS machine. With the advent of the MIT Lisp Machines, with their greater speed and *much* greater address space, the crowd that had once advocated a small, powerful execution environment with separate programming tools embraced the strategy of writing programming tools in Lisp and turning the Lisp environment into a complete programming environment.) In the end only a trivial exchange of features resulted from "the great MacLisp/Interlisp summit": MacLisp adopted from Interlisp the behavior `(CAR NIL)` → `NIL` and `(CDR NIL)` → `NIL`, and Interlisp adopted the concept of a read table.

By the mid-1970s it was becoming increasingly apparent that the address space limitation of the PDP-10—256K 36-bit words, or about one megabyte—was becoming a severe constraint as the size of Lisp programs grew. MacLisp by this time had enjoyed nearly ten years of strong use and acceptance within its somewhat small but very influential user community. Its implementation strategy of a large assembly language core proved to be too much to stay with the dialect as it stood, and intellectual pressures from other dialects, other languages, and the language design aspirations of its implementors resulted in new directions for Lisp.

To many, the period of stable MacLisp use was a golden era in which all was right with the world of Lisp. (This same period is also regarded today by many nostalgics as the golden era of Artificial Intelligence.) By 1980 the MacLisp user community was on the decline—the funding for MACSYMA would not last too long. Various funding crises in AI had depleted the ranks of the AI Lab Lisp wizards, and the core group of wizards from MIT and MIT hangers-on moved to new institutions.

6.2.3 Interlisp

Interlisp (and BBN-Lisp before it) introduced many radical ideas into Lisp programming style and methodology. The most visible of these ideas are embodied in programming tools, such as the spelling corrector, the file package, DWIM, CLISP, the structure editor, and MASTERSCOPE.

The origin of these ideas can be found in Warren Teitelman's Ph.D. dissertation on man-computer symbiosis [Teitelman 1966]. In particular, it contains the roots of structure editing (as opposed to "text" or "tape" editing [Rudloe 1962]), breakpointing, advice, and CLISP. (William Henneman in 1964 described a translator for the A-language [Henneman 1964], an English-like or ALGOL-like surface syntax for Lisp (see Section 6.3.5.1), but it was not nearly as elaborate or as flexible as CLISP. Henneman's work does not appear to have directly influenced Teitelman; at least, Teitelman does not cite it, though he cites other papers in the same collection containing Henneman's paper [Berkeley 1964].)

The spelling corrector and DWIM were designed to compensate for human foibles. When a symbol had no value (or no function definition), the Interlisp spelling corrector [Teitelman 1974] was invoked, because the symbol might have been misspelled. The spelling corrector compared a possibly misspelled symbol with a list of known words. The user had options for controlling the behavior of the system with respect to spelling correction. The system would do one of three things: (a) correct automatically; (b) pause and ask whether a proposed correction were acceptable; or (c) simply signal an error.

The spelling corrector was under the general control of a much larger program, called DWIM, for "Do What I Mean." Whenever an error of any sort was detected by the Interlisp system, DWIM was invoked to determine the appropriate action. DWIM was able to correct some forms of parenthesis errors, which, along with the misspelling of identifiers, comprised the most common typographical errors by users.

DWIM fit in well with the work philosophy of Interlisp. The Interlisp model was to emulate an infinite login session. In Interlisp, the programmer worked with source code presented by a *structure editor*, which operated on source code in the form of memory-resident Lisp data structures. Any changes to the code were saved in a file, which served as a persistent repository for the programmer's code. DWIM's changes were saved also. The memory-resident structure was considered the primary representation of the program; the file was merely a stable backup copy. (The MacLisp model, in contrast, was for the programmer to work with ASCII files that represented the program, using a character-oriented editor. Here the file was considered the primary representation of the program.)

CLISP (Conversational LISP) was a mixed ALGOL-like and English-like syntax embedded within normal Interlisp syntax. Here is a valid definition of **FACTORIAL** written in Interlisp CLISP syntax:

```
DEFINEQ((FACTORIAL
  (LAMBDA (N) (IF N=0 THEN 1 ELSE N*(FACTORIAL N-1)))))
```

CLISP also depended on the generic DWIM mechanism. Note that it not only must, in effect, rearrange tokens and insert parentheses, but also must split atoms such as **N=0** and **N*** into several appropriate tokens. Thus the user need not put spaces around infix operators.

CLISP defined a useful set of iteration constructs. Here is a simple program to print all the prime numbers p in the range $m \leq p \leq n$:

```
(FOR P FROM M TO N DO (PRINT P) WHILE (PRIMEP P))
```

CLISP, DWIM, and the spelling corrector could work together to recognize the following as a valid definition of **FACTORIAL** [Teitelman 1973]:

```
DEFINEQ((FACTORIAL
  (LAMBDA (N) (IFFN=0 THENN 1 ESLE N*8FACTTORIALNN-1))))
```

Interlisp eventually "corrects" this mangled definition into the valid form shown previously. Note that shift-8 is left parenthesis on the Model 33 teletype, which had a bit-paired keyboard. DWIM had to be changed when typewriter-paired keyboards (on which left parenthesis was shift-9, and shift-8 was the asterisk) became common.

MASTERSCOPE was a facility for finding out information about the functions in a large system. MASTERSCOPE could analyze a body of code, build up a data base, and answer questions interactively. MASTERSCOPE kept track of such relationships as which functions called which others (directly or indirectly), which variables were bound where, which functions destructively altered certain data structures, and so on. (MacLisp had a corresponding utility called INDEX, but it was not nearly as general or flexible, and it ran only in batch mode, producing a file containing a completely cross-indexed report.)

Interlisp introduced to the Lisp community the concept of *block compilation*, in which multiple functions are compiled as a single block; this resulted in faster function calling than would otherwise have been possible in Interlisp.

Interlisp ran on PDP-10s, Vaxen (plural of VAX [Raymond 1991]), and a variety of special-purpose Lisp machines developed by Xerox and BBN. The most commonly available Interlisp machines were the Dolphin, the Dorado, and the Dandelion (collectively known as D-machines). The Dorado was the fastest of the three and the Dandelion the most commonly used. It is interesting that different Interlisp implementations used different techniques for handling special variables: Interlisp-10 (for the PDP-10) used shallow binding, whereas Interlisp-D (for D-machines) used deep binding. These two implementation techniques exhibit different performance profiles—a program with a certain run time under one regime could take ten times longer under the other.

This situation of unexpected performance is prevalent with Lisp. One can argue that programmers produce efficient code in a language only when they understand the implementation. With C, the implementation is straightforward because C operations are in close correspondence to the machine operations on a von Neumann architecture computer. With Lisp, the implementation is not straightforward, but depends on a complex set of implementation techniques and choices. A programmer would need to be familiar with not only the techniques selected but the performance ramifications of using those techniques. It is little wonder that good Lisp programmers are harder to find than good C programmers.

Like MacLisp, Interlisp extended the function-calling mechanisms in Lisp 1.5 with respect to how arguments can be passed to a function. Interlisp function definitions specified arguments as the cross product of two attributes: **LAMBDA** versus **NLAMBDA**, and spread versus nospread.

LAMBDA functions evaluate each of their arguments; **NLAMBDA** functions evaluate none of their arguments (that is, the unevaluated argument *subforms* of the call are passed as the arguments). Spread functions require a fixed number of arguments; nospread functions accept a variable number. These two attributes were not quite orthogonal, because the parameter of a nospread **NLAMBDA** was bound to a list of the unevaluated argument forms, whereas the parameter of a nospread **LAMBDA** was bound to the number of arguments passed and the **ARG** function was used to retrieve actual argument values. There was thus a close correspondence between the mechanisms of Interlisp and MacLisp:

Interlisp		*MacLisp*
LAMBDA	spread	**EXPR**
LAMBDA	nospread	**LEXPR**
NLAMBDA	spread	no equivalent
NLAMBDA	nospread	FEXPR

There was another important difference here between MacLisp and Interlisp, however. In MacLisp, "fixed number of arguments" had a quite rigid meaning; a function accepting three arguments must be called with exactly three arguments, neither more nor less. In Interlisp, any function could legitimately be called with any number of arguments; excess argument forms were evaluated and their values discarded, and missing argument values were defaulted to `NIL`. This was one of the principal irreconcilable differences separating the two sides at their 1974 summit. Thereafter MacLisp partisans derided Interlisp as undisciplined and error-prone, while Interlisp fans thought MacLisp awkward and inflexible, for they had the convenience of optional arguments, which did not come to MacLisp until **`&optional`** and other complex lambda-list syntax was retrofitted, late in the game, from Lisp-Machine Lisp.

One of the most innovative of the language extensions introduced by Interlisp was the *spaghetti stack* [Bobrow 1973]. The problem of retention (by closures) of the dynamic function-definition environment in the presence of special variables was never completely solved until spaghetti stacks were invented.

The idea behind spaghetti stacks is to generalize the structure of stacks to be more like a tree, with various branches of the tree subject to retention whenever a pointer to that branch is retained. That is, parts of the stack are subject to the same garbage collection policies as are other Lisp objects. Unlike closures, the retained environment captures both the control environment and the binding environment.

One of the minor, but interesting, syntactic extensions that Interlisp made was the introduction of the superparenthesis, or superbracket. If a right square bracket `]` is encountered during a read operation, it balances all outstanding open left parentheses, or back to the last outstanding left square bracket `[`. Here is a simple example of this syntax:

```
DEFINEQ((FACTORIAL
  (LAMBDA (N)
   (COND [(ZEROP N) 1]
         (T (TIMES N (FACTORIAL (SUB1 N]
```

MacLisp and Interlisp came into existence about the same time and lasted about as long as each other. They differed in their user groups, though any generic description of the two groups would not distinguish them: both groups were researchers at AI labs funded primarily by ARPA (later DARPA) and were educated by MIT, CMU, and Stanford. The principal implementations ran on the same machines; one had cachet as the Lisp with the friendly environment and the other was the lean, mean, high-powered Lisp. The primary differences came from different philosophical approaches to the problem of programming. There were also different pressures from their user groups; MacLisp users, particularly the Mathlab group, were willing to use a less integrated programming environment in exchange for a good optimizing compiler and having a large fraction of the PDP-10 address space left free for their own use. Interlisp users preferred to concentrate on the task of coding by using a full, integrated development environment.

6.2.4 The Early 1970s

Though MacLisp and Interlisp dominated the 1970s, there were several other major Lisp dialects in use during this period. Most were more similar to MacLisp than to Interlisp. The two most widely used dialects were Standard Lisp [Marti 1979] and Portable Standard Lisp [Utah 1982]. Standard Lisp was defined by Anthony Hearn and Martin Griss, along with their students and colleagues. The motivation was to define a subset of Lisp 1.5 and other Lisp dialects that could serve as a medium for porting Lisp programs, most particularly the symbolic algebra system REDUCE.

Later, Hearn and his colleagues discovered that for good performance they needed more control over the environment and the compiler, so Portable Standard Lisp (PSL) was born. Standard Lisp attempted to piggyback on existing Lisps, whereas PSL was a complete new Lisp implementation with a retargetable compiler [Griss 1981], an important pioneering effort in the evolution of Lisp compilation technology. By the end of the 1970s, PSL ran—and ran well—on more than a dozen different types of computers.

PSL was implemented using two techniques. First, it used a system implementation language called SYSLISP to code operations on raw, untyped representations. Second, it used a parameterized set of assembly-level translation macros called c-macros. The Portable Lisp Compiler (PLC) compiled Lisp code into an abstract assembly language. This language was then converted to a machine-dependent LAP (Lisp Assembly Program) format by pattern-matching the c-macro descriptions with the abstract instructions in context. For example, different machine instructions might be selected, depending on the sources of the operands and the destination of the result of the operation.

In the latter half of the 1970s and on into the mid-1980s, the PSL environment was improved by adapting editors and other tools. In particular, a good multiwindow Emacs-like editor called Emode was developed that allowed fairly intelligent editing and the passing of information back and forth between the Lisp and the editor. Later, a more extensive version of Emode called Nmode was developed by Martin Griss and his colleagues at Hewlett-Packard in Palo Alto, California. This version of PSL and Nmode was commercialized by Hewlett-Packard in the mid-1980s.

At Stanford in the 1960s, an early version of MacLisp was adapted for their PDP-6; this Lisp was called Lisp 1.6 [Quam 1972]. The early adaptation was rewritten by John Allen and Lynn Quam; later compiler improvements were made by Whit Diffie. Lisp 1.6 disappeared during the mid-1970s, one of the last remnants of the Lisp 1.5 era.

UCI Lisp [Bobrow 1972] was an extended version of Lisp 1.6 in which an Interlisp style editor and other programming environment improvements were made. UCI Lisp was used during the early to mid-1970s by some folks at Stanford, as well as at other institutions.

In 1976 the MIT version of MacLisp was ported to the WAITS operating system by Gabriel at the Stanford AI Laboratory (SAIL), which was directed at that time by John McCarthy.

6.2.5 The Demise of the PDP-10

By the middle of the 1970s it became apparent that the 18-bit address space of the PDP-10 would not provide enough working space for AI programs. The PDP-10 line of computers (KL-10s and DEC-20s) was altered to permit an extended addressing scheme, in which multiple 18-bit address spaces could be addressed by indexing relative to 30-bit base registers.

However, this addition was not a smooth expansion to the architecture as far as the Lisp implementor was concerned; the change from two pointers per word to only one pointer per word required a complete redesign of nearly all internal data structures. Only two Lisps were implemented for extended addressing: ELISP (by Charles Hedrick at Rutgers) and PSL.

One response to the address space problem was to construct special-purpose Lisp machines (see Section 6.2.6). The other response was to use commercial computers (*stock hardware*) with larger address spaces; the first of these was the VAX [DEC 1981].

Vaxen presented both opportunities and problems for Lisp implementors. The VAX instruction set provided some good opportunities for implementing the low level Lisp primitives efficiently, though it required clever—perhaps too clever—design of the data structures. However, Lisp function calls could not be accurately modeled with the VAX function-call instructions. Moreover, the VAX, despite its theoretically large address space, was apparently designed for use by many small programs, not several large ones. Page tables occupied too large a fraction of memory; paging overhead for large Lisp programs was a problem never fully solved on the VAX. Finally, there was the problem of prior investment; more than one major Lisp implementation at the time had a large assembly-language base that was difficult to port.

The primary VAX Lisp dialects developed in the late 1970s were VAX Interlisp, PSL (ported to the VAX), Franz Lisp, and NIL.

Franz Lisp [Foderaro 1982] was written to enable research on symbolic algebra to continue at the University of California at Berkeley, under the supervision of Richard J. Fateman, who was one of the principal implementors of MACSYMA at MIT. Fateman and his students started with a PDP-11 version of Lisp written at Harvard, and extended it into a MacLisp-like Lisp that eventually ran on virtually all Unix-based computers, thanks to the fact that Franz Lisp is written almost entirely in C.

NIL [Burke 1983], intended to be the successor to MacLisp, was designed by Jon L White, Steele, and others at MIT, under the influence of Lisp-Machine Lisp, also developed at MIT. Its name was a too-cute acronym for "New Implementation of Lisp" and caused a certain amount of confusion because of the central role already played in the Lisp language by the atomic symbol named **NIL**. NIL was a large Lisp, and efficiency concerns were paramount in the minds of its MacLisp-oriented implementors; soon its implementation was centered around a large VAX assembly-language base.

In 1978, Gabriel and Steele set out to implement NIL [Brooks 1982a] on the S-1 Mark IIA, a supercomputer being designed and built by the Lawrence Livermore National Laboratory [Correll 1979; Hailpern 1979]. Close cooperation on this project was aided by the fact that Steele rented a room in Gabriel's home. This Lisp was never completely functional, but served as a testbed for adapting advanced compiler techniques to Lisp implementation. In particular, the work generalized the numerical computation techniques of the MacLisp compiler and unified them with mainstream register allocation strategies [Brooks 1982b].

In France in the mid-1970s, Patrick Greussay developed an interpreter-based Lisp called Vlisp [Greussay 1977]. At the level of the base dialect of Interlisp, it introduced a couple of interesting concepts, such as the *chronology*, which is a sort of dynamic environment for implementing interrupts and environmental functions like **trace** and **step**, by creating different incarnations of the evaluator. Vlisp's emphasis was on having a fast interpreter. The concept was to provide a virtual machine that was used to transport the evaluator. This virtual machine was at the level of assembly language and was designed for easy porting and efficient execution. The interpreter got a significant part of its speed from two things: a fast function dispatch using a function type space that distinguished a number of functions of different arity, and tail recursion removal. (Vlisp was probably the first production-quality Lisp to support general tail recursion removal. Other dialects of the time, including MacLisp, did tail recursion removal in certain situations only, in a manner not guaranteed predictable.) Vlisp was the precursor to Le_Lisp, one of the important Lisp dialects in France and Europe during the 1980s; though the dialects were different, they shared some implementation techniques.

At the end of the 1970s, no new commercial machines suitable for Lisp were on the horizon; it appeared that the VAX was all there was. Despite years of valiant support by Glenn Burke, VAX NIL never achieved widespread acceptance. Interlisp/VAX was a performance disaster. "General-purpose" workstations (those intended or designed to run languages other than Lisp) and personal computers hadn't quite appeared yet. To most Lisp implementors and users, the commercial hardware situation looked quite bleak.

But from 1974 onward there had been research and prototyping projects for Lisp machines, and at the end of the decade it appeared that Lisp machines were the wave of the future.

6.2.6 Lisp Machines

Though ideas for a Lisp machine had been informally discussed before, Peter Deutsch seems to have published the first concrete proposal [Deutsch 1973]. Deutsch outlined the basic vision of a single-user minicomputer-class machine that would be specially microcoded to run Lisp and support a Lisp development environment. The two key ideas from Deutsch's paper that have had a lasting impact on Lisp are the duality of load and store access based on functions, and the compact representation of linear lists through "**CDR**-coding."

All Lisp dialects up to that time had one function **CAR** to read the first component of a dotted pair and a nominally unrelated function **RPLACA** to write that same component. Deutsch proposed that functions like **CAR** should have both a "load" mode and a "store" mode. If $(f\ a_1 \dots a_n)$ is called in load mode, it should return a value; if called in store mode, as in $(f\ a_1 \ldots a_n\ v)$, the new value v should be stored in the location that would be accessed by the load version. Deutsch indicated that there should be two internal functions associated with every accessor function, one for loading and one for storing, and that the store function should be called when the function is mentioned in a particular set of special forms. However, his syntax is suggestive; here is the proposed definition of **RPLACA**:

```
(LAMBDA (X Y) (SETFQ (CAR X) Y))
```

Deutsch commented that the special form used here is called **SETFQ** because "it quotes the function and evaluates everything else." This name was abbreviated to **SETF** in Lisp-Machine Lisp. Deutsch attributed the idea of dual functions to Alan Kay.

6.2.6.1 *MIT Lisp Machines: 1974–1978*

Richard Greenblatt started the MIT Lisp Machine project in 1974; his proposal [Greenblatt 1974] cites the Deutsch paper. The project also included Thomas Knight, Jack Holloway, and Pitts Jarvis. The machine they designed was called CONS, and its design was based on ideas from the Xerox PARC Alto microprocessor, the DEC PDP-11/40, the PDP-11/40 extensions done by CMU, and some ideas on instruction modification suggested by Sam Fuller at DEC.

This machine was designed to have good performance while supporting a version of Lisp upwards-compatible with MacLisp but augmented with "Muddle-Conniver" argument declaration syntax. Its other goals included nonprohibitive cost (less than $70,000 per machine), single-user operation, a common target language along with standardization of procedure calls, a factor of three better storage efficiency than the PDP-10 for compiled programs, hardware support for type checking and garbage collection, a largely Lisp-coded implementation (less reliance on assembly language or other low-level implementation language), and an improved programming environment exploiting large, bit-mapped displays.

The CONS machine was built; then a subsequent improved version named the CADR (an in-joke—**CADR** means "the second one" in Lisp) was designed and some dozens of them were built. These became the computational mainstay within the MIT AI Lab and it seemed sensible to spin off a company to commercialize this machine. Because of disagreements among the principals, however, *two* companies were formed: LISP Machine, Inc. (LMI) and Symbolics. Initially each manufactured CADR clones. Soon thereafter, Symbolics introduced its 3600 line, which became the industry leader in Lisp machine performance for the next five years.

Although Greenblatt had paid particular care to providing hardware mechanisms to support fast garbage collection, the early MIT Lisp Machines in fact did not implement a garbage collector for quite some years; or rather, even when the garbage collector appeared, users preferred to disable it. Most of the programming tools (notably the compiler and program text editor) were designed to avoid consing (heap allocation) and to explicitly reclaim temporary data structures whenever possible; given this, the Lisp Machine address spaces were large enough, and the virtual memory system good enough, that a user could run for several days or even a few weeks before having to save out the running "world" to disk and restart it. Such copying back and forth to disk was equivalent to a slow, manually triggered copying garbage collector. (Although there was a great deal of theoretical work on interleaved and concurrent garbage collection during the 1970s [Steele 1975; Gries 1977; Baker 1978; Cohen 1981], continuous garbage collection was not universally accepted until David Moon's invention of ephemeral garbage collection and its implementation on Lisp Machines [Moon 1984]. Ephemeral garbage collection was subsequently adapted for use on stock hardware.)

The early MIT Lisp-Machine Lisp dialect [Weinreb 1978] was very similar to MacLisp. It lived up to its stated goal of supporting MacLisp programs with only minimal porting effort. The most important extensions beyond MacLisp included:

- An improved programming environment, consisting primarily of a resident compiler, debugging facilities, and a text editor. Although this brought Lisp-Machine Lisp closer to the Interlisp ideal of a completely Lisp-based programming environment, it was still firmly file-oriented. The text editor was an EMACS clone, first called EINE (EINE Is Not EMACS) and then ZWEI (ZWEI Was EINE Initially), the recursive acronyms of course being doubly delicious as version numbers in German.
- Complex lambda lists, including `&optional`, `&key`, `&rest`, and `&aux`
- Locatives, which provided a C-like ability to point into the middle of a structure
- `DEFMACRO`, a much more convenient macro definition facility (see Section 6.3.3)
- Backquote, a syntax for constructing data structures by filling in a template
- Stack groups, which provided a coroutine facility
- Multiple values, the ability to pass more than one value back from a function invocation without having to construct a list. Prior to this, various ad hoc techniques had been used; Lisp-Machine Lisp was the first dialect of Lisp to provide primitives for it. (Other languages such as POP-2 have also provided for multiple values.)
- `DEFSTRUCT`, a record structure definition facility (compare the Interlisp record package)
- Closures over special variables. These closures were not like the ones in Scheme; the variables captured by the environment must be explicitly listed by the programmer, and invocation of the closure required the binding of `SPECIAL` variables to the saved values.
- Flavors, an object-oriented, nonhierarchical programming system with multiple inheritance, was designed by Howard Cannon and David A. Moon and integrated into parts of the Lisp Machine programming environment (the window system, in particular, was written using Flavors [Weinreb 1981]).
- `SETF`, a facility for generalized variables

The use of `SETF` throughout Common Lisp—a later dialect of Lisp and the most popular—can be traced through Symbolics Zetalisp and MacLisp to the influence of MIT Lisp-Machine Lisp and then back through Greenblatt's proposal to Peter Deutsch and thence to Alan Kay.

The uniform treatment of access—reading and writing of state—has made Common Lisp more uniform that it might otherwise be. It is no longer necessary to remember both a reader function (such as `CAR`) and also a separate writer or update function (such as `RPLACA`), nor to remember the order of arguments. (For `RPLACA`, which comes first, the dotted pair or the new value for its car?) If the general form of a read operation is `(`*f*...`)`, then the form of the write is `(setf (`*f*...`)` *newvalue*`)`, and that is all the programmer needs to know about reading and writing data.

Later, in the Common Lisp Object System (CLOS), this idea was extended to methods. If a method *M* is specified to act as a reader and is invoked as `(`*M object*`)`, then it is possible to define a writer method that is invoked as `(setf (`*M object*`)` *newvalue*`)`.

That CLOS fits this idiom so well is no surprise. If Alan Kay was the inspiration for the idea around 1973, he was in the midst of his early involvement with Smalltalk, an early object-oriented language. Reading and writing are both methods that an object can support, and the CLOS adaptation of the Lisp version of Kay's vision was a simple reinvention of the object-oriented genesis of the idea.

6.2.6.2 *Xerox Lisp Machines: 1973–1980*

The Alto was a microcodable machine developed in 1973 [Thacker 1982] and used for personal computing experimentation at Xerox, using Interlisp and other languages such as Mesa [Geschke 1977]. The Alto version of the Interlisp environment first went into use at Xerox PARC and at Stanford University around 1975.

The Alto was standardly equipped with 64K 16-bit words of memory, expandable up to 256K words, which was quite large for a single-user computer but still only half the memory of a PDP-10. The machine proved to be underpowered for the large Interlisp environment, even with all the code density tricks discussed by Deutsch [1973], so it was not widely accepted by users.

The Alto was also used to build the first Smalltalk environment—the "interim Dynabook"—and here it was relatively successful.

In 1976, Xerox PARC undertook the design of a machine called the Dorado (or Xerox 1132), which was an ECL (Emitter Coupled Logic, an at-the-time fast digital logic implementation technology) machine designed to replace the Alto. A prototype available in 1978 ran all Alto software. A redesign was completed in 1979 and a number of them were built for use within Xerox and at certain experimental sites such as Stanford University. The Dorado was specifically designed to interpret byte codes produced by compilers and this is how the Dorado ran Alto software. The Dorado was basically an emulation machine.

Interlisp was ported to this machine using the Interlisp virtual machine model [Moore 1976]. The Dorado running Interlisp was faster than a KL-10 running single-user Interlisp and it would have proved a very nice Lisp machine if it had been made widely available commercially.

Interlisp was similarly ported to a smaller, cheaper machine called the Dolphin (1100), which was made commercially available as a Lisp machine in the late 1970s. The performance of the Dolphin was better than that of the Alto, but bad enough that the machine was never truly successful as a Lisp engine.

In the early 1980s, Xerox built another machine called the Dandelion (1108), which was considerably faster than the Dolphin but still not as fast as the Dorado. Because the names of these three machines all began with the letter "D," they became collectively known as the "D-machines."

All the Xerox Lisp machines used a reference-count garbage collector [Deutsch 1976] that was incremental: a few steps of the garbage collection process would execute each time storage was allocated. Therefore there was a short, bounded amount of work done for garbage collection per unit time.

In the late 1970s BBN also built a machine, the Jericho, that was used as an Interlisp engine. It remained internal to BBN.

6.2.6.3 *Comments on Early Lisp Machine History*

Freed from the address-space constraints of previous architectures, all the Lisp machine companies produced greatly expanded Lisp implementations, adding graphics, windowing capabilities, and mouse interaction capabilities to their programming environments. The Lisp language itself, particularly on the MIT Lisp Machines, also grew in the number and complexity of features. Though some of these ideas originated elsewhere, their adoption throughout the Lisp community was driven as much by the success and cachet of the Lisp machines as by the quality of the ideas themselves.

Nevertheless, for most users the value lay ultimately in the software and not in its enabling hardware technology. The Lisp machine companies ran into difficulty in the late 1980s, perhaps because they didn't fully understand the consequences of this fact. General-purpose hardware eventually became good enough to support Lisp once again, and Lisp implementations on such machines began to compete effectively.

6.2.7 IBM Lisps: Lisp360 and Lisp370

Although the first Lisps were implemented on IBM computers, IBM faded from the Lisp scene during the late 1960s, for two reasons: better cooperation between MIT and DEC and a patent dispute between MIT and IBM.

In the early 1960s, Digital Equipment Corporation discussed with MIT the needs MIT had for computers and features were added to help Lisp implementations. As on the 7094, each 36-bit word could hold two addresses to form a dotted pair, but on the PDP-6 (and its successor, the PDP-10) each address was 18 bits instead of 15. The PDP-10 halfword instructions made **CAR**, **CDR**, **RPLACA**, and **RPLACD** particularly fast and easy to implement. The stack instructions and the stack-based function calling instructions improved the speed of of Lisp function calls. (The MIT AI Laboratory received the first—or second—PDP-6, and it was the lab's mainstay computing engine until it was replaced by a PDP-10.)

Moreover, in the early 1960s, IBM and MIT disputed who had invented core memory and IBM insisted on enforcing its patents against MIT. MIT responded by declining to use IBM equipment as extensively as it had in the past. This provided further impetus to use DEC equipment instead, particularly for Lisp and AI.

Nevertheless, Lisp was implemented at IBM for the IBM 360 and called Lisp360. When the IBM 370 came out, Lisp370 implementation began. Lisp370 was later called Lisp/VM.

Lisp360 was basically a batch Lisp, and it was used fairly extensively for teaching in universities.

Lisp370 began with the definition of a core Lisp based on a formal semantics expressed in the SECD model [Landin 1964]. This definition fit on one or two pages. The Lisp370 project was under the direction of Fred Blair (who developed the SECD definition) at the IBM Thomas J. Watson Research Center in Yorktown Heights, New York. Other members of the group included Cyril Alberga, Martin Mikelsons, Richard W. Ryniker II, and Mark Wegman; they served primarily themselves and a few research groups, such as the SCRATCHPAD symbolic computation group and some AI groups at Yorktown.

Lisp370 supported both special binding and lexical binding, as well as closures over both lexical and special variables, using a technique similar to spaghetti stacks. Jon L White spent calendar year 1977 at Yorktown Heights working on Lisp370 and then returned to MIT; his experience at IBM had some influence on subsequent MacLisp development and on the NIL dialect.

Lisp370 had an Interlisp-like programming environment written to operate on both hardcopy terminals and the ubiquitous IBM 3270 character-display terminal. The Interlisp-10 model was ideal because it was developed with slow terminals in mind and the half-duplex nature of most IBM mainframe interactions had a similar feel. During the summer of 1976, Gabriel wrote the first version of this environment as a duplicate of the environment he had written for MacLisp at the Stanford AI Lab. Later, Mark Wegman and his colleagues at Yorktown extended this environment to include screen-based—rather than line-based—interaction and editing.

Improvements were made to the underlying Lisp system, such as good performance and the separation of the compilation and run-time environments (which was accomplished through the use of separate Lisp images).

Other Lisps later appeared on the 360/370 line of computers, including several Common Lisps. The first Common Lisp to appear on the IBM 370 was written by Intermetrics and featured good compilation technology. However, the Lisp was not well-constructed and never made much of an impact in the Lisp world. Several years later, Lucid ported its Common Lisp to the 370 under contract to IBM. IBM withdrew its support of Lisp370 in the late 1980s in favor of Common Lisp.

6.2.8 Scheme: 1975–1980

The dialect of Lisp known as Scheme was originally an attempt by Gerald Jay Sussman and Steele during the Autumn of 1975 to explicate for themselves some aspects of Carl Hewitt's theory of *actors* as a model of computation. Hewitt's model was object-oriented (and influenced by Smalltalk); every object was a computationally active entity capable of receiving and reacting to messages. The objects were called actors, and the messages themselves were also actors. An actor could have arbitrarily many *acquaintances*; that is, it could "know about" (in Hewitt's language) other actors and send them messages or send acquaintances as (parts of) messages. Message-passing was the only means of interaction. Functional interactions were modeled with the use of continuations; one might send the actor named "factorial" the number 5 and another actor to which to send the eventually computed value (presumably 120).

Sussman and Steele had some trouble understanding some of the consequences of the model from Hewitt's papers and language design, so they decided to construct a toy implementation of an actor language in order to experiment with it. Using MacLisp as a working environment, they wrote a tiny Lisp interpreter and then added the necessary mechanisms for creating actors and sending messages. The toy Lisp would provide the necessary primitives for implementing the internal behavior of primitive actors.

Because Sussman had just been studying ALGOL [Naur 1963], he suggested starting with a lexically scoped dialect of Lisp. (Some of the issues and necessary mechanisms had already been explored by Joel Moses [Moses 1970].) It appeared that such a mechanism would be needed anyway for keeping track of acquaintances for actors. Lexical scoping allowed actors and functions to be created by almost identical mechanisms. Evaluating a form beginning with the word **lambda** would capture the current variable-lookup environment and create a closure; evaluating a form beginning with the word **alpha** would also capture the current environment but create an actor. Message passing could be expressed syntactically in the same way as function invocation. The difference between an actor and a function would be detected in the part of the interpreter traditionally known as **apply**. A function would return a value, but an actor would never return; instead, it would typically invoke a *continuation*, another actor that it knows about. Thus one might define the function

```
(define factorial
  (lambda (n) (if (= n 0)
                  1
                  (* n (factorial (- n 1))))))
```

or the equivalent actor

```
(define actorial
  (alpha (n c) (if (= n 0)
                   (c 1)
                   (actorial (- n 1) (alpha (f) (c (* f n)))))))
```

Note in this example that the values of **c** and **n**, passed in the message that invokes the outer **alpha** expression, become acquaintances of the continuation actor created by the inner **alpha** expression. This continuation must be passed explicitly because the recursive invocation of **actorial** is not expected to return a value.

Sussman and Steele were very pleased with this toy actor implementation and named it "Schemer" in the expectation that it might develop into another AI language in the tradition of Planner and Conniver. However, the ITS operating system had a six-character limitation on file names and so the name was truncated to simply "Scheme" and that name stuck.

Then came a crucial discovery—one that, to us, illustrates the value of experimentation in language design. On inspecting the code for `apply`, once they got it working correctly, Sussman and Steele were astonished to discover that the codes in `apply` for function application and for actor invocation were identical! Further inspection of other parts of the interpreter, such as the code for creating functions and actors, confirmed this insight: the fact that functions were intended to return values and actors were not made no difference anywhere in their implementation. The difference lay purely in the primitives used to code their bodies. If the underlying primitives return values, then the user can write functions that return values; if all primitives expect continuations, then the user can write actors. But the **`lambda`** and **`alpha`** mechanisms were themselves identical, and from this Sussman and Steele concluded that actors and closures were the same concept. (Hewitt later agreed with this assessment, noting, however, that two types of primitive actor in his theory, namely cells (which have modifiable state) and synchronizers (which enforce exclusive access), cannot be expressed as closures in a lexically scoped pure Lisp without adding equivalent primitive extensions.)

Sussman and Steele did not think any less of the actors model—or of Lisp—for having made this discovery; indeed, it seemed to them that Scheme still might well be the next AI language, capturing many of the ideas then floating around about data and control structure but in a much simpler framework. The initial report on Scheme [Sussman 1975b] describes a very spare language, with a minimum of primitive constructs, one per concept. (Why take two when one will do?) There was a function constructor **`lambda`**, a fixpoint operator **`labels`**, a condition **`if`**, a side effect **`aset`**, a continuation accessor **`catch`**, function application, variable references, and not too much else. There was an assortment of primitive data structures such as symbols, lists, and numbers, but these and their associated operations were regarded as practical conveniences rather than theoretical requirements.

In 1976 Sussman and Steele wrote two more papers that explored programming language semantics using Scheme as a framework. *Lambda: The Ultimate Imperative* [Steele 1976a] demonstrated how a wide variety of control structure ideas could be modeled in Scheme. Some of the models drew on earlier work by Peter Landin, John Reynolds, and others [Landin 1965; Reynolds 1972; Friedman 1975]. The paper was partly tutorial in intent and partly a consolidated catalog of control structures. (This paper was also notable as the first in a long series of "Lambda: The Ultimate *X*" papers, a running gag that is as well-known in the Lisp community as the "*X* Considered Harmful" titles are in the broader programming-languages community.) *Lambda: The Ultimate Declarative* [Steele 1976b] concentrated on the nature of **`lambda`** as a renaming construct; it also provided a more extensive comparison of Scheme and Hewitt's PLASMA (see Section 6.4), relating object-oriented programming generally and actors specifically to closures. This in turn suggested a set of techniques for constructing a practical compiler for Scheme, which this paper outlined in some detail. This paper was a thesis proposal; the resulting dissertation discussed a Scheme compiler called RABBIT [Steele 1978a]. Mitchell Wand and Daniel Friedman were doing similar work at Indiana University [Wand 1977] and they exchanged papers with Sussman and Steele during this period.

Subsequently, Steele and Sussman wrote a revised report on Scheme [Steele 1978c]; the title of the report was intended as a tribute to ALGOL but in turn inspired another increasingly silly series of titles [Clinger 1985a, 1985b; Rees 1986]. Shortly thereafter they wrote an extended monograph, whose title was a play on *The Art of the Fugue*, illustrating numerous small Lisp interpreters with variations. The monograph was never finished; only parts Zero, One, and Two were published [Steele 1978b]. Part Zero introduced a tiny first-order dialect of Lisp modeled on recursion equations. Part

One discussed procedures as data and explored lexical and dynamic binding. Part Two addressed the decomposition of state and the meaning of side effects. Part Three was to have covered order of evaluation (call-by-value versus call-by-name) and Part Four was intended to cover metalanguage, macro processors, and compilers. That these last two parts were never written is no great loss, as these topics were soon treated adequately by other researchers. Although *The Art of the Interpreter* achieved some notoriety in the Scheme underground, it was rejected by an ACM journal.

A great deal in all these papers was not new; their main contribution was to bridge the gap between the models used by theoreticians (studying actors and the lambda calculus [Church 1941]) and practitioners (Lisp implementors and users). Scheme made theoretical contributions in such areas as denotational semantics much more accessible to Lisp hackers; it also provided a usable operational platform for experimentation by theoreticians. There was no need for a centralized implementation group to support Scheme at a large number of sites or on a wide variety of machines. Like Standard Lisp but even smaller and simpler, Scheme could be put up on top of some other Lisp system in a very short time. Local implementations and dialects sprang up at many other sites (one good example is Scheme 311 at Indiana University [Fessenden 1983; Clinger 1984]); it was several years before anyone made a serious attempt to produce a portable stand-alone Scheme system.

Extensive work on Scheme implementations was carried on at Yale and later at MIT by Jonathan Rees, Norman Adams, and others. This resulted in the dialect of Scheme known as T; this name was a good joke all around, because T was to Scheme approximately what the NIL dialect was to MacLisp. The goal was to be a simple dialect with an especially efficient implementation [Rees 1982]:

> T centers around a small core language, free of complicated features, thus easy to learn .... [We] have refrained from supporting features that we didn't feel completely right about. T's omissions are important: we have avoided the complicated argument list syntax of Common Lisp, keyword options, and multiple functionality overloaded on single functions. It's far easier to generalize on something later than to implement something now that one might later regret. All features have been carefully considered for stylistic purity and generality.

The design of T therefore represented a conscious break not only from the Lisp tradition but from earlier versions of Scheme in places where Steele and Sussman had relied on tradition rather than cleaning things up. Names of built-in functions were regularized. T replaced the traditional `-P` suffix with universal use of the question mark; thus `numberp` became `number?` and `null` became `null?`. Similarly, every destructive operation had a name ending with an exclamation point; thus `nconc`, the MacLisp name for the destructive version of `append`, became `append!`. (Muddle [Galley 1975] had introduced the use of question mark to indicate predicates and Sussman had used this convention over the years in some of his writing. Interlisp had had a more consistent system of labeling destructive operations than MacLisp, using the letter `d` as a prefix.)

T was initially targeted to the VAX (under both Unix and VMS) and to Apollo workstations. Most of the system was written in T and bootstrapped by the T compiler, TC. The evaluator and garbage collector, in particular, were written in T and not in machine language. The T project started with a version of the S-1 Lisp compiler [Brooks 1982b] and made substantial improvements; in the course of their work they identified several bugs in the S-1 compiler and in the original report on RABBIT [Steele 1978a]. Like the S-1 Lisp compiler, it relied heavily on optimization strategies from the mainstream compiler literature, most notably the work by Wulf and others on the BLISS-11 compiler [Wulf 1975].

A second generation of T compiler, called ORBIT [Kranz 1986], integrated a host of mainstream and Lisp-specific optimization strategies, resulting in a truly production-quality Scheme environment. RABBIT was organized around a principle of translating Lisp code by performing a source-to-source conversion into "continuation-passing style" (CPS); ORBIT generalized and extended this strategy to handle assignments to variables. The register allocator used trace scheduling to optimize register usage across forks, joins, and procedure calls. ORBIT also supported calls to procedures written in languages other than Lisp. (This was contemporaneous with efforts at CMU and elsewhere to develop general "foreign function call" mechanisms for Common Lisp.)

6.2.9 Prelude to Common Lisp: 1980–1984

In the Spring of 1981, the situation was as follows. Two Lisp machine companies had sprung up from the MIT Lisp machine project: LISP Machine, Inc. (LMI) and Symbolics, Inc. The former was founded principally by Richard Greenblatt and the latter by a larger group including David A. Moon. Both initially productized the CADR, the second MIT Lisp machine, and each licensed the Lisp machine software from MIT under an arrangement that included passing back any improvements made by the companies. Symbolics soon embarked on designing and building a follow-on Lisp machine, the 3600. The language Lisp-Machine Lisp had evolved greatly since the first definition published in 1978, acquiring a variety of new features, most notably an object-oriented extension called Flavors.

The Xerox Lisp machines, Dolphin and Dorado, were running Interlisp and were in use in research laboratories mostly located on the West Coast. BBN was constructing its Interlisp machine, the Jericho, and a port of Interlisp to the VAX was under way.

At MIT a project had started to define and implement a descendant of MacLisp called NIL on the VAX and S-1 computers.

At CMU, Scott Fahlman and his colleagues and students were defining and implementing a MacLisp-like dialect of Lisp called Spice Lisp, which was to be implemented on the SPICE machine (Scientific Personal Integrated Computing Environment).

6.2.10 Early Common Lisp

If there had been no consolidation in the Lisp community at this point, Lisp might have died. ARPA was not interested in funding a variety of needlessly competing and gratuitously different Lisp projects. And there was no commercial arena—yet.

6.2.10.1 *Out of the Chaos of MacLisp*

In April 1981, ARPA called a "Lisp Community Meeting," in which the implementation groups got together to discuss the future of Lisp. ARPA sponsored a lot of AI research, and their goal was to see what could be done to stem the tide of an increasingly diverse set of Lisp dialects in its research community.

The day before the ARPA meeting, part of the Interlisp community got together to discuss how to present a picture of a healthy Interlisp community on a variety of machines. The idea was to push the view of a standard language (Interlisp) and a standard environment existing on an ever-increasing number of different types of computers.

The day of the meeting, the Interlisp community successfully presented themselves as a coherent group with one goal and mission.

The MacLisp-descended groups came off in a way that can be best demonstrated with an anecdote. Each group stood up and presented where they were heading and why. Some questions arose about the ill-defined direction of the MacLisp community in contrast to the Interlisp community. Scott

Fahlman said, "The MacLisp community is *not* in a state of chaos. It consists of four well-defined groups going in four well-defined directions." There was a moment's pause for the laughter to subside [Steele 1982].

Gabriel attended the Interlisp powwow the day before the ARPA meeting, and he also witnessed the spectacle of the MacLisp community at the meeting. He didn't believe that the differences between the MacLisp groups were insurmountable, so he began to try to sell the idea of some sort of cooperation among the groups.

First he approached Jon L White. Second, Gabriel and White approached Steele, then at CMU and affiliated with the SPICE Lisp project. The three of them were all associated one way or another with the S-1 NIL project. A few months later, Gabriel, Steele, White, Fahlman, William Scherlis (a colleague of Gabriel's then at CMU), and Rodney Brooks (part of the S-1 Lisp project) met at CMU, and some of the technical details of the new Lisp were discussed. The new dialect was to have the following basic features:

- Lexical scoping, including full closures
- Multiple values, like those in Lisp-Machine Lisp, but perhaps with some modifications for single-value-forcing situations
- Separate value and function cells (a Lisp-2) [Gabriel 1988] (See Section 6.2.12.4.)
- **DEFSTRUCT**
- **SETF**
- Fancy floating point numbers, including complex and rational numbers (This was the primary influence of S-1 Lisp.)
- Complex lambda-list declarations, similar to those of Lisp-Machine Lisp
- No dynamic closures (closures over "special" variables, which are dynamically bound; also called "flexures" in NIL)

After a day and a half of technical discussion, this group went off to the Oakland Original, a greasy submarine-sandwich place not far from CMU. During and after lunch the topic of the name for the Lisp came up, and such obvious names as NIL and Spice Lisp were proposed and rejected—as giving too much credit to one group and not enough to others—and such nonobvious names as Yu-Hsiang Lisp were also proposed and reluctantly rejected.

The name felt to be best was "Standard Lisp" but another dialect was known by that name already. In the search for similar words, the name "Common Lisp" came up. Gabriel remarked that this wasn't a good name because we were trying to define an Elitist Lisp, and "Common Lisp" sounded too much like "Common Man Lisp." (Such names as "Vulgar Lisp" were then bandied about.)

The naming discussion resumed at dinner at the Pleasure Bar, an Italian restaurant in another Pittsburgh district, but no luck was had by all.

Later in e-mail, Moon referred to "whatever we call this common Lisp" and this time, among great sadness and consternation that a better name could not be had, it was selected.

The next step was to contact more groups. The key was the Lisp machine companies, which would be approached last. In addition, Gabriel volunteered to visit the Franz Lisp group in Berkeley and the PSL group in Salt Lake City.

The PSL group did not fully join the Common Lisp group and the Franz group did not join at all. The Lisp370 group was, through oversight, not invited. The Interlisp community sent an observer. ARPA was successfully pulled into supporting the effort.

The people and groups engaged in this grassroots effort were, by and large, on the ARPANET—because they were affiliated or associated with AI labs—so it was natural to decide to do most of the work over the network through electronic mail, which was automatically archived. In fact this was the first major language standardization effort carried out nearly entirely by e-mail.

A meeting with Symbolics and LMI took place at Symbolics in June 1981. Steele and Gabriel drove from Pittsburgh to Cambridge for the meeting. The meeting alternated between a deep technical discussion of what should be in the dialect and a political discussion about why the new dialect was a good thing. From the point of view of the Lisp machine companies, the action was with Lisp machines and the interest in the same dialect running more places seemed academic. Of course, there were business reasons for getting the same dialect running in many places, but people with business sense did not attend the meeting.

At the end, both Lisp machine companies decided to join the effort, and the Common Lisp Group was formed:

Alan Bawden	Richard P. Gabriel	William L. Scherlis
Rodney A. Brooks	Joseph Ginder	Richard M. Stallman
Richard L. Bryan	Richard Greenblatt	Barbara K. Steele
Glenn S. Burke	Martin L. Griss	Guy L. Steele Jr.
Howard I. Cannon	Charles L. Hedrick	William vanMelle
George J. Carrette	Earl A. Killian	Walter van Roggen
David Dill	John L. Kulp	Allan C. Weschler
Scott E. Fahlman	Larry M. Masinter	Daniel L. Weinreb
Richard J. Fateman	John McCarthy	Jon L White
Neal Feinberg	Don Morrison	Richard Zippel
John Foderaro	David A. Moon	Leonard Zubkoff

As a compromise, it was agreed that it was worth defining a family of languages in such a way that any program written in the language defined would run in any language in the family. Thus, a sort of subset was to be defined, though it wasn't clear anyone would implement the subset directly.

Some of the Lisp machine features that were dropped were Flavors, window systems, multiprocessing (including multitasking), graphics, and locatives.

During the Summer of 1981, Steele worked on an initial Common Lisp manual based on the Spice Lisp manual. His initial work was assisted by Brooks, Scherlis, and Gabriel. Scherlis provided specific assistance with the type system, mostly in the form of informal advice to Steele. Gabriel and Steele regularly discussed issues because Gabriel was living at Steele's home during that summer.

The draft, called the Swiss Cheese Edition—because it was full of large holes—was partly a ballot in which various alternatives and yes/no questions were proposed. Through a process of e-mail–based discussion and voting, the first key decisions were made. This was followed by a face-to-face meeting in November of 1981, where the final decisions on the more difficult questions were settled.

This led to another round of refinement with several other similar drafts and ballots.

The e-mail discussions were often in the form of proposals, discussions, and counterproposals. Code examples from existing software or proposed new syntax were often exchanged.

All e-mail was archived on-line, so everything was available for quick review by people wishing to come up to speed or to go back to the record.

This style also had some drawbacks. Foremost was that it was not possible to observe the reactions of other people, for example, to see whether some point angered them, which would mean the point was important to them. There was no way to see that an argument had gone too far or had little support.

This meant that some time was wasted and that carefully crafted written arguments were required to get anything done.

Once the process began, the approach to the problem changed from just a consolidation of existing dialects, which was the obvious direction to take, to trying to design The Right Thing [Raymond 1991]. Some people took the view that this was a good time to rethink some issues and to abandon the goal of strict MacLisp compatibility, which was so important to the early Lisp-Machine Lisp designs. Some issues, such as whether **NIL** is both a symbol and a **CONS** cell, were not rethought, though it was generally agreed that they should be.

One issue that came up early on is worth mentioning, because it is at the heart of one of the major attacks on Common Lisp, which was mounted during the ISO work on Lisp. (See Section 6.2.12.) This is the issue of modularization, which had two aspects: whether Common Lisp should be divided into a core language plus modules, and whether there should be a division into the so-called white, yellow, and red pages. These topics appear to have been blended in the discussion.

"White pages" refers to the manual proper, and anything that is in the white pages must be implemented somehow by a Lisp whose developers claim it is a Common Lisp. "Yellow pages" refers to implementation-independent packages that can be loaded in, for example, **TRACE** and scientific subroutine packages. The "red pages" were intended to describe implementation-dependent routines, such as device drivers.

Common Lisp was not broken into a core language plus layers, and the white/yellow/red pages division never materialized.

Four more drafts were made—the Colander Edition (July 29, 1982), the Laser Edition (November 16, 1982), the Excelsior Edition (July 15, 1983), and the Mary Poppins Edition (November 29, 1983).

Three of the cute names are explained by their subtitles:

Colander: Even More Holes Than Before—But They're Smaller!
Laser Edition: Supposed to be Completely Coherent
Mary Poppins Edition: Practically Perfect in Every Way

As for the Excelsior Edition, recall that "excelsior" is not only a term of exhortation but also a name for shredded wood or paper suitable for use as packing material.

Virtually all technical decisions were completed by early 1983, but it was almost a year before the book *Common Lisp: The Language* would be available, even with a fast publishing job by Digital Press.

The declared goals of the Common Lisp Group, paraphrased from CLTL1 [1984], were the following:

- Commonality: Common Lisp originated in an attempt to focus the work of several implementation groups, each of which was constructing successor implementations of MacLisp for different computers. Although the differences among the several implementations will continue to force some incompatibilities, Common Lisp should serve as a common dialect for these implementations.
- Portability: Common Lisp should exclude features that cannot be easily implemented on a broad class of computers. This should serve to exclude features requiring microcode or hardware on one hand as well as features generally required for stock hardware, for example, declarations.
- Consistency: The interpreter and compiler should exhibit the same semantics.
- Expressiveness: Common Lisp should cull the best experience from a variety of dialects, including not only MacLisp but Interlisp.

- Compatibility: Common Lisp should strive to be compatible with Zetalisp, MacLisp, and Interlisp, in that order.
- Efficiency: It should be possible to write an optimizing compiler for Common Lisp.
- Power: Common Lisp should be a good system-building language, suitable for writing Interlisp-like user-level packages, but it will not provide those packages.
- Stability: Common Lisp should evolve slowly and with deliberation.

6.2.10.2 *Early Rumblings*

The Common Lisp definition process was not all rosy. Throughout there was a feeling among some that they were being railroaded or that things were not going well. The Interlisp group had input in the balloting process, but at one point they wrote:

> The Interlisp community is in a bit of a quandary about what our contribution to this endeavor should be. It is clear that Common Lisp is not going to settle very many language features in Interlisp's favor. What should we do?

Part of the problem was the strength of the Lisp machine companies and the need for the Common Lisp Group to keep them within the fold, which bestowed on them a particularly strong brand of power. On this point, as one of the people in the early Common Lisp Group put it,

> Sorry, but the current version [draft] really gives a feeling of 'well, what's the largest subset of Lisp-Machine Lisp we can try to force down everyone's throat, and call a standard?'

The Lisp machine folks had a flavor of argument that was hard to contend with, namely, that they had had experience with large software systems and in that realm the particular solutions they had come up with were, according to them, The Right Thing. The net effect was that Common Lisp grew and grew.

One would think that the voices of the stock machine crowd, who had to write compilers for Common Lisp, would have objected, but the two strongest voices—Steele and Gabriel—were feeling their oats over their ability to write a powerful compiler to foil the complexities of Common Lisp. One often heard them, and later Moon, remark that a "sufficiently smart compiler" could solve a particular problem. Pretty soon the core group was quoting this "SSC" argument regularly. (Later, in the mouths of the loyal opposition, it became a term of mild derision.)

The core group eventually became the "authors" of CLTL1: Fahlman, Gabriel, Moon, Steele, and Weinreb. This group shouldered the responsibility for producing the language specification document and conducting its review. The self-adopted name for the group was the "Quinquevirate" or, more informally, the "Gang of Five."

6.2.10.3 *The Critique of Common Lisp*

At the 1984 ACM Symposium on Lisp and Functional Programming, Rod Brooks and Gabriel broke rank and delivered the stunning opening paper, "A Critique of Common Lisp" [Brooks 1984]. This was all the more stunning because Brooks and Gabriel were founders of a company whose business plan was to become the premier Common Lisp company. Fahlman, on hearing the speech delivered by Gabriel, called it traitorous.

This paper was only the first in a string of critiques of Common Lisp; many of those critiques quoted this first one. The high points of the paper reveal a series of problems that would plague Common Lisp throughout the decade.

This theme reappeared in the history of Common Lisp through the emergence of a number of "unCommon" Lisps, straining, perhaps, the tolerance of even the most twisted lovers of overused puns. Each unCommon Lisp proclaimed its better approaches to some of the shortcomings of Common Lisp. Examples of Lisp dialects that have officially or unofficially declared themselves "unCommon Lisps" at one time or another are Lisp370, Scheme, EuLisp, and muLisp. This was clearly an attempt to distance themselves from the perceived shortcomings of Common Lisp, but, less clearly, their use of this term attests to the apparent and real strength of Common Lisp as the primary Lisp dialect. To define a Lisp as standing in contrast to another dialect is to admit the supremacy of that other dialect. (Imagine Ford advertising the Mustang as "the unCorvette.")

More than any other single phenomenon, this behavior demonstrates one of the key ingredients of Lisp diversification: extreme—almost juvenile—rivalry between dialect groups.

We have already seen Lisp370 and Scheme. EuLisp is the European response to Common Lisp, developed as the lingua franca for Lisp in Europe. Its primary characteristics are that it is a Lisp-1 (no separate function and variable namespaces), has a CLOS-style generic-function–type object-oriented system integrated from the ground up, has a built-in module system, and is defined in layers to promote the use of the Lisp on small, embedded hardware and educational machines. Otherwise, EuLisp is Common-Lisp–like. The definition of EuLisp took a long time; started in 1986, it wasn't until 1990 that the first implementation was available (interpreter-only) along with a nearly complete language specification. Nevertheless, the layered definition, the module system, and the object-orientedness from the start demonstrate that new lessons can be learned in the Lisp world.

6.2.11 Other Lisp Dialects: 1980–1984

The rest of the world did not stand still while Common Lisp was developed, though Common Lisp was the focus of a lot of attention.

6.2.11.1 *Lisp Dialects on Stock Hardware*

Portable Standard Lisp spread to the VAX, DECsystem-20, a variety of MC68000 machines, and the Cray-1. Its Emode environment (later Nmode) proved appealing to Hewlett-Packard, which "productized" it in the face of a growing Common Lisp presence.

Franz Lisp was ported to many systems and it became the workhorse stock hardware Lisp for the years leading up to the general availability of Common Lisp in 1985–1986.

In the market, the Dolphin was taking a beating in the performance sweepstakes, primarily because it was a slow machine that ran the Interlisp virtual machine. The efforts of Xerox were aimed at porting and performance, with little attention to improving the dialect or the environment, though work continued in this area. The main Interlisp developers were busy tuning.

Interlisp/VAX made an appearance, but has to be regarded as a failure with three contributing causes: (1) it provided compatibility with Interlisp-10, the branch of the Interlisp family doomed by the eventual demise of the PDP-10, rather than with Interlisp-D; (2) it provided only a stop-and-copy garbage collector, which has particularly bad performance on a VAX; and (3) as the rest of the Lisp world, including the Interlisp world, flocked to personal Lisp machines, the VAX was never taken seriously for Lisp purposes except by a small number of businesses.

In France, Jérôme Chailloux and his colleagues developed a new dialect of Lisp called Le_Lisp. The dialect was reminiscent of MacLisp and focused on portability and efficiency. It needed to be portable because the computer situation in Europe was not as clear as it was in the U.S. for Lisp. Lisp machines were dominant for Lisp in the U.S., but in Europe these machines were not as available and often were prohibitively expensive. Research labs in Europe frequently acquired or were given a range of peculiar machines (from the U.S. perspective). Therefore, portability was a must.

The experience with Vlisp taught Chailloux that performance and portability can go together, and, extending some of the Vlisp techniques, his group was able to achieve their goals. By 1984 their dialect ran on about ten different machines and demonstrated performance very much better than that of Franz Lisp, the most comparable alternative. On a VAX-11/780, Le_Lisp performed about as well as Zetalisp on a Symbolics 3600.

In addition, Le_Lisp provided a full-fledged programming environment called Ceyx. Ceyx had a full set of debugging aids, a full-screen, multi-window structure editor and pretty printer, and an object-oriented programming extension, also called Ceyx.

The Scheme community grew from a few aficionados to a much larger group, characterized by an interest in the mathematical aspects of programming languages. Scheme's small size, roots in lambda calculus, and generally compact semantic underpinnings began to make it popular as a vehicle for research and teaching. In particular, strong groups of Scheme supporters developed at MIT, Indiana University, and Rice University. Most of these groups were started by MIT or Indiana graduates who joined the faculty at these schools.

At MIT, under the guidance of Hal Abelson and Gerry Sussman, Scheme was adopted for teaching undergraduate computing. The book *Structure and Interpretation of Computer Programs* [Abelson 1985] became a classic and vaulted Scheme to notoriety in a larger community.

Several companies sprang up that made commercial implementations of Scheme. Cadence Research Systems was started by R. Kent Dybvig; its Chez Scheme ran on various workstations. At Semantic Microsystems, Will Clinger, Anne Hartheimer, and John Ulrich produced MacScheme for the Apple Macintosh. PC Scheme, from Texas Instruments, ran on the IBM PC and clones such as the one TI built and sold.

The original *Revised Report on Scheme* was taken as a model for future definitions of Scheme, and a self-selected group of so-called "Scheme authors" took on the role of evolving Scheme. The rule they adopted was that features could be added only by unanimous consent. After a fairly short period in which certain features such as `call-with-current-continuation` were added, the rate of change of Scheme slowed down because of this rule. Only peer pressure in a highly intellectual group could convince any recalcitrant author to change his blackball. As a result there is a widely held belief that whenever a feature is added to Scheme, it is clearly The Right Thing. For example, only in late 1991 were macros added to the language in an appendix—as a partially standardized facility.

There emerged a series of Revised Reports, called *The Revised, . . . , Revised Report on Scheme*. In late 1991, *The Revised, Revised, Revised, Revised Report on Scheme* was written and approved; it is affectionately called "R^4RS."

Many of those who later became members of the Common Lisp Group proclaimed a deep-seated love of Scheme and a not-so-secret desire to see something like it become the next Lisp standard. However, parts of the Scheme and Common Lisp communities sometimes became bitter rivals in the latter part of the decade.

6.2.11.2 *Zetalisp*

Zetalisp was the name of the Symbolics version of Lisp-Machine Lisp. Because the 3600—the Symbolics second-generation Lisp machine, which is described in the following—was programmed almost entirely in Lisp, Zetalisp came to require a significant set of capabilities not seen in any single Lisp before this point. Not only was Zetalisp used for ordinary programming, but the operating system, the editor, the compiler, the network server, the garbage collector, and the window system were all programmed in Zetalisp, and because the earlier Lisp-Machine Lisp was not quite up to these tasks, Zetalisp was expanded to handle them.

The primary addition to Lisp-Machine Lisp was Flavors, a so-called nonhierarchical object-oriented language, a multiple inheritance, message-passing system developed from some ideas of Howard Cannon. The development of the ideas into a coherent system was largely due to David A. Moon, though Cannon continued to play a key role.

The features of Flavors were driven by the needs of the Lisp Machine window system, which, for a long time, was regarded as the only example of a system whose programming required multiple inheritance.

Other noteworthy additions were **FORMAT** and **SETF**, complex arrays, and complex lambda-lists for optional and keyword-named arguments. (**FORMAT** is a mechanism for producing string output conveniently by, basically, taking a predetermined string with placeholders and substituting computed values or strings for those placeholders—though it became much more complex than this because the placeholders included iteration primitives for producing lists of results, plurals, and other such exotica. It may be loosely characterized as FORTRAN **FORMAT** statements gone berserk. **SETF** is discussed in Section 6.2.6.)

One of the factors in the acceptance and importance of Zetalisp was the acceptance of the Lisp machines, which is discussed in the next section. Because Lisp machines—particularly Symbolics Lisp machines—were the most popular vehicles for real Lisp work in a commercial setting, there would grow to be an explicit belief, fostered by Symbolics itself, that Lisp-Machine Lisp (Zetalisp) was the primary dialect for Lisp. Therefore, the Symbolics folks were taken very seriously as a strong political force and a required political ally for the success of a wider Lisp standard.

6.2.11.3 *Early Lisp Machine Companies*

There were five primary Lisp machine companies: Symbolics; LISP Machine, Inc. (LMI); Three Rivers Computer, later renamed PERQ after its principal product; Xerox; and Texas Instruments (TI).

Of these, Symbolics, LMI, and TI all used basically the same software licensed from MIT as the basis of their offerings. The software included the Lisp implementation, the operating system, the editor, the window system, the network software, and all the utilities. There was an arrangement wherein the software would be cheaply (or freely) available as long as improvements were passed back to MIT. Therefore, the companies competed primarily on the basis of hardware performance but secondarily on the availability of advances in the common software base before that software passed back to the common source. Some of the companies also produced proprietary extensions, such as C and FORTRAN implementations from Symbolics.

Xerox produced the D-machines, which ran Interlisp-D.

Three Rivers sold a machine, the PERQ, that ran either a Pascal-based operating system and language or Spice Lisp (and later a Common Lisp based on Spice Lisp).

Thus, all the Lisp-machine companies started out with existing software and all the MacLisp-derived Lisp-machine companies licensed their software from a university.

Of these companies, Symbolics was most successful (as measured by number of installations at the end of the pre-Common-Lisp era), followed by Xerox and TI, though TI possibly could have claimed the most installed machines on the basis of one or two large company purchases.

Symbolics is the most interesting of these companies because of the extreme influence of Symbolics on the direction of Common Lisp; however, we do not want to claim that the other companies did not have strong significance. The popularity of Zetalisp—or at least its apparent influence on the other people in the Common Lisp group—stemmed largely from the popularity of the 3600.

The 3600 was a second-generation Lisp machine, the first being a version of the CADR called the LM-2. Both Symbolics and LMI started their businesses by producing essentially the CADR. However, Symbolics's business plan was to produce a much faster Lisp machine and to enter the workstation sweepstakes.

Sometimes it is easy to forget that in the early 1980s workstations were an oddity, and they were generally so computationally underpowered that many people did not take them seriously. The PDP-10 still offered vastly better performance than the workstations and it simply was not obvious that engineers would ever warm up to them or that they would form a large new market. Furthermore, it was not clear that a Unix-based/C-based workstation was necessarily the winner either, because it was thought that applications would drive the market more than software development. Therefore, it was not foolish for Symbolics to have the business plan it did.

Symbolics and LMI were founded by rivals at the MIT AI Lab, with Richard Greenblatt founding LMI and almost everyone else founding Symbolics, notably hackers Howard Cannon, Tom Knight, David Moon, and Dan Weinreb.

One of the factors in the adoption of Symbolics Lisp machines and Zetalisp was the fact that the first 3600s did not have a garbage collector, which meant that the performance penalty of garbage collecting a large address space was not observed. Originally the 3600 was to have a Baker-style incremental stop-and-copy collector [Baker 1978], but because the address space was so large, ordinary programs did not exhaust memory for several days and intensive ones could run for about eight hours. There was a facility for saving the running image, which basically did a stop-and-copy garbage collection to disk, and this image could be resumed. Therefore, instead of garbage collecting on the fly, a programmer would run until memory was exhausted, then he would start up the lengthy (up to several hours) process of disk-saving, and he would restart his program after dinner or the next day.

The incremental garbage collector was released several years after the first 3600s. It proved to have relatively bad performance, possibly due to paging problems. Instead, Moon developed an ephemeral garbage collector that is similar to the Ungar generation scavenger collector developed for Smalltalk [Ungar 1984]. With generation scavenging, objects are promoted from one generation to the next by a stop-and-copy process. After several generations objects are promoted (tenured) to long-term storage. The idea is that an object will become garbage soon after its creation, so if you can look at the ages of objects and concentrate on only young objects, you will get most of the garbage, and because a small working set is maintained, paging performance is good.

Ephemeral garbage collection [Moon 1984] is similar, but it maintains a few consing areas representing generations and a list of regions of memory where pointers to objects in the consing areas were created, and those regions are scanned in a stop-and-copy operation, moving from one generation to the other. Because objects in Smalltalk are created less frequently than in Lisp, the tradeoffs are a little different and the data structures are different.

The ephemeral garbage collector proved effective, and several years after the first 3600 was sold, an effective garbage collector was operational. It took a while for users to get used to the performance differences, but by then the 3600 was already established and the position of the 3600 was firmly implanted.

PERQ entered the market with a poorly performing microcoded machine that had been used as a document preparation computer. Scott Fahlman was involved with the company and when Common Lisp made its debut, the Spice Lisp code was a nearly compliant Common Lisp, so PERQ's was the first Common Lisp available on a Lisp machine.

The original PERQ and its later versions never made much of a commercial impact outside the Pittsburgh area, probably because its performance and price-performance were relatively poor.

The early history of the Xerox D-machines is discussed in the preceding. Before the Common Lisp era, their use became widespread in former InterLisp-10 circles.

Texas Instruments began to enter the Lisp machine business just before CLTL1 was published, in early 1984. They began with the Viking project (no relation to their current implementation of the SPARC microprocessor architecture!), which ran Spice Lisp on a Motorola MC68020 microprocessor. Later, they decided to go the pure Lisp machine route and introduced the Explorer, a microcoded machine that also ran the MIT software. Later, TI joined with LMI to trade some technology, which seemed to have little or no effect on the business fortunes of either company except to inject some capital into LMI, prolonging its existence. The Explorer had good price-performance and decent absolute performance. The high favor in which TI was held by the Department of Defense resulted in good sales for TI during the early Common Lisp era.

6.2.11.4 *MacLisp on the Decline*

Though MacLisp was still in widespread use and spreading a bit, development halted in the early 1980s. At this point, MacLisp ran on ITS, Multics, Tenex, TOPS-10, TOPS-20, and WAITS. (All but Multics were various operating systems for the PDP-10.)

Funding for MacLisp development had been provided by the MACSYMA Group, because the primary client for MacLisp, from the point of view of MIT, was the people who used MACSYMA—the MACSYMA Consortium. From the point of view of the rest of the world, however, although MACSYMA was an interesting application of Lisp, MacLisp itself was of much wider appeal as a research and development tool for AI, particularly vision and robotics. However, these groups were not flush with funding and, in any event, none found any reason to do other than to accept the use of a freely available MacLisp as MIT saw fit to provide.

The funding for MacLisp was supplanted by funding for NIL on the VAX by the Department of Energy. The Department of Energy oversaw such things as research and development of nuclear weapons in addition to its more benign projects such as civilian energy. Therefore, the DOE was an alternative source of defense funding and it funded such projects as S-1 Lisp.

In general, each site that used MacLisp had a local wizard who was able to handle most of the problems encountered, possibly by consulting Jon L White. In at least one case, funding was made available to MIT to do some custom work. For instance, the single-segment version of MacLisp on WAITS was paid for by the Stanford AI Lab and the work was done on site by Howard Cannon.

MacLisp was the host for a variety of language development and features over the years, including MicroPlanner, Conniver, Scheme, Flavors, Frames, Extends, Qlisp, and various vision-processing features. The last major piece of research in MacLisp was the multi-program programming environment done by Martin E. Frost and Gabriel at Stanford [Gabriel 1984a]. This environment defined a protocol that allowed MacLisp and E, the Stanford display editor that had operating-system support, to communicate over a mailbox-style operating system mechanism. With this mechanism, the code devoted to editing was shared by any users using E (even for non-Lisp tasks) by using the time sharing mechanism of the underlying host computer, and frequently code executed for the purpose of editing was executed within the operating system, requiring no code to be swapped in or paged in. It was also possible for Lisp programs to control the editor, so that very powerful "editor macros" written in Lisp could be used instead of the arcane E macro language. This environment predated similar Lisp/Emacs environments by a few years.

However, in the early days of the Common Lisp group, funding for NIL for the VAX by DOE and the MACSYMA Consortium was halted, perhaps fueled by the belief that Lisp machines would run

MACSYMA well, perhaps fueled by the belief that the development of Common Lisp would provide the common base for MACSYMA.

Around the same time that DOE funding stopped, Symbolics started a MACSYMA Group to sell Lisp-machine-based MACSYMA. This group remained profitable until its dissolution in the late 1980s or early 1990s.

With NIL funding stoppage, Jon L White joined Xerox to work on Interlisp. A stranger situation is difficult to imagine. First, White was so clearly an Easterner that the California lifestyle would seem too foreign for him to accept. Second, the intense rivalry between MacLisp and InterLisp over the years would seem to prevent their working together.

6.2.12 Standards Development: 1984–1992

The period just after the release of *Common Lisp: The Language* [CLTL1 1984] marked the beginning of an era of unprecedented Lisp popularity. In large part this popularity was coupled with the popularity of AI, but not entirely. Let's look at the ingredients:

- For the first time there was a commonly agreed standard for Lisp, albeit a flawed one.
- AI was on the rise, and Lisp was the language of AI.
- There appeared to be a burgeoning workstation market, and the performance of the workstations on Lisp was not far from that of the Lisp machines.
- The venture capital community, which, looking at the success of companies like Sun, was awed by the prospects of AI, and had a lot of money as a result of the booming economy in the first half of the Reagan presidency.
- Computer scientists were turning into entrepreneurs in droves, spurred by the near-instant success of their colleagues in such companies as Sun and Valid.

Articles about Lisp were being written for popular magazines, requests for Common Lisp were streaming into places like CMU (Fahlman) and Stanford (Gabriel), and otherwise academic-only people were asked to speak at industry conferences and workshops on the topics of AI and Lisp and were regarded as sages of future trends.

The key impetus behind the interest by industry in Lisp and AI was that the problems of hardware seemed under control and the raging beast of software was about to be tamed. More traditional methods seemed inadequate and there was always the feeling that the new thing, the radical thing, would have a more thorough effect than the old, conservative thing. The allure of AI and Lisp attracted both businessmen and venture capitalists.

As early as 1984—the year CLTL1 was published—several companies were founded to commercialize Common Lisp. These included Franz Inc.; Gold Hill Computers, Inc.; and Lucid, Inc. Other companies on the fringe of Lisp joined the Lisp bandwagon with Common Lisp or with Lisps that were on the road to Common Lisp. These included Three Rivers (PERQ) and TI. Some mainstream computer manufacturers joined in the Lisp business. These included DEC, HP, Sun, Apollo, Prime, and IBM. Some European companies joined the Common Lisp bandwagon, including Siemens and Honeywell Bull. And the old players began work on Common Lisp. These included the Lisp machine companies and Xerox. A new player from Japan—Kyoto Common Lisp (KCL)—provided a bit of a spoiler: KCL had a compiler that compiled to C, which was compiled by the C compiler. This Lisp was licensed essentially free, and the Common Lisp companies suddenly had a surprising competitor. (Surprising, because it appeared just as CLTL1 came out—the implementation was based on the Mary Poppins draft. KCL was also notable because it was implemented by outsiders, Taiichi Yuasa and

Masami Hagiya, solely on the basis of the specification. This effort exposed quite a number of holes and mistakes in the specification that had gone unnoticed by those who, having participated in the historical development of Common Lisp, consciously or unconsciously corrected for such mistakes as they went along on the basis of additional shared knowledge.)

Though one might think a free, good-quality product would easily beat an expensive better-quality product, this proved false and the Common Lisp companies thrived despite their no-cost competitor. It turned out that better performance, better quality, commitment by developers to moving ahead with the standard, and better service were more important than no price tag.

6.2.12.1 *Common Lisp Companies*

Franz, Inc., was already in business selling Franz Lisp, the MacLisp-like Lisp dialect used to transport a version of MACSYMA called Vaxima. Franz Lisp was the most popular dialect of Lisp on the VAX until plausible Common Lisps appeared. Franz decided to go into the Common Lisp market, funding the effort with the proceeds from its Franz Lisp sales. The principal founders of Franz are Fritz Kunze, John Foderaro, and Richard Fateman. Kunze was a Ph.D. student of Fateman's at the University of California at Berkeley in the mathematics department; Foderaro, having already obtained his Ph.D. under Fateman, became the primary architect and implementor of the various Lisps offered by Franz, Inc. Fateman, one of the original implementors of MACSYMA at MIT, carried the MacLisp/Lisp torch to Berkeley; he was responsible for the porting of MACSYMA to the VAX. Franz adopted a direct-sales strategy, in which the company targeted customers and sold directly to them.

Gold Hill was a division of a parent company named Apiary Inc., which was founded by Carl Hewitt and his student Jerry Barber. Barber had spent the year before founding Apiary/Gold Hill at INRIA in France, where he wrote a MacLisp/Zetalisp-like Lisp for the IBM PC. This work was partly funded by INRIA. When he returned, it was close enough to Common Lisp that he and Hewitt thought they could capitalize on the wave of Common interest by selling the existing Lisp as a Lisp about to become Common Lisp. Because the PC was believed to be an important machine for AI, it seemed to be an ironclad business plan, in which a variety of glamorous East-coast venture capitalists invested. Gold Hill's Lisp was not a Common Lisp and in the early years the company endured some criticism for false advertising; worse yet, as the Lisp was transformed into a Common Lisp, its quality apparently dropped. At the same time, the so-called "AI winter" hit and Gold Hill was not able to survive at the level it once had. It was abandoned by its venture capitalists, laid off just about all its employees, and continues today as a two-man operation. Gold Hill sold direct as well.

"AI winter" is the term first used in 1988 to describe the unfortunate commercial fate of AI. From the late 1970s until the mid-1980s, artificial intelligence was an important part of the computer business—many companies were started with the then-abundant venture capital available for high-tech start-ups. By 1988 it became clear to business analysts that AI would not experience meteoric growth and there was a backlash against AI and, with it, Lisp as a commercial concern. AI companies started to have substantial financial difficulties and so did the Lisp companies.

Lucid, Inc., was founded by Gabriel (Stanford), Rod Brooks (MIT), Eric Benson (Utah/PSL), Scott Fahlman (CMU), and a few others. Backed by venture capital, Lucid adopted a different strategy from that of the other Common Lisp companies. Instead of starting with the Spice Lisp source code, Lucid wrote an implementation of Common Lisp from scratch; moreover, it adopted an OEM strategy. (The OEM idea is to make arrangements with a computer (hardware) company to market and sell Lisp under its own name. However, the Lisp is implemented and maintained by an outside company, in this case, Lucid, which collects royalties.) Lucid quickly struck OEM deals with Sun, Apollo, and Prime. This was possible because Lucid traded on the strength of the names of its founders and the fact that it was writing a Common Lisp from scratch and would, therefore, be the first true Common Lisp.

Eventually Lucid ported its Lisp and established OEM arrangements with IBM, DEC, and HP. Though the royalties were relatively small per copy, the OEM route established Lucid as the primary stock-hardware Lisp company. Because the hardware companies were enthusiastic about the business opportunities for AI and Lisp, they invested a lot in the business. Often they would pay a large porting fee, a fixed-price licensing fee, and maintenance fees as well as royalties. Getting Sun as an OEM was the key to Lucid's survival, because Sun workstations developed the cachet that was needed to attract customers to the Lisp. Sun was always regarded as leading-edge, so people interested in leading-edge AI technology headed first to Sun. Sun also employed a number of engineers who did their own Lisp development, mostly in the area of programming environments.

Before the AI winter hit, Lucid began diversifying into other languages (C and C++) and programming environments.

6.2.12.2 *Big Companies with Their Own Lisps*

DEC and HP implemented their own Lisps. DEC started with the Spice Lisp code and HP with PSL. Each company believed that AI would take off and that having a Lisp was an essential ingredient for success in the AI business. Both DEC and HP made arrangements with the original implementors of those Lisps, both by hiring students who had worked on them and by arranging for on-going consulting. Both DEC and HP grew fairly large businesses out of these Lisp groups, large by the standards of other Lisp companies. At the peak of Lisp in the last quarter of the 1980s, the main players in the Lisp business, by revenue, were Symbolics, TI, DEC, HP, Sun, and Lucid.

DEC and HP put a lot of effort into their Lisp offerings, primarily in the area of environments but also in the performance of the Lisp system itself.

In the last quarter of the 1980s, HP realized that PSL was not the winner and they needed to provide a Common Lisp. They chose Lucid to provide it and reduced their own engineering staff, choosing to focus more on marketing. Because the AI winter was just about upon them when they made the decision, it is not clear whether their perception of this situation forced them to cut back on their Lisp investment.

In the early 1990s, in the midst of AI winter, DEC also decided to abandon its own efforts and also chose Lucid.

IBM had a number of platforms suitable for Lisp: the PC, the mainframe, and the RT. Of these, IBM initially decided to put a Common Lisp only on the RT. IBM funded a pilot program to put Spice Lisp (Common Lisp) on the RT, which was to be IBM's first real entry into the workstation market. Because of Fahlman's relationship with Lucid (a founder), a contract was eventually written for Lucid to port its Lisp to the RT for IBM.

Later, IBM reentered the workstation market with its RS6000, which has good performance, and Lucid did the Common Lisp for it. IBM eventually contracted with Lucid to provide the same Lisp on the 370 and PS-2 running AIX, a version of Unix.

Xerox produced a Common Lisp compatibility package on top of Interlisp. This package was never really a strong success for Xerox, which in the late 1980s got out of the Lisp business, licensing its Lisp software 1989 to a spinoff started by Xerox called Envos.

Envos put out a real Common Lisp implementation and sold the InterLisp-D environment. But Envos went out of business three years after it was founded. What was left of Envos became the company Venue, which essentially was granted the rights to continue marketing the same software Envos had been, but without direct funding. The funding was provided by servicing Xerox's Lisp customer base (maintenance).

6.2.12.3 *DARPA and the SAIL Mailing Lists*

Right after CLTL1 was published in 1984, ARPA (renamed DARPA) took a real interest in Common Lisp. They sponsored a community meeting and encouraged further development of Common Lisp into a full development system, including an object-oriented extension, multitasking, window systems, graphics, foreign function interfaces, and iteration. It seemed that DARPA wished for a resurgence of Lisp and was willing to provide some funds to help fulfill its wish.

After the meeting, new mailing lists were set up at SAIL for discussion of these topics and, though most of the lists were quiet, some witnessed interesting discussions.

6.2.12.4 *The Start of ANSI Technical Committee X3J13*

In a follow-up meeting one year later—December 1985 in Boston, Massachusetts—an apparently benign technical meeting was interrupted by a shocking announcement: Common Lisp must be standardized, DARPA announced, and Robert Mathis, the convenor of the ISO working group on the Ada programming language, was to head up this effort.

The reason for this sudden need was that the European Lisp community was planning to launch their own Lisp standardization effort at ISO to head off the spread of Common Lisp. Mathis, with his storehouse of international experience, seemed to DARPA the natural choice to head up the response, and the stunned, confused, and soon-to-be-previously-pastoral Common Lisp group could think of little else to do but go along.

The period from Spring of 1986 until Spring of 1992 was a combination of political wrangling and interesting Lisp development. As usual, the impetus behind the Lisp development was to increase the expressive power of Lisp. The political wrangling centered around two different objectives: within Common Lisp, each individual strived to put his or her mark on the language; outside Common Lisp, various groups tried to minimize the size of Lisp to guarantee its survival—both academic and commercial.

A few months after the December 1985 meeting there was a meeting at CBEMA (the Computer and Business Equipment Manufacturers Association) in Washington, D. C. (CBEMA serves as the secretariat for X3, an Accredited Standard Committee for Information Processing Systems operating under the procedures of ANSI, the American National Standards Institute. Among the better-known technical committees under X3 are X3H3 (computer graphics, including PHIGS), X3J3 (programming language FORTRAN), X3J4 (programming language COBOL), and X3J11 (programming language C).) The goals of standardization were discussed, and the most important topic, which was pushed by DARPA, was whether to merge with the Scheme activities—the technical issues surrounded the treatment of macros and whether there was a separate namespace for functions separate from ordinary variables. The goals of the new group, soon to become Technical Committee X3J13 for Programming Language Common Lisp, were also discussed.

The point about namespaces is important to understanding the debate between Lisp dialect proponents. A namespace is a mapping between an identifier (string of characters) and its meaning. In Common Lisp there are a number of namespaces—variables, functions, types, tags, blocks, and catch tags, among others. If a Lisp has separate namespaces for variables and functions, users are allowed to use variable names that also name functions, because the evaluation rules specify the namespace in which to look for the meaning. In a Lisp with a single namespace, the user must be careful when creating variable names to avoid shadowing a function name. This issue is important for macros, which in effect must carefully decide what a free variable is intended to mean. Although there are many namespaces in Lisp, because the variable and function namespaces are where the problems lie in practice, this issue reduces to the question of whether variable names and function names belong to one namespace or two separate namespaces. It is therefore often referred to as the "Lisp-1 versus Lisp-2 debate." A Lisp-1 is a Lisp where functions and variables are in the same namespace, and a Lisp-2 is a Lisp where they are in separate namespaces.

The effort to merge the Scheme and Common Lisp communities was launched on two fronts. One was to try to come up with a solution to the macro problem that a Lisp-1 causes. This problem is that with only one namespace it is relatively easier to stumble across an unintended name conflict leading to incorrect code. The key Common Lisp leaders felt that if the macro problem could be solved, Common Lisp could survive a transition from Lisp-2 to Lisp-1. The other front was to try to convince the Scheme community that this was a good idea.

On the first front, Gabriel and Kent Pitman produced a report detailing the technical issues involved in macros [Gabriel 1988]. Several technical solutions appeared around the same time, the most promising being described in Kohlbecker's dissertation [Kohlbecker 1986b].

On the second front, Gabriel and Will Clinger approached the Scheme community, which soundly rejected any association with the Common Lisp community. (Sadly, though there were several other attempts to bring the two communities together, there has never been any serious dialogue between the two groups.)

By the end of 1986, it was clear that the European Lisp community would eventually produce a new Lisp dialect, which would be informally called EuLisp, and that the same community intended to start an ISO effort to standardize this dialect.

EuLisp is a dialect of Lisp defined in layers, with a very small kernel language and increasingly larger ones, the goal being to have a Common-Lisp-sized layer. EuLisp has an object-oriented facility, modules, multitasking, and a condition system. It is a Lisp-1. (A *condition system* is a facility for defining and handling user exceptions and for handling system exceptions. In Common Lisp, this facility provides a mechanism for executing user-defined code in the dynamic context of the error.)

The most important technical development during this period was the Common Lisp Object System (CLOS). In 1986 four groups began to vie for defining the object-oriented programming part of Common Lisp: New Flavors (Symbolics) [Symbolics 1985], CommonLoops (Xerox) [Bobrow 1986], Object Lisp (LMI) [Drescher 1987], and Common Objects (HP) [Kempf 1987]. After a six-month battle, a group was formed to write the standard for CLOS based on CommonLoops and New Flavors. This group was David A. Moon (Symbolics), Daniel G. Bobrow (Xerox), Gregor Kiczales (Xerox), Sonya Keene (Symbolics, a writer), Linda DeMichiel (Lucid), and Gabriel (Lucid). Also, certain others contributed informally to the group: Patrick Dussud (TI), Jim Kempf (HP), and Jon L White (Lucid). The CLOS specification took two years, and the specification was adopted in June of 1988 with no changes.

CLOS has the following features:

- Multiple inheritance using a linearization algorithm to resolve conflicts and to order methods. Multiple inheritance provides a mechanism to build new classes by combining *mixins*, which are classes that provide some structure and behavior. Programming with multiple inheritance enables the designer to combine desired behaviors without having either to select the closest existing class and modify it or to start a fresh single inheritance chain.
- Generic functions whose methods are selected based on the classes of all required arguments. This is in contrast to the message-passing model in which a message is sent to a single object whose class selects the method to invoke.
- Method combination, which provides the mechanism to take behaviors from component parts and blend them together. Method combination is an important aspect of multiple inheritance,

because each combined class can provide part of the behavior needed, and the programmer need not code up a combining method to use existing methods.

- Metaclasses, whose instances are classes and which are used to control the representation of instances of classes.
- Meta-objects, which control the behavior of CLOS itself. CLOS can be viewed as a program written in CLOS. Because any CLOS program can be customized, so can CLOS itself.
- An elaborate object creation and initialization protocol that can be used to provide user customization of the instance creation, change class, reinitialization, and class redefinition processes.

During the deliberations of X3J13, a number of other additions were made to Common Lisp: an iteration facility, a condition system, a better specification of compilation and evaluation semantics, and several hundreds of small cleanups.

The X3J13 process was unlike the Scheme process. The Scheme process allowed any person to veto an addition. The X3J13 process went by majority vote. This allowed a great deal of log-rolling, and some committee members were eager to put their mark on Common Lisp.

The iteration facility, called **LOOP**, consists of a single macro that has an elaborate pseudo-English or COBOL-like syntax. The debate on this facility was at times intense, especially when Scott Fahlman was still active in Common Lisp. Because of its non-Lispy syntax, it was (and remains) easy to ridicule. (See Sections 6.3.2 and 6.3.5.1.)

The condition system further developed the exception handling capabilities of Common Lisp by introducing first-class conditions and mechanisms for defining how conditions of certain classes are to be handled—either automatically or with human intervention. Adoption of this facility was made easier by the adoption of CLOS, which paved the way for a cleaner formulation of the basic mechanisms. Nevertheless, the condition system was not completely CLOSified and cleaned up. For example, clauses that appear syntactically to be method definitions and hence should be selected based on class specificity are actually treated like **COND** clauses.

In 1987 ISO created a working group called WG 16 to begin the process of standardizing Lisp at the international level. The two primary contenders were EuLisp and Common Lisp.

The political goal of EuLisp was to displace Common Lisp from Europe. Because U.S. standards had such a strong influence in Europe and because the only standards organization with real clout in Europe was ISO, this route was dictated.

The intellectual goal was a clean, commercial-quality, layered Lisp dialect for the future. EuLisp appears to have met its goals and many consider it one of the nicer Lisp definitions, though there are still no commercial implementations of it.

For five years, the U.S. managed to keep any progress from being made in the ISO committee until, in 1992, a compromise was worked out in which, essentially, a near subset of Common Lisp and of CLOS would form the basis of a kernel Lisp dialect.

In 1988, DARPA called another Lisp meeting to discuss bringing the Scheme and Common Lisp communities together but, as with earlier attempts, this failed primarily because the Scheme community did not want to have anything to do with Common Lisp. Attending this meeting were Daniel G. Bobrow, Scott Fahlman, Gabriel, Bill Scherlis, Steve Squires, and Gerry Sussman.

In 1989, Scheme began an IEEE standardization process, which culminated in 1991 with both an IEEE and ANSI standard [IEEE 1991], the latter after a virtually unannounced public review period. The structure of the Scheme standards is that the official standard lags the informal R^n Report, so that the standard corresponds to the R^{n-1} Report when the R^n Report is current.

Also in 1989, the first non-intrusive garbage collectors appeared from the companies Lucid and Franz. The Lucid collector is an ephemeral garbage collector based on a combination of ideas from Smalltalk-generation scavengers and the Symbolics ephemeral garbage collector [Sobalvarro 1988].

The appearance of these collectors seemed to have the effect of increasing the legitimacy of stock-hardware Lisp companies to the same or higher level than the Lisp machine companies. This was because the Lisp machine companies encouraged the belief that stock-hardware Lisps could never have the performance—particularly for garbage collection—that the special-purpose-computer Lisps could have. When this was proven wrong, the Lisp machine companies suffered.

In 1991, the R^4 Report included a specification of hygienic macros, the first partially standardized macro facility in Scheme.

As X3J13 progressed and the power of general purpose workstations increased—largely due to development of fast RISC processors—stock hardware Lisp companies dominated, forcing most of the Lisp machine companies either out of business or out of their leadership position. Also, the deterioration of the Lisp market and the general decline of the economy in the U.S. combined to enable the smaller software-based Lisp companies to survive—customers were not willing to buy expensive "dedicated" computers and then spend money maintaining them.

In April of 1992 X3J13 delivered to X3 SPARC (the authorizing body for X3J13—no relation to the microprocessor architecture of the same name) its draft for Common Lisp. At the same time, ISO WG 16 produced the first draft of its kernel Lisp.

The ANSI draft for Common Lisp is immensely large—well over 1000 pages. We are told that one official at X3 SPARC, on first seeing it, gasped: "It's bigger than COBOL! *Much* bigger!"

Though this might seem funny, it shows how increasing desire for expressiveness, intensified attention to getting the details right (even for details that almost never matter), the need for individuals to make their mark, and a seemingly deliberate blind eye towards commercial realities can lead to an unintended result—a large, unwieldy language that few can completely understand.

6.3 EVOLUTION OF SOME SPECIFIC LANGUAGE FEATURES

In this section we discuss the evolution of some language features that are either unique to Lisp or uniquely handled by Lisp.

But for the constraints of space, we would also have addressed many other topics that have figured prominently in the technical development of Lisp or have been addressed in unusual ways in the context of the Lisp language:

continuations
reification and reflection
garbage collection
stack management
record structures
oblist, obarray, packages, modules
hash tables vs. property lists
structure editors
pretty-printing
program tracing and debugging
closures (lexical and dynamic)
nonlocal exits and `UNWIND-PROTECT`
parallel processing
object-oriented programming

Each of these topics has a story that spans decades and interacts with the development of language theory and other programming languages. Here we must content ourselves with a few topics that are representative of the concerns of the Lisp community.

6.3.1 The Treatment of NIL (and T)

Almost since the beginning, Lisp has used the symbol **nil** as the distinguished object that indicates the end of a list (and which is therefore itself the empty list); this same object also serves as the *false* value returned by predicates. McCarthy has commented that these decisions were made "rather lightheartedly" and "later proved unfortunate." Furthermore, the earliest implementations established a tradition of using the zero address as the representation of **NIL**; McCarthy also commented that "besides encouraging pornographic programming, giving a special interpretation to the address 0 has caused difficulties in all subsequent implementations" [McCarthy 1978].

The advantage of using address 0 as the representation of **NIL** is that most machines have a "jump if zero" instruction or the equivalent, allowing a quick and compact test for the end of a list. As an example of the implementation difficulties, however, consider the PDP-10 architecture, which had 16 registers, or "accumulators," which were also addressable as memory locations. Memory location 0 was therefore register 0. Because address 0 was **NIL**, the standard representation for symbols dictated that the right half of register 0 contain the property list for the symbol **NIL** (and the left half contain the address of other information, such as the character string for the name "**NIL**"). The implementation tradition thus resulted in tying up a register in an architecture where registers were a scarce resource.

Later, when MacLisp adopted from Interlisp, the convention that **(CAR NIL) = (CDR NIL) = NIL**, register 0 was still reserved; its two halves contained the value 0 so that the **car** and **cdr** operations did not need to special-case **NIL**. But all operations on symbols had to special-case **NIL**, for it no longer had the same representation as other symbols. This led to some difficulties for Steele, who had to find every place in the assembly-language kernel of MacLisp where this mattered.

Nowadays, some Common Lisp implementations use a complex system of offset-data representations to avoid special cases for either conses or symbols; *every* symbol is represented in such a way that the data for the symbol does not begin at the memory word addressed by a symbol pointer, but two words after the word addressed. A cons cell consists of the addressed word (the cdr) and the word after that (the car). In this way the same pointer serves for both **NIL**, the symbol and **()**, the empty list pseudo-cons whose car and cdr are both **NIL**.

There is a danger in using a quick test for the end of a list; a list might turn out to be improper, that is, ending in an object that is neither the empty list nor a cons cell. Interlisp split the difference, giving the programmer a choice of speed or safety [Teitelman 1978, p. 2.2]:

> Although most lists terminate in **NIL**, the occasional list that ends in an atom, e.g., **(A B . C)**, or worse, a number or string, could cause bizarre effects. Accordingly, we have made the following implementation decision:
>
> *All functions that iterate through a list, e.g.,* **member**, **length**, **mapc**, *etc., terminate by an* **nlistp** *check, rather than the conventional null-check, as a safety precaution against encountering data types which might cause infinite* **cdr** *loops* . . . [their italics]
>
> For users with an application requiring extreme efficiency, [footnote: A **NIL** check can be executed in only one instruction; an **nlistp** on Interlisp-10 requires about 8, although both generate only one word of code.] we have provided fast versions of **memb**, **last**, **nth**, **assoc**, and **length**, which compile open and terminate on **NIL** checks . . .

Fischer Black commented as early as 1964 on the difference between **NIL** and **()** as a matter of programming style [Black 1964]. There has been quite a bit of discussion over the years of whether to tease apart the three roles of the empty list, the false value, and the otherwise uninteresting symbol whose name is "`NIL`"; such discussion was particularly intense in the Scheme community, many of whose constituents are interested in elegance and clarity. They regard the construction

```
(if (car x) (+ (car x) 1))
```

as a bad pun, preferring the more explicit

```
(if (not (null (car x))) (+ (car x) 1))
```

The Revised Revised Report on Scheme [Clinger 1985b] defined three distinct quantities `nil` (just another symbol); `()`, the empty list; and `#!false`, the Boolean false value (along with `#!true`, the Boolean true value). However, in an interesting compromise, all places in the language that tested for true/false values regarded both `()` and `#!false` as false and all other objects as true. The report comments:

> The empty list counts as false for historical reasons only, and programs should not rely on this because future versions of Scheme will probably do away with this nonsense.
>
> Programmers accustomed to other dialects of Lisp should beware that Scheme has already done away with the nonsense that identifies the empty list with the symbol `nil`.

The *Revised^3 Report on the Algorithmic Language Scheme* [Rees 1986] shortened `#!false` and `#!true` to `#f` and `#t`, and made a remark that is similar but more refined (in both senses):

> The empty list counts as false for compatibility with existing programs and implementations that assume this to be the case.
>
> Programmers accustomed to other dialects of Lisp should beware that Scheme distinguishes false and the empty list from the symbol `nil`.

The recently approved IEEE standard for Scheme specifies that `#f` and `#t` are the standard false and true values, and that all values except `#f` count as true, "including `#t`, the empty list, symbols, numbers, strings, vectors, and procedures" [IEEE 1991]. So the Scheme community has, indeed, overcome long tradition and completely separated the three notions of the false value, the empty list, and the symbol `NIL`. Nevertheless, the question continues to be debated.

The question of `NIL` was also debated in the design of Common Lisp, and at least one of the directly contributing implementations, NIL, had already made the decision that the empty list `()` would not be the same as the symbol `NIL`. (A running joke was that NIL (New Implementation of Lisp) unburdened `NIL` of its role as the empty list so that it would be free to serve as the name of the language!) Eventually the desire to be compatible with the past [Raymond 1991] carried the day.

It is worth noting that Lisp implementors have not been tempted to identify `NIL` with the *number* 0 (as opposed to the internal *address* 0), with one notable exception, a Lisp system for the PDP-11 written in the 1970s by Richard M. Stallman, in which the number 0 rather than the symbol `NIL` was used as the empty list and as false. Compare this to the use of 0 and 1 as false and true in APL [Iverson 1962], or the use of 0 as false and as the null pointer in C [Kernighan 1978]. Both these languages have provoked the same kinds of comments about puns and bad programming practice that McCarthy made about Lisp.

This may seem to the reader a great deal of discussion on such a small point of language design. However, the space taken here reflects accurately the proportion of time and energy in debate actually expended on this point by the Lisp community over the years. It is a debate about expressiveness versus cleanliness and about different notions of clarity. Even if Lisp does not enforce strong typing, some programmers prefer to maintain a type discipline in their code, writing `(if (not (null` `(car x))) ...)` instead of `(if (car x) ...)`. Others contend that such excess clutter detracts from clarity rather than improving it.

6.3.2 Iteration

Although Lisp, according to its PR, has traditionally used conditionals and recursively defined functions as the principal means of expressing control structure, there have in fact been repeated and continuing attempts to introduce various syntactic devices to make iteration more convenient. In some cases this was driven by the desire to emulate styles of programming found in ALGOL-like languages [Abrahams 1966] and by the fact that, although some compilers would sometimes optimize tail-recursive calls, the programmer could not rely on this until the era of good Scheme and Common Lisp compilers in the 1980s, so performance was an issue.

Perhaps the simplest special iteration construct is exemplified by the first **do** loop introduced into MacLisp (in March of 1969):

```
(do var init step test . body)
```

means the same as

```
(let ((var init))
  (block (when test (return))
         (progn . body)
         (setq var step)))
```

Thus the FORTRAN DO loop

```
      DO 10 J=1,100
      IF (A(J) .GT. 0) SUM = SUM + A(J)
 10   CONTINUE
```

could be expressed as

```
(DO J 1 (+ J 1) (> J 100)
  (WHEN (PLUSP (A J))
    (SETQ TOTAL (+ TOTAL (AREF A J)))))
```

(except, of course, that Lisp arrays are usually 0-origin instead of 1-origin, so

```
(DO J 0 (+ J 1) (= J 100)
  (WHEN (PLUSP (A J))
    (SETQ TOTAL (+ TOTAL (AREF A J)))))
```

is actually a more idiomatic rendering).

This "old-style" MacLisp **do** loop was by no means the earliest iteration syntax introduced to Lisp; we mention it first only because it is the simplest. The Interlisp CLISP iterative statements were the earliest examples of the more typical style that has been reinvented ever since:

```
(FOR J←0 TO 99 SUM (A J) WHEN (PLUSP (A J)))
```

This returns the sum as its value rather than accumulating it into the variable **TOTAL** by side effect. (See Section 6.3.5.1 for further discussion of ALGOL-style syntax.)

Macros or other code-transformation facilities such as CLISP make this kind of extension particularly easy. Although the effort in Interlisp was centralized, in other Lisp dialects (MacLisp not excepted) there have been repeated instances of one local wizard or another cobbling up some fancy syntax for iterative processes in Lisp. Usually it is characterized by the kind of pseudo-English keywords found in the ALGOL-like languages, although one version at Stanford relied more on the extended-ASCII character set available on its home-grown keyboards. This led to a proliferation of closely related syntaxes, typically led off by the keyword **FOR** or **LOOP**, that have attracted many programmers but turned the stomachs of others as features accreted.

Because of these strong and differing aesthetic reactions to iteration syntax, the question of whether to include a `loop` macro became a major political battle in the early design of Common Lisp, with the Lisp Machine crowd generally in favor of its adoption and Scott Fahlman adamantly opposing it, seconded perhaps more weakly by Steele. The result was a compromise. The first definition of Common Lisp [CLTL1 1984] included a `loop` macro with absolutely minimal functionality: it permitted no special keywords and was good only for expressing endless repetition of a sequence of subforms. It was understood to be a placeholder, reserving the name `loop` for possible extension to some full-blown iteration syntax. ANSI committee X3J13 did eventually agree upon and adopt a slightly cleaned-up version of `loop` [CLTL2 1990] based on the one used at MIT and on Lisp Machines (which was not very much different from the one in Interlisp).

In the process, X3J13 also considered two other approaches to iteration that had cropped up in the meantime: series (put forward by Richard Waters) and generators and gatherers (by Pavel Curtis and Crispin Perdue) [CLTL2 1990; Waters 1984, 1989a, 1989b]. The example FORTRAN `DO loop` shown would be rendered using series as

```
(collect-sum (choose-if #'plusp
                        (#M(lambda (j) (a j))
                         (scan-range :start 0 :below 100))))
```

The call to `scan-range` generates a series of integers from 0 (inclusive) to 100 (exclusive). The notation `#M` means "map"—the following function is applied to every element of a series, producing a new series. The function `choose-if` is a *filter*, and `collect-sum` returns the sum of all the elements in a series. Thus series are used in a functional style, reminiscent of APL:

```
+/(T>0)/T←A[ι100]
```

The definition of the series primitives and their permitted compositions is cleverly constrained so that they can always be compiled into efficient iterative code without the need for unboundedly large intermediate data structures at run time. Generators and gatherers are a method of encapsulating series (at the cost of run-time state) so that they look like input or output streams, respectively, that serve as sources or sinks of successive values by side effect. Thus

```
(generator (scan-range :start 0 :below 100))
```

produces an object that delivers successive integers `0` through `99` when repeatedly given to the extraction function `next-in`. The complete example might be rendered as

```
(let ((num (generator (scan-range :start 0 :below 100))))
  (gathering ((result collect-sum))
    (loop (let ((j (next-in num (return result))))
            (if (plusp j) (next-out result j))))))
```

This reminds one of the possibilities lists of Conniver [McDermott 1974] or of the generators of Alphard [Shaw 1981], though we know of no direct connection. Generators and gatherers emphasize use of control structure rather than functional relationships.

After much debate, X3J13 applauded the development of series and generators but rejected them for standardization purposes, preferring to subject them first to the test of time.

One other iteration construct that deserves discussion is the MacLisp "new-style" **do** loop, introduced in March of 1972:

```
(do ((var1 init1 step1)
     (var2 init2 step2)
     ...
     (varn initn stepn))
    (test . result)
    body)
```

This evaluates all the *init* forms and binds the corresponding variables *var* to the resulting values. It then iterates the following sequence: if evaluating the *test* form produces a true value, evaluate the *result* forms and return the value of the last one; otherwise execute the *body* forms in sequence, give the variables of the values of the **step** forms, and repeat.

The beauty of this construct is that it allows the initialization and stepping of multiple variables without use of pseudo-English keywords. The awful part is that it uses multiple levels of parentheses as delimiters and you have to get them right or endure strange behavior; only a diehard Lisper could love such a syntax.

Arguments over syntax aside, there is something to be said for recognizing that a loop that steps only one variable is pretty useless, in *any* programming language. It is almost always the case that one variable is used to generate successive values while another is used to accumulate a result. If the loop syntax steps only the generating variable, then the accumulating variable must be stepped "manually" by using assignment statements (as in the FORTRAN example) or some other side effect. The multiple-variable **do** loop reflects an essential symmetry between generation and accumulation, allowing iteration to be expressed without explicit side effects:

```
(define (factorial n)
  (do ((j n (- j 1))
       (f 1 (* j f)))
      ((= j 0) f)))
```

It is indeed not unusual for a **do** loop of this form to have an empty body, performing all its real work in the *step* forms.

Although there is a pretty obvious translation of this **do** construct in terms of **prog** and **setq**, there is also a perspicuous model free of side effects:

```
(labels ((the-loop
           (lambda (var1 var2 ... varn)
             (cond (test . result)
                   (t (progn . body)
                      (the-loop step1 step2 ... stepn))))))
  (the-loop init1 init2 ... initn))
```

Indeed, this is equivalent to the definition of **do** adopted by Scheme [IEEE 1991], which resolves an outstanding ambiguity by requiring that the variables be updated by binding rather than by side effect. Thus the entire iteration process is free of side effects. With the advent of good Scheme compilers such as ORBIT [Kranz 1986] and good Common Lisp compilers, compiling the result of this side-effect-free translation produces exactly the same efficient machine-language code one would expect from the **PROG**-and-**SETQ** model.

6.3.3 Macros

Macros appear to have been introduced into Lisp by Timothy P. Hart in 1963 in a short MIT AI Memo [Hart 1963], which we quote here in its entirety (with permission):

> In LISP 1.5 special forms are used for three logically separate purposes: a) to reach the alist, b) to allow functions to have an indefinite number of arguments, and c) to keep arguments from being evaluated.
>
> New LISP interpreters can easily satisfy need (a) by making the alist a **SPECIAL**-type or **APVAL**-type entity. Uses (b) and (c) can be replaced by incorporating a **MACRO** instruction expander in **define**. I am proposing such an expander.
>
> 1. The property list of a macro definition will have the indicator **MACRO** followed by a function of one argument, a form beginning with the macro's name, and whose value will replace the original form in all function definitions.
> 2. The function **macro[l]** will define macros just as **define[l]** defines functions.
> 3. **define** will be modified to make macro expansions.
>
> Examples:
>
> 1. The existing **FEXPR csetq** may be replaced by the macro definition:
>
> ```
> MACRO ((
> (CSETQ (LAMBDA (FORM) (LIST (QUOTE CSET) (LIST (QUOTE QUOTE) (CADR FORM))
> (CADDR FORM))))
> ))
> ```
>
> 2. A new macro **stash** will generate the form found frequently in **PROG**'s:
>
> ```
> x := cons[form;x]
> ```
>
> Using the macro **stash**, one might write instead of the above:
>
> ```
> (STASH FORM X)
> ```
>
> **Stash** may be defined by:
>
> ```
> MACRO ((
> (STASH (LAMBDA (FORM) (LIST (QUOTE SETQ) (CADAR FORM)
> (LIST (CONS (CADR FORM) (CADAR FORM))) )))
> ))
> ```
>
> 3. New macros may be defined in terms of old. **Enter** is a macro for adding a new entry to a table (dotted pairs) stored as the value of a program variable.
>
> ```
>                   MACRO
> enter[form]      ≡    list[STASH;list[CONS;cadr[form];
> caddr[form];cadddr[form]]
> ```
>
> Incidentally, use of macros will alleviate the present difficulty resulting from the 90 LISP compiler's only knowing about those fexprs in existence at its birth.
>
> The macro defining function **macro** is easily defined:
>
> ```
> macro[l] ≡ deflist[l;MACRO]
> ```
>
> The new **define** is a little harder:
>
> ```
> define[l] ≡ deflist[mdef[l];EXPR]
> mdef[l] ≡ [
>     atom[l] → l;
> ```

```
eq[car[l];QUOTE] → l;
member[car[l];(LAMBDA LABEL PROG)] →
    cons[car[l];cons[cadr[l];mdef[caddr[l]]]];
get[car[l];MACRO] → mdef[get[car[l];MACRO][l]];
T → maplist[l;λ[[j];mdef[car[j]]]]]
```

4. The macro for `select` illustrates the use of macros as a means of allowing functions of an arbitrary number of arguments:

```
                MACRO
select[form]    ≡    λ[[g];
    list[list[LAMBDA;list[g];cons[COND;
    maplist[cddr[form];λ[[l];
         [null[cdr[l]] → list[T;car[l]];
          T → list[list[EQ;g;caar[l]];cadar[l]]]]]
]];cadr[form]]][gensym[]]
```

There are a number of points worth noting about Hart's proposal. It allows the macro expansion to be computed by an arbitrary user-defined function, rather than relying on substitution into a template, as so many other macro processors of the day did. He noted that macros, unlike fexprs, require no special knowledge for each one on the part of the compiler. Macros are expanded at function definition time, rather than on the fly as a function is interpreted or compiled. Note the switching off between S-expression and M-expression syntax. The **STASH** macro is the equivalent of the **PUSH** macro found in Interlisp [Teitelman 1978] and later in Common Lisp by way of Lisp-Machine Lisp; the verb "stash" was commonly used in the 1960s. There are two minor bugs in the definition of **mdef**: first, **PROG** is not properly handled, because it fails to process all the statements in a **PROG** form; second, **COND** is not handled specially, which can lead to mistakes if a variable has the same name as a macro and the variable is used as the test part of a **COND** clause. (Perhaps this was an oversight, or perhaps it never occurred to Hart that anyone would have the bad taste to use a name for two such different purposes.) The last example illustrates the technique of generating a new name for a temporary binding to avoid multiple evaluations of an argument form. Finally, Hart achieved an amazing increase in expressive power with a deceptively simple change to the language, by encouraging the user to exploit the power of Lisp to serve as its own metalanguage.

Hart's macro language was subsequently used in the Lisp system for the Q-32 [Saunders 1964b]. Inspection of the **MDEF** function in the compiler code [Saunders 1964a, p. 311] reveals that the error in processing **PROG** statements had been repaired: **mdef[caddr[l]]** was replaced by **mdef[cddr[l]]**. (In fact, this may be what Hart had originally intended; in Hart 1963 the "**a**" appears to have been written in by hand as a correction over another letter. Perhaps the typist had made the typographical error **mdef[ccddr[l]]** and subsequently a wrong correction was made.) Unfortunately, the use of **mdef[cddr[l]]** has its own problems: a variable whose value is returned by a **LAMBDA** expression or a tag at the head of a **PROG** might be incorrectly recognized as the name of a macro, thereby treating the body of the **LAMBDA** or **PROG** form as a macro call. Picky, picky—but nowadays we do try to be careful about that sort of thing.

Macros of this kind were an integral part of the design of Lisp 2. Abrahams *et al.* remark that by 1966 macros were an accepted part of Lisp 1.5 as well [Abrahams 1966].

A similar sort of computed macro appeared in the MIT PDP-6 Lisp, but macro calls were expanded on the fly as they were encountered by the compiler or the interpreter. In the case of the interpreter, if an explicitly named function in a function call form turned out to have a **MACRO** property on its property list (rather than one of the function indicators **EXPR**, **SUBR**, **LSUBR**, **FEXPR**, or **FSUBR**) then the function definition was given the original macro call form as an argument and was expected to return another form to be evaluated in place of the call. The example given in the PDP-6 Lisp memo [PDP-6 Lisp 1967] was

```
(DEFPROP CONSCONS
         (LAMBDA (A)
                 (COND ((NULL (CDDR A)) (CADR A))
                       ((LIST (QUOTE CONS)
                              (CADR A)
                              (CONS (CAR A)
                                    (CDDR A))))))
         MACRO)
```

This defined a macro equivalent in effect to the Common Lisp function **list***. Note the use of **DEFPROP** to define a function, the use of **QUOTE** rather than a single quote character, and the omission of the now almost universally customary **T** in the second **COND** clause.

An advantage of this scheme was that one could define some functions that use macros and later define (or redefine) the macro; a macro call would always use the latest macro definition. A drawback, however, was that the interpreter must constantly re-expand the same macro call every time it is repeated, reducing speed of execution. A device called *displacing macros* soon became common among MacLisp users; it involved the utility function **DISPLACE**:

```
(DEFUN DISPLACE (OLD NEW)
  (RPLACA OLD (CAR NEW))
  (RPLACD OLD (CDR NEW))
  OLD)
```

One would then write

```
(DEFPROP CONSCONS
         (LAMBDA (A)
            (DISPLACE A
                 (COND ...)))
         MACRO)
```

The effect was to destructively alter the original list structure of the macro call so as to replace it with its expansion.

This all-too-clever trick had drawbacks of its own. First, it failed if a macro needed to expand to an atom (such as a number or variable reference); macro writers learned to produce **(PROGN FOO)** instead of **FOO**. Second, if a macro were redefined after a call to it had been displaced, subsequent executions of the call would not use the new definition. Third, the code was modified; the pretty-printing code that originally contained a macro call would display the expansion, not the original macro call. This last drawback was tolerable only because the MacLisp environment was so firmly file-based: displacing macros modified only the in-core copy of a program; it did not affect the master definition, which was considered to be the text in some file. Displacing macros of this kind would have been intolerable in Interlisp.

Around 1978, Lisp-Machine Lisp introduced an improvement to the displacement technique:

```
(defun displace (old new)
  (rplacd new (list (cons (car old) (cdr old)) new))
  (rplaca old 'si:displaced)
  new)

(defmacro si:displaced (old new) new)
```

The idea is that the macro call is displaced by a list `(si:displaced` *macro-call expansion*`)`. The macro **`si:displaced`** transparently returns its second argument form, so everything behaves as if the expansion itself had replaced the macro call. Although expanding the call to **`si:displaced`** is not free, it is presumably cheaper than continually re-expanding the original macro call (if not, then the macro writer shouldn't use **`displace`**). The Lisp Machine pretty-printer recognizes calls to **`si:displace`** and prints only the original macro call.

BBN-Lisp [Teitelman 1971] had *three* kinds of macro: *open*, *computed*, and *substitution* (described later). A macro definition was stored in the property list of its name under the **MACRO** property; the form of the property value determined which of three types of macro it was. Originally all three types were effective only in compiled code. Eventually, however, after BBN-Lisp became Interlisp [Teitelman 1978], a DWIM hack called MACROTRAN was added that made all three types of macro effective in interpreted code. If interpreting a function call resulted in an "undefined function" error, the DWIM system would step in. MACROTRAN would gain control, expand the macro, and evaluate the resulting expansion. The Interlisp manual duly notes that interpreted macros will work only if DWIM is enabled. Contrast this with the MIT approach of building macros directly into the interpreter (as well as the compiler) as a primitive language feature.

A BBN-Lisp *open* macro simply caused the macro name to be replaced by a lambda expression, causing the function to be compiled "open" or in-line. Here is an open macro definition for **ABS**:

```
(LAMBDA (X) (COND ((GREATERP X 0) X) (T (MINUS X))))
```

Of course, this has exactly the same form as a function definition.

A BBN-Lisp *computed* macro was similar to the kind in MIT PDP-6 Lisp, except that the expander function received the **CDR** of the macro call rather than the entire macro call. Here is a computed macro for **LIST**:

```
(X (LIST (QUOTE CONS)
         (CAR X)
         (AND (CDR X)
              (CONS (QUOTE LIST)
                    (CDR X]
```

The leading **X** is the name of a variable to be bound to the **CDR** of the macro call form. Note also the use of a closing superbracket in the definition. (See Section 6.2.3.)

A BBN-Lisp *substitution* macro consisted of a simple pattern (a parameter list) and a substitution template; subforms of the macro call were substituted for occurrences in the template of corresponding parameter names. A substitution macro for **ABS** would look like this:

```
((X) (COND ((GREATERP X 0) X) (T (MINUS X))))
```

However, the call `(ABS (FOO Z))` would be expanded to

```
(COND ((GREATERP (FOO Z) 0) (FOO Z)) (T (MINUS (FOO Z))))
```

leading to multiple evaluations of `(FOO Z)`, which would be unfortunate if `(FOO Z)` were an expensive computation or had side effects. By way of contrast, with an open macro the call `(ABS (FOO Z))` would be expanded to

```
((LAMBDA (X) (COND ((GREATERP X 0) X) (T (MINUS X)))) (FOO Z))
```

which would evaluate `(FOO Z)` exactly once.

Despite the care sometimes required to avoid multiple evaluation, however, the pattern/template methodology for defining macros is very convenient and visually appealing. Indeed, pattern matching and template methodologies were a pervasive topic in the development of languages for Artificial Intelligence throughout the 1960s and 1970s. (See Section 6.4.) We return to the topic of template-based macros later.

Muddle [Galley 1975], not surprisingly, had a macro facility very much like that of PDP-6 Lisp, with one slight difference. The macro expansion function, rather than being called with the macro form as its argument, was applied to the **CDR** of the form. This allowed Muddle's complex argument-list keywords to come into play, allowing certain simple kinds of pattern matching as for Interlisp's substitution macros:

```
<DEFMAC INC (ATM "OPTIONAL" (N 1))
        <FORM SET .ATM <FORM + <FORM LVAL .ATM> .N>>>
```

It was nevertheless necessary to laboriously construct the result as for a computed macro. The result of expanding **<INC X>** would be **<SET X <+ .X 1>>** (Note that in Muddle **.X** is merely a readmacro abbreviation for **<LVAL X>**, the local value of **X**.)

As MacLisp grew out of PDP-6 Lisp, the MacLisp community diversified, producing a variety of methodologies for defining macros. Simple macros such as **INC** were conceptually straightforward to write, if a bit cumbersome (certainly more clumsy than in Muddle or Interlisp):

```
(DEFUN INC MACRO (X)
       (LIST 'SETQ
             (CADR X)
             (LIST 'PLUS
                   (CADR X)
                   (COND ((CDDR X) (CADDR X)) (T 1)))))
```

Note that the lack of automatic decomposition ("destructuring") of the argument forms leads to many uses of **CAR**, **CDR**, and **COND** within the code that constructs the result. One can use **LET** to separate the destructuring from the construction:

```
(DEFUN INC MACRO (X)
  (LET ((VAR (CADR X))
        (N (COND ((CDDR X) (CADDR X)) (T 1))))
    (LIST 'SETQ VAR (LIST 'PLUS VAR N))))
```

but **LET**—itself a macro first invented and reinvented locally at each site—was a late-comer to the MacLisp world; according to Lisp Archive, it was retroactively absorbed into PDP-10 MacLisp from Lisp-Machine Lisp in 1979, at the same time as **DEFMACRO** and the complex Lisp Machine **DEFUN** argument syntax. About the best one could do during the 1970s was to use a **LAMBDA** expression:

```
(DEFUN INC MACRO (X)
  ((LAMBDA (VAR N)
     (LIST 'SETQ VAR (LIST 'PLUS VAR N)))
   (CADR X)
   (COND ((CDDR X) (CADDR X)) (T 1))))
```

and many programmers found this none too attractive. As a result, the writing of complex macros was a fairly difficult art, and wizards developed their own separate styles of macro definition.

To see how easily this can get out of hand, consider a macro for a simple **FOR** loop. A typical use would be this:

```
(for a 1 100
  (print a)
  (print (* a a)))
```

This should expand to

```
(do a 1 (+ a 1) (> a 100)
  (print a)
  (print (* a a)))
```

This is a trivial syntactic transformation, simple but convenient, defining a FORTRAN–DO-loop–like syntax in terms of the slightly more general "old-style" MacLisp **DO** loop. (See Section 6.3.2.) In the MacLisp of the early 1970s one might define it as follows:

```
(defun for macro (x)
  (cons 'do
        (cons (cadr x)
              (cons (caddr x)
                    (cons (list '+ (cadr x) 1)
                          (cons (list '> (cadr x) (cadddr x))
                                (cddddr x)))))))
```

That's a lot to write for such a simple transformation.

Eventually the gurus at various MacLisp sites developed dozens of similar but not quite compatible macro-defining macros. It was not unusual for several such packages to be in use at the same site, with the adherents of each sect using whatever their wizard had developed. Such packages usually included tools for destructuring argument forms and for constructing result forms. The tools for constructing result forms fell into two major categories: substitution and pseudo-quoting. Substitution techniques required separate mention in a template of certain symbols that were to be replaced by specified values. Pseudo-quoting allowed the code to compute a replacement value to occur within the template itself; it was called pseudo-quoting because the template was surrounded by a call to an operator that was "just like `quote`" except for specially marked places within the template.

Macros took a major step forward with Lisp-Machine Lisp, which consolidated the various macro-defining techniques into two standardized features that were adopted throughout the MacLisp community and eventually into Common Lisp. The macro-defining operator **DEFMACRO** provided list-structure destructuring to arbitrary depth; the backquote feature provided a convenient and concise pseudo-quoting facility. Here is the definition of the **FOR** macro using **DEFMACRO** alone:

```
(defmacro for (var lower upper . body)
  (cons 'do
        (cons var
              (cons lower
                    (cons (list '+ var 1)
                          (cons (list '> var upper)
                                body))))))
```

Notice that we can name the parts of the original form. Using the backquote pseudo-quoting syntax, which makes a copy of a template, filling in each place marked by a comma with the value of the following expression, we get a very concise and easy-to-read definition:

```
(defmacro for (var lower upper . body)
  `(do ,var ,lower (+ ,var 1) (> ,var ,upper) ,@body))
```

Note the use of `,@` to indicate *splicing*.

The backquote syntax was particularly powerful when nested. This occurred primarily within macro-defining macros; because these were coded primarily by wizards, the ability to write and interpret nested backquote expressions was soon surrounded by a certain mystique. Alan Bawden of MIT acquired a particular reputation as backquote-meister in the early days of the Lisp Machine.

Backquote and **DEFMACRO** made a big difference. This leap in expressive power, made available in a standard form, began a new surge of language extension because it was now much easier to define new language constructs in a standard, portable way so that experimental dialects could be shared. Some, including David Moon, have opined that the success of Lisp as a language designer's kit is largely due to the ability of the user to define macros that use Lisp as the processing language and list structure as the program representation, making it easy to extend the language syntax and semantics. In 1980 Kent Pitman wrote a very good summary of the advantages of macros over **FEXPR**'s in defining new language syntax [Pitman 1980].

Not every macro was easy to express in this new format, however. Consider the **INC** macro discussed above. As of November of 1978, the Lisp Machine **DEFMACRO** destructuring was not quite rich enough to handle "optional" argument forms:

```
(DEFUN INC MACRO (VAR . REST)
  `(SETQ ,VAR (+ ,VAR ,(IF REST (CAR REST) 1))))
```

The optional part must be handled with an explicitly programmed conditional (expressed here using **IF**, which was itself introduced into Lisp-Machine Lisp, probably under the influence of Scheme, as a macro that expanded into an equivalent **COND** form). This deficiency was soon noticed and quickly remedied by allowing **DEFMACRO** to accept the same complex lambda-list syntax as **DEFUN**:

```
(DEFUN INC MACRO (VAR &OPTIONAL (N 1))
  `(SETQ ,VAR (+ ,VAR ,N)))
```

This occurred in January of 1979, according to Lisp Archive, at which time MacLisp absorbed **DEFMACRO** and **DEFUN** with **&**-keywords from Lisp-Machine Lisp.

An additional problem was that repetitive syntax, of the kind that might be expressed in extended BNF with a Kleene star, was not captured by this framework and had to be programmed explicitly. Contemplate this simple definition of **LET**:

```
(defmacro let (bindings . body)
  `((lambda ,(mapcar #'car bindings) ,@body)
    ,@(mapcar #'cadr bindings)))
```

Note the use of **MAPCAR** for iterative processing of the bindings. This difficulty was not tackled by Lisp-Machine Lisp or Common Lisp; in that community **DEFMACRO** with **&**-keywords is the state of the art today. Common Lisp did, however, generalize **DEFMACRO** to allow recursive nesting of such lambda-lists.

Further development of the theory and practice of Lisp macros was carried forward primarily by the Scheme community, which was interested in scoping issues. Macros are fraught with the same kinds of scoping problems and accidental name capture that had accompanied special variables. The problem with Lisp macros, from the time of Hart in 1963 to the mid-1980s, is that a macro call expands into an expression that is composed of symbols that have no attached semantics. When substituted back into the program, a macro expansion could conceivably take on a quite surprising meaning depending on the local environment. (Macros in other languages—the C preprocessor [Kernighan 1978; Harbison 1991] is one example—have the same problem if they operate by straight substitution of text or tokens.)

One practical way to avoid such problems is for the macro writer to try to choose names that the user is unlikely to stumble across, either by picking strange names such as `%%foo%%` (though it is surprising how often great minds will think alike), by using **gensym** (as Hart did in his **select** example, shown in the preceding), or by using multiple obarrays or packages to avoid name clashes. However, none of these techniques provides an iron-clad guarantee. Steele pointed out that careful use of thunks could probably eliminate the problem, though not in all situations [Steele 1978a].

The proponents of Scheme regarded all of these arrangements as too flawed or too clumsy for "official" adoption into Scheme. The result was that Scheme diversified in the 1980s. Nearly every implementation had some kind of macro facility but no two were alike. Nearly everyone agreed that macro facilities were invaluable in principle and in practice but looked down upon each particular instance as a sort of shameful family secret. If only The Right Thing could be found! This question became more pressing as the possibility of developing a Scheme standard was bandied about.

In the mid-1980s two new sorts of proposals were put forward: hygienic macros and syntactic closures. Both approaches involve the use of special syntactic environments to ensure that references are properly matched to definitions. A related line of work allows the programmer to control the expansion process by explicitly passing around and manipulating expander functions [Dybvig 1986]. All of these were intended as macro facilities for Scheme, previous methods being regarded as too deeply flawed for adoption into such an otherwise elegant language.

Hygienic macros were developed in 1986 by Eugene Kohlbecker with assistance from Daniel Friedman, Matthias Felleisen, and Bruce Duba [Kohlbecker 1986a]. The idea is to label the occurrences of variables with a tag indicating whether it appeared in the original source code or was introduced as a result of macro expansion; if multiple macro expansions occur, the tag must indicate which expansion step was involved. The technique renames variables so that a variable reference cannot refer to a binding introduced at a different step.

Kohlbecker's Ph.D. dissertation [Kohlbecker 1986b] carried this a step further by proposing a pattern matching and template substitution language for defining macros; the underlying mechanism automatically used hygienic macro expansion to avoid name clashes. The macro-defining language was rich enough to express a wide variety of useful macros, but provided no facility for the execution of arbitrary user-specified Lisp code; this restriction was thought necessary to avoid subversion of the guarantee of good hygiene. This little language is interesting in its own right. Although not as general as the separate matching and substitution facilities of **DEFMACRO** and backquote (with the opportunity to perform arbitrary computations in between), it does allow for optional and repetitive forms by using a BNF-like notation, and allows for optional situations by permitting multiple productions and using the first one that matches. For example, **INC** might be defined as

```
(extend-syntax (inc) ()
  ((inc x) (inc x 1))
  ((inc x n) (setq x (+ x n))))
```

and **LET** as

```
(extend-syntax (let) ()
  ((let ((var value) ...) body ...)
   ((lambda (var ...) body ...) value ...)))
```

The ellipsis "`...`" serves as a kind of Kleene star. Note the way in which variable-value pairs are implicitly destructured and rearranged into two separate lists in the expansion.

The first list given to **extend-syntax** is a list of keywords that are part of the macro syntax and not to be tagged as possible variable references. The second list mentions variables that may be introduced by the macro expansion but are *intended* to interact with the argument forms. For example, consider an implementation (using the Scheme call-with-current-continuation primitive) of a slight generalization of the n+½ loop attributed to Dahl [Knuth 1974]; it executes statements repeatedly until its **while** clause (if any) fails or until **exit** is used.

```
(extend-syntax (loop while repeat) (exit)
  ((loop e1 e2 ... repeat)
   (call/cc (lambda (exit)
              ((label foo
                 (lambda () e1 e2 ... (foo)))))))
  ((loop e1 ... while p e2 ... repeat)
   (call/cc (lambda (exit)
              ((label foo
                 (lambda () e1 ...
                           (unless p (exit #f))
                           e2 ...
                           (foo))))))))
```

In this example **loop**, **while**, and **repeat** are keywords and should not be confused with possible variable references; **exit** is bound by the macro but is intended for use in the argument forms of the macro call. The name **foo** is not intended for such use, and the hygienic macro expander will rename it if necessary to avoid name clashes. (Note that you have to try hard to make a name available; the default is to play it safe, which makes **extend-syntax** easier and safer for novice macro writers to use.) Note the use of the idiom "**e1 e2 ...**" to require that at least one form is present if there is no **while** clause.

Syntactic closures were proposed in 1988 by Alan Bawden and Jonathan Rees [Bawden 1988]. Their idea bears a strong resemblance to the expansion-passing technique of Dybvig, Friedman, and Haynes [Dybvig 1986] but is more general. Syntactic contexts are represented not by the automatically managed tags of hygienic macro expansion but by environment objects; one may "close" a piece of code with respect to such a syntactic environment, thereby giving the macro writer explicit control over the correspondence between one occurrence of a symbol and another. Syntactic closures provide great power and flexibility but put the burden on the programmer to use them properly.

In 1990, William Clinger (who used to be at Indiana University) joined forces with Rees to propose a grand synthesis that combines the benefits of hygienic macros and syntactic closures, with the added advantage of running in linear rather than quadratic time. Their technique is called, appropriately enough, "macros that work" [Clinger 1991]. The key insight may be explained by analogy to reduction in the lambda calculus [Church 1941]. Sometimes the rule of α-conversion must be applied to rename variables in a lambda-calculus expression so that a subsequent β-reduction will not produce a name clash. One cannot do such renaming all at once; it is necessary to intersperse renaming with the β-reductions, because a β-reduction can make two copies of a lambda-expression (hence both bind the same name) and bring the binding of one into conflict with that of the other. The same is true of macros: it is necessary to intersperse renaming with macro expansion. The contribution of Clinger and Rees was to clarify this problem and provide a fast, complete solution.

The Scheme standard [IEEE 1991] was adopted without a macro facility, so confusion still officially reigns on this point. Macros remain an active research topic.

Why are macros so important to Lisp programmers? Not merely for the syntactic convenience they provide, but also because they are programs that manipulate programs, which has always been a central theme in the Lisp community. If FORTRAN is the language that pushes numbers around, and C is the language that pushes characters and pointers around, then Lisp is the language that pushes programs around. Its data structures are useful for representing and manipulating program text. The macro is the most immediate example of a program written in a metalanguage. Because Lisp is its own metalanguage, the power of the entire programming language can be brought to bear on the task of transforming program text.

By comparison, the C preprocessor is completely anemic; the macro language consists entirely of substitution and token concatenation. There are conditionals, and one may conditionally define a macro, but a C macro may not expand into such a conditional. There is neither recursion nor metarecursion, which is to say that a C macro can neither invoke itself nor define another macro.

Lisp users find this laughable. They are very much concerned with the programming process as an object of discourse and an object of computation, and they insist on having the best possible means of expression for this purpose. Why settle for anything less than the full programming language itself?

(We say this not only to illustrate the character of Lisp, but also to illustrate the character of Lispers. The Lisp community is motivated, in part, by a attitude of superiority to the competition, which might be another programming language or another dialect of Lisp.)

6.3.4 Numerical Facilities

In Lisp 1.6 and through PDP-6 Lisp, most Lisp systems offered at most single-word fixnums (integers) and single-word flonums (floating-point numbers). (PDP-1 Lisp [Deutsch 1964] had only fixnums; apparently the same is true of the M-460 Lisp [Hart 1964]. Lisp 1.5 on the 7090 had floating-point [McCarthy 1962], as did Q-32 Lisp [Saunders 1964b] and PDP-6 Lisp [PDP-6 Lisp 1967].)

We are still a little uncertain about the origin of bignums (a data type that uses a variable amount of storage to represent arbitrarily large integer values, subject to the total size of the heap, which is where bignums are stored). They seem to have appeared in MacLisp and Stanford Lisp 1.6 at roughly the same time, and perhaps also in Standard Lisp. They were needed for symbolic algebra programs such as REDUCE [Hearn 1971] and MACSYMA [Mathlab Group 1977]. Nowadays the handling of bignums is a distinguishing feature of Lisp, though not an absolute requirement. Both the Scheme Standard [IEEE 1991] and Common Lisp [CLTL2 1990] require them. Usually the algorithms detailed in Knuth Volume 2 are used [Knuth 1969, 1981]. Jon L White wrote a paper about a set of primitives that allow one to code most of bignum arithmetic efficiently in Lisp, instead of having to code the whole thing in assembly language [White 1986].

There is also a literature on BIGFLOAT arithmetic. It has been used in symbolic algebra systems [Mathlab Group 1977], but has not become a fixture of Lisp dialects. Lisp is often used as a platform for this kind of research because having bignums gets you 2/3 of the way there [Boehm 1986; Vuillemin 1988]. The MacLisp functions **HAULONG** and **HAIPART** were introduced to support MACSYMA's bigfloat arithmetic; these became the Common Lisp functions **INTEGER-LENGTH** and (by way of Lisp-Machine Lisp) **LDB**.

In the 1980s the developers of Common Lisp grappled with the introduction of the IEEE floating-point standard [IEEE 1985]. (It is notable that, as of this writing, most other high-level programming languages have *not* grappled seriously with the IEEE floating-point standard. Indeed, ANSI X3J3 (FORTRAN) rejected an explicit request to do so.)

Although Lisp is not usually thought of as a numerical programming language, there were three strong influences in that direction: MACSYMA, the S-1 project, and Gerald Sussman.

The first good numerical Lisp compiler was developed for the MACSYMA group [Golden 1970; Steele 1977b, 1977c]; it was important to them and their users that numerical code be both fast and compact. The result was a Lisp compiler that was competitive with the DEC PDP-10 FORTRAN compiler [Fateman 1973].

The S-1 was initially intended to be a fast signal processor. One of the envisioned applications was detection of submarines, which seemed to require a mix of numerical signal processing and artificial intelligence techniques. The project received advice from W. Kahan in the design of its floating-point arithmetic, so it ended up being quite similar to the eventual IEEE standard. It seemed appropriate to refine the techniques of the MacLisp compiler to produce good numerical code in S-1 Lisp [Brooks 1982b]. The S-1 offered four different floating-point formats (18, 36, 72, and 144 bits) [Correll 1979]. Influenced by S-1 Lisp, Common Lisp provides an expanded system of floating-point data types to accommodate such architectural variation.

The inclusion of complex numbers in Common Lisp was also an inheritance from the S-1. This was something of a sticking point with Scott Fahlman. A running joke was an acceptance test for nascent Common Lisp implementations developed by Steele. It was in three parts. First you type `T`; if it responds `T`, it passes part 1. Second, you define the `factorial` function and then calculate

```
(/ (factorial 1000) (factorial 999))
```

If it responds `1000`, it passes part 2. Third, you try `(atanh -2)`. If it returns a complex number, it passes; extra credit if it returns the *correct* complex number. It was a long time before any Common Lisp implementation passed the third part. Steele broke an implementation or two on the trade-show floor with this three-part test.

Gerald Sussman and his students (including Gerald Roylance and Matthew Halfant) became interested in numerical applications and in the use of Lisp to generate and transform numerical programs [Sussman 1988; Roylance 1988]. Sussman also spent a fair amount of time at MIT teaching Lisp to undergraduates. Sussman thought it was absolutely crazy to have to tell students that the quotient of `10.0` and `4.0` was `2.5` but the quotient of `10` and `4` was `2`. Of course, nearly all other programming languages have the same problem (Pascal [Jensen 1974] and its derivatives being notable exceptions), but that is no excuse; Lisp aspires to better things, and centuries of mathematical precedent should outweigh the few decades of temporary aberration in the field of computers. At Sussman's urging, the `/` function was defined to return rationals when necessary, so `(/ 10 4)` in Common Lisp produces `5/2`. (This was not considered a radical change to the language. Rational numbers were already in use in symbolic algebra systems. The developers of Common Lisp were simply integrating into the language functionality frequently required by their clients, anyway.)

All this provoked another debate, for in MacLisp and its descendants the slash was the character-quoter; moreover, backslash was the remainder operator. The committee eventually decided to swap the roles of slash and backslash, so that slash became alphabetic and backslash became the character quoter, thus allowing the division operation to be written "`/`" instead of "`//`" and allowing rational numbers to be written in conventional notation. This also solved some problems caused by a then little-known and little-loved (in the Lisp community) operating system called Unix, which used backslash as a character-quoter and slash in file names. However, it was a major incompatible change from MacLisp and Zetalisp, which left Common Lisp open to criticism.

Of course, this left Common Lisp without a truncating integer division operation, which *is* occasionally useful. Inspired by the many rounding modes of the S-1 [Correll 1979; Hailpern 1979] (which were influenced in turn by Kahan), Steele added *four* versions of the integer division operation to Common Lisp— `truncate`, `round`, `ceiling`, and `floor`, each of which accepts either one or two arguments and returns a quotient and remainder—thus bettering even Pascal. Overall, Common Lisp provides a much richer set of numerical primitives, and pays even closer attention to such details as the branch cuts of complex trigonometric functions, than FORTRAN ever has.

6.3.5 Some Notable Failures

Despite Lisp's tendency to absorb new features over time, both from other programming languages and from experiments within the Lisp community, there are a few ideas that have been tried repeatedly in various forms but for some reason simply don't catch on in the Lisp community. Notable among these ideas are ALGOL-style syntax, generalized multiple values, and logic programming with unification of variables.

6.3.5.1 *Algol-Style Syntax*

Ever since Steve Russell first hand-coded an implementation of **EVAL**, S-expressions have been the standard notation for writing programs. In almost any Lisp system of the last thirty years, one could write the function **UNION** (which computes the union of two sets represented as lists of elements) in roughly the following form:

```
(defun union (x y)
  (cond ((null x) y)
        ((member (car x) y) (union (cdr x) y))
        (t (cons (car x) (union (cdr x) y)))))
```

The original intention, however, in the design of Lisp was that programs would be written as M-expressions; the S-expression syntax was intended only for representation of data. The **UNION** function in M-expression notation looks like this:

```
union[x;y] = [null[x]→y;
              member[car[x];y]→union[cdr[x];y];
              T→cons[car[x];union[cdr[x];y]]]
```

But as McCarthy [1981] noted:

> The unexpected appearance of an interpreter tended to freeze the form of the language . . . . The project of defining M-expressions precisely . . . was neither finalized nor completely abandoned. It just receded into the indefinite future, and a new generation of programmers appeared who preferred internal notation [i.e., S-expressions] to any Fortran-like or Algol-like notation that could be devised.

Yet that was not the end of the story. Since that time there have been many other efforts to provide Lisp with an ALGOL-like syntax. Time and again a Lisp user or implementor has felt a lack in the language and provided a solution—and not infrequently attracted a substantial group of users—and yet in the long run none of these has achieved acceptance.

The earliest example of this—after M-expressions, of course—appears to have been Henneman's A-language [Henneman 1964]. Henneman gives the following definition of **UNION**:

```
(DEFINE UNION (OF AND) (8)
  (UNION OF X AND Y) (IF X IS
  EMPTY THEN Y ELSE IF FIRST OF
  X IS A MEMBER OF Y THEN UNION
  OF REST OF X AND Y ELSE
  CONNECT FIRST OF X TO BEGIN
  UNION OF REST OF X AND Y
  END))
```

The number **8** in this definition is the precedence of the **UNION** operator; note the use of **BEGIN** and **END** as parenthetical delimiters, necessary because the **CONNECT** . . . **TO** . . . operator (which means **CONS**) has higher precedence.

We find it curious that Henneman went to the trouble of pretty-printing the M-expressions and S-expressions in his paper but presented all his examples of A-language in the sort of run-on, block-paragraph style often seen in the S-expressions of his contemporaries. Nowadays we would format such a program in this manner for clarity:

```
(DEFINE UNION (OF AND) (8)
  (UNION OF X AND Y)
  (IF X IS EMPTY THEN Y
   ELSE IF FIRST OF X IS A MEMBER OF Y
         THEN UNION OF REST OF X AND Y
   ELSE CONNECT FIRST OF X TO
           BEGIN UNION OF REST OF X AND Y END
  ))
```

Such formatting was not unheard of; the ALGOL programmers of the day used similar indentation conventions in their published programs.

The ARPA-supported LISP 2 project aimed at providing Lisp with a syntax resembling that of ALGOL 60, citing the advantage that "ALGOL algorithms can be utilized with little change" [Abrahams 1966]. LISP 2 code for **UNION** in the style of our running example would look like this:

```
SYMBOL FUNCTION UNION(X, Y); SYMBOL X, Y;
  IF NULL X THEN Y
  ELSE IF MEMBER(CAR X, Y) THEN UNION(CDR X, Y)
  ELSE CAR X . UNION(CDR X, Y);
```

However, contemporary examples of LISP 2 code seem to emphasize the use of loops over recursion, so the following version might be more typical of the intended style:

```
SYMBOL FUNCTION UNION(X, Y); SYMBOL X, Y;
BEGIN
  SYMBOL Z ← Y;
  FOR A IN X DO
    IF NOT MEMBER(A, Y) THEN Z ← A . Z;
   RETURN Z;
END;
```

(Of course, this version produces a result that is different when regarded as a list, although the same when regarded as a set.)

The EL1 language was designed by Ben Wegbreit as part of his Ph.D. research [Wegbreit 1970]. It may be loosely characterized as a Lisp with an ALGOL-like surface syntax and strong data typing. A complete programming system called ECL was built around EL1 at Harvard in the early 1970s [Wegbreit 1971, 1972, 1974]. The **UNION** function in EL1 looks like this:

```
union <- EXPR(x: FORM, y: FORM; FORM)
  [) x=NIL => y;
     MEMBER(CAR(x), y) => union(CDR(x), y);
     CONS(CAR(X), union(CDR(x), y)) (];
```

Note the type declarations of **x**, **y**, and the result as type **FORM** (pointer to dotted pair). The digraphs **[)** and **(]** are equivalent to **BEGIN** and **END** (they looked better on a Model 33 Teletype than they do here). Within a block the arrow **=>** indicates the conditional return of a value from the block, resulting in a notation reminiscent of McCarthy's conditional notation for M-expressions.

Lisp itself was not widely used at Harvard's Center for Research in Computing Technology at that time; EL1 and PPL (Polymorphic Programming Language, a somewhat more JOSS-like interactive system) may have been Harvard's answer to Lisp at the time. ECL might have survived longer if Wegbreit had not left Harvard for Xerox in the middle of the project. As it was, ECL was used for research and course work at Harvard throughout the 1970s.

We have already discussed Teitelman's CLISP (Conversational Lisp), which was part of Interlisp [Teitelman 1974]. The function **UNION** was built into Interlisp, but could have been defined using CLISP in this manner:

```
DEFINEQ((UNION (LAMBDA (X Y)
    (IF ~X THEN Y
     ELSEIF X:1 MEMBER Y THEN UNION X::1 Y
     ELSE <X:1 !(UNION X::1 Y)>]
```

In CLISP, ~ is a unary operator meaning **NOT** or **NULL**. **X:n** is element *n* of the list **X**, so **X:1** means **(CAR X)**; similarly **X::1** means **(CDR X)**. The function **MEMBER** is predefined by CLISP to be an infix operator, but **UNION** is not (though the user may so define it if desired). Angle brackets indicate construction of a list; **!** within such a list indicates splicing, so **<A !B>** means **(CONS A B)**. Finally, the use of a final **]** to indicate the necessary number of closing parentheses (four, in this case), although not a feature of CLISP proper, is consistent with the Interlisp style.

MLISP was an ALGOL-like syntax for Lisp, first implemented for the IBM 360 by Horace Enea and then re-implemented for the PDP-10 under Stanford Lisp 1.6 [Smith 1970]. It provided infix operators; a complex **FOR** construct for iteration; various subscripting notations such as **A(1,3)** (element of a two-dimensional array) and **L[1,3,2]** (equivalent to **(cadr (caddr (car L)))**); "vector" operations (a concise notation for **MAPCAR**); and destructuring assignment.

```
EXPR UNION (X,Y);                          %MLISP version of UNION
   IF ¬X THEN Y ELSE
   IF X[1] ∊ Y THEN UNION(X↓1,Y)
   ELSE X[1] CONS UNION(X↓1,Y);
```

Vaughan Pratt developed an ALGOL-style notation for Lisp called CGOL [Pratt 1973]. Rather than embedding algebraic syntax within S-expressions, CGOL employed a separate full-blown tokenizer and parser. This was first implemented for Stanford Lisp 1.6 in 1970 when Pratt was at Stanford; at this time there was an exchange of ideas with the MLISP project. After Pratt went to MIT shortly thereafter, he implemented a version for MacLisp [Pratt 1976]. Versions of this parser were also used in the symbolic algebra systems SCRATCHPAD at IBM Yorktown and MACSYMA at MIT's Project MAC; Fred Blair, who also developed LISP370, did the reimplementation for SCRATCHPAD, and Michael Genesereth did it for MACSYMA.

Our CGOL version of the **UNION** function defines it as an infix operator (the numbers 14 and 13 are left and right "binding powers" for the parser):

```
define x "UNION" y, 14, 13;
  if not x then y
  else if member(car x, y) then cdr x union y
  else car x . cdr x union y  ◊
```

Here we have assumed the version of CGOL implemented at MIT, which stuck to the standard ASCII character set; the same definition using the Stanford extended character set would be:

```
define x "∪" y, 14, 13;
  if ¬x then y else if αx ∈ y then βx ∪ y else αx . βx ∪ y ◊
```

The "**.**" represents **CONS** in both preceding examples; the delimiter ◊ (actually the ASCII "altmode" character, nowadays called "escape") indicates the end of a top level expression. All unary Lisp functions are unary operators in CGOL, including **CAR** and **CDR**. In the definition preceding we have relied on the fact that such unary operators have very high precedence, so `cdr x union y` means `(cdr x) union y`, not `cdr (x union y)`. We also carefully chose the binding powers for **UNION** relative to "**.**" so that the last expression would be parsed as `(car x) . ((cdr x) union y))`. It is not obvious that this is the best choice; Henneman chose to give **CONS** (in the form of **CONNECT** . . . **TO** . . .) higher precedence than **UNION**. Pratt remarked [1976]:

> If you want to use the CGOL notation but don't want to have anything to do with binding powers, simply parenthesize every CGOL expression as though you were writing in Lisp. However, if you omit all parentheses . . . you will not often go wrong.

Compare this to Henneman's remark [1964]:

> The one great cause of most of the incorrect results obtained in practice is an incorrect precedence being assigned to a function.

During the 1970s a number of "AI languages" were designed to provide specific programming constructs then thought to be helpful in writing programs for AI applications. Some of these were embedded within Lisp and therefore simply inherited Lisp syntax (and in some cases influenced Lisp syntax—see Section 6.4 for a discussion of these). Those that were not embedded usually had a syntax related to that of ALGOL, while including some of the other features of Lisp (such as symbolic data structures and recursive functions). Among these were POP-2 [Burstall 1971], SAIL [Feldman 1972], and the Pascal-based TELOS [Travis 1977].

The idea of introducing ALGOL-like syntax into Lisp keeps popping up and has seldom failed to create enormous controversy between those who find the universal use of S-expressions a technical advantage (and don't mind the admitted relative clumsiness of S-expressions for numerical expressions) and those who are certain that algebraic syntax is more concise, more convenient, or even more *natural* (whatever that may mean, considering that all these notations are artificial).

We conjecture that ALGOL-style syntax has not really caught on in the Lisp community as a whole for two reasons. First, there are not enough special symbols to go around. When your domain of discourse is limited to numbers or characters, there are only so many operations of interest, so it is not difficult to assign one special character to each and be done with it. But Lisp has a much richer domain of discourse, and a Lisp programmer often approaches an application as yet another exercise in language design; the style typically involves designing new data structures and new functions to operate on them—perhaps dozens or hundreds—and it's too hard to invent that many distinct symbols (though the APL community certainly has tried). Ultimately one must always fall back on a general function-call notation; it's just that Lisp programmers don't wait until they fail.

Second, and perhaps more important, ALGOL-style syntax makes programs look less like the data structures used to represent them. In a culture where the ability to manipulate representations of programs is a central paradigm, a notation that distances the appearance of a program from the appearance of its representation as data is not likely to be warmly received (and this was, and is, one of the principal objections to the inclusion of `loop` in Common Lisp).

On the other hand, precisely because Lisp makes it easy to play with program representations, it is always easy for the novice to experiment with alternative notations. Therefore we expect future generations of Lisp programmers to continue to reinvent ALGOL-style syntax for Lisp, over and over and over again, and we are equally confident that they will continue, after an initial period of infatuation, to reject it. (Perhaps this process should be regarded as a rite of passage for Lisp hackers.)

6.3.5.2 *Generalized Multiple Values*

Many Lisp extenders have independently gone down the following path. Sometimes it is desirable to return more than one item from a function. It is awkward to return some of the results through global variables, and inefficient to cons up a list of the results (pushing the system that much closer to its next garbage collection) when we know perfectly well that they could be returned in machine registers or pushed onto the machine control stack. Curiously, the prototypical example of a function that ought to return two results is not symbolic but numerical: integer division might conveniently return both a quotient and a remainder. (Actually, it would be just as convenient for the programmer to use two separate functions, but we know perfectly well that the computation of one produces the other practically for free—again it is an efficiency issue.)

Suppose, then, that some primitive means of producing multiple values is provided. One way is to introduce new functions and/or special forms. Common Lisp, for example, following Lisp-Machine Lisp, has a primitive function called **VALUES**; the result of `(values 3 4 5)` is the three numbers 3, 4, and 5. The special form

```
(multiple-value-bind (p q r) (foo) body)
```

executes its *body* with the variables `p`, `q`, and `r` locally bound to three values returned as the value of the form `(foo)`.

But this is all so *ad hoc* and inelegant. Perhaps multiple values can be made to emerge from the intrinsic structure of the language itself. Suppose, for example, that the body of a lambda expression were an implicit **VALUES** construct, returning the values of all its subforms, rather than an implicit **PROGN**, returning the values of only the last subform. That takes care of producing multiple values. Suppose further that function calls were redefined to use all the values returned by each subform, rather than just one value from each subform. Then one could write

```
((lambda (quo rem) ...) (/ 44 6))
```

thereby binding `quo` to the quotient `7` and `rem` to the remainder `2`. That takes care of consuming multiple values. All very simple and tidy! Oops, two details to take care of. First, returning to lambda expressions, we see that, for consistency, they need to return all the values of all the subforms, not just one value from each subform. So the form

```
((lambda (quo rem) (/ quo rem) (/ rem quo)) (/ 44 6))
```

returns four values: `3`, `1`, `0`, and `2`. Second, there is still a need for sequencing forms that have side effects such as assignment. The simple solution is to make such forms as `(setq x 0)` and `(print x)` return zero values, so that

```
((lambda (quo rem) (print quo) rem) (/ 44 6))
```

returns only the remainder `2` after printing the quotient `7`. This all has a very simple and attractive stack-based implementation. Primitives simply push all their values, one after another, onto the stack. At the start of the processing for a function call, place a marker on the stack; after all subforms have been processed, simply search the stack for the most recent marker; everything above it should be used as arguments for the function call—but be sure to remove or cancel the marker before transferring control to the function.

Yes, this is all very neat and tidy—and as soon as you try to use it, you find that code becomes much, much harder to understand, both for the maintainer and for the compiler. Even if the programmer has the discipline not to write

```
(cons (/ 44 6) (setq x 0))
```

which returns `(7 . 2)` after setting `x` to 0, the compiler can never be sure that no such atrocities lurk in the code it is processing. In the absence of fairly complete information about how many values are produced by each function, including all user-defined functions, a compiler cannot verify that a function call will supply the correct number of arguments. An important practical check for Lisp programming errors is thus made all but impossible.

Conditionals introduce two further problems. First: what shall be the interpretation of

```
(if (foo) (bar))
```

if `(foo)` returns two values? Shall the second value be discarded, or treated as the value to be returned if the first value is true? Perhaps the predicate should be required to return exactly one value. Very well, but there remains the fact that the two subforms might return different numbers of values: `(if (foo) 3 (/ 44 6))` might return the single value `3` or the multiple values `7` and `2`. It follows immediately that no compiler, even if presented with a complete program, can deduce in general how many values are returned by each function call; it is formally undecidable.

Now all this might seem to be entirely in the spirit of Lisp as a weakly typed language; if the types of the values returned by functions may not be determinable until run time, why not their very cardinality? And declarations might indicate the number of values where efficiency is important, just as type declarations already assist many Lisp compilers. Nevertheless, as a matter of fact, nearly everyone who has followed this path has given up at this point in the development, muttering, "This way madness lies," and returned home rather than fall into the tarpit.

We ourselves have independently followed this line of thought and have had conversations with quite a few other people who have also done so. There are few published sources we can cite, however, precisely because most of them eventually judged it a bad idea before publishing anything about it. (This is not to say that it actually *is* a bad idea, or that some variation cannot eliminate its disadvantages; here we wish merely to emphasize the similarity of thinking among many independent researchers.) Among the most notable efforts that did produce actual implementations before eventual abandonment are SEUS and POP-2 [Burstall 1971]. The designers and implementors of SEUS (Len Bosack, Ralph Goren, David Posner, William Scherlis, Carolyn Talcott, Richard Weyhrauch, and Gabriel) never published their results, although it was a novel language design, and had a fast, compiler- and microcode-based implementation, complete with programming environment. POP-2 was regarded by its designers as an AI language, one of the many produced in the late 1960s and early 1970s, rather than as a variant of Lisp; it enjoyed some popularity in Europe and was used to implement the logic programming language POPLOG [Mellish 1984].

6.3.5.3 *Logic Programming and Unification*

During the 1970s and on into the 1980s there have been a number of attempts to integrate the advantages of the two perhaps foremost AI programming language families, Lisp and Prolog, into a single language. Such efforts were a feature of the software side of the Japanese Fifth Generation project. Examples of this are Robinson's LOGLISP [Robinson 1982], the TAO project [Takeuchi 1983; Okuno 1984], and TABLOG [Malachi 1984]. There have also been related attempts to integrate functional programming and Prolog. (All these should be contrasted with the use of Lisp as a convenient language for *implementing* Prolog, as exemplified by Komorowski's QLOG [Komorowski 1982] and the work of Kahn and Carlsson [Kahn 1984].)

We conjecture that this idea has not caught on in the Lisp community because of unification, the variable-matching process used in Prolog. Indeed one can easily design a language that has many of the features of Lisp but uses unification during procedure calls. The problem is that unification is sufficiently different in nature from lambda-binding that the resulting language doesn't really feel like Lisp any more. To the average Lisp programmer, it feels like an extension of Prolog but not an extension of Lisp; you just can't mess around that much with something as fundamental as procedure calls. On the other hand, one can leave Lisp procedure calls as they are and provide unification as a separate facility that can be explicitly invoked. But then it is just another Lisp library routine, and the result doesn't feel at all like Prolog.

6.4 LISP AS A LANGUAGE LABORATORY

An interesting aspect of the Lisp culture, in contrast to those surrounding most other programming languages, is that toy dialects are regarded with a fair amount of respect. Lisp has been used throughout its history as a language laboratory. It is trivial to add a few new functions to Lisp in such a way that they look like system-provided facilities. Given macros, CLISP, or the equivalent, it is pretty easy to add new control structures or other syntactic constructs. If that fails, it is the work of only half an hour to write, in Lisp, a complete interpreter for a new dialect. To see how amazing this is, imagine starting with a working C, FORTRAN, Pascal, PL/I, BASIC, or APL system—you can write and run any program in that language, but have no access to source code for the compiler or interpreter—and then tackling these exercises:

1. Add a new arithmetic operator to the language similar to the one for Pythagorean addition in Knuth's Metafont language [Knuth 1986]: **`a++b`** computes $\sqrt{a^2+b^2}$. The language is to be augmented in such a way that the new operator is syntactically similar to the language operators for addition and subtraction. (For C, you may use **`+++`** or **`@`** rather than **`++`**; for APL, use one of the customary awful overstrikes such as ⊞.)
2. Add a **`case`** statement to the language. (If it already has a **`case`** statement, then add a statement called **`switch`** that is just like the **`case`** statement already in the language, except that when the selected branch has been executed, control falls through to succeeding branches; a special **`break`** statement, or dropping out of the last branch, must be used to terminate execution of the **`switch`** statement.)
3. Add full lexically scoped functional closures to the language.

Without source code for the compiler or interpreter, all three projects require one practically to start over from scratch. That is part of our point. But even given source code for a FORTRAN compiler or APL interpreter, all three exercises are much more difficult than in Lisp. The Lisp answer to the first one is a one-liner (shown here in Common Lisp):

```
(defun ++ (x y) (sqrt (+ (* x x) (* y y))))
```

Lisp does not reserve special syntax (such as infix operators) for use by built-in operations, so user-defined functions look just like system-defined functions to the caller.

The second requires about a dozen lines of code (again, in Common Lisp, using backquote syntax as described in the discussion of macros):

```
(defmacro switch (value &rest body)
  (let* ((newbody (mapcar #'(lambda (clause)
                               '(,(gensym) ,@(rest clause)))
                             body))
         (switcher (mapcar #'(lambda (clause newclause)
                                '(,(first clause) (go ,(first newclause))))
                              body newbody)))
    `(block switch
       (tagbody (case ,value ,@switcher)
                (break)
                ,@(apply #'nconc newbody)))))
(defmacro break () '(return-from switch))
```

Here we use two macros, one for **switch** and one for **break**, which together cause the statement

```
(switch n
  (0 (princ "none") (break))
  (1 (princ "one "))
  (2 (princ "too "))
  (3 (princ "many")))
```

(which always prints either **many**, **too many**, **one too many**, **none**, or nothing) to expand into

```
(block switch
  (tagbody (case n
             (0 (go G0042))
             (1 (go G0043))
             (2 (go G0044))
             (3 (go G0045)))
           (return-from switch)
   G0042   (princ "none")
           (return-from switch)
   G0043   (princ "one ")
   G0044   (princ "too ")
   G0045   (princ "many")))
```

which is not unlike the code that would be produced by a C compiler.

For examples of interpreters that solve the third problem in about 100 lines of code, see Steele 1978c and 1978b.

There is a rich tradition of experimenting with augmentations of Lisp, ranging from "let's add just one new feature" to inventing completely new languages using Lisp as an implementation language. This activity was carried on particularly intensively at MIT during the late 1960s and the 1970s and also at other institutions such as Stanford University, Carnegie-Mellon University, and Indiana University. At that time it was customary to make a set of ideas about programming style concrete by putting forth a new programming language as an exemplar. (This was true outside the Lisp community as well; witness the proliferation of ALGOL-like, and particularly Pascal-inspired, languages around the same time period. But Lisp made it convenient to try out little ideas with a small amount of overhead, as well as tackling grand revampings requiring many man-months of effort.)

One of the earliest Lisp-based languages was METEOR [Bobrow 1964], a version of COMIT with Lisp syntax. COMIT [MIT RLE 1962a, 1962b; Yngve 1972] was a pattern-matching language that repeatedly matched a set of rules against the contents of a flat, linear workspace of symbolic tokens; it was a precursor of SNOBOL and an ancestor of such rule-based languages as OPS5 [Forgy 1977]. METEOR was embedded within the MIT Lisp 1.5 system that ran on the IBM 7090. The Lisp code for METEOR is a little under 300 80-column cards (some with more whitespace than others). By contrast, the 7090 implementation of the COMIT interpreter occupied about 10,000 words or memory, according to Yngve; assuming this reflects about 10,000 lines of assembly language code, we can view this as an early example of the effectiveness of LISP as a high-level language for prototyping other languages.

Another of the early pattern-matching languages built on Lisp was CONVERT [Guzman 1966]. Whereas METEOR was pretty much a straight implementation of COMIT represented as Lisp data structures, CONVERT merged the pattern-matching features of COMIT with the recursive data structures of Lisp, allowing the matching of recursively defined patterns to arbitrary Lisp data structures.

Carl Hewitt designed an extremely ambitious Lisp-like language for theorem-proving called Planner [Hewitt 1969, 1972]. Its primary contributions consisted of advances in pattern-directed invocation and the use of automatic backtracking as an implementation mechanism for goal-directed search.

It was never completely implemented as originally envisioned, but it spurred three other important developments in the history of Lisp: Micro-Planner, Muddle, and Conniver.

Gerald Jay Sussman, Drew McDermott, and Eugene Charniak implemented a subset of Planner called Micro-Planner [Sussman 1971], which was embedded within the MIT PDP-6 Lisp system that eventually became MacLisp. The semantics of the language as implemented were not completely formalized. The implementation techniques were rather *ad hoc* and did not work correctly in certain complicated cases; the matcher was designed to match two patterns, each of which might contain variables, but did not use a complete unification algorithm. (Much later, Sussman, on learning about Prolog, remarked to Steele that Prolog appeared to be the first correct implementation of Micro-Planner.)

A version of Planner was also implemented in POP-2 [Davies 1984].

The language Muddle (later MDL) was an extended version of Lisp and in some ways a competitor, designed and used by the Dynamic Modeling Group at MIT, which was separate from the MIT AI Laboratory but in the same building at 545 Technology Square. This effort was begun in late 1970 by Gerald Jay Sussman, Carl Hewitt, Chris Reeve, and David Cressey, later joined by Bruce Daniels, Greg Pfister, and Stu Galley. It was designed "... as a successor to Lisp, a candidate vehicle for the Dynamic Modeling System, and a possible base for implementation of Planner-70" [Galley 1975]. To some extent, the competition between Muddle and Lisp, and the fact that Sussman had a foot in each camp, resulted in cross-fertilization. The I/O, interrupt handling, and multiprogramming (that is, coroutining) facilities of Muddle were much more advanced than those of MacLisp at the time. Muddle had a more complex garbage collector than PDP-10 MacLisp ever had, as well as a larger library of application subroutines, especially for graphics. (Some Lisp partisans at the time would reply that Muddle was used entirely to code libraries of subroutines but no main programs! But in fact some substantial applications were coded in Muddle.) Muddle introduced the lambda-list syntax markers OPTIONAL, REST, and AUX that were later adopted by Conniver, Lisp-Machine Lisp, and Common Lisp.

The language Conniver was designed by Drew McDermott and Gerald Jay Sussman in 1972 in reaction to perceived limitations of Micro-Planner and in particular of its control structure. In the classic paper *Why Conniving Is Better Than Planning* [Sussman 1972a, 1972b], they argued that automatic nested backtracking was merely an overly complicated way to express a set of FORALL loops used to perform exhaustive search:

> It is our contention that the backtrack control structure that is the backbone of Planner is more of a hindrance in the solution of problems than a help. In particular, automatic backtracking encourages inefficient algorithms, conceals what is happening from the user, and misleads him with primitives having powerful names whose power is only superficial.

The design of Conniver put the flow of control very explicitly in the hands of the programmer. The model was an extreme generalization of coroutines; there was only one active locus of control, but arbitrarily many logical threads and primitives for explicitly transferring the active locus from one to another. This design was strongly influenced by the "spaghetti stack" model introduced by Daniel Bobrow and Ben Wegbreit [Bobrow 1973] and implemented in BBN-Lisp (later to be known as Interlisp). Like spaghetti stacks, Conniver provided separate notions of a data environment and a control environment and the possibility of creating closures over either. (Later work with the Scheme language brought out the point that data environments and control environments do not play symmetrical roles in the interpretation of Lisp-like languages [Steele 1977d].) Conniver differed from spaghetti stacks in ways stemming primarily from implementation considerations.

The main point of Conniver was generality and ease of implementation; it was written in Lisp and represented control and data environments as Lisp list structures, allowing the Lisp garbage collector to handle reclamation of abandoned environments. The implementation of spaghetti stacks, on the other hand, involved structural changes to a Lisp system at the lowest level. It addressed efficiency issues by allowing stack-like allocation and deallocation behavior wherever possible. The policy was pay as you go but don't pay if you don't use it: programs that do not create closures should not pay for the overhead of heap management of control and data environments.

At about this time Carl Hewitt and his students began to develop the actor model of computation, in which every computational entity, whether program or data, is an actor: an agent that can receive and react to messages. The under-the-table activity brought out by Conniver was made even more explicit in this model; everything was message-passing; everything ran on continuations. Hewitt and his student Brian Smith commented on the interaction of a number of research groups at the time [Smith 1975]:

> The early work on PLANNER was done at MIT and published in IJCAI-69 [Hewitt 1969]. In 1970 a group of interested researchers (including Peter Deutsch, Richard Fikes, Carl Hewitt, Jeff Rulifson, Alan Kay, Jim Moore, Nils Nilsson, and Richard Waldinger) gathered at Pajaro Dunes to compare notes and concepts. . . .
>
> In November 1972, Alan Kay gave a seminar at MIT in which he emphasized the importance of using intentional definitions of data structures and of passing messages to them such as was done to a limited extent for the "procedural data structures" in the lambda calculus languages of Landin, Evans, and Reynolds and extensively in SIMULA-67. His argument was that only the data type itself really "knows" how to implement any given operation. We had previously given some attention to procedural data structures in our own research. . . . However, we were under the misconception that procedural data structures were too inefficient for practical use although they had certain advantages.
>
> Kay's lecture struck a responsive note . . . We immediately saw how to use his idea . . . to extend the principle of procedural embedding of knowledge to data structures. In effect each type of data structure becomes a little *plan* of what to do for each kind of request that it receives. . . .
>
> Kay proposed a language called SMALLTALK with a token stream oriented interpreter to implement these ideas. . . .

[At that time,] Peter Bishop and Carl Hewitt were working to try to obtain a general solution to the control structure problems which had continued to plague PLANNER-like problem solving systems for some years. Sussman had proposed a solution oriented around "possibility lists" which we felt had very serious weaknesses. . . . Simply looking at their contents using `try-next` can cause unfortunate global side-effects . . . [which] make Conniver programs hard to debug and understand. The token streams of Smalltalk have the same side-effect problem as the possibility lists of Conniver. After the lecture, Hewitt pointed out to Kay the control structure problems involved in his scheme for a token stream oriented interpreter.

By December 1972, we succeeded in generalizing the message mechanism of Smalltalk and SIMULA-67; the port mechanism of Krutar, Balzer, and Mitchell; and the previous CALL statement of PLANNER-71 to a universal communication mechanism. Our generalization solved the control structure problems that Hewitt pointed out to Kay in the design of SMALLTALK. We developed the actor transmission communication primitive as part of a new language-independent, machine-independent, behavioral model of computation. The development of the actor model of computation and its ramifications is our principal original contribution to this area of research. . . .

The following were the main influences on the development of the actor model of computation:

- The suggestion by [Alan] Kay that procedural embedding be extended to cover data structures in the context of our previous attempts to generalize the work by Church, Landin, Evans, and Reynolds on "functional data structures."
- The context of our previous attempts to clean up and generalize the work on coroutine control structures of Landin, Mitchell, Krutar, Balzer, Reynolds, Bobrow-Wegbreit, and Sussman.
- The influence of Seymour Papert's "little man" metaphor for computation in LOGO.
- The limitations and complexities of capability-based protection schemes. Every actor transmission is in effect an inter-domain call efficiently providing an intrinsic protection on actor machines.
- The experience developing previous generations of PLANNER. Essentially the whole PLANNER-71 language (together with some extensions) was implemented by Julian Davies in POP-2 at the University of Edinburgh.

In terms of the actor model of computation, control structure is simply a pattern of passing messages. . . . Actor control structure has the following advantages over that of Conniver:

- A serious problem with the Conniver approach to control structure is that the programmer (whether human or machine) must think in terms of low level data structures such as activation records or possibility links. The actor approach allows the programmer to think in terms of the behavior of objects that naturally occur in the domain being programmed. . . .
- Actor transmission is entirely free of side-effects. . . .
- The control mechanisms of Conniver violate principles of modularity. . . . Dijkstra has remarked that the use of the `goto` is associated with badly structured programs. We concur in this judgement but feel that the reason is that the `goto` is not a sufficiently powerful primitive. The problem with the `goto` is that a message cannot be sent along with control to the target. . . .
- Because of its primitive control structures, Conniver programs are difficult to write and debug. . . . Conniver programs are prone to going into infinite loops for no reason that is very apparent to the programmer.

Nevertheless Conniver represents a substantial advance over Micro-Planner in increasing the generality of goal-oriented computations that can be easily performed. However, this increase in generality comes at the price of lowering the level of the language of problem solving. It forces users to think in low level implementation terms such as "possibility lists" and "a-links." We propose a shift in the paradigm of problem solving to be one of a society of individuals communicating by passing messages.

We have quoted Smith and Hewitt at length for three reasons: because their comparative analysis is very explicit; because the passage illustrates the many connections among different ideas floating around in the AI, Lisp, and other programming language communities; and because this particular point in the evolution of ideas represented a distillation that soon fed back quickly and powerfully into the evolution of Lisp itself. (For a more recent perspective, see [Hewitt 1991].)

Hewitt and his students (notably Russ Atkinson, Peter Bishop, Mike Freiling, Irene Greif, Roger Hale, Ken Kahn, Benjamin Kuipers, Todd Matson, Marilyn McLennan, Keith Nishihara, Howie Shrobe, Brian Smith, Richard Stieger, Kathy Van Sant, and Aki Yonizawa) developed and implemented in MacLisp a new language to make concrete the actor model of computation. This language was first called Planner-73 but the name was later changed to PLASMA (PLAnner-like System Modeled on Actors) [Hewitt 1975; Smith 1975].

Although the syntax of PLASMA was recognizably Lisp-like, it made use of several kinds of parentheses and brackets (as did Muddle) as well as many other special characters. It is reasonable to assume that Hewitt was tempted by the possibilities of the then newly available Knight keyboard and Xerox Graphics Printer (XGP) printer. (The keyboards, designed by Tom Knight of the MIT AI Lab, were the MIT equivalent of the extended-ASCII keyboards developed years earlier at the Stanford AI Laboratory. Like the Stanford keyboards, Knight keyboards had Control and Meta keys (which were soon pressed into service in the development of the command set for the EMACS text editor) and a set of graphics that included such exotic characters as α, β, and ≡. The XGP, at 200 dots per inch, made possible the printing of such exotic characters.) The recursive factorial function looked like this in PLASMA:

```
[factorial ≡
   (cases
      (≡> [0] 1)
      (≡> [=n] (n * (factorial (n - 1))))))]
```

Note the use of infix arithmetic operators. This was not merely clever syntax, but clever semantics; `(n - 1)` really meant that a message containing the subtraction operator and the number 1 was to be sent to the number/actor/object named by `n`.

One may argue that Lisp development at MIT took two distinct paths during the 1970s. In the first path, MacLisp was the workhorse tool, coded in assembly language for maximum efficiency and compactness, serving the needs of the AI Laboratory and the MACSYMA group. The second path consisted of an extended dialogue/competition/argument between Hewitt (and his students) and Sussman (and his students), with both sides drawing in ideas from the rest of the world and spinning some off as well. This second path was characterized by a quest for "the right thing," where each new set of ideas was exemplified in the form of a new language, usually implemented on top of a Lisp-like language (MacLisp or Muddle) for the sake of rapid prototyping and experimentation.

The next round in the Hewitt/Sussman dialogue was, of course, Scheme (as discussed in Section 6.2.8); in hindsight, we observe that this development seems to have ended the dialogue, perhaps because it brought the entire path of exploration full circle. Starting from Lisp, they sought to explicate issues of search, of control structures, of models of computation, and finally came back simply to good old Lisp, but with a difference: lexical scoping—closures, in short—were needed to make Lisp compatible with the lambda calculus, not merely in syntax but also in semantics, thereby connecting it firmly with various developments in mathematical logic and paving the way for the Lisp community to interact with developments in functional programming.

Hewitt had noted that the actor model could capture the salient aspects of the lambda calculus; Scheme demonstrated that the lambda calculus captured nearly all salient aspects (excepting only side effects and synchronization) of the actor model.

Sussman and Steele began to look fairly intensely at the semantics of Lisp-like as well as actor-based languages in this new light. Scheme was so much simpler even than Lisp 1.5, once one accepted the overheads of maintaining lexical environments and closures, that one could write a complete interpreter for it in Lisp on a single sheet of paper (or in two 30-line screenfuls). This allowed for extremely rapid experimentation with language and implementation ideas; at one point Sussman and Steele were testing and measuring as many as ten new interpreters a week. Some of their results were summarized in *The Art of the Interpreter* [Steele 1978b]. A particular point of interest was the comparison of call-by-name and call-by-value parameters; in this they were influenced by work at Indiana University discussed in the paper *CONS Should Not Evaluate Its Arguments* [Friedman 1975].

Besides being itself susceptible to rapid mutation, Scheme has also served as an implementation base for rapid prototyping of yet other languages. One popular technique among theoreticians for formally describing the meaning of a language is to give a denotational semantics, which describes the meaning of each construct in terms of its parts and their relationships; lambda calculus is the glue of this notation.

Although Scheme showed that a properly designed Lisp gave one all the flexibility (if not all the syntax) one needed in managing control structure and message-passing, it did not solve the other goal of the development of Lisp-based AI languages: the automatic management of goal-directed search or of theorem proving. After Scheme, a few new Lisp-based languages were developed in this direction by Sussman and his students, including constraint-based systems [Sussman 1975a; Stallman 1976; Steele 1979; de Kleer 1978b] and truth maintenance systems [de Kleer 1978a; McAllester 1978] based on nonmonotonic logic. The technique of dependency-directed backtracking eliminated the "giant nest of FORALL loops" effect of chronological backtracking. Over time this line of research became more of a database design problem than a language design problem, and has not yet resulted in feedback to the mainstream evolution of Lisp.

Development of languages for artificial intelligence applications continued at other sites, however, and Lisp has remained the vehicle of choice for implementing them. During the early 1980s C became the alternative of choice for a while, especially where efficiency was a major concern. Improvements in Lisp implementation techniques, particularly in compilation and garbage collection, have swung that particular pendulum back a bit.

During the AI boom of the early 1980s, "expert systems" was the buzzword; this was usually understood to mean rule-based systems written in languages superficially not very different from METEOR or CONVERT. OPS5 was one of the better-known rule-based languages of this period; XCON (an expert system for configuring VAX installations, developed by Carnegie-Mellon University for Digital Equipment Corporation) was its premier application success story. OPS5 was first implemented in Lisp; later it was recoded for efficiency in BLISS [Wulf 1971] (a CMU-developed and DEC-supported systems implementation language at about the same semantic level as C).

Another important category of AI languagess was frame-based; a good example was KRL (Knowledge Representation Language), which was implemented in Interlisp.

Another line of experimentation in Lisp is in the area of parallelism. Although early developments included facilities for interrupt handling and multiprogramming, true multiprocessing evolved only with the availability of appropriate hardware facilities (in some cases built for the purpose). S-1 Lisp [Brooks 1982a] was designed to use the multiple processors of an S-1 system, but (like so many other features of S-1 Lisp) that part never really worked. Some of the most important early "real" parallel Lisp implementations were Multilisp, Qlisp, and Butterfly PSL.

Multilisp [Halstead 1984, 1985] was the work of Bert Halstead and his students at MIT. Based on Scheme, it relied primarily on the notion of a *future*, which is a sort of laundry ticket, a promise to deliver a value later once it has been computed. Multilisp also provided a `pcall` construct, essentially a function call that evaluates the arguments concurrently (and completely) before invoking the function. Thus `pcall` provides a certain structured discipline for the use of futures that is adequate for many purposes. Multilisp ran on the Concert multiprocessor, a collection of 32 Motorola 68000 processors. MultiScheme, a descendant of Multilisp, was later implemented for the BBN Butterfly [Miller 1987].

Butterfly PSL [Swanson 1988] was an implementation of Portable Standard Lisp [Griss 1982] on the BBN Butterfly. It also relied entirely on futures for the spawning of parallel processes.

Qlisp [Gabriel 1984b; Goldman 1988] was developed by Richard Gabriel and John McCarthy at Stanford. It extended Common Lisp with a number of parallel control structures that parallel (pun intended) existing Common Lisp control constructs, notably `qlet`, `qlambda`, and `qcatch`. The computational model involved a global queue of processes and a means of spawning processes and controlling their interaction and resource consumption. For example, `qlambda` could produce three kinds of functions: normal ones, as produced by `lambda`; eager ones, which would spawn a separate process when created; and delayed ones, which would spawn a separate process when invoked. Qlisp was implemented on the Alliant FX8 and was the first compiled parallel Lisp implementation.

Connection Machine Lisp [Steele 1986] was a dialect of Common Lisp extended with a new data structure, the *xapping* intended to support fine-grain data parallelism. A xapping was implementationally a strange hybrid of array, hash table, and association list; semantically it is a set of ordered index-value pairs. The primitives of the language are geared toward processing all the values of a xapping concurrently, matching up values from different xappings by their associated indices. The idea was that indices are labels for virtual processors.

To recapitulate: Lisp is an excellent laboratory for language experimentation for two reasons. First, one can choose a very small subset, with only a dozen primitives or so, that is still recognizably a member of the class of Lisp-like languages. It is very easy to bootstrap such a small language, with variations of choice, on a new platform. If it looks promising, one can flesh out the long laundry list of amenities later. Second, it is particularly easy—the work of an hour or less—to bootstrap such a new dialect within an existing Lisp implementation. Even if the host implementation differs in fundamental ways from the new dialect, it can provide primitive operations such as arithmetic and I/O as well as being a programming language that is just plain convenient for writing language interpreters. If you can live with the generic, list-structure-oriented syntax, you can have a field day reprogramming the semantics. After you get that right there is time enough to re-engineer it and, if you must, slap a parser on the front.

6.5 WHY LISP IS DIVERSE

In this history of the evolution of Lisp, we have seen that Lisp seems to have a more elaborate and complex history than languages with wider usage. It would seem that almost every little research group has its own version of Lisp and there would appear to be as many Lisps as variations on language concepts. It is natural to ask what is so special or different about Lisp that explains it.

There are six basic reasons: its theoretical foundations, its expressiveness, its malleability, its interactive and incremental nature, its operating system facilities, and the people who choose it.

Its theoretical foundations. Lisp was founded on the footing of recursive function theory and the theory of computability. The work on Scheme aligned it with Church's lambda calculus and denotational semantics. Its purest form is useful for mathematical reasoning and proof. Therefore, many theoretically minded researchers have adopted Lisp or Lisp-like languages in which to express their ideas and to do their work. We thus see many Lisp-oriented papers with new language constructs explained, existing constructs explained, properties of programs proved, and proof techniques explored.

The upshot is that Lisp and Lisp-like languages are always in the forefront of basic language research. And it is common for more practically minded theoretical researchers to also implement their ideas in Lisp.

Its expressiveness. Lisp has proved itself concerned more with expressiveness than anything else. We can see this more obliquely by observing that only a person well-versed with how a particular Lisp is implemented can write efficient programs. Here is a perfectly nice piece of code:

```
(defun make-matrix (n m)
  (let ((matrix ()))
    (dotimes (i n matrix)
      (push (make-list m) matrix))))

(defun add-matrix (m1 m2)
  (let ((l1 (length m1))
        (l2 (length m2)))
    (let ((matrix (make-matrix l1 l2)))
      (dotimes (i l1 matrix)
        (dotimes (j l2)
          (setf (nth i (nth j matrix))
                (+ (nth i (nth j m1))
                   (nth i (nth j m2)))))))))
```

The expression to read and write a cell in a matrix looks perfectly harmless and fast as anything. But it is slow, because `nth` takes time proportional to the value of its first argument, essentially `CDR`ing down the list every time it is called. (An experienced Lisp coder would iterate over the cells of a list rather than over numeric indices, or would use arrays instead of lists.)

Here expressiveness has gone awry. People tend to expect that operations in the language cost a small unit time, not something complicated to figure out. But this expectation is false for a sufficiently expressive language. When the primitives are at a sufficiently high level, there is enough wiggle room underneath to permit a choice of implementation strategies. Lisp implementors continue to explore that space of strategies. Precisely *because* Lisp is so expressive, it can be very hard to write fast programs (though it is easy to write pretty or clear ones).

Its malleability. It is easy with Lisp to experiment with new language features, because it is possible to extend Lisp in such a way that the extensions are indistinguishable to users from the base language. Primarily this is accomplished through the use of macros, which have been part of Lisp since 1963 [Hart 1963]. Lisp macros, with their use of Lisp as a computation engine to compute expansions, have proved to be a more effective way to extend a language than the string-processing mechanisms of other languages. Such macro-based extensions are accepted within the Lisp community in a way that is not found in other language communities.

Furthermore, more recent Lisp dialects have provided mechanisms to extend the type system. This enables people to experiment with new data types. Of course, other languages have had this mechanism, but in Lisp the data typing mechanism combines with the powerful macro facility and the functional nature of the language to allow entirely new computing paradigms to be built in Lisp. For example, we have seen data-driven paradigms [Sussman 1971], possible-worlds paradigms [McDermott 1974], and object-oriented paradigms [Moon 1986; Bobrow 1986] implemented in Lisp in such a way that the seams between Lisp and these new paradigms are essentially invisible.

Its interactive and incremental nature. It is easy to explore the solutions to programming problems in Lisp, because it is easy to implement part of a solution, test it, modify it, change design, and debug the changes. There is no lengthy edit-compile-link cycle. Because of this, Lisp is useful for rapid prototyping and for constructing very large programs in the face of an incomplete—and possibly impossible to complete—plan of attack. Therefore, Lisp has often been used for exploring territory that is too imposing with other languages. This characteristic of Lisp makes it attractive to the adventuresome and pioneering.

Its operating system facilities. Many Lisp implementations provide facilities reminiscent of operating systems: a command processor, an automatic storage management facility, file management, display (windows, graphics, mouse) facilities, multitasking, a compiler, an incremental (re)linker/loader, a symbolic debugger, performance monitoring, and sometimes multiprocessing.

It is possible to do operating system research in Lisp and to provide a complete operating environment. Combined with its interactive and incremental nature, it is possible to write sophisticated text editors and to supplant the native operating system of the host computer. A Lisp system can provide an operating environment that provides strong portability across a wide variety of incompatible platforms. This makes Lisp an attractive vehicle for researchers and thereby further diversifies Lisp.

Its people. Of course, languages do not diversify themselves; people diversify languages. The five preceding factors merely serve to attract people to Lisp and provide facilities for them to experiment with Lisp. If the people attracted to Lisp were not interested in exploring new language alternatives, then Lisp would not have been diversified, so there must be something about Lisp that attracts adventuresome people.

Lisp is the language of artificial intelligence, among other things. And AI is a branch of computer science that is directed towards exploring the most difficult and exotic of all programming tasks: mimicking or understanding cognition and intelligence. (Recall that symbolic computation, now a field of its own, was at many institutions originally considered a branch of AI.) The people who are attracted to AI are generally creative and bold, and the language designers and implementors follow in this mold, often being AI researchers or former AI researchers themselves.

Lisp provides its peculiar set of characteristics because those features—or ones like them—were required for the early advances of AI. Only when AI was the subject of commercial concerns did AI companies turn to languages other than Lisp.

Another attraction is that Lisp is a language of experts, which for our purposes means that Lisp is not a language designed for inexpert programmers to code robust reliable software. Therefore, there is little compile-time type checking, there are few module systems, there is little safety or discipline built into the language. It is an "anarchic" language, whereas most other languages are "fascist" (as hackers would have it [Raymond 1991]).

Here are how some others have put it:

> LISP is unusual, in the sense that it clearly deviates from every other type of programming language that has ever been developed. . . . The theoretical concepts and implications of LISP far transcend its practical usage.
>
> —Jean E. Sammet [1969, p. 406]

This is one of the great advantage of Lisp-like languages: They have very few ways of forming compound expressions, and almost no syntactic structure. . . . After a short time we forget about syntactic details of the language (because there are none) and get on with the real issues.

—Abelson and Sussman [1985, p. xvii]

Syntactic sugar causes cancer of the semicolon.

—Alan Perlis

What I like about Lisp is that you can feel the bits between your toes.

—Drew McDermott [1977]

Lisp has such a simple syntax and semantics that parsing can be treated as an elementary task. Thus parsing technology plays almost no role in Lisp programs, and the construction of language processors is rarely an impediment to the rate of growth and change of large Lisp systems.

—Alan Perlis (forward to Abelson [1985])

APL is like a beautiful diamond—flawless, beautifully symmetrical. But you can't add anything to it. If you try to glue on another diamond, you don't get a bigger diamond. Lisp is like a ball of mud. Add more and it's still a ball of mud—it still looks like Lisp.

—Joel Moses [1978?]

Pascal is for building pyramids—imposing, breathtaking, static structures built by armies pushing heavy blocks into place. Lisp is for building organisms. . . .

—Alan Perlis (forward to Abelson [1985])

Lisp is the medium of choice for people who enjoy free style and flexibility.

—Gerald Jay Sussman (introduction to Friedman [1987], p. ix)

Hey, Quux: Let's quit hacking this paper and hack Lisp instead!

—rpg (the final edit) [Gabriel 1992]

REFERENCES

[Abelson, 1985] Abelson, Harold and Sussman, Gerald Jay, with Sussman, Julie. *Structure and Interpretation of Computer Programs.* Cambridge, MA: MIT Press, 1985.

[Abrahams, 1966] Abrahams, Paul W., Barnett, Jeffrey A., Book, Erwin, Firth, Donna, Kemeny, Stanley L., Weissman, Clark, Hawkinson, Lowell, Levin, Michael I., and Saunders, Robert A. The LISP 2 programming language and system. In *Proceedings of the 1966 AFIPS Fall Joint Computer* Conference, vol. 29, San Francisco, CA, Nov. 1966, pp. 661–676. American Federation of Information Processing Societies. Washington, D. C.: Spartan Books, 1966.

[ACM AIPL, 1977] Association for Computing Machinery. *Proceedings of the Artificial Intelligence and Programming Languages Conference*, Rochester, NY, Aug. 1977. *ACM SIGPLAN Notices*, 12:8, Aug. 1977. *ACM SIGART Newsletter*, 64, Aug. 1977.

[ACM LFP, 1982] Association for Computing Machinery. *Proceedings of the 1982 ACM Symposium on Lisp and Functional Programming*, Pittsburgh, PA, Aug. 1982.

[ACM LFP, 1984] Association for Computing Machinery. *Proceedings of the 1984 ACM Symposium on Lisp and Functional Programming*, Austin, Texas, Aug. 1984.

[ACM LFP, 1986] Association for Computing Machinery. *Proceedings of the 1986 ACM Conference on Lisp and Functional Programming*, Cambridge, MA, Aug. 1986.

[ACM LFP, 1988] Association for Computing Machinery. *Proceedings of the 1988 ACM Conference on Lisp and Functional Programming*, Snowbird, Utah, July 1988.

[ACM OOPSLA, 1986] Association for Computing Machinery. *Proceedings of the ACM Conference on Objected-Oriented Programming, Systems, Languages, and Applications (OOPSLA '86)*, Portland, OR, Oct. 1986. *ACM SIGPLAN Notices*, 21:11, Nov. 1986.

[ACM PLDI, 1990] Association for Computing Machinery. *Proceedings of the 1990 ACM SIGPLAN '90 Conference on Programming Language Design and Implementation*, White Plains, NY, June 1990. *ACM SIGPLAN Notices* 25:6, June 1990.

[ACM PSDE, 1984] Association for Computing Machinery. *Proceedings of the ACM SIGSOFT/SIGPLAN Symposium on Practical Software Development Environments*, Pittsburgh, PA, Apr. 1984. *ACM SIGPLAN Notices*, 19:5, May 1984; also *ACM Software Engineering Notes*, 9:3, May 1984.

[Backus, 1978] Backus, John. Can programming be liberated from the von Neumann style? A functional style and its algebra of programs. *Communications of the ACM*, 21:8, Aug. 1978, pp. 613–641, 1977 ACM Turing Award Lecture.

[Baker, 1978] Baker, Jr., Henry B. List processing in real time on a serial computer. *Communications of the ACM*, 21:4, Apr. 1978, pp. 280–294.

[Bartley, 1986] Bartley, David H. and Jensen, John C. The implementation of PC Scheme. In [ACM LFP, 1986], pp. 86–93.

[Bawden, 1988] Bawden, Alan and Rees, Jonathan. Syntactic closures. In [ACM LFP, 1988], pp. 86–95.

[Berkeley, 1964] Berkeley, Edmund C., and Bobrow, Daniel G., Eds. *The Programming Language LISP: Its Operation and Applications*. Information International, Inc., and Cambridge, MA: MIT Press, 1964.

[Black, 1964] Black, Fischer. Styles of programming in LISP. In [Berkeley, 1964], pp. 96–107.

[Bobrow, 1964] Bobrow, Daniel G. METEOR: A LISP interpreter for string transformations. In [Berkeley, 1964], pp. 161–190.

[Bobrow, 1972] Bobrow, Robert J., Burton, Richard R., and Lewis, Daryle. 1972 *Manual* (An Extended Stanford LISP *1.6* System). Information and Computer Science Technical Report 21, University of California, Irvine, Irvine, CA, Oct. 1972.

[Bobrow, 1973] Bobrow, Daniel G. and Wegbreit, Ben. A model and stack implementation of multiple environments. *Communications of the ACM*, 16:10, Oct. 1973, pp. 591–603.

[Bobrow, 1986] Bobrow, Daniel G., Kahn, Kenneth, Kiczales, Gregor, Masinter, Larry, Stefik, Mark, and Zdybel, Frank. CommonLoops: Merging Lisp and object-oriented programming. In [ACM OOPSLA, 1986], pp. 17–29.

[Boehm, 1986] Boehm, Hans-J., Cartwright, Robert, Riggle, Mark, and O'Donnell, Michael J. Exact real arithmetic: A case study in higher order programming. In [ACM LFP, 1986], pp. 162–173.

[Brooks, 1982a] Brooks, Rodney A., Gabriel, Richard P., and Steele, Jr., Guy L. S-1 Common Lisp implementation. In [ACM LFP, 1982], pp. 108–113.

[Brooks, 1982b] Brooks, Rodney A., Gabriel, Richard P., and Steele, Guy L., Jr. An optimizing compiler for lexically scoped LISP. In *Proceedings of the 1982 Symposium on Compiler Construction*, Boston, June 1982, pp. 261–275. Association for Computing Machinery. *ACM SIGPLAN Notices*, 17:6, June 1982.

[Brooks, 1984] Brooks, Rodney A. and Gabriel, Richard P. A critique of Common Lisp. In [ACM LFP, 1984], pp. 1–8.

[Burke, 1983] Burke, G. S., Carrette, G. J., and Eliot, C. R. *NIL Reference Manual*. Report MIT/LCS/TR-311, MIT Laboratory for Computer Science, Cambridge, Massachusetts, 1983.

[Burstall, 1971] Burstall, R. M., Collins, J. S., and Popplestone, R. J., Eds. *Programming in POP-2*. Edinburgh University Press, 1971.

[Campbell, 1984] Campbell, J. A., Ed. *Implementations of Prolog*. Chichester: Ellis Horwood Limited, 1984. Also published by John Wiley & Sons, New York.

[Church, 1941] Church, Alonzo. *The Calculi of Lambda Conversion*. Annals of Mathematics Studies 6. Princeton, NJ: Princeton University Press, 1941. Reprinted by Klaus Reprint Corp., New York, 1965.

[Clark, 1982] Clark, K. L. and Tärnlund, S.-Å., Eds. *Logic Programming*. New York: Academic Press, 1982.

[Clinger, 1984] Clinger, William. The Scheme 311 compiler: An exercise in denotational semantics. In [ACM LFP, 1984], pp. 356–364.

[Clinger, 1985a] Clinger, William, Ed. *The Revised Revised Report on Scheme; or, An Uncommon Lisp*. AI Memo 848, MIT Artificial Intelligence Laboratory, Cambridge, MA, Aug. 1985.

[Clinger, 1985b] Clinger, William, Ed.. *The Revised Revised Report on Scheme; or, An Uncommon Lisp*. Computer Science Department Tech. Rep. 174, Indiana University, Bloomington, June 1985.

[Clinger, 1988] Clinger, William D., Hartheimer, Anne H., and Ost, Eric M. Implementation strategies for continuations. In [ACM LFP, 1988], pp. 124–131.

[Clinger, 1990] Clinger, William D. How to read floating point numbers accurately. In [ACM PLDI, 1990], pp. 92–101.

[Clinger, 1991] Clinger, William, and Rees, Jonathan. Macros that work. In *Proceedings of the Eighteenth Annual ACM Symposium on Principles of Programming Languages*, Orlando, Florida, January 1991, pp. 155–162. Association for Computing Machinery.

[CLTL1, 1984] *Common Lisp: The Language.* By Guy L. Steele, Jr., Scott E. Fahlman, Richard P. Gabriel, David A. Moon, and Daniel L. Weinreb. Burlington, MA: Digital Press, 1984.

[CLTL2, 1990] *Common Lisp: The Language (Second Edition).* By Guy L. Steele, Jr., Scott E. Fahlman, Richard P. Gabriel, David A. Moon, Daniel L. Weinreb, Daniel G. Bobrow, Linda G. DeMichiel, Sonya E. Keene, Gregor Kiczales, Crispin Perdue, Kent M. Pitman, Richard C. Waters, and Jon L White. Bedford, MA: Digital Press, 1990.

[Cohen, 1981] Cohen, Jacques. Garbage collection of linked data structures. *ACM Computing Surveys*, 13:3, Sept. 1981, pp. 341–367.

[Correll, 1979] Correll, Steven. S-1 uniprocessor architecture (SMA-4). In *The S-1 Project 1979 Annual Report*, Vol. I, Chap. 4. Lawrence Livermore Laboratory, Livermore, CA, 1979.

[Davies, 1984] Davies, J. POPLER: Implementation of a POP-2–based PLANNER. In [Campbell, 1984], pp. 28–49.

[DEC, 1964] Digital Equipment Corporation, Maynard, MA. *Programmed Data Processor–6 Handbook*, 1964.

[DEC, 1969] Digital Equipment Corporation, Maynard, MA. *PDP-10 Reference Handbook*, 1969.

[DEC, 1981] Digital Equipment Corporation, Maynard, MA. *VAX Architecture Handbook*, 1981.

[de Kleer, 1978a] de Kleer, Johan, Doyle, Jon, Rich, Charles, Steele, Guy L., Jr., and Sussman, Gerald Jay. *AMORD: A Deductive Procedure System.* AI Memo 435, MIT Artificial Intelligence Laboratory, Cambridge, MA, Jan. 1978.

[de Kleer, 1978b] de Kleer, Johan, and Sussman, Gerald Jay. *Propagation of Constraints Applied to Circuit Synthesis.* AI Memo 485, MIT Artificial Intelligence Laboratory, Cambridge, MA, September 1978. Also in *Circuit Theory and Applications*, 8, 1980, pp. 127–144.

[Deutsch, 1964] Deutsch, L. Peter, and Berkeley, Edmund C. The LISP implementation for the PDP-1 computer. In [Berkeley, 1964], pp. 326–375.

[Deutsch, 1973] Deutsch, L. Peter. A LISP machine with very compact programs. In [IJCAI, 1973], pp. 697–703.

[Deutsch, 1976] Deutsch, L. Peter, and Bobrow, Daniel G. An efficient, incremental, automatic garbage collector. *Communications of the ACM*, 19:9, Sept. 1976, pp. 522–526.

[Drescher, 1987] Drescher, Gary. *ObjectLISP User Manual.* LMI (LISP Machine, Inc.), Cambridge, Massachusetts, 1987.

[Dybvig, 1986] Dybvig, R. Kent, Friedman, Daniel P., and Haynes, Christopher T. Expansion-passing style: Beyond conventional macros. In [ACM LFP, 1986], pp. 143–150.

[Eastlake, 1968] Eastlake, D., Greenblatt, R., Holloway, J., Knight, T., and Nelson, S. *ITS 1.5 Reference Manual.* AI Memo 161, MIT Artificial Intelligence Laboratory, Cambridge, MA, June 1968. Revised as AI Memo 161A, July 1969.

[Eastlake, 1972] Eastlake, Donald E. *ITS Status Report.* AI Memo 238, MIT Artificial Intelligence Laboratory, Cambridge, MA, Apr. 1972.

[Fateman, 1973] Fateman, Richard J. Reply to an editorial. *ACM SIGSAM Bulletin*, 25, March 1973, pp. 9–11. This reports the results of a test in which a compiled MacLisp floating-point program was faster than equivalent FORTRAN code. The numerical portion of the code was identical and MacLisp used a faster subroutine-call protocol.

[Feldman, 1972] Feldman, J. A., Low, J. R., Swinehart, D. C., and Taylor, R. H. Recent developments in SAIL. In *Proceedings of the 1972 AFIPS Fall Joint Computer Conference* 41, Stanford, CA, Nov. 1972, pp. 1193–1202. American Federation of Information Processing Societies.

[Fessenden, 1983] Fessenden, Carol, Clinger, William, Friedman, Daniel P., and Haynes, Christopher. *Scheme 311 Version 4 Reference Manual.* Tech. Rep. 137, Indiana University, Feb. 1983.

[Foderaro, 1982] Foderaro, J. K., and Sklower, K. L. *The FRANZ Lisp Manual.* University of California, Berkeley, CA, Apr. 1982.

[Forgy, 1977] Forgy, C., and McDermott, J. OPS, a domain-independent production system language. In *Proceedings of the Fifth International Joint Conference on Artificial Intelligence (IJCAI-77)*, Cambridge, MA, 1977, pp. 933–935. International Joint Council on Artificial Intelligence.

[Friedman, 1975] Friedman, Daniel P., and Wise, David S. *CONS Should Not Evaluate Its Arguments.* Tech. Rep. 44, Indiana University, Nov. 1975.

[Friedman, 1987] Friedman, Daniel P., and Felleisen, Matthias. *The Little LISPer.* Trade edition. Cambridge, MA: MIT Press, 1987. Also published by Science Research Associates, Chicago, 3rd ed., 1989.

[Gabriel, 1982] Gabriel, Richard P. and Masinter, Larry M. Performance of Lisp systems. In [ACM LFP, 1982], pp. 123–142.

[Gabriel, 1984a] Gabriel, Richard P. and Frost, Martin E. A programming environment for a timeshared system. In [ACM PSDE, 1984], pp. 185–192.

[Gabriel, 1984b] Gabriel, Richard P. and McCarthy, John. Queue-based multiprocessing Lisp. In [ACM LFP, 1984], pp. 25–44.

[Gabriel, 1985] Gabriel, Richard P. *Performance and Evaluation of Lisp Systems.* Cambridge, MA: MIT Press, 1985.

[Gabriel, 1988] Gabriel, Richard P. and Pitman, Kent M. Technical issues of separation in function cells and value cells. *Lisp and Symbolic Computation*, 1:1, June 1988, pp. 81–101.

[Gabriel, 1992] Gabriel, Richard P. Personal communication to Guy L. Steele, Jr., Nov. 30, 1992 (two hours before handing off this manuscript to Federal Express).

[Galley, 1975] Galley, S.W. and Pfister, Greg. *The MDL Language*. Programming Technology Division Document SYS.11.01, MIT Project MAC, Cambridge, MA, Nov. 1975.

[Geschke, 1977] Geschke, Charles M., Morris, Jr., James H., and Satterthwaite, Edwin H. Early experience with Mesa. *Communications of the ACM*, 20:8, Aug. 1977, pp. 540–553.

[Golden, 1970] Golden, Jeffrey P. *A User's Guide to the A. I. Group LISCOM Lisp Compiler: Interim Report*. AI Memo 210, MIT Project MAC, Cambridge, MA, Dec. 1970.

[Goldman, 1988] Goldman, Ron and Gabriel, Richard P. Preliminary results with the initial implementation of Qlisp. In [ACM LFP, 1988], pp. 143–152.

[Greenblatt, 1974] Greenblatt, Richard. *The LISP Machine*. Working Paper 79, MIT Artificial Intelligence Laboratory, Cambridge, MA, Nov. 1974.

[Greussay, 1977] Greussay, P. *Contribution à la définition interprétive et à l'implémentation des lambda-langages*. Thèse d'Etat, Université de Paris VI, Nov. 1977.

[Gries, 1977] Gries, David. An exercise in proving parallel programs correct. *Communications of the ACM*, 20:12, Dec. 1977, pp. 921–930.

[Griss, 1981] Griss, Martin L. and Hearn, Anthony C. A portable LISP compiler. *Software Practice and Experience*, 11, 1981, pp. 541–605.

[Griss, 1982] Griss, Martin L., Benson, Eric, and Maguire, Gerald Q., Jr. PSL: A portable LISP system. In [ACM LFP, 1982], pp. 88–97.

[Guzman, 1966] Guzman, Adolfo and McIntosh, Harold V. *CONVERT*. AI Memo 99, MIT Project MAC, Cambridge, MA, June 1966.

[Hailpern, 1979] Hailpern, Brent T. and Hitson, Bruce L. *S-1 Architecture Manual*. Tech. Rep. 161 (STAN-CS-79-715), Department of Electrical Engineering, Stanford University, Stanford, California, Jan. 1979.

[Halstead, 1984] Halstead, Robert H., Jr., Implementation of Halstead, 1985: Lisp on a multiprocessor. In [ACM LFP, 1984], pp. 9–17.

[Halstead, 1985] Halstead, Robert H., Jr., Multilisp: A language for concurrent symbolic computation. *ACM Transactions on Programming Languages and Systems*, 7:4, Oct. 1985, pp. 501–538.

[Harbison, 1991] Harbison, Samuel P. and Steele, Jr., Guy L. *C: A Reference Manual*. 3rd ed., Englewood Cliffs, NJ: Prentice-Hall, 1991.

[Hart, 1963] Hart, Timothy P. *MACRO Definitions for LISP*. AI Memo 57, MIT Artificial Intelligence Project—RLE and MIT Computation Center, Cambridge, MA, Oct. 1963.

[Hart, 1964] Hart, Timothy P. and Evans, Thomas G. Notes on implementing LISP for the M-460 computer In [Berkeley, 1964], pp. 191–203.

[Hearn, 1971] Hearn, A. C. REDUCE 2: A system and language for algebraic manipulation. In *Proceedings of the Second Symposium on Symbolic and Algebraic Manipulation*, Los Angeles, Mar. 1971, pp. 128–133.

[Henneman, 1964] Henneman, William. An auxiliary language for more natural expression—The A-language. In [Berkeley, 1964], pp. 239–248.

[Hewitt, 1969] Hewitt, Carl. PLANNER: A language for proving theorems in robots. In *Proceedings of the [First] International Joint Conference on Artificial Intelligence (IJCAI)*, Washington, DC, May 1969, pp. 295–301. International Joint Council on Artificial Intelligence.

[Hewitt, 1972] Hewitt, Carl. *Description and Theoretical Analysis (Using Schemata) of PLANNER: A Language for Proving Theorems and Manipulating Models in a Robot*. MIT, Cambridge, MA, Apr. 1972. MIT Artificial Intelligence Laboratory TR-258. Ph.D. thesis.

[Hewitt, 1975] Hewitt, Carl. How to use what you know. In *Proceedings of the Fourth International Joint Conference on Artificial Intelligence*, vol. 1, pp. 189–198, Tbilisi, Georgia, USSR, Sept. 1975. International Joint Council on Artificial Intelligence. Originally circulated as Working Paper 93, MIT Artificial Intelligence Laboratory, Cambridge, MA, May 1975.

[Hewitt, 1991] Hewitt, Carl and Inman, Jeff. DAI betwixt and between: From "intelligent agents" to open systems science. *IEEE Transactions on Systems, Man, and Cybernetics*, 21:6, Nov./Dec. 1991, pp. 1409–1419.

[Hieb, 1990] Hieb, Robert, R., Dybvig, Kent, and Bruggeman, Carl. Representing control in the presence of first-class continuations. In [ACM PLDI, 1990], pp. 66–77.

[IEEE, 1985] IEEE, New York. *IEEE Standard for Binary Floating-Point Arithmetic*, ANSI/IEEE STD 754-1985, 1985. An American National Standard.

[IEEE, 1991] IEEE Computer Society, New York. *IEEE Standard for the Scheme Programming Language*, IEEE STD 1178-1990, 1991.

[IJCAI, 1973] International Joint Council on Artificial Intelligence. *Proceedings of the Third International Joint Conference on Artificial Intelligence (IJCAI3)*, Stanford, CA, Aug. 1973.

[Iverson, 1962] Iverson, Kenneth E. *A Programming Language*. New York: Wiley,1962.

[Jensen, 1974] Jensen, Kathleen, and Wirth, Niklaus. *Pascal User Manual and Report*. New York: Springer-Verlag, 1974.

[Kahn, 1984] Kahn, K. M., and Carlsson, M. How to implement Prolog on a LISP machine. In [Campbell, 1984], pp. 117–134.

[Kempf, 1987] Kempf, James, Harris, Warren, D'Souza, Roy, and Snyder, Alan. Experience with CommonLoops. In *Proceedings of the ACM Conference on Objected-Oriented Programming Systems, Languages, and Applications (OOPSLA '87)*, Orlando, FL, Oct. 1987, pp. 214–226. Association for Computing Machinery. *ACM SIGPLAN Notices*, 22:12, Dec. 1987.

[Kernighan, 1978] Kernighan, Brian W. and Ritchie, Dennis. *The C Programming Language*. Englewood Cliffs, NJ: Prentice-Hall, 1978.

[Knuth, 1969] Knuth, Donald E. *Seminumerical Algorithms*, Vol. 2 of *The Art of Computer Programming*. Reading, MA: Addison-Wesley, 1969.

[Knuth, 1974] Knuth, Donald E. Structured programming with GO TO statements. *Computing Surveys*, 6:4, Dec. 1974, pp. 261–301.

[Knuth, 1981] Knuth, Donald E. *Seminumerical Algorithms (Second ed.)*, Vol. 2 of *The Art of Computer Programming*. Reading, MA: Addison-Wesley, 1981.

[Knuth, 1986] Knuth, Donald E. *The METAFONT Book*, volume C of *Computers and Typesetting*. Reading, MA: Addison-Wesley, 1986.

[Kohlbecker, 1986a] Kohlbecker, Eugene, Friedman, Daniel P., Felleisen, Matthias, and Duba, Bruce. Hygienic macro expansion. In [ACM LFP, 1986], pp. 151–161.

[Kohlbecker, 1986b] Kohlbecker, Eugene E., Jr., *Syntactic Extensions in the Programming Language Lisp*. Tech. Rep. 109, Indiana University, Aug. 1986. Ph.D. thesis.

[Komorowski, 1982] Komorowski, H. J. QLOG: The programming environment for PROLOG in LISP. In [Clark, 1982], pp. 315–322.

[Kranz, 1986] Kranz, David, Richard Kelsey, Rees, Jonathan, Hudak, Paul, Philbin, James, and Adams, Norman. ORBIT: An optimizing compiler for Scheme. In *Proceedings of the 1986 ACM SIGPLAN '86 Symposium on Compiler Construction*, Palo Alto, CA, June 1986. Association for Computing Machinery. *ACM SIGPLAN Notices*, 21:7, July 1986, pp. 219–233.

[Landin, 1964] Landin, Peter J. The mechanical evaluation of expressions. *Computer Journal*, 6:4, 1964.

[Landin, 1965] Landin, Peter J. A correspondence between ALGOL 60 and Church's lambda-notation. *Communications of the ACM*, 8:2–3, Feb.–Mar. 1965.

[Lisp Archive] **LISP ARCHIV**. On-line archive of MacLisp release notes, 1969–1981, with entries by Jon L White, Guy L. Steele Jr., Howard I. Cannon, Richard P. Gabriel, Richard M. Stallman, Eric C. Rosen, Richard Greenblatt, and Robert W. Kerns.

[Lisp Conference, 1980] *Conference Record of the 1980 LISP Conference*, Stanford, CA, Aug. 1980. Republished by Association for Computing Machinery.

[Malachi, 1984] Malachi, Yonathan, Manna, Zohar, and Waldinger, Richard. TABLOG: The deductive-tableau programming language. In [ACM LFP, 1984], pp. 323–330.

[Marti, 1979] Marti, J., A. C. Hearn, Griss, M. L., and Griss, C. Standard Lisp report. *ACM SIGPLAN Notices*, 14:10, Oct. 1979, pp. 48–68.

[Mathlab Group, 1977] Mathlab Group, The. *MACSYMA Reference Manual (Version Nine)*. MIT Laboratory for Computer Science, Cambridge, MA, 1977.

[McAllester, 1978] McAllester, David A. *A Three Valued Truth Maintenance System*. AI Memo 473, MIT Artificial Intelligence Laboratory, Cambridge, MA, May 1978.

[McCarthy, 1962] McCarthy, John, Abrahams, Paul W., Edwards, Daniel J., Hart, Timothy P., and Levin, Michael I. *LISP 1.5 Programmer's Manual*. Cambridge, MA: MIT Press, 1962.

[McCarthy, 1980] McCarthy, John. Lisp: Notes on its past and future. In [Lisp Conference, 1980], pp. v–viii.

[McCarthy, 1981] McCarthy, John. History of LISP. In Wexelblat, Richard L., Ed., *History of Programming Languages*, ACM Monograph Series, Chapter IV, pp. 173–197. New York: Academic Press, 1981. (Final published version of the Proceedings of the ACM SIGPLAN History of Programming Languages Conference, Los Angeles, CA, June 1978.)

[McDermott, 1974] McDermott, Drew V., and Sussman, Gerald Jay. *The CONNIVER Reference Manual*. AI Memo 295a, MIT Artificial Intelligence Laboratory, Cambridge, MA, Jan. 1974.

[McDermott, 1977] McDermott, Drew V. Oral remark at the ACM Symposium on Artificial Intelligence and Programming Languages, Rochester, NY, Aug. 1977, as recollected by Guy L. Steele, Jr.

[McDermott, 1980] McDermott, Drew. An efficient environment allocation scheme in an interpreter for a lexically-scoped LISP. In [Lisp Conference, 1980], pp. 154–162.

[Mellish, 1984] Mellish, C. and Hardy, S. Integrating Prolog in the POPLOG environment. In [Campbell, 1984], pp. 147–162.

[Miller, 1987] Miller, James Slocum. *MultiScheme: A Parallel Processing System Mased on MIT Scheme*. Ph.D. thesis, MIT, Cambridge, MA, Aug. 1987.

[MIT RLE, 1962a] MIT Research Laboratory of Electronics. Cambridge, MA: MIT Press. *COMIT Programmers Reference Manual*, June 1962.

[MIT RLE, 1962b] MIT Research Laboratory of Electronics. Cambridge, MA: MIT Press. *An Introduction to COMIT Programming*, June 1962.

[Moon, 1974] Moon, David A. *MacLISP Reference Manual*. MIT Project MAC, Cambridge, MA, Apr. 1974.

[Moon, 1984] Moon, David A. Garbage collection in a large Lisp system. In [ACM LFP, 1984], pp. 235–246.

[Moon, 1986] Moon, David A. Object-oriented programming with flavors. In [ACM OOPSLA, 1986], pp. 1–8.

[Moore, 1976] Moore, J. Strother, II. *The InterLISP Virtual Machine Specification*. Tech. Rep. CSL 76-5, Xerox Palo Alto Research Center, Palo Alto, California, Sept. 1976.

[Moses, 1970] Moses, Joel. *The Function of FUNCTION in LISP*. AI Memo 199, MIT Artificial Intelligence Laboratory, Cambridge, MA, June 1970.

[Moses, 1978?] Moses, Joel, as recalled (and probably paraphrased) by Guy L. Steele, Jr. There has been a persistent confusion in the literature about this remark. Some have reported that Moses said it while on a panel at the ACM APL 79 Conference. Moses denies having ever made that particular remark, however, and indeed Steele has heard him deny it. Steele, however, is equally certain that Moses *did* make such a remark—not at the APL conference, but while standing in the doorway of Steele and White's office, MIT room number NE43-834, circa 1978. Jon L White [personal communication to Steele, November 30, 1992] independently recalls having heard Moses comparing APL to a diamond and Lisp to a ball of mud on at least three separate occasions in that office building, once in NE43-834. The confusion will undoubtedly persist.

[Naur, 1963] Naur, Peter, Ed., *et al.* Revised report on the algorithmic language ALGOL 60. *Communications of the ACM*, 6:1, Jan. 1963, pp. 1–20.

[Okuno, 1984] Okuno, Hiroshi G., Takeuchi, Ikuo, Osato, Nobuyasu, Hibino, Yasushi, and Watanabe, Kazufumi. TAO: A fast interpreter-centered Lisp system on Lisp machine ELIS. In [ACM LFP, 1984], pp. 140–149.

[Organick, 1972] Organick, Elliot I. *The Multics System: An Examination of Its Structure*. Cambridge, MA: MIT Press, 1972.

[Padget, 1986] Padget, Julian, *et al.* Desiderata for the standardisation of Lisp. In [ACM LFP, 1986], pp. 54–66.

[PDP-6 Lisp, 1967] *PDP-6 LISP (LISP 1.6)*. AI Memo 116, MIT Project MAC, Cambridge, MA, Jan. 1967. Revised as Memo 116A, April 1967. The report does not bear the author's name, but Jeffrey P. Golden [Golden, 1970] attributes it to Jon L White.

[Pitman, 1980] Pitman, Kent M. Special forms in Lisp. In [Lisp Conference, 1980], pp. 179–187.

[Pitman, 1983] Pitman, Kent M. *The Revised MacLISP Manual*. MIT/LCS/TR 295, MIT Laboratory for Computer Science, Cambridge, MA, May 1983.

[Pratt, 1973] Pratt, Vaughan R. Top down operator precedence. In *Proceedings of the ACM Symposium on Principles of Programming Languages*, Boston, Oct. 1973, pp. 41–51. Association for Computing Machinery.

[Pratt, 1976] Pratt, Vaughan R. *CGOL: An Alternative External Representation for LISP Users*. AI Working Paper 121, MIT Artificial Intelligence Laboratory, Cambridge, MA, Mar. 1976.

[Quam, 1972] Quam, Lynn H., and Diffie, Whitfield. *Stanford LISP 1.6 Manual*. SAIL Operating Note 28.6, Stanford Artificial Intelligence Laboratory, Stanford, CA, 1972.

[Raymond, 1991] Raymond, Eric, Ed. *The New Hacker's Dictionary*. Cambridge, MA: MIT Press, 1991.

[Rees, 1982] Rees, Jonathan A. and Adams, Norman I., IV, T: A dialect of Lisp; or, LAMBDA: The ultimate software tool. In [ACM LFP, 1982], pp. 114–122.

[Rees, 1986] Rees, Jonathan, Clinger, William, *et al.* The revised^3 report on the algorithmic language Scheme. *ACM SIGPLAN Notices*, 21:12, Dec. 1986, pp. 37–79.

[Reynolds, 1972] Reynolds, John C. Definitional interpreters for higher order programming languages. In *Proceedings of the ACM National Conference*, Boston, Aug. 1972, pp. 717–740. Association for Computing Machinery.

[Robinson, 1982] Robinson, J. A. and Sibert, E. E. LOGLISP: Motivation, design, and implementation. In [Clark, 1982], pp. 299–313.

[Roylance, 1988] Roylance, Gerald. Expressing mathematical subroutines constructively. In [ACM LFP, 1988], pp. 8–13.

[Rudloe, 1962] Rudloe, H. *Tape Editor*. Program Write-up BBN-101, Cambridge, MA: Bolt Beranek and Newman Inc., Jan. 1962.

[Sabot, 1988] Sabot, Gary W. *The Paralation Model: Architecture-Independent Parallel Programming*. Cambridge, MA: MIT Press, 1988.

[Sammet, 1969] Jean E. Sammet. *Programming Languages: History and Fundamentals*. Englewood Cliffs, NJ: Prentice-Hall, 1969.

[Saunders, 1964a] Saunders, Robert A. The LISP listing for the Q-32 compiler, and some samples. In [Berkeley, 1964], pp. 290–317.

[Saunders, 1964b] Saunders, Robert A. The LISP system for the Q-32 computer. In [Berkeley, 1964], pp. 220–238.

[Shaw, 1981] Shaw, Mary, Wulf, William A., and London, Ralph L. Abstraction and verification in Alphard: Iteration and generators. In Mary Shaw, Ed., *ALPHARD: Form and Content*, Chapter 3, pp. 73–116. New York: Springer-Verlag, 1981.

[Smith, 1970] Smith, David Canfield. *MLISP*. Technical Report AIM-135, Stanford Artificial Intelligence Project, Oct. 1970.

[Smith, 1973] Smith, David Canfield and Enea, Horace J. Backtracking in MLISP2: An efficient backtracking method for LISP. In [IJCAI, 1973], pp. 677–685.

[Smith, 1975] Smith, Brian C. and Hewitt, Carl. *A PLASMA Primer*. Working Paper 92, MIT Artificial Intelligence Laboratory, Cambridge, MA, Oct. 1975.

[Sobalvarro, 1988] Sobalvarro, Patrick G. A Lifetime-based Garbage Collector for LISP Systems on General-Purpose Computers. Bachelor's Thesis, MIT, Cambridge, MA, Sept. 1988.

[Stallman, 1976] Stallman, Richard M. and Sussman, Gerald Jay. *Forward Reasoning and Dependency-Directed Backtracking in a System for Computer-Aided Circuit Analysis*. AI Memo 380, MIT Artificial Intelligence Laboratory, Cambridge, MA, Sept. 1976. Also in *Artificial Intelligence*, 9, 1977, pp. 135-196.

[Steele, 1975] Steele, Guy Lewis, Jr. Multiprocessing compactifying garbage collection. *Communications of the ACM*, 18:9, Sept. 1975, pp. 495–508.

[Steele, 1976a] Steele, Guy Lewis, Jr., and Sussman, Gerald Jay. *LAMBDA: The Ultimate Imperative*. AI Memo 353, MIT Artificial Intelligence Laboratory, Cambridge, MA, Mar. 1976.

[Steele, 1976b] Steele, Guy Lewis, Jr. *LAMBDA: The Ultimate Declarative*. AI Memo 379, MIT Artificial Intelligence Laboratory, Cambridge, MA, Nov. 1976.

[Steele, 1977a] Steele, Guy Lewis, Jr. *Compiler Optimization Based on Viewing LAMBDA as Rename plus Goto*. Master's thesis, MIT, May 1977. Published as [Steele, 1978a].

[Steele, 1977b] Steele, Guy Lewis, Jr. Data representations in PDP-10 MacLISP. In *Proceedings of the 1977 MACSYMA Users' Conference*, Washington, DC, July 1977, pp. 203–214. NASA Scientific and Technical Information Office. Also published as AI Memo 420, MIT Artificial Intelligence Laboratory, Cambridge, MA, Sept. 1977.

[Steele, 1977c] Steele, Guy Lewis, Jr. Fast arithmetic in Maclisp. In *Proceedings of the 1977 MACSYMA Users' Conference*, Washington, DC, July 1977, pp. 215–224. NASA Scientific and Technical Information Office. Also published as AI Memo 421, MIT Artificial Intelligence Laboratory, Cambridge, MA, Sept. 1977.

[Steele, 1977d] Steele, Guy L., Jr. Macaroni is better than spaghetti. In [ACM AIPL, 1977], pp. 60–66.

[Steele, 1977e] Steele, Guy Lewis, Jr. Debunking the 'expensive procedure call' myth; or, Procedure call implementations considered harmful; or, LAMBDA: The ultimate GOTO. In *Proceedings of the ACM National Conference*, Seattle, Oct. 1977, pp. 153–162. Association for Computing Machinery. Revised version published as AI Memo 443, MIT Artificial Intelligence Laboratory, Cambridge, MA, Oct. 1977.

[Steele, 1978a] Steele, Guy Lewis, Jr. *A Compiler for SCHEME (A Study in Compiler Optimization)*. Tech. Rep. 474, MIT Artificial Intelligence Laboratory, May 1978. This is a revised version of the author's master's thesis [Steele, 1977a].

[Steele, 1978b] Steele, Guy Lewis, Jr., and Sussman, Gerald Jay. *The Art of the Interpreter; or, The Modularity Complex (Parts Zero, One, and Two)*. AI Memo 453, MIT Artificial Intelligence Laboratory, Cambridge, Massachusetts, May 1978.

[Steele, 1978c] Steele, Guy Lewis, Jr. and Sussman, Gerald Jay. *The Revised Report on SCHEME: A Dialect of LISP*. AI Memo 452, MIT Artificial Intelligence Laboratory, Cambridge, MA, Jan. 1978.

[Steele, 1979] Steele, Guy Lewis, Jr. and Sussman, Gerald Jay. Constraints. In *Proceedings of the APL 79 Conference*, Rochester, NY, June 1979, pp. 208–225. Association for Computing Machinery. *APL Quote Quad*, 9:4, June 1979. Also published as AI Memo 502, MIT Artificial Intelligence Laboratory, Cambridge, MA, Nov. 1978.

[Steele, 1980] Steele, Guy Lewis, Jr. and Sussman, Gerald Jay. The dream of a lifetime: A lazy variable extent mechanism. In [Lisp Conference, 1980], pp. 163–172.

[Steele, 1982] Steele, Guy L., Jr. An overview of Common Lisp. In [ACM LFP, 1982], pp. 98–107.

[Steele, 1986] Steele, Guy L., Jr. and Hillis, W. Daniel. Connection Machine Lisp: Fine-grained parallel symbolic processing. In [ACM LFP, 1986], pp. 279–297.

[Steele, 1990a] Steele, Guy L., Jr. Making asynchronous parallelism safe for the world. In *Proceedings of the Seventeenth Annual ACM Symposium on Principles of Programming Languages*, San Francisco, Jan. 1990, pp. 218–231. Association for Computing Machinery.

[Steele, 1990b] Steele, Guy L., Jr. and White, Jon L. How to print floating-point numbers accurately. In [ACM PLDI, 1990], pp. 112–126.

[Sussman, 1971] Sussman, Gerald Jay, Winograd, Terry, and Charniak, Eugene. *Micro-PLANNER Reference Manual*. AI Memo 203A, MIT Artificial Intelligence Laboratory, Cambridge, MA, Dec. 1971.

[Sussman, 1972a] Sussman, Gerald Jay and McDermott, Drew Vincent. From PLANNER to McDermott, 1974—A genetic approach. In *Proceedings of the 1972 Fall Joint Computer Conference*, Montvale, NJ, Aug. 1972, pp. 1171–1179. AFIPS Press. This is the published version of [Sussman, 1972b].

[Sussman, 1972b] Sussman, Gerald Jay and McDermott, Drew Vincent. *Why Conniving is Better than Planning*. AI Memo 255A, MIT Artificial Intelligence Laboratory, Cambridge, MA, April 1972.

[Sussman, 1975a] Sussman, Gerald Jay and Stallman, Richard M. *Heuristic Techniques in Computer-Aided Circuit Analysis*. AI Memo 328, MIT Artificial Intelligence Laboratory, Cambridge, MA, Mar. 1975.

[Sussman, 1975b] Sussman, Gerald Jay and Steele, Guy Lewis, Jr., *SCHEME: An Interpreter for Extended Lambda Calculus*. AI Memo 349, MIT Artificial Intelligence Laboratory, Cambridge, MA, Dec. 1975.

[Sussman, 1988] Sussman, Gerald Jay and Halfant, Matthew. Abstraction in numerical methods. In [ACM LFP, 1988], pp. 1–7.

[Swanson, 1988] Swanson, Mark R., Kessler, Robert R., and Lindstrom, Gary. An implementation of Portable Standard Lisp on the BBN Butterfly. In [ACM LFP, 1988], pp. 132–142.

[Swinehart, 1972] Swinehart, D. C. and Sproull, R. F. *SAIL*. SAIL Operating Note 57.2, Stanford Artificial Intelligence Laboratory, Stanford, CA, 1972.

[Symbolics, 1985] Symbolics, Inc., Cambridge, MA. *Reference Guide to Symbolics-Lisp*, Mar. 1985.

[Takeuchi, 1983] Takeuchi, Ikuo, Okuno, Hirochi, and Ohsato, Nobuyasu. TAO: A harmonic mean of Lisp, Prolog, and Smalltalk. *ACM SIGPLAN Notices*, 18:7, July 1983, pp. 65–74.

[Teitelman, 1966] Teitelman, Warren. *PILOT: A Step toward Man-Computer Symbiosis*. Tech. Rep. MAC-TR-32, MIT Project MAC, Sept. 1966. Ph.D. thesis.

[Teitelman, 1971] Teitelman, W., Bobrow, D. G., Hartley, A. K., and Murphy, D. L. *BBN-LISP: TENEX Reference Manual*. Cambridge, MA: Bolt Beranek and Newman Inc., 1971.

[Teitelman, 1973] Teitelman, Warren. CLISP: Conversational LISP. In [IJCAI, 1973], pp. 686–690.

[Teitelman, 1974] Teitelman, Warren, *et al. InterLISP Reference Manual*. Xerox Palo Alto Research Center, Palo Alto, CA, 1974. First revision.

[Teitelman, 1978] Teitelman, Warren, *et al. InterLISP Reference Manual*. Xerox Palo Alto Research Center, Palo Alto, CA, Oct. 1978. Third revision.

[Tesler, 1973] Tesler, Lawrence G., Enea, Horace J., and Smith, David C. The LISP70 pattern matching system. In [IJCAI, 1973], pp. 671–676.

[Thacker, 1982] Thacker, C. P., McCreight, E. M., Lampson, B. W., Sproull, R. F., and Boggs, D. R. Alto: A personal computer. In Siewiorek, Daniel P., C. Gordon Bell, and Allen Newell, Eds., *Computer Structures: Principles and Examples*, Computer Science Series, Chap. 33, pp. 549–572. New York: McGraw-Hill, 1982.

[Travis, 1977] Travis, Larry, Honda, Masahiro, LeBlanc, Richard, and Zeigler, Stephen. Design rationale for TELOS, a Jensen, 1974-based AI language. In [ACM AIPL, 1977], pp. 67–76.

[Ungar, 1984] David Ungar. Generation scavenging: A non-disruptive high performance storage reclamation algorithm. In [ACM PSDE, 1984], pp. 157–167.

[Utah, 1982] Utah Symbolic Computation Group. *The Portable Standard LISP Users Manual*. Tech. Rep. TR-10, Department of Computer Science, University of Utah, Salt Lake City, Jan. 1982.

[Vuillemin, 1988] Vuillemin, Jean. Exact real computer arithmetic with continued fractions. In [ACM LFP, 1988], pp. 14–27.

[Wand, 1977] Wand, Mitchell and Friedman, Daniel P. *Compiling Lambda Expressions Using Continuations and Factorization*. Tech. Rep. 55, Indiana University, July 1977.

[Waters, 1984] Waters, Richard C. Expressional loops. In *Proceedings of the Eleventh Annual ACM Symposium on Principles of Programming Languages*, Salt Lake City, Utah, Jan. 1984, pp. 1–10. Association for Computing Machinery.

[Waters, 1989a] Waters, Richard C. *Optimization of Series Expressions, Part I: User's Manual for the Series Macro Package*. AI Memo 1082, MIT Artificial Intelligence Laboratory, Cambridge, MA, Jan. 1989.

[Waters, 1989b] Waters, Richard C. *Optimization of Series Expressions, Part II: Overview of the Theory and Implementation*. AI Memo 1083, MIT Artificial Intelligence Laboratory, Cambridge, MA, Jan. 1989.

[Wegbreit, 1970] Wegbreit, Ben. *Studies in Extensible Programming Languages*. Ph.D. thesis, Harvard University, Cambridge, MA, 1970.

[Wegbreit, 1971] Wegbreit, Ben. The Wegbreit, 1974 programming system. In *Proceedings of the 1971 Fall Joint Computer Conference*, pp. 253–262, Montvale, NJ: AFIPS Press, Aug. 1971.

[Wegbreit, 1972] Wegbreit, Ben, Brosgol, Ben, Holloway, Glenn, Prenner, Charles, and Spitzen, Jay. *ECL Programmer's Manual*. Tech. Rep. 21-72, Harvard University Center for Research in Computing Technology, Cambridge, MA, Sept. 1972.

[Wegbreit, 1974] Wegbreit, Ben, Holloway, Glenn, Spitzen, Jay, and Townley, Judy. *ECL Programmer's Manual*. Tech. Rep. 23-74, Harvard University Center for Research in Computing Technology, Cambridge, MA, Dec. 1974.

[Weinreb, 1978] Weinreb, Daniel, and Moon, David. *LISP Machine Manual, Preliminary Version*. MIT Artificial Intelligence Laboratory, Cambridge, Massachusetts, Nov. 1978.

[Weinreb, 1981] Weinreb, Daniel and Moon, David. *LISP Machine Manual, Third ed.* MIT Artificial Intelligence Laboratory, Cambridge, MA, Mar. 1981.

[White, 1980] White, Jon L. Address/memory management for a gigantic LISP environment; or, GC considered harmful. In [Lisp Conference, 1980], pp. 119–127.

[White, 1986] White, Jon L. Reconfigurable, retargetable bignums: A case study in efficient, portable Lisp system building. In [ACM LFP, 1986], pp. 174–191.

[Wulf, 1971] Wulf, W.A., Russell, D.B., and Habermann, A.N. Bliss: A language for systems programming. *Communications of the ACM*, 14:12, Dec. 1971, pp. 780–790.

[Wulf, 1975] Wulf, William, Johnsson, Richard K., Weinstock, Charles B., Hobbs, Steven O., and Geschke, Charles M. *The Design of an Optimizing Compiler*, Vol. 2 of *Programming Language Series*. New York: American Elsevier, 1975.

[Yngve, 1972] Yngve, Victor H. *Computer Programming with COMIT II*. Cambridge, MA: MIT Press, 1972.

TRANSCRIPT OF PRESENTATION

STEELE: We're very happy to be here this morning at the HOPL conference. We've worked very hard on this paper. We began work on it almost *two years* ago. So this has been a long time in the making and we're ready to do it this morning.

GABRIEL: Yes, and we have also worked very hard on the presentation for this conference today. We've been working on the presentation for almost *two days* now. [*laughter*]

STEELE: This extreme range, a difference of orders of magnitude, is typical of various things that go on in the Lisp community. Let me give you a couple of examples. One is that there is an ANSI standard for the dialect of Lisp known as Scheme. It is a mere 50 pages long. It is a model of concision.

GABRIEL: The ANSI Common Lisp draft specification is at the opposite extreme, currently weighing in at 1,350 pages.

STEELE: That is a difference of 27 to 1. Another example is that with merely a stone knife, a block of wood, and a working C compiler, you can put together a working Lisp interpreter in less than a day if you know what you are doing.

GABRIEL: And, if you want to put together a fairly decent, but not outstanding, Common Lisp system, you should plan on 20 to 30 man-years. [*laughter*]

STEELE: We worked very hard putting this paper together. We polished it and polished it and got it as perfect as we could and there is no way we can present all of that material this morning in a space of 35 minutes. So we are not even going to try.

GABRIEL: So what we are going to do instead is try to take different slices through this complicated and very difficult to understand history of Lisp, and try to show you some themes that we've discovered over the years.

STEELE: We are assuming that you have read or probably will read the paper [in this book]. But that's not a prerequisite for what we're going to do this morning. Instead, we're going to show you a graphical presentation of the various Lisp projects and we're going to show you everything on this two-dimensional graphical plot [Figure 6.1], in which the vertical axis is time, extending from a little before 1960 to about the present. On the horizontal axis we've put geography running East and West. There is no reason why this should have turned out to be a useful axis, but it did, coincidentally, and so we're going to lay things out that way. You will find over here on the left projects occurring in

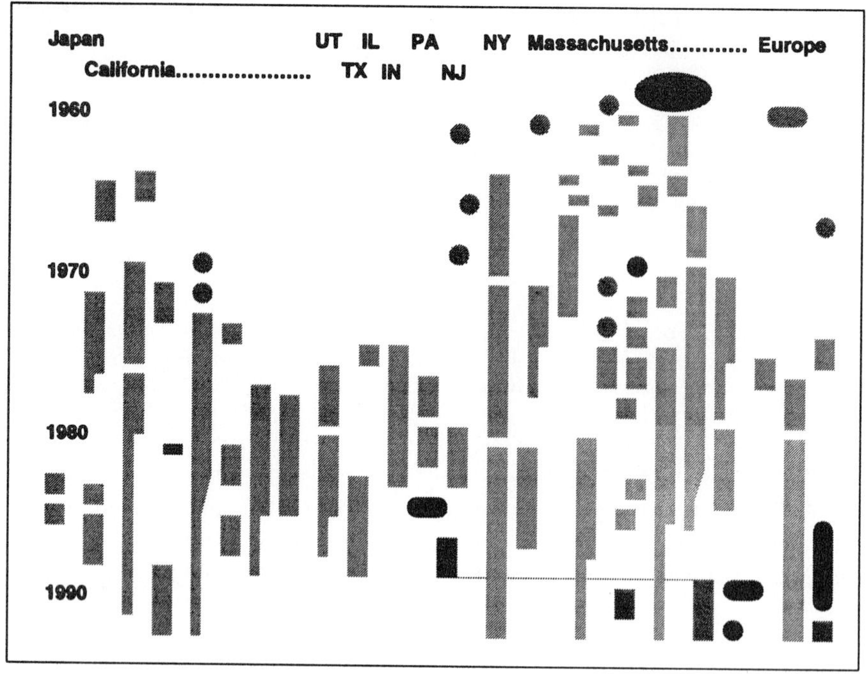

FIGURE 6.1

Japan. There is a large cluster of stuff that happened in California; a variety of things that happened between the coasts in the U.S. at various scattered locations that we will talk about later—they are labeled by state on this plot; a whole pile of stuff that happened in Massachusetts, particularly centered around MIT where Lisp got started; and then there are a number of projects over in Europe.

GABRIEL: As often happens, you can learn quite a bit by plotting the relationships among the various languages and dialects. So we did that with the Lisp family graph and we came up with this intuitive [*laughter*] look at the history of Lisp [Figure 6.2].

In this diagram the black arrows indicate a direct relationship, for example, either using the implementation to bootstrap a further one or to use part of the implementation later on. The magenta arrows [*gray in this book*], which took us three hours to draw in, represent an influence that is significant. Rather than show you all of this, we are going to show you different slices through this that illustrate some particular points.

STEELE: It would be helpful if I explained our color coding system. The red [*lightest gray*] rectangles represent specific Lisp implementation projects, and we have attempted to show the geographic location at which the implementation occurred, not necessarily the sites of their use. Where some of these bars are first wider, then narrow, we have intended the wide part to indicate roughly the time span of the heyday of those implementations, although use continued after their heyday for some time in some instances. The green [*light gray*] ovals indicate language specifications for languages that are not of the Lisp family but which we have included on the chart because they have an influence on the development of Lisp. The blue [*darkest gray*] ovals indicate language specifications within the Lisp family, but specifications as opposed to implementations. The cyan [*dark gray*] rectangles indicate official standards projects under ANSI or ISO.

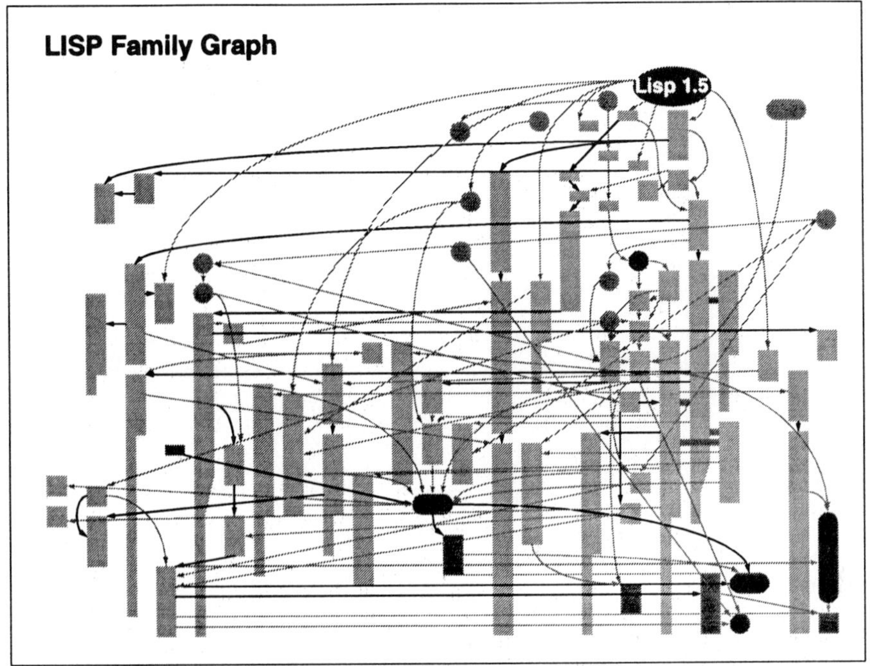

FIGURE 6.2

There's no way in the world that we could possibly make intelligible sense out of this network of boxes and arrows. We're going to show you different subsets of that. Let's begin by looking at the Lisp 1.5 family [Figure 6.3].

This all stems from the original idea, shown here as a blue oval, of Lisp 1.5 as reflected in the *Lisp 1.5 Programmer's Manual* and earlier documents. This spawned a number of implementations. Perhaps the most direct descendants are the Lisp 1.5 implementations on IBM machines on the 7090 and the 7094 at MIT. There are a number of implementations early on on other machines, notably several different PDP-1 implementations that happened in different geographic locations; implementations on the M-460 and the Q-32, which you can read about in references that are cited in our paper; and also, notably, an implementation on the PDP-6, which was arguably the first real hardware Lisp machine. It was the first architecture that included instructions specifically for the support of the Lisp language and this turned out to have a great influence on the rest of the development of Lisp, as we will see later. There is also a version of Lisp developed in Cambridge, in England, and Lisp 1.5, after about ten or fifteen years, resulted in implementations in Utah (Standard Lisp) and the Stanford Lisp 1.6 and UCI Lisp configuration.

The most notable characteristic of this slide is that there is an important idea and suddenly there was a quick spawning of a bunch of implementations. Lisp was still a fairly small language, and at the time it was very easy for a project at another university or another company to say, "Hey, let's build us a Lisp, too." You could within a day, or a week, or a month, get some kind of Lisp working on whatever machine you had there locally.

GABRIEL: Now we are going to look at a later family, the MacLisp family [Figure 6.4]. This family was developed here at MIT. Again, as Guy pointed out, it started off with the PDP-6 Lisp, which soon turned into MacLisp. MacLisp ran primarily on the PDP-10, which was again sort of a Lisp machine.

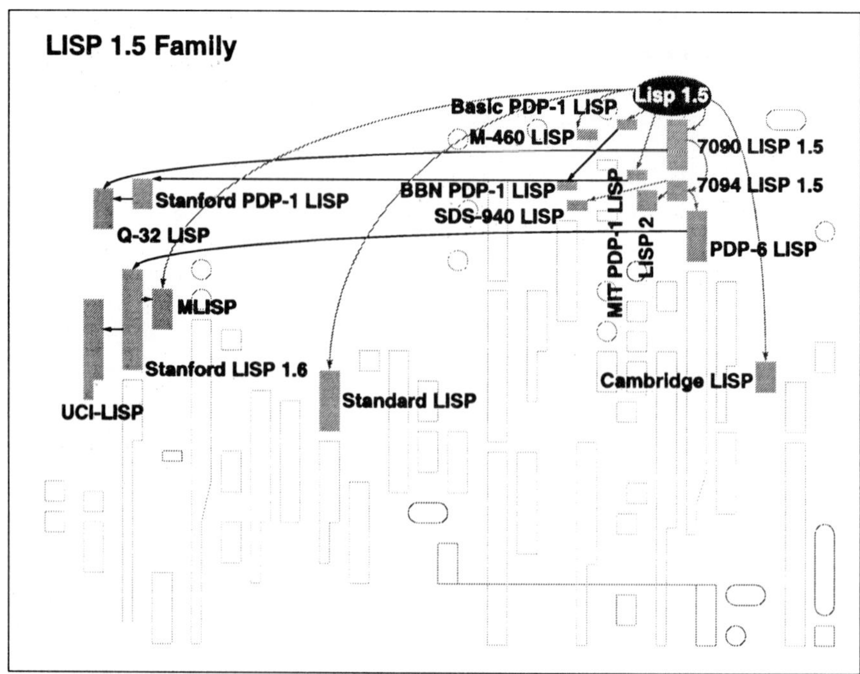

FIGURE 6.3

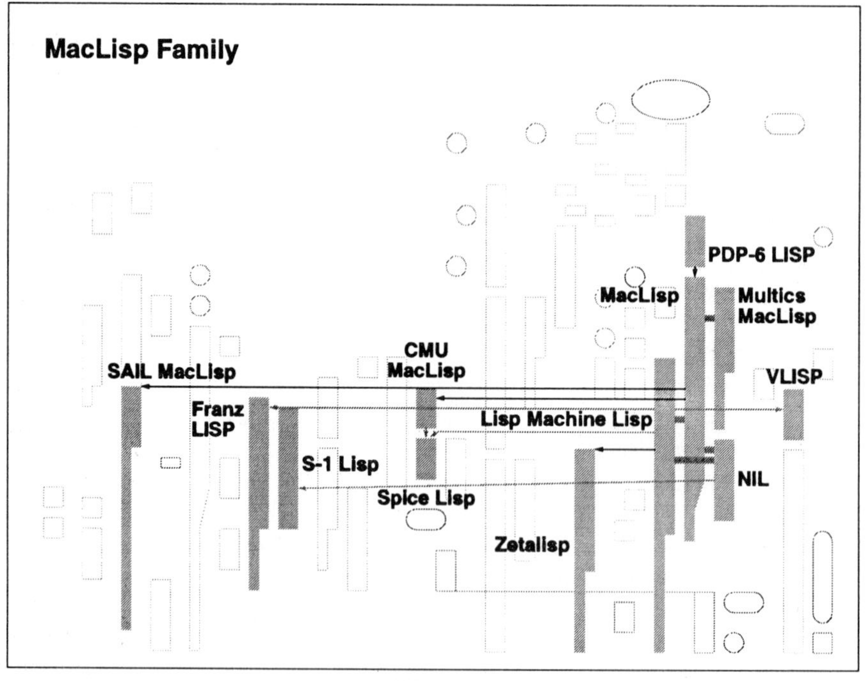

FIGURE 6.4

It had special instructions for doing **CAR** and **CDR** and good stack instructions for fast function call. This work was primarily done by a fellow named Jon L White, whom we see again and again in our story. He worked on this fairly continuously up until the beginning of the demise of MacLisp. As we can see by the direction of the arrows, MacLisp kind of spread; even though most people think of MacLisp as having remained at MIT, it moved across country, particularly when Scott Fahlman and Dave Touretzky moved from MIT to CMU. They, along with Guy Steele, did a port of it to the local system, where they did some extensions. I'm not sure what sort of adaptations they did, but they did some adaptations so that it became one of the standard Lisps at CMU.

Similarly, when I moved across country, MacLisp came with me and we did some significant adaptations to it on the West Coast. And, in particular, one thing you can see is that MacLisp was used for quite a long time at Stanford, way beyond where it was used at MIT. Other MacLisp-like dialects spawned off, for example, Lisp-Machine Lisp, which was kind of a response to the limited address space that the PDP-10 had. In fact, one of the significant events was running into the limit of basically a one-megabyte, one-MIPS machine. Keep in mind that people were trying to do AI research in this Lisp on this machine. There are several dialects of Lisp-Machine Lisp that we will see later.

One of the points we want to make here is a little bit surprising. We didn't know it until we saw these graphs. One of the things that you can see is that MacLisp kind of spread throughout the country and it did it for a couple of reasons. For one, MIT is relatively unstable in the sense that, when you are there, your funding may end at any time, so you might have to leave. So the tendency is for people to leave the area and take what they know with them. The, ah . . . I forget what the second point was!

STEELE: Instead of your second point, let me point out one block you missed: Richard Fateman left MIT when he went to Berkeley (as opposed to Stanford); the Franz Lisp effort got started, and this was another important offshoot of the MacLisp family.

I'll make a contrast with Dick's first point by looking at the IBM Lisp family [Figure 6.5]. Here there is a fairly direct relationship of taking at least the ideas, if not some of the implementation code, from the 7090 Lisp. Notice that this is the 7090 Lisp and not the 7094 Lisp—the difference between those is that the 7090 Lisp was running under the IBM operating system; the 7094 Lisp was running under MIT's CTSS operating system. It became Lisp360, and once it got there at Yorktown, or somewhere in New York, there was a fairly direct implementation line. It stayed in one place because IBM, at least compared to MIT, is a relatively stable place. Once you are there, you are set; there is less of a need to publish outside. There are more controls, for good reason: you have a product you are selling, as opposed to just doing it as an academic exercise. There are reasons to maintain central control over an implementation. Notice this is not the locale of use; this is the locale of implementation. There were, of course, users wherever IBM computers were.

There is one interesting connection here with Interlisp and with MacLisp, which is that there was a programming environment that—actually, Interlisp developed a great programming environment, and when Dick Gabriel happened to be at Illinois and he read about the Interlisp programming environment, he was greatly impressed and decided to bring a version of it up in MacLisp. He did that, and then when he went to Stanford, he carried that with him, brought it up there, and it became the programming environment of choice at Stanford, completely displacing the old Stanford Lisp 1.6. That programming environment then got ported back to the IBM environment and became the programming environment that was standard within VM Lisp. But except for that one strong outside influence, it was pretty much a self-contained series of projects there at IBM.

GABRIEL: Another example of a stable situation is with Interlisp [Figure 6.6]. Interlisp actually had its roots a little bit higher up in this diagram with the Basic PDP-1 Lisp that Peter Deutsch wrote as

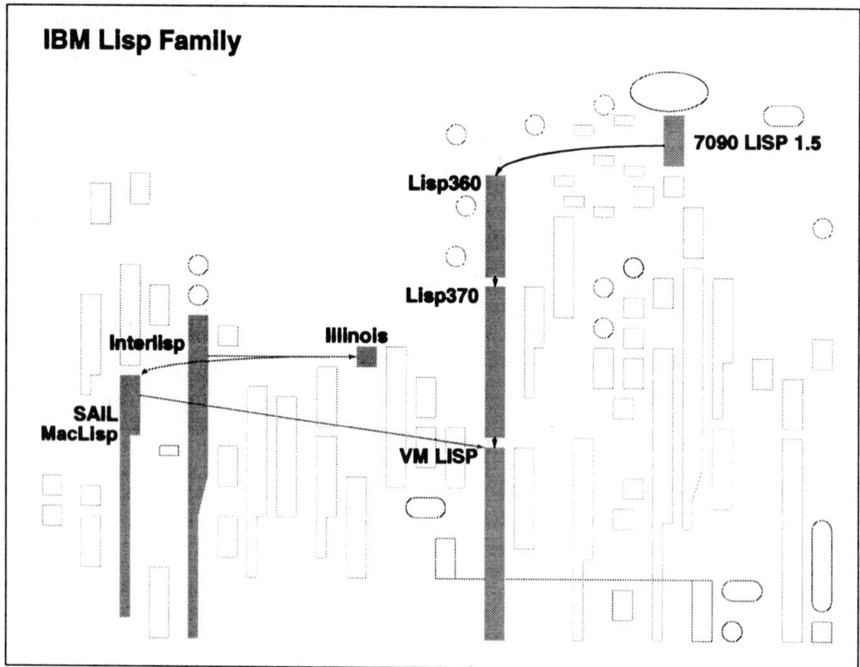

FIGURE 6.5

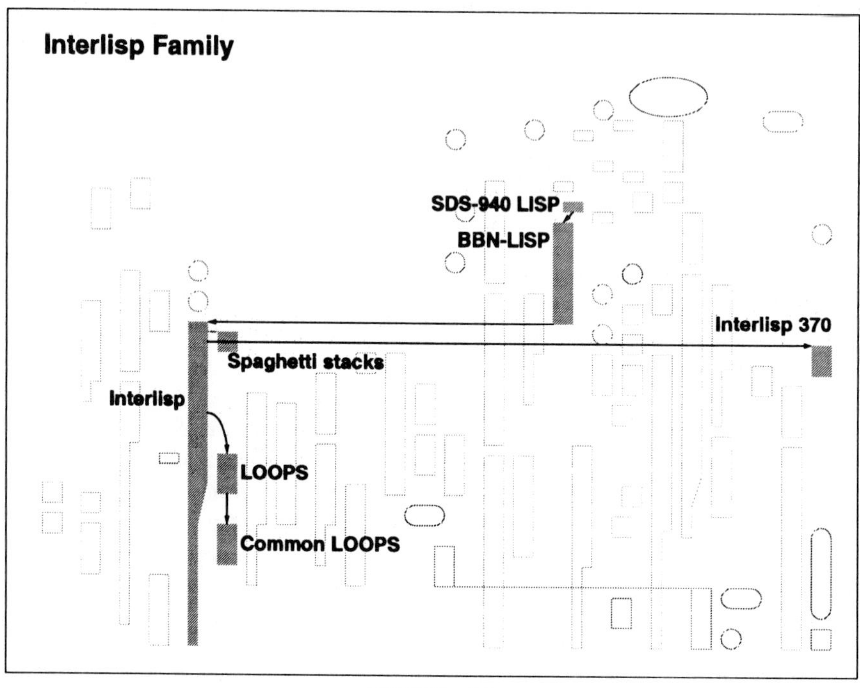

FIGURE 6.6

a high school student in this area. This was later expanded into the SDS 940 Lisp, which was done, at least in part, by Danny Bobrow, who will, again, appear in many places in this story.

The interesting developments, from our point of view, start with BBN-Lisp. Now BBN-Lisp, which later became Interlisp, is interesting because it developed a notion of a very elaborate, cushy, comfortable programming environment. So, in contrast to MacLisp, which was concerned with performance and small size (in order to write large programs in the small address space of the PDP-10), Interlisp was more concerned about making the programming task easier, so there was a non-file-based structure editor, "Do What I Mean," Conversational Lisp type of programming environment. At some point, BBN passed over the responsibility of maintaining BBN-Lisp to Xerox, partly coinciding with the departure of the principals, for example, Danny Bobrow, to the West Coast.

Interlisp has sort of a long history. As you can see, it doesn't exist in very many places except for this box you can't see, which is Interlisp 370, which was developed in Sweden, and I'm not sure how widely it was used. But if you ignore that, we can see a similar situation to IBM where there is sort of a narrow but long use. Again, because of the stability of the place, people didn't tend to leave, they didn't need to publish outside, so the ideas didn't spread very much. There are a couple of interesting spawns here into LOOPS and CommonLoops, the Lisp Object-Oriented Programming System. We'll see that later when we talk about the object-oriented programming aspects of this.

Danny Bobrow did quite a lot of work all over this map. One of the interesting things he did was a concept called spaghetti stacks, which were a kind of a coroutining facility, a way of saving state and going back and forth between different threads of control.

STEELE: Its important to realize that the Interlisp implementation, like the MacLisp implementation, was trying to run on a machine that had one megabyte of address space and ran at 1 MIPS; and that there were necessarily some severe engineering tradeoffs to be made. It's not that the MacLisp group would not have liked to have had a good programming environment; it's not as if the Interlisp group would not have liked to focus on compiler development and so forth, and good numerical performance, as the MacLisp group did; it is just that, when you are running under those kind of machine constraints, you have to make some hard choices. There was a time, in 1974, when the two implementation groups got together, at what we sometimes called a MacLisp-Interlisp summit, where the implementors got together and tried to agree on a set of features that they could exchange in order to encourage portability between the two platforms, and ultimately we agreed only on a few trivial things. At the time, I remember thinking, "Boy, those people are really pigheaded—they won't take all our good ideas!" and I'm sure they felt very much the same way about us. Looking back on it, I'm inclined to the more generous interpretation that each of us, consciously or unconsciously thinking about our severe budgetary constraints of memory space and machine speed, simply felt that we couldn't afford anything that wasn't on our main program. But what broke this logjam was the development of the Lisp machines [Figure 6.7].

It became clear in the mid-70s that the PDP-10 wasn't going to cut it for too much longer, and that it seemed to be more cost-effective to build custom-designed Lisp hardware—this was a point where you could just begin to afford to design special-purpose personal workstations. I think the original inspiration for this was the Alto at Xerox, although it wasn't initially running Lisp. Then Tom Knight and Richard Greenblatt at MIT proposed to build these things called Lisp Machines, of which first a few dozen were built at MIT, and this then proceeded to spawn two companies, LMI and Symbolics, which then commercialized those. At the same time, Xerox produced a series of machines designed for both Lisp and Smalltalk, and some other languages, such as Mesa. So they had a series of personal workstations such as the Alto and the so called "D machines," the Dorado, the Dolphin, and the Dandelion, and Interlisp was brought up on all those machines. There was also a machine that was

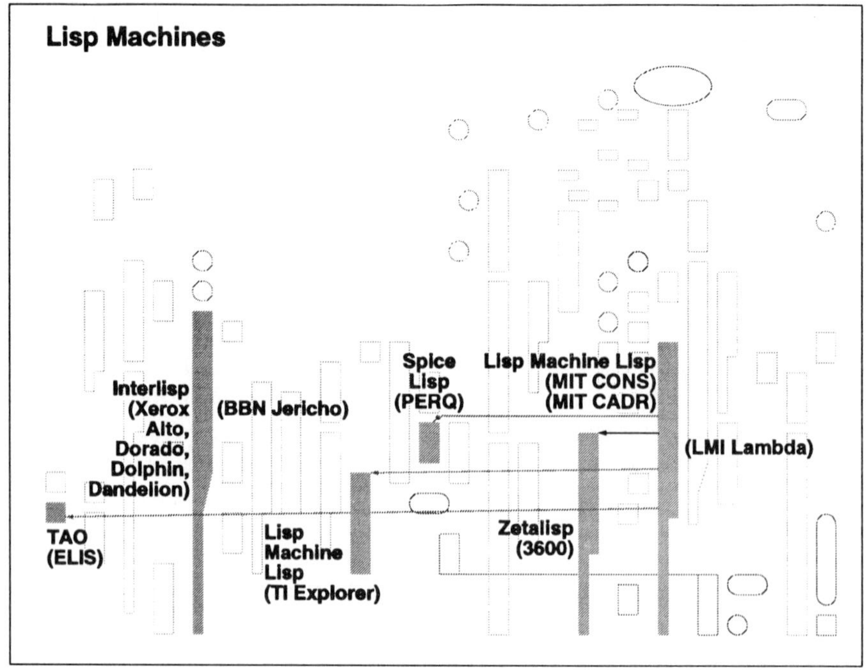

FIGURE 6.7

done at BBN, called the Jericho. The machine was geographically over here, but it used Interlisp, so I've notated it next to the box there for Interlisp. There was also some work done on Lisp machines in Japan, of which I think the most notable was the ELIS machine, which ran a dialect that was a combination of Lisp and Prolog, and this dialect was called Tao. The Lisp Machines lasted for quite a while and some of them are still in use today. There are Lisp Machines running over at Thinking Machines, doing diagnostic debugging of Connection Machines—that's just the software we happen to run on them right now. They are still considered workhorses in some places.

On the other hand, by the mid-80s, it became clear that machines that were custom-built to run just one language weren't necessarily cost-effective anymore, because the general-purpose workstation market had exploded and you could just go to Sun, or HP, or whatever place you liked, and buy a stock workstation, put up an implementation of Lisp on it, and the overall combination would be just as effective as having a custom-built piece of hardware.

GABRIEL: The next major development is Common Lisp [Figure 6.8]. Common Lisp is an interesting development in the sense that it is, I think, the first time that the Lisp community tried to work together. What happened was, basically, as you will recall from the MacLisp slide, all of the MacLisp people kind of split up, went to the four winds, and started working on their own various dialects of Lisp. Here are some of these dialects: NIL, ZetaLisp, Spice Lisp, S-1 Lisp are the primary ones. In April 1981, there was a DARPA meeting at SRI in California, sort of another Lisp summit meeting. The purpose of that meeting was for DARPA to find out whether it was going to be able to have a consolidated Lisp to use in its research. What happened at that meeting was that the Interlisp community, being sort of unified anyway, appeared very unified and the MacLisp community seemed kind of scatterbrained. So what we did was, we all got together and said, "Let's beat those guys." We got together and we started to define a description of a family of langages called Common Lisp.

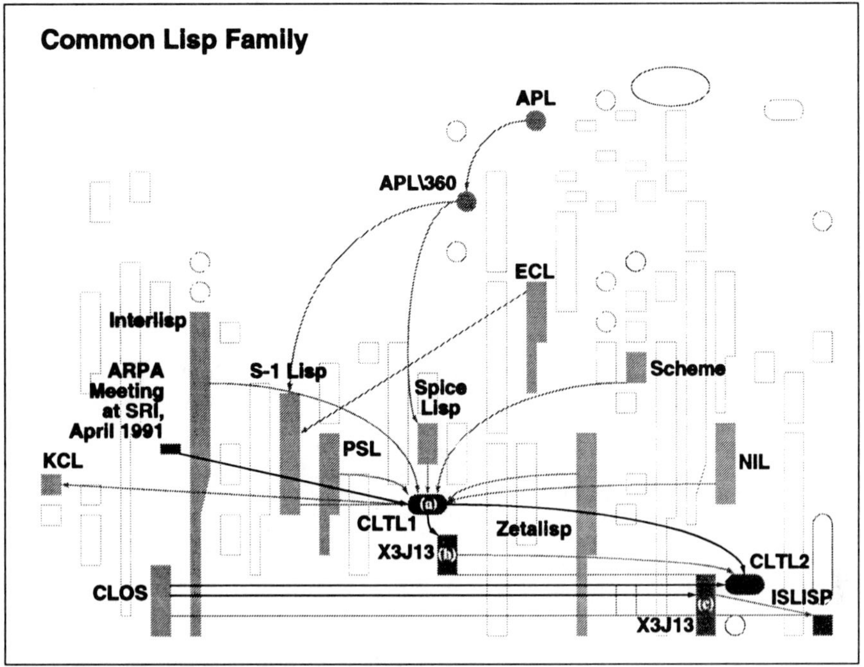

FIGURE 6.8

Now Common Lisp has gone through a somewhat lengthy history. As mentioned, it takes quite a while to implement the Lisp. That's because it's a fairly large definition; a large, what most languages call library was included. This box here [*points to* (a) in Figure 6.8] represents the publication of CLTL1—*Common Lisp: The Language*, first edition—which represented the work of two or three years of informal standardization, which happened over the network, primarily. It was one of the first designs that happened over the network, and in fact, the e-mail traffic has been studied by various sociologists to figure out what was going on with us. [*laughter*] Later on, an ANSI standards committee was formed, called X3J13, to do a formal ANSI standardization of that. These boxes here represent the location of the chairman, Guy Steele, over here [*points to* (b)], and [*puzzled*] Guy Steele over there [*points to* (c)].

STEELE: [The diagram is] kinda crunched.

GABRIEL: [to audience] Okay, so we switched chairmen. The other interesting thing, which is not noted on here, is the extreme reaction against Common Lisp; we'll come back to that later. [*In fact, they didn't.*]

STEELE: Here is a picture of the Scheme extended family [Figure 6.9], and there are three points to be noted here. One is that this is a two-part story where Scheme represents a very sudden left-hand turn. Everything that happened before Scheme was a series of developments of a series of AI-oriented languages, actually going all the way back to COMIT, which was a very early string processing, pattern matching language at MIT. One of the notable offshoots of COMIT is that it had an influence on SNOBOL, but SNOBOL then did not have a lot of direct influence on Lisp; but it's interesting to note it is a cousin of Scheme though a very distant connection. COMIT also spawned an implementation of COMIT in Lisp, which was called Meteor—there is an obvious pun there—that was done by Danny

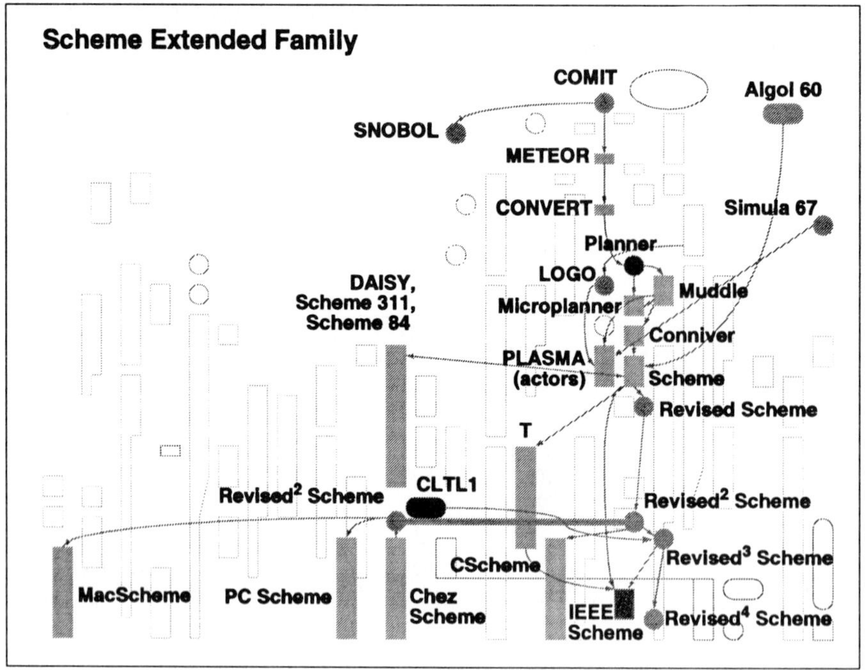

FIGURE 6.9

Bobrow also, actually—and then after that there was a version of a pattern matching language called Convert, done by Adolfo Guzman at MIT, which was a redesign as a Lisp-embedded pattern matching language; it was used for some AI applications. Convert then had an influence on Carl Hewitt's Planner, as described in his doctoral dissertation, and then Planner spawned a bunch of ideas, and what then began was what can be characterized as a debate, or an argument, between Carl Hewitt and Gerry Sussman and their respective students about how languages to support AI should be designed and how complicated control structure should be done. Sussman worked on the Muddle project, which was inspired by some of the ideas of Planner, and also on MicroPlanner and some others. Conniver was a response to Planner, suggesting that all the automated mechanisms of Planner that happened under the table to do coroutining and backtracking should be brought out and made explicit and put under the control of the programmer. And so Conniver was a coroutinist's dream.

Scheme was originally called Schemer, and it was conceived of as another in the series of Planner and Conniver and so forth, and the name got truncated because file names on the PDP-10 were limited to six characters. [*loud laughter and applause*] And we decided that that was an okay name, too.

Scheme was an attempt to implement some of the actors ideas that Carl Hewitt had put in his language PLASMA, which had a very complicated and elaborate syntax. We were trying to strip it down to its barest essentials. After we had implemented a version of Lisp, we decided to give it lexical scoping as in ALGOL—there's the ALGOL 60 influence—rather than the dynamic scoping that had been typical of Lisp 1.5, largely because Sussman had been studying ALGOL 60 and teaching it in a course and wanted to try that idea, too, and he thought it would work with actors.

When we got the whole thing implemented, we discovered that the code for implementing lexical closures and the code for implementing actors were identical—and this was discovered empirically—and we said, "Oh, I see! Actors are just closures of lambda expressions." Well, there is a little bit more to it than that, but suddenly we realized that Scheme was just a dialect of Lisp, rather than a complicated AI language. And at the point below that is the second part of the story, which is that Scheme, being a very small, simple version of Lisp, spawned a bunch of new dialects. There is a version at Yale called T, and there are a bunch of others that I haven't shown; there's work done at Indiana, by Dan Friedman and Dave Wise and their students, which was actually quite a hotbed of Scheme activity, and actually some Lisp activity even before Scheme got started—they influenced some of the early ideas of Scheme.

And we see a pattern here, hanging below Scheme, that is very much like the pattern that appears below Lisp 1.5, which is that a small simple idea suddenly could be implemented by a bunch of people and they could start to play with it, and we saw a large spawning of a bunch of implementations, which then got together and began to try to do some standards efforts. These green ovals, which are not on the master slide, show a series of revised Scheme reports—which are informal standards—and the third revision spawned the effort to produce the IEEE Scheme standard.

GABRIEL: The next thing we're going to see is the object-oriented influence, and this slide [Figure 6.10] is interesting for a couple of reasons. It's one of the few slides that show ideas and influence going one way and then the other, geographically. So, as we can see, one of the things that spawned all this off, of course, is the Simula 67 work, which influenced the Smalltalk work that we will hear about from Alan Kay later today. There is some question here about exactly how the Smalltalk work influenced the PLASMA and the Flavors work. The way that we interpreted it is that Smalltalk 71, as it's called, was the thing that influenced Carl Hewitt in a meeting that you can read about in our paper *and* in Alan's paper, where they got together and talked about the implementation of these sorts of languages. The later Smalltalk, which we call Smalltalk 72, had sort of a direct influence on Flavors;

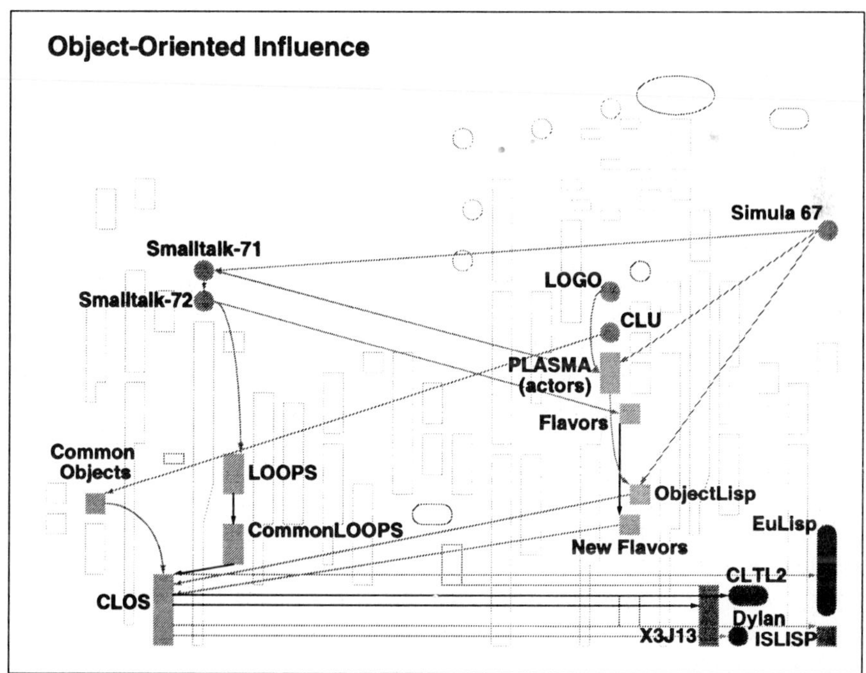

FIGURE 6.10

several of the MIT folks had visited Xerox PARC, seen the idea, and said, "Yeah, we can do that a little bit better."

Now, one of the things this made us think about is, a lot of the other slides that you've seen have shown ideas originating here [at MIT] and spreading out. And we think that it's not so much because there's so many great ideas that come from MIT; rather, that MIT is a little more parochial, a little more inbred, and doesn't pay attention as much as the rest of the world to what's going on, so ideas tend to move away from here because ideas don't move *in* so much. [*laughter*] Sort of an extreme way of putting it. [*laughter*] The other thing is, MIT—well, you don't get a high salary, so people leave, and so they take their ideas with them. This is a contrast here, where we see the ideas coming back over.

Now, LOOPS, the Lisp Object-Oriented Programming System, is kind of an offshoot of Interlisp and is relatively Smalltalk-like. CommonLoops and CLOS [Gabriel consistently pronounced this "see-loss"], on the other hand, are very different. CommonLoops and CLOS attempt to merge the pseudo-functional programming style of Lisp with the object-oriented style, so that you have generic functions rather than message passing. In addition, from Flavors and New Flavors, CommonLoops and CLOS have multiple inheritance, also method combination, and a lot of other exotic object-oriented technology.

CLOS itself was an activity of X3J13, and I've listed a couple of other influences, namely Object Lisp and Common Objects. Object Lisp is probably a relatively direct decendent of actors—it's a delegation-based object-oriented system. And Common Objects, done by Alan Snyder, is sort of an encapsulation-heavy type of system. I have listed influences here, but they are negative influences. The CLOS group decided to explicitly ignore Object Lisp Common Objects. CLOS, as you can see, has influenced quite a lot of work, both here and in Europe. Dylan, ISLisp (which is the ISO standard Lisp), and EuLisp all use a variant of CLOS.

STEELE: Now I'd like to discuss the influence of the lambda calculus [Figure 6.11] on the development of Lisp. Those who have not studied Lisp very closely are aware that Lisp has lambda expressions, and that lambda calculus started that, and so forth. If you read McCarthy's paper in the first HOPL conference, he explains there that primarily what was borrowed from the lambda calculus was the lambda *notation* but not its precise *semantics*; rather, it was used in a slightly different way. Functions in Lisp 1.5 give dynamic scoping to their variables, rather than lexical scoping adhering to something like the ALGOL copy rule. So the notation came in there.

A second influence sort of focuses down here on Scheme and also on Lisp370, where through a series of influences—including Peter Landin's work on SECD machines and on ISWIM, and Evans' work on PAL, and Reynolds' work (particularly the "Definitional Interpreters" paper at the ACM '72 conference, which was a very strong influence on Sussman and me)—by these various intermediaries, Scheme and Lisp370 were led to implement lexical scoping, thereby preserving substitutability of expressions in a way that Lisp 1.5 did not.

The third influence of the lambda calculus is that, more recently, purely functional languages appeared, the so-called "functional languages," some of which are Lisp-like in syntax and some are not, but they are very clearly Lisp-like in spirit. I think the current culmination may be described as Haskell, which is a project that was done at Yale and other places, and that was in turn influenced by implementations of ML and Hope, which were in turn influenced by Landin. The influence coming in from lambda calculus is normal order reduction, that is, guaranteeing that if there is a normal form result for your computation, the interpreter will find it; this is not guaranteed in the case of Scheme or Lisp 1.5.

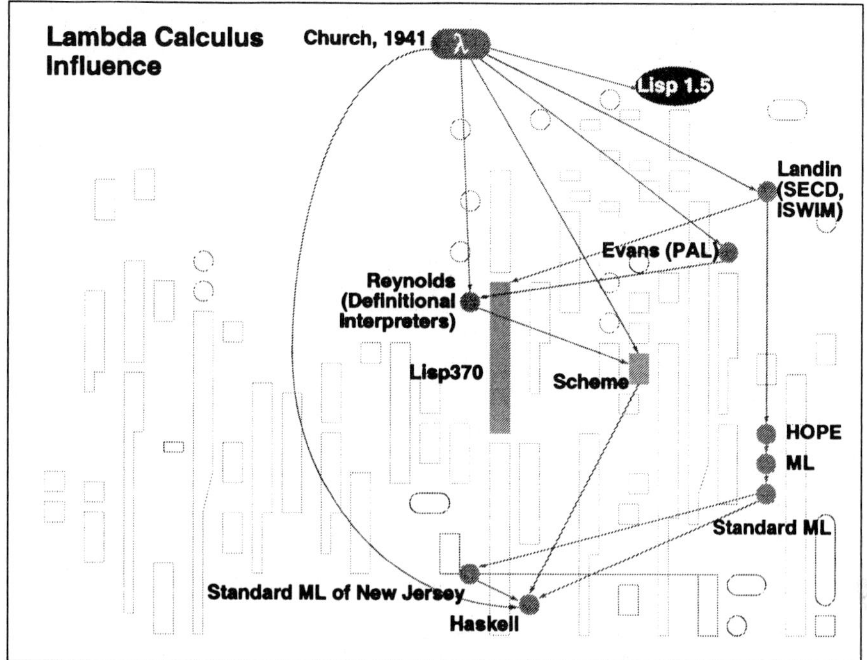

FIGURE 6.11

I guess the point to be made is that there is an interesting progression as Lisp moves onward, going back to its roots in lambda calculus, and discovering, in several cycles, there is more there in lambda calculus than we thought and the closer we get to lambda calculus, the better the language gets.

GABRIEL: Moving from the sublime to the ridiculous, [*laughter*] the influence of FORTRAN [Figure 6.12] is relatively minor. This influence up here is merely that the first Lisp was the FORTRAN List Processing Language [FLPL], implemented in FORTRAN. The second influence is basically complex numbers. [*For lack of time, Gabriel omitted mention of the influence of FORTRAN on* **FORMAT** *in Lisp-Machine Lisp.*]

[to Steele] I guess we've got four minutes.

STEELE: [to Gabriel] Right, okay.

[to audience] I've been on a number of standards committees where people say, "Well, this is an issue that can be decided in the FORTRAN community, because only FORTRAN worries about, say, complex numbers." And I'd pop up and say, "Well, there's also Common Lisp." And [when they'd add] "Only FORTRAN has **FORMAT**," I'd say, "Well, there's also Common Lisp."

Now we'd like to show you a series of peregrinations of some key individuals who were involved with Lisp projects. First we'd like to show you what happened with John McCarthy [Figure 6.13]. He worked at MIT for some time, and then in the mid-to-late-60s moved to Stanford. The important thing there is that he took PDP-1 Lisp with him, and this is how Lisp got started on the West Coast. That was a key migration, even if a short story.

GABRIEL: The next guy is Danny Bobrow [Figure 6.14], who started here at MIT, worked on another PDP-1 Lisp, worked on a PDP-6 Lisp, worked on BBN-Lisp, and moved to the West Coast, where he

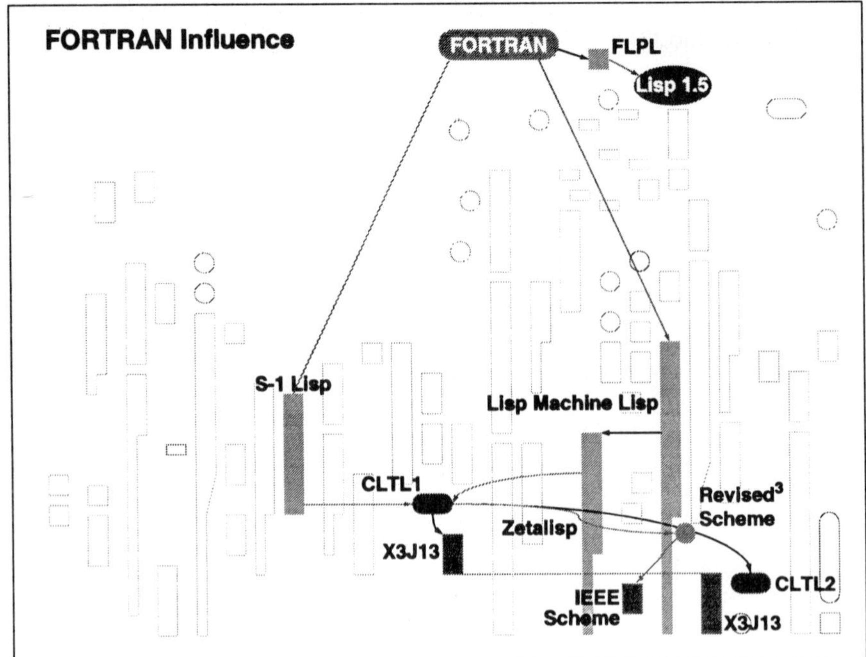

FIGURE 6.12

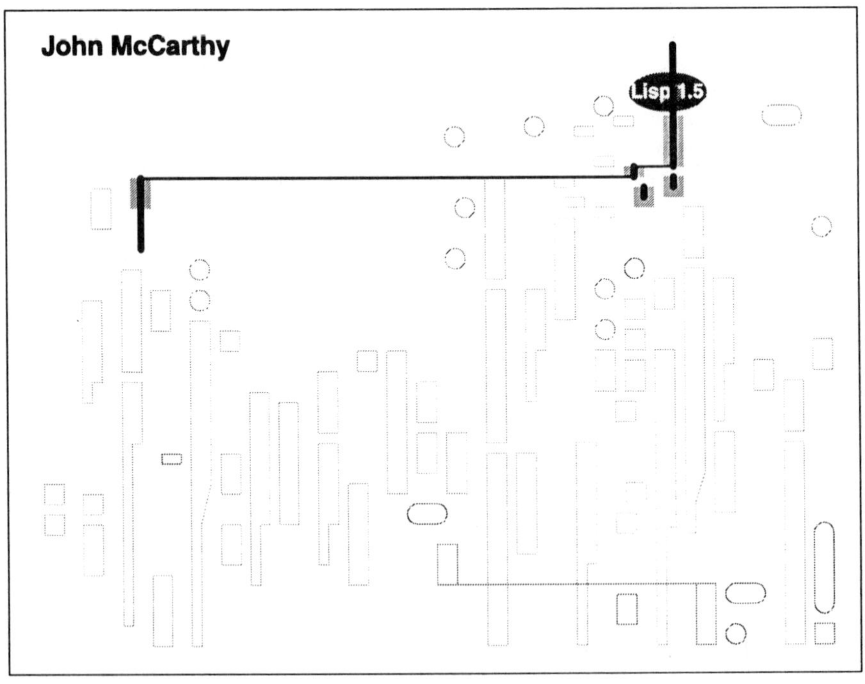

FIGURE 6.13

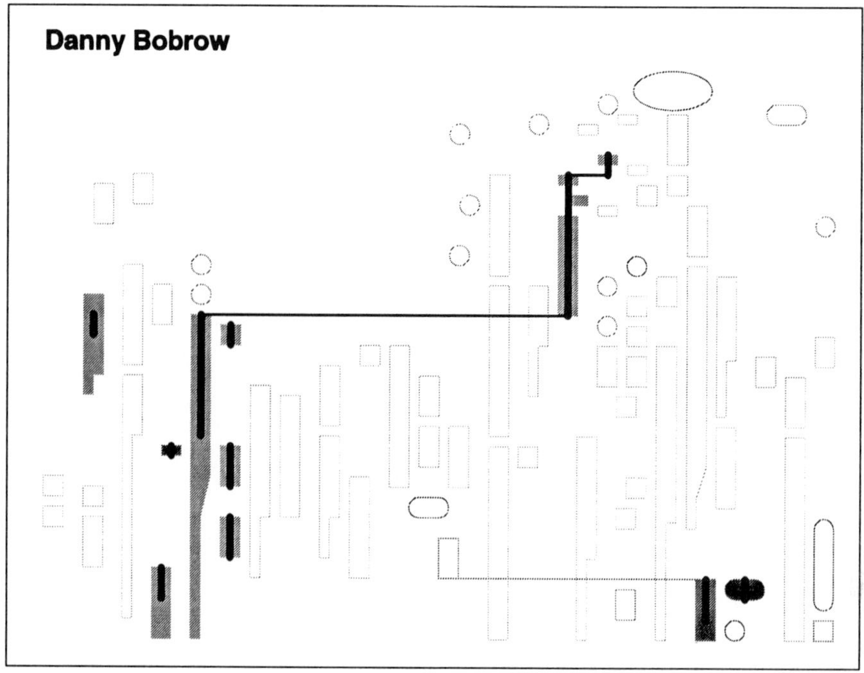

FIGURE 6.14

still is. This shows that he worked on UCI Lisp, spaghetti stacks, LOOPS, CommonLoops, and CLOS. He was involved in X3J13 and also worked on CLTL2.

STEELE: There is another individual whose path parallels Danny Bobrow's to some extent, which is Warren Teitelman, who also went from MIT and worked on Interlisp at Xerox; those two were the very strong influence from MIT on the Interlisp effort.

Here's the path of Dick Gabriel [Figure 6.15], who got started on MacLisp at MIT, moved to Illinois—I've already discussed the influence of his Illinois presence, eventually, on IBM Lisp there—and from Illinois he went to Stanford and has been on the West Coast ever since then, except for a diversion for one summer to CMU, where he and I worked together on S-1 Lisp, which is shown here [in California] geographically, but actually, wherever we were, we were working on that. He was also involved in a large number of standards efforts, in Europe as well as in the U.S.

GABRIEL: From the ridiculous to the sublime, Guy Steele. [*laughter*] Guy Steele [Figure 6.16] started here at MIT and then, through a series of trips out to the West Coast to work with me on S-1 Lisp, sort of bounced back and forth, and eventually went back to CMU and worked on Common Lisp. He was involved in a lot of the standards activities, worked on NIL, worked on Scheme, did a lot of stuff—but you know that.

STEELE: Here are the travels of David Moon [Figure 6.17], and while he's geographically been in Cambridge, he's moved from project to project and carried a bunch of ideas back and forth. He got started working on Multics MacLisp. He was supporting the Multics implementation at the same time that I was working on the PDP-10 implementation. Then he was one of the principal implementors of the software for the Lisp Machine, and then moved over to Symbolics, and then has recently gone to Apple, where he's been working on the Dylan project.

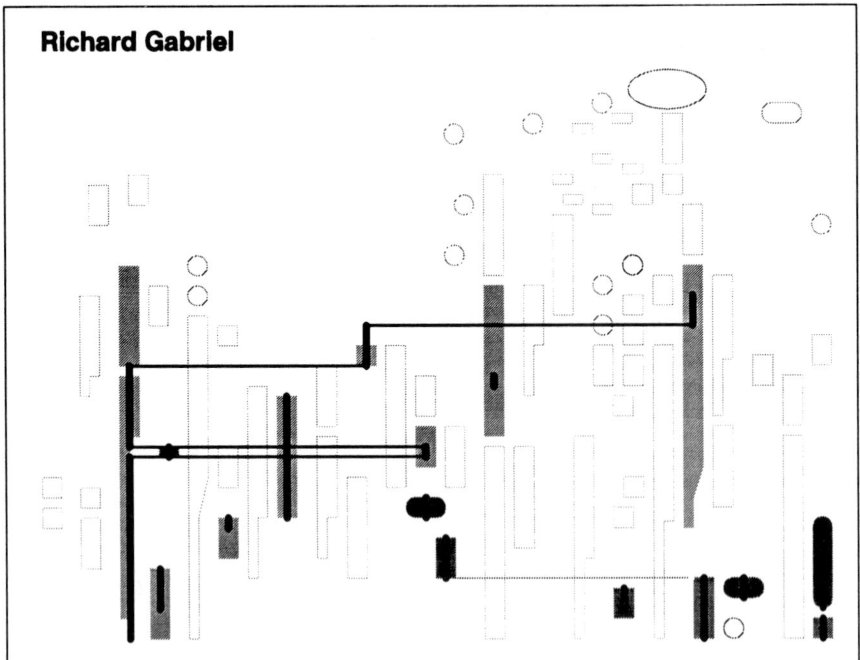

FIGURE 6.15

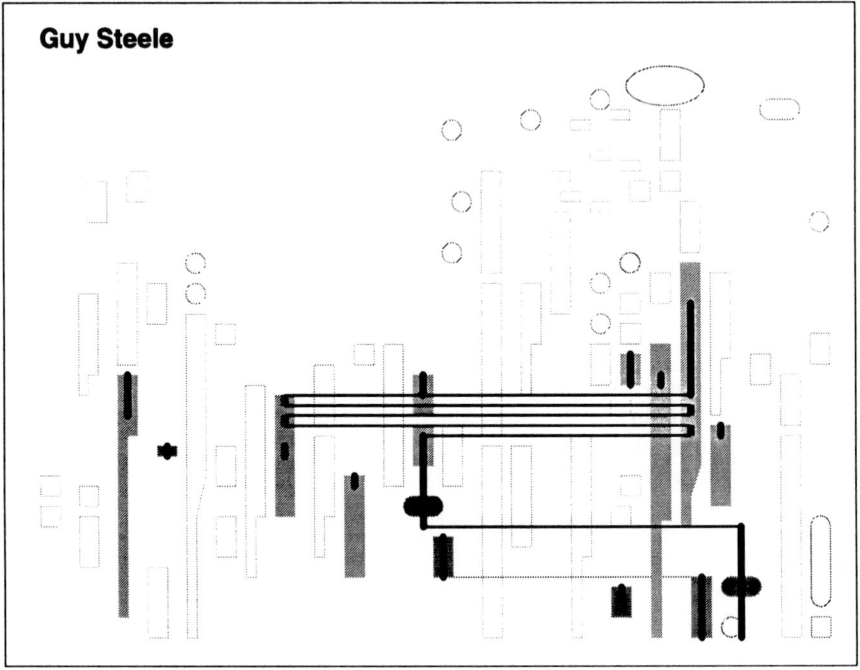

FIGURE 6.16

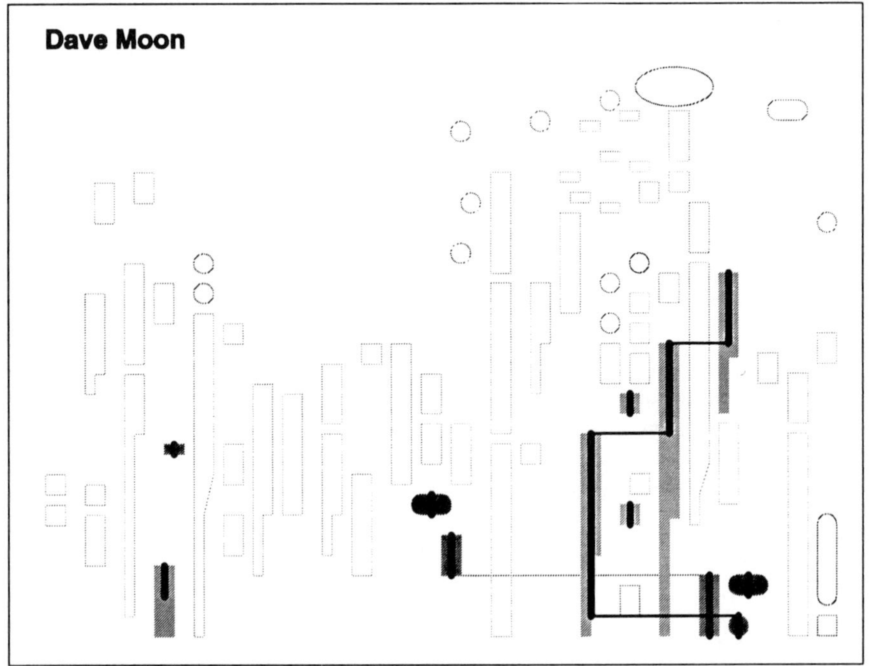

FIGURE 6.17

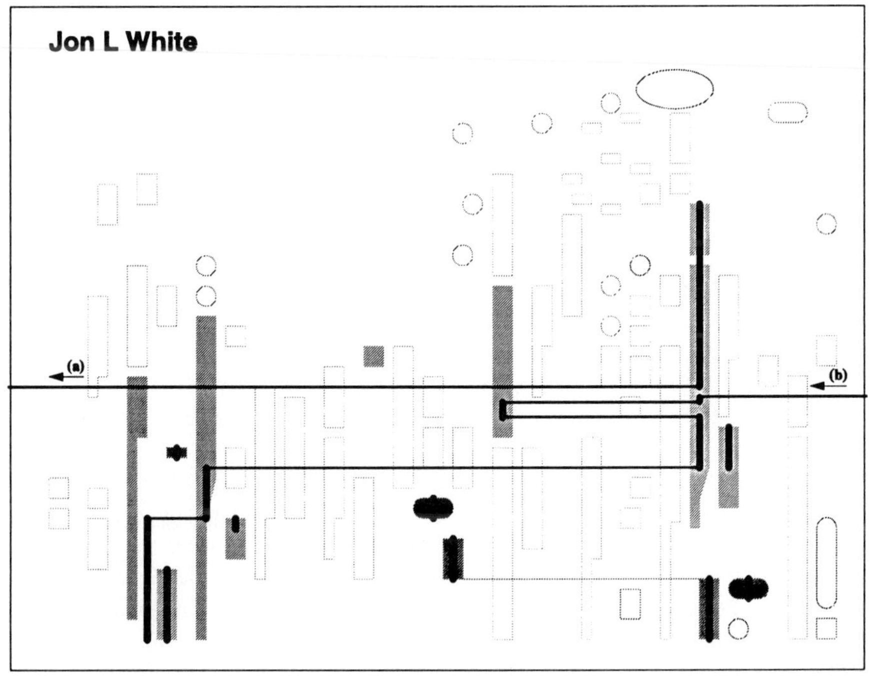

FIGURE 6.18

GABRIEL: Finally, there's Jon L White [Figure 6.18], who kind of disappears. He started here at MIT; he was the progenitor primarily of MacLisp. He took a trip to India [*points to* (a)] [*laughter*], came back [*points to* (b)] [*laughter and applause*] to work on MacLisp, went to IBM Yorktown to work on Lisp370, came back to work on MacLisp, went to Xerox to work on Interlisp, then left there and went to work for Lucid, where he works on Common Lisp. He has worked on all of these things—one of the few people who has switched among major families.

STEELE: Okay, do your sliding slot; I think we need to finish.

GABRIEL: [*During this last bit, Gabriel took a piece of opaque paper with a narrow horizontal slot cut in it and moved it over the overhead for Figure 6.1 from top to bottom so as to reveal horizontal slices through the diagram, thereby converting the vertical axis representing time into an actual time axis.*] One of the things that we've noticed is that if you look at the history as a little bit of a slice, you can see what things look like at different times [*bell rings, indicating end of allotted time, but Gabriel is allowed to finish his sentence*]—the number of implementations and dialects is scattered, kind of blooms in the middle of the 70s, starts to taper off, and ends up with a lot of standards activities (which never happened before) and only a very few dialects, showing that, possibly, the history is dying off. [*applause*]

TRANSCRIPT OF DISCUSSANT'S REMARKS

RANDY HUDSON: John Foderaro received a B.S. in Computer Science and Mathematics from the Pennsylvania State University in 1977. That year he began his graduate work at the University of California at Berkeley. His research focus was programming languages for symbolic algebraic systems. He worked on the design and implementation of Franz Lisp and on the design and implementation and testing of RISC in microprocessors. In 1983 he received his Ph.D. from Berkeley. The following year he co-founded Franz Inc. to support the Franz Lisp language and to implement Common Lisp.

JOHN FODERARO: Franz Lisp began in 1978 when DEC introduced the VAX minicomputer. I was at Berkeley at this point working with Richard Fateman on symbolic algebra systems. We had been using the MACSYMA system at MIT through the ARPANET. In fact, we had a very slow connection to the ARPANET, a 300-baud modem. So we wanted a version of Lisp and a version of MACSYMA on a local machine so we could actually do a little research on it.

The VAX was a great machine. It is a 32-bit flat-address-space machine, and it looked ideal for Lisp. At the time MIT had also received a VAX and we assumed they would come up with a Lisp and we would simply use their Lisp and get on with our work on symbolic algebra. Their Lisp was called NIL. As a stopgap we decided to work on Lisp anyway. It began as a port of Harvard Lisp. I am not sure where its origins are. Harvard Lisp ran on a PDP-11, written in an assembler language and was a very tiny interpreter in Lisp. A bunch of grad students took that, rewrote it in C, and brought it up on the VAX.

When it came time to give a name to this Lisp, we assumed this Lisp would be thrown away in a year so we were not thinking seriously about a name. Richard Fateman suggested the name Franz Lisp as a joke. We said, "It sounds pretty funny; let's use that name." We never thought the Lisp would ever leave Berkeley. It turned out that NIL never got out. I am not sure what its current state is now. It was lacking a garbage collector the last time I checked. NIL was more of an idea than a real implementation, probably because at MIT they had Lisp machines that were more interesting to play with than VAX's. So Franz Lisp actually was successful. A couple of names were not in the paper and

I want to mention their contribution: Keith Sklower was a staff programmer working for Richard Fateman. He did a lot of the work on the interpreter on Franz Lisp and the garbage collector and the bignum package and so on. Kevin Layer came on a little later. He was the first person to port Franz Lisp with another architecture. He ported it to a 68K and then went on to add a lot of Common-Lisp type features like packages and so on to it. They made significant contributions. There are other people throughout the world who added to Franz Lisp, too numerous to mention. But one I would like to mention is Tom London of Bell Labs who wrote the first compiler for Franz Lisp, a really excellent piece of work. My interest was actually in compilers. I actually wrote a few more compilers for Franz Lisp. That was my main focus.

I guess I should point out that Franz Lisp was actually successful. We ported MACSYMA to the VAX using it, basically adding MacLisp-like features to it. We were able to do a lot of work in symbolic algebra using Franz Lisp. When we first got our VAX it was only a half megabyte of memory and ran a swapping version of Unix, which came from Bell Labs. Both of these things meant it was really painful to use Lisp on this machine. It was a multi-user machine. We were trying to maybe share the machine with 20 people, and a half megabyte of memory doesn't give you much room. So we desperately needed a virtual memory, large address space Unix system. A couple of grad students at the university got interested in writing one, one of them being Bill Joy. They did a very good job of that, and as a result, this version of Unix, which was called Vmunix was distributed around the world. The everyday distribution of that Vmunix came with a set of tools from Berkeley, one of them being Franz Lisp. As a result of that, Franz Lisp ended up being installed as a standard piece of software on about 40,000 machines around the world. Contrast this to the other Lisp you saw in that diagram: most of them are either ones or twos, maybe they worked on one machine, maybe they were someone's idea of a Lisp, but this one actually got around. As a result of that, I think we helped propagate the idea of Lisp to a lot of people who never would have thought of using it. Even though on many of those machines, I would admit, people didn't actually use Lisp, on some of the machines, there were classes given. We estimate probably around 20,000 people actually used Franz Lisp throughout its lifetime—maybe more.

The paper mentioned that Franz Lisp was written entirely in C. Actually, it was written about 1/3 in C and 2/3 in Lisp, as typical for Lisp at that time. The fact that it was written in C is kind of unusual. At the time, most Lisp systems had an assembler language base. In fact, the NIL Lisp that was sort of our contemporary, I think, was designed with an assembler language kernel. We used C because that is what you did in Unix. C is the base for everything. I think nowadays people would sort of hesitate about starting out any large project written in an assembly language.

One particular feature of Franz Lisp that I want to mention is the foreign function interface. I think that is a major contribution and that its effects really have not been fully realized in the Lisp community. But I think it will be in the years to come. We had a symbolic algebra system, but we also did numerical work. We wanted access to large FORTRAN libraries, namely the IMSL libraries. We didn't want to have to decode them in Lisp, as people were doing, I understand, for Lisp machines. So we developed a system by which we could dynamically load in programs written in other languages, such as FORTRAN, C, or Pascal, and create automatic linkage functions from Lisp to those functions and call them just as if they were normal Lisp functions. We coined the phrase *foreign function interface* to describe this idea of talking to other languages. This has had a major effect on how I use the Lisp and how I think others have. First of all, no longer is the Lisp programmer kind of isolated. There are a lot more C programmers out there than there are Lisp programmers, and they are developing libraries, both math and graphic libraries. Lisp programmers used to have to sit by themselves and either recode the algorithms in Lisp or else just not use them. But with the foreign function interface people can actually load in C code well as the C programmer can. It is actually easier for Lisp people to use C code than a C programmer because Lisp programmers can dynamically call out to the C functions through the interpreter. We could actually test C code and get back and try different values without having to recode the main program. So we had a really good connection to all the C functions. We could actually start with what the C programmer had and quickly build on it and generate nice environments.

The second effect is Lisp has always had a problem doing numerical work. Lisp is a great language for symbolic systems; it is a great language for doing object-oriented programming. It has the best object-oriented programming system now; CLOS is the most flexible but it has always had a problem doing numerical work because Lisp wants to keep track of all the types of all the objects at run time so we can do run-time dispatching, debugging, and so on.

There have been stabs at making good numerical compilers for Lisp but it requires the user to do lots of declarations and ensure that inside a loop he doesn't do strange things that would cause values that have to be boxed and stored in the heap.

Through using the foreign function interface, users can now think of their applications in chunks. There is a numerical part, which they can code in their favorite numerical language be it C or FORTRAN, and the control portion, which they can code in Lisp. No longer does the Lisp compiler have to be large and massive and have great knowledge of great compilation. They can divide that portion off and let the C or FORTRAN compiler worry about that. Lisp systems, in particular Common Lisp, are really a huge language. I think needlessly so. Common Lisp has a huge numerical component. It is not a Common Lisp program unless it can do inverse hyperbolic arc tangent. This is just ridiculous. It was put in there because some people thought it might be interesting, but I bet not one person in ten thousand has ever used that for the reason it was there, other than to test on whether it works. That never should have been put in Common Lisp. If the designers of Common Lisp had gotten the idea that we should separate out what Lisp can do well from what FORTRAN and C do well, then we could let programs be built as a combination of the two languages. I think in the future Lisp will be used more as a control language for computational systems than as a whole complete language.

TRANSCRIPT OF QUESTION AND ANSWER SESSION

HUDSON: We have time for some questions now. Our first question is from Alan Kay of Apple: When and how did you realize how great Lisp is in the meta sense?

STEELE: I can report that I first cut my teeth on APL and thought that was the world's most wonderful programming language. I still have a great deal of respect for it, and this is one of the reasons it had so much influence on the design on Common Lisp and some other dialects. I was convinced that Lisp was completely wrong-headed and made no sense at all. I tried to read the Lisp 1.5 manual and discovered it was trying to define the language in terms of itself; it was just not at all well-founded, and made no sense at all. A year later I had this sudden conversion, decided on an implementation, and then understood what the real idea was. So I would say that it was about 1972 when I suddenly realized how it hung together. It was difficult to glean from the 1.5 manual.

GABRIEL: My answer is the same, but with different details.

HUDSON: (From Stavros Macrakis, OSF Research Institute): Earlier Lisps tend to have one dialect per architecture since interpreters weren't portable. Ideas had to move by re-implementation. How have portable implementations changed the dynamics of innovation?

STEELE: I would say that innovation has decreased as portability has increased, but I think there is a chicken and egg problem there. I am not sure which is the effect.

GABRIEL: I think that people, now that they are trying to do portable systems, spend more time trying to make sure that they are implementing the same dialect, time that otherwise they would spend on great new ideas, so I think it has tended to slow things down. Also, standardization is freezing progress, and portability kind of implies standardization.

STEELE: A lot of the intellectual ferment in the Lisp community was with the InterLisp and MacLisp groups during the 70s. Once Common Lisp got started, that tended to freeze the MacLisp ideas, as you might expect. We saw the epicenter of this intellectual ferment and innovation transferred into the Scheme community. And Scheme proceeded to innovate in a number of ways, including the development of hygienic macros and some other things. Once the IEEE and then ANSI Scheme standardization efforts got going, that set of ideas tended to gel. I would say that now the locus of intellectual activity is probably within the Haskell group. This worries me a little bit, because while I think there are some really good ideas going on in Haskell, they have also abandoned some ideas that made Lisp very usable. I have been trying to use Haskell myself for the last year and have had mixed results. I have been very happy with some aspects of the language, particularly support for automatic currying. That is a much more expressive device than I thought I understood in the 70s. On the other hand, I found it very frustrating that I was trying to write program-transforming programs in Haskell and it doesn't come with a built-in parser the way Lisp does. So the first thing I had to do was to reinvent a bunch of tools in Haskell that I was used to having with the Lisp system before I could even get started. I am hoping that Haskell implementers will take that to heart.

HUDSON: (A question from Scott Guthrey of Schlumberger): A chart you didn't show is the use of Lisp in commercial systems. What would that chart look like?

STEELE: We actually thought of that chart and ran out of steam last night. That chart would look like this one, and you would see companies appear in the late 70s and early 80s and you would see more and more of them progressing towards the 90s. We are beginning to see some of them die off again in the computational marketplace. What are some of the ones that have disappeared, Dick?

GABRIEL: Teknowledge has kind of disappeared. They are down to a very small number. A whole raft of them disappeared.

STEELE: They came and they are going!

BIOGRAPHY OF GUY L. STEELE JR.

Guy L. Steele Jr. received his A.B. in applied mathematics from Harvard College (1975), and his S.M. and Ph.D. in computer science and artificial intelligence from M.I.T. (1977 and 1980). He has been an assistant professor of computer science at Carnegie-Mellon University; a member of technical staff at Tartan Laboratories in Pittsburgh, Pennsylvania; and a senior scientist at Thinking Machines Corporation.

He is author or coauthor of three books: *Common Lisp: The Language* (Digital Press); *C: A Reference Manual* (Prentice-Hall); and The Hacker's Dictionary (Harper&Row), which has been revised as The New Hacker's Dictionary, edited by Eric Raymond with introduction and illustrations by Guy Steele (MIT Press).

He has published more than two dozen papers on the subject of the Lisp language and Lisp implementation, including a series with Gerald Jay Sussman that defined the Scheme dialect of Lisp. One of these, "Multiprocessing Compactifying Garbage Collection," won first place in the ACM 1975 George E. Forsythe Student Paper Competition. Other papers published in are "Design of a

LISP–Based Microprocessor" with Gerald Jay Sussman (November 1980) and "Data Parallel Algorithms" with W. Daniel Hillis (December 1986). He has also published papers on other subjects, including compilers, parallel processing, and constraint languages. One song he composed has been published in the *Communications of the ACM* ("The Telnet Song," April 1984).

The Association for Computing Machinery awarded him the 1988 Grace Murray Hopper Award. He was elected a Fellow of the American Association for Artificial Intelligence in 1990. He led the team that received a 1990 Gordon Bell Prize honorable mention for achieving the fastest speed to that date for a production application: 14.182 Gigaflops.

He has served on accredited standards committees X3J11 (C language) and X3J3 (FORTRAN) and is currently chairman of X3J13 (Common Lisp). He was also a member of the IEEE committee that produced the IEEE Standard for the Scheme Programming Language, IEEE Std 1178-1990. He represents Thinking Machines Corporation in the High Performance FORTRAN Forum.

He has served on Ph.D. thesis committees for seven students. He has served as program chair for the 1984 ACM Conference on Lisp and Functional Programming and for the 15th ACM Symposium on Principles of Programming Languages (1988); he also served on program committees for 30 other conferences. He served a five-year term on the ACM Turing Award committee, chairing it in 1990. He served a five-year term on the ACM Grace Murray Hopper Award committee, chairing it in 1992.

He has had chess problems published in *Chess Life and Review* and is a Life Member of the United States Chess Federation. He has sung in the bass section of the MIT Choral Society (John Oliver, conductor) and the Masterworks Chorale (Allen Lannom, conductor) as well as in choruses with the Pittsburgh Symphony Orchestra at Great Woods (Michael Tilson Thomas, conductor) and with the Boston Concert Opera (David Stockton, conductor). He has played the role of Lun Tha in *The King and I* and the title role in *Li'l Abner*. His "Crunchly" cartoons appear in *The New Hacker's Dictionary*. He designed the original EMACS command set and was the first person to port TeX.

BIOGRAPHY OF RICHARD P. GABRIEL

Richard P. Gabriel received his Ph.D. in Computer Science from Stanford University in 1981. He has been a researcher at Stanford University, a company president and Chief Technical Officer of Lucid, Inc., and a Consulting Professor of Computer Science at Stanford University.

He helped design and implement a variety of dialects of Lisp. He is author of one book, *Performance and Evaluation of Lisp Systems* (MIT Press). He has published more than 100 scientific, technical, and semi-popular papers, articles, and essays on computing.

He is the lead guitarist in a working rock 'n' roll band and a poet.

VII

Prolog Session

Chair: *Randy Hudson*
Discussant: *Jacques Cohen*

THE BIRTH OF PROLOG

Alain Colmerauer

Faculté des Sciences de Luminy
163 avenue de Luminy
13288 Marseille cedex 9, France

Philippe Roussel

Université de Nice–Sophia Antipolis, CNRS, Bat 4
250 Avenue Albert Einstein
06560 Valbonne, France

ABSTRACT

The programming language, Prolog, was born of a project aimed not at producing a programm3ing language but at processing natural languages; in this case, French. The project gave rise to a preliminary version of Prolog at the end of 1971 and a more definitive version at the end of 1972. This article gives the history of this project and describes in detail the preliminary and then the final versions of Prolog. The authors also felt it appropriate to describe the Q-systems because it was a language that played a prominent part in Prolog's genesis.

CONTENTS

7.1 INTRODUCTION

As is well known, the name "Prolog" was invented in Marseilles in 1972. Philippe Roussel chose the name as an abbreviation for "PROgrammation en LOGique" to refer to the software tool designed to implement a man-machine communication system in natural language. It can be said that Prolog was the offspring of a successful marriage between natural language processing and automated theorem-proving. The idea of using a natural language such as French to reason and communicate directly with a computer seemed like a crazy idea, yet this was the basis of the project set up by Alain Colmerauer in the summer of 1970. Alain had some experience in the computer processing of natural languages and wanted to expand his research.

We have now presented the two coauthors of this article—Alain Colmerauer and Philippe Roussel—but clearly, as in any project of this kind, many other people were involved. To remain objective in our account of how Prolog—a language that is now already twenty years old—came to be, we took a second look at all the documents still in our possession, and played the part of historians. To begin with, we followed the chronology in order to present the facts and describe the participants over the time from the summer of 1970 until the end of 1976. This constitutes the first part of the article. The other parts are of a more technical nature. They are devoted to three programming languages that rapidly succeeded one another: Q-systems, conceived for machine translation; the preliminary version of Prolog, created at the same time as its application; and the definitive version of Prolog, created independently of any application.

This paper is not the first to be written about the history of Prolog. We must mention the paper written by Jacques Cohen [1988], which directly concerns Prolog, and the paper by Robert Kowalski [1988] about the birth of "Logic Programming" as a discipline. Also worthy of attention are the history of automated theorem-proving as described by Donald Loveland [1984] and the prior existence of the Absys language, a possible competitor with Prolog in the opinion of E. Elcok [1988].

7.2 PART I. THE HISTORY

At the beginning of July 1970, Robert Pasero and Philippe arrived in Montreal. They had been invited by Alain who was then Assistant Professor of Computer Science at the University of Montreal and was leading the automatic translation project, TAUM (Traduction Automatique de l'Université de Montréal). All were at turning points in their careers. Robert and Philippe were then 25 years old and had just been awarded teaching positions in Computer Science at the new Luminy Science Faculty. Alain was 29 years old and, after a three-year stay in Canada, was soon to return to France.

During their two-month stay in Montreal, Robert and Philippe familiarized themselves with the computer processing of natural languages. They wrote several nondeterministic context-free analyzers in Algol 60 and a French paraphrase generator using Q-systems, the programming language which Alain had developed for the translation project (see Part II).

At the same time, Jean Trudel, a Canadian researcher and a doctoral student of Alain's, had chosen to work on automated theorem-proving. His point of reference was Alan Robinson's article [1965] on the resolution principle. It was a difficult article to understand in 1970, but Jean had the advantage of having taken a course in logic given by Martin Davis in New York. He had already developed a complete theorem prover in which unification was written in an up-to-date programming style: all the computations consisted in modifying pointers.

7.2.1 1971: The First Steps

At the beginning of 1971, everyone was back in Marseilles. Alain had obtained a teaching position in Computer Science (maître de conférence) and Jean Trudel had been able to accompany him, thanks to a two-year grant from Hydro-Quebec. The project was to make deductions based on texts written in French. The work was divided up as follows: Jean Trudel and Philippe worked on the deduction part, Robert Pasero and Alain on the natural language part.

We had access to a machine at the Marseilles university computing center: an IBM 360-44 installed in our department, offering approximately 900Kb of internal memory and equipped with an operating system without virtual memory. By means of an interactive monitor developed by Jean Trudel and by using the machine at night to take advantage of all the available memory, we were able to work under conditions which, in France at that time, were exceptionally good: practically 1Mb of memory to execute the programs and an interactive mode for communications between users and programs via the operator's console.

Jean Trudel improved his prover and then, beginning in May, Philippe produced a whole series of provers written in Algol-W. A primitive natural-language communication system was then developed by the entire team [Colmerauer 1971]. The interfaces between the logical formulæ and French consisted of 50 Q-system rules for the input and 17 Q-system rules for the output. The reasoning part was implemented through one of Philippe's provers. It was thus possible to have the following conversation with the computer:

```
User
Cats kill mice.
Tom is a cat who does not like mice who eat cheese.
Jerry is a mouse who eats cheese.
Max is not a mouse.
What does Tom do?
Computer
Tom does not like mice who eat cheese.
Tom kills mice.
User
Who is a cat?
Computer
Tom.
User
What does Jerry eat?
Computer
Cheese.
User
Who does not like mice who eat cheese?
Computer
Tom.
User
What does Tom eat?
Computer
What cats who do not like mice who eat cheese eat.
```

The logical formulæ created made use of: (i) constants representing elements,

```
Tom, Jerry, Max, Cheese;
```

(ii) constants representing sets,

```
Cats, Mice, MiceWhoEatCheese, CatsWhoDoNotLikeMiceWhoEatCheese;
```

(iii) constants representing binary relations between sets,

```
Kill, DoesNotLike, Eat;
```

(iv) a functional symbol of arity 1 and two relational symbols of arity 2 and 3,

`The, Subset, True.`

A term of the form `The(a)` was taken to represent the set consisting only of the element `a`. A formula of the form `Subset(x,y)` expressed the inclusion of set `x` in set `y` and a formula of the form `True(r,x,y)` expressed that the sets `x` and `y` were in the relation `r`. To the clauses that encoded the sentences, Jean Trudel added four clauses relating the three symbols `The, Subset, True`:

```
(∀x)[Subset(x,x)],
(∀x)( ∀y)(∀z)[Subset(x,y)∧Subset(y,z) ⇒ Subset(x,z)],
(∀a)(∀b)[Subset(The(a),The(b)) ⇒ Subset(The(b),The(a))],
(∀x)(∀y)(∀r)(∀x')(∀y')
[True(r,x,y)∧Subset(x,x')∧Subset(y,y') ⇒ True(r,x',y')].
```

The main problem was to avoid untimely production of inferences due to the transitivity and reflexivity axioms of the inclusion relation `Subset`.

While continuing his research on automated theorem-proving, Jean Trudel came across a very interesting method: SL-resolution [Kowalski 1971]. He persuaded us to invite one of its inventors, Robert Kowalski, who came to visit us for a week in June 1971. It was an unforgettable encounter. For the first time, we talked to a specialist in automated theorem-proving who was able to explain the resolution principle, its variants, and refinements. As for Robert Kowalski, he met people who were deeply interested in his research and who were determined to make use of it in natural language processing.

While attending an IJCAI convention in September 1971 with Jean Trudel, we met Robert Kowalski again and heard a lecture by Terry Winograd on natural language processing. The fact that he did not use a unified formalism left us puzzled. It was at this time that we learned of the existence of Carl Hewitt's programming language, Planner [Hewitt 1969]. The lack of formalization of this language, our ignorance of Lisp and, above all, the fact that we were absolutely devoted to logic meant that this work had little influence on our later research.

7.2.2 1972: The Application that Created Prolog

The year 1972 was the most fruitful one. First of all, in February, the group obtained a grant of 122,000 FF (at that time about $20,000) for a period of 18 months from the Institut de Recherche d'Informatique et d'Automatique, a computer research institution affiliated with the French Ministry of Industry. This contract made it possible for us to purchase a teletype terminal (30 characters per second) and to connect it to the IBM 360-67 (equipped with the marvelous operating system CP-CMS, which managed virtual machines) at the University of Grenoble using a dedicated 300-baud link. For the next three years, this was to be by far the most convenient computing system available to the team; everyone used it, including the many researchers who visited us. It took us several years to pay Grenoble back the machine-hour debt thus accumulated. Finally, the contract also enabled us to hire a secretary and a researcher, Henry Kanoui, a post-graduate student who would work on the French morphology. At his end, Kowalski obtained funding from NATO, which financed numerous exchanges between Edinburgh and Marseilles.

Of all the resolution systems implemented by Philippe, the SL-resolution of R. Kowalski and D. Kuehner seemed to be the most interesting. Its stack-type operating mode was similar to the management of procedure calls in a standard programming language and was thus particularly well-suited to processing nondeterminism by backtracking à la Robert Floyd [1967] rather than by copying and saving the resolvents. SL-resolution then became the focus of Philippe's thesis on the processing of formal equality in automated theorem-proving [Roussel 1972]. Formal equality is less expressive than standard equality but it can be processed more efficiently. Philippe's thesis would lead to the introduction of the `dif` predicate (for ≠) into the very first version of Prolog.

We again invited Robert Kowalski but this time for a longer period: April and May. Together, we then all had more computational knowledge of automated theorem-proving. We knew how to axiomatize small problems (addition of integers, list concatenation, list reversal, etc.) so that an SL-resolution prover computed the result efficiently. We were not, however, aware of the Horn clause paradigm; moreover, Alain did not yet see how to do without Q-systems as far as natural language analysis was concerned.

After the departure of Robert, Alain ultimately found a way of developing powerful analyzers. He associated a binary predicate $N(x,y)$ with each nonterminal symbol N of the grammar, signifying that x and y are terminal strings for which the string u defined by $x = uy$ exists and can be derived from N. By representing x and y by lists, each grammar rule can then be encoded by a clause having exactly the same number of literals as occurrences of nonterminal symbols. It was thus possible to do without list concatenation. (This technique is now known as "The difference lists technique.") Alain also introduced additional parameters into each nonterminal to propagate and compute information. As in Q-systems, the analyzer not only verified that the sentence was correct but also extracted a formula representing the information that it contained. Nothing now stood in the way of the creation of a man-machine communication system entirely in "logic."

A draconian decision was made: at the cost of incompleteness, we chose linear resolution with unification only between the heads of clauses. Without knowing it, we had discovered the strategy that is complete when only Horn clauses are used. Robert Kowalski [1973] demonstrated this point later and together with Maarten van Emden, he would go on to define the modern fixed point semantics of Horn clause programming [Kowalski 1974].

During the fall of 1972, the first Prolog system was implemented by Philippe in Niklaus Wirt's language Algol-W; in parallel, Alain and Robert Pasero created the eagerly awaited man-machine communication system in French [Colmerauer 1972]. There was constant interaction between Philippe, who was implementing Prolog, and Alain and Robert Pasero, who programmed in a language that was being created step by step. This preliminary version of Prolog is described in detail in Part III of this paper. It was also at this time that the language received its definitive name following a suggestion from Philippe's wife based on keywords that had been given to her.

The man-machine communication system was the first large Prolog program ever to be written [Colmerauer 1972]. It had 610 clauses: Alain wrote 334 of them, mainly the analysis part; Robert Pasero 162, the purely deductive part, and Henry Kanoui wrote a French morphology in 104 clauses, which makes possible the link between the singular and plural of all common nouns and all verbs, even irregular ones, in the third person singular present tense. Here is an example of a text submitted to the man-machine communication system in 1972:

```
Every psychiatrist is a person.
Every person he analyzes is sick.
Jacques is a psychiatrist in Marseille.
Is Jacques a person?
Where is Jacques?
Is Jacques sick?
```

and here are the answers obtained for the three questions at the end:

```
Yes.
In Marseille.
I don't know.
```

The original text followed by the three answers was in fact as follows:

```
TOUT PSYCHIATRE EST UNE PERSONNE.
CHAQUE PERSONNE QU'IL ANALYSE, EST MALADE.
*JACQUES EST UN PSYCHIATRE A *MARSEILLE.
EST-CE QUE *JACQUES EST UNE PERSONNE?
OU EST *JACQUES?
EST-CE QUE *JACQUES EST MALADE?
OUI. A MARSEILLE. JE NE SAIS PAS.
```

All the inferences were made from pronouns (he, she, they, etc.), articles (the, a, every, etc.), subjects and complement relations with or without prepositions (from, to, etc.). In fact, the system knew only about pronouns, articles, and prepositions (the vocabulary was encoded by 164 clauses); it recognized proper nouns from the mandatory asterisk that had to precede them as well as verbs and common nouns on the basis of the 104 clauses for French morphology.

In November, together with Robert Pasero, we undertook an extensive tour of the American research laboratories after a visit in Edinburgh. We took with us a preliminary report on our natural language communication system and our very first Prolog. We left copies of the report almost everywhere. Jacques Cohen welcomed us in Boston and introduced us at MIT, where we received a warm welcome and talked with Minsky, Charniak, Hewitt, and Winograd. We also visited Woods at BBN. We then went to Stanford, visited the SRI and John McCarthy's AI laboratory, met Cordell Green, presented our work to a very critical J. Feldman, and spent Thanksgiving at Robert Floyd's home.

7.2.3 1973: The Final Prolog

At the beginning of the year or, to be exact, in April, our group attained official status. The CNRS recognized us as an "associated research team" entitled "Man-machine dialogue in natural language," and provided financial support in the amount of 39,000 FF (about $6,500) for the first year. This sum should be compared to the 316,880 FF (about $50,000) we received in October from IRIA to renew the contract for "man-machine communication in natural language with automated deduction" for a period of two and a half years.

Users of the preliminary version of Prolog at the laboratory had now done sufficient programming for their experience to serve as the basis for a second version of Prolog, a version firmly oriented toward a programming language and not just a kind of automated deductive system. Besides the communication system in French in 1972, two other applications had been developed using this initial version of Prolog: a symbolic computation system [Bergman 1973a, 1973b; Kanoui 1973] and a general problem-solving system called Sugiton [Joubert 1974]. Also, Robert Pasero continued to use it for his work on French semantics, leading to the successful completion of his thesis in May [Pasero 1973].

Between February and April 1973, at the invitation of Robert Kowalski, Philippe visited the School of Artificial Intelligence at the University of Edinburgh, which was within the Department of Computational Logic directed by Bernard Meltzer. Besides the many discussions with the latter and with David Warren, Philippe also met Roger Boyer and Jay Moore. They had constructed an implementation of resolution using an extremely ingenious method based on a structure-sharing technique to represent the logical formulæ generated during a deduction. The result of this visit and the laboratory's need to acquire a true programming language prompted our decision to lay the foundations for a second Prolog.

In May and June 1973, we laid out the main lines of the language, in particular the choice of syntax, basic primitives, and the interpreter's computing methods, all of which tended toward a simplification of the initial version. From June to the end of the year, Gérard Battani, Henry Meloni, and René Bazzoli, postgraduate students at the time, wrote the interpreter in FORTRAN and its supervisor in Prolog.

As the reader will see from the detailed description of this new Prolog in Part IV of this paper, all the new basic features of current Prologs were introduced. We observe in passing that this was also the time when the "occur check" disappeared as it was found to be too costly.

7.2.4 1974 and 1975: The Distribution of Prolog

The interactive version of Prolog which operated at Grenoble using teletype was in great demand. David Warren, who stayed with us from January to March, used it to write his plan generation system, Warplan [Warren 1974]. He notes:

> The present system is implemented partly in Fortran, partly in Prolog itself and, running on an IBM 360-67, achieves roughly 200 unifications per second.

Henry Kanoui and Marc Bergman used it to develop a symbolic manipulation system of quite some size called Sycophante [Bergman 1975; Kanoui 1976]. Gérard Battani and Henry Meloni used it to develop a speech recognition system enabling questions to be asked about the IBM operating system CP-CMS at Grenoble [Battani 1975; Meloni 1975]. The interface between the acoustic signal and the sequence of phonemes was borrowed from the CNET at Lannion and was obviously not written in Prolog.

Early in 1975, Alain Colmerauer had completely rewritten the supervisor keeping the infix operator declarations in Prolog but adding a compiler of the so-called "metamorphosis" grammars. This time, in contrast to René Bazzoli, he used a top-down analyzer to read the Prolog rules. This was a good exercise in metaprogramming. David Warren later included grammar rules of this sort in his compiled version of Prolog [Warren 1977] and together with Fernando Pereira rechristened a simplified variant of metamorphosis grammars with the name, "definite clause grammars" [Pereira 1980]. Metamorphosis grammars enabled parameterized grammar rules to be written directly as they were in Q-systems. The supervisor compiled these rules into efficient Prolog clauses by adding two additional parameters. To prove the efficiency and expressiveness of the metamorphosis grammars, Alain wrote a small model compiler from an Algol-style language to a fictitious machine language and a complete man-machine dialogue system in French with automated deductions. All this work was published in Colmerauer [1975], along with the theoretical foundations of the metamorphosis grammars.

Gérard Battani and Henry Meloni were kept very busy with the distribution of Prolog. They sent it to Budapest, Warsaw, Toronto, and Waterloo (Canada) and traveled to Edinburgh to assist David Warren in installing it on a PDP 10. A former student, Hélène Le Gloan, installed it at the University of Montreal. Michel Van Caneghem did the same at the IRIA in Paris before coming to work with us. Finally, Maurice Bruynooghe took Prolog to Leuven (Belgium) after a three-month stay in Marseilles (October through December 1975).

Indeed, as David Warren has pointed out, Prolog spread as much, or more, by people becoming interested and taking away copies either directly from Marseilles or from intermediaries such as Edinburgh. Thus, Prolog was not really distributed; rather it "escaped" and "multiplied."

During 1975, the whole team carried out the porting of the interpreter onto a 16-bit mini-computer: the T1600 from the French company, Télémécanique. The machine only had 64K bytes and so a virtual memory management system had to be specially written. Pierre Basso undertook this task and also won the contest for the shortest instruction sequence that performs an addressing on 32 bits while also testing the page default. Each laboratory member then received two pages of FORTRAN to translate into machine language. The translated fragments of program were reassembled and it worked! After five years, we at last had our very own machine and, what is more, our cherished Prolog ran; slowly, but it ran all the same.

7.3 PART II. A FORERUNNER OF PROLOG, THE Q-SYSTEMS

The history of the birth of Prolog thus comes to a halt at the end of 1975. We now turn to more technical aspects and, first of all, describe the Q-systems, the result of a first gamble: to develop a very high-level programming language, even if the execution times it entailed might seem bewildering [Colmerauer 1970b]. That gamble, and the experience acquired in implementing the Q-systems was determinative for the second gamble: Prolog.

7.3.1 One-Way Unification

A Q-system consists of a set of rewriting rules dealing with sequences of complex symbols separated by the sign +. Each rule is of the form

$$e_1 + e_2 + ... + e_m \rightarrow f_1 + f_2 + ... + f_n$$

and means: in the sequence of trees we are manipulating, any subsequence of the form $e_1 + e_2 + ... + e_m$ can be replaced by the sequence $f_1 + f_2 + ... + f_n$. The e_is and the f_is are parenthesized expressions representing trees, with a strong resemblance to present Prolog terms but using three types of variables. Depending on whether the variable starts with a letter in the set {A,B,C,D,E,F}, {I,J,K,L,M,N}, or {U,V,W,X,Y,Z} it denotes either a label, a tree, or a (possibly empty) sequence of trees separated by commas. For example, the rule

$$P + A^*(X^*,I^*,Y^*) \rightarrow I^* + A^*(X^*,Y^*)$$

(variables are followed by an asterisk) applied to the sequence

```
P + Q(R,S,T) + P
```

produces three possible sequences

```
R + Q(S,T) + P,
S + Q(R,T) + P,
T + Q(R,S) + P.
```

The concept of unification was therefore already present but it was one-way only; the variables appeared in the rules but never in the sequence of trees that was being transformed. However, unification took account of the associativity of the concatenation and, as in the preceding example, could produce several results.

7.3.2 Rule Application Strategy

This relates to the unification part. Concerning the rule application strategy, Alain Colmerauer [1970b] wrote:

> It is difficult to use a computer to analyze a sentence. The main problem is combinatorial in nature: taken separately, each group of elements in the sentence can be combined in different ways with other groups to form new groups which can in turn be combined again and so on. Usually, there is only one correct way of grouping all the elements but to discover it, all the possible groupings must be tried. To describe this multitude of groupings in an economical way, I use an oriented graph in which each arrow is labeled by a parenthesized expression representing a tree. A Q-system is nothing more than a set of rules allowing such a graph to be transformed into another graph. This information may correspond to an analysis, to a sentence synthesis or to a formal manipulation of this type.

For example the sequence

```
A + A + B + B + C + C
```

is represented by the graph

and the application of the four rules

```
A + B + C → S
A + S + X + C → S
X + C → C + X
B + B → B + X
```

produces the graph

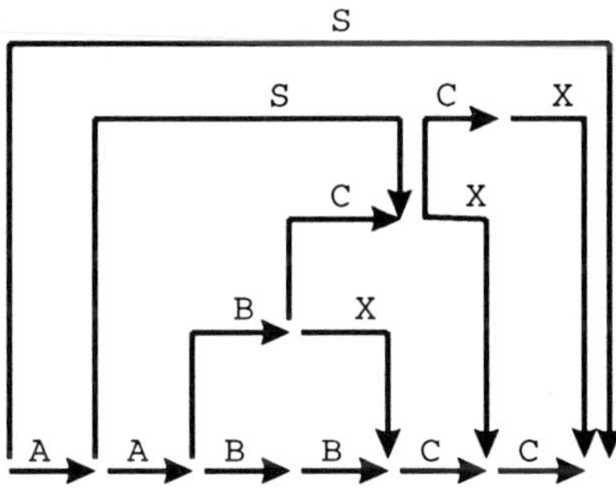

One retains all the paths that lead from the entry point to the end point and do not contain any arrows used in the production of other arrows. One thus retains the unique arrow

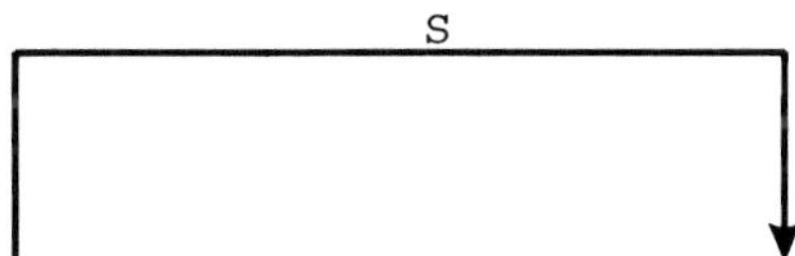

that is, the sequence reduced to the single symbol S.

This procedure is relatively efficient, because it retains the maximum number of common parts in all the sequences. Another aspect of the Q-systems is that they can be applied one after the other. Each one takes as input the graph resulting from the previous system. This technique was widely used in the automatic translation project, where an English sentence would undergo no fewer than fifteen Q-systems before being translated into French. Two Q-systems dealt with morphology, another with the analysis of English, two more with the transfer from an English structure to a French structure, one with the synthesis of French, and nine with French morphology [TAUM 1971].

Let us draw attention to the reversibility of the Q-systems. The rewriting sign that we have represented by → was in fact written == and, depending on which specified option was chosen at the start of the program, it was interpreted as either a rewriting from left to right or from right to left. That is, the same program could be used to describe a transformation and its reverse transformation such as the analysis and the synthesis of a sentence.

It is interesting to note that in contrast to the analyzers written in Prolog that used a top-down strategy, the analyzers written in Q-systems used a bottom-up strategy. In fact, Alain had extensive experience with this type of strategy. The subject of his thesis done in Grenoble (France) had been bottom-up analyzers which, however, operated by backtracking [Colmerauer 1970a]. Nondeterminism was then reduced by precedence relations very similar to those of Robert Floyd [1963]. In addition, just before developing the Q-systems, and still as part of the automatic translation project, Alain had written an analyzer and a general synthesizer for W-grammars, the formalism introduced by A. van Wijngaarden to describe ALGOL 68 [van Wijngaarden 1968]. Here again a bottom-up analyzer was used to find the structure of complex symbols (defined by a metagrammar) as well as a second bottom-up analyzer for analysis of the text itself [Chastellier 1969].

7.3.3 Implementation

The Q-systems were written in ALGOL by Alain Colmerauer and were operational by October 1969. Michel van Caneghem and François Stellin, then completing a master's degree, developed a FORTRAN version, and Gilles Steward developed an ultra-fast version in machine language for the CDC 6400 computer of the University of Montreal.

These Q-systems were used by the entire TAUM project team to construct a complete chain of automatic English-French translations. The English morphology was written by Brian Harris, Richard Kittredge wrote a substantial grammar for the analysis of English, Gilles Stewart wrote the transfer phase, Jules Danserau wrote the grammar for the French synthesis, and Michel van Caneghem developed a complete French morphology [Taum 1971]. The Q-systems were also used a few years later to write the METEO system, a current industrial version of which produces daily translations of Canadian weather forecasts from English into French.

7.4 PART III. THE PRELIMINARY PROLOG

Let us now turn to the preliminary version of Prolog which was created in the fall of 1972 in connection with the development of the man-machine communication system [Colmerauer 1972].

Recall that the objective we had set for ourselves was extremely ambitious: to have a tool for the syntactic and semantic analysis of natural language, by considering first order logic not only as a programming language but also as a knowledge representation language. In other words, the logical formulation was to serve not only for the different modules of the natural language dialogue system but also for the data exchanged between them, including the data exchanged with the user.

The choice having settled on first order logic (in clausal form) and not on a higher order logic, it then seemed that we were faced with an insurmountable difficulty in wanting programs to be able to manipulate other programs. Of course, this problem was solved using nonlogical mechanisms. In fact, this initial version of Prolog was conceived more as an application tool than as a universal programming language. Nevertheless, the basis for such a language was already there.

7.4.1 Reasons for the Choice of Resolution Method

The success of the project hinged on the decision concerning the choice of the logic system and on the basic inference mechanism to be adopted. Although Robinson's resolution principle naturally suggested itself by the simplicity of its clausal form, the uniqueness of the inference rule, and its similarity with procedure calls in standard languages, it was difficult to decide what type of adaptation was necessary to fulfill our requirements. Among the considerations to be taken into account were the validity and logical completeness of the system, the problems for implementation on the machine, and, especially, the risks of combinatorial explosion, which we were well aware of from our experiments.

Among the question-answering systems and the problem-solving techniques that we had explored, there were those of D. Luckam [1971] and N.J. Nilson, of J.L. Darlington [1969] and of Cordell Green [1969]. Our exploration, the tests by Jean Trudel and Robert Pasero using experimental versions of Philippe's provers, Alain's research on the logical formulation of grammars and numerous discussions with Robert Kowalski: all these elements led us to view the resolution principle from a point of view different from the prevailing one. Rather than demonstrating a theorem by reduction ad absurdum, we wanted to calculate an "interesting" set of clauses that were deducible from a given set of clauses. Because, to our way of thinking, such sets constituted programs, we would thus have programs generating other programs. This idea constantly underlay the conception of this preliminary version of the language as it did the realization of the application.

The final choice was an adaptation of the resolution method similar to those of the subsequent Prologs but comprising some very novel elements, even compared with modern Prologs. Each execution was performed with a set of clauses constituting the "program" and a set of clauses constituting the "questions." Both of them produced a set of clauses constituting the "answers." The literals of the clauses were ordered from left to right and the resolution was performed between the head literal of the resolvent and the head literal of one of the program clauses. The novelty resided in the fact that in each clause a part of the literals, separated by the "/" sign, was not processed during the proof. Instead, they were accumulated to produce one of the answer clauses at the end of deduction. In addition, certain predicates (such as `DIF`) were processed by delayed evaluation and could also be transmitted as an answer. Finally, it was decided that nondeterminism should be processed by backtracking, meaning that only a single branch of the search tree was stored at any given time in the memory.

Formally, the chosen deduction method can be described by the three deduction rules below, where "question," "chosen clause," and "answer" denote three clauses taken respectively from the sets "questions," "program," and "answers" and "resolvent" denotes the current list of goals.

Deduction initialization rule

$$\frac{\text{question: } L_1 \ldots L_m \;/\; R_1 \ldots R_n}{\text{resolvent: } L_1 \ldots L_m \;/\; R_1 \ldots R_n}$$

Basic deduction rule

$$\frac{\text{resolvent: } L_0\, L_1 \ldots\ /\ R_1 \ldots R_n,\ \text{chosen clause: } L'_0\, L'_1 \ldots L'_{m'}\ /\ R'_1 \ldots R'_{n'}}{\text{resolvent } \sigma(L'_1) \ldots \sigma(L'_{m'})\sigma(L_1) \ldots \sigma(L_m)\ /\ \sigma(R'_1) \ldots \sigma(R'_{n'})\sigma(R_1) \ldots \sigma(R_n)}$$

End of deduction rule

$$\frac{\text{resolvent: } /\ R_1 \ldots R_n}{\text{answer: } R_1 \ldots R_n}$$

where of course, L_0 and L'_0 are complementary unifiable literals and s is the most general substitution that unifies them. (An example is given later.)

The first reason for choosing this linear resolution technique with a predefined order of literal selection was its simplicity and the fact that we could produce clauses that were logically deducible from the program, which thus guaranteed, in a way, the validity of the results. To a large extent, we were inspired by Robert Kowalski's SL-Resolution which Philippe had implemented for his thesis on formal equality. However, despite its stack-like functioning analogous to procedure calling in standard languages, we knew that this method introduced computations that were certainly necessary in the general case but unnecessary for most of our examples. We therefore adopted the extremely simplified version of SL-Resolution described by the preceding three rules, which continues to serve as the basis for all Prologs.

The choice of the treatment of nondeterminism was basically a matter of efficiency. By programming a certain number of methods, Philippe had shown that one of the crucial problems was combinatorial explosion and a consequent lack of memory. Backtracking was selected early on for management of nondeterminism, in preference to a management system of several branch calculations simultaneously resident in memory, whose effect would have been to considerably increase the memory size required for execution of the deductions. Alain had a preference for this method, introduced by Robert Floyd [1967] to process nondeterministic languages, and was teaching it to all his students. Although, certainly, the use of backtracking led to a loss of completeness in deductions comprising infinite branches, we felt that, given the simplicity of the deduction strategy (the execution of literals from left to right and the choice of clauses in the order they were written), it was up to the programmer to make sure that the execution of his or her program terminated.

7.4.2 Characteristics of the Preliminary Prolog

Apart from the deduction mechanism we have already discussed, a number of built-in predicates were added to the system as Alain and Robert Pasero required them: predicates to trace an execution, `COPY` to copy a term, `BOUM` to split an identifier into a list of characters or reconstitute it and `DIF` to process the symbolic (that is, syntactic) equality of Philippe's thesis. It should be noted that we refused to include input-output predicates in this list as they were considered to be too far removed from logic. Input-output, specification of the initial resolvents, and chaining between programs were specified in a command language applied to sets of clauses (read, copy, write, merge, prove, etc.). This language, without any control instructions, allowed chainings to be defined only statically but had the virtue of treating communications uniformly by way of sets of clauses. It should be emphasized that this first version already included lazy evaluation (or coroutined evaluation, if you prefer) of certain predicates; in this case `DIF` and `BOUM`. The `DIF` predicate was abandoned in the next version but reappeared in modern Prologs. The only control operators were placed at the end of clauses as punctuation marks, and their function was to perform cuts in the search space. The annotations:

.. performed a cut after the head of the clause,
.; performed a cut after execution of the whole rule,
;. performed a cut after production of at least one answer,
;; had no effect.

These extra-logical operators were exotic enough to cause their users problems and were therefore subsequently abandoned. Curiously, this punctuation had been introduced by Alain following his discovery of the optional and mandatory transformation rules of the linguist, Noam Chomsky [1965].

On the syntactic level, the terms were written in functional form although it was possible to introduce unary or binary operators defined by precedences as well as an infixed binary operator that could be represented by an absence of sign (like a product in mathematics and very useful in string input-output). Here is an example of a sequence of programs that produced and wrote a set of clauses defining the great-nephews of a person named `MARIE`:

```
READ
   RULES
   +DESC(*X,*Y) -CHILD(*X,*Y);;
   +DESC(*X,*Z) -CHILD(*X,*Y) -DESC(*Y,*Z);;
   +BROTHERSISTER(*X,*Y) -CHILD(*Z,*X) -CHILD(*Z,*Y) -DIF(*X,*Y);;
   AMEN

READ
   FACTS
   +CHILD(PAUL,MARIE);;
   +CHILD(PAUL,PIERRE);;
   +CHILD(PAUL,JEAN);;
   +CHILD(PIERRE,ALAIN);;
   +CHILD(PIERRE,PHILIPPE);;
   +CHILD(ALAIN,SOPHIE);;
   +CHILD(PHILIPPE,ROBERT);;
   AMEN

READ
 QUESTION
 -BROTHERSISTER(MARIE,*X) -DESC(*X,*Y) / +GREATNEPHEW(*Y) -MASC(*Y)..
 AMEN

CONCATENATE(FAMILYTIES,RULES,FACTS)

PROVE(FAMILYTIES,QUESTION,ANSWER)

WRITE(ANSWER)

AMEN
```

The output from this program was thus not a term but instead the following set of binary clauses:

```
+GREATNEPHEW(SOPHIE) -MASC(SOPHIE);.
+GREATNEPHEW(ROBERT) -MASC(ROBERT);.
```

The `READ` command read a set of clauses preceded by a name x and ending with AMEN and assigned it the name x. The command `CONCATENATE`$(y,x_1,\ldots,x_n)$ computed the union y of the sets of clauses

$x_1,\ldots,x_n$. The command PROVE(x,y,z) was the most important one; it started a procedure where the program is x, the initial resolvent is y, and the set of answers is z. Finally, the command WRITE(x) printed the set of clauses x .

The man-machine communication system operated in four phases and made use of four programs, that is, four sets of clauses:

- C1 to analyze a text T0 and produce a deep structure T1,
- C2 to find in T1 the antecedents of the pronouns and produce a logical form T2,
- C3 to split the logical formula T2 into a set T3 of elementary information,
- C4 to carry out deductions from T3 and produce the answers in French T4.

The sequence of commands was therefore

```
PROVE(C1,T0,T1)
PROVE(C2,T1,T2)
PROVE(C3,T2,T3)
PROVE(C4,T3,T4),
```

where T0, the French text to process, and T4, the answers produced, were represented by elementary facts over lists of characters.

7.4.3 Implementation of the Preliminary Prolog

Because the Luminy computing center had been moved, the interpreter was implemented by Philippe in ALGOL-W, on the IBM 360-67 machine of the University of Grenoble computing center, equipped with the CP-CMS operating system based on the virtual machine concept. We were connected to this machine via a special telephone line. The machine had two unique characteristics almost unknown at this time, characteristics that were essential for our work: it could provide a programmer with a virtual memory of 1Mb if necessary (and it was), and it allowed us to write interactive programs. So it was, that, on a single console operating at 300 baud, we developed not only the interpreter but also the question-answering system itself. The choice of ALGOL-W was imposed on us, because it was the only high-level language we had available that enabled us to create structured objects dynamically, while also being equipped with garbage collection.

The basis for the implementation of the resolution was an encoding of the clauses into interpointing structures with anticipated copying of each rule used in a deduction. Nondeterminism was managed by a backtracking stack and substitutions were performed only by creating chains of pointers. This approach eliminated the copying of terms during unifications, and thus greatly improved the computing times and memory space used. The clause analyzer was also written in ALGOL-W, in which the atoms were managed by a standard "hash-code" technique. This analyzer constituted a not insignificant part of the system which strengthened Alain's desire to solve these syntax problems in Prolog itself. However, experience was still lacking on this topic, because the purpose of the first application was to reveal the very principles of syntactic analysis in logic programming.

7.5 PART IV. THE FINAL PROLOG

Now that we have described the two forerunners at length, it is time to lay out the fact sheet on the definitive Prolog of 1973. Our major preoccupation after the preliminary version was the reinforcement of Prolog's programming language aspects by minimizing concepts and improving its interactive capabilities in program management. Prolog was becoming a language based on the resolution principle alone and on the provision of a set of built-in predicates (procedures) making it possible to do everything in the language itself. This set was conceived as a minimum set enabling the user to:

- create and modify programs in memory,
- read source programs, analyze them and load them in memory,
- interpret queries dynamically with a structure analogous to other elements of the language,
- have access dynamically to the structure and the elements of a deduction,
- control program execution as simply as possible.

7.5.1 Resolution Strategy

The experience gained from the first version led us to use a simplified version of its resolution strategy. The decision was based not only on suggestions from the first programmers but also on criteria of efficiency and on the choice of FORTRAN to program the interpreter which forced us to manage the memory space. The essential differences with the previous version were:

- no more delayed evaluation (`DIF`, `BOUM`),
- replacement of the `BOUM` predicate by the more general `UNIV` predicate,
- the operations assert and retract, at that time written `AJOUT` and `SUPP`, are used to replace the mechanism that generates clauses as the result of a deduction,
- a single operator for backtracking management, the search space cut operator "!" , at that time written "/",
- the meta-call concept to use a variable instead of a literal,
- use of the predicates `ANCESTOR` and `STATE`, which have disappeared in present Prologs, to access ancestor literals and the current resolvent (considered as a term), for programmers wishing to define their own resolution mechanism.

Backtracking and ordering the set of clauses defining a predicate were the basic elements retained as a technique for managing nondeterminism. The preliminary version of Prolog was quite satisfactory in this aspect. Alain's reduction of backtracking control management to a single primitive (the cut), replacing the too numerous concepts in the first version, produced an extraordinary simplification of the language. Not only could the programmer reduce the search space size according to purely pragmatic requirements but also he or she could process negation in a way, which, although simplified and reductive in its semantics, was extremely useful in most common types of programming.

In addition, after a visit to Edinburgh, Philippe had in mind the basis for an architecture that is extremely simple to implement from the point of view of memory management and much more efficient in terms of time and space, if we maintained the philosophy of managing nondeterminism by backtracking. In the end, all the early experiences of programming had shown that this technique allowed our users to incorporate nondeterminism fairly easily as an added dimension to the control of the execution of the predicates.

Concerning the processing of the implicit "or" between literals inside a clause, sequentiality imposed itself there again as the most natural interpretation of this operator because, in formal terms, the order of goal execution has no effect at all on the set of results (modulo the pruning of infinite branches), as Robert Kowalski had proved concerning SL-resolution.

To summarize, these two choices concerning the processing of "and" and "or", were fully justified by the required objectives:

- employ a simple and predictable strategy that the user can control, enabling any extra-logical predicate (such as input-output) to be given an operational definition,
- provide an interpreter capable of processing deductions with thousands or tens of thousands of steps (an impossible objective in the deductive systems existing at that time).

7.5.2 Syntax and Primitives

On the whole, the syntax retained was the same as the syntax of the preliminary version of the language. On the lexical level, the identifier syntax was the same as that of most languages and therefore lower-case letters could not be used (the keyboards and operating systems at that time did not systematically allow this). It should be noted that among the basic primitives for processing morphology problems, one single primitive `UNIV` was used to create dynamically an atom from a character sequence, to construct a structured object from its elements, and, conversely, to perform the inverse splitting operations. This primitive was one of the basic tools used to create programs dynamically and to manipulate objects whose structures were unknown prior to the execution of the program.

Enabling the user to define his own unary and binary operators by specifiying numeric precedences proved very useful and flexible although it complicated somewhat the clause analyzers. It still survives as such in the different current Prologs.

In the preliminary version of Prolog, it was possible to create clauses that were logically deducible from other clauses. Our experience with this version had showed us that sometimes it was necessary to manipulate clauses for purposes very far removed from first order logic: modeling of temporal type reasoning, management of information persisting for an uncertain lifetime, or simulation of exotic logics. We felt that much research would still be needed in the area of semantics in order to model the problems of updating sets of clauses. Hence, we made the extremely pragmatic decision to introduce extra-logical primitives acting by side effect to modify a program (`ADD`, `DELETE`). This choice seems to have been the right one because these functions have all been retained.

One of the missing features of the preliminary Prolog was a mechanism that could compute a term that could then be taken as a literal to be resolved. This is an essential function needed for metaprogramming such as a command interpreter; this feature is very easy to implement from a syntactic point of view. In any event, a variable denoting a term can play the role of a literal.

In the same spirit—and originally intended for specialists in computational logic—various functions giving access to the current deduction by considering it as a Prolog object appeared in the basic primitives (`STATE`, `ANCESTOR`). Similarly, the predicate " / " (pronounced "cut " by Edinburghers) became parametrizable in a very powerful manner by access to ancestors.

7.5.3 A Programming Example

To show the reader what an early Prolog program looked like, we introduce an old example dealing with flights between cities. From a base of facts that describes direct flights, the program can calculate routes which satisfy some scheduling constraints.

Direct flights are represented by unary clauses under the following format:

```
+FLIGHT(<departure city>,<arrival city>,
        <departure time>,<arrival time>,<flight identifier>)
```

where time schedules are represented by pairs of integers under the format `<hours>:<minutes>`. All flights are supposed to be completed in the same day.

The following predicate will be called by the user to plan a route.

```
PLAN(<departure city>,<arrival city>,<departure time>,<arrival time>,
     <departure min time>,<arrival max time>)
```

It enumerates (and outputs as results) all pairs of cities connected by a route that can be a direct flight or a sequence of flights. Except for circuits, the same city cannot be visited more than once. Parameters `<departure min time>` and `<arrival max time>` denote constraints given by the user about departure and arrival times. The first flight of the route should leave after `<departure min time>` and the last one should arrive before `<arrival max time>`.

In order to calculate PLAN, several predicates are defined. The predicate:

```
ROUTE(<departure city>,<arrival city>,<departure time>,<arrival time>,
    <plan>, <visits>, <departure mini time>,<arrival maxi time>)
```

is similar to the `PLAN` predicate, except for two additional parameters: the input parameter `<visits>` is given represents the list (`Ck.Ck-1...C1.NIL`) of already visited cities (in inverse order), the output parameter `<plan>` is the list (`F1....Fk.NIL`) of calculated flight names. The predicates `BEFORE(<t1>,<t2>)` and `ADDTIMES(<t1>,<t2>,<t3>)` deal with arithmetic aspects of time schedules. The predicate `WRITEPLAN` writes the sequence of flight names. Finally, `NOT(<literal>)` defines negation by failure, and `ELEMENT(<element>,<elements)` succeeds if `<element>` is among the list `<elements>`.

Here then is the complete program, including data and the saving and execution commands.

```
* INFIXED OPERATORS
--------------------.
-AJOP( ".", 1, "(X|X)|X")  -AJOP(":",  2, "(X|X)|X") !
*  USER PREDICATE
-----------------.
+PLAN(*DEPC, *ARRC, *DEPT, *ARRT, *DEPMINT, *ARRMAXT)
   -ROUTE(*DEPC, *ARRC, *DEPT, *ARRT, *PLAN, *DEPC.NIL, *DEPMINT,
                                                        *ARRMAXT)
   -SORM("---------------------------------------------")
   -LIGNE
   -SORM("FLYING ROUTE BETWEEN:  ")
   -SORT(*DEPC)
   -SORM(" AND: ")
   -SORT(*ARRC)
   -LIGNE
   -SORM("---------------------------------------------")
   -LIGNE
   -SORM(" DEPARTURE TIME:   ")
   -SORT(*DEPT)
   -LIGNE
   -SORM("ARRIVAL TIME:      ")
   -SORT(*ARRT)
   -LIGNE
   -SORM(" FLIGHTS:    ")
   -WRITEPLAN(*PLAN) -LIGNE -LIGNE.
* PRIVATE PREDICATES
```

```
---------------------.
+ROUTE(*DEPC, *ARRC, *DEPT, *ARRT, *FLIGHTID.NIL, *VISITS, *DEPMINT,
                                                            *ARRMAXT)R
-FLIGHT(*DEPC, *ARRC, *DEPT, *ARRT, *FLIGHTID)
   -BEFORE(*DEPMINT, *DEPT)
   -BEFORE(*ARRT, *ARRMAXT).
+ROUTE(*DEPC,*ARRC, *DEPT,*ARRT, *FLIGHTID.*PLAN, *VISITS,*DEPMINT,
                                                           *ARRMAXT)
   -FLIGHT(*DEPC, *INTC, *DEPT, *INTT, *FLIGHTID)

   -BEFORE(*DEPMINT, *DEPT)
   -ADDTIMES(*INTT, 00:15, *INTMINDEPT)
   -BEFORE(*INTMINDEPT, *ARRMAXT)
   -NOT( ELEMENT(*INTC, *VISITS)
   -ROUTE(*INTC,*ARR,*INTDEPT,*HARR, *PLAN, *INTC.*VISITS,
                                          *INTMINDEPT, *ARRMAXT).

+BEFORE(*H1:*M1, *H2:*M2) -INF(H1, H2).
+BEFORE(*H1:*M1, *H1:*M2) -INF(M1, M2).
+ADDTIMES(*H1:*M1, *H2:*M2, *H3:*M3)
   -PLUS(*M1, *M2, *M)
   -RESTE(*M, 60, *M3)
   -DIV(*M, 60,*H)
   -PLUS(*H, *H1, *HH)
   -PLUS(*HH,*H2,*H3).
+WRITEPLAN( *X. NIL) -/ -SORT(*X).
+WRITEPLAN( *X.*Y) -SORT(*X) -ECRIT(-) -WRITEPLAN(*Y).
+ELEMENT(*X, *X.*Y).
+ELEMENT(*X, *Y.*Z) -ELEMENT(*X, *Z).
+NOT(*X) -*X -/ -FAIL.
+NOT(*X).
* LIST OF FLIGHTS
-----------------.
+FLIGHT(PARIS, LONDON, 06:50, 07:30, AF201).
+FLIGHT(PARIS, LONDON, 07:35, 08:20, AF210).
+FLIGHT(PARIS, LONDON, 09:10, 09:55, BA304).
+FLIGHT(PARIS, LONDON, 11:40, 12:20, AF410).
+FLIGHT(MARSEILLES, PARIS, 06:15, 07:00, IT100).
+FLIGHT(MARSEILLES, PARIS, 06:45, 07:30, IT110).
+FLIGHT(MARSEILLES, PARIS, 08:10, 08:55, IT308).
+FLIGHT(MARSEILLES, PARIS, 10:00, 10:45, IT500).
+FLIGHT(MARSEILLES, LONDON, 08:15, 09:45, BA560).
+FLIGHT(MARSEILLES, LYON, 07:45, 08:15, IT115).
+FLIGHT(LYON, LONDON, 08:30, 09:25, TAT263).
* SAVING THE PROGRAM
--------------------.
-SAUVE!
* QUERYING
----------.
-PLAN(MARSEILLES, LONDON, *HD, *HA, 00:00, 09:30)!
```

This is the ouput of the program:

```
-----------------------------------------------------
 FLYING ROUTE BETWEEN:   MARSEILLES  AND: LONDON
-----------------------------------------------------
DEPARTURE TIME:      06:15
ARRIVAL TIME:       08:20
FLIGHTS:     IT100-AF210

-----------------------------------------------------
 FLYING ROUTE BETWEEN:   MARSEILLES  AND: LONDON
-----------------------------------------------------
DEPARTURE TIME:      07:45
ARRIVAL TIME:       09:25
FLIGHTS:     IT115-TAT263
```

7.5.4 Implementation of the Interpreter

The resolution system, in which nondeterminism was managed by backtracking, was implemented using a very novel method for representing clauses, halfway between the technique based on structure sharing used by Robert Boyer and Jay Moore in their work on the proofs of programs [Boyer 1972; Moore 1974] and the backtracking technique used in the preliminary version of Prolog. Philippe came up with this solution during his stay in Edinburgh after many discussions with Robert Boyer. In this new approach, the clauses of a program were encoded in memory as a series of templates, which can be instantiated without copying, several times in the same deduction, by means of contexts containing the substitutions to be performed on the variables. This technique had many advantages compared to those normally used in automated theorem-proving:

- in all known systems, unification was performed in times that were, at best, linear in relation to the size of the terms unified. In our system, most of the unifications could be performed in constant time, determined not by the size of the data, but by that of the templates brought into action by the clauses of the called program. As a result, the concatenation of two lists was performed in a linear time corresponding to the size of the first and not in quadratic time as in all other systems based on copying techniques;
- in the same system, the memory space required for one step in a deduction is not a function of the data, but of the program clause used. Globally therefore, the concatenation of two lists used only a quantity of memory space proportional to the size of the first list;
- the implementation of nondeterminism did not require a sophisticated garbage collector in the first approach but simply the use of several stacks synchronized on the backtracking, thus facilitating rapid management and yet remaining economical in the use of interpreter memory.

Concerning the representation of the templates in memory, we decided to use prefix representation (the exact opposite of Polish notation). The system consisted of the actual interpreter (i.e., the inference machine equipped with a library of built-in predicates), a loader to read clauses in a restricted syntax, and a supervisor written in Prolog. Among other things, this supervisor contained a query evaluator, an analyzer accepting extended syntax, and the high level input-output predicates.

Alain, who like all of us disliked FORTRAN, succeeded nonetheless in persuading the team to program the interpreter in this language. This basic choice was based primarily on the fact that

FORTRAN was widely distributed on all machines and that the machine we had access to at that time supported no other languages adapted to our task. We hoped in that way to have a portable system, a prediction that proved to be quite correct.

Under Philippe's supervision, Gérard Battani [Battani 1973] and Henri Meloni developed the actual interpreter between June 1973 and October 1973 on a CII 10070 (variant of the SIGMA 7) while René Bazzoli, under Alain's direction, was given the task of writing the supervisor in the Prolog language itself. The program consisted of approximately 2000 instructions, of roughly the same size as the ALGOL-W program of the initial version.

The machine had a batch operating system with no possibility of interaction via a terminal. Hence, data and programs were entered by means of punched cards. That these young researchers could develop as complex a system as this under such conditions and in such short time is especially remarkable in light of the fact that none of them had ever written a line of FORTRAN before in their lives. The interpreter was finally completed in December 1973 by Gérard Battani and Henry Meloni after porting it onto the IBM 360-67 machine at Grenoble, thus providing somewhat more reasonable operating conditions. Philippe Roussel wrote the reference and user's manual for this new Prolog two years later [Roussel 1975].

7.6 CONCLUSION

After all these vicissitudes and all the technical details, it might be interesting to take a step back and to place the birth of Prolog in a wider perspective. The article published by Alan Robinson in January 1965, "A machine-oriented logic based on the resolution principle," contained the seeds of the Prolog language. This article was the source of an important stream of works on automated theorem-proving and there is no question that Prolog is essentially a theorem prover "à la Robinson."

Our contribution was to transform that theorem prover into a programming language. To that end, we did not hesitate to introduce purely computational mechanisms and restrictions that were heresies for the existing theoretical model. These modifications, so often criticized, assured the viability, and thus the success, of Prolog. Robert Kowalski's contribution was to single out the concept of the "Horn clause," which legitimized our principal heresy: a strategy of linear demonstration with backtracking and with unifications only at the heads of clauses.

Prolog is so simple that one has the sense that sooner or later someone had to discover it. Why did we discover it rather than anyone else? First of all, Alain had the right background for creating a programming language. He belonged to the first generation of Ph.D.s in computer science in France and his specialty was language theory. He had gained valuable experience in creating his first programming language, Q-systems, while on the staff of the machine translation project at the University of Montreal. Then, our meeting, Philippe's creativity, and the particular working conditions at Marseilles did the rest. We benefitted from freedom of action in a newly created scientific center and, having no outside pressures, we were able to devote ourselves fully to our project.

Undoubtedly, this is why that period of our lives remains one of the happiest in our memories. We have had the pleasure of recalling it for this paper over fresh almonds accompanied by a dry martini.

ACKNOWLEDGMENTS

We would like to thank all those who contributed to the English version of this paper: Andy Tom, Franz Günther, Mike Mahoney, and Pamela Morton.

BIBLIOGRAPHY

[Battani, 1973] Battani, Gérard and Henry Meloni, *Interpréteur du langage PROLOG*, DEA report, Groupe Intelligence Artificielle, Faculté des Sciences de Luminy, Université Aix-Marseille II, France, 1973.

[Battani, 1975] Battani, Gérard, *Mise en oeuvre des contraintes phonologiques, syntaxiques et sémantiques dans un système de compréhension automatique de la parole*, 3ème cycle thesis, Groupe Intelligence Artificielle, Faculté des Sciences de Luminy, Université Aix-Marseille II, France, June 1975.

[Bergman, 1973a] Bergman, Marc and Henry Kanoui, Application of mechanical theorem proving to symbolic calculus, *Third International Colloquium on Advanced Computing Methods in Theoretical Physics*, Marseilles, France, June 1973.

[Bergman, 1973b] *Résolution par la démonstration automatique de quelques problèmes en intégration symbolique sur calculateur*, 3ème cyle thesis, Groupe Intelligence Artificielle, Faculté des Sciences de Luminy, Université Aix-Marseille II, France, Oct. 1973.

[Bergman, 1975] Bergman, Marc and Henry Kanoui, *SYCOPHANTE, système de calcul formel sur ordinateur*, final report for a DRET contract (Direction des Recherches et Etudes Techniques), Groupe Intelligence Artificielle, Faculté des Sciences de Luminy, Université Aix-Marseille II, France, 1975.

[Boyer, 1972] Boyer, Roger S. and Jay S. Moore, The sharing of structure in theorem proving programs, *Machine Intelligence 7*, edited by B. Melzer and D. Michie, New York: Edinburgh University Press, 1972, pp. 101–116.

[Chastellier, 1969] Chastellier (de), Guy and Alain Colmerauer, W-Grammar. *Proceedings of the ACM Congress*, San Francisco, Aug., New York: ACM, 1969, pp. 511–518.

[Chomsky, 1965] Chomsky, Noam, *Aspects of the Theory of Syntax*, MIT Press, Cambridge, 1965.

[Cohen, 1988] Cohen, Jacques, A view of the origins and development of Prolog, *Commun. ACM 31*, 1, Jan. 1988, pp. 26–36.

[Colmerauer, 1970a] Colmerauer, Alain, Total precedence relations, *J. ACM 17, 1*, Jan. 1970, pp. 14–30.

[Colmerauer, 1970b] Colmerauer, Alain, *Les systèmes-q ou un formalisme pour analyser et synthétiser des phrases sur ordinateur,* Internal publication 43, Département d'informatique de l'Université de Montréal, Sept. 1970.

[Colmerauer, 1971] Colmerauer, Alain, Fernand Didier, Robert Pasero, Philippe Roussel, Jean Trudel, *Répondre à*, Internal publication, Groupe Intelligence Artificielle, Faculté des Sciences de Luminy, Université Aix-Marseille II, France, May 1971. This publication is a computer print-out with handwritten remarks.

[Colmerauer, 1972] Colmerauer, Alain, Henry Kanoui, Robert Pasero and Philippe Roussel, *Un système de communication en français*, rapport préliminaire de fin de contrat IRIA, Groupe Intelligence Artificielle, Faculté des Sciences de Luminy, Université Aix-Marseille II, France, Oct. 1972.

[Colmerauer, 1975] Colmerauer, Alain, *Les grammaires de métamorphose GIA*, Internal publication, Groupe Intelligence Artificielle, Faculté des Sciences de Luminy, Université Aix-Marseille II, France, Nov. 1975. English version, Metamorphosis grammars, *Natural Language Communication with Computers, Lectures Notes in Computer Science 63*, edited by L. Bolc, Berlin, Heidelberg, New York: Springer Verlag, 1978, pp. 133–189.

[Darlington, 1969] Darlington, J. L. Theorem-proving and information retrieval. *Machine Intelligence 4*, Edinburgh University Press, 1969, pp. 173–707.

[Elcok, 1988] Elcok, E., W. Absys: the first logic programming language—A restrospective and a commentary. *The Journal of Logic Programming.*

[Floyd, 1963] Floyd, Robert W., Syntactic analysis and operator precedence. *J.ACM 10*, 1963, pp. 316–333.

[Floyd, 1967] Floyd, Robert W., Nondeterministic algorithms. *J. ACM 14, 4*, Oct. 1967, pp. 636–644.

[Green, 1969] Green, Cordell C., Application of theorem-proving to problem-solving, *Proceedings of First International Joint Conference on Artificial Intelligence*, Washington D.C., 1969, pp. 219–239.

[Hewitt, 1969] Hewitt, Carl, PLANNER: A language for proving theorems in robots, *Proceedings of First International Joint Conference on Artificial Intelligence*, Washington D.C., 1969, pp. 295–301.

[Joubert, 1974] Joubert, Michel, *Un système de résolution de problèmes à tendance naturelle*, 3ème cycle thesis, Groupe Intelligence Artificielle, Faculté des Sciences de Luminy, Université Aix-Marseille II, France, Feb. 1974.

[Kanoui, 1973] Kanoui, Henry, *Application de la démonstration automatique aux manipulations algébriques et à l'intégration formelle sur ordinateur*, 3ème cycle thesis, Groupe Intelligence Artificielle, Faculté des Sciences de Luminy, Université Aix-Marseille II, France, Oct. 1973.

[Kanoui, 1976] Kanoui, Henry, Some aspects of symbolic integration via predicate logic programming. *ACM SIGSAM Bulletin*, 1976.

[Kowalski, 1971] Kowalski, Robert A. and D. Kuehner, *Linear resolution with selection function*, memo 78, University of Edinburgh, School of Artificial Intelligence, 1971. Also in *Artificial Intelligence 2, 3*, pp. 227–260.

[Kowalski, 1973] Kowalski, Robert A., *Predicate Logic as Programming Language*, memo 70, University of Edimburgh, School of Artificial Intelligence, Nov. 1973. Also in *Proceedings of IFIP 1974*, Amsterdam: North Holland, Amsterdam, 1974, pp. 569–574.

[Kowalski, 1974] Kowalski, Robert A. and Maarten van Emden, *The semantic of predicate logic as programming language*, memo 78, University of Edinburgh, School of Artificial Intelligence, 1974. Also in *JACM* 22, 1976, pp. 733–742.

[Kowalski, 1988] Kowalski, Robert A., The early history of logic programming, *CACM vol. 31, no. 1*, 1988, pp 38–43.

[Loveland, 1984] Loveland, D.W. Automated theorem proving: A quarter-century review. *Am. Math. Soc. 29* , 1984, pp. 1–42.

[Luckam, 1971] Luckam, D. and N.J. Nilson, Extracting information from resolution proof trees, *Artificial Intelligence 12, 1*, 1971, pp. 27–54.

[Meloni, 1975] Meloni, Henry, *Mise en oeuvre des contraintes phonologiques, syntaxiques et sémantiques dans un système de compréhension automatique de la parole*, thèse de 3ème cycle, Groupe Intelligence Artificielle, Faculté des Sciences de Luminy, Université Aix-Marseille II, France, June 1975.

[Moore, 1974] Moore, Jay, *Computational logic : Structure sharing and proof of program properties, part I and II*, memo 67, University of Edinburgh, School of Artificial Intelligence, 1974.

[Pasero, 1973] Pasero, Robert, *Représentation du français en logique du premier ordre en vue de dialoguer avec un ordinateur*, thèse de 3ème cycle, Groupe Intelligence Artificielle, Faculté des Sciences de Luminy, Université Aix-Marseille II, France, May 1973.

[Pereira, 1980] Pereira, Fernando C. and David H.D. Warren, Definite clause grammars for language analysis, *Artificial Intelligence. 13*, 1980, pp. 231–278.

[Robinson, 1965] Robinson, J.A., A machine-oriented logic based on the resoulution principle, *J. ACM 12, 1*, Jan. 1965, pp. 23–41.

[Roussel, 1972] Roussel, Philippe, *Définition et traitement de l'égalité formelle en démonstration automatique*, thèse de 3ième cycle, Groupe Intelligence Artificielle, Faculté des Sciences de Luminy, Université Aix-Marseille II, France, May 1972.

[Roussel, 1975] Roussel, Philippe, *Prolog, manuel de référence et d'utilisation*, Groupe Intelligence Artificielle, Faculté des Sciences de Luminy, Université Aix-Marseille II, France, Sept. 1975.

[Taum, 1971] *TAUM 71*, Annual report, Projet de Traduction Automatique de l'Université de Montréal, Jan. 1971.

[Warren, 1974] Warren, David H. D.,Warplan, *A System for Generating Plans*, research report, University of Edimburgh, Department of Computational Logic, memo 76, June 1974.

[Warren 1977] Warren, David H. D., Luis M. Pereira and Fernando Pereira, Prolog the language and its implementation, *Proceedings of the ACM, Symposium on Artificial Intelligence and Programming Languages*, Rochester, N.Y., Aug. 1977.

[Wijngaarden, 1968] van Wijngaarden, A., B. J. Mailloux, J. E. L. Peck, and G. H. A. Koster, *Final Draft Report on the Algorithmic Language Algol 68*, Mathematish Centrum, Amsterdam, Dec. 1968.

TRANSCRIPT OF PRESENTATION

ALAIN COLMERAUER: (SLIDE 1) I was supposed to give this talk with Philippe Roussel but he could not come. I won't speak so much about Prolog but about the circumstances which brought about the birth of the language. Unlike other programming languages, there was no institution which decided to create Prolog. Prolog was born in a spontaneous way, as a software tool for natural language processing.

These are the succesive topics of my talk:

(SLIDE 2) After my PhD in Grenoble, I went, as Assistant Professor, to the University of Montreal where I got involved in an automatic translation project. It was within the framework of this project that I developed a software tool, called "Q-systems", which in fact turned out to be a forerunner of Prolog. The letter "Q" stood for Quebec. At the end of the 70s, I went back to France where I got a position as Professor in Marseilles. There I met Philippe Roussel and we started to develop a natural language communication system involving logical inferences.

After a first "primitive" system, we developed a more sophisticated one, which led us to design and implement a preliminary version of Prolog, which I will call, "Prolog 0." We then developed a full version of the language, which I will call "Prolog 1". This version had a wide distribution. After describing all this in detail, I will conclude by giving information about direct and indirect contributions of various people to the birth of Prolog.

The Birth of Prolog

Alain Colmerauer
and
Philippe Roussel

University of Marseille

SLIDE 1

- 1970 Automantic translation project
- 1970 Q-systems, a forerunner
- 1971 Primitive natural language communication system
- 1972 Natural language communication system

SLIDE 2

(SLIDES 3 and 4) First let us talk about the automatic translation project which was given the name TAUM, for "Traduction Automatique Université de Montréal". We were supposed to translate texts from English into French, and here is a typical example of a sentence to be translated.

(SLIDES 5 and 6) Slide 5 shows the input and slide 6 shows the output. The input sentence was translated using Q-sytems rules which were essentially rewriting rules on sequences of complex symbols.

(SLIDE 7) You would take the input sentence and cut it into pieces separated by plus signs. The "–1–" indicated the beginning of the sentence and "–2–" the end. Then you would apply rules on subsequences of elements. You would apply a first set of rules and then you would obtain this.

(SLIDE 8) "The" has been transformed into a definite article, "expansion" is a noun and so on. This makes up the first step in morphology. Then you would add another phase and you would end up with just one complex symbol.

(SLIDE 9) What results is, in fact, a tree, in which you would have all the information contained in the sentence. Then you would have another set of Q-system rules which would take the tree and cut it into little pieces of complex symbols. While cutting it into little pieces you would start to produce some French.

(SLIDE 10) Then you would parse this output, obtain a French deep structure . . .

(SLIDE 11) . . . and then you would produce a French sentence.

- 1972 Prolog 0
- 1973 Prolog 1
- 1974–1975 Distribution of Prolog
- Contributions of people

SLIDE 3

Automatic translation
project: TAUM
Montréal, 1970

SLIDE 4

```
THE EXPANSION OF
GOVERNMENT ACTIVITIES IN
CANADA AS IN MANY OTHER
COUNTRIES IS NOT SOMETHING
NEW.
```

SLIDE 5

```
L'EXPANSION DES ACTIVITES
GOUVERNEMENTALES AU CANADA
COMME DANS PLUSIEURS
AUTRES PAYS N'EST PAS
QUELQUE CHOSE DE NOUVEAU.
```

SLIDE 6

```
  -1- THE + EXPANSION + OF
+ GOVERNMENT + ACTIVITIES
+ IN + CANADA + AS + IN +
MANY + OTHER + COUNTRIES
+ IS + NOT + SOMETHING +
NEW + . -2-
```

SLIDE 7

```
-1- ART(DEF) + N(EXPANSION
,/,*AB,*DV) + ... + NP(N(C
ANADA),/,*C,*PROP,*NT) -2-
-2- SCONJ(AS) -3-
-2- P(AS) -3-
-3- P(IN) ... + *(.) -4-
```

SLIDE 8

```
-1- SENTENCE(PH(GOV(T(PRS3
S),OPS(INV(NOT)),NP(N(SOME
THING),...,ADJ(OTHER,/),/,
*H,*C,*GP,*PL,*LOC),/,*C,*
LOC,*LOC)),/,*AB,*PL)),/,*
AB,*DV),/)) -2-
```

SLIDE 9

```
-1- [(PH) + [(GOV) + [(T)
+ *GPR + [(OPS) + [(INV)
+ NE + PAS + ... + *PL +
] + ^ + ] + / + *AB + * +
] + ^ + NO(1) + ^ + / + ]
+ . -2-
```

SLIDE 10

```
-1- PH(GOV(T(*IPR),OPS(INV
(NE,PAS)),SN(N(QUELQUE,CHO
SE),ADJ(GOUVERNEMENTAL,/).
GP(P(DANS),SN(CONJ(COMME),
SN(N(CANADA),...,)),/,/,*F
,*AB,*PL,3)),/,/*F,*AB,*S,3
,),/) + . -2-
```

SLIDE 11

```
-1- L + ' + EXPANSION + DE
S + ACTIVITES + GOUVERNEME
NTALES + AU + CANADA +COMM
E + DANS + PLUSIEURS + AUT
RES + PAYS + N + ' + EST +
 PAS + QUELQUE + CHOSE + D
E + NOUVEAU + . -2-
```

SLIDE 12

(SLIDE 12) This is just to give an idea of what we were doing.

(SLIDE 13) I would like to say a few words about the Q-systems. Essentially a Q-system is a set of rewriting rules.

(SLIDE 14) Here the third rule states that the subsequence **X + C** can be rewritten as the sequence **C + X**. When you apply the rewriting rules on an input sequence like **A + A + B + B + C + C**, you want to be very efficient and avoid a large search space. The way we did it, was to represent each symbol occurrence by an arrow labeled by that symbol and thus to represent the input sequence by a graph. Then the result of applying the different rewriting rules becomes the following graph.

(SLIDE 15) This graph representation leads to an efficient bottom-up parser which keeps most common parts together.

The important thing was that, within a rule, you were allowed to speak about complex symbols and complex symbols were just trees, like the ones we now have in Prolog. To denote complex symbols, that is, trees, we were using formulae, similar to Prolog terms, with the difference that there were three kinds of variables, each represented by a single letter followed by an asterisk. A variable with a letter from the beginning of the alphabet, like "A," was used to denote an unknown label of a node, a variable with a letter in the middle of the alphabet, like "I," was used to denote a whole unknown tree and a variable with a letter at the end of the alphabet, like "X" and "Y," was used to denote an unknown sequence of trees.

Q-Systems

Montréal, 1970

SLIDE 13

```
    A + B + C -> S
A + S + X + C -> S
        X + C -> C + X
        B + B -> B + X

A + A + B + B + C + C
```

SLIDE 14

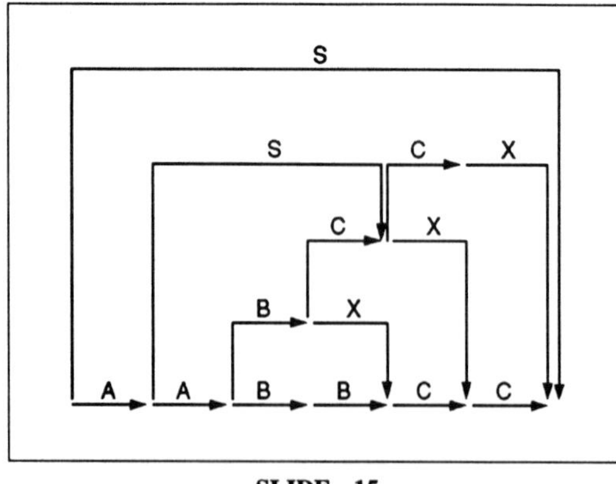

SLIDE 15

```
P + Q(R,S,T) + P

P + A*(X*,I*,Y*) ->
            I* + A*(X*,Y*)

R + Q(S,T) + P
S + Q)R,T) + P
T + Q(R,S) + P
```

SLIDE 16

(SLIDE 16) So, for example, if you apply the rule in the middle of this slide, to the sequence at the top of the slide you obtain the three different sequences at the bottom of the slide, according to the fact that the variable "I*" matches "R," "S," or "T." Here we have a nondeterministic unification, but it is not a true unification, it is more like a pattern matching because it just works in one direction. But, the status of the variables here was already the same as in Prolog. They were true unknowns.

(SLIDE 17) The Q-systems were very efficient and they are still used in a program which every day translates Canadian weather reports from English to French. This slide shows an example of such a translation made in 1978.

(SLIDE 18) During my stay at the University of Montréal, I was surrounded by a large team of linguists and I had to spend a lot of energy to make the computer scientists work together with them. Also, I was working more on syntactical aspects of natural languages than on semantical aspects, and my knowledge of English was, and is still, too poor to work on English syntax. So I wanted to stop working on automatic translation and do research in the processing of information contained in French sentences.

Just before I went to Marseilles I was introduced to the "Resolution Principle" paper by Alan Robinson about automatic theorem proving. I was very impressed and then saw the possibility of designing a system able to "understand" statements and questions written in French and able to do the right logical inferences for answering the questions. So, I arrived in Marseilles together with Jean Trudel, a Canadian doctoral student, in the winter of 1971. Both Jean and Philippe Roussel started to write different theorem provers à la Robinson. But, instead of proving mathematical theorems, Jean always tried to do inferences on little stories.

(SLIDES 19 and 20) This is the kind of logical axiom he was writing for this purpose: reflexivity (axiom 1) and transitivity (axiom 2) of the subset relation as shown: if the sets "x" and "y" are in the relation "r", and if "x" prime is a subset of "x" and "y" prime is the subset of y then "x" prime and "y" prime are also in the relation "r" (axiom 4). For example, if the boys love the girls, then if you take a boy and a girl then that boy will love that girl.

It's very naive but if you work on natural languages, you always have the problem of plural noun phrases which denote sets. Thus all your relations are on sets and you have to make a connection between sets, subsets, and your relations. We also had a lot of trouble with the subset relation because the addition of a communitivity axiom was producing a lot of unnecessary inferences. So we only allowed communitivity in the case where we were sure that every subset was a singleton (axiom 3).

TAUM METEO 1978

```
CLOUDY WITH A CHANCE OF
SHOWERS TODAY AND THURSDAY
------
NUAGEUX AVEC POSSIBILITE
D AVERSES AUJOURD HUI ET
JEUDI.
```

SLIDE 17

Primitive natural language communication system

Marseille, 1971

SLIDE 18

1

$(\forall x)[\text{Subset}(x,x)]$,

2

$(\forall x)(\forall y)(\forall z)[\text{Subset}(x,y) \wedge \text{Subset}(y,z) \Rightarrow \text{Subset}(x,z)]$,

SLIDE 19

3

$(\forall a)(\forall b)[\text{Subset}(\text{The }(a)], \text{The }(b)) \Rightarrow \text{Subset}(\text{The}(b), \text{The}(a))]$,

4

$(\forall x)(\forall y)(\forall r)\ (\forall x')\ (\forall y')$
$[\text{True}(r,x,y) \wedge \text{Subset}(x',x) \wedge \text{Subset}(y',y) \Rightarrow \text{True}(r,x',y')]$.

SLIDE 20

```
CATS KILL MICE.
TOM IS A CAT WHO DOES NOT
LIKE MICE WHO EAT CHEESE.
JERRY IS A MOUSE WHO EATS
CHEESE.
MAX IS NOT A MOUSE.
WHAT DOES TOM DO?
```

SLIDE 21

```
> TOM DOES NOT LIKE MICE
  WHO EAT CHEESE.
> TOM KILLS MICE.
WHO IS A CAT?
> TOM.
WHAT DOES JERRY EAT?
> CHEESE.
```

SLIDE 22

```
WHO DOES NOT LIKE MICE WHO
EAT CHEESE?
> TOM.
WHAT DOES TOM EAT?
> WHAT CATS WHO DO NOT
  LIKE MICE WHO EAT
  CHEESE EAT.
```

SLIDE 23

- 50 Q-systems rules to translate sentences into logical statements.
- 4 added logical statements.
- 17 Q-systems rules to translate the deduced logical statements into sentences.

SLIDE 24

(SLIDES 21, 22, 23, and 24) By putting together the four axioms, a whole theorem prover, a little Q-system to parse sentences in French, another one to produce answers, we were able to have the conversation shown in the slides and in which sentences starting with a ">" prompt are answers generated by the computer. Our taste for embedded relative clauses must be noticed when, to the query "What does Tom eat?" the computer replies "What cats, who do not like mice who eat cheese, eat."

(SLIDE 25) We thought maybe we could use the theorem prover not only for making inferences, but also for the parsing and for the synthesis of the sentences. I spent a long time solving this problem.

(SLIDE 26) I think it was in the summer of 1971 that I found the trick for writing a context-free parser using logical statements. It is a trick that is now well known under the name "difference lists". If you consider the first context-free rule of slide 26, you would like to write roughly: if "x" is of type "B" and if "y" is of type "C", then "x" concatenated with "y" is of type A. You would then have to run a concatenation subprogram and the parser would be very inefficient. So you just write: if the list "x" minus "y" (that is, the list "x" from which you have suppressed the ending list "y") is of type B and if the list "y" minus "z" is of type "C" then the list "x" minus "z" is of type "A."

After this discovery, I decided that from now on we should program everything by just writing logical statements and use a kind of theorem prover to execute our statements. So we wrote a special theorem prover that I have called Prolog 0 and we wrote the first Prolog program which was already large.

Natural language communication system

Marseille, 1972.

A Prolog program of 610 clauses.

SLIDE 25

$A \rightarrow BC,$

$A \rightarrow a.$

$(\forall x)(\forall y)(\forall z)$

$[A(x,z) \Leftarrow B(x,y) \wedge C(y,z)],$

$(\forall x)[A(\text{list}(a,x),x)].$

SLIDE 26

- 164 clauses to encode pronouns, articles, and prepositions,
- 104 clauses for linking singular and plural,
- 334 clauses for the parsing,
- 162 clauses for the deductive and answering part.

SLIDE 27

```
EVERY PSYCHIATRIST IS A
PERSON.
EVERY PERSON HE ANALYZES
IS SICK.
*JACQUES IS A PSYCHIATRIST
IN *MARSEILLE.
```

SLIDE 28

(SLIDE 27) This is the size of the different parts of the program: a dictionary of pronouns, articles and prepositions, a small morphology of French, a large parser of French sentences and finally a part for computing and generating answers.

(SLIDES 28 and 29) These are the kinds of sentences you were able to give as input to the computer. In these sentences the computer knows only the words "every," "is," "a," "he," "in" (that is, prepositions, articles and pronouns) and recognizes the proper nouns "Jacques" and "Marseille" because of the asterisk in front of them. With this input, you asked the questions : "Is Jack a person?", "Where is Jack?" "Is Jack sick?" and then you got the answers.

(SLIDE 30) This system was written using Prolog 0, the very first Prolog.

(SLIDE 31) For the syntax of Prolog 0 programs, this gives an idea. I was using an asterisk in front of the variables (in the Q-systems I used to put an asterisk after the variables). The minus sign denotes negation, the plus sign is used otherwise and all the atomic formula are implictly connected by "or" connectors. At the bottom of the slide you can see the way you would write the same program now if you use the normalized Prolog which I hope will come out soon.

There were some main differences between Prolog 0 and current versions of Prolog. There was not a simple cut operation but there were different double punctuation marks at the end of each clause to perform different types of search space reductions.

```
IS *JACQUES A PERSON?
WHERE IS *JACQUES?
IS JACQUES SICK?

> YES.
> IN *MARSEILLE.
> I DO NOT KNOW.
```

SLIDE 29

Prolog 0
Marseille, 1972.

SLIDE 30

```
+APPEND(NIL,*Y,*Y).
+APPEND(*A.*X,*Y,*A.*Z)
        -APPEND(*X,*Y,*Z).

append([],Y,Y).
append([A|X],Y,[A|Z] :-
        append(X,Y,Z).
```

SLIDE 31

No cut operation but double punctuation marks at the end of the clause:

.. cuts after the clause head,
.; cuts after the whole clause,
;. gives only the first answer,
;; do not cut.

SLIDE 32

(SLIDE 32) For example you would put a double dot if you wanted to perform a cut after the head of the clause. There were very few predefined predicates.

(SLIDE 33) There was a "DIF" predicate to write nonequal constraints. You could write "X" is not equal to "Y" and it would delay the test until "X" and "Y" were enough known. So Prolog 0 already had features which we later put in Prolog II. There was a primitive called "BOUM" to split or create an identifier into, or from, a string of characters. And somebody wanted to have a strange thing which was to copy terms and rename the variables.

We didn't like it but we were forced to add the "COPY" predicate. There was no explict input and output instructions. For the ouput, what you were supposed to do was to put a slash in some clauses and then all the literals after the slash would be delayed and accumulated. At the end the Prolog 0 interpreter would print the sequence of all these literals. What you would input, would in fact be a set of clauses and the output would be another set of clauses which would be entailed by the first set of clauses. This was Prolog 0.

(SLIDE 34) Then we decided to make a full programming language which I have called Prolog 1. This language was very close to the actual Prolog programming language.

(SLIDE 35) With Prolog 1, there was the introduction of a unique cut operation and no more not-equal constraints. There were all the classical built-in predicates like input, output, assert, retract. The names of the last two ones were "AJOUT" and "SUPPRIMER". There was a metacall: you could

Predefined predicates:

- DIF for the $\neq$ constraint of Philippe's dissertation,
- BOUM to split or create an identifier,
- COPY to copy a term.

SLIDE 33

Prolog 1
Marseille, 1973

SLIDE 34

- Introduction of the unique cut operation.
- Suppresion of ≠ constraints.
- Classical predefined predicates: input, output, assert, retract ...
- Meta-call: use of a variable instead of a literal.

SLIDE 35

"The present system is implemented partly in Fortran, partly in Prolog itself and, running on an IBM 360-67, achieves roughly 200 unifications per second."

David Warren

SLIDE 36

use a variable instead of a literal. This was because a large part of Prolog was written in Prolog itself and thus we needed some meta level.

(SLIDE 36) We had a visit from David Warren. This was in January 1973. After his visit, David wrote the sentence shown, which among others gives the speed of our implementation. In fact, an early version of Prolog 1 was running on a Sigma 7. This computer was sold in France by BULL, but under a different name.

(SLIDE 37) The fact that the interpreter was written in FORTRAN was very helpful in the distribution of the language. We had a lot of visitors who came and took a copy away with them. First what happened was that different people started using Prolog to do something other than natural language processing.

(SLIDE 38) The first other application was a plan generation system made by David Warren who was visiting us. Then there were people like Marc Bergman and Henry Kanoui who started to write a symbolic computation system. Then Henri Meloni started to make a speech recognition system using Prolog.

(SLIDE 39) At the same time people came and took Prolog away to Budapest, University of Warsaw, Toronto, University of Waterloo, University of Edinburgh, University of Montreal, and INRIA in Paris. I was later told that David Warren took a copy from Marseilles and brought it to Stanford. From there Koichi Furakawa took a copy to Tokyo. This story was related in an issue of *The Washington Post*.

The distribution of Prolog
1974–1975

SLIDE 37

- Plan generation system
- Symbolic Computation system
- Speech recognition system

SLIDE 38

- Budapest,
- University of Warsaw,
- Toronto,
- University of Waterloo,
- University of Edinburgh,
- University of Montréal,
- IRIA, research center in Paris.

SLIDE 39

People and papers who influenced the work on Prolog

SLIDE 40

(SLIDE 40) I wanted to talk about the people and papers who influenced the work around Prolog. First, it sounds strange but Noam Chomsky had a strong influence on my work. When I did my thesis, I worked on context-free grammars and parsing and I spent a long time on this subject. At that time, Noam Chomsky was like a god for me because he had introduced me to the context-free grammars in his paper mentioned at the top of this next slide.

(SLIDE 41) Also, when I was in Montreal, I discussed with people who were working in linguistics and these people were very influenced by the second paper mentioned in the same slide. If you look at this second paper from the point of view of a computer scientist, you understand that you can do everything in a nice way if you just use trees and transform them. I think this is what we are all doing. We are doing this in Lisp; we are doing this in Prolog. Trees are really good data structures.

(SLIDE 42) Another person who is not a linguist but a computer scientist and who had a strong influence was Robert Floyd. He visited me when I was still a student in Grenoble and I was very impressed by him. I did my thesis starting from the first paper mentioned in the slide. I knew about the work described in the second paper before it was published. So I understood the way to implement a nondeterministic language, how to do the back-tracking, how to save information in a stack, and so on, and how to do it in an efficient way.

(SLIDE 43) Another person who influenced me was A. van Wijngaarden. I was influenced in two ways. First, as a student I participated in different meetings to design a new ALGOL 60. I was very

Noam Chomsky

On certain formal properties of grammars, *Information and Control*, 1959.

Aspects of the Theory of Syntax, *MIT Press*, 1965.

SLIDE 41

Robert Floyd

Syntactic analysis and operator precedence. J. *ACM*, 1963.

Nondeterministic algorithms. *J. ACM*, 1967.

SLIDE 42

A. van Wijngaarden	Alan Robinson
Final Draft Report on the Algorithmic Language Algol 68, Mathematisch Centrum, Amsterdam, 1968 (with B.J. Mailloux, J.E.L. Peck, and G.H.A. Koster).	A machine-oriented logic based on the resolution principle. *J. ACM*, 1965.
SLIDE 43	**SLIDE 44**

impressed to see that people, starting from nothing, were creating a whole language. It's hard to believe that you can just take a sheet of paper and design a new language which will be used by many people. Secondly, I was very strongly influenced by the W-grammars, which is my name for the formalism introduced by A. van Wijngaarden to describe ALGOL 68. And in fact, I wrote a complete parser for languages that are generated by W-grammars. I also wrote a complete generator and I used both for performing automatic translation before using the Q-systems.

(SLIDE 44) Of course, I think that Prolog would not have been born without Alan Robinson. I did not get the paper mentioned in the slide directly. I was still at the University of Montreal, and a student came, Jean Trudel, and showed me the paper. I looked at it and I didn't understand anything. I was not trained in logic at all. Jean Trudel spent a lot of time working on the paper and explaining it to us. This was a very important paper.

(SLIDE 45) There was another influence: Robert Kowalski. When we arrived in Marseilles, we were not trained in logic and we were looking at all the papers written on automatic theorem proving. But we didn't exactly have a feeling for why things were made in such a way. So we invited people who knew a lot about automatic theorem proving. Robert Kowalski came to visit us and of course something clicked. He talked about logic, we wanted to do inferences and he did not know a lot about computers. So we began a very close collaboration. He had a very nice prover which was essentially

Robert Kowalski	People who contributed directly to the work around Prolog
Linear resolution with selection function, *Artificial Intelligence*, 1972, (with D. Kuehner).	
SLIDE 45	**SLIDE 46**

- Richard Kittredge,
  University of Montréal,
- Jean Trudel,
  Hydro Québec, Montréal,
- Robert Pasero,
  University of Marseille.

SLIDE 47

- Gérard Battani,
- Henri Meloni,
- René Bazzoli.

SLIDE 48

a resolution prover and the first Prolog was somehow an imitation of his complete SL-resolution method mentioned in the slide.

(SLIDE 46) These are people who were more directly involved with the implementation or discussion which were next door.

(SLIDE 47) First, I learned a lot from Richard Kittredge at the University of Montréal. He was a linguist who had received his Ph.D. from Zelleg Harris. I wanted to thank Jean Pierre Trudel because he was really the person who filled the gap between Robinson's paper and our own work. Robert Pasero is the person who was always involved on the natural language processing side of Prolog.

(SLIDE 48) And there are three other people who really were the implementors of Prolog 1 which was written in FORTRAN: they are Gerard Battani, Henri Meloni, and René Bazzoli. The first Prolog interpreter was their first FORTRAN program!

That is all I have to tell.

TRANSCRIPT OF DISCUSSANT'S REMARKS

SESSION CHAIR RANDY HUDSON: Jacques Cohen is a Professor in the Michtom School of Computer Science at Brandeis University. He has two Doctorates, one from the University of Illinois, the other from the University of Grenoble, France. He has held visiting positions at MIT, Brown, and at the University of Marseilles where the Prolog language originated. From 1963 to 1967 he was a colleague of Alain Colmerauer as a Doctoral student at the University of Grenoble. At that time, they had similar interests in syntax-directed compilation and nondeterminism. Jacques interacted only informally with Alain in the 1970s. In 1980, he was invited by Alain, now the head of the Artificial Intelligence group at the University of Marseilles, to teach a yearly course on compilers. Since the early 1980s, Jacques has been an aficionado of Prolog and has written several papers on logic programming including one on its early history. Jacques' current research interests are in the areas of compiler development using logic programming, parallelism, and constraint languages. He is currently Editor in Chief of Communications of the ACM. Jacques is a member of the Program Committee of this conference.

JACQUES COHEN: In the first HOPL Conference the discussant for the Lisp language was Paul Abrams who rightly pointed out that LISP was unusual in the sense that it had not been designed by a committee, but it was an invention or, if you want, a discovery of a single individual, John McCarthy. Abrams also mentioned that he knew only one other language with a similar origin. That was APL, the brain child of Ken Iverson. One can state that Prolog also belongs to that category of languages. Prolog had a principal inventor, Alain Colmerauer, who contributed to most of the ideas underlying that language.

Robert Kowalski and Philippe Roussel also played key roles. The first one, as an expert of automatic theorem proving, the second one as a doctoral student of Alain's who implemented the first version of Prolog. Alain and Philippe admit in their paper that had Prolog not been discovered by them, it would have certainly appeared later under a form which would be recognizable as a variant of Prolog as it is known nowadays. I wish to emphasize that this in no way diminishes the amazing feat of having been the first to discover this beautiful language. Again, a parallel with Lisp is in order. Prolog, like Lisp, has a very simple syntax and embodies an elegant set of primitives and rules. In my view, both languages appear to be so simple and effective for expressing symbolic computation, that they would have come into existence sooner or later.

In the 1960s I was a colleague of Alain as a doctoral student at the University of Grenoble. I remember that one of his first research projects was to write a syntax-directed error detector for COBOL programs. Alain avoided reading many technical papers because at the time he had some difficulties with English. I am sure that when he located a key paper he read it with great care. I believe that two papers from Robert Floyd had a considerable impact on Prolog. The first was on parsing and the second was on backtracking.

Prolog rules can be viewed as grammar rules and parsing corresponds to the equivalent Prolog program. Furthermore, the subject of parsing is closely related to Alain's interest in natural language processing. It is relevant to point out that Alain became aware of Alan Robinson's seminal paper of resolution and unification five years after that paper had been published in the *Journal of the Association for Computing Machinery*. As happened in the case of the Floyd papers, Alain realized the importance of Robinson's work and that prompted him to contact experts in theorem proving like Robert Kowalski.

In the conclusion of their paper, Colmerauer and Roussel state that their first Prolog interpreter was essentially a theorem prover à la Robinson. The great merit of the inventors is to transform a theorem prover into an interpreter for a novel programming language and that in itself represents a formidable task. To illustrate that transformation, let us consider the following experiment: Submit a set of current Prolog programs to Robinson's theorem prover. (A parenthetic remark is in order. That set of Prolog examples actually took several years to develop. It would not be available without the experience gained in programming in the new language.) Robinson's prover would perhaps provide the needed answers to the current Prolog programs. But, it would be excruciatingly slow or it would run out of memory, even using present-day workstations.

The heart of Colmerauer's quest was how to make Robinson's prover work practically. Efficiency became of paramount importance and the Prolog designers were willing to use all sorts of compromises provided that they could solve the class of problems they had in mind. In Prolog's case the problem was natural language understanding using computers. The compromises that Alan Colmerauer was willing to make would stupefy even the most open-minded logician. First, they dropped completeness by performing only certain steps needed to prove a theorem. Therefore, they had no guarantee that if it was known that the theorem was provable, that the prover would inevitably find that proof. They also dropped an important test which is called "the occur-test," which insures that the unification works properly. In other words, they were willing to eliminate these costly tests even though certain programs would automatically result in an infinite loop. Finally, they introduced annotations (mainly to cut operations) that bypass certain computations in an effort to further increase the speed at the expense of missing certain solutions of a problem.

All this was done for the sake of increasing efficiency. But the gained efficiency was precisely what enabled Alain to experiment with the prover by concentrating on expressing problems in their embryonic language. That experience was crucial in making the transition from a theorem prover to an interpreter of a new programming language.

The role of Robert Kowalski in cleaning up the rudimentary language that preceded Prolog is considerable. Kowalski's main contribution was the discovery that most of the sample problems that he and Alain were submitting to the general theorem prover were of a particular kind. They simply did not need all the power of the general prover. I have had the opportunity to discuss that discovery with Robert Kowalski. According to Robert, it was a moment in which the main faults in Alain's implementation actually became a superior advantage. It avoided the combinatorial explosion of Robinson's approach by restricting the form of the theorem submitted to the prover to the so-called Horn clauses. In so doing, we would then regain the formal advantages of dealing with logic. One can also state that the limitation of the occur-test and the introduction of cut were premonitions of the designers of the new language and the fertile new areas of research extending Prolog.

In my view, the development of Prolog reflects Polya's advice for solving difficult problems. If you cannot solve a difficult problem, try to solve a particular version of it. In the case of Prolog, the particular version of the problem developed into a rich area of logic programming. Polya's approach seems to underline Prolog's historical development and it can be summarized by: first specialize then generalize.

A discussion about the history of Prolog would be incomplete without a few remarks about implementation. I believe that the lack of a fast mainframe in Colmerauer's actually slowed down the development of Prolog. As I recall, even in 1980, Alain and his colleagues implemented one version of the first Prologs on an Apple II. It is known that Prolog interpreters have a voracious appetite for memory. The designers had to implement a virtual memory on the Apple II, using a floppy disk as slow memory. According to Alain and his colleagues the hardest part of this implementation was temporarily stopping a program using Control C and making sure that the information in memory was not destroyed. Fortunately, the visit to Marseilles of David H. Warren from Edinburgh enabled him to implement the first fairly efficient compiler for the PDP 10. It is fair to state that it was that compiler that contributed to a wider acceptence of Prolog.

Finally, I would like to mention that in my view, the recent contributions that Alain has made in the area of constraint logic programming, equal or surpass his previous contributions as an inventor of Prolog. One can only hope that in HOPL III, he or one of his colleagues will present a paper on the evolution of Prolog into the new class of constraint logic programming languages.

TRANSCRIPT OF QUESTION AND ANSWER SESSION

GUY STEELE from Thinking Machines: Q-systems seem reminiscent of the COMIT language. Was there any influence of one language on the other?

COLMERAUER: I am not familiar with COMIT but I am familiar with SNOBOL. But in SNOBOL there is no parsing. Furthermore, in the Q-system the rules are not context free. They are general rules specifying the rewriting of trees. So, the answer is no.

BIOGRAPHY OF ALAIN COLMERAUER

Alain Colmerauer was born in 1941 in Carcassonne, France. After receiving a graduate degree in computer science from the Institut Polytechnique de Grenoble, he received a doctorat from the

University of Grenoble in 1967. The subject of his thesis was: precedences, syntactic analysis, and programming languages.

His interest then turned from computer languages to natural languages. As an assistant professor at the University of Montréal, he worked for three years on a project for automatic translation from English into French. Upon returning to France in 1970, he was appointed professor in computer science at the Faculty of Sciences of Luminy. There, together with Philippe Roussel, he designed the programming language Prolog which has become indispensable in the field of Artificial Intelligence.

His work centers on natural language processing, logic programming, and constraint programming. A good introduction to his recent work is the article: An Introduction to Prolog III, in *Communications of the ACM*, July 1990.

He has received these prizes and honors:

- Lauréat de la Pomme d'Or du Logiciel français 1982, an award from Apple France shared with Henry Kanoui and Michel Van Caneghem.
- Lauréat for 1984 of the Conseil Régional, Provence Alpes et Côte d'Azur.
- Prix Michel Monpetit 1985, awarded by the Académie des Sciences.
- Chevalier de la Légion d'Honneur in 1986.
- Fellow of the American Association for Artificial Intelligence in 1991.
- Correspondant de l'Académie des Sciences in mathematics.

BIOGRAPHY OF PHILIPPE ROUSSEL

Philippe Roussel is presently Associate Professor at the University of Nice, Sophia Antipolis, and member of the I3S-CNRS Laboratory of the same university.

He is the coauthor, with Alain Colmerauer, of the Prolog language. He implemented it for the first time in 1972, while he was a researcher at the University of Marseilles. He received his doctoral degree the same year, in the field of automatic theorem-proving. After spending six years in this university as an Assistant Professor in Computer Science, he joined the Simon Bolivar University in Caracas, Venezuela. He took charge of a cooperative program for developing a master's program in computer sciences, working on logic programming and deductive data bases. He returned to France in 1984, first as manager of the Artificial Intelligence Department of the BULL Company and later, as a scientific director of the Elsa Software Company. During this time, he conceived the LAP language, an object-oriented language based upon logic programming paradigms.

His major research interest is knowledge representation languages for information system modeling.

Discrete Event Simulation Languages Session

Chair: *Tim Bergin*

A HISTORY OF DISCRETE EVENT SIMULATION PROGRAMMING LANGUAGES

Richard E. Nance

Director, Systems Research Center
Professor of Computer Science
Virginia Polytechnic Institute and State University
Blacksburg, Virginia 24061-0251

ABSTRACT

The history of simulation programming languages is organized as a progression in periods of similar developments. The five periods, spanning 1955–1986, are labeled: The Period of Search (1955–1960); The Advent (1961–1965); The Formative Period (1966–1970); The Expansion Period (1971–1978); and The Period of Consolidation and Regeneration (1979–1986). The focus is on recognizing the people and places that have made important contributions in addition to the nature of the contribution. A balance between comprehensive and in-depth treatment has been reached by providing more detailed description of those languages that have or have had major use. Over 30 languages are mentioned, and numerous variations are described. A concluding summary notes the concepts and techniques either originating with simulation programming languages or given significant visibility by them.

CONTENTS

8.1 INTRODUCTION

This introductory section is intended to explain the different types of computer simulation and to identify the key issues in simulation programming languages (SPLs). The approach to this survey is the subject of a concluding subsection.

8.1.1 Computer Simulation

Analog (or analogue) simulation, that is, simulation on analog computers, is not addressed in this survey because no major "language" or language issues are associated with this early form. However, analog simulation was much in evidence during the 1950s and earlier. Digital simulation, that is, simulation on digital computers, is considered synonymous with "computer simulation" for this history of SPLs.

8.1.1.1 *Taxonomy and Terminology*

Computer simulation is an application domain of programming languages that permits further division into three partitions:

1. discrete event simulation,
2. continuous simulation, and
3. Monte Carlo simulation.

Discrete event simulation utilizes a mathematical/logical model of a physical system that portrays state changes at precise points in simulated time. Both the nature of the state change and the time at which the change occurs mandate precise description. Customers waiting for service, the management of parts inventories, or military combat are typical application domains for discrete event simulation.

Continuous simulation uses equational models, often of physical systems, which do not portray precise time and state relationships that result in discontinuities. The objectives of studies using such models do not require the explicit representation of state and time relationships. Examples of such systems are found in ecological modeling, ballistic reentry, or large-scale economic modeling.

Monte Carlo simulation, the name given by John von Neumann and Stanislaw M. Ulam [Morgenthaler 1961, p. 368] to reflect its gambling similarity, utilizes models of uncertainty where representation of time is unnecessary. The term is originally attributed to "a situation in which a difficult nonprobablistic problem is solved through the invention of a stochastic process that satisfies the relations of the deterministic problem" [Morgenthaler 1961]. A more recent characterization is that Monte Carlo is "the method of repetitive trials" [Shreider 1966, p.1]. Typical of Monte Carlo simulation is the approximation of a definite integral by circumscribing the region with a known geometric shape, then generating random points to estimate the area of the region through the proportion of points falling within the region boundaries.

Simulation as a problem-solving technique precedes the appearance of digital computers by many years. However, the emergence of digital technology exerted an influence far more than adding the term "computer" as an adjectival descriptor of this method of problem solving. The oppressive manual computational burden was now off-loaded to a much faster, more tolerant processor—the digital computer.

Three related forms of simulation are commonly noted in the literature. *Combined simulation* refers generally to a model that has both discrete event and continuous components (see [Law 1991, p. 112]). Typically, a discrete event submodel runs within an encapsulating continuous model. *Hybrid simulation* refers to the use of an analytical submodel within a discrete event model (see [Shantikumar 1983]).

Finally, *gaming* or *computer gaming* can have discrete event, continuous, and/or Monte Carlo modeling components.

8.1.1.2 *Language Requirements for Discrete Event Simulation*

In her description of programming languages, Sammet [1969, p. 650] justifies the categorization of simulation languages as a specialization warranting limited description with the statement that, "their usage is unique and presently does not appear to represent or supply much carry-over into other fields." The impact of the object-oriented paradigm, and the subsequent clamor over object-oriented programming languages, first represented by SIMULA, would appear in hindsight to contradict this opinion, which accurately represented the attitude of the programming language research community at that time.

A simulation language must provide a model representation that permits analysis of execution behavior. This provision entails six requirements:

1. generation of random numbers, so as to represent the uncertainty associated with an inherently stochastic model;
2. process transformers, to permit uniform random variates obtained through the generation of random numbers to to be transformed to a variety of statistical distributions;
3. list processing capability, so that objects can be created, deleted, and manipulated as sets or as members, added to and removed from sets;
4. statistical analysis routines, to provide the descriptive summary of model behavior so as to permit comparison with system behavior for validation purposes and the experimental analysis for both understanding and improving system operation;
5. report generation, to furnish an effective presentation of potentially large reams of data to assist in the decision making that initially stimulates the use of simulation; and
6. timing executive or a time flow mechanism, to provide an explicit representation of time.

Every simulation programming language provides these components to some degree.

Many simulation applications are undertaken in general purpose languages. Strongly influenced by this fact, simulation "languages" have taken three forms: package, preprocessor, and conventional programming language. A package is a set of routines in language X that can be called or invoked to meet the six requirements listed previously. The user (programmer) might develop additional routines in X to provide needed capabilities or a tailored treatment. Although such packages are not truly languages, some have had major influence, perhaps leading to descendants that take one of the other two forms. For example, the evolution of GASP, a package, produced SLAM, a preprocessor. All three "language" forms are included because examples of each have played significant roles in shaping the simulation scene.

8.1.1.3 *Conceptual Frameworks for Discrete Event Modeling*

Very early, Lackner [1962, p. 3] noted the importance of a modeling perspective as a "WELTANSICHT" or world view that "must be implicitly established to permit the construction of a simulation language." In a subsequent work, he attempted to lay the groundwork for a theory of discrete event simulation and used the differing world views to categorize SPLs [Lackner 1964]. Lackner's categorization differentiates between event-oriented and activity-oriented SPLs. Kiviat [1967; 1969] expanded the categories to identify three world views: event-oriented, activity-oriented, and process-oriented.

Fishman [1973] helped to clarify the distinction among the categories, which he labeled "event scheduling," "activity scan," and "process interaction." These labels have become more or less the conventions in the literature. A recent thesis by Derrick [1988] expanded the three to 13, doing so in a manner that encompassed more than SPL discrimination.

The differentiation among world views characterized by languages is captured best using the concept of locality [Overstreet 1986, p. 171]:

> *Event scheduling* provides locality of time: each event routine in a model specification describes related actions that may all occur in a single instant.
>
> *Activity scanning* provides locality of state: each activity routine in a model specification describes all actions that must occur due to the model assuming a particular state (that is, due to a particular condition becoming true).
>
> *Process interaction* provides locality of object: each process routine in a model specification describes the entire action sequence of a particular model object.

8.1.2 Historical Approach

Although fundamental in distinguishing the modeling differences among SPLs, the world views do not suggest a basis for historical description for the following reasons:

1. the origins and initial development of the language(s) promoting a particular view took place concurrently without a clear progression of conceptual convergence, and
2. remarkably parallel development patterns are evident throughout the major SPLs, irrespective of world view ties.

However, the extent and range of activity in SPLs mandates an organizational thesis, and a chronological presentation is used.

A chronological depiction of SPL development could proceed in several ways. One could provide a vertical trace of developments within each SPL. The tack taken in this paper is more of a horizontal cut across periods of time, which are noted in the genealogical tree of SPLs, shown in Figure 8.1:

1955–1960: The Period of Search
1961–1965: The Advent
1966–1970: The Formative Period
1971–1978: The Expansion Period
1979–1986: The Period of Consolidation and Regeneration

Each major language originating in a period is described in terms of its background and rationale for language content. Description of that language in subsequent time periods is limited to changes in that language, particularly those that mark the designated time period. Descriptions of GPSS and SIMULA are limited also; since both languages are treated extensively in the first conference devoted to programming language history (see [Wexelblatt 1981]). No attempt is made to describe language developments since 1986; sufficient time has yet to elapse to permit a historical perspective.

Figure 8.1 is organized vertically to distinguish languages according to world view. This categorization cannot be precise, for the language developer in most instances was unaware of the distinguishing characteristic. Crookes [1982, p. 1] places the number of SPLs as 137, although giving

FIGURE 8.1

The Geneological Tree for Simulation Programming Languages.

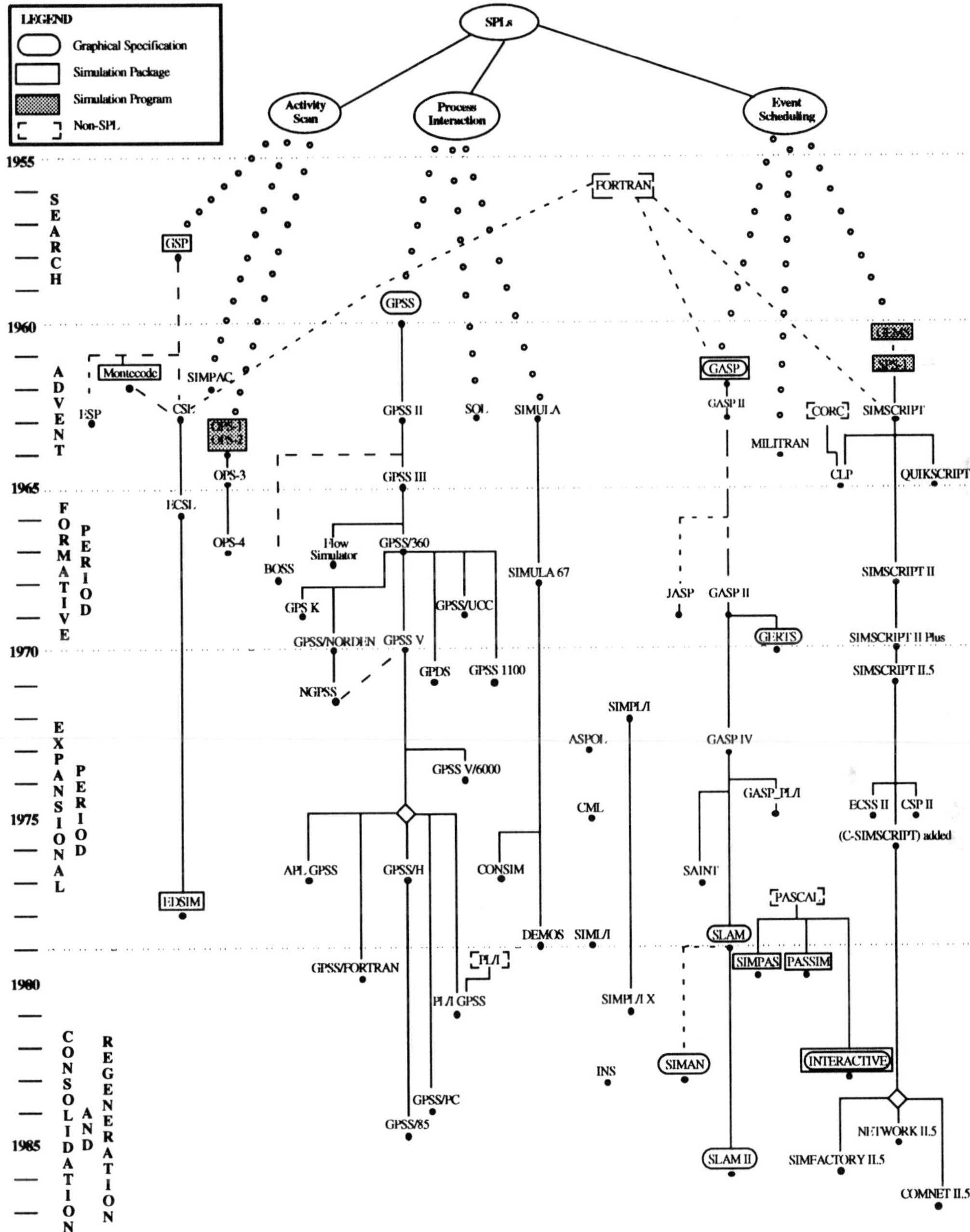

no source, and attributes this overpopulation to a lack of standardization in general purpose computer languages. More likely, the excess in SPLs can be attributed to a combination of root causes:

1. perceived differences among application domains, requiring language features not provided in extant SPLs;
2. lack of awareness of SPLs or the reliance on the general purpose language "crutch" leading to package development;
3. educational use of a well known language in which components are provided so that learning time is reduced and the cost of an additional translator is avoided; and
4. competition among language vendors to exploit particular features or selected application domains.

The degree to which each of these causes has proved influential is quite dependent on time. The first and second tend to mark the early periods; the fourth, the later periods.

One further point concerns the unfortunate but all too common instances of incomplete references, primarily missing dates. In the attempt to provide as much historical information as possible, dates are given if suggested by other sources, added notes (time stamps), or personal recollection. In those cases where the data is uncertain, a "?" suffix is placed in the citation, for example, [Meyerhoff 1968?] indicates that the recollection of Paul Roth is that this undated manual was completed in 1968 [Roth 1992].

8.2 THE PERIOD OF SEARCH (1955–1960)

The title of this subsection is derived from the efforts during this period to discover not only concepts of model representation but to facilitate the representational needs in simulation modeling. Simulation languages came into being with the recognition of the power of the technique in solving problems that proved intractable to closed-form mathematical solution. The most prominent examples of such problems are the early manufacturing simulations by a group at General Electric; Jackson, Nelson, and Rowe at UCLA; and Baker and Dzielinski cited in Conway [1967, p. 219].

K.D. Tocher is generally credited with the first simulator described in a 1960 publication jointly with D.G. Owen [Tocher 1960]. The simulator, later called GSP (General Simulation Program), introduced the three-phase method of timing control generally adopted by activity scan languages. Significantly, Tocher characterized his work as "searching for a simulation structure," rather than merely providing a "simulation language," [Tocher 1960, p.51]. Excerpts from the GSP example given in the appendix of the 1960 paper are shown in Figure 8.2. Although lacking the format regularity of assembly language programs, the syntactic structure of GSP seems to fall far short of the descriptor "automatic programming of simulations," [Tocher 1960, p.51]. However, this seemingly inflated claim was typically applied to languages other than basic machine coding, including assemblers (see [Rosen 1967] for examples).

In the United States interest in simulation was emerging rapidly in the late 1950s; however, the recognition of concepts and the assistance of languages in dealing with them was less recognized. Gordon [1981] describes his own efforts prior to 1960 as the writing of simulation programs for message switching systems. The Sequence Diagram Simulator, described in a conference in 1960, indicates some appreciation of language support for the application task [Gordon 1981, p. 405].

The treatment given to computer simulation in the 1961 issue of *Progress in Operations Research* [Ackoff 1961] demonstrates the perceived importance of the technique. However, the issue of manual

FIGURE 8.2
Excerpts from a GSP Program.

```
EXAMPLE FOR I.F.O.R.S. PAPER              Title of Job.
R1-5  B1  0   0   0    B3                 Initial values
T1-5   1  0   0   0    1440               for time-dependent
U5                     1440               machines, 1-5
Z

PARAMETERS
R-U11 +.462   +1000  +.576     +.4                  Parameters
L                                                   for routines
R-W12 +.529   +46913 +75859 +129459 -5612 +3095     SAMPLE and
L                                                   NEGEXP,
R-W13 +.371 +228219 -98655 +260848 -9995 +9162      defining
L                                                   distributions,
R-W14 +.293 +120440 -30872  +45456 -4360 +2879      etc.
L
R-W15 +.801  +76869 +18834 +176332 -7907 +2895
L
R-W16 +.427 +228218 -98632 +228080 -9993 +9161
L
R-W17 +.516  +28675 +61077  +66404 -3897 +3295
L
Z

DURATION  14400   Simulation to run for 10 days at a
time.

TRANSLATE         (End of Initial Conditions.)

C1 PROCESSING                        Activity C1
x ≠ 0                           If there is a non-zero queue, and an
n/2, A(n + 2), U = 0.           available unloaded machine, select
Q(n + 2) XYZ TII                process time for m/c and quality,
v → SAMPLE R(n+Q (n+2) + 12)    record which quality this item
is,
V(n + 2) - T + TIME, U → 1, D   up-date idle time, start processing,
x - 1                           and reduce queue by one.

K                               ('K' marks end of Activity.)


C2 UNLOADING                          Activity C2

A4                              If the crane is available, and if there is
n/2, A(n + 2), U = 1.           an available loaded machine, set
v  3                            (constant) unloading time, up-date
W - T + TIME, U → 0, D          waiting time, start unloading, record
Q4 → Q(n + 2), D                quality, and commit the crane.
THEN B2

K
Z                               (End of C-Activities.)
```

```
B1 ARRIVALS                   Activity B1
v → NEGEXP R11/S           Select next arrival interval, up-date
Pn + 1, D                  no. of items in system, add 1 to
x + 1, x  W,               queue, and if it now exceeds previous
W → X                       maxiumu, record new maximum.
K

B2 TRANSPORT TO STOCK        Activity B2
v → SAMPLE R(14 + Qn)      Select transport time for given quality,
Rn → 0, D                   cancel B2, and start transporting. Reduce
H, P1 - 1                  items in system by 1, and check for con-
H, P ≠ U2 + U3 + X          sistency with m/c-states. (Note: 'H' allows
H, STOP                    operator to suppress these statements.
K

B3 REPORT RESULTS             Activity B3
PRINT.C  W1                Print:
PRINT.A  V2
PRINT.E  W2
PRINT.A  V3                TIME, MAX.QUEUE TODAY
PRINT.E  W3                IDLE TIME, WAITING TIME (m/c 1)
Wn → (V2+W2+V3+W3)          IDLE TIME, WAITING TIME (m/c 2)
Wn → MULTIPLY Wn/50        PER CENT LOST TIME SO FAR
Wn → DIVIDE.B Wn/T
PRINT.A  Wn                Reset reporting m/c to operate again after
v → Un                     one day.
Dn                         Reset max. queue for tomorrow.
W1 → x
 K
Z                          (End of B-Activities.)

COMPILE                    (End of Activities.)

XYZ
5.6  700
6     100
0    0717
0.1 1037
0     600
5.1  162                   Subroutine XYZ
1.4  600
5.1  060                   Here, the text of the subroutine is supplied in
3     000.                 Pegasus order-code. It will be incorporated
0                          in the specification of the model.
+0                         (The routine produces one of two results:  the
+0                         quality '3' or the quality 'zero.'  The former
+0                         appears with probability given by element
14    600                   U11. A pesudo-random number stored in T11
5.1  610                   is used.)
5.6  710
0.0 7007
1.6  720
7     650
F
```

versus computer execution is still a matter of consideration [Morgenthaler 1961, pp. 406–407], and little consideration of language needs is indicated.

8.3 THE ADVENT (1961–1965)

The period of 1961–1965 marks the appearance of the forerunners of the major simulation programming languages currently in use. This claim is documented to some extent in the genealogical tree for SPLs (Figure 8.1).

The historical development of GPSS and SIMULA are described in detail in Wexelblatt [1981]. Herein, each is described sufficiently to furnish a trace of the evolution of the language through the subsequent time periods. More detailed description is provided for other languages emerging during this period, although none can be described to the extent permitted in the first conference.

8.3.1 GPSS

Beginning with the Gordon simulator in 1960, the General Purpose System Simulator (GPSS) was developed on various IBM computers, for example, 704, 709, and 7090, during 1960–1961. With the later name change to the General Purpose Simulation System, GPSS developments continued under the version labeled GPSS II, which transitioned from table-oriented to list processing techniques. The GPSS III version released in 1965 was made available primarily for the large IBM systems (7090/94 and 7040/44) [IBM 1965]. A major issue was the lack of compatibility between GPSS II and GPSS III.

GPSS has the distinction of being the most popular SPL. Uses and users of the language outnumbered all others during the early years (prior to 1975). No doubt, this popularity was due in part to the position of IBM as the premier marketing force in the computing industry, and GPSS during this era of unbundled software was the discrete event SPL for IBM customers. That fact alone, however, does not explain the appeal of GPSS. The language readily gained proponents in the educational community because of the speed with which noncomputer-oriented students could construct a model of a queueing system and obtain numerical results. Originating in the problem domain of communication systems, the GPSS block semantics were ideally suited for queueing models (although logic switches might have puzzled many business students).

The importance of graphical output for on-line validation was demonstrated in 1965 using an IBM 2250 interactive display terminal tied to a GPSS model [Reitman 1992]. Boeing (Huntsville) was the first to employ this device to enable the observation of model behavior and the interruption and restart during execution.

8.3.2 SIMULA I

The selection of GPSS and SIMULA by the program committee for the first conference on the History of Programming Languages (HOPL I) is notable in that the two represent opposite poles in several measurement scales that could be proposed for languages. Within the simulation community in the United States (US), GPSS was viewed as easy to learn, user friendly (with the symbolic interface), highly used, limited (in model size and complexity), inflexible (especially so prior to the introduction of the HELP block), and expensive to run (the interpretive implementation). On the contrary, SIMULA was considered difficult to learn (lack of ALGOL knowledge in the US), lacking in its human interface (with input/output being an implementation decision following ALGOL 60), little used (in the US), but conceptually innovative and broadly applicable. The discovery of SIMULA by the programming language research community in the 1970s was probably the influencing factor in its selection for HOPL I rather than the regard held for the language by simulation practitioners (notwithstanding its excellent reputation among a small cadre of simulation researchers in the US and a larger group in Europe).

Originating as an idea in the spring of 1961, SIMULA I represented the work primarily of Ole-Johan Dahl and Kristen Nygaard. The language was developed for the Univac 1107 as an extension of Univac's ALGOL 60 compiler. Nygaard and Dahl [1981] described the development of the language during this period as progressing through four main stages: (1) a discrete event network concept, (2) basing of the language on Algol 60, (3) modification and extensions of the Univac ALGOL 60 compiler, and the introduction of the "process concept," and (4) the implementation of the SIMULA I compiler.

The technical contributions of SIMULA are impressive, almost awesome. Dahl and Nygaard, in their attempt to create a language where objects in the real world could be accurately and naturally described, introduced conceptual advances that would be heralded as a paradigmatic shift almost two decades later. Almost lost in the clamor over the implementation of abstract data types, the class concept, inheritance, the coroutine concept, and quasi-parallel execution were the solution of significant problems in the extension of ALGOL 60. The creation, deletion, and set manipulation operations on objects are but one example. A second is that the sharing of attribute values by interacting processes required a means for breaking down the scoping restrictions of ALGOL 60. During the luncheon with language presenters at HOPL I in 1978, Nygaard remarked that only those who had programmed simulations really understood the power of the language (see [Wexelblat 1981, p. 485]).

8.3.3 SIMSCRIPT

SIMSCRIPT, in its original form was an event scheduling SPL. Two ancestors contributing to SIMSCRIPT are identified in the Preface to Markowitz [1963]: GEMS (General Electric Manufacturing Simulator) developed by Markowitz at the General Electric Manufacturing Services and SPS-1 developed at RAND. Morton Allen was identified as a major contributor to GEMS, and contributors to SPS-1 included Jack Little of RAND and Richard W. Conway of Cornell University.

8.3.3.1 *Background*

The RAND Corporation developed SIMSCRIPT under the auspices of the U.S. Air Force. The IBM 709/7090 computer was the target machine, and copies of SIMSCRIPT were distributed through SHARE (the IBM user's group). Harry Markowitz, whose broad contributions in several areas were to earn him a Nobel Prize, is generally attributed with the major design, and Bernard Hausner was the sole programmer, actually for both SPS-1 and the SIMSCRIPT translators. Herbert Karr authored the SIMSCRIPT manual [Markowitz 1963, p. iii].

SIMSCRIPT was considered a general programming system that could treat nonsimulation problems, but the major purpose of the language was to reduce the model and program development times that were common in large efforts. Users were intended to be noncomputing experts, and the descriptive medium for model development was a set of forms: (1) a SIMSCRIPT definition form in which variables, sets, and functions are declared, (2) an initialization form to define the initial system state, and (3) a report generation layout, for prescribing the format and content of simulation output. Accompanying the forms in the model definition is a routine for each endogenous and exogenous event and for any other decisions that prescribe the model logic. The applications context was machine or job shop scheduling and the initial examples reflect this focus.

8.3.3.2 *Rationale for Language Content*

Influencing Factors The first version of SIMSCRIPT provided a set of commands that included FORTRAN statements as a subset. The syntax of the language and program organization were influenced considerably by FORTRAN. Basically, the language was transformed by a preprocessor into FORTRAN before compilation into the executable object program version. Insertion of a SIMULATION or NON-SIMULATION card in the compile deck differentiated between the intended uses, permitting omission of the events list and timing routines for nonsimulation purposes. A control routine designated as MAIN replaced the timing routine.

SIMSCRIPT I.5, a version proprietary to CACI [Karr 1965], is described by Markowitz [1979, pp. 27–28] as a "slightly cleaner version of SIMSCRIPT I" that did not appear much different externally. However, the SIMSCRIPT I.5 translator did not generate FORTRAN statements but produced assembly language. SIMSCRIPT I.5 is also described as germinating many of the ideas that later appeared in SIMSCRIPT II.

Language Design and Definition SIMSCRIPT I (and SIMSCRIPT I.5) describe the world in terms of entities, attributes, and sets. Entities can be either permanent (available throughout the simulation duration) or temporary (created and destroyed during the simulation). Attributes define the properties of entities, and are distinguished by their *values*. Sets provide a convenience to the modeler for description of a class of entities (permanent entities), and set ownership and membership are defined relationships among entities.

The model structure is described in terms of a listing of events to prescribe the dynamic relationships, coupled with the entity and attribute definitions that provide a static description. Figure 8.3 taken from Markowitz [1963, p. 21] shows the declaration of exogenous and endogenous events for a job shop model. Figure 8.4 shows one exogenous input-an event with the name ORDRIN, also taken from Markowitz [1963, p. 22]. The event declarations create event notices that enable the timing executive to manipulate the events list, advancing time to the next imminent event. System-defined variables and functions such as TIME, RANDM, and PAGE are accessible by the modeler.

Nontechnical Influences Shortly after SIMSCRIPT I appeared, Karr left RAND to form Consolidated Analysis Centers, Incorporated (CACI). CACI was the major force behind SIMSCRIPT I.5, and implementations were done by Claude M. Delfosse, Glen Johnson, and Henry Kleine (see the Preface to [CACI 1983]).

Referring to the language requirements described in section 8.1, Figure 8.5 gives examples of each of the six language requirements. The terminology used in the middle column of Figure 8.5 follows that of the first version of SIMSCRIPT. Upper case in the examples shows the required syntax.

8.3.4 CSL

Control and Simulation Language (CSL) was a joint venture of Esso Petroleum Company, Ltd. and IBM United Kingdom, Ltd. The purpose of the language was to aid in the solution of complex logical and decision making problems in the control of industrial and commercial undertakings [Esso 1963].

8.3.4.1 *Background*

[Buxton 1962] describes the simulation capabilities of CSL as based on the General Simulation Program [Tocher 1960] and Montecode [Kelly 1962]. The language is described as experimental in

FIGURE 8.3

Events List for Example—Job Shop Simulation in SIMSCRIPT.

	STATEMENT NUMBER		STATEMENT
1	2 5	6	7 72
			EVENTS
			3 EXOGENOUS
			ORDRIN (1)
			ANALYZ (2)
			ENDSIM (3)
			1 ENDOGENOUS
			EPROC
			END

FIGURE 8.4

Exogenous Event Routine Describing the Receipt of an Order.

	STATEMENT NUMBER		STATEMENT
1	2 5	6	7 72
			EXOGENOUS EVENT ORDRIN
			SAVE EVENT CARD
			CREATE ORDER
			LET DATE(ORDER) = TIME
			READ N
			FORMAT (I4)
			DO TO 10, FOR I = (1) (N)
			CREATE DESTN
			READ MGDST(DESTN), PTIME(DESTN)
			FORMAT (I4, H3.2)
			FILE DESTN IN ROUT(ORDER)
		10	LOOP
			CALL ARRVL(ORDER)
			RETURN
			END

FIGURE 8.5

The SIMSCRIPT Capabilities for Meeting the Six Requirements.

Language Requirement	Basis for Provision	Examples
Random Number Generation	Automatically generated functions Integers uniformly distributed from I to J	RANDI (I,J)
	Restart random number stream (odd integer) Uniform variates from 0.0 to 1.0	RANDR(17319) RANDM
Process Transformers	Automatically generated functions Table look-up with step functions (discrete) and linear interpolation (continuous)	
List Processing Capability	Entity Operations	CREATE temporary entity DESTROY temporary entity
	Control Constructs	FOR EACH OF set
Statistical Analysis	Miscellaneous Commands	ACCUMULATE COMPUTE
Report Generation	Form produced reports with specification of lines, text headings, spacing, etc.	
Timing Executive	Events Scheduling with Events List and Event Notices	EX06 EVENT ARRVL

nature with an intentional provision of redundancy. This experimental approach also influenced the design of the compiler, emphasizing modifiability over other factors such as reliability.

Buxton and Laski [1962, p. 198] attribute contributions to CSL from Tocher and his colleagues at United Steel Companies, Ltd., D.F. Hartley of Cambridge University, and I.J. Cromar of IBM, who had major responsibility in writing the compiler. They also acknowledge becoming aware of SIMSCRIPT only on the completion of the CSL definition.

No estimates are given for the language design effort, but the compiler is estimated to have required about nine man-months. The object program produced is described as "fairly efficient," both in terms of storage and execution time [Buxton 1962, p. 198]. A second version of CSL, described by Buxton [1966] and labeled C.S.L. 2 by Clementson [1966], attributed to P. Blunden, P. Grant, and G. Parncutt of IBM UK the major credit for the compiler design that resulted in the product described by [IBM UK 1965]. This version, developed for the IBM 7094, provided extensive dynamic checking to aid program verification and offered some capability for parameter redefinition without forcing recompilation [Buxton 1966, p. 140].

8.3.4.2 *Rationale for Language Content*

Influencing Factors The following factors appear to have influenced CSL:

1. the intended use for decision making beyond simulation models prompted the adoption of a predicate calculus approach [Buxton 1962, p. 194],
2. the reliability on FORTRAN for intermediate translation, and
3. the dependence on techniques advanced by Tocher in GSP promoting the focus on activity as the basic descriptive unit.

The terminology of CSL resembles that of SIMSCRIPT in that entities, attributes, and sets are primary static model descriptors. The T-cells of CSL provide the basis for dynamic description, that is, representation of time associated with the initiation and completion of activities.

Language Design and Definition To the FORTRAN arithmetic and matrix manipulation capability, the developers of CSL added set manipulation operations, statistical utilities, and some logical operations to support the predicate calculus requirements intended for activity tests. The term ACTIVITIES both signals the use of CSL for simulation purposes (adding of timing requirements) as well as marking the beginning of activity description.

With reference to the six language requirements for discrete event simulation, CSL provided all, but some in limited form as shown in Figure 8.6. The CSL manual contains no explicit identification of the random number generation technique although a linear congruential method is implied by the requirement of an odd integer initialization. Only the normal and negative exponential transformation techniques were supplied in addition to a user defined specification for table look-up. Class definition of entities gave a major descriptive advantage over programming in the host language (FORTRAN II or FAP). The class definition example in Figure 8.6 shows a driver class with two attributes where entities belong to one of two sets, either local or long distance (LD). The use of TIME prescribes a T-cell associated with each driver. Set manipulation is illustrated in the FIND statement which shows that a customer entity has two attributes and the search is intended to find the first in the queue that

FIGURE 8.6

The CSL Capabilities for Meeting the Six Requirements.

Language Requirement	Basis for Provision	Examples
Random Number Generator	Automatically Generated Function Rectangular: variable = RANDOM (stream,range) (Type of generator not specified)	TM1=RANDOM(STREAMB,2)
Process Transformers	Automatically Generated Functions Normal: variable = DEVATE (stream,stddev,mean) Negative Exponential: variable = NEGEXP (stream,mean) User Defined: variable = SAMPLE (cell name, dist,name,stream)	SERV.T = DEVIATE(STRMC,3,30) X = NEGEXP(BASE,MEAN(2)) T.MACH.K = SAMPLE(1, POISSON, STRM)
List Processing Capability	Class definition of objects having the same attributes that can be referenced as a set or sets with the use of TIME assigning a clock (T.cell) to each entity. Additions to (GAINS) and deletions from (LOSES) set, and searching based on FIRST, LAST, MAX (expression), MIN (expression), ANY	CLASS TIME DRIVER.10(2) SET LOCAL,LD FIND CUST QUEUE FIRST &120
Statistical	Provides only a HIST statement for accumulating data during program execution. FORTRAN II or FAP subroutines can be called	
Report Generation	FORTRAN input/output and formatting	
Timing Executive	Conditions specified which are tested. Time cells provide the link between time and state. Based primarily on GSP [Tocher 1960]	WAIT.CUST(1) GE 10 WAIT.CUST(2) GE 35

FIGURE 8.7

Problem Statement and Example of CSL Code [Buxton 1962, p. 199].

Initial statements in the program read in a two-dimensional data array of mileages between all airports in a given part of the world, and establish three sets that hold subgroups of airports. The first of these, AIRPORTS, holds the names of those airports between which possible transfer routings involving one change of aeroplane are required. The second set, TRANSFERPORTS, holds the names of the major airports where transfer facilities are possible. The third set, USED, is used during the program as a working-space set. A transfer routing is permissible provided that the total mileage flown does not exceed the direct mileage by more than 15%. The following program establishes valid transfer routings. The initial statements are omitted and the output statements are stylized to avoid the introduction of detail which has not been fully described in the paper. The transfer airports for each airport pair are written out in the order of increasing total mileage.

```
        FOR A AIRPORTS
            FOR B AIRPORTS
                 A LT B & 2
                WRITE A, B
                 ZERO USED
1               FIND X TRANSFERPORTS MIN
                    (MILEAGE (A, X)+MILEAGE (X, B))
                    & 2
                X NE A
                 X NE B
                100* (MILEAGE(A, X)+MILEAGE (X, B))
                    LE 115*MILEAGE (A, B)
                AIRPORT.X NOTIN USED
                WRITE X
                AIRPORT. X HEAD USED
                GO TO 1
2               DUMMY
        EXIT
```

has attribute 1 value greater than or equal to 10 and attribute 2 value greater than or equal to 35. Basically, conditions were tested to determine if an activity could initiate; the termination was usually prescribed through the assignment of T-cell value. The timing executive was very similar to that used by Tocher in GSP [Buxton 1962, p. 197].

Activities had a test and an action section. The test could be prescribed in rather complex logical statements comprising a chain. An evaluation of the chain would lead to the proper actions within the activity specification.

Translation was accomplished in four phases. An intermediate phase produced a FORTRAN II program as output on an IBM 1401 (serving as input tape creator for an IBM 7090). Despite the multiphase translation with repetitive passes, the authors felt the process to be efficient, easy to modify, and easy to extend [Buxton 1962, p. 198]. A ratio of CSL to FORTRAN statements is "of the order of one to five." The authors also claim that an equivalent CSL program can be written in approximately 20 percent of the time required for a FORTRAN program.

The problem statement and example of CSL code shown in Figure 8.7 are taken from Buxton [1962, p. 199].

Nontechnical Influences CSL continued the GSP organization of a model through activities. It also continued the use of activity scan but provided a simpler two-phase as opposed to a three-phase executive, probably because the application domain stressed contingent (state conditioned) events more than determined (time dependent) events. Following both precedents kept CSL in the mainstream of British simulation efforts, and it soon became a favorite for program generation techniques based on the entity-cycle or activity cycle diagrams, the successors to the wheel charts. Examples of these early graphical modeling aids are shown in Figure 8.8.

8.3.5 GASP

GASP (General Activity Simulation Program) was developed by Philip J. Kiviat at the Applied Research Laboratory of the United States Steel Corporation. Kiviat came to U.S. Steel in June of 1961 and began work on the steel mill simulation project shortly thereafter [Kiviat 1991a].

8.3.5.1 *Background*

The initial draft of GASP and a large part of the coding occurred during 1961, originally in ALGOL. Early on (presumably in 1961) the decision was made to base the GASP simulator on FORTRAN II. By February 1962, the design of the language was completed sufficiently so that Kiviat received approval for a seminar presentation entitled, "A Simulation Approach to the Analysis of a Complex Large Scale Industrial System," in the Department of Industrial and Engineering Administration at Cornell University. The invitation was extended by Professors Richard W. Conway and William L. Maxwell, both significant contributors to simulation conceptual development.

Developed for internal use within United States Steel, GASP was intended to run on several machines, for example, the IBM 1410, IBM 1620, Control Data 1604, and Bendix G-20. A preliminary version of the Programmer's Manual, dated January 16, 1963, also showed intended execution on the IBM 7070 and 7090 with erasures of pencil inclusions of the IBM 7074 and 7094. Editorial markings by Kiviat noted that an update of the target machines would be necessary at final typing [Kiviat 1963a].

A report during the same time period [Kiviat 1963c] clearly casts GASP as the key ingredient in a method for utilizing computer simulation in the analysis of steel industry operations. The intended report was to educate potential users as to the benefits derived from simulation studies and to serve as an introduction to the use of the technique with a GASP "simulation-programming system that greatly reduces the time required for problem analysis, computer programming, and computer use" [Kiviat 1963c, Abstract].

8.3.5.2 *Rationale for Language Content*

Exposed to the subject in his graduate study at Cornell, Kiviat was both knowledgeable in simulation techniques and aware of other language developments. The completed version of the report describing GASP [Kiviat 1963b] (a revision of the earlier titled "Programmers' Manual") contained references to SIMSCRIPT, Tocher's GSP, SIMPAC, and industrial dynamics [Forrester 1961]. An incomplete reference contains the name "Gordon, Geoffery [sic]," but nothing more.

Influencing Factors GASP was designed to "bridge the gap" between two groups: operating or engineering personnel, unfamiliar with computer programming, and computer programmers unknowledgeable of the application domain. Like GPSS, flow-chart symbols were intended to be used by the operational personnel in defining the system. The symbols followed the conventions for general purpose use. An example, taken from [Kiviat 1963a], is shown in Figure 8.9. The sketch of language capabilities, provided in Figure 8.10, is supplemented by the following explanation.

FIGURE 8.8

Wheel Chart and Activity Cycle Diagrams.

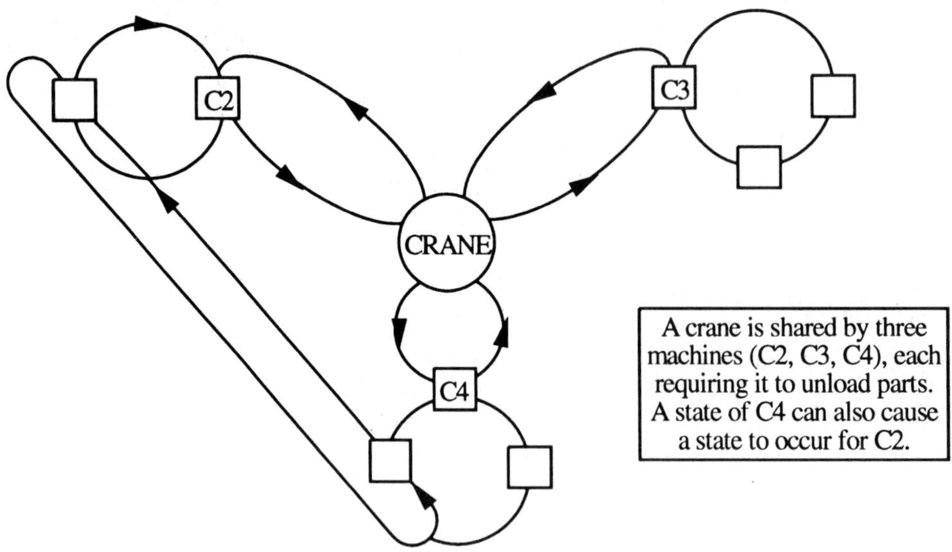

(a) The Wheel Chart Example (from [Tocher 1966, p. 129])

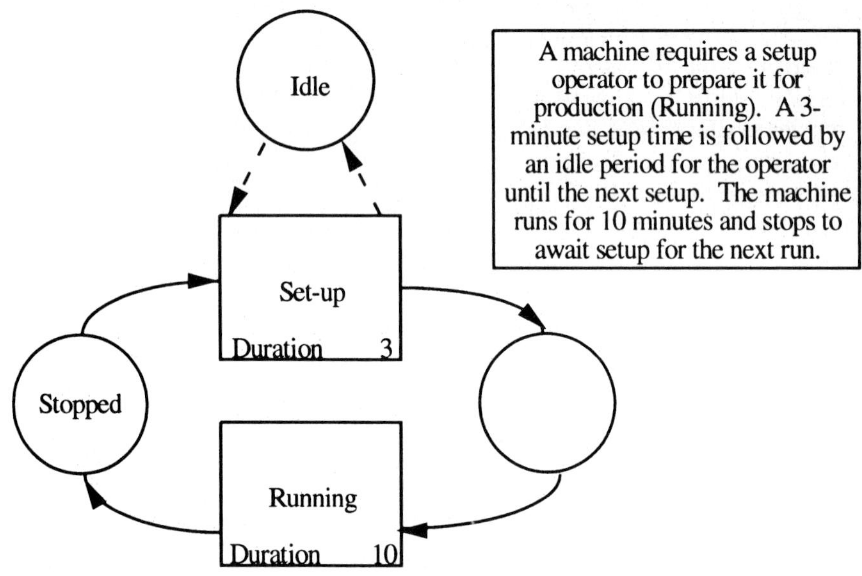

(b) The Activity Cycle Example (from [ECSL-CAPS Reference Manual 1978, p. 9])

FIGURE 8.9

The Flow-Chart Representation of an Event (EJOBIN) in GASP.

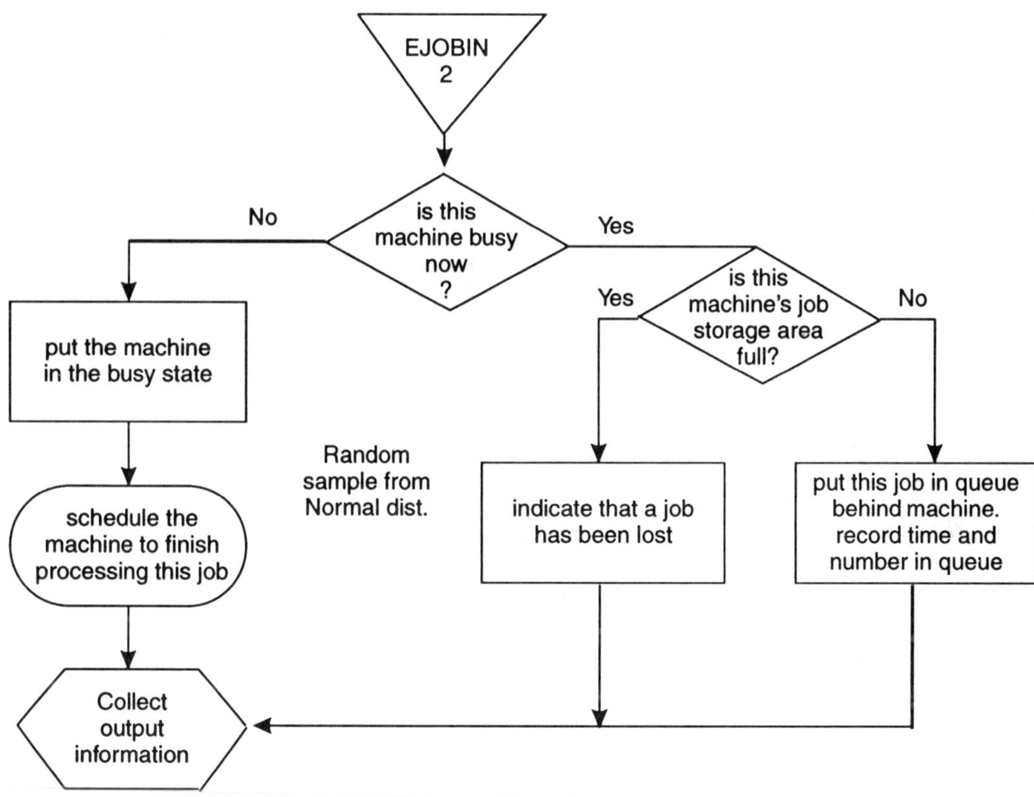

A GASP model was made up of elements—people, machines, orders—with elements described in terms of *attributes*. A list of attributes describing an element corresponded to the later concept of a record. Changes in the value of attributes occur through *activities*, which could either be instantaneous or require a time duration. Event routines were described by the user or the operating personnel, through flow charts subsequently translated into executable representations by programmers.

Subroutines written in FORTRAN II provided the list processing capabilities (queue insertion, item removal, etc.) relying on the array data structure completely. Reporting was centralized in a single subroutine (OUTPUT) to which transfers were made, depending on the data being collected.

The FORTRAN II resident library provided the random number generator, and GASP utilized transformations for the generation of variates following the uniform, Poisson, normal, and Erlang distributions. In addition, sampling could produce a value from an empirical distribution (based on sample data).

A rather unique feature of GASP was the provision of a regression equation from which sampling could be used primarily to produce input values. The number of arguments for the regression equation was limited to 10 or less, and the error term was expected to follow a normal distribution.

Timing was the responsibility of the GASP EXECUTIVE, which utilized the data supplied by the modeler's use of scheduling (SCHED) calls to sequence events properly. Debugging was also a major concern, and features were provided in a special subroutine (MONITR) that assisted in this effort. A routine for error determination reported 13 types of errors.

Nontechnical Influences A revision to GASP, labeled GASP II, was underway in early 1963. No doubt, further developments were hindered by the departure of Kiviat who took a position at the RAND Corporation. A later version of the GASP User's Manual, which is believed to be in the 1965 time frame, was authored by Jack Belkin and M.R. Rao [Belkin 1965?].

8.3.6 OPS-3

OPS-3 is classed as a major SPL, not because of conceptual influences but because it was an innovative and technical effort considerably ahead of its time. Growing out of classroom instruction at MIT during the spring, 1964, OPS-3 was a prototyping effort building on two earlier versions, each the result of classroom experiments. The MIT time sharing system, CTSS, stimulated the experiments in interactive model building and simulation programming.

8.3.6.1 *Background*

The major contributors to OPS-3 were Martin Greenberger, Malcolm M. Jones, James H. Morris, Jr., and David N. Ness. However, a number of others are cited in the preface of Greenberger [1965]: M. Wantman, G.A. Gorry, S. Whitelaw, and J. Miller. The implication is that all in this second group were students in the Alfred P. Sloan School of Management.

The OPS-3 *system* was intended to be a multi-purpose, open-ended, modular, compatible support for creative researchers. The users were not intended to be computing experts, but persons involved in problem solving and research that necessitated model building. Additions to OPS-3 could be from a variety of programming languages or represent a synthesis of subprograms without modification [Greenberger 1965, pp. 1–2].

8.3.6.2 *Rationale for Language Content*

OPS-3 was intended to be a general programming tool with extended capabilities for handling modeling and simulation to support research users. As pointed out before, OPS-3 was viewed as a system and not simply a language.

Influencing Factors The major influence on OPS-3 was the interactive, time-sharing environment provided by CTSS. For the first time simulation modeling was to be done in a quasi-real-time mode, but not necessarily with interactive assistance beyond that provided by CTSS. The AGENDA, provided as a compound operation (KOP), enabled the scheduling, cancellation, and rescheduling activities following the "spirit of simulation languages such as SOL and SIMSCRIPT," [Greenberger 1965, p. 7]. The power of interactive model execution was recognized as something totally new.

Language Design and Definition OPS-3 is structured in a hierarchical fashion with a basic calculation capability furnishing the lowest level of support. The system provides five modes or user states: Execute, Store, Store and Execute, Run, and Guide. Simple operators such as PRINT are available in *execute mode*. Cascading a series of operations into a program is enabled with *store mode*. If single operators are to execute within a program then *store and execute* mode was used. *Run* mode enabled execution of compound operations (KOPs) without interruption. The assistance or help was accessible in *guide mode*. In the terminology typical of the time, OPS-3 would be categorized as emphasizing

FIGURE 8.10

The GASP Capabilities for Meeting the Six Requirements.

Language Requirement	Basis for Provision	Examples
Random Number Generation	FORTRAN II resident library, NRANDM(d) with d = 1, 2, 3, or 4 gives an integer $[1,10^d]$	JDGT = NRANDM(I) – 1
Process Transformers	Uniform, Poisson, Normal, and Erlang distributions. An empirical distribution also could be defined.	NUM = NPOISN (3) (where 3 specifics the row of the input parameter list which contains the actual parameter value)
List Processing Capability	Subroutines provided the capability for filing (FILEM) and retrieving (FETCHM) elements using FIFO or LIFO disciplines in a FORTRAN array.	CALL FILEM (TMDUE,JDDLR, KMATL,QUEUE,1) CALL FETCHM (FLOATF(JDOLR), XINTF(TMDUE),KMATL,QUEUE,1) (Note: first argument is the basis for insertion and removal)
Statistical	Subroutines COLECT: the sum, sum of squares, extreme values, and sample size for up to 20 designated variables HISTOG: forms a histogram for each up to 20 designated variables	
Report Generation	The OUTPUT subroutine must be written by the user but the statistical subroutines above and PRINTQ provide the functionality.	
Timing Executive	Event scheduling with a scheduling subroutine and using an associated list organization developed by Kiviat [1962a, 1962b]	CALL SCHDL(ARVTM,JARVL,KCUST)

operators rather than data structures. An operator took the form of a closed subroutine written in MAD (Michigan Algorithmic Decoder), FORTRAN, FAP (an assembler), or any other source language available under CTSS. Over 90 operators were provided in the language, and 75 subroutines were provided in the library.

In terms of the six language requirements for simulation, Figure 8.11 shows the capabilities provided by OPS-3. Especially impressive were the statistical capabilities for input data modeling and output analysis through an operator set that provided linear least-squares fit, intercorrelation and partial correlation, tests of homogeneity, contingency table analysis, and others. A guided form of each test ushered the novice user through the requirements for performing the test. A short form was available for the experienced user.

The determination of the next activity is based on a three-phase method resembling that used in Tocher's GSP [Tocher 1960]. The contingent event is placed on the AGENDA in an order dictated by TIME, the system clock, in the sequence of conditional events. Parameters can be passed with the SCHED operator, and the AGENDA can be accessed by the user as a debugging aid.

Nontechnical Influences This period in MIT computing was certainly one of the most exciting. Time sharing and interactive computation were in their infancies. Innovative thinkers such as J.C.R. Licklider, John McCarthy, and R.M. Fano were pushing the boundaries of computing technology to

FIGURE 8.11

The OPS-3 Capabilities for Meeting the Six Requirements.

Language Requirement	Basis for Provision	Examples
Random Number Generation	Defined function, presumably a linear congruential method. DRAW arguments: returned val, distribution, parm1, parm2 Initialization possible with SEED odd integer	DRAW PRIORITY RANDOM 1 7 SEED 6193
Process Transformers	The second argument of DRAW specified the distribution: exponential, normal, or modeler specified. Default parameters of 0 (mean) and 1 (std. dev.) for normal.	DRAW SERVTM EXPONE THETA DRAW MEMRY DEMAND CLASS
List Processing Capability	Major control through user-accessible symbol table. Major data structure is array but with more flexible manipulation than with FORTRAN. Stack operators permit entry, removal, and examination of values.	RESETQ WLINE Empties the queue WLINE GETOLD REDYQ PROCQ Places oldest item in REDYQ into PROCQ
Statistical	Extensive statistical operators with capability for input data modeling and output analysis	CNTING X 2-way contingency table with X a floating-point matrix. TTESTS X N1 N2 A t-test between two samples of size N1 and N2 with the values in the matrix X
Report Generation	Nothing beyond the usual interactive input and output	
Timing Executive	A three-phase method built around the KOP AGENDA. SCHED activity option basis CANCEL option activity variable	SCHED SRVCE AT 100 SCHED ENDSV NOW CANCEL FIRST ARRVL ATIME

the utmost. Consider the insightful perspective of Licklider concerning the future role of languages for dynamic interactive modeling [Licklider 1967, p. 288–289].

> In their static form, computer-program models are documents. They preserve and carry information just as documents printed in natural language do, and they can be read and understood by recipients who know the modeling language. In their dynamic form, however, computer-program models appeal to the recipient's understanding directly through his perception of dynamic behavior. That model of appeal is beyond the reach of ordinary documents. When we have learned how to take good advantage of it, it may—indeed, I believe it will—be the greatest boon to scientific and technical communication, and to the teaching and learning of science and technology, since the invention of writing on a flat surface.

Within less than two years of publication, the DEC PDP-10 would supply even more advanced facilities than afforded to the developers of OPS-3. The efforts of Greenberger, Jones, and others with OPS-3 deserve recognition for the perceptions and demonstration of technology potential rather than the effect on SPL developments.

8.3.7 DYNAMO

The DYNAMO (DYNAmic MOdels) language served as the executable representation for the industrial dynamics systems models developed by Jay Wright Forrester and others at MIT during the late 1950s and into the 1960s and beyond. DYNAMO is the lone nondiscrete event simulation language included in this history. Justification for this departure is that concept, techniques, and approaches utilized by the MIT group had a significant impact on those working in the development of discrete event SPLs [Kiviat 1991b].

8.3.7.1 *Background*

The predecessor of DYNAMO, a program called SIMPLE (Simulation of Industrial Management Problems with Lots of Equations), was developed by Richard K. Bennett for the IBM 704 computer in the spring of 1958. (Note that this is a contemporary of GSP in the discrete-event SPL domain.) SIMPLE possessed most of the basic features of DYNAMO, but the model specifications from which the program was derived were considered to be rather primitive [Pugh 1963, p.2]. DYNAMO is attributed to Dr. Phyllis Fox and Alexander L. Pugh, III with assistance from Grace Duren and David J. Howard. Modifications and improvement of the original SIMPLE graphical plots was provided by Edward B. Roberts [Forrester 1961, p.369].

Originally written for an IBM 704 computer, the DYNAMO compiler, consisting of about 10,000 instructions, was converted to an IBM 709 and then an IBM 7090 by Pugh. The DYNAMO compiler as described in the User's Manual represented about six staff-years of effort (including that required to develop SIMPLE), and the maximum model size was about 1500 equations. A FORTRAN simulator (FORDYN), intended for users who did not have access to the large IBM 7090 or 7094, was developed by Robert W. Llewellyn of North Carolina State University in 1965 [Llewellyn 1965]. (Note that neither DYNAMO nor FORDYN are included in Figure 8.1.)

8.3.7.2 *Rationale for Language Content*

Although applicable to the modeling of any information feedback system, DYNAMO was developed as the means of implementing industrial dynamics models, which addressed the application of simulation to large scale economic and social systems. The level of modeling granularity does not address the individual items or events typically associated with the job shop models of that time. A thorough understanding of the basis for systems dynamics modeling, the term later employed, is beyond the scope of this paper (see [Forrester 1961]).

Influencing Factors The design of DYNAMO was strongly influenced by the following desirable properties [Pugh 1963, p.2]:

1. The language should be easily understood and easy to learn by the user group, who in general might not be professional programmers. Flexibility would be sacrificed for both ease of use and correctness.
2. A very efficient (at the time) compilation phase, with no object language production, eliminated the usual practice at the time of saving object text.
3. Output in the form of graphical plots was recognized as more useful than extensive numerical results; however, both were provided to the user.

4. Error detection and error correction were considered a primary responsibility. Both initial conditions and the order of computation were subject to detection and correction. The claim was that DYNAMO checked for almost every logical inconsistency, and provided comments on errors that were easily understood.

Language Design and Definition DYNAMO is described as a language expressing zero- and first-order difference equations. A system is described in terms of flows and accumulations. Flows in orders, material, personnel, money, capital equipment, and most importantly information, affect the decision making that leads to changes in the rate of flow occurring in subsequent time periods. Over time the changes in flow contribute to the redefinition of levels (of money, materials, information) that have subsequent influence on future rates of flow. Each model must begin with an initial state definition, and the constant increment of time (DT) is selected to be sufficiently small to avoid inherent instability.

Figure 8.12 portrays the timing sequence for each set of DYNAMO computations. The present time (K), has values determined based on levels of accumulation at J modified by rates of flow over the JK interval. Levels at present time (K) then contribute to the definition of rates over the interval KL, where L = K + DT.

Figure 8.13 is an example taken from [Pugh 1963, p.17] showing the model of a retail store that illustrates the DYNAMO representation. The equational representation in Figure 8.13 is understood by noting that the number of each equation is suffixed by the type of equation: L for level; A for auxiliary; R for rate; N for initial value. NOTE is a comment statement, and special statements such as PRINT, PLOT, and SPEC provide instructions on the execution process. The subscripting enables not only a determination of direct statement formulation, but also of statement ordering and typing. Although discontinuities were permitted in systems dynamics, and could be represented in DYNAMO, they were discouraged unless absolutely necessary as a modeling technique.

The graphical output produced on a lineprinter consisted of letters showing the relative values for designated variables. The use of plotters with smoothed curvilinear, coded representations is provided in the book by Forrester, but was not available with the early version of DYNAMO. The fixed format field definition required by the translator was to be replaced in later versions.

FIGURE 8.12

Time Notation (from [Pugh 1963, p.4].

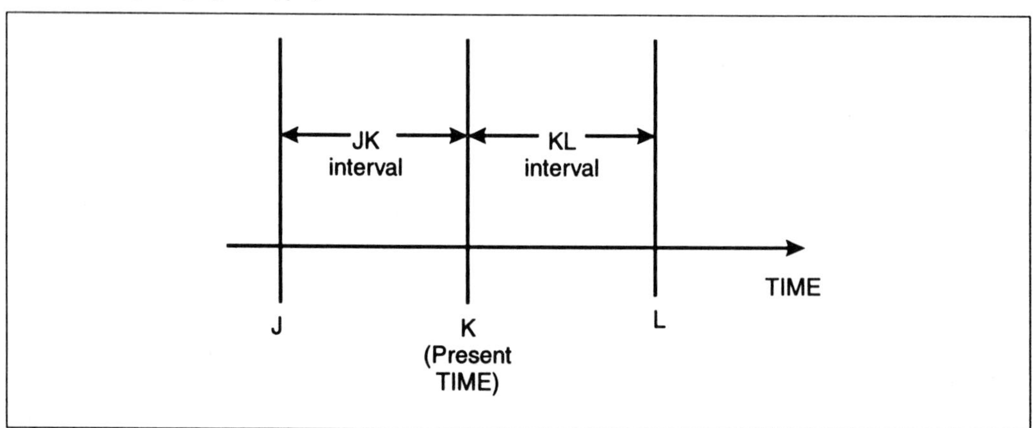

FIGURE 8.13

Listing of model.

```
*       M478-248,DYN,TEST,1,1,0,0
RUN     2698JP
NOTE    MODEL OF RETAIL STORE
NOTE
1L      IAR.K=IAR.J+(DT) (SRR.JK-SSR.JK)          INVENTORY ACTUAL
1L      UOR.K=UOR.J+(DT) (RRR.JK-SSR.JK)          UNFILLED ORDERS
20A     NIR.K=IAR.K/DT                            NEGATIVE INVENTORY
20A     STR.K=UOR.K/DFR                           SHIPMENTS TRIED
54R     SSR.KL=MIN(STR.K,NIR.K)                   SHIPMENTS SENT
40R     PSR.KL=RRR.JK+(1/DIR) (IDR.K-IAR.K)       PURCHASE ORDERS SENT
12A     IDR.K=(AIR) (RSR.K)                       INVENTORY DESIRED
3L      RSR.K=RSR.J+(DT) (1/DRR) (RRR.JK-RSR.J)   REQUISITIONS SMOOTHED
39R     SSR.KL=DELAY3(PSR.JK,DTR)                 SHIPMENTS RECEIVED
NOTE
NOTE    INITIAL CONDITIONS
NOTE
12N     UOR=(DFR) (RRR)
6N      RSR=RRR
6N      IAR=IDR
NOTE
NOTE    INPUT
NOTE
7R      RRR.KL=RRI+RCR.K                       REQUISITIONS RECEIVED
45A     RCR.K=STEP(STH,5)                      REQUISITION CHANGE
NOTE
NOTE    CONSTANTS
NOTE
C       AIR=8 WKS                              CONSTANT FOR INVENTORY
C       DFR=1 WK                               DELAY IN FILLING ORDERS
C       DIR=4 WKS                              DLY REFILLING INVENTORY
C       DRR=8 WKS                              REQUISITION SMTHNG T C
C       DTR=2 WKS                              DELAY IN TRANSIT
C       RRI=1000 ITEMS/WK                      REQ. RECEIVED INITIALLY
C       STH=100 ITEMS/WK                       STEP HEIGHT
NOTE
PRINT   1)IAR,IDR/2)UOR/3)RRR,SSR/4)PSR,SRR
PLOT    IAR=I,UOR=U/RRR=R,SSR=S,PSR=P,SRR=Q
SPEC    DT=0.1/LENGTH=10/PRTPER=5/PLTPER=0
```

Nontechnical Influences Systems dynamics and DYNAMO, although developed totally at MIT, attracted considerable nationwide interest. Financial support from the Ford Foundation and the Sloan Research Fund are acknowledged in the Preface of Forrester [1961]. Additional support from a number of sources is identified there also.

Since DYNAMO was not a discrete event SPL, and because its influence was limited to the developmental period, successive versions of the language are not described. However, the language continued, both in refined versions [Pugh 1973] and extensions [Pugh 1976].

8.3.8 Other Languages

Numerous SPLs emerged during this advent period. Most, experienced some use and disappeared. A few had distinctive characteristics that deserve some note in a paper of this type.

MILITRAN was produced by the Systems Research Group for the Office of Naval Research [Systems Research Group, Inc. 1964]. Krasnow [1967, p. 87] states that little concession to military subject matter was given in MILITRAN. Event scheduling was the world view promoted, and a distinction between permanent (synchronous) and contingent events was made.

The Cornell List Processor (CLP) was a list processing language used extensively for simulation instruction. The developers had the goal of producing a list processing language that required no more than a "FORTRAN level" knowledge of programming [Conway 1965]. CLP relying on CORC, a general algebraic language used at Cornell also for instructional purposes, enabled students to define entities, and use them in set manipulation (INSERT, REMOVE) without the major effort of learning a language such as SIMSCRIPT [Conway 1965, p. 216]. The student still had to write his or her own timing, statistical analysis, and report generation routines.

QUIKSCRIPT was a SIMSCRIPT derivative simulator, a set of subroutines, based on the 20-GATE algebraic language used at Carnegie Institute of Technology [Tonge 1965]. The GATE subroutines did not provide all the facilities of SIMSCRIPT (e.g., no report generation), and the definitional forms of the latter were omitted.

SIMPAC, produced at the System Development Corporation, was distinguished by its fixed-time-increment timing routine. This would appear to make it the only US language to adhere completely to the activity scan world view [Bennett 1962]. (OPS-4 departed from OPS-3 by accommodating all three world views.)

SOL (Simulation Oriented Language) was developed by Knuth and McNeley as an extension to ALGOL. The language is structured much like GPSS, even using terms such as SEIZE, RELEASE, and ENTER. Sets are represented as subscripted variables. In contrast with SIMULA, SOL focused on the dynamic interaction of temporary objects, again much like GPSS [Knuth 1964a, 1964b]. Of note in SOL was the explicit use of a *wait on state condition* that was not present in GPSS or in SIMULA, because the prevailing view was that such an indeterminate expression could lead to gross inefficiencies (see [Nygaard 1981, p. 452] for a discussion specific to SIMULA and [Nance 1981] for a more general discussion). A second, more anecdotal, item related to SOL was the response of Knuth when asked at the IFIP Conference what were the plans for SOL; he replied that there were no plans for he found SIMULA to have all the capabilities of SOL (except for the *wait on state condition*) and more [Knuth 1992].

8.3.9 Language Comparisons

The end of the advent period marked the beginning of a period of intense interest in simulation programming language comparison and evaluation. Such interest was manifested in the publication of a number of papers during the 1964–1967 timeframe that reviewed and compared existing languages with respect to many criteria [Young 1963; Krasnow 1964; Tocher 1965; Kiviat 1966; Teichrow 1966; Krasnow 1967; Reitman 1967]. These sources also refer to lesser known languages that are not mentioned here.

Interest in comparison and evaluation was likely stimulated by the perceived cost associated with using "another language." The cost of acquiring the translator was minor; the cost of training people, maintaining the language, and supporting its migration to subsequent hardware systems could be very high. For that reason, packages in a general purpose language had considerable appeal.

This sharp interest in language comparisons is also marked by the number of workshops, symposia, and conferences addressing SPL issues. Daniel Teichrow and John F. Lubin are cited by Philip Kiviat as the "honest brokers" in that they had no commitment to a particular language but were instrumental in developing forums for the exchange of concepts, ideas, and plans. A workshop organized by them and held at the University of Pennsylvania on March 17–18, 1966 refers to an earlier one at Stanford in 1964 [Chrisman 1966]. Session chairs at the 1966 workshop included Kiviat, R. L. Sisson (University of Pennsylvania), Julian Reitman (United Aircraft), and J.F. Lubin. Comparison papers were presented by Harold G. Hixson (Air Force Logistics Command), Bernard Backhart (General Services Administration), and George Heidorn (Yale University). Among the 108 attendees were several who were involved in SPL development: W.L. Maxwell of Cornell (CLP), Malcolm M. Jones of MIT (OPS), Howard S. Krasnow and Robert J. Parente of IBM, and Julian Reitman of Norden (GPSS/Norden).

In between the two workshops described was the IBM Scientific Computing Symposium on Simulation Models and Gaming held at the T.J. Watson Research Center in Yorktown Heights, New York on December 7–9, 1964. A session entitled, "Simulation Techniques" included a paper by Geoffrey Gordon that compares GPSS and SIMSCRIPT [Gordon 1966] and a paper by Tocher that presents the wheel chart as a conceptual aid to modeling [Tocher 1966]. In another session, the Programming by Questionnaire (PBQ) technique for model specification is described [Geisler 1966]. (More about PBQ is to follow.) The Symposium took a broad applications view of simulation, and among the 175 attendees at this conference were Jay W. Forrester (MIT), who described the principles of industrial dynamics, Richard M. Cyert (CIT), Herbert A. Simon (CIT), Philip Morse (MIT), J.C.R. Licklider (MIT), Harold Guetzkow (Northwestern), Richard W. Conway and William L. Maxwell (Cornell), Oscar Morgenstern (Princeton), and Guy H. Orcutt (Wisconsin).

The most notable technical conference on simulation languages was the IFIP Working Conference on Simulation Programming Languages, chaired by Ole-Johan Dahl and held in Oslo, 22–26 May 1967. The *Proceedings* were edited by John N. Buxton and appeared the following year. The list of presenters and attendees reads like a "Who's Who," not only in computer simulation but also in computer science. The "by invitation only" participants, with their role or presentation subject in parentheses, included Martin Greenberger and Malcolm M. Jones (OPS-4), Michael R. Lackner (graphic forms for conversational modeling), Howard S. Krasnow (process view), Donald E. Knuth (Session Chair), Jan V. Garwick (Do we need all these languages?), R.D. Parslow (AS: an Algol language), Ole-Johan Dahl and Kristen Nygaard (class and subclass declaration), L. Patrone (SPL: a simulation language based on PL/I), John G. Laski (interactive process description and modeling languages), G.K. Hutchison (multiprocessor system modeling), Robert J. Parente (simulation-oriented memory allocation), G. Molner (self-optimizing simulation), G.P. Blunden (implicit interaction), John L. McNeley (compound declarations), C.A.R. Hoare (Session Chair), A.L. Pugh III (DYNAMO II), T.B. Steel, Jr. (standardization), and Evzen Kindler (COSMO). The highly interactive group of participants included: Richard W. Conway, Douglas T. Ross, Christopher Strachey, Robin Hills, and John N. Buxton. Issues and problems surfacing in this symposium on occasion resurface, for example, in the annual Winter Simulation Conferences.

In November 1967, Harold Hixson, Arnold Ockene, and Julian Reitman collaborated to produce the Conference on Applications of Simulation Using GPSS held in New York. Hixson, representing SHARE (the IBM User Group), served as General Chair, Ockene of IBM served as Publicity Chair, and Reitman of Norden Systems was the Program Chair. In the following years this conference expanded its programming language scope (beyond GPSS) and became known as the Winter Simulation Conference (WSC), which celebrated its twenty-fifth anniversary in December 1992, in Washington. The three individuals named above, together with other pioneers in the early years of the

WSC, were brought together in a panel session entitled "Perspectives of the Founding Fathers" [Wilson 1992].

8.4 THE FORMATIVE PERIOD (1966–1970)

Following the bustle of activity surrounding the emergence of new SPLs, the period from 1966–1970 marked a consolidation in conceptual clarification. The concepts, possibly subjugated earlier in the necessities of implementation, were reviewed and refined to promote more consistent representation of a world view and improve clarity in its presentation to users. Nevertheless, rapid hardware advancements and vendor marketing activities forced some languages, notably GPSS, to undergo major revisions.

8.4.1 GPSS

GPSS II and III are included in the advent period as is the ZIP/ZAP compiled version of the language translator. With the introduction of SYSTEM/360 in the 1960s, GPSS/360 represented an improved and extended version of GPSS III that appeared in two versions (see [Schriber 1974, p. 496]). An RCA version of the language, called *Flow Simulator*, represents a combined version of the two [Greenberg 1972, p. 8]. *Flow Simulator* appeared in 1967 [Flow Simulator, RCA 1967] [Flow Simulator Information Manual, RCA 1967]. A Honeywell version, GPS K appeared in 1969 [GPS K 1969]. Two versions of a User's Manual for GPSS V appeared in 1970–1971 [GPSS V 1970, 1971]. GPSS/UCC, corresponding closely to GPSS/360, was developed by the University Computing Corporation in the late 1960s.

GPSS/360 extended the prior version (GPSS III) by increasing the number of block types from 36 to 44. Set operations were expanded by the introduction of groups. Extensions to the GENERATE block improved storage use. A HELP block permitting access to routines in other languages was provided. Comparisons of the language versions for GPS K, *Flow Simulator*, and GPSS III with GPSS/360 can be found in the Appendices of Greenberg [1972].

GPSS V provided more convenience features but made no major changes in the language. A run timer could be set by the modeler, extensions were made to the HELP block, and free format coding (removal of statement component restrictions to particular fields) was permitted. A detailed comparison of differences in GPSS/360 and GPSS V is provided in Appendix A of Schriber [1974].

8.4.2 SIMULA 67

The realization of shortcomings in SIMULA I and the influences of language and translator developments during the mid-1960s led to an extensive revision of the language. This revision, described in detail in Nygaard [1981], is not repeated here. Needless to say, the class concept was a major innovative contribution. Clearly, SIMULA 67 served to crystallize the process concept, the coroutine and quasi-parallel processing capabilities and demonstrate the implementation of abstract data types. The result was a language well beyond the power of most of its contemporaries.

8.4.3 SIMSCRIPT II

SIMSCRIPT II, although dependent on SIMSCRIPT I.5 for its basic concepts of entity, attribute, and set, was clearly a major advancement over the earlier version. SIMSCRIPT II is intended to be a general purpose language whereas SIMSCRIPT I.5 was intended to be a simulation programming language. SIMSCRIPT II in appearance looks much different from SIMSCRIPT I [Markowitz 1979, p. 28]. An expressed goal of SIMSCRIPT II was to be a self-documenting language. SIMSCRIPT II was written in SIMSCRIPT II, just as its predecessor was written, for the most part, in SIMSCRIPT I.5.

8.4.3.1 *Background*

The RAND Corporation provided the organizational support and financial underpinnings for SIMSCRIPT II. Philip J. Kiviat, having come from the United States Steel Company, took over the leading role in the design and development of the language from Harry Markowitz, who had started the project. Markowitz, whose ideas had formed the basis for SIMSCRIPT I and SIMSCRIPT I.5, was in the process of leaving RAND during the major part of the language project. Bernard Hausner, the principal programmer on SIMSCRIPT I.5, had departed, and Richard Villanueva assumed this role.

Although the claim was made that SIMSCRIPT II was a general purpose language, RAND's principal interest in developing SIMSCRIPT II was to enhance its capability within discrete event simulation and to offer greater appeal to its clients [Kiviat 1968, p. vi]. Many of RAND's models were military and political applications, necessitating extremely large complex descriptions. The intent was to create a language that, through its free-form and natural language appearance, would encourage more interaction with application users.

Contributions to the language are acknowledged in the preface to the aforementioned book. George Benedict and Bernard Hausner were recognized as contributing much of the basic compiler design and programming. Joel Urman of IBM influenced the language design as well as programmed much of the I/O and operating system interface routines. Suggestions and criticisms were attributed to a number of persons, including Bob Balzer, John Buxton, John Laski, Howard Krasnow, John McNeley, Kristen Nyggard, and Paula Oldfather [Kiviat 1968, p. vii].

In addition to a free-form, English-like mode of communication, the language designers desired a compiler to be "forgiving," and to correct a large percentage of user syntax errors. Furthermore, forced execution of a program was felt to reduce the number of runs to achieve a correct model implementation. Debugging statements and program control features were central to the translator.

8.4.3.2 *Rationale for Language Content*

Influencing Factors Certainly, SIMSCRIPT I.5 and the entity, attribute, and set concepts had the major influence on the language design. Nevertheless, the intent to involve application users and to provide a language working within SYSTEM/360 and OS/360, both still somewhat in development, had some impact. At one point, the language designers considered writing SIMSCRIPT II in NPL (the New Programming Language), subsequently PL/I, but the idea was rejected because of the instability of NPL [Kiviat 1992]. Kiviat [1991b] acknowledges that ideas and information came from interaction with other language developers and designers. The Working Conference on Simulation and Programming Languages, cited above, was a primary source of such ideas [Buxton 1968].

Language Design and Definition The design of SIMSCRIPT II can be represented by the reverse analogy of "peeling the onion." The language designers refer to "levels of the language," and use that effectively in describing the rather large language represented by SIMSCRIPT II.

Level 1 is a very simple programming language for doing numerical operations. It contains only unsubscripted variables and the simplest of control structures with only rudimentary input (READ) and output (PRINT) statements.

Level 2 adds subscripted variables, subroutines, and extended control structures to offer a language with roughly the capability of FORTRAN 66 but lacking the FORTRAN rigidities.

Level 3 adds more general logical expressions with extended control structures, and provides the capability for storage management, function computations, and statistical operations.

Level 4 introduces the entity, attribute, set concepts needed for list processing. The pointer structures, implied subscripting, and text handling go well beyond the capabilities of SIMSCRIPT I.5.

Level 5 contains the dynamic capabilities necessary for simulation: time advance, event processing, generation of statistical variates, and output analysis.

Nontechnical Influences Markowitz [1979] attributes the lack of interest by RAND in developing SIMSCRIPT II as more than a simulation language to dictating the limitation of five levels in the implementation. He identifies Level 6 as that which dealt with database entities, and Level 7 as a language writing "language," used in the implementation of SIMSCRIPT II so that a user could define the syntax of statements and the execution of more complex commands [Markowitz 1979, p. 29]. Kiviat recalls discussion of the extension but that no concrete proposal was ever made [Kiviat 1992].

8.4.3.3 *Variants*

SIMSCRIPT I.5 was developed as a commercial product by Consolidated Analysis Centers, Incorporated (CACI). SIMSCRIPT II became a commercial product in SIMSCRIPT II Plus through Simulation Associates, Incorporated, cofounded by P.J. Kiviat and Arnold Ockene, formerly IBM GPSS Administrator. CACI purchased the rights to SIMSCRIPT II Plus and marketed it as SIMSCRIPT II.5. Markowitz [1979, p. 29] also describes a SHARE version of the translator.

8.4.4 ECSL

ECSL, or E.C.S.L. as Clementson [1966] preferred, was developed for Courtaulds Ltd. by the originators of CSL [Buxton 1964]. The extensions that distinguish ECSL from its predecessor are likened to those of CSL2 developed by IBM United Kingdom, but the provision of the features took forms quite different on the Honeywell 400 and 200 series machines. A single man-year of effort was required for each of the Honeywell versions (400 and 200) [Clementson 1966, p. 215].

The most striking difference in CSL and ECSL is the departure from FORTRAN taken with the latter. This decision was based on the desire to facilitate use of ECSL by those having no knowledge of any other programming language [Clementson 1966, p. 215]. The approach taken was to adopt a columnar field formatting akin to that used in GPSS. Abandonment of FORTRAN also led to a richer I/O capability. The FORTRAN I/O was felt to be "the major shortcoming of C.S.L., as originally conceived," [Clementson 1966, p. 218]. ECSL became the target language for the Computer Aided Programming System (CAPS), the first *interactive* program generator, developed by Clementson in 1973 [Mathewson 1975].

A contrary argument to the separation from FORTRAN was raised almost a decade later in the simulation package EDSIM, which claimed both to emulate ECSL and to be event based [Parkin 1978]. In actuality, EDSIM closely followed the ECSL design as an activity scan language.

8.4.5 GASP II

GASP II appears twice in the genealogical tree in Figure 8.1. A preliminary description of the revised version appears in manual form available from Pritsker at Arizona State University [Pritsker 1967]. Although the published description appears in the book by Pritsker and Kiviat [1969], a listing of FORTRAN subprograms designated as a GASP II compilation on the IBM 7090 is dated "3/13/63." This early revision, the work of Kiviat alone, predates his departure from U.S. Steel by only a few months.

An examination of the 1963 and 1967 versions of GASP II reveals both the addition and elimination of routines. The most prominent addition is the routine SET. The use of NSET as the primary data structure improved the organization of the package. A basic and extended version of GASP II are described [Pritsker 1967, pp. 22–23].

A version of GASP II, written in the JOSS interactive language, called JASP was developed by Pritsker during the summer of 1969 at RAND. Pritsker notes that memory limitations of 2000 words forced data packing and overlay techniques developed by Lou Miller of RAND. JASP is the only example of a time-sharing simulation language developed outside of MIT prior to 1970.

8.4.6 OPS-4

Defined in the Ph.D. thesis of Malcolm M. Jones [1967], the description of OPS-4 is taken here primarily from [Greenberger 1968]. Based on PL/I, OPS-4 encouraged the incremental construction and test of model components. All three world views (event scheduling, activity scan, and process interaction) were supported in the language. Additional routines for the generation of random variates were provided, and the numerous statistical routines of OPS-3 were continued. Extensive debugging and tracing capabilities were available along with immediate on-line diagnostic explanations for error detection. Model execution could be interrupted for examination and redefinition of values.

OPS-4 was described as a project in the planning stage. Intended for operation under the MULTICS operating system, OPS-4 raised the issue of the degree to which an SPL might use underlying operating systems support for simultaneous execution and asychronous processing [Greenberger 1968, p. 22, 24]. Ambitious in scope, OPS-4 did not become a commercial language, and little is known about its eventual use.

8.4.7 Other Languages

BOSS (Burroughs Operational Systems Simulator) was initiated in 1967 as the generalization of a gun placement simulator developed by the Defense, Space, and Special Systems Group of the Burroughs Corporation. Principals in the development of BOSS were Albert J. Meyerhoff, the informal group leader, Paul F. Roth, the conceptual designer, and Philip E. Shafer, the programmer. Supported at a high level by independent research and development funds, BOSS was viewed as a potential competitor with GPSS. The first prototypes for external use were completed in early 1969. Roth [1992] acknowledges experience with GPSS II as contributing to his design of BOSS, and the

FIGURE 8.14
The GERT Family Tree (from [Pritsker 1990, p. 243]).

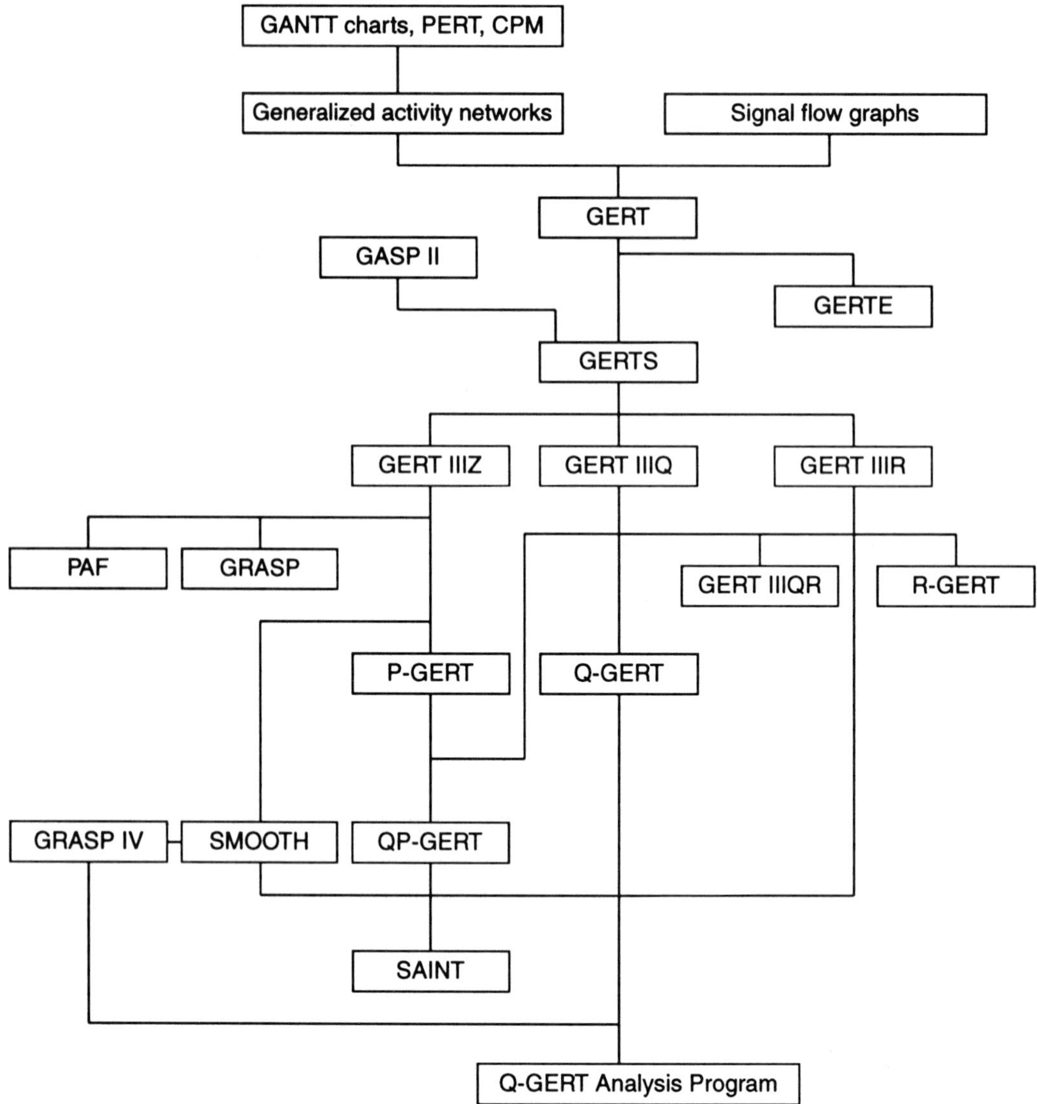

transaction flow and diagrammatic specification of GPSS are evident in the language description [Meyerhoff 1968?]. An extensive set of symbols enabled a wide variety of graphical structures to be represented, and the subsequent diagram was transformed into an executable ALGOL program. Roth [1992] attributes an internal competition with SIMULA as the reason that BOSS was never converted into a marketable product, which was the motivation of the developing group. A very interesting application of BOSS during the 1970s was to message/communication processing by CPUs in a network model developed by Scotland Yard. Roth [1992] believes the language continued in use until approximately 1982.

Q-GERT, appearing in the early 1970s, is described by Pritsker as the first network-oriented simulation language [Pritsker 1990, p. 246]. It is based on the GERT network analysis technique developed by Pritsker, and is first reported in Pritsker and Burgess [1970]. The intent with Q-GERT was to provide a user friendly modeling interface with a limited number of node types that could be combined through edge definition to describe routing conditions. Obviously, Pritsker's experience with GASP II had an influence, and the GERT family tree shown in Figure 8.14 shows the mutual influence between GERT and GASP.

Buxton [1968] contains descriptions of several languages offered in concept or perhaps developed to some extent during this period. Presentations at the 1967 IFIP workshop included: SPL (Petrone), AS (Parslow), SLANG (Kalinichenko).

8.5 THE EXPANSION PERIOD (1971–1978)

The title for this period in SPL development emanates from the major expansions and extensions to GPSS, SIMSCRIPT II.5, and GASP. The program generator concept, initiated in the U.S., took hold in the U.K. and became a major model development aid.

8.5.1 GPSS

The major advances in GPSS came from outside IBM as the success of the language caused others to extend either its capabilities or the host machine environment.

8.5.1.1 *GPSS/NORDEN and NGPSS*

Advances in GPSS were underway by the Norden Division of United Aircraft Corporation in the late 1960s. Labeled GPSS/NORDEN, this version of the language is an interactive, visual, on-line environment for executing GPSS models. Programmed in COBOL (the language known best by the programming team) [Reitman 1977?], GPSS/NORDEN permitted the user to interact through a CRT terminal, examining the behavior of the model (queues forming at facilities, storages filling and emptying, etc.) during execution. The user could interrupt model execution and redefine certain standard numerical attributes and then resume execution. The NORDEN report generator was described as a radically new free format English-like compiler that provides an ideal method for intermixing data, text, and titles [GPSS/NORDEN 1971, pp. 1–3].

GPSS/NORDEN in effect was a redesign around the matrix organization of GPSS. Model redefinition was accomplished through manipulation of matrices, and interactive statistical display and manipulation routines enabled both the inspection and alteration of matrix data, supported by the VP/CSS time sharing system. A film showing the use of this version of the language was distributed by the United Aircraft Corporation during the 1970s.

A version of the language entitled NGPSS (Norden GPSS) is described in a report dated 15 December 1971. Characterized as a superset of GPSS/360 and GPSS V for both batch and interactive versions, the User's Guide attributes the translator with the capability of handling very large databases, utilizing swapping capability to IBM 2311 or 2314 disk drives. A limited database capability is provided through the GPSS language to permit a modeler's access to matrix savevalues so that model components can be created and stored in a library [NGPSS 1971]. The User's Guide is replete with CRT displays of program block structures, data input, and model execution. A light pen is illustrated as used with the display [NGPSS 1971, p. 71].

8.5.1.2 *GPSS V/6000*

A version of GPSS V was developed by Northwestern University for Control Data Corporation in a project completed in 1975. Program copyright is shown in [GPSS V/6000 1975]. GPSS V/6000 was intended to be fully compatible with the IBM product bearing the name GPSS V. In some cases perceived restrictions imposed in the IBM version were removed in order to allow compatibility with an earlier version GPSS III/6000 [GPSS V/6000 1975, p. v-1]. The translator resided under the SCOPE 3.3 operating system (or later versions) and was a one-pass assembler in contrast to the two-pass IBM version. Differences between the two versions are described in detail in Appendix B of [GPSS V/6000 1975].

8.5.1.3 *GPDS and GPSS 1100*

A version of GPSS, based apparently on GPSS/360, called the General Purpose Discrete Simulator, was a program product of Xerox Data Systems for the Sigma Computer line. Little is known about it beyond the identification in [Reifer 1973]. Similarly, a UNIVAC product labeled GPSS 1100 is referenced with a 1971 date [UNIVAC 1971a, 1971b]. Little else is known about this version, particularly, if it was related in any way to GPSS/UCC, which was also implemented on a UNIVAC 1108.

8.5.1.4 *GPSS/H*

In 1975, James O. Henriksen published a description of a compiler for GPSS that produced a 3:1 performance enhancement [Henriksen 1976]. With the announcement of the termination of support for GPSS V by IBM in the mid-1970s, Henriksen was poised to market his version of the language which was already gaining proponents. In 1977 GPSS/H was released by Wolverine Software Corporation, which have supported the language with extensive enhancements since that time [Schriber 1991, p. 17]. Other versions of the language have been developed, both on PCs and mainframes, but GPSS/H (the "H" for Henriksen) remains to date the most popular version.

8.5.2 SIMULA 67

The historical description in [Wexelblatt 1981] describes the period of expansion for SIMULA as the development of a pure system description language called DELTA [Holbaek-Hanssen 1977]. Beginning from the SIMULA platform, the DELTA Project sought to implement system specification for simulation execution through a series of transformations from the high-level user perspective, represented in the DELTA specification language, through an intermediate language called BETA, culminating with an executable language called GAMMA. Probably due to lack of funding, the project is not viewed as having been successful.

Beyond the recognition of the lack of success of the DELTA project, little can be said conceptually about SIMULA during this period. However, the originating organization (Norwegian Computing Center) issued publications that noted comparisons of the language with other SPLs and sought to promote the language in this way [Virjo 1972; Røgeberg 1973]. Houle and Franta [1975, pp. 39–45] published an article showing that the structural concepts of SIMULA encompassed those of other languages, notably GPSS and SIMSCRIPT, and included a comparison with the language ASPOL [MacDougall 1973]. They specifically claim that GPSS and SIMSCRIPT concepts are a subset of the structural capabilities of SIMULA.

8.5.3 SIMSCRIPT

As the decade of the seventies opened, simulation languages provided contrasting positions in the representation of world views identified by Kiviat in the classic RAND report [1969]:

event scheduling—SIMSCRIPT II, GASP II,
activity scan—ECSL, and
process interaction—GPSS V, SIMULA 67.

However, those studying model and language representation concepts readily recognized a major distinction between GPSS and SIMULA in the representation of the process interaction world view, that is, GPSS lacked the flexibility of SIMULA in portraying interactions among permanent entities, which made the former cumbersome for problems where such relationships must be represented.

The expansion period marked the beginnings of the breakdown in conceptual distinctions among languages. Nowhere was this more apparent than with SIMSCRIPT II.

Supported by the U.S. Department of Agriculture, Agricultural Research Service, CACI completed the extension of SIMSCRIPT II.5 to include continuous simulation components in 1976. This effort is documented with a report authored by Claude M. Delfosse [1976] describing C-SIMSCRIPT. This report describes the definitions and program structure for continuous simulation and integration control variables within SIMSCRIPT II.5. Examples of both continuous and combined models are given.

Almost concurrently, the process view with focus on temporary entities was added to the language. Using the distinction of processes to describe the typical GPSS transaction and resources to represent facilities and storages, the modeling approach enabled a definition of resources as passive (permanent) entities and temporary entities represented as processes. Process instances are created similar to the creation and scheduling of events. An ACTIVE or CREATE statement is used. Within the process a WORK or WAIT statement provides for time passage, the latter with a process in a passive, the former an active, state. Processes may SUSPEND, INTERRUPT, or RESUME other processes.

A second form of expansion took place in the form of computer system modeling languages based on SIMSCRIPT. Two such vehicles were ECSS [Kosy 1975] and CSP II [Iwata 1975]. Developed at the RAND Corporation, ECSS became a favored language for computer system performance evaluation studies.

8.5.4 GASP

During this period GASP was the subject of notable changes and considerable experimentation by Pritsker and his graduate students at Purdue. These activities are described extensively in Pritsker [1990].

8.5.4.1 *GASP IV*

GASP IV became available on a published basis with a book in 1974 [Pritsker 1974]. The contributions of Nicholas R. Hurst and C. Elliott Sigal are noted in the preface to the book. GASP IV proceeded philosophically in the differentiation between state and time as modeling characterizations. State events and time events became means of describing the event scheduling concept of an event and the activity scan concept of a condition. However, the concept of state variables was used to extend the discrete event capability to a continuous representation.

Mirroring the SIMSCRIPT II strategy, GASP augmented the transaction flow world view in the 1975–1976 time period [Washam 1976a, 1976b]. In [Pritsker 1990, p. 252] GASP is described as an on-going language development that is intended to produce subsequent versions at least up to GASP VI.

The increased capability and flexibility of treating both continuous and discrete models within the same language provided a claimed advantage for GASP over its contemporaries. This advantage was short-lived because SIMSCRIPT followed with the capability in 1976 [Delfosse 1976].

8.5.4.2 *GASP_PL/I*

In the early 1970s, several efforts were made to map a simulation language onto PL/I. Some of these are noted in the final section describing this period. GASP_PL/I, developed by Pritsker and Young [Pritsker 1975] produced a version of GASP. A doctoral student examining the coded subroutines commented at the time that it appeared as if a FORTRAN programmer had done a statement by statement syntactic translation of FORTRAN into PL/I, and none of the PL/I features were utilized. Kiviat notes that preoccupation with a PL/I implementation was rather widespread at this time [Kiviat 1992].

8.5.5 Program Generators

Simulation program generators were intended to accept a model definition in a nonexecutable form and produce an executable program or one that would admit execution after slight modification. In a sense the early definitional forms of SIMSCRIPT suggested such an approach, replacing the 80-column card specification with custom forms for entity definition and report generator layout. The first program generator was Programming By Questionnaire (PBQ), developed at the RAND Corporation [Ginsberg 1965; Oldfather, 1966]. With PBQ model definition was accomplished through a user's completion of a questionnaire. The questionnaire, with the user's responses, forms a specification that produces a SIMSCRIPT program.

While PBQ was under development at RAND, K.D. Tocher was showing the utility of "wheel charts" for model description in GSP [Tocher 1966]. The "wheel chart," based on the UK "machine based" (permanent entity) approach, pictured the cyclic activity of machines going from idle to busy as they interacted with material requiring the machine resource. In this same paper Tocher comments on the potential for real-time simulation for process control.

Interactive program generators, those permitting an interactive dialogue between modeler and program generator, appeared in the early 1970s in the UK. CAPS-ECSL (Computer Aided Programming System/Extended Control and Simulation Language), developed by Alan T. Clementson at the University of Birmingham, is generally considered the first [Mathewson 1975]. DRAFT, developed by Stephen Mathewson at Imperial College, appeared in several versions in which the activity cycle diagrams (also known as entity cycle diagrams), successors to the "wheel charts," are translated into DRAFT/FORTRAN, DRAFT/GASP, DRAFT/SIMON, or DRAFT/SIMULA programs [Mathewson 1977].

Two efforts, not specifically program generators but related to them, deserve mention in this section. The first is HOCUS, a very simple representational form for simulation model specification, first suggested by Hills and Poole in 1969 but subsequently marketed both in the U.S. and the U.K. in the early to mid-1970s [Hills 1969]. The second is the natural language interface to GPSS, a project of George E. Heidorn at the Naval Postgraduate School in the early 1970s. Heidorn's work actually began at Yale University in 1967 as a doctoral dissertation [Heidorn 1976]. The project had as its eventual goal to enable an analyst working at a terminal to carry on a two-way dialogue with the computer about his simulation problem in English. The computer would then develop the model, execute the simulation, and report the results, all in an English dialect [Heidorn 1972, p.1].

8.5.6 Other Languages

8.5.6.1 *The PL/I Branch*

The cessation of support for GPSS V coincided with a decision by IBM to create the language SIMPL/I, a PL/I preprocessor [SIMPL/I 1972]. SIMPL/I has the distinct flavor of GPSS in its provision of the list processing, random number generation, and statistical routines, to assist in the modeling and simulation studies. Later, SIMPL/I and GPSS V commands were made interchangeable, with the translation of both into PL/I. Such a package, described as SIMPL/I X or PL/I GPSS, provided even greater flexibility to the modeler [Metz 1981]. Only a few IBM 360/370 Assembly Language routines augmented the PL/I implementation.

SIMPL is a descendent of OPS-4, created by Malcolm W. Jones and Richard C. Thurber [Jones 1971a, 1971b]. Implemented on the MULTICS time sharing system, SIMPL was envisioned as a simulation system consisting of both a programming language and a run-time support system, quite similar to its ancestors. Again, PL/I provided the underlying translation capability with SIMPL source code being compiled into PL/I. Use of SIMULATE (model name) set up the special environment for simulation and initiated the model. Like OPS-4, the interactive time sharing environment, now provided by MULTICS, served as the major vehicle.

A third member of the PL/I family, SIML/I, actually appeared in 1979 [MacDougall 1979]. Intended for computer system modeling, as was one of its predecessors ASPOL [MacDougall 1973], SIML/I provided representational capability "which extends into the gap between system-level and register-transfer-level simulation languages," [MacDougall 1979, p. 39]. The process interaction world view is apparent, perhaps influenced more by SOL than SIMULA. Process communication occurs via signals that can be simple or synthesized into more complex expressions. The influence of the application domain is readily apparent in the representation of signals.

8.5.6.2 *The Pritsker Family*

A. Alan B. Pritsker and Pritsker and Associates, Incorporated have contributed significantly to the development of simulation languages. In addition to GASP II and subsequent versions, GERTS (GERT Simulation program) provided a network modeling capability for simulation solutions to activity network models and queueing network formulations based on GERT, created earlier by Pritsker. Extensions to the network modeling capability resulted in a family of programs generally identifiable as one form of GERT or another. The GERT family tree is shown in Figure 8.14 which also shows the relationship to GASP [Pritsker 1990, pp. 242–243].

SAINT (Systems Analysis for Integrated Networks of Tasks) was developed by Pritsker and Associates under an Air Force contract that sought a modeling capability that enabled the assessment of contributions of system components especially human operators to overall performance [Wortman 1977a]. SAINT utilized a graphical approach to modeling, similar to Q-GERT, and depended on an underlying network representation. The continuous component was similar to the provided in GASP IV [Wortman 1977a, p.532]. Like GASP IV, SAINT is actually a simulator consisting of callable FORTRAN sub-routines and requiring approximately 55,000 decimal words of internal storage [Wortman 1977b, 1977c]. The contributions of numerous students and employees are generously described in Pritsker [1990].

8.5.6.3 *Interactive Simulation Languages*

The rapid acceptance and increased availability of time-sharing operating systems led to the emergence of interactive modeling systems based on user dialogue or conversational style. Two such languages during this period are CML (Conversational Modeling Language) developed by Ronald E. Mills and Robert B. Fetter of Yale University [undated]. CML was intended for language creation as well as a language for simulation purposes. The reference describes the use of CML for creation of a simulation language used to study hospital resource utilization. The power of CML was found in its ability to provide deferred run-time definition of model parameters and its ability for model modification and redefinition. The creators describe CML as equally useful as a simulation language, a general purpose programming tool, a specialized "package" for certain tasks, and an environment for systems programming.

CONSIM was developed as a doctoral dissertation by Sallie Sheppard Nelson at the University of Pittsburgh. Considered a prototype conversational language, CONSIM is patterned after SIMULA 67 because of the recognized advanced capabilities of the language [Sheppard Nelson 1977, p. 16]. Coroutine sequencing, process description, and dynamic interaction in the CONSIM interpreter follow the design found in SIMULA 67.

8.6 CONSOLIDATION AND REGENERATION (1979–1986)

The period from 1979 to 1986 might be characterized as one in which predominant simulation languages extended their implementation to many computers and microprocessors while keeping the basic language capabilities relatively static. On the other hand, two major descendants of GASP (in a sense) appeared to play major roles: SLAM II and SIMAN.

8.6.1 Consolidation

Versions of GPSS on personal computers included GPSS/PC developed by Springer Cox and marketed by MINUTEMAN Software [Cox 1984] and a Motorola 68000 chip version of GPSS/H [Schriber 1984, p.14]. Joining the mapping of GPSS to PL/I are a FORTRAN version [Schmidt 1980] and an APL version [IBM 1977].

CACI extended SIMSCRIPT II.5 even further by providing application dependent interfaces: NETWORK II.5 for distributed computing in September 1985 and SIMFACTORY II.5 for the modeling of manufacturing problems in October 1986 [Annino 1992]. An added interface in November 1987, COMNET II.5, addressed the modeling of wide and local area communications networks.

An extension of SIMULA, to capture an explicit transaction world view, called DEMOS, was introduced by Birtwistle [1979]. DEMOS was intended to provide modeling conveniences (built in resource types, tracing, report generation capability) that were lacking in SIMULA [Birtwistle 1981, p. 567].

8.6.2 SLAM AND SLAM II

The Simulation Language for Alternative Modeling (SLAM), a GASP descendent in the Pritsker and Associates, Inc. software line, sought to provide multiple modeling perspectives: process, event, or state variables, each of which could be utilized exclusively or joined in a combined model [Pritsker 1979]. SLAM appeared in 1979; SLAM II, in 1983 [O'Reilly 1983]. (Note that the acronym SLAM is also used for a continuous simulation language developed in the mid-1970s [Wallington 1976]. The two are not related.)

8.6.2.1 *Background*

The background for SLAM introduction included the coding of processes as an addition to GASP IV in a version called GASPPI. This work was done as a master's thesis by Ware Washam [Washam 1976a]. Jerry Sabuda in a master's thesis at Purdue did the early animation work for Q-GERT networks that led to its incorporation eventually in the SLAM II PC animation program and SLAMSYSTEM® [Pritsker 1990, p. 292]. Pritsker [1990, p.290–293] describes the long, evolutionary process in developing highly usable simulation languages.

The intended purpose of SLAM was to join diverse modeling perspectives in a single language that would permit a large degree of flexibility as well as strong capability to deal with complex systems. Modeling "power" was considered the primary support capability influencing the design of the language and the later evolution of SLAMSYSTEM® [Pritsker 1991].

8.6.2.2 *Rationale for Language Content*

Clearly, GASP, Q-GERT, SAINT, and several variations of each contributed to the creation of SLAM. In fact, many of the identical subroutine and function names in GASP IV are repeated in SLAM.

8.6.2.3 *Language Design and Definition*

Unlike its predecessors which were simulators, SLAM is a FORTRAN preprocessor, with the preprocessing requirements limited to the network modeling perspective. The simulator aspect is preserved in the representation of continuous and discrete event models. Improvements were made to the functions and subroutines making up the discrete event and continuous components, but the major structure of the SLAM design followed that of GASP.

8.6.2.4 *Nontechnical Influences*

After the completion and delivery of SLAM as a product, differences occurred between Pritsker and Pegden over the rights to the language and a court case ensued. Settlement of the case dictated neither party should say more about the relationship of SLAM to SIMAN, a language developed in 1980–1983 by Pegden. The statements below are taken from Prefaces to the most current sources for each language.

> C. Dennis Pegden led in the development of the original version of SLAM and did the initial conception, design, and implementation. Portions of SLAM were based on Pritsker and Associates' proprietary software called GASP and Q-GERT. Since its original implementation, SLAM has been continually refined and enhanced by Pritsker and Associates [Pritsker 1986, p. viii].

> Many of the concepts included in SIMAN are based on the previous work of other simulation language developers. Many of the basic ideas in the process-orientation of SIMAN can be traced back to the early work of Geoffrey Gordon at IBM who developed the original version of GPSS. Many of the basic ideas in the discrete-event portion of SIMAN can be traced back to the early work by Philip Kiviat at U.S. Steel who developed the original version of GASP. SIMAN also contains features which Pegden originally developed for SLAM. Some of the algorithms in SIMAN are based on work done by Pritsker and Associates. The combined discrete-continuous features of SIMAN are in part based on SLAM [Pegden 1990, p. xi].

8.6.3 SIMAN

The name SIMAN derives from SIMulation ANalysis for modeling combined discrete event and continuous systems. Originally couched in a manufacturing systems application domain, SIMAN possesses the general modeling capability for simulation found in languages such as GASP IV and SLAM II.

8.6.3.1 *Background*

Developed by C. Dennis Pegden, while a faculty member at Pennsylvania State University, SIMAN was essentially a one-person project. A Tektronix was used as the test bed for the language, which originated as an idea in 1979 and moved rapidly through initial specifications in 1980, to final specification and a prototype in 1981. A full version of the language was completed in 1982, and the release date was in 1983.

8.6.3.2 *Rationale for Language Content*

SIMAN incorporates multiple world views within a single language:

1. a process orientation utilizing a block diagram similar to that of GPSS,
2. an event orientation represented by a set of FORTRAN subroutines defining instantaneous state transitions, and
3. a continuous orientation, utilizing dependent variables representing changes in state over time (state variables).

Thus, SIMAN is either a FORTRAN preprocessor or a FORTRAN package depending on the selected world view. The use of FORTRAN as the base for SIMAN was justified by the wide availability of the latter language on mainframes and minicomputers. Pegden [1991] acknowledges that in today's technical market place it would be much easier if written in C or C++.

Influencing Factors SIMAN draws concepts from GPSS, SIMSCRIPT, SLAM, GASP, and Q-GERT [Pegden 1991]. The primary contributions are the combined process, next event, and continuous orientation from SLAM and the block diagram and process interaction concepts from GPSS.

New concepts introduced in SIMAN include general purpose features embedded in specialized manufacturing terminology, for example, stations, conveyors, transporters. SIMAN has claimed to be the first major simulation language executable on the IBM PC and designed to run under MS-DOS constraints [Pegden 1991]. Macro submodels provide convenient repetition of a set of objects without replication of entire data structures.

Nontechnical Influences Systems Modeling Corporation in marketing SIMAN recognized the major advantage of output animation and created a "companion" product called CINEMA.

8.6.4 The PASCAL Packages

The emergence of yet another popular general purpose language—Pascal—stimulated a repetition of history in the subsequent appearance of simulation packages based on the language. Bryant [1980; 1981] developed SIMPAS as an event scheduling language through extensions of Pascal that met the six requirements for simulation (described in section 8.1.1.2). Implemented as a preprocessor,

SIMPAS was designed to be highly portable yet complete in its provision of services. In contrast, PASSIM [Uyeno 1980] provided less services, requiring more knowledge of Pascal by the modeler.

INTERACTIVE, described as a network simulation language, used graphical symbols in a four-stage model development process that supported interactive model construction and execution [Lakshmanan 1983]. The implementation on microcomputers, coupled with the ability of Pascal to support needed simulation capabilities, motivated the development of the package [Mourant 1983, p. 481].

8.6.5 Other Languages

INSIGHT (INS) was developed by Stephen D. Roberts to model health care problems and as a general simulation modeling language [Roberts 1983a]. Utilizing the world view of a network of processes, INSIGHT adopts the transaction flow characterization of object interaction with passive resources. Described as a simulation modeling language rather than a programming language or parameterized model [Roberts 1983b, p. 7], INSIGHT provides a graphical model representation that must be translated manually into INSIGHT statements. INSIGHT provides the usual statistical utilities for random number generation but also provides assistance for output analysis. A default output of model behavior can be supplemented through a TABLE statement, and the utilization of FORTRAN is always available for the user of this preprocessor.

8.7 CONCLUDING SUMMARY

The history of simulation programming languages is marked by commercial competition, far more intense than that of general purpose languages. Perhaps that single fact explains the identifiable periods of remarkably similar behavior. Such competition might also be the motivator for the numerous concepts and techniques that either originated with an SPL or gained visibility through their usage in the language. Among the most significant are:

- the process concept,
- object definition as a record datatype,
- definition and manipulation of sets of objects,
- implementation of the abstract data type concept,
- quasi-parallel processing using the coroutine concept,
- delayed binding with run-time value assignment,
- English-like syntactic statements to promote self-documentation,
- error detection and correction in compilation,
- dynamic storage allocation and reclaim, and
- tailored report generation capabilities.

Acknowledged as the first object-oriented programming language, SIMULA 67 with its combination of features such as encapsulation, inheritance, the class and coroutine concepts, still remains a mystery to the large majority of the programming language community. Moreover, it remains an unknown to the majority of those hailing the object-oriented paradigm, irrespective of their knowledge in discrete event simulation.

Although the ALGOL roots are often cited as the cause of SIMULA's relative obscurity, what dooms SIMSCRIPT to a similar fate? Is it the FORTRAN roots? Addressing the issue more seriously, the entity-attribute-relational view of data was both implicitly and explicitly enunciated in SIMSCRIPT fully ten years before Peter Chen's landmark paper in database theory [Chen 1976]. Yet, neither the database systems nor the programming languages community took notice.

Given the early prominence attached to simulation programming languages, reflected by the significance of meetings such as the IFIP Working Conference [Buxton 1968] and the eminence of the attendees, what has led to the appearance of lack of interest by the larger community (be it programming languages or computer science)? Has this subdisciplinary insularity been counter-productive in the development of current general purpose languages? Is this insularity a two-way phenomenon and, if so, is MODSIM (a recently developed object-oriented SPL) likely to suffer for it? Although a series of questions might be thought unseemly to close a paper such as this, the answers to them seem crucial to answering a more fundamental question of the programming language community:

Is the past only a prologue?

ACKNOWLEDGMENTS

I am deeply indebted to Philip J. Kiviat for his guidance throughout the development of this paper. I am grateful also to those who provided personal information on various languages and other topics: Joseph Annino, Nick Cooper, Donald E. Knuth, C. Dennis Pegden, A. Alan B. Pritsker, and Paul F. Roth. My thanks also to my colleagues, James D. Arthur, for his help in language and translator characteristics, and Osman Balci, for discussions of language and model representational issues.

REFERENCES

[Ackoff, 1961] Ackoff, Russell L., ed., *Progress in Operations Research, Volume 1*, New York: John Wiley and Sons, 1961, pp. 375–376.

[Annino, 1992] Annino, Joseph, Personal Communication, April 1992.

[Belkin, 1965?] Belkin, J. and M.R. Rao, *GASP User's Manual*, United States Steel Corporation, Applied Research Laboratory, Monroeville, PA, undated (believed to be in 1965).

[Bennett, 1962] Bennett, R.P., P.R. Cooley, S.W. Hovey, C.A. Kribs, and M.R. Lackner, *Simpac User's Manual*, Report #TM-602/000/00, System Development Corporation, Santa Monica, CA, April 1962.

[Birtwistle, 1979] Birtwistle, Graham M., *DEMOS: A System for Discrete Event Modeling on SIMULA*, London: New York: Macmillan, 1979.

[Birtwistle, 1981] Birtwistle, Graham M., Introduction to Demos, In *Proceedings of the 1981 Winter Simulation Conference*, T.I. Øren, C.M. Delfosse, C.M. Shub, Eds., 1981, pp. 559–572.

[Bryant, 1980] Bryant, R.M., SIMPAS—A simulation language based on PASCAL, In *Proceedings of the 1980 Winter Simulation Conference*, T.I. Øren, C.M. Shub, and P.F. Roth, Eds., 1980, pp. 25–40.

[Bryant, 1981] Bryant, R.M., A tutorial on simulation programming with SIMPAS, In *Proceedings of the 1981 Winter Simulation Conference*, T.I. Øren, C.M. Delfosse, and C.M. Shub, Eds., 1981, pp. 363–377.

[Buxton, 1966] Buxton, J.N., Writing simulations in CSL, *The Computer Journal*, 9:2, 1966, pp. 137–143.

[Buxton, 1968] Buxton, J.N., Ed., Simulation programming languages, In *Proceedings of the IFIP Working Conference on Simulation Programming Languages*, North-Holland Publishing Company, 1968.

[Buxton, 1962] Buxton, J.N. and J.G. Laski, Control and simulation language, *The Computer Journal*, 5:3, 1962, pp. 194–199.

[Buxton, 1964] ———, Courtaulds All Purpose Simulator, Programming Manual, Courtaulds Ltd., 1964.

[CACI, 1983] CACI, *SIMSCRIPT II.5 Programming Language*, CACI, Los Angeles, 1983.

[Chen, 1976] Chen, P.P., The entity-relationship model—toward a unified view of data, *ACM Transactions on Database Systems*, 1:1, 1976, pp. 9–36.

[Chrisman, 1966] Chrisman, J.K., *Summary of the Workshop on Simulation Languages Held March 17–18, 1966*, University of Pennsylvania, Sponsored by the IEEE Systems Services and Cybernetics Group and the Management Center, April 28, 1966.

[Clementson, 1966] Clementson, A.T., Extended control and simulation language, *The Computer Journal*, 9:3, 1966, pp. 215–220.

[Conway, 1965] Conway, R.W., J.J. Delfausse, W.L. Maxwell, and W.E. Walker, CLP—The Cornell LISP processor, *Communications ACM*, 8:4, Apr. 1965, pp. 215–216.

[Conway, 1967] Conway, Richard W., William L. Maxwell, and Louis W. Miller, *Theory of Scheduling*, Reading MA: Addison-Wesley, 1967.

[Cox, 1984] Cox, Springer, *GPSS/PC User's Manual*, MINUTEMAN Software, Stowe, MA, 1984.

[Crookes, 1982] Crookes, John G., Simulation in 1981, *European Journal of Operational Research*, 9: 1, 1982, pp. 1–7.

[Delfosse, 1976] Delfosse, Claude M., Continuous Simulation and Combined Simulation in SIMSCRIPT II.5, Arlington, VA: CACI, Mar. 1976.

[Derrick, 1988] Derrick, Emory Joseph, Conceptual Frameworks for Discrete Event Simulation, Master's Thesis, Department of Computer Science, Virginia Polytechnic Institute and State University, Blacksburg, Virginia, Aug. 1988.

[Esso, 1963] C.S.L.: Reference Manual/Control and Simulation Language, Esso Petroleum Company, Ltd. and IBM United Kingdom, Ltd., 1 Mar. 1963.

[Fishman, 1973] Fishman, George S., *Concepts and Methods in Discrete Event Digital Simulation*, New York: John Wiley and Sons, 1973, pp. 22–58.

[Flow Simulator, RCA , 1967] Flow Simulator, RCA publication #70-05-008, Oct. 1967.

[Flow Simulator Information Manual, RCA, 1967] Flow Simulator Information Manual, RCA publication #70-35-503, Oct. 1967.

[Forrester, 1961] Forrester, Jay W., *Industrial Dynamics*, Cambridge, MA: The MIT Press, 1961.

[Geisler, 1966] Geisler, Murray A. and Allen S. Ginsberg, Man-machine simulation experience, In *Proceedings IBM Scientific Computing Symposium on Simulation Models and Gaming*, White Plains, New York, 1966, pp. 225–242.

[Ginsberg, 1965] Ginsberg, Allen S., Harry M. Markowitz, and Paula M. Oldfather, Programming by Questionnaire, Memorandum RM-4460-PR, RAND Corporation, Apr. 1965.

[Gordon, 1966] Gordon, Geoffrey, Simulation languages for discrete systems, In *Proceedings IBM Scientific Computing Symposium on Simulation Models and Gaming*, White Plains, New York, 1966, pp. 101–118.

[Gordon, 1981] ———, The development of the general purpose simulation system (GPSS), *History of Programming Languages*, Richard L. Wexelblatt Ed., New York: Academic Press, 1981, pp. 403–437.

[GPS K, 1969] General Purpose Simulator K, Honeywell publication, file #123.8405.001 K, April 1969.

[GPSS/NORDEN, 1971] GPSS/NORDEN Simulation Language, Norden Division of United Aircraft Corporation, form 910-1, Mar. 1971, pp. 1–3.

[GPSS V, 1970] General Purpose Simulation System V, User's Manual, IBM publication #SH20-0851-0, Oct. 1970.

[GPSS V, 1971] General Purpose Simulation System V, Introductory User's Manual, IBM publication #SH20-0866-0, Oct. 1971.

[GPSS V/6000, 1975] GPSS V/6000 General Information Manual, Control Data Corporation, 84003900, 1 Dec. 1975.

[Greenberg, 1972] Greenberg, Stanley, *GPSS Primer*, New York: John Wiley and Sons, 1972.

[Greenberger, 1968] Greenberger, Martin and Malcolm M. Jones, *On-Line Incremental Simulation, in Simulation Programming Languages*, J.N. Buxton, Ed., North-Holland, 1968, pp. 13–32.

[Greenberger, 1965] Greenberger, Martin, Malcolm M. Jones, James H. Morris, and David N. Ness, *On Dash Line Computation and Simulation: The OPS-3 System*, Cambridge, MA: MIT Press, 1965.

[Heidorn, 1972] Heidorn, George E., Natural Language Inputs to a Simulation Programming System, Naval Postgraduate School, NPS-55HD72101A, Oct. 1972.

[Heidorn, 1976] ———, Automatic programming through natural language dialogue, a survey, *IBM Journal of Research and Development*, July 1976, pp. 302–313.

[Henriksen, 1976] Henriksen, James O., Building a better GPSS: a 3:1 enhancement, In *Proceedings of the 1975 Winter Simulation Conference*, Montvale, NJ: AFIPS Press, 1976, pp. 465–469.

[Hills, 1969] Hills, B.R. and T.G. Poole, A Method for Simplifying the Production of Computer Simulation Models, TIMS Tenth American Meeting, Atlanta, Georgia, Oct. 1–3, 1969.

[Holbaek-Hanssen, 1977] Holbaek-Hanssen, Erik, Peter Händlykken, and Kristen Nygaard, System Description and the DELTA Language, DELTA Project Report No. 4, Second Printing, Norwegian Computing Center, Feb. 1977.

[Houle, 1975] Houle, P.A. and W.R. Franta, On the structural concepts of SIMULA, *The Australian Computer Journal*, 7:1, Mar. 1975, pp. 39–45.

[IBM, 1965] International Business Machines, General Purpose Simulator III: Introduction, Application Program, Technical Publications Department, White Plains, New York, 1965.

[IBM, 1977] International Business Machines, APL GPSS, Form #G320-5745 and SH20-1942, Armonk, NY, 1977.

[IBMUK, 1965] IBM United Kingdom Ltd., CSL Reference Manual, 1965.

[Iwata, 1975] Iwata, H.Y. and Melvin M. Cutler, CSP II— A universal computer architecture simulation system for performance evaluation, *Symposium on the Simulation of Computer Systems*, 1975, pp. 196–206.

[Jones, 1967] Jones, Malcolm M., Incremental Simulation on a Time-Shared Computer, unpublished Ph.D. dissertation, Alfred P. Sloane School of Management, Massachusetts Institute of Technology, Jan. 1967.

[Jones, 1971a] Jones, Malcolm M. and Richard C. Thurber, The SIMPL Primer, Oct. 4, 1971.

[Jones, 1971b] ———, SIMPL Reference Manual, Oct. 18, 1971.

[Karr, 1965] Karr, H.W., H. Kleine, and H.M. Markowitz, SIMSCRIPT 1.5, CACI 65-INT-1, Los Angeles: CACI, Inc., 1965.

[Kelly, 1962] Kelly, D.H. and J.N. Buxton, Montecode—an interpretive program for Monte Carlo simulations, *The Computer Journal*, 5, p. 88.

[Kiviat, 1962a] Kiviat, Philip J., Algorithm 100: add item to chain-linked list, *Communications of the ACM*, 5:6, June 1962, p. 346.

[Kiviat, 1962b] ———, Algorithm 100: remove item from chain-linked list, *Communications of the ACM*, 5:6, June 1962, p. 346.

[Kiviat, 1963a] ———, GASP: General Activities Simulation Program Programmer's Manual, Preliminary Version, Applied Research Laboratory, Monroeville, PA: United States Steel Corporation, Jan. 16, 1963.

[Kiviat, 1963b] ———, GASP—A General Purpose Simulation Program, Applied Research Laboratory 90.17-019(2), United States Steel Corporation, undated (believed to be around Mar. 1963).

[Kiviat, 1963c] ———, Introduction to Digital Simulation, Applied Research Laboratory 90.17-019(1), United States Steel Corporation, Apr. 15, 1963 (stamped date).

[Kiviat, 1966] ———, Development of new digital simulation languages, *Journal of Industrial Engineering*, 17:11, Nov. 1966, pp. 604–609.

[Kiviat, 1967] ———, Digital Computer Simulation: Modeling Concepts, RAND Memo RM-5378-PR, RAND Corporation, Santa Monica, California, Aug. 1967.

[Kiviat., 1968] Kiviat, Philip J., R. Villanueva, and H.M. Markowitz, *The SIMSCRIPT II Programming Language*, Englewood Cliffs, NJ: Prentice Hall, Inc., 1968.

[Kiviat, 1969] ———, Digital Computer Simulation: Computer Programming Languages, RAND Memo RM-5883-PR, RAND Corporation, Santa Monica, CA, Jan. 1969.

[Kiviat, 1991a] ———, Personal Communication, May 13, 1991.

[Kiviat, 1991b] ———, Personal Communication, July 5, 1991.

[Kiviat, 1992] ———, Personal Communication, Feb. 3, 1992.

[Knuth, 1992] Knuth, Donald E., Personal Communication, Nov. 24, 1992.

[Knuth, 1964a] Knuth, D.E. and McNeley, J.L., SOL—a symbolic language for general purpose system simulation, *IEEE Transactions on Electronic Computers*, EC-13:4, Aug. 1964, pp. 401–408.

[Knuth, 1964b] ———, A formal definition of SOL, *IEEE Transactions on Electronic Computers*, EC-13:4, Aug. 1964, pp. 409–414.

[Kosy, 1975] Kosy, D.W., The ECSS II Language for Simulating Computer Systems, RAND Report R1895-GSA, Dec. 1975.

[Krasnow, 1967] Krasnow, H.S., Dynamic presentation in discrete interaction simulation languages, *Digital Simulation in Operational Research*, S.H. Hollingsdale, Ed., American Elsevier, 1967, pp. 77–92.

[Krasnow, 1964] Krasnow, H.S. and R.A. Merikallio, The past, present, and future of general simulation languages, *Management Science*, 11:2, Nov. 1964, pp. 236–267.

[Lackner, 1962] Lackner, Michael R., Toward a general simulation capability, In *Proceedings of the SJCC*, San Francisco, CA, 1–3 May 1962, pp. 1–14.

[Lackner, 1964] ———, Digital Simulation and System Theory, System Development Corporation, SDC SP-1612, Santa Monica, CA, 6 Apr. 1964.

[Lakshmanan, 1983] Lakshmanan, Ramon, Design and Implementation of a PASCAL Based Interactive Network Simulation Language for Microcomputers, unpublished Ph.D. dissertation, Oakland University, Rochester, MI, 1983.

[Law, 1991] Law, Averill M. and David Kelton, *Simulation Modeling and Analysis*, Second Edition, New York: McGraw-Hill, Inc., 1991.

[Licklider, 1967] Licklider, J.C.R., Interactive dynamic modeling, *Prospects for Simulation and Simulators of Dynamic Systems*, George Shapiro and Milton Rogers, eds., Spartan Books, 1967.

[Llewellyn, 1965] Llewellyn, Robert W., *FORDYN: An Industrial Dynamics Simulator*, Typing Service, Raleigh, NC, 1965.

[MacDougall, 1979] MacDougall, M.H., The simulation language SIML/I, In *Proceedings of the National Computer Conference*, 1979, pp. 39–44.

[MacDougall, 1973] MacDougall, M.H. and J. Stuart MacAlpine, Computer simulation with ASPOL, In *Proceedings Symposium on the Simulation of Computer Systems*, 1973, pp. 92–103.

[Markowitz, 1979] Markowitz, Harry M., SIMSCRIPT: past, present, and some thoughts about the future, *Current Issues in Computer Simulation*, N.R. Adam and Ali Dogramaci, Eds., New York: Academic Press, pp. 27–60, 1979.

[Markowitz, 1963] Markowitz, Harry M., Bernard Hausner, and Herbert W. Karr, SIMSCRIPT: A Simulation Programming Language, The RAND Corporation, Englewood Cliffs, NJ: Prentice Hall, Inc., 1963.

[Mathewson, 1975] Mathewson, Stephen C., Interactive simulation program generators, In *Proceedings of the European Computing Conference on Interactive Systems*, Brunel University, UK, 1975, pp. 423–439.

[Mathewson, 1977] Mathewson, Stephen C. and John A. Alan, DRAFT/GASP—A program generator for GASP, In *Proceedings of the Tenth Annual Simulation Symposium*, Tampa, Florida, W.G. Key, *et al.*, Eds., 1977, pp. 211–228.

[Metz, 1981] Metz, Walter C., Discrete event simulation using PL/I based general and special purpose simulation languages, In *Proceedings of the Winter Simulation Conference*, T.I. Øren, C.M. Delfosse, C.M. Shub, Eds., 1981, pp. 45–52.

[Meyerhoff, 1968?] Meyerhoff, Albert J., Paul F. Roth, and Philip E. Shafer, BOSS Mark II Reference Manual, Burroughs Corporation, Defense, Space, and Special Systems Group, Document #66099A, undated.

[Mills, undated] Mills, Ronald E. and Robert B. Fetter, CML: A Conversational Modeling Language, Technical Report #53, undated.

[Morgenthaler, 1961] Morgenthaler, George W., The theory and application of simulation and operations research, *Progress in Operations Research I*, New York: John Wiley and Sons, 1961.

[Mourant, 1983] Mourant, Ronald R. and Ramon Lakshmanan, INTERACTIVE—a user friendly simulation language, In *Proceedings of the 1983 Winter Simulation Conference*, S. Roberts, J. Banks, and B. Schmeiser, Eds., 1983, pp. 481–494.

[Nance, 1981] Nance, Richard E., 1981, The time and state relationships in simulation modeling, *Communications ACM*, 24:4, Apr. 1981, pp. 173–179.

[NGPSS, 1971] User's Guide to NGPSS, Norden Report 4339 R 0003, Norden Division of United Aircraft Corporation, 15 Dec. 1971.

[Nygaard, 1981] Nygaard, Kristen and Ole-Johan Dahl, The development of the SIMULA languages, *History of Programming Languages*, Richard L. Wexelblatt, Ed., New York: Academic Press, 1981, pp. 439–491.

[Oldfather, 1966] Oldfather, Paula M., Allen S. Ginsberg, and Harry M. Markowitz, Programming by Questionnaire: How to Construct a Program Generator, Memorandum RM-5129-PR, Nov. 1966.

[O'Reilly, 1983] O'Reilly, Jean J., SLAM II User's Manual, Pritsker and Associates, Inc., West Lafayette, IN, 1983.

[Overstreet, 1986] Overstreet, C. Michael and Richard E. Nance, World view based discrete event model simplification, *Modeling and Simulation Methodology in the Artificial Intelligence Era*, Maurice S. Elzas, Tuner È. Øren, and Bernard P. Zeigler, Eds., North Holland, 1986, pp. 165–179.

[Parkin, 1978] Parkin, A. and R.B. Coats, EDSIM—Event based discrete event simulation using general purpose languages such as FORTRAN, *The Computer Journal*, 21:2, May 1978, pp. 122–127.

[Pegden, 1991] Pegden, C. Dennis, Personal Communication, June 11, 1991.

[Pegden, 1990] Pegden, C. Dennis, R.E. Shannon, and Randall P. Sadowski, *Introduction to Simulation Using SIMAN*, New York: McGraw-Hill, 1990.

[Pritsker, 1967] Pritsker, A. Alan B., GASP II User's Manual, Arizona State University, 1967.

[Pritsker, 1969] Pritsker, A. Alan B. and Philip J. Kiviat, *Simulation with GASP II: A FORTRAN Based Simulation Language*, Englewood Cliffs, NJ: Prentice Hall, 1969.

[Pritsker, 1970] Pritsker and R.R. Burgess, The GERT Simulation Programs: GERTs III, GERTs III-Q, GERTs, III-R, NASA/ERC contract NAS12-2113, Virginia Polytechnic Institute and State University, Blacksburg, VA, 1970.

[Pritsker, 1974] Pritsker, A. Alan B., *The GASP IV Simulation Language*, New York: John Wiley and Sons, 1974.

[Pritsker, 1975] Pritsker, A. Alan B. and R.E. Young, *Simulation with GASP_PL/I*, New York: John Wiley and Sons, 1975.

[Pritsker, 1979] Pritsker, A. Alan B. and Claude Dennis Pegden, *Introduction to Simulation and SLAM*, John Wiley and Sons, 1979.

[Pritsker, 1986] ———, *Introduction to Simulation and SLAM II*, Systems Publishing Corporation, 1986.

[Pritsker, 1990] ———, *Papers, Experiences, Perspectives*, Systems Publishing Company, 1990.

[Pritsker, 1991] ———, Personal Communication, 13 June, 1991.

[Pugh, 1963] Pugh, Alexander L., III, DYNAMO User's Manual, Cambridge, MA: The MIT Press, Second Edition, 1963.

[Pugh, 1973] ———, DYNAMO II User's Manual, including DYNAMO II (Subscript F), Cambridge, MA: The MIT Press, Forth Edition, 1973.

[Pugh, 1976] ———, DYNAMO User's Manual, including DYNAMO II/370, DYNAMO II/F, DYNAMO III, Gaming DYNAMO, Cambridge, MA: The MIT Press, Fifth Edition, 1976.

[Reifer, 1973] Reifer, Donald J., Simulation Language Survey, Hughes Aircraft Corporation, Interdepartmental Correspondence, Ref. 2726.54/109, 24 July, 1973.

[Reitman, 1967] Reitman, Julian, The user of simulation languages—the forgotten man, In *Proceedings ACM 22nd National Conference*, 1967, pp. 573–579.

[Reitman, 1977?] Reitman, Julian, Personal Communication, around 1977.

[Reitman, 1992] Reitman, Julian, How the software world of 1967 conspired (interacted?) to produce the first in the series of Winter Simulation Conferences, In *Proceedings of the 1992 Winter Simulation Conference*, James J. Swain, Robert C. Crain, and James R. Wilson, Eds., 1992, pp. 52–57.

[Roberts, 1983a] Roberts, Stephen D., Simulation Modeling and Analysis with INSIGHT, Regenstrief Institute for Health Care, Indianapolis, IN, 1983.

[Roberts, 1983b] Roberts, Stephen D., Simulation modeling with INSIGHT, In *Proceedings of the 1983 Winter Simulation Conference*, Stephen D. Roberts, Jerry Banks, Bruce Schmeiser, Eds., 1983, pp. 7–16.

[Røgeberg, 1973] Røgeberg, Thomas, Simulation and Simulation Languages, Norwegian Computing Center, Publication No. S-48, Oslo, Norway, Oct. 1973.

[Rosen, 1967] Rosen, Saul, Programming systems and languages: a historical survey, *Programming Systems and Languages*, S. Rosen, Ed., New York: McGraw-Hill, 1967.

[Roth, 1992] Roth, Paul F. Personal Communication, Feb. 1992.

[Sammet, 1969] Sammet, Jean E., *Programming Languages: History and Fundamentals*, First Edition, Englewood Cliffs, NJ: Prentice-Hall, 1969, p. 650.

[Schmidt, 1980] Schmidt, Bernd, *GPSS _ FORTRAN*, New York: John Wiley and Sons, 1980.

[Schriber, 1974] Schriber, Thomas J., *Simulation Using GPSS*, New York: John Wiley and Sons, 1974.

[Schriber, 1984] ———, Introduction to GPSS, In *Proceedings of the 1984 Winter Simulation Conference*, Sallie Sheppard, Udo W. Pooch, C. Dennis Pegden, Eds., 1984, pp. 12–15.

[Schriber, 1991] ———, *An Introduction to Simulation*, New York: John Wiley and Sons, 1991.

[Shantikumar, 1983] Shantikumar, J.G. and R.G. Sargent, A unifying view of hybrid simulation/analytic models and modeling, *Operations Research*, 31:6, Nov.–Dec. 1983, pp. 1030–1052.

[Sheppard Nelson, 1977] Sheppard Nelson, Sallie, Control Issues and Development of a Conversational Simulation Language, unpublished Ph.D. dissertation, University of Pittsburgh, 1977.

[Shreider, 1966] Schrieder, Yu A., Ed., *The Monte Carlo Method: The Method of Statistical Trials*, Tarrytown, NY: Pergamon Press, 1966.

[SIMPL/I, 1972] SIMPL/I (Simulation Language Based on PL/I), Program Reference Manual, IBM publication number SH19-5060-0, June 1972.

[Systems Research Group, Inc., 1964] Systems Research Group, Inc. MILITRAN Programming Manual, Prepared for the Office of Naval Research, Washington, DC, June 1964.

[Teichrow, 1966] Teichrow, Daniel and John Francis Lubin, Computer simulation—discussion of the technique and comparison of languages, *Communications of the ACM*, 9:10, Oct. 1966, pp. 723–741.

[Tocher, 1965] Tocher, K.D., Review of simulation languages, *Operational Research Quarterly*, 16:2, June 1965, pp. 189–217.

[Tocher, 1966] ———, Some techniques of model building, In *Proceedings IBM Scientific Computing Symposium on Simulation Models and Gaming*, White Plains, New York, 1966, pp. 119–155.

[Tocher, 1960] Tocher, K.D. and D.G. Owen, 1960, The automatic programming of simulations, In *Proceedings of the Second International Conference on Operational Research*, pp. 50–68.

[Tonge, 1965] Tonge, Fred M., Peter Keller, and Allen Newell, Quikscript—a simscript-like language for the G-20, *Communications of the ACM*, 8:6, June 1965, pp. 350–354.

[UNIVAC 1100, 1971a] *UNIVAC 1100 Series General Purpose Simulator (GPSS 1100) Programmer Reference*, UP-7883, 1971.

[UNIVAC 1100, 1971b] *UNIVAC 1100 General Purpose Systems Simulator II Reference Manual*, UP 4129, 1971.

[Uyeno, 1980] Uyeno, D.H. and W. Vaessen, PASSIM: a discrete-event simulation package for PASCAL, *Simulation* 35:6, Dec. 1980, pp. 183–190.

[Virjo, 1972] Virjo, Antti, A Comparative Study of Some Discrete Event Simulation Languages, Norwegian Computing Center Publication #S-40 (reprint of a presentation at the Nord Data 1972 Conference, Helsinki).

[Wallington, 1976] Wallington, Nigel A. and Richard B. Were, SLAM: a new continuous-system simulation language, In *SCS Simulation Councils Proceedings Series: Toward Real-Time Simulation (Languages, Models, and Systems)*, Roy E. Crosbie and John L. Hays, Eds., 6:1, Dec. 1976, pp. 85–89.

[Washam, 1976a] Washam, W.B., GASPPI: GASP IV with Process Interaction Capabilities, unpublished Master's thesis, Purdue University, West Lafayette, IN, 1976.

[Washam, 1976b] Washam, W.B. and A. Alan B. Pritsker, Putting Process Interaction Capability into GASP IV, ORSA/TIMS Joint National Meeting, Philadelphia, 1976.

[Wexelblatt, 1981] Wexelblatt, Richard L. *History of Programming Languages*, New York: Academic Press. This is the Proceedings of the ACM SIGPLAN History of Programming Languages Conference, 1–3 June 1978. It is a volume in the ACM Monograph Series.

[Wilson, 1992] Wilson, James R., The winter simulation conference: perspectives of the founding fathers, twenty-fifth anniversary panel discussion, In *Proceedings of the 1992 Winter Simulation Conference*, James J. Swain, Robert C. Crain, and James R. Wilson, Eds., 1992 (to appear).

[Wortman, 1977a] Wortman, David B., Steven D. Duket, and Deborah J. Siefert, Modeling and analysis using SAINT: a combined discrete/continuous network simulation language, In *Proceedings of the 1977 Winter Simulation Conference,* Harold J. Highland, Robert G. Sargent, J. William Schmidt, Eds., 1977, pp. 528–534.

[Wortman, 1977b] Wortman, David B., Steven D. Duket, R.L. Hann, G.P. Chubb, and Deborah J. Siefert, Simulation Using SAINT: A User-Oriented Instruction Manual, AMRL-TR-77-61, Aerospace Medical Research Laboratory, Wright-Patterson Air Force Base, Ohio, 1977.

[Wortman, 1977c] Wortman, David B., Steven D. Duket, R.L. Hann, G.P. Chubb, and Deborah J. Siefert, The SAINT User's Manual, AMRL-TR-77-62, Aerospace Medical Research Laboratory, Wright-Patterson Air Force Base, Ohio, 1977.

[Young, 1963] Young, Karen, A User's Experience with Three Simulation Languages (GPSS, SIMSCRIPT, and SIMPAC), System Development Corporation, Report #TM-1755/000/00, 1963.

TRANSCRIPT OF PRESENTATION

DICK NANCE: I'm going to stand a little closer to the projector and carry you through a number of slides fairly rapidly. I encourage you to read the paper, since obviously I am not covering anywhere near the extent of the material that's provided in the paper. I'm skating, and pulling material that appears to me to be perhaps the most interesting to you.

(SLIDE 1) I'll talk about the technical background very briefly, give you some idea of the historical perspective, the organization of the talk, and how periods arose as a way of organizing the material here. In other words, I've taken a horizontal cut in time, in talking about all simulation languages during that horizontal period. The reason for it is that they went through a number of very similar experiences, and then there will be selected language sketches; I cannot talk about all the languages. I will pick and choose just a few, and then give a concluding summary.

(SLIDE 2) In terms of simulation, I think the term is often associated with three different forms: *discrete event* simulation portrays state changes at particular points in time, *continuous* simulation is typically thought of as state equations for solutions of differential equations or equational models, and *Monte Carlo* simulation, which is a sequence of repetitive trials in which you have a very simple state representation, nothing like the complexity you can have in a discrete event model. And then there are, as I have shown across the bottom, three sorts of different forms based on how you view the relationship with the three above. A hybrid model will fall within a discrete event simulation model, typically. Combined simulation deals with combined discrete event and continuous modeling, and then gaming is an area where simulation is very crucial, but there are other factors too that need

Presentation Outline

- Technical Background
- Historical Perspective and Organization
- Periods of Partitioning
  - ❑ General Description
  - ❑ Selected Language Sketches
- Concluding Summary

SLIDE 1

Simulation Taxonomy and Terminology

- Discrete Event:
  State changes at precise points in simulated time.
- Continuous:
  Equational models without explicit time and state relationships
- Monte Carlo:
  Repetitive trials (simple state representation)

❑ Hybrid ❑ Combined ❑ Gaming

SLIDE 2

Language Perspectives for Discrete Event Simulation (DES)

(1) Requirements for a DES language

(2) Language forms

(3) Conceptual frameworks

SLIDE 3

Requirements for a DES Language

(1) Random number generation

(2) Process transformers U (0, 1) ⇨ G (__, __)

(3) List processing capability

(4) Statistical analysis of output

(5) Report generation

(6) Timing executive (time flow mechanism)

SLIDE 4

to be considered. In the red or magenta, are shown the two forms that I will concentrate on, both here and in the paper, the discrete event and the combined.

(SLIDE 3) There are three different perspectives that I advance in the paper for looking at discrete event simulation and languages for discrete event simulation: the requirements for a language, the different forms for a language, and then something that is very important to people working in the field of discrete event simulation, the conceptual framework that a language supports.

(SLIDE 4) Each simulation language must meet these six requirements: a means of random number generation, some way of transforming the random numbers (from the U(0,1) to a more general set of distributions), a capability for list processing (creating, deleting, and manipulating objects), a basis for statistical analysis of output, some means of report generation (so that behavior can be characterized), and then a timing executive or a time-flow mechanism.

(SLIDE 5) In terms of language forms, we find simulation packages being a very predominant form. Now I know that a language purist doesn't view a package as a language *per se*, but I had to include them here, because they have had such a major effect historically. GSP, the general simulation program, GASP, the general activities simulation program, and the Control and Simulation Language—three packages from the very early days that, in fact, have influenced—and continue to influence—languages today.

Pre-processors are another form, and two of the current languages, SLAM, Simulation Language for Alternative Modeling and SIMAN simulation analysis language, represent preprocessors. Then the more typical programming languages themselves, GPSS (was represented at the first conference by Geoffrey Gordon), Simscript II from the Rand Corporation—Phil Kiviat and Harry Markowitz—you've already heard Harry Markowitz mentioned; you'll hear Phil Kiviat mentioned a great deal. And in fact, at this point, let me say, that I am in debt to Phil Kiviat for his help in preparing both the paper and the presentation. Phil is a tremendous resource and a great individual to work with. And then SIMULA, which needs no introduction—you've already heard several people in the conference and preceding speakers discuss the effect SIMULA has had in areas like LISP, and Per Brinch Hansen noted its effect in operating systems and Concurrent Pascal.

(SLIDE 6) To explain conceptual frameworks, this third perspective, let me start with a very simple example of a type of model that is used in discrete event simulation, a single server queuing model—if you like to think in applications, think of a single barber in a barber shop. In such a model, you will have a process model of jobs or customers arriving and a queue formed if the server is busy. You will have a first-come first-served order to the service, and a server idle if that queue is empty. The objective

Language Forms

- Simulation packages:
  GSP (Tocher), GASP (Kiviat), CSL (Buxton and Laski)
- Preprocessors:
  SLAM (Pritsker), SIMAN (Pegden)
- Simulation Programming Languages (SPLs):
  GPSS (Gordon), SIMSCRIPT II (Kiviat and Markowitz), SIMULA (Dahl and Nygaard)

SLIDE 5

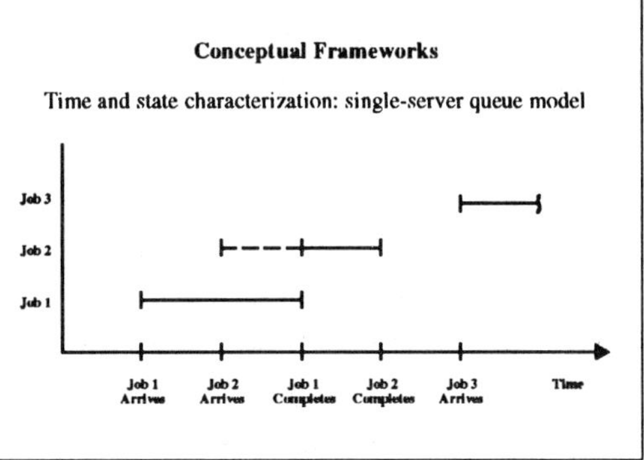

SLIDE 6

there may be to compute the job wait versus the server idle time, because they represent costs that you are trying to balance. Now, the views that are exemplified by the time and state characterizations of such a model, might be when events occur, when jobs arrive, or when services end.

(SLIDE 7) This has been characterized by Mike Overstreet as temporal locality and the US refers to where it geographically was considered the way to describe a system: in this case, the United States. Event scheduling or next event languages were typical of the US view of how to do simulation modeling.

Activity duration, where you concentrated on the state of the simulation over some period of time, was more popular in the United Kingdom—there you might look at the state of a model, of a job waiting, or a job in service, for the period where the server is idle.

The third framework, the object existence, the encapsulation here of locality of object as Overstreet characterized it, in contrast with locality of state or locality of time. You look at all that occurs with respect to the job; its entire experience as it goes through a system, as we have described above.

(SLIDE 8) Now, the event scheduling conceptual framework focused on the epochs marking state change. What happens or what are the consequences of a job arriving? Well, I have to describe them as "what is the next thing that will happen to this job—it will be served if the server is available?" But, you notice here, there are points in time which are pulled out for emphasis in the description;

Conceptual Frameworks
(Alternative Characterization)

Framework	Technical (Locality)	Geographical
Event Scheduling	Temporal	U.S.
Activity Scan	State (Machine)	U.K.
Process Interaction	Object	Europe
PI: Transaction	Temporary Object (Material)	U.S.

SLIDE 7

Conceptual Frameworks

Time and state characterization: event scheduling

Job 3
Job 2
Job 1
Job 1 Arrives
Job 2 Arrives
Job 1 Completes
Job 2 Completes
Job 3 Arrives
Time
Epochs Marking State Change:

SLIDE 8

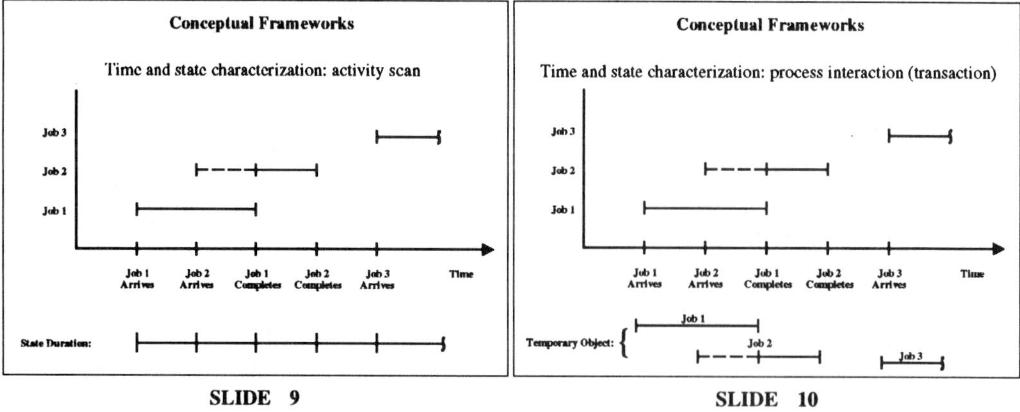

SLIDE 9

SLIDE 10

those points in time relate to the job, very obviously, but also to something not so obviously and that is the server.

(SLIDE 9) The activity-scan or class of languages concentrated on state, and described the state duration for the separation of the two events that either initiated or terminated the two state activities: job one arrives, and job one completes, but in between that time, job two arrives and must wait until the server is available.

(SLIDE 10) Now in the process interaction, the third form described as locality of object, we really have two subforms—the first process interaction or transaction view, as it was characterized in GPSS, was that you looked at the temporary objects, the customers or jobs, as they came into the system—you focused on what happened to that job. But behind the scenes, was the server, the permanent object, which is not well characterized.

(SLIDE 11) In fact, the problem, or the difference between the transaction view and the more traditional process interaction view, is the explicit representation of the server as a process as well as jobs as processes. Now you're characterizing what's happening with the server and jobs, and the points where they interact.

(SLIDE 12) What are some of the influences and consequences we see for having these differing conceptual frameworks that underlay the whole development of simulation languages? Well, the conceptual frameworks sort of created conceptual communities in and of themselves, and as we heard our friends talk about LISP, these communities were equally isolated—they didn't talk to each other much. Phil Kiviat characterized this, in his Rand Report of 1967, as an inversion of theory and interpretation. Where the language should be an interpretation of the theory, it became the theory, and so people working in SIMULA didn't talk to people working in SIMSCRIPT II. On the other hand, there was knowledge of the work going on, in many cases. I would say that the people working on the languages had far more knowledge of the other language forms than the people actually using the languages. There were differences because of application domains, and the frameworks themselves were at least stimulated by the application domains. And then there was a contrast in educational and industrial desires and constraints. Many simulation languages were developed because of a desire to use them in an educational setting. They had very different constraints and very different objectives from those developed to use in a business or industrial setting.

The consequence, of course, is that we ended up with numerous simulation languages—however you wish to define "language." In 1966–1967, two reviews at that time identified 21 different discrete event simulation languages—that does not include the continuous (simulation) languages. In 1981,

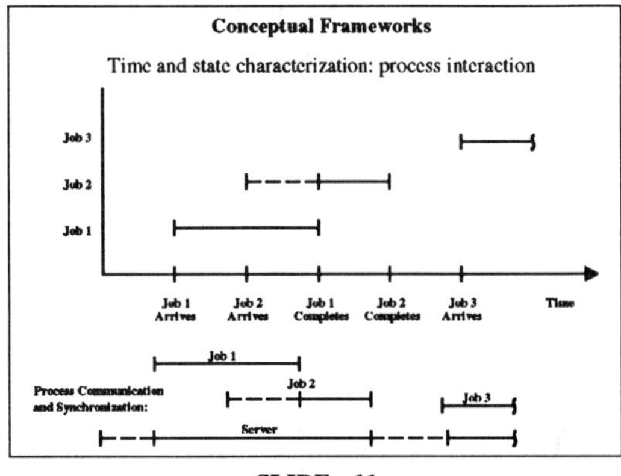

SLIDE 11

Influencers and Consequences

- Differing conceptual frameworks
- Application domain dependent perspectives
- Contrast in educational and industrial desires/constraints

{Consequences} ⇒ Numerous simulation "languages"

1) 21 [Teichroew and Lubin, 1966; Krasnow, 1967]
2) 137 [Crookes, 1981]

SLIDE 12

John Crooks said that he could count 137 different simulation programming languages (SPLs). If the estimate of a thousand programming langauges is correct, then SPLs number over 10 percent—that's a very healthy number. Now, I'm sure that many of these are dead, and some of those that aren't perhaps should be.

(SLIDE 13) When I started preparing for this talk, I thought about different ways I could present the material. I could talk about, for instance, the different languages within a framework family. What were the activity scan languages? What were the event scheduling languages,etc.

(SLIDE 14) I could also talk about a genealogy of a particular language following GPSS or SIMULA or SIMSCRIPT and follow it through its rather interesting history of spinning off and creating others.

(SLIDE 15) But I chose a different way, I chose probably a horizontal perspective, where I cut across in periods of time and I did that because there are very interesting similarities that occur in all the languages during that period of time.

I think it is interesting to ask why do they occur? What is driving that?

(SLIDE 16) So there are the five periods that I will talk about.

(SLIDE 17) The period of search. That was the period prior to the existence of any simulation language, per se, from roughly 1955 to 1960. There were new general purpose languages appearing in that period of time, and there were some simulation models that were done in assembly language

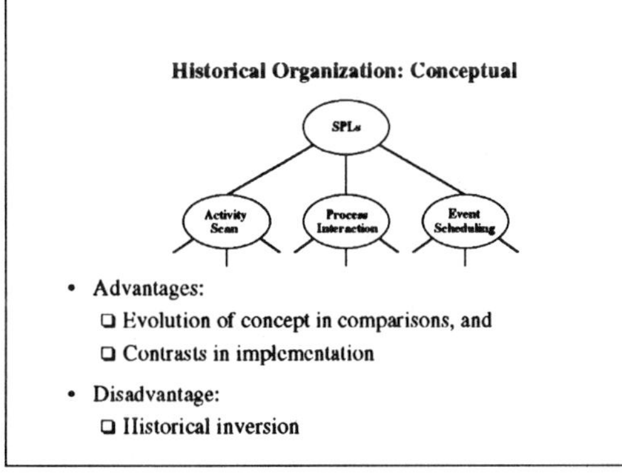

SLIDE 13

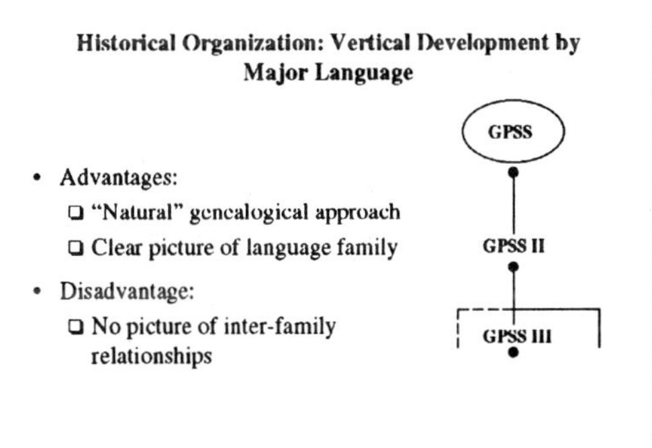

SLIDE 14

Historical Organization: Horizontal Development by Period

- Advantages:
  - ❑ Clear picture of inter-family relationships
  - ❑ Striking similarities
- Disadvantages:
  - ❑ Less than "natural"
  - ❑ More difficult, even argumentative

SLIDE 15

Periods of Partitioning

- The Period of Search (1955–1960)
- The Advent (1961–1965)
- The Formative Period (1966–1970)
- The Expansion Period (1971–1978)
- Consolidation and Regeneration (1979–1986)

SLIDE 16

and the new general purpose languages. General Electric was one place, and the study of scheduling rules by Jackson, Nelson, and Rowe at UCLA around the 1958 or 1959 time period.

Then, around 1958, Tocher and Owen in the UK published a paper on the General Simulation Program.

(SLIDE 18) The General Simulation Program was essentially a search for a simulation structure. K.D. Tocher realized when he did programming of a simulation model he repeatedly did several things. He developed an initialization form or an initialization routine. He developed the description of what he called state-based activities or events and time-based events. Then he also had a report generator. So what he began to do, as every programmer does, is to create his set of routines which he reuses as he programs later simulation models. This became known as the General Simulation Program.

(SLIDE 19) When we move into The Advent (of real languages), we find some interesting things, at least I find them interesting, for today. For instance, this continuing legacy. All the major simulation programming languages of today can trace their roots back to the languages developed in the period of 1960 to 1965. With Control and Simulation Language, it was an activity scan language, a FORTRAN preprocessor and graphical input was provided for. One drew a picture of the model. GASP was an event scheduling language, also a FORTRAN package, and again a graphical interface was provided. GPSS was a process interaction, transaction language, interpretive in terms of its

The Period of Search (1955–1960)

- Programming in assembly languages
- Appearance of new general purpose languages (GPLs), e.g., FORTRAN
- Specific models in GPLs
  - ❑ General Electric
  - ❑ UCLA: Jackson, Nelson, Rowe
- General Simulation Program (GSP): K.D. Tocher, D.G. Owen (1958)

SLIDE 17

General Simulation Program

- Purpose: "Searching for a simulation structure"
- Program organization
  - ❑ Initialization (Parameters for process transformers, termination)
  - ❑ C Activities (Contingent: state-based events)
  - ❑ B Activities (Bound: time-based events)
  - ❑ Report Generation (Could be "C" or "B" activity)
  - ❑ Subroutine(s)

SLIDE 18

The Advent (1960–1965)

- Continuing Legacy
  - CSL: AS, FORTRAN Preprocessor, Graphical
  - GASP: ES, FORTRAN Package, Graphical
  - GPSS: PI/T, Interpreter, Graphical
  - SIMSCRIPT: ES, FORTRAN Preprocessor, Textual
  - SIMULA: PI, ALGOL Extension, Textual
- Others: DYNAMO, OPS-3

SLIDE 19

SPL Sketches

- Creator(s), Developer(s)
- Organization(s)
- Contributors
- Predecessors/Influencers
- Level of Effort
- Distinctive Characteristics/Points

SLIDE 20

translation and was also graphical. SIMSCRIPT, event scheduling, again a FORTRAN preprocessor and textual in nature, no graphical interface. SIMULA, the process interaction ALGOL extension, is textual. There were others: DYNAMO and OPS-3.

You might ask why are you including DYNAMO? DYNAMO was not a discrete event simulation language. That's true. But according to the persons who have contributed so much to the development of languages that are discrete event, they go back to claim many interesting influences, many interesting discussions with the developers of DYNAMO, and also, that they watched very carefully what was happening at MIT during the period of DYNAMO's development.

(SLIDE 20) In trying to provide a language sketch, I both apologize and ask your understanding about the brevity of the sketches. I'll try to identify the creators or developers of each language that I include, the organization or organizations here, contributors to the language, the predecessors or influencers, that is, preceding language or language versions. In some cases information about the level of effort is included, although it is not easy to pull that out. And then, any distinctive characteristics or points about the language.

(SLIDE 21) Control and Simulation Language (CSL), originating in 1962, John Buxton and John Laski were the developers. It was a joint development of Esso Petroleum and IBM UK. They cite Tocher and Hartley in Cambridge and Cromar of IBM as persons influential on them in the development of the language. The predecessors include Tocher's GSP, Montecode, and FORTRAN—Montecode being a simulation model that was developed in the 1960 time frame.

CSL eventually became a compiled language, taking about nine staff-months in the development of the language. I could find no indication of how much effort was devoted to design. The second version of the language in 1965, called by some, C.S.L.2, provided dynamic checking of array subscripts, which I thought was an interesting capability at that point in time.

(SLIDE 22) GASP, the General Activity Simulation Program, began in 1961 with Philip Kiviat's arrival at US Steel. It was basically a one-person effort although Belkin and Rao authored the GASP Users Manual, we think around 1965. It was done as a FORTRAN or FORTRAN package and had a lot of influence from the steel-making application domain. It took approximately 12 staff-months for both design and code, and was viewed principally as a problem-solving tool, not really a language for doing simulation. For instance, it had a regression model of input that was very capable for that period of time. It indicated an understanding of dependencies in the input stream, which you don't find in other languages of that period.

CSL: Control and Simulation Language

- John N. Buxton and John G. Laski (1962)
- Jointly: Esso Petroleum + IBM U.K.
- K.D. Tocher, D.F. Hartley (Cambridge), I.J. Cromar (IBM)
- GSP, Montecode, FORTRAN
- Compiler: 9 staff-months; Design : ?
- Second version (1965) ·▷ C.S.L. 2 — Dynamic checking

SLIDE 21

GASP: General Activity Simulation Program

- Philip J. Kiviat
- United States Steel
- Jack Belkin and M.R. Rao (GASP User's Manual, 1965?)
- FORTRAN, Application domain
- Approximately 12 staff months: Design + Code
- Problem-solving focus, regression model of input

SLIDE 22

(SLIDE 23) GPSS is described in detail in HOPL I, so I include it here only for completeness. (SLIDE 24) SIMSCRIPT, whose conceptual father was Harry Markowitz, a Nobel Laureate in Economics, was based on the entity, attribute, and set discriptors. Much of what is later included in the entity-relationship model is found in SIMSCRIPT.

(SLIDE 25) SIMULA, Dahl and Nygaard, 1961—and as those of you who have read the proceedings from HOPL I know, this has had a major influence on simulation programming languages, general purposes languages, and computer science. I would like to say that if there is any question about it, as far as I am concerned—and I think I could defend this—SIMULA *was* the first and *is* the first object-oriented language. It was developed at the Norwegian Computing Center. Jan Garwick, the father of Norwegian computing, is identified as a major influence.

SIMSCRIPT and ALGOL, of course, were mutual influencers in their own right. Bernard Hausner, who was one of the early developers of SIMSCRIPT 1.5—in fact, he was the chief programmer—actually joined the team in 1963 at the Norwegian Computing Center. As the report in the 1981 HOPL proceedings indicate, Dahl and Nygard suddenly discovered the event scheduling view of the world that they had never even thought about. You notice the effort here is considerable, 68 staff-months, and this was just for SIMULA I. Key here are the process and code routine concepts. You immediately say, "what about the inheritance, what about class?" That really came with SIMULA 67 about four years later.

GPSS: General Purpose System Simulation

- Geoffrey Gordon (1960)
- IBM
- R. Barbieri, R. Efron
- Sequence Diagram Simulator (D.L. Dietmeyer), Gordon Simulator
- Approximately 24 staff-months
- Block diagram, Interpreter, GPSS II, GPSS III

SLIDE 23

SIMSCRIPT

- Harry Markowitz, Bernard Hausner, Herbert Karr
- U.S. Air Force Project RAND
- R. Conway (Cornell)
- GEMS (Morton Allen), SPS-1 (Jack Little)
- Approximately 36 staff-months
- Entity/Attribute/Set Description

SLIDE 24

SIMULA

- Ole-Johan Dahl and Kristen Nygaard (1961)
- Norwegian Computing Center
- Jan V. Garwick
- SIMSCRIPT, ALGOL
- Approximately 68 staff-months
- Process and co-routine concepts

SLIDE 25

OPS-3: On-Line Programming System (Process Synthesizer)

- M. Greenberger, M.M. Jones, J.H. Morris, Jr., and D.N. Ness
- Sloan School of Management, MIT
- M. Wantman, G.A. Gorry, S. Whitelaw, J. Miller
- CTSS, OPS
- Unknown
- System, not simply a SPL: Interactive

SLIDE 26

(SLIDE 26) OPS-3, a very interesting language, not because of the influence it had, but because of what it set as goals for the future. OPS-3, developed at MIT, Martin Greenburger and Mal Jones, major influences there, at the Sloan School of Management. I always found it referred to as the "On-Line Programming System," however, Jean Sammet in her book in 1969 indicated that it was actually the "On-Line Process Synthesizer" and that is why I have shown that title in parentheses.

Using CTSS, the creators of OPS-3 showed us what a language and a capability for simulation could look like in a kind of time-sharing domain that few had at their disposal at that time. I cannot say much about the level of effort. The distinctive point here is that OPS-3 was considered a system not a language. It was a system for doing interactive development and model execution. As such, it really pushed into a domain that sort of defined a path or identified a path.

(SLIDE 27) To summarize: In the period of the advent, there were numerous simulation programming languages other than the ones that I have sketched—SIMPAC at SDC, Simulation Oriented Language, that Knuth and McNeley created. There were also several interesting comparison papers; I note seven papers during that period of 1963 to 1967. People were interested in what others were doing; what alternatives were being taken—I think in part because the simulation language and simulation modeling was such an intensive effort, both in development and in execution. There were many workshops, and Dan Teichrow—at Case at the time, and John Lubin at Pennsylvania were called by Kiviat "the honest brokers," the people who did not have vested interests in language but kept trying to move along the whole technology of language development. There was an IBM symposium in 1964 on simulation models and gaming. Tocher and Geoff Gordon spoke at that. There were several conferences. The 1967 IFIP Working Conference on SPLs, Doug Ross was at least one person there. There could be others here that attended that conference. It read like a "who's who" of personages in computer science. Tony Hoare was there. An interesting anecdote from this conference asked what were the plans for SOL. Knuth said, "We have no plans for SOL, I found everything save the wait-on-state condition that is provided in SOL provided in SIMULA, and I would encourage you to go to SIMULA."

In 1967, there also was the conference entitled Applications of Simulation Using GPSS that later expanded into Simulation Applications and then finally the Winter Simulation Conference, that's what WSC stands for. And today it remains as the premier conference for discrete event simulation.

(SLIDE 28) During the next period, which I have called the Formative Period, we find all the languages beginning to really focus on their concepts—to revise and refine these concepts and set forth what really distinguished that language from others. The Extended Control and Simulation

The Advent (1960–1965)

- Numerous SPLs: SIMPAC (SDC); SOL (Knuth & McNeley)
- Language Comparisons: Seven papers (1963–1967)
- Conferences and Workshops
  - ❑ Workshops (1964–1966): D. Teichroew, J. Lubin
  - ❑ Symposia: IBM — Simulation Models and Gaming (1964)
  - ❑ Conferences:
    IFIP Working Conference on SPLs (22–26 May 1967)
    Applications of Simulation Using GPSS (November 1967)
    ⇨ WSC

SLIDE 27

The Formative Period (1966–1970)

- Concept Extraction, Revision, Refinement
  - ❑ ECSL (Clementson):
    FORTRAN abandoned
    CAPS (Computer Aided Programming System)
  - ❑ GASP II (Pritsker and Kiviat):
    Target ⇨ Small computers
  - ❑ GPSS/360 and GPSS V:
    Expanded set operations
    External access (HELP)
    Free-format coding

SLIDE 28

Language (ECSL), now Allen Clementson became the major mover and FORTRAN was abandoned. A front end, which was called the Computer Aided Programming System (CAPS), was added. GASP II by Alan Pritsker and Phil Kiviat—really Alan Pritsker—becoming the mover and its target was simulation capability on small computers. GPSS-360 and then GPSS-V expanded the set operations, provided the external access to other languages through HELP, and then provided free-format coding.

(SLIDE 29) In concept extraction, revision, and refinement, we see that SIMULA now includes the object and class concept and the virtual concept. SIMSCRIPT II comes into being and OPS-4 provides a PL1 based language with all three world views.

(SLIDE 30) During this period, no language had really more effect than SIMSCRIPT. SIMSCRIPT II by Kiviat, Markowitz, and Villanueva at RAND became a prime competitor with GPSS. It took approximately 150 staff-months. It was interesting in that it had five different levels and an English-like forgiving compiler.

(SLIDE 31) Other languages, the Burroughs Operational System Simulator (BOSS), Q-GERT, a network modeling language proposed by Pritsker, and SIMPL/I, a language from IBM based on PL/I.

(SLIDE 32) During 1971 to 1978 we find the period of extensions and enhancements (Period of Expansion). Now languages previously described in terms to distinguish them began to effect a blurring of these distinctions. GASP from Pritsker emerged as GASP IV in 1974, which had the capability for doing combined discrete event/ continuous modeling, and then also provided a process

The Formative Period (1966–1970)

- Concept Extraction, Revision, Refinement
  - ❑ SIMULA 67
    Object/class concepts
    Virtual concept
  - ❑ SIMSCRIPT II
  - ❑ OPS-4
    PL/I based
    Three world views

SLIDE 29

SIMSCRIPT II

- P.J. Kiviat, H. Markowitz, R. Villanueva
- RAND
- G. Benedict, B. Haussner, J. Urman (IBM)
- SIMSCRIPT I.5
- Approximately 150 staff-months
- Levels 1–5, English-like, "Forgiving" compiler

SLIDE 30

The Formative Period (1966–1970)

- Other Languages
  - ❑ BOSS: Burroughs Operational System Simulator (1967)
    A.J. Meyerhoff, P.F. Roth, P.E. Shafer
  - ❑ Q-GERT — Network-modeling (1970)
    A.A.B. Pritsker
  - ❑ SIMPL/I: IBM, Based on PL/I (1967)
    N. Cooper, K. Blake, U. Gross

SLIDE 31

The Expansion Period (1971–1978)

- Extensions and Enhancements
  - ❑ GASP (Pritsker)
    GASP IV (1974): Combined capability, PI
    GASP_PL/I
  - ❑ GPSS
    NGPSS and /NORDEN: J. Reitman (1971–73)
    Interactive, Animation (crude)
    Numerous versions: GPSS V/6000, GPDS,
    GPSS 1100, GPSS/UCC
    GPSS-H: Compiled version

SLIDE 32

interaction—that is, GASP provided a vehicle to look much like GPSS in terms of its view of the world. GPSS took a different form in the Norden GPSS and GPSS/NORDEN versions, Julian Reitman being a major mover here. It actually had interactive capability, and provided some basis for rather crude animation to look at the output. Then there were other versions of GPSS.

(SLIDE 33) During this period, SIMSCRIPT II.5 develops a combined view for discrete event/continuous models and also adopts a transaction view like GPSS. And then extensions for computer system modeling emerge. SIMULA 67 really moves away from the machine and toward the user with this idea of a pure system description language called Delta.

(SLIDE 34) Then ECSL moves into program generators. Program generators are an interesting concept—they actually began at RAND in 1965, but interactive generators in the UK became the major means of creating models. They were based on the original Tocher Wheel Charts, but became well known as activity or entity cycle diagrams. They were not intended to provide a complete model description but a draft. And, in fact, that is what Mathenson at Imperial College called his generator DRAFT of a model that can then be transformed into different implementation forms.

(SLIDE 35) This is just one example of a single server queue shown as an entity cycle diagram, where you see jobs arriving from the world, going into a queue, then meeting the server in the period of service, and then going back to the world. This became a way of describing a model. It could be automatically translated into a draft or outline of an executable program.

The Expansion Period (1971–1978)

- Extensions and Enhancements
  - ❑ SIMSCRIPT II.5
    Combined — C-SIMSCRIPT (C.M. Delfosse)
    Transaction View — Limited PI concept
    Computer system modeling: ECSS (Kosy 1975) and CSP II (Iwata 1975)
  - ❑ SIMULA 67
    Pure system description language: DELTA
  - ❑ ECSL
    Program Generators

SLIDE 33

Program Generators

- Initiated with Programming by Questionnaire (PBQ)
  - ❑ A. Ginsberg, H. Markowitz, P. Oldfather (1965–1966) at RAND
  - ❑ Job shop model for batch execution
- Interactive generators in U.K. (1972–1977)
  - ❑ Based on Tocher's Wheel Charts:
    {Activity / Entity} Cycle Diagrams
  - ❑ Provided a "draft" to be completed
    CAPS-ECSL (Clementson, Birmingham)
    DRAFT {FORTRAN / GASP / SIMON / SIMULA} (Mathewson, Imperial College)

SLIDE 34

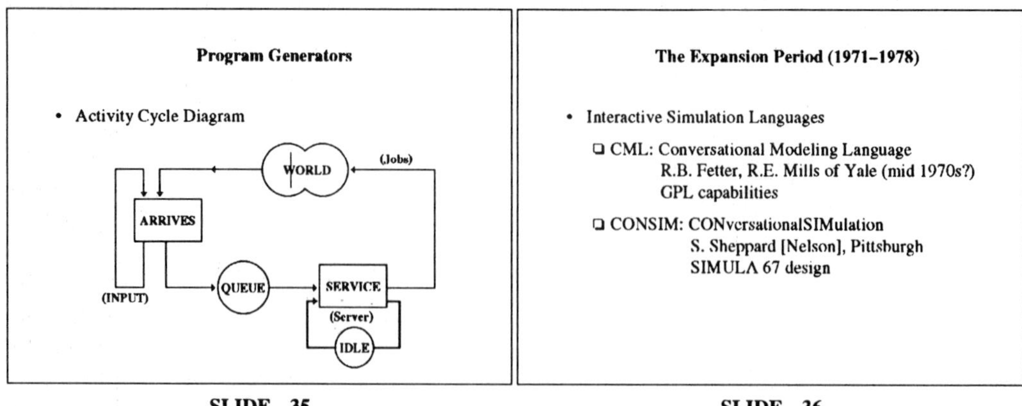

SLIDE 35

SLIDE 36

(SLIDE 36) We also had interactive simulation languages, the Conversational Modeling Language from Yale and the Conversational Simulation Language by Sallie Sheppard at Pittsburgh based on SIMULA 67.

(SLIDE 37) Other simulation languages were created; I have identified some of them here. You notice that SIMPL is a descendent of OPS-4. SIML/I, by MacDougall was primarily for computer system modeling. Then there was a family of languages introduced by Pritsker Corporation or Pritsker and Associates that included the GERTS language and the SAINT languages—Systems Analysis for Integrated Systems of Tasks (I think that is what SAINT stood for).

(SLIDE 38) In '79 to '86 we had the period that I called the Consolidation and Regeneration. Now we have different versions of GPSS appearing on personal computers; we have a GPSS FORTRAN in Germany, and we have a GPSS/APL. Did you know that there was such a beast? We had different application domain dialects being developed for SIMSCRIPT II.5, SIMFACTORY II.5, NETWORK II.5, and COMNET II.5. There is even a LanNet II.5. Then with SIMULA 67, we have an extension DEMOS that makes it look again like GPSS, in that it takes a transaction world view which is viewed as a much simpler approach for teaching.

(SLIDE 39) In terms of regeneration we find two languages, SLAM and SIMAN. Of interest here is that the people creating these two languages worked together, and then worked separately and you

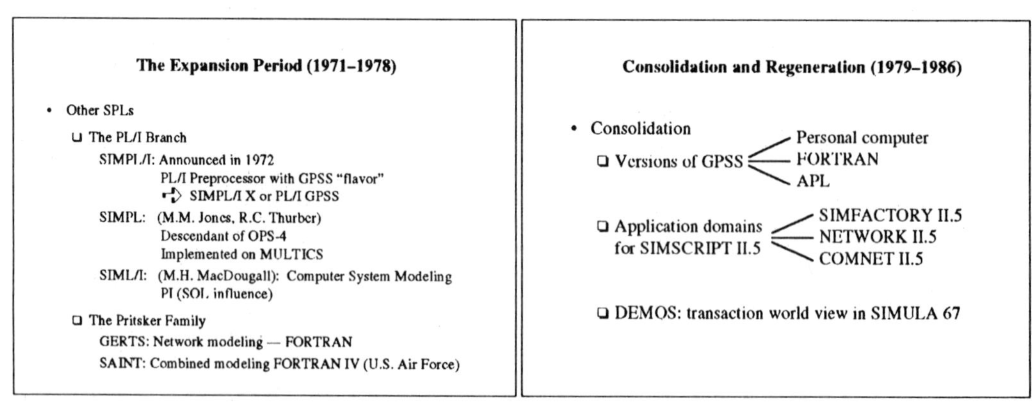

SLIDE 37

SLIDE 38

Consolidation and Regeneration (1979–1986)

- Regeneration
  - ❑ SLAM (Pritsker Corporation): Simulation Languge for Alternative Modeling SLAM (1979) and SLAM II (1983)
  - ❑ SIMAN (Systems Modeling Corporation): SIMulation ANalysis Initial idea: 1979 Released: 1983
  - ❑ Litigation

SLIDE 39

SLAM and SLAM II

- A.A.B. Pritsker and C.D. Pegden
- Pritsker and Associates, Inc.
- J. Sabuda, W. Washam
- GASP, Q-GERT, SAINT
- Effort through GASP evolution (graduate students)
- FORTRAN preprocessor, Graphical, Multiple world views, Combined simulation

SLIDE 40

notice the third bullet. You can read in the paper what is said about the result of the court suit between SIMAN and SLAM.

(SLIDE 40) SLAM developed by Prisker and Pegden, was a natural evolution of GASP. It became a preprocessor though, as opposed to a language package. It consolidated a lot of things developed by Prisker's graduate students. It still is a FORTRAN preprocessor, using a graphical input, and providing multiple world views and combined simulation.

(SLIDE 41) Pegden's SIMAN, was a faculty project at Penn State—really a single person effort that took approximately 24 staff-months over a four-year period. It drew from a lot of different languages but I would have to say notably from SLAM since Pegden was a codeveloper there. It was the first major simulation programming language on a PC. It showed the PC as a viable platform. It had manufacturing applications features and provided a CINEMA animation report capability.

(SLIDE 42) In conclusion I find that simulation programming language history is characterized by a number of things. First of all, a large number of languages—long lived major languages, those that have been with us for thirty years—and very spirited commercial competition. Pick up a copy of *Industrial Engineering* and note the number of advertisements for simulation software.

In part, this spirited competition contributed to the similarities in SPL development during the recognized periods used for organizational division. While the advent of a new general purpose language, such as Pascal or C, typically led to simulation packages in that language, a mutual

SIMAN

- C. Dennis Pegden (1979–1983)
- Faculty project (Penn State)
- Single person
- GPSS, SIMSCRIPT, SLAM, GASP, Q-GERT
- Approximately 24 staff-months (over four-year period)
- FORTRAN preprocessor, Graphical, Multiple world views, Combined simulation, CINEMA animation

SLIDE 41

Concluding Summary

- SPL history characterized by
  - ❑ Large number of languages
  - ❑ Long-lived major languages
  - ❑ Spirited commercial competition
  - ❑ Periods of comparatively similar development
  - ❑ Progressive mutual disinterest (Simulation ⇔ Programming languages)

SLIDE 42

indifference has characterized the relations between the two language communities. Hopefully the recognition of programming as a form of modeling and the evolution of model development environments will produce a more symbiotic relationship.

TRANSCRIPT OF QUESTION AND ANSWER SESSION

HERBERT KLAEREN (Univ. of Tubingen): It seems to me that your six requirements for a discrete event simulation language can be fulfilled using a library for any general purpose programming language. What are the drawbacks of the "library approach" that justify the development of dedicated simulation languages?

NANCE: Perhaps my paper makes it clearer than the presentation that packages in GPLs have always been major contributors, and my conjecture is that, during the period covered (1955–1986) more simulation models have been developed in GPLs than in SPLs. However, there are major advantages to using an SPL: (1) statistics collection can be made much simpler for the user, (2) the user interface can accommodate nonprogrammers more readily, and (3) application domain knowledge can be incorporated, or the provisions made for doing so, with less difficulty.

ROSS HAMILTON (Univ. of Warwick): Your categorization of periods in the development of simulation languages seems to infer that they have "evolved" and that they have now completed their evolution. Would you please care to comment on this?

NANCE: That inference is certainly not intended. However, my perhaps biased (by my own research interests) view is that current emphasis is on model specification at a more abstract level, with transformation to an execution specification that remains hidden from the user. This emphasis follows the "automation based paradigm" of [Balzer 1983], and attempts to move the model development responsibility to users more expert in the application domain that are not programmers. Nevertheless, problems remain that motivate new implementation concepts, and specification techniques will be offered commercially that are tied to existing SPLs or their progeny. As I note in my paper, developments after 1986 are so recent as to defy a historical perspective.

CHARLES LINDSEY (U. of Manchester): Has there been any standardization activity in the field (ANSI or ISO), and would such be desirable?

NANCE: Yes, there is a standard for Simula67, and those standards activities are well managed from what I see. GPSS/H and Simscript II.5 are proprietary and have active user groups. For other SPLs, whether increased standardization would be welcomed and by whom is not clear.

JAN RUNE HOLMEVIK (Univ. of Trondheim): Do you see any difficulties in explaining historical developments genealogically, like in Figure 8.1 on page 373 of your paper?

NANCE: First, I would not characterize the genealogical tree as an "explanation" of historical developments. The tree shows chronological relationships that furnish a perspective on a large body of work. Clearly, an understanding of historical developments requires far more in the way of textual and graphical material; else, I might have supplied you with a paper containing a single figure.

TOM MARLOWE (Seton Hall Univ.): Does the move to make symbolic languages work in a standard interface/environment, such as Windows, address your concerns about language extension in any way (at least as far as the issues of familiarity and "front-end")?

NANCE: Most definitely, and my colleague Osman Balci and I have been working for the last ten years on research in model development environments. Specification of model behavior must be done at a higher level of abstraction than the implementation level. Further, our expectations are producing models far larger and more complex than we can hope to deal with successfully unless we can call upon automated support for diagnosis of specifications for correctness, component reuse at both design and program levels, etc. You might wish to examine a summary paper that describes this work [Balci 1992].

REFERENCES (for Questions and Answers)

[Balci, 1992] Balci, Osman and Richard E. Nance, The simulation model development environment: An overview, In *Proceedings of the 1992 Winter Simulation Conference,* James J. Swain, Robert C. Crain, and James R. Wilson, Eds., 1992, pp. 726–736.

[Balzer, 1983] Balzer, Robert, Thomas E. Cheatham and Cordell Green, Software technology in the 1990s: Using a new paradigm, *Computer,* 16:11, Nov. 1983, pp. 39–45.

BIOGRAPHY OF RICHARD E. NANCE

Richard E. Nance is the RADM John Adolphus Dahlgren Professor of Computer Science and the Director of the Systems Research Center at Virginia Polytechnic Institute and State University. He received B.S. and M.S. degrees from N.C. State University in 1962 and 1966, the Ph.D. degree from Purdue University in 1968. He has served on the faculties of Southern Methodist University and Virginia Tech, where he was Department Head of Computer Science, 1973–1979. Dr. Nance has held research appointments at the Naval Surface Weapons Center and at the Imperial College of Science and Technology (UK). Within the Association for Computing Machinery (ACM), he has chaired two special interest groups: Information Retrieval (SIGIR), 1970–1971 and Simulation (SIGSIM), 1983–1985. He has served as Chair of the External Activities Board and several ACM committees. The author of over 100 papers on discrete event simulation, performance modeling and evaluation, computer networks, and software engineering, Dr. Nance has served on the Editorial Panel of *Communications ACM* for research contributions in simulation and statistical computing, 1985–1989, as Area Editor for Computational Structures and Techniques of *Operations Research*, 1978–1982, and as Department Editor for Simulation, Automation, and Information Systems of *IIE Transactions*, 1976–1981. He served as Area Editor for Simulation, 1987–1989 and as a member of the Advisory Board, 1989–1992, *ORSA Journal on Computing*. He is the founding Editor-in-Chief of the ACM *Transactions on Modeling and Computer Simulation* and currently serves as the US representative to TC-7: System Modeling and Optimization of the International Federation for Information Processing. He served as Program Chair for the 1990 Winter Simulation Conference. Dr. Nance received a Distinguished Service Award from the TIMS College on Simulation in 1987 and was inducted as an ACM Fellow in 1996. He is a member of Sigma Xi, Alpha Pi Mu, Upsilon Pi Epsilon, ACM, IIE, and INFORMS.

FORMAC Session

Chair: *Thomas J. Bergin*
Discussant: *Joel Moses*

THE BEGINNING AND DEVELOPMENT OF FORMAC (FORmula MAnipulation Compiler)

Jean E. Sammet

Programming Language Consultant
P. O. Box 30038
Bethesda, MD 20824

ABSTRACT

The first widely available programming language for symbolic mathematical computation to have significant practical usage was FORMAC (FORmula MAnipulation Compiler). This paper discusses the earliest conceptual work in detail, and then provides information about later developments of the language. Other languages and systems of the early and mid-1960s are described briefly, with emphasis on their relation to FORMAC. There are also a few glimpses into the software management process at IBM. Finally there is an evaluation of FORMAC and its influence.

CONTENTS

9.1 INTRODUCTION

The language FORMAC (standing for both **FOR**mula **MA**nipulation **C**ompiler and **FORM**al **A**lgebra **C**ompiler) was the first language for symbolic mathematics that had significant use. Its development really involved three phases, in which the following versions of the language were developed:

1. 7090/94 FORTRAN-based version,
2. System/360 PL/I-based version, and
3. FORMAC 73.

The first two phases took place in IBM in Cambridge, Massachusetts, and the third occurred entirely outside of IBM, and largely in Europe. This paper emphasizes the first two phases and provides some information on the third. The paper also provides some details about two other formula manipulation languages (ALTRAN and Formula ALGOL), which were developed around the same time or only slightly after FORMAC. There is also some information about the general milieu of computation in symbolic mathematics (known then as formula manipulation). I will use the latter term throughout much of the paper for consistency with the early documents.

9.2 PROJECT PLANNING AND ORGANIZATION

9.2.1 Initial Activity in IBM

On October 9, 1961, I joined IBM's Data Systems Division (DSD) with an assignment to establish and manage a group in the Boston, Massachusetts area to do applied research/advanced development in software. The reason for establishing the Boston Advanced Programming Department was the feeling within IBM that there were probably very good people in the Boston area who would be interested in joining the company but who would not be interested in working in Poughkeepsie, New York, which is where the bulk of the DSD software people were located. It was also felt that having a high-quality software group (even if small), which was involved with R&D rather than production software, would make it easier to establish informal and useful contacts with the faculty at MIT and Harvard.

My immediate manager was Nathaniel Rochester, who was in charge of a department called Advanced Computer Utilization, whose mission was to take a forward look at software for the division. At that time, DSD was responsible for the large computers (e.g., 7090, 7080), operating systems (e.g., IBSYS), and the major language compilers (i.e., FORTRAN and COBOL). Rochester initially reported to Bob Evans (the Division Vice-President, who later managed the System/360 development). Throughout most of the work on FORMAC, Rochester reported to Carl Reynolds, who was in charge of almost all the programmers in the division—many hundreds and perhaps as many as a thousand. Thus I had the advantage of reporting to a relatively high level in spite of having a small department (which never exceeded 30 people).

9.2.2 Early Thoughts

Rochester's instructions to me were rather general, but he did say that I should plan a project in the area of *symbol manipulation*. This term was not defined by him, and it was left to me to decide how to interpret it. For the first six months, I was very busy with organizational problems such as recruiting a staff, finding appropriate offices, etc. In the spring of 1962, I proposed to Rochester that we do an evaluation of various symbol manipulation systems which then existed. In the terminology of that time, those systems included LISP, COMIT (a string processing language), as well as various others. Rochester replied that he preferred that we do something that would produce a practical—even if experimental—system.

I then came up with the idea of developing an extension to the FORTRAN language, which would enable people to do "formula manipulation"—although the more accurate term is "formal algebraic manipulation"—of the type done in high school and college (e.g., expansion of expressions, formal differentiation, and substitution). *The two key aspects of this idea were that the system was to be an extension of the FORTRAN language, and that it was to be practical.* My reasoning was that the people who might use such a proposed system were engineers and mathematicians already using FORTRAN for numeric work, and thus they would find it easier to absorb these new ideas.

At the time I was starting these considerations, the pendulum of mathematical work had gone from the precomputer era of analytic solutions to the computer era of numeric solutions. The reason for this was very simple—the early facilities, such as subroutines for trigonometric functions, square root, etc., all applied to numeric information, as of course did FORTRAN. What I was proposing (although not stating it so specifically) was to swing the pendulum back to the precomputer era, but *using the full power of the computer.* This point is important, because throughout the 1960s, and to a lesser extent even into the 1990s, there was an intellectual selling job that needed to be done to make the potential users realize that they really could use the computer in a practical way to do analytic work. The general state of the art around that time is described in Sammet [1966a, 1966c].

9.2.3 Initial Project Description

One of the people I hired in 1962 was Robert G. Tobey, who was finishing his Ph.D. in Applied Mathematics at Harvard University. With his assistance, I sent a formal project description to Rochester [Sammet 1962a]. What follows is a quotation from parts of that memorandum (which was seven pages single-spaced). The word "provide" was used as a synonym for "develop" because at this stage I certainly was *not* thinking about issues of distribution or support.

OBJECTIVES

. . . To provide a system which has basic Fortran capabilities and also the ability to do symbolic mathematics.

. . . To provide a system which can be used for production runs of problems involving both symbolic and numeric mathematics.

. . . To provide a system which can be useful to application areas which have previously used numerical approximations because the analytic methods were too time-consuming and prone to errors. . . .

METHOD

. . . The system has two parts: a language and a compiler to translate the language. The language will consist of

(a) control statements

(b) arithmetic statements

(c) symbol manipulation statements

(d) declarative statements for the compiler usage

(e) subprogram statements

(f) input/output statements

Parts (a) and (b) will be upward compatible with FORTRAN IV. Parts (d), (e), and (f) will be as upward compatible with FORTRAN IV as possible. . . .

Among the symbol manipulation capabilities will be the following:

> . . . substitution . . . rearrange a given symbolic expression . . . simplify . . . extract specific coefficients . . . expand an expression . . .

JUSTIFICATION

. . . Preliminary investigations show that there are groups which could use a system of the kind being planned. Among these are astronomers, aerodynamic engineers, and molecular chemists. . . .

9.2.4 Constant Need for Justification

Because the idea of producing a practical system to do this type of symbolic mathematics was new, there was a constant need for both quantitative and conceptual justification. After all, we were providing a system for people to do something they had never done before, and it wasn't clear how many of them would be receptive. This need for justification continued throughout the project's first two phases. In August 1962, I sent a memo to Rochester [Sammet 1962b], which contained estimates of potential usage, as well as the planned name for the system—SYMACOM (SYmbol MAnipulation COMpiler).

One of the examples we cited as justification for the project was the following [Bond 1964, p. K2.1–1]:

> Of 4 months spent on a project in perturbation theory, a senior physicist spent 2 months trying to correctly complete manipulations in tedious algebra. Many algebraic errors were found only after the programmer had debugged the program for the numeric calculations and had sought futilely for several weeks for additional programming errors.

We generally provided information on intended usage from two angles: application areas and mathematical areas. Included in the former were astronomy, hydrodynamics, physics, and stress analysis. The latter included curve fitting, elliptic functions, quaternions, and series operations. Tables 9.1a and 9.1b, from Sammet [1962b], show the full list of application areas and mathematical areas that we identified at that time. These were not idealistic or abstract lists, but were based on actual interviews with individuals who had specific applications. This same memo included an estimate that almost 2000 man-years were being spent in doing symbolic manipulation of this kind by hand; I believe this estimate was based on work by scientists and engineers in the United States.

It should be remembered that in those days there was no consideration of "selling software." The justification of the project was needed to make sure that IBM's resources were being spent in a way that would benefit customers.

9.2.5 Start of Work

Rochester was enthusiastic about this project, and gave me a hearty "go-ahead." By then I had recruited more people, and we started developing the detailed language specifications. In December, 1962, we issued the *FORMAC Preliminary Language Specifications* with the authors R. J. Evey, S. F. Grisoff, J. E. Sammet, and R. G. Tobey [Evey 1962]. By that time, the name had been changed to FORMAC (**FOR**MULA **MA**nipulation **C**ompiler or **FORM**al **A**lgebra **C**ompiler or **FOR**mal **MA**thematics **C**ompiler; the first became the official name associated with the acronym). Several other names had been considered, and a vote had actually been taken within the group earlier; the other names considered were ALMACOM (ALgebraic MAnipulation COMpiler), MAMACOM (MAthematical MAnipulation COMpiler), APS (Algebraic Programming System), MAPS (MAthematical Programming System), ALMANAC (ALgebraic MANipulation Automatic Compiler), ALMANS (ALgebraic MANipulation System), and FORMAN (FORmula MANipulator).

The following footnote from the first page of the preliminary language specifications ([Evey 1962]) highlights the terminology of that time period:

> The terms 'symbol manipulation', 'tedious algebra', 'formal algebra', 'formal mathematical computations', and 'non-numeric mathematics' are all to be considered equivalent for the purposes of this report. The use of the word 'algebra' does not preclude other mathematical elements, e.g., trigonometric expressions, formal differentiation, etc.

TABLE 9.1a

List of application areas needing formula manipulation. (Source: [Sammet 1962b])

Astronomy
Chemistry (theoretical)
Economic models
Flight simulation (missile and plane)
Heat transfer
High frequency vibration of quartz crystals
Hydrodynamics
Logical circuit design
Meteorology
Missile and aircraft design
Perturbation problems of higher order
Physics (theoretical and mathematical)
lens design
molecular physics
nuclear physics
Prediction of radioactive fallout
Reactor physics—neutron and gamma ray distributions
Stress analysis
War gaming

TABLE 9.1b

List of mathematical areas needing formula manipulation. (Source: [Sammet 1962b])

Algebraic and trigonometric expression simplification
Analytic differentiation (ordinary and partial)
Analytic solution of linear equations
Boolean matrices
Calculus of variations
Continued fractions
Curve fitting
Differential equations (solution by successive iterations)
Eigenfunctions
Elliptic functions
Laplace and Fourier transforms
Linear dependence tests on vectors
Matrix manipulations
Numerical analysis
Quaternions
Recurrence equations (computation of functions)
Rewrite functions to permit integration around a singularity
Series operations (e.g., expansion of series coefficients, polynomial manipulation, Fourier series)
Stability analysis
Symbolic determinants

These were terms we used ourselves, but I believe they were also used by others in the field at that time. The current terms for the same concepts tend to be "symbolic computation" or "symbolic mathematics."

The objectives stated for the system in Evey [1962] were essentially the same as those in my August 1962 memo, except that two additional objectives were added:

To provide a tool useful in improving numerical analysis techniques.

To provide for eventual usage with remote terminals on a time-sharing basis, thus permitting man-machine interaction.

(In today's environment, with a computer on every desk, it is hard to remember that in 1963 the only personal interactions with the computer were primitive systems involving typewriters connected to mainframes, which could be used in a time-sharing mode. Very very few people had access to these systems, and almost everyone "communicated" with a computer via physical media such as punched cards or paper tape.)

9.2.6 Consultant and Joint Study Agreement

Early in the considerations of this system, I talked to Professor Michael Barnett of the MIT Physics Department. He was one of several physicists who needed more computer software than was normally available in order for him to do his work in physics. Barnett became involved in the development of the software, and actually became more interested in that than in the physics. In any case, as he was both a potential user and someone with significant knowledge of software, he became an unofficial, and later an official, consultant to the project. Because there were others at MIT who might be interested in using an early version of FORMAC, we negotiated a joint-study agreement in January 1963 between IBM and MIT to enable various faculty members to use the system as it was being developed. There were certain political difficulties inherent in this, because Barnett was MIT's Principal Investigator on this contract, and he ran a computing laboratory that was different from, and sometimes in conflict with, the main computing facility at MIT. (The latter group developed the Compatible Time-Sharing System [CTSS] on the 7090 [Crisman 1965], and it appears to have been the first general time-sharing system to have had substantial use.)

9.2.7 Project Personnel and Operation

By June 1963, I had hired or had IBM transfers of several more people, namely Marc Auslander, Elaine R. Bond, and Stephen Zilles. Somewhat later, Robert Kenney and Matthew Myszewski joined the project. With those people, as well as Evey, Grisoff, and Tobey, who had worked with me on the preliminary language specifications, we had a full team. However, we did use several students from MIT and Harvard on either a part-time and/or summer basis, namely A. Anger, R. Bobrow, S. Bollt, R. Gruen, and A. Rosenberg. Other IBM employees who participated in the later stages of the work were Larry Bleiweiss and Jim Baker.

With the shift of the work from language design to the implementation, Bond became essentially the technical leader. I remained as the project manager, but I was also responsible for other projects, as well as running an off-site department (i.e., located in a city distant from any IBM laboratory or administrative facility).

To make sure that everybody was kept informed, I started a series of internal memos dealing with the language and its implementation; we issued more than 100 of these memos.

9.2.8 Planned Schedules and Costs

The planned schedule (following the basic defining memo [Sammet 1962a]) was to produce language specifications by December 1962, do the system design from January to June 1963, and do most of the coding by December 1963. The system was scheduled to be fully operational by April 1964. I specifically established early completion rather than efficiency as a major objective. We met the April 1964 completion date with a reasonably tested, running system!

Although the project originally had no intention of releasing FORMAC in any way, we did want to get feedback and experience. We initiated a number of joint-study contracts with various organizations to permit them to use the system and get some assistance from us. In addition to MIT, joint-study contracts existed with Raytheon, Jet Propulsion Lab, United Aircraft, and others. Word quickly spread, and as a result of various lectures by our staff and informal dissemination of information, there was strong pressure to release the system in some way.

In November 1964, FORMAC was released as an official Type III program for the 7090/94 family of computers [Bond 1965a, p. 1; IBM 1965]. That gave it more status than merely an experiment, and meant that the tape would be distributed by the normal IBM distribution center, rather than by us. However, there was no guarantee of support to the users. In that time period, Type I programs were those systems that IBM was fully committed to support (e.g., FORTRAN and COBOL compilers). Type II were application programs also receiving full support. The Type III programs were those developed by IBM personnel but released on a "user beware" basis. This meant that IBM was *not* responsible for supporting them in any way, although the development group frequently did so. My group provided support because we were very anxious to learn about the successes and problems of our users to see if we had achieved our objectives and produced a useful system.

The cost to produce the operational prototype (i.e., the expenditures in the period from 1962 to April 1964) are as follows, where the information is based on a typed—but otherwise unidentified sheet—in my files.

Manpower	$ 181.1K
Machine Time	55.7K
Miscellaneous	9.5K
Total for prototype	$ 246.3K

Additional costs of $256.4K were incurred from May to December 1964, resulting in a total cost of $502.7K, essentially through the initial Type III release.

The manpower expended was around 20 man-years, including:

- conception, design, implementation, testing, etc.
- preliminary specifications for the System/360
- modified CTSS versions
- some interaction with users
- participation in forecasts of potential FORMAC usage
- much documentation (manuals, technical reports, and published papers)

9.2.9 Interaction with Users

We felt it was extremely important to work closely with the users—helping them and learning from them—because this would assist in justifying our work to IBM management.

Because of the constant need to justify the work on both the 7090/94 and proposed System/360 systems, I issued several detailed memos describing actual usage (e.g., [Sammet 1965a]). In addition to our work, SHARE (the users' group for IBM scientific computers at that time) set up a project with which we cooperated strongly. The heavy involvement with SHARE continued for many years, including their eventually "taking over" the system after IBM dropped it.

In June 1965, we held a user symposium attended by more than 30 non-IBM users, as well as numerous IBM personnel. Critique forms we requested be filled in provided us with useful information. Generally, the users' comments were favorable, but since the details differ in each case it is not feasible to summarize them here. Over a period of more than a year, various internal memos were written summarizing user interest and accomplishments (e.g., [Sammet 1965a]). A number of reports and journal articles by people outside IBM were published describing the use of FORMAC in practical problems. Some of them are listed in Section 9.7.1 (points 3 and 6).

9.2.10 Desk Calculator Version

In January 1965, we developed a "desk calculator FORMAC," which essentially allowed people to use a simplified version of FORMAC in the context of a time-sharing system, where each statement was executed immediately after it was typed in. It was installed on an IBM system, under the MIT Project MAC CTSS [IBM 1966]. Details of the system are in Bleiweiss [1966].

9.2.11 Publications and Lectures

Because part of our task was "selling" the concept—intellectually although not financially—we had a fairly ambitious set of publication and lecture activities. The first full journal publication was in an *IEEE Transactions* [Sammet 1964a], and this was followed shortly by a paper in the *ACM Conference Proceedings* [Bond 1964]; this was the first presentation at a conference. Numerous lectures were given at universities and user organizations. Other publications are shown in the reference list (e.g., [Sammet 1967]), and referred to elsewhere in this paper. Many more publications are not even mentioned here, to avoid an even longer paper!

9.3 OTHER EARLY LANGUAGES AND SYSTEMS

In considering other languages and systems known at the time I started the FORMAC project, it is crucial to distinguish between a *language* and a *system*, where the latter generally involves an integrated package of routines, but not a programming language connecting them. As will be seen later, there were several of the latter, but only one of the former.

9.3.1 ALGY

By 1962, when the project description was written, there was only one programming language that had ever been developed to do formula manipulation, and that was ALGY, developed for the Philco 2000 [Bernick 1961]. ALGY contained commands for removing parentheses, substitution, factoring with respect to a single variable, and a few other commands. It did *not* have any relation to an existing language. As I stated in my book: "Although ALGY apparently never received too much usage or publicity, I consider it a major contribution to the field because it was the first system to try to provide multiple capabilities on a general class of expressions all in one system. In fact, for some ideas, ALGY was a conceptual forerunner of FORMAC." [Sammet 1969, p. 474].

My reason for the last sentence is that ALGY helped me realize that what would be most helpful to users was a *language* rather than a set of subroutines. The only other effect that ALGY had on my thinking was the actual commands; however, since the ALGY commands are all obviously necessary, I am sure that I would have derived them independently even if I had never seen ALGY. Thus, ALGY's primary influence was the concept of a language with commands operating on the formal expressions.

9.3.2 Other Systems (Not Languages)

There were several formula manipulation systems known around the time FORMAC started, although many of them were either experimental and used only by their developers, or based on a specific, relatively narrow, class of applications. A fairly detailed description of these systems is given in Sammet [1966a], and a very detailed annotated bibliography is in Sammet [1966b]. (A retrospective look at that time period, from the hindsight of 25 years, is given in Sammet [1990]).

The more widely mentioned or used nonlanguage systems of that time included ALPAK (developed at Bell Labs) [Brown 1963–1964], and PM (developed at IBM Research Center) [Collins 1966]; both dealt with polynomials or rational functions and emphasized efficiency for those classes of expressions. (The evolution of ALPAK into the language ALTRAN is discussed in the next section.) ALPAK and PM were probably developed in parallel with FORMAC. Information on other efforts was difficult to obtain since the field was not cohesive, and the people involved generally did not know each other at this early stage nor was there an effective methodology for communication. As will be indicated later in Section 9.7.1 (point 7), solving this communication problem was one of the major motivations for my forming the ACM **S**pecial **I**nterest **C**ommittee on **S**ymbolic and **A**lgebraic **M**anipulation—SICSAM.

9.3.3 Other (Later) Languages

By the time FORMAC was made available to users, as described in Section 9.2.9, two other *languages* were also under development, namely ALTRAN (based on ALPAK) [Brown 1966] and Formula ALGOL [Perlis 1964, 1966], although documents for these systems were not available to us at that time. Knowledge of both these languages was certainly available to us as we started the PL/I version of FORMAC (as described in Section 9.5).

It is worth noting the difference in philosophy among the three languages in the period 1964–1965. All three were languages. ALTRAN was essentially an extension of FORTRAN (as FORMAC was) and was based on the existing ALPAK system. A version called "Early ALTRAN" was running on the 7090/94 sometime in the period 1964–1966, but the date is unclear due to discrepancies among the ALTRAN documents I have seen. However, ALTRAN dealt only with polynomials and rational functions, whereas FORMAC permitted trigonometric, exponential, and logarithmic functions as well. The greater generality allowed for FORMAC expressions resulted in FORMAC having less object time efficiency than ALTRAN when handling problems involving polynomials or rational functions.

Formula ALGOL, as a language, was a superset of ALGOL 60 and permitted manipulation of transcendental functions. The first major difference in philosophy between FORMAC and Formula ALGOL was the selection of the base language, which was an obvious choice in both cases, since IBM had initially developed and promulgated FORTRAN, and Perlis had been on the ALGOL 58 and ALGOL 60 committees. Formula ALGOL provided the user with more elementary/basic capabilities and let the user build up the type of capability desired. This is best illustrated by considering simplification. FORMAC had a well-defined set of rules, which did certain things automatically (e.g.,

A*1 was automatically replaced by **A**—see Section 9.4.3.2), whereas Formula ALGOL provided facilities for doing this replacement but did not force it on the user. Those of us involved (particularly Al Perlis and his group, as well as myself and people in my group) had many long, albeit informal, debates on this issue at various times and places, and each group stuck to its technical philosophy. The best analogy is that in Formula ALGOL the facilities for manipulating formal algebraic expressions are similar in spirit to an assembly language; the user has the ability—but also the requirement—to write and hand-tailor many facilities that are provided automatically in FORMAC. It was the classical debate between the merits of an assembly language and a high-level language such as FORTRAN. Formula ALGOL also had facilities for dealing with strings and lists, which made it the most general of the languages that could be used for formula manipulation.

Other more minor *languages*, which were implemented by 1965–1966, were Magic Paper [Clapp 1963], MATHLAB [Engelman 1965], Symbolic Mathematical Laboratory [Martin 1967], and FLAP [Morris 1967]. A brief summary of these is given in Sammet [1969, Chapter VII]. Of this set, I consider MATHLAB to be the most interesting, as it was the first complete on-line system with formal algebraic manipulation facilities, and it was written in Lisp. Furthermore, MATHLAB, and its later version MATHLAB 68 [Engelman 1971], were precursors for the major system MACSYMA [Martin 1971; Moses 1974].

A representation of the state of the art in languages and systems as of 1965–1966 occurred in the first SYMSAM (ACM **SYM**posium on **S**ymbolic and **A**lgebraic **M**anipulation) held March 29–31, 1966; a full issue of the *ACM Communications* [ACM 1966] represented the proceedings. SYMSAM was followed shortly by a small IFIP conference held in September 1966 in Pisa, Italy; the book that served as the proceedings of that conference also provided a good representation of the state of the art at that time [Bobrow 1968]. An updated bibliography [Sammet 1968] was included in that book. The milieu of five years later is reflected in the second symposium—SYMSAM 1971 [Petrick 1971].

For those readers familiar with more current systems such as MACSYMA, MAPLE, Mathematica, and REDUCE, they did not exist in 1965. The initial version of REDUCE was not a language but rather a set of routines [Hearn 1966, 1967]. (Partially at my urging, REDUCE was eventually developed into a language based on ALGOL 60, even though it was implemented in Lisp [Hearn 1971].)

9.3.4 FORMAC Not Influenced by Other Languages

It should be clear from the preceding remarks that the 7090 FORMAC was *not* influenced at all by the work occurring around the same time. The primary inspiration for the language was the desire to provide reasonable capability within the framework of a good syntactic and semantic extension of FORTRAN. (Knowledge of ALGY was only minimally useful to us, because the information about it was too sketchy, and the language itself too primitive to have more than a minor effect. Furthermore, it was a "stand-alone" language, which was contrary to my basic objective of a FORTRAN extension.) By the time the PL/I-FORMAC version was developed, we were too convinced of the correctness of our approach, and also had the confirming experience of our users, to make major conceptual changes or use many ideas from other systems.

9.3.5 Involvement with LISP

The preceding discussion has not yet mentioned LISP. That language was a "low-level language" *from the viewpoint of actually doing formal algebraic manipulation*. LISP could be—and was—used to develop routines such as differentiation, simplification, and so on, but it did not provide those basic capabilities *ab initio*. Considerable work in various aspects of symbolic computation was done using LISP, including programs for doing simplification and integration, as well as specific applications in physics [Sammet 1966a, 1966c].

One of the early considerations was whether to use LISP to implement FORMAC. I made the decision not to do so, because I didn't see any great advantage to using LISP. We implemented FORMAC in MAP (the 7090 assembly language). The developers of the SCRATCHPAD/I [Griesmer 1971] and REDUCE [Hearn 1966] systems clearly did not agree with me; they used LISP as the implementation language and were also able to incorporate some existing LISP routines to build up their systems.

One of the obvious questions about the operational FORMAC concerned its efficiency. Unfortunately, we had no basis of comparison as there was no other system remotely resembling it. I hired Joel Moses for the summer of 1964, because he was then a graduate student at MIT and thoroughly familiar with LISP. Moses later became the leader of the large, major MACSYMA system development [Moses 1974]. It was not surprising that the results of all the comparisons we ran in 1964 were mixed. In those cases that made use of LISP capabilities (e.g., sublists), the problem ran faster on LISP than on FORMAC, whereas in other cases the converse was true. In some instances the coding of FORMAC problems was trivial (e.g., 15 statements long) versus the LISP coding which took two weeks, because LISP did not have existing routines, such as EXPAND, that might be needed in a specific problem. (Note that the comparisons were made to "pure LISP" and not to LISP-based symbolic mathematical systems.)

9.4 RATIONALE FOR THE CONTENT OF THE LANGUAGE

9.4.1 Fundamental Concepts

The fundamental concept introduced by FORMAC was that of a *general language* rather than a package of routines. It was felt from the very beginning—see Section 9.2.3 regarding the Initial Project Description—that the intended users were undoubtedly already familiar with FORTRAN and thus we should build on that rather than introduce a brand new language. In fact, the development of FORMAC as a "superset" required that the user know FORTRAN (or at least learn it). For the time period, this was quite logical, as the only other significant numerical language at the time was ALGOL 60, and that certainly was not in wide use in the United States nor (I have been told) even in industrial companies in Europe.

To clarify the difference between FORTRAN and FORMAC, note the following two very simple examples:

FORTRAN

```
A = 5
B = 3
C = (A + B) * (A - B)
```

These statements result in the value **16** being assigned to **C**.

FORMAC

```
LET A = X
LET B = Y
LET C = (A + B) * (A - B)
```

These statements result in the *expression* **(X + Y) * (X – Y)** being assigned to **C**.

In both cases, the evaluation occurs when the object code for the third statement is executed.

A more complete example, namely a program to produce the symbolic roots of a quadratic equation, is provided in Figure 9.1.

The language was defined using the same metalanguage as had been used for COBOL and which can be seen in any early COBOL manual.

Considering the time period, however, the system obviously had to be batch-oriented. Some experimental work was done to make FORMAC available on a terminal, but this was never significantly used. That work was mentioned in Section 9.2.10.

FIGURE 9.1

Example of FORMAC program to find the symbolic roots of three quadratic equations where coefficients can be either expressions or numbers.

```
INPUT TO FORMAC PREPROCESSOR (FOR FORTRAN ON IBM 709/7090)
      $IBFMC QUDIST NODECK
      C         THIS PROGRAM FINDS THE SYMBOLIC ROOTS OF A
      C         QUADRATIC EQUATION WHERE THE COEFFICIENTS
      C         CAN BE EXPRESSIONS OR NUMBERS.
      C         ALTHOUGH THIS WAS SET UP TO RUN ONLY 3 CASES IT
      C         COULD OBVIOUSLY BE GENERALIZED BY USING A
      C         SUBROUTINE AND READING EXPRESSIONS IN AT
      C         OBJECT TIME
            SYMARG
            ATOMIC X,Y,K
            DIMENSION CASE (3), X1(3),X2(3)
            LET CASE(1) = X**2 + 2*X*(Y+1) + (Y+1}**2
            LET CASE(2) = 2 + X**2 - 4*X
            LET CASE(3) = 3*X**2 + K*(X+X**2+1) +4
            N=3
            DO 88 I = 1, N
            LET RVEXPR = EXPAND CASE (1)
      C                 REMOVE PARENTHESES
            LET A = COEFF RVEXPR,X**2
            LET B = COEFF RVEXPR,X
             LET C = COEFF RVEXPR, X**0
      C                 THE EXPANSIONS IN THE NEXT THREE STATEMENTS
      C                 ARE DONE BECAUSE THE PARENTHESES MUST BE
      C                 REMOVED TO PERMIT MAXIMUM COLLAPSING OF
      C                 EXPRESSIONS
            LET DISCRM = EXPAND B**2 - 4*A*C
            LET X1(I) = EXPAND (-B + DISCRM**(1/2))/(2*A)
            LET X2(I) = EXPAND (-B - DISCRM**(1/2))/(2*A)
      88 CONTINUE
          FMCDMP
          STOP
          END
```

9.4.2 Key Elements of the FORMAC Language

Since FORMAC was to be an extension of FORTRAN IV, we introduced a new data type, known as a "FORMAC variable." This was really a symbolic data type, to contrast with the normal numeric data types in FORTRAN. This basic concept was crucial, and no symbolic commands could adequately be developed without it. The commands and functions provided in FORMAC are shown in Table 9.2.

Noticeable (perhaps) by their absence from this list are commands or functions for integration and general factoring. The reason for their omission is merely that both those capabilities were well beyond the state of the art at the time the first FORMAC was developed.

A few general comments are worth making here. First, the philosophy of automatic simplification is discussed in Section 9.4.3.2. Second, there is a differentiation operator, but not an integration operator. This reflects the state of the art in the early 1960s. Differentiation is a relatively straightforward task (sometimes assigned to freshmen as homework today). Differentiation was in fact the first known use of a computer to do any type of symbolic computation—see Sammet [1966a]. However, in 1962 when we started FORMAC, integration was an extremely difficult task. It was not until the development of the integration system SIN (Symbolic INtegration) by Joel Moses for his Ph.D. thesis [Moses 1967] that sufficient algorithms and techniques were developed to enable symbolic integration to be implemented effectively. From a language viewpoint, the inclusion of an integration function

TABLE 9.2

FORMAC executable statements and functions.

Statements yielding FORMAC Variables	
LET	construct specified expressions (essentially an assignment statement for the symbolic variables)
SUBST	replace variables with expressions or other variables
EXPAND	remove parentheses
COEFF	obtain the coefficient of a variable, or a variable raised to a power
PART	separate expressions into terms, factors, exponents, arguments of functions, etc.
Statements yielding FORTRAN variables	
EVAL	evaluate expression for numerical values of the variables
MATCH	compare two expressions for equivalence or identity [yields a FORTRAN logical variable]
FIND	determine dependence relations or existence of variables
CENSUS	count words, terms, or factors
Miscellaneous Statements	
BCDCON	convert to BCD form from internal form [needed for output]
ALGCON	convert to internal form from BCD form [needed for input]
ORDER	specify sequencing of variables within expressions
AUTSIM	control arithmetic done during automatic simplification [a few options were available]
ERASE	eliminate expressions no longer needed
FMCDMP	symbolic dump
Functions	
FMCDIF	differentiation
FMCOMB	combinatorial
FMCFAC	factorial
FMCDFA	double factorial

Note: FORMAC also contained trigonometric, logarithmic, and exponential functions.

(or command) in the earliest FORMAC would have been trivial, but the difficulty of the object time routine to handle this was utterly beyond the scope of our project—or even our knowledge! There was a 1961 Ph.D. thesis at MIT by J. R. Slagle (later published in Slagle [1963]), that identified heuristic techniques for integration, but I don't recall whether I was even aware of his 1961 thesis when I started the FORMAC work.

It was recognized that debugging might be difficult, but we did not realize just *how* difficult until practical output of many pages of algebraic expressions were produced. There was a command to permit a useful dump, and there were numerous diagnostic messages generated at both compile and object time.

9.4.3 Other Language Issues

9.4.3.1 *General*

We were constantly influenced throughout the entire project, and specifically during the language design, by the realization that we had to persuade engineers and scientists that they could use a computer for their nonnumeric computations in a way that none of them had ever done before. (Some of our relationship with potential and actual users was discussed in Section 9.2.9) We tried to do this in two ways—first, by providing an easy way of going back and forth between the numeric and symbolic computations, and second by providing adequate capabilities for the nonnumeric work. In actual practice, an application often requires massive symbolic computation to create an expression, which must then be numerically evaluated for a wide variety of values. FORMAC achieved this interaction by providing an EVAL command, which operated at object time by examining the expression just created, and generating object code for it "on the fly," which was then evaluated for the desired parameters. The alternative would have been to produce the expressions as FORMAC output and then require the user to reintroduce them into FORTRAN to do the numeric computation. We felt it was crucial to avoid that extra step. However, we eventually did have to provide that facility automatically when many problems took too long to execute the numeric evaluation (after finishing the symbolic computation) because it was interpretive. In those cases the FORMAC system generated symbolic output in exactly the form that FORTRAN needed as input, generated the FORTRAN commands to do the numerical computations indicated by the EVAL command, and automatically fed this back into the FORTRAN compiler to obtain a pure numeric compilation and computation.

With respect to providing "adequate capabilities," the question has arisen as to whether the lack of integration or complete factoring was a serious problem in persuading users to try FORMAC. While this might have been true in a few cases—obviously those involving complex integration—I do not think it was a significant deterrent in most cases. I know that there were many problems where what was needed was only the ability to perform the four arithmetic operations on massive expressions, and then simplify and/or evaluate them. In fact, one of our earliest test cases for debugging involved generating a series that involved nothing more than addition, multiplication, and simplification of expressions; but the first few terms could be done easily by hand, each additional term required many hours to generate it, and the time required grew with each term!

We certainly expected that programs would only be written by a single person. As far as libraries were concerned, we planned to use the capability in FORTRAN but nothing beyond that. There was no intention of trying to achieve significant portability—the system was meant to be implemented as a preprocessor to FORTRAN IV using the operating system on the 7090/94, namely IBSYS/IBJOB.

The users did not seem to have much difficulty learning the FORMAC facilities once they understood the basic difference between the numeric computations of FORTRAN and the symbolic computations of FORMAC.

9.4.3.2 *Simplification*

One of the major technical/philosophical issues in any formula manipulation system is the amount, type, and style of simplification. It is obvious from high school algebra that the expression **AB – BA** simplifies to **0**, and that $\mathbf{A^2 * A^3}$ simplifies to $\mathbf{A^5}$. It is not at all obvious in a computerized system that these simplifications will—or even should—occur; if one wants them to occur, then routines must be coded and properly invoked. The FORMAC group decided on a specific set of rules for automatic simplification, and these are described in Tobey [1965b].

In considering simplification, the language specifications must specify exactly which simplifications the system will perform automatically and which the programmer can request, since simplification is a relative term that depends on the intent of the user at a particular point in the program.

Most people would agree that in normal scientific and engineering work:

A * 0 should result in **0**
A ** 1 should result in **A**
AB – BA should result in **0**

but it is less obvious whether **A(B + C)** should be left alone or automatically expanded to **AB + AC**. Conversely, the existence of **AB + AC** could be factored into **A(B + C)** by the system, but the user might not want that. It is also not obvious whether **(A – B) * (A + B)** should be left in that form, or expanded to produce $\mathbf{A^2 - B^2}$. These particular decisions were left for the user to specify in the program through the **EXPAND** command. There was also a command (**AUTSIM**) that gave the user control over whether factorials and/or trigonometric functions should be evaluated or left in symbolic form; for example, the user could decide whether to leave **FAC(4)** in that symbolic form or have it evaluated to produce the number **24**.

As discussed in Section 9.3.3, the amount of simplification that should be done automatically versus the amount that should be controlled by the user was an issue of much philosophical debate among those of us developing differing systems throughout this period. Even within the FORMAC project itself we didn't always agree!

9.4.3.3 *Rational Arithmetic*

One of the more interesting features of FORMAC is its ability to permit mixed-mode expressions and, of even more importance, rational arithmetic. The latter simply means that if we add the fractions **(A/B) + (C/D)** we obtain **(AD + BC)/BD**. Thus, **5/12 + 1/3** yields **3/4** when the result is reduced to lowest terms. While this may seem obvious, and is of course consistent with elementary school arithmetic, it was actually a rather innovative idea in software systems at the time. This feature was not in the original design ideas, nor even in the Preliminary Language Specs. I personally realized this was crucial when I was doing a hand formula calculation to check the computer runs. The latter produced either a floating-point number or an incorrect answer (e.g., in FORTRAN **1/3 + 1/3** produced either **.666 . . .** rounded to **.7** or produced **0**). Neither of these is acceptable in expressions that are often of the form

$$\mathbf{x/3 + x^2 * (2/3) \ + x^3 * (4/3) \ldots}$$

In a few cases, FORMAC was used primarily (or even exclusively) because of its rational arithmetic capability, which I believe was not available in any other system of that time period.

9.4.3.4 *Effect of the Implementation on Language Design*

Although the basic plan for implementation did not have a *major* impact on the language, it did have some. For that reason it is worth briefly indicating the overall plan. Details may be found in Bond [1965a].

The basic concept of the implementation was to use a preprocessor, which changed FORMAC statements into **COMMENT** statements and generated **CALL** statements for each FORMAC executable statement. The preprocessor built various tables of information and inserted pertinent FORTRAN executable and declarative statements. The output of the preprocessor became input to the regular FORTRAN IV compiler. However, it is crucial to understand that from the user's viewpoint this was transparent, and the user had a truly respectable language to work with, rather than just a series of **CALL** statements.

Thus, the user might write something of the following form, following the normal FORTRAN conventions for fixed- and floating-point arithmetic:

```
LET A = B + 3 * C
M = 4
LET Z = SUBST A, (B, M), (C, FMCDIF(X ** 2, X, 1))
```

At object time the result would be that **Z** was assigned the value

```
X * 6. + 4.
```

This is achieved because initially the **SUBST** command causes the variable **M** to replace the variable **B** in the expression **A**, and then **M** is assigned the value **4.** (in floating point because **B** is a floating-point variable). Finally, the differentiation operator **FMCDIF** causes the value **X * 2.** to be substituted into **C** since **X * 2** is the derivative of **X ** 2**. (Note again that the distinction between a FORTRAN integer [e.g., **2**] and a floating-point number [e.g., **2.**] is kept in the FORMAC statements and in the results.)

The preceding example was implemented by the preprocessor which generated a series of FORTRAN statements of the form

```
CALL LET (A, (B + 3 * C))
M = 4
CALL SUBST (Z, (A, (B, M), (C, FMCDIF(X ** 2, X, 1))))
```

Note that the key word **LET** was used to identify the executable FORMAC statements, which were transformed into legal FORTRAN **CALL** statements that invoked the appropriate subroutines and which were then handled by the regular compiler. In the previous example, the original statement

```
M = 4
```

remains unchanged, because it is a pure FORTRAN statement. The execution time subroutines for arithmetic on formal variables (i.e., **LET**), for substitution (**SUBST**), and the differentiation function (**FMCDIF**) are generated with the appropriate parameters.

The language design was not significantly affected by concerns about object code efficiency, although we certainly had major concerns about this. Some of our projections about where the object time would be spent turned out to be wrong. For example, we were deathly afraid that the system would spend most of its time doing the automatic simplification, but this did not turn out to be true.

The biggest difficulty in implementation was something that we did not foresee, and could not have prevented in the language even if we had known it earlier. The biggest problem was running out of storage space because the expressions became very large; the initial implementation frequently expanded everything before using simplification or any other means to contract the size of the resulting expression. Thus, although the final result of multiplying two expressions might be quite small, the "intermediate expression swell" could exceed the storage capacity of the machine.

An illustration of this storage problem can be seen in the following simple example:

```
EXPAND (A - B) * (A + B) - A ** 2 + B ** 2
```

This results in the system generating (internally at object time) the expression

```
A * A + A * B - B * A - B * B - A ** 2 + B ** 2,
```

which the simplification routine automatically reduces to **0**.

Thus, the expression being expanded might be very large in its intermediate (fully expanded) form, but actually result in a small final expression. This intermediate form could exceed the storage capacity of the computer and thus cause trouble before the simplification reduction occurred. This problem, and the solution of continuously compressing the intermediate results, is well described in Tobey [1966a]. In other words, we modified the system to perform frequent simplification to reduce the size of the partially expanded expressions. (This is somewhat analogous to frequently using a garbage collection routine in a list-processing program to improve object time efficiency.)

9.5 THE PL/I-FORMAC DEVELOPMENT

9.5.1 Initial Planning

Before even seeing the early somewhat successful reception of our experimental version on the 7090/94, we were naturally anxious to provide a production version for the IBM System/360, which was (to be) announced in April 1964. I felt we could make significant improvements based on user experience without changing the basic model, which seemed to be quite satisfactory.

I decided that we should develop the second version with PL/I as a base, rather than FORTRAN. In selecting PL/I for the second version of the language, I was truly operating as a "good corporate citizen." There was a strong plan and intent by the IBM programming managers responsible for PL/I for it to replace COBOL and FORTRAN and become the single major language for users. Since I believed this was a worthwhile goal, and definitely wanted to support it, the logical choice was to apply the same symbolic concepts to PL/I that were applied to FORTRAN. (For the sake of accuracy in nomenclature, I wish to point out that at the time these considerations were under way, the initial name for PL/I—i.e., NPL—was in use. Hence, all the memos referred in some way to a FORMAC associated with NPL. I have chosen to use the term PL/I in this paper for ease of reading by people who don't know what NPL was, but the references themselves accurately reflect the usage of "NPL" at the time.)

As early as May 1963 [Sammet 1963a], consideration of a FORMAC version for the System/360 using PL/I started. This was long before the 7090/94 FORMAC system was fully implemented (and certainly long before there was any experience with it), and it was even before the existence of any preliminary specifications for PL/I. Additional considerations for a System/360 version of FORMAC were expressed in Sammet [1963b]. My basic intent—expressed a year later, after some experience—was to emphasize and develop the system in a time-sharing environment. I wrote, "Furthermore, I have stated from the very beginning that the most effective use of FORMAC would be in a terminal system where the user can see the results of a statement before going on to the next." [Sammet 1964b]. However, later funding decisions forced me to change that plan back into developing a batch version.

One of the characteristics of that time period is that estimating development costs for software was a difficult (or nonexistent) activity. Since I naturally had to provide a proposed budget for the development of the PL/I-FORMAC, I decided that the easiest way to do this was to develop the estimate as a percentage of the cost of developing a FORTRAN compiler. When I provided that percentage, I was told that nobody knew what it cost to develop a FORTRAN compiler!

As is almost always true, it was essential to fight for budget and staff. At the time, there were numerous projects competing for the "software support" dollars for the System/360. Rochester and I made a presentation in April 1965 to John W. Haanstra (President of the Data Systems Division). Our objective was to persuade him to authorize the PL/I-FORMAC as a Type I (i.e., fully supported) program, and *also* to allow us to prepare an experimental version of a conversational FORMAC (also based on PL/I).

Haanstra was fully supportive and sent a memo [Haanstra 1965] to his immediate manager Paul W. Knaplund. This memo said in part: "I have had a more thorough review of FORMAC and am convinced that we must proceed with this work." We were allocated budget and head count. Unfortunately, as time went on, the requirements for other software (e.g., OS/360—the operating system for the mid/high-end System/360 machines) became very large, and the full support for a Type I program for formula manipulation was dropped. We were allowed to continue as a Type III program, and the PL/I-FORMAC system was released in November 1967.

Management discussions continued for many months in 1964 and 1965 over such issues as (a) whether to emphasize a batch or a time-shared version, (b) whether it was to be a production version or another advanced technology version, or (c) whether a production version would be done in my Boston department or somewhere else. The paper flow on these subjects is too large to even summarize here! These discussions are of interest because they indicate some of the issues being faced by the software development and technology transfer activities in IBM in that time period. Many of the discussions applied to other software projects as well as FORMAC, and some of these technology transfer issues exist even into the 1990s.

By January 1965, we had a 350-page document [Tobey 1965a] containing preliminary specifications for a batch version as an extension to PL/I on the System/360, with new implementation approaches. Both the language and implementation ideas were significant advances over the 7090/94 version, but retained the fundamental concept of adding the formula manipulation capability to an existing programming language. This document also contained ideas for even further extensions—specifically, integration, complex variables, and non-Abelian simplification, among others. It also contained a proposal for a separate object time subsystem to handle polynomials. Unfortunately, due to a lack of resources, none of these ideas—or several others—was ever implemented.

In the latter part of 1965, I relinquished management of the Boston Advanced Programming Department to Rochester, who wanted to move to Boston from White Plains. That gave me the time to write my book on programming languages [Sammet 1969]. The manager for the PL/I-FORMAC project was Elaine Bond; she had been appointed manager for the 7090 work in the latter part of 1964. Thus, I had virtually no direct involvement with the development of the PL/I-FORMAC.

9.5.2 Technical Approach

Later in 1965, many of the ideas for the PL/I-FORMAC were modified and coalesced into the description given in Bond [1968], which was actually written in 1967. Although this proposal was not the description of the actual version implemented, it is an interesting published version of the type of thinking involved. The following highlights *did* appear in the final system. They are all based on the plan to (1) extend PL/I as little as necessary and (2) incorporate lessons learned from usage of the 7090/94 FORMAC:

a. introduce a new category, **Domain**, which included the PL/I arithmetic variables and a new formal data type for formula manipulation; extend the PL/I declarations as needed;
b. provide additional functions to control the expansion of expressions (which is, of course, a form of simplification);
c. provide alternative commands for *simultaneous* versus *iterative* substitution into an expression;
d. provide additional factoring capability (but still only with respect to a single variable or its powers);
e. provide fraction-handling functions to allow expressions to be written in the general form **a/b** (which requires developing a common denominator); and
f. provide better primitives with which the user could build new formula manipulation routines. Such primitives include lead operator functions, ways to count arguments, several ways to partition expressions, search for a particular expression, and various ways to use the pointer capabilities of PL/I but applied to formal variables and expressions.

A published paper describing the system that was actually implemented is in Xenakis [1971], and the official manual is that of IBM [1967]. The PL/I-FORMAC system was implemented by using a preprocessor to the PL/I compiler, just as the FORTRAN version had been.

It is interesting to note that one of the most important improvements made was not actually a language feature, but was to the format of the output. The 7090 FORMAC produced expressions printed in a completely linear fashion using FORTRAN notation. It is an understatement to say that they were not really readable except by dedicated users who really needed the output! As can be seen in Figure 9.2a, the normal rules of arithmetic precedence apply and parentheses are used where necessary. Given the expression:

```
((X + 1) * (X - 1))/(X - 1)
```

the System/360 version produced two-dimensional output with the exponents appearing as superscripts, although fractions were still indicated via parentheses and the "/" (see Figure 9.2b).

9.5.3 Market Forecast Activity

In this time period, the forecasting of potential software usage or demand was generally not done. Remember that software was given away with the hardware, and all that was required to start new software projects was a management judgment that the software was worth developing in the context of increasing the sales of hardware. In 1965, attempts were just starting to get a handle on how to forecast software usage, as had traditionally been done for hardware. (I don't know if the upper management of IBM already had in mind what became known as IBM's "1969 unbundling decision," although I have reason to think that they did.)

When it came time to consider a new and upgraded version for the System/360, an unusual step was taken. While I can't be certain that it was the first of its kind in IBM, it certainly was one of the earliest. We commissioned Arthur D. Little to do a study of "the utility and marketability of FORMAC," and they produced an interesting report [A. D. Little 1965]. They interviewed more than

60 people in more than 20 organizations, and they tried the 7090/94 system themselves. Their recommendations were basically positive; i.e., they felt a system like FORMAC would be quite useful.

In any case, I was asked if I would be willing to be a "guinea pig" and allow the existing primitive IBM techniques for forecasting software usage to be applied to the potential System/360 FORMAC. (The Arthur D. Little study was not considered an official IBM forecast.) I agreed, and various numbers were produced. They were not conclusive, in the sense that they didn't prove that a PL/I-FORMAC would significantly increase hardware sales, but they did indicate there would be *some* increase. Part of the problem was that some of the FORMAC users were doing their work without the knowledge of the systems people who were responsible for their organization's computer systems; those systems people were the ones normally contacted by the IBM marketing representatives. Until this became understood, the numbers of future usage were actually lower than our current usage on the 7090/94! As a result, the eventual decisions regarding FORMAC funding were made "the old-fashioned way"—by management fiat!

9.5.4 Availability, Usage, and Other Systems

Although the higher-management decision was made not to provide PL/I-FORMAC as a Type I program (i.e., fully supported), it was (again) released as a Type III program, and did receive considerable usage. By the time of the Second Symposium on Symbolic and Algebraic Manipulation sponsored by ACM SIGPLAN [Petrick 1971], newer languages were under construction, namely MACSYMA and SCRATCHPAD/I. Further work was also reported at that conference on earlier systems, such as ALTRAN, MATHLAB, and REDUCE.

FIGURE 9.2a

Example of high-speed printer output from 7090/94 FORMAC. (Same problem as in Figure 9.2b, but in the original output format.)

Taylor series for e^x sin(x) to 20th degree

(Normal rules of arithmetic precedence apply, and parentheses are used where necessary)

```
X/1!+2*X**2/2!+2*X**3/3!-4*X**5/5!-8*X**6/6!-8*X**7/7!
+16*X**9/9!+32*X**10/10!+32*X**11/11!-64*X**13/13!-128*X**14/14!
-128*X**15/15!+256*X**17/17!+512*X**18/18!+512*X**19/19!
```

FIGURE 9.2b

Example of high-speed printer output from PL/I-FORMAC. (Source: [Xenakis 1971, p. 106])

Taylor series for e^x sin(x) to 20th degree

TAYLOR = $X \;/\; 1! + 2\, X^2 \;/\; 2! + 2\, X^3 \;/\; 3! - 4\, X^5 \;/\; 5! - 8\, X^6 \;/\; 6!$

$- 8\, X^7 \;/\; 7! + 16\, X^9 \;/\; 9! + 32\, X^{10} \;/\; 10! + 32\, X^{11} \;/\; 11!$

$- 64\, X^{13} / \; 13! - 128\, X^{14} \;/\; 14! - 128\, X^{15} \;/\; 15! + 256\, X^{17} \;/\; 17!$

$+ 512\, X^{18} / \; 18! + 512\, X^{19} \;/\; 19!$

9.6 FORMAC 73

By 1970, IBM no longer had anybody involved with FORMAC, and released the source code. The SHARE project in Europe prepared a list of known errors and proposed extensions, and several people developed a new preprocessor. Although several people worked on providing improvements, the key individual to do this was Knut Bahr (of the GMD, Institut für Datenfernverarbeitung in Darmstadt, Germany). Among the improvements planned or implemented in 1974 [Bahr 1974], and referred to as "novelties" in Bahr [1975], are the following:

- the **EVAL** function permitted the use of the phrase "for any x," denoted **$x**;
- the user could write functions as procedures;
- the function **CODEM**, which put an expression over a common denominator, was made more powerful by having the system attempt to remove or make use of common factors; and
- the **REPLACE** function was made more general by permitting the user to specify integration rules and thus apply **REPLACE** to do some integration.

In addition, Bahr created a new FORTRAN-FORMAC on the System/360, which was compatible with the PL/I-FORMAC [van Hulzen 1974]. A revised manual was issued in several stages, a later one of which is SHARE [1983]. Furthermore, a Conversational FORMAC was developed in the early 1980s at Pennsylvania State University [Penn State 1983], where the key individual was H. D. (Skip) Knoble, who was the Chairman of the SMC Committee in the SHARE Math Software Project.

FORMAC 73 continues to be used, but certainly is far behind the current technology.

9.7 EVALUATION OF FORMAC

In examining the objectives set forth in the original project description [Sammet 1962a], and excerpted in Section 9.2.3, it seems fair to say that FORMAC met its objectives. On the other hand, in terms of some of the larger objectives that I personally had for FORMAC, it has not been that successful. It is appropriate to be much more specific about this mixed evaluation, and these issues are the focus of this section.

9.7.1 Influence of FORMAC

FORMAC had significant, although sometimes indirect, influence in a number of areas and on other systems. There is certainly a difference between the influence of FORMAC as a language and a system, and my own personal influence (manifested largely, but not entirely, through establishing ACM SIGSAM). Both these factors are mentioned in this section.

1. FORMAC made clear that a *language*—as contrasted with a package of subroutines—was important to the user. In that sense both FORMAC and I influenced REDUCE and subsequent systems, which were developed as real programming languages for symbolic mathematics.

   Memories of the key participants, as well as later documents, apparently differ over whether our work had any influence in causing ALPAK to evolve into the language ALTRAN. The ALTRAN documents do not mention FORMAC, but nevertheless I have a strong recollection that we had at least an indirect effect on their work; unfortunately, I cannot find a document to support my recollection. Circumstantial evidence exists in the sense that we published two significant papers describing FORMAC in 1964 [Sammet 1964a; Bond 1964]. The Early ALTRAN version seems to have been developed in the 1964–1966 period [Brown 1971, p. A3], but (as stated earlier) there is a conflict in the dates given in the numerous ALTRAN documents that I have.

In my own view, the development of a *language* was the most significant contribution of FORMAC. Furthermore, I believe that the concept of adding to an existing major language was a large contribution, although clearly the workers in this field do not agree with me. (See point 1 in Section 9.7.2.) These are the contributions of which I am the proudest.

2. Because of our fairly large "publicity campaign" of publications, talks, and direct work with users, a significant number of scientists and engineers realized that a computer could be used quite effectively to save them the manual labor of formal mathematics. Along with ALTRAN in the mid-1960s, FORMAC made it clear to users that this was a viable approach to solve many problems.
3. One of our test cases—known as the "f and g series" [Sconzo 1965] became a benchmark for performance comparison for almost all systems for many years. (This certainly was not an objective, or our intent; it just happened.)
4. We introduced—I believe for the first time—the significant use of rational number arithmetic. (See Section 9.4.3.3 for a fuller description of this.)
5. We made it clear that the users really needed more than just polynomials and rational functions.
6. Numerous early practical uses of FORMAC [Cuthill 1965; Duby 1968; Howard 1967; Neidleman 1967; Walton 1967] clearly demonstrated that many practical problems could and should be solved in a batch mode. A broader summary of real applications developed using FORMAC is given in Tobey [1966b]. While many problems absolutely need interactive user decisions to direct the course of the symbolic computation as it proceeds, there are also many other problems that don't need that interaction and hence can be done in a pure batch mode.
7. Because of the desire to be able to interact freely with others working in this area (which was normally prevented by IBM policies unless there was an external organizational "umbrella"), I founded (and chaired) the ACM Special Interest *Committee* on Symbolic and Algebraic Manipulation (SICSAM) in 1965. I defined and charted its scope to be primarily formal algebraic manipulation. In accordance with ACM procedures, this group evolved into the Special Interest *Group* (SIGSAM) in 1967. At that time, I declined to continue as Chairman because I was no longer actively involved in this field and was concentrating on finishing my programming languages book [Sammet 1969]. SIGSAM has been, and still is, a major organizational focus of work in this area.
8. I organized the first real technical conference in this subject area (namely SYMSAM—ACM Symposium on Symbolic and Algebraic Manipulation, held in March 1966) and served as both General Chair and Program Chair. The August 1966 issue of the *Communications of the ACM* [ACM 1966] represented its proceedings. This was the initial activity of SICSAM, and started a long series of conferences organized by different groups, including (but not limited to) ACM SIGSAM.
9. The PL/I-FORMAC version on the IBM System 360/370 is still in use today, in spite of a lack of support by IBM or anybody else. PL/I-FORMAC is distributed through SHARE.

In summary, it seems reasonable to suggest that FORMAC and the creation of ACM SIGSAM were the major—although by no means the only—activities that started significant practical work in the field of symbolic computation.

9.7.2 Problems, Difficulties, Failures

1. I am personally most disappointed that no other significant language development has chosen to follow the philosophy of adding on to an existing scientific language. The more modern systems are completely independent languages (e.g., MACSYMA, Maple, and Mathematica).
2. Early FORMAC usage was significantly hindered by people who were not used to thinking of using computers for formula manipulation, particularly in a batch mode. By the time there were significant numbers of people interested in doing symbolic computation, FORMAC had been overtaken by more modern systems, most of which are interactive.
3. Although FORMAC is still being used in the 1990s, it has been a minor language since the 1970s. The failure of IBM (or any other organization) to provide major technology updates means that it will never be widely used.
4. Although not the fault of the FORMAC effort, I find it disappointing that the people concerned with scientific and mathematical computation continued for many years to prefer numerical to nonnumerical calculations. The conference on Mathematical Software held in April 1970 contained only one paper that was not purely numerical—namely, mine [Sammet 1971]. Fortunately, since then, there has been more realization of the usefulness of symbolic computation in the general field of mathematical software.

9.7.3 Mistakes or Desired Changes

For its time, I think FORMAC did moderately well. Aside from minor points, I don't think we made many mistakes *within the scope of our basic intent and resources*, nor would I make many changes (except minor ones) if I had it to do all over again. That sounds self-serving, and perhaps it is, but FORMAC represented a particular philosophy that I continue to believe was a reasonable one. Obviously, in today's environment, FORMAC is obsolescent because there was no organization with sufficient support to modernize it as symbolic mathematical technology progressed.

One indication of the types of faults that Rochester perceived at the time of the 7090/94 FORMAC is recorded in Sammet [1965b]. Quoting from that memo:

> 1. FORMAC is quite inefficient compared to ALPAK in the handling of polynomials.
> 2. The output is terrible.
> 3. FORMAC handles expressions and not equations. This causes difficulties in problems.
> 4. FORMAC is not open ended.
>
> In a slightly different category, but equally valid, are two major capabilities which are lacking—namely, integration and vector and matrix handling.

My own reactions to these points, based on 25 years of hindsight, are about the same as they were then, namely:

1. Since FORMAC had no special capabilities to make polynomial handling efficient, it was indeed inefficient when the application involved polynomials or rational functions. I tried strongly to get this into PL/I-FORMAC, even to the extent of issuing a memo to Bond indicating that this must be done [Sammet, 1965c]. However, by the time the work was actually under way, I was no longer responsible for the activity and could not enforce this.
2. Rochester's criticism was certainly true, and the output format was significantly improved in the PL/I-FORMAC version.

3. Point 3 is not terribly significant because the intent of FORMAC was to handle formal mathematical expressions and not equations. This is an interesting semantic distinction but I never found any cases where it made any difference. In practice, it was "expressions" that were being manipulated and not "equations."
4. I really can't recall exactly what Rochester meant about not being open ended, and so I am not sure of its importance. However, I do remember vividly that he criticized FORMAC for not having the language features needed to write its own compiler. I protested vigorously to him that compiler writing was a specific type of application, just as was symbolic mathematics, and that it was unreasonable (and made no sense) to expect a system such as FORMAC to do both.

   With regard to the basic scope of FORMAC, certainly the absence of integration and vector/matrix handling, and the inefficient handling of polynomials and rational functions were weaknesses, but they certainly could have been corrected if FORMAC had become a system supported by IBM. The obstacle was not the language itself but the resources needed to implement the object time routines; after all, it was trivial to add a command called INTEGRATE to the language! Stated another way, I don't feel there was anything in the language, or in the basic concepts, that would have prevented the correction of any perceived technical deficiencies or omissions in FORMAC, had there been an appropriate management decision to do so.

9.7.4 Major Problem—Storage Space

The major problem that actually occurred was clearly not a language issue, but rather one of performance in terms of running out of storage space. The large machines of the 1960s were small compared to the personal computers of today. FORMAC users frequently suffered because of the enormous amount of storage needed to run some of their applications. Fortunately, some tricks and techniques were found to alleviate some of the difficulties of that time period. This was discussed in Section 9.4.3.4.

9.7.5 Why Didn't FORMAC Become a Major System?

As part of the evaluation, it is appropriate to examine the question of why FORMAC did not become a major system. After all, it *was* the *first* formula manipulation *language* that was used for real problems, and even the first version did receive significant usage. It seems to me—albeit with obvious bias—that there are two main reasons that FORMAC is of more interest historically than as a current viable system.

Certainly the first and most important reason is that IBM never supported it, beyond allowing the developers to provide rudimentary help to the users. It was never a fully supported Type I system (pre-1969 unbundling) and certainly never became a program product (after 1969). In spite of the fact that we had a large early technical lead in this area, it was never possible to persuade the management that formula manipulation/symbolic computation in general, and FORMAC in particular, was more important than other software systems competing for resources. The net result of this lack of support is that FORMAC was not able to improve as better technology became known and available. It is worth noting that various users did become interested enough to upgrade the PL/I-FORMAC to FORMAC 73 (as discussed in Section 9.6). However, in that time period, it was difficult for users to take a large complex system and make major improvements.

The second reason is perhaps the very fact that FORMAC was very early in a relatively new and unknown technical area. An enormous amount of our effort throughout the 7090/94 development had to be spent explaining to people what the system could do for them, and how it would enhance their productivity and the accuracy of their results. Although this activity was crucial, it deflected a large portion of our resources from making significant improvements to the system.

A third possible reason for FORMAC's lack of growth is the fact that newer systems—which had far more functional capability—were "stand-alone" languages. Some users became persuaded that this was a better approach than adding to an existing language. Naturally I feel otherwise, but I don't believe there have been any studies comparing the merits of the two approaches.

A fourth reason is FORMAC's tie-in to PL/I, which never became a major language. Clearly, PL/I never achieved its goal of replacing FORTRAN and COBOL. Because FORTRAN was much more widely used than PL/I for scientific computation, our initial decision to build the System/360 version on PL/I (instead of on FORTRAN) limited its use. The later development of the user-developed version of FORTRAN-FORMAC on the System/360 was not sufficient to overcome the other difficulties.

9.8 IMPLICATIONS FOR THE FUTURE OF LANGUAGES FOR SYMBOLIC MATHEMATICS

As I have tried to indicate in this paper, FORMAC played a leading role in the initial stages of the field of symbolic mathematical computation. By the 1970s, the field of symbolic mathematics (including users, language designers, and implementors) had learned all that could be learned from FORMAC in both positive and negative directions—most notably that a language (rather than just a package of routines) is important, but that adding the symbolic computation facilities to an existing scientific language is not crucial. The field has progressed very far beyond FORMAC now, and so there is nothing more that it can contribute. FORMAC will probably continue to be used by a small group of people, but certainly it has no significant future.

ACKNOWLEDGMENTS

I am extremely grateful to James H. Griesmer, who reviewed several drafts of this lengthy paper with great patience and great diligence. He did a superb job of pointing out both conceptual problems as well as small errors of fact and typographical errors. Seldom have I seen such care exerted in helping someone else write a paper!

I am also very grateful to Michael Mahoney, the HOPL-II conference consulting historian, for helping me clarify issues, sharpen various points, and include material I might otherwise have overlooked. Brent Hailpern, Robert Rosin, and unknown referees were also very helpful in pointing out various flaws and omissions. Tim Bergin provided significant editing assistance. However, all flaws remaining in the paper are due to me and not to the very helpful referees.

REFERENCES

[A. D. Little, 1965] *FORMAC MARKET STUDY*. Report to IBM, C-66891, Arthur D. Little, Inc., March 1965.

[ACM, 1966] *Comm. ACM. Vol. 9, No. 8, Aug. 1966, entire issue.*

[Bahr, 1974] Bahr, Knut and Smith, Jasp. Tuning an Algebraic Manipulation System through Measurements, in *Proceedings of EUROSAM 74, ACM SIGSAM Bulletin*, Vol. 8, No. 3, Aug. 1974, pp. 17–23.

[Bahr, 1975] Bahr, Knut. Utilizing the FORMAC Novelties, *ACM SIGSAM Bulletin*, Vol. 9, No. 1, Feb. 1975, pp. 21–24.

[Bernick, 1961] Bernick, M. D., Callender, E. D., and Sanford, J. R. ALGY—An Algebraic Manipulation Program, in *Proceedings of the Western Joint Computer Conference*, Vol. 19, 1961, pp. 389–392.

[Bleiweiss, 1966] Bleiweiss, L. *et al.* A Time-Shared Algebraic Desk Calculator Version of FORMAC, IBM Corp., TR00.1415, Systems Development Division, Poughkeepsie, NY Mar. 1966.

[Bobrow, 1968] Bobrow, D. G., Ed. *Symbol Manipulation Languages and Techniques, Proceedings of the IFIP Working Conference on Symbol Manipulation Languages, Pisa*, Amsterdam: North-Holland, 1968.

[Bond, 1964] Bond, E. R. *et al., FORMAC—An Experimental FORmula MAnipulation Compiler, in Proceedings of the ACM 19th National Conference*, 1964, pp. K2.1-1–K2.1-11.

[Bond, 1965a] Bond, E. *et al.* Implementation of FORMAC, TR00.1260, IBM Systems Development Division, Poughkeepsie Laboratory, NY, March 1965.

[Bond, 1968] Bond, E. R. and Cundall, P. A. A Possible PL/I Extension for Mathematical Symbol Manipulation, in *Symbol Manipulation Languages and Techniques, Proceedings of the IFIP Working Conference on Symbol Manipulation Languages*, D. G. Bobrow, Ed., Amsterdam: North-Holland, 1968, pp. 116–132.

[Brown, 1963–1964] Brown, W. S., Hyde, J. P., and Tague, B. A. The ALPAK System for Nonnumerical Algebra on a Digital Computer, *Bell System Technical Journal*, Vol. 42, No. 5, Sept. 1963, pp. 2081–2119; Vol. 43, No. 2, Mar. 1964, pp. 785–804; Vol. 43, No. 4, Part 2, July 1964, pp. 1547–1562.

[Brown, 1966] Brown, W. S. A Language and System for Symbolic Algebra on a Digital Computer, in *Proceedings of the IBM Scientific Computing Symposium on Computer-Aided Experimentation*, IBM Corp., 320-0936-0 Data Processing Division, White Plains, NY 1966, pp. 77–114.

[Brown, 1971] _____, *ALTRAN USER'S MANUAL* (Second Edition), Bell Telephone Laboratories, Inc., Murray Hill, NJ, 1971.

[Clapp, 1963] Clapp, L. C. and Kain, R. Y. A Computer Aid for Symbolic Mathematics, in *Proceedings of the Fall Joint Computer Conference*, Vol. 24, Nov. 1963, pp. 509–517.

[Collins, 1966] Collins, G. E. PM, A System for Polynomial Manipulation, *Comm. ACM*, Vol. 9, No. 8, Aug. 1966, pp. 578–589.

[Crisman, 1965] Crisman, P. A., Ed., *The Compatible Time-Sharing System, A Programmer's Guide*, Second Edition, Cambridge, MA: MIT Press, 1965.

[Cuthill, 1965] Cuthill, E., Voigt, S., and Ullom, S. *Use of Computers in the Solution of Boundary Value and Initial Value Problems*, Annual Progress Report, SR011-01-01 Task 0401 AML Problem 821–911, David Taylor Model Basin, Washington, DC, June 1965.

[Duby, 1968] Duby, J. J. Sophisticated Algebra on a Computer—Derivatives of Witt Vectors, in *Symbol Manipulation Languages and Techniques, Proceedings of the IFIP Working Conference on Symbol Manipulation Languages*, D. G. Bobrow, Ed., Amsterdam: North-Holland, 1968, pp. 71–85.

[Engelman, 1965] Engelman, C. MATH-LAB: A Program for On-Line Machine Assistance in Symbolic Computations, in *Proceedings of the Fall Joint Computer Conference*, Vol. 27, Part 2, 1965, pp. 413–422.

[Engelman, 1971] _____, The Legacy of MATHLAB 68, in *Proceedings of the Second Symposium on Symbolic and Algebraic Manipulation*, S. R. Petrick, Ed., New York: ACM, Mar. 1971, pp. 29–41.

[Evey, 1962] Evey, R. J., Grisoff, S. F., Sammet, J. E., and Tobey, R. G. *FORMAC Preliminary Language Specifications*, IBM, Boston Advanced Programming, Advanced Computer Utilization Dept., Data Systems Division, Dec. 14, 1962.

[Griesmer, 1971] Griesmer, J. H. and Jenks, R. D. SCRATCHPAD/I—An Interactive Facility for Symbolic Mathematics, in *Proceedings of the Second Symposium on Symbolic and Algebraic Manipulation*, S. R. Petrick, Ed., New York: ACM, 1971, pp. 42–58.

[Haanstra, 1965] Haanstra, J. W. FORMAC, Memo to P. W. Knaplund, IBM, April 12, 1965.

[Hearn, 1966] Hearn, Anthony C. Computation of Algebraic Properties of Elementary Particle Reactions Using a Digital Computer, *Comm. ACM*, Vol. 9, No. 8, Aug. 1966, pp. 573–577.

[Hearn, 1967] _____, *REDUCE USERS' MANUAL*, Memo No. 50, Stanford Artificial Intelligence Project, Feb. 1967.

[Hearn, 1971] _____, REDUCE 2, A System and Language for Algebraic Manipulation, in *Proceedings of the Second Symposium on Symbolic and Algebraic Manipulation*, S. R. Petrick, Ed., New York: ACM, 1971, pp. 128–133.

[Howard, 1967] Howard, J. C. Computer Formulation of the Equations of Motion Using Tensor Notation, *Comm. ACM*, Vol. 10, No. 9, Sept. 1967, pp. 543–548.

[IBM, 1965] *FORMAC (Operating and User's Preliminary Reference Manual)*, IBM Corp., No. 7090 R2IBM 0016, IBM Program Information Dept., Hawthorne, NY, Aug. 1965.

[IBM, 1966] *DESCRIPTION OF TIME-SHARED FORMAC*, IBM, Boston Programming Center, No. CC-257, Computation Center, MIT, March 1966,

[IBM, 1967] *PL/I-FORMAC Interpreter*, IBM Corp., Contributed Program Library, 360D 03.3.004, Program Information Dept., Hawthorne, NY, Oct. 1967.

[Martin, 1967] Martin, W. A. *Symbolic Mathematical Laboratory*, MIT, MAC-TR-36 (Ph.D. thesis), Project MAC, Cambridge, MA, Jan. 1967.

[Martin, 1971] Martin, W. A. and Fateman, R. J. The MACSYMA System, in *Proceedings of the Second Symposium on Symbolic and Algebraic Manipulation*, S. R. Petrick, Ed., New York: ACM, 1971, pp. 59–75.

[Morris, 1967] Morris, A. H., Jr. *The FLAP Language—A Programmer's Guide*, U.S. Naval Weapons Lab., K-8/67, Dahlgren, VA, Jan. 1967.

[Moses, 1967] Moses, Joel. *Symbolic Integration*, MAC-TR-47, Project MAC, MIT, Dec. 1967.

[Moses, 1974] _____, MACSYMA—The Fifth Year, in *Proceedings of the Eurosam Conference, ACM SIGSAM Bulletin*, Vol. 8, No. 3, Aug. 1974, pp. 105–110.

[Neidleman, 1967] Neidleman, L. D. An Application of FORMAC, *Comm. ACM*, Vol. 10, No. 3, Mar. 1967, pp. 167–168.

[Penn State, 1983] *CFORMAC: CONVERSATIONAL FORMAC*, The Pennsylvania State University Computation Center, Aug. 1983.

[Perlis, 1964] Perlis, A. J. and Iturriaga, R. An Extension to ALGOL for Manipulating Formulae, *Comm. ACM*, Vol. 7, No. 2, Feb. 1964, pp. 127–130.

[Perlis, 1966] Perlis, A. J., Iturriaga, R., and Standish, T. A. *A Definition of Formula ALGOL*, Carnegie Inst. of Tech., Pittsburgh, PA, Aug. 1966.

[Petrick, 1971] Petrick, S. R., Ed., *Proceedings of the Second Symposium on Symbolic and Algebraic Manipulation*, New York: ACM, 1971.

[Sammet, 1962a] Sammet, Jean E. Project Description for Symbol Manipulation Compiler, internal memo, IBM, Aug. 1, 1962.

[Sammet, 1962b] _____, Numerical Estimates for Justification of SYmbol MAnipulation COMpiler, internal memo, IBM, Aug. 13, 1962.

[Sammet, 1963a] _____, FORMAC and NPL, internal memo, IBM, May 20, 1963.

[Sammet, 1963b] _____, Implementation of FORMAC for NPL, internal memo, IBM, Nov., 23, 1963.

[Sammet, 1964a] _____, and Elaine R. Bond, Introduction to FORMAC, *IEEE Trans. Elec. Comp.*, Vol. EC-13, No. 4, Aug. 1964, pp. 386–394.

[Sammet, 1964b] _____, Proposed FORMAC Activity in 1965, internal memo, IBM, Oct. 12, 1964.

[Sammet, 1965a] _____, Updated Summary of Interest on FORMAC, internal memo, IBM, Sept. 27, 1965.

[Sammet, 1965b] _____, Faults with FORMAC, internal memo, IBM, May 28, 1965.

[Sammet, 1965c] _____, Efficient polynomial manipulation capability for OS/360 FORMAC, internal memo, IBM, Mar. 23, 1965.

[Sammet, 1966a] _____, Survey of Formula Manipulation, *Comm. ACM*, Vol. 9, No. 8, Aug. 1966, pp. 555–569.

[Sammet, 1966b] _____, An Annotated Descriptor Based Bibliography on the Use of Computers for Non-Numerical Mathematics, *Computing Reviews*, Vol. 7, No. 4, July–Aug., 1966, pp. B-1–B-31.

[Sammet, 1966c] _____, Survey of the Use of Computers for Doing Non-Numerical Mathematics, IBM Systems Development Division, Poughkeepsie Laboratory, NY, TR 00.1428, Mar. 1966.

[Sammet, 1967] _____, Formula Manipulation by Computer, in *Advances in Computers*, Vol. 8, F. L. Alt and M. Rubinoff, Eds., New York: Academic Press, 1967, pp. 47–102.

[Sammet, 1968] _____, Revised Annotated Descriptor Based Bibliography on the Use of Computers for Non-Numerical Mathematics, in *Symbol Manipulation Languages and Techniques*, D. G. Bobrow, Ed., Amsterdam: North-Holland, 1968, pp. 358–484.

[Sammet, 1969] _____, *PROGRAMMING LANGUAGES: History and Fundamentals*, Englewood Cliffs, NJ: Prentice Hall, 1969.

[Sammet, 1971] _____, Software for Nonnumerical Mathematics, in *MATHEMATICAL SOFTWARE*, John Rice, Ed., New York: Academic Press, 1971, pp. 295–330.

[Sammet, 1990] _____, Symbolic Computation: The Early Days (1950–1971), in *Computers in Mathematics*, David V. Chudnovsky and Richard D. Jenks, Eds., New York: Marcel Dekker, 1990, pp. 351–366.

[Sconzo, 1965] Sconzo, P., LeSchack, A. R., and Tobey, R. G. Symbolic Computation of f and g Series by Computer, *Astronomical Journal*, Vol. 70, No. 4, May 1965, pp. 269–271.

[SHARE, 1983] SHARE-FORMAC, No. 360D-03.3.013 II, Aug. 1983.

[Slagle, 1963] Slagle, J. R. A Heuristic Program that Solves Symbolic Integration Problems in Freshman Calculus, *J. ACM*, Vol. 10, No. 4, Oct. 1963, pp. 507–520.

[Tobey, 1965a] Tobey, R. G. *et al.* Preliminary Specifications for FORMAL NPL (System/360 FORMAC), internal report, IBM, Jan. 28, 1965.

[Tobey, 1965b] Tobey, R. G., Bobrow, R. J., and Zilles, S. N. Automatic Simplification in FORMAC, in *Proceedings of the AFIPS Fall Joint Computer Conference*, Vol. 27, Nov. 1965, pp. 37–52.

[Tobey, 1966a] Tobey, R. G. Experience with FORMAC Algorithm Design, *Comm. ACM*, Vol. 9, No. 8, Aug. 1966, pp. 589–595.

[Tobey, 1966b] ______, Eliminating Monotonous Mathematics with FORMAC, *Comm. ACM*, Vol. 9, No. 10, Oct. 1966, pp. 742–751.

[van Hulzen, 1974] van Hulzen, J. A. FORMAC Today, or What Can Happen to an Orphan, *ACM SIGSAM Bulletin*, Vol. 8, No. 1, Feb. 1974, pp. 5–7.

[Walton, 1967] Walton, J. J. Tensor Calculations on Computer: Appendix, *Comm. ACM*, Vol. 10, No. 3, Mar. 1967, pp. 183–186.

[Xenakis, 1971] Xenakis, J. The PL/I—Formac Interpreter, in *Proceedings of the Second Symposium on Symbolic and Algebraic Manipulation*, S. R. Petrick, Ed., New York: ACM, Mar. 1971, pp. 105–114.

TRANSCRIPT OF PRESENTATION

JEAN SAMMET: I want to start by expressing thanks to two people. One is Jim Griesmer, formerly from IBM, who was an enormous help in the preparation of the paper, and I want to give my thanks to Dick Wexelblat who prepared—from a physical point of view—the foils that you are about to see. He has far better capability than I do. If the intellectual content is bad, that's my fault but if the physical format is nice, it's his credit.

(SLIDE 1, SLIDE 2) There are three phases of the work on FORMAC that I want to discuss. The first and major one from my point of view was on the 7090/94 in the time period of 1962 to 1965. Then, somewhat briefly, the System/360 on PL/I for some years after that, and then a little on the FORMAC 73, which was done outside IBM.

(SLIDE 3) When I joined IBM, aside from being told to set up a group to do advanced R&D work in software, my boss said to me, "Do something in symbol manipulation." And that was the extent of the directive I got from him, and, in particular, that term was not defined. So I made a couple of false starts and then came up with an idea as described in the next slide.

(SLIDE 4) The basic objectives I had for the system that eventually became known as FORMAC, were to provide a system that *extended* FORTRAN from a *language* point of view, with capabilities for symbolic math. It was to be *practical*, not experimental. I guess it was experimental in the sense that it was brand new and was something that had never been tried before because it was to allow for both symbolic and numerical mathematics. Finally, what I wanted to do all along—and I'm not sure I ever said this explicitly—was to sort of reverse the clock. What had happened was that prior to the use of computers, a great deal of analytic mathematical work had been done by people by hand. Then computers came along and they were obviously great number crunchers. So the analytic work that had been done by people in using formal differentiation or any kind of mathematical expressions or integration then reverted to being done as numerical computations because that was what was being done on computers, and I wanted to reverse that.

"The Beginning and Development of FORMAC (FORmula MAnipulation Compiler)"

Jean E. Sammet
Programming Language Consultant

ACM SIGPLAN HOPL-II Conference
April 1993

SLIDE 1

THREE PHASES OF WORK

Version	Major Time Period
7090/94 (FORTRAN)	(1962-1965)
System/360 (PL/I)	(1964-1968)
FORMAC 73 (PL/I) *(outside IBM)*	(1970 ff. —

SLIDE 2

DIRECTIVE TO ME FROM MY MANAGER

"Plan a symbol manipulation project"

but...

the term *"symbol manipulation"* was undefined

SLIDE 3

MY BASIC OBJECTIVES FOR THE PROPOSED PROJECT (1962)

Provide a system that is—

- **a language extension of FORTRAN with capabilities for symbolic mathematics.**
- **practical for problems involving symbolic *and* numerical mathematics**
- **useful to applications being done with numerical approximations where analytic techniques are preferable**

SLIDE 4

(SLIDE 5) There were a lot of terms that we used then and which were all pretty much equivalent. It depended on what you wrote or spoke, and who you talked to, but you can see the list that was there. The more common current terms are "symbolic mathematics" and "symbolic computation," but if I use any or all of these in the course of the talk, they are all meant to be equivalent. Many of you are saying, "What the devil is FORMAC, and why is it different?" So the next slide is going to attempt to explain this.

(SLIDE 6) On the left we have a real complicated FORTRAN Program. [sarcasm] If I take **(9 + 4)** × **(9 – 4)**, unless I've made a gross mistake, we'll get **65**. So what? FORMAC is very different. We are dealing with symbols here; we are dealing with mathematical expressions. The word **LET** was simply a key word that we used from a language or compiling point of view. We said suppose that the variable **A** has the value of the symbolic variable **X**; **B** was assigned **Y**; and, now **C** was going to be **(A + B) * (A – B)**. And the result would be, depending on which form you preferred, $X^2 - Y^2$ or **(X + Y) * (X – Y)**. There was an internal representation for that, but **C** was assigned the value of $X^2 - Y^2$.

Now, for almost any project—regardless of whether you are in a large company like IBM, or applying for a grant, or even trying to get some seed money from any organization—you need to justify what it is that you are doing.

SOME EQUIVALENT TERMS

Then

- **Symbol manipulation**
- **Formula manipulation**
- **Tedious algebra**
- **Formal algebra**
- **Nonnumerical mathematics**

Current

- **Symbolic mathematics**
- **Symbolic computation**

SLIDE 5

FORTRAN vs. FORMAC EXAMPLE

FORTRAN	*FORMAC*
`A = 9`	`LET A = X`
`B = 4`	`LET B = Y`
`C = (A+B)*(A-B)`	`LET C = (A+B)*(A-B)`
C ← 65	C ← (X+Y)*(X-Y)
	C ← $X^2 - Y^2$

SLIDE 6

SLIDE 7a

SLIDE 7b

(SLIDE 7a) So we did a lot of exploring of areas in which such a system might be useful, and I've listed four or five here. There is a longer list in the paper. Here, they are specifically listed by application areas, as distinguished from the next slide, which shows the mathematical areas, which, of course, can be used in any or all of the preceding application areas. (SLIDE 7b)

Now, the next slide will give you a time scale and some cost information.

(SLIDE 8) I wrote the proposal for this earlier in 1962, and we had fairly detailed and complete language specifications by December 1962. We did most of the system design in the first half of 1963, and had almost all of the coding finished in December 1963. The integration and testing went on over the next year, as you would expect, and it was operational in December 1964. As best my records will indicate, and I have boxes and boxes of records on this, there were approximately 20 person-years involved. But, that included a lot of documentation, and we really *did do* a lot of documentation, because implicit in that was some of the justification that we also had to do. There were lots of other activities—for example, user interaction forecasts, and attempts to explain to people what it was we were doing, because this was brand new and therefore it was very hard for people to understand what such a system could do in any way, shape, or form.

(SLIDE 9) I want to talk about systems that existed at the time. Before I even get to these, let me point out that all the systems that you have heard of today are not on this list, because they didn't exist. The earliest of them came into existence in the mid-60s and by that time we were well on our way; we had finished the 7090 version, and as you will see in a few minutes, we had started on the PL/I version. So if you note the absence of MACSYMA or Mathematica, or Maple or REDUCE, or anything else, it is because they all came afterwards. But, I do want to talk somewhat about some of the systems on the slide, *none* of which had any real influence on what we did.

The first, interestingly enough, is called ALGY, which almost nobody has heard of. It is described very briefly in my 1969 book on programming languages, and if anything had an influence, it was that. It was a really neat little system that had some interesting commands in it. I think they implemented it, but they certainly never did anything with it.

Then there were two *systems* and I—as many of you know—am a purist with regard to language, and something is either a language or it is not. And just because it is not a language doesn't mean it's bad—it's just not a language. It's a taxonomy issue, not a value judgment.

ALPAK was a system to manipulate polynomials. It was a series of subroutines added to FAP (an assembler on the 7090) that was being done at Bell Labs. PM was being done initially at IBM, and

SCHEDULE AND COSTS

Language specifications . . Dec. 1962
System design . . . . Jan. – June 1963
Coding (basically finished) Dec. 1963
Integration & testing. . . . . . Jan. – April 1964
Operational . . . . Dec. 1964

Approximately 20 person-years, including

- much documentation
- other activities
  (e.g., user interaction & forecasts)

SLIDE 8

RELATED SYSTEMS
(...though none had real influence!)

- Early language:
  ALGY
- Systems (not languages):
  ALPAK, PM
- Contemporary languages:
  ALTRAN, Formula ALGOL
- Minor contemporary languages:
  Magic Paper, MATHLAB,
  Symbolic Mathematical Laboratory

SLIDE 9

that was another system to manipulate polynomials. And those people were very concerned about algorithms for how you handle polynomials efficiently.

Then the ALPAK people at Bell Labs moved into the language concept and, as we did, added concepts to FORTRAN to produce ALTRAN, but still limiting the capability to the handling of polynomials or rational functions. It turns out that has a profound effect on what you do internally and from an implementation point of view. Polynomials, for those of you who maybe don't remember the mathematics, are simply something of the form $\mathbf{A^n + B^m}$—you are simply dealing with variables to powers, products, and divisions of that, but it does not allow for trigonometric functions such as sine or cosine or exponential functions, like $\mathbf{e^x}$ or any of those things. The implementation of dealing *just* with polynomials or rational functions is orders of magnitude easier than allowing for these other things. The other major contemporary language research work that was going on at this time, was Formula ALGOL. That was done under the guidance of Al Perlis at Carnegie Mellon. It is certainly not a surprise that, when I started this, I decided to add the language capabilities to FORTRAN, and when Al Perlis started this, he decided to add the language capabilities to ALGOL. I think both of those are quite obvious. Formula ALGOL was the closest in concept to what we were doing, but even then we had very many differences—in particular, a different philosophy on simplification, which I will talk about a little later. There were some other minor contemporary languages that never became overly significant: Magic Paper done by Lew Clapp here in the Boston area, MATHLAB was done by Carl Engelman at MITRE, and Symbolic Mathematical Laboratory being done by Bill Martin as a Ph.D. thesis at MIT. MATHLAB and Symbolic Mathematical Laboratory had significant influences and eventually—I think, although Joel Moses might disagree with me—sort of metamorphosed and in some way eventually became the MACSYMA system.

Now, let me show you, in the next few charts, the kind of capability that existed.

(SLIDE 10a) The statements on the left are the FORMAC commands, and they were put in the middle of the FORMAC programs. The **LET** statement was really just an assignment statement for symbolic variables. **SUBST** allowed you to do what you would expect, namely replace any variable by any other variable or an expression. **EXPAND** was to remove parentheses. **COEFF** obtained the coefficient, and the **PART** was a shorthand for partition, and allows you to chop up expressions in various ways.

(SLIDE 10b) The first of these, the **EVAL**, is probably the most important of the commands that are in there aside from the **LET** commands, which are just the symbolic assignment statements. **EVAL**

FORMAC Executable statements and functions (1 of 4)

Statements yielding FORMAC variables

LET ...... construct specified expressions (assignment statement for symbolic variables)

SUBST .... replace variables with expressions or other variables

EXPAND ... remove parentheses

COEFF .... obtain the coefficient of a variable

PART ..... separate expressions into terms, factors, exponents, arguments of functions, etc.

SLIDE 10a

FORMAC Executable statements and functions (2 of 4)

Statements yielding FORTRAN variables

EVAL ..... evaluate expression for numerical values

MATCH .... compare two expressions for equivalence or identity

FIND ..... determine dependence relations or existence of variables

CENSUS ... count words, terms, or factors

SLIDE 10b

allowed us to evaluate the expressions for numerical values. The **EVAL** command was crucial, because our philosophy said that one wanted to generate these formal mathematical expressions, but then in many cases—in the practical engineering and mathematical examples—one wanted to evaluate them. And in essence, what we did was implement **EVAL** as an interpreter at object time. I will have something to say about that at the banquet tonight. The point of the **EVAL** command was to provide a seamless capability to the user wherein he/she put in the problem, generated these vast mathematical expressions, and then evaluated them numerically and came out with a number. The point being that they could not do the *algebra* by hand. There were many cases in which people spent not only hours but days, weeks, months, and in some cases even years, doing what we call "tedious algebra." The same kind of things that people did numerically before there were computers, were still being done by hand from an algebraic point of view. The **MATCH** command allowed you to do what it indicates, trying to compare expressions for equivalence or identity; there is a big difference, and it is quite significant in systems of this kind, as to whether you really have identical expressions or whether they are just mathematically equivalent. **FIND** and **CENSUS** are not very interesting; they are important to us, but they are not overly interesting.

(SLIDE 10c) The first two of these just got us over a hurdle—to get to and from BCD (Binary Coded Decimal), which was the internal format of the machine—and these were needed for the input and output. The **ORDER** was to do some kind of sequencing. **AUTSIM** was a very crucial thing and I'll say more about that later, because it had something to do with the automatic simplification. **ERASE** was to get rid of expressions which we didn't need. In that sense, it's like garbage collection in Lisp or something like that. And the last one (**FMCDMP**) was just a debugging tool.

(SLIDE 10d) The FORMAC differentiation was crucial; that may be of some interest to you. As early as *1954*—that's not an oral misprint, 1954, before there were many computers around—there were two master's theses done to do formal differentiation on a computer. One was done at Temple University by a student under the guidance of Grace Hopper, and it was done on a UNIVAC I. The other was done at MIT on Whirlwind. These were master's theses; now I think they are given as overnight homework exercises to freshmen. But at that time, it was quite a *tour de force*. We had differentiation, we had these other things, trig functions and so forth. You note the complete absence of integration. That *was far* beyond the state of the art at the time we started this—the heuristics and the algorithms came much later, first with Jim Slagle, then with Joel Moses, then with Robert Risch. So that's why we never had integration. It was far too difficult, and for any of you who remember college calculus, you will perhaps recall that differentiation is a very straightforward algorithmic

FORMAC Executable statements and functions (3 of 4)

Miscellaneous Statements

BCDCON . . . convert to BCD form from internal form [needed for output]
ALGCON . . . convert to internal form from BCD form [needed for input]
ORDER . . . . specify sequencing of variables within expressions
AUTSIM . . . control arithmetic done during automatic simplification
ERASE . . . . eliminate expressions no longer needed
FMCDMP . . . symbolic dump

SLIDE 10c

FORMAC Executable statements and functions (4 of 4)

Functions

FMCDIF . . . differentiation
FMCOMB . . . combinatorial
FMCFAC . . . factorial
FMCDFA . . . double factorial

Trigonometric, logarithmic, and exponential functions

SLIDE 10d

process, in which you write down a whole bunch of rules and therefore you can easily program a computer to do. At that time, at least, to integrate required a fair amount of intellectual gestalt as to what rules you were going to apply to the expressions.

(SLIDE 11) Simplification is one of the issues in which people who work in these systems have a lot of difference of opinion. Most people would agree that if you end up in a situation where you are multiplying by **0**, you want the result to be **0**. If you multiply by **1** you want to get rid of the **1**, and if the internal representation turns out that these variables are not in the same order, there should be something which will put them in the right order and have the system recognize this as being the same, and get 0.

Now you get down to something like **A * (B + C)**, and it's not clear what simplification means in that case. It may mean nothing; you may want it in that form, or you may want it in this expanded form **(AB + AC)**, and it depends on the particular point in the activity in the program that you are doing this. One of the major differences in philosophy between Formula ALGOL and FORMAC was that we did a large amount of this automatically and gave the user a little bit of control over what could be done. Formula ALGOL insisted that the user specify exactly what it was that he wanted done throughout.

(SLIDE 12) There are some special issues and some special problems that we encountered. The first one had to do with exceeding available storage, and we coined a version of Parkinson's Law. You know that the original Parkinson's Law said that "costs expand to exceed the amount of money available." A later version then became "the workload expands to exceed the amount of time available." And we had one that said "the size of the expression expanded to exceed the amount of storage available" because these things ate up storage like it was going out of style. Eventually we developed some better techniques and this is described in the paper. Even though we developed some better techniques to help save some storage, nevertheless they did eat up an enormous amount of storage. The next issue was the philosophy of simplification and I've already described that. Now, with respect to interactivity, I ask you to try and put yourself mentally back in the period of 1962 or 1963. There essentially were no terminals. By around 1964 there was one—I think it was the 2741. There were some terminals you could hook up to a mainframe, but they were really just typewriters, albeit connected to the mainframe; it was all very primitive. So what we were doing was in batch. There was some debate on whether anybody could really do this kind of problem in a batch mode. Well, I'm here to tell you that there were an awful lot of people, hundreds of them, who knew enough about what their problem was, that they could indeed write a batch program to get reasonable answers,

SLIDE 11

SLIDE 12

either in a truly symbolic form or in numeric form. Some problems you couldn't because you needed to know what the expression looked like as you went along to know what the devil to do with it. And for that, you needed an interactive version, and as part of our experimental work, we developed a fairly simple version. We took the FORMAC on the 7090, and we did enough manipulation that people could do this on an interactive version.

Market forecasting may strike you as being a strange thing to occur in this paper, but there is some more significant discussion about it in the paper. At the time, there was no forecasting for software, at least not within IBM and I assume nowhere else. They were very busy going around to determine if they were going to build some kind of a new box, how many people might buy it, and what they should charge. But since there was no charging for software, there wasn't much forecasting about its use either. And we were asked to be a "guinea pig" for some of this, and indeed we were. The results were not very conclusive, but at least we helped get IBM and others involved in the forecasting business. The form of output I will come back to with a couple of horrendous examples in a few minutes.

(SLIDE 13) Now, let me go on and talk about the PL/I version. Naturally, before you finish the first version, you've got to be looking at the second one. Our objective was to use what we had learned with our experience on the original one, to improve the basic approach, add new commands, and clean up some of the ones that we had. And, more importantly, to add the language capability to PL/I instead of to FORTRAN. The reason for doing that, was at that time—as you may recall Fred Brooks noting in his keynote address—the original IBM strategy was to replace FORTRAN and COBOL by PL/I, and I felt we ought to be good corporate citizens and support that goal, which I thought was a pretty good goal; I'm not trying to knock it in any way. It didn't succeed for a whole variety of reasons, but that's a different issue. We wanted to support that strategy so we were going to add this capability to PL/I.

(SLIDE 14a) Imagine if you can, the time when you got pages and pages of output from a high-speed printer—and I saw engineers getting 20 pages of stuff that looked like that, or worse because it went further across the width of the paper. And they were absolutely delighted because they could go in and find some coefficients of some expressions and some new patterns that they didn't know about, and they could see. And they were thrilled with this stuff. It gives me a headache every time I look at it. But, I'm not exaggerating when I say that lots of engineers and mathematicians with problems would get 20 pages of output for a single computer run, and be thrilled because it told them things about their problems and gave them data that they didn't have. These were the cases in which people did not want to evaluate—they really wanted to see what the expressions looked like. We

PL/I VERSION ON IBM SYSTEM/360

Objective—

- **Use experience to improve basic approach**
- **Add to PL/I instead of FORTRAN**

Reason for changing languages—

- **Support the IBM strategy of supplying PL/I to replace FORTRAN and COBOL**

SLIDE 13

recognized this was pretty gruesome no matter how happy they were. We certainly weren't happy. After all, we had to do some debugging with this stuff ourselves.

(SLIDE 14b) So, we improved matters a lot with regard to the PL/I format, because we got the exponents up where they belong and we got rid of the asterisks to denote the implicit multiplication. Things were a little bit better.

Now, there were other people around that time who were doing much more work, and in fact better work, on getting better output, but that's not where our main thrust was. We wanted to get something that was rather more readable, but we weren't prepared, and we simply didn't have the resources to go as far as some other groups were doing at that time.

(SLIDE 15) Let me go on to the last chart, which is my attempt at evaluation here. FORMAC, I think, had somewhat of an influence, but it was rather indirect. And I'm not sure what Joel is going to say; he may or may not choose to comment on that particular aspect of it. FORMAC was the first real formula manipulation language to receive significant usage. And I emphasize the word language because ALPAK at that time, which was the polynomial manipulation system developed at Bell Labs, was getting significant usage. But that was a series of subroutines added to an assembly language. The language that was represented by FORMAC was the first of the languages. Even ALTRAN came somewhat after. I became convinced—and I believe everybody else that followed us in any way agreed—that it was a language, not just subroutines, that was important. One of the areas that I felt

High-speed printer output from 7090/94

```
X/1!+2*X**2/2!+2*X**3/3!
  -4*X**5/5!-8*X**6/6!
  -8*X**7/7!+16*X**9/9!
  +32*X**10/10!+32*X**11/11!
  -64*X**13/13!-128*X**14/14!
  -128*X**15/15!+256*X**17/17!
  +512*X**18/18!+512*X**19/19!
-----------------------------
```

SLIDE 14a

High-speed printer output from PL/I-FORMAC

TAYLOR = x / 1! + 2 x^2 / 2! + 2 x^3 / 3!

- 4 x^5 / 5! - 8 x^6 / 6! - 8 x^7 / 7!

+ 16 x^9 / 9! + 32 x^{10} / 10!

+ 32 x^{11} / 11! - 64 x^{13}/ 13!

- 128 x^{14} / 14! - 128 x^{15} / 15!

+ 256 x^{17} / 17! + 512 x^{18}/ 18!

+ 512 x^{19} / 19!

SLIDE 14b

EVALUATION

- **Influence—some was only indirect**
- **A language (not just subroutines) is *important***
- **Symbolic mathematics *can* be done in a practical way**
- **Rational arithmetic**
- **ACM SIGSAM**

SLIDE 15

strongly about, and essentially nobody that followed us did, was that I felt that the language capability for the symbolic computation should be added to an existing language. I may have said that earlier, but I want to emphasize it here. One of the basic philosophies that we had was that we wanted to add this type of formal capability to an existing language. The issue was not so much *which* language but to *a* language. I believe that all of the people who followed us supported the concept of using a language but, I believe, in almost every case used a stand-alone language. That is to say, they did not choose to add to an existing language. And that's a matter of belief. I continue to believe that all these systems should add to an existing language because the user of these systems tends to be doing both numeric and nonnumeric work. And if the user is familiar with an existing language—and I don't care if it's FORTRAN or PL/I or Ada or whatever—then I think they ought to have this kind of formula manipulation capability added to that language rather than as a stand-alone language. But again, that is a matter of a philosophy that I have, that most people simply do not agree with.

The next thing that was clear from what we did, was that symbolic mathematics could be done in a practical way. Primitive as this system was, and as dreadful as its 7090 output was, it really did produce useful results for a number of users. Before I talk about the last two points, I want to mention something which is not on a slide. I want to say something about what turned out to be FORMAC 73. After the PL/I FORMAC was done, IBM dropped all interest. In both cases, the systems (7090/94 and the PL/I version) were made available as what were then called Type III programs. This is before the days of unbundling, so these systems were being given away. IBM at that time, categorized software systems into a number of groups. Type I programs were the compilers and the operating systems, which were the major systems given away and had full major support. Type II systems were some application programs that got good support. Type III programs were given away on a "user beware" basis. That is to say, if the developing group in IBM wanted to make it available to the users, they could do that. No problem, but the user had to understand that they were not going to get any support *officially* from IBM. Again, if the developing group chose to provide support, then that was all right too. That was a management decision, and we supported this to the hilt. After the PL/I-FORMAC was done and released, IBM really dropped all interest. The development group, which by that time I was no longer managing, ceased to exist and it sort of faded. Then people in SHARE picked this up, modified it, improved it for PL/I, and made it available through SHARE. Some people in SHARE-Europe also put the PL/I version back onto FORTRAN. In other words, using the additional capabilities they put that back onto FORTRAN.

Now, let me talk briefly about rational arithmetic, which I confess to feeling very proud of as being one of the contributions that had been made, because it's something people don't think of very often.

One third (**1/3**) is a rational number, but **.33333** is not. And the reason that this got put into the system was that when we did the original testing, all we had were some very primitive examples where you didn't need anything but assignment statements. So you were multiplying and dividing expressions, and the coefficients for many of these systems are of the kind of things that you saw before—they had a pattern. They may have had something factorial as the coefficient, or they go up as **3 * 5** and then **5 * 7**, and things of that kind. I did the hand calculations to check out what it was that the systems were generating, and nothing matched. So, finally it turned out that my arithmetic was wrong in most cases, but it also became perfectly clear that the output that we were getting was virtually useless because in expressions of this kind—and if we could go back for a minute to slide 14B—you will notice that the denominators are all factorial while the numerators are simply single digits. In many of these kinds of expressions, they turn out to be things where you are multiplying. As I say, one coefficient might be **4 * 5** and the next is **5 * 6** and so on. If you multiply that out, you lose all the pattern that is inherent in things of that kind. So we put the rational arithmetic in because we felt you couldn't see what was going on without it.

The last factor (on Slide 15) that I think was significant that came out of the FORMAC effort—and you may be surprised that I list that—is ACM SIGSAM. That came about for the following reasons. IBM then, was very concerned about who its employees spoke to in a technical and professional sense. They were concerned about giving away secrets and this kind of thing. Unlike academia, and unlike some of the research-oriented organizations that existed, I couldn't really—legally—just pick up the phone and call someone at a university. That was too bad, but I also couldn't really just pick up the phone and call Stan Brown at Bell Labs and discuss something—that was sort of a "no no." I felt there needed to be an umbrella organization of some kind which would enable us to legally meet, discuss, have technical meetings, and so forth. So I eventually (through a series of other circumstances) wrote to George Forsythe, who was then the President of ACM, and said, "I don't know what a Special Interest Group is, but I think that maybe I'd like to see what has to be done to form one." He wrote back and said "you are now the Chairman." Things are a little more formal now! And so, I founded the ACM SICSAM, which is what it was called at that time. We started with a newsletter of which Peter Wegner was the first editor. We held a conference in 1966, which produced an entire issue of the *ACM Communications*; this was the first real major attempt in getting all these kinds of people together in one group to present what they were doing. Since then, the community has been fairly cohesive under the leadership of a number of people that came after me with regard to SIGSAM. There have been other organizations, other activities, and so forth. But I'd like to think that SIGSAM—which was certainly motivated by my desire to discuss FORMAC with other people in a legal sense—was one of the contributions that came out of the FORMAC effort.

TRANSCRIPT OF DISCUSSANT'S REMARKS

SESSION CHAIR, TIM BERGIN: Our discussant is Joel Moses, who was a graduate student in the AI group of Project MAC from 1963 to 1967. He worked on FORMAC in the summer of 1964 and did his Ph.D. research on symbolic integration, from both a theoretical and practical perspective. He is now the Dean of Engineering at MIT, having been department head of Electrical Engineering and Computer Science from '81 through '89, and associate head for Computer Science and Engineering from '78 to '81. He was also a Visiting Professor at the Harvard Business School in '89 and '90. Joel is a member of the National Academy of Engineering and a fellow of the American Academy of Arts and Sciences. He is an IEEE Fellow and the developer of the MACSYMA system. His current interests are the architectures of large and complex systems.

JOEL MOSES: I am pleased to be allowed to make comments on Jean's paper. Actually, having been here all morning, there are some other papers I would like to comment on too! Let me start off with the Lisp paper. Guy Steele made the point that we had unstable funding at MIT and that's the reason people left. Well, I don't know about that. I was responsible for funding for much of that time, and we had relatively stable funding, between '68 and '82. The only reason we stopped funding the MACSYMA project is because I became department head in '81 and I just couldn't hold the group together while fulfilling my administrative duties. MIT licensed it; unfortunately it was to Symbolics, but that is another story. But in the meantime we had very good funding and were able to maintain a lot of support of Lisp development. Of course, MIT is an educational institution and we do train people who are supposed to leave—most of them in any case.

The major emphasis in Jean's paper is that FORMAC was different because it was a language rather than a collection of subroutines for formula manipulation. Anybody who has known Jean as long as I have, which is now about 30 years, is always concerned about Jean's interest in what's a language and what's not a language. In any case, I thought long and hard about why my colleagues in the early '60s who worked in formula manipulation, Tony Hearn, George Collins, and Stan Brown, did things in terms of packages rather than as languages. I think it has something to do with who they thought the users would be.

Tony was building REDUCE for his friends who were theoretical physicists. They needed to do Feynman diagrams; Feynman diagrams are this great discovery in the late '40s of how to do work in quantum electro-dynamics, essentially by doing integration of rational functions. And then you get logs and you integrate these logs, and things get very complicated very quickly. In any case, he had a very clear-cut user community.

George Collins was building a system largely for himself. His Ph.D. thesis, in 1956, was essentially on a system which proved theorems in plane geometry by converting the theorems into systems of polynomial equations. I don't know who Stan Brown viewed as his community; probably his theoretical colleagues at Bell Labs. In any case, in each of those three situations one could conveniently make the assumptions that the user was relatively sophisticated, the problems were extremely time consuming and had a relatively simple formulaic structure such as polynomials and rational functions.

I think FORMAC was interested in a different community. I think they were interested more in engineers than scientists, at least engineers as well as scientists and mathematicians. These are users whose problems were more diverse and possibly not quite so gigantic all the time. Mathematicians can generate problems which are unbelievably large. I once calculated the number of terms in a solution, if we could ever figure it out, of a particular problem to be 10 to the 120. This is not the assumption that I think could be made about the majority of users of FORMAC. To attract such users, a good front end was needed, in order to make the experience not too cumbersome. We can argue about whether the front end has to be an extension of a popular language, as Jean indicated just now, or whether it could be a special-purpose language. Nevertheless, I think it was very important to attract the variety of users, the small- or medium-size users as well as some large users, to have an attractive front end in the system. Remember that when FORMAC was implemented, computing was done in a batch environment, and, therefore, I think an extension of PL/I or FORTRAN makes a lot of sense in that context. Most of us who worked a little bit later, when we did have nice linguistic front ends, basically recognized that in a time-sharing environment you really want to have a different kind of a language. Since there wasn't a particularly appropriate language to extend, we built our own.

Eventually, many of us gravitated to Jean's view about the user community and the need for front ends, especially so in the MACSYMA system. I'll talk a little bit about that later. I think Jean rightfully complains that IBM didn't give her and FORMAC sufficient support to continue to develop the system. On the other hand, the imprimatur that IBM did give FORMAC helped the rest of us obtain support for our activities, because IBM was a monopoly and everybody then knew that if IBM said this was OK, then it must be so.

Jean is correct in pointing out the precursors of MACSYMA were MATHLAB, Carl Engelman's package; the Symbolic Mathematical Laboratory, Bill Martin's work; and the program that I did on integration. The first talk I ever gave was titled "Moses on SIN." My program was called SIN for Symbolic Integrator, because my predecessor's program was called SAINT. Slagle is a Catholic and I am not. Anyway, it was clear to Martin, Engelman, and me in '68, that we were aiming at both a large number of potential users from engineering as well as education. We had as our goal, even then, that college students and even high school students would use these systems, as, of course, they do now. At the same time, we wanted a system which was as fast as the fastest of the existing packages, REDUCE and ALTRAN, and, therefore, could attract mathematicians and physicists with their gigantic problems. So we built a front-end language with an expression display by Bill Martin, which was the state of the art for many years, and we concentrated on very efficient formula representations. We also built an enormous amount of code for the various algorithms we felt were necessary in a universally useful algebraic system.

We worked in Lisp as did Tony Hearn with REDUCE. His work was done at Stanford, and later at Utah. Jim Griesmer and Dick Jenks worked for IBM at Yorktown Heights on the SCRATCHPAD system in Lisp as well. This gave us great programming flexibility at an admitted cost of possible a factor of 2 in space, and a comparably large factor of time. We, as I think is noted in the Lisp paper, developed MacLisp to deal with the time issue. We couldn't live with the original cost of doing arithmetic in Lisp, which was, I think, a factor of 30 slower than FORTRAN when we started. We got it down to maybe a factor of 2 or so by making appropriate declarations. We were memory hogs, some of the largest memory hogs in the world. In fact, the big physical memories that were bought by MIT in the '70s, were bought for us. Although other people used them, the excuse was always the MACSYMA project. Memory prices were declining, and address spaces were growing, although not as fast as we liked. All of that allowed us to continue forefront research for a long time. Some of the more recent systems, such as Maple and Mathematica, are written in C, rather than Lisp, getting some greater efficiency than we got with Lisp. Mathematica initially had a nicer front end than any of the other systems. That attracted a very broad class of users, some of whom have very little interest in formula manipulation. The key advantage that these two systems have is that the algorithms stabilized over the last 30 years, and the programming flexibility in Lisp is not as critical today as it was for us. For example, in MACSYMA, we created three new algorithms for the greatest common divisor of two polynomials. We continually had to develop things, and we wanted to have a system which gave us the ease of programming that Lisp provides.

Let me get back to FORMAC. Jean's memory of the summer of 1964 is that I spent it on this project, working for Jean, running comparisons between FORMAC and Lisp base code. My memory was of my attempts to convince Bob Tobey and others in the group to add more functionality to FORMAC. In particular, I wanted to have a pattern-matching facility so that users could program their own simplification rules in addition to the built-in ones. Alan Perlis was doing something like this at CMU in Formula ALGOL, but I didn't know this, since there was so little communication between groups at the time. And, as Jean pointed out, one of her achievements in the FORMAC period was to create a group called SICSAM—a Special Interest Committee, before the Special Interest Group—and to lead the 1966 conference where the community met for the very first time. You can all see now how Jean accomplished all this. She doesn't take "no" for an answer. I recall that once she got a gift. I don't know what the name of it is, but it is a toy where you have four of these aluminum balls, which knock each other out of position. I thought this was a perfectly appropriate gift for Jean because she was always great at knocking heads together. And I believe FORMAC represents the best of the head knocking. Thank you.

TRANSCRIPT OF QUESTION AND ANSWER SESSION

CHARLES LINDSEY—UNIVERSITY OF MANCHESTER: Was the **MATCH** operation equivalent to what we now know as unification?

SAMMET: I'm not sure what he means by unification so I can't answer the question.

MOSES: Robinson's paper on unification came out in '63 and by that time the FORMAC design was pretty much frozen.

SAMMET: The **MATCH** command was really very trivial. Remember that when you are generating expressions in this kind of thing, you have no idea what the expression is going to look like. It's the symbolic equivalent of an equals test in a numeric computation. You generate a number, you don't know what the number is, so you ask whether it is equal to 17, if that happens to be of interest to you. Well, we would generate two expressions and try and find out whether or not they were the same. And there are two different ways in which they could be the same. One is that they are physically identical, that is to say, bit matching. And the other is whether they are logically the same, for example, **A * (B + C)** is logically equivalent to **AB + AC** but is certainly not equivalent on a bit match. So the **MATCH** is just really elementary conceptually.

HERBERT KLAEREN—UNIVERSITY OF TUBINGEN: During the FORMAC preprocessor development, was it ever discussed to make the translation process to FORTRAN user programmable, so people could extend or change the formula manipulation capabilities?

SAMMET: I can't honestly remember whether we discussed it, but if we did, we certainly would have said no. That is to say, we were not trying to make an extensible system in any meaning of that word whatsoever. The user was going to get what we thought the user ought to have—with a few exceptions. There was some flexibility in the automatic simplification and there were some things that the user could put in or block. I think, for example, the expansion of a factorial was one of them. So, for example, the user had the option of asking for **7 factorial** to be displayed as **7!**—or whether the user wanted that multiplied out. That was one of the options that the user had in the automatic simplification. But, no, we weren't going to give the user the chance to extend this.

TOM MARLOW—SETON HALL: Does the move to make symbolic languages work in a standardized interface/environment such as Windows address your concerns about language extension in any way, at least as far as the issues of familiarity in front end?

SAMMET: I'm not sure. Either one has a standard language or one doesn't. Whether it runs under Windows or UNIX or DOS strikes me as being a separate issue. The whole issue of the portability of environments and whether a particular language or compiler (or anything else) runs under that environment, in my mind is a separate issue.

BIOGRAPHY OF JEAN E. SAMMET

Miss Sammet has a B.A. (Mathematics) from Mount Holyoke College and an M.A. (Mathematics) from the University of Illinois.

From 1955 to 1958, Miss Sammet was the first group leader for programmers in the engineering organization of the Sperry Gyroscope Company on Long Island. She taught what were among the earliest computer courses given for academic credit. In 1956–1957, she organized and taught graduate courses entitled "Digital Computer Programming" and "Advanced Digital Computer Programming" in the Graduate Applied Mathematics Department at Adelphi College on Long Island. (By today's standards, those were very elementary courses in basic programming and coding, using UNIVAC and the IBM 704.) During the second year she taught those courses (1957–1958), she used FORTRAN, which had just been released.

In 1958, she joined Sylvania Electric Products in Needham, Massachusetts, as Section Head for MOBIDIC Programming. The primary task of the section was the preparation of the basic programming package for MOBIDIC (a large-scale computer of that time frame) under a contract to the Signal Corps as part of the Army FIELDATA program. She held that position at the time the COBOL effort started in 1959. She was a key member of the COBOL (then called Short Range) Committee, and continued COBOL committee work until she joined IBM in 1961.

Her mission in joining IBM was to organize and manage the Boston Advanced Programming Department in Cambridge, MA, to do advanced development work in programming. One of the key projects of that department was the development of FORMAC, the first programming language for symbolic mathematics.

She later held various technical management and staff positions at IBM until the end of 1988 when she took early retirement. Most of the positions and activities involved programming languages, including originating and directing the development of the first FORMAC (FORmula MAnipulation Compiler), and organizing the strategy and activities for the use of Ada in the IBM Federal Systems Division.

She has given numerous lectures and talks on the subjects of symbolic computation and programming languages, including the historical aspects of both. She has published over 50 papers on these subjects. In 1969, her 785-page book *PROGRAMMING LANGUAGES: History and Fundamentals* was published by Prentice Hall and has been described by others as "the standard work on programming languages" and an "instant computer classic."

She has been very active in professional society activities, including serving as ACM SIGPLAN Chair (1971–1972), ACM Vice-President (1972–1974), and ACM President (1974–1976). From January 1979 to January 1987 she was Editor-in-Chief of ACM *Computing Reviews* and of the *ACM Guide to Computing Literature*. She served on several standards committees. She organized and chaired the first AFIPS History of Computing Committee (1977–1979). She conceived the idea, and served as General and Program Chair, for the very successful ACM SIGPLAN History of Programming Languages Conference in 1978, and was the Program Chair for the Second ACM SIGPLAN History of Programming Languages Conference (HOPL-II) in April 1993. From 1983 to 1993 she was a member of the Board of Directors of the Computer Museum and has been on its Collections Committee. She is on the Executive Committee of the Software Patent Institute and was the first Chair of its Education Committee.

She received an honorary Sc.D. from Mount Holyoke in 1978. Some of her honors and awards include membership in the National Academy of Engineering (1977), the ACM Distinguished Service Award (1985), and the Augusta Ada Lovelace Award from the Association for Women in Computing (1989).

She is currently a programming language consultant.

CLU Session

Chair: *Barbara Ryder*

A HISTORY OF CLU

Barbara Liskov

Laboratory for Computer Science
Massachusetts Institute of Technology
Cambridge, MA 02139

ABSTRACT

The idea of a data abstraction has had a significant impact on the development of programming languages and on programming methodology. CLU was the first implemented programming language to provide direct linguistic support for data abstraction. This paper provides a history of data abstraction and CLU. CLU contains a number of other interesting and influential features, including its exception handling mechanism, its iterators, and its parameterized types.[1]

CONTENTS

10.1 INTRODUCTION

The idea of a data abstraction arose from work on programming methodology. It has had a significant impact on the way modern software systems are designed and organized and on the features that are provided in modern programming languages. In the early and mid-1970s, it led to the development of new programming languages, most notably CLU and Alphard. These language designs were undertaken to flesh out the idea and to provide direct support for new techniques for developing software.

This paper provides a history of CLU and data abstraction. CLU provides linguistic support for data abstraction; it was the first implemented language to do so. In addition, it contains a number of

1 This research was supported in part by the Advanced Research Projects Agency of the Department of Defense, monitored by the Office of Naval Research under contract N00014-89-J-1988, in part by the National Science Foundation under Grant CCR-8822158, and in part by the NEC Corporation of Tokyo, Japan.

other interesting and influential features, including its exception handling mechanism, its iterators, and its parameterized types.

The paper is organized as follows. Section 10.2 describes the work that led to the concept of data abstraction and how this concept came into existence. It also describes the beginning of the work on CLU, and discusses some of the later work on programming methodology that was based on data abstraction. Section 10.3 provides a history of the CLU development process, with emphasis on the design issues related to the technical features of CLU; the section contains material about related work in other languages as well. The paper concludes with an evaluation of CLU and a discussion of its influence on programming languages and methodology.

10.2 DATA ABSTRACTION

In my early work on data abstraction, in the latter part of 1972 through the summer of 1973, I was concerned with figuring out what the concept was, rather than designing a programming language. This section traces the development of the concept and describes the environment in which the work occurred and the related work that was going on at that time.

A data abstraction, or abstract data type, is a set of objects and operations. Programs that access the objects can do so only by calling the operations, which provide means to observe an object's state and to modify it. The objects contain within them a storage representation that is used to store their state, but this representation is encapsulated: it is not visible to programs that use the data abstraction. For example, a "set of integers" type might have operations to create an empty set, to insert and delete elements from a set, to determine the cardinality of a set, and to determine whether a particular integer is a member of a set. A set might be represented by an array or a linked list, but because users can interact with it only by calling operations, the particular representation is not visible. One important benefit of such encapsulation is that it allows decisions about implementation to be changed without any need to modify programs that use the data abstraction.

The idea of a data abstraction developed in the early seventies. It grew out of work on programming methodology. At that time, there was a great deal of interest in methods for improving the efficiency of the programming process and also the quality of the product. There were two main approaches: structured programming and modularity. Structured programming [Dijkstra 1969] was concerned with program correctness (or reliability, as it was called in those days):

> The goal of structured programming is to produce program structures which are amenable to proofs of correctness. The proof of a structured program is broken down into proofs of the correctness of each of the components. Before a component is coded, a specification exists explaining its input and output and the function which it is supposed to perform [Liskov 1972a, p. 193].

Not using gotos [Dijkstra 1968a] was a part of structured programming because the resulting program structures were easier to reason about, but the idea of reasoning about the program at one level using specifications of lower-level components was much more fundamental. The notion of stepwise refinement as an approach to constructing programs was also a part of this movement [Wirth 1971].

The work on modularity [Liskov 1972a; Parnas 1971, 1972a; Randell 1969] was concerned with what program components should be like. For example, I proposed the idea of partitions:

> The system is divided into a hierarchy of partitions, where each partition represents one level of abstraction, and consists of one or more functions which share common resources. . . . The connections in data between partitions are limited to the explicit arguments passed from the functions of one partition to the (external)

> functions of another partition. Implicit interaction on common data may only occur among functions within a partition [Liskov 1972a, p. 195].

This notion of partitions was based on Dijkstra's ideas about levels of abstraction [Dijkstra 1968b] and my own work on the Venus operating system [Liskov 1972b]. Venus was organized as a collection of partitions, each with externally accessible functions and hidden state information, which communicated by calling one another's functions.

The papers on programming methodology were concerned with system structure rather than with programming language mechanisms. They provided guidelines that programmers could use to organize programs but did not describe any programming language constructs that would help in the organization. The work on data abstraction arose from an effort to bridge this gap. Data abstraction merged the ideas of modularity and encapsulation with programming languages by relating encapsulated modules to data types. As a result, programming languages that provided direct support for modular programming came into existence, and a much clearer notion of what a module is emerged.

By the fall of 1972, I had become dissatisfied with the papers on programming methodology, including my own, because I believed it was hard for readers to apply the notions to their own programs. The idea of a module was somewhat nebulous in these papers (some operations with hidden state information). Even less obvious was how to do modular design. The designer was supposed to identify modules, but it was not at all clear how this was to be done, and the papers provided relatively little guidance on this crucial point.

I noticed that many of the modules discussed in the papers on modularity were defining data types. For example, I had suggested that designers look for abstractions that hid the details of interacting with various hardware resources, and that hid the storage details of data structures [Liskov 1972a]. This led me to think of linking modules to data types and eventually to the idea of abstract types with an encapsulated representation and operations that could be used to access and manipulate the objects. I thought that programmers would have an easier time doing modular design in terms of abstract types (instead of just looking for modules) because this was similar to deciding about data structures, and also because the notion of an abstract type could be defined precisely. I referred to the types as "abstract" because they are not provided directly by a programming language but instead must be implemented by the user. An abstract type is abstract in the same way that a procedure is an abstract operation.

I gave a talk [Liskov 1973a] on abstract data types at a workshop on Programming Languages and Operating Systems held in Savannah on April 9–12, 1973. This talk merged the ideas of structured programming and modularity by relating the components of a structured program to either abstract operations (implemented by procedures) or abstract types. An abstract type provides

> a group of related functions whose joint actions completely define the abstraction as far as its users are concerned. The irrelevant details of how the abstraction is supported are completely hidden from the users [Liskov 1973a, p. 6].

Furthermore, the language should support a syntactic unit that can be used to implement abstract types, and "the language must be strongly typed so that it is not possible to make use of an object in any other way" [Liskov 1973a, p. 7] except by calling its operations.

At about the time of the Savannah meeting, I began to work with Steve Zilles, who was also at MIT working on a similar idea. Steve published his ideas at Savannah [Zilles 1973], and there were a number of other related talks given there, including a talk on monitors by Mike McKeag [1973] and a talk on LIS by Jean Ichbiah [1973].

Steve and I worked on refining the concept of abstract types over the spring and summer of 1973; Austin Henderson was involved to a lesser extent as an interested listener and critic. Our progress report for that year [Liskov 1973b] describes a slightly later status for the work than what was reported at the Savannah meeting. In the progress report, we state that an abstract type should be defined by a "function cluster" containing the operations of the type. By the end of the summer, our ideas about language support for data abstraction were quite well established, and Steve and I described them in a paper published in September [Liskov 1973c]; a slightly later version of this paper appeared in the conference on very high level languages held in April 1974 [Liskov 1974a]. The September paper states that an abstract data type is implemented by a "cluster" containing a description of the representation and implementations of all the operations. It defines structured programming:

> In structured programming, a problem is solved by means of a process of successive decomposition. The first step is to write a program which solves the problem but which runs on an abstract machine, i.e., one which provides just those data objects and operations which are suitable to solving the problem. Some or all of those data objects and operations are truly abstract, i.e., not present as primitives in the programming language being used [Liskov 1973c, p. 3].

CLU was chosen as the name of the language in the fall of 1973. The name was selected because it is the first three letters of "cluster."

10.2.1 Related Early Work

Programming languages that existed when the concept of data abstraction arose did not support abstract data types, but some languages contained constructs that were precursors of this notion. (An analysis of language support for other languages was done by Jack Aiello, a student in the CLU group, in the fall of 1973 and the spring of 1974 [Aiello 1974].) The mechanism that matched the best was the class mechanism of Simula 67 [Dahl 1970]. A Simula class groups a set of procedures with some variables. A class can be instantiated to provide an object containing its own copies of the variables; the class contains code that initializes these variables at instantiation time. However, Simula classes did not enforce encapsulation (although Palme proposed a change to Simula that did [Palme 1973]), and Simula was lacking several other features needed to support data abstraction, as discussed further in section 10.3.2.

Extensible languages contained a weak notion of data abstraction. This work arose from a notion of "uniform referents" [Balzer 1967; Earley 1971; Ross 1970]. The idea was that all data types ought to be referenced in the same way so that decisions about data representation could be delayed and changed. This led to a notion of a fixed set of operations that every type supported. For example, every type in EL1 [Wegbreit, 1972, 1973] was permitted to provide five operations (conversion, assignment, selection, printing, and generation). However, the new type was not abstract; instead it was just an abbreviation for the chosen representation, which could be accessed everywhere, so that there was no encapsulation.

PL/I provides multi-entry procedures, which can be used to implement data abstractions, and in fact I have used PL/I in teaching how to program using abstract data types when languages with more direct support were not available. The PL/I mechanism allows the description of the representation chosen for objects of the new type to be grouped with the code for the operations; the representation is defined at the beginning of the multi-entry procedure, and the entry points serve as the operations. However, users of the type can access the representations of objects directly (without calling the operations), so again there is no enforcement of encapsulation. Furthermore, multi-entry procedures have other peculiarities; for example, if control falls off the end of one entry point, it does not return to the caller but instead continues in the entry point that follows textually within the multi-entry procedure.

Jim Morris' paper on protection in programming languages [Morris 1973a] appeared in early 1973. This paper contains an example of an abstract data type implemented by a lambda expression that returns a list of operations to be used to access and manipulate the new object. The paper also describes how encapsulation can be enforced dynamically by means of a key that is needed to access the representation and whose value is known only to the type's operations (this notion is elaborated in Morris [1973b]). In the early design of CLU, we thought that this kind of dynamic checking would be needed in some cases, but as the design progressed we came to realize that complete static type checking is possible.

Bill Wulf and Mary Shaw published a paper concerning the misuse of global variables [Wulf 1973] in 1973. One point made in this paper is that there is no way in a block structured language to limit access to a group of variables to just the group of procedures that need such access. This paper represents some of the early thinking of the people who went on to develop Alphard [Shaw 1981; Wulf 1976].

Also in 1973 Tony Hoare published an important paper about how to reason about the correctness of a data type implementation [Hoare 1972]. This paper pointed the way to future work on specification and verification of programs built with data abstractions.

A timely and useful meeting was organized by Jack Dennis and held at the Harvard Faculty Club on October 3–5, 1973 to discuss issues in programming language design; a list of attendees is contained in Appendix A. The topics discussed were: types, semantic bases, concurrency, error handling, symbol identification, sharing and assignment, and relation to systems. Most attendees at the meeting gave brief talks describing their research. I spoke about clusters and the current state of the CLU design, and Bill Wulf discussed the work on Alphard. (Neither of the language names existed at this point.) Ole-Johan Dahl discussed Simula classes and their relationship to clusters. Steve Zilles described his early work on specifying abstract data types. Carl Hewitt discussed his work on Actors, and Tony Hoare described monitors. Also, Jim Mitchell described his early work on error handling, which led to the exception handling mechanism in Mesa [Mitchell 1978].

10.2.2 Programming Methodology

The identification of data abstractions as an organizing principle for programs spurred work in programming methodology. This work is discussed briefly in this section.

As mentioned, the concept of data abstraction arose out of work on structured programming and modularity that was aimed at a new way of organizing programs. Traditionally, programs had been organized using procedures or subroutines. The new idea was to organize around modules that consisted of a number of related procedures, and, with the advent of data abstraction, these modules defined data types or objects. The hope was that this would lead to better organized programs that would be easier to implement and understand, and, as a result, easier to get right.

The resulting programming methodology [Liskov 1979a, 1986] is object-oriented: programs are developed by thinking about the objects they manipulate and then inventing a modular structure based on these objects. Each type of object is implemented by its own program module. Although no studies have shown convincingly that this methodology is superior to others, the methodology has become widespread and people believe that it works. (I believe this; I also believe that it is impossible to run a controlled experiment that will produce a convincing result.)

A keystone of the methodology is its focus on independence of modules. The goal is to be able to deal with each module separately: a module can be implemented independently of (the code of) others, it can be reasoned about independently, and it can be replaced by another module implementing the same abstraction, without requiring any changes in the other modules of the program. Thus, for example, if a data abstraction were implemented too inefficiently, it could be reimplemented and the result would be a program that ran better, but whose externally visible behavior was otherwise unchanged. What is really interesting is that client programs don't have to be changed, and yet will run better.

Achieving independence requires two things: encapsulation and specification. Encapsulation is needed because if any other module depends on implementation details of the module being replaced, it will not be possible to do the replacement without changing that other module. Just having code in some other module that accesses (but does not modify) an object's representation is enough to make replacement impossible, because that code is dependent on implementation details. To keep programmers from writing such code, Dave Parnas advocated hiding code from programmers of other modules so that they would be unable to write code that depended on the details [Parnas 1971]. I believe this position is too extreme, because it conflicts with other desirable activities such as code reading. Encapsulation makes it safer for programmers to read code.

Specifications are needed to describe what the module is supposed to do in an implementation-independent way so that many different implementations are allowed. (Code is not a satisfactory description because it does not distinguish what is required from ways of achieving it. One of the striking aspects of much of the work on object-oriented programming has been its lack of understanding of the importance of specifications; instead the code is taken as the definition of behavior.) Given a specification, one can develop an implementation without needing to consider any other part of the program. Furthermore, the program will continue to work properly when a new implementation is substituted for the old, providing the new implementation satisfies the specification (and assuming the old implementation did, too). Specifications also allow code that uses the abstraction to be written before code that implements the abstraction, and therefore are necessary if you want to do top-down implementation.

Work on specifications of data abstractions and on the related area of reasoning about correctness in programs that use and implement data abstraction started in the early seventies [Hoare 1972; Parnas 1972b; Zilles, 1974a, 1975] and continued for many years (see, e.g., [Wulf 1976; Goguen 1975; Guttag 1975, 1977; Berzins 1979; Parnas 1972b; Spitzen 1975; Guttag 1980]). Verification methods work only when the type's implementation is encapsulated (actually, protection against modification of the representation from outside the module is sufficient), because otherwise it would not be possible to limit one's attention to just a single module's implementation. If a language enforces encapsulation, independent reasoning about modules is on a sound foundation. Otherwise, it is not and a complete proof requires a global analysis. In essence, having a language enforce encapsulation means that the compiler proves a global property of a program; given this proof, the rest of the reasoning can be localized.

Languages that enforce encapsulation are based on a "less is more" kind of philosophy. The idea is that something can be gained by having a programmer give up some freedom. What is gained is global: increased ease in reasoning about an entire, multimodule program. What is lost is local: a programmer must live by the rules, which can sometimes be inconvenient.

10.3 CLU

Although I was not thinking about developing a complete, implemented programming language when I first worked on data abstraction, I took this next step quite soon, sometime in the spring or summer of 1973. By the time work began in earnest on the language design in the fall of 1973, many details of the language were already set. For example, we had already decided to implement abstract types with clusters, to keep objects in the heap, and to do complete type checking. However, there was lots of work left to do to design all the language features and their interactions.

In this section I provide a history of the CLU development. I begin by describing our goals (section 10.3.1), the design process (section 10.3.2), and our design principles (section 10.3.3). The remaining sections discuss what I consider to be the important technical decisions made during the project. Details about project staffing and the phases of the project can be found in Appendices B and C, respectively.

10.3.1 Language Goals

The primary goal of the project was to do research on programming methodology:

> We believe the best approach to developing a methodology that will serve as a practical tool for program construction is through the design of a programming language such that problem solutions developed using the methodology are programs in the language. Several benefits accrue from this approach. First, since designs produced using the methodology are actual programs, the problems of mapping designs into programs do not require independent treatment. Secondly, completeness and precision of the language will be reflected in a methodology that is similarly complete and precise. Finally, the language provides a good vehicle for explaining the methodology to others [Liskov 1974b, p. 35].

We recognized early on that implementations are not the same as abstractions. An implementation is a piece of code; an abstraction is a desired behavior, which should be described independently from the code, by means of a specification. Thus, our original proposal to NSF says: "An abstract data type is a concept whose meaning is captured in a set of specifications, while a cluster provides an implementation of a data type" [Dennis 1974, p. 21]. An implementation is correct if it "satisfies" the abstraction's specification. There was a great deal of interest in the group in specification and verification techniques, especially for data abstractions. This started with Steve Zilles' early work on algebraic specifications, which was mentioned in the proposal and also in the progress report for 1973–1974 [Liskov 1974b]; work on specifications was discussed briefly in section 10.2.2. However, unlike the Alphard group, we chose to separate the work on specifications from the language definition. I believed that the language should contain only declarations that the compiler could make use of, and not statements that it would treat simply as comments. I think this decision was an important factor in our ability to make quick progress on the language design.

The work on CLU occurred at MIT within the Laboratory for Computer Science with support from the National Science Foundation and DARPA. We believed that our main "product" was concepts rather than the language. We thought of our primary output as being publications, and that success would be measured by our influence on programming methodology and practice, and on future programming languages. We did not think of CLU as a language that would be exported widely. Instead, we were concerned primarily with the export of ideas.

CLU was intended to be a general purpose programming language, although it was geared more toward symbolic than numerical computing. It was not oriented toward low-level system programming (for example, of operating systems), but it can be used for this purpose by the addition of a few data types implemented in assembler, and the introduction of some procedures that provide "unsafe features." This is the technique that we have used in our implementations. For example, we have a procedure in the library called "_cvt" that can be used to change the type of an object. Such features are not described in the CLU reference manual; most users are not supposed to use them. I believe this is a better approach than providing a generally unsafe language like C, or a language with unsafe features, like Mesa [Mitchell 1978], because it discourages programmers from using the unsafe features casually.

CLU was intended to be used by "experienced" programmers. Programmers would not have to be wizards, but they were not supposed to be novices either. Although CLU (unlike Pascal) was not designed to be a teaching language, we use it this way and it seems to be easy to learn (we teach it to MIT sophomores).

CLU was geared toward developing production code. It was intended to be a tool for "programming in the large," for building big systems (for example, several hundred thousand lines) that require many programmers to work on them. (Such large systems have not been implemented in CLU, but systems containing 40–50 thousand lines of code have been.) As the work on CLU went on, I developed a programming methodology for such systems [Liskov 1979a, 1986]. CLU favors program readability and understandability over ease of writing, because we believed that these were more important for our intended users.

10.3.2 The Design Process

There were four main language designers: myself, and three graduate students, Russ Atkinson, Craig Schaffert, and Alan Snyder. Steve Zilles was deeply involved in the early work on the language, but by 1974 Steve was concentrating primarily on his work on specifications of abstract types, and acted more as an interested onlooker and critic of the developing design. As time went by, other students joined the group including Bob Scheifler and Eliot Moss. (A list of those who participated in the design is given in Appendix B.)

The design was a real group effort. Usually it is not possible to identify an individual with a feature (iterators are the exception here, as discussed in section 10.3.10). Instead, ideas were developed in meetings, worked up by individuals, evaluated in later meetings, and then reworked.

I was the leader of the project and ultimately made all the decisions, although often we were able to arrive at a consensus. In our design meetings we sometimes voted on alternatives, but these votes were never binding. I made the actual decisions later.

Russ, Craig, and Alan (and later Bob and Eliot) were implementers as well as designers. All of us acted as "users"; we evaluated every proposal from this perspective (considering its usability and expressive power), as well as from a designer's perspective (considering both implementability, and completeness and well-definedness of semantics).

We worked on the implementation in parallel with the design. We did not allow the implementation to define the language, however. We delayed implementing features until we believed that we had completed their design, and if problems were discovered, they were resolved in design meetings. Usually, we did not introduce any new features into the language during the implementation, but there were a few exceptions (in particular, own data).

We provided external documentation for the language through papers, reference manuals, and progress reports. We documented the design as it developed in a series of internal design notes [PMG 1979a]. There were 78 notes in all; the first was published on December 6, 1973 and the last on July 30, 1979. The notes concentrated on the utility and semantics of proposed language features. Typically, a note would describe the meaning of a feature (in English) and illustrate its use through examples. Syntax was introduced so that we could write code fragments, but was always considered to be of secondary importance. We tended to firm up syntax last, at the end of a design cycle.

The group held weekly design meetings. In these meetings we evaluated proposed features as thoroughly as we could. The goal was to uncover any flaws, both with respect to usability and semantics. This process seemed to work well for us: we had very few surprises during implementation. We published (internal) design meeting minutes for most of our meetings [PMG 1979b].

The design notes use English to define the semantics of proposed constructs. We did not use formal semantics as a design tool because I believed that the effort required to write the formal definitions of all the many variations we were considering would greatly outweigh any benefit. We relied on our very explicit design notes and thorough analysis instead. I believe our approach was wise, and I would recommend it to designers today. During design what is needed is precision, which can be achieved by doing a careful and rigorous, but informal, analysis of semantics as you go along. It is the analysis process that is important; in its absence, a formal semantics is probably not much help. We provided a formal semantics (in several forms) when the design was complete [Schaffert 1978; Scheifler 1978]. It validated our design but did not uncover errors, which was gratifying. For us, the main virtue of the formal definition was as *ex post facto* documentation.

The group as a whole was quite knowledgeable about languages that existed at the time. I had used Lisp extensively and had also programmed in FORTRAN and ALGOL 60, Steve Zilles and Craig Schaffert had worked on PL/I compilers, and Alan Snyder had done extensive programming in C. In addition, we were familiar with ALGOL 68, EL/1, Simula 67, Pascal, SETL, and various machine languages. Early in the design process we did a study of other languages to see whether we should use one of them as a basis for our work [Aiello 1974]. We ultimately decided that none would be suitable as a basis. None of them supported data abstraction, and we wanted to see where that idea would lead us without having to worry about how it might interact with pre-existing features. However, we did borrow from existing languages. Our semantic model is largely borrowed from Lisp; our syntax is ALGOL-like.

We also had certain negative influences. We felt that Pascal had made too many compromises to simplify its implementation. We believed strongly in compile-time type checking but felt it was important for the language to support types in a way that provided adequate expressive power. We thought Pascal was deficient here, for example, in its inability (at the time) to support a procedure that could be passed different size arrays on different calls. We felt that ALGOL 68 had gone much too far in its support for overloading and coercions. We believed that a language must have very simple rules in this area or programs would be hard for readers to understand. This led us ultimately to our ideas about "syntactic sugar" (see section 10.3.8).

Simula 67 was the existing language that was closest to what we wanted, but it was deficient in several ways, some of which seemed difficult to correct:

1. Simula did not support encapsulation, so its classes could be used as a data abstraction mechanism only if programmers obeyed rules not enforced by the language.
2. Simula did not provide support for user-defined type "generators." These are modules that define groups of related types, for example, a user-defined set module that defines set[int], set[real], etc.
3. It did not group operations and objects in the way we thought they should be grouped, as discussed in section 10.3.4.
4. It treated built-in and user-defined types nonuniformly. Objects of user-defined types had to reside in the heap, but objects of built-in type could be in either the stack or the heap.

In addition, we felt that Simula's inheritance mechanism was a distraction from what we were trying to do. Of course, this very mechanism was the basis for another main language advance of the seventies, Smalltalk. The work on Smalltalk was concurrent with ours and was completely unknown to us until around 1976.

10.3.3 Design Principles

The design of CLU was guided by a number of design principles, which were applied quite consciously. The principles we used were the following:

1. Keep focused. The goal of the language design was to explore data abstraction and other mechanisms that supported our programming methodology. Language features that were not related to this goal were not investigated. For example, we did not look at extensible control structures. Also, although I originally intended CLU to support concurrency [Dennis 1974], we focused on sequential programs initially to limit the scope of the project, and eventually decided to ignore concurrency entirely. (We did treat concurrency in a successor language, Argus [Liskov 1983, 1988].)
2. Minimality. We included as few features as possible. We believed that we could learn more about the need for a feature we were unsure of by leaving it out: if it was there, users would use it without thinking about whether they needed it, but if it was missing, and they really needed it, they would complain.
3. Simplicity. Each feature was as simple as we could make it. We measured simplicity by ease of explanation; a construct was simple if we could explain it (and its interaction with other features) easily.
4. Expressive power. We wanted to make it easy for users to say the things we thought they needed to say. This was a major motivation, for example, for the exception mechanism. To a lesser extent, we wanted to make it hard to express things we thought should not be expressed, but we did not pay too much attention to this; we knew that users could write (what we thought were) bad programs in CLU if they really wanted to.
5. Uniformity. As much as possible, we wanted to treat built-in and user-defined types the same. For example, operations are called in the same way in both cases; user-defined types can make use of infix operators, and built-in types use our "`type_name$op_name`" syntax to name operations that do not correspond to operator symbols just like the user-defined types.
6. Safety. We wanted to help programmers by ruling out errors or making it possible to detect them automatically. This is why we have strong type checking, a garbage collected heap, and bounds checking.
7. Performance. We wanted CLU programs to run quickly, for example, close to comparable C programs. (Performance measurements indicate that CLU programs run at about half the speed of comparable C programs.) We also wanted fast compilation, but this was of secondary importance.

As usual, several of these goals are in conflict. Expressive power conflicts with minimality; performance conflicts with safety and simplicity. When conflicts arose we resolved them as best we could, by trading off what was lost and what was gained in following a particular approach. For example, we based our semantics on a garbage collected heap—even though it may require more expense at runtime—because it improves program safety and simplifies our data abstraction mechanism. A second example is our iterator mechanism; we limited the expressive power of the mechanism so that we could implement it using a single stack.

Concern for performance pervaded the design process. We always considered how proposed features could be implemented efficiently. In addition, we expected to make use of compiler optimizations to improve performance. Programming with abstractions means there are lots of procedure calls, for example, to invoke the operations of abstract types. In our September 1973 paper, Steve and I noted:

> The primary business of a programmer is to build a program with a good logical structure—one which is understandable and leads to ease in modification and maintenance. . . . We believe it is the business of the compiler to map good logical structure into good physical structure. . . . Each operator-use may be replaced either by a call upon the corresponding function in the cluster or by inline code for the corresponding function. . . . Inline insertion of the code for a function allows that code to be subject to the optimization transformations available in the compiler [Liskov 1973c, p. 32–33].

Thus we had in mind inline substitution followed by other optimizations. Bob Scheifler did a study of how and when to do inline substitution for his BS thesis [Scheifler 1976, 1977], but we never included it in our compiler because of lack of manpower.

10.3.4 Implementing Abstract Types

In CLU an abstract data type is implemented by a cluster, which is a program module with three parts (see Figure10.1): (1) a header listing the operations that can be used to create and interact with objects of that type; (2) a definition of the storage representation, or rep, that is used to implement the objects of the type; (3) procedures (and iterators—see section 10.3.10) that implement the operations listed in the header (and possibly some additional internal procedures and iterators as well). Only procedures inside the cluster can access the representations of objects of the type. This restriction is enforced by type checking.

There are two different ways to relate objects and operations:

1. One possibility is to consider the operations as belonging to the type. This is the view taken in both CLU and Alphard. (Alphard "forms" are similar to clusters.) In this case, a type can be thought of as defining both a set of objects and a set of operations. (The approach in Ada is a variation on this. A single module defines both the type and the operations. Operations have access to the representation of objects of their type because they are defined inside the module that defines the type. Several types can be defined in the same modules, and operations in the module can access the representations of objects of all these types.)
2. A second possibility is to consider the operations as belonging to the objects. This is the view taken in Simula, and also in Smalltalk and C++.

These two approaches have different strengths and weaknesses. The "operations in type" approach works well for operations like "+" or "union" that need to access the representations of two or more

FIGURE 10.1

The Structure of a Cluster

```
int_set = cluster is create, member, size, insert, delete, elements

    rep = array[int]

    % implementations of operations go here

end int_set
```

objects at once, because with this approach, any operation of the type can access the representation of any object of the type. The "operations in object" approach does not work so well for such operations because an operation can only access the representation of a single object, the one to which it belongs. On the other hand, if there can be more than one implementation for a type in existence within a program, or if there is inheritance, the "operations in object" approach works better, because an operation knows the representation of its object, and cannot rely on possibly erroneous assumptions about the representation of other objects, as it is unable to access these representations.

We believed that it was important to support multiple implementations but even more important to make binary operations like "+" work well. We did not see how to make the "operations in object" approach run efficiently for binary operations. For example, we wanted adding two integers to require a small number of machine instructions, but this is not possible unless the compiler knows the representation of integers. We could have solved this problem by treating integers specially (allowing just one implementation for them), but that seemed inelegant, and it conflicted with our uniformity goal. Therefore, a program in CLU can have only a single implementation for any given type (built-in or user-defined); this case is discussed further in section 10.3.11.

People have been working for the last 15 years to make integers run fast in object-oriented languages (see, for example, the work of Dave Ungar and Craig Chambers [Chambers 1990]). So in retrospect, it was probably just as well that we avoided this problem. During the design of CLU, we hypothesized that it might be sufficient to limit different implementations to different regions of a program [Liskov 1975a]. This idea was incorporated into Argus [Liskov 1983, 1988], the language we developed after CLU. In Argus the regions are called "guardians" and the same type can have different implementations in different guardians within the same program. Guardians can communicate using objects of a type where the implementations differ because the representation can change as part of the communication [Herlihy 1982].

10.3.5 Semantic Model

CLU looks like an ALGOL-like language, but its semantics is like that of Lisp: CLU objects reside in an object universe (or heap), and a variable just identifies (or refers to) an object. We decided early on to have objects in the heap, although we had numerous discussions about the cost of garbage collection. This decision greatly simplified the data abstraction mechanism (although I do not think we appreciated the full extent of the simplification until quite late in the project). A language that allocates objects only on the stack is not sufficiently expressive; the heap is needed for objects whose sizes must change and for objects whose lifetime exceeds that of the procedure that creates them. (Of course, it is possible for a program to do everything using a stack—or FORTRAN common—but only at the cost of doing violence to the program structure.) Therefore, the choice is: just heap, or both.

Here are the reasons why we chose the heap approach (an expanded discussion of these issues can be found in [Moss 1978]):

1. Declarations are simple to process when objects are on the heap: the compiler just allocates space for a pointer. When objects are on the stack, the compiler must allocate enough space so that the new variable will be big enough to hold the object. The problem is that knowledge about object size ought to be encapsulated inside the code that implements the object's type. There are a number of ways to proceed. For example, in Alphard, the plan was to provide additional operations (not available to user code) that could be called to determine how much space to allocate; the compiler would insert calls to these operations when allocating space for variables. Ada requires that size information be made available to the compiler; this is why

type definitions appear in the "public" part of a module. However, this means that the type's representation must be defined before any modules that use the type can be compiled, and also, if the representation changes, all using modules must be recompiled. The important point is that with the heap approach the entire problem is avoided.

2. The heap approach allows us to separate variable and object creation: variables are created by declarations, and objects are created explicitly by calling an operation. The operation can take arguments if necessary and can ensure that the new object is properly initialized so that it has a legitimate state. (In other words, the code can ensure that the new object satisfies the rep invariant [Hoare 1972; Guttag 1975].) In this way we can avoid a source of program errors. Proper initialization is more difficult with the stack approach because arguments are often needed to do it right. Also, the heap approach allows many creation operations, for example, to create an empty set, or a singleton set; having many creation operations is more difficult with the stack approach.
3. The heap approach allows variable and object lifetimes to be different. With the stack approach they must be the same; if the object is to live longer than the procedure that creates it, a global variable must be used. With the heap approach, a local variable is fine; later a variable with a longer lifetime can be used, for example, in the calling procedure. Avoiding global variables is good because they interfere with the modular structure of the program (as was pointed out by Wulf and Shaw [Wulf 1973]).
4. Assignment has a type-independent meaning with the heap approach;

   ```
   x := e
   ```

   causes x to refer to the object obtained by evaluating expression e. With the stack approach, evaluating an expression produces a value that must be copied into the assigned variable. To do this right requires a call on the object's assignment operation, so that the right information is copied. In particular, if the object being copied contains pointers, it is not clear whether to copy the objects pointed at; only the implementer of the type knows the right answer. The assignment operation needs access to the variable containing the object being copied; really call-by-reference is required. Alphard did copying right because it allowed the definers of abstract types to define the assignment operation using by-reference parameters. Ada did not allow user-defined operations to control the meaning of assignment; at least this is, in part, because of the desire to treat call-by-reference as an optimization of call-by-value/result, which simply will not work in this case.

One unusual aspect of CLU is that our procedures have no free (global) variables (this is another early decision that is discussed in our September, 1973 paper [Liskov, 1973c]). The view of procedures in CLU is similar to that in Lisp: CLU procedures are not nested (except that procedures can be local to a cluster) but instead are defined at the "top" level, and can be called from any other module. In Lisp such procedures can have free variables that are scoped dynamically, a well-known source of confusion. We have found that free variables are rarely needed. This is probably attributable partly to data abstraction itself, because it encourages grouping related information into objects, which can then be passed as arguments.

In fact, CLU procedures do not share variables at all. In addition to there being no free variables, there is no call-by-reference. Instead arguments are passed "by object"; the (pointer to the) object resulting from evaluating the actual argument expression is assigned to the formal. (Thus passing a parameter is just doing an assignment to the formal.) Similarly, a pointer to a result object is returned to the caller. We have found that ruling out shared variables seems to make it easier to reason about programs.

A CLU procedure can have side effects only if the argument objects can be modified (because it cannot access the caller's variables). This led us to the concept of "mutable" objects. Every CLU object has a state. The states of some objects, such as integers and strings, cannot change; these objects are "immutable." Mutable objects (e.g., records and arrays) can have a succession of states. We spent quite a bit of time discussing whether we should limit CLU to just immutable objects (as in pure Lisp) but we concluded that mutable objects are important when you need to model entities from the real world, such as storage. (Probably this discussion would not have been so lengthy if we had not had so many advocates of dataflow attending our meetings!) It is easy to define a pure subset of CLU by simply eliminating the built-in mutable types (leaving their immutable counterparts, e.g., sequences are immutable arrays).

CLU assignment causes sharing: after executing "x := y," variables x and y both refer to the same object. If this object is immutable, programs cannot detect the sharing, but they can if the shared object is mutable, because a modification made via one variable will be visible via the other one. People sometimes argue that sharing of mutable objects makes reasoning about programs more difficult. This has not been our experience in using CLU. I believe this is true in large part because we do not manipulate pointers explicitly. Pointer manipulation is clearly both a nuisance and a source of errors in other languages.

The cost of using the heap is greatly reduced by keeping small immutable objects of built-in types, such as integers and Booleans, directly in the variables that refer to them. These objects fit in the variables (they are no bigger than pointers) and storing them there is safe because they are immutable: Even though in this case, assignment does make a copy of the object, no program can detect it.

10.3.6 Issues Related to Safety

Our desire to make it easy to write correct programs led us to choose constructs that either ruled out certain errors entirely or made it possible to detect them automatically.

We chose to use garbage collection because certain subtle program errors are not possible under this semantics. Explicit deallocation is unattractive from a correctness point of view, because it can lead to both dangling references and storage leaks; garbage collection rules out these errors. The decision to base CLU on a garbage-collected heap was made during the fall of 1973 [Liskov 1974a].

Another important effect of the safety goal was our decision to have static type checking. We included here both checking within a module (e.g., a procedure or a cluster) and intermodule type checking; the interaction of type checking with separate compilation is discussed in section 10.3.11. Originally we thought we would need to do run-time checking [Liskov 1973c] and we planned to base our technique on that of Morris [Morris 1973a]. By early 1974, we realized that we could do compile-time checking [Liskov 1974a]; this issue is discussed further in section 10.3.7.

We preferred compile-time checking to run-time checking because it enabled better runtime performance and allowed us to find errors early. We based our checking on declarations, which we felt were useful as a way of documenting the programmer's intentions. (This position differs from that of ML [Milner 1990], in which type information is inferred from the way variables are used. We were not aware of work on ML until the late seventies.) To make the checking as effective as possible, we ruled out coercions (automatic type conversions). We avoided all declarative information that could not be checked. For example, we discussed declaring within a cluster whether the type being implemented was immutable. We rejected this because the only way the compiler could ensure that this property held was to disallow mutable representations for immutable types. We wanted to allow an immutable type to have a mutable representation. One place where this is useful is in supporting "benevolent side effects" that modify the representation of an object to improve performance of future operation calls without affecting the visible value of the object.

Type checking in CLU uses both structure and name equality. Name equality comes from clusters. If "foo" and "bar" are the names of two different clusters, the two types are not equal. (This is true even if they have the same representations; it is also true even if they have the same operations with the same signatures.) Structure equality comes from "equates." For example, if we have the two equates

```
t = array[int]
s = array[int]
```

then t = s. We decided not to allow recursion in equates on the grounds that recursion can always be accomplished by using clusters. Although this reasoning is correct, the decision was probably a mistake; it makes certain programs awkward to write because extraneous clusters must be introduced just to get the desired recursion.

Another decision made to enhance safety was not to require that variables be initialized by their declarations. CLU allows declarations to appear anywhere; they are not limited to just the start of a block. Nevertheless, sometimes when a variable is declared there is no meaningful object to assign to it. If the language requires such an assignment, it misses a chance to notice automatically if the variable is used before it is assigned. The definition of CLU states that this situation will be recognized. It is recognized when running under the debugger, but the necessary checking has never been implemented by the compiler. (This is the only thing in CLU that was not implemented.) Checking for proper variable initialization can usually be done by the compiler (using simple flow analysis), which would insert code to do run-time checks only for the few variables where the analysis is inconclusive. However, we never added the checking to the compiler (because of lack of manpower), and we did not want to do run-time checking at every variable use.

By contrast, we require that all parts of an object be initialized when the object is created, thus avoiding errors arising from missing components. We believed that meaningful values for all components exist when an object is created; in part this is true because we do not create the object until we need to, in part because creation happens as the result of an explicit call with arguments, if necessary, and in part because of the way CLU arrays are defined (see the following). This belief has been borne out in practice.

The differing positions on variable and object component initialization arose from an evaluation of performance effects as well as from concerns about safety. As mentioned, checking for variable initialization can usually be done by the compiler. Checking that components are initialized properly is much more likely to need to be done at run-time.

Finally, we took care with the definitions of the built-in types both to rule out errors and to enable error detection. For example, we do bounds checking for ints and reals. Arrays are especially interesting in this regard. CLU arrays cannot have any uninitialized elements. When they are created, they contain some elements (usually none) provided as arguments to the creation operation. Thereafter they can grow and shrink on either end; each time an array grows, the new element is supplied. Furthermore, bounds checking is done on every array operation that needs it (for example, when the ith element is fetched, we check to be sure that the index i is legal). Finally, arrays provide an iterator (see section 10.3.10) that yields all elements and a second iterator that yields all legal indices, allowing a programmer to avoid indexing errors altogether.

10.3.7 Parametric Polymorphism

I mentioned earlier that we wanted to treat built-in and user-defined types alike. Because built-in types could make use of parameters, we wanted to allow them for user-defined types too. At the same time we wanted to provide complete type checking for them.

For example, CLU arrays are parameterized. An "array" is not a type by itself. Instead it is a "type generator" that, given a type as a parameter, produces a type. Thus, given the parameter int, it produces the type array[int]. We say that providing the parameter causes the type to be "instantiated." It is clearly useful to have parameterized user-defined types; for example, using this mechanism we could define a set type generator that could be instantiated to provide set[int], set[char], set[set[char]], and so on.

The problem with type generators is how to type-check the instantiations. We limit actual values of parameters to compile time constants such as "3," "int," and "set[int]." However, when the parameter is a type, the type generator may need to use some of its operations. For example, to test for set membership requires the ability to compare objects of the parameter type for equality. Doing this requires the use of the "equal" operation for the parameter type.

Our original plan was to pass in a type-object (consisting of a group of operations) as an argument to a parameterized module, and have the code of the module check (at run-time) whether the type had the operations it needed with the proper signatures. Eventually we invented the "where" clause [Liskov 1977a], which describes the names and signatures of any operations the parameter type must have, for example,

```
set = cluster [t: type] is create, member, size, insert, delete, elements
      where t has equal: proctype (t, t) returns (bool)
```

Inside the body of a parameterized module, the only operations of a type parameter that can be used are those listed in the where clause. Furthermore, when the type is instantiated, the compiler checks that the actual type parameter has the operations (and signatures) listed in the where clause. In this way, complete compile-time checking occurs.

CLU was way ahead of its time in its solution for parameterized modules. Even today, most languages do not support parametric polymorphism, although there is growing recognition of the need for it (for example, [Cardelli 1988]).

10.3.8 Other Uniformity Issues

In the previous section I discussed how user-defined types can be parameterized just like built-in ones. In this section I discuss two other uniformity issues, the syntax of operation calls and syntax for expressions. I also discuss the way CLU views the built-in types, and what built-in types it provides.

A language such as CLU that associates operations with types has a naming problem: many types will have operations of the same name (e.g., "create," "equal," "size"), and when an operation is called we need some way of indicating which one is meant. One possibility is to do this with overloading, for example, "equal" denotes many procedures, each with a different signature, and the one intended is selected by considering the context of the call. This rule works fairly well (assuming no coercions) when the types of the arguments are sufficient to make the determination, for example, equal(s, t) denotes the operation named "equal" whose first argument is of s's type and whose second argument is of t's type. It does not work so well if the calling context must be considered, which is the case for all creation operations. For example, we can tell that set create is meant in the following code:

```
s: set[int] := create( )
```

but it is more difficult (and sometimes impossible) if the call occurs within an expression.

We wanted a uniform rule that applied to all operations of a type, including creation operations. Also, we were vehemently opposed to using complicated rules to resolve overloading (e.g., as in ALGOL 68). This led us to require instead that every call indicate explicitly the exact operation being called, for example,

```
s: set[int] := set[int]$create( )
```

In doing so, we eliminated overloading altogether: the name of an operation is always of the form t$o, where t is the name of its type, and o is its name within its type. This rule is applied uniformly to both built-in and user-defined types.

We also allow certain short forms for calls. Most languages provide an expression syntax that allows symbols such as "+" to be used and allows the use of infix notation. We wanted to provide this too. To accomplish this we used Peter Landin's notion of "syntactic sugar" [Landin 1964]. We allow common operator symbols but these are only short forms for what is really happening, namely a call on an operation using its full t$o name. When the compiler encounters such a symbol, it "desugars" it by following a simple rule: it produces t$o where t is the type of the first argument, and o is the operation name associated with the symbol. Thus "x + y" is desugared to "t$add(x, y)" where t is the type of x. Once the desugaring has happened, the compiler continues processing using the desugared form (it even does type checking using this form). In essence the desugared form is the canonical form for the program.

Not only is this approach simple and easy to understand, it applies to both built-in and user-defined types uniformly. To allow sugars to be used with a new type, the type definer need only choose the right names for the operations. For example, to allow the use of +, he or she names the addition operation "add." This notion of desugaring applies to all the arithmetic operations, to equality and related operations (e.g., <), and also to the operations that access and modify fields of records and elements of arrays.

We did not succeed in making built-in and user-defined types entirely alike, however. Some built-in types have literals (e.g., ints). Although we considered having a special literal notation for user-defined types, in the end we concluded that it offered very little advantage over regular calls of creation operations. Another difference is that there is more power in our parameterization mechanism for records than exists for user-defined types. A record type generator is parameterized by the names and types of its fields; different instantiations can have different numbers of fields, and the operation names are determined by the field names. User-defined type generators must have a fixed number of parameters, and the operation names are fixed when the type generator is defined.

Nevertheless, we achieved a design with a high degree of uniformity. This ultimately colored our view of the built-in types. We ceased to think of them as something special; instead they were just the types we provided. This led us to decide that we need not be parsimonious with the built-in types. For example, all the type generators come in mutable/immutable pairs, for example, array/sequence, record/struct, variant/oneof (these are tagged unions), although just providing the mutable generators would have been sufficient (and the decision to provide both mutable and immutable generators was made very late in the design). Naturally we thought of the built-in types in terms of their operations, because this was how we thought about all types. We were generous with the operations for built-in types: we provided all operations that we thought users might reasonably need, rather than a small subset that would have been semantically complete. I believe this is the proper view when defining a type (either built-in or user-defined) that is expected to be used by many different people.

The built-in types of CLU are similar to those of other modern languages. Procedures are first class values in CLU; we permit them to be passed as arguments, returned as results, and stored in data structures. We have an easy time with procedures because they are not allowed to have free variables and therefore we do not need to create closures for them. Recursive calls are permitted.

CLU provides a type called "any" that is the union of all types. An object of type any can be "forced" at run-time to its underlying type, but this does not lead to type errors, because an attempt to force the object to the wrong type will fail. A type such as "any" is needed in a statically typed language; in essence it provides an escape to run-time type-checking.

10.3.9 Exception Handling

I have already discussed the fact that the main goal of the work on CLU was to support a programming methodology. We had a strong belief that some kind of exception mechanism was needed for this. We wanted to support

> "robust" or "fault-tolerant" programs, i.e., programs that are prepared to cope with the presence of errors by attempting various error recovery techniques [Liskov 1975b, p. 9].

This means they must be prepared to check for "exceptional" conditions and to cope with them when they occur; a majority of the code is often dedicated to this. Without a good mechanism, this code is both hard to write and difficult to read. Also, we believed that support for exceptions

> strengthens the abstraction power of the language. Each procedure is expected to be defined over all possible values of its input parameters and all possible actions of the procedures it calls. However, it is not expected to behave in the same way in all cases. Instead, it may respond appropriately in each case [Liskov 1975b, p. 11].

Therefore, we decided that CLU ought to have an exception mechanism. Support for such a mechanism was already a goal in early 1974 [Zilles 1974b]. In doing the design, we were aware of mechanisms in PL/I, Mesa [Mitchell 1978; Lampson 1974], and also Roy Levin's thesis [Levin 1977] and the paper by John Goodenough [Goodenough 1975].

CLU provides an exception mechanism based on the termination model of exceptions: A procedure call terminates in one of a number of conditions; one is the "normal" return and the others are "exceptional" terminations. We considered and rejected the resumption model present in both PL/I and Mesa because it was complex and also because we believed that most of the time, termination was what was wanted. Furthermore, if resumption were wanted, it could be simulated by passing a procedure as an argument (although closures would be useful here).

CLU's mechanism is unusual in its treatment of unhandled exceptions. Most mechanisms pass these through: if the caller does not handle an exception raised by a called procedure, the exception is propagated to its caller, and so on. We rejected this approach because it did not fit our ideas about modular program construction. We wanted to be able to call a procedure knowing just its specification, not its implementation. However, if exceptions are propagated automatically, a procedure may raise an exception not described in its specification.

Although we did not want to propagate exceptions automatically, we also did not want to require that the calling procedure handle all exceptions raised by the called procedure, because often these represented situations in which there was nothing the caller could do. For example, it would be a nuisance to have to provide handlers for exceptions that ought not to occur, such as a bounds exception for an array access when you have just checked that the index is legal. Therefore, we decided to turn all unhandled exceptions into a special exception called "failure" and propagate it. This mechanism seems to work well in practice.

The main decisions about our exception mechanism had been made by June 1975 [Liskov 1975b], but we noted that

> The hardest part of designing an exception handling mechanism, once the basic principles are worked out, is to provide good human engineering for catching exceptions [Liskov 1975b, p. 13].

We worked out these details over the following two years. We had completed the design by the fall of 1977; the mechanism is described in [Liskov 1977b, 1978a, 1979b].

CLU exceptions are implemented efficiently [Liskov 1978b]. As a result, they are used in CLU programs not just to indicate when errors occur but as a general way of conveying information from a called procedure to its caller.

10.3.10 Iterators

One of the tenets of the CLU design was that we were not going to do research on control structures. However, we did such work in defining the exception mechanism, and also in designing certain other control structures to make up for the lack of gotos (e.g., the **break** statement, which terminates a loop). We also did it in defining iterators.

Iterators were inspired by a construct in Alphard called a "generator" [Shaw 1976, 1977]. We first learned about this in the summer of 1975 when we visited the Alphard group at CMU. We were intrigued by generators because they solved some problems with data abstractions, but we thought they were too complicated. Russ Atkinson designed iterators on the airplane going back to Boston after this meeting and described them in a design note in September 1975 [Atkinson 1975].

The problem solved by both generators and iterators is the following: many data abstractions are collections of elements, and the reason for collecting the elements is so that later you can do something to them. Examples of such collections are arrays, sets, and lists. The problem is that for some types there is no obvious way to get to the elements. For arrays, you can use indexes; for lists, you can follow links. But for sets it is not clear what to do. What you would like is an operation of the type that provides the elements. Such an operation could be a procedure that returns an array containing the elements, but that is expensive if the collection is large. Instead, it would be nice to get at the elements one at a time. A generator does this by providing a group of operations, containing at least an operation to get the generation started, an operation to get the next element, and an operation to determine whether there are any more elements. Alphard generators had several more operations, and the Alphard designers worked out a way to use the for statement to call these operations at appropriate points.

A CLU iterator is a single operation that yields its results incrementally. For example,

```
elements = iter (s: set[t]) yields (t)
```

produces all the elements in set s, but it yields them one at a time. An iterator is called in a **for** statement:

```
for x: int in set[int]$elements(coll) do
    ...
```

The **for** loop begins by calling the iterator. Each time the iterator yields a result, the loop body is executed; when the body finishes, control resumes in the iterator, and when the iterator returns, the loop terminates. Also, if the loop body causes the loop to terminate, the iterator terminates.

Iterators are related to coroutines; the iterator and the body of the **for** loop pass control back and forth. However, their use is limited so that CLU programs can make do with a single stack. They are inexpensive: a yield effectively calls the loop body, which returns to the iterator when it is finished.

(Calls are very cheap in CLU.) Imposing the limitations on iterators was done to get the efficient, single stack implementation, albeit at the expense of some expressive power. For example, iterators cannot be used to compute whether two lists have the same elements, because to do this you need to iterate through the two lists side by side, and CLU only allows iterator calls to be nested.

10.3.11 Putting Programs Together

From the start, we believed that modules should be compiled separately and linked together to form programs. Furthermore we wanted to be able to compile programs that used abstractions before the used abstractions had been implemented or even fully defined (in the case of an abstract type, only some of the type's operations may be known when the type is invented). Nevertheless, we wanted to have complete intermodule type checking, and we wanted the checking to be accurate: when compiling a using module, we wanted to check the actual interface of the used module rather than some local definitions that might be wrong. (CLU modules are procedures, clusters, and iterators.)

By September 1973, we had already decided that CLU programs should be developed within a program library [Liskov 1973c]. The library contained "description units," each of which represented an abstraction. A description unit contained an interface specification for its abstraction; for a data abstraction, this consisted of the names and signatures of the operations. The description unit also contained zero or more implementations. Its interface specification could not be changed (after an initial period when the abstraction is being defined), but new implementations could be added over time.

When compiling a module, the compiler would use the interface specifications in description units in the library to type check all its uses of other modules. The module uses local names to refer to other modules:

> However, using the entire library to map a module-name provides too much flexibility and leads to the possibility of name conflicts. Instead the compiler interprets module-names using a directory supplied by the user [Liskov 1973c, p. 29].

The description units used in this way did not need to contain any implementations. Implementations would be selected in a separate step, at link time. In this way we could support top-down program construction, and we could change the implementation of a used module without having to recompile using modules. The library is described in the reference manual [Liskov 1979c, 1984].

The CLU library was never implemented because we never had enough time; it was finally implemented for Argus [Liskov 1983, 1988]. However, our compiler and linker provide an approximation to what we wanted. The compiler can be run in "spec" mode to produce interface specifications of a module or modules and store them in a file. One or more spec files can be supplied when compiling a module and the compiler will use the information in them to do intermodule type checking. Implementations are selected using the linker, which combines (object) files produced by the compiler into a program.

Our insistence on declared interface specifications contrasts with work on type inference, for example, in ML [Milner 1990]. I believe specifications are crucial because they make it possible for programmers to work independently; one person can implement an abstraction while others implement programs that use it. Furthermore, the compiler should use the information in the specification because this makes top-down implementation possible. Inference could still be used within the body of a module, however.

10.4 EVALUATION

The main goal of the work on CLU was to contribute to research in programming methodology. We hoped to influence others through the export of ideas rather than by producing a widely used tool. In this section I discuss the success of CLU as a programming tool and a programming language, and also its influence on programming methodology.

CLU has been used in a number of applications including a text editor called TED that is still in use today, a WYSIWYG editor called ETUDE, a browser for database conceptual schemas, a circuit design system, a gate array layout system, and the LP theorem-proving system [Garland 1990] and other related work in rewriting systems [Anantharaman 1989]. These projects vary in size; some were large projects involving several programmers and lasting several years. CLU is still being used in the work on LP.

CLU has also been used in teaching; this is probably its main use today both at MIT and elsewhere (for example, at the Tokyo Institute of Technology where it is "the language" in the Information Science department [Kimura 1992]). It is the basis of a book on programming methodology that I wrote with John Guttag [Liskov 1986]. It is used at MIT in our software engineering course and also in our compiler construction course.

In addition, CLU has been used in research. There have been follow-on projects done elsewhere including a CLU-based language developed in Finland [Arkko 1989], and a parallel version of CLU called CCLU [Bacon 1988a; Cooper 1987] developed at Cambridge University in England. CCLU grew out of the Swift project at MIT [Clark 1985], in which CLU was extended and used as a system programming language. It has been widely used in research at Cambridge [Bacon 1988b; Craft 1983]. CLU was also the basis of my own later work on Argus [Liskov 1983, 1988], a programming language for distributed systems.

Although CLU has been exported to several hundred sites over the years, it is not used widely today. In retrospect, it is clear that we made a number of decisions that followed from our view of CLU as a research vehicle but made it highly unlikely that CLU would succeed in the marketplace. We did not take any steps to promote CLU or to transfer it to a vendor to be developed into a product. Furthermore, in developing our compiler, we emphasized performance over portability, and the compiler is difficult to port to new machines. (This problem is being corrected now with our new portable compiler.) Finally, we were very pure in our approach to the language; a practical tool might need a number of features we left out (for example, formatted I/O).

In spite of the fact that it is not widely used, I believe that CLU was successful as a language design. CLU is neat and elegant. It makes it easier to write correct programs. Its users like it (to my surprise, they even like the "t$o" notation because they believe it enhances program correctness and readability). CLU does not contain features that we would like to discard, probably because we were so parsimonious in what we put in. Its features have stood the test of time. It is missing some desirable features including recursive type definitions and a closure mechanism. (Some of these features have been put into Argus.)

CLU has been an influence on programming languages both directly and indirectly. Many of the features of CLU were novel; in addition to the support for data abstraction through clusters, there are iterators, the exception mechanism, and the mechanism for parametric polymorphism. These ideas have had an important impact on programming language design and CLU's novel features have made their way into many modern languages. Among the languages influenced by CLU are Ada, Cedar/Mesa [Horning 1991], C++, ML, Modula 3 [Nelson 1991], and Trellis/Owl [Schaffert 1986].

CLU is an object-oriented language in the sense that it focuses attention on the properties of data objects and encourages programs to be developed by considering abstract properties of data. It differs from what are more commonly called object-oriented languages in two ways. The first difference is relatively small: CLU groups operations with types whereas object-oriented languages group them with objects. The other is more significant: CLU lacks an inheritance mechanism. Object-oriented languages use inheritance for two purposes. Inheritance is used to achieve "subtype polymorphism," which is the ability to design by identifying a generic abstraction and then defining more specific variants of that abstraction as the design progresses (for example, "windows" with "bordered windows" as a subtype). Inheritance is also used to develop code by modifying existing code, and in most object-oriented languages, encapsulation can be violated, because the designer of the subclass can make use of implementation details of the superclass. Of course, this means that if the superclass implementation is changed, all the subclasses will need to be reimplemented. I think this use of inheritance is not desirable in production programs or in programs developed by many people.

I believe that subtype polymorphism is a useful program development idea. If CLU were being designed today, I would probably try to include it. I am doing such a design in my current research on an object-oriented database system called Thor [Liskov, 1992].

The work on CLU, and other related work such as that on Alphard, served to crystallize the idea of a data abstraction and make it precise. As a result, the notion is widely used as an organizing principle in program design and has become a cornerstone of modern programming methodology.

ACKNOWLEDGMENTS

I consulted a number of people about historical matters, including Russ Atkinson, Austin Henderson, Jim Horning, Eliot Moss, Greg Nelson, Bob Scheifler, Mary Shaw, Alan Snyder, and Steve Zilles. In addition, several people gave me comments about earlier drafts of this paper, including Mark Day, Dorothy Curtis, John Guttag, Jim Horning, Daniel Jackson, Butler Lampson, Eliot Moss, Rishiyur Nikhil, Bob Scheifler, and Alan Snyder, and the referees.

APPENDIX A. PEOPLE WHO ATTENDED THE HARVARD MEETING

There were about twenty attendees at the Harvard meeting, including: Brian Clark, Ole-Johan Dahl, Jack Dennis, Nico Habermann, Austin Henderson, Carl Hewitt, Tony Hoare, Jim Horning, Barbara Liskov, Jim Mitchell, James H. Morris, John Reynolds, Doug Ross, Mary Shaw, Joe Stoy, Bill Wulf, and Steve Zilles.

APPENDIX B. PEOPLE INVOLVED IN THE CLU EFFORT

CLU originated in joint work between myself and Steve Zilles, with Austin Henderson acting as an interested observer and critic. Most of the work on the CLU design was done by myself, Russ Atkinson, Craig Schaffert, and Alan Snyder, but others also contributed to the design, including Toby Bloom, Deepak Kapur, Eliot Moss, Bob Scheifler, and Steve Zilles. Over the course of the CLU project, the CLU group also included Jack Aiello, Valdis Berzins, Mark Laventhal, and Bob Principato. In addition to members of the CLU group, the CLU meetings in the first two years were attended by Nimal Amersinghe, Jack Dennis, Dave Ellis, Austin Henderson, Paul Kosinski, Joe Stoy, and Eiiti Wada.

The first CLU implementation was done by Russ Atkinson, Craig Schaffert, and Alan Snyder. Eliot Moss and Bob Scheifler worked on later implementations. Still later implementation work was done by Paul Johnson, Sharon Perl, and Dorothy Curtis.

APPENDIX C. PROJECT SCHEDULE

From the time the design started in 1973 until we had our production compiler in 1980, I estimate that approximately fourteen person-years were spent on CLU. Until 1978, all of this work was done by myself and students. In June of 1978, Bob Scheifler became a member of the full-time technical staff, and Paul Johnson joined the group in March, 1979. By then, the research group was working on the Argus project [Liskov 1983, 1988]. Bob and Paul worked on the CLU implementation, but they also spent part of their time contributing to our work on Argus.

The work on CLU proceeded in several stages:

CLU .5

The first stage was the design and implementation of a preliminary version of CLU called CLU .5. This work started in the fall of 1973. At first language design issues were considered at meetings of a group that included both people interested in CLU and people working on Jack Dennis' dataflow language [Dennis 1975]. In fact, our initial plan was to use the dataflow work as a basis for the CLU definition [Dennis 1974], but this plan was dropped sometime in 1974. The two groups began to meet separately in January 1974, although members of the data flow group continued to attend CLU meetings. Most of the work between meetings was done by members of the CLU group, especially Russ, Craig, Alan, and myself; Steve and Austin also joined in some of this work.

The goal over the first year was to define a preliminary version of CLU that could be implemented as a proof of concept. Work on the compiler started in summer 1974 and was done by Alan (the parser), Russ (the code generator), and Craig (the type checker). At first the code generator produced Lisp; later, for political reasons, it was changed to produce MDL [Falley 1977]. (MDL was a dialect of Lisp that contained a richer set of data structures and did some compile-time type checking.) The compiler was initially implemented in Lisp, but was soon rewritten in CLU. Using CLU to implement its own compiler was very helpful to us in evaluating its expressive power. The implementation was done for the PDP-10.

CLU .5 is described in [Liskov 1974c] and also in the preliminary reference manual, which was published (internally only) in January 1975 [Snyder 1975]. It included all of current CLU (in some form) except for exception handling and iterators. It had parameterized types (type definitions that take types as parameters and can be instantiated to produce types), but the mechanism required type checking at run-time. At that point it was unclear to us whether parameterized types really could be type-checked statically.

CLU

At the same time that we were implementing CLU .5, we continued work on the design of CLU. All the features of CLU were designed and integrated into the language by the end of 1976. A paper documenting CLU at this stage appeared in early 1976 [Liskov 1976] and another one in early 1977 [Liskov 1977c]. After we felt that we understood every part of CLU, we spent most of 1977 reviewing the design and made lots of small changes, for example, to the syntax. As we went along, we changed the compiler to match the language. The CLU reference manual was published in July 1978 [Liskov 1978a].

In 1977, we reimplemented the compiler so that it generated instructions in macro-assembler rather than MDL, leading to both faster run-time execution and faster compilation. (MDL had a very slow compiler and we found the time taken to do double compilation—from CLU to MDL to assembler—very annoying.) Going directly to assembler meant that we had to write our own standalone run-time system, including the garbage collector. In addition, we had to provide our own debugger. In doing the move we designed new implementation techniques for iterators, exception handling, and parameterized modules; these are described in [Liskov 1978b]. Bob Scheifler did the compiler front end, Russ Atkinson implemented the run-time system (as macros) and the debugger, and Eliot Moss wrote the garbage collector.

Finishing Up

We did a final pass at the language design during 1979. We had quite a bit of user experience by then and we added some features that users had requested, most notably the "resignal" statement (this is part of our exception mechanism), and "own" data. Our last design note appeared in July, 1979. The final version of the reference manual was published in October 1979 [Liskov 1979c, 1984].

The compiler was changed to accept the new features, and also to produce machine code rather than macros; the compiler produced code for DEC System 20. Only at this point did we provide static instantiation of parameterized modules (in the linker, written by Paul Johnson); earlier implementations had used a dynamic approach, in which information about the parameters was passed to the code at run-time. We also finally provided an intermodule type-checking mechanism (see section 10.3.11). By 1980 we had a high quality compiler that could be exported to other groups with confidence.

Later we retargeted the compiler for VAXes and still later for M68000 machines (Sharon Perl did this port). Today we are moving CLU again, but this time we are changing the compiler to generate C so that it will be easy to port from now on; Dorothy Curtis is doing this work.

REFERENCES

[Aiello, 1974] Aiello, Jack, An investigation of current language support for the data requirements of structured programming, Technical Memo MIT/LCS/TM-51, MIT Laboratory for Computer Science, Cambridge, MA, September 1974.

[Anantharaman, 1989] Anantharaman, S., J. Hsieng, and J. Mzali, SbReve2: A term rewriting laboratory with AC-Unfailing completion, in *Proceedings of the 3rd International Conference on Rewriting Techniques and Applications*, 1989. Lecture Notes in Computer Science, 355, Springer-Verlag.

[Arkko, 1989] Arkko, J., V. Hirvisalo, J. Kuusela, E. Nuutila and M. Tamminen, XE reference manual (XE version 1.0), 1989. Dept. of Computer Science, Helsinki University of Technology, Helsinki, Finland.

[Atkinson, 1975] Atkinson, Russell, Toward more general iteration methods in CLU, CLU Design Note 54, Programming Methodology Group, MIT Laboratory for Computer Science, Cambridge, MA, Sept. 1975.

[Bacon, 1988a] Bacon J., and K. Hamilton, Distributed computing with RPC: The Cambridge approach, in Barton, M., et al., eds., *Proceedings of IFIPS Conference on Distributed Processing*, North Holland, 1988.

[Bacon, 1988b] Bacon J., I. Leslie, and R. Needham, Distributed computing with a processor bank, in *Proceedings of Workshop on Distributed Computing*, Berlin: 1988. Also Springer Verlag Lecture Notes in Computer Science, 433, 1989.

[Balzer, 1967] Balzer, Robert M., Dataless programming, in *Fall Joint Computer Conference*, 1967.

[Berzins, 1979] Berzins, Valdis, Abstract model specifications for data abstractions, Technical Report MIT/LCS/TR-221, MIT Laboratory for Computer Science, Cambridge, MA, July 1979.

[Cardelli, 1988] Cardelli, Luca, A semantics of multiple inheritance, *Information and Computation*, 76, 1988, 138–164.

[Chambers, 1990] Chambers, Craig, and David Ungar, Iterative type analysis and extended message splitting: Optimizing dynamically-typed object-oriented programs, in *Proceedings of the ACM SIGPLAN '90 Conference on Programming Language Design and Implementation*, June 1990.

[Clark, 1985] Clark, David, The structuring of systems using upcalls, in *Proceedings of the Tenth ACM Symposium on Operating Systems Principles*, Orcas Island, WA: ACM 1985.

[Cooper, 1987] Cooper, R., Pilgrim: A debugger for distributed systems, in *Proceedings of IEEE 7th ICDCS*, Berlin: 1987.

[Craft, 1983] Craft, D., Resource management in a decentralised system, *Operating Systems Review*, 17:5, June 1983, 11–19.

[Dahl, 1970] Dahl, O.-J., B. Myhrhaug, and K. Nygaard, The Simula 67 common base language, Publication No. S-22, Norwegian Computing Center, Oslo, 1970.

[Dennis, 1974] Dennis, Jack, and Barbara Liskov, Semantic foundations for structured programming, Proposal to National Science Foundation, 1974.

[Dennis, 1975] Dennis, Jack, A first version of a data flow procedure language, Project MAC Technical Memorandum 66, Cambridge, MA: MIT Laboratory for Computer Science, May 1975. Also published in *Proceedings of Symposium on Programming*, Institut de Programmation, University of Paris, Paris, France, Apr. 1974, 241–271.

[Dijkstra, 1968a] Dijkstra, Edsger W., Go To statement considered harmful, *Communications of the ACM*, 11:3, Mar. 1968, 147–148.

[Dijkstra, 1968b] Dijkstra, Edsger W., The structure of the "THE"-multiprogramming system, *Communications of the ACM*, 11:5, May 1968, 341–346.

[Dijkstra, 1969] Dijkstra, Edsger W., Notes on structured programming, in *Structured Programming*, Academic Press, 1969.

[Earley, 1971] Earley, Jay, Toward an understanding of data structures, *Communications of the ACM*, 14:10, October 1971, 617–627.

[Falley, 1977] Falley, Stuart W., and Greg Pfister, *MDL—Primer and Manual*, MIT Laboratory for Computer Science, Cambridge, MA, 1977.

[Garland, 1990] Garland, Stephen, John Guttag, and James Horning, Debugging Larch shared language specifications, *IEEE Transactions on Software Engineering*, 16:9, Sept. 1990, 1044–1057.

[Goguen, 1975] Goguen, J. A., J. W. Thatcher, E. G. Wagner, and J. B. Wright, Abstract data-types as initial algebras and correctness of data representations, in *Proceedings of Conference on Computer Graphics, Pattern Recognition and Data Structure*, May 1975.

[Goodenough, 1975] Goodenough, John, Exception handling: Issues and a proposed notation, *Communications of the ACM*, 18, Dec. 1975, 683–696.

[Guttag, 1975] Guttag, John, The specification and application to programming of abstract data types, Technical Report CSRG-59, Computer Systems Research Group, University of Toronto, Canada, 1975.

[Guttag, 1977] Guttag, John, Abstract data types and the development of data structures, *Communications of the ACM*, 20:6, June 1977. Also in *Proceedings of Conference on Data: Abstraction, Definition and Structure*, Salt Lake City, UT, Mar. 1976.

[Guttag, 1980] Guttag, John, Notes on Type Abstraction (Version 2), *IEEE Transactions on Software Engineering*, SE-6:1, Jan. 1980, 13–23.

[Herlihy, 1982] Herlihy, Maurice, and Barbara Liskov, A value transmission method for abstract data types, *ACM Transactions on Programming Languages and Systems*, 4:4, Oct. 1982, 527–551.

[Hoare, 1972] Hoare, C. A. R., Proof of correctness of data representations, *Acta Informatica*, 4, 1972, 271–281.

[Horning, 1991] Horning, James, Private communication, 1991.

[Ichbiah, 1973] Ichbiah, Jean, J. Rissen, and J. Heliard, The two-level approach to data definition and space management in the LIS system implementation language, in *Proceedings of ACM SIGPLAN-SIGOPS Interface Meeting—Programming Languages-Operating Systems*, Savannah, GA: ACM, Apr. 1973.

[Kimura, 1992] Kimura, Izumi, Private communication, 1992.

[Lampson, 1974] Lampson, Butler, James Mitchell, and Edward Satterthwaite, On the transfer of control between contexts, in *Proceedings of Symposium on Programming*, Institut de Programmation, University of Paris, Paris, France: 1974.

[Landin, 1964] Landin, Peter, The mechanical evaluation of expressions, *Computer Journal*, 6:4, Jan. 1964, 308–320.

[Levin, 1977] Levin, Roy, Program structures for exceptional condition handling, Ph.D. dissertation, Dept. of Computer Science, Carnegie Mellon University, Pittsburgh, PA, 1977.

[Liskov, 1972a] Liskov, Barbara, A design methodology for reliable software systems, in *Proceedings of Fall Joint Computer Conference 41*, Part 1, IEEE, Dec. 1972. Also published in *Tutorial on Software Design Techniques*, Peter Freeman and A. Wasserman, Eds., IEEE, 1977, 53–61.

[Liskov, 1972b] Liskov, Barbara, The design of the Venus operating system, *Communications of the ACM*, 15:3, Mar. 1972. Also published in *Software Systems Principles: A Survey*, Peter Freeman, SRA Associates, Inc., Chicago 1975, 542–553.

[Liskov, 1973a] Liskov, Barbara, Report of session on structured programming, in *Proceedings of ACM SIGPLAN-SIGOPS Interface Meeting—Programming Languages-Operating Systems*, Savannah, GA: ACM, Apr. 1973.

[Liskov, 1973b] Liskov, Barbara, Fundamental studies group progress report, in *Project MAC Progress Report X*, Cambridge, MA: MIT Laboratory for Computer Science 1973.

[Liskov, 1973c] Liskov, Barbara, and Stephen Zilles, An approach to abstraction, Computation Structures Group Memo 88, MIT Laboratory for Computer Science, Cambridge, MA, September 1973.

[Liskov, 1974a] Liskov, Barbara, and Stephen Zilles, Programming with abstract data types, in *Proceedings of ACM SIGPLAN Conference on Very High Level Languages*, ACM 1974.

[Liskov, 1974b] Liskov, Barbara, Fundamental studies group progress report, in Project MAC Progress Report XI, Cambridge, MA: MIT Laboratory for Computer Science 1974.

[Liskov, 1974c] Liskov, Barbara, A note on CLU, Computation Structures Group Memo 112, Laboratory for Computer Science, MIT, Cambridge, MA, Nov. 1974.

[Liskov, 1975a] Liskov, Barbara, Multiple implementation of a type, CLU Design Note 53, Cambridge, MA: MIT Laboratory for Computer Science, July 1975.

[Liskov, 1975b] Liskov, Barbara, Fundamental studies group progress report, in Laboratory for Computer Science Progress Report XII, Cambridge, MA: MIT Laboratory for Computer Science 1975.

[Liskov, 1976] Liskov, Barbara, Introduction to CLU, in S. A. Schuman, Ed., *New Directions in Algorithmic Languages 1975*, INRIA, 1976.

[Liskov, 1977a] Liskov, Barbara, Programming methodology group progress report, in Laboratory for Computer Science Progress Report XIV, Cambridge, MA: MIT Laboratory for Computer Science 1977.

[Liskov, 1977b] Liskov, Barbara, and Alan Snyder, Structured exception Handling, Computation Structures Group Memo 155, MIT Laboratory for Computer Science, Cambridge, MA, Dec. 1977.

[Liskov, 1977c] Liskov, Barbara, Alan Snyder, Russell Atkinson, and J. Craig Schaffert, Abstraction mechanisms in CLU, *Communications of the ACM*, 20:8, Aug. 1977, 564–576. Also published as Computation Structures Group Memo 144-1, MIT Laboratory for Computer Science, Cambridge, MA, Jan. 1977.

[Liskov, 1978a] Liskov, Barbara, Russell Atkinson, Toby Bloom, J. Eliot Moss, J. Craig Schaffert, Robert Scheifler, and Alan Snyder, CLU reference manual, Computation Structures Group Memo 161, MIT Laboratory for Computer Science, Cambridge, MA, July 1978.

[Liskov, 1978b] Liskov, Barbara, Russell Atkinson, and Robert Scheifler, Aspects of implementing CLU, in *Proceedings of the Annual Conference*, ACM 1978.

[Liskov, 1979a] Liskov, Barbara, Modular program construction using abstractions, Computation Structures Group Memo 184, MIT Laboratory for Computer Science, Cambridge, MA, Sept. 1979.

[Liskov, 1979b] Liskov, Barbara, and Alan Snyder, Exception Handling in CLU, *IEEE Transactions on Software Engineering*, SE-5:6, Nov. 1979, 546–558.

[Liskov, 1979c] Liskov, Barbara, Russell Atkinson, Toby Bloom, J. Eliot Moss, J. Craig Schaffert, Robert Scheifler, and Alan Snyder, CLU reference manual, Technical Report MIT/LCS/TR-225, MIT Laboratory for Computer Science, Cambridge, MA, Oct. 1979.

[Liskov, 1983] Liskov, Barbara, and Robert Scheifler, Guardians and actions: Linguistic support for robust, distributed programs, *ACM Transactions on Programming Languages and Systems*, 5:3, July 1983, 381–404.

[Liskov, 1984] Liskov, Barbara, Russell Atkinson, Toby Bloom, J. Eliot Moss, J. Craig Schaffert, Robert Scheifler, and Alan Snyder, *CLU Reference Manual*, Springer-Verlag, 1984. Also published as Lecture Notes in Computer Science 114, G. Goos and J. Hartmanis, Eds., Springer-Verlag, 1981.

[Liskov, 1986] Liskov, Barbara, and John Guttag, *Abstraction and Specification in Program Development*, Cambridge MA: MIT Press and McGraw Hill, 1986.

[Liskov, 1988] Liskov, Barbara, Distributed programming in Argus, *Communications of the ACM*, 31:3, Mar. 1988, 300–312.

[Liskov, 1992] Liskov, Barbara, Preliminary design of the Thor object-oriented database system, Programming Methodology Group Memo 74, MIT Laboratory for Computer Science, Cambridge, MA, March 1992.

[McKeag, 1973] McKeag, R. M., Programming languages for operating systems, in *Proceedings of ACM SIGPLAN-SIGOPS Interface Meeting—Programming Languages-Operating Systems*, Savannah, GA: ACM, Apr. 1973.

[Milner, 1990] Milner, Robin, M. Tofte, and R. Harper, *The Definition of Standard ML*, Cambridge, MA: MIT Press, 1990.

[Mitchell, 1978] Mitchell, James G., W. Maybury, and R. Sweet, Mesa language manual, Technical Report CSL-78-1, Xerox Research Center, Palo Alto, CA, Feb. 1978.

[Morris, 1973a] Morris, James H., Jr., Protection in programming languages, *Communications of the ACM*, 16:1, Jan. 1973, 15–21.

[Morris, 1973b] Morris, James H., Jr., Types are not sets, in *Proceedings of the Symposium on Principles of Programming Languages*, ACM 1973.

[Moss, 1978] Moss, J. Eliot, Abstract data types in stack based languages, Technical Report MIT/LCS/TR-190, Cambridge, MA: MIT Laboratory for Computer Science, Feb. 1978.

[Nelson, 1991] Nelson, Greg, Private communication, 1991.

[Palme, 1973] Palme, Jacob, Protected program modules in Simula 67, FOAP Report C8372-M3 (E5), Stockholm, Sweden: Research Institute of National Defence, Division of Research Planning and Operations Research, July 1973.

[Parnas, 1971] Parnas, David, Information distribution aspects of design methodology, in *Proceedings of IFIP Congress*, North Holland Publishing Co., 1971.

[Parnas, 1972a] Parnas, David, On the Criteria to be used in decomposing systems into modules, *Communications of the ACM*, 15:12, Dec. 1972, 1053–1058.

[Parnas, 1972b] Parnas, David, A Technique for the specification of software modules with examples, *Communications of the ACM*, 15, May 1972, 330–336.

[PMG, 1979a] Programming Methodology Group, *CLU Design Notes*, MIT Laboratory for Computer Science, Cambridge, MA, 1973–1979.

[PMG, 1979b] Programming Methodology Group, *CLU Design Meeting Minutes*, MIT Laboratory for Computer Science, Cambridge, MA, 1974–1979.

[Randell, 1969] Randell, Brian, Towards a methodology of computer systems design, in *Software Engineering*, P. Naur and B. Randell, Eds., NATO Science Committee, 1969.

[Ross, 1970] Ross, Douglas T., Uniform referents: An essential property for a software engineering language, in J. T. Tou, Ed., *Software Engineering*, Academic Press, 1970.

[Schaffert, 1978] Schaffert, J. Craig, A formal definition of CLU, Technical Report MIT/LCS/TR-193, MIT Laboratory for Computer Science, Cambridge, MA, Jan. 1978.

[Schaffert, 1986] Schaffert, Craig, T. Cooper, B. Bullis, M. Kilian and C. Wilpolt, An introduction to Trellis/Owl, in *Proceedings of ACM Conference on Object Oriented Systems, Languages and Applications*, Portland, OR: Sept. 1986.

[Scheifler, 1976] Scheifler, Robert, An analysis of inline substitution for a structured programming language, S.B. Thesis, Department of Electrical Engineering and Computer Science, Massachusetts Institute of Technology, Cambridge, MA, 1976.

[Scheifler, 1977] Scheifler, Robert, An analysis of inline substitution for a structured programming language, *Communications of the ACM*, 20:9, Sept. 1977.

[Scheifler, 1978] Scheifler, Robert, A denotational semantics of CLU, Technical Report MIT/LCS/TR-201, MIT Laboratory for Computer Science, Cambridge, MA, June 1978.

[Shaw, 1976] Shaw, Mary, William Wulf, and Ralph London, Carnegie Mellon University and USC Information Sciences Institute Technical Reports, Abstraction and verification in Alphard: Iteration and generators, Aug. 1976.

[Shaw, 1977] Shaw, Mary, William Wulf, and Ralph London, Abstraction and verification in Alphard: Defining and specifying iteration and generators, *Communications of the ACM*, 20:8, Aug. 1977.

[Shaw, 1981] Shaw, Mary, Ed., *ALPHARD: Form and Content*, Springer-Verlag, 1981.

[Snyder, 1975] Snyder, Alan and Russell Atkinson, Preliminary CLU reference manual, CLU design note 39, Programming Methodology Group, MIT Laboratory for Computer Science, Cambridge, MA, Jan. 1975.

[Spitzen, 1975] Spitzen, Jay, and Ben Wegbreit, The verification and synthesis of data structures, *Acta Informatica*, 4, 1975, 127–144.

[Wegbreit, 1972] Wegbreit, Ben, D. Brosgol, G. Holloway, Charles Prenner, and Jay Spitzen, *ECL Programmer's Manual*, Center for Research in Computing Technology, Harvard University, Cambridge, MA, 1972.

[Wegbreit, 1973] Wegbreit, Ben, *The Treatment of Data Types in EL1*, Center for Research in Computing Technology, Harvard University, Cambridge, MA, 1973.

[Wirth, 1971] Wirth, Niklaus, Program development by stepwise refinement, *Communications of the ACM*, 14:4, Apr. 1971, 221–227.

[Wulf, 1973] Wulf, William, and Mary Shaw, Global variables considered harmful, *SIGPLAN Notices*, 8:2, Feb. 1973, 28–34.

[Wulf, 1976] Wulf, William, Ralph London, and Mary Shaw, An introduction to the construction and verification of Alphard programs, *IEEE Transactions on Software Engineering*, SE-2:4, Dec. 1976, 253–265. Presented at Second International Conference on Software Engineering, Oct. 1976.

[Zilles, 1973] Zilles, Stephen, Procedural encapsulation: A linguistic protection technique, in *Proceedings of ACM SIGPLAN-SIGOPS Interface Meeting—Programming Languages-Operating Systems*, Savannah, GA: ACM, Apr. 1973.

[Zilles, 1974a] Zilles, Stephen, Computation structures group progress report, in Project MAC Progress Report XI, Cambridge, MA: MIT Laboratory for Computer Science 1974.

[Zilles, 1974b] Zilles, Stephen, Working notes on error handling, CLU design note 6, Cambridge, MA: MIT Laboratory for Computer Science, Jan. 1974.

[Zilles, 1975] Zilles, Stephen, Algebraic specification of data types, Computation Structures Group Memo 119, Cambridge, MA: MIT Laboratory for Computer Science, March 1975.

TRANSCRIPT OF PRESENTATION

BARBARA LISKOV: (SLIDE 1) I'm going to talk today about CLU, which is a programming language that I developed in the early to mid 1970s. I undertook the design of CLU because of my interest in program methodology. The work was motivated by the desire to improve the state of the art in methodology by coming to a better understanding of some of the main principles.

(SLIDE 2) In my talk today I'm going to begin by talking about some of the events that occurred before and during the development of CLU. Then I'll spend the second half of the talk on a technical history of some of the main ideas.

(SLIDE3) As I said before, CLU was motivated by work in programming methodology, and in the late sixties and early seventies, there was a lot of work going on in this area. There were two major directions that were important. The first was Dijkstra's notion of structured programming, where the idea was that you ought to organize your programs in a way that made them easy to understand and

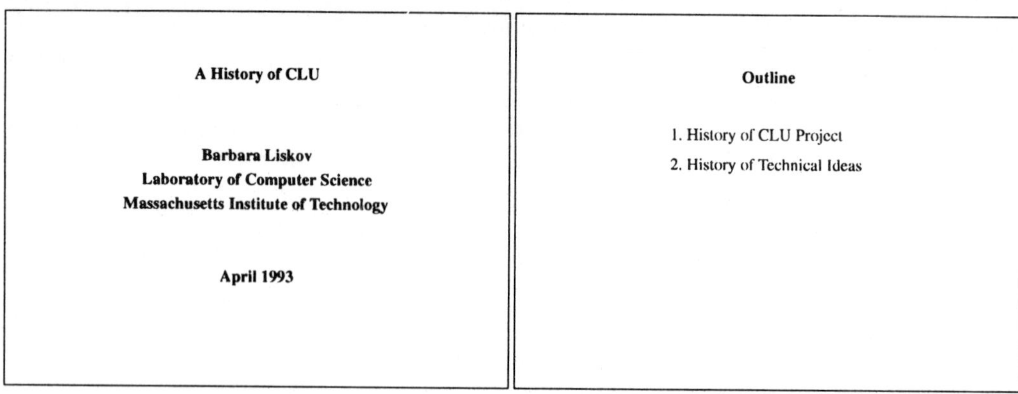

SLIDE 1

SLIDE 2

easy to reason about. This approach also led to the idea of the development of programs by step-wise refinement, where you would start with an abstract skeleton of your program and then gradually put more and more detail into the abstraction so you finally have running code. The other main direction was the idea of modularity using units larger than functions. Parnas was one of the main people who was working on this idea, but there were a number of other people as well. People interested in this kind of modularity acknowledged that procedures were a very important modularity concept, but they weren't sufficient for the building of programs. You also wanted to have units that were larger than individual procedures, that encapsulated state within them, and provided a number of procedures as an interface to the users. That's what I have illustrated at the bottom of the slide. I called these units "partitions" and there were numerous other names for them. The idea is that inside the box is a lot of hidden information that can be accessed only by calling the procedures that are represented as the lines going up.

(SLIDE 4) I had been working on this notion of programming methodology and had written a paper on it. I was concerned, however, that it seemed quite difficult to go from the papers that described the idea in the abstract, and maybe showed you how to apply it to a particular example, to a system of your own where you were trying to identify those kinds of modules in your own system. So, I was casting around for a way to make this idea more accessable to programmers. This is what I was

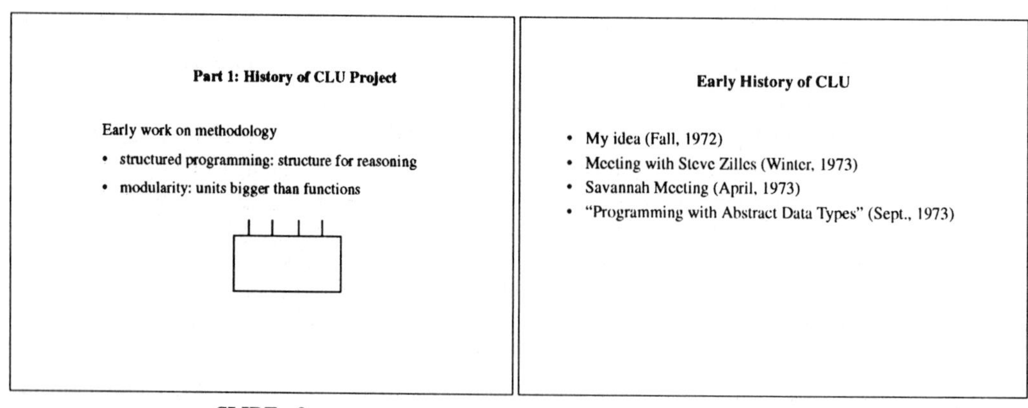

SLIDE 3

SLIDE 4

interested in at the time I joined the faculty at MIT in the fall of 1972. Sometime during that fall I got the idea that you could merge this idea of multiprocedure modules with the idea of a data type. So the idea was that the module itself would then become an abstract object. Inside the object there would be some hidden state information. And access to the object would happen through a set of operations that belonged to the object's type, which allowed the users to do whatever they wanted to with that object but hid from them how the object was actually represented in storage. I was very excited when I realized that I could put these two ideas together, because I felt that people were used to programming using data types. So, adding this idea of an abstract type wasn't going to change the way they went about their business very much. They just had to abstract a bit from the way they were used to doing things, so they could think about types that matched the objects in their application domain. In this way, they would achieve a modular structure of the sort that seemed good.

This work was something that I did in the fall of 1972. At that time, Steve Zilles was a graduate student at MIT and he had been working on similar ideas. We didn't actually meet until sometime in the late winter of that year, maybe around March. We started to talk together in April when there was a very interesting meeting held in Savannah, the SIGPLAN-SIGOPS Interface Meeting on Operating Systems and Programming Languages. At that meeting I gave a talk on my ideas on data abstraction and Steve had a paper. And there were several other papers there that were also related. For example, Mike McKeag had a paper on monitors. I found that meeting to be a very useful one for focusing attention on these ideas.

As a result of that meeting, Steve and I started to work together. We worked together through 1973. There was another student, Austin Henderson, also a graduate student, who sometimes acted as a consultant for us. We tried out our ideas on him. By the end of the summer of 1973, Steve and I had written a paper called "Programming with Abstract Data Types," that described our ideas on how to use data abstraction in programming. We submitted this to the Conference on Very High Level Languages at the end of that summer.

(SLIDE 5) Now, I hadn't really started on the design of CLU at this point. What happened was, after we had finished this work in the summer and had identified the outlines of a programming language construct, I made a decision to try and work on a full-fledged programming language. I decided that it was worth doing this for three reasons. First of all, to put something into a programming language you had to really work out the rules. So this was a way of making sure that I really understood what was going on with these abstract types, what the rules really were. Secondly, I felt that a language would be a really good way of communicating to programmers because programmers were used to thinking about programs in terms of programming language constructs. And then finally, of course, there was always the chance that you might have a language that was a useful tool at the end.

So, I decided that Fall to form the CLU group and three new graduate students joined that group: Russ Atkinson, Craig Schaffert, and Alan Snyder. They were all first-year graduate students. They, together with me, became the principle designers of the CLU language. Steve was still involved in the CLU design, but at that time he was working on his thesis which was concerned with the algebraic specifications of abstract types. He would listen to our discussions and make suggestions, but he really wasn't working on the language design.

During the course of the language design, we did several implementations including one of a subset of a language in 1974. One of things that was interesting about the design process, was that we were continually implementing as we went. As you can see, the most recent implementation was in 1990; it was done by a member of my group, Dorothy Curtis. This is a portable implementation that allows CLU to run on many different platforms.

(SLIDE 6) I wanted to talk a bit about what the state of the art in data types was at the time I started to work on CLU. There had been some early work on uniform referents and extensible languages,

CLU Design (1973—1979)

Russ Atkinson
Barbara Liskov
Craig Schaffert
Alan Snyder

Several Implementations (1974, 1977, 1980, 1986, 1990)

SLIDE 5

Data Types in 1972

- Uniform Referents (e.g., Balzer 1967)
- Extensible Languages (e.g., EL1, Wegbreit 1972)
- "Types are not Sets" (Morris 1973)
- "Global Variable Considered Harmful" (Wulf & Shaw 1973)
- Simula 67 (Dahl 1970, Hoare 1972)

SLIDE 6

which was getting at the idea of data abstractions by identifying the notion that there were certain operations associated with data types. This early work didn't get all the way to the idea of an abstract data type because the researchers had in mind a sort of fixed set of operations, but still, it was a step in that direction. In 1973, Jim Morris wrote a very influential paper called, "Types Are Not Sets," in which he pointed out that there was more to a data type than just the structure of the object. The objects also had a semantics that ought to be captured by their operations. In 1973, Bill Wulf and Mary Shaw published a paper called "Global Variable Considered Harmful." They were working on the Alphard Project, which along with CLU, was the other major project at that time exploring the idea of data abstraction. This paper gave some of the rationale as to why they were doing their work. And then, underlying all of this work, was Simula 67. Simula 67 was an amazing language that was way ahead of its time. Its class mechanism was a limited abstraction mechanism. At the time I started working on CLU, there was no encapsulation in Simula 67. But, you could use its classes to support abstract data types.

(SLIDE 7) This slide shows some of the work that went on at the same time as the CLU work. I have already mentioned the work on Alphard. Alphard went through many different designs, but it was never implemented. The work on Smalltalk was concurrent. Of course you will hear about that later in the session. I didn't know about the work on Smalltalk until the mid seventies, well after the CLU design was quite far underway. The work on monitors was contemporaneous; you heard Brinch Hansen talk about that yesterday. Monitors are a kind of limited data abstraction mechanism that includes synchronization concepts along with other things. The slide lists language-related work; in addition, that was a lot of work on programming methodology that was given a boost because of the work on CLU and Alphard: work on how to specify abstract data types, how to verify the implementation on abstract type; simply the idea that a type was distinct from any implementation of it was a major step forward. I did some of this work, and John Guttag and Steve Zilles were also working on this. It all came back to Tony Hoare's original paper, "Proofs of Correctness of Data Representations," published in 1972. And then, I was always very interested in the question of program methodology; that's where I came from. I built up a methodology based on data abstraction that developed into a course that I taught at MIT, and still teach. As a result of work on the course, I wrote a book with John Guttag explaining the methodology [Liskov 1986].

(SLIDE 8) I want to tell you what the design process for CLU was like. We had group meetings every week. One of the things we did at these meetings was to keep minutes. I don't know what led us to do this, but it was a very smart decision. Of course, I found these minutes extremely valuable

Contemporary Work

- Alphard
- Smalltalk
- Monitors
- Specification and Verification of Abstract Data Types
- Programming Methodology

SLIDE 7

The Design Process

- Weekly group meetings with minutes
- All points discussed in written design notes (1973–1979)
- Consensus with a leader
- Informal, not formal, semantics

SLIDE 8

when I came to write this paper. At the time, they were useful because you could go back and look at the details of an argument and see what problems people were concerned with. Of course, they were good for people who missed the meetings, to find out what had happened. The group meetings were quite large, because in addition to myself and Russ, Craig, and Alan, and a couple of other interested bystanders like Steve Zilles and Austin Henderson, there were other graduate students who joined the project later. And in addition, in the early stages, we were looking at things jointly with Jack Dennis' data flow language group. So a lot of people from the data flow group attended our meetings.

In the early stages of design, there was a lot of argument about whether CLU would or would not be a language with side effects. That influence on having a language without side effects was coming from the data flow group. Ultimately, pragmatic heads prevailed, namely, mine and those of my three students, because we believed that a practical programming language ought to be based on a paradigm that allowed state changes.

Of course, most of the work about the design of the language didn't happen in the meetings; it happened in between the meetings. We also adopted a philosophy of always writing up our design decisions in design notes written over a period of six years. There were, at the end of that time, 78 such design notes in all. In these design notes, we would pick up a problem, propose a number of solutions, and then try to analyze their strengths and weaknesses. In doing these arguments, we were focused on the semantics of the mechanisms. We weren't too concerned about the syntax, although we would usually propose a syntax so we would have something to talk about. This philosophy that semantics was much more important than syntax pervaded our design, so that at the very end of the design, in 1977 and 1978, we had a series of design meetings in which we argued about syntactic matters. It turned out to be surprisingly difficult to work out all the final details about what the syntax ought to be. Of course, syntax isn't as important as semantics, but it is nevertheless very important because it is the way people come to perceive your ideas.

In our design notes we did not use formal semantics, we used informal semantics. I believe that was a very good decision. What really matters in doing a design is getting a precise, complete understanding of the features that you are working on. It doesn't matter whether that understanding is expressed formally or informally. So we relied on a process of written and verbal presentation and analysis, and we treated our group meetings as problem-solving sessions where everybody attempted to probe the mechanisms that were being proposed, in order to decide whether there were any problems with them. We did do some formal semantics of the language, but after the fact. Our process was very successful because we didn't find errors in the language later. We did find one small error in an obscure part of the parameterized modules mechanism, but that was the only problem that was uncovered either by the implementation or by the formal semantics.

One final point about this process is that we tried to make decisions by consensus in these meetings. We even had votes about whether this mechanism was more desirable than that one. But, ultimately I made all the decisions. These votes were only advisory. They had no standing otherwise. Of course, we were a group working closely together, and we were pretty much in synch. Often my decisions went with the consensus but sometimes they didn't.

(SLIDE 9) Finally, we had a set of design principles that we kept in mind. These were explicitly stated, although we never actually wrote them down. The first one was very important: we decided to limit our goals. The purpose of the language design was to explore the idea of data abstraction, and we refrained from doing additional language design on other things that were not going to add to that goal. For example, we did not think about mechanisms for concurrency, and we did not think about control extensions. I think that decision contributed to the success of the project, because it allowed us to make progress and complete the work on the language design.

The other goals were what you would see in any language. By simplicity, what we meant was the ease with which you could explain a concept to people who were not involved in the design, but nevertheless programmers; and so ease of explanation, simplicity or shortness of explanation were the criteria we used. Uniformity meant to us the treatment of the abstract types with respect to the treatment of the built-in types. There were both kinds of types in the language and we wanted to treat them the same. We didn't want to have special things you could do with the built-in types that would not have worked for the abstract types. Of course, we wanted expressive power; everybody does. We wanted to allow people to say the right things easily. We knew that we couldn't keep them from saying the wrong things, but we tried to avoid mechanisms that made it easy for them to say the wrong things. Safety was a really important goal for us. We thought the language should prevent errors. For example, CLU's a garbage-collected language, so it's not possible to have dangling references. If you can't prevent errors altogether, the next best thing is to catch them at compile-time. For that reason, CLU is statically type checked. If you can't catch errors at compile time, the next best thing is to catch them automatically at run-time. And so, for that reason, we do automatic bounds checking for arrays. This concern with safety was so important that we sometimes made decisions that made the language more safe even though it was at the expense of a slower execution. However, performance was also an important goal. We always thought about how to implement our mechanisms efficiently. We did sometimes change mechanisms to enhance the speed of the possible implementation, but when there was a conflict among goals, particularly between performance and safety, which is where the biggest conflicts came in, the rule was that safety prevailed. I should say, by the way, that we didn't have explicit performance goals. But when the language was finally implemented by a high-quality compiler late in the game, we did compare performance using a set of standard benchmarks. It was half the speed of C, which we thought was quite good for a language that was garbage collected.

(SLIDE 10) Now I want to move on to the second part of the talk, the technical history. As I said, CLU is a heap-based language, with garbage collection, static type checking, and separate compilation. In fact, one thing I forgot to mention earlier was how knowledgeable the group was about programming languages that were extant at the time. I, of course, coming out of AI, had extensive experience using LISP, and other members of the group had extensive experience with other languages like PL/I, ALGOL 60; they knew about Pascal, ALGOL 68, and so on. I would say that CLU really is LISP clothed in ALGOL 60-like syntax. Like LISP, CLU is a heap-based language with garbage collection and separation compilation. Also, as in LISP you build a program by writing procedure after procedure, and you put the whole thing together later. Of course, LISP is not a statically typed

Design Principles

- Limited Goals
- Simplicity
- Uniformity
- Expressive Power
- Safety
- Good Performance

SLIDE 9

Part 2: Technical History

CLU is a heap-based language with garbage collection, static type checking, and separate compilation

Major innovations:

- abstract data types
- parametric polymorphism
- iterators
- exception handling

SLIDE 10

language and that was my reaction to LISP, because I had been so annoyed while working on my thesis at the errors that would show up at run-time that could have been caught at compile-time.

CLU was really ahead of its time. There were four major innovations: abstract data types, parametric polymorphism, iterators, and exception handling. And what I am going to do in the rest of the talk is explain a little about each of these.

(SLIDE 11) This is how we implemented an abstract data type in CLU, using a mechanism type called a "cluster." And in fact, the name CLU is the first three letters of "cluster." The word cluster was invented in the summer of 1973, and we finally chose the word CLU sometime in the late fall of 1973.

The header of the cluster says that we are implementing a type named **intset** (integer set), and that the operations we are going to provide on objects of that type are create, member, size, insert, and a bunch of others I haven't bothered to list. Then if you look inside the body of the cluster, first you see a line that describes how objects of the **intset** type are going to be represented. In this case, I've chosen to represent them with an array of integers. The remainder of the cluster gives you the implementations of the different operations. There has to be an implementation of every operation listed in the header, and there can be some additional private operations as well. If you look at the definition of the create operation, you will see that its header says that it's a procedure that doesn't take any arguments, and returns an **intset**. Here I have this funny word **cvt**; what's going on is there are actually two types involved. On the outside, there is this abstract type **intset**; on the inside, there is the representation type array of integers. On the outside, it's not possible to ever see the representation type. But on the inside, in order to implement the operations, you need to have access to the real representation. And so, the **cvt** expresses the fact that you have special privileges inside the cluster. What it means when it appears in the result clause is that although I'm working with an array of integers on the inside, as the object passes out to the caller, it turns into an integer set. You can see in the size procedure header that what is coming in from the outside is an integer set and now I'm going to turn it in to an array of integers so I can have access to the details of its representation. The only other thing to notice in this slide, is the use of **rep$new** in the return clause of the create operation. What we are doing there is solving a naming problem. Many different types will have operations of the same name. You probably could figure out which one was wanted by looking at the context of the call. But, we were opposed to overloading and having the compiler figure out what is going on. We wanted an explicit mechanism that said exactly what operation is being called. That position was a reaction to overloading in ALGOL 68.

Abstract data types are implemented by clusters:

```
intset = cluster is create, member, size, insert, . . .
      rep = array[int]
      create = proc () returns (cvt)
            return (rep$new())
            end create
      size = proc (s: cvt) returns (int)
            return (rep$size(s))
            end size
      end intset
```

SLIDE 11

Operations are in the type not the objects.

- Abstract data type view: operations in type
- Object-oriented view: operations in objects

Op 1
Op 2
. . .
Obj 1 Obj 2

Obj 1 Obj 2

binary operations
fast calls

multiple implementations
inheritance

SLIDE 12

(SLIDE 12) One thing I want to point out is that the notion of the abstract types is different in CLU than it is in object-oriented languages like Smalltalk and C++. In CLU, the idea is that the operations belong to the type rather than the objects; because they belong to the type, they have special privileges. A type has operations and objects; its operations have the right to look inside the type's objects, and nothing else in the system does. That is how we do things in CLU. In a language like Smalltalk or C++, the idea is that the operations are attached to the objects. When you call a message, you run inside your object, and that is what gives you the access to the representation. We actually spent quite a bit of time in the CLU design trying to figure out which of these two views we wanted to have. The view that we ended up with has two advantages: it is easy to do binary operations, for example, set union, because the operation can easily look inside two objects of its type. It is also very cheap to do operation calls because they are just procedure calls. A disadvantage of our view is that you can not easily have multiple implementations of the type, for the very same reasons that it was easy to do binary operations. If you can look inside many different objects, you will have a problem if they can have different implementations. We decided that it was more important to have good support for binary operations and fast procedure calls than to support multiple implementations of a type, and that's why we chose our mechanism.

(SLIDE 13) Now I want to move on to parametric polymorphism. This is a mechanism still being worked on by the research community in computer science. It came out of our uniformity goal. When you have a notion like an array, this is not a single type, but rather a class of related types: The class contains an array of integers, an array of reals, and so forth. We wanted to be able to do the same thing with abstract types that you can do with built-in types. So we wanted to be able to define, for example, a set. Then you could have a specific set of integers, and set of reals, and so on. When we started the language design in 1973, we thought we could not have such parameterized modules and also have compile-time type checking with separate compilation. So in the initial version of the language, called CLU.5, which was implemented in 1974, we left this mechanism out. We returned to the problem later, around 1976, and figured out a solution that allowed us to have compile-time type checking. We can define something like a set with a single cluster. Then when a user wanted to use it, they would say "I want a set of integers," or "I want a set of Booleans," or whatever.

(SLIDE 14) So here is how the mechanism works. The slide shows a cluster implementing sets. Its header says that set is going to be parameterized by a type "T." "T" is just a place-holder in this definition. Whenever you instantiate the definition, you'll replace it with whatever the real type is, so you will have for example, a set of integers, and it's as if you just rewrite the definition, replacing "T"

Parametric Polymorphism (1974–1977)

e.g., want sets (like arrays)

- define with a single cluster
- instantiate when used, e.g., set[int]

SLIDE 13

```
set = cluster [ T: type ] is create, insert, member, ...
        where T has equal: proctype (T, T) returns (bool)

    rep = array[ T ]
    member = proc (s: set[ T ], x: T) returns (bool)
        ...
        if x = s[i] ...
    end set
```

SLIDE 14

with integer. It almost like a macro mechanism although it is not implemented that way. Then you can see that the **rep**, instead of being an array of integers, is an array of "T"s and so on. The problem that we didn't know how to solve in 1973, was that it doesn't make sense to instantiate a cluster like set with just any old type. It only makes sense to instantiate it if you have a type that has an equal operation and semantically, of course, that equal operation ought to be an equality operator on the elements of that type. We didn't know how to express this information in a way that would allow us to check at compile-time that everything would work out all right. In 1976, we invented the **where** clause, sitting there on the second line of the slide. What the **where** clause does is express that constraint. What it's saying is that you can only instantiate a set with a type that has an operation named equal with the signature given on the slide. When the CLU compiler compiles a module, such as the set cluster, it makes sure that inside that module, the only operations of the parameter type that are used are the ones that are listed explicitly in the **where** clause. And then, furthermore, when the clusters are instantiated, the compiler makes sure that the type used in the instantiation has the operations that are needed. And in that way, you can compile, separately, both the instantiation and the definition and still be sure that no run-time errors will arise from the use of the parameters. Inside the member operation, you can see the use of the equal operation where it says, **x= s[i]**; what's going on there is something we call "syntactic sugar,"which provides a short form for the real syntax, **T$ equal (x, s[i])**, which is awkward. So we established a relationship between certain symbols and operation names. When you define operations with those names, the associated short forms can be used for them. That's why we are able to use the equal sign to call the equal operation.

(SLIDE 15) Now, the next mechanism I want to talk about is the exception mechanism. This is one place that we broke our rule about not looking at control structures, because this is a control structure mechanism. The reason we included an exception mechanism in the language was because of our interest in programming methodology. If you look at production programs, you discover that an awful lot of the code in them is concerned with the handling of errors. In the absence of an exception mechanism, it can be quite awkward to write that code. You have to go to the trouble of picking out explicit ways to pass the information about errors around, and then you have to insert code that checks for them; and possibly at places where is not very convenient to do that checking. So, we thought it was really very important to have an exception mechanism as a way of making it easier to write error-checking code, ending up with programs that are easier to read, and encouraging people to do a good job error checking. That was the motivation for the exception mechanism.

Exceptions (1975–1977)

Termination model: a call can terminate in one of a number of conditions, one of which is normal

- Results in all cases
- Unhandled exceptions aren't propragated automatically

```
choose = proc (s: cvt) returns (T) signals (empty)
   if rep$empty(s) then signal empty end
   return (s[rep$bottom(s)])
   end choose
```

SLIDE 15

Iterators (designed in 1975)

Need a way of iterating through a collection that is both efficient and abstract

for x ∈ C do S end

SLIDE 16

At the time we did the design, there was a lot of debate about what is a good exception mechanism. For example, PL/I had the resumption model of exceptions. So, we spent a lot of time thinking about what was the right kind of exception mechanism. We ultimately decided that we wanted a termination model, which means that the procedure terminates, but in one of a number of conditions, one of which is designated as the normal condition. In each termination condition, you can have results, and they don't have to be the same in the different cases. So I can have a procedure that terminates normally with an integer or maybe raises the "foo" exception with a real; and that would be OK. We don't propagate or handle exceptions automatically, and I'll explain that in just a minute. What I have on the rest of the slide is an example of a procedure that signals an exception. This is another operation of the set type that I showed you before. The choose procedure is supposed to return some arbitrary element of the set except, of course, it can't do that if the set is empty. So in that case it signals empty. The implementation of choose is straightforward. We check to see if the rep is empty. If it is, we signal; otherwise we remove the bottom element and return it.

There are a couple of points about CLU syntax that I should point out. Notice the closing end. All CLU statements are self-terminating like this. Also notice the absence of semicolons. At the time we designed CLU, there was a debate raging about semicolons as separators versus semicolons as terminators. And there was also the missing semicolon problem; if you didn't watch out and put your semicolons in the right places, your program wouldn't compile. We considered it a major coup to design our syntax so that we didn't need semicolons. They are in our language as an option, but in fact, we have adopted a style of never using them.

Now I want to talk about unhandled exceptions. Suppose that the call to bottom signaled "bounds," even though it shouldn't as we know the array is not empty. I wouldn't want to require the code to catch that exception. But I also don't want to tell the caller of choose about the exception, because that would mean the caller would have to prepare for any exception to be signalled. So in CLU, the run-time system catches exceptions that aren't caught explicitly, and turns them into a special exception called "failure." Every procedure can potentially signal failure.

In CLU, exceptions are implemented very efficiently: signaling an exception is no more expensive than returning normally. Therefore, we actually program with exceptions, and I wouldn't write the implementation of choose the way it is shown on the slide. Instead, I would just try to return the bottom element, and if that failed, then I would signal the empty exception.

I believe an exception mechanism need not be implemented so that signaling is as cheap as returning normally. But, it is very important that a procedure that might potentially signal exceptions is cheap when it returns normally. Otherwise people are unlikely to use exceptions. They will find cheaper ways of doing their job. So, it's nice when you can do it the way CLU does it; it's not essential. But what is really essential is that you make sure it's cheap to return normally for programs that might signal exceptions.

(SLIDE 16) The final mechanism I want to talk about is iterators. This is another place where we violated our rule about control structures. What happened was that as we went on with our design, we came to realize that we needed a way of iterating over a collection that was both abstract and efficient. For certain kinds of data types, like sets, for example, you have a mechanism where you gather things together. The reason you gather a bunch of things together is because later you want to do something with them. You might want to print all of them, or you might want to look at them to find ones that satisfy certain use properties, or whatever. So access to elements is going to be an important use of collections. And it is equally important that you access elements in a way that doesn't expose the representation or cause you to change the abstraction to something more complicated.

We were wondering about what to do about this problem when we went to visit the Alphard people at CMU in the summer of 1975. I went there with Russ, Craig, and Alan, the three students who worked with me on the project. The Alphard people had invented a mechanism called the "generator" which solved the element access problem by providing a group of operations, one of which started the iteration, another one that got you the next element, another one that told you whether you were done. I think there were six or seven such operations in their mechanism. We could see that this was a solution to the iteration problem, but we thought it was inelegant. On the airplane home, Russ Atkinson got the idea of iterators. Iterators are a limited coroutine facility; the limitations allow us to implement them on a single stack. This was the place where we decided to limit the expressive power of the language so we could get an efficient implementation.

Now let me show you what iterators are like.

(SLIDE 17) On the top of the slide, I have an example of an operation of the set cluster that will give you all the members of the set, one at a time. The header says it is an iterator, and that it is going to yield type "T." An iterator is like a procedure except that rather than returning just once, it yields results multiple times. It will yield something, run some more and yield another thing, and so on.

An iterator is called in the **for** loop; an example of a **for** loop is at the bottom of the slide. When you enter the **for** loop, the iterator is called. When the iterator yields, you run the body of the **for** loop. When the body is finished, you go back into the iterator where you left off and continue processing from there. When the iterator terminates, that will terminate the loop. Or, if the loop terminates before the iteration is done, that will terminate both the loop and the iterator. So that is the simple idea of an iterator. What is nice about it is that you can write an iterator as a single procedure rather than having to write a whole bunch of procedures to accomplish the same thing (as in a generator).

Iterators are implemented very efficiently in CLU. When you enter the loop body after yielding, that is essentially calling the loop body. When the loop body completes, you return to the iterator. So each iteration is a procedure call. Procedure calls are very cheap in CLU. Of course, you can go even further and do inline substitutions and get rid of the cost of the call. So this turns out to be an elegant mechanism and it doesn't cost you much.

(SLIDE 18) I want to end with an evaluation of CLU. CLU is not a widely used language. It does have its enthusiastic users. It does have two compilers, and we have exported it to a number of sites—over several hundred sites have received CLU. And we have used it for some large projects. Larch, which is a specification and analysis system, and Argus, which is the language I developed after CLU, are two examples. These implementations happened at MIT, but some implementations were done at other places. Nevertheless, CLU isn't in widespread use today. On the other hand, that is not actually what it was developed for. The purpose for the design, as I said at the beginning, was

```
members = iter (s: cvt) yields (T)
   i: int := rep$low(s)
   while i <= rep$high(s) do
      yield (s[i])
      i := i + 1
      end
   end members

for x: int in set[int]$member(s) do
   if is_prime(x) then return (true) end
   end
```

SLIDE 17

Evaluation

Not widely used

- Vax and PCLU compilers
- Some large projects: Larch and Argus

Ideas have been influential

- On other languages (Ada, Trellis/Owl, Modula 3)
- On programming methodology

SLIDE 18

to explore ideas in programming methodology in the hope of making advances in the state of the art. What I hoped for the language was that it would have an impact on programming methodology and on the design of future languages, and I think it has been successful from that point of view. Thank you.

TRANSCRIPT OF QUESTION AND ANSWER SESSION

TOM MARLOWE (Seton Hall): Did the process of writing up design notes ever result in changing a consensus decision?

LISKOV: I can't remember specific instances, but I'm sure that it did. It's the combination of oral and verbal analysis that leads to success. When you write things down, you tend to discover things that you hadn't thought about when it was just an idea that you were talking about. Then, if you go into a meeting where everybody is troubleshooting the ideas, a whole bunch of other issues that you may have overlooked will come up. I really think that it was the way that we did things, with the design notes, followed by the design meetings where we did troubleshooting, that led to pinning down the semantics.

GUY STEELE (Thinking Machines): You described CLU as being much like LISP but with some key changes, such as static typing and clusters. Do these changes make CLU more suitable or less suitable for the traditional applications areas of LISP such as AI research and symbolic algebra.

LISKOV: I don't think that CLU is well suited for the traditional applications of LISP. CLU was intended to be used in building production systems, which were built and used over a long period of time. It is not a language in which you can build by experimentation. It's not that it isn't easy to modify CLU programs, but that was not the goal of the language, to build in that prototyping style. Furthermore, as you know, there are certain kinds of applications that would be very difficult to implement in CLU because of the strong type checking and the lack of dealing with programs as data at run-time. I wasn't trying to compete with LISP when I designed CLU, but LISP was a very important influence on the language.

HERBERT KLAEREN (University of Tubingen): Can you comment on the Ada exception handling model on the ground of your thoughts and decisions about CLU exception handling?

LISKOV: I think the Ada mechanism is like CLU's mechanism in many respects. In fact, my understanding of the history is that it came from CLU. I was involved as a consultant in some of the early Ada designs and CLU's mechanism was in one of those designs and got into Ada from there. But, in my opinion, the Ada designers threw away the most important thing, which is not propagating the exceptions automatically when they are not handled by the caller.

DAN HALBERT (DEC): Why were you opposed to overloading, though not to the "syntactic sugar" operators?

LISKOV: I think if I were going to do it today, I would probably change that decision. But, it was partly in reaction to ALGOL 68. Now, those of you who weren't there in the early seventies probably don't understand fully the impact that ALGOL 68 had on the research community. It wasn't until Dr. Lindsey's revised book came out, in 1977, that it was possible to understand fully what was going on in ALGOL 68. In the meantime, what you saw was this combination of mechanisms with what seemed like unbounded power. I think the overloading decision in CLU was an overreaction to that. I think that limited overloading where you make decisions based on the types of the arguments but not the types of the results, is a perfectly plausible thing to do.

ELLEN SPERTUS (MIT): Because of its safety, especially with heap memory, one might expect development and debugging in CLU to be faster than in less safe languages. Have studies been done on whether this is the case? And if so, why isn't CLU more widely used?

LISKOV: Studies have not been done. Throughout the history of programming methodology there has always been a desire to do studies, to try and prove whether or not a particular methodology or language is more effective than another. But they have never been very successful, because if you tried to tackle this with a large project, it was too much work. I certainly have enthusiastic testimonials from satisfied users. The question about why isn't it more widely used: that has a lot to do with whether the language is widely supported. If you are building a big project, you don't want to risk the project on a language that is only supported by a research lab at a university. For example, you are concerned about how you are going to move your product to the next machine, and so forth. There is a lot more to making a decision about what language you are going to use than just its technical merits.

BJARNE STROUSTRUP (Bell Labs): To what extent did you understand Simula at the start of the CLU design, (and) had you written a Simula program?

LISKOV: I have never written a Simula program, but I certainly pored over that little black book, *Structured Programming* by Dahl, Dijkstra, and Hoare. So, my understanding of Simula was based on reading that book. What I saw in Simula confused me, because the class mechanism in Simula is used for so many different things. One of the things I forgot to say in my talk was that I did make an explicit decision at one point early in the CLU design about whether to base CLU on an existing language or whether to design a new language. I ultimately decided to do a new language because I felt that would give me the best chance of really getting to some of the fundamentals of the mechanism I was trying to explore. The obvious language on which to have based CLU was Simula. That was the only one that had a mechanism at all like what I was interested in studying. But the class mechanism was used for so many different things that I felt that it would distract us. It was used not only for inheritance, but also for a kind of parametric polymorphism. I don't think I fully understood that at the time, and I did feel it would have been a distraction to try to deal with all that stuff at once.

DICK GABRIEL (Lucid): What is the influence or relationship between iterators and the au revoir mechanism in Conniver?

LISKOV: I don't know. Generators came from IPL and we got iterators from generators. I certainly knew about Conniver, but I don't remember such a mechanism.

GUY STEELE: Why dollar sign as opposed, say, to dot?

LISKOV: We were using dot for another purpose. We were using dot to give access to fields of records and that's actually a "syntactic sugar." So, **x.foo** really means record type dollar **get_foo** of the record. We didn't want to use the dot in those two distinct ways. So, in fact, there really was a reason why it wasn't dot, but it could have been many other things other than the dollar sign.

HERBERT KLAEREN (University of Tubingen): Would you agree that the object-oriented concept has superseded the abstract data type idea. And if you were to redo the CLU development right now, would it become an object-oriented language?

LISKOV: Well, I guess I have a lot of answers to that question. One is that I believe the most important thing about object-oriented programming is data abstraction. It happens to be expressed in a slightly different form in object-oriented languages, with the notion that the operations belong to the objects rather than to the type. But, I don't believe that's a very important difference. I believe the important idea, grouping objects and operations together, is supported by both approaches. On the other hand, I am now designing an object-oriented language and it does have an inheritance mechanism and it does have a type hierarchy mechanism. And I have to say that even today I am not a hundred percent convinced about the utility of these mechanisms. But I'm thinking about it.

BIOGRAPHY OF BARBARA LISKOV

Barbara Liskov was born in Los Angeles and grew up in San Francisco. She attended the University of California at Berkeley, where she majored in mathematics. Barbara did not go directly to graduate school but instead worked for a couple of years. Because she couldn't find an interesting job as a mathematician, she took a job as a programmer, and that is how she got into the field of computer science.

Barbara did graduate work at Stanford University. The computer science department at Stanford was formed after she started graduate work, and she was a member of the first group of students to take the computer science qualifying examination. She did thesis work in artificial intelligence with John McCarthy; her Ph.D. thesis was on a program to play chess endgames.

After finishing at Stanford, Barbara returned to work at the Mitre Corporation, where she had worked before going to graduate school. At Mitre, she switched from AI to systems. Four years later, she joined the faculty at the Massachusetts Institute of Technology, where she is the NEC Professor of Software Science and Engineering.

Barbara's research and teaching interests include programming languages, programming methodology, distributed computing, and parallel computing. She is a member of the ACM, the IEEE, the National Academy of Engineering, and a fellow of the American Academy of Arts and Sciences. Barbara is married and the mother of a son who is now in college.

Smalltalk Session

Chair: *Barbara Ryder*
Discussant: *Adele Goldberg*

THE EARLY HISTORY OF SMALLTALK

Alan C. Kay

Apple Computer
kay2@applelink.apple.com@Internet#

ABSTRACT

Most ideas come from previous ideas. The sixties, particularly in the ARPA community, gave rise to a host of notions about "human-computer symbiosis" through interactive time-shared computers, graphics screens, and pointing devices. Advanced computer languages were invented to simulate complex systems such as oil refineries and semi-intelligent behavior. The soon to follow paradigm shift of modern personal computing, overlapping window interfaces, and object-oriented design came from seeing the work of the sixties as something more than a "better old thing." That is, more than a better way: to do mainframe computing; for end-users to invoke functionality; to make data structures more abstract. Instead the promise of exponential growth in computing/$/volume demanded that the sixties be regarded as "*almost* a new thing" and to find out what the actual "new things" might be. For example, one would compute with a handheld "Dynabook" in a way that would not be possible on a shared main-frame; millions of potential users meant that the user interface would have to become a learning environment along the lines of Montessori and Bruner; and needs for large scope, reduction in complexity, and end-user literacy would require that data and control structures be done away with in favor of a more biological scheme of protected universal cells interacting only through messages that could mimic any desired behavior.

Early Smalltalk was the first complete realization of these new points of view as parented by its many predecessors in hardware, language, and user interface design. It became the exemplar of the new computing, in part, because we were actually trying for a qualitative shift in belief structures—a new Kuhnian paradigm in the same spirit as the invention of the printing press—and thus took highly extreme positions that almost forced these new styles to be invented.

CONTENTS

—To Dan Ingalls, Adele Goldberg and the rest of the Xerox PARC LRC gang

—To Dave Evans, Bob Barton, Marvin Minsky, and Seymour Papert

—To SKETCHPAD, JOSS, LISP and SIMULA, the four great progrmming conceptions of the sixties

INTRODUCTION

I am writing this introduction in an airplane at 35,000 feet. On my lap is a five-pound notebook computer—1992's "Interim Dynabook"—by the end of the year it sold for under $700. It has a flat, crisp, high-resolution bitmap screen, overlapping windows, icons, a pointing device, considerable storage and computing capacity, and its best software is object-oriented. It has advanced networking built in and there are already options for wireless networking. Smalltalk runs on this system, and is one of the main systems I use for my current work with children. In some ways this is more than a Dynabook (quantitatively), and some ways not quite there yet (qualitatively). All in all, pretty much what was in mind during the late sixties.

Smalltalk was part of this larger pursuit of ARPA, and later of Xerox PARC, that I called personal computing. There were so many people involved in each stage from the research communities that the accurate allocation of credit for ideas is intractably difficult. Instead, as Bob Barton liked to quote Goethe, we should "share in the excitement of discovery without vain attempts to claim priority."

I will try to show where most of the influences came from and how they were transformed in the magnetic field formed by the new personal computing metaphor. It was the attitudes as well as the great ideas of the pioneers that helped Smalltalk get invented. Many of the people I admired most at this time—such as Ivan Sutherland, Marvin Minsky, Seymour Papert, Gordon Moore, Bob Barton, Dave Evans, Butler Lampson, Jerome Bruner, and others—seemed to have a splendid sense that their creations, though wonderful by relative standards, were not near to the absolute thresholds that had to be crossed. Small minds try to form religions, the great ones just want better routes up the mountain. Where Newton said he saw further by standing on the shoulders of giants, computer scientists all too often stand on each other's toes. Myopia is still a problem when there are giants' shoulders to stand on—"outsight" is better than insight—but it can be minimized by using glasses whose lenses are highly sensitive to esthetics and criticism.

Programming languages can be categorized in a number of ways: imperative, applicative, logic-based, problem-oriented, and so on. But they all seem to be either an "agglutination of features" or a "crystalization of style." COBOL, PL/1, Ada, and the like, belong to the first kind; LISP, APL—and Smalltalk—are the second kind. It is probably not an accident that the agglutinative languages all seem to have been instigated by committees, and the crystalization languages by a single person.

Smalltalk's design—and existence—is due to the insight that everything we can describe can be represented by the recursive composition of a single kind of behavioral building block that hides its combination of state and process inside itself and can be dealt with only through the exchange of messages. Philosophically, Smalltalk's objects have much in common with the monads of Leibniz and the notions of 20th century physics and biology. Its way of making objects is quite Platonic in that some of them act as idealizations of concepts—*Ideas*—from which *manifestations* can be created. That the Ideas are themselves manifestations (of the Idea-Idea) and that the Idea-Idea is a-kind-of Manifestation-Idea—which is a-kind-of itself, so that the system is completely self-describing—would have been appreciated by Plato as an extremely practical joke [Plato].

In computer terms, Smalltalk is a recursion on the notion of computer itself. Instead of dividing "computer stuff" into things each less strong than the whole—such as data structures, procedures, and functions that are the usual paraphernalia of programming languages—each Smalltalk object is a recursion of the entire possibilities of the computer. Thus its semantics are a bit like having thousands and thousands of computers all hooked together by a very fast network. Questions of concrete representation can thus be postponed almost indefinitely because we are mainly concerned that the computers behave appropriately, and are interested in particular strategies only if the results are off or come back too slowly.

Though it has noble ancestors indeed, Smalltalk's contribution is a new design paradigm—which I called *object-oriented*—for attacking large problems of the professional programmer, and making small ones possible for the novice user. Object-oriented design is a successful attempt to qualitatively improve the efficiency of modeling the ever more complex dynamic systems and user relationships made possible by the silicon explosion.

"We would know what they thought when they did it"
—Richard Hamming

"Memory and imagination are but two words for the same thing"
—Thomas Hobbes

In this history I will try to be true to Hamming's request as moderated by Hobbes' observation. I have had difficulty in previous attempts to write about Smalltalk because my emotional involvement has always been centered on personal computing as an amplifier for human reach—rather than programming system design—and we haven't got there yet. Though I was the instigator and original designer of Smalltalk, it has always belonged more to the people who made it work and got it out the door, especially Dan Ingalls and Adele Goldberg. Each of the LRGers contributed in deep and remarkable ways to the project, and I wish there was enough space to do them all justice. But I think all of us would agree that for most of the development of Smalltalk, Dan was the central figure. Programming is at heart a practical art in which real things are built, and a real implementation thus has to exist. In fact, many if not most languages are in use today not because they have any real merits but because of their existence on one or more machines, their ability to be bootstrapped,and so on. But Dan was far more than a great implementer; he also became more and more of the designer, not just of the language but also of the user interface as Smalltalk moved into the practical world.

Here, I will try to center focus on the events leading up to Smalltalk-72 and its transition to its modern form as Smalltalk-76. Most of the ideas occurred here, and many of the earliest stages of OOP are poorly documented in references almost impossible to find.

This history is too long, but I was amazed at how many people and systems that had an influence appear only as shadows or not at all. I am sorry not to be able to say more about Bob Balzer, Bob Barton, Danny Bobrow, Steve Carr, Wes Clark, Barbara Deutsch, Peter Deutsch, Bill Duvall, Bob Flegal, Laura Gould, Bruce Horn, Butler Lampson, Dave Liddle, William Newman, Bill Paxton, Trygve Reenskaug, Dave Robson, Doug Ross, Paul Rovner, Bob Sproull, Dan Swinehart, Bert Sutherland, Bob Taylor, Warren Teitelman, Bonnie Tennenbaum, Chuck Thacker, and John Warnock. Worse, I have omitted to mention many systems whose design I detested, but that generated considerable, useful ideas and attitudes in reaction. In other words, "histories" should not be believed very seriously but considered as "FEEBLE GESTURES OFF" done long after the actors have departed the stage.

Thanks to the numerous reviewers for enduring the many drafts they had to comment on. Special thanks to Mike Mahoney for helping so gently that I heeded his suggestions and so well that they greatly improved this essay—and to Jean Sammet, an old, old friend, who quite literally frightened me into finishing it—I did not want to find out what would happen if I were late. Sherri McLoughlin and Kim Rose were of great help in getting all the materials together.

11.1 1960–1966—EARLY OOP AND OTHER FORMATIVE IDEAS OF THE SIXTIES

Though OOP came from many motivations, two were central. The large-scale one was to find a better module scheme for complex systems involving hiding of details, and the small-scale one was to find a more flexible version of assignment, and then to try to eliminate it altogether. As with most new ideas, it originally happened in isolated fits and starts.

New ideas go through stages of acceptance, both from within and without. From within, the sequence moves from "barely seeing" a pattern several times, then noting it but not perceiving its "cosmic" significance, then using it operationally in several areas; then comes a "grand rotation" in which the pattern becomes the center of a new way of thinking, and finally, it turns into the same kind of inflexible religion that it originally broke away from. From without, as Schopenhauer noted, the new idea is first denounced as the work of the insane, in a few years it is considered obvious and mundane, and finally the original denouncers will claim to have invented it.

True to the stages, I "barely saw" the idea several times circa 1961 while a programmer in the Air Force. The first was on the Burroughs 220 in the form of a style for transporting files from one Air Training Command installation to another. There were no standard operating systems or file formats back then, so some (to this day unknown) designer decided to finesse the problem by taking each file and dividing it into three parts. The third part was all the actual data records of arbitrary size and format. The second part contained the B220 procedures that knew how to get at records and fields to copy and update the third part. And the first part was an array of relative pointers into entry points of the procedures in the second part (the initial pointers were in a standard order representing standard meanings). Needless to say, this was a great idea, and was used in many subsequent systems until the enforced use of COBOL drove it out of existence.

The second barely seeing of the idea came just a little later when ATC decided to replace the 220 with a B5000. I did not have the perspective to really appreciate it at the time, but I did take note of its segmented storage system,

FIGURE 11.1 USAF ATG Randolph AFB B220 File Format ca. 1961

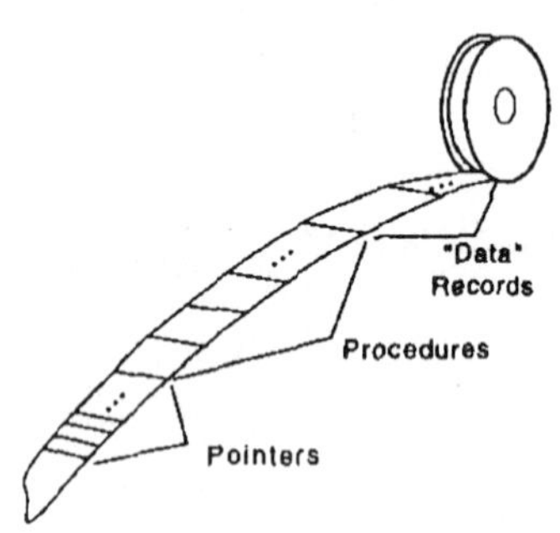

FIGURE 11.2 Gordon Moore's "Law"

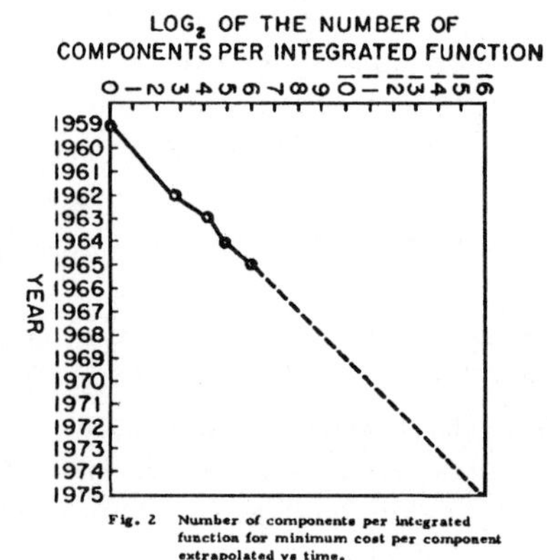

its efficiency of HLL compilation and byte-coded execution, its automatic mechanisms for subroutine calling and multiprocess switching, its pure code for sharing, its protection mechanisms, and the like. And, I saw that the access to its Program Reference Table corresponded to the 220 file system scheme of providing a procedural interface to a module. However, my big hit from this machine at this time was not the OOP idea, but some insights into HLL translation and evaluation [Barton 1961; Burroughs 1961].

After the Air Force, I worked my way through the rest of college by programming mostly retrieval systems for large collections of weather data for the National Center for Atmospheric Research. I got interested in simulation in general—particularly, of one machine by another—but aside from doing a one-dimensional version of a bit-field block transfer (bitblt) on a CDC 6600 to simulate word sizes of various machines, most of my attention was distracted by school, or I should say the theatre at school. While in Chippewa Falls helping to debug the 6600, I read an article by Gordon Moore that predicted that integrated silicon on chips was going to exponentially improve in density and cost over many years. At that time in 1965, standing next to the room-sized freon-cooled 10 mip 6600, his astounding predictions had little projection into my horizons.

11.1.1 Sketchpad and Simula

Through a series of flukes, I wound up in graduate school at the University of Utah in the Fall of 1966, "knowing nothing." That is to say, I had never heard of ARPA or its projects, or that Utah's main goal in this community was to solve the "hidden line" problem in 3D graphics, until I actually walked into Dave Evans's office looking for a job and a desk. On Dave's desk was a foot-high stack of brown covered documents, one of which he handed to me: "Take this and read it."

Every newcomer got one. The title was "Sketchpad: A man-machine graphical communication system"[Sutherland 1963]. What it could do was quite remarkable, and completely foreign to any use of a computer I had ever encountered. The three big ideas that were easiest to grapple with were: it was the invention of modern interactive computer graphics; things were described by making a "master drawing" that could produce "instance drawings"; control and dynamics were supplied by "constraints," also in graphical form, that could be applied to the masters to shape and interrelate parts. Its data structures were hard to understand—the only vaguely familiar construct was the embedding of pointers to procedures and using a process called reverse indexing to jump though them

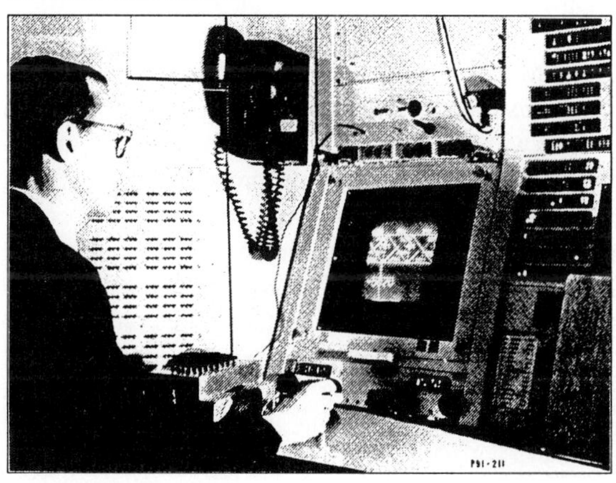

FIGURE 11.3 When there was only one personal computer. Ivan at the TX-2 ca. 1962

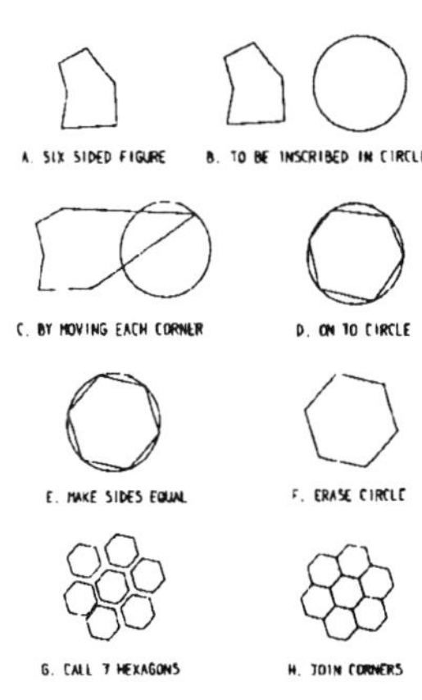

FIGURE 11.4 Drawing in Sketchpad

FIGURE 11.5 Programming with constraints

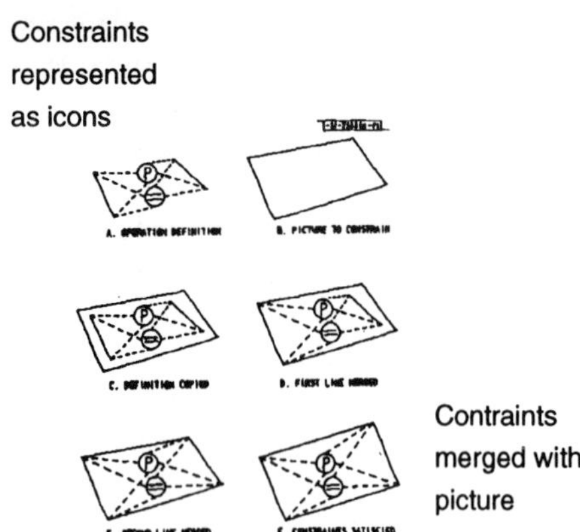

FIGURE 11.6 Sketchpad Structures

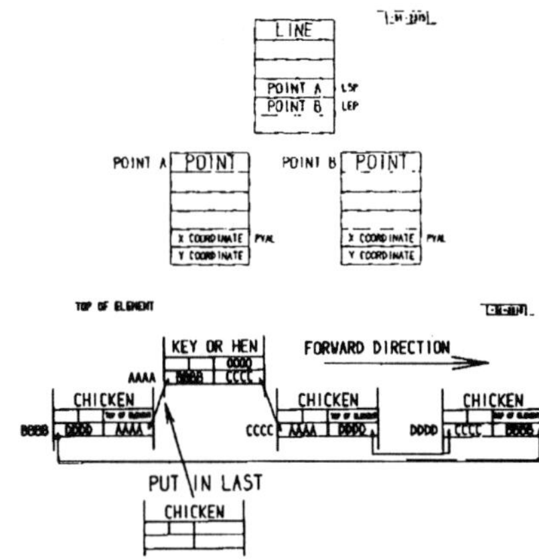

to routines, like the 220 file system [Ross1961]. It was the first to have clipping and zooming windows—one "sketched" on a virtual sheet about one third mile square!

Head whirling, I found my desk. On it was a pile of tapes and listings, and a note: "This is the Algol for the 1108. It doesn't work. Please make it work." The latest graduate student gets the latest dirty task.

The documentation was incomprehensible. Supposedly, this was the Case-Western Reserve 1107 ALGOL—but it had been doctored to make a language called Simula; the documentation read like Norwegian transliterated into English, which in fact it was. There were uses of words like *activity* and *process* that did not seem to coincide with normal English usage.

Finally, another graduate student and I unrolled the program listing 80 feet down the hall and crawled over it yelling discoveries to each other. The weirdest part was the storage allocator, which did not obey a stack discipline as was usual for ALGOL. A few days later, that provided the clue. What Simula was allocating were structures very much like the instances of Sketchpad. There were descriptions that acted like masters and they could create instances, each of which was an independent entity. What Sketchpad called masters and instances, Simula called activities and processes. Moreover, Simula was a procedural language for controlling Sketchpad-like objects, thus having considerably more flexibility than constraints (though at some cost in elegance) [Nygaard1966, 1983].

This was the big hit, and I have not been the same since. I think the reason the hit had such impact was that I had seen the idea enough times in enough different forms that the final recognition was in such general terms to have the quality of an epiphany. My math major had centered on abstract algebras with their few operations generally applying to many structures. My biology major had focused on both cell metabolism and larger scale morphogenesis with its notions of simple mechanisms controlling complex processes and one kind of building block able to differentiate into all needed building blocks. The 220 file system, the B5000, Sketchpad, and finally Simula, all used the same idea for different purposes. Bob Barton, the main designer of the B5000 and a professor at Utah, had said in one of his talks a few days earlier: "The basic principle of recursive design is to make the parts have the same power as the whole." For the first time I thought of the whole as the entire computer and wondered why anyone would want to divide it up into weaker things called data structures and procedures. Why not divide it up into little computers, as time-sharing was starting to? But not in dozens. Why not thousands of them, each simulating a useful structure?

FIGURE 11.7 "Generic block" showing procedural attachment

24	4	VARIABLES	TYPE
-2		0000	SPECB
TYPEWRITER CODE NAME			NAME
SUBROUTINE ENTRY			DISPLAY
FIT SCOPE AROUND IT			HOWBIG
APPLY TRANSFORMATION			MOVIT
24.16..			SIZE
NORMAL PICTURE KIND			KIND
FOUR COMPONENTS			TUPLE
VALUE AT IVAL			VARLOC

FIGURE 11.8 Sketchpad's "inheritance" hierarchy

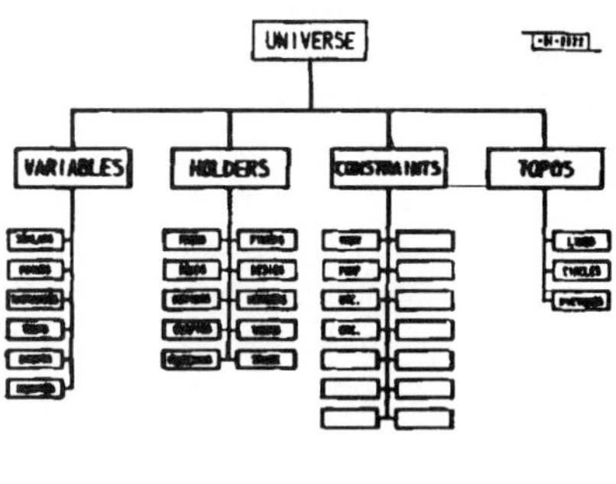

I recalled the monads of Leibniz, the "dividing nature at its joints" discourse of Plato, and other attempts to parse complexity. Of course, philosophy is about opinion and engineering is about deeds, with science the happy medium somewhere in between. It is not too much of an exaggeration to say that most of my ideas from then on took their roots from Simula—but not as an attempt to improve it. It was the promise of an entirely new way to structure computations that took my fancy. As it turned out, it would take quite a few years to understand how to use the insights and to devise efficient mechanisms to execute them.

11.2 1967–69—THE FLEX MACHINE, A FIRST ATTEMPT AT AN OOP-BASED PERSONAL COMPUTER

Dave Evans was not a great believer in graduate school as an institution. As with many of the ARPA "contractors" he wanted his students to be doing "real things"; they should move through graduate school as quickly as possible; and their theses should advance the state of the art. Dave would often get consulting jobs for his students, and in early 1967, he introduced me to Ed Cheadle, a friendly hardware genius at a local aerospace company who was working on a "little machine." It was not the first personal computer—that was the LINC of Wes Clark—but Ed wanted it for noncomputer professionals; in particular, he wanted to program it in a higher level language, like BASIC. I said: "What about JOSS? It's nicer." He said: "Sure, whatever you think," and that was the start of a very pleasant collaboration we called the FLEX machine. As we got deeper into the design, we realized that we wanted to dynamically *simulate* and *extend*, neither of which JOSS (or any existing language that I knew of) was particularly good at. The machine was too small for Simula, so that was out. The beauty of JOSS was the extreme attention of its design to the end-user—in this respect, it has not been surpassed [Joss 1964, 1978]. JOSS was too slow for serious computing (but see also [Lampson 1966]), and did not have real procedures, variable

FIGURE 11.9 "The LINC was early and small" Wes Clark and the LINC, ca. 1962

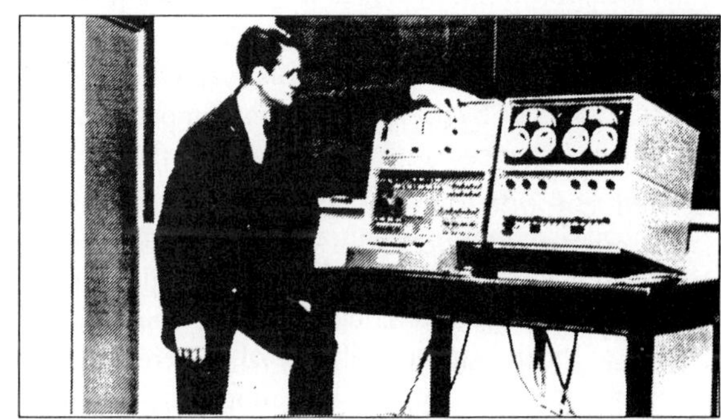

scope, and so forth. A language that looked a little like JOSS but had considerably more potential power was Wirth's EULER [Wirth 1966]. This was a generalization of Algol along lines first set forth by van Wijngaarden [van Wijngaarden 1968] in which types were discarded, different features consolidated, procedures were made into first-class objects, and so forth—actually kind of LISPlike, but without the deeper insights of LISP.

But EULER was enough of "an almost new thing" to suggest that the same techniques be applied to simplify Simula. The EULER compiler was a part of its formal definition and made a simple conversion into B5000-like byte-codes. This was appealing because it suggested that Ed's little machine could run byte-codes emulated in the longish slow microcode that was then possible. The EULER compiler, however, was torturously rendered in an "extended precedence" grammar that actually required concessions in the language syntax (for example, "," could only be used in one role because the precedence scheme had no state space). I initially adopted a bottom-up Floyd-Evans parser (adapted from Jerry Feldman's original compiler-compiler [Feldman 1977]) and later went to various top-down schemes, several of them related to Schorre's META II [Schorre 1963] that eventually put the translator in the name space of the language.

The semantics of what was now called the FLEX language needed to be influenced more by Simula than by ALGOL or EULER. But it was not completely clear how. Nor was it clear how the user should interact with the system. Ed had a display (for graphing, and so forth) even on his first machine, and the LINC had a "glass teletype," but a Sketchpad-like system seemed far beyond the scope of what we could accomplish with the maximum of 16k 16-bit words that our cost budget allowed.

11.2.1 Doug Engelbart and NLS

This was in early 1967, and while we were pondering the FLEX machine, Utah was visited by Doug Engelbart. A prophet of Biblical dimensions, he was very much one of the fathers of what on the FLEX machine I had started to call "personal computing." He actually traveled with his own 16mm projector with a remote control for starting and stopping it to show what was going on (people were not used to seeing and following cursors back then). His notion of the ARPA dream was that the destiny of oNLine Systems (NLS) was the "augmentation of human intellect" via an interactive vehicle navigating through "thought vectors in concept space." What his system could do then—even by today's standards—was incredible. Not just hypertext, but graphics, multiple panes, efficient navigation and command input, interactive collaborative work, and so on. An entire conceptual world and world view [Engelbart 1968]. The impact of this vision was to produce in the minds of those who were "eager to be augmented" a compelling metaphor of what interactive computing should be like, and I immediately adopted many of the ideas for the FLEX machine.

In the midst of the ARPA context of human-computer symbiosis and in the presence of Ed's "little machine," Gordon Moore's "Law" again came to mind, this time with great impact. For the first time I made the leap of putting the room-sized interactive TX-2 or even a 10 mip 6600 on a desk. I was almost frightened by the implications; computing as we knew it could not survive—the actual meaning of the word changed—it must have been the same kind of disorientation people had after reading Copernicus and first looked up from a different Earth to a different Heaven.

Instead of at most a few thousand *institutional* mainframes in the world—even today in 1992 it is estimated that there are only 4000 IBM mainframes in the entire world—and at most a few thousand users trained for each application, there would be millions of *personal* machines and users, mostly outside of direct institutional control. Where would the applications and training come from? Why should we expect an applications programmer to anticipate the specific needs of a particular one of the millions of potential users? An *extensional* system seemed to be called for in which the end-users

FIGURE 11.10 A very modern picture: Doug Englebart, ca. 1967

would do most of the tailoring (and even some of the direct construction) of their tools. ARPA had already figured this out in the context of their early successes in time-sharing. Their larger metaphor of human-computer symbiosis helped the community avoid making a religion of their subgoals and kept them focused on the abstract holy grail of "augmentation."

One of the interesting features of NLS was that its user interface was parametric and could be supplied by the end-user in the form of a "grammar of interaction" given in their compiler-compiler TreeMeta. This was similar to William Newman's early "Reaction Handler" work in specifying interfaces by having the end-user or developer construct through tablet and stylus an iconic regular expression grammar with action procedures at the states (NLS allowed embeddings via its context-free rules). This was attractive in many ways, particularly William's scheme, but to me there was a monstrous bug in this approach. Namely, these grammars forced the user to be in a system state that required getting out of before any new kind of interaction could be done. In hierarchical menus or "screens" one would have to backtrack to a master state in order to go somewhere else. What seemed to be required were states in which there was a transition arrow to every other state—not a fruitful concept in formal grammar theory. In other words, a much "flatter" interface seemed called for—but could such a thing be made interesting and rich enough to be useful?

Again, the scope of the FLEX machine was too small for a miniNLS, and we were forced to find alternate designs that would incorporate some of the power of the new ideas, and in some cases to improve them. I decided that Sketchpad's notion of a general window that viewed a larger virtual world was a better idea than restricted horizontal panes and with Ed came up with a clipping algorithm

FIGURE 11.11 Multiple Panes and View Specs in NLS

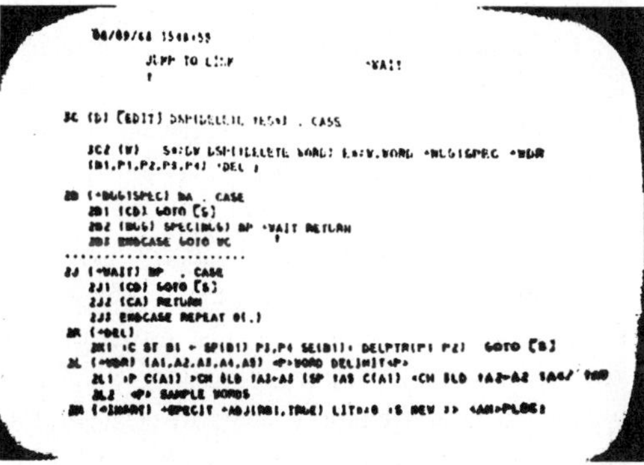

FIGURE 11.12 Collaborative work using NLS

very similar to that under development at the same time by Sutherland and his students at Harvard for the 3D "virtual reality" helmet project [Sutherland 1968].

Object references were handled on the FLEX machine as a generalization of B5000 descriptors. Instead of a few formats for referencing numbers, arrays, and procedures, a FLEX descriptor contained two pointers: the first to the "master" of the object, and the second to the object instance (later we realized that we should put the master pointer in the instance to save space). A different method was taken for handling generalized assignment. The B5000 used l-values and r-values [Strachey] which worked for some cases but could not handle more complex objects. For example: *a[55] := 0*, if *a* was a sparse array whose default element was *0* would still generate an element in the array because := is an "operator" and *a[55]* is dereferenced into an l-value before anyone gets to see that the r-value is the default element, regardless of whether *a* is an array or a procedure fronting for an array. What is needed is something like: *a(55, ':=', 0)*, which can look at all relevant operands before any store is made. In other words, := is not an operator, but a kind of an index that can select a behavior from a complex object. It took me a remarkably long time to see this, partly I think because one has to invert the traditional notion of operators and functions, and the like, to see that objects need to privately own all of their behaviors: *that objects are a kind of mapping whose values are its behaviors*. A book on logic by Carnap [Carnap 1947] helped by showing that "intensional" definitions covered the same territory as the more traditional extensional technique and were often more intuitive and convenient.

As in Simula, a coroutining control structure [Conway 1963] was used as a way to suspend and resume objects. Persistent objects such as files and documents were treated as suspended processes and were organized according to their ALGOL-like static variable scopes. These were shown on the screen and could be opened by pointing at them. Coroutining was also used as a control structure for looping. A single operator **while** was used to test the generators which returned **false** when unable to furnish a new value. Booleans were used to link multiple generators. So a "for-type" loop would be written as:

```
while i <= 1 to 30 by 2 ^ j <= 2 to k by 3 do j<- j * i;
```

where the ... **to** ... **by**... was a kind of coroutine object. Many of these ideas were reimplemented in a stronger style in Smalltalk later on.

Another control structure of interest in FLEX was a kind of event-driven "soft interrupt" called **when**. Its Boolean expression was compiled into a "tournament sort" tree that cached all possible

FIGURE 11.13 Flex when statement [Kay 1969]

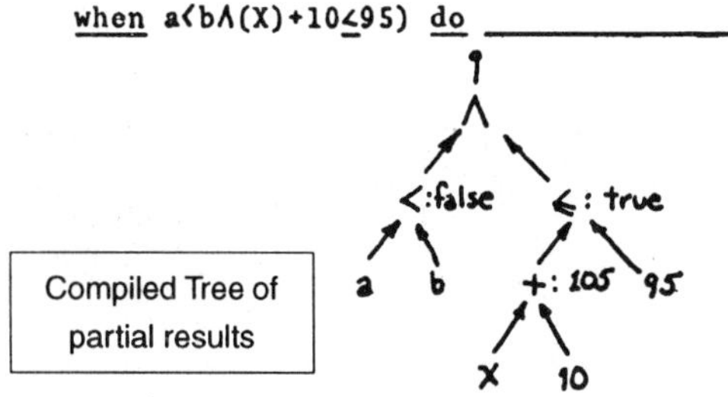

FIGURE 11.14 The first plasma panel

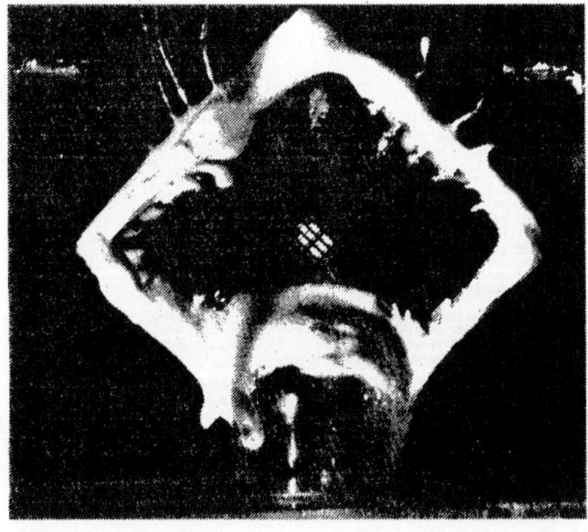

FIGURE 11.15 The FLEX machine self portrait, c. 1968 [Kay 1969]

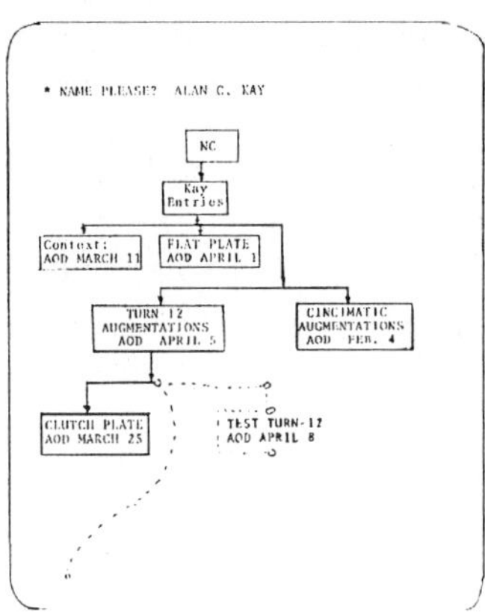

FIGURE 11.16 FLEX user interface. "Files" as suspended processes [Kay 1969]

intermediate results. The relevant variables were threaded through all of the sorting trees in all of the **when**s so that any change only had to compute through the necessary parts of the Booleans. The efficiency was very high and was similar to the techniques now used for spreadsheets. This was an embarrassment of riches with difficulties often encountered in event-driven systems. Namely, it was a complex task to control the *context* of just when the **when**s should be sensitive. Part of the Boolean expression had to be used to check the contexts, where I felt that somehow the structure of the program should be able to set and unset the event drivers. This turned out to be beyond the scope of the FLEX system and needed to wait for a better architecture.

Still, quite a few of the original FLEX ideas in their proto-object form did turn out to be small enough to be feasible on the machine. I was writing the first compiler when something unusual happened: the Utah graduate students got invited to the ARPA contractors' meeting held that year at Alta, Utah. Toward the end of the three days, Bob Taylor, who had succeeded Ivan Sutherland as head of ARPA-IPTO, asked the graduate students (sitting in a ring around the outside of the 20 or so contractors) if they had any comments. John Warnock raised his hand and pointed out that since the

FIGURE 11.17 FLEX machine window clipping [Kay 1969]

FIGURE 11.18 FLEX machine object structure [Kay 1969]

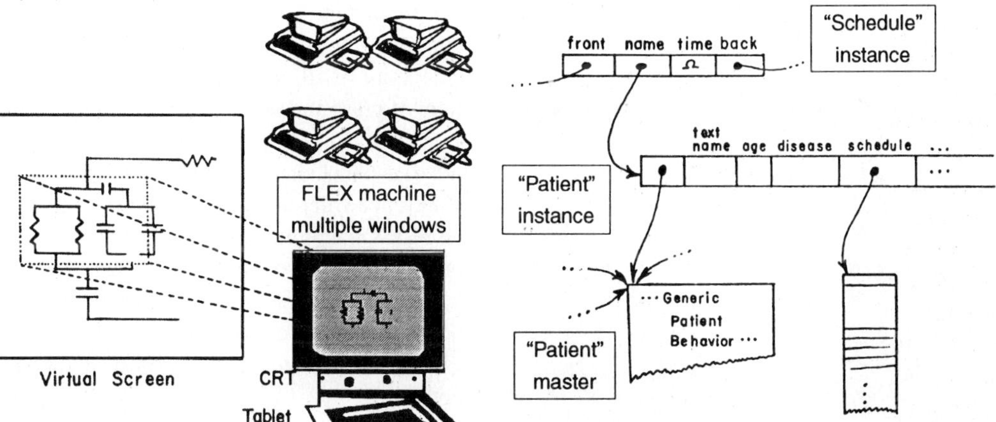

FIGURE 11.19 GRAIL

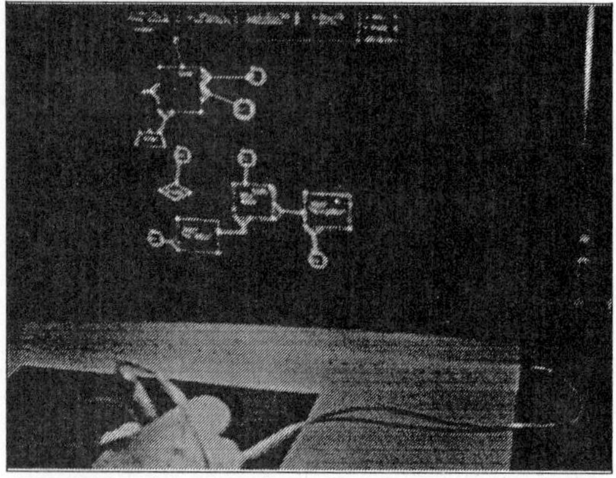

FIGURE 11.20 Seymour Papert and LOGO Turtle

FIGURE 11.21 The Dynabook model

ARPA grad students would all soon be colleagues (and since we did all the real work anyway), ARPA should have a contractors-type meeting each year for the grad students. Taylor thought this was a great idea and set it up for the next summer.

Another ski-lodge meeting happened in Park City later that spring. The general topic was education and it was the first time I heard Marvin Minsky speak. He put forth a terrific diatribe against traditional educational methods, and from him I heard the ideas of Piaget and Papert for the first time. Marvin's talk was about how we think about complex situations and why schools are really bad places to learn these skills. He did not have to make any claims about computers+kids to make his point. It was clear that education and learning had to be rethought in the light of 20th century cognitive psychology and how good thinkers really think. Computing enters as a new representation system with new and useful metaphors for dealing with complexity, especially of systems [Minsky 1970].

For the summer 1968 ARPA grad students meeting at Allerton House in Illinois, I boiled all the mechanisms in the FLEX machine down into one 2'x3' chart. This included all of the "object structures," the compiler, the byte-code interpreter, i/o handlers, and a simple display editor for text and graphics. The grad students were a distinguished group that did indeed become colleagues in subsequent years. My FLEX machine talk was a success, but the big whammy for me came during a tour to the University of Illinois where I saw a 1" square lump of glass and neon gas in which individual spots would light up on command—it was the first flat-panel display. I spent the rest of the conference calculating just when the silicon of the FLEX machine could be put on the back of the display. According to Gordon Moore's "Law," the answer seemed to be sometime in the late seventies or early eighties. A long time off—it seemed too long to worry much about it then.

But later that year at RAND I saw a truly beautiful system. This was GRAIL, the graphical followon to JOSS. The first tablet (the famous RAND tablet) was invented by Tom Ellis [Davis 1964] in order to capture human gestures, and Gabe Groner wrote a program to efficiently recognize and respond to them [Groner 1966]. Though everything was fastened with bubble gum and the system crashed often, I have never forgotton my first interactions with this system. It was direct manipulation, it was analogical, it was modeless, it was beautiful. I realized that the FLEX interface was all wrong, but how could something like GRAIL be stuffed into such a tiny machine since it required all of a stand-alone 360/44 to run in?

A month later, I finally visited Seymour Papert, Wally Feurzig, Cynthia Solomon, and some of the other original researchers who had built LOGO and were using it with children in the Lexington schools. Here were children doing real programming with a specially designed language and environment. As with Simula leading to OOP, this encounter finally hit me with what the destiny of personal computing *really* was going to be. Not a personal dynamic *vehicle*, as in Engelbart's metaphor opposed to the IBM "railroads," but something much more profound: a personal dynamic *medium*. With a vehicle one could wait until high school and give "drivers ed," but if it was a medium, it had to extend into the world of childhood.

Now the collision of the FLEX machine, the flat-screen display, GRAIL, Barton's "communications" talk, McLuhan, and Papert's work with children all came together to form an image of what a personal computer really should be. I remembered Aldus Manutius who 40 years after the printing press put the book into its modern dimensions by making it fit into saddlebags. It had to be no larger than a notebook, and needed an interface as friendly as JOSS's, GRAIL's, and LOGO's, but with the reach of Simula and FLEX. A clear romantic vision has a marvelous ability to focus thought and will. Now it was easy to know what to do next. I built a cardboard model of it to see what it would look and feel like, and poured in lead pellets to see how light it would have to be (less than two pounds). I put a keyboard on it as well as a stylus because, even if handprinting and writing were recognized perfectly (and there was no reason to expect that it would be), there still needed to be a balance between the lowspeed tactile degrees of freedom offered by the stylus and the more limited but faster keyboard. Because ARPA was starting to experiment with packet radio, I expected that the Dynabook when it arrived a decade or so hence, would have a wireless networking system.

Early the next year (1969) there was a conference on Extensible Languages which almost every famous name in the field attended. The debate was great and weighty—it was a religious war of unimplemented, poorly thought out ideas. As Alan Perlis, one of the great men in Computer Science, put it with characteristic wit:

> It has been such a long time since I have seen so many familiar faces shouting among so many familiar ideas. Discovery of something new in programming languages, like any discovery, has somewhat the same sequence of emotions as falling in love. A sharp elation followed by euphoria, a feeling of uniqueness, and ultimately the wandering eye (the urge to generalize) [ACM 1969].

But it was all talk—no one had *done* anything yet. In the midst of all this, Ned Irons got up and presented IMP, a system that had already been working for several years and was more elegant than most of the nonworking proposals. The basic idea of IMP was that you could use any phrase in the grammar as a procedure heading and write a semantic definition in terms of the language as extended so far [Irons 1970].

I had already made the first version of the FLEX machine syntax-driven, but the meaning of a phrase was defined in the more usual way as the kind of code that was emitted. This separated the compiler-extensor part of the system from the end-user. In Irons' approach, every procedure in the system defined its own syntax in a natural and useful manner. I incorporated these ideas into the second version of the FLEX machine and started to experiment with the idea of a direct interpreter rather than a syntax-directed compiler. Somewhere in all of this, I realized that the bridge to an object-based system could be in terms of each object as a syntax-directed interpreter of messages sent to it. In one fell swoop this would unify object-oriented semantics with the ideal of a completely extensible language. The mental image was one of separate computers sending requests to other computers that had to be accepted and understood by the receivers before anything could happen. In today's terms, every object would be a server offering services whose deployment and discretion depended entirely on the server's notion of relationship with the servee. As Liebniz said: "To get everything out of nothing, you only need to find one principle." This was not well thought out enough to do the FLEX machine any good, but formed a good point of departure for my thesis [Kay 1969], which as Ivan Sutherland liked to say, was "anything you can get three people to sign."

After three people signed it (Ivan was one of them), I went to the Stanford AI project and spent much more time thinking about notebook KiddyKomputers than AI. But there were two AI designs that were very intriguing. The first was Carl Hewitt's PLANNER, a programmable logic system that formed the deductive basis of Winograd's SHRDLU [Hewitt 1969]. I designed several languages based on a combination of the pattern matching schemes of FLEX and PLANNER [Kay 1970]. The second design was Pat Winston's concept formation system, a scheme for building semantic networks and comparing them to form analogies and learning processes [Winston 70]. It was kind of "object-oriented." One of its many good ideas was that the arcs of each net which served as attributes in AOV triples should themselves be modeled as nets. Thus, for example, a first order arc called LEFT-OF could be asked a higher order question such as "What is your converse?" and its net could answer: RIGHT-OF. This point of view later formed the basis for Minsky's frame systems [Minsky 1975]. A few years later I wished I had paid more attention to this idea.

That fall, I heard a wonderful talk by Butler Lampson about CAL-TSS, a capability-based operating system that seemed very "object-oriented" [Lampson 1969]. Unforgeable pointers (àla B5000) were extended by bit-masks that restricted access to the object's internal operations. This confirmed my "objects as server" metaphor. There was also a very nice approach to exception handling that reminded me of the way failure was often handled in pattern matching systems. The only problem—which the CAL designers did not see as a problem at all—was that only certain (usually large and slow) things were "objects." Fast things and small things, and the like, were not. This needed to be fixed.

The biggest hit for me while at SAIL in late '69 was to *really understand* LISP. Of course, every student knew about *car*, *cdr*, and *cons*, but Utah was impoverished in that no one there used LISP and hence, no one had penetrated the mysteries of *eval* and *apply*. I could hardly believe how beautiful and wonderful the *idea* of LISP was [McCarthy 1960]. I say it this way because LISP had not only been around enough to get some honest barnacles, but worse, there were deep flaws in its logical foundations. By this, I mean that the pure language was supposed to be based on functions, but its most important components—such as lambda expressions, quotes, and conds—were not functions at all, and instead were called special forms. Landin and others had been able to get quotes and conds in terms of lambda by tricks that were variously clever and useful, but the flaw remained in the jewel. In the practical language things were better. There were not just EXPRS (which evaluated their arguments), but FEXPRS (which did not). My next question was, why on earth call it a functional language? Why not just base everything on FEXPRS and force evaluation on the receiving side when needed? I could never get a good answer, but the question was very helpful when it came time to invent Smalltalk, because this started a line of thought that said "take the hardest and most profound thing you need to do, make it great, and then build every easier thing out of it." That was the promise of LISP and the lure of lambda—needed was a better "hardest and most profound" thing. Objects should be it.

11.3 1970–1972—XEROX PARC: THE KIDDIKOMP, MINICOM, AND SMALLTALK-71

In July 1970, Xerox, at the urging of its chief scientist, Jack Goldman, decided to set up a long-range research center in Palo Alto, California. In September, George Pake, the former chancellor at Washington University where Wes Clark's ARPA project was sited, hired Bob Taylor (who had left the ARPA office and was taking a sabbatical year at Utah) to start a "Computer Science Laboratory." Bob visited Palo Alto and we stayed up all night talking about it. The Mansfield Amendment was threatening to blindly muzzle the most enlightened ARPA funding in favor of direct military research, and this new opportunity looked like a promising alternative. But work for a company? He wanted me to consult and I asked for a direction. He said: follow your instincts. I immediately started working up a new version of the KiddiKomp that could be made in enough quantity to do experiments leading to the user interface design for the eventual notebook. Bob Barton liked to say that "good ideas don't often scale." He was certainly right when applied to the FLEX machine. The B5000 just did not directly scale down into a tiny machine. Only the byte-codes did, and even these needed modification. I decided to take another look at Wes Clark's LINC, and was ready to appreciate it much more this time [Clark 1965].

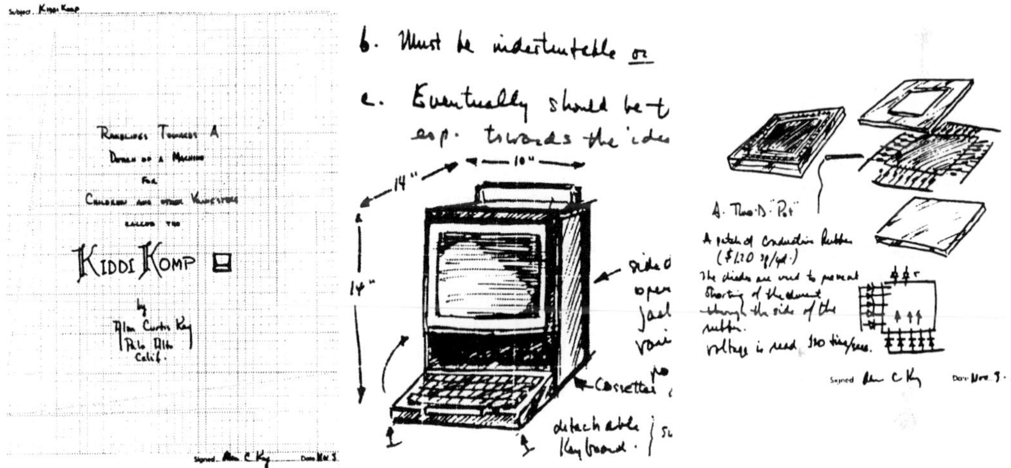

I still liked pattern-directed approaches and OOP so I came up with a language design called "Simulation LOGO" or SLOGO for short (I had a feeling the first versions might run nice and slow). This was to be built into a SONY "tummy trinitron" and would use a coarse bit-map display and the FLEX machine rubber tablet as a pointing device.

Another beautiful system that I had come across was Peter Deutsch's PDP-1 LISP (implemented when he was only 15) [Deutsch 1966]. It used only 2K (18-bit words) of code and could run quite well in a 4K machine (it was its own operating system and interface). It seemed that even more could be done if the system were byte-coded, run by an architecture that was hospitable to dynamic systems, and stuck into the ever larger ROMs that were becoming available. One of the basic insights I had gotten from Seymour was that you did not have to do a lot to make a computer an "object for thought" for children, but what you did had to be done well and be able to apply deeply.

Right after New Year's 1971, Bob Taylor scored an enormous coup by attracting most of the struggling Berkeley Computer Corp. to PARC. This group included Butler Lampson, Chuck Thacker, Peter Deutsch, Jim Mitchell, Dick Shoup, Willie Sue Haugeland, and Ed Fiala. Jim Mitchell urged the group to hire Ed McCreight from CMU and he arrived soon after. Gary Starkweather was there already, having been thrown out of the Xerox Rochester Labs for wanting to build a laser printer (which was against the local religion). Not long after, many of Doug Englebart's people joined up—part of the reason was that they want to reimplement NLS as a distributed network system, and Doug wanted to stay with time-sharing. The group included Bill English (the co-inventor of the mouse), Jeff Rulifson, and Bill Paxton.

Almost immediately we got into trouble with Xerox when the group decided that the new lab needed a PDP-10 for continuity with the ARPA community. Xerox (which had bought SDS essentially sight unseen a few years before) was horrified at the idea of their main competitor's computer being used in the lab. They balked. The newly formed PARC group had a meeting in which it was decided that it would take about three years to do a good operating system for the XDS SIGMA-7 but that we could build "our own PDP-10" in a year. My reaction was "Holy Cow!" In fact, they pulled it off with considerable panache. MAXC was actually a microcoded emulation of the PDP-10 that used for the first time the new integrated chip memories (1K bits!) instead of core memory. Having practical in-house experience with both of these new technologies was critical for the more radical systems to come.

One little incident of LISP beauty happened when Allen Newell visited PARC with his theory of hierarchical thinking and was challenged to prove it. He was given a programming problem to solve while the protocol was collected. The problem was: given a list of items, produce a list consisting of all of the odd indexed items followed by all of the even indexed items. Newell's internal programming language resembled IPL-V in which pointers are manipulated explicitly, and he got into quite a struggle to do the program. In 2 seconds I wrote down:

```
oddsEvens(x) = append(odds(x), evens(x))
```

the statement of the problem in Landin's LISP syntax—and also the first part of the solution. Then a few seconds later:

```
where odds(x)  =  if null(x) v null(tl(x)) then x
                  else hd(x) & odds(ttl(x))
      evens(x) =  if null(x) v null(tl(x)) then nil
                  else odds(tl(x))
```

FIGURE 11.22 "Pendery Paper Display Transducer" design

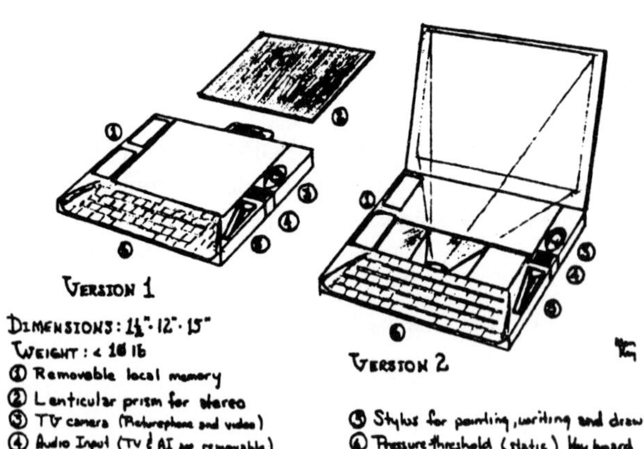

This characteristic of writing down many solutions in declarative form and have them also be the programs is part of the appeal and beauty of this kind of language. Watching a famous guy much smarter than I struggle for more than 30 minutes to not quite solve the problem his way (there was a bug) made quite an impression. It brought home to me once again that "point of view is worth 80 IQ points." I wasn't smarter but I had a much better internal thinking tool to amplify my abilities. This incident and others like it made it paramount that any tool for children should have great thinking patterns *and* deep beauty "built-in."

Right around this time we were involved in another conflict with Xerox management, in particular with Don Pendery, the head "planner." He really did not understand what we were talking about and instead was interested in "trends" and "what was the future going to be like" and how could Xerox "defend against it." I got so upset I said to him, "Look. *The best way to predict the future is to invent it.* Don't worry about what all those other people might do; this is the century in which almost any clear vision can be made!" He remained unconvinced, and that led to the famous "Pendery Papers for PARC Planning Purposes," a collection of essays on various aspects of the future. Mine proposed a version of the notebook as a "Display Transducer," and Jim Mitchell's was entitled "NLS on a Minicomputer."

Bill English took me under his wing and helped me start my group as I had always been a lone wolf and had no idea how to do it. One of his suggestions was that I should make a budget. I am afraid that I really did ask Bill, "What's a budget?" I remembered at Utah, in pre-Mansfield Amendment days, Dave Evans saying to me as he went off on a trip to ARPA, "We're almost out of money. Got to go get some more." That seemed about right to me. They give you some money. You spend it to find out what to do next. You run out. They give you some more. And so on. PARC never quite made it to that idyllic standard, but for the first half-decade it came close. I needed a group because I had finally realized that I did not have all the temperaments required to completely finish an idea. I called it the Learning Research Group (LRG) to be as vague as possible about our charter. I only hired people who got stars in their eyes when they heard about the notebook computer idea. I did not like meetings: did not believe brainstorming could substitute for cool sustained thought. When anyone asked me what to do, and I did not have a strong idea, I would point at the notebook model and say, "Advance that." LRG members developed a very close relationship with each other—as Dan Ingalls was to say later: "...the rest has enfolded through the love and energy of the whole Learning Research Group." A lot of daytime was spent outside of PARC, playing tennis, bike riding, drinking beer, eating Chinese food, and constantly talking about the Dynabook and its potential to amplify human reach and bring new ways of thinking to a faltering civilization that desperately needed it (that kind of goal was common in California in the aftermath of the sixties).

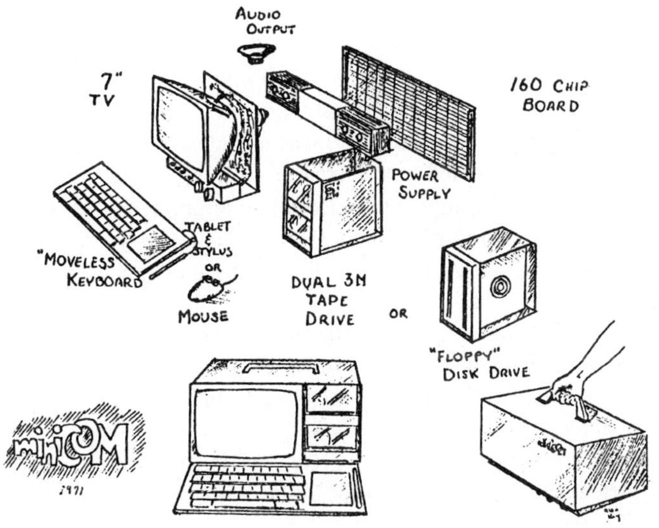

FIGURE 11.23 Smalltalk-71 programs

```
to T 'and' :y do 'y'
to F 'and' :y do F

to 'factorial' 0 is 1
to 'factorial' :n do 'n*factorial n-1'

to 'fact' :n do 'to 'fact' n do factorial n. ^ fact n'

to :e 'is-member-of [] do F
to :e 'is-member-of :group
        do 'if e = first of group then T
                 else e is-member-of rest of group'

to 'cons' :x :y is self
to 'hd' ('cons' :a :b) do 'a'
to 'hd' ('cons' :a :b) '<-' :c do 'a <- c'
to 'tl' ('cons' :a :b) do 'b'
to 'tl' ('cons' :a :b) '<-' :c do 'b <- c'

to :robot 'pickup' :block
       do 'robot clear-top-of block.
       robot hand move-to block.
       robot hand lift block 50.
       to 'height-of block do 50'
```

In the summer of '71 I refined the KiddiKomp idea into a tighter design called miniCOM. It used a bit-slice approach like the NOVA 1200, had a bit-map display, a pointing device, a choice of "secondary" (really tertiary) storages, and a language I now called "Smalltalk"—as in "programming should be a matter of ..." and "children should program in ...".The name was also a reaction against the "IndoEuropean god theory" where systems were named Zeus, Odin, and Thor, and hardly did anything. I figured that "Smalltalk" was so innocuous a label that if it ever did anything nice people would be pleasantly surprised.

This Smalltalk language (today labeled –71) was very influenced by FLEX, PLANNER, LOGO, META II, and my own derivatives from them. It was a kind of parser with object-attachment that executed tokens directly. (I think the awkward quoting conventions came from META.) I was less interested in programs as algebraic patterns than I was in a clear scheme that could handle a variety of styles of programming. The patterned front-end allowed simple extension, patterns as "data" to be retrieved, a simple way to attach behaviors to objects, and a rudimentary but clear expression of its *eval* in terms that I thought children could understand after a few years experience with simpler programming. Program storage was sorted into a discrimination net and evaluation was straightforward pattern-matching.

As I mentioned previously, it was annoying that the surface beauty of LISP was marred by some of its key parts having to be introduced as "special forms" rather than as its supposed universal building block of functions. The actual beauty of LISP came more from the *promise* of its metastructures than its actual model. I spent a fair amount of time thinking about how objects could be characterized as universal computers without having to have any exceptions in the central metaphor. What seemed to be needed was complete control over what was passed in a message send; in particular, *when* and in *what environment* did expressions get evaluated?

An elegant approach was suggested in a CMU thesis of Dave Fisher [Fisher 1970] on the synthesis of control structures. ALGOL60 required a separate link for dynamic subroutine linking and for access to static global state. Fisher showed how a generalization of these links could be used to simulate a wide variety of control environments. One of the ways to solve the "funarg problem" of LISP is to associate the proper global state link with expressions and functions that are to be evaluated later so that the free variables referenced are the ones that were actually implied by the static form of the language. The notion of "lazy evaluation" is anticipated here as well.

Nowadays this approach would be called *reflective design*. Putting it together with the FLEX models suggested that all that should be required for "doing LISP right" or "doing OOP right" would be to handle the mechanics of invocations between modules without having to worry about the details of the modules themselves. The difference between LISP and OOP (or any other system) would then be what the modules could contain. A universal module (object) reference—à la B5000 and LISP—and a message holding structure—which could be virtual if the senders and receivers were simpatico—that could be used by all would do the job.

If all of the fields of a messenger structure were enumerated according to this view, we would have:

```
GLOBAL:                 the environment of the parameter values
SENDER:                 the sender of the message
RECEIVER:               the receiver of the message
REPLY-STYLE:            wait, fork, ...?
STATUS:                 progress of the message
REPLY:                  eventual result (if any)
OPERATION SELECTOR:     relative to the receiver
# OF PARAMETERS:
P1
...
PN
```

This is a generalization of a stack frame, such as is used by the B5000, and very similar to what a good intermodule scheme would require in an operating system such as CAL-TSS—a lot of state for every transaction, but useful to think about.

Much of the pondering during this state of grace (before any workable implementation) had to do with trying to understand what "beautiful" might mean with reference to object-oriented design. A subjective definition of a beautiful thing is fairly easy but is not of much help: we think a thing beautiful because it evokes certain emotions. The cliche has it lie "in the eye of the beholder" so that it is difficult to think of beauty as other than a relation between subject and object in which the predispositions of the subject are all-important.

If there are such things as universally appealing forms, then we can perhaps look to our shared biological heritage for the predispositions. But, for an object like LISP, it is almost certain that most of the basis of our judgment is learned and has much to do with other related areas that we think are beautiful, such as much of mathematics.

One part of the perceived beauty of mathematics has to do with a wondrous synergy between parsimony, generality, enlightenment, and finesse. For example, the Pythagorean Theorem is expressible in a single line, is true for all the infinite number of right triangles, is incredibly useful in understanding many other relationships, and can be shown by a few simple but profound steps.

When we turn to the various languages for specifying computations we find many to be general and a few to be parsimonious. For example, we can define universal machine languages in just a few

FIGURE 11.24 The "Old Character Generator"—early 1972

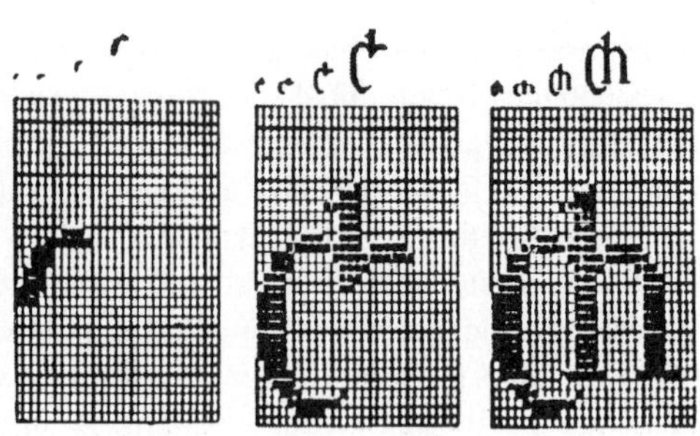

Use a Special Font

instructions that can specify anything that can be computed. But most of these we would not call beautiful, in part because the amount and kind of code that has to be written to do anything interesting is so contrived and turgid. A simple and small system that can do interesting things also needs a "high slope"—that is, a good match between the degree of interestingness and the level of complexity needed to express it.

A fertilized egg that can transform itself into the myriad of specializations needed to make a complex organism has parsimony, generality, enlightenment, and finesse—in short, beauty, and a beauty much more in line with my own esthetics. I mean by this that Nature is wonderful at *both* elegance and practicality—the cell membrane is partly there to allow useful evolutionary kludges to do their necessary work and still be able to act as components by presenting a uniform interface to the world.

One of my continual worries at this time was about the size of the bit-map display. Even if a mixed mode was used (between fine-grained generated characters and coarse-grained general bit-map for graphics) it would be hard to get enough information on the screen. It occurred to me (in a shower, my favorite place to think) that FLEXtype windows on a bit-map display could be made to appear as overlapping documents on a desktop. When an overlapped one was refreshed it would appear to come to the top of the stack. At the time, this did not appear as the wonderful solution to the problem but it did have the effect of magnifying the effective area of the display enormously, so I decided to go with it.

To investigate the use of video as a display medium, Bill English and Butler Lampson specified an experimental character generator (built by Roger Bates) for the POLOS (PARC OnLine Office System) terminals. Gary Starkweather had just gotten the first laser printer to work and we ran a coax over to his lab to feed him some text to print. The "SLOT machine" (Scanning Laser Output Terminal) was incredible. The only Xerox copier Gary could get to work on went at 1 page per second and could not be slowed down. So Gary just made the laser run at that rate with a resolution of 500 pixels to the inch!

The character generator's font memory turned out to be large enough to simulate a bit-map display if one displayed a fixed "strike" and wrote into the font memory. Ben Laws built a beautiful font editor and he and I spent several months learning about the peculiarities of the human visual system (it is decidedly nonlinear). I was very interested in high-quality text and graphical presentations because I

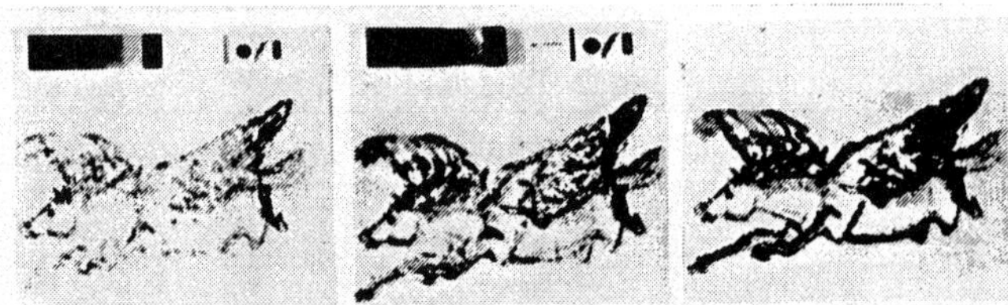

FIGURE 11.25 The first painting system—Summer '72

FIGURE 11.26 Portrait of the Xerox "RISK" executive

thought it would be easier to get the Dynabook into schools as a "trojan horse" by simply replacing school books rather than to try to explain to teachers and school boards what was really great about personal computing.

Things were generally going well all over the lab until May of 1972 when I tried to get resources to build a few miniCOMs. A relatively new executive ("X") did not want to give them to me. I wrote a memo explaining why the system was a good idea (see Appendix I), and then had a meeting to discuss it. "X" shot it down completely, saying among other things that we had used too many green stamps getting Xerox to fund the time-shared MAXC and this use of resources for personal machines would confuse them. I was shocked. I crawled away back to the experimental character generator and made a plan to get four more made and hooked to NOVAs for the initial kid experiments.

I got Steve Purcell, a summer student from Stanford, to build my design for bit-map painting so the kids could sketch as well as display computer graphics. John Shoch built a line-drawing and gesture recognition system (based on Ledeen's [Newman and Sproull 1972]) that was integrated with the painting. Bill Duvall of POLOS built a miniNLS that was quite remarkable in its speed and power. The first overlapping windows started to appear. Bob Shur (with Steve Purcell's help) built a 2 1/2 D animation system. Along with Ben Laws' font editor, we could give quite a smashing demo of what we intended to build for real over the next few years. I remember giving one of these to a Xerox executive, including doing a portrait of him in the new painting system, and wound it up with a flourish, declaring: "And what's really great about this is that it only has a 20% chance of success. We're taking a risk just like you asked us to!" He looked me straight in the eye and said, "Boy, that's great, but just make sure it works." This was a typical executive notion about risk. He wanted us to be in the "20%" one hundred percent of the time.

That summer while licking my wounds and getting the demo simulations built and going, Butler Lampson, Peter Deutsch, and I worked out a general scheme for emulated HLL machine languages. I liked the B5000 scheme, but Butler did not want to have to decode bytes, and pointed out that in as much as an 8-bit byte had 256 total possibilities, what we should do is map different meanings onto different parts of the "instruction space." This would give us a "poor man's Huffman code" that would be both flexible and simple. All subseqent emulators at PARC used this general scheme.

I also took another pass at the language for the kids. Jeff Rulifson was a big fan of Piaget (and semiotics) and we had many discussions about the "stages" and what iconic thinking might be about. After reading Piaget and especially Jerome Bruner, I was worried that the directly symbolic approach taken by FLEX, LOGO (and the current Smalltalk) would be difficult for the kids to process because evidence existed that the symbolic stage (or mentality) was just starting to switch on. In fact, all of the educators that I admired (including Montessori, Holt, and Suzuki) all seemed to call for a more

FIGURE 11.27 Children with Dynabooks from "A Personal Computer for Children of All Ages" [Kay 1972]

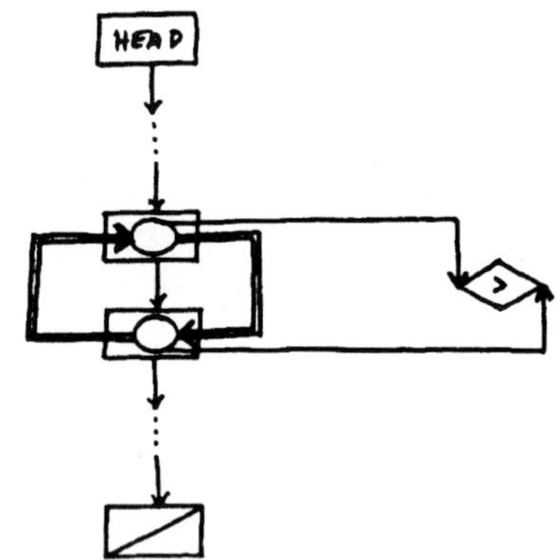

FIGURE 11.28 Iconic Bubble Sort from 1972 LRG Plan [Kay 1972b]

figurative, more iconic approach. Rudolph Arnheim [Arnheim 1969] had written a classic book about visual thinking, and so had the eminent art critic Gombrich [Gombrich 1960]. It really seemed that something better needed to be done here. GRAIL wasn't it, because its use of imagery was to portray and edit flowcharts, which seemed like a great step backwards. But Rovner's AMBIT-G held considerably more promise [Rovner 1968]. It was kind of a visual SNOBOL [Farber 1964] and the pattern matching ideas looked like they would work for the more plannerlike scheme I was using.

Bill English was still encouraging me to do more reasonable-appearing things to get higher credibility, such as making budgets and writing plans and milestone notes, so I wrote a plan that proposed over the next few years that we would build a real system on the character generators *cum* NOVAs that would involve OOP, windows, painting, music, animation, and "iconic programming." The latter was deemed to be hard and would be handled by the usual method for hard problems, namely, give them to grad students.

"Simple things should be simple, complex things should be possible."

11.4 1972–76—THE FIRST REAL SMALLTALK (–72), ITS BIRTH, APPLICATIONS, AND IMPROVEMENTS

In Sepember, within a few weeks of each other, two bets happened that changed most of my plans. First, Butler and Chuck came over and asked: "Do you have any money?" I said, "Yes, about $230K for NOVAs and CGs. Why?" They said, "How would you like us to build your little machine for you?" I said, "I'd like it fine. What is it?" Butler said: "I want a '$500 PDP-10,' Chuck wants a '10 times faster nova,' and you want a 'kiddicomp.' What do you need on it?" I told them most of the results we had gotten from the fonts, painting, resolution, animation, and music studies. I asked where this had come from all of a sudden and Butler told me that they wanted to do it anyway, that Executive "X" was away for a few months on a "task force" so maybe they could "sneak it in," and that Chuck had a bet with Bill Vitic that he could do a whole machine in just three months. "Oh," I said.

The second bet had even more surprising results. I had expected that the new Smalltalk would be an iconic language and would take at least two years to invent, but fate intervened. One day, in a typical PARC hallway bull session, Ted Kaehler, Dan Ingalls, and I were standing around talking about programming languages. The subject of power came up and the two of them wondered how large a language one would have to make to get great power. With as much panache as I could muster, I asserted that you could define the "most powerful language in the world" in "a page of code." They said. "Put up or shut up."

Ted went off to CMU but Dan was still around egging me on. For the next two weeks I got to PARC every morning at four o'clock and worked on the problem until eight, when Dan, joined by Henry Fuchs, John Shoch, and Steve Purcell showed up to kibbitz the morning's work.

I had originally made the boast because McCarthy's self-describing LISP interpreter was written in itself. It was about "a page," and as far as power goes, LISP was the whole nine-yards for functional languages. I was quite sure I could do the same for object-oriented languages *plus* be able to do a reasonable syntax for the code à la some of the FLEX machine techniques.

It turned out to be more difficult than I had first thought for three reasons. First, I wanted the program to be more like McCarthy's second nonrecursive interpreter—the one implemented as a loop that tried to resemble the original 709 implementation of Steve Russell as much as possible. It was more "real." Second, the intertwining of the "parsing" with message receipt—the evaluation of parameters that was handled separately in LISP—required that my object-oriented interpreter re-enter itself "sooner" (in fact, much sooner) than LISP required. And, finally, I was still not clear how *send* and *receive* should work with each other.

The first few versions had flaws that were soundly criticized by the group. But by morning 8 or so, a version appeared that seemed to work (see Appendix II for a sketch of how the interpreter was designed). The major differences from the official Smalltalk-72 of a little bit later were that in the first version symbols were byte-coded and the receiving of return-values from a send was symmetric—that is, receipt could be like parameter binding—this was particularly useful for the return of multiple values. For various reasons, this was abandoned in favor of a more expression-oriented functional return style.

Of course, I had gone to considerable pains to avoid doing any "real work" for the bet, but I felt I had proved my point. This had been an interesting holiday from our official "iconic programming" pursuits, and I thought that would be the end of it. Much to my surprise, only a few days later, Dan Ingalls showed me the scheme *working* on the NOVA. He had coded it up (in BASIC!), added a lot of details, such as a token scanner, a list maker, and the like, and there it was—running. As he like to say: "You just do it and it's done."

It evaluated 3+4 *v e r y s l o w l y* (it was "glacial," as Butler liked to say) but the answer always came out 7. Well, there was nothing to do but keep going. Dan loved to bootstrap on a system that "always ran," and over the next ten years he made at least 80 major releases of various flavors of Smalltalk.

In November, I presented these ideas and a demonstration of the interpretation scheme to the MIT AI lab. This eventually led to Carl Hewitt's more formal "Actor" approach [Hewitt 1973]. In the first Actor paper the resemblence to Smalltalk is at its closest. The paths later diverged, partly because we were much more interested in making things than theorizing, and partly because we had something no one else had: Chuck Thacker's Interim Dynabook (later known as the "ALTO").

Just before Chuck started work on the machine I gave a paper to the National Council of Teachers of English [Kay 1972c] on the Dynabook and its potential as a learning and thinking amplifier—the paper was an extensive rotogravure of "20 things to do with a Dynabook" [Kay 1972c]. By the time I got back from Minnesota, Stewart Brand's *Rolling Stone* article about PARC [Brand 1972] and the surounding hacker community had hit the stands. To our enormous surprise it caused a major furor at Xerox headquarters in Stamford, Connecticut. Though it was a wonderful article that really caught the spirit of the whole culture, Xerox went berserk, forced us to wear badges (over the years many were printed on t-shirts), and severely restricted the kinds of publications that could be made. This was particularly disastrous for LRG, because we were the "lunatic fringe" (so-called by the other computer scientists), were planning to go out to the schools, and needed to share our ideas (and programs) with our colleagues such as Seymour Papert and Don Norman.

Executive "X" apparently heard some harsh words at Stamford about us, because when he returned around Christmas and found out about the interim Dynabook, he got even more angry and tried to kill it. Butler wound up writing a masterful defense of the machine to hold him off, and he went back to his "task force."

Chuck had started his "bet" on November 22, 1972. He and two technicians did all of the machine except for the disk interface which was done by Ed McCreight. It had a ~500,000 pixel (606x808) bitmap display, its microcode instruction rate was about 6MIPs, it had a grand total of 96kb, and the entire machine (exclusive of the memory) was rendered in 160 MSI chips distributed on two cards. It was beautiful [Thacker 1972, 1986]. One of the wonderful features of the machine was "zero-overhead" tasking. It had 16 program counters, one for each task. Condition flags were tied to interesting events (such as "horizontal retrace pulse," and "disk sector pulse," and so on). Lookaside logic scanned the flags while the current instruction was executing and picked the highest priority program counter to fetch from next. The machine never had to wait, and the result was that most hardware functions (particularly those that involved I/O (such as feeding the display and handling the disk) could be replaced by microcode. Even the refresh of the MOS dynamic RAM was done by a task. In other words, this was a coroutine architecture. Chuck claimed that he got the idea from a lecture I had given on coroutines a few months before, but I remembered that Wes Clark's TX-2 (the Sketchpad machine) had used the idea first, and I probably mentioned that in the talk.

In early April, just a little over three months from the start, the first Interim Dynabook,

FIGURE 11.29 BILBO, the first "Interim Dynabook," and "Cookie Monster," the first graphics it displayed. April 1973

1. Everything is an *object*
2. Objects communicate by sending and receiving *messages* (in terms of objects)
3. Objects have their *own memory* (in terms of objects)

---

4. Every object is an *instance* of a *class* (which must be an object)
5. The class holds the shared *behavior* for its instances (in the form of objects in a program list)
6. To eval a program list, control is passed to the first object and the remainder is treated as its message

known as "Bilbo," greeted the world and we had the first bit-map picture on the screen within minutes: the Muppets' Cookie Monster that I had sketched on our painting system.

Soon Dan had bootstrapped Smalltalk across, and for many months it was the sole software system to run on the Interim Dynabook. Appendix III has an "acknowledgements" document I wrote from this time that is interesting in its allocation of credits and the various priorities associated with them. My $230K was enough to get 15 of the original projected 30 machines (over the years some 2000 Interim Dynabooks were actually built). True to Schopenhauer's observation, Executive "X" now decided that the Interim Dynabook was a good idea and he wanted *all but two* for his lab (I was in the other lab). I had to go to considerable lengths to get our machines back, but finally succeeded.

By this time most of Smalltalk's schemes had been sorted out into six main ideas that were in accord with the initial premises in designing the interpreter. The first three principles are what objects "are about"—how they are seen and used from "the outside." These did not require any modification over the years. The last three—objects from the inside—were tinkered with in every version of Smalltalk (and in subsequent OOP designs). In this scheme, (1 and 4) imply that classes are objects and that they must be instances of themself. (6) implies a LISPlike universal syntax, but with the receiving object as the first item followed by the message. Thus c_i <– *de* (with subscripting rendered as "°" and multiplication as "*") means:

receiver	| *message*
c	| ° *i* <– *d**e*

The *c* is bound to the receiving object, and *all* of ° *i* <– *d**e* is the message to it. The message is made up of a literal token "°", an expression to be evaluated in the sender's context (in this case *i*), another literal token <–, followed by an expression to be evaluated in the sender's context (*d**e*). Because "LISP" pairs are made from two element objects they can be indexed more simply: *c hd*, *c tl*, and *c hd* <– *foo*, and so on.

"Simple" expressions like a+b and 3+4 seemed more troublesome at first. Did it really make sense to think of them as:

receiver	| *message*
a	| + *b*
3	| + *4*

It seemed silly if only integers were considered, but there are many other metaphoric readings of "+", such as:

"*kitty*"	| + "*kat*"	=>	"*kittykat*"
$\begin{bmatrix} 3 & 4 & 5 \\ 6 & 7 & 8 \end{bmatrix}$	| + 4	=>	$\begin{bmatrix} 7 & 8 & 9 \\ 10 & 11 & 12 \end{bmatrix}$

This led to a style of finding *generic behaviors* for message symbols. "Polymorphism" is the official term (I believe derived from Strachey), but it is not really apt as its original meaning applied only to functions that could take more than one type of argument. An example class of objects in Smalltalk-72, such as a model of cons pairs, would look like:

```
          temporary variable
            |   instance variables
            ↓   ↓
to Pair b | h t          "b is temp. h, t are internal instance vars"
   (ISNEW   » (:h. :t)   "cons—if no explicit return is given, SELF is returned"
   ¤hd      » (<- » (^:h)^h)     "replaca and car"
   ¤tl      » (<- » (:t)^t)      "replacd and cdr"
   ¤isPair » (^true)
   ¤print   » ('(print. SELF mprint)
   ¤mprint » (h print. t isNil » (')print t isPair » (t mprint) »
         '•print. t print.') print)
   ¤length » (t isPair » (^1+t length) 1))
```

to like LOGO, except makes a class from its message

ISNEW is true if a new instance has been created

true any object not false acts as true

true » m n will evaluate m and escape from surrounding ()

false » m n will evaluate n

: evals the next part of message and binds result to the variable in its message

¤ eyeball looks to see if its message is a literal token in the message stream

^ send-back returns its value to sender

. "statement separator" value is following message

Because control is passed to the class before any of the rest of the message is considered—the class can decide *not* to receive at its discretion—complete protection is retained. Smalltalk-72 objects are "shiny" and impervious to attack. Part of the environment is the binding of the SENDER in the "messenger object" (a generalized activation record) that allows the receiver to determine differential privileges (see Appendix II for more details). This looked ahead to the eventual use of Smalltalk as a network OS (see [Goldstein and Bobrow 1980]), and I don't recall it being used very much in Smalltalk-72.

One of the styles retained from Smalltalk-71 was the comingling of function and class ideas. In other words, Smalltalk-72 classes looked like and could be used as functions, but it was easy to produce an instance (a kind of closure) by using the object *ISNEW*. Thus factorial could be written "extensionally" as:

```
to fact n (^if :n=0 then 1 else n*fact n-1)
```

or "intensionally", as part of class integer:

```
(... ¤! » (^:n=0 » (1) (n-1)! )
```

Of course, the whole idea of Smalltalk (and OOP in general) is to define everything *intensionally*. And this was the direction of movement as we learned how to program in the new style. I never liked this syntax (too many parentheses and nestings) and wanted something flatter and more grammar-like as in Smalltalk-71. To the right is an example syntax from the notes of a talk I gave around then. We will see something more like this a few years later in Dan's design for Smalltalk-76. I think something similar happened with LISP—that the "reality" of the straightforward and practical syntax **you could program in** prevailed against the flights of fancy that never quite got built.

FIGURE 11.30 Proposed Smalltalk-72 syntax

```
Pair :h :t
   hd <- :h
   hd         » h
   tl <- :t   » t
   isPair     » true
   print      » '(print. SELF mprint.
   mprint     » h print. if t isNil then ') print
                    else if t isPair then t mprint
                    else '•print. t print. ') print.
   length     » 1 + if t isList then t length else 0
```

11.4.1 Development of the Smalltalk-72 System and Applications

The advent of a real Smalltalk on a real machine started off an explosion of parallel paths that are too difficult to intertwine in strict historical order. Let me first present the general development of the Smalltalk-72 system up to the transistion to Smalltalk-76, and then follow that with the several years of work with children who were the primary motivation for the project. The Smalltalk-72 interpreter on the Interim Dynabook was not exactly zippy ("majestic" was Butler's pronouncement), but was easy to change and quite fast enough for many real-time interactive systems to be built in it.

Overlapping windows were the first project tackled (with Diana Merry) after writing the code to read the keyboard and create a string of text. Diana built an early version of a bit field block transfer (bitblt) for displaying variable pitch fonts and generally writing on the display. The first window versions were done as real 2 1/2D draggable objects that were just a little too slow to be useful. We decided to wait until Steve Purcell got his animation system going to do it right, and opted for the style that is still in use today, which is more like "2 1/4D." Windows were perhaps the most redesigned and reimplemented class in Smalltalk because we did not quite have enough compute power to just do the continual viewing to "world coordinates" and refreshing that my former Utah colleagues were starting to experiment with on the flight simulator projects at Evans & Sutherland. This is a simple powerful model but it is difficult to do in real-time even in 2 1/2D. The first practical windows in

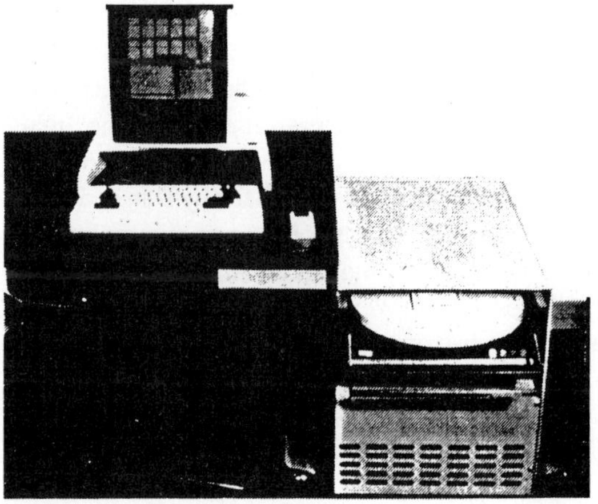

FIGURE 11.31 One of the "first build" ALTOs

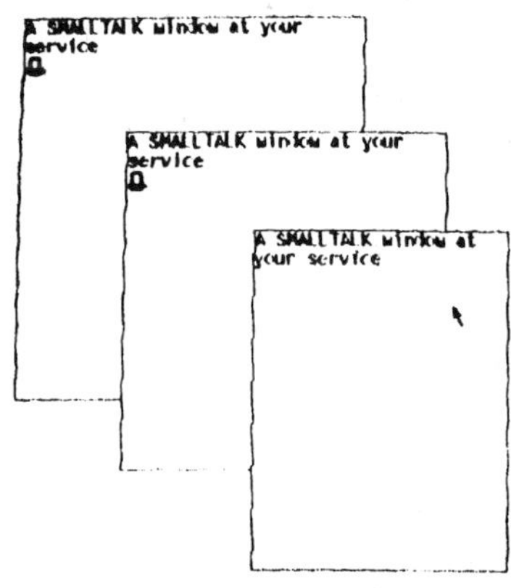

FIGURE 11.32 Early Smalltalk Windows on Interim Dynabook

FIGURE 11.33 Turtles

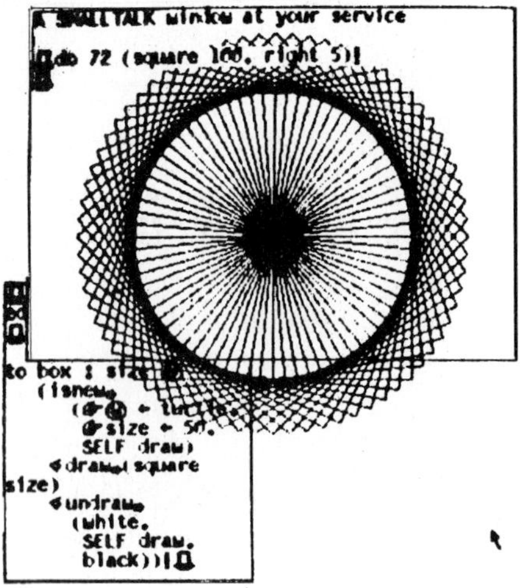

Smalltalk used the GRAIL conventions of sensitive corners for moving, resizing, cloning, and closing. Window scheduling used a simple "loopless" control scheme that threaded all the windows together.

One of the next classes to be implemented on the Interim Dynabook (after the basics of numbers, strings, and so on) was an object-oriented version of the LOGO turtle implemented by Ted. This could make many turtle instances that were used both for drawing and as a kind of value for graphics transformations. Dan created a class of "commander" turtles that could control a troop of turtles. Soon the turtles were made so they could be clipped by the windows.

John Shoch built a mouse-driven structured editor for Smalltalk code.

Larry Tesler (then working for POLOS) did not like the modiness and general approach of NLS, and he wanted both to show the former NLSers an alternative and to conduct some user studies (almost unheard of in those days) about editing. This led to his programming *miniMOUSE* in Smalltalk, the first real WYSIWYG galley editor at PARC. It was modeless (almost) and fun to use, not just for us, but for the many people he tested it on. (I ran the camera for the movies we took and remember their delight and enjoyment.) *miniMOUSE* quickly became an alternate editor for Smalltalk code and some of the best demos we ever gave used it.

One of the "small program" projects I tried on an adult class in the Spring of '74 was a one-page paragraph editor. It turned out to be too complicated, but the example I did to show them was completely modeless (it was in the air) and became the basis for much of the Smalltalk text work over the next few years. Most of the improvements were made by Dan and Diana Merry. Of course, objects mean multimedia documents; you almost get them for free. Early on we realized that in such a document, each component object should handle its own editing chores. Steve Weyer built some of the earliest multimedia documents, whose range was greatly and variously expanded over the years by Bob Flegal, Diana Merry, Larry Tesler, Tim Mott, and Trygve Reenskaug.

FIGURE 11.33 Findit retrieval by example

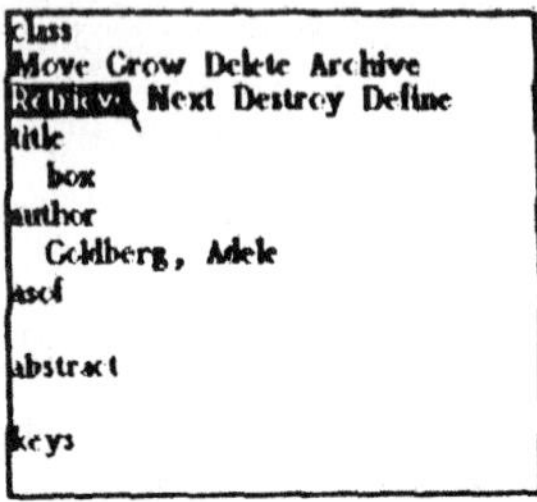

Steve Weyer and I devised *Findit*, a "retrieval by example" interface that used the analogy of classes to their instances to form retrieval requests. This was used for many years by the PARC library to control circulation.

The sampling synthesis music I had developed on the NOVA could generate three high-quality real-time voices. Bob Shur and Chuck Thacker transfered the scheme to the Interim Dynabook and achieved 12 voices in real-time. The 256 bit generalized input that we had specified for low speed devices (used for the mouse and keyboard) made it easy to connect 154 more to wire up two organ keyboards and a pedal. Effects such as portamento and decay were programmed. Ted Kaehler wrote TWANG, a music capture and editing system, using a tabulature notation that we devised to make music clear to children [Kay 1977a]. One of the things that was hard to do with sampling was the voltage controlled operator (VCO) effects that were popular on the "Well Tempered Synthesizer." A summer later, Steve Saunders, another of our bright summer students, was challenged to find a way to accomplish John Chowning's *very* non-real-time FM synthesis in real-time on the ID. He had to find a completely different way to think of it than "FM," and succeeded brilliantly with eight real-time voices that were integrated into TWANG [Saunders 1977].

Chris Jeffers (who was a musician and educator, not a computer scientist) knocked us out with OPUS, the first real-time score capturing system. Unlike most systems today it did not require metronomic playing but instead took a first pass looking for strong and weak beats (the phrasing) to establish a local model of the likely tempo fluctuations and then used curve fitting and extrapolation to make judgments about just where in the measure, and for what time value, a given note had been struck.

The animations on the NOVA ran 3–5 objects at about 2–3 frames per second. Fast enough for the *phi* phenomenon to work (if double buffering was used), but we wanted "Disney rates" of 10–15 frames per second for 10 or more large objects and many more smaller ones. This task was put into the ingenious hands of Steve Purcell. By the Fall of '73 he could demo 80 ping-pong balls and 10 flying horses running at 10 frames per second in 2 1/2 D. His next task was to make the demo into a general

FIGURE 11.34 Retrieved HyperDocument

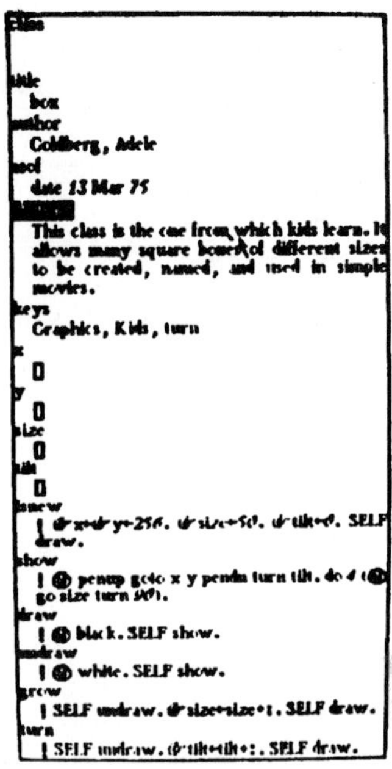

FIGURE 11.35 TWANG Music System

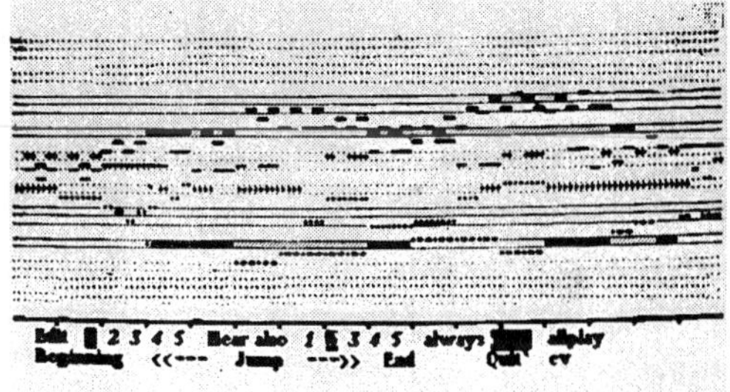

FIGURE 11.36 FM Timbre Editor

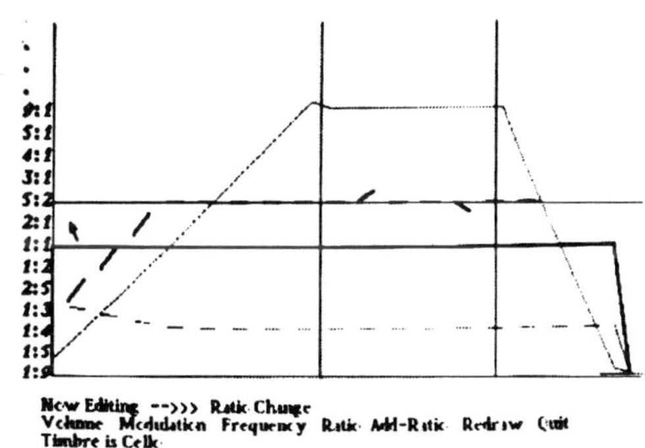

FIGURE 11.37 OPUS Score Capture

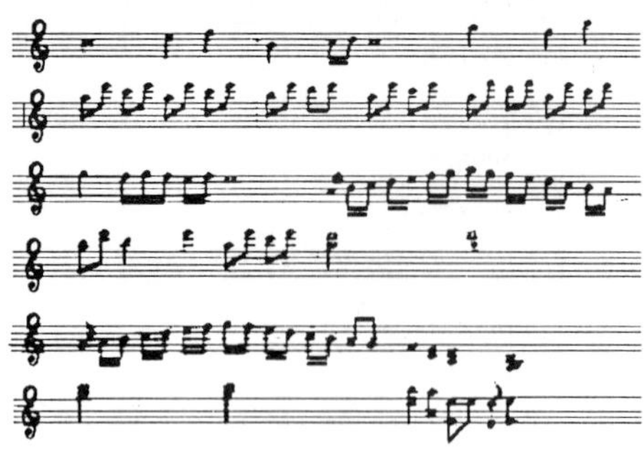

FIGURE 11.38 Shazam iconic user interface

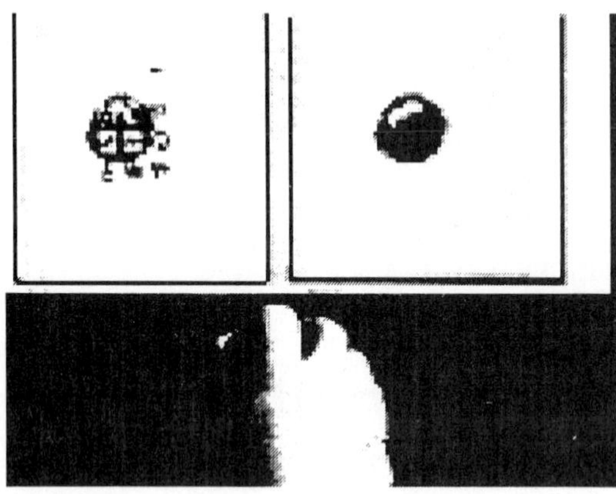

FIGURE 11.39 A sample animation

systems facility from which we could construct animation systems. His chaos system started working in May '74, just in time for summer visitors Ron Baecker, Tom Horseley, and professional animator Eric Martin to visit and build Shazam, a marvelously capable and simple animation system based on Ron's GENESYS thesis project on the TX-2 in the late sixties [Baecker 1969].

The main thesis project during this time was Dave Smith's PYGMALION [Smith 1975], an essay into iconic programming (no, we hadn't quite forgotten). One programmed by showing the system how changes should be made, much as one would illustrate on a blackboard with another programmer. This program became the starting place from which many subsequent "programming by example" systems took off.

I should say something about the size of these programs. PYGMALION was the largest program ever written in Smalltalk-72. It was about 20 pages of code—all that would fit in the interim dynabook ALTO—and is given in full in Smith's thesis. All the other applications were smaller. For example, the Shazam animation system was written and revised several times in the summer of 1974, and finally wound up as a 5–6 page application that included its icon-controlled multiwindowed user interface.

Given its roots in simulation languages, Simpula, a simple version of the SIMULA sequencing set approach to schedulingwas easy to write in a few pages. By this time we had decided that coroutines could be rendered more cleanly by scheduling individual methods as separate simulation phases. The generic SIMULA example was a job shop. This could be generalized into many useful forms, such as a hospital with departments of resources serving patients (see to the right). The children did not care for hospitals but saw they could model amusement parks, such as Disneyland, their schools, the stores they and their parents shopped in, and so forth. Later this model formed the basis of the Smalltalk Sim-kit, a high-level end-user programming environment (described ahead).

FIGURE 11.40 PYGMALION iconic programming

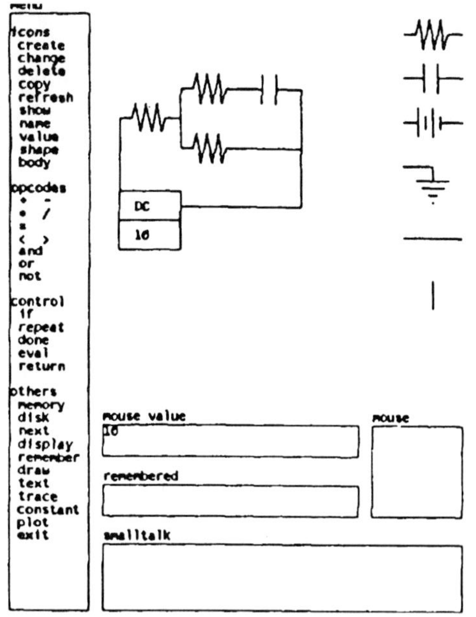

FIGURE 11.41 "Simpula" hospital simulation

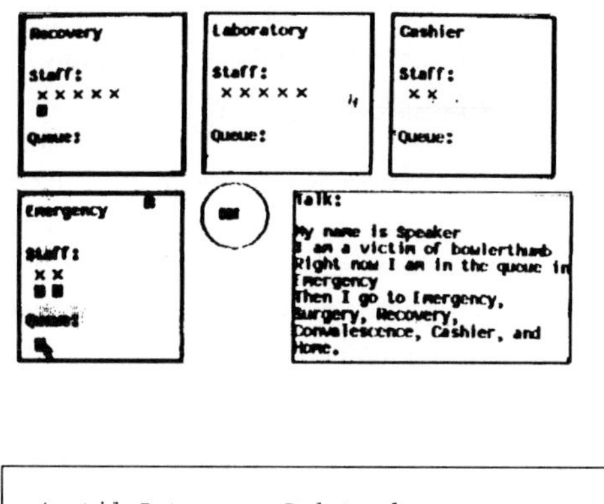


```
(until Return or Delete do
  ('character <- display <- keyboard.
  character = ret » (Return)
  character = del » (Delete)
  )
then case
  Return : ('deal with this normal exit')
  Delete : ('handle the abnormal exit'))
```

Many nice "computer sciency" constructs were easy to make in Smalltalk-72. For example, one of the controversies of the day was whether to have **goto**s or not (we did not), and if not, how could certain very useful control structures—such as multiple exits from a loop—be specified? Chuck Zahn at SLAC proposed an *event-driven case* structure in which a set of events could be defined so that when an event is encountered, the loop will be exited and the event will select a statement in a case block [Zahn 1974; Knuth 1974]. Suppose we want to write a simple loop that reads characters from the keyboard and outputs them to a display. We want it to exit normally when the <return> key is struck and with an error if the <delete> key is hit. Appendix IV shows how John Shoch defined this control structure.

11.4.2 The Evolution Of Smalltalk-72

Smalltalk-74 (sometimes known as FastTalk) was a version of Smalltalk-72 incorporating major improvements that included providing a real "messenger" object, message dictionaries for classes (a step toward real class objects), Diana Merry's bitblt (the now famous 2D graphics operator for bitmap graphics) redesigned by Dan and implemented in microcode, and a better, more general window interface. Dave Robson, while a student at UC Irvine, had heard of our project and made a pretty good stab at implementing an OOPL. We invited him for a summer and never let him go back—he was a great help in formulating an official semantics for Smalltalk.

The crowning addition was the OOZE (Object-Oriented Zoned Environment) virtual memory system that served Smalltalk-74, and more importantly, Smalltalk-76 [Ingalls 1978; Kaehler 1981]. The ALTO was not very large (128–256K), especially with its page-sized display (64k), and even with small programs, we soon ran out of storage. The 2.4 megabyte model 30 disk drive was faster and larger than a floppy and slower and smaller than today's hard drives. It was quite similar to the HP direct contact disk of the FLEX machine on which I had tried a fine-grain version of the B5000 segment swapper. It had not worked as well as I wanted, despite a few good ideas as to how to choose objects when purging. When the gang wanted to adapt this basic scheme, I said: "But I never got it to work well." I remember Ted Kaehler saying, "Don't worry, we'll make it work!"

The basic idea in all these systems is to be able to gather the most comprehensive possible working set of objects. This is most easily accomplished by swapping individual objects. Now the problem becomes the overhead of purging nonworking set objects to make room for the ones that are needed. (Paging sometimes works better for this part because you can get more than one object (**OOZE**) in each disk touch.) Two ideas help a lot. First, Butler's insight in the GENIE OS that it was worthwhile to expend a small percentage of time purging dirty objects to make core as clean as possible [Lampson 1966]. Thus crashes tend not to hurt as much and there is always clean storage to fetch pages or objects from the disk into. The other is one from the FLEX system in which I set up a stochastic decision mechanism (based on the class of an object) that determined during a purge whether to throw an object out. This had two benefits: important objects tended not to go out, and a mistake would just bring it back in again with the distribution, ensuring a low probablity that the object would be purged again soon.

The other problem that had to be taken care of was object-pointer integity (and this is where I had failed in the FLEX machine to come up with a good enough solution). What was needed really was a complete *transaction*, a brand new technique (thought up by Butler?) that ensured recovery regardless of when the system crashed. This was called "cosmic ray protection" as the early ALTOs had a way of just crashing once or twice a day for no discernable good reason. This, by the way did not particularly bother anyone as it was fairly easy to come up with *undo* and *replay* mechanisms to get around the cosmic rays. For pointer-based systems that had automatic storage management, this was a bit more tricky.

Ted and Dan decided to control storage using a Resident Object Table that was the only place machine addresses for objects would be found. Other useful information was stashed there as well to help LRU ageing. Purging was done in background by picking a class, positioning the disk to its instances (all of a particular class were stored together), then running through the ROT to find the dirty ones in storage and stream them out. This was pretty efficient and, true to Butler's insight, furnished a good-sized pool of clean storage that could be overwritten. The key to the design though (and the implementation of the transaction mechanism) was the checkpointing scheme. This ensured that there was a recoverable image no more than a few seconds old, regardless of when a crash might occur. OOZE swapped objects in just 80KB of working storage and could handle about 65K objects (up to several megabytes worth, more than enough for the entire system, its interface, and its applications).

11.4.3 "Object-oriented" Style

This is probably a good place to comment on the difference between what we thought of as OOP-style and the superficial encapsulation called "abstract data types" that was just starting to be investigated in academic circles . Our early "LISP-pair" definition is an example of an abstract data type because it preserves the "field access" and "field rebinding" that is the hallmark of a data structure. Considerable work in the 1960s was concerned with generalizing such structures. The "official" computer science world started to regard Simula as a possible vehicle for defining *abstract data types* (even by one of its inventors [Dahl 1970]), and it formed much of the later backbone of ADA. This led to the ubiquitous stack data-type example in hundreds of papers. To put it mildly, we were quite amazed at this, because to us, what Simula had whispered was something much stronger than simply reimplementing a weak and *ad hoc* idea. What I got from Simula was that you could now replace bindings and assignment with *goals*. The last thing you wanted any programmer to do is mess with internal state even if presented figuratively. Instead, the objects should be presented as *sites of higher level behaviors more appropriate for use as dynamic components.*

Even the way we taught children (see also ahead) reflected this way of looking at objects. Not too surprisingly, this approach has considerable bearing on the ease of programming, the size of the code needed, the integrity of the design, and so on. It is unfortunate that much of what is called "object-oriented programming" today is simply old style programming with fancier constructs. Many programs are loaded with "assignment-style" operations now done by more expensive attached procedures.

Where does the special efficiency of object-oriented design come from? This is a good question given that it can be viewed as a slightly different way to apply procedures to data structures. Part of the effect comes from a much clearer way to represent a complex system. Here, the constraints are as useful as the generalities. Four techniques used together—persistant state, polymorphism, instantiation, and methods-as-goals for the object—account for much of the power. None of these requires an "object-oriented language" to be employed—ALGOL 68 can almost be turned to this style—an OOPL merely focuses the designer's mind in a particular, fruitful direction. However, doing encapsulation right is a commitment not just to abstraction of state, but to eliminate state-oriented metaphors from programming.

Perhaps the most important principle—again derived from operating system architectures—is that when you give someone a structure, rarely do you want them to have unlimited privileges with it. Just doing type-matching is not even close to what is needed. Nor is it terribly useful to have some objects protected and others not. Make them all first class citizens and protect all.

I believe that the much smaller size of a good OOP system comes not just by being gently forced to come up with a more thought-out design. I think it also has to do with the "bang per line of code" you can get with OOP. The object carries with it a lot of significance and intention, its methods suggest the strongest kinds of goals it can carry out, and its superclasses can add up to much more code-functionality being invoked than most procedures-on-data-structures. Assignment statements—even abstract ones—express very low-level goals, and more of them will be needed to get anything done. Generally, we don't want the programmer to be messing around with state, whether simulated or not. The ability to instantiate an object has a considerable effect on code size as well. Another way to think of all this is: though the late-binding of automatic storage allocation does not do anything a programmer cannot do, its presence leads to both simpler and more powerful code. OOP is a late binding strategy for many things and all of them together hold off fragility and size explosion much longer than the older methodologies. In other words, human programmers are not Turing machines—and the less their programming systems require Turing machine techniques the better.

11.4.4 Smalltalk And Children

Now that I have summarized the "adult" activities (we were actually only semiadults) in Smalltalk up to 1976, let me return to the summer of '73, when we were ready to start experiments with children. None of us knew anything about working with children, but we knew that Adele Goldberg and Steve Weyer who were then with Pat Suppes at Stanford had done quite a bit and we were able to entice them to join us.

Because we had no idea how to teach object-oriented programming to children (or anyone else), the first experiments Adele did mimicked LOGO turtle graphics, and she got what appeared to be very similar results. That is to say, the children could get the turtle to draw pictures on the screen, but there

FIGURE 11.42 Adele holding forth at Jordan Middle School

seemed to be little happening beyond surface effects. At that time I felt that because the content of personal computing was interactive tools, the content of this new kind of authoring literacy should be the creation of interactive *tools* by the children. Procedural turtle graphics just wasn't it.

Then Adele came up with a brilliant approach to teaching Smalltalk as an object-oriented language: the "Joe Book." I believe this was partly influenced by Minsky's idea that you should teach a programming language holistically from working examples of serious programs.

Several instances of the class box are created and sent messages, culminating in a simple multiprocess animation. After getting kids to guess what a box might be like—they could come surprisingly close—they would be shown:

```
to box | x y size tilt
(¤draw    »   (@ place x y turn tilt. square size.)
¤undraw   »   (@ white. SELF draw. @ black)
¤turn     »   (SELF undraw. 'tilt <- tilt + :. SELF draw)
¤grow     »   (SELF undraw. 'size <- size + :. SELF draw)
ISNEW     »   (SELF undraw. 'size <- size + :. SELF draw)
```

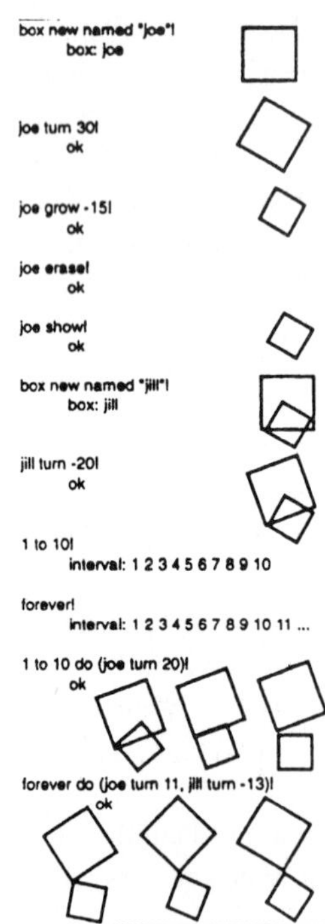

What was so wonderful about this idea were the myriad children's projects that could spring off the humble boxes. And some of the earliest were tools! This was when we got really excited. For example, Marion Goldeen's (12 years old) painting system was a full-fledged tool. A few years later, so was Susan Hamet's (12 years old) OOP illustration system (with a design that was like the MacDraw to come). Two more were Bruce Horn's (15 years old) music score capture system and Steve Putz's (15 years old) circuit design system. Looking back, this could be called another example in computer science of the "early success syndrome." The successes were real, but they were not as general as we thought. They would not extend into the future as strongly as we hoped. The children were chosen from the Palo Alto schools (hardly an average background) and we tended to be much more excited about the successes than the difficulties. In part, what we were seeing was the "hacker phenomenon," that, for any given pursuit, a particular 5% of the population will jump into it naturally, whereas the 80% or so who can learn it in time do not find it at all natural.

We had a dim sense of this, but we kept on having relative successes. We could definitely see that learning the mechanics of the system was not a major problem. The children could get most of it themselves by swarming over the ALTOS with Adele's JOE book. The problem seemed more to be that of design.

It started to hit home in the Spring of '74 after I taught Smalltalk to 20 PARC nonprogrammer adults. They were able to get through the initial material faster than the children, but just as it looked like an overwhelming success was at hand, they started to crash on problems that did not look to me to be much harder than the ones on which they had just been doing well. One of them was a project thought up by one of the adults, which was to make a little database system that could act like a card file or rolodex. They could not even come close to programming it. I was very surprised because I "knew" that such a project was well below the mythical "two pages" for end-users within we were working. That night I wrote it out, and the next day I showed all of them how to do it. Still, none of them were able to do it by themselves. Later, I sat in the room pondering the board from my talk. Finally, I counted the number of nonobvious ideas in this little program. They came to 17. And some of them were like the concept of the arch in building design: very hard to discover, if you do not already know them.

The connection to literacy was painfully clear. It is not enough to just learn to read and write. There is also a *literature* that renders *ideas*. Language is used to read and write about them, but at some point the organization of ideas starts to dominate mere language abilities. And it helps greatly to have some powerful ideas under one's belt to better acquire more powerful ideas [Papert 1971, 1971a, 1973]. So, we decided we should teach *design*. And Adele came up with another brilliant stroke to deal with this. She decided that what was needed was an intermediary between the vague ideas about the problem and the very detailed writing and debugging that had to be done to get it to run in Smalltalk. She called the intermediary forms *design templates*.

Using these, the children could look at a situation they wanted to simulate, and decompose it into classes and messages without having to worry just how a method would work. The method planning

FIGURE 11.43 The suthor in the Interim Dynabook playroom. Working with the kids was my favorite part of this Romance

FIGURE 11.44 Adele's planning template for Smalltalk (top) New behavior added by child (bottom)

Message the box can receive	English description of the action the box will carry out	Smalltalk description
new	It creates a new box that needs its own *pen* to draw the new box on the display, and that must remember its **size** whose first value is 50. Then it draws itself on the display screen	**pen new name "pal". number new name "size". size value 50. SELF draw.**
draw	The box has its pen draw a square on the screen at the pen's current location and orientation. The length of its four sides is **size**.	**do 4 (pal draw size. pal turn 90).**
undraw	Erase the box.	**pal white. SELF draw. pal black.**
grow	After erasing itself, the box instance retrieves a message which is interpreted as an increment of its size. It then redraws itself as a bigger or smaller square.	**SELF undraw. size increase by :. SELF draw.**
turn	After erasing itself, the box instance retrieves a message which is interpreted as an increment of its orientation. Note, since the pen, rather than the box, remembers the orientation, the box has to tell the pen to turn.	**SELF undraw. pal turn :. SELF draw.**

Message the box can receive	English description of the action the box will carry out	Smalltalk description
moveto	After erasing itself, the box instance retrieves two messages which are interpreted as the new coordinates of the box. Note, since the pen, rather than the box, remembers the location, the box has to tell the pen to place itself at the new location.	**SELF undraw. pal place at :. SELF draw.**

FIGURE 11.45 Marion Goldeen's painting program (top) Susan Hamet's OO Illustrator (bottom)

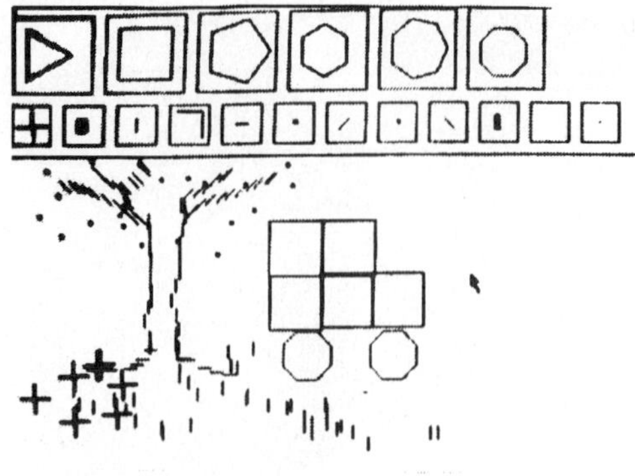

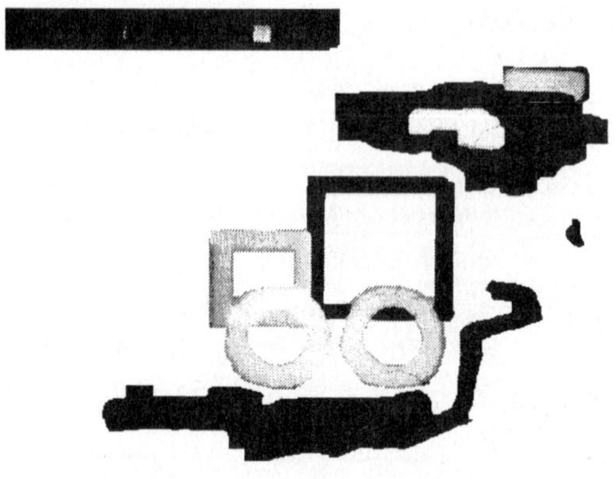

FIGURE 11.46 Cirrcuit design system by Steve Putz (age 15)

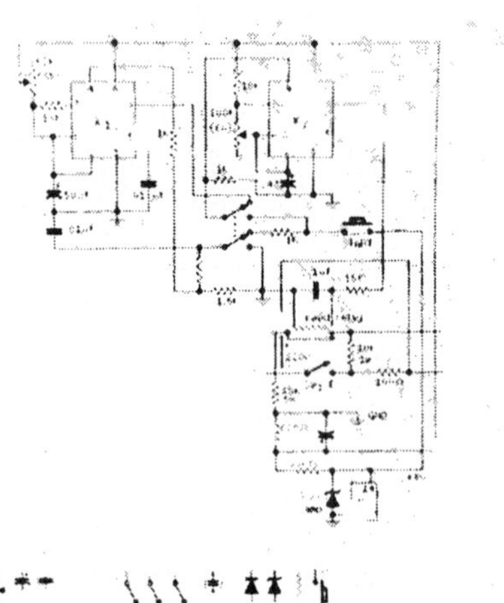

could then be done informally in English, and these notes would later serve as commentaries and guides to the writing of the actual code. This was a terrific idea, and it worked very well.

But not enough to satisfy us. As Adele liked to point out, it is hard to claim success if only some of the children are successful—*and* if a maximum effort of both children and teachers was required to get the successes to happen. Real pedagogy has to work in much less idealistic settings and be considerably more robust. Still, *some* successes are qualitatively different from *no* successes. We wanted more, and started to push on the inheritance idea as a way to let novices build on frameworks that could only be designed by experts. We had good reason to believe that this could work because we had been impressed by Lisa van Stone's ability to make significant changes to Shazam (the five or six page Smalltalk animation tool done by relatively expert adults). Unfortunately, inheritance—though an incredibly powerful technique—has turned out to be very difficult for novices (and even professionals) to deal with.

At this point, let me do a look back from the vantage point of today. I am now pretty much convinced that our design template approach was a good one after all. We just did not apply it longitudinally enough. I mean by this that there is now a large accumulation of results from many attempts to teach novices programming [Soloway 1989]. They all have similar stories that seem to have little to do with the various features of the programming languages used, and everything to do with the difficulties novices have thinking the special way that good programmers think. Even with a much better interface than we had then (and have today), it is likely that this area is actually more like writing than we wanted it to be. Namely, for the "80%," it really has to be learned gradually over a period of years in order to build up the structures that need to be there for design and solution look-ahead.

The problem is not to get the kids to do stuff—they love to *do*, even when they are not sure exactly what they are doing. This correlates well with studies of early learning of language, when much rehearsal is done regardless of whether content is involved. Just *doing* seems to help. What is difficult is to determine *what* ideas to put forth and how *deeply* they should penetrate at a given child's developmental level. This confusion still persists for reading and writing of natural language—and for mathematics—despite centuries of experience. And it is the main hurdle for teaching children programming. When, in what order and depth, and how should the powerful ideas be taught?

Should we even try to teach programming? I have met hundreds of programmers in the last 30 years and can see no discernable influence of programming on their general ability to think well or to take an enlightened stance on human knowledge. If anything, the opposite is true. Expert knowledge often remains rooted in the environments in which it was first learned—and most metaphorical extensions result in misleading analogies. A remarkable number of artists, scientists, and philosophers are quite dull outside of their specialty (and one suspects within it as well). The first siren's song we need to be wary of is the one that promises a connection between an interesting pursuit and interesting thoughts. The music is not in the piano, and it is possible to graduate Julliard without finding or feeling it.

I have also met a few people for whom computing provides an important new metaphor for thinking about human knowledge and reach. But something else was needed besides computing for enlightenment to happen.

Tools provide a path, a context, and almost an excuse for developing enlightenment, but no tool ever contained it or can dispense it. Cesare Pavese observed: to know the world we must construct it. In other words, *we make not just to have, but to know*. But the having can happen without most of the knowing taking place.

Another way to look at this is that knowledge is in its least interesting state when it is first being learned. The representations—whether

FIGURE 11.47 Tangram designs are created by selecting shapes from a "menu" displayed at the top of the screen. This system was implemented in Smalltalk by a fourteen-year old girl [Kay 1977a]

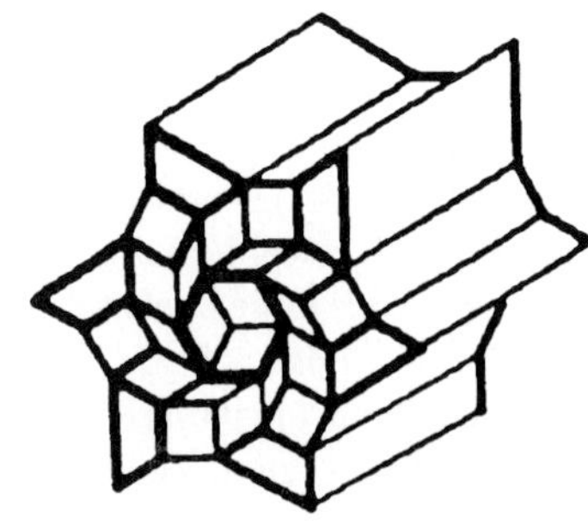

FIGURE 11.48 SpaceWar by Dennis (age 12)

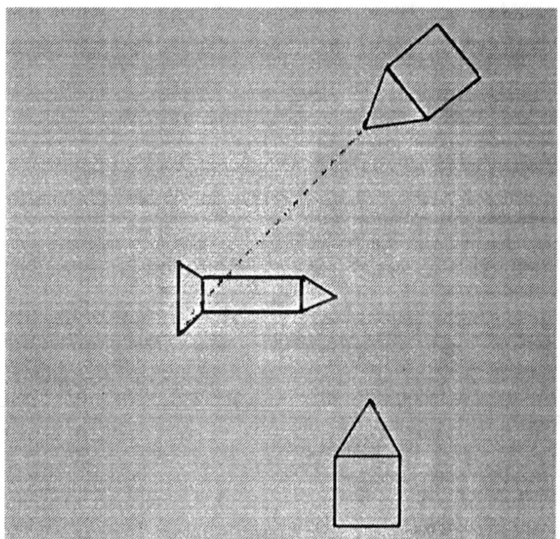

FIGURE 11.49 Shazam modified to "group" multiple images by Lisa van Stone (age 12)

markings, allusions, or physical controls—get in the way (almost take over as goals) and must be laboriously and painfully interpreted. From here there are several useful paths, two of which are important and intertwined.

The first is *fluency*, which in part is the process of building mental structures that make the interpretations of the representations disappear. The letters and words of a sentence are experienced as meaning rather than markings, the tennis racquet or keyboard becomes an extension of one's body, and so forth. If carried further one eventually becomes a kind of expert—but without deep knowledge in other areas, attempts to generalize are usually too crisp and ill-formed.

The second path is toward taking the knowledge as a *metaphor* than can illuminate other areas. But without fluency it is more likely that prior knowledge will hold sway and the metaphors from this side will be fuzzy and misleading.

The "trick," and I think that this is what liberal arts eduation is supposed to be about, is to get fluent *and* deep while building relationships with other fluent deep knowledge. Our society has lowered its aims so far that it is happy with "increases in scores" without daring to inquire whether any important threshold has been crossed. Being able to read a warning on a pill bottle or write about a summer vacation is not literacy and our society should not treat it so. Literacy, for example, is being able to fluently read and follow the 50-page argument in Paine's *Common Sense* and being able (and happy) to fluently write a critique or defense of it. Another kind of 20th century literacy is being able to hear about a new fatal contagious incurable disease and instantly know that a disastrous exponential relationship holds and early action is of the highest priority. Another kind of literacy would take citizens to their personal computers where they can fluently and without pain build a systems simulation of the disease to use as a comparison against further information.

At the liberal arts level we would expect that connections between each of the fluencies would form truly powerful metaphors for considering ideas in the light of others.

The reason, therefore, that many of us want children to understand computing deeply and fluently is that like literature, mathematics, science, music, and art, it carries special ways of thinking about situations that, in contrast with other knowledge and other ways of thinking critically, boost our ability to understand our world.

We did not know then, and I am sorry to say from 15 years later that these critical questions still do not yet have really useful answers. But there are some indications. Even very young children can understand and use interactive *transformational tools*. The first ones are their hands! They can readily extend these experiences to computer objects and making changes to them. They can often imagine what a proposed change will do and not be surprised at the result. Two- and three-year-olds can use the Smalltalk-style interface and manipulate object-oriented graphics. Third graders can (in a few days) learn more than 50 features—most of these are transformational tools—of a new system including its user interface. They can answer any question whose answer requires the application of just *one* of these tools. But it is extremely difficult for them to answer any question that requires *two* or more transformations. Yet they have no problem applying sequences of transformations, exploring "forward." It is for conceiving and achieving even modest goals requiring several changes that they almost completely lack navigation abilities.

It seems that what needs to be learned and taught is how to package transformations in two's and three's in a manner similar to learning a strategic game such as checkers. The vague sense of a "threesome" pointing toward one's goal can be a setup for the more detailed work that is needed to accomplish it. This art is possible for a large percentage of the population, but for most, it will need to be learned gradually over several years.

11.5 1976–1980—THE FIRST MODERN SMALLTALK (-76), ITS BIRTH, APPLICATIONS, AND IMPROVEMENTS

By the end of 1975 I felt that we were losing our balance—that the "Dynabook for children" idea was slowly dimming out—or perhaps starting to be overwhelmed by professional needs. In January 1976, I took the whole group to Pajaro Dunes for a three-day offsite to bring up the issues and try to reset the compass. It was called "Let's Burn Our Disk Packs." There were no shouting matches; the group liked (I would go so far to say: *loved*) each other too much for that. But we were troubled. I used the old aphorism that "no biological organism can live in its own waste products" to plead for a really fresh start: an hw-sw system very different from the ALTO and Smalltalk. One thing we all did agree on was that the current Smalltalk's power did not match our various levels of aspiration. I thought we needed something different, as I did not see how OOP by itself was going to solve our end-user problems. Others, particularly some of the grad students, really wanted a better Smalltalk that was faster and could be used for bigger problems. I think Dan felt that a better Smalltalk could be the vehicle for the different system I wanted, but could not describe clearly. The meeting was not a disaster, and we went back to PARC still friends and colleagues, but the absolute cohesiveness of the first four years never re-jelled. I started designing a new small machine and language I called the *NoteTaker* and Dan started to design Smalltalk-76.

The reason I wanted to "burn the disk packs" is that I had a very McLuhanish feeling about media and environments: that once we have shaped tools, in his words, they turn around and "reshape us." Of course this is a great idea if the tools are *really* good and aimed squarely at the issues in question. But the other edge of the sword cuts as deep—that inadequate tools and environments still reshape our thinking in spite of their problems, in part, because we *want* paradigms to guide our goals. Strong paradigms such as LISP and Smalltalk are so compelling that they *eat their young*: when you look at an application in either of these two systems, they resemble the systems themselves, not a new idea. When I looked at Smalltalk in 1975, I was looking at something great, but I did not see an end-user language; I did not see a solution to the original goal of a "reading" and "writing" computer medium for children. I wanted to stop, dynamite everything, and start from scratch again.

The *NoteTaker* was to be a "laptop" that could be built in a few years using the (almost) available 16K RAMs (a vast improvement over the 1K RAMs that the ALTO employed). A laptop could not use a mouse (which I hated anyway) and a tablet seemed awkward (not a lot of room and the stylus could flop out of reach when let go), so I came up with an embedded pointing device I called a "tabmouse." It was a relative pointer and had an *up* sensor so it could be stroked like a mouse and would also stay where you left it, but it felt like a stylus and used a pantograph mechanism that eliminated the annoying hysteresis bias in the x and y directions that made it hard to use a mouse as a pen. I planned to use a multiprocessor architecture of slow but highly integrated chips as originally specified for the Dynabook and wanted a new bytecoded interpreter for a friendlier and simpler system than Smalltalk-72.

Meanwhile Dan was proceeding with his total revamp of Smalltalk and along somewhat similar lines [Ingalls 1978]. The first major thing that needed to be done was to get rid of the function/class dualism in favor of a completely intensional definition with every piece of code as an intrinsic method. We had wanted that from the beginning (and most of the code was already written that way). There was a variety of strong desires for a real inheritance mechanism from Adele and me, from Larry Tesler, who was working on desktop publishing, and from the grad students. Dan had to find a better way than Simula's very rigid compile-time conception. It was time to make good on the idea that

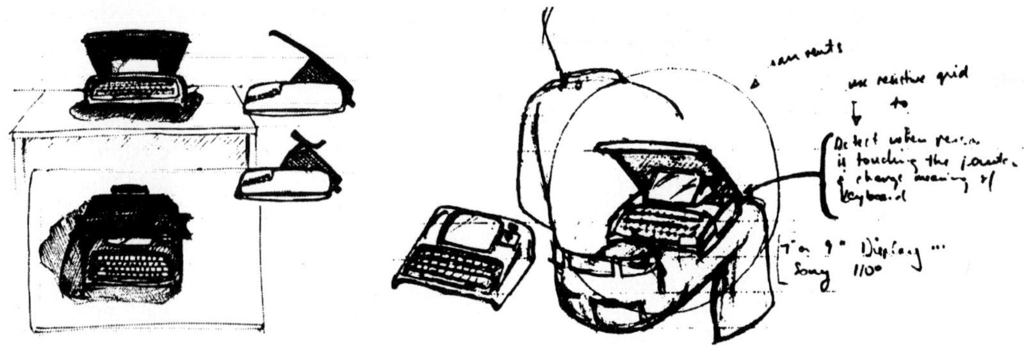

"everything was an object," which included all of the internal "systems" objects like "activation records," and the like. We were all agreed that the flexible syntax of the earlier Smalltalks was too flexible, and this level of extensibility was not desirable. All the extensions we liked used various keyword schemes, so Dan came up with a combination keyword/operator syntax that was very flexible, but allowed the language to be read unambiguously by both humans and the machine. This allowed a FLEX machine-like byte-code compiler and efficient interpreter to be defined that ran up to 180 times as fast as the previous direct interpreter. The OOZE VM system could be modified to handle the new objects and its capacity was well matched to the ALTO's RAM and disk.

11.5.1 Inheritance

A word about inheritance. Simula-I had neither classes as objects nor inheritance. Simula-67 added the latter as a generalization to the ALGOL-60 <block> structure. This was a great idea. But it did have some drawbacks: minor ones, like name clashes in multiple threaded lists (no one uses threaded lists anymore), and major ones, like a rigidity in the extended type structures, a need to qualify types, only a single path of inheritance, and difficulty in adapting to an interactive development system with incremental compiling and other needs for instant changes. Then there were a host of problems that were really outside the scope of Simula's goals: having to do with various kinds of modeling and inferencing that were of interest in the world of artificial intelligence. For example, not all useful questions could be answered by following a static chain. Some of them required a kind of "inheritance" or "inferencing" through dynamically bound "parts" (that is, instance variables). Multiple inheritance also looked important but the corresponding possible clashes between methods of the same name in different superclasses looked difficult to handle, and so forth.

On the other hand, because things can be done with a dynamic language that are difficult with a statically compiled one, I just decided to leave inheritance out as a feature in Smalltalk-72, knowing that we could simulate it back using Smalltalk's LISPlike flexibility. The biggest contributer to these AI ideas was Larry Tesler, who used what is now called "slot inheritance" extensively in his various versions of early desktop publishing systems. Nowadays, this would be called a "delegation-style" inheritance scheme [Lieberman]. Danny Bobrow and Terry Winograd during this period were designing a "frame-based" AI language called KRL which was "object-oriented" and I believe was influenced by early Smalltalk. It had a kind of multiple inheritance—called *perspectives*—that permitted an object to play multiple roles in a very clean way. Many of these ideas a few years later went into PIE, an interesting extension of Smalltalk to networks and higher level descriptions by Ira Goldstein and Bobrow [Goldstein and Bobrow 1980].

By the time Smalltalk-76 came along, Dan Ingalls had come up with a scheme that was Simula-like in its semantics but could be incrementally changed on the fly to be in accord with our goals of close interaction. I was not completely thrilled with it because it seemed that we needed a better theory about inheritance entirely (and still do). For example, inheritance and instancing (which is a kind of inheritance) muddles both pragmatics (such as factoring code to save space) and semantics (used for way too many tasks such as: specialization, generalization, speciation, and so forth). Alan Borning employed a multiple inheritance scheme in Thinglab [Borning 1977] which was implemented in Smalltalk-76. But no comprehensive and clean multiple inheritance scheme appeared that was compelling enough to surmount Dan's original Simula-like design.

Meanwhile, the running battle with Xerox continued. There were now about 500 ALTOs linked with Ethernets to each other and to Laserprinter and file servers, that used ALTOs as controllers. I wrote many memos to the Xerox planners trying to get them to make plans that included personal computing as one of their main directions. Here is an example:

A Simple Vision of the Future

A Brief Update of My 1971 Pendery Paper

In the 1990's there will be millions of personal computers. They will be the size of notebooks of today, have high-resolution flat-screen reflective displays, weigh less than ten pounds, have ten to twenty times the computing and storage capacity of an *Alto*. Let's call them *Dynabooks*.

The purchase price will be about that of a color television set of the era, although most of the machines will be given away by manufacturers who will be marketing the content rather than the container of personal computing.

...

Though the *Dynabook* will have considerable local storage and will do most computing locally, it will spend a large percentage of its time hooked to various large, global information utilities which will permit communication with others of ideas, data, working models, as well as the daily chit-chat that organizations need in order to function. The communications link will be by private and public wires and by packet radio. Dynabooks will also be used as servers in the information utilities. They will have enough power to be entirely shaped by software.

The Main Points of This Vision

- There need only be a few hardware types to handle almost all of the processing activity of a system.
- Personal Computers, Communications Links, and Information Utilities are the three critical components of a Xerox future.

...

In other words, the *material* of a computer system is the computer itself, *all* of the *content* and *function* is fashioned in software.

There are two important guidelines to be drawn from this:

» Material: If the design and development of the hardware computer material is done as carefully and completely as Xerox's development of special light-sensitive alloys, then only one or two computer designs need to be built... Extra investment in development here will be vastly repaid by simplifying the manufacturing process and providing lower costs through increased volume.

» Content: Aside from the wonderful generality of being able to continously shape new content from the same material, *software* has three important characteristics:

- the *replication* time and cost of a content-function is *zero*
- the *development* time and cost of a content-function is *high*
- the *change* time and cost of a content-function can be *low*

Xerox ***must*** take these several points seriously if it is to survive and prosper in its new business area of information media. If it does, the company has an excellent chance for several reasons:

- Xerox has the financial base to cover the large development costs of a small number of very powerful computer-types and a large number of software functions.
- Xerox has the marketing base to sell these functions on a wide enough scale to garner back to itself an incredible profit.
- Xerox has working for it an impressively large percentage of the best software designers in the world.

In 1976, Chuck Thacker designed the ALTO III that would use the new 16k chips and be able to fit on a desktop. It could be marketed for about what the large cumbersome special purpose "word-processors" cost, yet could do so much more. Nevertheless, in August of 1976, Xerox made a fateful decision: not to bring the ALTO III to market. This was a huge blow to many of us—even me, who had never really really thought of the ALTO as anything but a stepping stone to the "real thing." In 1992, the world market for personal computers and workstations was $90 million—twice as much as the mainframe and mini market, and many times Xerox's 1992 gross. The most successful company of this era—Microsoft—is not a hardware company, but a software company.

11.5.2 The Smalltalk User Interface

I have been asked by several of the reviewers to say more about the development of the "Smalltalk-style" overlapping window user interface in as much as there are now more than 20 million computers in the world that use its descendents. A decent history would be as long as this chapter, and none has been written so far. There is a summary of some of the ideas in [Kay 1989]—let me add a few more points.

All of the elements eventually used in the Smalltalk user interface were already to be found in the sixties—as different ways to access and invoke the functionality provided by an interactive system. The two major centers of ideas were Lincoln Labs and RAND Corporation—both ARPA funded. The big shift that consolidated these ideas into a powerful theory and long-lived examples came because the LRG focus was on children. Hence, we were thinking about learning as being one of the main effects we wanted to have happen. Early on, this led to a 90-degree rotation of the purpose of the user interface from "access to functionality" to "environment in which users learn by doing." This new stance could now respond to the echos of Montessori and Dewey, particularly the former, and got me, on rereading Jerome Bruner, to think beyond the children's curriculum to a "curriculum of the user interface."

The particular aim of LRG was to find the equivalent of writing—that is, learning and thinking by doing in a medium—our new "pocket universe." For various reasons I had settled on "iconic programming" as the way to achieve this, drawing on the iconic representations used by many ARPA projects in the sixties. My friend Nicholas Negroponte, an architect, was extremely interested in how environments affected people's work and creativity. He was interested in embedding the new computer

FIGURE 11.50 Paul Rovner showing the iconic "Lincoln Wand" ca. 1968

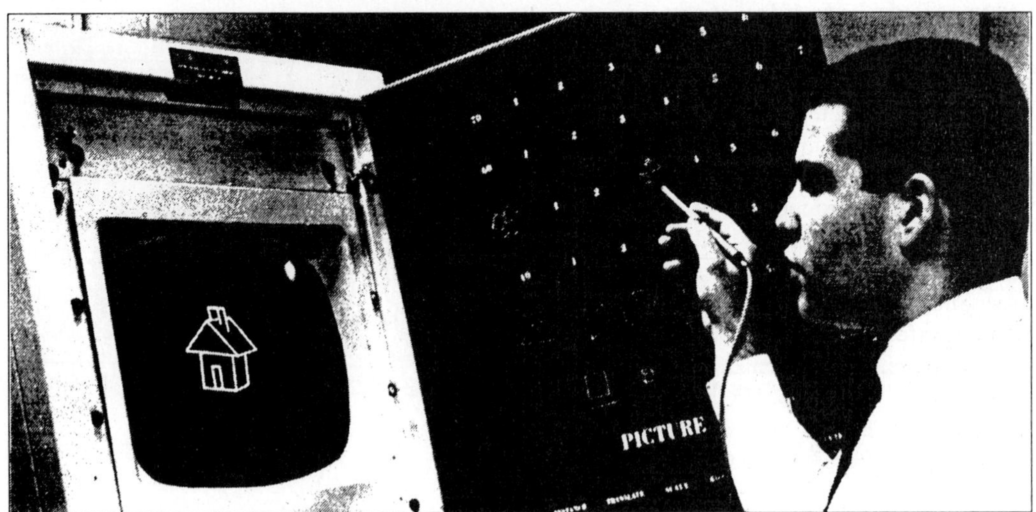

magic in familar surroundings. I had quite a bit of theatrical experience in a past life, and remembered Coleridge's adage that "people attend 'bad theatre' hoping to forget, people attend 'good theatre' *aching to remember*." In other words, it is the ability to evoke the audience's own intelligence and experiences that makes theatre work.

Putting all this together, we want an apparently free environment in which exploration causes desired sequences to happen (Montessori); one that allows kinesthetic, iconic, and symbolic learning—"*doing* with *images* makes *symbols*" (Piaget and Bruner); the user is never trapped in a mode (GRAIL); the magic is embedded in the familiar (Negroponte); and which acts as a magnifying mirror for the user's own intelligence (Coleridge). It would be a great finish to this story to say that having articulated this we were able to move straightforwardly to the design as we know it today. In fact, the UI design work happened in fits and starts in between feeding Smalltalk itself, designing children's experiments, trying to understand iconic construction, and just playing around. In spite of this meandering, the context almost forced a good design to turn out anyway. Just about everyone at PARC at this time had opinions about the UI, ours and theirs. It is impossible to

FIGURE 11.51 The last Smalltalk-72 interface

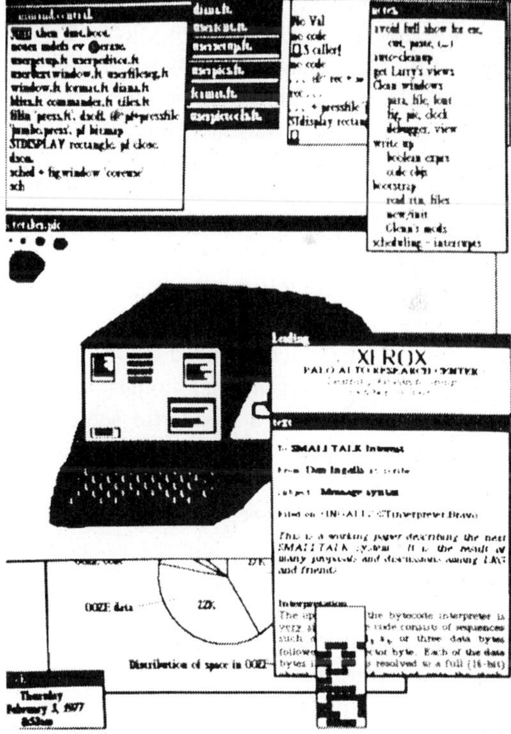

give detailed credit for the hundreds of ideas and discussions. However, the consolidation can certainly be attributed to Dan Ingalls, for listening to everyone, contributing original ideas, and constantly building a design for user testing. I had a fair amount to do with setting the context, inventing overlapping windows, and so on, and Adele and I designed most of the experiments. Beyond that, Ted Kaehler and visitor, Ron Baecker, made highly valuable contributions. Dave Smith designed SmallStar, the prototype iconic interface for the Xerox Star product.

Meanwhile, I had gotten Doug Fairbairn interested in the *Notetaker*. He designed a wonderful "smart bus" that could efficiently handle slow multiple processors and the system looked very promising, even though most of the rest of PARC thought I was nuts to abandon the fast bipolar hw of the ALTO. But I could not see that bipolar was ever going to make it into a laptop or Dynabook. On the other hand, I hated the 8-bit micros that were just starting to appear, because of the silliness and naivete of their designs—there was no hint that anyone who had ever designed software was involved.

FIGURE 11.52 Ted Kaehler's iconic painting interface

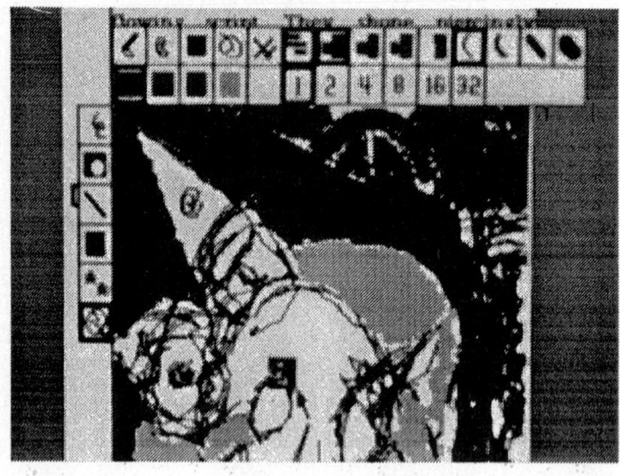

FIGURE 11.53 Smalltalk-76 User Interface with a variety of applications, including a clock, font editor, painting and illustration editor with iconic menus and programmable radio buttons, a word processor document editor, and a class editor showing window interface code.

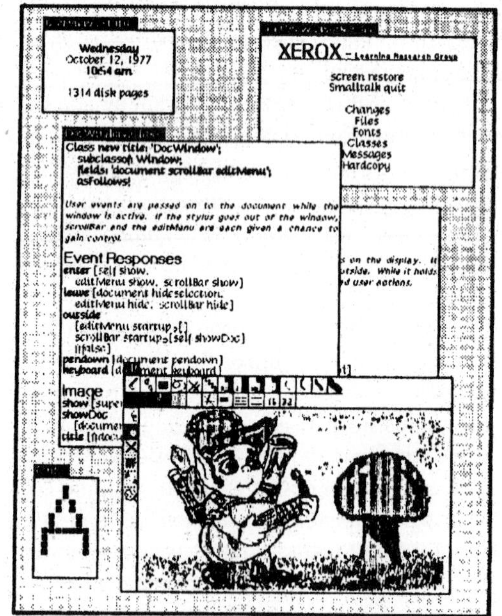

11.5.3 Smalltalk-76

Dan finished the Smalltalk-76 design in November, and he, Dave Robson, Ted Kaehler, and Diana Merry successfully implemented the system from scratch (which included rewriting all the existing class definitions) in just seven months. This was such a wonderful achievement that I was bowled over in spite of my wanting to start over. It was fast, lively, could handle "big" problems, and was great fun. The system consisted of about 50 classes described in about 180 pages of source code. This included all of the OS functions, files, printing, and other Ethernet services, the window interface, editors, graphics and painting systems, and two new contributions by Larry Tesler, the famous browsers for static methods in the inheritance hierarchy, and dynamic contexts for debugging in the run-time environment. In every way it was the consolidation of all our

```
Class new title: 'Window';
  fields: 'frame';
  asFollows!
```

This is a superclass for presenting windows on the display. It holds control until the stylus is depressed outside. While it holds control, it distributes messages to itself based on user actions.

```
Scheduling
startup
  [frame contains: stylus =>
    self enter.
    repeat:
      [frame contains: stylus loc =>
        [keybard active => [self keyboard]
        stylus down => [self pendown]]
      self outside => []
      stylus down => [^self leave]]]
  ^false]
Default Event Responses
enter [self show]
leave
outside [^false]
pendown
keyboard [keyboard next. frame flash]
Image
show
  [frame outline: 2.
  titleframe put: self title at: frame origin + title loc.
  titleframe complement]
... etc.
```

: means keyword whose following expression will be sent "by value"

: means keyword whose following expression will be sent "by name"

^ means "send back"

=> means "then"

```
Class new title: 'DocWindow';
  subclassof: Window;
  fields: 'document scrollbar edit Menu';
  asFollows!
```

User events are passed on to the document while the window is active. If the stylus goes out of the window, scrollbar and the editMenu are each given a chance to gain control.

```
Event Responses
enter [self show.editMenu show.scrollbar
show]
leave [document hideselection.editMenu
hide.scrollbar hide]
outside
  [editMenu startup => []
  scrollbar startup => [self showDoc]
  ^flase]
pendown [document pendown]
keyboard [document keyboard]
Image
show [super show.self showDoc]
showDoc [doucument showin: frame at: scrollbar position]
title [^document title]
```

super means delegate message to next higher superclass

FIGURE 11.54 Smalltalk-76 Metaphysics

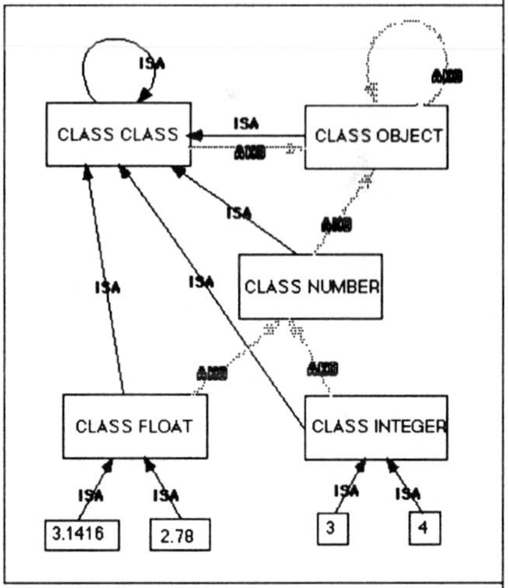

FIGURE 11.55 Dan Ingalls, the main implementer of Smalltalk, creator of Smalltalk-76, and his implementation plan (right)

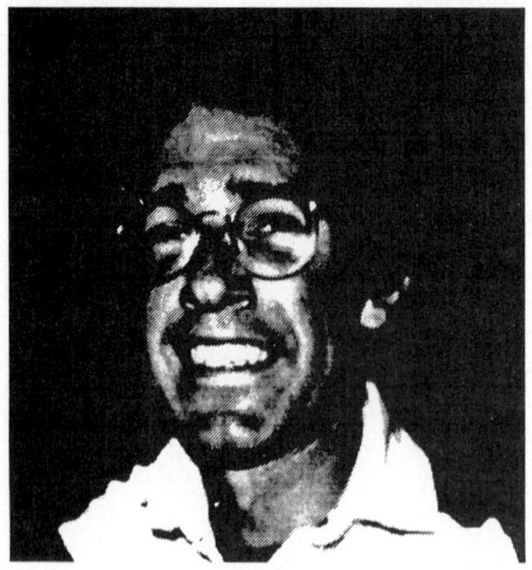

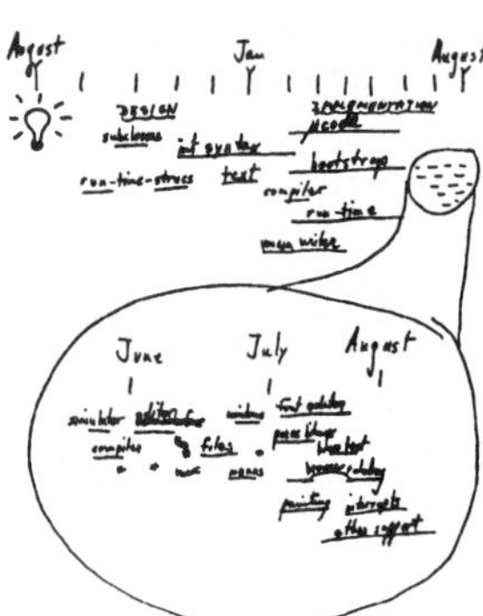

ideas and yearnings about Smalltalk in one integrated package. All Smalltalks since have resembled this conception very closely. In many ways, as Tony Hoare once remarked about ALGOL, Dan's Smalltalk-76 was a great improvement on its successors!

Here are two stylish ST-76 classes written by Dan. Notice, particularly in class Window, how the code is expressed as goals for other objects (or itself) to achieve. The superclass Window's main job is to notice events and distribute them as messages to its subclasses. In the example, a document window (a subclass of DocWindow) is going to deal with the effects of user interactions. The Window class will notice that the keyboard is active and send a message to itself that will be intercepted by the subclass method. If there is no method the character will be thrown away and the window will flash. In this case, it finds DocWindow method: **keyboard**, which tells the held document to check it out.

In January of 1978 Smalltalk-76 had its first real test. CSL had invited the top ten executives of Xerox to PARC for a two-day seminar on software, with a special emphasis on complexity and what could be done about it. LRG got asked to give them a hands-on experience in end-user programming so "they could do 'something real' over two 1 1/2 hour sessions." We immediately decided *not* to teach them Smalltalk-76 (my "burn our disk packs" point in spades), but to create in two months in Smalltalk-76 a rich system especially tailored for adult nonexpert users (Dan's point in trumps). We took our "Simpula" job shop simulation model as a starting point and decided to build a user interface for a generalized job shop simulation tool that the executives could make into specific dynamic simulations that would act out their changing states by animating graphics on the screen. We called it the Smalltalk SimKit. This was a maximum effort and everyone pitched in. Adele became the design leader in spite of the very recent appearance of a new baby. I have a priceless memory of her debugging away on the SimKit while simultaneously nursing Rachel!

There were many interesting problems to be solved. The system itself was straightforward but it had to be completely sealed off from Smalltalk proper, particularly with regard to error messages. Dave Robson came up with a nice scheme (almost an expert system) to capture complaints from the bowels of Smalltalk and translated them into meaningful SimKit terms. There were many user interface details—some workaday, such as making new browsers that could only look at the four SimKit classes (Station, Worker, Job, Report), and some more surprising as when we tried it on ten PARC nontechnical adults of about the same age and found that they could not read the screen very well. The small fonts our thirtysomething year-old eyes were used to did not work for those in their

FIGURE 11.56 Jack Goldman finally uses the system he paid for all those years (with Alan Borning helping)

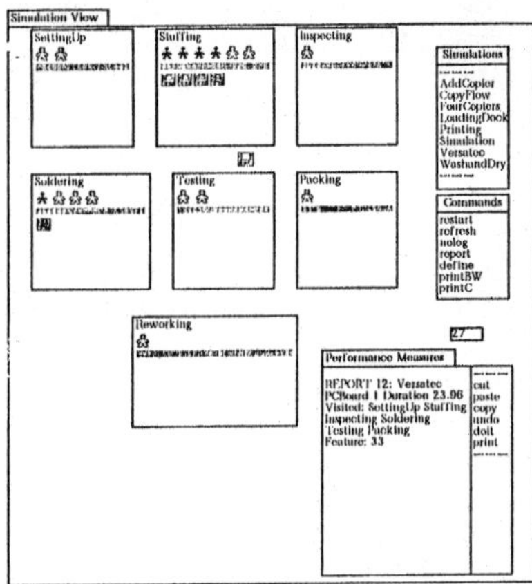

FIGURE 11.57 An end-user simulation by a Xerox executive, in SimKit. Total time including training: 3 hours

fifties. This led to a nice introduction to the system in which the executives were encouraged to customize the screen by choosing among different fonts and sizes with the side effect that they learned how to use the mouse unselfconsciously.

On the morning of the "big day" Ted Kaehler decided to make a change in the virtual memory system OOZE to speed it up a little. We all held our breaths, but such was the clarity of the design and the confidence of the implementers that it did work, and the executive hands-on was a howling success. About an hour into the first session one of the VPs (who had written a few programs in FORTRAN 15 years before) finally realized he was programming and mused "so it's finally come to this." Nine out of the ten executives were able to finish a simulation problem that related to their specific interests. One of the most interesting and sophisticated was a PC board production line done by the head of a Xerox-owned company using actual figures (that he carried around in his head) to prime a model that could not be solved easily by closed form mathematics—it revealed a serious flaw in the disposition of workers, given the line's average probability of manufacturing defects.

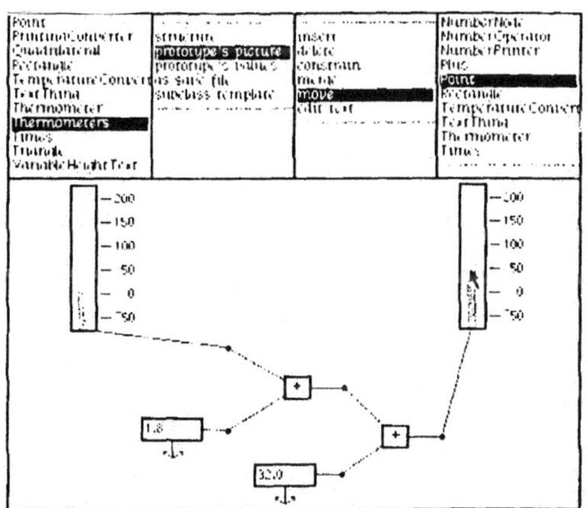

FIGURE 11.58 Alan Borning's Thinglab, a constraint-based iconic problem solver

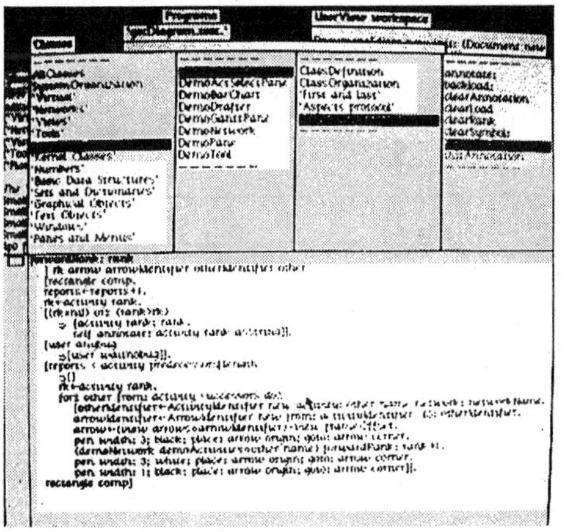

FIGURE 11.59 Smalltalk-76 hierarchical class browser designed and built by Larry Tesler

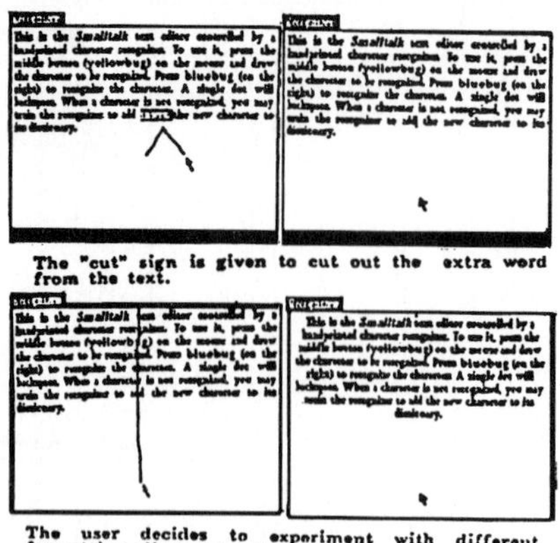

FIGURE 11.60 The author' pen-based interface for ST-

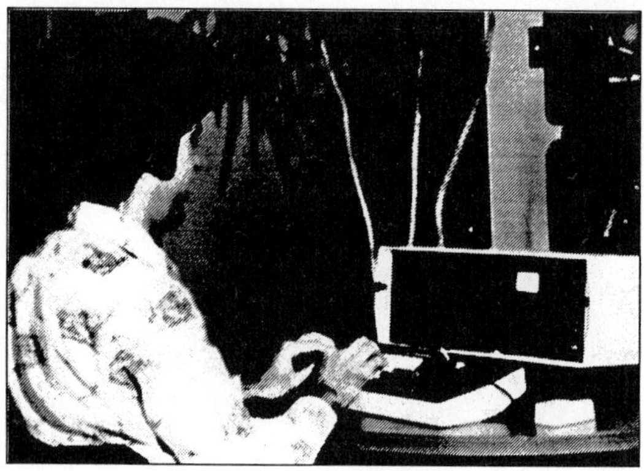

FIGURE 11.61 Doug Fairbain using his *NoteTaker*

Another important system done at this time was Alan Borning's Thinglab [Borning1979]—the first serious attempt to go beyond Ivan Sutherland's Sketchpad. Alan devised a very nice approach for dealing with constraints that did not require the solver to be omniscient (or able to solve Fermat's last theorem).

We could see that the "pushing" style of Smalltalk could eventually be relaced by a "pulling" style that was driven by changes to values that different methods were based on. This was an old idea but Thinglab showed how the object-oriented definition could be used to automatically limit the contexts for event-driven processing. And we soon discovered that "prototypes" were more hospitable than classes and that multiple inheritance would be well served if there were classes for methods that knew generally what they were supposed to be about (inspired by Pat Winston's second order models).

Meanwhile, the *NoteTaker* was getting more real, bigger, and slower. By this time the Western Digital emulation-style chips I hoped to use showed signs of being "diffusion-ware," and did not look like they would really show up. We started looking around for something that we could count on, even if it did not have a good architecture. In 1978, the best candidate was the Intel 8086, a 16-bit chip (with many unfortunate remnants of the 8008 and 8080), but with (barely) enough capacity to do the job—we would need three of them to make up for the ALTO, one for the interpreter, one for bitmapped graphics, and one for I/O (networking, and so on).

Dan had been interested in the *NoteTaker* all along and wanted to see if he could make a version of Smalltalk-76 that could be the *NoteTaker* system. In order for this to happen, it would have to run in 256K (the maximum amount of RAM that we had planned for the machine. None of the NOVA-like emulated "machine-code" from the ALTO could be brought over, and it had to fit in memory as well—there would only be floppies, no swapping memory existed. This challenge led to some excellent improvements in the system design. Ted Kaehler's system tracer (which could write out new virtual memories from old ones) was used to clone Smalltalk-76 into the *NoteTaker*. The indexed object table (as was used in early Smalltalk-80) first appeared here to simplify object access. An experiment in stacking contexts contiguously was tried: to save space and gain speed. Most of the old machine code was rewitten in Smalltalk and the total machine kernel was reduced to 6K bytes of (the not very strong) 8086 code.

All the re-engineering had an interesting effect. Though the 8086 was not as good at bitblt as the ALTO (and much of the former machine code to assist graphics was now in Smalltalk), the overall

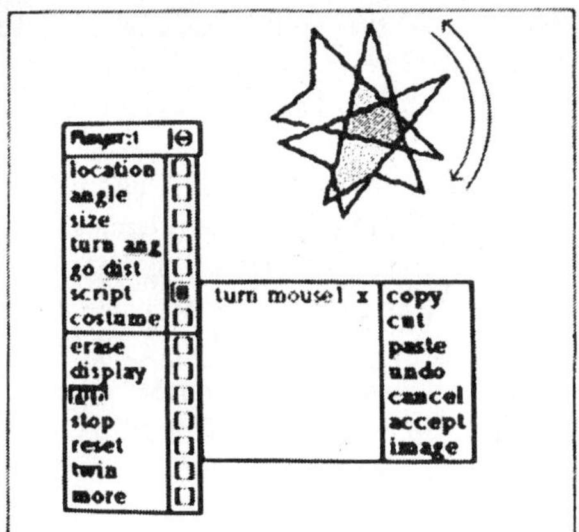

FIGURE 11.62 Design for *NoteTaker* Interface [Kay 1979]

FIGURE 11.63 Diana Merry at her trusty ALTO

interpreter was about twice as fast as the ALTO version (because not all the Smalltalk byte-code interpreter would fit into the 4K microcode memory on the ALTO). With various kinds of tricks and tuning, graphics display was "largely compensated" (in Dan's words). This was mainly because the ALTO did not have enough microcode memory to take in all of the Smalltalk emulation code—some of it had to be rendered in emulated "NOVA" code which forced two layers of interpretation. In fact, the *NoteTaker* worked extremely well, though it would have crushed any lap. It had hopped back on the desk, and looked suspiciously like miniCOM (and several computers that would appear a few years later). It really did run on batteries and several of us had the pleasure of taking *NoteTaker* on a plane and running an object-oriented system with a windowed interface at 35,000 feet.

We eventually built about 10 of the machines, and though in many senses an engineering success, what had to be done to make them had once again squeezed out the real end-users for whom it was originally aimed. If Xerox (and PARC) as a whole had believed in these smaller scale ideas, we could have put much more silicon muscle behind the dreams and successfully built them in the '70s when

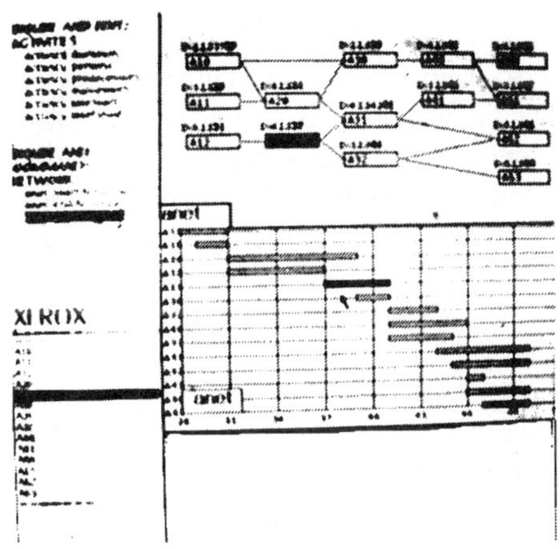

FIGURE 11.64 What Steve Jobs saw. Multiviews on complex structures by Trygve Reenskaug

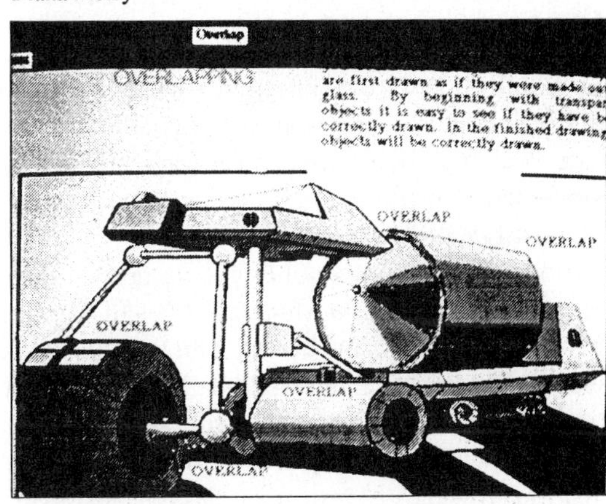

FIGURE 11.65 Multimedia documents by Bob Flegal and Diana Merry

FIGURE 11.66 Dave Robson

they were first possible. It was a bitter disappointment to have to get the wrong kind of CPU from Intel and the wrong kind of display from HP because there was not enough corporate will to take advantage of internal technological expertise.

By now it was already 1979, and we found ourselves doing one of our many demos, but this time for a very interested audience: Steve Jobs, Jeff Raskin, and other technical people from Apple. They had started a project called *Lisa* but were not quite sure what it should be like, until Jeff said to Steve, "You should really come over to PARC and see what they are doing." Thus, more than eight years after overlapping windows had been invented and more than six years after the ALTO started running, the people who could really do something about the ideas finally got to see them. The machine used was the Dorado, a very fast "big brother" of the ALTO, whose Smalltalk microcode had been largely written by Bruce Horn, one of our original "Smalltalk kids" who was still only a teenager. Larry Tesler gave the main part of the demo with Dan sitting in the copilot's chair and Adele and I watched from the rear. One of the best parts of the demo was when Steve Jobs said he did not like the blt-style scrolling we were using and asked if we could do it in a smooth continuous style. In less than a minute Dan found the methods involved, made the (relatively major) changes, and scrolling was now continuous! This shocked the visitors, especially the programmers among them, as they had never seen a really powerful incremental system before.

Steve tried to get and/or buy the technology from Xerox (which was one of Apple's minority venture capitalists), but Xerox would neither part with it nor come up with the resources to continue to develop it in-house by funding a better *NoteTaker* cum Smalltalk.

"The greatest sin in Art is not Boredom, as is commonly supposed, but lack of Proportion"
—Paul Hindemith

11.6 1980–1983—THE RELEASE VERSION OF SMALLTALK (-80)

As Dan said, "The decision not to continue the *NoteTaker* project added motivation to release Smalltalk widely." But not for me. By this time I was both happy about the cleanliness and elegance of the Smalltalk conception as realized by Dan and the others, and sad that it was farther away than ever from the children—it came to me as a shock that no child had programmed in any Smalltalk since Smalltalk-76 made its debut. Xerox (and PARC) were now into "workstations" as things in themselves—but I still wanted "playstations." The romance of the Dynabook seemed less within grasp, paradoxically, just when the various needed technologies were starting to be commercially feasible—some of them, unfortunately, like the flat-screen display, were abandoned to the Japanese by the US companies who had invented them. This was a major case of "snatching defeat from the jaws of victory." Larry Tesler decided that Xerox was never going to "get it" and was hired by Steve Jobs in May 1980 to be a principal designer of the *Lisa*. I agreed, had a sabbatical coming, and took it.

Adele decided to drive the documentation and release process for a new Smalltalk that could be distributed widely almost regardless of the target hardware. Only a few changes had to be made to the *NoteTaker* Smalltalk-78 to make a releasable system. Perhaps the change that was most ironic was to turn the custom fonts that made Smalltalk more readable (and were a hallmark of the entire PARC culture) back into standard pedestrian ASCII characters. According to Peter Deutsch this "met with heated opposition within the group at the time, but has turned out to be essential for the acceptance of the system in the world." Another change was to make blocks more like lambda expressions; as Peter Deutsch was to observe nine years later: "In retrospect, this proliferation of different kinds of instantiation and scoping was probably a bad idea." The most puzzling idea—at least to me as a new outsider—was the introduction of metaclasses (really just to make instance initialization a little easier—a very minor improvement over what Smalltalk-76 did quite reasonably already). Peter's 1989 comment is typical and true: "Metaclasses have proven confusing to many users, and perhaps in the balance more confusing than valuable." In fact, in their PIE system, Goldstein and Bobrow had already implemented in Smalltalk an "observer language," somewhat following the view-oriented approach I had been advocating and in some ways like the "perspectives" proposed in KRL [Goldstein]. Once one can view an instance via multiple perspectives, even "semi-metaclasses" such as Class Class and Class Object are not really necessary because the object-role and instance-of-a-class-role are just different views and it is easy to deal with life-history issues including instantiation. This was there for the taking (along with quite a few other good ideas), but it was not adopted. My guess is that Smalltalk had moved into the final phase I mentioned at the beginning of this story, in which a way of doing things finally gets canonized into an inflexible belief structure.

11.6.1 Coda

One final comment. Hardware is really just software crystallized early. It is there to make program schemes run as efficiently as possible. But far too often the hardware has been presented as a given and it is up to software designers to make it appear reasonable. This has caused low-level techniques and excessive optimization to hold back progress in program design. As Bob Barton used to say: "Systems programmers are high priests of a low cult."

One way to think about progress in software is that a lot of it has been about finding ways to *late-bind*, then waging campaigns to convince manufacturers to build the ideas into hardware. Early hardware had wired programs and parameters; random access memory was a scheme to late-bind them. Looping and indexing used to be done by address modification in storage; index registers were a way to late-bind. Over the years software designers have found ways to late-bind the locations of computations—this led to base/bounds registers, segment relocation, paging MMUs, migratory processes, and so forth. Time-sharing was held back for years because it was "inefficient"—but the manufacturers would not put MMU's on the machines; universities had to do it themselves! Recursion late-binds parameters to procedures, but it took years to get even rudimentary stack mechanisms into CPUs. Most machines still have no support for dynamic allocation and garbage collection, and so forth. In short, most hardware designs today are just re-optimizations of moribund architectures.

From the late-binding perspective, OOP can be viewed as a comprehensive technique for late-binding as many things as possible: the *mix* of state and process in a set of behaviors, *where* they are located, *what* they are called, *when* and *why* they are invoked, *which* HW is used, and so on, and more subtle, the strategies used in the OOP scheme itself. The art of the wrap is the art of the trap.

Consider the two cases that must be handled efficiently in order to completely wrap objects. It would be terrible if $a+b$ incurred *any* overhead if a and b were bound, say, to "3" and "4" in a form that could be handled by the ALU. The operation should occur full speed using look-aside logic (in the simplest scheme a single *and* gate) to trap if the operands are not compatible with the ALU. Now all elementary operations that have to happen fast have been wrapped without slowing down the machine.

The second case happens if the trap has determined the objects in question are too complicated for the ALU. Now the HW has to dynamically find a method that can handle the objects. This is very similar to indexing—the class of one of the objects is "indexed" by the desired method-selector in a slightly more general way. In other words, the VIRTUAL-ADDRESS of a method is <class><selector>. Because most HW today does a virtual address translation of some kind to find the real address—a trap—it is quite possible to hide the overhead of the OOP dispatch in the MMU overhead that has already been rationalized.

Again, the whole point of OOP is *not* to have to worry about what is *inside* an object. Objects made on different machines and with different languages *should* be able to talk to each other—and will *have to* in the future. Late-binding here involves trapping incompatibilities into *re*compatibility methods—a good discussion of some of the issues is found in [Popek 1984].

Staying with the metaphor of late-binding, what further late-binding schemes might we expect to see? One of the nicest late-binding schemes that is being experimented with is the *metaobject protocol* work at Xerox PARC [Kiczales 1991]. The notion is that the language designer's choice for the internal representation of instances, variables, and the like, may not cover what the implementer needs. So within a *fixed* semantics they allow the implementer to give the system strategies—for example, using a hashed lookup for slots in an instance instead of direct indexing. These are then efficiently compiled and extend the base implementation of the system. This is a direct descendant of similar directions from the past of Simula, FLEX, CDL, Smalltalk, and Actors.

Another late-binding scheme that is already necessary is to get away from direct protocol matching when a new object shows up in a system of objects. In other words, if someone sends you an object from halfway around the world it will be unusual if it conforms to your local protocols. At some point it will be easier to have it carry even more information about itself—enough so its specifications can be "understood" and its configuration into your mix done by the more subtle matching of *inference*.

A look beyond OOP as we know it today can also be done by thinking about late-binding. Prolog's great idea is that it does not need bindings to values in order to carry out computations. The variable is an object, and a web of partial results can be built to be filled in when a binding is finally found. Eurisko constructs its methods—and modifies its basic strategies—as it tries to solve a problem. Instead of a problem looking for methods, the methods look for problems—and Eurisko looks for the methods of the methods. This has been called "opportunistic programming"—I think of it as a drive for more enlightenment, in which problems get resolved as part of the process.

This higher computational finesse will be needed as the next paradigm shift—that of pervasive networking—takes place over the next five years. Objects will gradually become active agents and will travel the networks in search of useful information and tools for their managers. Objects brought back into a computational environment from halfway around the world will not be able to confugure themselves by direct protocol matching as do objects today. Instead, the objects will carry much more information about themselves in a form that permits *inferential* docking. Some of the ongoing work in specification can be turned to this task.

Tongue in cheek, I once characterized progress in programming languages as a kind of "sunspot" theory, in which major advances took place about every 11 years. We started with machine code in 1950, then in 1956 FORTRAN came along as a "better old thing" which, if looked at as "almost a new thing," became the precursor of ALGOL-60 in 1961. In 1966, SIMULA was the "better old thing," which if looked at as "almost a new thing" became the precursor of Smalltalk in 1972.

Everything seemed set up to confirm the "theory" once more: In 1978, Eurisko was in place as the "better old thing" that was "almost a new thing." But 1983—and the whole decade—came and went without the "new thing." Of course, such a theory is silly anyway—and yet, I think the enormous commercialization of personal computing has smothered much of the kind of work that used to go on in universities and research labs, by sucking the talented kids towards practical applications. With companies so risk-adverse towards doing their own HW, and the HW companies betraying no real understanding of sw, the result has been a great step backwards in most repects.

A twentieth century problem is that technology has become too "easy." When it was hard to do *anything*, whether good or bad, enough time was taken so that the result was usually good. Now we can make things almost trivially, especially in software, but most of the designs are trivial as well. This is inverse vandalism: the making of things because you can. Couple this to even less sophisticated buyers and you have generated an exploitation marketplace similar to that set up for teenagers. A counter to this is to generate enormous dissatisfaction with one's designs, using the entire history of human art as a standard and goad. Then the trick is to decouple the dissatisfaction from self-worth—otherwise it is either too depressing or one stops too soon with trivial results.

I will leave the story of early Smalltalk in 1981 when an extensive series of articles on Smalltalk-80 was published in *Byte* magazine [Byte 1981], followed by Adele's and Dave Robson's books [Goldberg 1983] and the official release of the system in 1983. Now programmers could easily implement the virtual machine without having to reinvent it, and, in several cases, groups were able to roll their own *image* of basic classes. In spite of having to run almost everywhere on moribund hw architectures, Smalltalk has proliferated amazingly well (in part because of tremendous optimization efforts on these machines) [Deutsch 1989]. As far as I can tell, it still seems to be the most widely used system that claims to be object-oriented. It is incredible to me that no one since has come up with a qualitatively better idea that is as simple, elegant, easy to program, practical, and comprehensive. (It is a pity that we did not know about PROLOG then or vice versa; the combinations of the two languages done subsequently are quite intriguing.)

While justly applauding Dan, Adele, and the others who made Smalltalk possible, we must wonder at the same time: where are the Dans and Adeles of the '80s and '90s who will take us to the next stage?

APPENDIX I: PERSONAL COMPUTER MEMO

Smalltalk Program Evolution

From a Memo on the "KiddiKomputer":

To: Butler Lampson, Chuck Thacker, Bill English, Jerry Elkind, George Pake

Subject: "KiddiKomputer"

Date: May 15, 1972

****

4. January 1972

The Reading Machine. Another attempt to work on the actual problem of a personal computer. Every part of this gadget (except display) is buildable now but requires some custom chip design and fabrication. This is discussed more completely later on. A meeting was held with all three labs to try to stimulate invention of the display.

B. Utility

1. I think the uses for a personal gadget as an editor, reader, take-home-context, intelligent terminal, etc. are fairly obvious and greatly needed by adults. The idea of having kids use it implies (possibly) a few more constraints having to do with size, weight, cost, and capacity. I have been begging this question under the assumptions that a size and weight that are good for kids will be super acceptable to adults, and that the gadget will almost inescapably have CPU power to burn (more than PDP-10): implies larger scale use by adults can be gotten by buying more memory and maybe a cache.

2. Although there are many "educational" things that can be done once the device is built, I have had four basic projects in mind from the start.

a. Teaching "thinking" (à la Papert) through giving the kids a franchise for the strategies, tactics, and model visualization that are the fun (and important) part of the design and debugging of programs. Fringe benefits include usage as a medium for symbols allowing editing of text and pictures.

b. Teaching "models" through "simulation" of systems with similar semantics and different syntax. This could be grouped with (a) although the emphasis is a bit different. The initial two systems would be music and programming and would be an extension of some stuff I did at Utah in 1969-1970 with the organ/computer there.

c. Teaching "interface" skills such as "seeing" and "hearing." The initial "seeing" project would be an investigation into how reading might be taught via combining iconic and audible representation of works in a manner reminiscent of Bloomfield and Moore. This would require a corollary inquiry into why good readers do so much better than average readers. A farther off project in the domain of sight would be an investigation into the nature and topology of kids' internal models for objects and an effort to perserve iconic imagery from being totally replaced by a relational model.

d. Finding out what children would do (if anything) "unofficially" during non-school hours with such a gadget through invisible 'demons", which are little processes that watch surreptitiously.

3. Second Level Projects

a. The notion of evaluation (partly an extension of 2.a.) represents an important plateau in "algorithmic thinking."

b. Iconic programming. If we believe Piaget and Bruner, kids deal mostly with icons before the age of 8 rather than symbolic references. Most people who teach programming say there is a remarkable difference between 3rd and 4th grades. Whatever an iconic programming language is, it had better be considerably more stylish and viable than GRAIL and AMBIT/G. I feel that this is a way to reach very young kids and is tremendously important.

****

C. The Viability Of miniCOM

It was noted earlier that miniCOM is only barely portable for a child. Does it have a future for adults and/or as a functional testbed for kids? If only one is needed, the answer seems to be no since ~$15k will simulate its function in a non-portable fashion. If more than one is necessary (say 10 or more), then the cheapest way to get functions of this kind is to design and build it.

Rationalizations for building a bunch of them:

1. It will allow us to find out some things not predictable or discoverable by any other path.

A perfect case in point is our character generator through which we have found some absolutely astounding and unsuspected things about human perception and raster scan television which will greatly further display design. It has paid its way already.

2. The learning experiments not involving portability can be done for a reasonable cost and will allow us to get into the real world which is absolutely necessary for the future of learning research at PARC.

3. It will foster some new thoughts in small computer system design.

It has already sparked the original "jaggies" investigation. The minimal nice serifed character fonts were done because of cost and space limitations. There are some details which have been handwaved into the woodwork which really neeed to be solved seriously: philosophy of instruction set, compile or interpret, mapping, and I/O control.

4. It will be a useful "take home" editor and terminal for PARC people. It is absurd to think of using a multidimensional medium during the day (NLS, etc.), then at night going home to a 1D AJ or worse: dumping structured ideas on paper.

5. It is not unreasonable to think of the gadget as an attempt at a cost-effective node for a future office system. As such, it should be developed in parallel with the more exotic and greatly more expensive luxury system.

6. It is not clear that the more ideal device (A.4.), requiring custom chip design, can be done well without us knowing quite a bit more about this kind of system.

APPENDIX II: SMALLTALK INTERPRETER DESIGN

When I set out to win the bet, I realized that many of the details that have to be stated explicitly in McCarthy's elegant scheme can be *finessed.* For example, if there were objects that could handle various kinds of partial message receipt, such as *evaluated, unevaluated, literal,* and the like, then there would be no need to put any of those details in the *eval.* This is analogous to not having cond as a "special form," but instead to finding a basic building block in which COND can be defined like any other subpart.

One way to do this was to use the approach of Dave Fisher, in which the no-man's land of control structures is made accessable by providing a protected way to access and change the relationships of the static and dynamic environment [Fisher 1970]. In an object-based scheme, the protection can be provided by the objects themselves and many of Fisher's techniques are even easier to use. The effect of all this is to extend the *eval* by *distributing* it: both to the individual objects that participate in it and dynamically as the language is extended.

I also decided to ignore the metaphysics of objects even though it was clear that, unlike Simula, in a full blown OOPL classes had to exist at run-time as "first-class" objects—indeed, there should be nothing but first-class objects. So there had to be a "class-class" whose instances were classes, class-class had to be an instance of itself, there had to be a "class-object" that would terminate any subclassing that might be done, and so forth. All of this could be part of the argument concerning what I *didn't* have to show to win the bet.

The biggest problem remaining was that I wanted to have a much nicer syntax than LISP and I did not want to use any of my precious "half-page" to write even a simple translator. Somehow the *eval* had to be designed so that syntax got specified as part of the use of the system, not in its basic definition.

I wanted the interpretation to go from left to right. In an OOP, we can choose to interpret the syntax rule for expressions as meaning: the first element will be evaluated into the instance that will receive the message, and *everything* that follows will be the message. What should expressions like $a+b$ and c_i <– *de* mean? From past experience with FLEX, the second of these had a clear rendering in object-oriented terms. The *c* should be bound to an object, and *all* of $_i$ <– *de* would be thought of as the message to it. Subscripting and multiplication are implicit in standard mathematical orthography—we need explicit symbols, say "°" and "*". This gives us:

receiver | message
c | ° *i* <– *d***e*

The message is made up of a literal token "°", an expression to be evaluated in the sender's context (in this case *i*), another literal token <–, followed by an expression to be evaluated in the sender's context (*d***e*). "LISP" pairs are made from two element objects and can be indexed more simply: *c hd*, *c tl*, and *c hd* <– *foo*, and so forth.

The expression *3+4* seemed more troublesome at first. Did it really make sense to think of it as:

receiver | message
3 | +*4*

We are so used to thinking of "+" and "*" as operators, function machines. On the other hand, there are many senses of "+" and "*" that go beyond simple APLish generalizations of scalar operators to arrays—for example in matrix and string algebras. From this standpoint it makes great sense to let the objects in question decide what the token "+" means in a particular context. This means that *3+4*5...* should be thought of as *3|+4*5...*, and that the way class number chooses to receive messages should be arranged so that the next subexpression is handled properly. For example, 3 could check to see if a token (like +, or *) follows and then ask to have the rest of the message evaluated to get its next input. This would force *4*5...* to be the new sending , as *4|*5*, and so on. Not only are fewer parentheses needed but proglike sequential evaluation is a byproduct.

By this point I had been able to finesse and argue away most of the programming that seemed to be required of the *eval*. To summarize:

- message receipt would be done by objects in the midst of normal code
- control structures would be handled by objects that could addess the context objects
- the context objects (that acted like stack frames, schedulers, and so on) could be simulated by standard objects and thus wouldn't have to be specified in the eval
- variable dereferencing and storage would be done by having variables be objects and sending them the messages *value* and <-.
- the evaluation of a code body would be done by starting evaluation of its first item
- methods would be realized by the control structure in the cl6.alss code body. This would implement protection, would make the externals of an object entirely virtual, and permit very flexible messaging schemes
- Smalltalk's metaphysics would be covered by making everything an object, and didn't have to be specified now
- and so forth

This also means that useful elements such as lists, atoms, control structures, quote, receivers (such as "receive evaluated," "is the next token this?," and so on), and the like do not have to be defined in the kernel interpreter, as they can be realized quite simply as instances of normal classes with escapes to metacode.

What seemed to remain for the *eval* was simply to show of what a message send actually consisted. For this system a send is the equivalent not of a postman delivering a letter, but simply delivering a notice of where the letter was to be found. It is up to the receiving object to do something about it. In fact, it could ignore the request, complain about it, invoke inferential processes elsewhere, or simply handle it with one of its own messages.The final thing I had to do was to extend the uniform syntax idea of *receiver message* to cover all cases, including message receipt and simple control structures. So, we need some objects to pattern match and evaluate, to return and define, and so on.

The "LISP" code body would not need any escapes to lower-level code and could look something like:

```
(¤hd     » (¤<-   (^:h)^h)   "replaca and car where h is an instance variable"
¤tl      » (¤<-   (:t)^t)    "replaca and cdr where t is an instance variable"
¤isPair  » (^true)
¤length  » (t isPair  (^1+t length) 1)
...)                         "etc"
```

I hope this is clear enough. For example, if *c* is bound to a cons pair,

c hd <– 3+4

FIGURE 11A.1 Used in the first interpreter definition

¤	eyeball	looks to see if its message is a literal token in the message stream
:	evl-bind	evals the next part of message and binds result to its message
:	unval-bind	picks up next part of message unevaled and binds to its message
^	send-back	returns its value to the sender
'	quote	overides any metainterpretation of its message

would be dealt with as follows: Control is passed to that object and the first test is to see if the symbol *hd* appears in the message (¤*hd* »). It does. The next check is for an "assignment" token (¤<– »). It is there. Last, we want to evaluate the rest of the message (we get 7), bind the value to the internal instance variable t and, finally, return this value to the sender (^:*t*). So this is like: (REPLACA C (PLUS 3 4)).

This is getting a little ahead of the story in that not all of these ideas were thought out in this detail, but I want to show the context in which I was thinking, and it seemed quite clear at the time that things would come out all right if I pushed in this direction. This stuff is similar to mathematical or musical thinking where many things can be done "ahead of time" if one's intuition whispers that "you're on the right track." The compass setting felt right; I could "see" that all these things would eventually work out just because of "what objects were."

To motivate the next part, let us examine the classic evaluation of *3+4* using a *nonrecursive* evaluator. For code, we use *arrays* of pointers and expect that some of the pointers will be encoded for literal objects (an old LISP trick). We need good old program counters "PC" that we can bump along over the code. The wrinkle of delayed receipt of message (not evaling and passing arguments at *send* time) will require us to manipulate *both* the program counter of the sender and the receiver as the message is reeled in. One way I worked it out was as a before-after diagram for "3+4".

We start in the middle of a method of some class of objects and we need to evaluate "3+4". The essentials of the *eval* are those that successfully take us into the method of "3" in class integer. Because all methods are only in terms of sends and all sends are done in a similar manner, this is enough. It is like an induction proof in which we assume "n" and show how to get to "n+1".

Note that the various auxiliary objects (such as 'peek') have to responsibly move the sender's program counter when receiving part of the message.

I have hand-evaluated this nonrecursive version in a number of cases and it seems to work pretty well, but there are probably some bugs. If a reader feels prompted to come up with an even nicer, tidier, and smaller scheme, I would be glad to look at it.

FIGURE 11A.2 Defined when the first "real" implementation was done

to	define	likeLOGO, except can make a class from it message
ISNEW	testinst	is true if a new instance has been created
=	equals	true only if its receiver and parameter are the same object
»	then	receiver=true: evals next part of message and exits receiver=false: skips over the next part of message and continues evaling
.	fence	"statement" separator. Quits applying its receiver; starts evaling its arg

FIGURE 11A.3 The One Pager

e (the environment) will be bound to the current Messenger object

result holds the result of a send, usually to be *applied* to next part of message

"Before"

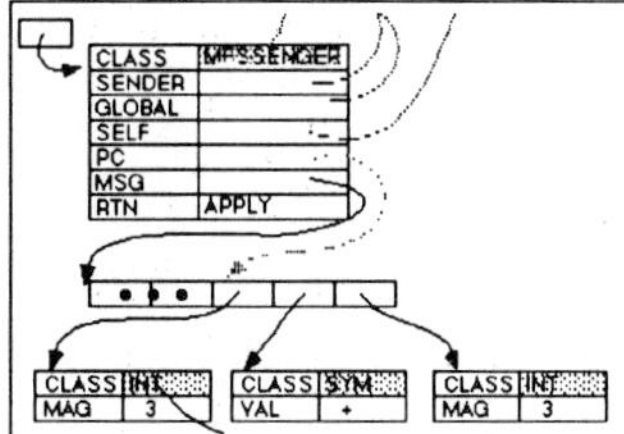

```
eval: if null(•MSG)      then 'reuslt <- nil; goto apply;
      if escale(e•MSG)   then goto escapes;
      if atom(•MSG)      the 'result <- lookupvalue(e,e•MSG); goto apply;
      if notlist(e•MSG)  the 'result <- e•MSG; goto apply;
evlist: 'e <- Table(CLASS, MESSENGER,
                    SENDER, e,
                    GLOBAL, e•GLOBAL,
                    SELF,   e•SELF,
                    PC,     1,
                    MSG,    e•MSG•PC)
                    RTN,    APPLY);
              goto eval;

apply: 'e <- e•SENDER;
        e•PC <- e•PC + 1
        if e•PC > length(MSG) then goto dispathrtn;
        if e•MSG•PC = '.      then e•PC <- e•PC + 1; goto evlist;
        if e•MSG•PC = '»      then if result = 'false
                                      then e•PC <- e•PC + 2; goto evlist;
                                      else e•PC <- e•PC + 1;
                                          'e <- Table(CLASS   MESSENGER,
                                                      SENDER, e,
                                                      GLOBAL, GLOBAL,
                                                      SELF    result,
                                                      PC,     t,
                                                      MSG,    e•MSG•PC,
                                                      RTN,    FROMTTRUE);
                                          goto eval;
        'e <- Table( CLASS,  MESSENGER,
                     SENDER, e,
                     GLOBAL, GLOBAL,
                     SELF,   reuslt,
                     PC,     1,
                     MSG,    reuslt•CLASS•CODE,
                     RTN,    APPLY);

fromTURE: 'e <- e•SENDER•SENDER; goto dispatchrtn;

fromEYE: putvalue(E•GLOBAL, e•p, reuslt); goto apply;

dispatchrtn: select e•RTN
                    case APPLY:    goto apply;
                    case FROMTRUE: goto fromTRUE;
                    case FROMEYE:  goto fromEYE;
escapes: select e•MSG•PC+1
                    etc...
```

"During"

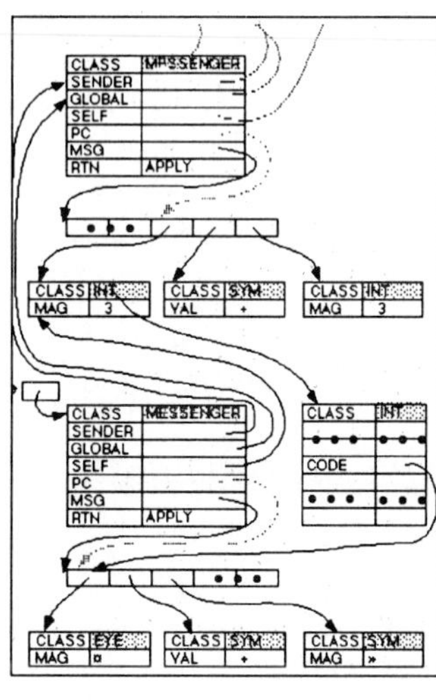

FIGURE 11A.3 The "One Pager" *(cont.)*

"After"

```
to ¤ (metacodefor(if e•SNDR•MSG(PC)=e•SNDR•SNDR•MSG(PC)
                    then bump(e•SNDR•SNDR•PC);result <- TRUE
                    else result <- FALSE;
                    goto apply))
to : p (: p. metacodefor(set up a new context and eval sender))
to : p v (metacodefor('v <- e•SNDR•SNDR•MSG•PC;
                    if nil(e•'p <- e•SNDR•MSG•PC)
                         then result <- v
                          else e•p <- result <- v;
                    goto apply;))
to ^ b (: b. metacodefor('return <- e•b; goto apply))
```

APPENDIX III: ACKNOWLEDGMENTS

1971

Chris Jeffers, + ?

1972

Chris Jeffers, John Shoch, Steve Purcell, Bob Shur, Bonny Tennenbaum, Barbara Deutsch

1973

A document written by me shortly after Smalltalk-72 started working

ACKNOWLEDGMENTS

Latest revision: March 23, 1973

Much of the philosophy on which our work is based was inspired by the ideas of Seymour Papert and his group at MIT.

The Dynabook (ka 71) is a godchild of Wes Clark's LINC (cl 1962) and a lineal descendent of the FLEX machine (ka 67, 68, 69).

The "interim Dynabook" (known as the ALTO (Th 71, Mc 71) is the beautiful creation of Chuck Thacker and Ed McCreight of the Computer Science Lab. at PARC.

SMALLTALK is basically a synthesis of wellknown ideas for programming languages and machines which have appeared in the last 15 years.

The Burroughs B5000 (ba 61) (B60) had many design ideas well in advance of its time (and still not generally appreciated): compact "addressless code; a uniform semantics for names (the PRT), automatic coprocesses, "capability" protection (also by the PRT and Descriptors_, virtual segmented memory, the ability to call a subroutine from "either side" of the assignment arrow, etc.

The notions of code as a data structure; intensional properties of names (property lists of attribute-value pairs on atoms); evaluation with respect to arbitrary environments; etc., are found in LISP, probably the greatest single design for a programming language yet to appear. SMALLTALK is definitely "LISPlike".

The SIMULAs ('65 and '67) combined Conway's notions of software coroutines (1963—hardware version had appeared in the B5000 3 years earlier), ALGOL-60, and Hoare's ideas about record classes (ca.1964) into an epistemology that allowed a class to have any number of parallel instantiations (or activation records) containing local state including a separate program counter. Most of the operations for a SIMULA '67 class are held intrinsically as procedures local to the class definition.

The FLEX machine and its language ('67-69) took the SIMULA ideas (discarding most of the AGOLishness), moved "type" from a variable onto the objects (ala B5000 and EULER), formed a total identification between "coprocesses" and "data", consolidating notions such as arrays, files, lists, "subroutine" files (ala SDS-940) etc., into one idea. The "user as a process" also appeared here. A start was made to allow proccesses to determine their own input syntax, an idea held by many (notably Irons, Leavenworth, etc.)

The Control Definition Language of Dave Fisher (1970) provided many ideas, solutions and approaches to the notion of control. It, with FLEX, is the major source for the semantics of SMALLTALK. It is a "soulmate" to FLEX; independently worrying about many of the same problems and very frequently arriving at cleaner, neater ways to do things. Many of Dave;s ideas are used including the provision for many orthogonal paths to external environments, and that control is basically a matter of organizing these environments. SMALLTALK removes Fisher's need for a compiler to provide a mapping between nice syntax and semantics and offers other improvements over his schemes such as total local control of the format of an instance, etc.

An extemporaneous talk by R.S. Barton at Alta ski lodge (1968) about computers as communications devices and how everything one does can easily be portrayed as sending messages to and fro, was the real genesis of the current version of SMALLTALK.

The fact that kids were to be the users, and the simplicity and ease of use of the already existing LOGO, whose own parents were LISP and JOSS (which set a standard for the esthetics for interaction that has not yet been surpassed), provided lots of motivation to have programs and transactions appear as simple as possible—i.e. moving from left to right, procedures gather their own messages, etc. It is no accident that simple SMALLTALK programs look a bit like LOGO!

Problems discovered years ago in "lefthand calls" prompted SMALLTALK to make "store" intensional—i.e. a <- b, means "call 'a' with a message consisting of the token'<-' and symbol 'b'. If anyone can make the right decision for what this means, it must be the object bound to 'a'. The early fall of 1972 saw an evaluator for SMALLTALK, and the idea that '+', '-', etc., should also be intensional. This led to an entire philosophy of use (unlike SIMULA '67) to put EVERYTHING in class definitions including the so-called "infix operators". This message idea allows messages to have a wide range of form since all messages can be received incrementally.

"Control of control" allows control structures to be defined, The language SMALLTALK itself thus avoids "primitives" such as "loop...pool", synchronous and asynchronous "ports", interrupts, backtracking, parallel evel and return, etc. All of these can be easily simulated when needed.

****

These are the main influences on our language. There were many other minor and negative influences from other existing languages and ideas too numerous to mention except briefly in the references,

****

This particular version of SMALLTALK was designed through the summer and early fall of 1972 and was aided by discussions with Steve Purcell, Dan Ingalls, Henry Fuchs, Ted Kaehler, and John Schoch. From the proceeding acknowledgements it can be seen as a consolidation of good ideas into one simple ides:

Make the PARTS (object, subroutines, I/O, etc.) have the same properties and power as the WHOLE (such as a computer).

This is the basic principle of recursive design, SMALLTALK recurs on the notion of "computer" rather than of "subroutine."

A talk on SMALLTALK was given at the AI lab at MIT (Nov 1972) which discussed the process structure and the new, intentional way to look at properties, messages, and "infix operators". This led to the just published formal "actors model of computation" of Hewitt, *et. al.* (1973).

****

Dan Ingalls of our group at PARC, the implementor of SMALLTALK, has revealed many design flaws through his several, excellent quick "throw away" implementation of the language. SMALLTALK could not have existed without his help, virtuosity, and good cheer.

The original design of the "painting editor" was by Alan Kay. It was implented and tremendously improved by Steve Purcell.

The "Animator" was designed and implemented by Bob Shur and Steve Purcell.

Line graphics and the hand-character recognizer were done by John Shoch.

"Music:" was designed and implemented by Alan Kay.

The design and implementation of the font editor was by Ben Laws (POLOS).

We would like to thank CSL and POLOS in general for a great deal of all kinds of help.

1976

Learning Research Group

Alan Kay, Head, Adele Goldberg, Dan Ingalls, Chris Jeffers, Ted Kaehler, Diana Merry, Dave Robson, John Shoch, Dick Shoup, Steve Weyer

Students

Barbara Deutsch, Tom Horsley, Steve Purcell, Steve Saunders, Bob Shur, David C. Smith, Radia Perlman

Child Interns

Dennis Burke (age 12), Marian Goldeen (age 13), Susan Hammet (age 12), Bruce Horn (age 15), Lisa Jack (age 12), Kathy Mansfield (age 12), Steve Putz (age 15)

Visitors

Ron Baecker, Eric Martin, Bonnie Tenenbaum

Help from Other Groups at PARC

Patrick Baudelaire, Dave Boggs, Bill Bowman, Larry Clark, Jim Cucinitti, Peter Deutsch, Bill English, Bob Flegal, Ralph Kimball, Butler Lampson, Bob Metcalfe, Mike Overton, Alvy Ray Smith, Bob Sproull, Larry Tesler, Chuck Thacker, Truett Thach

APPENDIX IV: EVENT DRIVEN LOOP EXAMPLE

First we make a class for events:

```
to event | mycode

(ISNEW    »  ('mycode <- array 3.
              mycode[2] <- 'done.)
¤newcode »  (mycode[1] <- :.)
¤is       »  (ISIT eval)
mycode eval)
```

Each event stores away code to be executed later (the *done* will eventually cause an exit from the driving loop in the *until* structure, defined next:

```
to until tempatom statement
    (repeat ('tempatom <- :.      "this loop picks up all the event identifiers
(unevaled)"
               tempatom <- event."an indirect store to whatever was in the message"
               ¤or » (again) done)
   (¤do    »  ('statement <- :))       "the loop body to be evaled"
   (¤case  »  (repeat ('tempatom <- :. "pick up an event-case label"
                    (tempatom eval is event »
                      (¤:. tempatom eval newcode :.)"pick up the corresponding code"
                    done)))
   repeat (statement eval)) "execute body until an event is encountered and run"
                        "the event will then force exit from the until loop"
```

This kind of playing around was part of the general euphoria that came with having a really extensible language. It is like the festooning of type faces that happens when many fonts are suddenly available. We had both, and our early experimentation sometimes got pretty baroque. Eventually we calmed down and started to focus on fewer, simpler structures of higher power.

APPENDIX V: SMALLTALK-76 INTERNAL STRUCTURES

This shows how Smalltalk-76 was implemented. In the center, between "static" and "dynamic" lies a byte-compiled method of Class Rectangle. Slightly above it is the source text string written by the programmer. The method tests to see whether a point is contained in the rectangle. In the dynamic part, the program counter is just starting to execute the first less-than. This general scheme goes all the way back to the B5000 and the FLEX machine, but is considerably more refined.

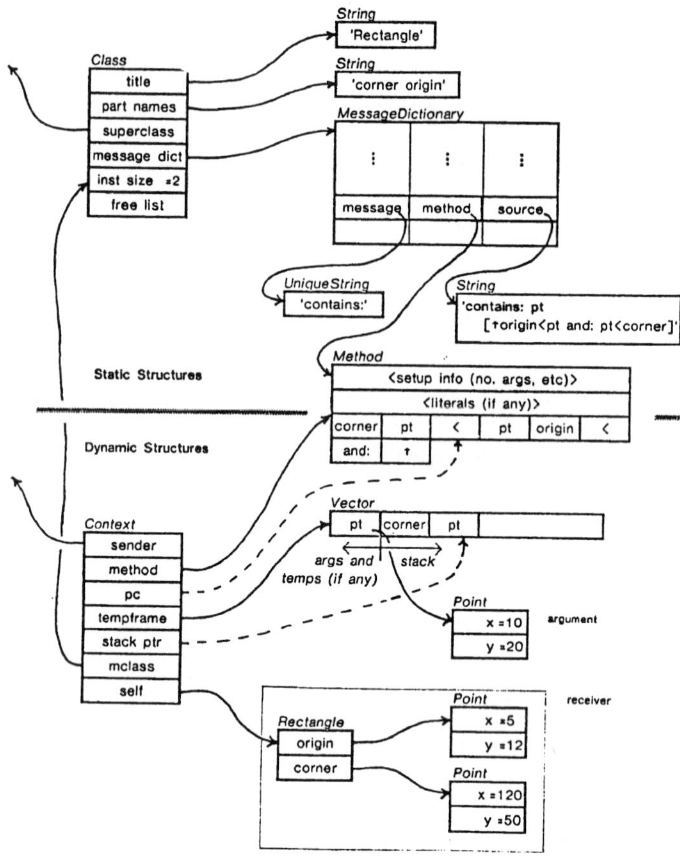

APPENDIX VI: SMALLTALK INTERPRETER DESIGN DOCUMENTATION

General Landscape of the Sixties

The almost-OOP idea started early, as designers found that the straightforward material-and-recipe metaphors of data structures and procedures broke down all too readily under stress.

1962–1964	representation independence (wrapping)	USAF ATG file system	unknown
1960–1964	protection, HLL Arch, many firsts	B5000	Barton
1962–1963	graphics, simulation, classes, instances	Sketchpad	Sutherland
1962–1963	coroutines	B220 COBOL Comp.	Conway

1964–1967	general simulation: proc classes & instances	Simula	Nygaard, Dahl
1967–1969	subsuming programming constructs	FLEX	Kay
1967–*	inheritance	Simula-67	Nygaard, Dahl
1967	"dataless programming"	??	Balzer
1969–1971	capability operating system	CAL-TSS	Lampson-Sturgis

What these designers had in common—and what set them apart from others in the field—was an interest in finding simple general structures to *finesse* difficulties, rather than expending enormous efforts to produce large amounts of code.

In addition to these initial gropings towards the OOP idea, several other early nonOOP systems contributed important ideas and stylistic directions.

1959–1963	kernel elegance, self-describing, etc.	LISP	McCarthy
1959–1966	ease of end-user authoring	JOSS	Shaw
1961–1966	generalizations of PLs	GA, EULER, APL, etc.	vanWijn..., Wirth
1967–1969	pattern-based inferencing	PLANNER	Hewitt
1968–1970	definition of control structures	CDL	Fisher

The other major set of cross-currents at work in the sixties was Licklider's dream of man-machine symbiosis. This led to the formation of the ARPA IPT office that in the sixties funded most of the advanced computer research in the US. Perhaps as important is that these visions were also adopted by other funders such as ONR and NIH. Shortly there appeared on the scene time-sharing, computer graphics, advanced networking, and many other new ways to think about the technology. In addition to several of the above listings (for example, Sketchpad, JOSS), specific contributions to the invention of personal computing were:

1962	first true personal computer	LINC	Clark
1962–1967?	metaphor of personal computing	NLS	Englebart
1964–1966	modern operating system	GENIE	Lampson
1964–	programming for children	LOGO	Feurzig, Papert
1967–1969	first OO desktop PC	FLEX machine	Cheadle-Kay
196?–?	conceptions of end-user interaction	ARC-MACH	Negroponte
1967–1969	gesture/modeless GUI, iconic prog.	GRAIL	Ellis, Groner, *et al.*
1968	early iconic programming	AMBIT-G	Rovner

Finally, there was a considerable background radiation of ideas generated by the enormous productivity of the sixties. It was still possible back then to be aware of just about everything that was going on and most ideas contributed, even if only to help avoid unpromising paths. For example:

1960–1969	syntax dir. proc., extensible lang., etc.	FSL, META II, IMP, EL1	Feldman, Shorre, Irons, Wegbreit
1960–1969	formal models of prog.	CPL, ISWIM, GEDANKEN	Strachey, Landin, Reynolds
1963–1969	postALGOL, DS definitions	ALGOL-W, -X,-68, etc.	Wirth, Hoare, vanWijn..., etc.
1963–1970	AI representation development	GAS, ***, QA4, etc.	Minsky, Evans, Winston, Hewitt

In other words, there was an entire landscape of activity going on even when the filter is restricted to the 10% or so that was actually interesting.

Smalltalk Documentation

After PARC got set up, it was customary to write a report every six months and a two-year plan every September. I have many of these, but will not list them specifically. All the things described in the text of this chapter were documented in the six-month report that followed, which (in our case) always contained lots of screen shots of the latest wonders. I should also mention that there is an extensive collection of slides, 16mm film (most of it shot by me) both in my files and at Xerox, and many hours of video tapes of all aspects of our work.

Nov 1970	KiddiKomp notebook
Spring 1971	First of several SLOGO documents
June 1971	Display Transducers, (A Pendery Paper for PARC Planning Purposes)
Sum 1971	"Brown Lab Book" (lost or mislaid)
Sum 1971	miniCOM documents
Sum 1971	early Smalltalk-71 programs
Sum 1971	first LRG plan
Fall 1971	first LRG report
Fall 1971	**FJCC panel abstract on mainframes as dinosaurs that will be replaced by personal computers**
Win 1972	report on the wonderful world of fonts (lost or mislaid, most material duped in "May 1972")
May 1972	formal miniCOM proposal (per "X"), I have first draft
Sum 1972	Drafts of A Personal Computer For Children Of All Ages, many Smalltalk-71 programs
Aug 1972	**Final Draft of APCFCOAA (Smalltalk-71 programs removed as per D. Bobrow suggestion)** ACM Nat'l Conf. Boston
Sept 1972	LRG plan about "iconic programming," etc. Xerox probably still has. (Jack Goldman files?)
Sept 1972	First Smalltalk-72 "one page" interpreter demonstration
Oct 1972	First Smalltalk-72 programs run (D. Ingalls)
Nov 1972	**A Dynamic Medium For Creative Thought, NCTE Conference** "20 things to do with a Dynabook" This was pretty much what I wanted the group to accomplish (except for music, etc.)
Nov 1972	Presentation to MIT AI Lab of Smalltalk and its interpreter
Nov 1972	Stewart Brand *Rolling Stone* article on PARC—caused blackout of LRG pubs until 1975.
Win 1973	Smalltalk "Bluebook": general documentation, teaching sequences, alternate syntaxes, etc
Win 1973	First of many Smalltalk bootstrap files (D. Ingalls)—so readable, they were used as a manual
1973–1975	Many application documentation notes, written by Ted Kaehler, Diana Merry, etc.
1974	minimouse (Larry Tesler)
??	
1975	**Blackout lifted. Smalltalk-72 Handbook (with Adele), PARC TR-?**
1975	Dynamic Personal Media (with Adele) proposal to NSF for funding longitudinal studies of children
1975	**PYGMALION *** (David Canfield Smith), Ph.D. Thesis, Stanford, also as ???**
1976	**Dynamic Personal Media (with Adele)** PARC TR-?, a fairly complete rendering of work through 1975
1976	First *NoteTaker* documents
1976	*Findit* (with Steve Weyer), presented at "Dulles" learning center
1977	**Smalltalk in the Classroom (with Adele), PARC TRs, report on work with kids**
???	**Marion Goldeen, etc., articles on her experiences (*Creative Computing*?)**
1977	**Personal Dynamic Media (with Adele) *IEEE Computer*, March.**
1977	Smalltalk-76 Listing (Dan Ingalls + Dave Robson, Ted Kaehler, Diana Merry) The first complete running system
1977	Smalltalk-76 Documentation (Larry Tesler) with included applications

1977	More *NoteTaker* documents (with Doug Fairbairn)
1977	**THINGLAB *** (Alan Borning), Ph.D. Thesis, Stanford**
1977	**Microelectronics and the personal computer, *Scientific American*, Sept.**
1978	**Smalltalk-76 (Dan Ingalls), ACM POPL Conference, January**
1979	**TinyTalk (Larry Tesler and Kim McCall) where?**
1979	**Programming Your Own Computer, Science Year '79, *World Book* Computer Infotech State of the Art Report**
1979	**The Programming Language Smalltalk-72 (John Shoch), *****, Paris**
1980	**Infotech State of the Art Report**
1981	**Smalltalk Issue, *Byte* Magazine**
1983	**Goldberg and Robson**

+ ca 1975–1966 ???, 3D masters thesis in ST-72
+ ca 1978–1980 Gould and Finzer, Rehearsal World
+ ca 1978 Ingalls, Horn, etc., Smalltalk-78, Dorado Smalltalk, etc.
+ ca 1979ish Goldstein & Bobrow, PIE documents
+ ca 1980 Steve Weyer Thesis

Historical Views Of PARC and LRG

19**	Ted Nelson Ravings
19**	Tim Rentsch paper
1984	Smalltalk Implementation History, D. Ingalls
198**	Tools for Thought, H. Rheingold, good profile on early ARPA, Engelbart, etc.
198**	IEEE Computer, Tekla Perry, et al., excellent portrait of PARC
1989	Smalltalk, Past, Present, and Future, P. Deutsch
19**	*Fumbling the Future*, disorganized, and inaccurate portrait of PARC

Smalltalk Spinoffs

Hewitt Actors papers
D-LISP (User interface)
MIT LISP machines
Rosetta Smalltalk
Methods and Smalltalk-V
etc.

REFERENCES

[ACM, 1969] ACM SIGPLAN, *Conference on Extensible Languages*, May 1969.

[Arnheim,1969] Arnheim, Rudolf, *Visual Thinking*, Berkeley: University of California Press, 1969.

[Balzer, 1967] Balzer, R.M. Dataless programming. *Proceedings of the FJCC*, July 1967.

[Barton, 1961] Barton, R.S. A new approach to the functional design of a digital computer, in *Proceedings of the WJCC*, May 1961.

[Baecker, 1969] Baecker, Ronald M. Interactive computer-mediated animation, Dept. of Electrical Engineering, Ph.D. thesis, MIT, 1969, Supervisor: Edward L. Glaser.

[Borning, 1979] Borning, Alan. Thinglab—A constraint-oriented simulation laboratory, Xerox Palo Alto Research Center, #SSL-79-3, July 1979.

[Brand, 1972] Brand, Stewart. Fanatic life & symbolic death among the computer bums, *Rolling Stone Magazine*, Dec. 1972.

[Burroughs,1961] Burroughs Corp. The Descriptor—a definition of the B5000 information processing system, Detroit, Michigan, Bulletin No. 5000-20002-P, Feb. 1961.

[Byte, 1981] *Byte Magazine*, Issue on Smalltalk , Christopher Morgan, Ed., Vol. 6, No. 8, Aug. 1981.

[Carnap, 1947] Carnap, Rudolf. *Meaning and Necessity, A Study in Semantics and Modal Logic*, Chicago:University of Chicago Press, 1947.

[Clark, 1962] Clark, Wesley A. The General Purpose Computer in the Life Sciences Laboratory, in *Engineering and the Life Sciences*, NAS-NRC Report, Washington DC, Apr. 1962.

[Clark ,1965] _______, and Molnar, C.E. A Description of the LINC, in *Computers in Biomedical Research*, Vol. 1, Chapter 2, R.W. Stacy and B.D. Waxman, Ed., New York: Academic Press, 1965.

[Conway, 1963] Conway, Melvin E. Design of a separable transition-diagram compiler, in *Communications of the ACM*, Vol. 6, No. 7, July 1963, pp. 396–408.

[Dahl, 1970] Dahl, O.-J., Decomposition and Classification in Programming Languages, in *Linguaggi nella Società e nella Tecnica*. Milan: Edizioni di Comunita, 1972.

[Dahl, 1970] Dahl, O.-J. and Hoare, C. A. R., Hierarchical Program Structures, in Dahl, O.-J., Dijkstra, E. W., and Hoare, C. A. R., *Structured Programming*, New York: Academic Press, pp. 175–220.

[Davis, 1964] Davis, M. R., and Ellis, T. O. The RAND tablet: A man-machine graphical communication device, report .#RM-4122-ARPA, CA: RAND, 1964.

[Deutsch, 1966] Deutsch, L.P. LISP for the PDP-1, in *The Programming Language LISP; Its Operation and Applications*, Edmund C. Berkeley and Daniel G. Bobrow, Eds., Cambridge, MA: M.I.T. Press, ix, p. 382.

[Deutsch, 1989] ______. The past, present, and future of smalltalk, in *Proceedings of the 3rd European Conference on Object Oriented Programming*, Cambridge University Press, 1989.

[Engelbart, 1968] Engelbart, Douglas C. and English, William K., A research center for augmenting human intellect, in *Proceedings of the FJCC*, Vol. 33, Part one, Dec. 1968, pp. 395–410.

[Farber,1964 Farber, D. J., Griswald, R. E. and Polensky, F. P., "*SNOBOL, a string manipulation language*" JACM 11, 1964, pp. 21–30.

[Feldman, 1977] Feldman, Jerome A. A formal semantics for computer languages and its application in a compiler-compiler, in *Communications of the ACM*, Jan. 1977, pp. 3–9.

[Fisher, 1970] Fisher, David Allen. Control structures for programming languages, Ph.D. thesis, Department of Computer Science, Carnegie Mellon University, 1970.

[Goldberg, 1983] Goldberg, Adele, Kay, Alan C. and Robson, D. *Smalltalk-80: The Language and its Implementation*, Reading, MA: Addison Wesley, 1983.

[Goldstein, 1980] Goldstein, I. and Bobrow, D., PIE Papers.

[Gombrich,1960] Gombrich, E. H. *Art & Illusion: A Study in the Psychology of Pictorial Representation*, New York: Pantheon Books, 1960.

[Groner, 1966] Groner, Gabriel. Real-time recognition of hand printed text, CA: RAND, Report #RM-5016-ARPA, Oct. 1966.

[Hewitt, 1969] Hewitt, Carl E. Planner: A language for manipulating models and proving theorems in a robot, Cambridge: MIT, Project MAC., AI memo #168, 1969.

[Hewitt, 1973] ______, P. Bishop, Greif, I. Smith, B. Matson, T. and Steiger, R. ACTOR induction and meta-evaluation, in *Conference Record of ACM Symposium on Principles of Programming Languages*, 1–3 Oct. 1973, New York: ACM, 1973, pp.153–168.

[Ingalls 1978] Ingalls, D. The Smalltalk-76 Programming System, Design and Implementation, in 5th ACM *Symposium on Principles of Programming Languages*, Tucson, AZ, Jan. 1978

[Irons, 1970] Irons, E. T. Experience with an extensible language, in *Communications of the ACM*, vol. 13, no. 1, Jan. 1970, pp. 31–40.

[Joss,1964] Shaw, J. C. JOSS: *A Designer's View of an Experimental Online Computer System*, CA: RAND, #P-2922, 1964.

[Joss, 1978] _______, JOSS Session, in *History of Programming Languages*, ed. Richard L. Wexelblat, New York: Academic Press, xxiii, Chapter X, 1981. Conference: History of Programming Languages Conference, Los Angeles, CA, 1978.

[Kaehler, 1981] Kaehler, Edwin B. Virtual memory for an object-oriented langauge, *Byte*, Aug. 1981.

[Kay, 1968] Kay, Alan C. FLEX: a flexible extensible language, M.S. thesis, University of Utah, May 1968.

[Kay, 1969] ______. The reactive engine, Ph.D. thesis, University of Utah, September 1969.

[Kay, 1970] ______. Ramblings towards a KiddiKomp, in *Stanford AI Project Lab Notebook*, Nov. 1970.

[Kay, 1972b ______. Learning research group 3 year plan, Xerox Palo Alto Research Center, May 1972.

[Kay, 1972c] ______. A personal computer for children of all ages, in *Proceedings of the ACM National Conference*, Boston, Aug. 1972.

[Kay, 1977a] ______ and Goldberg, Adele Personal dynamic media, *IEEE Computer*, Vol. 10, March 1977, pp. 31–41. Reprinted in *A History of Personal Workstations*, New York: Academic Press, 1988.

[Kay, 1979] ______. Programming your own computer, Science Year 1979, *World Book Encyclopedia*, 1979.

[Kiczales, 1991] Kiczales, Gregor, Des Rivieres, Jim Bobrow, Daniel G. *The Art of the Metaobject Protocol*, Cambridge, MA: MIT Press, viii, 335 p. 1991.

[Knuth, 1971] Knuth, Donald E. and Floyd, Robert W. Notes on avoiding 'go to'statements, in *Information Processing Letters*, Vol., 1, No. 1, Feb. 1971.

[Lampson, 1966] Lampson, B.T. Project GENIE documentation, Computer Center, U.C.Berkeley, Oct. 1966.

[Lampson, 1969] ______. An overview of the CAL time-sharing system, Computer Center, U.C. Berkeley, Sept. 1969. Originally entitled On reliable and extendable operating systems, Sept. 5, 1969.

[McCarthy, 1960] McCarthy, John P. Part 1, Recursive functions of symbolic expressons and their computation by machine, in *Communications of the ACM*, Vol. 3, Number 4, April 1960, pp. 184–195.

[Minsky, 1974] Minsky, Marvin. A framework for representing knowledge, MIT, Artificial Intelligence Laboratory Memo No. 306, June 1974. Reprinted in *The Psychology of Computer Vision*, New York: McGraw-Hill, 1975.

[Newman, 1973] Newman, W. M., and Sproull, R. F. *Principles of interactive computer graphics*, New York: McGraw-Hill, 1973.

[Nygaard, 1966] Nygaard, Kristen, and Dahl, Ole-Johan. Simula—an ALGOL-based simulation language, in *Communicatons of the ACM*, IX, 9, Sept. 1966, pp. 671–678.

[Plato] Plato. Timaeus & Phaedrus: *The Dialogues of Plato*, translated by Benjamin Jowett, Great Books of the Western World, Robert Maynard Hutchins, Ed., Encyclopedia Britannica, Inc., 1952.

[Popek, 1984] Popek, G., *et al.*, *The Locus Distributed Operating System*, Cambridge: MIT Press, 1984.

[Ross, 1960] Ross, D.T., and Ward, J. E. Picture and pushbutton languages, chapter 8 of *Investigations in Computer-Aided Design*, interim engineering report 8436-IR-1, Electrical Systems Lab, MIT, May 1960.

[Ross, 1961] ________. A generalized technique for symbol manipulation and numerical calculation, in *Communications of the ACM*, Vol. 4, No. 3, March 1961, pp. 147–150.

[Rovner, 1968] Rovner, P. D. An AMBIT/G programming language implementation, MIT Lincoln Laboratory, Lexington, MA, June 1968.

[Schorre, 1963] Shorre, D. V. META II— A syntax-oriented compiler writing language, UCLA computing facility,

[Shoch, 1979] Shoch, J. F. 1979, An overview of the programming language Smalltalk-72, in *SIGPLAN Notices*, vol. 14, no. 9, Sept. 1979, pp. 64–73.

[Soloway, 1989] Soloway, Elliot and James C. Spohrer, Ed., *Studying the Novice Programmer*, New Jersey: Lawrence Erlbaum Associates, Inc., 1989.

[Smith, 1975] Smith, David Canfield. *Pygmallion*, Ph.D. thesis, Stanford University, 1975.

[Strachey,*] Strachey, Christopher. Toward a formal semantics, United Kingdom.

[Sutherland, 1963] Sutherland, Ivan C. Sketchpad: A man-machine graphical communication system, MIT Lincoln Laboratory, Technical Report 296, Jan. 1963.

[Sutherland, 1963a ______. ibid, in *Proceedings of the SJCC*, Vol. 23, 1963, pp. 329–346.

[Sutherland, 1968] ______. A head-mounted three dimensional display, in *Proceedings of the FJCC*, 1968, p. 757.

[Thacker, 1972] Thacker, C.P. A personal computer with microparallel processing, Xerox Palo Alto Research Center, Dec. 1972.

[Thacker, 1986] ______. Personal distributed computing: the ALTO and ethernet hardware, in *A History of Personal Workstations*, Adele Goldberg, Ed., New York: ACM Press, 1988, pp. 267–290.

[Van Wijngaarden, 1968] Van Wijngaarden, A., Ed., Draft Report on ALGOL 68, Mathematisch Centrum, MR 93, Amsterdam, The Netherlands, 1968.

[Wirth, 1966] Wirth, N.K. and Weber, H. EULER: A generalization of ALGOL, and its formal definition: Part I, in *Communications of the ACM*, Vol. 9, No. 1, Jan. 1966, pp. 13–25.

[Winston, 1970] Winston, Patrick H. Learning structural descriptions from examples, Ph.D. thesis, MIT, Jan. 1970.

[Zahn, 1974] Zahn, C. T, Jr. A control statement for natural top-down structured programming, in *Proceedings of the Colloque sur la Programmation*, April 1974, Paris. A revised version of this paper appears, under the same title, in *Programming Symposium*, vol. 19 of the Lecture notes in Computer Science, B. Robinet, Ed., Berlin: Springer Verlag, 1974, pp. 170–180.

TRANSCRIPT OF PRESENTATION

SESSION CHAIR BARBARA RYDER: This interesting biography was given to me by Dr. Kay. Alan Kay is a former professional musician, who majored in mathematics and molecular biology while an undergraduate at the University of Colorado, but spent most of his time working on theatrical productions, and as a systems programmer for the National Center of Atmospheric Research. In 1966 he joined the University of Utah's ARPA Project under Dave Evans and Bob Barton. First contributions were as a member of the original continuous-tone, 3D graphics group. Early on, the confluence of Sketchpad and Simula, with his background in math and biology, brought forth a vision of what he later called object-oriented programming. Then, with Ed Cheadle at Memcor and Montec Corporation, he designed and built the FLEX Machine, the first object-oriented personal computer. He received his masters and Ph.D. degrees in 1968 and 1969 (both with distinction) for this work. In 1968, struck by the first flat panel display, the GRAIL system at Rand, and Papert's work on LOGO, Kay conceived of the Dynabook, a notebook-sized intimate computer "For Children of All Ages," and set out to realize it. He spent his first post-doc year at the Stanford AI project, and became one of the founders of Xerox PARC when it was set up in 1970. Between the years of 1971 and 1981, Kay was at Xerox PARC serving as the head of the Learning Research Group, principal scientist, and finally Xerox Fellow. In his own terms, he invented, co-invented, inspired, admired, coerced,and tantrumed, with a host of great colleagues, much of personal computing or as he called it—a new paradigm for human–computer collaboration. He was the original designer of the bit-mapped screen, overlapping window interface, painting graphics, and Smalltalk, the first completely object-oriented language. From 1982 to 1984, he was the Chief Scientist, and then Senior Vice President, of Atari, where he set up a large scale research organization. From 1984 to the present, he has been at Apple Computer Corporation, where he currently is an Apple Fellow. There he started, and is currently the head, of the Vivarium Project, a large scale, long-range investigation of children's learning and ability to be amplified by computers. He is codesigner of a number of language environments, including Playground and Constructo. Beyond computers, music is Kay's special passion. He has been a professional jazz musician, a composer, an amateur classical pipe organist, harpsichordist, and chamber pianist. And the last is, according to him, in a decreasing order of ability and interest. His sole professional membership is in the International Society of Organ Builders. He has built several musical instruments, including a collaboration with a master organ builder on a late 17th century instrument for his home.

ALAN C. KAY My job is to get to the ten-minute video tape in twenty-five minutes. I'm going to give a different kind of talk, I think. The paper I wrote "The Early History of Smalltalk" was written to be readable and to be read, and I hope that you will read it at some point, if you haven't already. It is fairly detailed, and I can't actually cover that ground today. It's probably just as well. There is also an interesting ACM policy in writing papers, I discovered, and that is that they won't let you put footnotes in. So the idea is that you either put them in the body of the text or leave them out. So I left them out, because the reason for footnotes is so you can have a nice flow of writing. But what I thought I would do, is do the footnotes in this talk. I'm a little worried about the time limit. I remember after graduate school I was going around looking for jobs and somebody asked me, "Can you give a two-hour lecture on the FLEX machine?" I said, "I don't know. I'd never been that brief."

One of the things I discovered about this exercise is what Henry Ford said, which is "history is bunk," because every time I tried writing the paper, I wrote a different one. Every time I worked on this talk, I came up with a different one. They are all sort of true, and they are all sort of false. There's not only revisionism here, but there's also the emotional tinge that you have from day to day, in how you remember things.

(SLIDE 1) At PARC in 1974—forget about these firsts—the word "first" doesn't matter; arguably, we had the first PC workstation, first overlapping window interface, first modern OOP, first laser printer, and first packet-switching LAN. One of the interesting things about PARC—and I'm going to get into this a little bit—is that, for example, the PC workstation was done by a couple of people in the Computer Science Lab with some data from me. Our group, the Learning Research Group, did the user interface and Smalltalk. The Ethernet was done by one person in one lab and one person in another lab. And the laser printer was done by a person in yet a third lab. And in fact, there was no supreme plan of any kind, having to do with management coordination. The whole shebang was done

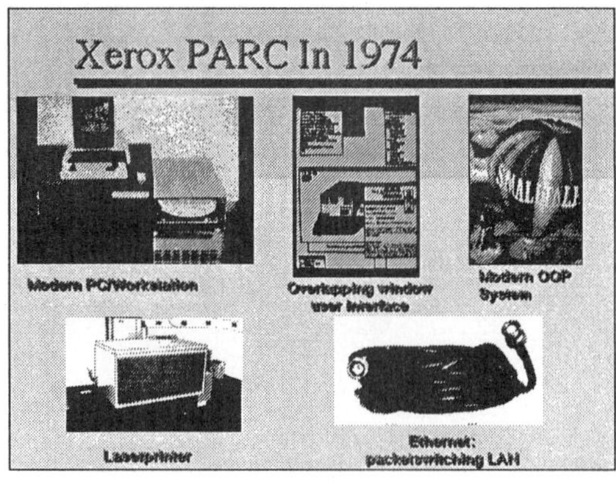

SLIDE 1

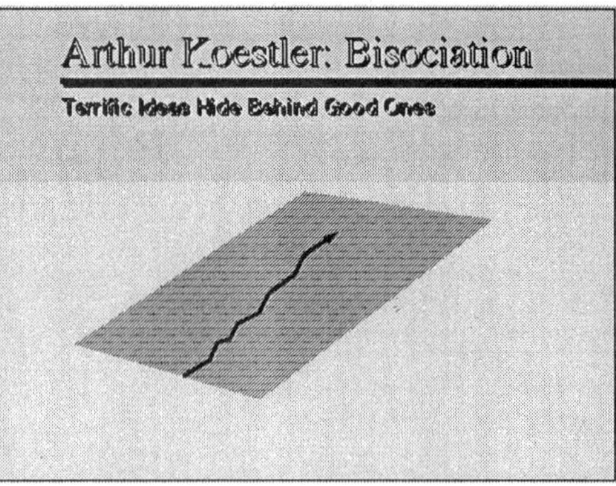

SLIDE 2a

by a bunch of people who were actually kind of friendly and just decided to do it. It wasn't to say that there wasn't a dream or a vision; there was a very strong dream from ARPA, and a very strong vision. One of the joys at PARC is that, for many years, we got along without a lot of management. There was a *romance* about this, and what I want to talk to you about, is the romance of design, or how do you actually do it, or why do things sometimes turn out in a completely different way than normal improvement.

(SLIDE 2a) Arthur Koestler wrote a book called *The Act of Creation* which had quite a bit of influence on us. One of his models was that we think relative to contexts, which are more or less consistent sets of beliefs. Kuhn calls them "paradigms." Creativity-in-a-context normally happens and turns out results that are improvements on the kinds of things that you are doing that are in accord with your belief structures. Now, he calls this "normal science" or "evolutionary science." I'd like to explore the other kind, what he calls "revolutionary science." The way I think about this is, the two things that make life worth living are love and "holy shits." Once you have a "holy shit," it's hard not to want to find more. And in Koestler's diagram, a "holy shit" is sort of represented like this.

(SLIDE 2b) It is a funny thing that terrific ideas tend to hide behind good ones. The real enemy of a terrific idea is a good one, because the good ones have so many reasons for staying with them. But, all of a sudden something happens, and all of a sudden you are catapulted into a completely different

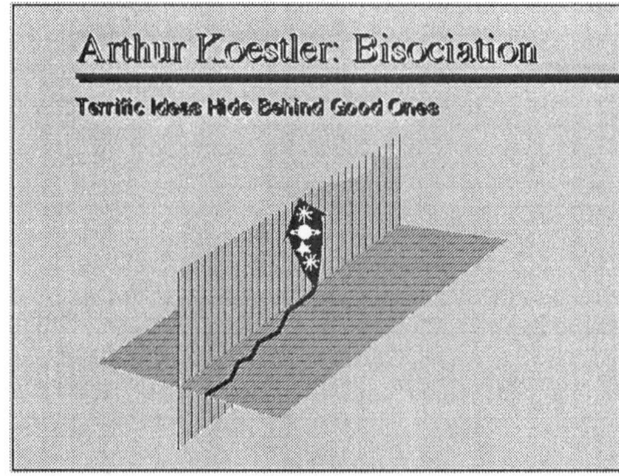

SLIDE 2b

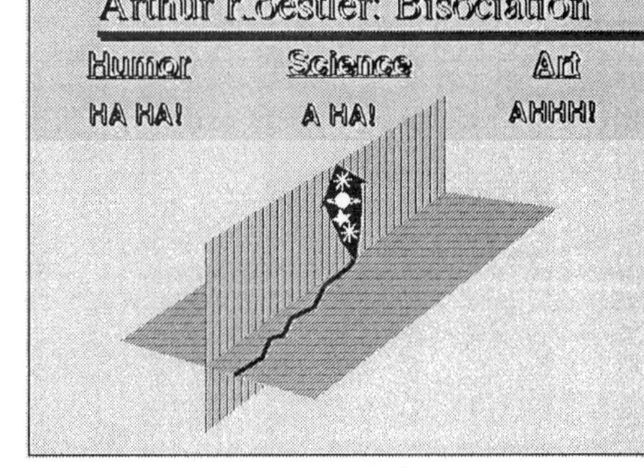

SLIDE 2c

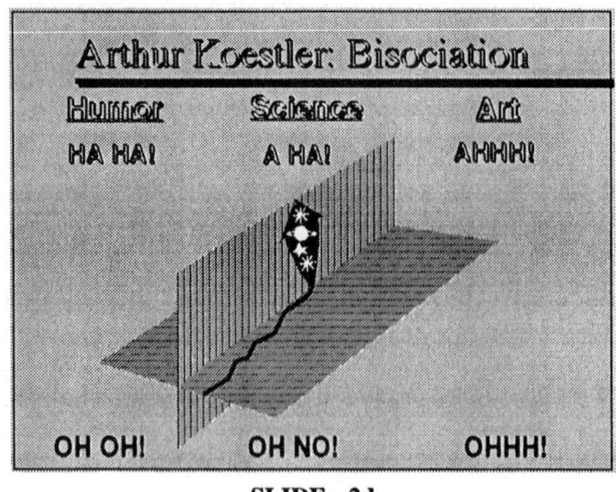

SLIDE 2d

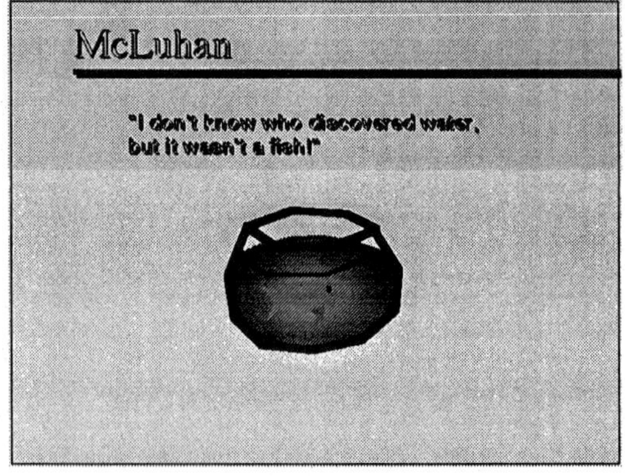

SLIDE 3a

set of beliefs. Koestler's theory of creation is that most creation is sort of like a joke—a joke is where you are led around one path and all of a sudden it reveals you are in a completely different situation.

(SLIDE 2c) He even came up with emotional reactions: like if it's a joke it's "ha," if it's science, its "a ha," and if it's art, it's "aah." I thought I would balance that, because that was too optimistic.

(SLIDE 2d) There was also "uh oh," "oh no" and "oh!" So there is a surprise of being catapulted into a different context.

(SLIDE 3a) McLuhan had a different way of looking at this. He said "I don't know who discovered water but it wasn't a fish." So the fish doesn't know what color water he is in, because his nervous system has normalized away what's in his environment. We can think of that water as being beliefs.

(SLIDE 3b) One of the things that humans have learned to do is to use better goldfish bowls. Some of them are called culture. The cultural beliefs that we have can be much more powerful than what our brains are born with. Going from being situated in one goldfish bowl to another is about as tough as being totally creative; maybe it's tougher. Many people who make the jump become even more religious about the new bowl; they forget it's a bowl.

(SLIDE 3c) And of course, one of the things that we do occasionally in science, is that we make a better goldfish bowl. So as we're jumping, we are sketching away at the bowl, and we hope that we get all the water in there before we hit.

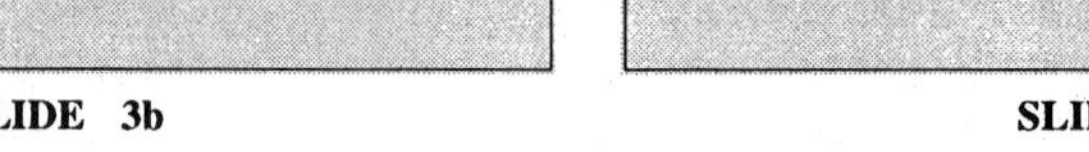
SLIDE 3b

SLIDE 3c

SLIDE 4

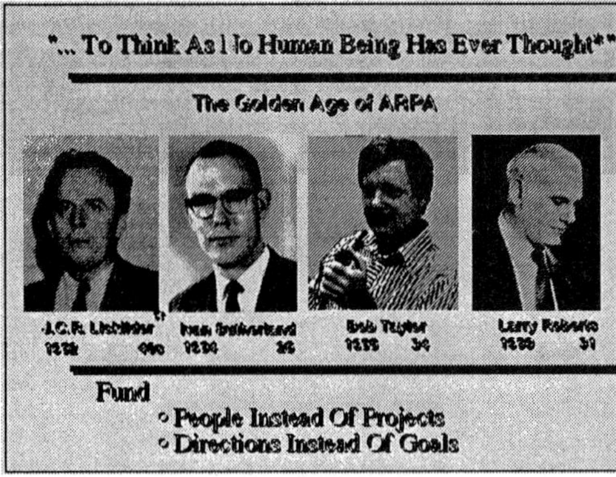

SLIDE 5

Now this one is mainly done by crazy people, and by a few scientists, and some artists. One of the problems with this is that when you go from one goldfish bowl to another—particularly when you make the goldfish bowl yourself—every goldfish bowl forces you to see things its way. It's like the man in Moliere's play, who suddenly discovered that he had been speaking prose all of his life; it changed his realization of what he had been doing. So, the idea is that if you are going to do this, you better make sure that the end result is really good, because the religious feeling you are going to get when you get over here is going to be the same regardless of whether it is good or bad. It is just the self-confirming seductiveness that a belief-structure has.

(SLIDE 4) Another metaphor I like is frogs. In fact, here at MIT they discovered that the frog's eyes do not tell the frog's brain about much. If you take the frog's normal food, paralyze it (the frog) with a little bit of chloroform, (and then) put flies out in front of the frog, the frog will not eat them, because it can't see that a fly is food. If you flip a little piece of cardboard at the frog that is organized longitudinally, the frog will try and eat it every time, because the food is an oblong moving shape. I think that for us scientists, one of the ways of looking at this, is thinking of these flies as ideas. They are in front of us all the time, but we can't see the darn things.

So there's a fundamental principle in all this stuff, and that is that all nervous systems are unconscious with regard to most of the environment, all of the time. One of the most important things to realize, when you are trying to do this stuff, is that whatever you think you believe in almost certainly is not going to help you. You somehow have to make the bowl that you are in, visible, and there are various ways of doing it. You can only learn to see, when you realize that you are blind. Of course, one of the things we know about eyes is that they don't evolve when there is no light.

(SLIDE 5) Here are some candle bearers. This is one of the most amazing decades I think in this century for funding that these four guys created in the sixties. Notice that only Lick (Licklider) was over forty when he took over. Ivan (Sutherland) was twenty-six, Bob Taylor was thirty-four, and Larry Roberts was thirty-one. They were taken out of the ARPA community, and their basic idea is that we will fund people instead of projects, because we can't really judge projects. So we will fund people instead, and we will fund directions instead of goals. That way, these guys didn't have to do a lot of peer-review stuff. But, what they were interested in, was the energy and verve, and probability of success, of the people that they were funding. In spite of the fact that this is one of the best examples of success in funding, very few companies and very few institutions do it this way.

(SLIDE 6) There are lots of cool characters out there that helped the future happen. Here is Dave Evans. One of the most important things about Dave Evans is that he, like most of the ARPA

SLIDE 6

SLIDE 7

Contractors, treated his graduate students as absolute colleagues. If you couldn't be a colleague, he would ease you out. For instance, I flew 140,000 miles as a graduate student; he actually had a travel budget for graduate students. His idea was (that) we had to go around and find out what people are doing; don't wait to read it in a paper. He had been an architect of one of the earliest tagged architectures, the Bendix G-20, in the the '50s. And one of the things I got from him, is this idea that, whenever you are working on what appears to be the main part of a problem, you are probably off, because that's the most obvious path. What you should be worrying about are the exception conditions. So one of his ideas was basically always leave an "extra bit." That extra bit is all you need, because if you can trap anywhere, then whatever you are trying to do straightforwardly won't kill you in the end. This is a terrific general metaphor.

(SLIDE 7) The context at Utah was large scale 3-D. It wasn't just inventing continuous tone graphics. It was large-scale architecture and CAD. The size of the data structures and stuff they were talking about was many, many orders of magnitude larger than any of the computing that was going on at the time. One of the first things that struck me, was the disparity between what Evans wanted to do, and the way computing was being done then. Which reminded me of how you can make a dog house out of pretty much anything except maybe match sticks, because the materials are so strong compared to the size and structure you are building. Programming in the '50s, particularly in the '60s, could get away with having fragile data structures and procedures, because they weren't that complicated; it wasn't that big a deal; you could track down things. When I learned how to program in the early '60s we only got the machine for five minutes every other day, and you couldn't touch it. So you had to do everything by desk checking.

(SLIDE 8) But this isn't what they are talking about. So this is the mechanistic view that still persists today. Probably the worst thing you ever could do is to teach somebody algorithms as their first programming course, because it gives people a completely limited idea of what computers are about. It's like anybody could do physics in the middle ages, you just get a hat. There is not that much to know.

(SLIDE 9) But, if you want to do something that has hundreds and hundreds of thousands, or millions and millions of parts, you need something like a principle of architecture. That set up some stress.

One of the most fortunate things that happened to me when I went to Utah, was that I got there too late for one semester and too early for another semester. So there were actually two months when I had nothing to do. Dave Evans did something really amazing; he said, "What would you like to do in

SLIDE 8

SLIDE 9

those two months?" I'd never had anybody ask me that in any school situation. I said, "Well, I'd like to actually read things. I'd like to try to understand what's going on," because I actually didn't know anything.

(SLIDE 10) Now, go back to Koestler a second. Why is general education important? Well, if you don't have general education, you don't have any blue ideas, because when you are thinking along, what actually happens is your little thought patterns in one context are bumping into these other contexts. There are little excursions in there, and then rejections usually, and they come back to earth. You need some sort of forcing function. When a forcing function happens, you have two choices. One is you can decide to keep on going and automate the old stuff that you are working on using the new technique better, or there might be this possibility that this is an entirely new way of doing things—and you can actually leap up into this new context and the world is not the same again. For instance, in Maxwell's equations, the cruxpoint was Lorentz's transform, which was a solution of Maxwell's equations that didn't make any sense in a Newtonian world, and Einstein had to go to a different context in order to make sense of them.

Simula, I think, was one of the greatest cruxpoints that we have had in many years, certainly the best one since LISP. The question is, what was it?

The most normal way was to think of it as a better old thing, and it certainly was—certainly better than ALGOL and ALGOL-X. One of the things you could do—as Barbara talked about—is we could use this as a stimulus to construct something that was better than the better old things, and get abstract data types. Fortunately, I didn't know anything about computer science then. I've not been that innocent since. So, I actually had no interest in improving ALGOL because I didn't even know ALGOL very well. I had only programmed in machine code and a little bit of FORTRAN. And so, when I saw Simula, it immediately made me think of tissues. There are lots of little independent things—Simula called them processes—floating around in communication with each other, and my little bump transformed me from thinking of computers as mechanisms, to thinking of them as things that you could make biological-like organisms in, that is, things were up in the ten^9 to ten^{13} level of complexity.

So, my path from then on, was this way—towards something that was a different way. It's not necessarily that this was a better way of going, but I am just trying to say that I just couldn't look a regular programming language in the face after that encounter with Simula—procedures seemed now to be the worst possible way of doing anything.

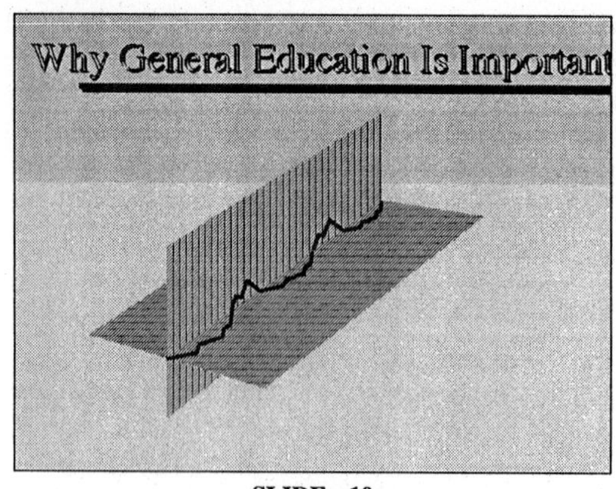

SLIDE 10

SLIDE 11

And I had some aiders and abetters: Bob Barton, who is known as the "ghost who walks" at Utah, because he was seen outside of the Merrill Engineering building and inside of Merrill Engineering building, but he was never seen entering or leaving Merrill Engineering Building.

(SLIDE 11) This is actually not a picture of him, because I don't think he has ever been photographed. I'm not sure that he would actually show up on film. So, I actually found a picture of somebody else that looked like him, and I processed it. Barton was this big huge guy who spoke his mind. I remember the first course I took from him. He came stomping into the room and said, "Well, there are a few things known about advanced systems design. I expect you to read them and learn them. But my job is to firmly disabuse you of all the fondly held notions that you might have brought into this classroom." And so what he proceeded to do was to shoot down everything that we believed in. This is something I believe Marvin did that was a service to MIT students. It was extremely liberating. Because by the time you got done with this, those of us who would still survive, there was nothing that was sacred. We could do anything we wanted. Just because other people were doing it didn't mean anything. He was so obnoxious, that even the faculty complained about him to Dave Evans. And Dave Evans said to them: "We don't care if they are prima donnas, as long as they can sing."

That was Bob Barton.

(SLIDE 12) Here is Ivan. I once asked him, "How could you possibly have done the first object-oriented software system, the first graphics system, and the first constraint solving system, all in one year?" He said, "Well, I didn't know it was hard." In fact, according to Wes Clark, the genesis of Sketchpad was when Ivan went out to Lincoln Labs and saw how bad the display was on the TX-2. And instead of rejecting it like other people had, he asked, "What else can it do?" That's a question we could all try asking for ourselves. And what else it could do, it could simulate the things it was showing pictures of, not just these thick papers, but to actually simulate.

(SLIDE 13) Marvin (Minsky). "You have to form the habit of not being right for very long." One of the things that Marvin used to say is you should never just form distinctions, you should form "tri-stinctions." So, don't just divide it up into two things, try to find a third way to divide it up, and that's probably the way you should go.

The reason I am showing things, is, because this stuff is more a matter of attitude than intelligence. The attitude that these guys had led to really good results. Classical science we think of as being given a universe and we work to discover its rules.

(SLIDE 14) The best book on complex system design. Think about it.

SLIDE 12

SLIDE 13

(SLIDES 15 and 16) Just two more people here.

I want to say that when you are doing something real, you've got to have some real people make it happen; and in many ways, Smalltalk is more of Dan's language than mine. I gave you some of the basis for the way we did it. I should mention one other thing, and that is that one of the great things about PARC is that we didn't have to worry about anybody's hardware. We just built everything. When you do that, you don't have to worry about certain efficiency things. Dan, if you know him, is one of the most even-tempered guys I've ever met. I only saw him really angry once, and that was right after he had done Smalltalk-76. I went into him and said, "Dan, now I know what we really should do." He just could not believe I would do this, after he had spent seven months getting this new system going. That was the kind of relationship we had.

And then finally, Adele, who said, "Isn't this illegal?" when we wanted to take the ALTOs down to the school, and PARC wouldn't let us—even though that was in the plan. We got our station wagon and loaded up some ALTOs in that station wagon, and took them down to the school. I called up George Pake and said, "Guess what I just did?" So, I'm the person who corrupted Adele.

(VIDEO) I want to show you a quick video montage of things in Smalltalk. This goes quickly, so I'll just talk as fast as I can. Here is the early ALTOs, with the cardboard protector on the display.

Here is one of the earliest groups of children, and I wonder who that might be, watching what they are doing. I don't recognize the hair style.

SLIDE 14

SLIDE 15

SLIDE 16

Here is how we taught—this was devised by Adele—here's how we taught kids Smalltalk. We gave them an instance of a class, which is called traditionally "Joe." We said, "Joe, grow fifty," now we say "Joe grow minus fifty." "Joe turn thirty-five." And now we make another instance of box called "Jill". That shows up too and we can talk to it separately. So, we say, "Jill, turn whatever." Then we can make a little infinite repeat loop, that gives messages to them. Ultimately, we get a little movie. This gives the kids the idea that these are separate entities but have similar behavior. Make a more complicated movie, has them changing size as well as rotating. They could play around with these. What was interesting about this way of going about it, is you could build many interesting things from these boxes.

Here is one of the very first Smalltalk classes, Marion Goldeen, age twelve. One of the things she discovered was that if you took out the erase part in the draw methods, that you could make little brushes out of things. Each one of those is a box at the top. She has generalized them from squares into polygons. What it is doing now is following the mouse. Now she is getting a hexagon, and again it follows the mouse; it's a particular brush type. As you can see, she has made quite a few . . . . This is like MacPaint; it wasn't completely original; she had seen one of the early painting systems that we had done. This is a very short Smalltalk program done by a twelve-year old.

Then, we got this idea to have Marion teach the class. She is a year older here. She is thirteen, teaching twelve-year olds.

Here is an example from 1975, done by Susan Hamet who is also age twelve. This is a little bit more elaborate; this is like MacDraw, yet in the future, because instead of painting here, what she has is objects being maintained on the screen, (so) she can talk to them separately. She has a little menu over there, and a little window for feeding back and getting parameters. So she is going to change the size of this box on the left, make it small, and give it a lot of sides so she will get a circle. Each one of these things is actually an instance of a single class. This is the kind of thing we were shooting for, which is to have kids do their own tools, their own applications.

Now, the grownups are also doing things. This is the animation system done by Steve Purcell—unfortunately, quite superior to what you can still do on the Macintosh. The ALTO is very powerful doing this.

And then some adult animators and computer people did this system that is called Shazam. This is about a five and a half to six page program in Smalltalk 72. On the left there is an animation window, on the right is a painting window, little iconic menus there. What he is going to do is give the thing he just drew a path to follow. Now it's following the path. What he is going to do is single step it now.

He is pointing to the stair steps. What he wants, is to get it down to the bottom, and he wants to replace the bottom one with a squashed one. Now, now he starts the animation again. And he has gotten a transparent cell; it's overlaid on the one he's got there. So he has actually not destroyed the old one; he is painting on another transparent layer. He is using that as the center. You can see that the painting is being inserted in, as he is painting. What animators want to do is put in enough similarity so you will think that the ball is deforming continuously, even though it's just one frame.

Another twelve-year old. Now she added a feature to the adult system. The feature is to be able to take two animated images and to combine them into one, which is not in the original system. So she picks that up; when she lets it go it's going to merge with the thing there, so now she gets a jockey and a race horse that will animate together.

One more thing in Smalltalk-72. This is a timbre editing system for frequency modulation. This was the first real-time FM system. It was done by Steve Saunders and Ted Kaehler. What you are doing is producing that timbre as a woodwind, and here it is as a kind of a bowed string. The ALTO could do eight real-time voices without any special hardware at all. So here is the C minor Fugue by Bach. This is about 1975.

Now, transition to Smalltalk-76, which is actually much more of a language for adult programmers. One of the first really nifty things that was done in it, was this "simulation kit," which was a tool for novices. This grew out of our work going all the way back to Simula. It's kind of a job shop simulation where you can design the icons. This happened to be done by a Xerox Versatech executive, and represented a production line in the Versatech, and would automatically animate the simulation as it went along.

This was mainly designed by Adele. It was done in 1978. This is a system that was done in Smalltalk, called Playground. The ideas are very similar to stuff we were doing at PARC, except we decided that instead of just having the kids do applications, we wanted them to do complex systems. Because one of the things that the computer does better than anything else is (it can be) a medium for understanding complex systems.

This is all done by children. It is a clownfish that has about twenty-five separate processes running in it. This is all highly parallel programming. What the clownfish is doing is acclimating itself to see an enemy. It also forages for food, tries to mate in the spring, it does shelter. It has four or five drives and only one body. In this foraging path, it attracts the attention of the shark. The shark chases it, its predator avoidance routine takes over the body and it goes for its sea anemone, which it has gotten acclimated to. The shark will not go there because the sea anemone will sting it. That was a more complicated program than most college people ever write, because they almost never write anything that is highly parallel or even parallel at all. One of the ways of thinking about this, my last sentence, is that the Greeks held that the visual arts were the imitation of life; we know that creativity is a lot more than that. But the computer arts are the imitation of creation itself. That's what we should aspire to when we try and design these systems.

TRANSCRIPT OF DISCUSSANT'S REMARKS

Session Chair Barbara Ryder: Adele Goldberg joined Xerox PARC in June 1973, working with Alan Kay in the Learning Research Group as a new Ph.D. with experience in the use of computers and education, both for young children, college students, and adults. Her initial responsibility was to determine how to effectively teach children and adults about the various Smalltalk systems, and to plan and manage experiential projects as feedback to the language and environment design groups. When Kay left on sabbatical, Goldberg became group manager for the System Concepts Group. One goal for the group was to create a Smalltalk system that would run on standard workstations and be distributed outside Xerox. This goal was accomplished in 1983. At this time, Goldberg authored and coauthored several books on the Smalltalk-80 system. Earlier in 1981, Goldberg served as guest editor of the August 1981 issue of *Byte Magazine*, which introduced the general public to the ideas behind Smalltalk. In the early 1980s, Goldberg became manager of the System Concepts Laboratory, one of six research labs at PARC. This lab was located both in Palo Alto and in Portland. Research programs were pursued on the use of video to facilitate group design when members of the group are located in remote sites, essentially initiating research on collaborative computing. While working at Xerox PARC, Goldberg was active in the ACM. She served as Editor-in-Chief of *Computing Surveys* from 1979 until 1982, National Secretary from 1982 to 1984, and President from 1984 to 1986. During that time, she founded ACM Press, initiated the History Series, edited the ACM Press Book on *The History of Personal Workstations*, and helped found the OOPSLA Conference now managed by SIGPLAN. In 1987, Goldberg convinced Xerox to form a separate business to leverage the research on object-oriented technology. ParcPlace Systems was founded in 1988. From 1988 through 1992, she served as CEO and President of ParcPlace. She is currently Chairman of the Board. Goldberg's current technical activities focus on organizational and cultural issues in the introduction of new technology into large organizations' software engineering groups.

ADELE GOLDBERG: As Alan has pointed out in his paper and presentation, Smalltalk is not the story of the evolution of the design of a language or language mechanisms. But rather, it's a story of culture, of organization and vision.

Early in my acquaintance with Alan, I recall someone asking him to give a talk to predict the future of computing. He said, "No, I'm not going to do that. I don't predict the future—I make it."

Lesson number one from Alan. Pick a dream, make it happen.

In this first regard, the Smalltalk invention and development history is different from many other languages. It represents an attempt to realize a dream.

(SLIDE 1) The dream starts with the idea, startling for those days, that computers are simply *not* interesting. What is interesting is what people can do with computers, and what they can access with them.

(SLIDE 2) The scheme then, the key to flexible information access and use, would be software, and that software we named Smalltalk.

Of course, to make dreams happen, you have to be empowered, and you have to empower. Alan once told us, that to his dismay, his vision of the future was hard, and he simply could not do it by

THE PERSONAL WORKSTATION
IS OF INTEREST BECAUSE OF
WHAT IT CAN ACCESS.

SLIDE 1

THE SMALLTALK SYSTEM
IS OF INTEREST BECAUSE IT
IS DESIGNED FOR FLEXIBLE
INFORMATION ACCESS AND USE.

SLIDE 2

SLIDE 3

SLIDE 4

himself. So he went to Xerox and set out to hire an unorthodox set of people—each one too naive and full of the dream, to know the problem was hard—and each one some expansion of some part of Alan. In private, we use to joke about which part each of us represented. I suppose that in truth, we weren't supposed to be a part of his body, but of his mind—sort of an early form of Vulcan mind meld.

Lesson number two from Alan. Hire people who don't know that what you want them to do is hard.

In the early days, I was the representative user. Maybe you could call me the Learning Police. Is what we have created learnable outside the group? Lots of clever computer science can't live up to that requirement.

(SLIDE 3) In a way, it was very fortunate that the research was set in the context of working with kids, because it introduced pedagogy as a quality objective. It motivated a number of significant language changes to support learning by doing, and learning by reading. Doing meant refining from existing useful objects—at every layer of the system. This readability as a quality objective allowed us to see the software problem that we were trying to solve—not as a problem in creating a programming language—but rather as a problem of creating a system for creating systems. These systems would define a higher-level language, created by their developers to be writeable and readable by anyone who understood the domain in which it was going to be used. Aiding readability became a critical challenge for us and any user interface and other environment support.

(SLIDE 4) One of my self-imposed tasks was to get people to understand that the ability to teach Smalltalk to children in no way implied that we had solved the learnability problem for adults. Kids could be guided through the system as it was constructed. The several educational resource centers I created convinced me of this point.

But adults would come to the system with their own ideas of what they wanted to do. We would have to be responsive to their way of thinking—of helping them to create appropriate models for their worlds. Clearly, the simulation or information modeling capabilities of our system would be the key determiner of success. I still believe this today. I do not believe I succeeded, however, in getting the group to understand the unfortunate distinction between so-called kids and so-called adults.

(SLIDE 5) By 1979, we were in systems programming mode, trying to move software ideas forward without a similar change in hardware capability. As Alan pointed out in his paper, the *NoteTaker* project had been canceled despite—in our eyes—major proof-of-concepts success. We created the Smalltalk Hall of Shame that same year, and we inducted as the first member the then head of PARC, who declared that no one was interested in carrying computers around.

SLIDE 5

SLIDE 6

It was time to publish what we knew, and reorganize the research project. Perhaps it was time to admit the problem was hard, and find some more naive people to help us. Also, this form of completion was important as a morale builder, since considerable frustration was building up at the lack of, at least, internal Xerox acknowledgment of the group's contributions.

(SLIDE 6) Larry Tesler and I made another run at the business players that year—a project called Monk. Simple idea and it was very doable. Xerox technicians were not using up-to-date manuals, nor good diagnostic tools when repairing copiers. We wanted to give them an interim Dynabook, with a world of copier information literally under the machine with them. They didn't get the idea and the project did not get funded.

Steve Jobs came to visit. He did get the idea. He came back—with the entire Lisa programming team. After a two-hour hallway argument, I was forced by my managers' manager (the head of the then divided PARC) to give them an in-depth demo. They took the idea. This manager, too, was inducted into the Smalltalk Hall of Shame.

(SLIDE 7) These experiences communicated one hard lesson—we did not have a coherent act. We had lots of bits and pieces for good demos, but, the integrated whole was still in our heads. The best way to share was going to be by publishing the Smalltalk system itself, not a book or papers about a dream where we would risk people getting the schemes wrong. Of course, this was very risky. It violated Alan's critical admonishment, "Do not have customers; they expect support."

> Lesson number three from Alan. If you don't share your results, you can burn the disk packs and start over.

But as individuals, and as a group, we wanted to feel that we finished something in a form that would get a fair evaluation in the computing world. We knew Smalltalk would run on the new "personal" computers because the *NoteTaker* was 8086-based. And we know we could not, alone, do all the work to take Smalltalk to people using these personal computers.

(SLIDE 8) To put out a system meant stopping research and doing enough work to have something we could release to people like us—researchers at universities and advanced development people in commercial companies. But which companies? Burt Sutherland suggested the answer—companies with the ability to create the hardware we wanted. We wanted to influence hardware extensions that would enhance the media accessible by a Smalltalk-like system.

So, we picked companies that built hardware systems, but which had in-house software teams. We signed up Apple, Hewlett-Packard, DEC, and Tektronix. Thus began the saga of creating the shareable

SLIDE 7

Participants in Release Process

APPLE COMPUTER
David Casseres
Dan Cochran
Bruce Daniels
Steven Jobs
Richard Meyers

DIGITAL EQUIPMENT CORPORATION
Stony Ballard
Larry Samberg
Stephen Shirron

HEWLETT-PACKARD
Bob Ballance
David Crockett
Alec Dara-Abrams
Richard L. Dellinger
Joe Falcone
Bob Shaw
Jim Stinger

TEKTRONIX, INC.
Joe Eckardt
Jack D. Grimes
Tom Kloos
Paul McCullough
Jasen Penney
John Theus
Allen Wirfs-Brock

SLIDE 8

version of the system called Smalltalk-80, as a multivendor project. Again, Alan wasn't there to tell us the next lesson, although I'm sure it's something he would say.

Lesson number four from Alan. You have to be careful what you wish for—because you *will* get it.

(SLIDE 9) The release process had three parts to it. We redesigned the language and environment subsystem by subsystem, giving the engineers in the other companies access as we proceeded. We were able to rebuild the system in this manner partially because of the ability to cause all existing objects of one class to, essentially and instantaneously, *become* objects of another class.

(SLIDE 10) Ted Kaehler, the group cartoonist, likened this to the process of launching a ship while it was still being constructed.

The engineers in the four companies worked with us to define the formal specification of the virtual machine architecture. They each implemented the bytecode interpreter and devised various memory management schemes. Later these efforts were published in the book *Smalltalk 80: Bits of Wisdom, Words of Advice*, edited by Glenn Krasner, who managed the systems work in our research laboratory.

Dave Robinson and I acted as documenters, writing the description of the system as it unfolded, and making sure each part was sufficiently explainable. We wrote three books about the language. We only published the third.

SLIDE 9

SLIDE 10

SLIDE 11

Requests For Purchase 1981-1983

University of Michigan
Harvard University
Colby College
InterFace
GMD
Asolv Limited
University of Otago
N.V. Philips' Glogilampenfabrieken
DIKU
Laboratoires De Marcoussis
Entwicklungsbüro
ICL
National University of Singapore
Open University
Rockefeller University
University of Oregon
ATARI
University of Rochester
Three Rivers Computer
Bell Laboratories
AVANT-GARDE Computing, Inc.
Object Oriented Systems
Rosemount Inc.
Bolt Beranek and Newman, Inc.
Loyola University
Hawaiian Telephone
St. Luke's Hospital Medical Center
Cybertroncis International, Inc.
University of British Columbia

Korea Institute of Electronics Technology
SYDIS
NCR Corporation
Datagraph
Child Incorporated
Brown University
Rand
National Information Systems, Inc.
Spatial Tool Co.
BNR Inc.
RCA
CHROMA
Microsoft, Inc.
Lakeside Press, R.R. Donnelley & Sons Company
Motorola Corporation
Fritz-Howard Clapp, Information Systems Consultant
Logical Systems Design, Ltd.
Westinghouse Electric Corporation
SRI International
Zilog
Future Computer Systems
Valtion Teknillinen Tutkimuskeskus
Prime Computer, Inc.
IBM
Viewdata Corporation of America, Inc.
Scott K. Warren (Rosetta)
Massachusetts Institute of Technology
University of Washington
California Institute of Technology

Corgraphics Corporation
Rutherford Appleton Laboratory
Verac Inc.
University of Toronto
University of Iowa
Queen Mary College
TDI Limited
Brigham Young University
Net Computers Inc.
Langages Et Systemes Informatiques
Lanier Business Products, Inc.
Canadian Educational Microprocessor Corporation
MicroMart
Kuras-Alterman Corporation
University of Southern California
NEC Systems Laboratory, Inc.
Fortune Systems Corporation
University of Texas
Solaster Corporation
United States Department of Commerce
University of Manchester
University of Nevada, Las Vegas
Software Investment Research Corporation
MITRE Corporation
SCC International Inc.
Standard Elektrik Lorenz Aktiengesellschaft
Wormald Vigilant Limited
Berry Research
University of Canterbury

SLIDE 12

(SLIDE 11) The earliest practice in publication came in 1981. Chris Morgan, then Editor-in-Chief of *Byte Magazine*, offered me all the feature pages of the August 1981 issue. Dan Ingalls liked hot air balloons as a way to announce that Smalltalk was finally traveling off its isolated island, an island Chris had described two years before.

(SLIDE 12) The result was shocking. I started to get letters from around the world—from universities and commercial organizations—asking to purchase the Smalltalk system. There was even an article called "Mostly Smalltalk" in the TWA *Ambassador Magazine*.

(SLIDE 13) Two more Xerox disappointments clouded the work effort. Because of some problems with the introduction of the Star system in 1981, we were asked to join another group in making recommendations. On July 21, 1982, Dan Ingalls and I formally submitted a plan to build a low-cost 68000-based Smalltalk-80 machine, that would serve as the entry level system of the Star family. We called it *Twinkle*. The proposal was ignored. It reappeared in 1984 as a variety of Apple. Apparently suggesting freehand graphics and a Smalltalk base was too controversial for Xerox. The Xerox manager responsible for delivering the proposal had simply not bothered, and he too was inducted into the Smalltalk Hall of Shame.

In order to share the Smalltalk-80 result, the then head of the Office Systems Group obligated us to build a version for the Star workstation. The project was started in (September) 1982 by Frank Zdybel, and joined later by Paul Mc Cullough. It was completed in the spring of 1984. It was written

November 15, 1982

SLIDE 13

SLIDE 14

in the Mesa programming environment and was our first experiment in creating an environment within an environment. In honor of how it ran, we called it Molasses. Early in the development process, the business head tried to renege on the deal to release Smalltalk, and earned his position in the Smalltalk Hall of Shame.

(SLIDE 14) It took until May of 1983 to finish the first of the Smalltalk-80 books, and to start rolling out the first of commercial implementations done by the vendors participating in the release process. This slide shows the Tekronix Magnolia, with a Smalltalk-80 system, created in Tek Labs, primarily by Allen Wirfs-Brock. The Magnolia was designed by Roger Bates, who had left Xerox a short time before. The next version was sold commercially as the Tekronix 4400. We ourselves had done a native system port to the first Sun workstation which I had borrowed from the Fairchild AI Lab because we were, in those days, not allowed to buy non-Xerox machines.

Meanwhile, Xerox Special Information Systems, a unit of Xerox which does government contract work, had taken early Smalltalk releases and used them to create an office automation system called the Analyst. The Analyst-84 was being readied for broad deployment in the CIA. And so by 1985, we tried to get Xerox to face up to a cold truth: the CIA was in production using an Analyst workstation based on a research result. This was *not* a good idea. The base system had to be engineered; a real business investment was needed. Visits from the Administrative Head of the CIA to PARC did not change the mind of any Xerox business decision maker.

But, in 1986, with a new head of the Office Systems Group, and some friendly ears, an internal task force set out to evaluate the marketplace for Smalltalk. Their conclusion? Do it! Bill Spencer, then head of PARC, approved an experiment to start a business internally, while Xerox sorted out what to do. We moved three engineers from the Dallas Development Center in July, and some of the researchers refocused on rethinking the implementation technology. In November of 1986, Peter Deutsch and shortly after, Allan Shiffman, joined and started the complete redesign of the virtual machine technology. In February 1987, myself and two of the research team formed ParcPlaceHolders, a corporate shell that began a 13-month negotiation to form ParcPlace Systems, Inc., as an independent company.

(SLIDE 15) After five years, the language base has not changed a lot, although the implementation technology has been completely redesigned and implemented. It is the first truly reusable, fully-compiled, Smalltalk system. Creating an application on one of 11 ParcPlace platforms means that your application runs on 11, without your doing any more work. But those ports are compiled to the host instruction set, access host operating system features, and host windowing and graphics. We have

Smalltalk-80 Environment Development

Object Engine

Lazy Machine Code Generation
- Fast execution speed
- Space efficiency
- Binary portability

Memory Management
- Segregates objects according to age
- Apply radically different reclamation algorithms to each
  - Generation scavaging
  - Incremental interruptable garbage collection
  - Mark sweep

Portable Architecture

Execution Environment

Uniform I/O
- File system independence

Host Window System Integration
- Conventional imaging model
  - Graphics code independence
- Host window manager independence

Policy Interfaces
- Paint
- Font selection
- Widgets
- Memory manager

SLIDE 15

Smalltalk-80 Language Development/Libraries

Full block Closure

Exception Handling

Graphics, User Interface Libraries

Visual Interface Painter/Definer
- Specification based

Bridges to/from Other Systems
- C programming call/call back interface
- Database isolation framework
  - Embedded SQL
- Database independence framework
  - Persistent object world
  - Automatic SQL generation
  - Automatic forms extraction
  - Automatic navigation over relational world

SLIDE 16

Smalltalk Trainers and Consultants

Cunningham & Cunningham
EDP Consultants
First Class Software
Greystone Group Inc.
Icon Computing, Inc.
Information Fountain Inc.
Inwood Systems Associates
KBSI.
Knowledge Systems Corporation
Object Oriented Computing Solutions
The Object People
Object Trainers

Pantheon Systems, Inc.
QA Training Ltd.
Reusable Solutions
Rothwell International
Semaphore
smOO dynamics
Synergistics
System Development Guild
VC Software Construction
WhetStone
XSIS

Smalltalk Vendors

Digitalk
Easel/ENFIN
GNU
Object Technology International
ParcPlace Systems, Inc.
QKS

SLIDE 17

changed the virtual machine and the object engine; we have extended the notion of late binding to run-time compilation and execution in the context of late binding of application-level specification of policies for graphics and for user interaction.

(SLIDE 16) The language was modified to have closure of blocks. An exception handling capability was added. And a number of libraries, as well as bridges to C, and to external databases, were built. We ship two different development environments, two additional kits of libraries and tools, on all 11 platforms. Since the fall of 1986, we have released five complete revisions of the system.

(SLIDE 17) Today, there are numerous Smalltalk vendors and service companies. A few months ago, ANSI created X3J20 as the official Smalltalk Standards Committee. According to last week's *Business Week* article, "The Buzz is About Smalltalk," and the Analyst workstation is still alive and well in the CIA.

So, 10 years, almost to the month, after its first publication, and two months short of a 20-year anniversary of my arrival at Xerox, Smalltalk continues to be a surprisingly persistent object.

TRANSCRIPT OF QUESTION AND ANSWER SESSION

For ALAN KAY and ADELE GOLDBERG from JEFF SUTHERLAND (Object Databases): Smalltalk is used by 10 percent of software product developers, C++ by 50 percent. What do you see as the future mind-share for Smalltalk, particularly in end-users SWOPS?

ALAN KAY: Like AV equipment, which should have a grenade put in them with a 20-year timer, programming languages should be forced to blow themselves up because the problem with the mind-share is that they actually pollute further ideas. I mean, I think one of our biggest problems is that programming languages hang around for too long, and I see absolutely no correlation between the number of people who use a particular language or how long it's been around, with how good the language is. So the fact that people are using Smalltalk now, doesn't mean it's any good either. I think the thing that I left out in my talk, that was the most important reason to use a language like Smalltalk or LISP, is the meta-definition facility. You should not take the language any more as a collection of features done by some designer, but you should take it as a way of enabling the language that you actually need, to write a system. From that standpoint, I think Smalltalk and LISP actually are going to hang on for a long time. I think writing in the language as the original designers envisioned them is really silly after all this time.

ADELE GOLDBERG: Let me add to this. I really despise all these statistics. Languages are designed for specific purposes. Each one of them has its role to meet the design objectives. If you take a market segment where the language is appropriate, then you talk about penetration, you'll have some interesting numbers. The market segment that's interesting for Smalltalk, is the current COBOL community of MIS people, where C++ has zero penetration, where Smalltalk has now got about five percent, which I think is at least four and a half percent more than anybody expected, maybe more. What is going on here, is that people invent languages to express their ideas. And what really needs to happen, is to make it easier and easier for people who know their domain to know what they want to do, to express their ideas, and invent their own programming language. That's why that simulation kit that Alan showed you is so interesting. It is a framework for expressing the adventure of simulation, in which people who know something about the events and the domains that they are interested in could express their own ideas about what they want to see happen.

For ALAN KAY from JIM KIRK (Affiliation not mentioned): In your talk, you nominated object-oriented programming as a programming system with thousands of parts. In your paper you endorsed object-oriented programming as a way for children and others to think about computers. Are these two notions, in fact, related? Are these two notions, in fact, the same?

KAY: Give me a few minutes, and I can relate any two things. One of the ways of boiling down what our aspirations were, was that every time we come along with a new medium for capturing our ideas, it also has some modes of thought that go along with it. I think the modes of thought that are fallacious about computing, have to do with complex systems with many interacting parts. And that's something that's very hard to think about in using old mathematics, and old medium(s). I think that one of the aims for teaching children thinking, is that one of the good modes for them to think about are very complex things that have ecological relationships to each other. So, I think giving children a way of attacking complexity, even though for them complexity may be having a hundred simultaneously executing objects—which I think is complex enough for anybody—gets them into that space in thinking about things that I think is more interesting than just simple input/output mechanisms.

SCOTT GUTHREY (Schlumberger): Did the D machine initiative help or hinder Smalltalk?
(Ryder: Perhaps in your answer, you'll explain what the D machines were)

KAY: The D machines were talked about this morning a bit. They were a series of follow-ons to the ALTP. I think in many ways, one of the things that hurt Smalltalk—and this is absolutely my own personal view—is that the first D machine was late. And it was late, partially because Xerox just did not want to put hundreds of ALTOs in there and we came right back and said now we need machines that are five times faster. They just didn't understand the implications of things. And part of what happened when we did Smalltalk-76 was not just a cleanup, but we actually regressed—if I can use that word—back towards some of the Simula formations, to get more efficiency. I think what we should have done was kept on building faster and faster machines until we understood what object-oriented design was really about.

BIOGRAPHY OF ALAN C. KAY

Dr. Alan Kay is best known for the idea of personal computing, the conception of the intimate laptop computer, and the inventions of the now ubiquitous overlapping-window interface and modern object-oriented programming. These were catalyzed by his deep interests in education and children. He led one of several groups in the early '70s at the Xerox Palo Alto Research Center that together developed these ideas into: modern workstations and the forerunners of the Macintosh, Smalltalk, EtherNet, Laserprinting, and network "client-servers."

Before Xerox, Kay was a member of the University of Utah ARPA research team that developed 3D graphics. His Ph.D. in 1969 was awarded for the development of the first graphical object-oriented personal computer. His undergraduate degrees were in Mathematics and Molecular Biology (from the University of Colorado in 1966). As a member of the ARPA community, he also participated in the early design of the ARPANet (which became the Internet). After Xerox he was Chief Scientist of Atari, and from 1984 has been a Fellow at Apple Computer.

He is a Fellow of the American Academy of Arts and Sciences, and the Royal Society of Arts. He has received numerous awards and prizes including the J-D Warnier Prix D'Informatique and the ACM Systems Software Award.

A former professional jazz guitarist and composer, he is now an amateur classical pipe-organist.

Icon Session

Chair: *Helen Gigley*

HISTORY OF THE ICON PROGRAMMING LANGUAGE

Ralph E. Griswold and Madge T. Griswold

Department of Computer Science
The University of Arizona
Tucson, AZ 85721

ABSTRACT

The Icon programming language, which was conceived in 1977, was strongly influenced by the earlier SNOBOL languages and the subsequent SL5. This paper concentrates primarily on the early development of Icon, but also discusses subsequent versions. The motivation, design philosophy, and environmental factors that shaped Icon are emphasized in this paper.

CONTENTS

12.1 BACKGROUND

12.1.1 Source and Motivation

Icon is the latest in a series of programming languages that started with the string-manipulation language SNOBOL [Farber 1964]. Evolution of the SNOBOL languages led to SNOBOL4 [Griswold 1968a], which has patterns as first-class values, and augments string-processing facilities with sophisticated data structures. Several problems are evident in SNOBOL4. The ones of most concern in subsequent research are its lack of conventional control structures and a dichotomy between conventional computation and pattern matching [Griswold 1980a].

A subsequent language, SL5 ("SNOBOL Language 5") [Griswold 1977d], integrates SNOBOL4's success/failure signalling mechanism with conventional control structures. SL5 also has a very general procedure mechanism, in which coroutines follow as a natural consequence [Hanson 1978b]. A feature similar to SNOBOL4's pattern matching is provided in terms of scanning environments [Griswold 1976b]. Although SL5 is an improvement over SNOBOL4 in some ways, it is unsatisfactory in others. In particular, its very general procedure mechanism is overbearing in some respects, leading to unnecessarily complex programs.

A spark of insight inspired Icon: SL5's very general procedure mechanism is not necessary for pattern matching—a much simpler suspension/resumption mechanism will do.

Icon was conceived in the form of a proposed return to "old values." It was envisioned by Ralph Griswold [1977a] as

> . . . a programming language "successor" to SNOBOL4, having the following properties:
>
> SNOBOL4 philosophic and semantic basis
> SL5 syntactic basis
> SL5 features, excluding the generalized procedure mechanism.

The concept of *generators*, expressions that can produce a sequence of results by suspension and resumption, is the key to expression evaluation in Icon. Generators, in combination with goal-directed evaluation, allow pattern matching to take place in a conventional computational context [Griswold 1981a].

Icon turned out to be considerably different from what was envisioned in 1977, but that was the starting point.

12.1.2 The Name

"SNOBOL5" was the first name used for the language that was to become Icon [Griswold 1977a]. One issue in the choice of a name was the degree of connection it would imply with the SNOBOL languages. "Product identification" with the SNOBOL languages was viewed as giving the new language credibility and visibility, but it had the disadvantage of looking backward instead of forward. More significantly, the use of "SNOBOL" in the name would be misleading if the language turned out to be (as it did) very different from the SNOBOL languages.

So a new name was needed. Dave Hanson suggested "s"—a homage to "C" with its mimimalistic one-character name, but in lowercase, reflecting a distaste for computer-generated text that, at the time, still was frequently printed in all uppercase. As an abstraction from "SNOBOL" and "SL5", "s" made some sense without drawing too close a connection between the old languages and the new one. But "s" wasn't a happy choice for several reasons, not least of which was its typographical difficulties in documentation (which forced the awkward quoting used here).

Over a period of months, the name "s" was disparaged and sometimes ridiculed ("ssssssss"). Other names were suggested ("irving," "bard," and "TL" ("The Language")), but nothing stuck until Madge and Ralph Griswold suggested "icon" (then with the initial lowercase).

The name "icon" is not an acronym, nor was any particular meaning attached to it, although the word "iconoclast" was immediately offered as describing the flavor of the new language.

This choice of name was made before Xerox started to use it for little screen images. It was only later that confusion arose between "Icon, the programming language" and screen icons. By then, it was too late. It didn't help that the programming language significantly predated the usage that is so common now.

Although an occasional person has mistaken Icon as a programming language for manipulating screen images, the confusion has been less than might be suspected and has never been a serious problem. Perhaps this is because so many company and product names now include the substring "icon" [Griswold 1989a].

12.1.3 Versions of Icon

In order to put the Icon programming language in perspective, it is necessary to understand that there have been eight versions of the language, spanning a period of more than 12 years. The first version of the language captured the essential ideas [Griswold 1978c]. Version 2 took some of the rough edges off the first version and added a few new features [Griswold 1979].

After completion of the second version of Icon, it became clear that there were many possibilities for further refinements and extensions. Some of the new features in subsequent versions were the consequence of research. Other new features were provided in response to requests from a growing user community. Figure 12.1 shows the chronology of Icon language versions and Table 12.1 shows the main differences between versions.

As is typical with programming languages that mature through a series of versions, Icon's computational repertoire increased substantially over time, mostly in response to requests from users for additional facilities. The number of operations, functions, and keywords gives a rough measure

FIGURE 12.1

Version Release Dates.

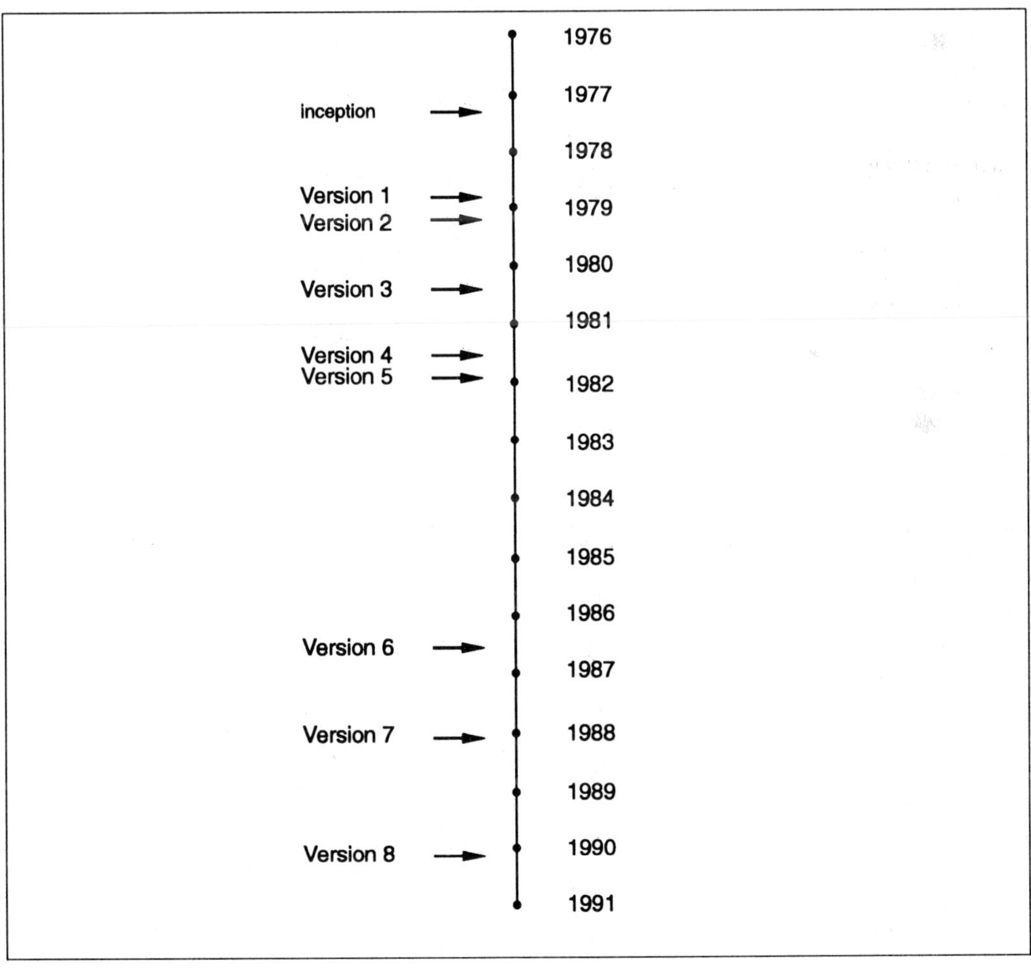

TABLE 12.1

Feature Changes.

Version	Features	Functions	Operators	Keywords	Total
1	The original language [Griswold 1978c].	45	27	15	87
2	*Added:* assignment to matching functions and reversible assignment [Griswold 1979].	47	33	19	99
3	*Added:* string transformations, augmented assignment, and external functions. *Removed:* post-fix operators [Coutant 1980a].	51	45	19	115
4	*Added:* mutual evaluation, repeated alternation, and limitation. *Changed:* stack and queue access to lists [Coutant 1981a].	44	54	20	118
5	*Added:* co-expressions. *Removed:* string transformation and assignment to matching functions [Wampler 1983b; Coutant 1981b].	43	70	20	133
6	*Added:* link declarations, set data type, new sorting options, programmer-defined control operations, and string invocation. *Removed:* external functions [Griswold 1983c, 1986b].	48	76	35	159
7	*Added:* functions to access operating-system facilities, bit functions, variable-length argument lists, error conversion, error trace back, and access to storage management information [Griswold 1988a].	65	76	35	176
8	*Added:* mathematical functions, keyboard functions, arbitrary-precision integer arithmetic, list invocation, external call interface, and instrumentation of storage management [Griswold 1990b].	89	76	36	201

of the size of Icon's computational repertoire. (The measure is only rough, since some operations, functions, and keywords have more computational functionality than others.) Table 1 shows the size of Icon's computational repertoire for the different versions of the language. Note that the repertoire more than doubled between the first version and the last.

12.1.4 Project Organization and Staffing

The Icon programming language was designed and implemented in the Department of Computer Science at The University of Arizona. It was funded primarily by grants from the National Science Foundation, with supplementary support from the University of Arizona.

From an organizational point of view, Icon actually was a by-product of research whose primary goal was the design of new linguistic facilities for non-numeric computation. Icon brought together new ideas from this research, in the context of a complete programming language, allowing the ideas to be evaluated and refined in a real computational context.

The initial design team consisted of faculty members Ralph E. Griswold and David R. Hanson, and Ph.D. student John T. "Tim" Korb. Walter J. Hansen, also a Ph.D. student, provided support. Cary

A. Coutant and Stephen B. Wampler, Ph.D. students in Computer Science, played major roles in the design and implementation of Versions 3 and 4.

As the Icon project developed, several other graduate students participated in significant ways. These included David Gudeman, Clinton L. Jeffery, William H. Mitchell, Kelvin Nilsen, Janalee O'Bagy, and Kenneth Walker.

In the later stages of the development, support also was provided by the laboratory staff of the Department of Computer Science. Gregg M. Townsend contributed to both design and implementation, while Sandra L. Miller and Phillip Kaslo assisted with various aspects of the implementation.

Many persons outside the University of Arizona participated in a variety of ways. This participation was informal, out of personal interest, and on a voluntary basis. The most significant outside contributions were made by Robert J. Alexander, Alan Beale, Mark B. Emmer, Owen R. Fonorow, Robert E. Goldberg, Andrew P. Heron, Robert McConeghy, Jerry Nowlin, John Polstra, Christopher Smith, and Cheyenne Wills.

The backgrounds and technical experience of the participants in the development of Icon were varied. Ralph Griswold had many years of experience in the design and implementation of programming languages, starting at Bell Telephone Laboratories in 1962. Dave Hanson had worked at Western Electric Engineering Research, prior to his doctoral work, which was completed at the University of Arizona in 1976 with a dissertation related to SL5. Gregg Townsend received his master's degree in computer science at the University of Arizona and also had considerable professional experience in programming. The graduate students who participated had varying backgrounds.

As in most academic environments, the organization of the design team was somewhat informal. As time passed, some individuals left the project and others joined it. In particular, students participated during their degree programs. Ralph Griswold and Dave Hanson led the project at the beginning. Ralph Griswold continued to lead the project in later versions.

Unlike the development of many programming languages, the design and implementation of Icon were not distinctly separated. Instead, the major participants viewed themselves as designers, implementors, and users of Icon. Design and implementation were, in fact, strongly coupled with results from experimental implementations affecting the design. Almost all of the persons who contributed to the design of Icon also contributed to the implementation.

The initial implementation of Icon was done by Dave Hanson and Tim Korb, with assistance from Walt Hansen. A second and entirely different implementation was done by Cary Coutant and Steve Wampler. This implementation was later refined by Bill Mitchell, Ralph Griswold, and others. As the implementation matured, many of the persons mentioned above contributed in various ways.

12.1.5 Costs and Schedules

Since Icon was a by-product of a research program, the primary goal of which was the design of new programming language features and not the production of a new programming language *per se*, it is not possible to determine accurately the costs involved.

The funding, provided largely by grants from the National Science Foundation, strongly influenced both the nature of the work and the time frame under which it was undertaken. There were no fixed schedules, nor was the scope of the project ever clearly specified. Many developments were the consequence of new research ideas and feedback from users.

For similar reasons, it is not possible to determine accurately the manpower expended on the design and implementation of Icon. All participants divided their time, as is customary in academic environments. Averaged over the period of Icon development, one faculty member and two graduate students devoted about half their time to Icon. A number of persons, outside the University of Arizona, devoted significant amounts of time on an irregular basis, but the total amount of their contribution is impossible to determine.

Since language design and implementation were closely coupled, it is not possible to assign specific portions of the effort. In the early part of the project, effort on design dominated implementation. As the language matured, the opposite was true. On the whole, probably three or four times as much effort was devoted to implementation as was devoted to design.

Other related activities—documentation, distribution, and support—accounted for a considerable amount of the total effort. The effort expended on these activities was irregular and primarily associated with different releases of Icon. In recent years, these supporting activities have dominated the work, as implementations have proliferated and an increasingly large user community has made greater demands.

Because of the "co-mingling" of more fundamental research, and the specific activities related to programming-language design and implementation, it is not possible to determine the "cost" of producing Icon with any degree of accuracy. Perhaps $100,000 was expended before the first working version was distributed to the public. Perhaps $600,000 has been expended in the development, implementation, and distribution of subsequent versions.

12.1.6 The Influence of Other Programming Languages

The developers of Icon had extensive experience with other programming languages. Ralph Griswold's early work on SNOBOL had been influenced by SCL [Lee 1962], COMIT [Yngve 1958], and IPL-V [Newell 1965]. By the time work on Icon was initiated, he had been influenced by BCPL [Richards 1969], Bliss [Wulf 1971], EL1 [Wegbreit 1970], APL [Iverson 1962], and C precursors [Johnson 1973]. And, of course, he had a working knowledge of the more widely known programming languages. Dave Hanson had considerable experience with SNOBOL4, a broad knowledge of most other programming languages, and had been a principal in the design of SL5. Graduate-student knowledge of programming languages came primarily from their academic contact and work with their colleagues.

Since Icon developed over several years, other newly developing programming languages, such as Prolog [Cohen 1985] and C [Ritchie 1978] became known to the persons working on Icon.

While knowledge of other programming languages inevitably influenced the design of Icon, there was a conscious attempt not to be influenced unduly by other programming languages, but instead to do something distinctly different. Clearly, SNOBOL4 and the subsequent SL5 had profound influence and were shaping forces in the design of Icon. Nevertheless, there was a deliberate attempt not to copy from other languages or to develop refined versions of their features. A philosophy of language design, more than the nature of existing languages, was the driving force.

12.1.7 Design Philosophy

The design of Icon was driven by a philosophy of what a programming language should be. Although this philosophical basis was never formalized, it was generally agreed that Icon should be easy to use. This goal was based on the view that programming is largely a human activity and that human beings are more important than computers.

Closely related to this view was the desire to develop fundamentally new linguistic mechanisms, instead of refining and improving the existing ones. This inevitably meant Icon should be distinctly different from other programming languages, as the SNOBOL languages were. Frequent references were made to the work being "orthogonal to the mainstream." These references were not entirely in jest.

12.1.8 Intended Use

Icon was not designed for any specific application area, although non-numeric computation (the manipulation of strings and structures) was its primary focus and SNOBOL4's widespread use of computing in the Humanities was suggestive for Icon [Griswold 1982a]. Instead, Icon was viewed as a tool that would be suitable to certain programming *contexts*. There were two main contexts of interest, influenced largely by the designers' experience: (1) situations in which quick-and-easy programming solutions were needed; and (2) very complex research applications that strained the capabilities of other programming languages. It is interesting that, although these two contexts are so different, they did not produce tension in language design.

Although Icon is now widely used for an enormous range of applications, many of which do not occur in the contexts originally envisioned, it remains the case that many uses of Icon are either "one-shot," quick-and-dirty applications, or very sophisticated ones. This sometimes gives Icon a rather schizoid appearance to potential users—they may hear that Icon is good for simple tasks and then see powerful and sophisticated applications written in Icon. It is partly for this reason, also, that Icon often is compared to programming languages such as Awk [Aho 1988], REXX [Cowlishaw 1985], and Perl [Wall 1991], even though Icon is very different from them.

As expected, Icon has come into widespread use for computing in the Humanities, supplanting SNOBOL4 in many cases, although SNOBOL4 still retains many staunch supporters.

Just as Icon was not designed with a specific application area in mind, neither was it designed for any particular programmer profile. It was expected that the persons who used Icon would have some prior programming experience with a procedural language (C is the current referent).

No specific compromises were made in the design of Icon to cater to particular kinds of programmers or specific programming and application experience. It was realized, from the beginning, that trying to design a language that would be significantly different from other languages would lead to some problems for experienced programmers. The need to "unlearn" concepts from other programming languages was foreseen. On the other hand, the designers of Icon did not attempt to make it particularly accessible to programming novices or to make it suitable as a first programming language.

12.1.9 Implementation

The initial development of Icon took place in a mainframe environment. The envisioned language features clearly required extensive resources and no concessions in design were made so that Icon could run on smaller computers.

The language design probably was influenced, even if unconsciously, by the physical environment in which its first implementation was done—a DEC-10 running in a time-sharing environment. The primary mode of operation was interactive text entry and editing, but not interactive programming *per se*. Thus, Icon programs could be run in batch mode as well.

Portability was a central concern in the implementation [Hanson 1980]. Considerable thought was given to the language in which Icon would be implemented. Since portability was a major issue, assembly language was ruled out. Languages commonly used at that time for the implementation of other programming languages, especially C, BCPL, and Minimal [Dewar 1977], were given serious consideration but rejected, partly for technical reasons but mainly for concern about their availability and support, as well as lack of local experience in their use.

The possibility of designing an implementation language was also considered but rejected on the basis of experience with the implementation of SL5, which was done this way [Korb 1977]. This approach was viewed as too much work, especially since the implementation language would have to be transported, also.

The decision finally was made to use FORTRAN with the Ratfor preprocessor [Hanson 1978a] to support better program structure. The choice of FORTRAN was not embraced with enthusiasm by all members of the project. FORTRAN was not viewed as particularly suitable as an implementation language. It was almost a question of proving such an implementation was *possible*.

The Ratfor implementation of Icon generated FORTRAN code, which then was compiled and linked with a run-time system written in Ratfor. This implementation of Icon proved to be quite portable, although large and somewhat inefficient. However, it required a robust FORTRAN compiler and considerable computational resources. Consequently, this implementation of Icon turned out to be limited to large computers—the CDC 6000, the DEC-10, the IBM 370, and the VAX. Ironically, newer FORTRAN compilers for smaller machines proved a barrier to this implementation of Icon. Their more rigorous error checking often rejected FORTRAN code produced by the Icon compiler that, nonetheless, corresponded to *de facto* FORTRAN IV.

Initially the only computer facilities available to the Icon project were the DEC-10 and CDC 6600 in the Computer Center at the University of Arizona. The Department of Computer Science acquired its first computer, a PDP-11/70, in 1979 and began to run UNIX. This local computer, albeit limited in resources, was very appealing for program development, and in the same year the C implementation of Icon was started on the department's computer [Coutant 1980b].

This implementation effort was necessarily very concerned about memory requirements, since the PDP-11/70's combined I and D spaces allowed only 128K bytes of memory to be addressed. At this point, portability was discarded as an implementation goal in favor of obtaining a workable and easily accessible implementation of Icon for local use. This change in emphasis was greeted with considerable relief, since much of the effort expended in the Ratfor implementation had been the consequence of portability concerns.

Although the C implementation of Icon on the PDP-11 was not designed with portability in mind, the implementation was based on a virtual machine that had instructions suitable for the implementation of Icon language features [Coutant 1980b; Wampler 1983c; Griswold 1986a]. An Icon program was translated into virtual machine instructions, which then were interpreted, interfacing a run-time system written in C. This conceptual framework eventually proved important for C implementations on other platforms and became the basis for tools for measuring the performance and behavior of Icon programs [Coutant 1983].

It is worth noting that, at the time the C implementation of Icon was started, there was no way of knowing that C would become available on most computers, running under most operating systems.

The C implementation was successful, despite the limited address space available. By the time it was running, implementations of C had begun to proliferate, and other persons expressed an interest in adapting the C implementation of Icon to their platforms. This began the process of making the C implementation of Icon portable. It is a story in itself, involving not just Icon but the maturation of C compilers and the evolving ANSI C Standard [American 1990].

At the time of this writing, the C implementation of Icon runs on nearly 60 different UNIX platforms, as well as the Acorn Archimedes, the Amiga, the Atari ST, CMS, the Macintosh, MS-DOS, MVS, OS/2, OS-9, and VMS. It is particularly ironic that an implementation that disregarded portability as a goal has, in fact, become highly portable.

12.1.10 Documentation

Documentation was a major consideration from the initial design of Icon. In fact, while Dave Hanson and Tim Korb took the major responsibility for the first implementation effort, Ralph Griswold was the official amanuensis for the project.

Since Icon was developed in a research environment within an academic organization, the initial documentation was primarily for internal use, first by the designers themselves, and then by other local users [Griswold 1977b, 1977c, 1978a, 1978b]. As the early design progressed to a working implementation, more attention was given to user manuals [Griswold 1978c].

As Icon came into widespread use, the demand for documentation led to books on the language [Griswold 1983a] and its implementation [Griswold 1986a]. The language book was revised in 1990 to correspond to Version 8 of Icon [Griswold 1990a, 1990b].

Starting in 1978, many aspects of Icon were documented in the technical report series, published by the Department of Computer Science at the University of Arizona. To date, there have been over 100 such technical reports. As use of Icon spread and the amount of documentation related to it grew, it became necessary to develop a system to keep track of less formal and more specialized documentation, such as user manuals for specific platforms. At the same time, it became important to be able to identify communications concerning Icon. The Icon Project became a semi-official entity and a series of numbered Icon Project Documents (IPDs) was started in 1986. More recently, technical documentation about Icon, too specialized for general distribution as technical reports, has also appeared in Icon Project Documents. To date, there have been over 200 IPDs.

The Icon Newsletter was started in 1978 [Griswold 1978d] to provide information to interested parties outside the University of Arizona. This newsletter was essentially a redirection of an earlier SL5 newsletter [Griswold 1976a], which in turn was an offshoot of *The SNOBOL4 Information Bulletin* [Griswold 1968b], which started in 1968. Thus, there was a ready community of interested persons when Icon came on the scene, many of whom had prior knowledge of SNOBOL4 and SL5.

The Icon Newsletter initially provided both news of topical interest and technical information about Icon. In 1990, a second newsletter, *The Icon Analyst* [Griswold 1990e], was started to cover material of a more technical nature, while *The Icon Newsletter* took on a more topical role.

12.2 RATIONALE FOR THE CONTENT OF THE LANGUAGE

12.2.1 Environmental Factors

12.2.1.1 *Program Size*

Little thought was given to the potential size of Icon programs during the initial design phases. Because of the programming contexts envisioned, it was expected that many Icon programs would be small and that larger ones usually would be written by one person. No specific attention was given to very large programs written by teams of programmers and no language facilities were included specifically to deal with the problems of writing such programs.

The lack of facilities to support the development of large programs did not pose significant problems in the early use of Icon. As Icon became more widely known, however, programmers started to use it for larger projects, where the lack of program structuring facilities began to pose problems.

This is just one of several cases where extensive use exposes limitations that were not foreseen. In fact, use of a programming language tends to produce requirements for facilities that even may be inappropriate at the time of its initial design. Conversely, if a programming language does not have significant use, such considerations are irrelevant.

12.2.1.2 *Program Libraries*

Little thought was given to program libraries initially, but the need for separate compilation of program modules was recognized and supported, starting with Version 3 of Icon.

More attention was given to program libraries as the community of users increased and wanted to share program material. An Icon program library was established by the Icon project in 1983 [Griswold 1983e] and was placed on a subscription basis in an expanded form in 1990 [Griswold 1990f].

As of this writing, the Icon program library contains 132 complete programs and 152 packages of procedures.

12.2.1.3 *Portability*

Portability was a significant concern in the design of the Icon programming language, as well as its implementation, as mentioned earlier.

There are several views about portability, as it concerns language features. At one extreme, a language can be viewed as portable only if it provides ready access to all the features of any platform on which it runs. This is a tall order for platforms that have libraries of hundreds, if not thousands, of graphical and audio routines.

At the other extreme, a language can be viewed as portable if any program written in it runs on any platform on which the language is implemented. This is more likely to be the case if the language supports few, if any, platform-specific facilities. On the other hand, lack of support for platform-dependent facilities limits what can be done with the language on some platforms.

The initial design of Icon tended toward the latter view, providing only simple, sequential input and output, for example. As use of Icon increased on different platforms, users needed more capabilities for input, output, and file manipulation, as well as access to operating-system capabilities from within Icon programs.

The C implementation of Icon attempted to deal with these problems largely by passing the buck to C, casting its system operations in terms of those of C. For example, the system() function was added to allow commands to be executed in a shell.

At the time the C implementation of Icon was started, C was only readily available on UNIX platforms. As C implementations proliferated, its "UNIXisms" brought an alien flavor to other platforms. This problem was dealt with, to some extent, in the ANSI C Standard [American 1990].

The last version of Icon retains the C flavor in its interface to operating-system capabilities, but looks less like a "UNIX language" now than it did before C came into widespread use on many platforms.

As anticipated at the beginning of the language design, extensions have been added to the language to meet the needs of those using different platforms. Of course, such extensions render programs that use them nonportable on platforms that do not have them.

One approach that was considered to minimize these problems, was the design of platform-independent facilities to subsume platform-specific ones. The problem with this approach is that a particular facility cannot be cast in the "native" way for all platforms. Graphics and window management are particularly difficult in this respect.

Nonetheless, portability is not a concern of most users, who would rather have a facility available in the way that is natural on their platforms. The designers of Icon decided in favor of the majority of users, leaving platform-specific facilities to be provided in platform-specific ways.

12.2.1.4 *Efficiency*

Speed of execution was never a significant factor in the design of Icon; rather the opposite. Part of the reason for largely disregarding efficiency was the philosophical goal of designing a programming language that would be easy to use and minimize programming time and effort. This goal is in essential conflict with execution speed. Another reason for largely disregarding efficiency was the view that such concerns inhibited creativity and the invention of new linguistic mechanisms during the design process. Past experience had shown that features whose initial implementation was slow could be implemented efficiently once they were better understood [Dewar 1977, 1985]. In this sense, many efficiency considerations were deferred with the expectation that clever implementation techniques would be developed to overcome otherwise slow execution speed.

It is virtually impossible, however, for language designers who also are programmers to entirely ignore considerations related to efficiency—these considerations enter design decisions unconsciously, if not consciously. On a few occasions, efficiency was a specific factor in language design. One of these concerned matching expressions in string scanning. Starting with Version 2, strings could be assigned to matching functions to change the value of the scanned subject. This capability significantly slowed string scanning, even when the capability was not used. Assignment to matching functions was removed in Version 5, partly because of efficiency considerations but also because it was not widely used and because changing the subject, especially its length, during string scanning, tended to be confusing and conceptually ill-formed.

12.2.1.5 *Programming Ease*

Ease of programming was a major concern in the design of Icon. This was a natural consequence of the philosophical position that human beings were more valuable than computers. Particular attention was given to expressiveness—the ease and brevity with which computations could be formulated.

Another consideration was avoiding aspects of programming languages that are designed either to assist in generating good object code or to prevent bad programming. The intention in the design of Icon was to make it easy to write good programs, rather than difficult to write bad ones. The lack of a compile-time type system in Icon is a reflection of these views.

12.2.1.6 *Character Set*

Since string manipulation was a major component of Icon, the choice of a character set was given careful consideration. The possibility of using an internal character set different from that of host computers on which Icon ran, was considered. In particular, a very large character set offered the possibility of representing internally the large number of characters needed in problem domains such as linguistics and typesetting. This idea was rejected, however, because of the lack of peripheral devices to represent such characters and potential implementation problems.

An eight-bit character set was chosen because it naturally fits most computer architectures and because it provides enough different characters for most applications. It is important to know that Icon allows all characters in the underlying character set to occur in strings, including the null character, control characters, and other characters with no external graphic representations.

The question of *which* eight-bit character set to use was more difficult. The problem involved language design, implementation, and the interface between programs and the systems on which they run. In the discussion of character sets, Dave Hanson [1977] retorted "ASCII rules the world! What's an EBCDIC?" The ASCII character set was eventually selected for the first version of Icon.

For the C implementation of Icon, which initially disregarded portability, the choice of a character set was easy—it obviously was ASCII. As portability of the C implementation became a concern, the issue of the character set for use on EBCDIC-based platforms arose. The first edition of the Icon language book [Griswold 1983a, p. 234] stated that the underlying internal character set for Icon is ASCII, regardless of the native character set of the platform on which Icon is implemented. This statement was based largely on the incorrect assumption that implementations in C for EBCDIC-based computers would most naturally use ASCII internally.

Several design issues arose regarding character sets, even for character sets of the same size:

1. Availability of characters used to represent programs on peripheral devices such as keyboards and printers;
2. Differences in graphics;
3. Collating (sorting) sequences.

When the first EBCDIC implementation of Icon was started, one of the obvious problems was that Icon, from ASCII heritage, used braces, square brackets, and other such characters to represent important syntactic structures in programs, while many EBCDIC peripherals did not support these characters. These problems were solved by providing alternative characters and digraphs. For portability, these constructions are supported on ASCII-based Icon implementations as well.

Collating sequence is a somewhat more troublesome problem, since upper- and lowercase letters and digits appear in quite different relative positions in the ASCII and EBCDIC collating sequences.

There are two obvious choices—using the native collating sequence or translating to a standard internal character set on input and output. In the former case, string comparison and sorting are done in the native manner for the platform. In the latter case, string comparison and sorting are the same for all platforms, but "unnatural" on EBCDIC platforms. This, again, is a trade-off between what best suits most users (results that are the same as for other programs on the local platform) and portability (results that are the same for all platforms).

There are, in fact, two EBCDIC implementations of Icon, both based on the implementation of Icon that originally supported ASCII. One of these takes the former view of collating sequences [Beale 1989] and one takes the latter [Schiller 1989].

12.2.1.7 *Standardization*

Standardization was not an issue in the design of Icon. It was felt that considerations of standardization would stifle innovation in a programming language in which innovation was a prime concern.

On the other hand, the availability of the highly portable public-domain implementation discouraged other essentially different implementations that would have been a potential source of major dialectic differences, providing a kind of *de facto* standardization of the central part of Icon.

It is easy to make extensions to Icon, especially additions to its function repertoire, and there are many of these. Some are platform-specific and in general use, while others have been done by individuals for their own use.

12.2.2 Functionality

The primary concern in designing the functionality of Icon was a repertoire of features for processing nonnumerical data—strings and structures. At the same time, it was expected that Icon would be a general-purpose programming language and, therefore, would have a large repertoire of conventional operations. As shown in Table 12.1, both aspects of the functionality of Icon increased over time, with new versions. Because of the growing user community, it became impractical in later versions of Icon to remove or substantially change functionality.

Except for the expansion of the function repertoire, the most notable changes in functionality occurred in Version 4 of Icon, with new control structures [Coutant 1981a]; in Version 5 of Icon, with co-expressions [Coutant 1981b]; in Version 6 of Icon, with sets [Griswold 1986b]; and in Version 8, with arbitrary-precision integer arithmetic [Griswold 1990a].

The addition of sets shows how capricious major additions to the functionality of a programming language can be. The first version of Icon provided tables with associative look up as one of the major data structures carried forward from SNOBOL4. Sets, which are in some sense more natural to programming, came about much later as a class project for a graduate "language internals" course on the implementation of Icon. Since tables already existed, most of the mechanism for implementing sets was available and most students were able to complete the project satisfactorily. The results of one of the best projects were added to Version 6 of Icon.

If tables had not existed, adding sets to Icon would have been impractical in the context of the course, and they probably would not have been added to Icon. Yet, sets had never been considered as a language feature for Icon before this class.

12.2.3 The Design Process

The design of Icon was dominated by the goals mentioned earlier: the development of new features for string and list processing, innovation rather then refinement, and ease of use. Because of the importance placed on these goals, the design of Icon was not done by systematically applying any particular principles or methodologies. Instead, the design process emphasized informality and encouraged "brainstorming." The designers met frequently, often on a daily basis, to discuss issues and work out the details of language design. Much of the communication was via electronic mail. This electronic mail was informal, often brash or funny, and sometimes zany. Occasionally it even bordered on lunacy.

A central, even dominating, aspect of early Icon language design was experimentation. Ideas for language features were implemented almost at once, using modified versions of SL5 and high-level interpreters designed for quickly testing new ideas.

Although Icon made a significant break with SL5 and SNOBOL4, these earlier languages had considerable influence on the design of Icon, sometimes suggesting that things be done differently and sometimes suggesting that they be done in similar ways. Thus, the experience with SNOBOL4 and SL5 had a major impact on Icon.

There were two areas of major concern: (1) pattern matching and control structures; and (2) data structures. The design of features for these two areas did not interact significantly. In fact, attempts at integrating the two failed. Sometimes work proceeded more on one and sometimes more on the other.

Although the initial design of Icon was not governed by any specific design methodologies, later work was influenced by the abstract characterization of sequences [Wampler 1983a] and formal semantic models [Gudeman 1991].

12.2.4 Distribution

The distribution of Icon was a major factor in its acceptance. Since Icon was developed in an academic setting, the normal commercial forms of distribution were unavailable and inappropriate.

One question was the legal status of Icon. In the tradition of the SNOBOL languages [Griswold 1981b, pp. 612–614] and SL5, Icon was placed in the public domain without any of the usual restrictions (such as proprietary notices, copyrights that permit unlimited copying, and licensing requirements). Since Icon originated in an academic environment and was funded primarily by grants from the National Science Foundation, public-domain status, without any qualifications, was viewed as appropriate and desirable. It was in the best interests of the computing community and it would contribute to Icon's acceptance. The public-domain status applies to source code as well as to executable files, and no attempt was made to prevent individuals from modifying the source code for their own purposes.

Early versions of Icon were distributed on magnetic tape, at no charge to recipients. In some cases, persons interested in Icon were asked to provide a magnetic tape on which Icon was then written. In the case of persons likely to make a contribution to the design or implementation of Icon, tapes usually were provided free of charge. Similarly, documentation was provided at no cost during the early years of Icon.

As Icon matured and attracted a larger group of interested persons, it became impractical for the Icon project to underwrite the costs of media, printing, and shipping—what can be given freely to 100 persons is impractically expensive for 1,000.

Gradually, a system was developed to provide Icon on various magnetic media for a nominal charge. The charge was somewhat more than actual costs. The net revenue was used to purchase software and hardware needed to support Icon, to underwrite the (free) *Icon Newsletter*, and so forth.

In a time of rapid evolution of computer systems, distribution formats became an increasing problem. While magnetic tapes in a few formats sufficed in the early days of Icon, later there was a need for various floppy disk formats and data cartridges. While it was not feasible to supply Icon for every conceivable media format and packaging, many packages were eventually developed for its distribution. As of this writing, the Icon Project provides Icon for 13 different platforms, in 12 different formats, on magnetic tape, data cartridges, and three kinds of floppy disks.

In 1987, Icon material was made available via FTP for network transfer, and an electronic bulletin board (RBBS) was established to allow persons to download Icon material via telephone. In addition, Icon is available on many other electronic bulletin boards and conferencing systems.

Consequently, Icon is widely available for a nominal cost. Combined with its public-domain status, this makes Icon accessible to most interested persons. This has contributed, substantially, both to its usefulness and its acceptance in the computing community.

While there is no way to determine the number of persons who use Icon, the size of the Icon-user community can be estimated from the fact that over 13,000 copies of Icon have been distributed by the Icon Project on magnetic media and more than 30,000 copies of Icon-related files are downloaded via FTP annually.

Feedback from users indicates a large user population in the academic community, primarily in computer science and the humanities. Icon also is used extensively in companies that produce software, as well as in industrial and governmental research laboratories. Perhaps the largest community of users consists of individuals using Icon on personal computers for diverse applications.

12.3 A POSTERIORI EVALUATION

12.3.1 Meeting of Objectives

It is not surprising that the design of a language that stressed innovation and language characteristics over specific applications, users, or markets, turned out to be somewhat different from what was originally envisioned.

12.3.1.1 *Icon and SNOBOL4*

Icon is, to a certain degree, a successor to SNOBOL4, as was originally anticipated. Icon is appropriate for the same kinds of applications as SNOBOL4. In fact, Icon has much the same kind of clientele as SNOBOL4. Icon, however, strongly resembles SNOBOL4 only in its types and their handling: strings as atomic data objects, structures with pointer semantics, associative look up in tables, and so forth.

Icon has a much larger repertoire of low-level string-processing operations than SNOBOL4. String scanning in Icon, unlike pattern matching in SNOBOL4, is integrated into the rest of the language. String scanning is, however, lower-level and more imperative in nature than pattern matching in SNOBOL4.

Icon has a syntax typical of modern imperative programming languages, making Icon programs much different in appearance from SNOBOL4 programs. Icon also lacks some of the most powerful features of SNOBOL4—run-time compilation and operator redefinition.

The most significant fundamental difference between Icon and SNOBOL4 is in expression evaluation. Icon's generators and goal-directed evaluation have a profound effect on programming techniques [Griswold 1981a, 1982b, 1988c]. They not only remove the dichotomy between conventional computation and pattern matching found in SNOBOL4 [Griswold 1980a], thus allowing conventional computation during pattern matching, but they also greatly increase the expressiveness of conventional computation. As a consequence, the approaches to programming in Icon are much different from those in SNOBOL4—which is what makes the two languages so different in practice.

12.3.1.2 *Icon and SL5*

While SNOBOL4 still is generally available and in widespread use, SL5 is a dead language. Consequently, the differences and similarities between SL5 and Icon are less significant than those between SNOBOL4 and Icon.

As originally envisioned, Icon has a syntax that is similar to that of SL5. And, as planned, it lacks SL5's very general procedure mechanism. Much of Icon's repertoire of operations and functions consists of a refinement to SL5's. Again, the big difference between Icon snd SL5 lies in expression evaluation.

12.3.2 An Evaluation of Icon

An evaluation of Icon can be divided into three general categories: pleasant surprises, results as expected, and disappointments.

12.3.2.1 *Pleasant Surprises*

As mentioned earlier, prior research, as well as the insight that sparked the design of Icon, revolved around issues of expression evaluation and, in particular, around ways of providing conventional computational facilities during pattern matching.

Generators and goal-directed evaluation solved these problems, but they did much more. It was quite a while before it was apparent that the converse was true: generators and goal-directed evaluation greatly enrich all kinds of computation. In fact, pattern matching (cast as string scanning) is an almost trivial by-product of a general expression-evaluation mechanism that supports generators and goal-directed evaluation.

12.3.2.2 *Results as Expected*

Icon's handling of types and values, as well as its data structures, satisfies the original design goals. They provide substantial, but not revolutionary, advances over those of SNOBOL4 and SL5 [Griswold 1989b].

Coupled with better control structures than those of SNOBOL4, Icon's data-structuring capabilities have proven to be popular for rapid prototyping [Fonorow 1988; Fraser 1989]—an application that was not anticipated or considered in the design of Icon. In fact, in such applications Icon often is used in a style that can be characterized as "C with automatic storage management." The higher-level features of Icon provide programming leverage that allows prototypes to be built quickly, and changed easily, while retaining much of the program structure and organization of C.

The choice of an expression-based syntax for Icon was given careful consideration and chosen for the generality it provided. The results of this decision were largely as expected, with an expression-based syntax making the identification of syntax errors more difficult. An expression-based syntax, on the other hand, allowed more expressiveness, albeit with a potential loss of clarity [Griswold 1992].

12.3.2.3 *Disappointments*

String scanning is one portion of Icon that did not achieve the design objectives. By integrating backtracking control structures with conventional ones, many of the problems with pattern matching in SNOBOL4 were solved, but at a considerable expense. The higher-level, declarative nature of patterns and their status as first-class values is lost in Icon. String analysis in Icon is much more imperative than pattern matching in SNOBOL4. The programmer has more flexibility, but must deal with more detail at a lower level. Furthermore, the increased flexibility in string scanning brings with it problems in program structure. String scanning expressions often are poorly organized. While there are disciplines to overcome these problems [Griswold 1980c, 1983d, 1990d], they are somewhat demanding and are rarely used.

It is worth noting that the somewhat unsatisfactory nature of string scanning in Icon was recognized during the early development of the language. Several attempts were made to solve the problem, but they were unsuccessful. At the time that the first edition of the Icon language book was being written, it was recognized that the book, by its existence, would inevitably limit future language changes. The book was deferred for a while in hope that some improvement could be made to string scanning, but eventually the effort was abandoned with the recognition that the problems with string scanning would not be solved in the context of Icon.

12.3.3 Contributions

A programming language makes contributions in many ways, ranging from concepts, to specific features, to providing a useful tool. The most important conceptual contribution in Icon is its method of expression evaluation with generators and goal-directed evaluation. This method of expression evaluation allows searching, in pattern matching and other applications, to be integrated with conventional computation. As a result, many computational tasks can be expressed more easily and concisely in Icon than in other programming languages.

It is difficult to quantify ease of use in a particular programming language. It is a subjective and somewhat personal matter, but it is nonetheless important. Icon programmers who also program in C often contrast the two languages. For programming tasks of moderate size, an Icon program often is about one tenth the size of a corresponding C program and usually can be done in about one tenth the time. For larger tasks, the difference usually is less, with a factor of one half to one third being more typical.

Another, even more subjective, factor is psychological. Programmers often characterize Icon as a "fun language." Programming is, after all, largely a human activity. If the programming process is enjoyable, programmers are more motivated and productive.

One measure of the success of a language like Icon is whether it allows programmers to do things they otherwise would not attempt. This has been repeatedly reported by Icon programmers.

12.3.3.1 *Other Implementations and Dialects*

The ready availability of the highly portable interpreter for Icon [Griswold 1986a, 1990c] eliminated the usual motivation for most alternative implementations of programming languages—the need for the language on a platform for which there is no implementation. Instead, other implementations of Icon have focused mainly on two issues: efficiency and conceptual models for the implementation of generators and goal-directed evaluation.

Thomas Christopher [1985] addressed both issues in an implementation for the VAX-11. This implementation was brought to the point where the design could be evaluated, but it was not completed. Andrew Freeman [1985] proposed a stackless implementation model for generators and expressions. David Gudeman [1986] produced a prototype implementation of a subset of Icon in T, using continuation semantics as an implementation model. Mark Bailey [1990] implemented a similar idea in Scheme.

O'Bagy [1987] designed a conceptual model for implementing generators and goal-directed evaluation in which recursion was a central aspect of interpretation. She subsequently cast this model in the context of compilation and designed a framework for optimizing the generated code for expression evaluation in Icon [O'Bagy 1988].

The first commercial implementation of Icon, based on the implementation done at the University of Arizona, was done for the Macintosh [ProIcon 1989]. This implementation supports the standard Macintosh visual interface and includes a number of language extensions. A second commercial implementation was done for UNIX 386/486 platforms [ISI 1991]. It also includes several language extensions.

Recently Ken Walker developed techniques for type inference and liveness analysis in Icon and combined these with O'Bagy's expression-evaluation model in a production-quality optimizing compiler for Icon [Walker 1991].

Other implementation work related to Icon includes Kelvin Nilsen's on-the-fly garbage collection algorithm for producing constant-time execution speed [Nilson 1988b], and his related work on Conicon [Nilson 1988a]. Kelvin Nilsen and John Martinek also designed a temporary variable model for the virtual machine that underlies the Icon interpreter [Martinek 1989a, 1989b, 1989c].

12.3.4 Mistakes

The original design of Icon, as mentioned earlier, stressed elimination of unnecessary "baggage." As a result, defaults were provided so that programmers would not have to specify the typical or obvious usage. In most cases, these defaults work well, but the default scoping for local identifiers proved to be misguided. If an identifier is not declared otherwise, its scope is taken to be local. While this is a reasonable choice for programs that are compiled from a single file, it can introduce mysterious errors in the case of the separate compilation of a program from several files: A global declaration in one file may change the scope of an otherwise undeclared identifier in another. In retrospect, it would have been better to require scope declarations for all identifiers.

It also probably was a mistake not to consider facilities to aid in the development of very large Icon programs. This problem is addressed in a commercial version of Icon [ISI 1991].

12.3.5 Problems

Programmers have had problems with several aspects of Icon. In most cases, these problems are not mistakes in the design of Icon, but rather a consequence of its difference from most other programming languages and a necessary by-product of its valuable characteristics.

Programmers who have learned programming languages, like Basic and Pascal, before learning Icon, sometimes have difficulty with Icon's concepts of success and failure. They tend to feel that success and failure are merely hidden Boolean true and false values. The consequence of this misconception can be difficulty in learning Icon and using it properly.

Icon's pointer semantics for structures, also, sometimes cause problems. Problems with unintentional aliasing in this regard are well known. More subtle problems occur when a structure is the default value for a table and is not replicated when used for different new table keys. Despite these problems, the usefulness of pointer semantics in efficiently handling large and complex data structures, as well as the ability to produce program data structures that are isomorphic to abstract structures in the problem domain, outweigh the problems.

As mentioned earlier, programmers have trouble using string scanning in a well-structured manner. There also is a tension between Icon's low-level string operations and its higher-level string scanning. The two linguistic levels clash, but programmers nonetheless often mix them; in fact the language provides no alternative to this in some cases. SNOBOL4 programmers often have more difficulty with string scanning than other programmers. SNOBOL4 programmers, in particular, miss the ability to compose complex patterns out of simpler ones.

SNOBOL4 programmers also often lament Icon's lack of SNOBOL4's CODE and EVAL functions that allow strings to be compiled and executed during program execution.

The lack of a conversational, interactive interpreter for Icon, also, is frequently cited as a deficiency. This problem is being addressed by Blanchard [1991].

12.4 IMPLICATIONS FOR CURRENT AND FUTURE LANGUAGES

12.4.1 Direct Influence

Several programming languages have been inspired, at least in part, by various aspects of Icon. Generators have had the greatest influence. They have been incorporated in dialects of several existing languages: Cg: for C [Budd 1982], Little Smalltalk [Budd 1987], and Π for Pascal [Gallesio 1986]. Generators also appear in the multi-paradigm languages Leda [Budd 1992], and G [Placer 1991], and in the "hacker's language" SPLASH [Abrahams 1989].

The relationship between generators and sequences of values is evident in programming languages that manipulate "streams," such as those formulated by Nakata and Sassa [Nakata 1991]. At a higher level, Seque developed the idea of generators to the level of first-class values [Griswold 1988b].

Several other programming languages have been based on Icon or strongly influenced by it in more general ways. EZ [Fraser 1983, 1985] adapted several aspects of Icon in a language that subsumes facilities normally provided by operating systems. Rebus [Griswold 1985] recast SNOBOL4 with a syntax derived from Icon. Logicon [Lapalme 1986] is a hybrid formed by combining many of the features of Icon and Prolog. CommSpeak [Nilsen 1986], a programming language designed for real-time string-processing applications, also contains several features of Icon. CommSpeak evolved into Conicon [Nilsen 1988a], which augments Icon with a stream data type [Nilsen 1990a] and control structures for handling concurrency [Nilsen 1990b]. Walker [1989] added patterns to Icon as first-class data objects. Idol [Jeffery 1990] adds object-oriented facilities on top of Icon.

12.4.2 Indirect Influence

Icon's indirect influence on other programming languages, current and future ones, can be viewed in terms of the specific linguistic characteristics of Icon or in more general terms.

In the areas of specific linguistic characteristics, Icon's expression-evaluation mechanism is certainly its most influential feature. In addition to the inclusion of generators in the languages mentioned previously, Icon's control structures have influenced work such as Leichter [1984], Magma2 [Turini 1984], and Grandi [1986]. The view of strings and string operations used in Icon also has influenced work on string handling [Hansen 1992], and Icon's use of character sets has led to new programming techniques [Griswold 1980b].

The philosophy and character of Icon may have more far-reaching, if less identifiable, influences. In many respects, Icon runs contrary to the current conventional wisdom about programming-language design. It favors the programmer over computational efficiency, it attempts to make it easy to write good programs rather than imposing barriers to bad programming practices, and it is fun to use. Icon is a reminder that programming need not be excessively encumbered with restrictions in order to produce good programs.

The philosophy and mechanism of the distribution of Icon certainly are influential. In a time when commercial considerations influence programming languages in major ways, there are significant social and legal concerns and an essential tension between creativity, access, and proprietary rights. The proliferation of various pseudo-legalisms, such as shareware and freeware, reflects conflicts between access, intellectual property rights, and computation.

Icon is relatively unusual in being entirely in the public domain (except for commercial implementations) and in being very accessible. The evident contribution that unrestricted and ready access has made to the acceptance of Icon will surely have some influence on the complicated and difficult issues related to software distribution.

ACKNOWLEDGMENTS

As noted throughout this paper, many persons contributed to the design and implementation of the Icon programming language. The persons cited are by no means all of those who participated in one way or another in the development of Icon—there are literally hundreds of others.

The authors would like to express their appreciation to Dave Hanson for many helpful suggestions on the presentation of material in this paper.

REFERENCES

[Abrahams, 1989] Abrahams, Paul W. *SPLASH: A Systems Programming Language for Software Hackers*, Abstract submitted to SIGPLAN '90, 1989.

[Aho, 1988] Aho, Alfred V., Kernighan, Brian W., andWeinberger, Peter J. *The AWK Programming Language*, Reading, MA: Addison-Wesley, 1988.

[American, 1990] *American National Standard for Information Systems—Programming Language—C*, New York: American National Standards Institute, 1990.

[Bailey, 1990] Bailey, Mark. *A Continuating-Passing Implementation of Icon*, Technical Report, Department of Computer Science, University of Arizona, July 1990.

[Beale, 1989] Beale, Alan. *User's Guide for Version 7.5 of Icon for MVS*, Technical Report IPD101, SAS Institute, Inc., September 3, 1989.

[Blanchard, 1991] Blanchard, Heather. *Master's Thesis Proposal: A Multi-language Conversational Interpreter Based on the Icon Translator*, Department of Engineering and Computer Science, Division of Computer Science, University of California, Davis, 1991.

[Budd, 1982] Budd, Timothy A. An implementation of generators in C, *Computer Languages*, Vol. 7, 1982, pp. 69–87.

[Budd, 1987] ———. *A Little Smalltalk*, Reading, MA: Addison-Wesley, 1987, p. 91 and pp. 194–195.

[Budd, 1992] ———. *Multiparadigm Data Structures in Leda*, IEEE Computer Society 1992 International Conference on Computer Languages, Oakland, California, April 1992, pp.165–173.

[Christopher, 1985] Christopher, Thomas C. *Efficient Evaluation of Expressions in Icon*, Technical Report, Illinois Institute of Technology, 1985.

[Cohen, 1985] Cohen, Jacques. Describing Prolog by its interpretation and compilation, *Communications of the ACM*, Vol. 28, No. 12, Dec. 1985, pp. 1311–1324.

[Coutant, 1980a] Coutant, Cary A., Griswold, Ralph E., and Wampler, Stephen B. *Reference Manual for the Icon Programming Language, Version 3*, Technical Report TR 80-2, Department of Computer Science, University of Arizona, May 1980.

[Coutant, 1980b] Coutant, Cary A., and Wampler, Stephen B. *A Tour Through the C Implementation of Icon*, Technical Report TR 80-9, Department of Computer Science, University of Arizona, June 1980.

[Coutant, 1981a] Coutant, Cary A., Griswold, Ralph E., and Wampler, Stephen B. *Reference Manual for the Icon Programming Language, Version 4*, Technical Report TR 81-4, Department of Computer Science, University of Arizona, July 1981.

[Coutant, 1981b] ———. *Reference Manual for the Icon Programming Language, Version 5*, Technical Report TR 81-4a, Department of Computer Science, University of Arizona, Dec. 1981, Corrected July 1982.

[Coutant, 1983] Coutant, Cary A., Griswold, Ralph E., and Hanson, David R. Measuring the performance and behavior of Icon programs, *IEEE Transactions on Software Engineering*, Vol. SE-9, No. 1, Jan. 1983, pp. 93–103.

[Cowlishaw, 1985] Cowlishaw, M. F. *The REXX Language; A Practical Approach to Programming*, Englewood Cliffs, NJ: Prentice-Hall, 1985.

[Dewar, 1977] Dewar, Robert B. K., and McCann, Anthony P. MACRO SPITBOL—A SNOBOL4 compiler, *Software—Practice and Experience*, Vol. 7, 1977, pp. 95–113.

[Dewar, 1985] Dewar, Robert B. K. PC SNOBOL, panel discussion, *1985 International Conference on English Language and Literature Applications of SNOBOL and SPITBOL*, Jun. 1981.

[Farber, 1964] Farber, David J., Griswold, Ralph E., and Polonsky, Ivan P. SNOBOL, A string manipulation language, *Journal of the ACM*, Vol. 11, No. 1, Jan. 1964, pp. 21–30.

[Fonorow, 1988] Fonorow, O. Richard. *Modeling Software Tools With Icon*, AT&T, Naperville, Illinois, Jan. 1988.

[Fraser, 1983] Fraser, Christopher W., and Hanson, David R. A high-level programming and command language, *Proceedings of the SIGPLAN '83 Symposium on Programming Language Issues in Software Systems, SIGPLAN NOTICES*, Vol. 18, No. 6, June 1983, pp. 212–219.

[Fraser, 1985] ———. High-level language facilities for low-level services, *Conference Record of the Twelfth Annual ACM Symposium on Principles of Programming Languages*, New Orleans, Louisiana, Vol. 18, No. 6, Jan. 1985, pp. 217–224.

[Fraser, 1989] Fraser, Christopher W. A language for writing code generators, *Proceedings of the SIGPLAN Conference on Programming Language Design and Implementation, SIGPLAN NOTICES*, Vol. 24, No. 7, July 1989, pp. 238–245.

[Freeman, 1985] Freeman, J. Andrew. *Generators and Co-Routines: A Stackless Implementation Technique*, draft report, Computer Science Department, Stanford University, 1985.

[Gallesio, 1986] Gallesio, Erick. *Inclusion de l'evaluation dirigée par le but dans un langage de programmation monomorphique*, doctoral dissertation, University of Nice, France, June, 1986.

[Grandi, 1986] Grandi, Piercarlo. *A Small C Macros Package to Define Generators and Procedure Instances with Arbitrary Lifetime and Control Flow*, source unknown.

[Griswold, 1968a] Griswold, Ralph E., Poage, James F., and Polonsky, Ivan P. *The SNOBOL4 Programming Language*, Englewood Cliffs, NJ: Prentice-Hall, 1968.

[Griswold, 1968b] Griswold, Ralph E. *SNOBOL4 Information Bulletin*, Murray Hill, New Jersey: Bell Laboratories S4B1-S4B7, 1968–1971, Tucson, Arizona: University of Arizona, S4B8-No. 31, 1972–1987.

[Griswold, 1976a] ———. *SL5 Newsletter*, Tucson, Arizona: University of Arizona, S5NL1-S5NL4, 1976–1978.

[Griswold, 1976b] ———. String analysis and synthesis in SL5, *Proceedings of the ACM Conference*, Houston, Texas, Oct. 1976, pp. 410–414.

[Griswold, 1977a] ———. Research Notebooks, March 15, 1977 to August 14, 1977.

[Griswold, 1977b] ———. *Types and Data Structures in Icon*, Technical Report, Department of Computer Science, University of Arizona, December 26, 1977.

[Griswold, 1977c] ———. *The Icon Programming Language*, draft report, Department of Computer Science, The University of Arizona, Dec. 26, 1977.

[Griswold, 1977d] Griswold, Ralph E., and Hanson, David R. An overview of SL5, *SIGPLAN Notices*, Vol. 12, No. 4, April 1977, pp. 40–50.

[Griswold, 1978a] Griswold, Ralph E. *Unresolved Issues in the Design of Icon*, Technical Report, Department of Computer Science, University of Arizona, May 1, 1978.

[Griswold, 1978b] ———. *Icon Reference Manual Outline*, Technical Report, Department of Computer Science, University of Arizona, May 7, 1978.

[Griswold, 1978c] ———. *User's Manual for the Icon Programming Language*, Technical Report TR 78-14, Department of Computer Science, University of Arizona, Oct. 6, 1978.

[Griswold, 1978d] Griswold, Ralph E., and Hanson, David R. *The Icon Newsletter*, Department of Computer Science, University of Arizona, No. 1, Dec. 1978.

[Griswold, 1979] ———. *Reference Manual for the Icon Programming Language*, Technical Report TR 79-1, Department of Computer Science, University of Arizona, Jan. 1979.

[Griswold, 1980a] ———. An alternative to the use of patterns in string processing, *ACM Transactions on Programming Languages and Systems*, Vol. 2, No. 2, April 1980, pp. 153–172.

[Griswold, 1980b] Griswold, Ralph E. The use of character sets and character mappings in Icon, *The Computer Journal*, Vol. 23, No. 2, 1980, pp. 107–114.

[Griswold, 1980c] ———. *Pattern Matching in Icon*, Technical Report TR 80-25, Department of Computer Science, University of Arizona. Oct. 1980.

[Griswold, 1981a] Griswold, Ralph E., Hanson, David R., and Korb, John T. Generators in Icon, *ACM Transactions on Programming Languages and Systems*, Vol. 3, No. 2, April 1981, pp. 144–161.

[Griswold, 1981b] Griswold, Ralph E. *A History of the SNOBOL Programming Languages*, History of Programming Languages, Richard L. Wexelblat, Ed., New York: Academic Press, 1981, pp. 601–660.

[Griswold, 1982a] ———. The Icon programming language; an alternative to SNOBOL5 for computing in the humanities, *Computing in the Humanities*, Richard W. Bailey, Ed., Amsterdam: North Holland Publishing Company, 1982, pp. 7–17.

[Griswold, 1982b] ———. The evaluation of expressions in Icon, *ACM Transactions on Programming Languages and Systems*, Vol. 4, No. 4, Oct. 1982, pp. 563–384.

[Griswold, 1983a] Griswold, Ralph E., and Griswold, Madge T. *The Icon Programming Language*, Englewood Cliffs, NJ: Prentice-Hall, Inc., 1983.

[Griswold, 1983c] Griswold, Ralph E., and Novak, Michael. Programmer-defined Control Operations, *The Computer Journal*, Vol. 26, No. 2, 1983, pp. 175–184.

[Griswold, 1983d] Griswold, Ralph E. Implementing SNOBOL4 pattern matching in Icon, *Computer Languages*, Vol. 8, No. 2, 1983, pp. 77–92.

[Griswold, 1983e] ———. *The Icon Program Library*, Technical Report TR 83-6, Department of Computer Science, University of Arizona, June 29, 1983.

[Griswold, 1985] ———. Rebus—A SNOBOL5/Icon hybrid, *SIGPLAN Notices*, Vol. 20, No. 2, Feb. 1985, pp. 7–16.

[Griswold, 1986a] Griswold, Ralph E., and Griswold, Madge T. *The Implementation of the Icon Programming Language*, Princeton, NJ: Princeton University Press, 1986.

[Griswold, 1986b] Griswold, Ralph E., Mitchell, William H., and O'Bagy, Janalee. *Version 6 of Icon*, Technical Report TR 86-10b, Department of Computer Science, University of Arizona, June 8, 1986.

[Griswold, 1988a] Griswold, Ralph E., Townsend, Gregg M., and Walker, Kenneth. *Version 7 of Icon*, Technical Report TR 88-5a, Department of Computer Science, University of Arizona, January 16, 1988.

[Griswold, 1988b] Griswold, Ralph E., and O'Bagy, Janalee. Seque: A Programming Language for Manipulating Sequences, *Computer Languages*, Vol. 13, No. 1, 1988, pp. 13–22.

[Griswold, 1988c] Griswold, Ralph E. Programming with Generators, *The Computer Journal*, Vol. 31, No. 3, 1988, pp. 220–228.

[Griswold, 1989a] ———. *The Words of Icon*, Technical Report IPD88, Department of Computer Science, University of Arizona, July 15, 1989.

[Griswold, 1989b] ———. Data Structures in the Icon Programming Language, *Computing Systems*, Vol. 2, No. 4, 1989, pp. 339–365.

[Griswold, 1990a] Griswold, Ralph E., and Griswold, Madge T. *The Icon Programming Language*, Second Edition, Englewood Cliffs, NJ: Prentice Hall, 1990.

[Griswold, 1990b] Griswold, Ralph E. *Version 8 of Icon*, Technical Report TR 90-1, Department of Computer Science, University of Arizona, January 1, 1990.

[Griswold, 1990c] ———. *Supplementary Information for the Implementation of Version 8 of Icon*, Technical Report IPD112, Department of Computer Science, University of Arizona, February 27, 1990.

[Griswold, 1990d] ———. String scanning in the Icon programming language, *The Computer Journal*, Vol 33, No. 2, April 1990, pp. 98–106.

[Griswold, 1990e] Griswold, Madge T., and Griswold, Ralph E. *The Icon Analyst*, University of Arizona and The Bright Forest Company, No. 1, Aug. 1990.

[Griswold, 1990f] Griswold, Ralph E. *The Icon Program Library*, Technical Report IPD151, Department of Computer Science, University of Arizona, September 11, 1990.

[Griswold, 1992] Griswold, Madge T., and Griswold, Ralph E. *The Icon Analyst*, University of Arizona and The Bright Forest Company, No. 11, April 1992.

[Gudeman, 1986] Gudeman, David. *The T Implementation of Icon*, Technical Report, Department of Computer Science, University of Arizona, May 1986.

[Gudeman, 1991] ———. Denotational Semantics of the Icon Programming Language, *ACM Transactions on Programming Languages and Systems*, Vol. 14, No. 1, 1992, pp. 107–125.

[Hansen, 1992] Hansen, Wilfred J. Subsequence references: first-class values for substrings, *Transactions on Programming Languages and Systems*, Vol. 14, No. 4, pp. 471–489, 1992.

[Hanson, 1977] Hanson, David R. letter to Ralph E. Griswold, April 1977.

[Hanson, 1978a] ———. *Conventions and Restrictions in the Ratfor Implementation of Icon*, Technical Report, Department of Computer Science, University of Arizona, 1978.

[Hanson, 1978b] Hanson, David R., and Griswold, Ralph E. The SL5 procedure mechanism, *Communications of the ACM*, Vol. 21, No. 5, May 1978, pp. 392–400.

[Hanson, 1980] Hanson, David R. A Portable Storage Management System for the Icon Programming Language, *Software—Practice and Experience*, Vol. 10, 1980, pp. 489–500.

[ISI, 1991] Iconic Systems Inc. Icon from ISI, *The Icon Newsletter*, Madge T. Griswold and Ralph E. Griswold Eds., No. 36, July 1, 1991, p. 6.

[Iverson, 1962] Iverson, Kenneth. E. *A Programming Language*, New York: John Wiley & Sons, 1962.

[Jeffery, 1990] Jeffery, Clinton. *Programming in Idol: An Object Primer*, Technical Report TR 90-10, Department of Computer Science, University of Arizona. January 24, 1990. Last revision, July 17, 1990.

[Johnson, 1973] Johnson, Stephen C., and Kernighan, Brian W. *The Programming Language B*, Technical Report, Bell Laboratories, Murray Hill, New Jersey, Jan. 1973.

[Korb, 1977] Korb, John T. *Sil/2 Compiler; Version 3*. technical report S5WD102, Department of Computer Science, University of Arizona, March 30, 1977.

[Lapalme, 1986] Lapalme, Guy, and Chapleau, Suzanne. Logicon: An Integration of Prolog into Icon, *Software—Practice and Experience*, Vol. 16, No. 10, Oct. 1986, pp. 925–944.

[Lee, 1962] Lee, C. Y. *A Language for Symbolic Communication*, Unpublished technical memorandum 62-3344-4, Holmdel, New Jersey: Bell Laboratories, 1962.

[Leichter, 1984] Leichter, Jerrold S. *Generalized Control Constructs—Some Threads and Thoughts*, research report YALEU/DCS/RR-318, Yale University Department of Computer Science, Sept. 1984.

[Martinek, 1989a] Martinek, John. *A Temporary Variable Implementation of the Icon Virtual Machine*, Technical Report TR#89-14, Department of Computer Science, Iowa State University, Aug. 1989.

[Martinek, 1989b] ———. *The Instruction Set of the Temporary Variable Icon Virtual Machine*, Technical Report TR#89-15, Department of Computer Science, Iowa State University, September, 1989.

[Martinek, 1989c] Martinek, John, and Nilsen, Kelvin. *Code Generation for the Temporary-Variable Icon Virtual Machine*, Technical Report TR#89-9, Department of Computer Science, Iowa State University, December 6, 1989.

[Nakata, 1991] Nakata, Ikuo, and Sassa, Masataka. Programming with Streams in a Pascal-like Language, *IEEE Transactions on Software Engineering*, Vol. 12, No. 1, Jan. 1991, pp. 1–9.

[Newell, 1965] Newell, Allen *et al.*, *Information Processing Language-V Manual*, Second Edition, Englewood Cliffs, NJ: Prentice-Hall, 1965.

[Nilsen, 1986] Nilsen, Kelvin. *The CommSpeak Programming Language Reference Manual*. Technical Report, Department of Computer Science, University of Arizona, October 21, 1986.

[Nilsen, 1988a] ———. *The Design and Implementation of High-Level Programming Language Features for Pattern Matching in Real Time*, doctoral dissertation, Department of Computer Science, University of Arizona, July 15, 1988.

[Nilsen, 1988b] ———. Garbage Collection of String and Linked Data Structures in Real Time, *Software—Practice and Experience*, Vol. 18, No. 7, 1988, pp. 613–640.

[Nilsen, 1990a] ———. A Stream Data Type that Supports Goal-Directed Pattern Matching on Unbounded Sequences of Values, *Computer Languages*, Vol. 15, No. 1, 1990, pp. 41–54.

[Nilsen, 1990b] ———. High-level Goal-directed Concurrent Processing in Icon, *Software—Practice and Experience*, Vol. 20, No. 12, Dec. 1990, pp. 1273–1290.

[O'Bagy 1987] O'Bagy, Janalee, and Griswold, Ralph E. A recursive interpreter for the Icon Programming Language, *Proceedings of the SIGPLAN '87 Symposium on Interpreters and Interpretive Techniques*, St. Paul, Minnesota, June 24–26, 1987, pp. 138–149.

[O'Bagy 1988] O'Bagy, Janalee. *The Implementation of Generators and Goal-Directed Evaluation in Icon*, doctoral dissertation, Department of Computer Science, University of Arizona, August 4, 1988.

[Placer, 1991] Placer, John. R. The multiparadigm language G, *Computer Languages*, Vol. 16, No. 3/4, 1991, pp. 235–258.

[ProIcon, 1989] *The ProIcon Programming Language for Apple Macintosh Computers*. Salida, Colorado, and Tucson, Arizona: The ProIcon Group, 1989.

[Richards, 1969] Richards, Martin. A Tool for Compiler Writing and Systems Programming, *Proceedings of the Spring Joint Computer Conference*, Vol. 34, 1969, pp. 557–566.

[Ritchie, 1978] Ritchie, Dennis M., and Johnson, Stephen C. The C Programming Language, *Bell System Technical Journal*, Vol. 57, No. 6, July 1978, pp. 1991–2019.

[Schiller, 1989] Schiller, Walter H. *The Icon Compiler for the IBM-370 Systems (VM/CMS)*, Paderborn, West Germany, June 26, 1989.

[Turini, 1984] Turini, Franco. Magma2: A Language Oriented Toward Experiments in Control, *ACM Transactions on Programming Languages and Systems*, Vol. 6, No. 4, Oct. 1984, pp. 468–486.

[Walker, 1989] Walker, Kenneth W. First-class Patterns for Icon, *Computer Languages*, Vol. 14, No. 3, 1989, pp. 153–163.

[Walker, 1991] ———. *The Implementation of an Optimizing Compiler for Icon*, doctoral dissertation, Department of Computer Science, University of Arizona, 1991.

[Wall, 1991] Wall, Larry, and Schwartz, Randal L. *Programming perl*, O'Reilly and Associates, Inc., 1990.

[Wampler, 1983a] Wampler, Stephen B., and Griswold, Ralph E. Result Sequences, *Computer Languages*, Vol. 8, No. 1, 1983, pp. 1–14.

[Wampler, 1983b] ———. Co-expressions in Icon, *The Computer Journal*, Vol. 26, No. 1, 1983, pp. 72–78.

[Wampler, 1983c] ———. The Implementation of Generators and Goal-directed Evaluation in Icon, *Software—Practice and Experience*, Vol. 3, 1983, pp. 495–518.

[Wegbreit, 1970] Wegbreit, Ben. *Studies in Extensible Programming Languages*, doctoral dissertation, Harvard University, 1970.

[Wulf, 1971] Wulf, William A., Russell, David B., and Haberman., A. N. Bliss: A Language for Systems Programming, *Journal of the ACM*, Vol. 14, No. 12, Dec. 1971, pp. 780–790.

[Yngve, 1958] Yngve, Victor H. A Programming Language for Mechanical Translation, *Mechanical Translation*, Vol. 5, No. 1, 1958, pp. 25–41.

TRANSCRIPT OF PRESENTATION

Editor's note: Ralph Griswold's presentation closely followed his paper, and we have omitted it, with his permission, due to page limitations.

TRANSCRIPT OF QUESTION AND ANSWER SESSION

JOHN QUIDY (Jackson Laboratory): Is there any truth to the rumor that the name "Icon" was derived from a regional pronunciation of the phase "I can, I con, Icon"?

RALPH GRISWOLD: The name Icon didn't come from anywhere actually. I've been quoted earlier as saying finding a good name for programming languages is a lot harder than designing a good programming language. And I seem to have some evidence of that. The name doesn't stand for anything; it seemed nice at the time. I suppose "iconoclast" came to mind, but that really wasn't where it came from. Incidently, the use of "icon" for a little image on the screen, wasn't in general use. If we had known that, we wouldn't have picked it, because it has caused some confusion. Having picked the name, people have made various attempts to integrate it into a presumptive history of the origin of the name. But, no, there is nothing to that rumor.

CHRISTIAN HORN (Turtwangen): Had you some Prolog features in mind when designing Icon, or do you regard the generate-test paradigm, for structuring algorithms using backtracking techniques, as a universal multi-purpose language feature?

GRISWOLD: There are really two questions. Let me address the first one, did we have Prolog features in mind. No, at the time we started designing Icon, which was somewhat before the implementation that came out in 1978, we were not aware of Prolog, nor was Prolog aware of Icon. I remember being on a panel about languages, giving short talks at an ACM Conference. A person got up and described Prolog, I got up and described Icon, and we looked at each other. Someone in the audience stood up and saids "What's the difference?" And neither of us had heard about the other's efforts. There is quite a bit in common, actually, between Icon and Prolog, though they are cast very differently. Down inside, at some more fundamental level, there is a great deal in common. I think that it is basically something that was an idea that was going to happen. Our background came from pattern matching and SNOBOL4, and we generalized that kind of search and backtrack capability; that dates all the way back to 1968, and that was where we were coming from. But our language is in, of course, an imperative context, which gives the programmer a considerable amount of control over what actually goes on. It is possible to limit generation and control structures in various ways. The two kinds of things are different; but no, the two languages didn't even know about each other, initially. So it was, I think, a historical accident that two somewhat similar features, at least to the core, happened at approximately the same time.

JAY CONNE (Consultant): You spoke of Icon combining data structures with string manipulation, added to the other functions. Do you have any published guidelines for maintaining good structure?

GRISWOLD: The question concerns the quality of programs, the way the programs are structured. In Icon, they use string scanning, and that is the only context in which my remark was made. The problem really is that it allows too much freedom. The pattern-matching facilities of SNOBOL4 limited you, pretty much, to string analysis and generation of alternatives and goal-directed evaluation. Icon string analysis lets you do arithmetic, I/O, and everything else right there in the middle of string analysis. Yes, we do have published guidelines, which really constitute a program methodology on how one should write string processing using string scanning in Icon. We encourage people to follow those, but it is very much a learned kind of a thing. It took us a while to figure out how to write well-structured string scanning; what to do, what not to do. It doesn't come naturally from the language, and that's where I consider the result wasn't as successful as we had hoped.

RONALD FISHER (No affiliation given): You also designed, as far as this person remembers, Rebus. Was that a precursor of, or a parallel development to, Icon?

GRISWOLD: Rebus was an attempt to provide some of the nice modern syntax in Icon for SNOBOL4 users. It followed Icon. One of the things we discovered, when we designed Icon, was there were a lot of SNOBOL4 fans out there and they really didn't want to give up SNOBOL4. But they were dealing with a language whose only control structure, beside the procedure call, was the conditional "goto," and they had to fabricate loops with labels and gotos. So Rebus was an attempt to give SNOBOL4 an Icon-like syntax with ordinary looping control structures, and things like that. It was done with a pre-processor that translated Rebus into SNOBOL4. It was an experimental implementation, although we don't support it anymore. But it definitely followed Icon, because we used Icon syntax to try to recast the very old language semantics of SNOBOL4 in a more modern and acceptable package.

DANIEL SOLOMON (University of Manitoba): Do you have a new language in the works, so that you can present it at HOPL III?

GRISWOLD: No!

BIOGRAPHY OF RALPH E. GRISWOLD

Ralph E. Griswold received his Ph.D. in Electrical Engineering from Stanford University in 1962. His doctoral work was in the area of switching theory and his dissertation dealt with iterative switching networks. Dr. Griswold also holds a B.S. in Physics with honors and great distinction and an M.S. in Electrical Engineering, both from Stanford University.

In 1962 Dr. Griswold joined the staff of Bell Laboratories, where he worked in the Programming Research Department on symbolic computation and the design and implementation of high-level languages for nonnumerical applications.

In 1967 Dr. Griswold was appointed supervisor of the Computer Languages Research Group and in 1969 was appointed head of the Programming Research and Development Department. Groups under his supervision were engaged in programming language research, minicomputer interfaces, and the development of large application programs for the Bell System. His personal research continued in the areas of program portability, programming language design and implementation, software engineering, and computer-based document preparation systems.

In 1971, Dr. Griswold left Bell Laboratories to start the Department of Computer Science at the University of Arizona, where he served as department head until 1981. At the University of Arizona, he has continued to conduct and direct research with emphasis on programming languages, nonnumeric data processing, program portability, and programming methodology. In 1990 he was appointed Regents' Professor of Computer Science.

Dr. Griswold is author, or co-author, of several programming languages, including SNOBOL, SL5, and Icon. He is the author, or co-author, of six books on programming languages and programming language implementation.

BIOGRAPHY OF MADGE T. GRISWOLD

Madge T. Griswold received a BA in History and Journalism from Syracuse University in 1962 and an MA in history from the University of Arizona in 1974.

Ms. Griswold joined Bell Telephone Laboratories at Holmdel, N.J. in 1962 as a technical editor. From 1962 to 1968 she served as an editor for Bell Laboratories technical documentation, including book production. In addition, she was responsible for maintenance and programming modifications for early document-preparation systems.

In 1968, Ms. Griswold became a member of the Programming Research and Development Department at Bell Laboratories, Holmdel. She served as editorial and technical advisor, and documentation writer for document preparation systems. She also was a member of the research group investigating the interface of document-preparation systems with computerized typesetting systems.

Since 1971, Ms. Griswold has been a consultant and free-lance writer specializing in computing applications and computer-based publication techniques. She has served as consultant to the Department of Computer Science at the University of Arizona for computer-assisted document preparation, computer-assisted typesetting, and desktop publishing. She has also served as editorial consultant for book creation and production. She is coauthor of four books on computer programming languages and is president of The Bright Forest Company, Tucson, Arizona, which specializes in advanced software tools and book publishing.

Forth Session

Chair: *Helen Gigley*

THE EVOLUTION OF FORTH

Elizabeth D. Rather
FORTH, Inc.
111 N. Sepulveda Blvd., #300
Manhattan Beach, CA 90266

Donald R. Colburn
Creative Solutions, Inc.
4701 Randolph Rd., Suite #12
Rockville, MD 20853

Charles H. Moore
Computer Cowboys
410 Star Hill Road
Woodside, CA 94062

ABSTRACT

Forth is unique among programming languages in that its development and proliferation has been a grass-roots effort unsupported by any major corporate or academic sponsors. Originally conceived and developed by a single individual, its later development has progressed under two significant influences: professional programmers who developed tools to solve application problems and then commercialized them, and the interests of hobbyists concerned with free distribution of Forth. These influences have produced a language markedly different from traditional programming languages.

CONTENTS

13.1 CHUCK MOORE'S PROGRAMMING LANGUAGE

Forth was invented by Charles H. (Chuck) Moore. A direct outgrowth of Moore's work in the 1960s, the first program to be called Forth was written in about 1970 [Moore 1970a]. This section covers the early work leading to Forth.

13.1.1 Early Development

Moore's programming career began in the late 1950s at the Smithsonian Astrophysical Observatory with programs to compute ephemerides, orbital elements, satellite station positions, and so forth

[Moore 1958; Veis, 1960]. His source code filled two card trays. To minimize recompiling this large program, he developed a simple interpreter to read cards controlling the program. This enabled him to compose different equations for several satellites without recompiling. This interpreter featured several commands and concepts that survived into modern Forth, principally a command to read "words" separated by spaces, and one to convert numbers from external to internal form, plus an **IF ... ELSE** construct. He found free-form input to be both more efficient (smaller and faster code) and reliable than the more common FORTRAN practice of formatting into specific columns, which had resulted in numerous reruns due to misaligned columns.

In 1961, Moore received his BA in Physics from MIT and entered graduate school at Stanford. He also took a part-time programming position at the Stanford Linear Accelerator (SLAC), writing code to optimize beam steering for the (then) pending two-mile electron accelerator, using an extension of some of his prior work with least-squares fitting. A key outgrowth of this work was a program called **CURVE**, coded in ALGOL (1964), a general-purpose nonlinear differential-corrections data fitting program. To control this program, he used an enhanced version of his interpreter, extended to manage a push-down stack for parameter passing, variables (with the ability to explicitly fetch and store values), arithmetic and comparison operators, and the ability to define and interpret procedures.

In 1965, he moved to New York City to become a free lance programmer. Working in FORTRAN, ALGOL, JOVIAL, PL/I and various assemblers, he continued to use his interpreter as much as possible, literally carrying around his card deck and recoding it as necessary. Minicomputers appeared in the late '60s, and with them teletype terminals, for which Moore added operators to manage character input and output. One project involved writing a FORTRAN-ALGOL translator and file-editing utilities. This reinforced for him the value of spaces between words, which were not required in FORTRAN source.

Newly married and seeking a small town environment, Moore joined Mohasco Industries in Amsterdam, NY, in 1968. Here he developed computer graphics programs for an IBM 1130 minicomputer with a 2250 graphic display. This computer had a 16-bit CPU, 8K RAM, his first disk, keyboard, printer, card reader/punch (used as disk backup!), and FORTRAN compiler. He added a cross-assembler to his program to generate code for the 2250, as well as a primitive editor and source-management tools. This system could draw animated 3-D images, at a time when IBM's software for that configuration drew only static 2-D images. For fun, he also wrote a version of *Spacewar*, an early video game, and converted his ALGOL Chess program into the new language, now (for the first time) called FORTH. He was impressed by how much simpler it became.

The name FORTH was intended to suggest software for the fourth (next) generation computers, which Moore saw as being characterized by distributed small computers. The operating system he used at the time restricted file names to five characters, so the "U" was discarded. FORTH was spelled in upper case until the late '70s because of the prevalence of upper-case-only I/O devices. The usage "Forth" was generally adopted when lower case became widely available, because the word was not an acronym.

Moore found the Forth-based 1130 environment for programming the 2250 superior to the FORTRAN environment in which the 1130 software was developed, so he extended it into an 1130 compiler. This added looping commands, the concept of keeping source in 1024-byte blocks and tools for managing them, and most of the compiler features we recognize in Forth today.

Most important, there was now a dictionary. Procedures now had names, and the interpreter searched a linked list of names for a match. Names were compiled with a count and three characters, a practice learned from the compiler writers of Stanford and which prevailed in Forth until the 1980s. Within a dictionary entry was a "code field" containing the address of code to be executed for that routine. This was an indirect threaded code implementation (see Section 13.5.2) and was in use five years before Dewar's paper on indirect threaded code appeared in *Communications of the ACM* [Dewar 1975]. The use of indirect threaded code was an important innovation, because an indirect jump was the only overhead once a word had been found. Dictionary entries could consist either of pointers to other "high-level" routines or of machine instructions.

Finally, in order to provide a simple mechanism for nesting routines, a second stack called the "return stack" was added. The benefit of having a stack reserved for return addresses was that the other stack could be used freely for parameter passing, without having to be "balanced" before and after calls.

The first paper on Forth was written at Mohasco [Moore 1970a].

In 1970, Mohasco assigned Moore to an ambitious project involving a new Univac 1108, handling a network of leased lines for an order-entry system. He ported Forth onto the 1108, and arranged for it to interface to COBOL modules that did the transaction processing. The 1108 Forth was coded in assembler. It buffered input and output messages and shared the CPU among tasks handling each line. It also interpreted the input and executed the appropriate COBOL modules. This version of Forth added mechanisms for defining and managing tasks, and also added an efficient scheme for managing disk block buffers similar to schemes in use today.

Unfortunately, an economic downturn led Mohasco to cancel the 1108 project before completion. Moore immediately gave notice, then wrote an angry poem and a book on Forth [Moore 1970b] that was never published. It described how to develop Forth software and encouraged simplicity and innovation.

13.1.2 Philosophy and Goals

To Moore, Forth was a personal response to his frustration with existing software tools, which he viewed as a sort of "Tower of Babel":

> The software provided with large computers supplies a hierarchy of languages: the assembler defines the language for describing the compiler and supervisor; the supervisor the language for job control; the compiler the language for application programs; the application program the language for its input. The user may not know, or know of, all these languages: but they are there. They stand between him and his computer, imposing their restrictions on what he can do and what it will cost.
>
> And cost it does, for this vast hierarchy of languages requires a huge investment of man and machine time to produce, and an equally large effort to maintain. The cost of documenting these programs and of reading the documentation is enormous. And after all this effort the programs are still full of bugs, awkward to use and satisfying to no one. [Moore 1970a]

Moore conceived of Forth as replacing the entire "vast hierarchy" with a single layer, requiring only two elements: a programmer-to-Forth interface, consisting of minimal documentation (minimal because the interface should be simple and natural), and the Forth-machine interface, consisting of the program itself.

His view was entirely personal, considering his own needs in light of his own experience. The following excerpts from his unpublished book [Moore 1970b], describe this view:

> I've written many programs over the years. I've tried to write *good* programs, and I've observed the manner in which I write them rather critically. My goal has been to decrease the effort required and increase the quality produced.

> In the course of these observations, I've found myself making the same mistakes repeatedly. Mistakes that are obvious in retrospect, but difficult to recognize in context. I thought that if I wrote a prescription for programming, I could at least remind myself of problems. And if the result is of value to me, it should be of value to others....

Above all, his guiding principle, which he called the "Basic Principle," was, "Keep it simple!" Throughout his career he has observed this principle with religious dedication.

> As the number of capabilities you add to a program increases, the complexity of the program increases exponentially. The problem of maintaining compatibility among these capabilities, to say nothing of some sort of internal consistency in the program, can easily get out of hand. You can avoid this if you apply the Basic Principle. You may be acquainted with an operating system that ignored the Basic Principle.
>
> It is very hard to apply. All the pressures, internal and external, conspire to add features to your program. After all, it only takes a half-dozen instructions, so why not? The only opposing pressure is the Basic Principle, and if you ignore it, there is no opposing pressure.

The main enemy of simplicity was, in his view, the siren call of generality that led programmers to attempt to speculate on future needs and provide for them. So he added a corollary to the Basic Principle: "Do not speculate!"

> Do not put code in your program that *might* be used. Do not leave hooks on which you can hang extensions. The things you might want to do are infinite; that means that each has 0 probability of realization. If you need an extension later, you can code it later—and probably do a better job than if you did it now. And if someone else adds the extension, will he notice the hooks you left? Will you document this aspect of your program?

This approach flew in the face of accepted practice then, as now. A second corollary was even more heretical: "Do it yourself!"

> The conventional approach, enforced to a greater or lesser extent, is that you shall use a standard subroutine. I say that you should write your own subroutines.
>
> Before you can write your own subroutines, you have to know how. This means, to be practical, that you have written it before; which makes it difficult to get started. But give it a try. After writing the same subroutine a dozen times on as many computers and languages, you'll be pretty good at it.

Moore followed this to an astounding extent. Throughout the '70s, as he implemented Forth on eighteen different CPUs (Table 13.1). He invariably wrote for each his own assembler, his own disk and terminal drivers, even his own multiply and divide subroutines (on machines that required them, as many did). When there were manufacturer-supplied routines for these functions, he read them for ideas, but never used them verbatim. By knowing exactly how Forth would use these resources, by omitting hooks and generalities, and by sheer skill and experience (he speculated that most multiply/divide subroutines were written by someone who had never done one before and never would again), his versions were invariably smaller and faster, usually significantly so.

Moreover, he was never satisfied with his own solutions to problems. Revisiting a computer, or an application, after a few years, he often rewrote key code routines. He never reused his own code without re-examining it for possible improvements. This later became a source of frustration to Rather, who, as the marketing arm of FORTH, Inc. (see Section 13.2.2), often bid jobs on the assumption that inasmuch as Moore had just done a similar project, this one would be easy—only to watch helplessly as he tore up all his past code and started over.

Today, Moore is designing Forth-based microprocessors using his own Forth-based CAD system, which he has rewritten (and sometimes rebuilt, with his own hardware) almost continuously since 1979.

TABLE 13.1

Table showing computers for which Chuck Moore personally implemented Forth systems. In 1978, his implementations of Forth on the Level 6 and 8086 represented the first resident software on both CPUs, anticipating their manufacturers' systems by many months.

Year	Model	Customer	Forth Applications
1970–71	Honeywell H316	National Radio Astronomy Observatory (NRAO)	Data acquisition, on-line analysis w/ graphics terminal
1971	Honeywell DDP116	NRAO	Radio telescope control
1971–2	IBM 370/30	NRAO	Data analysis
1972	Varian 620	Kitt Peak National Observatory (KPNO)	Optical telescope control and instrumentation
1972	HP2100	KPNO	Instrumentation
1972–3	Modcomp	NRAO	Data analysis
1973	PDP-11	NRAO	Radio telescope control, data acquisition, analysis, graphics
1973	DG Nova	Steward Observatory	Data acquisition and analysis
1974	SPC-16	Steward Observatory	Ground control of balloon-borne telescope
1975	SDS920	Aerospace Corp.	Antenna control
1975	Prime	Gen'l Dynamics, Pomona	Environmental controls
1976	Four-Phase	Source Data Systems	Data entry and database management
1977	Interdata Series 32	County of Alameda, CA	Database management
1977	CA LSI-4	MICOA	Business systems
1978	Honeywell Level 6	Source Data Systems	Data entry and database management
1978	Intel 8086	Aydin Controls	Graphics and Image Processing
1980	Raytheon PTS-100	American Airlines	Airline display and workstations

Moore considered himself primarily an applications programmer, and regarded this as a high calling. He perceived that "systems programmers" who built tools for "applications programmers" to use had a patronizing attitude toward their constituents. He felt that he had spent a great portion of his professional life trying to work around barriers erected by systems programmers to protect the system from programmers and programmers from themselves, and he resolved that Forth would be different. Forth was designed for a programmer who was intelligent, highly skilled, and professional; it was intended to empower, not constrain.

The net result of Moore's philosophy was a system that was small, simple, clean—and extremely flexible: in order to put this philosophy into practice, flexible software is essential. The reason people leave hooks for future extensions is that it's generally too difficult and time-consuming to re-implement something when requirements change. Moore saw a clear distinction between being able to teach a computer to do "anything" (using simple, flexible tools) and attempting to enable it to do "everything" with a huge, general-purpose OS. Committing himself to the former, he provided himself with the ideal toolset to follow his vision.

13.2 DEVELOPMENT AND DISSEMINATION

By the early 1970s, Forth had reached a level of maturity that not only enabled it to be used in significant applications, but that attracted the attention of other programmers and organizations. Responding to their needs, Moore implemented it on more computers and adapted it to handle ever larger classes of application.

13.2.1 Forth at NRAO

Moore developed the first complete, stand-alone implementation of Forth in 1971 for the 11-meter radio telescope operated by the National Radio Astronomy Observatory (NRAO) at Kitt Peak, Arizona. This system ran on two early minicomputers (a 16 KB DDP-116 and a 32 KB H316) joined by a serial link. Both a multiprogrammed system and a multiprocessor system (in that both computers shared responsibility for controlling the telescope and its scientific instruments), it was responsible for pointing and tracking the telescope, collecting data and recording it on magnetic tape, and supporting an interactive graphics terminal on which an astronomer could analyze previously recorded data. The multiprogrammed nature of the system allowed all these functions to be performed concurrently, without timing conflicts or other interference.

The system was also unique for that time in that, all software development took place on the minis themselves, using magnetic tape for source. Not only did these Forth systems support application development, they even supported themselves. Forth itself was written in Forth, using a "metacompiler" to generate a new system kernel when needed.

To place these software capabilities in context, it's important to realize that manufacturer-supplied system software for these early minicomputers was extremely primitive. The main tools were cross-assemblers and FORTRAN cross-compilers running on mainframes (although the FORTRAN cross-compilers were too inefficient to do anything complex, given the tiny memories on the target machines). On-line programming support was limited to assemblers loaded from paper tape, with source maintained on paper tape. Digital Equipment Corporation had just announced its RT-11 OS for its PDP-11 line, which offered limited foreground-background operation; no form of concurrency was available for the H316 family. Multi-user operation of the sort that enabled NRAO's astronomers to graphically analyze data while an operator controlled the telescope and live data was flowing in, was unheard of.

Edward K. Conklin, head of the Tucson division of NRAO, which operated the 11-meter telescope, found it difficult to maintain the software as Moore was based at NRAO's headquarters in Charlottesville, VA. So, in 1971, he brought in Elizabeth Rather, a systems analyst at the University of Arizona, to provide local support on a part time basis. Rather was appalled to find this critical system written in a unique language, undocumented, and known to only one human. Her instinctive reaction was to rewrite the whole thing in FORTRAN to get it under control. Alas, however, there was neither time nor budget for this, so she set out to learn and document the system, as best she could.

After about two months, Rather began to realize that something extraordinary was happening: despite the incredibly primitive nature of the on-line computers, despite the weirdness of the language, despite the lack of any local experts or resources, she could accomplish more in the few hours she spent on the Forth computers once a week than in the entire rest of the week when she had virtually unlimited access to several large mainframes.

She wondered why. The obvious answer seemed to lie in the interactive nature of Forth. (The programmer's attention is never broken by the procedural overhead of opening and closing files, loading and running compilers, linkers, loaders, debuggers, and the like. But there's more to it than that. For example, all the tools used by Forth's OS, compiler, and other internal functions are available to the programmer. And, as Chuck Moore intended, its constraints are minimal and its attitude is permissive. Forth devotees still love to debate the source and magnitude of such productivity increases!)

Rather immediately left the University and began working for NRAO jointly with Kitt Peak National Observatory (KPNO), an optical observatory with which NRAO shared facilities, maintaining the Forth system for NRAO and developing one for KPNO (which was later used on KPNO's 156" Mayall telescope and other instruments [Phys. Sci. 1975]). During the next two years she wrote the first Forth manual [Rather 1972] and gave a number of papers and colloquia within the observatory and related astronomical organizations [Moore 1974a].

In 1973, Moore and Rather replaced the twin-computer system by a single disk-based PDP-11 computer [Moore 1974a&b]. This was a multi-user system, supporting four terminals, in addition to the tasks of controlling the telescope and taking data. It was so successful that the control portions of it were still in use in 1991 (data acquisition and analysis functions are more dependent on experimental equipment and techniques, which have changed radically over the years). The system was so advanced that astronomers from all over the world began asking for copies of the software. Versions were installed at Steward Observatory, MIT, Imperial College (London), the Cerro Tololo (Chile) Inter-American Observatory, and the University of Utrecht (Netherlands). Its use spread rapidly, and in 1976 Forth was adopted as a standard language by the International Astronomical Union.

13.2.2 Commercial Minicomputer Systems

Following completion of the upgraded system in 1973, Moore and his colleagues Rather and Conklin formed FORTH, Inc. to explore commercial uses of the language. FORTH, Inc. developed multi-user versions of Forth [Rather 1976a] for most of the minicomputers then in use (see Table 13.1), selling these as components of custom applications in a widely diverse market, ranging from database applications to scientific applications, such as image processing. The minicomputers and applications of the '70s provided the environment in which Forth developed and stabilized, to the extent that all the innovations contributed by independent implementors in the years that followed, represented relatively minor variants on this theme. Because of this, we shall take a close look at the design and structure of these systems.

13.2.2.1 *Environmental constraints*

Minicomputers of the 1970s were much less powerful than the smallest microcomputers of today. In the first half of the decade not all systems even had disks—1/2" tape was often the only mass storage available. Memory sizes ranged from 16 to 64 Kbytes, although the latter were considered large. In the early '70s, most programming for minis was done in assembly language. By the middle of the decade, compilers for FORTRAN and BASIC were available, and manufacturer-supplied executives such as DEC's RT-11 supported foreground-background operation. Multi-user systems were also becoming common: a PDP-11 or Nova could be expected to support up to eight users, although the performance in a system with eight active users was poor.

On this hardware, Moore's Forth systems offered an integrated development toolkit including interactive access to an assembler, editor, and the high-level Forth language, combined with a multitasking, multi-user operating environment supporting 64 users without visible degradation, all resident without run-time overlays.

Although time-critical portions of the system were written in assembler, as most applications required very high performance, Moore could port an entire Forth development environment to a new computer in about two weeks. He achieved this by writing Forth in Forth—any Forth computer could generate Forth for another, given the target system's assembler and code for about 60 primitives. Because the first step in a port was designing and writing the target assembler, it is possible that Moore has written more assemblers for different processors than anyone else.

Being able to port the system easily to new architectures was important, as the minicomputer market was extremely fragmented. A large number of CPUs was available, and each was supported by a large number of possible disk controller and drive combinations. Today, by contrast, the microcomputer market is dominated by a very short list of processor families, and adherence to *de facto* standards such as the PC/AT is the norm.

Installations were done on site, because it was impractical to ship the minicomputers. When LSI-11s first became available, Moore bought one and mounted it in a carry-on suitcase, with a single 8" floppy drive in a second suitcase. This portable personal computer accompanied him everywhere until 1982, acting as a "friendly" host for generating new Forths.

13.2.2.2 *Application Requirements*

If the principal environmental constraints were memory limitations and a need to serve a broad spectrum of CPU architectures, the application requirements were dominated by a need for performance. Here are some of the principal application areas in which Forth achieved success in this period:

1. **Commercial/business data base systems:** First developed for Cybek Corporation under the guidance of Arthur A. Gravina, these systems supported multiple terminals on a Data General Nova, handling high-speed transaction processing. The first was written for Vernon Graphics, Inc., a service bureau to Pacific Telephone, in 1974. It supported 32 terminals processing transactions against a 300 MB database. In its first week the system handled over 100,000 transactions a day (40,000 was the requirement). The system was subsequently upgraded to support 64 terminals and a 600 MB database, with no discernable degradation in response times, which remained under one second.

   Cybek subsequently marketed this system for business applications in banking and hospital management; its current version is marketed by a division of McDonnell Douglas. A similar effort by Source Data Systems in Iowa produced a multi-terminal data-entry system marketed by NCR Corp. for hospital management and similar applications.

   The performance of such a system is overwhelmingly dominated by operating system issues, principally the ability of the native Forth block-based file system to read and write data files very quickly.

2. **Image Processing:** FORTH, Inc. developed a series of image processing applications for the Naval Weapons Research Center, NASA's Goddard Space Flight Center, the Royal Greenwich Observatory in England, and others. Central to these was a need for performing standardized operations (e.g., enhancement, windowing, etc.) on images residing on different kinds of hardware. The approach taken included many features now associated with object-oriented programming: encapsulation (the basic object was an "image," with characteristic parameters and methods), inheritance (you could add new images that would inherit characteristics of previously defined classes of images) and dynamic binding of manipulation methods. Moore, the principal architect of this approach, was unaware of any academic work in this area. Striving to achieve the same goals as later OOPS writers, he independently derived similar solutions.

Image processing systems are also distinguished by a need to manipulate and move large quantities of data very fast; a 512x512x16 image, for example, occupies 512 KB. In addition to the high-speed disk performance that characterized Forth database systems, these also required fast processing speed and the ability to handle algorithms such as FFTs. As many minicomputers lacked hardware floating-point arithmetic, Forth included flexible integer and fixed-point fraction operators, as well as specialized array primitives.

3. **Instrumentation and control:** Forth was first developed and used for this purpose at NRAO, and Forth is widely used for instrumentation and controls today. FORTH, Inc. produced several more astronomical systems (for the Universities of Wyoming [Gehrz 1978], Minnesota, Hawaii and Illinois; Cal Tech; plus the Royal Greenwich Observatory and St Andrews University in the UK). In addition, a number of commercial instrument manufacturers, such as Princeton Applied Research (now a division of EG&G) and Nicolet Instruments, adopted Forth as a language for internal development.

   These applications are characterized by high data rates, as much as 20 KHz in some cases, which really strained the CPU speed of the processors available. Fast interrupt response was essential, along with high-speed multitasking to allow data acquisition to proceed concurrently with operator activity and instrument control.

13.2.2.3 *Influences*

The evolution of Forth prior to 1978 was completely dominated by Moore himself. As we have seen, Moore was, and is, a fanatic minimalist, dedicated to the principle of zero-based design in which every feature, and every instruction, must justify its existence or be ruthlessly scrapped.

Moore originally developed the system for his own use. It surprised him a little to find that Rather, and the other early users, also liked it and found it enhanced their productivity as much as it did his. But even after the formation of FORTH, Inc. and its open marketing of the system, the selection and design of support tools and the general programming interface was dominated by his personal tastes.

Moore was working primarily as a consultant, supported by others within FORTH, Inc., installing a Forth system on a customer's computer as the first step in developing a custom application. Because the customer was primarily interested in the application, it was imperative that the port be completed quickly and inexpensively. The extreme simplicity of Forth made this possible without compromising the performance of the application.

Each of these projects contributed its own lessons, tools, and techniques. Moore carried microfiche listings of all previous projects in his briefcase, and often referred to them to get the code for some unique primitive or driver from the past. Frequently used words might become a standard fixture of the system. Also, improved techniques for solving common problems were integrated into the system.

This pattern of continual evolution created customer support headaches for FORTH, Inc., however, as no two installed systems were the same. In most cases the installation included a five-day Forth programming course taught by Rather, who had to check every evening to make sure that the system still behaved the way it was being taught.

13.2.3 Early Microprocessor Systems

In 1976, Robert O. Winder, of RCA's Semiconductor Division, engaged FORTH, Inc. to implement Forth on its new CDP-1802 8-bit microprocessor [Rather 1976b; Electronics 1976]. The new product, called "microFORTH," was subsequently implemented on the Intel 8080, Motorola 6800, and Zilog Z80, and sold by FORTH, Inc. as an off-the-shelf product. microFORTH was successfully used in numerous embedded microprocessor instrumentation and control applications in the United States, Britain, and Japan.

13.2.3.1 *Environment and Applications*

microFORTH was FORTH, Inc.'s first experience with off-the-shelf, mail-order software packages; the minicomputer systems were all installed on-site. The mail-order operation was made possible by the rapid standardization of the industry on 8" "IBM-format" floppy disks, and the relatively small number of development systems for each CPU type.

These microprocessors were all 8-bit devices, typically with 16K bytes of memory in the development system. The target systems were usually custom boards (although Intel's Single Board Computer series quickly became popular), and the software was expected to run from PROM in an embedded environment without disk or (usually) terminal. This was significantly different from the minicomputer environment, where there was always a disk, and a program was expected to run on the same (or identical) computer as the one used for development.

Most microprocessor manufacturers offered development platforms consisting of the same microprocessor as in the target, up to 64K bytes of RAM, a serial line for a terminal, a parallel printer port, and two 8" floppy disk drives. Software support was mainly assembler, although Intel soon introduced PL/M. In-circuit emulators and separate utilities were introduced for debugging.

microFORTH was principally marketed as an interactive alternative to assembler which, unlike PL/M, was available across most microprocessor families and therefore offered a higher degree of transportability.

13.2.3.2 *Language Definition*

Following some initial experimentation with 8-bit stack width and 128-byte block buffers, it was quickly decided to maintain the same basic internal architecture as on the minicomputer systems. The organization of the program changed significantly, however.

microFORTH came with a target nucleus designed to run from PROM. This nucleus was only 1K in size, containing primitives such as single-precision arithmetic and other very basic functions. The development environment supported writing and testing code interactively, and then compiling a version of that code designed to mate to the run-time nucleus. A version of **VARIABLE** was provided to support segregated ROM/RAM data space (**CONSTANT**s were in PROM), and defining words were adapted so that user-defined structures could be made to reside in either. And whereas previously, **VARIABLE**s could be initialized at compile time, that capability was removed, as it is difficult to initialize target RAM when a ROM is being compiled without setting up a "shadow" table: ROM space was considered too precious for that.

The multiprogramming support was initially stripped out, although it later came back using a new, faster task-swapping algorithm, and the database tools vanished completely.

FORTH, Inc. never released the metacompiler used to generate Forth on new minicomputer CPUs. A variant of this metacompiler became an integral part of microFORTH, however, as it was used to generate the ROMable code for the target application. This was significant, as we shall see in the next section.

13.2.3.3 *Influences*

The principal architect of microFORTH was Dean Sanderson. Although Sanderson worked closely with Moore and shared most of his basic philosophies, differences in style and approach were inevitable. But the major new influence came from the broader customer base that resulted from the wider marketing of microFORTH. It was customer pressure that brought back multiprogramming, and this larger customer base also caused standards groups to form.

13.2.4 Language Definition

The commercial mini and microcomputer implementations produced by FORTH, Inc. in the early- and mid-1970s, for the first time encapsulated the principles and elements of Forth as it is used today. For this reason, we shall summarize these briefly.

13.2.4.1 *Design Principles*

Much as algebra was the "metaphor" for FORTRAN, Forth was conceived on the model of English prose (though some have suggested that its postfix notation tends to resemble verb-at-the-end languages such as German). Its elements ("words") are named data items (roughly equivalent to nouns), named procedures (equivalent to verbs), and defining words (special kinds of verbs capable of creating data items with customized characteristics). Words may be defined in terms of previously defined words or in machine code (using the embedded assembler).

Forth "words" are functionally analogous to subroutines in other languages. They are also equivalent to commands in other languages—Forth blurs the distinction between linguistic elements and functional elements.

Words are referenced (either from the keyboard or in program source) by name. As a result, the term "word" is applied both to program (and linguistic) units and to their text names. In parsing text, Forth considers a word to be any string of characters bounded by spaces (or "white space" characters in some file-based systems). Except for these, there are no special characters that cannot be included in a word or start a word, although many programming teams adopt naming conventions to improve readability. Words encountered in text fall into three categories: defined words (i.e., Forth routines), numbers, and undefined words.

There are no explicit typing mechanisms in Forth, a feature that sometimes surprises newcomers, but is generally admired by experienced Forth programmers.

13.2.4.2 *Structured Programming Disciplines*

Architecturally, Forth words adhere strictly to the principles of "structured programming" as articulated by Dijkstra [Dijkstra 1970] and "modular programming" [Parnas 1972]. These principles may be summarized as follows:

- Every program is described as a linear sequence of self-contained modules;
- A module has one entry point, one exit point, and ideally performs one function, given a set of inputs and a set of outputs;
- A module can contain:
  - — references to other modules;
  - — decision structures (**IF THEN** statements);
  - — looping structures.

Top-down design and bottom-up coding and testing are strongly encouraged by Forth's structure.

As was the case with Moore's independent development of OOPs-like features in his image processing system, Moore was unfamiliar with the contemporary literature on structured programming. These principles were first called to his attention in 1973 by Rather, who received several comments on the apparent relationship between Forth and structured programming in seminars she was giving on Forth. On reading one of Djikstra's papers, Moore observed, "it just seems like good programming practice to me."

In fact, advanced Forth programmers with knowledge of the underlying implementation know ways of "cheating," but such practices are frowned upon, and definitely not supported or encouraged by the structure of the language.

13.2.4.3 *Elements of Forth*

Moore's Forth systems of the early 1970s were built on a nucleus of only 4K bytes. This tiny program included disk (or tape) and terminal drivers and the ability to search and build the dictionary. This nucleus was then used to compile from source the balance of the programming environment, including the assembler, editor, multiuser support, and several hundred general commands. Booting the system, including compiling most of it from source into executable form, took only a few seconds.

A metacompiler, also written in Forth, was used to compile the nucleus. The entire source for the system was about 40 pages long.

These systems were "native," that is, running without any host OS or executive. This was a necessity in the early days, as OSs weren't available. Later, it was regarded as a significant advantage, as I/O services in a native Forth environment were much faster than could be supplied by a general purpose OS.

The principal elements of Forth are discussed briefly in the sections that follow.

Dictionary: A Forth program is organized into an extensible dictionary that occupies almost all the memory used by the system. The dictionary is classically implemented as a linked list of variable-length items, each of which defines a word. The content of each definition depends upon the type of word (data item, constant, sequence of operations, etc.). On multi-user Forth systems, individual users may have private dictionaries, each of which is connected to a shared, re-entrant system dictionary.

Push-Down Stacks: Forth maintains two push-down stacks, or LIFO lists (on a multiprogrammed version, a pair for each task). These are used to pass data between Forth words and for controlling logical flow. A stack contains one-cell items, where a cell is 16 bits wide on 8-bit and 16-bit computers, and 32 bits wide on most implementations for 32-bit processors such as the 680x0 family. Extended-precision numbers occupy two stack positions, with the most significant part on top. Items on either stack may be addresses or data items of various kinds. Stacks are of indefinite size, and usually grow towards low memory.

Forth's explicit use of stacks leads to a "postfix" notation in which operands precede operators. Because results of operations are left on the stack, operations may be strung together effortlessly, and there is little need to define variables to use for temporary storage.

Interpreters: Forth is an interpretive system, in that program execution is typically controlled by a small machine-code routine (often only two or three instructions) interpreting lists of pointers or tokens for abstract machine functions. This architecture is much faster than classical interpreters, as used in BASIC and PROLOG for example, enabling it to perform satisfactorily in the real-time applications for which it was designed.

This internal engine is often referred to as the "inner" or "address" interpreter, as distinct from Forth's more traditional text interpreter which processes source and user input. The text interpreter extracts strings separated by spaces from the terminal or mass storage, looking each word up in the dictionary. If a word is found it is executed by invoking the address interpreter, which processes a string of addresses compiled in a word definition by executing the definition pointed to by each. The text is not stored in memory, even in condensed form. If a word is not found, the system attempts to convert it as a number and push it onto the stack. If number conversion fails (due to a nonnumeric character), the interpreter aborts with an error message.

The address interpreter has two important properties. First, it is fast, often requiring as few as one or two machine instructions per address. Second, it makes Forth definitions extremely compact, as each reference requires only one cell (or computer word; Forth users prefer to avoid the use of "word" as a hardware unit because of its use to denote an element in the language). In contrast, a subroutine call constructed by most compilers requires instructions for handling the calling sequence before and after a **CALL** or **JSR** instruction and address, and typically, **save** and **restore** registers within the subroutine. Forth's stack architecture obviates the need for an explicit calling sequence, and most implementations make global register assignments, in which certain system state variables are assigned to dedicated registers, and all other registers are designated scratch registers for use in code words.

Assembler: Most Forth systems include a macro assembler for the CPU on which they run. When using **CODE**, the programmer has full control over the CPU, as with any other assembler, and **CODE** definitions run at full machine speed. The assembler lets the programmer use explicit CPU-dependent code in manageable pieces with machine-independent interfacing conventions. To move an application to a different processor requires recoding only the **CODE** words, which will interact with other Forth words in exactly the same manner.

Forth assemblers feature an unusual design, which has two goals: (1) to improve transportability between processors by standardizing assembler notation as much as possible without impairing the programmer's control of the processor; and (2) to yield a compact assembler that can be resident at all times to facilitate interactive programming and debugging.

In a classical Forth assembler, the op-code itself is a Forth word that assembles the instruction according to operands passed on the stack giving the addressing information. This leads to a format in which the addressing mode specifiers precede the op-code (consistent with the postfix notation used elsewhere in Forth). Moore also standardized notation for addressing modes, although he usually used the manufacturer's instruction mnemonics. Registers were generally referred to by number, except for registers assigned to key internal system functions. For example, the stack pointer is usually in a register called **S**. One would address the second item on a two-byte wide stack using the phrase **2 S)** .

Forth assemblers support structured programming in the same way that high-level Forth does. Arbitrary branching to labeled locations is discouraged; on the other hand, structures such as **BEGIN ... UNTIL** and **IF ... ELSE ... THEN** are available in the assembler (implemented as macros that assemble appropriate conditional and unconditional branches). Such structures are easy to implement because the stack is available during assembly to carry addressing information.

Conventional assemblers leave the code in a file, which must be integrated with code in files from high-level language compilers (if any) by a linker, before the resultant program can be loaded into memory for testing. The resident Forth assembler assembles the code directly into memory in executable form, thus avoiding the linking step.

The Forth assembler is used to write short, named routines that function just like high-level Forth words: when the name of the routine is invoked, it will be executed. Like other Forth routines, code routines expect their arguments on the stack and leave their results there. Within code, a programmer may refer to constants (to get a value), variables (to get an address) or other defined data types. Code routines may be called from high-level definitions just as other Forth words, but do not themselves call high-level or code definitions.

These features enable Forth programmers to write code in short, easily testable modules that are automatically integrated into an application. Programming is fully structured, with consistent rules of usage and user interface for both assembler and high-level programming. Words are tested incrementally, while the desired behavior is fresh in the programmer's mind. Most new words can be tested simply by placing input values on the stack, typing the word to be tested and validating the result left on the stack by displaying it.

The result is complete control of the computer, high performance where needed, and overall shortening of development time due to interactive programming at all levels.

Disk Support: Classical Forth divides mass storage into "blocks" of 1024 bytes each. The block size was chosen as a convenient standard across disks whose sector sizes vary. At least two block buffers are maintained in memory, and the block management algorithm makes it appear that all blocks are in memory at all times. The command **n BLOCK** returns the memory address of block *n*, having read it if necessary. A buffer, the contents of which are changed, is marked so that when it needs to be reused, its block is automatically written out. This algorithm provides a convenient form of virtual memory for data and source storage, with a minimum number of physical disk accesses required. FORTH, Inc.'s database applications build data files out of blocks, with a file defined as spanning a specified range of blocks; data access is through operations performed against named fields within selected files.

In native Forths, the block system is both fast and reliable, as the disk driver computes the physical address of the block from its number—no directory is required. In disk-intensive applications, performance can be enhanced by adding more buffers, so more blocks will be found in memory; the buffers become a disk cache.

In the 1980s, Forth systems became available running under conventional OSs, as we shall see. Many of these support blocks within host OS files, although some have abandoned blocks altogether. As blocks provide a compatible means of accessing mass storage across both native and non-native systems, ANS Forth (Section 13.5.1) requires that blocks be available if any mass storage support is available.

Multiprogramming: The earliest Forth systems supported multiprogramming, in that the computer could execute multiple concurrent program sequences. In 1973, Moore extended this capability to support multiple users, each with a terminal and independent subdictionaries and stacks. The entity executing one of these program sequences or supporting a user is referred to as a task. Many of today's Forths support multiprogramming, and most of these use variants of Moore's approach.

This approach allocates CPU time using a cooperative, nonpreemptive algorithm: a task relinquishes the CPU while awaiting completion of an I/O operation or, upon use of the word **PAUSE**, which relinquishes the CPU for exactly one lap around the round-robin task queue.

Moore's systems used interrupts for I/O. Interrupts were directly vectored to the response code using an assembler macro, without intervention by the Forth executive. Interrupt code performed only the most time-critical operations (e.g., read a number, increment a counter), then reenabled the task

TABLE 13.2

Performance comparisons of several real-time OSs on a M68010 [Cox 1987]. Times are averages, given in μs. Times were normalized to a 10 MHz 68010. polyFORTH's use of nonpreemptive task scheduling accounts for its performance advantage.

Event:	VRTX	OS9	PDOS	polyFORTH
Interrupt response	91	43.75	93.4	7.0
Context switch	128	186.25	93.4	36
Suspend task	180	316.25	184.7	6.8
Copy memory (80 bytes)		212.5		97

that had been suspended pending the interrupt. The task would actually resume operation the next time it was encountered in the round-robin task loop, at which time it would complete any high-level processing occasioned by the event and continue its work.

In theory this nonpreemptive algorithm is vulnerable to a task monopolizing the CPU with logically or computationally intensive activity, but in practice, real-time systems are so dominated by I/O that this is rarely a problem. Where CPU-intensive operations do occur, **PAUSE** is used to "tune" performance.

Consultant Bill Cox pointed out [Cox 1987] that a nonpreemptive algorithm such as this has several advantages. First, the task scheduler itself is simpler and faster, taking as little as one machine instruction per task. Second, inasmuch as a task is suspended only at known, well-defined times, it has less "context" to be saved and restored, so the context-switch itself is faster. Third, task code can be written with the knowledge of exactly when the task does or does not control the CPU, and management of shared resources is considerably simplified. Cox compared the performance of several real-time OSs; the results are given in Table 13.2.

Tasks were constructed when the system was booted, and each was given a fixed memory allocation adequate to the functions it was intended to perform. As rebooting took only a few seconds, it was easy to reconfigure a task.

Computation: Until the late 1970s, few minicomputers offered floating point arithmetic—indeed, many lacked hardware multiply and divide. From the beginning, however, Forth was used for computationally intensive work. Controlling the radio telescope, for example, required converting wanted positions from the celestial coordinates, in which astronomical objects are located, to an azimuth/elevation coordinate system once per second and interpolating intermediate positions five times per second, with data acquisition and operator activity proceeding concurrently.

Moore's approach was to build into Forth the ability to manipulate integers effectively. For example, the command ***/** multiplies two single-cell integers and divides by a third, with a double-length intermediate product. This reflects the way most multiply and divide machine instructions work, and enables calculations such as:

```
12345 355 113 */
```

This phrase multiplies 12345 by the ratio 355/113, which represents π with an error of 8.5×10^{-8} [Brodie 1981]. The ability to multiply by a ratio is ideal for calibration and scaling, as well as rational approximations. Similarly, the word **/MOD** performs a single division, returning both the quotient and remainder. A rich set of single, double, and mixed-precision operations, such as these, make integer arithmetic much more usable than it is in most languages.

Moore expressed angles internally as 14-bit, 15-bit, or 30-bit fixed-point binary fractions. He provided a set of primitives to convert to and from angle formats (e.g., dd:mm:ss), and a math library supporting transcendental functions for these formats based largely on algorithms from Hart [1968]. Operations, such as the Fast Fourier Transform, were provided in some applications, built on specialized primitives supporting complex numbers as scaled integer pairs.

Today, fast floating-point processors are common. Many Forths support floating point, as does ANS Forth. But in many cases, such as embedded systems on simple microcontrollers, Forth's integer arithmetic still provides simpler, faster solutions.

Data Types: Perhaps, nowhere was Moore's personal philosophy more in evidence than in his approach to data typing. Basically, he wanted to assume full responsibility for manipulating data objects in whatever way he wished. If pressed on this point, he would say, "If I want to add 1 to the letter A, it's none of the compiler's business to tell me I can't."

Standard words in Forth support single and double-precision **CONSTANT**s, which return their values on the stack, and **VARIABLE**s, which return a pointer. **CREATE** names the beginning of a data region in which space can be reserved. The pointer returned by a **CREATE**d entity can be incremented to index into an array. The nature of the values kept in constants and variables was entirely arbitrary; there is normally no explicit type checking. Strings are normally kept in memory with their length in the first byte. The address of this structure, or the address and length of the actual string, can be passed on the stack.

CONSTANT, **VARIABLE**, and **CREATE** are "defining words," that is, they define new words with characteristic behaviors. Forth also provides tools to enable the programmer to build new defining words, specifying a custom behavior both at compile time (e.g., setting up and initializing a table) and run-time (e.g., accepting an index and automatically applying it to the base address of the structure).

13.3 FORTH WITHOUT CHUCK MOORE

microFORTH was heavily marketed, and attracted a lot of attention in the late '70s. One side effect of this, was the growth of an active and enthusiastic group of hobbyists who fell in love with Forth. In their wake came new companies marketing versions of Forth in competition with FORTH, Inc. At the same time, Moore himself was becoming increasingly drawn toward hardware implementations of Forth, and less involved in software production at FORTH, Inc. (which he left in 1982 to pursue his hardware interests full time). In this section, we examine the development of Forth under these diverse new influences.

13.3.1 The Forth Interest Group

In the late 1970s, Northern California was afire with the early rumblings of the Computer Revolution. Groups of interested individuals, such as the "Home Brew Computer Club," were meeting to share interests and experiences. Magazines, such as *Radio Electronics*, published step-by-step instructions on how to build your own video display terminal, and even how to build your own microcomputer system.

Due to the high cost of memory and low level of VLSI integration, typical "homebrew" computers were very resource-constrained environments. Echoing back to the first generation computers, there was insufficient memory to concurrently support an editor, assembler, and linker. Mass storage was slow and expensive, so many homebrew systems used paper tape or audio cassette tapes for I/O.

Although some BASIC language products were available, they were typically very slow, and incapable of supporting significant programs. The stage was thus set for something else to meet the expanding needs of these hardy explorers and "early adopters."

Forth had been born and bred to exploit the minimal facilities of resource-constrained systems. It carried neither the excess baggage of a general solution, nor a requirement for an existing file, or operating system, or significant mass storage. As Forth was used to tackle more and more difficult embedded computer applications, it started to claim the attention of the Northern California homebrew computer enthusiasts.

Bill Ragsdale, a successful Bay Area security system manufacturer, became aware of the benefits of microFORTH, and in 1978 asked FORTH, Inc. to produce a version of microFORTH for the 6502. FORTH, Inc. declined, seeing much less market demand for microFORTH on the 6502 than the more popular 8080, Z80 and 6800 CPUs.

Ragsdale then looked for someone with the knowledge of microFORTH and intimate familiarity with the 6502 to port a version of microFORTH to the 6502. He found Maj. Robert Selzer, who had used microFORTH for an AMI 6800 development system on an Army project and was privately developing a stand-alone editor/assembler/linker package for the 6502. Selzer wrote a 6502 Forth assembler, and used the Army's microFORTH metacompiler to target compile the first 6502 stand-alone Forth for the Jolt single board computer.

Selzer and Ragsdale subsequently made substantial modifications and improvements to the model, including exploitation of page zero and stack-implicit addressing architectural features in the 6502. Many of the enhancements that characterized the later public-domain versions were made during this period, including variable-length name fields and modifications to the dictionary linked-list threading. A metacompiler on the Jolt could target a significantly changed kernel to a higher address in memory. A replacement bootable image would then be recompiled by the new kernel into the lower boot address, which could then be written out to disk. At this point, Ragsdale had a system with which to meet his professional needs for embedded security systems.

During this period, the Forth Interest Group (FIG) was started by Ragsdale, Kim Harris, John James, David Boulton, Dave Bengel, Tom Olsen, and Dave Wyland [FIG 1978]. They introduced the concept of a "FIG Forth Model," a publicly available Forth system that could be implemented on popular computer architectures.

The FIG Forth Model was derived from Ragsdale's 6502 system. In order to simplify publication and rapid implementation across a wide variety of architectures, a translator was written to convert Forth metacompiler source code into text that, when input into a standard 6502 assembler, would replicate the original kernel image. In this way, neither the metacompiler nor its source code needed to be published. This is an important point. Forth metacompilation is a difficult process to understand completely. It requires the direct manipulation of three distinct execution phases and object areas, and is not something that a casual user wanted or needed.

By publishing assembler listings, the Forth Interest Group was able to encapsulate a Forth run-time environment in a manner that could be easily replicated and/or translated into the assembly language of a different computer architecture. It was the intention of the original team of implementors to thus stimulate the development of compatible Forth systems and the appearance of new vendors of Forth products.

After the 6502 FIG Model was published, FIG implementors published compatible versions for the 8080 and 6800 microcomputers and the PDP-11 and Computer Automation minicomputers. Over the years, volunteers added other platforms and documentation. The 1982 *Forth Encyclopedia* by Mitch Derick and Linda Baker [Derick 1982] provided an exhaustive 333-page manual on FIG Forth, with flow charts of most words. In 1983, an ad in *Forth Dimensions*, the FIG newsletter [FIG 1983], listed: RCA 1802, 8080, PACE, 6502, 8086/88, 6800, 6809, 9900, Nova, Eclipse, VAX, Alpha Micro, Apple II, 68000, PDP11/LSI11 and Z80.

Today, there are several thousand members of the Forth Interest Group in over fifteen countries. Since 1980, FIG has sponsored an annual conference called FORML (Forth Modification Laboratory), an educational forum for sharing and discussing new or unproven proposals intended to benefit Forth, and for discussion of technical aspects of Forth. Its proceedings are available from the Forth Interest Group (P. O. Box 8231, San Jose, CA 95155).

13.3.2 Commercial and Public Domain Systems for Personal Computers

Apple Computer grew out of the bubbling computer enthusiasm in the San Francisco Bay area, and with it, a whole new generation of resource-constrained computers. Although BASIC was available in ROM, Forth was used to write a number of popular text editors and games on the Apple II, allowing resident development of significant programs within its scarce memory and disk constraints. It is hard now, with ubiquitous megabytes of memory and disk, to imagine what it was like to develop significant programs on a 40-column wide screen within 16K of memory and 100K of disk storage.

Vendors of low cost Forth systems sprang up almost overnight, each supporting their favorite personal computer, most of them basing their systems on the FIG model. In 1979, for example, Miller Microcomputer Services announced MMSFORTH for the TRS-80 [TRS-80 1979], and by 1980 *Computerworld* reported [Taylor 1980], that MMS had over 100 user groups for its product.

When IBM entered the personal computer business, with their original PC product offering, they chose to distribute a version of the popular Apple II text editor EasyWriter, written in Forth, as an IBM product. Laboratory Microsystems (LMI) introduced a commercial IBM PC Forth system in 1982. Numerous commercial and public domain Forth products followed, and significant software product development began.

Following its introduction of the first commercial Forth for the IBM-PC, LMI has maintained a continuing strategy of producing cutting-edge Forth systems for the PC, including a 32-bit real-mode implementation (February, 1983), an OS/2-based Forth (February, 1988) and a Windows version (1992). Along the way LMI's founder, Ray Duncan, became an acknowledged authority on Microsoft OSs [e.g., Duncan 1988].

FORTH, Inc.'s PC offering was polyFORTH, which combined the multi-user support and database tools of its minicomputer products with the ROMable architecture of microFORTH. By 1984 FORTH, Inc. was supporting up to 16 users on a PC with no visible degradation, and running polyFORTH —first as a native OS and later as a coresident OS with MS-DOS. By the late '80s polyFORTH users, such as NCR, were supporting as many as 150 users on a single 80386-based PC.

In 1978, Major Seltzer gave Don Colburn a copy of the 6502 Forth he wrote for Ragsdale in exchange for Colburn's writing two articles on Selzer's 6502 work. Colburn subsequently used this as a basis for a version based on the preliminary FORTH-77 standard (the only FORTH-77 implementation of which the authors are aware). In the Fall of 1979, Colburn generated a FIG-compatible system for prototypes of the 68000. A multitasking, multiuser version of this product called MultiForth was demonstrated to Motorola in January, 1980, well ahead of production shipments of the 68000. When Hewlett Packard's desktop-computer division designed a new generation of desktop computers around the 68000 in 1982, the first available third-party language product they distributed under an HP part number was MultiForth.

Colburn's company "Creative Solutions" also introduced MacForth, the first resident development system for the 128K Apple Macintosh, immediately after the Mac's debut in January of 1984. Because MacForth uniquely provided direct access to the entire Macintosh "Toolbox ROM" (routines in a

TABLE 13.3

Some major suppliers of Forth systems, services and related products.

System(s)	Company	Primary Products & Markets
CFORTH83, Forthmacs, SunForth	Bradley Forthware	Portable Forth written in C; versions for Atari, Macintosh, Sun; consulting and services related to the Sun Microsystems Open Boot.
cmFORTH	Silicon Composers and others	Public-domain system for Novix Forth processor by C. Moore, ported to the Harris and SC-32 Forth processors by others.
Cyrano	Opto-22	Forth for a proprietary embedded controller
F-PC	T. Zimmer et al.	Extensive public-domain system for the IBM-PC family
F83	Laxen and Perry	Public-domain system for the IBM-PC family, later ported by others to other platforms
HS/Forth	Harvard Softworks	IBM-PC family
JForth	Delta Research	Amiga
MacForth	Creative Solutions, Inc.	Apple Macintosh, NuBus interface boards
Mach2	Palo Alto Shipping	Apple Macintosh
mmsFORTH	Miller Microcomputer Services	IBM-PC family; business and commercial applications
MPEForth	MicroProcessor Engineering (UK)	PCs and embedded systems
mvpFORTH	Mountain View Press	Public-domain system on a variety of platforms
Open Boot	Sun Microsystems	Programmable ROM-based Forth on SPARC workstations
polyFORTH	FORTH, Inc.	Industrial systems on PCs and other platforms; interactive cross-compilers; consulting and custom programming services
UR/Forth	Laboratory Microsystems, Inc. (LMI)	IBM-PC family running DOS, OS2 and Windows; also cross compilers for a variety of systems

resident programming environment, along with comprehensive application examples), a majority of the first generation of Macintosh application programmers learned how to create, and use, pull-down menus, windows, graphics and mice with MacForth. Significant large-volume spreadsheets, 2D and 3D rendering and design packages, CAD/CAM design tools, games, medical diagnostics, image enhancement programs, accounting packages, desktop planetariums, and process control applications were written on early Macintoshes in MacForth.

Byte Magazine dedicated its August, 1980 issue to Forth. It was their largest-selling issue to date, and was reprinted several times.

By 1985, there were over 70 vendors of Forth systems, ranging from single individuals to multimillion dollar organizations.

In 1982, Lawrence Forsley founded the Institute for Applied Forth Research, now called simply the Forth Institute. This organization sponsors an annual Conference on Forth Applications at the University of Rochester, Rochester, NY, and publishes the *Journal of Forth Application and Research*, a refereed technical periodical on applications of Forth, new developments and techniques, and surveys of specific areas of Forth.

In 1989, George Shaw and others formed an ACM Special Interest Group on Forth called SIGForth, which also sponsors a newsletter and an annual conference.

13.3.2.1 *Design principles*

FIG Forth was optimized for portability rather than performance. Only a very few primitives were coded in assembler, and the rest of the logic was implemented using high-level Forth. As a result, it was fairly slow—some operations, such as dictionary searches, were a factor of ten slower than representative commercial implementations.

Other internal decisions were similarly made with the neophyte in mind. For example, the earlier FORTH, Inc. systems compiled word names as the length of the name and the first three characters. This gave a lower collision rate than simple truncation, and was adequate most of the time. But, the FIG model used variable-length names up to 31 characters, thereby trading size for user-friendliness. This was somewhat controversial at the time (see Fig. 13.1), but by the mid 1980s, most systems had converted to this usage.

The advent of personal computers provided Forth implementors with the incentive to learn to run under a host OS. The first non-native systems were developed in 1980 by Martin Tracy of Micromotion (for the Apple II) and Ray Duncan of Laboratory Microsystems, Inc. (for CP/M on Z80s). LMI's system, also featured a full-screen editor. In 1981, LMI added support for a software and hardware floating point, and also pioneered performance enhancements, such as native code translation and caching dictionary lookups in a hash table to accelerate dictionary searches.

The advent of non-native Forth implementations introduced an issue that remains controversial in Forth practice today, the use of host OS files for mass storage. There are two main approaches: abandoning traditional blocks altogether in favor of directly manipulating source and data in files, and mapping blocks to host OS files. The former approach is favored by implementors who are concentrating on systems for a particular OS (e.g., MS-DOS), whereas the latter is preferred by organizations such as FORTH, Inc. that support both native and non-native products.

FIGURE 13.1

"Letter to the Editor" of *Forth Dimensions* [Moore 1983] concerning the practice of storing names of Forth words as a count and first three characters.

```
DEA- EDI---

I AM AFR--- THA- THE LET--- IN THE LAS- ISS-- ABO--
FOR-- INC- USI-- ONL- THR-- LET--- NAM- FIE--- HAS
HAD THE OPP----- EFF--- FRO- WHA- THE WRI--- WAN---

HIS LET--- ( LIK- THI- ONE ) SHO-- THA- SAV--- ONL-
THR-- LET---- AND COU-- IS JUS- ABO-- OPT---- IN
TER-- OF A TRA-- OFF BET---- SAV--- MEM--- AND
KEE---- LEG-------

WE STI-- DON-- SEE THE NEE- FOR 31 CHA------ NAM--
IN THE GEN---- CAS-

YOU-- TRU--

CHU-- MOO--

FOR-- INC-
```

Creative Solutions' MacForth used very compact object image strategies, including token threading and separated name heads to maximize the amount of memory available for program development on the original 128K Macintoshes. Other novel features included run-time relocation of the executable image and exclusion of word names in run-time systems without metacompilation. MacForth included a seamless programming environment, incorporating screen based text editor, compiler, interpreter, and assembler in under 20k bytes of memory.

13.3.2.2 *Influences*

The FIG Model was in the public domain, and was ported to a wide variety of computer systems. Because the internal design of FIG Forth was essentially the same across all machines, programs written in FIG Forth enjoyed a substantial degree of portability, even for "system-level" programs that directly manipulated the internals of dictionary entries and other implementation-dependent features. Because FIG Forth was the first introduction to Forth for many people, it is widely associated with "the nature of Forth."

However, FIG Forth was not representative of all commercial implementations of this era. Commercial vendors tended to be much more performance-conscious, and elected implementation strategies that optimized performance or size rather than porting ease, as we have seen.

The first major effort to standardize Forth was at a meeting in Utrecht in 1977, attended by several astronomical Forth users and FORTH, Inc. (at that time the only commercial vendor). They produced a preliminary standard called FORTH-77, and agreed to meet the following year. Meetings in 1978 and 1979 on Catalina Island in California, now including representatives from the Forth Interest Group and other producers, yielded a more comprehensive standard called FORTH-79. Although FORTH-79 was very influential, many Forth users and vendors found flaws in it; in 1982 two meetings were held to update the standard, and in 1983 a new standard was released called FORTH-83. Both FORTH-79 and FORTH-83 specified a 16-bit, twos-complement, unaligned, linear byte-addressed virtual machine, and included a number of assumptions about implementation techniques.

Unfortunately, some of the changes in FORTH-83 produced grave incompatibilities with existing code. For example, the formal representation of a "true" flag had always been 1, and the word **NOT** inverted a Boolean flag. In FORTH-83, "true" became –1 and **NOT** became a bit-wise complement. Other problems involved the specification for floored division in FORTH-83 and a serious ambiguity in the specification of parameters for certain loop structures. The effect of these incompatibilities was divisive. Although most implementors agreed that FORTH-83 was an improvement and adopted the new standard, there remains a vocal group who never converted, and who remain skeptical of the whole standards process. Of the systems listed in Table 13.3, for example, most are fairly close to FORTH-83 compatibility; notable exceptions are MacForth, mmsFORTH and mvpFORTH, all of which stayed with FORTH-79.

In 1981, Prentice Hall published *Starting FORTH*, by Leo Brodie [Brodie 1981], then an employee of FORTH, Inc. Both lucid and entertaining (Brodie drew memorable cartoon figures representing important Forth primitives), *Starting FORTH* was also a thorough introduction to the language. It sold over 110,000 copies (for a time it was the best-seller in Prentice Hall's computer line) and exerted a powerful influence on many people learning about Forth for the first time, as well as on vendors scrambling to be compatible with it. Although the first edition was primarily based on FORTH, Inc.'s polyFORTH, it included many footnotes and examples in FIG Forth and other dialects. The second edition (1987) was based on the FORTH-83 standard.

Another major influence in the personal computer marketplace has been the competition between public-domain and commercial versions of Forth. In the mid-1980s, the FIG model was gradually replaced by the public domain F83 (produced by Henry Laxen, Mike Perry, and others, operating under the name "No Visible Support Software"), a multitasking system originally released on the IBM-PC. Versions have been developed by many independent programmers on a wide variety of other platforms. This system is so widespread that many people are led by its name to confuse it with the FORTH-83 standard. In fact, although it is largely compatible with FORTH-83, F83 goes well beyond the limited FORTH-83 standard in its features. In the late '80s, Tom Zimmer and others produced an even more extensive public-domain system for PCs called F-PC, which includes several megabytes of source code and utilities. But, except for these, most public-domain Forths are rather limited.

Public-domain Forths have certainly helped to ensure that Forth is widely known. But their influence isn't entirely benign. According to Tyler Sperry, editor of *Embedded Systems Programming Magazine* [Sperry 1991]:

> The problem is that it is relatively easy to implement your own minimal Forth system. The kernel, after all, is only a few hundred bytes of code.... Unfortunately, bringing up a Forth interpreter is like writing a Small C compiler: it's only a toy without a well-developed library. One of the biggest problems with public-domain and shareware systems is that their libraries are often only partially completed, with sketchy documentation. And that's putting the situation kindly.

People who have only seen or used limited public-domain Forth implementations often perceive that Forth itself is a toy. And suppliers of high-quality commercial systems must deal with prospective customers' assumptions that all Forths are the same, an assumption that naturally creates considerable price resistance, given that the public-domain versions are extremely inexpensive. The standing joke within the Forth community, however, is "when you've seen one Forth ... you've seen one Forth." The range in quality of code and documentation, nature and extent of libraries, as well as product support, is enormous. A prospective user is well advised to evaluate a number of both public domain and commercial offerings.

13.3.3 Embedded Systems

13.3.3.1 *Environment and applications*

Forth's ability to make maximum use of limited hardware resources made it a natural choice for embedded uses of microprocessors. Some of these have been small: an RCA 1802-based cardiac monitor (1979) that performed a detailed waveform analysis of heart beats was not much larger than the 1" x 2" tape cassette it used to record abnormalities. Some were large, such as the 750-ton stretch press used by Lockheed to form panels for the C5B airplane wings in the early '80s. Some were distributed, such as the roughly 500 networked processors used for an extensive facility management system at the King Khaled International Airport at Ryadh, Saudi Arabia [Rather 1985]. Forth has been especially successful in developing firmware for hand-held devices made by companies such as Itron and MSI Data. In 1990, Federal Express won the prestigious Malcolm Baldridge quality award for its package-tracking system, data entry of which is performed by Forth-based hand-held devices carried by Federal's 50,000 couriers and agents world-wide.

Forth's extreme modularity facilitates thorough, systematic testing, which has made it attractive for applications requiring high reliability. As a result, it has been used in a number of satellites and Space Shuttle experiments. McDonnell Douglas used polyFORTH in their Electrophoresis in Space project [Wood 1986] to control the cargo bay factory itself (multiple 68000 VME-bus boards), the astronaut's control console (a laptop PC), and their ground-based analysis computer (a Compaq PC).

The November, 1990 Columbia shuttle flight carried four astronomy payloads, of which three were programmed in Forth [Ballard 1991], and the January, 1992, Spacelab flight featured a Microgravity Vestibular Investigation (MVI) experiment using a polyFORTH system for on-board control and analysis [Paloski 1986] and MACH2 in a ground-based Macintosh for analysis.

Probably the most prolific single purveyor of embedded Forths is Sun Microsystems, whose SPARC workstations all use a programmable Forth-based monitor called Open Boot, developed by Mitch Bradley and associates. Bradley believes [Bradley 1991] that Forth was successful for this purpose because it offered:

1. a CPU-independent "virtual machine" to use for the byte-coded portable drivers;
2. a debugging environment for those drivers;
3. an interactive command language, with complete programming language capability, that was useful for hardware startup and debugging;
4. a built-in debugging environment for the firmware itself (firmware is otherwise rather painful to debug);
5. a debugging environment for the operating system software;
6. extensibility, allowing easy support of new hardware requirements and features; and
7. great flexibility in tuning the implementation for speed/space tradeoffs.

At least one other major board-level CPU vendor has adopted Open Boot firmware across their product line, and there is a working group developing an IEEE standard for it.

13.3.3.2 *Design principles*

From the minis of the '70s to the PCs of the '80s, most Forth systems have supported development on the same computer on which the completed application is to run. Even the microprocessor systems of the late '70s and early '80s were developed on the same CPU (as opposed to cross-development), with development software features for stripping the development tools and producing a ROMable target.

Most embedded systems lack a disk, a terminal, or both, thereby rendering themselves inhospitable to even the leanest Forth programming environment. Nonetheless, some vendors do provide on-board Forths in microcontrollers. Examples include the Rockwell AIM 65 mentioned before, and microcontroller boards sold by New Micros, Inc. of Texas; Vesta Technologies, Inc., in Colorado; and Opto-22 in California.

But as PCs became ubiquitous, they also became popular as hosts for more comfortable and powerful Forth cross-development environments. These have generally been based on modified versions of the classical Forth metacompilers, adapted to support cross development.

The traditional Forth dictionary is integrated: a "definition" includes the word's name (which can be found in a dictionary search performed by the text interpreter), an executable portion (typically a pointer to code that executes words of a particular class, such as colon definitions, variables, constants, etc.), and data space (containing one or more values or addresses of words that make up the content of the definition), all classically in contiguous memory locations. (However, see Section 13.5.2, Implementation Strategies). A metacompiler divides these structurally into portions that are used by the host system's compiler (equivalent to a symbol table) and portions required at run-time in the target. In order for a target program to be ROMable, the compiler must also manage separate ROM and RAM data spaces, usually using multiple sets of dictionary pointers.

13.4 HARDWARE IMPLEMENTATIONS OF FORTH

The internal architecture of Forth simulates a computer with two stacks, a set of registers, and other well-defined features. As a result, it was almost inevitable that someone would attempt to build a hardware representation of the actual Forth computer.

The first such effort was made in 1973 by John Davies of the Jodrell Bank Radio Astronomy Observatory near Manchester, England. Davies' approach was to re-design a Ferranti computer that had gone out of production to optimize its instruction set for Forth.

The first actual Forth computers were bit-sliced board-level products. The first of these was made by a California company called Standard Logic, in 1976. By making a minor modification in the instruction set of their board-level computer, Standard Logic's chief programmer Dean Sanderson was able to implement the precise instruction that Forth uses in its "address interpreter" to move from one high-level command to the next. Their system was used widely by the US Postal System.

In the early 1980s, Rockwell produced a microprocessor with Forth primitives in on-chip ROM, the Rockwell AIM 65F11 [Dumse 1984]. This chip has been used quite successfully in embedded microprocessor applications. However, no attempt was made to adapt the actual architecture of the processor (basically a 6502) for Forth support.

In 1981, Moore himself undertook design of an actual Forth chip. Working first at FORTH, Inc. and subsequently with a start-up company called Novix, formed to develop the chip, Moore completed the design in 1984, and the first prototypes were produced in early 1985 [Golden 1985]. This design was subsequently purchased and adapted by Harris Semiconductor Corp., and formed the basis of their line of RTX processors.

Starting in the early 1980s, a group at the John Hopkins Applied Physics Laboratory in Maryland developed a series of experimental Forth processors for use in space instrumentation [Hayes 1987]. The most successful of these, marketed as the SC-32 by Silicon Composers of Palo Alto, CA, was used to control the Hopkins Ultraviolet Telescope which flew in the Columbia Space Shuttle in November, 1990 [Ballard 1991]. It continues to be the basis for more space instruments under development.

Moore himself, working on his own, has continued to develop Forth-based processors for special applications.

The various Forth processors have had an influence on Forth software systems. In order to take full advantage of these architectures, Forth compilers were developed by Moore, FORTH, Inc., and Laboratory Microsystems that generated machine code optimized for the chip's internal architecture. A native looping structure in the Novix and Harris chips called **FOR ... NEXT** (which counted down from a single-argument upper limit to zero) led to adoption of this structure in other Forths as well.

13.5 PRESENT AND FUTURE DIRECTIONS

The computer industry has always been characterized by rapid and profound changes. Because Forth was last standardized in the early 1980s, the speed, memory size, and disk capacity of affordable personal computers have increased by factors of more than one hundred. 8-bit processors are now rare in PCs (although they are still widely used in embedded systems), and 32-bit processors are common. Operating systems, programming environments, and user interfaces are far more sophisticated. Many recent Forth implementations, both commercial and public-domain, have attempted to address these issues.

13.5.1 Standardization Efforts

At the time of writing (November, 1992), a Technical Committee X3J14 (of which authors Rather and Colburn are members) is nearing completion of an ANS Forth. Among the 20 voting members in the TC are vendors (FORTH, Inc., Creative Solutions, Sun Microsystems, and a division of NCR), some large user organizations (Ford Motor Co., NASA), and a number of smaller user organizations, consultants and experts. Starting in 1987, this group has addressed a number of problems with FORTH-79 and FORTH-83, as well as some contemporary issues. A few of the issues addressed in the draft standard follow, as they represent current areas of lively debate and technical activity among Forth users and implementors.

ANS Forth attempts to reconcile some of the divisions caused by the incompatibilities between FORTH-79 and FORTH-83. For example, it retains **0=** to perform the FORTH-79 **NOT** function, introduces **INVERT** to perform the FORTH-83 **NOT**, and removes the word **NOT**. This enables application writers who depend on either version to leave their programs unchanged, and achieve compatibility by adding a simple shell in which **NOT** is defined as a synonym for the preferred behavior.

The proposed standard also removes virtually all restrictions on implementation options, provides for independence from CPU word size, and offers a number of optional extension word-sets for functions such as host OS file compatibility, dynamic memory allocation, and floating point arithmetic. Some significant issues addressed by ANS Forth follow.

13.5.1.1 *Cell size*

FORTH-79 and FORTH-83 mandated a 16-bit architecture, including stack width, addresses, flags, and numbers. ANS Forth specifies sizes in terms of a "cell," the width of which is implementation-defined but must be at least 16 bits. Words have been added to increment addresses transportably by a cell, a character, or an integral number of cells or characters.

13.5.1.2 *Arithmetic*

Amid great controversy, FORTH-83 mandated floored division. Not only was this incompatible with prior usage (which didn't specify the algorithm for handling signed division), it was also at variance with hardware multiply/divide instructions on most processors. But many people felt strongly that floored division is mathematically more appropriate, and that it was important to specify. Recognizing that there were many implementations on both sides of this issue, the TC opted to allow either floored or truncated division. The implementation must specify which default it uses, and must provide primitives supporting both methods.

13.5.1.3 *Control structures*

One of the unique characteristics of Forth is the degree to which its own internal tools are accessible to the application programmer. For example, there is one lexical analyzer used by the compiler, assembler, and text interpreter; it is also available for command and text parsing in applications. Similarly, the tools that implement control structures, such as loops and conditionals, are available for making custom structure words. In 1986, Wil Baden demonstrated [Baden 1986] that the standard Forth structure words, plus a few extensions made from these underlying tools, are adequate to make any structure, including solutions to problems posed in D. E. Knuth's paper "Structured Programming with **go to** statements" [Knuth 1974].

TABLE 13.4

Standard control structures in Forth. ANS Forth allows programmers to form new structures by mixing the component words or using them to define new structure words.

Structure	Description
DO ... LOOP	Finite loop incrementing by 1
DO ... <n> +LOOP	Finite loop incrementing by **<n>**.
BEGIN ... <f> UNTIL	Indefinite loop terminating when **<f> is** 'true'
BEGIN ... <f> WHILE ... REPEAT	Indefinite loop terminating when **<f> is** 'false'
BEGIN ... AGAIN	Infinite loop
<f> IF ... ELSE ... THEN	Two-branch conditional; performs words following **IF** if **<f> is** 'true' and words following **ELSE** if it is 'false'. **THEN** marks the point at which the paths merge.
<f> IF ... THEN	Like the two-branch conditional, but with only a 'true' clause.

FORTH-79 and FORTH-83 provided syntactic specifications for the common structures listed in Table 13.4, as well as an "experimental" collection of structure primitives. The latter were not widely adopted, however, and few implementations perform the kind of syntax checking the standards anticipated. F83 offers a limited form of syntax checking, in that it requires the stack, which is used at compile-time for compiling structures, to have the same size before and after compiling a definition, the theory being that a stack imbalance would indicate an incomplete structure. Unfortunately, this technique prevents the very common practice of leaving a value on the compile-time stack which is to be compiled as a literal inside a definition.

Common practice often took advantage of knowledge about how the structure words worked at compile-time to manipulate them in creative ways. The ANS Forth Technical Committee sanctioned this by providing specifications of both the compile-time and run-time behaviors of the structure words, so that they may be combined in arbitrary order. A set of structure primitives is provided in a "programming tools" wordset, and the word **POSTPONE** is provided to enable programmers to write new structure words that reference existing compiler directives, in order to provide a portion of the desired new behavior.

13.5.2 Implementation Strategies

The original Forth systems, developed by Moore in the 1970s, compiled source from disk into an executable form in memory. This avoided the separate compile-link-load sequences characteristic of most compiled languages, and led to a very interactive programming style in which the programmer could use the resident Forth editor to modify source and recompile it, having it available for testing in seconds. The internal structure of a definition was as shown in Fig. 13.2, with all fields contiguous in memory. The FIG model and its derivatives modified the details of this structure somewhat, but preserved its essential character.

Forth systems implemented according to this model built a high-level definition by compiling pointers to previously defined words into its parameter field; the address interpreter, that executed such definitions, proceeded through these routines, executing the referenced definitions in turn by performing indirect jumps through the register used to keep its place. This is generally referred to as *indirect-threaded* code.

FIGURE 13.2

Diagram showing the logical components of a Forth definition. In classical implementations, these fields are contiguous in memory. The data field will hold values for data objects, addresses, or tokens for procedures, and the actual code for CODE definitions.

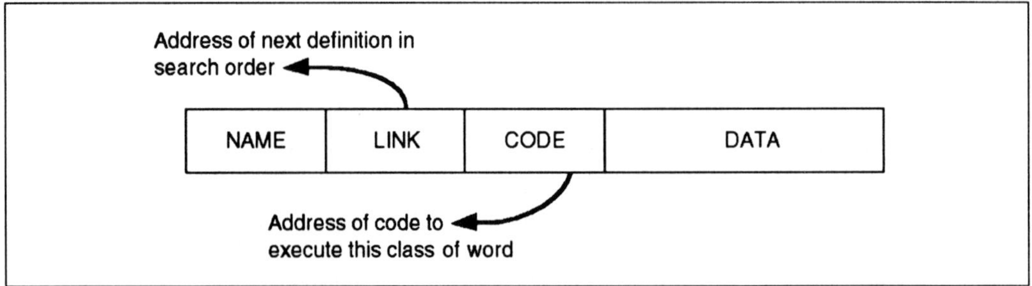

The need to optimize, for different conditions, has led to a number of variants in this basic implementation strategy, however. Some of the most interesting are:

1. **Direct threaded code.** In this model, the code field contains machine code instead of a pointer-to-machine code. This is somewhat faster, but typically costs extra bytes for some classes of words. It is most prevalent on 32-bit systems.
2. **Subroutine-threaded code.** In this model, the compiler places a jump-to-subroutine instruction with the destination address in-line. This technique costs extra bytes for each compiled reference on a 16-bit system. It is often slower than direct-threaded code, but it is an enabling technique to allow the progression to native code generation.
3. **Native code generation.** Going one step beyond subroutine-threaded code, this technique generates in-line machine instructions for simple primitives such as + and jumps to other high-level routines. The result can run much faster, at some cost in size and compiler complexity. Native code can be more difficult to debug than threaded code. This technique is characteristic of optimized systems for the Forth chips such as the RTX, and on 32-bit systems where code compactness is often less critical than speed.
4. **Optimizing compilers.** A variant of native code generation, these were invented for the Forth processors that can execute several Forth primitives in a single cycle. They looked for the patterns that could be handled in this way and automatically generated the appropriate instruction. The range of optimization was governed by the capabilities of the processor; for example, the polyFORTH compiler for the Novix and RTX processors had a four-element peephole window.
5. **Token threading.** This technique compiles references to other words using a token, such as an index into a table, which is more compact than an absolute address. Token threading was used in a version of Forth for a Panasonic hand-held computer developed in the early 1980s, for example, and is a key element in MacForth.
6. **Segmented architectures.** The 80x86 family supports segmented address spaces. Some Forths take advantage of this to enable a 16-bit system to support programs larger than 64K. Similarly, implementations for Harvard-architecture processors such as the 8051 and TI TMS320 series manage separate code and data spaces.

Although the early standards assumed the classical structure, ANS Forth makes a special effort to avoid assumptions about implementation techniques, resulting in prohibitions against assuming a relationship between the head and data space of a definition or accessing the body of a data structure other than by predefined operators. This has generated some controversy among programmers who prefer the freedom to make such assumptions over the optimizations that are possible with alternative implementation strategies.

13.5.3 Object-Oriented Extensions

Forth's support for custom data types with user-defined structure, as well as compile-time and run-time behaviors, has, over the years, led programmers to develop object-based systems such as Moore's approach to image processing described in Section 13.2.2.2, item 2. Pountain [1987] described one approach to object-oriented programming in Forth, which has been tried by a number of implementors. Several Forth vendors have taken other approaches to implementing object-based systems, and this is currently one of the most fertile areas of exploration in Forth.

In 1984, Charles Duff introduced an object-oriented system written in Forth called Neon [Duff 1984 a & b]. When Duff discontinued supporting it in the late '80s, it was taken over by Bob Lowenstein, of the University of Chicago's Yerkes Observatory, where it is available as a public-domain system under the name Yerk. More recently, Michael Hore re-implemented Neon using a subroutine-threaded code; the result is available (also in the public domain) under the name MOPS. Both Yerk and MOPS are available as down-loadable files on a number of Forth-oriented electronic bulletin boards listed at the end of this paper.

13.6 *A POSTERIORI* EVALUATION

The early development of FORTH was, in many ways, quite different from that of most other programming languages. Whereas they generally emerged full featured, with unambiguous formal specifications for language syntax and semantics, Forth enjoyed a lengthy, dynamic adolescence, in which each fundamental presupposition of the language was tested on the anvil of actual applications experience. During this period, Moore, unencumbered by a large following of users, often made revolutionary changes to the language on a daily basis, to suit his current view of what the language should be. He had complete control and responsibility for the machine at hand, from the first bootstrap loader to the completed application. The language converged toward the actual needs of one man solving a broad class of technically challenging problems in resource-constrained environments.

The resulting method of problem solving, expressed by the resulting *de facto* language specification, has proven useful to others. Given the complete flexibility to add syntax checking, data typing, and other more formal structures often considered essential to programming languages, most of the several hundred people who have independently implemented versions of Forth for their own use have not done so. The results of their efforts, as surveyed by the ANS Forth Technical Committee, represent a startlingly democratic ratification of Moore's personal vision.

13.6.1 Meeting Objectives

Without a formal language design specification citing clearly defined objectives, we can only evaluate the stated objectives of the inventor of the language and those who have used it. Personal productivity and intellectual portability were Moore's primary stated objectives. Forth has been ported across the vast majority of programmable computers and has been embodied in several different dedicated Forth computer architectures.

In 1979, Chuck Moore looked back on ten years' experience with Forth and observed [Moore 1979]:

> My original goal was to write more than 40 programs in my life. I think I have increased my throughput by a factor of 10. I don't think that throughput is program-language limited any longer, so I have accomplished what I set out to do. I have a tool that is very effective in my hands—it seems that it is very effective in others' hands as well. I am happy and proud that this is true.

Today he sees no reason to change this assessment.

The developers of FIG Forth saw their systems spread all over the world, along with chapters of their organization, and influence Forth programmers everywhere. Their goal of instantiating additional commercial vendors of Forth products was also achieved.

Of the many entrepreneurs who committed their careers and fortunes to Forth-based enterprises, few have become rich and famous for their efforts. But most have had the satisfaction of seeing their own productivity increased just as Moore did, and of having seen seemingly impossible project objectives met because of the power and flexibility of the language. They have also enjoyed prosperity in making this capability available to their clients and customers.

Given Moore's criteria of productivity and portability, perhaps the best measure of achieving these objectives is the very large quantity and range of application programs that have been written in Forth by a small number of programmers across a very broad variety of computers.

13.6.2 Major Contributions of Forth

In 1984, Leo Brodie wrote a book on designing Forth applications called *Thinking Forth* [Brodie 1984]. In it, he quoted a number of Forth programmers on their design and coding practices. In an Epilogue, several of them commented that Forth had significantly influenced their programming style in other languages, and indeed their approaches to problem solving in general. Here are two examples, which are typical of observations of Forth users in general:

> [The] essence of good Forth programming is the art of factoring procedures into useful free-standing words. The idea of the Forth word had unexpected implications for laboratory hardware design.
>
> Instead of building a big, monolithic, all-purpose Interface, I found myself building piles of simple little boxes which worked a lot like Forth words: they had a fixed set of standard inputs and outputs, they performed just one function, they were designed to connect up to each other without much effort, and they were simple enough that you could tell what a box did just by looking at its label. . . .
>
> Because Forth is small, and because Forth gives its users control over their machines, Forth lets humans control their applications. It's just silly to expect scientists to sit in front of a lab computer playing "twenty questions" with packaged software. Forth . . . lets a scientist instruct the computer instead of letting the computer instruct the scientist.
>
> — Mark Bernstein, president of Eastgate Systems, Inc., Cambridge, MA

> Forth has changed my thinking in many ways. Since learning Forth I've coded in other languages, including assembler, BASIC and FORTRAN. I've found that I used the same kind of decomposition we do in Forth, in the sense of creating words and grouping them together.
>
> More fundamentally, Forth has reaffirmed my faith in simplicity. Most people go out and attack problems with complicated tools. But simpler tools are available and more useful.
>
> — Jerry Boutelle, owner of Nautilus Systems, Santa Cruz, CA

Mitch Bradley reports [Bradley 1991] that the design of the Forth-based Open Boot has significantly influenced the thinking of the people at Sun Microsystems who are responsible for the low-level interfaces in the Unix kernel. Open Boot design philosophy is influencing driver interfaces, the device naming system, and the early startup and configuration mechanisms. There is even talk of unifying the syntax of several disparate kernel configuration files by using Forth syntax and including a subset Forth interpreter in the Unix kernel. People at Sun, who have worked with Open Boot, are impressed by the fact that the simple postfix syntax never "runs out of steam" or "paints you into a corner."

13.6.3 Mistakes or Desired Changes

Forth has a chameleon-like capacity to adapt to any particular application need. Indeed, the process of programming in Forth is to add to it application-oriented words at increasingly high levels until all the desired functionality is implemented. So, for any project, or even any particular programming group, any perceived needs will be promptly addressed. When looking for "mistakes" then, the most useful questions to ask are, "What were the things that a significant number of implementors have chosen to change or add?" and, "What are the characteristics of the language that may have prevented its wider acceptance?"

One of the first actions taken by the ANS Forth Technical Committee, when it formed in 1987, was to poll several hundred Forth implementors and users to determine their views on problems in the language that needed to be addressed. The issues cited fell into three categories: "mistakes" in one or both of the existing standards (e.g., incompatibilities introduced by FORTH-83 and anomalies such as an awkward specification for arguments to **DO**); obsolete restrictions in FORTH-83 (mainly the reliance on a 16-bit architecture); and a need for standards for such things as host file access, floating point arithmetic, and so forth. Features in the latter group were, by then, offered by most commercial and many public-domain systems, but as they had been developed independently, there was variance in usage and practice. ANS Forth has attempted to address all these concerns.

In retrospect, however, the lack of standard facilities for such things as floating-point arithmetic, which are covered by other languages, has probably impeded widespread acceptance of Forth. It's insufficient to point out that most commercial systems offer them, if the public perception of the language is formed by a standard that omits any mention of such features! From this perspective, the ANS Forth effort has come almost too late.

Another difficulty is that Forth's very identity is unclear: it is not only unconventional in appearance with its reliance on an overt stack architecture and postfix notation, but it broadly straddles territory conventionally occupied by not only languages, but also operating systems, editors, utilities, and the like, that most people are accustomed to viewing as independent entities. As a result, it's difficult to give a simple answer to the question of what it is.

The integrated character of Forth is viewed by its practitioners as its greatest asset. As Bradley [1991] expresses it,

> Forth has taught me that the 'firewalls' between different components of a programming environment (i.e., the different syntax used by compilers, linkers, command interpreters, etc.) are very annoying, and it is much more pleasant to have a uniform environment where you can do any thing at any level at any time, using the same syntax.

Duncan [1991], however, believes that this seamless integration of Forth the language, Forth the virtual machine, and Forth the programming environment is a significant barrier to mainstream acceptance. He notes that the same has been observed regarding Smalltalk versus C++:

> I have been using C++ for some months now, and the very things about C++ that frustrate me—the language is not written in itself (thus there is no way to use the building blocks for the programming environment as part of the application), the language is not truly extensible (e.g., the operators for the native data types cannot be overridden), and there is no programming environment that is smart about the language and class hierarchies—are the things that traditional language experts see as assets for C++ compared to Smalltalk!

As long as Forth users are convinced that its integrated, intrinsically interactive character is the key to their productivity as programmers, however, it is unlikely to change.

13.6.4 Problems

Some languages tend to be "levelers:" that is, a program written by an expert is unlikely to be significantly better (smaller, faster, and so forth) than one written by a novice. Chuck Moore once observed [Moore 1979], "...FORTH is an amplifier. A good programmer can do a fantastic job with FORTH; a bad programmer can do a disastrous one." Although never quantified, this observation has been repeated on many Forth projects across a broad programmer population, and has achieved the status of "folk wisdom" within the Forth community.

This tendency has given Forth the reputation of being "unmanageable," and there have been some highly publicized "Forth disasters" (notably Epson's VALDOCS project in the early 1980s). On close examination, however, the root causes of this, and other failed Forth projects, are the same problems that doom projects using other languages: inadequate definition, poor management, and unrealistic expectations.

There have also been a number of Forth successes, such as the facility management system for the Saudi Arabian airport mentioned before, in which a project that was estimated to contain 300,000 lines of executable FORTRAN, PLM, and assembly language software was totally redesigned, recoded in Forth, and tested to the satisfaction of the customer in only eighteen months [Rather 1985]. The result ran more than a factor of ten faster.

Jack Woehr, a senior project manager for Vesta Technologies, observes [Woehr 1991] that successful management of Forth projects demands nothing more than generally good management practices, plus, an appreciation of the special pride that Forth programmers take in their unusual productivity. Forth rewards a management style that believes a small team of highly skilled professionals can do a better job, in a shorter time, at less overall cost, than a large group of more junior programmers.

13.6.5 Implications for Current and Future Languages

What can be learned from 20 years experience with Forth? Forth stands as a living challenge to many of the assumptions guiding language developers. Its lack of rigid syntax and strong data typing, for example, are characteristically listed as major advantages by Forth programmers. The informal, interactive relationship between a Forth system and its programmer has been shown through many projects to shorten development times, in comparison with more conventional tools such as C. Despite the tremendous increases in the size and power of modern computers, Forth's combination of easy programming, compact size, and fast performance (characteristics often thought to be mutually exclusive) continues to earn a loyal following among software developers, especially for embedded systems.

REFERENCES

[ANS 1991] *Draft Proposed ANS Forth*, document number X3.215-199x, available from Global Engineering Documents, 2805 McGaw Ave., Irvine, CA, 92714.

[Baden, 1986] Baden, W., Hacking Forth, *Proceedings of the Eighth FORML Conference*, pub. by the Forth Interest Group, P. O. Box 8231, San Jose, CA 95155, 1986.

[Ballard, 1991] Ballard, B., and Hayes, J., Forth and space at the applied physics laboratory, in *Proceedings of the 1991 Rochester Forth Conference*, Rochester, NY: Forth Institute, 1991.

[Bradley, 1991] Bradley, M., private communication, 7/8/91.

[Brodie, 1981] Brodie, L., *Starting FORTH*, Englewood Cliffs, NJ: Prentice Hall, 1981.

[Brodie, 1984] Brodie, L., *Thinking FORTH*, Englewood Cliffs, NJ: Prentice Hall, 1984.

[Cox, 1987] Cox, William C., A case for NPOSs in real-time applications, *I&CS Magazine* (pub. by Chilton), Oct. 1987.

[Derick, 1982] Derick, M., and Baker, L., *The Forth Encyclopedia*. Mountain View, CA: The Mountain View Press, 1982.

[Dewar, 1970] Dewar, R., Indirect threaded code, *Communications of the ACM*, Vol. 18, No. 6, 1975.

[Dijkstra, 1970] Dijkstra, E. W., Structured programming, *Software Engineering Techniques*, Buxton, J. N., and Randell, B., eds. Brussels, Belgium, NATO Science Committee, 1969.

[Duff, 1984a] Duff, C., and Iverson, N., Forth meets Smalltalk, *Journal of Forth Application and Research*, Vol. 2, No. 1, 1984.

[Duff, 1984b] Duff, C., Neon—Extending Forth in new directions, *Proceedings of the 1984 Asilomar FORML Conference* pub. by the Forth Interest Group, P. O. Box 8231, San Jose, CA 95155, 1984.

[Dumse, 1984] Dumse, R., The R65F11 and F68K single chip FORTH computers, *Journal of Forth Application and Research*, Vol. 2, No. 1, 1984.

[Duncan, 1988] Duncan, R., (Gen'l Ed.). *The MS-DOS Encyclopedia*. Redmond, WA: Microsoft Press, 1988.

[Duncan, 1991] Duncan, R., private communication, 7/5/91.

[Electronics, 1976] RCA may offer memory-saving processor language. *Electronics*, Feb. 19, 1976, p. 26.

[FIG, 1978] *Forth Dimensions*, Vol. 1, No. 1, June/July 1978, pub. by the Forth Interest Group, P. O. Box 8231, San Jose, CA 95155.

[FIG, 1983] *Forth Dimensions*, Vol. 5, No. 3, Sept./Oct., 1983, pub. by the Forth Interest Group, P. O. Box 8231, San Jose, CA 95155.

[Gehrz, 1978] Gehrz, R. D., and Hackwell, J. A., Exploring the infrared universe from Wyoming. *Sky and Telescope* (June 1978).

[Golden, 1985] Golden, J., Moore, C. H., and Brodie, L., Fast processor chip takes its instructions directly from Forth, *Electronic Design*, Mar. 21, 1985.

[Hart, 1968] Hart, J. F. *et al.*, *Computer Approximations*. Malabar, FL: Krieger, 1968; (Second Edition), 1978.

[Hayes, 1987] Hayes, J. R., Fraeman, M. E., Williams, R. L., and Zaremba, T., A 32-bit Forth microprocessor, *Journal of Forth Application and Research*, Vol. 5, No. 1, 1987.

[Knuth, 1974] Knuth, D. E., Structured programming with **go to** statements. *Computing Reviews*, #4, 1974.

[Moore, 1958] Moore, C. H., and Lautman, D. A., Predictions for photographic tracking stations—APO Ephemeris 4 in *SAO Special Report #11*, G. F. Schilling, Ed., Cambridge, MA: Smithsonian Astrophysical Observatory, 1958.

[Moore, 1970a] Moore, C. H., and Leach, G. C., *FORTH—A Language for Interactive Computing*, Amsterdam, NY: Mohasco Industries Inc. (internal pub.) 1970.

[Moore, 1970b] Moore, C. H., *Programming a Problem-oriented Language*, Amsterdam, NY: Mohasco Industries Inc. (internal pub.) 1970.

[Moore, 1974a] Moore, C. H., FORTH: A new way to program a computer, *Astronomy & Astrophysics Supplement Series*, Vol. 15, No. 3, Jun. 1974. *Proceedings of the Symposium on Collection and Analysis of Astrophysical Data at NRAO*, Charlottesville, VA, Nov. 13–15, 1972.

[Moore, 1974b] Moore, C. H., and Rather, E. D., The FORTH program for spectral line observing on NRAO's 36 ft telescope, *Astronomy & Astrophysics Supplement Series*, Vol. 15, No. 3, June 1974, *Proceedings of the Symposium on the Collection and Analysis of Astrophysical Data*, Charlottesville, VA, Nov. 13–15, 1972.

[Moore, 1979] Moore, C. H., FORTH, The Last Ten Years and the Next Two Weeks..., Address at the first FORTH Convention, San Francisco, CA, October 1979, reprinted in *Forth Dimensions*, Vol. 1, No. 6, 1980.

[Moore, 1983] Moore, C. H., Letter to the Editor of *Forth Dimensions*, Vol. 3, No. 1, 1983.

[Paloski, 1986] Paloski, W. H., Odette, L., and Krever, A. J., Use of a Forth-based Prolog for real-time expert system, *Journal of Forth Application and Research*, Vol. 4, No. 2, 1986.

[Pountain, 1987] Pountain, R., *Object Oriented Forth*. New York: Academic Press, 1987.

[Parnas, 1971] Parnas, D. L., Information distribution aspects of design methodology, *Proceedings of IFIP 1971 Congress*. Ljubljana, Yugoslavia.

[Phys. Sci. 1975] Graphics in Kitt form, *Physical Science*, Nov. 1975, p. 10.

[Rather, 1972] Rather, E. D., and Moore, C. H., *FORTH programmer's guide*, NRAO Computer Division Internal Report #11, 1972. A later version, with J. M. Hollis added as a coauthor, was Internal Report #17, 1974.

[Rather, 1976a] Rather, E. D., and Moore, C. H., The FORTH approach to operating systems, *Proceedings of the ACM*, Oct. 1976, pp. 233–240.

[Rather, 1976b] Rather, E. D., and Moore, C. H., High-level programming for microprocessors, *Proceedings of Electro 76*.

[Rather, 1985] Rather, E. D., Fifteen programmers, 400 computers, 36,000 sensors and Forth, *Journal of Forth Application and Research*, Vol. 3, No. 2, 1985. Available from the Forth Institute, P.ÊO. Box 27686, Rochester, NY, 14627.

[Sperry, 1991] Sperry, T., An enemy of the people. *Embedded Systems Programming*, Vol. 4, No. 12, Dec. 1991.

[Taylor, 1980] Taylor, A., Alternative software making great strides. *Computerworld*, 12/?/80.

[TRS-80, 1979] Press release published in "Software and Peripherals" section of *Minicomputer News*, 8/30/79.

[Veis, 1960] Veis, G., and Moore, C. H., SAO differential orbit improvement program, *Tracking Programs and Orbit Determination Seminar Proceedings*, Pasadena, CA: Jet Propulsion Laboratories, 1960.

[Woehr, 1991] Woehr, J. J., Managing Forth projects, *Embedded Systems Programming*, May 1991.

[Wood, 1986] Wood, R. J., Developing real-time process control in space. *Journal of Forth Application and Research*, Vol. 4, No. 2, 1986.

BIBLIOGRAPHY

Brodie, L., *Starting FORTH*, Englewood Cliffs, NJ: Prentice Hall, 1981.

Brodie, L., *Thinking FORTH*, Englewood Cliffs, NJ: Prentice Hall, 1984.

Feierbach, G., and Thomas, P., *Forth Tools & Applications*, Reston, VA: Reston Computer Books, 1985.

Haydon, G. B., *All about Forth: An Annotated Glossary*, La Honda CA: Mountain View Press, 1990.

Kelly, M. G., and Spies, N., *FORTH: A Text and Reference*, Englewood Cliffs, NJ: Prentice Hall, 1986.

Knecht, K., *Introduction to Forth*, Howard Sams & Co., Indiana, 1982.

Kogge, P. M., An architectural trail to threaded code systems, *IEEE Computer*, Mar. 1982.

Koopman, P., *Stack Computers, The New Wave*, Chichester, West Sussex, England: Ellis Horwood Ltd. 1989

Martin, T., *A Bibliography of Forth References*, (Third Edition), Rochester, NY: Institute for Applied Forth Research, 1987.

McCabe, C. K., *Forth Fundamentals* (2 volumes), Oregon: Dilithium Press, 1983.

Moore, C. H., The evolution of FORTH—An unusual language, *Byte*, Aug. 1980.

Ouverson, M. (Ed)., *Dr. Dobbs Toolbook of Forth*, Redwood City, CA: M&T Press, Vol. 1, 1986; Vol. 2, 1987.

Pountain, R., *Object Oriented Forth*, New York: Academic Press, 1987.

Rather, E. D., Forth programming language, *Encyclopedia of Physical Science & Technology* (Vol. 5), New York: Academic Press, 1987.

Rather, E. D., FORTH, *Computer Programming Management*, Auerbach Publishers, Inc., 1985.

Terry, J. D., *Library of Forth Routines and Utilities*, New York: Shadow Lawn Press, 1986.

Tracy, M., and Anderson, A., *Mastering Forth* (Second Edition), New York: Brady Books, 1989.

Winfield, A., *The Complete Forth*, New York: Wiley Books, 1983.

Forth Organizations

ACM/SIGForth, Association for Computing Machinery, 1515 Broadway, New York, NY 10036. Publishers of the quarterly *SIGForth* newsletter, sponsor of annual conference (usually in March).

The Forth Institute, 70 Elmwood Dr., Rochester, NY 14611. Publishers of the *Journal of Forth Application and Research* and sponsors of the annual Rochester Forth Conference (usually in June). *Proceedings* of these Conferences are also published.

The Forth Interest Group, P. O. Box 8231, San Jose, CA 95155. Publishers of *Forth Dimensions* (newsletter), source of various books on Forth and public-domain Forth systems; also coordinator for worldwide chapters and sponsor of annual FORML conference (usually in November).

On-line Resources

BIX (ByteNet) (for information call 800-227-2983) Forth Conference. Access BIX via TymNet, then type **j Forth**. Type **FORTH** at the **:** prompt.

CompuServe (for information call 800-848-8990) Forth Forum sponsored by Creative Solutions, Inc. Type **GO FORTH** at the ! prompt.

GEnie (for information call 800-638-9636) Forth Round Table. Call GEnie local node, then type **FORTH**. Sponsored by the Forth Interest Group. Also connected via cross-postings with Internet (comp.lang.forth) and other Forth conferences.

AUTHORS' NOTE (7/95)

The purpose of this addendum is to present a few significant events that have occurred since its original presentation:

1. Concerning Table 13.3 (Section 13.3.2), the systems listed for Bradley Forthware are now available from FirmWorks, of Mountain View, CA, and Palo Alto Shipping is no longer in business.
2. The Forth-based underlying technology in Sun Microsystems' "Open Boot" (Section 13.3.3.1) was standardized as IEEE Std 1275-1994, *IEEE Standard for Boot (Initialization Configuration) Firmware: Core Requirements and Practices*, and is available from IEEE, 345 E. 47th St., New York, NY 10017, USA.
3. ANS Forth (Section 13.5.1) received final approval March 24, 1994, and is now available as *American National Standard for Information Systems—Programming Languages—Forth*, Document X3.215-1994, from American National Standards Institute, 11 W. 42nd St., 13th Floor, New York, NY 10036.
4. The BIX and GEnie bulletin boards are now replaced by the Internet newsgroup **comp.lang.forth**.

TRANSCRIPT OF PRESENTATION

SESSION CHAIR HELEN GIGLEY: Elizabeth Rather holds A.B. and M.A. degrees from the University of California, Berkeley, and an M.B.A. from Pepperdine University. Her programming experiences span FORTRAN, COBOL, BASIC, APL, NELIAC, over a dozen different assemblers, and of course, Forth. She met her first computer in 1962, the ORACLE, at Oak Ridge National Laboratory. It had vacuum tubes and reels of tape for memory. She managed data analysis for a physics group there, and went on to computing jobs in the Astronomy Department at UC, Berkeley. Later jobs included processing student records for the College of Letters and Science at Berkeley and the University of Arizona. Her first minicomputer experience was in 1971, at the National Radio Astronomy Observatory's, Tucson, Arizona, Division. Here she met Chuck Moore, the inventor of Forth, who was sitting on a high stool in front of the machine. This encounter, and the language called Forth, changed her career. Ms. Rather has been president of Forth Inc. since 1988, where she has managed the development of products and services for scientific and industrial computer applications. Currently, Forth Inc. is introducing a software development system for process control and automated manufacturing.

ELIZABETH RATHER: (SLIDE 1) I want to start out by introducing ourselves briefly. I'm sorry my two coauthors couldn't make it. They consist of Chuck Moore, who was the inventor of Forth—and with the discussion of "designed," with respect to languages and whatever, I will stick to "invention" as being the correct word in this case. He certainly never "designed" it in the sense of thinking it through. I'm not sure that if he had, he would have ever gotten started. He conceived of it, from the outset, as a personal productivity tool that, in the long run, got out of control, as some of them tend

SLIDE 1

History of the Forth Language

- 1969 — Forth name given to Chuck Moore's programming language at Mohasco Industries
- 1971 — First stand-alone Forth at National Radio Astronomy Observatory
- 1972 — First multiuser Forth
- 1973 — FORTH, Inc. founded
- 1977 — First off-the-shelf product from FORTH, Inc.
- 1978 — Forth Interest Group founded
- 1979 — First published standard (FORTH79)
- 1980 — *BYTE* special issue on Forth
- 1981 — *Starting FORTH* published; has sold 125,000 copies
- 1983 — Latest published standard (FORTH83) First issue of *Journal of Forth Applications and Research*
- 1987 — ANS Forth TC approved and started work
- 1989 — SIGForth holds first conference
- 1991 — dpANS Forth published for public review

Evolution of Forth 2

SLIDE 2

to do. For the last ten years, he has been involved in doing hardware implementations of various Forth based processors for general and specific applications, none of which have been commercially successful. Don Colburn, my other coauthor, was one of the founders of The Forth Interest Group, and one of the earliest independent developers of commercial Forth systems. He currently is the proprietor of a company that sells the most successful version of Forth for Macintoshes and also Nubus boards. He also works as a teacher's aide in an elementary school in Maryland one day a week.

(SLIDE 2) The history of Forth goes back, actually, a long way, as you can see in the paper—which I am not going to entirely summarize. Forth had precedents way back in the early '60s, in work that Chuck did at the Smithsonian Astrophysical Observatory and other places. It first acquired the name "Forth" in 1969. It was supposed to suggest a "fourth generation" computer. At the time, the "third generation" was big, and he saw the fourth generation as being distributed small computers—which in many respects was accurate. Just as "Schemer" became "Scheme," his compiler would only handle five. So the "u" went away. There has been a lot of history, much of which is covered in the paper. My talk, like others, is going to be in the form of footnotes. On the other hand, you can say that by seeing this slide, you can go home now or get ready for dinner. But, I do have a few more remarks.

(SLIDE 3) Chuck is an unusual person, and it's been a great treat knowing him. But I could not talk about Forth without talking a little bit about his philosophy and what some of his attitudes were. I have summarized it there, but just to give you a little flavor, I will read a couple of excerpts from a

Chuck's Philosophy & Goals

GOAL: Replace "vast hierarchy" of languages, compilers, /assemblers, OSs, editors ... with a single layer having 2 elements:

- programmer-to-Forth interface
- Forth-to-machine interface

PRINCIPLES:

- Keep it simple!
- Do not speculate!
- Do it yourself!

Evolution of Forth 3

SLIDE 3

Everything vs. Anything

CONVENTIONAL APPROACH:

You can't change your tools, so they must be able to handle *everything* you might do.

(big, slow, complex, hard to learn & maintain)

FORTH'S APPROACH:

Make the tool easily adaptable to do *anything* you need.

(small, fast, simple, flexible; application-oriented tool sets)

Evolution of Forth 4

SLIDE 4

book he wrote in about 1970, which was never published. He said, "In connection with these principles, do not put code in your program that might be used." He was very much opposed to the notion of "hooks"—people putting hooks in and making provisions for something that might come up in the future—he thinks that simply leads to unsanitary code. He says:

> Do not leave hooks on which you can hang extensions. The things you *might* want to do are infinite; that means that each has 0 probability of realization. If you need an extension later, you can code it later—and probably do a better job than if you did it now. And if someone else adds the extension, will he notice the hooks you left? Will you document this aspect of your program?

Well, certainly not. And even more "Chuckish" was his notion of writing everything himself. In the entire time I've known him, which is well over 20 years, he has yet to use any code that actually came from a manufacturer with their computer, including their assembler or their math (multiply and divide) routines. (In the '70s, you had to have software multiply, divide, and so on.) He said:

> The conventional approach, enforced to a greater or lesser extent, is that you should use a standard subroutine. I say you should write your own subroutines.
>
> Before you can write your own subroutines, you have to know how. This means, to be practical, that you've written it before; which makes it difficult to get started. But give it a try. After writing the same subroutine a dozen times on as many computers and languages you'll be pretty good at it.

(SLIDE 4) More particularly, his view was that the application programmer, who was the target of his effort, is an intelligent, responsible, creative person, who deserves and needs empowering tools. It was his perception, based on a number of years of experience, that the software tools that were provided, were generally designed with the view of the programmer as being simple minded, at best, and irresponsible in most cases (and possibly even with criminal intent), who needed externally imposed discipline, in order to stay out of trouble. He had quite the opposite approach.

(SLIDE 5) The language that he built over the years had some unique features. This is a summary of some of them. They were unique for Chuck in that, although he spent a good part of his career around academic science, it was not computer science, and he really has never been involved in the reading and writing of papers, where these kinds of ideas are disseminated. Nonetheless, he came up with a lot of them entirely on his own. I remember distinctly when I was giving papers on Forth in the early '70s, somebody said, "What you are talking about sounds an awful lot like structured programming;" and I said, "What's that?" And they directed me to the appropriate papers, which I read with great interest and passed along to Chuck. He said, "Well I don't see what all the fuss is about; it just looks like good programming to me." And I think that is fairly representative of his ideas. He was working empirically, trying to make the kinds of tools that he saw being necessary.

(SLIDE 6) The first running, full stand-alone Forth system at NRAO (National Radio Astronomy Observatory) that I worked on, which was really the first stand-alone Forth system, was controlling a radio telescope. I found out, much to my astonishment, last Fall, that system is still in use. Unfortunately, they are about to tear down the telescope. So for all I know, the program is going to outlive the telescope—which is kind of unusual.

(SLIDE 7) Relevant to Chuck's remark about writing the same program a number of times, he actually implemented Forth personally on over 17 computers. I tried to research this list as best I could; there may be some that aren't on it. But he wrote the entire system for this many computers, and other people have written many more since. In doing one of these implementations, you had to start off by designing the assembler and writing an assembler—and then coding about a hundred assembly language primitives using that assembler, then getting it all to work. Forth was written in Forth. You used a friendly Forth computer to generate Forth for the new computer that you were

Early Uses, Independent Discoveries and Heresies

- **"Structured Programming" — 196?-72**
- **"Type-free" data structures — 196?-70**
- **Postfix notation & dual stack operation — 1968**
- **Indirect threaded code — 1970**
- **Improved integer math operators (*/, /MOD, etc.) — 1970**
- **Completely self-contained environment — 1971**
- **Non-preemptive real-time multitasking/multiuser executive — 1972**
- **Object-oriented techniques — 1976-8**

Evolution of Forth 5

SLIDE 5

First Forths at NRAO

- **Two computers, connected by a 1-bit link (1971-2).**
- **Concurrent command & control of 36' radio telescope, plus data acquisition & graphical analysis.**
- **Upgraded to single PDP-11 w/ 4 terminals in 1973.**

Operator
Observer
H-316
DDP-116
Data acq. & anal.
Antenna & dome control

Evolution of Forth

SLIDE 6

working on. But nonetheless, that's a lot of work to do. What's really astonishing is that he did this in approximately two weeks for each one—including writing the software multiply and divide routines—which were invariably faster that the ones than came from the manufacturer, which is a great source of pride to him. I would also like to point out that on several of these computers: the Honeywell 316, the (Honeywell) DDP 116, the Varian 620, the Honeywell Level 6, the Intel 8086, and the Raytheon PTS-100—which is a pretty obscure computer—on all of these, Forth was the first high-level language running on that processor. We were working on the 8086, while it was still in prototype, and in fact, helped Intel find a couple of bugs in the part.

(SLIDE 8) This is a list of some of the early projects so that you will see what kinds of applications influenced the early growth of Forth. Unlike Icon, we very definitely had applications in mind. Forth has, from day one, been designed for use in applications, and the applications in which it was used in the early days had a lot of influence. So it's been very well integrated with the real world. We traveled a lot to do these systems. Chuck built a personal portable computer in the mid-70s out of one of the first LSI-11s, which he packaged in a suitcase, and put a floppy disk in another suitcase. We carried that with us to go and install the systems on these various computers.

(SLIDE 9) As a result of those applications, and the influences of those kinds of applications, the critical factors in Forth became: operating in a resource-constrained environment; placing a high degree of emphasis on size and compactness of code; operating with very high performance

Chuck's Forths

Year	Model	Forth Applications
1970-71	Honeywell H316	Data acquisition, on-line analysis w/ graphics terminal
1971	Honeywell DDP116	Radio telescope control
1971-2	IBM 370/30	Data analysis
1972	Varian 620	Optical telescope control and instrumentation
1972	HP2100	Instrumentation
1972-3	Modcomp	Data analysis
1973	PDP-11	Radio telescope ctrl., data acquisition, analysis, graphics
1973	DG Nova	Data acquisition and analysis
1974	SPC-16	Ground control of balloon-borne telescope
1975	SDS-920	Antenna control
1975	Prime	Environmental controls
1976	Four-Phase	Data entry and data base management
1977	Interdata Series 32	Data base management
1977	CA LSI-4	Business systems
1978	Honeywell Level 6	Data entry and data base management
1978	Intel 8086	Graphics and Image Processing
1980	Raytheon PTS-100	Airline display and workstations

Evolution of Forth 7

SLIDE 7

Early, Influential Projects

- **Business Data Base: Cybek Corp., 1974**
  DG/Nova, 32 terminals (upgraded to 64), 300 Mb disk
  >100,000 transactions/day, <1 sec. response times.
- **Image Processing: Navy, NASA, RGO, 1976-80**
  PDP-11s, various image processing equipment
  Independently derived OOPS
  High-speed processing, complex algorithms
- **Instrumentation & Control: NRAO, Univ.'s, EG&G, etc., 1970's**
  High data rates
  Fast multitasking, allowing analysis concurrent w/ data taking

Evolution of Forth 8

SLIDE 8

SLIDE 9

SLIDE 10

requirements, as the kinds of applications we were working on were very, very time critical; a lot of specialized custom I/O: it's very easy to write and add I/O drivers to a Forth system; and being an R&D environment, it was really important to be able to change things quickly.

(SLIDE 10) The internal design principles that arose out of that involved a very simple language with minimal syntax. In fact, very early on when I was working on Forth, Jean Sammet wrote a book on programming languages. I wrote to her and said, "You ought to know about Forth," and she wrote back and said, "Well it's not a language; it doesn't have syntax". It, in fact, *doesn't* have very much syntax. It is, nonetheless, quite useful. Certainly, now that we found out that it does structured programming, we can say that is what it does. It is extraordinarily modular, and out of that modularity there is an effect in that programming size is far from linear. You have words calling other words. You have, in a large application, perhaps thousands of them. A word is sort of like a routine; it's sort of like a command in a language; in fact, we blur the distinctions between the two—but you develop a very, very rich vocabulary of application-oriented words in Forth. They are organized in a sort of pyramiding structure, where at the very high level you have a huge amount of leverage—by writing a line or two of code, or using just a few words, you accomplish, in fact, quite a great deal. You can do very high level operations. And—perhaps the most controversial—there is no explicit data typing in Forth at all. That flies very much against a lot of conventional wisdom, I realize. And it is very astounding to people that meet Forth for the first time. But people that have used Forth extensively find that it is one of the most valued features of the languages. While working on the ANSI Standard Report for Forth, our Technical Committee had a lot of input from a lot of sources—people wanting all their favorite word-sets or whatever. We had very, very little pressure—almost none at all—to do anything about type-checking.

(SLIDE 11) I'm not going to try to teach you the language. I will mention briefly some of the principal elements of it. One of the more unusual features is that it does include an integrated assembler in it, so that you can drop down to the assembler level at any time. It doesn't look like the manufacturer's assembler, usually, but it does produce real code.

The next three slides are from the book, *Starting Forth*, probably one of the most influential books in Forth, written by Leo Brodie, published in the early '80s, and it sold about 120,000 copies. It was very popular, but in addition to being a light-hearted book, it also includes quite a great deal of information—such as an explanation of the relationship between the compiler, the interpreter, and execution in Forth.

Elements of Forth

- **Dictionary**
  Linked list of compiled word definitions
- **Push-down stacks**
  Data stack for parameter passing
  Return stack for return addresses & other uses
- **Interpreters**
  Text interpreter for commands, compiler, data
  Address interpreter for run-time
- **Assembler**
  Integrated, resident, interactive
- **Disk support**
  1024-byte blocks for source, data (OS independence)

Evolution of Forth 11

SLIDE 11

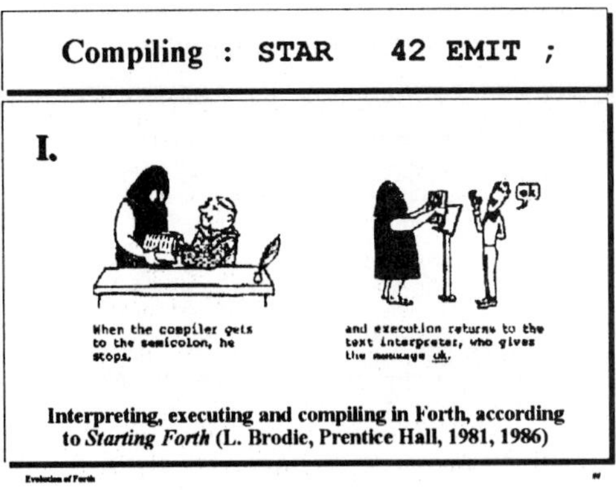

Interpreting, executing and compiling in Forth, according to *Starting Forth* (L. Brodie, Prentice Hall, 1981, 1986)

SLIDE 12

(SLIDE 12) This is our first occasion to see a Forth definition. A definition begins with colon and ends with semicolon. The word following the colon is the name of the new word being defined, and this is what it is going to do. 42 goes on a push-down stack and becomes the argument to EMIT which is going to send it to the terminal. This is how these things are put together.

(SLIDE 13) The compiler actually executes the word : (colon), which creates the definition. It goes on until it's terminated by a ; (semicolon).

(SLIDE 14) Finally, that's done, and execution returns to the interpreter which then tells you "OK," at the terminal. In fact, that word is now compiled and is available for execution immediately. This is an interactive system that supports incremental compilation and it makes it very easy to test programs.

(SLIDE 15) This is a look at one of the more unusual language features, which is the ability in Forth to make custom data-types of a sort. Such definitions have two parts: There is a *compile-time* behavior and a *run-time* behavior—which will be shared by all instances of a class of words that this is defining. Here is an example: we are making an array of pairs of cells and the size of the array comes in on the stack. We make the definition, make a copy of the size, and compile it so that you can use it if you want to for range checking at run-time (although I don't think I did in this example). Then, you multiply that size by two, because there are going to be two cells for each thing, and you allot that much space. That's all you do at compile-time. Now at run-time, when a member of this class executes, it begins executing with an index on the stack that's supplied externally, and the address

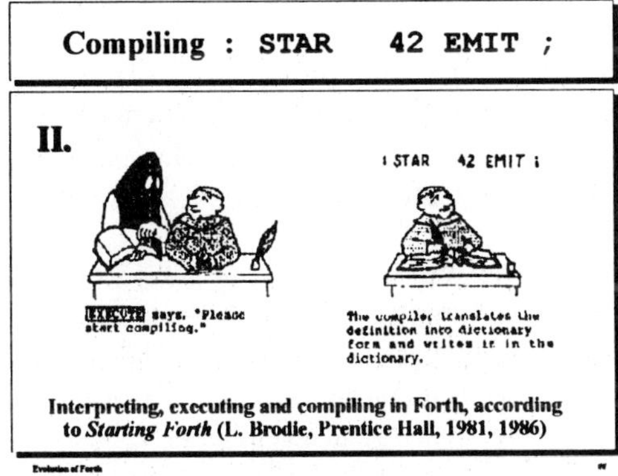

Interpreting, executing and compiling in Forth, according to *Starting Forth* (L. Brodie, Prentice Hall, 1981, 1986)

SLIDE 13

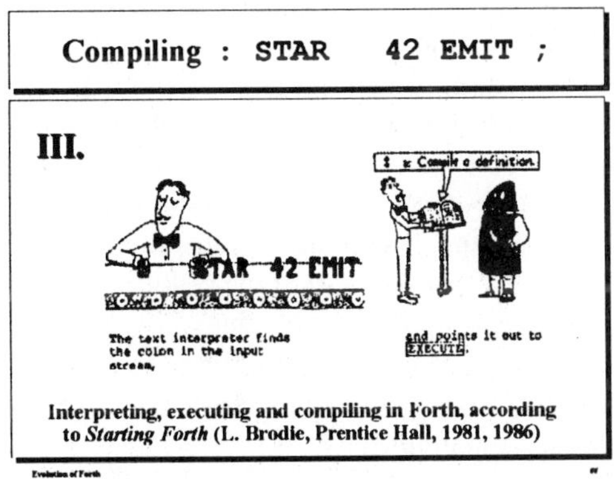

Interpreting, executing and compiling in Forth, according to *Starting Forth* (L. Brodie, Prentice Hall, 1981, 1986)

SLIDE 14

User-defined Data Structures

Syntax:

```
: name    <compile-time behavior>  DOES>  <run-
   time behavior> ;
```

Example:

```
: 2ARRAY ( n)   CREATE DUP ,   2* CELLS ALLOT
     DOES> ( i a - a')  SWAP 2* CELLS + ;
```

Use:

```
1000 CONSTANT N    N 2ARRAY DATA
: SHOW   N 0 DO   I 5 MOD 0= IF  CR THEN     I
     DATA 2@ 10 D.R   LOOP ;
```

SLIDE 15

User-defined Compiler Directives

- Used to perform actions at compile-time.
- Designated by the word IMMEDIATE.
- The bold words in the following definition are IMMEDIATE:

```
: SHOW    N 0 DO  I 5 MOD 0= IF  CR THENI
  DATA 2@ 10 D.R  LOOP ;
```

Example of new compiler directive:

```
: -IF    POSTPONE NOT   POSTPONE IF ;
  IMMEDIATE
```

SLIDE 16

at the beginning of the array that is supplied internally, and returns the address of the item. And it does it by multiplying the index by two, converting that to cells, and adding it the address. So these things are very simple and it shows how that's used in the definition. But some of these can be very complex. You can make datatypes that live as bits on an I/O interface or very elaborate things that are application dependent. It's very easy to define such structures.

(SLIDE 16) Another interesting feature is that it's easy to add compiler directives; compiler directives are structure words. And here, for example, we have `DO` and `LOOP`, and `IF` and `THEN`. If you wanted to make a negative `IF`, you could do that very simply by defining `POSTPONE NOT POSTPONE IF`. In these two cases, `POSTPONE` makes a definition which is going to compile a reference to `NOT` and a reference to `IF`. When the word containing `NOT IF` is executed, which is executed at compile-time to create the structure. So it is very easy for a programmer to add extensions, even to the compiler.

(SLIDE 17) Here is a somewhat more complex example. This shows a number of the different logical structures in it. It also has a number of application-dependent words in it. Without telling you all those words are, I think you can probably get the sense of the definition. But we have here, an indefinite `BEGIN UNTIL` loop; this will work until `FULL` returns `true`. The next loop is going to run from 0 to 24; it's a `DO LOOP` that begins *here*, and ends *there*. This is a !("Store") operator; it's going to store the value `BLACKBIRD` in the location `PIE`, and then do `BAKE`. Here is a `conditional`—when it is opened, then `BIRDS WILL SING`. After `PIE` is a @ ("fetch") operation. You fetch a value, compare it against the value `DAINTY`; if the result of the comparison is `true`, then you execute `KING` and `SERVE`, and so on.

(SLIDE 18) Many Forths have operating system capabilities. All of the Forths that I have personally ever worked on have been multi-tasking, multi-user systems, although not all Forths are that way. Many Forths are completely native, that is, they run with no host operating system. Many others run concurrently with another operating system, and there are versions available right now for most processors and most of the popular operating systems.

(SLIDE 19) These are some of the recent contemporary uses of Forth. The big areas where it is useful are, not surprisingly, those for which it was developed, that is, embedded systems and high performance control systems. Every Federal Express Courier carries one in his hand, when he picks up his package. Every Sun workstation has a Forth system on its mother-board. The "Open Boot" is currently the subject of an IEEE standard (1275) that's in development, and a number of VME system people are picking that up. There have been a lot of space applications; the control systems, just as

Is Forth Readable?

```
: SONG   6 PENCE  SING  BEGIN
   RYE POCKET !  FULL UNTIL
  24 0 DO  BLACKBIRD PIE ! LOOP  BAKE
  OPEN IF  BIRDS SING  THEN
     PIE @ DAINTY = IF
      KING SERVE THEN ;
```

Evolution of Forth 17

SLIDE 17

OS Issues

- **Native vs. co-resident operation**
  Native systems extremely fast
  Market pressures often demand OS compatibility
  Use of blocks provides transportability
- **Multitasking**
  Non-preemptive task scheduling
  Multitasking can run within a co-resident Forth

Evolution of Forth 18

SLIDE 18

an example, the King Khaled International Airport in Riyadh, Saudi Arabia, is a system that involves approximately 500 computers. That project was done actually here in the Boston area, in the mid 1980s. There was a program that was about 300,000 lines of FORTRAN and Assembly language, that did not work fast enough or well enough. That program was replaced with an all Forth system. The 300,000 line program was, in fact, replaced by a Forth system which was written from scratch, tested, and installed in about an 18-month period, and consisted of about 30,000 lines of code. The leverage I was speaking of earlier results in considerable compactness of code, even to do a very complex application. It supports rapid prototyping very easily and works out very well in those kinds of applications.

(SLIDE 20) Quantitatively, it is very hard to measure how many people are using Forth. Our best estimates are perhaps a few tens of thousands of people. But, it is very difficult to track them all. There have been two surveys. These two magazines do surveys every even numbered year. So, I assume they did it in 1992, but I haven't seen the results yet. I just wanted to give you some measure of where it is, and the answer is, it is a minority, but it is hanging in there.

(SLIDE 21) The purpose of listing some suppliers of Forth systems is really, as much as anything, to give you a feeling for some of the diversity of some of the implementations available. There is a very definite family tree here. I was admiring the work in the Lisp paper—which I heard about—sketching out a family tree. I would love to do this for Forth. There are several major sources

Contemporary Uses of Forth

- **Embedded Systems**
  Federal Express' "SuperTracker"
  Sun Microsystems' "Open Boot"
  Issues: efficiency in resource-constrained environments, easy debugging of custom hardware
- **Space**
  >30 known successful shuttle & satellite applications by NASA, Johns Hopkins APL, others
  Issues: flexibility, modularity (thorough testing)
- **Control systems**
  King Khaled International Airport
  GM/Saturn's HVAC system
  Issues: security, flexibility, quick development time

Evolution of Forth 19

SLIDE 19

Extent of Use

Source: Dr. Dobbs Journal Survey, 1990
- 12% of readers use Forth
- Forth places 15th of 20 languages, ahead of Modula 2, Smalltalk, APL, Actor, Eiffel

Source: EDN (Cahners Research) Report, 1990
- 11% of readers use Forth
- Forth places 10th of 15 languages, ahead of Prolog, Modula 2, PL/1, APL, Smalltalk

Evolution of Forth 20

SLIDE 20

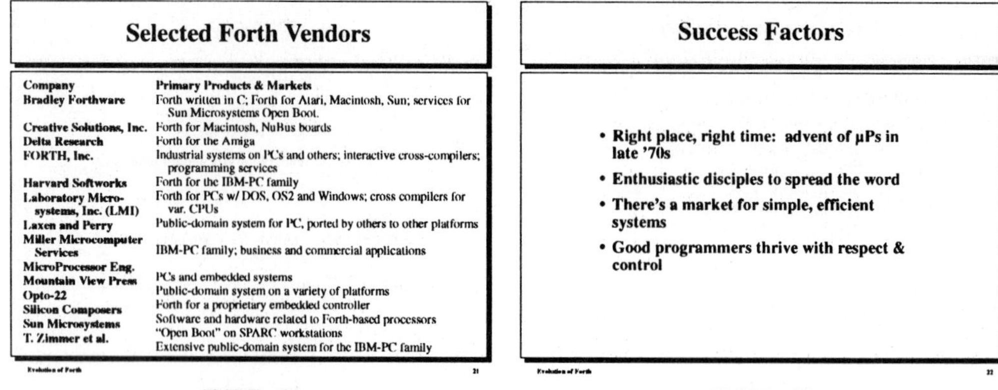

SLIDE 21

SLIDE 22

of things, ranging from some of the early commercial implementations to some of the public domain systems. There has been actually a considerable "war" in the Forth community between the vendors and suppliers of public domain systems. Remember, the early work on Forth was at a government laboratory so, therefore, the concept is public domain, but there have been a number of commercial applications. The fans of the public domain systems believe that it is in fact immoral to make money off it. Those of us who do make money off it, think that tends to contribute to language improvement and growth over time. So, it's sort of a "communist" versus "capitalist" issue that can be debated at length.

(SLIDE 22) Looking at a few success factors. Why has Forth survived now for over 20 years? It came along, in terms of its real promulgation, at the right time. In the late '70s, it was beginning to mature—and that was a time when microprocessors were there and available. They were more or less mother-naked as far as software was considered, and a lot of people became interested. A lot of very enthusiastic Forth users have spread the word, in spite of the fact that there has never been any major deep-pocket corporate or academic sponsorship at all—worse luck. And, I think, as much as anything else, the fact that it survived, means that there is a market for this kind of thing. And to look at what kind of market that is, I think it's fair to ask what kind of problem it's trying to solve. In the Ada talk, there was the issue of 2,500 line programs versus, say, 25 million line programs. And as I think I've said, these things in the world of Forth are not linear. Something that might be a 300,000 line FORTRAN and assembler program translates into 30,000 lines of Forth. It's very nonlinear there, and Forth does tend to shrink the problem. Nonetheless, it is probably true that for very, very large programs, Forth is not the best approach. I think there is the question of whether your programming philosophy, or the philosophy of your shop, really, is the theory that "a million monkeys with word processors can produce Shakespeare"—and that's going to lead to one kind of view of what software tools you need—versus the "Marine Corps" philosophy—"we need a few good programmers"—kind of thing. And that's really the philosophy that Forth is attempting to enable and support.

(SLIDE 23) So, why hasn't it taken over the world? Well, it's very different. You can write the language that looks a lot like all the other languages, and people say, "Oh yeah, I understand that." And Forth is really quite different. There are a lot of heresies, such as the lack of data typing—regardless of how well they work in practice. People are sometimes uncomfortable looking at it from the outside; it's hard to visualize how well it can work. As I said, there have never been any major corporate or academic sponsors of it, although it's used, you know we conduct guerilla warfare whenever we can; it's used in virtually all the major corporations and educational institutions. It's hanging in there!

Constraining Factors

- Too different, too many heresies
- No major corporate or academic sponsors
- Successful users regarded it as a "secret weapon"
- Unsuccessful users found it an easy scapegoat
- Diverse dialects prevented development of widely used libraries

Mixed blessing:

- Public domain versions were widely circulated in the '80s, but created a "hobbyist" image of Forth

SLIDE 23

Prognosis

- Adoption of ANS Forth will help several ways:
  - Standard interface will promote development of libraries
  - Management fears of "non-standard languages" defused
  - Opportunity for new textbooks and other support aids
  - More common culture for Forth programmers
- Forth will persist as a minority language, able to create "miracles" for those who need them.

SLIDE 24

But a lot of our users have, in fact, been reluctant to give away to the competition the secret to their success—why they can do so much more with so much less. There have also been a few projects that have not worked out, and it's been awfully easy in that case, when you have a failed project that was done in a minority language, to say, "Well of course it failed, you used that funny language." There has been some amount of publicity about a small number of "Forth disasters." I doubt that there have been any languages that haven't had their share of project disasters. If you are using the language that 99 percent of people use, however, and you have a disaster, it's a lot harder to blame it on the language, isn't it? In fact, I have looked at some of the publicized, so-called Forth disasters. I know a number of people that were involved in at least one of them, and the problems there were the same problems in just about all disaster projects, having to do with management problems, design problems, things like that. Then, finally, there has been the problem of diverse dialects. There have been several industry standards. There was one in 1979 called *FORTH-79*, that was picked up by several implementers, a much better one in 1983 called *FORTH-83*. For the last six years, there has been an ANS Forth committee (at) work.

I do want to extend my condolences to the new Smalltalk [ANS] committee. People shook their heads and clucked pityingly at me when we got started [on ANS Forth], and I'm going to do the same thing for you—and you'll find out why. We do have a draft standard out for public review—for the third time, right now—and most of us on the committee feel like "this is it!" I think that's going to help.

In the early '80s, there were a lot of public domain versions that were circulated, and that was, as I say, a mixed blessing. That got a lot of people familiar with Forth who might not have otherwise been. However, the Forth they became familiar with was of very limited functionality, sometimes poorly implemented, and certainly not a well-supported system. And if people have the notion that, "When you've seen one Forth, you've seen them all," they can hardly be blamed for getting a poor impression. However, there have been quite a number of very good implementations, both commercial systems and some of the public domain systems. I think that some people should have perhaps looked a little harder. It has been a factor in the history of the language.

(SLIDE 24) Finally, the prognosis. Adoption of ANS Forth is going to help a lot, I think, making up for some of the deficiencies. I think it's a very good standard—of course, being the chair of the committee—we've had a very, very diverse membership on the committee, from all of the dialects and so on. We have made some compromises in a number of places, but I think overall the standard is very clean and very strong. It's unfortunately about 250 pages long. *FORTH-79* was about 30 pages.

FORTH-83 was about 50 pages. At 250 (pages), this is becoming hefty. But we have done one thing that I think was very successful, and that I would recommend to some of you involved in this effort: that is, we've made it a layered standard; we have a number of optional word-sets. Since Forth was originally designed for resource-constrained environments, there's still strong feeling among Forth users that it should be possible to run Forth in a very small system. And in fact, there are Forths available that run on 8-bit single-chip micro-controllers. That is, the Forth runs on it. The whole thing, the compiler, the assembler, the whole nine yards, can run on an 8-bit single-chip micro-controller, in maybe 8 or 10K. Now, this is not one of the more full functioned Forths, but all the essentials are there. The core required word set in the ANSI standard can run in that kind of environment. Yet, you can put on optional word sets, for floating point, for host OS file access, for memory allocation, whatever you want. There are a number of these things available. I think that has been a very successful concept.

If you talked to a Forth programmer and asked him why he's so . . . people have accused Forth programmers of being sort of wild-eyed fanatics and there is some measure of accuracy in that. If you ask them why, the major reason is that they feel *empowered*. Your typical Forth programmer (and I'm not one—I have been, but I'm a mere manager now) feels that they are suddenly "superman": they've been in the phone booth and they've put on the cape. And all of a sudden, they have the power of ten. I was talking, just last night, to the local Boston Forth Interest Group, and I raised this question—and they all said that they keep getting this from customers and prospective customers, clients, whatever. A lot of them are consultants in corporations trying to persuade their bosses that they ought to be able to use Forth: that they could do in a few weeks what in C is going to take them months. There is a huge wealth of anecdotal evidence, to the effect that this is true. Certainly, as a business, we (Forth, Inc.) have succeeded by doing projects in weeks or months that were projected to take months or years. That has kept us economically viable over the years. We feel very strongly it is because of the tool, that the tool itself creates a productive environment. It's easy to point to a lot of the reasons why. But, with this amount of anecdotal evidence, we nonetheless have a credibility issue. We tell these stories and people say, "We don't believe you; all programming languages are pretty much the same, aren't they?"

I would like to close by urging somebody here, who has a sufficiently objective, respectable academic background and knows how to measure these things, and how to apply the metrics, to really take a look at this question. I know that proponents of functional programming make some of the same claims—of orders of magnitude improvement in productivity. Improvements this big deserve to be looked at. They deserve to be looked at honestly by somebody to see if there is something real there. And if so, what is it? What is the factor that makes it work? I'll be happy to supply the data if somebody wants to undertake that.

TRANSCRIPT OF QUESTION AND ANSWER SESSION

HERBERT KLAEREN (University of Tubingen): The first is, are there any significant differences between Forth and PostScript, apart from PostScript printer-specific dictionaries?

ELIZABETH RATHER: It is a very similar concept, and I'm not sure whether the developers of PostScript had seen Forth before or not. One could certainly believe that they might have. It is very similar concept; a lot of differences in detail, but I know of people who are strong in Forth or PostScript can go back and forth, so to speak, quite easily.

HERBERT KLAEREN (University of Tubingen): Can you remember how you came to base your language on the stack paradigm? Were you aware of stack-based code generation methods?

RATHER: I'm not sure. Certainly, Chuck had encountered stack somewhere along the line. I think what is really interesting about Forth, is not that it uses stacks, but in the way in which it uses stacks. The dual stack architecture has proved to be successful, probably not for any formal logical reason, but sort of the same reason the two party system in the United States works better than the 400 party system in some countries. It's a very useful number. People have experimented with different numbers of stacks and the dual stack architecture has persisted, using one stack for parameter passing and another stack for everything else—principally return information, but also a great deal else. I think, really, it's the way that it's used, as much as anything else that's been powerful.

BIOGRAPHY OF ELIZABETH RATHER

Ms. Rather was a cofounder of FORTH, Inc. and has been President since 1980. She was previously Chief Programmer for the Tucson Division of the National Radio Astronomy Observatory (NRAO), and has programmed and managed computer systems since 1962 at the University of Arizona, the University of California, and the Oak Ridge (Tennessee) National Laboratory.

She first worked with Chuck Moore, the inventor of the Forth programming language, at NRAO in 1971. Recognizing the potential capabilities of Forth, she began a campaign of talks and papers on the language that ultimately resulted in its being adopted as a standard in 1978, by the International Astronomical Union (IAU). She has authored, or coauthored, more than a dozen books and papers on Forth.

At FORTH, Inc., Ms. Rather has managed projects in a wide variety of fields, including scientific data acquisition and analysis, image processing, database management, networking, embedded systems, and industrial controls, in addition to Forth-based software development systems for over 20 platforms.

In 1987 Ms. Rather was instrumental in organizing a Technical Committee commissioned to develop an ANSI Standard for Forth. She was elected Chair of the TC, which in 1993 submitted a completed Standard (X3.215/1994) for final processing by ANSI.

Ms. Rather holds BA and MA degrees from the University of California, Berkeley, and an MBA from Pepperdine University.

BIOGRAPHY OF DONALD R. COLBURN

Don Colburn has been writing Forth Operating Systems since the late 1970s. He is the author of Multi-Forth™ and MacForth™, two popular Forth implementations for 68000 based computers. He has been active in the drafting of all Forth Standards-1979, 1983 and recent ANSI effort.

Don is a well-known developer for the Apple Macintosh family of computers. He has used the MacForth tools to write drivers for his company, Creative Solutions' popular hardware products, Hurdler™ and Hustler™. These peripherals add serial, parallel, and prototyping interfaces to the Macintosh.

Don is the father of two sons and enjoys volunteering at their schools—making them "well ahead of their time" in computerization. When he is not volunteering at the school, another very important organization he supports is the National Multiple Sclerosis Society. Don has MS and is an active source of encouragement for other MS patients.

BIOGRAPHY OF CHARLES H. MOORE

Chuck Moore was born Charles Havice Moore, II on September 9, 1938 in McKeesport, Pennsylvania. He grew up in Flint, Michigan and was Valedictorian of Central High School in 1956. He received a BS in Physics from MIT in 1960 and is a member of Kappa Sigma. While at MIT he learned FORTRAN and Lisp and programmed data reduction for Moonwatch satellite tracking and the Explorer-11 Gamma-ray Satellite. He studied mathematics at Stanford for several years, learned ALGOL and programmed electron-beam transport at SLAC.

After freelance programming on minicomputers, he learned COBOL and business programming and became an operating-system guru. In 1968, he invented Forth and used it at NRAO to program radio-telescopes. He, Elizabeth Rather, and Ned Conklin formed Forth, Inc. in 1973, to exploit the opportunities it provides. For 10 years he programmed applications in real-time control and database management. Today Forth, Inc. is a $3M firm selling software products and custom applications. Forth is particularly popular in China and Eastern Europe, where computer resources are still limited.

John Peers formed Novix in 1983, with funding from Sysorex. Its plan was to develop hardware implementations of Forth. With Bob Murphy of ICE, Moore designed a microprocessor with Forth primitives as its instruction set. Mostek produced a 4,000 gate array in 3μ CMOS that was an 8 Mips, 16-bit Forth engine. This NC4016 led to a modified NC6016 which was licensed to Harris Semiconductor in 1987. They marketed it as the RTX2000. Harris was granted two patents, with Moore and Murphy as inventors.

Computer Cowboys sold several hundred $400 Forth-Kits that incorporated the NC4016. In 1988, Russell Fish proposed a new microprocessor called ShBoom. Moore designed it and Oki Semiconductor produced prototypes on an 8,000 gate array in 1.2μ CMOS. This constituted a 50 Mips, 32-bit Forth engine.

With two technically successful gate-arrays, Moore wanted to produce a custom design. He was by now convinced that existing tools were inadequate. So in 1990 he started developing unique layout and simulation software. Layout is based upon five layers of square tiles that produce correct-by-design chips. A simple transistor model simulates the entire part and its connections. This was first implemented on ShBoom, and later ported to a 386.

He then designed MuP21 with a 20-bit bus and four 5-bit instructions/word as a way to minimize memory cost (only five 4-bit DRAMs). The internal buses are 21 bits to provide a 1M-word addresses for both DRAM and SRAM. MuP stands for Multi-uProcessor. The intent is to achieve parallelism with several independent microprocessors sharing memory. ShBoom had a DMA controller. MuP21 has a video generator—NTSC output with 16 colors—and a memory manager with DRAM, SRAM, and cache timing. Specialized processors can be very simple and effective.

Prototypes have been made by Orbit Technologies on their mosaic wafers, and by HP, through the MOSIS prototyping service where 12 to 25 chips cost $3,000 to $6,000 with two-month turn-around. This low cost makes possible iterative development, though project time can be long. After several tries, the design tools and architecture converged to a 100 Mips, 21-bit Forth engine. It is now being upgraded to 300 Mips.

C Session

Chair: *Brent Hailpern*

THE DEVELOPMENT OF THE C PROGRAMMING LANGUAGE

Dennis M. Ritchie

AT&T Bell Laboratories
Murray Hill, NJ 07974 USA

ABSTRACT

The C programming language was devised in the early 1970s as a system implementation language for the nascent Unix operating system. Derived from the typeless language BCPL, it evolved a type structure; created on a tiny machine as a tool to improve a meager programming environment, it has become one of the dominant languages of today. This paper studies its evolution.

CONTENTS

14.1 INTRODUCTION

This paper is about the development of the C programming language, the influences on it, and the conditions under which it was created. For the sake of brevity, I omit full descriptions of C itself, its parent B [Johnson 1973], and its grandparent BCPL [Richards 1979], and instead concentrate on characteristic elements of each language and how they evolved.

C came into being in the years 1969–1973, in parallel with the early development of the Unix operating system; the most creative period occurred during 1972. Another spate of changes peaked between 1977 and 1979, when portability of the Unix system was being demonstrated. In the middle of this second period, the first widely available description of the language appeared: *The C Programming Language*, often called the "white book" or "K&R" [Kernighan 1978]. Finally, in the middle 1980s, the language was officially standardized by the ANSI X3J11 committee, which made further changes. Until the early 1980s, although compilers existed for a variety of machine architectures and operating systems, the language was almost exclusively associated with Unix; more recently, its use has spread much more widely, and today it is among the languages most commonly used throughout the computer industry.

14.2 HISTORY: THE SETTING

The late 1960s were a turbulent era for computer systems research at Bell Telephone Laboratories [Ritchie 1978, 1984]. The company was pulling out of the Multics project [Organick 1975], which had started as a joint venture of MIT, General Electric, and Bell Labs; by 1969, Bell Labs management, and even the researchers, came to believe that the promises of Multics could be fulfilled only too late and too expensively. Even before the GE-645 Multics machine was removed from the premises, an informal group, led primarily by Ken Thompson, had begun investigating alternatives.

Thompson wanted to create a comfortable computing environment constructed according to his own design, using whatever means were available. His plans, it is evident in retrospect, incorporated many of the innovative aspects of Multics, including an explicit notion of a process as a locus of control, a tree-structured file system, a command interpreter as a user-level program, simple representation of text files, and generalized access to devices. They excluded others, such as unified access to memory and to files. At the start, moreover, he and the rest of us deferred to another pioneering (though not original) element of Multics, namely, writing almost exclusively in a higher-level language. PL/I, the implementation language of Multics, was not much to our tastes, but we were also using other languages, including BCPL, and we regretted losing the advantages of writing programs in a language above the level of assembler, such as ease of writing and clarity of understanding. At the time we did not put much weight on portability; interest in this arose later.

Thompson was faced with a hardware environment cramped and spartan even for the time: the DEC PDP-7 on which he started in 1968 was a machine with 8K (18-bit) words of memory and no software useful to him. While wanting to use a higher-level language, he wrote the original Unix system in PDP-7 assembler. At the start, he did not even program on the PDP-7 itself, but instead used a set of macros for the GEMAP assembler on a GE-635 machine. A postprocessor generated a paper tape readable by the PDP-7.

These tapes were carried from the GE machine to the PDP-7 for testing until a primitive Unix kernel, an editor, an assembler, a simple shell (command interpreter), and a few utilities (like the Unix *rm*, *cat*, *cp* commands) were completed. After this point, the operating system was self-supporting: programs could be written and tested without resorting to paper tape, and development continued on the PDP-7 itself.

Thompson's PDP-7 assembler outdid even DEC's in simplicity; it evaluated expressions and emitted the corresponding bits. There were no libraries, no loader or link editor: the entire source of a program was presented to the assembler, and the output file—with a fixed name—that emerged was directly executable. (This name, *a.out*, explains a bit of Unix etymology; it is the output of the assembler. Even after the system gained a linker and a means of specifying another name explicitly, it was retained as the default executable result of a compilation.)

Not long after Unix first ran on the PDP-7, in 1969, Doug McIlroy created the new system's first higher-level language: an implementation of McClure's TMG [McClure 1965]. TMG is a language for writing compilers (more generally, TransMoGrifiers) in a top-down, recursive-descent style that combines context-free syntax notation with procedural elements. McIlroy and Bob Morris had used TMG to write the early PL/I compiler for Multics.

Challenged by McIlroy's feat in reproducing TMG, Thompson decided that Unix—possibly it had not even been named yet—needed a system programming language. After a rapidly scuttled attempt at FORTRAN, he created, instead, a language of his own that he called B. B can be thought of as C without types; more accurately, it is BCPL squeezed into 8K bytes of memory and filtered through Thompson's brain. Its name most probably represents a contraction of BCPL, though an alternate theory holds that it derives from Bon [Thompson 1969], an unrelated language created by Thompson during the Multics days. Bon in turn was named either after his wife Bonnie, or (according to an encyclopedia quotation in its manual), after a religion whose rituals involve the murmuring of magic formulas.

14.3 ORIGINS: THE LANGUAGES

BCPL was designed by Martin Richards in the mid-1960s while he was visiting MIT, and was used during the early 1970s for several interesting projects, among them the OS6 operating system at Oxford [Stoy 1972], and parts of the seminal Alto work at Xerox PARC [Thacker 1979]. We became familiar with it because the MIT CTSS system [Corbato 1962], on which Richards worked, was used for Multics development. The original BCPL compiler was transported both to Multics and to the GE-635 GECOS system by Rudd Canaday and others at Bell Labs [Canaday 1969]; during the final throes of Multics's life at Bell Labs and immediately after, it was the language of choice among the group of people who would later become involved with Unix.

BCPL, B, and C all fit firmly in the traditional procedural family typified by FORTRAN and ALGOL 60. They are particularly oriented towards system programming, are small and compactly described, and are amenable to translation by simple compilers. They are 'close to the machine' in that the abstractions they introduce are readily grounded in the concrete data types and operations supplied by conventional computers, and they rely on library routines for input/output and other interactions with an operating system. With less success, they also use library procedures to specify interesting control constructs such as coroutines and procedure closures. At the same time, their abstractions lie at a sufficiently high level that, with care, portability between machines can be achieved.

BCPL, B, and C differ syntactically in many details, but broadly they are similar. Programs consist of a sequence of global declarations and function (procedure) declarations. Procedures can be nested in BCPL, but may not refer to nonstatic objects defined in containing procedures. B and C avoid this restriction by imposing a more severe one: no nested procedures at all. Each of the languages (except for earliest versions of B) recognizes separate compilation, and provides a means for including text from named files.

Several syntactic and lexical mechanisms of BCPL are more elegant and regular than those of B and C. For example, BCPL's procedure and data declarations have a more uniform structure, and it supplies a more complete set of looping constructs. Although BCPL programs are notionally supplied from an undelimited stream of characters, clever rules allow most semicolons to be elided after statements that end on a line boundary. B and C omit this convenience, and end most statements with semicolons. In spite of the differences, most of the statements and operators of BCPL map directly into corresponding B and C.

Some of the structural differences between BCPL and B stemmed from limitations on intermediate memory. For example, BCPL declarations may take the form

```
let P1 be command
and P2 be command
and P3 be command
 ...
```

where the program text represented by the commands contains whole procedures. The subdeclarations connected by and occur simultaneously, so the name P3 is known inside procedure P1. Similarly, BCPL can package a group of declarations and statements into an expression that yields a value, for example

```
E1 := valof $( declarations ; commands ; resultis E2 $) + 1
```

The BCPL compiler readily handled such constructs by storing and analyzing a parsed representation of the entire program in memory before producing output. Storage limitations on the B compiler demanded a one-pass technique in which output was generated as soon as possible, and the syntactic redesign that made this possible was carried forward into C.

Certain less pleasant aspects of BCPL owed to its own technological problems and were consciously avoided in the design of B. For example, BCPL uses a 'global vector' mechanism for communicating between separately compiled programs. In this scheme, the programmer explicitly associates the name of each externally visible procedure and data object with a numeric offset in the global vector; the linkage is accomplished in the compiled code by using these numeric offsets. B evaded this inconvenience initially by insisting that the entire program be presented all at once to the compiler. Later implementations of B, and all those of C, use a conventional linker to resolve external names occurring in files compiled separately, instead of placing the burden of assigning offsets on the programmer.

Other fiddles in the transition from BCPL to B were introduced as a matter of taste, and some remain controversial, for example the decision to use the single character `=` for assignment instead of :=. Similarly, B uses `/**/` to enclose comments, where BCPL uses `//`, to ignore text up to the end of the line. The legacy of PL/I is evident here. (C++ has resurrected the BCPL comment convention.) FORTRAN influenced the syntax of declarations: B declarations begin with a specifier like `auto` or `static`, followed by a list of names, and C not only followed this style but ornamented it by placing its type keywords at the start of declarations.

Not every difference between the BCPL language documented in Richards's book [Richards 1979] and B was deliberate; we started from an earlier version of BCPL [Richards 1967]. For example, the `endcase` that escapes from a BCPL `switchon` statement was not present in the language when we learned it in the 1960s, and so the overloading of the `break` keyword to escape from the B and C `switch` statement owes to divergent evolution rather than conscious change.

In contrast to the pervasive syntax variation that occurred during the creation of B, the core semantic content of BCPL—its type structure and expression evaluation rules—remained intact. Both languages are typeless, or rather have a single data type, the 'word,' or 'cell,' a fixed-length bit pattern. Memory in these languages consists of a linear array of such cells, and the meaning of the contents of a cell depends on the operation applied. The `+` operator, for example, simply adds its operands using the machine's integer add instruction, and the other arithmetic operations are equally unconscious of the actual meaning of their operands. Because memory is a linear array, it is possible to interpret the value in a cell as an index in this array, and BCPL supplies an operator for this purpose. In the original language it was spelled `rv`, and later `!`, whereas B uses the unary `*`. Thus, if `p` is a cell containing the index of (or address of, or pointer to) another cell, `*p` refers to the contents of the pointed-to cell, either as a value in an expression or as the target of an assignment.

Because pointers in BCPL and B are merely integer indices in the memory array, arithmetic on them is meaningful: if p is the address of a cell, then `p+1` is the address of the next cell. This convention is the basis for the semantics of arrays in both languages. When in BCPL one writes

```
let V = vec 10
```

or in B,

```
auto V[10];
```

the effect is the same: a cell named `V` is allocated, then another group of 10 contiguous cells is set aside, and the memory index of the first of these is placed into `V`. By a general rule, in B, the expression

```
*(V+i)
```

adds `V` and `i`, and refers to the `i`-th location after `V`. Both BCPL and B each add special notation to sweeten such array accesses; in B, an equivalent expression is

```
V[i]
```

and in BCPL

```
V!i
```

This approach to arrays was unusual even at the time; C would later assimilate it in an even less conventional way.

None of BCPL, B, or C supports character data strongly in the language; each treats strings much like vectors of integers and supplements general rules by a few conventions. In both BCPL and B, a string literal denotes the address of a static area initialized with the characters of the string, packed into cells. In BCPL, the first packed byte contains the number of characters in the string; in B, there is no count and strings are terminated by a special character, which B spelled `'*e'`. This change was made partially to avoid the limitation on the length of a string caused by holding the count in an 8- or 9-bit slot, and partly because maintaining the count seemed, in our experience, less convenient than using a terminator.

Individual characters in a BCPL string were usually manipulated by spreading the string out into another array, one character per cell, and then repacking it later; B provided corresponding routines, but people more often used other library functions that accessed or replaced individual characters in a string.

14.4 MORE HISTORY

After the TMG version of B was working, Thompson rewrote B in itself (a bootstrapping step). During development, he continually struggled against memory limitations: each language addition inflated the compiler so it could barely fit, but each rewrite, taking advantage of the feature, reduced its size. For example, B introduced generalized assignment operators, using `x=+y` to add `y` to `x`. The notation came from ALGOL 68 [Wijngaarden 1975] via McIlroy, who had incorporated it into his version of TMG. (In B and early C, the operator was spelled `=+` instead of `+=` ; this mistake, repaired in 1976, was induced by a seductively easy way of handling the first form in B's lexical analyzer.)

Thompson went a step further by inventing the `++` and `--` operators, which increment or decrement; their prefix or postfix position determines whether the alteration occurs before or after noting the value of the operand. They were not in the earliest versions of B, but appeared along the way. People often guess that they were created to use the auto-increment and auto-decrement address modes provided by the DEC PDP-11, on which C and Unix first became popular. This is historically impossible, inasmuch as there was no PDP-11 when B was developed. The PDP-7, however, did have a few "auto-increment" memory cells, with the property that an indirect memory reference through them incremented the cell. This feature probably suggested such operators to Thompson; the generalization to make them both prefix and postfix was his own. Indeed, the auto-increment cells were not used directly in implementation of the operators, and a stronger motivation for the innovation was probably his observation that the translation of `++x` was smaller than that of `x=x+1`.

The B compiler on the PDP-7 did not generate machine instructions, but instead "threaded code" [Bell 1972], an interpretive scheme in which the compiler's output consists of a sequence of addresses of code fragments that perform the elementary operations. The operations typically—in particular for B—act on a simple stack machine.

On the PDP-7 Unix system, only a few things were written in B except B itself, because the machine was too small and too slow to do more than experiment; rewriting the operating system and the utilities wholly into B was too expensive a step to seem feasible. At some point, Thompson relieved the address-space crunch by offering a "virtual B" compiler that allowed the interpreted program to occupy more than 8K bytes by paging the code and data within the interpreter, but it was too slow to be practical for the common utilities. Still, some utilities written in B appeared, including an early version of the variable-precision calculator *dc* familiar to Unix users [McIlroy 1979]. The most ambitious enterprise I undertook was a genuine cross-compiler that translated B to GE-635 machine instructions, not threaded code. It was a small *tour de force*: a full B compiler, written in its own language and generating code for a 36-bit mainframe, that ran on an 18-bit machine with 4K words of user address space. This project was possible only because of the simplicity of the B language and its run-time system.

Although we entertained occasional thoughts about implementing one of the major languages of the time such as FORTRAN, PL/I, or ALGOL 68, such a project seemed hopelessly large for our resources: much simpler and smaller tools were called for. All these languages influenced our work, but it was more fun to do things on our own.

By 1970, the Unix project had shown enough promise that we were able to acquire the new DEC PDP-11. The processor was among the first of its line delivered by DEC, and three months passed before its disk arrived. Making B programs run on it using the threaded technique required only writing the code fragments for the operators, and a simple assembler that I coded in B. Soon, *dc* became the first interesting program to be tested, before any operating system, on our PDP-11. Almost as rapidly, still waiting for the disk, Thompson recoded the Unix kernel and some basic commands in PDP-11 assembly language. Of the 24K bytes of memory on the machine, the earliest PDP-11 Unix system used 12K bytes for the operating system, a tiny space for user programs, and the remainder as a RAM disk. This version was only for testing, not for real work; the machine marked time by enumerating closed knight's tours on chess boards of various sizes. Once its disk appeared, we quickly migrated to it after transliterating assembly language commands to the PDP-11 dialect, and porting those already in B.

By 1971, our miniature computer center was beginning to have users. We all wanted to create interesting software more easily. Using assembler was dreary enough that B, despite its performance problems, had been supplemented by a small library of useful service routines and was being used for more and more new programs. Among the more notable results of this period was Steve Johnson's first version of the *yacc* parser-generator [Johnson 1979a].

14.5 THE PROBLEMS OF B

The machines on which we first used BCPL and then B were word-addressed, and these languages' single data type, the "cell," comfortably equated with the hardware machine word. The advent of the PDP-11 exposed several inadequacies of B's semantic model. First, its character-handling mechanisms, inherited with few changes from BCPL, were clumsy: using library procedures to spread packed strings into individual cells and then repack, or to access and replace individual characters, began to feel awkward, even silly, on a byte-oriented machine.

Second, although the original PDP-11 did not provide for floating-point arithmetic, the manufacturer promised that it would soon be available. Floating-point operations had been added to BCPL in our Multics and GCOS compilers by defining special operators, but the mechanism was possible only because on the relevant machines, a single word was large enough to contain a floating-point number; this was not true on the 16-bit PDP-11.

Finally, the B and BCPL model implied overhead in dealing with pointers: the language rules, by defining a pointer as an index in an array of words, forced pointers to be represented as word indices. Each pointer reference generated a run-time scale conversion from the pointer to the byte address expected by the hardware.

For all these reasons, it seemed that a typing scheme was necessary to cope with characters and byte addressing, and to prepare for the coming floating-point hardware. Other issues, particularly type safety and interface checking, did not seem as important then as they became later.

Aside from the problems with the language itself, the B compiler's threaded-code technique yielded programs so much slower than their assembly-language counterparts that we discounted the possibility of recoding the operating system or its central utilities in B.

In 1971, I began to extend the B language by adding a character type and also rewrote its compiler to generate PDP-11 machine instructions instead of threaded code. Thus the transition from B to C was contemporaneous with the creation of a compiler capable of producing programs fast and small enough to compete with assembly language. I called the slightly extended language NB, for "new B."

14.6 EMBRYONIC C

NB existed so briefly that no full description of it was written. It supplied the types `int` and `char`, arrays of them, and pointers to them, declared in a style typified by

```
int i, j;
char c, d;
int iarray[10];
int ipointer[];
char carray[10];
char cpointer[];
```

The semantics of arrays remained exactly as in B and BCPL: the declarations of `iarray` and `carray` create cells dynamically initialized with a value pointing to the first of a sequence of 10 integers and characters, respectively. The declarations for `ipointer` and `cpointer` omit the size, to assert that no storage should be allocated automatically. Within procedures, the language's interpretation of the pointers was identical to that of the array variables: a pointer declaration created a cell differing from an array declaration only in that the programmer was expected to assign a referent, instead of letting the compiler allocate the space and initialize the cell.

Values stored in the cells bound to array and pointer names were the machine addresses, measured in bytes, of the corresponding storage area. Therefore, indirection through a pointer implied no run-time overhead to scale the pointer from word to byte offset. On the other hand, the machine code for array subscripting and pointer arithmetic now depended on the type of the array or the pointer: to compute `iarray[i]` or `ipointer+i` implied scaling the addend `i` by the size of the object referred to.

These semantics represented an easy transition from B, and I experimented with them for some months. Problems became evident when I tried to extend the type notation, especially to add structured (record) types. Structures, it seemed, should map in an intuitive way onto memory in the machine, but in a structure containing an array, there was no good place to stash the pointer containing the base of the array, nor any convenient way to arrange that it be initialized. For example, the directory entries of early Unix systems might be described in C as

```
struct {
        int inumber;
        char name[14];
};
```

I wanted the structure not merely to characterize an abstract object but also to describe a collection of bits that might be read from a directory. Where could the compiler hide the pointer-to-name that the semantics demanded? Even if structures were thought of more abstractly, and the space for pointers could be hidden somehow, how could I handle the technical problem of properly initializing these pointers when allocating a complicated object, perhaps one that specified structures containing arrays containing structures to arbitrary depth?

The solution constituted the crucial jump in the evolutionary chain between typeless BCPL and typed C. It eliminated the materialization of the pointer in storage, and instead caused the creation of the pointer when the array name is mentioned in an expression. The rule, which survives in today's C, is that values of array type are converted, when they appear in expressions, into pointers to the first of the objects making up the array.

This invention enabled most existing B code to continue to work, despite the underlying shift in the language's semantics. The few programs that assigned new values to an array name to adjust its origin—possible in B and BCPL, meaningless in C—were easily repaired. More important, the new language retained a coherent and workable (if unusual) explanation of the semantics of arrays, while opening the way to a more comprehensive type structure.

The second innovation that most clearly distinguishes C from its predecessors, is this fuller type structure and especially its expression in the syntax of declarations. NB offered the basic types `int` and `char`, together with arrays of them, and pointers to them, but no further ways of composition. Generalization was required: given an object of any type, it should be possible to describe a new object that gathers several into an array, yields it from a function, or is a pointer to it.

For each object of such a composed type, there was already a way to mention the underlying object: index the array, call the function, use the indirection operator on the pointer. Analogical reasoning led to a declaration syntax for names mirroring that of the expression syntax in which the names typically appear. Thus,

```
int i, *pi, **ppi;
```

declare an integer, a pointer to an integer, a pointer to a pointer to an integer. The syntax of these declarations reflects the observation that `i`, `*pi`, and `**ppi` all yield an `int` type when used in an expression. Similarly,

```
int f(), *f(), (*f)();
```

declare a function returning an integer, a function returning a pointer to an integer, a pointer to a function returning an integer;

```
int *api[10], (*pai)[10];
```

declare an array of pointers to integers, and a pointer to an array of integers. In all these cases the declaration of a variable resembles its usage in an expression whose type is the one named at the head of the declaration.

The scheme of type composition adopted by C owes considerable debt to ALGOL 68, although it did not, perhaps, emerge in a form of which ALGOL's adherents would approve. The central notion I captured from ALGOL was a type structure based on atomic types (including structures), composed into arrays, pointers (references), and functions (procedures). ALGOL 68's concept of unions and casts also had an influence that appeared later.

After creating the type system, the associated syntax, and the compiler for the new language, I felt that it deserved a new name; NB seemed insufficiently distinctive. I decided to follow the single-letter style and called it C, leaving open the question whether the name represented a progression through the alphabet or through the letters in BCPL.

14.7 NEONATAL C

Rapid changes continued after the language had been named, for example the introduction of the `&&` and `||` operators. In BCPL and B, the evaluation of expressions depends on context: within if and other conditional statements that compare an expression's value with zero, these languages place a special interpretation on the `and` (`&`) and `or` (`|`) operators. In ordinary contexts, they operate bitwise, but in the B statement

```
if (e1 & e2) ...
```

the compiler must evaluate `e1` and if it is nonzero, evaluate `e2`, and if it too is nonzero, elaborate the statement dependent on the `if`. The requirement descends recursively on `&` and `|` operators within `e1` and `e2`. The short-circuit semantics of the Boolean operators in such "truth-value" context seemed desirable, but the overloading of the operators was difficult to explain and use. At the suggestion of Alan Snyder, I introduced the `&&` and `||` operators to make the mechanism more explicit.

Their tardy introduction explains an infelicity of C's precedence rules. In B one writes

```
if (a==b & c) ...
```

to check whether a equals b and c is nonzero; in such a conditional expression it is better that `&` have lower precedence than `==`. In converting from B to C, one wants to replace `&` by `&&` in such a statement; to make the conversion less painful, we decided to keep the precedence of the `&` operator the same relative to `==`, and merely split the precedence of `&&` slightly from `&`. Today, it seems that it would have been preferable to move the relative precedences of `&` and `==`, and thereby simplify a common C idiom: to test a masked value against another value, one must write

```
if ((a&mask) == b) ...
```

where the inner parentheses are required but easily forgotten.

Many other changes occurred around 1972–1973, but the most important was the introduction of the preprocessor, partly at the urging of Alan Snyder [Snyder 1974], but also in recognition of the utility of the file-inclusion mechanisms available in BCPL and PL/I. Its original version was exceedingly simple, and provided only included files and simple string replacements: `#include` and

`#define` of parameterless macros. Soon thereafter, it was extended, mostly by Mike Lesk and then by John Reiser, to incorporate macros with arguments and conditional compilation. The preprocessor was originally considered an optional adjunct to the language itself. Indeed, for some years, it was not even invoked unless the source program contained a special signal at its beginning. This attitude persisted, and explains both the incomplete integration of the syntax of the preprocessor with the rest of the language and the imprecision of its description in early reference manuals.

14.8 PORTABILITY

By early 1973, the essentials of modern C were complete. The language and compiler were strong enough to permit us to rewrite the Unix kernel for the PDP-11 in C during the summer of that year. (Thompson had made a brief attempt to produce a system coded in an early version of C—before structures—in 1972, but gave up the effort.) Also during this period, the compiler was retargeted to other nearby machines, particularly the Honeywell 635 and IBM 360/370; because the language could not live in isolation, the prototypes for the modern libraries were developed. In particular, Lesk wrote a "portable I/O package" [Lesk 1972] that was later reworked to become the C "standard I/O" routine. In 1978, Brian Kernighan and I published *The C Programming Language* [Kernighan1978]. Although it did not describe some additions that soon became common, this book served as the language reference until a formal standard was adopted more than ten years later. Although we worked closely together on this book, there was a clear division of labor: Kernighan wrote almost all the expository material, while I was responsible for the appendix containing the reference manual and the chapter on interfacing with the Unix system.

During 1973–1980, the language grew a bit: the type structure gained unsigned, long, union, and enumeration types, and structures became nearly first-class objects (lacking only a notation for literals). Equally important developments appeared in its environment and the accompanying technology. Writing the Unix kernel in C had given us enough confidence in the language's usefulness and efficiency that we began to recode the system's utilities and tools as well, and then to move the most interesting among them to the other platforms. As described in *Portability of C Programs ond the UNIX System* [Johnson 1978a], we discovered that the hardest problems in propagating Unix tools lay not in the interaction of the C language with new hardware, but in adapting to the existing software of other operating systems. Thus, Steve Johnson began to work on *pcc*, a C compiler intended to be easy to retarget to new machines [Johnson 1978b], while he, Thompson, and I began to move the Unix system itself to the Interdata 8/32 computer.

The language changes during this period, especially around 1977, were largely focused on considerations of portability and type safety, in an effort to cope with the problems we foresaw and observed in moving a considerable body of code to the new Interdata platform. C, at that time, still manifested strong signs of its typeless origins. Pointers, for example, were barely distinguished from integral memory indices in early language manuals or extant code; the similarity of the arithmetic properties of character pointers and unsigned integers made it hard to resist the temptation to identify them. The `unsigned` types were added to make unsigned arithmetic available without confusing it with pointer manipulation. Similarly, the early language condoned assignments between integers and pointers, but this practice began to be discouraged; a notation for type conversions (called "casts" from the example of ALGOL 68) was invented to specify type conversions more explicitly. Beguiled by the example of PL/I, early C did not tie structure pointers firmly to the structures they pointed to, and permitted programmers to write `pointer->member` almost without regard to the type of `pointer`; such an expression was taken uncritically as a reference to a region of memory designated by the pointer, whereas the member name specified only an offset and a type.

Although the first edition of K&R described most of the rules that brought C's type structure to its present form, many programs written in the older, more relaxed style persisted, and so did compilers that tolerated it. To encourage people to pay more attention to the official language rules, to detect legal but suspicious constructions, and to help find interface mismatches undetectable with simple mechanisms for separate compilation, Steve Johnson adapted his *pcc* compiler to produce *lint* [Johnson 1979b], which scanned a set of files and remarked on dubious constructions.

14.9 GROWTH IN USAGE

The success of our portability experiment on the Interdata 8/32 soon led to another by Tom London and John Reiser on the DEC VAX 11/780. This machine became much more popular than the Interdata, and Unix and the C language began to spread rapidly, both within AT&T and outside. Although by the middle 1970s Unix was in use by a variety of projects within the Bell System, as well as a small group of research-oriented industrial, academic, and government organizations outside our company, its real growth began only after portability had been achieved. Of particular note were the System III and System V versions of the system from the emerging Computer Systems division of AT&T, based on work by the company's development and research groups, and the BSD series of releases by the University of California at Berkeley that derived from research organizations in Bell Laboratories.

During the 1980s the use of the C language spread widely, and compilers became available on nearly every machine architecture and operating system; in particular it became popular as a programming tool for personal computers, both for manufacturers of commercial software for these machines, and for end-users interested in programming. At the start of the decade, nearly every compiler was based on Johnson's *pcc*; by 1985 there were many independently produced compiler products.

14.10 STANDARDIZATION

By 1982 it was clear that C needed formal standardization. The best approximation to a standard, the first edition of K&R, no longer described the language in actual use; in particular, it mentioned neither the `void` or `enum` types. It foreshadowed the newer approach to structures, but only after it was published did the language support assigning them, passing them to and from functions, and associating the names of members firmly with the structure or union containing them. Although compilers distributed by AT&T incorporated these changes, and most of the purveyors of compilers not based on *pcc* quickly picked them up, there remained no complete, authoritative description of the language.

The first edition of K&R was also insufficiently precise on many details of the language, and it became increasingly impractical to regard *pcc* as a "reference compiler"; it did not perfectly embody even the language described by K&R, let alone subsequent extensions. Finally, the incipient use of C in projects subject to commercial and government contract meant that the imprimatur of an official standard was important. Thus (at the urging of M. D. McIlroy), ANSI established the X3J11 committee under the direction of CBEMA in the summer of 1983, with the goal of producing a C standard. X3J11 produced its report [ANSI 1989] at the end of 1989, and subsequently this standard was accepted by ISO as ISO/IEC 9899-1990.

From the beginning, the X3J11 committee took a cautious, conservative view of language extensions. Much to my satisfaction, they took seriously their goal: "to develop a clear, consistent, and unambiguous Standard for the C programming language which codifies the common, existing definition of C and which promotes the portability of user programs across C language environments,"

[ANSI 1989]. The committee realized that mere promulgation of a standard does not make the world change.

X3J11 introduced only one genuinely important change to the language itself: it incorporated the types of formal arguments in the type signature of a function, using syntax borrowed from C++ [Stroustrup 1986]. In the old style, external functions were declared in this way:

```
double sin();
```

which says only that sin is a function returning a double (that is, double-precision floating-point) value. In the new style, this is better rendered

```
double sin(double);
```

to make the argument type explicit and thus encourage better type checking and appropriate conversion. Even this addition, though it produced a noticeably better language, caused difficulties. The committee justifiably felt that simply outlawing "old-style" function definitions and declarations was not feasible, yet also agreed that the new forms were better. The inevitable compromise was as good as it could have been, though the language definition is complicated by permitting both forms, and writers of portable software must contend with compilers not yet brought up to standard.

X3J11 also introduced a host of smaller additions and adjustments, for example, the type qualifiers `const` and `volatile`, and slightly different type promotion rules. Nevertheless, the standardization process did not change the character of the language. In particular, the C standard did not attempt to specify formally the language semantics, and so there can be dispute over fine points; nevertheless, it successfully accounted for changes in usage since the original description, and is sufficiently precise as a base for implementations.

Thus, the core C language escaped nearly unscathed from the standardization process, and the Standard emerged more as a better, careful codification than a new invention. More important changes took place in the language's surroundings: the preprocessor and the library. The preprocessor performs macro substitution, using conventions distinct from the rest of the language. Its interaction with the compiler had never been well-described, and X3J11 attempted to remedy the situation. The result is noticeably better than the explanation in the first edition of K&R; besides being more comprehensive, it provides operations, like token concatenation, previously available only by accidents of implementation.

X3J11 correctly believed that a full and careful description of a standard C library was as important as its work on the language itself. The C language itself does not provide for input/output or any other interaction with the outside world, and thus depends on a set of standard procedures. At the time of publication of K&R, C was thought of mainly as the system programming language of Unix; although we provided examples of library routines intended to be readily transportable to other operating systems, underlying support from Unix was implicitly understood. Thus the X3J11 committee spent much of its time designing and documenting a set of library routines required to be available in all conforming implementations.

By the rules of the standards process, the current activity of the X3J11 committee is confined to issuing interpretations on the existing standard. However, an informal group originally convened by Rex Jaeschke as NCEG (Numerical C Extensions Group) has been officially accepted as subgroup X3J11.1, and they continue to consider extensions to C. As the name implies, many of these possible extensions are intended to make the language more suitable for numerical use: for example, multidimensional arrays whose bounds are dynamically determined, incorporation of facilities for dealing with IEEE arithmetic, and making the language more effective on machines with vector or other advanced architectural features. Not all the possible extensions are specifically numerical; they include a notation for structure literals.

14.11 SUCCESSORS

C and even B have several direct descendants, though they do not rival Pascal in generating progeny. One side branch developed early. When Steve Johnson visited the University of Waterloo on sabbatical in 1972, he brought B with him. It became popular on the Honeywell machines there, and later spawned Eh and Zed (the Canadian answers to "what follows B?"). When Johnson returned to Bell Labs in 1973, he was disconcerted to find that the language whose seeds he had brought to Canada had evolved back home; even his own *yacc* program had been rewritten in C, by Alan Snyder.

More recent descendants of C proper include Concurrent C [Gehani 1989], Objective C [Cox 1986], C* [Thinking 1990], and especially C++ [Stroustrup 1986]. The language is also widely used as an intermediate representation (essentially, as a portable assembly language) for a wide variety of compilers, both for direct descendents such as C++, and independent languages such as Modula 3 [Nelson 1991] and Eiffel [Meyer 1988].

14.12 CRITIQUE

Two ideas are most characteristic of C among languages of its class: the relationship between arrays and pointers, and the way in which declaration syntax mimics expression syntax. They are also among its most frequently criticized features, and often serve as stumbling blocks to the beginner. In both cases, historical accidents or mistakes have exacerbated their difficulty. The most important of these has been the tolerance of C compilers to errors in type. As should be clear from the preceding history, C evolved from typeless languages. It did not suddenly appear to its earliest users and developers as an entirely new language with its own rules; instead we continually had to adapt existing programs as the language developed, and make allowance for an existing body of code. (Later, the ANSI X3J11 committee standardizing C would face the same problem.)

Compilers in 1977, and even well after, did not complain about usages such as assigning between integers and pointers, or using objects of the wrong type to refer to structure members. Although the language definition presented in the first edition of K&R was reasonably (though not completely) coherent in its treatment of type rules, that book admitted that existing compilers didn't enforce them. Moreover, some rules designed to ease early transitions contributed to later confusion. For example, the empty square brackets in the function declaration

```
int f(a) int a[]; { ... }
```

are a living fossil, a remnant of NB's way of declaring a pointer: `a` is, in this special case only, interpreted in C as a pointer. The notation survived in part for the sake of compatibility, in part under the rationalization that it would allow programmers to communicate to their readers an intent to pass `f` a pointer generated from an array, rather than a reference to a single integer. Unfortunately, it serves as much to confuse the learner as to alert the reader.

In K&R, C, supplying arguments of the proper type to a function call, was the responsibility of the programmer, and the extant compilers did not check for type agreement. The failure of the original language to include argument types in the type signature of a function was a significant weakness, indeed the one that required the X3J11 committee's boldest and most painful innovation to repair. The early design is explained (if not justified) by my avoidance of technological problems, especially cross-checking between separately compiled source files, and my incomplete assimilation of the implications of moving between an untyped and a typed language. The *lint* program, mentioned previously, tried to alleviate the problem: among its other functions, *lint* checks the consistency and coherency of a whole program by scanning a set of source files, comparing the types of function arguments used in calls with those in their definitions.

An accident of syntax contributed to the perceived complexity of the language. The indirection operator, spelled * in C, is syntactically a unary prefix operator, just as in BCPL and B. This works well in simple expressions, but in more complex cases, parentheses are required to direct the parsing. For example, to distinguish indirection through the value returned by a function from calling a function designated by a pointer, one writes `*fp()` and `(*pf)()`, respectively. The style used in expressions carries through to declarations, so the names might be declared

```
int *fp();
int (*pf)();
```

In more ornate but still realistic cases, things become worse:

```
int *(*pfp)();
```

is a pointer to a function returning a pointer to an integer. There are two effects occurring. Most important, C has a relatively rich set of ways of describing types (compared, say, with Pascal). Declarations in languages as expressive as C—ALGOL 68, for example—describe objects equally hard to understand, simply because the objects themselves are complex. A second effect owes to details of the syntax. Declarations in C must be read in an "inside-out" style that many find difficult to grasp [Anderson 1980]. Sethi [Sethi 1981] observed that many of the nested declarations and expressions would become simpler if the indirection operator had been taken as a postfix operator instead of prefix, but by then it was too late to change.

In spite of its difficulties, I believe that C's approach to declarations remains plausible, and am comfortable with it; it is a useful unifying principle.

The other characteristic feature of C, its treatment of arrays, is more suspect on practical grounds, though it also has real virtues. Although the relationship between pointers and arrays is unusual, it can be learned.

Moreover, the language shows considerable power to describe important concepts, for example, vectors whose length varies at run-time, with only a few basic rules and conventions. In particular, character strings are handled by the same mechanisms as any other array, plus the convention that a null character terminates a string. It is interesting to compare C's approach with that of two nearly contemporaneous languages, ALGOL 68 and Pascal [Jensen 1974]. Arrays in ALGOL 68 either have fixed bounds, or are "flexible": considerable mechanism is required both in the language definition, and in compilers, to accommodate flexible arrays (and not all compilers fully implement them). Original Pascal had only fixed-sized arrays and strings, and this proved confining [Kernighan 1981]. Later, this was partially fixed, though the resulting language is not yet universally available.

C treats strings as arrays of characters conventionally terminated by a marker. Aside from one special rule about initialization by string literals, the semantics of strings are fully subsumed by more general rules governing all arrays, and as a result the language is simpler to describe and to translate than one incorporating the string as a unique data type. Some costs accrue from its approach: certain string operations are more expensive than in other designs, because application code or a library routine must occasionally search for the end of a string, because few built-in operations are available, and because the burden of storage management for strings falls more heavily on the user. Nevertheless, C's approach to strings works well.

On the other hand, C's treatment of arrays in general (not just strings) has unfortunate implications both for optimization and for future extensions. The prevalence of pointers in C programs, whether those declared explicitly or arising from arrays, means that optimizers must be cautious, and must use careful dataflow techniques to achieve good results. Sophisticated compilers can understand what most pointers can possibly change, but some important usages remain difficult to analyze. For example, functions with pointer arguments derived from arrays are hard to compile into efficient code on vector machines, because it is seldom possible to determine that one argument pointer does not overlap data also referred to by another argument, or accessible externally. More fundamentally, the definition of C so specifically describes the semantics of arrays that changes or extensions treating arrays as more primitive objects, and permitting operations on them as wholes, become hard to fit into the existing language. Even extensions to permit the declaration and use of multidimensional arrays whose size is determined dynamically are not entirely straightforward [MacDonald 1989; Ritchie 1990], although they would make it much easier to write numerical libraries in C. Thus C covers the most important uses of strings and arrays arising in practice by a uniform and simple mechanism, but leaves problems for highly efficient implementations and for extensions.

Many smaller infelicities exist in the language and its description besides those discussed, of course. There are also general criticisms to be lodged that transcend detailed points. Chief among these is that the language and its generally expected environment provide little help for writing very large systems. The naming structure provides only two main levels, "external" (visible everywhere) and "internal" (within a single procedure). An intermediate level of visibility (within a single file of data and procedures) is weakly tied to the language definition. Thus there is little direct support for modularization, and project designers are forced to create their own conventions.

Similarly, C itself provides two durations of storage: "automatic" objects that exist while control resides in, or below, a procedure, and "static," existing throughout execution of a program. Off-stack, dynamically allocated storage is provided only by a library routine and the burden of managing it is placed on the programmer: C is hostile to automatic garbage collection.

14.13 WHENCE SUCCESS?

C has become successful to an extent far surpassing any early expectations. What qualities contributed to its widespread use?

Doubtless the success of Unix itself was the most important factor; it made the language available to hundreds of thousands of people. Conversely, of course, Unix's use of C and its consequent portability to a wide variety of machines was important in the system's success. But the language's invasion of other environments suggests more fundamental merits.

Despite some aspects mysterious to the beginner and occasionally even to the adept, C remains a simple and small language, translatable with simple and small compilers. Its types and operations are well-grounded in those provided by real machines, and for people used to computers and how they work, learning the idioms for generating time- and space-efficient programs is not difficult. At the same time the language is sufficiently abstracted from machine details that program portability can be achieved.

Equally important, C and its central library support always remained in touch with a real environment. It was not designed in isolation to prove a point, or to serve as an example, but as a tool to write programs that did useful things; it was always meant to interact with a larger operating system, and was regarded as a tool to build larger tools. A parsimonious, pragmatic approach influenced the things that went into C: it covers the essential needs of many programmers, but does not try to supply too much.

Finally, despite the changes that it has undergone since its first published description, which was admittedly informal and incomplete, the actual C language as seen by millions of users using many different compilers has remained remarkably stable and unified compared to those of similarly widespread currency, for example, Pascal and FORTRAN. There are differing dialects of C—most noticeably, those described by the older K&R and the newer Standard C—but on the whole, C has remained freer of proprietary extensions than other languages. Perhaps the most significant extensions are the "far" and "near" pointer qualifications intended to deal with peculiarities of some Intel processors. Although C was not originally designed with portability as a prime goal, it succeeded in expressing programs, even including operating systems, on machines ranging from the smallest personal computers through the mightiest supercomputers.

C is quirky, flawed, and an enormous success. Although accidents of history surely helped, it evidently satisfied a need for a system implementation language efficient enough to displace assembly language, yet sufficiently abstract and fluent to describe algorithms and interactions in a wide variety of environments.

ACKNOWLEDGMENTS

It is worth summarizing compactly the roles of the direct contributors to today's C language. Ken Thompson created the B language in 1969–1970; it was derived directly from Martin Richards's BCPL. Dennis Ritchie turned B into C during 1971–1973, keeping most of B's syntax, while adding types and many other changes, and writing the first compiler. Ritchie, Alan Snyder, Steven C. Johnson, Michael Lesk, and Thompson contributed language ideas during 1972–1977, and Johnson's portable compiler remains widely used. During this period, the collection of library routines grew considerably, thanks to these people and many others at Bell Laboratories. In 1978, Brian Kernighan and Ritchie wrote the book that became the language definition for several years. Beginning in 1983, the ANSI X3J11 committee standardized the language. Especially notable in keeping its efforts on track were its officers Jim Brodie, Tom Plum, and P. J. Plauger, and the successive draft redactors, Larry Rosler and Dave Prosser.

I thank Brian Kernighan, Doug McIlroy, Dave Prosser, Peter Nelson, Rob Pike, Ken Thompson, and HOPL's referees for advice in the preparation of this paper.

REFERENCES

[ANSI, 1989] American National Standards Institute, *American National Standard for Information Systems-Programming Language C*, X3.159-1989.

[Anderson, 1980] B. Anderson, Type syntax in the language C: an object lesson in syntactic innovation, *SIGPLAN Notices*, Vol. 15, No. 3, Mar. 1980, pp. 21–27.

[Bell, 1972] J. R. Bell, Threaded Code, C. *ACM*, Vol. 16, No. 6, pp. 370–372.

[Canaday, 19 69] R. H. Canaday and D. M. Ritchie, Bell Laboratories BCPL, AT&T Bell Laboratories internal memorandum, May 1969.

[Corbato, 1962] F. J. Corbato, M. Merwin-Dagget, and R. C. Daley, An Experimental Time-sharing System, *AFIPS Conference Proceedings SJCC*, 1962, pp. 335–344.

[Cox, 1986] B. J. Cox and A. J. Novobilski, *Object-Oriented Programming: An Evolutionary Approach*, Addison-Wesley: Reading, MA, 1986, Second edition, 1991.

[Gehani, 1989] N. H. Gehani and W. D. Roome, *Concurrent C*, Silicon Press: Summit, NJ, 1989.

[Jensen, 1974] K. Jensen and N. Wirth, Pascal User Manual and Report, Springer-Verlag: New York, Heidelberg, Berlin. Second Edition, 1974.

[Johnson, 1973] S. C. Johnson and B. W. Kernighan, The programming language B, *Computer Science Technical Report* No. 8, AT&T Bell Laboratories, Jan. 1973.

[Johnson, 1978a] S. C. Johnson and D. M. Ritchie, Portability of C programs and the UNIX system, *Bell Systems Technical J. 57*, Vol. 6, (part 2), July–Aug. 1978.

[Johnson, 1978b] S. C. Johnson, A portable compiler: Theory and practice, *Proceedings of the 5th ACM POPL Symposium*, Jan. 1978.

[Johnson, 1979a] S. C. Johnson, Yet another compiler-compiler, Unix Programmer's Manual, Seventh Edition, Vol. 2A, M. D. McIlroy and B. W. Kernighan, Eds. AT&T Bell Laboratories: Murray Hill, NJ, 1979.

[Johnson, 1979b] S. C. Johnson, Lint, a program checker, *Unix Programmer's Manual*, Seventh Edition, Vol. 2B, M. D. McIlroy and B. W. Kernighan, Eds. AT&T Bell Laboratories: Murray Hill, NJ, 1979.

[Kernighan, 1978] B. W. Kernighan and D. M. Ritchie, *The C Programming Language*, Prentice-Hall: Englewood Cliffs, NJ, 1978. Second edition, 1988.

[Kernighan, 1981]B. W. Kernighan, Why Pascal is not my favorite programming language, *Computer Science Technical Report* No. 100, AT&T Bell Laboratories, 1981.

[Lesk, 1973] M. E. Lesk, A portable I/O package, AT&T Bell Laboratories internal memorandum c. 1973.

[MacDonald, 1989]T. MacDonald, Arrays of variable length, *Journal of C Language Translation*, Vol. 1, No. 3, Dec. 1989, pp. 215–233.

[McClure, 1965] R. M. McClure, TMG—A syntax directed compiler, *Proceedings of the 20th ACM National Conference*, 1965, pp. 262–274.

[McIlroy, 1960] M. D. McIlroy, Macro instruction extensions of compiler languages, *C. ACM*, Vol. 3, No. 4, pp. 214–220.

[McIlroy, 1979] M. D. McIlroy and B. W. Kernighan, Eds., *Unix Programmer's Manual*, Seventh Edition, Vol. I, AT&T Bell Laboratories: Murray Hill, NJ, 1979.

[Meyer, 1988] B. Meyer, *Object-Oriented Software Construction*, Prentice-Hall: Englewood Cliffs, NJ, 1988.

[Nelson, 1991] G. Nelson, *Systems Programming with Modula-3*, Prentice-Hall: Englewood Cliffs, NJ, 1991.

[Organick, 1975] E. I. Organick, *The Multics System: An Examination of its Structure*, MIT Press: Cambridge, Mass., 1975.

[Richards, 1967] M. Richards, The BCPL Reference manual, MIT Project MAC Memorandum M-352, July 1967.

[Richards, 1979] M. Richards and C. Whitbey-Strevens, *BCPL: The Language and its Compiler*, Cambridge Univ. Press: Cambridge, 1979.

[Ritchie, 1978] D. M. Ritchie, UNIX: A retrospective, *Bell Systems Technical Journal*, Vol. 57, No. 6, (part 2), July–Aug. 1978.

[Ritchie, 1984]D. M. Ritchie, The evolution of the UNIX time- sharing system, *AT&T Bell Labs. Technical Journal*, Vol. 63, No. 8, (part 2), Oct. 1984.

[Ritchie, 1990] D. M. Ritchie, Variable-size arrays in C, *Journal of C Language Translation* 2, No. 2, Sept. 1990, pp. 81–86.

[Sethi, 1981] R. Sethi, Uniform syntax for type expressions and declarators, *Software Practice and Experience*, Vol. 11, No. 6, June 1981, pp. 623–628.

[Snyder, 1974] A. Snyder, *A Portable Compiler for the Language C*, MIT: Cambridge, Mass., 1974.

[Stoy, 1972] J. E. Stoy and C. Strachey, OS6-An experimental operating system for a small computer. Part I: General principles and structure, *Computer Journal*, Vol. 15, Aug. 1972, pp. 117–124.

[Stroustrup 86] B. Stroustrup, *The C++ Programming Language*, Addison-Wesley: Reading, Mass., 1986. Second edition, 1991.

[Thacker 79] C. P. Thacker, E. M. McCreight, B. W. Lampson, R. F. Sproull, D. R. Boggs, Alto: A Personal Computer, *Computer Structures: Principles and Examples*, D. Sieworek, C. G. Bell, A. Newell, McGraw-Hill: New York, 1982.

[Thinking 90] C* Programming Guide, Thinking Machines Corp.: Cambridge Mass., 1990.

[Thompson 69] K. Thompson, Bon-an interactive language, undated AT&T Bell Laboratories internal memorandum (c. 1969).

[Wijngaarden 75] A. van Wijngaarden, B. J. Mailloux, J. E. Peck, C. H. Koster, M. Sintzoff, C. Lindsey, L. G. Meertens, and R. G. Fisker, Revised report on the algorithmic language ALGOL 68, *Acta Informatica 5*, pp. 1–236.

TRANSCRIPT OF PRESENTATION

DENNIS RITCHIE: Thank you. Before I begin the talk, I will put forth a little idea I thought of in the last day or so. It's a programming problem having to do with graph theory: you have a graph. The nodes contain a record with a language and a person, and, just to make the example concrete: the nodes might be (C, Ritchie), (Ada, Ichbiah), (Pascal, Wirth), or (Concurrent Pascal, Brinch Hansen) perhaps. (Lisp, Steele), (C++, Stroustrup) might also be part of the population. There is an edge from X to Y, whenever X.Person will throw a barb in public at Y.Language. And the questions are: is this a complete graph? Does it have self-edges? If it's not complete, what cliques exist? There are all sorts of questions you can ask. I guess if it were a finite state machine, you could ask about diagnosability, too. Can you push at the people and get them to throw these barbs?

The Development of the C Language
or
Five Little Languages and How They Grew

Dennis M. Ritchie
AT&T Bell Laboratories

dmr@research.att.com

Ritchie *HOPL-II* *1*

SLIDE 1

Five Little Languages

Bliss
Pascal
Algol 68
BCPL
C

Ritchie *HOPL-II* *2*

SLIDE 2

(SLIDE 1) The paper itself tells the history of C, so I don't want to do it again. Instead, I want to do a small comparative language study, although it's not really that either. I'm going to talk about a bunch of 20-year old languages. Other people can discuss what the languages contain. These were things that were around at the time, and I'm going to draw some comparisons between them just to show the way we were thinking and perhaps explain some things about C. Indirectly, I want to explain why C is as it is. So the actual title of the talk, as opposed to the paper, is "Five Little Languages and How They Grew."

(SLIDE 2) Here are the five languages: Bliss, Pascal, ALGOL 68, BCPL, C. All these were developed in more or less the same period. I'm going to argue that they're very much similar in a lot of ways. And each succeeded in various ways, either by use or by influence. C succeeded really without politics in a sense that we didn't do any marketing, so there must have been a need for it. What about the rest of these? Why are these languages the same?

(SLIDE 3) In the first place, the things that they're manipulating, their atomic types, their ground-level objects, are essentially identical. They are simply machine words interpreted in various ways. The operations that they allow on these are actually very similar. This is in contrast to SNOBOL, for example, which has strings, or Lisp, which has lists. The languages I'm talking about are just cleverly designed ways of shuffling bits around; everybody knows about the operations once they've learned a bit about machine architecture. That's what I mean by concretely grounded. They're

Similarities

Atomic types similar
Concretely grounded
Procedural
Based on tradition of Algol 60 and Fortran
System programming

Ritchie *HOPL-II* *3*

SLIDE 3

Bliss

by Wulf et al. at CMU
PDP-10 and PDP-11 system language
Picked up by DEC
Word oriented: operator used to access bytes
< *start*, *len* >
Macros used for arrays and structures

Ritchie *HOPL-II* *4*

SLIDE 4

procedural, which is, to say, imperative. They don't have very fancy control structures, and they perform assignments; they're based on this old, old model of machines that pick up things, do operations, and put them someplace else. They are very much influenced by ALGOL 60 and FORTRAN and the other languages which were discussed in the first HOPL conference.

Mostly they were designed (speaking broadly) for "systems programming." Certainly some of them, like BCPL and C and Bliss, are explicitly system programming languages, and Pascal has been used for that. ALGOL 68 didn't really have that in mind, but it really can be used for the purpose; when Steve Bourne came to Bell Labs with the ALGOL 68C compiler, he made it do the same things that C could do; it had Unix system call interfaces and so forth. The point is, that "system" can be understood in a fairly broad sense, not just operating systems.

Let me very briefly characterize each language.

(SLIDE 4) Bliss is the one that hasn't been mentioned before at this conference. It was done by Bill Wulf and his students at Carnegie-Mellon. I believe it started as a PDP-10 system programming language, and it was then later used to do system programming on the PDP-11 for a variety of projects. It went somewhat beyond that—it was picked up in particular by Digital Equipment Corp., I suppose partly through the close connections between DEC and CMU at that time. And in fact it's been used, maybe still is used, for parts of VMS. Bliss is word oriented, by which I mean, there is only one data type, which is the machine word. So that's 36 bits in the case of the PDP-10 version; 16 bits in the case of the '11. You accessed individual bytes, or characters, by having a special operator notation where you mentioned the start bit and the length. So it is a special case that accessed characters of a slightly more general case, that accessed individual rows of bits.

Bliss was innovative in a variety of ways. It was goto-less; it was an expression language. A lot of things that are built into other languages were not built into Bliss; instead there were syntax macros used for giving meaning to arrays, particularly multidimensional arrays, and structures. An array or structure was represented by the programmer as a sort of in-line function to access the members, instead of being built in as a data type.

(SLIDE 5) But the thing that people really remember about Bliss is all those dots. Bliss is unusual in that the value of a name appearing in an expression is the address at which the associated value is stored. And to retrieve the value itself, you put a dot operator in front of the name. For example, in an ordinary assignment of a sum will be written as "C gets .A+.B." Here you're taking the value stored in A and the value stored in B, and adding them. (If you left off the dots, you would be adding the addresses.) On the other hand, the assignment operator wants an address on the left and a value on the right; that's why there's no dot in front of the C.

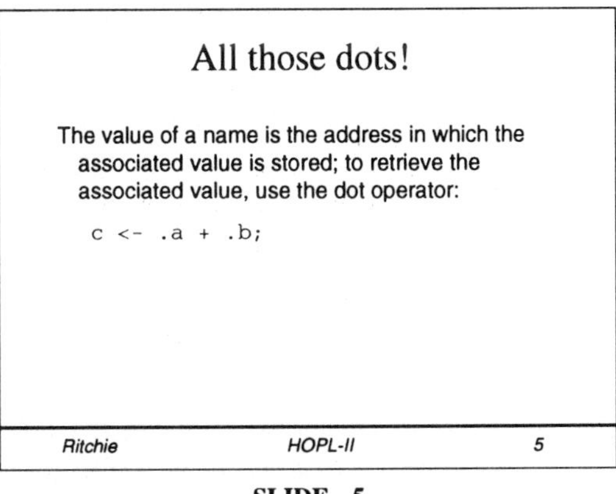

SLIDE 5

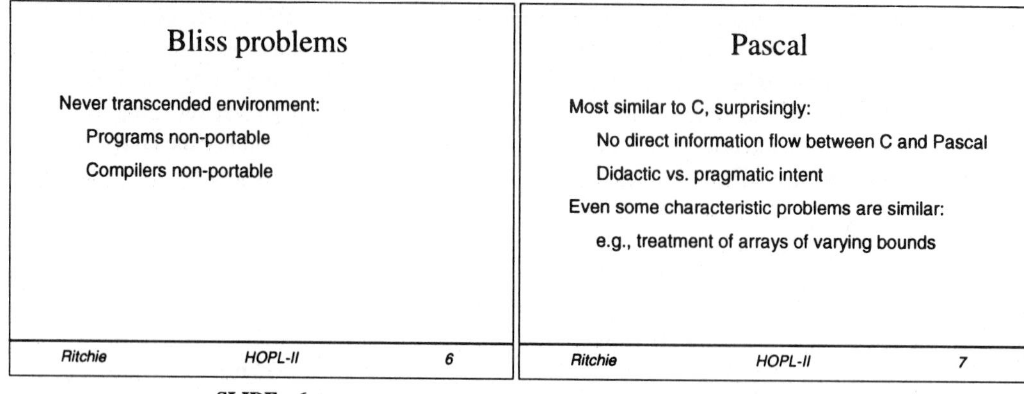

SLIDE 6 **SLIDE 7**

What were the problems of Bliss? Really, that it never transcended its original environments. The programs tended to be nonportable. There was a notation for the bit extraction to get characters, but there were also notations that created PDP-10 specific byte pointers, because they couldn't resist using this feature of the PDP-10. And this (and other things) made programs tend to be nonportable because they were either PDP-11 dialect, or the PDP-10 dialect. And perhaps equally important, the compilers were nonportable; in particular, the compiler never ran on the PDP-11.

(SLIDE 6) Whatever the motivation for Bliss as a language, much of the interest in it actually came because of a sequence of optimizers for its compilers created by a succession of students. In other words, its legacy is a multiphase optimizing compiler that ran on the PDP-10. It was a project that could be divided up into phases, in which each student gets a phase and writes a thesis on this particular kind of optimization. Altogether a very CMU-like way of operating—a series of programs that collectively could be called C.PhD. A good way of working, I think. [It was used as well in C.mmp and Mach, as well.]

(SLIDE 7) Let me move on to Pascal. I argue that Pascal is very similar to C; some people may be surprised by this, some not. C and Pascal are approximately contemporaneous. It's quite possible that there could have been mutual information flow in the design, but in fact, there wasn't. So it's interesting that they're so much the same. The languages differ much in detail but at heart are really the same; if you look at the actual types in the languages, and the operators on the types, there really is a very large degree of overlap. Some things are said differently—in particular Pascal's sets are in some ways a more interesting abstraction than unsigned integers, but they're still bit fields.

This is in spite of the fact Wirth's intent in creating Pascal was very different from ours in C. He was creating a language for teaching, so that he had a didactic purpose. And in particular, I take it both from Pascal, and from his later languages, that he's interested in trying to constrain expression as much as possible, although no more. In general, he explores where the line should go between constraints that are there for safety, and expressiveness. He's really a very parsimonious fellow, I think, and so am I.

Even some of the characteristic problems of Pascal and C are very similar. In particular, in treatment of arrays with varying bounds: this is worth discussing a bit.

C has always provided for open-ended, that is, variable-sized, arrays (one-dimensional arrays, or vectors). In particular, C has been able to subsume strings under the same set of general rules as integer arrays. Pascal, certainly in the original form, did not allow even that. In other words, even one-dimensional arrays had a fixed size known at compile-time. There have been, in at least some of the dialects, a notion of "conformant" arrays so that procedures can take arrays of different sizes. But still the issue isn't fully resolved; the status of this is not really clear.

C's solution to this has real problems, and people who are complaining about safety definitely have a point. Nevertheless, C's approach has in fact lasted, and actually does work. In Pascal's case, certainly in the original language, and perhaps even in some of the following ones, the language needs extensions in order to be really useful. You can't take the pure language and use it, for example, as a system programming language. It needs other things.

Here's an aphorism I didn't create for this conference, but several years ago. It seems particularly apt, given the people present [Stu Feldman and Niklaus Wirth]: "'Make' is like Pascal. Everybody likes it, so they want to change it." In both cases, a very good idea wasn't quite right at the start.

Here's another anecdote, based on something that happened yesterday afternoon. During the coffee break, Wirth said to me, "Sometimes you can be too strict . . . ." Interestingly, he was not talking about language design and implementation, but instead about the type- and bounds-checking that was occurring within the conference. [That is, to the insistence on written-down questions to speakers and strongly enforced time limits on speakers and questioners].

Pascal is very elegant. It's certainly still alive. It is prolific of successors and it has influenced language design profoundly.

(SLIDES 8 and 9) ALGOL 68 is definitely the odd member of the list. I wrote "designed by committee" on the original slide. I started to cross this out based on what Charles Lindsay said earlier, but I didn't cross it out completely because, the point I want to make here, is not so much that it was designed by a committee, but that it was "official." In other words, there was an international standards organization that was actually supporting the work and expecting something out of the design of ALGOL 68. Whatever the result, it was definitely not a small project. Of course, it was formally defined from the very beginning. The language was designed well before there were any compilers; this meant that, like most interesting languages done that way, it held surprises; even ALGOL 60 held surprises. ALGOL 60's call-by-name mechanism looked beautiful in the report, and then people came to implement it and realized that it had unexpected consequences. There were a few other things like this, even in ALGOL 60. Similarly, in ALGOL 68, there were things that were put in because they looked natural and orthogonal, and then when people came to implement the language they found that, although it was possible, it was difficult. It's a hard language, and big in some ways. It does have more concepts than the others, even if they're orthogonal. Things like flexible arrays, slices, parallelism, the extensibility features (especially operator identification), and so forth. Despite the

Pascal is . . .

elegant

still alive

prolific

Ritchie HOPL-II 8

SLIDE 8

Algol 68

Odd member of my list:

A 'big project' by committee

Formally defined

Held surprises
(e.g., operator identification)

A 'harder' language
(flexible arrays, slices, parallelism, extensible)

Ritchie HOPL-II 9

SLIDE 9

SLIDE 10

SLIDE 11

efforts of Charles Lindsay, I think the language really did suffer from its definition in terms of acceptance. Nevertheless, it was really quite practical.

(SLIDE 10) In some ways, ALGOL 68 is the most elegant of the languages I've been discussing. I think in some ways, it's even the most influential, although as a language in itself, it has nearly gone away. But the number of people at this conference who have said "This was influenced by ALGOL 68," is surprisingly quite large. As the accompanying paper points out, C was influenced by it in important ways. The reference on the slide to ALGOL 68C is to indicate that we had an A68C compiler on the early Unix system in the '70s, when Steve Bourne came from Cambridge and brought it with him. It didn't handle the complete language, but it was certainly enough to get the flavor. (It was kind enough to give me warnings whenever I said the wrong thing. The most common was, "Warning! Voiding a Boolean," which always struck me as amusing. Of course it meant that I had written "`A=B`" instead of "`A:=B`").

(SLIDE 11) BCPL was the direct predecessor to C. It is very much like Bliss because it's a typeless language, and it was intended for system programming. Unlike Bliss, it was designed to be portable. The compiler itself was written to be portable, and transportable; it produced a well-described intermediate code. And, in spite of the fact that the only type was the "word," it ran on machines with different word sizes. It was a small language, and its style was pragmatic. Its original purpose was to be the implementation language for CPL, a more ambitious undertaking by Strachey and his students that never quite materialized. BCPL was used in a variety of places. It was one of the early languages used at Xerox PARC on the Alto, for example.

(SLIDE 12) Let me compare. (This is the only technical part of the talk.) What is the meaning of a name, when it appears in an expression? There are three very different interpretations that happen in these languages.

First, a further example of the way Bliss works. In the first statement, you've simply assigned a value 1 to A. In the second statement when you say "B gets A," what you have assigned is the address at which A is located. So, if you print the value B at this point, you'll see a number representing some memory address. However, if you do this assignment with the dot, as in the third statement, then you have assigned the value 1 that came from the assignment on the first line. That means that "dereferencing" (a word that came from ALGOL 68) is always explicit in Bliss, and it's necessary because in Bliss a simple name is a reference, not a value.

In ALGOL 68, there is a more interesting situation. The meaning of a name, at heart, is often the same as in Bliss; in other words, it often denotes a location. In SLIDE 13 (first line of program), the

A Comparison: meaning of names

In Bliss, a name means a location; a dot must be used to dereference:

```
A <-1;
B <- A;     ! B is the address of A
C <- .A;    ! C holds 1
```

Ritchie HOPL-II 12

SLIDE 12

A Comparison: meaning of names

In Algol 68, a name often means a location; dereferencing is accomplished by semi-automatic coercions:

```
int A;    C  ref int A = loc int  C
ref int B;
int C;

A := 1;
B := A;   C  B gets address of A  C
C := A;   C  C gets 1  C
C := B;   C  C gets 1 again  C
```

Ritchie HOPL-II 13

SLIDE 13

declaration of `A` says that `A` is a reference to an integer stored in a local cell that can hold an integer. The notation "`int A`" is a shorthand for the more explicit declaration shown in the comment.

Later, you write, in line 4, "`A gets 1`." The rules of the language see a reference to an `int` on the left, an `int` on the right, and do the appropriate magic (called "coercion") that puts 1 into the cell referred to by `A`. In line 5, because `B` is declared as a reference to a reference to an integer, `B` is assigned the address of `A`, while in line 6, `C` gets the value (the number 1) stored in `A`. On the last line, the same 1 is stored again, this time indirectly through the reference in `B`.

So the two A's, on lines 5 and 6, are coerced in different ways, depending on the context in which they appear. "Dereferencing," or turning an address into the value stored in it, happens automatically, according to explicit rules, when appropriate; even though the underlying semantics resemble those of Bliss, one doesn't have have to write the dots.

(SLIDE 14) The next slide shows the way things work in BCPL and its descendants and also Pascal. Here we have the same kind of types, in that `A` holds an integer, `B` holds a reference to (or pointer to) an integer. However, in these languages, the value of the name (like `A`) that holds the integer, is the integer's value, and there is an explicit operator that generates the address. Similarly, if one has a variable (like `B`) that holds a reference to (pointer to) an integer, one uses an explicit operator to get to the integer. In line 4 of the program, where `A` gets 1, there's no coercion; instead the rules observe that there is an integer on the left, whose expression is a special form called an "`lvalue`," which can appear in this position. In line 5, the explicit "`&`" operator produces the address (reference value) of `A` and likewise assigns it to `B`; in line 7, the explicit "`*`" operator fetches the value from the reference (pointer) stored in `B`.

These languages (Bliss, ALGOL 68, and BCPL/B/C), show three different approaches to the question, "What is the meaning of a name when it appears in a program?" Bliss says, "It means the location of a value; to find the value itself, you must be explicit." ALGOL 68 says, "It means the location of a value; the language, however, supplies coercion rules such that you will always get the value itself, or its location, as appropriate. Otherwise you have made a error that will be diagnosed." BCPL, B, C, and Pascal say, "A name means a value. You must be explicit if you wish to get the location in which that value is stored, and also if the value happens to represent a reference to another value."

Naturally, I prefer the approach that C has taken, but I appreciate how ALGOL 68 has clarified thinking about these issues of naming and reference.

(SLIDE 15) Let's talk about the influences of these languages. While you ponder the slide, I'll digress to talk about characterizations of the languages along the lines of Fred Brooks's [keynote]

A Comparison: meaning of names

In Pascal, BCPL, and C, names refer to values in locations; indirect references are explicit

```
int A;
int *B;
int C;

A = 1;
B = &A;     /* B gets address of A */
C = *B;     /* C gets 1 */
```

Ritchie HOPL-II 14

SLIDE 14

Effects on the World

Bliss has sunk

Pascal is alive, along with its descendants

Algol 68 and BCPL are moribund, but their influence continues

C is lively, its descendants possibly livelier

Ritchie HOPL-II 15

SLIDE 15

talk, which mentioned empiricism versus rationalism, being pragmatic and utilitarian versus theoretical and doctrinal. How do we classify these languages? Some were created more to help their creators solve their own problems, some more to make a point. ALGOL 68 is unabashedly rationalist, even doctrinaire. Pascal is an interesting question—in some ways, the most interesting because it's clearly got the rationalistic spirit, but also some of the empiricism as well. BCPL and C are, in general, not pushing any "-ology," and belong clearly in the pragmatic camp. Bliss, a goto-less, expression language, with an unusual approach to the meaning of names, partakes heavily of the rationalist spirit, but, like Pascal, was created by the same people who intended to use it.

I'll make another side point, a comparison that doesn't have a slide either. Of these languages, only Pascal does anything interesting about numerical precision control. ALGOL 68 really thought about static semantics of names, and in most cases, dynamic semantics of things. But one thing it just didn't talk about at all in a meaningful sense, is: what numbers go out or go in? It has "ints" and "long ints" and "long long ints," and so forth, but the language doesn't tell you how big these things are; there's no control over them. In B and BCPL, there is nothing but the "word." What's a word? It depends on the machine. C is similar to ALGOL 68, in the sense that it has type modifiers like "long." The C standard does say, "Here is the minimal size you can expect for 'int,' for 'long,' for 'short.' " But this is still fairly weak. Pascal has ranges, so that you can be explicit about the range of values you expect to store. Of course, you hit against limits, and you can't have numbers that are too big.

Other languages allow you to use very big numbers. Various predecessors of these languages, like PL/1, were very explicit about numerical precision, and successors like Ada make it possible [to] say similar things in a different way. The question, "How can you be portable if you don't know how big an integer is?" is continually raised. The interesting fact, and it's one that's surprising to me, is how little this actually matters. In other words, though you have to do some thinking about program design, it's fairly seldom that this issue turns out to be the important source of bugs, at least in my experience.

Let me go back to talk about influences of these languages on the world. Bliss has pretty much disappeared. Its optimization ideas have remained useful, and some of the companies that worked with it have survived. Digital Equipment Corp. still has a lot of Bliss code that they're wondering what to do with.

Pascal is definitely alive, and it has many direct descendants and other languages strongly influenced by it. ALGOL 68 and BCPL as languages are moribund, but their influence continues: ALGOL 68 influences in a broad way, and BCPL rather directly through its influence on C. C remains lively, obviously.

How to Succeed in Language Without Really Trying

Neither elegance nor formality is enough
(do people understand it?)

Connection with what people need and can get:

Availability
(compiler technology, implemetation, distribution)

Appropriate interaction with environment
(usability as tool, adaptability to unexpected uses, ways of dealing with extra-linguistic issues)

Ritchie HOPL-II 16

SLIDE 16

How to Succeed in Language Without Really Trying

Ability to age gracefully
What is your standards committee doing?
What will the next one do?

It's best to get it mostly right the first time

Ritchie HOPL-II 17

SLIDE 17

C's own descendants, by which I mainly mean C++, may very well be even livelier in the next few years. Aside from languages that are directly descended from C, (particularly C++ but also some others), C's intellectual influence on the semantic design of new languages has been small. On the other hand, it has influenced notation: even pseudo-code these days tends to contain curly braces.

(SLIDE 16) Let me finish by trying to show how C succeeded in becoming so widely used, much more than any of the others I talked about. I can't give a real answer, because I don't know it, but I'll try.

Elegance and formality of definition may be necessary, according to some, but it's certainly not sufficient. It's important that people be able to understand the language. One of the problems with ALGOL 68, despite the efforts of Charles Lindsay and others, was that its definition was hard to read. More fundamentally, though, a language has to be able to connect with and facilitate what people need to do, and potential users have to be able to get an implementation of it.

So, you need to be able to get a compiler: the language has to be implementable in the compiler technology of the day, on the systems they have available to them.

When you design a language with new ideas before implementing it, you are taking a chance that you're pushing compiler technology. This may be a social good, but it may not do your language any good. It has to have an implementation, so that people can try it, and it needs distribution. As I've mentioned, the definition of both ALGOL 68, and ALGOL 60 before it, held surprises for implementers.

Also, languages need to provide appropriate interaction with a real environment. Computer languages exist to perform useful things that affect the world in some way, not just to express algorithms, and so their success depends in part on their utility. Environments vary. The one that we created in the Unix System had a particular flavor, and we took full advantage of the ability of the C language to express the software tools appropriate for the environment. As an old example, suppose you want to search many files for strings described by regular expressions, in the manner of the Unix "grep" program.

What languages could you write grep in? As an example, there are really neat ways of expressing the regular expression search algorithm in the APL language. However, traditional APL systems are usually set up as a closed environment, and give you no help in creating a tool for text searching in a more general setting.

[Lack of time prevented discussion of SLIDE 17].

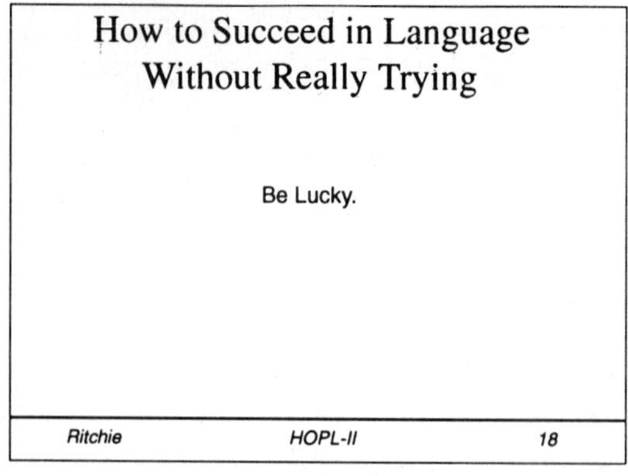

SLIDE 18

(SLIDE 18) Here's how to succeed: by being lucky. Grab on to something that's moving pretty fast. Let yourself be carried on when you're in the right place at the right time.

TRANSCRIPT OF QUESTION AND ANSWER SESSION

BERNIE GALLER (University of Michigan): In regard to referencing and dereferencing, you said ALGOL 68 made the distinctions clear. I would think that by suppressing the operators, ALGOL 68 buried the distinctions, thus obscuring the issue. Pascal and C made it clear, no?

RITCHIE: I failed to make myself clear. What I should have said more explicitly was that ALGOL 68 clarified the issue from the point of view of language design, not that it was necessarily easier for the users of the language to understand what was going on. You're quite right. The business of coercions, and when they occurred, is in fact one of the stumbling blocks for users of ALGOL 68. They're clear from the point of view of the language designer. Thinking about that sort of thing made the issues clearer.

ANDY MIKEL (MCAD Computer Center): Are you aware that the Apollo DOMAIN C compiler was hacked from the Apollo Pascal compiler (with type checking intact), and that when used to compile Unix, found uninitialized variables and pointers to nowhere, (but no instances of taking square roots of pointers)?

RITCHIE: I'm not surprised at the last! Yeah, C did not choose to be type-unsafe purely out of boastfulness, or something like that. In fact, the work that is currently being done in our group is using a compiler that is very much more strict than the original compilers. It enforces ANSI/ISO C rules, and demands function prototypes in particular, unless you ask it very kindly. And so a lot of type errors are, in fact, caught by this and other modern C compilers.

ROBERT THAU (MIT AI Lab): The BCPL "`resultof`" construct, made it into B; why did it vanish in C?

RITCHIE: It didn't make into B; that's discussed in the paper. B really was too small. Stu Feldman mentioned this yesterday. Remember, the first B compiler fit into 8K bytes. The first C compiler fit into about 16K bytes. Maybe it's like the cheetah; it's believed that the African cheetah was at some time down to 17 individuals or something like that. It squeezed through a very tight evolutionary space. C sort of did the same thing.

HERBERT KLAEREN (University of Tubingen): Do you welcome the clarifications made in ANSI C, or would you agree with that part of the C community that feels this should be called "Anti-C"? Do you program in ANSI C yourself?

RITCHIE: Absolutely not. [Interrupting before the last part of the question was asked.] The slide that I regret not having time to show says that one of the ways to succeed is to get yourself a good standards committee, and I did. Look, there are a lot of details that you can argue with, but they came out with a language that's actually better than when it went in. Certainly, no worse. And so, I do program in ANSI C, and I think they did a good job.

RICH MILLER (SHL System House): The book, K&R, became a *de facto* standard. How important was that, and how lucky was that?

RITCHIE: It was lucky for me. One of the facts about C is that for a long time it did not need extensions. And there was a *de facto* standard, even though there was no real standard. The reference manual was certainly not as precise as it could be, and it got out of date.

ANDREW BLACK (DEC CRL): C's declaration syntax has been called an interesting experiment. In your view, what are the results?

RITCHIE: I don't know; I still kind of like it. This is discussed somewhat in the paper. It was Ravi Sethi who observed that if C's unary star operator were a postfix operator instead of a prefix operator, suddenly everything becomes nice and linear and clear. That's as far as the syntax is concerned. The semantics, I think, are still interesting. I think it's a viable approach. It might not be the best, but I think it's reasonable.

GUY STEELE (Thinking Machines): If you had to do it all over again, would you do anything differently?

RITCHIE: I'd become a monk? No. that really is very hard to answer. Again, there is some discussion in the paper. There are lots of little decisions about which you can say, "Gee, that would have been better to do some other way." Broadly speaking, I would say no; I'm reasonably happy with the results. I think there is an inevitability about a lot of these issues; once you're committed, you have to continue on the same path. I don't want to go into the details about what I would do. Again, I guess I refer you to the paper—maybe if you ask a specific question.

JEFF SUTHERLAND (Object Databases): In your paper, you say, "Structures [in C] became nearly first-class objects." The notion of first-class objects is now coming up in the definition of SQL3 language (since I brought it up at the ANSI X3H7/X3H2 joint meeting). What is your precise definition of a first-class object?

RITCHIE: I suppose simply that all the appropriate operations are present. In particular, structures started out as not being values that could be returned by functions, or assigned to. But, even in the first book, there's clearly a place holder for that. But if there's some obvious orthogonality lacking, then that's what makes a second-class citizen.

NIKLAUS WIRTH (ETH): You mentioned the similarities of C and Pascal. Which do you consider to be the most important differences?

RITCHIE: I think I've already mentioned some. The important differences are that Pascal's definition (although the first design was not absolutely perfect) at some level defined completely the semantics of the language. Furthermore, equally or even more important, the style in which it was used encouraged checking the semantic rules, either in advance or during run-time. The fact is, if you read the definition of C (although it's not completely safe), it does say what is defined and what is undefined. In particular, subscript checking is perfectly possible; pointer and range checking are perfectly possible. All sorts of possibilities are there, yet most implementations do not provide them. One can attack that very easily. It's the style of use, I think, more than anything else, that determines the most significant difference between the languages, not the differences in their rules.

BERNIE GALLER (University of Michigan): Which style of referencing and dereferencing was easier to learn and use? Were there any empirical studies?

RITCHIE: I certainly don't know of any empirical studies. I do know that whenever you mention Bliss to somebody, they complain about dots. The style that remains in common use is the one used in C's family; the ALGOL 68 style of heavily implicit dereferencing and the Bliss idea of making it all very explicit are both unusual.

ADAM RIFKIN (Caltech): Did you expect C to be as widely used as it is today? Given its current popularity: at the time of design, would you have changed any design decisions?

RITCHIE: No, I didn't expect C to become so widely used; it was done as a tool for folks nearby. As for decisions: in retrospect, the worst lack in the original language was function prototypes (attachment of the types of parameters to the type of the function). This was by far the most important change made by the ANSI committee, and it should have been done earlier.

BILL MCKEEMAN (Digital): Is it possible to define C more clearly than the standard does?

RITCHIE: Yes, of course. There are several parts that I don't like much, including the explanation of the details of how macros are expanded, and the notion of 'linkage' and how it describes the visibility of static and external data. This is related to the fact that neither I, nor the committee came up with a clean, unified model of how these concepts should work, in the presence of differing existing implementations. Nevertheless, I give X3J11 good marks. If someone dislikes C they probably dislike it for itself, not for the formulation of its standard, and conversely.

BIOGRAPHY OF DENNIS M. RITCHIE

Dennis M. Ritchie is head of the Computing Techniques Research Department of AT&T Bell Laboratories.

He joined Bell Laboratories in 1968 after obtaining his graduate and undergraduate degrees from Harvard University. He assisted Ken Thompson in creating the Unix operating system, and is the primary designer of the C language, in which Unix, as well as many other systems, are written. He continues to work in operating systems and languages.

He is a member of the US National Academy of Engineering, is a Bell Laboratories Fellow, and has received several honors, including the ACM Turing award, the IEEE Piore, Hamming and Pioneer awards, and the NEC C&C Foundation award.

C++ Session

Chair: *Brent Halpern*
Discussant: *Stuart Feldman*

A HISTORY OF C++: 1979–1991

Bjarne Stroustrup

AT&T Bell Laboratories
Murray Hill, New Jersey 07974

ABSTRACT

This paper outlines the history of the C++ programming language. The emphasis is on the ideas, constraints, and people that shaped the language, rather than the minutiae of language features. Key design decisions relating to language features are discussed, but the focus is on the overall design goals and practical constraints. The evolution of C++ is traced from C with Classes to the current ANSI and ISO standards work and the explosion of use, interest, commercial activity, compilers, tools, environments, and libraries.

CONTENTS

15.1 INTRODUCTION

C++ was designed to provide Simula's facilities for program organization together with C's efficiency and flexibility for systems programming. It was intended to deliver that to real projects within half a year of the idea. It succeeded. At the time, I realized neither the modesty nor the preposterousness of that goal. The goal was modest in that it did not involve innovation, and preposterous in both its time scale and its Draconian demands on efficiency and flexibility. While a modest amount of innovation did emerge over the years, efficiency and flexibility have been maintained without compromise. While the goals for C++ have been refined, elaborated, and made more explicit over the years, C++ as used today directly reflects its original aims.

Most effort has been expended on the early years because the design decisions taken early determined the further development of the language. It is also easier to maintain an historical perspective when one has had many years to observe the consequences of decisions.

Essential language features are presented to make this paper approachable by a non-C++ specialist. However, the emphasis is on the people, ideas, and constraints that shaped C++ rather than on detailed descriptions of those language features or their use. For a description of what C++ is today and how to use it see [Stroustrup 1991].[1]

15.2 C WITH CLASSES

C++ evolved from an earlier version called "C with Classes." The work and experience with C with Classes from 1979 to 1983 determined the shape of C++.

15.2.1 Prehistory

The prehistory of C++—the couple of years before the idea of adding Simula-like features to C occurred to me—is important because during this time, the criteria and ideals that later shaped C++ emerged. I was working on my Ph.D. thesis in the Computing Laboratory of Cambridge University in England. My aim was to study alternatives for the organization of system software for a distributed system. The conceptual framework was provided by the capability-based Cambridge CAP computer and its experimental and continuously evolving operating system. The details of this work and its outcome [Stroustrup 1979a] are of little relevance to C++. What is relevant, though, was the focus on composing software out of well-delimited modules and that the main experimental tool was a relatively large and detailed simulator I wrote for simulating software running on a distributed system.

The initial version of this simulator was written in Simula and ran on the Cambridge University computer center's IBM 360/165 mainframe. It was a pleasure to write that simulator. The features of Simula were almost ideal for the purpose and I was particularly impressed by the way the concepts of the language helped me think about the problems in my application. The class concept allowed me to map my application concepts into the language constructs in a direct way, that made my code more readable than I had seen in any other language. The way Simula classes can act as co-routines made the inherent concurrency of my application easy to express. For example, an object of class *computer* could trivially be made to work in pseudo parallel with other objects of class *computer*. Class hierarchies were used to express variants of application level concepts. For example, different types of computers could be expressed as classes derived from class *computer* and different types of inter module communication mechanisms could be expressed as classes derived from class *IPC*. The use of class hierarchies was not heavy, though; the use of classes to express concurrency was much more important in the organization of my simulator.

During writing and initial debugging, I acquired a great respect for the expressiveness of Simula's type system and the ability of its compiler's ability to catch type errors. The observation was that a type error almost invariably reflected either a silly programming error or a conceptual flaw in the

1 **Author's note:** It is now 1995, four years since I first completed this paper. Rather than rewriting major sections of it for the final book, I have added footnotes where needed to reflect recent events. Most of the themes of this paper are explored further in [Stroustrup 1994]. This work also includes many issues related to the design and evolution of C++ that couldn't be included here.

design. The latter was by far the most significant and a help that I had not experienced in the use of more primitive "strong" type systems. In contrast, I had found Pascal's type system worse than useless—a strait jacket that caused more problems than it solved by forcing me to warp my designs to suit an implementation-oriented artifact. The perceived contrast between the rigidity of Pascal and the flexibility of Simula was essential for the development of C++. Simula's class concept was seen as the key difference, and ever since I have seen classes as the proper primary focus of program design.

I had used Simula before (during my studies at the University of Aarhus, Denmark), but was very pleasantly surprised by the way the mechanisms of the Simula language became increasingly helpful as the size of the program increased. The class and co-routine mechanisms of Simula and the comprehensive type checking mechanisms ensured that problems and errors did not (as I—and I guess most people—would have expected) grow linearly, or more than linearly, with the size of the program. Instead, the total program acted more like a collection of small (and therefore easy to write, comprehend, and debug) programs, rather than a single large program.

The implementation of Simula, however, did not scale in the same way and as a result the whole project came close to disaster. My conclusion at the time was that the Simula implementation (as opposed to the Simula language) was geared to relatively small programs and was inherently unsuited for larger programs [Stroustrup 1979a]. Link times for separately compiled classes were abysmal: It took longer to compile 1/30th of the program and link it to a precompiled version of the rest than it took to compile and link the program as a monolith. This I believe to be more a problem with the mainframe linker than with Simula, but it was still a burden. On top of that, the run-time performance was such that there was no hope of using the simulator to obtain real data. The poor run-time characteristics were a function of the language and its implementation, rather than a function of the application. The overhead problems were fundamental to Simula and could not be remedied. The cost arose from several language features and their interactions: run-time type checking, guaranteed initialization of variables, concurrency support, and garbage collection of both user-allocated objects and procedure activation records. For example, measurements showed that more than 80 percent of the time was spent in the garbage collector despite the fact that resource management was part of the simulated system so that no garbage was ever produced. Simula implementations are better these days (15 years later), but the order-of-magnitude improvement relative to systems programming languages still has not (to the best of my knowledge) materialized.

To avoid terminating the project, I rewrote the simulator in BCPL and ran it on the experimental CAP computer. The experience of coding and debugging the simulator in BCPL was horrible. BCPL makes C look like a very high-level language and provides absolutely no type checking or run-time support. The resulting simulator did, however, run suitably fast and gave a whole range of useful results that clarified many issues for me and provided the basis for several papers on operating system issues [Stroustrup 1978, 1979b, 1981a].

Upon leaving Cambridge, I swore never again to attack a problem with tools as unsuitable as those I had suffered while designing and implementing the simulator. The significance of this to C++ was the notion I had evolved of what constituted a "suitable tool" for projects such as the writing of a significant simulator, an operating system, and similar systems programming tasks:

1. A good tool would have Simula's support for program organization—that is, classes, some form of class hierarchies, some form of support for concurrency, and strong (that is, static) checking of a type system based on classes. This I saw as support for the process of inventing programs, as support for design rather than just support for implementation.
2. A good tool would produce programs that ran as fast as BCPL programs and shared BCPL's ability to easily combine separately compiled units into a program. A simple linkage convention

is essential for combining units written in languages such as C, ALGOL 68, FORTRAN, BCPL, assembler, and so on, into a single program and, thus, not to get caught by inherent limitations in a single language.

3. A good tool should also allow for highly portable implementations. My experience was that the "good" implementation I needed would typically not be available until "next year" and only on a machine I couldn't afford. This implied that a tool must have multiple sources of implementations (no monopoly would be sufficiently responsive to users of "unusual" machines and to poor graduate students), that there should be no complicated run-time support system to port, and that there should be only very limited integration between the tool and its host operating system.

Not all of these criteria were fully formed when I left Cambridge, but several were, and more matured on further reflection on my experience with the simulator, on programs written over the next couple of years, and on the experiences of others as learned through discussions and reading of code. C++ as defined at the time of release 2.0, strictly fulfills these criteria; the fundamental tensions in the effort to design templates and exception handling mechanisms for C++ arise from the need to depart from some aspects of these criteria. I think the most important aspect of these criteria is that they are only loosely connected with specific programming language features. Rather, they specify constraints on a solution.

My background in operating systems work and my interest in modularization and communication had permanent effects on C++. The C++ model of protection, for example, is based on the notion of granting and transferring access rights, the distinction between initialization and assignment has its root in thoughts about transferring capabilities, and the design of C++'s exception handling mechanism was influenced by work on fault tolerant systems done by Brian Randell's group in Newcastle in the seventies.

15.2.2 The Birth of C with Classes

The work, on what eventually became C++, started with an attempt to analyze the UNIX kernel to determine to what extent it could be distributed over a network of computers connected by a local area network. This work started in April of 1979 in the Computing Science Research Center of Bell Laboratories in Murray Hill, New Jersey, where I have worked ever since. Two subproblems soon emerged: how to analyze the network traffic that would result from the kernel distribution and how to modularize the kernel. Both required a way to express the module structure of a complex system and the communication pattern of the modules. This was exactly the kind of problem that I had become determined never to attack again without proper tools. Consequently, I set about developing a proper tool according to the criteria I had formed in Cambridge.

In October of 1979, I had a preprocessor, called Cpre, that added Simula-like classes to C; and in March of 1980, this preprocessor had been refined to the point where it supported one real project and several experiments. My records show the preprocessor in use on 16 systems by then. The first key C++ library, the task system supporting a co-routine style of programming [Stroustrup 1980b, 1987b; Shopiro 1987], was crucial to the usefulness of "C with Classes," as the language accepted by the preprocessor was called, in these projects.

During the April to October period the transition from thinking about a "tool" to thinking about a "language" had occurred, but C with Classes was still thought of primarily as an extension to C for expressing modularity and concurrency. A crucial decision had been made, though. Even though support of concurrency and Simula-style simulations was a primary aim of C with Classes, the language contained no primitives for expressing concurrency; rather, a combination of inheritance (class hierarchies) and the ability to define class member functions with special meanings recognized by the preprocessor was used to write the library that supported the desired styles of concurrency. Please note that "styles" is plural. I considered it crucial, as I still do, that more than one notion of concurrency should be expressible in the language. This decision has been reconfirmed repeatedly by me and my colleagues, by other C++ users, and by the C++ standards committee. There are many applications for which support for concurrency is essential, but there is no one dominant model for concurrency support; thus when support is needed it should be provided through a library or a special purpose extension so that a particular form of concurrency support does not preclude other forms.

Thus, the language provided general mechanisms for organizing programs rather than support for specific application areas. This was what made C with Classes, and later C++, a general-purpose language rather than a C variant with extensions to support specialized applications. Later, the choice between providing support for specialized applications or general abstraction mechanisms, has come up repeatedly. Each time the decision has been to improve the abstraction mechanisms.

An early description of C with Classes was published as a Bell Labs technical report in April 1980 [Stroustrup 1980a], and later in *SIGPLAN Notices.* The SIGPLAN paper was in April 1982, followed by a more detailed Bell Labs technical report, "Adding Classes to the C Language: An Exercise in Language Evolution" [Stroustrup 1982], that was later published in *Software: Practice and Experience.* These papers set a good example by describing only features that were fully implemented and had been used. This was in accordance with a long standing tradition of Bell Labs Computing Science Research Center; that policy has been modified only where more openness about the future of C++ became needed to ensure a free and open debate over the evolution of C++ among its many non-AT&T users.

C with Classes was explicitly designed to allow better organization of programs; "computation" was considered a problem solved by C. I was very concerned that improved program structure was not achieved at the expense of run-time overhead compared to C. The explicit aim was to match C in terms of run-time, code compactness, and data compactness. To wit: someone once demonstrated a three percent systematic decrease in overall run-time efficiency compared with C. This was considered unacceptable and the overhead promptly removed. Similarly, to ensure layout compatibility with C and thereby avoid space overheads, no "housekeeping data" was placed in class objects.

Another major concern was to avoid restrictions on the domain where C with Classes could be used. The ideal—which was achieved—was that C with Classes could be used for whatever C could be used for. This implied that in addition to matching C in efficiency, C with Classes could not provide benefits at the expense of removing "dangerous" or "ugly" features of C. This observation/principle had to be repeated often to people (rarely C with Classes users) who wanted C with Classes made safer by increasing static type-checking along the lines of early Pascal. The alternative way of providing "safety," inserting run-time checks for all unsafe operations, was (and is) considered reasonable for debugging environments, but the language could not guarantee such checks without leaving C with a large advantage in run-time and space efficiency. Consequently, such checks were not provided for C with Classes, though C++ environments exist that provide such checks for debugging. In addition, users can, and do, insert run-time checks (assertions [Stroustrup 1991]) where needed and affordable.

C allows quite low-level operations, such as bit manipulation and choosing between different sizes of integers. There are also facilities, such as explicit unchecked type conversions, for deliberately breaking the type system. C with Classes, and later C++, follow this path by retaining the low-level and unsafe features of C. In contrast to C, C++ systematically eliminates the need to use such features except where they are essential, and performs unsafe operations only at the explicit request of the programmer. I strongly felt then, as I still do, that there is no one right way of writing every program, and a language designer has no business trying to *force* programmers to use a particular style. The language designer does, on the other hand, have an obligation to encourage and support a variety of styles and practices that have proven effective and to provide language features and tools to help programmers avoid the well-known traps and pitfalls.

15.2.3 Feature overview

The features provided in the initial 1980 implementation can be summarized:

1. classes
2. derived classes
3. public/private access control
4. constructors and destructors
5. call and return functions (Section 15.2.4.8)
6. `friend` classes
7. type checking and conversion of function arguments

During 1981 three more features were added:

8. inline functions
9. default arguments
10. overloading of the assignment operator

Since a preprocessor was used for the implementation of C with Classes, only new features, that is, features not present in C, needed to be described and the full power of C was directly available to users. Both of these aspects were appreciated at the time. Having C as a subset dramatically reduced the support and documentation work needed. This was most important because for several years I did all of the C with Classes and later C++ documentation and support in addition to doing the experimentation, design, and implementation. Having all C features available further ensured that no limitations introduced through prejudice or lack of foresight on my part would deprive a user of features already available in C. Naturally, portability to machines supporting C was ensured. Initially, C with Classes was implemented and used on a DEC PDP/11, but soon it was ported to machines such as DEC, VAX, and Motorola 68000-based machines. C with Classes was still seen as a dialect of C. Furthermore, classes were referred to as "An Abstract Data Type Facility for the C Language" [Stroustrup 1980a]. Support for object-oriented programming was not claimed until the provision of virtual functions in C++ in 1983 [Stroustrup 1984a].

15.2.4 Feature Details

Clearly, the most important aspect of C with Classes and later of C++ was the class concept. Many aspects of the C with Classes class concept can be observed by examining a simple example from [Stroustrup 1980a]:

```
class stack {
    char   s[SIZE]; /* array of characters */
    char * min;     /* pointer to bottom of stack */
    char * top;     /* pointer to top of stack */
    char * max;     /* pointer to top of allocated space */
    void   new();   /* initialization function (constructor) */
```

```
public:
    void   push(char);
    char   pop();
};
```

A class is a user-defined data type. A class specifies the type of the class members that define the representation of a variable of the type (an object of the class), specifies the set of operations (functions) that manipulate such objects, and specifies the access users have to these members. Member functions are typically defined "elsewhere":

```
char stack.pop()
{
    if (top <= min) error("stack underflow");
    return *(--top);
}
```

Objects of class `stack` can now be defined and used:

```
class stack s1, s2;          /* two variables of class 'stack' */
class stack * p1 = &s2;      /* 'p1' points to 's2' */
class stack * p2 = new stack; /* 'p2' points to stack object
                                 allocated on free store */

s1.push('h');    /* use object directly */
p1->push('s');   /* use object through pointer */
```

Several key design decisions are reflected here:

1. C with Classes follows Simula in letting the programmer specify types from which variables (objects) can be created, rather than, say, the Modula approach of specifying a module as a collection of objects and functions. In C with Classes (as in C++), a class is a type. This is a key notion in C++. When `class` means user-defined type in C++ why didn't I call it type? I chose `class` primarily because I dislike inventing new terminology and found Simula's quite adequate in most cases.
2. The representation of objects of the user-defined type is part of the class declaration. This has far-reaching implications. For example, it means that true local variables can be implemented without the use of free store (heap store, dynamic store) or garbage collection. It also means that a function must be recompiled; the representation of an object it uses directly is changed. See Section 15.4.3 for C++ facilities for expressing interfaces that avoid such recompilation.
3. Compile time access control is used to restrict access to the representation. By default, only the functions mentioned in the class declaration can use names of class members. Members (usually function members) specified in the public interface, the declarations after the `public:` label, can be used by other code.
4. The full type (including both the return type and the argument types) of a function, is specified for function members. Static (compile-time) type checking is based on this type specification. This differed from C at the time, where function argument types were neither specified in interfaces nor checked in calls.
5. Function definitions are typically specified "elsewhere" to make a class more like an interface specification than a lexical mechanism for organizing source code. This implies that separate

compilation for class member functions and their users is easy and the linker technology traditionally used for C is sufficient to support C++.

6. The function `new()` is a constructor, a function with a special meaning to the compiler. Such functions provided guarantees about classes. In this case, the guarantee is that the constructor, known somewhat confusingly as a `new` function, at the time is guaranteed to be called to initialize every object of its class before the first use of the object.
7. Both pointers and nonpointer types are provided (as in both C and Simula).

Much of the further development of C with Classes and C++ can be seen as exploring the consequences of these design choices, exploiting their good sides, and compensating for the problems caused by their bad sides. Many, but by no means all, of the implications of these design choices were understood at the time; Stroustrup [1980a] is dated April 3, 1980. This section tries to explain what was understood at the time and give pointers to sections explaining later consequences and realizations.

15.2.4.1 *Run-time Efficiency*

In Simula, it is not possible to have local or global variables of class types; that is, every object of a class must be allocated on the free store using the new operator. Measurements of my Cambridge simulator had convinced me that this was a major source of inefficiency. Later, Karel Babcisky from the Norwegian Computer Centre presented data on Simula run-time performance that confirmed my conjecture [Babcisky 1984]. For that reason alone, I wanted global and local variables of class types.

In addition, having different rules for the creation and scope of built-in and user-defined types is inelegant, and I felt that on occasion my programming style had been cramped by an absence of local and global class variables in Simula. Similarly, I had on occasion missed the ability to have pointers to built-in types in Simula so I wanted the C notion of pointers to apply uniformly over user-defined and built-in types. This is the origin of the notion that over the years grew into a "principle" for C++: user-defined and built-in types should behave the same, relative to the language rules, and receive the same degree of support from the language and its associated tools. When the ideal was formulated, built-in types received by far the best support, but C++ has overshot that target so that built-in types now receive slightly inferior support compared to user-defined types.

The initial version of C with Classes did not provide inline functions to take further advantage of the availability of the representation. Inline functions were soon provided, though. The general reason for the introduction of inline functions was worry that the cost of crossing a protection barrier would cause people to refrain from using classes to hide representation. In particular, Stroustrup [1982] observes that people had made data members public to avoid the function call overhead incurred by a constructor for simple classes where only one or two assignments are needed for initialization. The immediate cause for the inclusion of inline functions into C with Classes was a project that couldn't afford function call overhead for some classes involved in real-time processing.

Over the years, considerations along these lines grew into the C++ "principle" that it was not sufficient to provide a feature, it had to be provided in an affordable form. Most definitely, "affordable" was seen as meaning "affordable on hardware common among developers" as opposed to "affordable to researchers with high-end equipment," or "affordable in a couple of years when hardware will be cheaper." C with Classes was always considered as something to be used *now* or *next month* rather than simply a research project to deliver something in a couple of years hence.

Inlining was considered important for the utility of classes and, therefore, the issue was more *how* to provide it than *whether* to provide it. Two arguments won the day for the notion of having the programmer select which functions the compiler should try to inline. First, I had poor experiences with languages that left the job of inlining to compilers "because clearly the compiler knows best." The compiler only knows best if it has been programmed to inline and it has a notion of time/space optimization that agrees with mine. My experience with other languages was that only "the next release" would actually inline and it would do so according to an internal logic that a programmer couldn't effectively control. To make matters worse, C (and therefore, C with Classes and later C++) has genuine separate compilation so that a compiler never has access to more than a small part of the program (Section 15.2.4.2). Inlining a function for which you don't know the source appears feasible given advanced linker and optimizer technology, but such technology wasn't available at the time (and still isn't in most environments). Furthermore, extensive global analysis and optimization easily become unaffordable for large systems where optimizations are most critical. C with Classes was designed to deliver efficient code given a simple portable implementation on traditional systems. Given that, the programmer had to help. Even today, the choice seems right.

15.2.4.2 *The Linkage Model*

The issue of how separately compiled programs are linked together is critical for any programming language and, to some extent, determines the features the language can provide. One of the critical influences on the development of C with Classes and C++ was the decision that

1. Separate compilation should be possible with traditional C/FORTRAN UNIX/DOS style linkers.
2. Linkage should in principle be type safe.
3. Linkage should not require any form of database (though one could be used to improve a given implementation).
4. Linkage to program fragments written in other languages such as C, assembler, and FORTRAN should be easy and efficient.

C uses "header files" to ensure consistent separate compilation. Declarations of data structure layouts, functions, variables, and constants are placed in header files that are typically textually included into every source file that needs the declarations. Consistency is ensured by placing adequate information in the header files and ensuring that the header files are consistently included. C++ follows this model up to a point.

The reason that layout information can be present in a C++ class declaration (though it doesn't *have* to be; see Section 15.4.3) is to ensure that the declaration and use of true local variables is easy and efficient. For example:

```
void f()
{
    stack s;
    int c;
    s.push('h');
    c = s.pop();
}
```

Using the stack declaration from Section 15.2.4, even a simple-minded C with Classes implementation can ensure that no use is made of free store for this example, that the call of `pop()` is inlined so that no function call overhead is incurred and that the non-inlined call of `push()` can invoke a separately compiled function `pop()`. In this, C++ resembles Ada [Ichbiah 1979].

At the time, I felt that there was a tradeoff between having separate interface and implementation declarations (as in Modula2), plus a tool (linker) for matching them up, and having a single class declaration plus a tool (a dependency analyzer) that considered the interface part separately from the implementation details for the purposes of re-compilation. It appears that I underestimated the complexity of the latter, and also, that the proponents of the former approach underestimate the cost (in terms of porting problems and run-time overhead) of the former.

The concern for simple-minded implementations was partly a necessity caused by the lack of resources for developing C with Classes and partly a distrust of languages and mechanisms that required "clever" techniques. An early formulation of a design goal was that C with Classes "should be implementable without using an algorithm more complicated than a linear search." Wherever that rule of thumb was violated, as in the case of function overloading (Section 15.3.3.3), it led to semantics that were more complicated than anyone felt comfortable with and typically also to implementation complications.

The aim—based on my Simula experience—was to design a language that would be easy enough to understand to attract users and easy enough to implement to attract implementers. Only if a relatively simple implementation could be used by a relatively novice user in a relatively unsupportive programming environment to deliver code that compared favorably with C code in development time, correctness, run-time speed, and code size, could C with Classes, and later C++, expect to survive in competition with C.

This was part of a philosophy of fostering self-sufficiency among users. The aim was always and explicitly to develop local expertise in all aspects of using C++. Most organizations must follow the exact opposite strategy. They keep users dependent on services that generate revenue for a central support organization and/or consultants. In my opinion, this contrast is a deep reason for some of the differences between C++ and many other languages.

The decision to work in the relatively primitive and almost universally available framework of the C linking facilities caused the fundamental problem that a C++ compiler must always work with only partial information about a program. An assumption made about a program could possibly be violated by a program written tomorrow in some other language (such as C, FORTRAN, or assembler) and linked in possibly after the program has started executing. This problem surfaces in many contexts. It is hard for an implementation to guarantee

1. that something is unique,
2. that (type) information is consistent,
3. that something is initialized.

In addition, C provides only the feeblest support for the notion of separate name spaces so that avoiding name space pollution by separately written program segments becomes a problem. Over the years, C++ has tried to face all of these challenges without departing from the fundamental model and technology that gives portability, but in the C with Classes days we simply relied on the C technique of header files.

Through the acceptance of the C linker came another "principle" for the development of C++: C++ is just one language in a system and not a complete system. In other words, C++ accepts the role of a traditional programming language with a fundamental distinction between the language, the operating system, and other important parts of the programmer's world. This delimits the role of the language in a way that is hard to do for a language, such as Smalltalk or Lisp, that was conceived as a complete system or environment. It makes it essential that a C++ program fragment can call program fragments written in other languages and that a C++ program fragment can itself be called by program fragments written in other languages. Being "just a language" also allows C++ implementations to benefit directly from tools written for other languages.

The need for a programming language and the code written in it to be just a cog in a much larger machine is of utmost importance to most industrial users, yet such co-existence with other languages and systems was apparently not a major concern to most theoreticians, would-be perfectionists, and academic users. I believe this to be one of the main reasons for C++'s success.

15.2.4.3 *Static Type Checking*

I have no recollection of discussions, no design notes, and no recollection of any implementation problems about the introduction of static ("strong") type checking into C with Classes. The C with Classes syntax and rules, the ones subsequently adopted for the ANSI C standard, simply appeared fully formed in the first C with Classes implementation. After that, a minor series of experiments led to the current (stricter) C++ rules. Static type checking was to me, after my experience with Simula and ALGOL 68, a simple *must* and the only question was exactly how it was to be added.

To avoid breaking C code, it was decided to allow the call of an undeclared function and not perform type checking on such undeclared functions. This was of course a major hole in the type system, and several attempts were made to decrease its importance as the major source of programming errors before finally, in C++, the hole was closed by making a call of an undeclared function illegal. One simple observation defeated all attempts to compromise, and thus maintain a greater degree of C compatibility: As programmers learned C with Classes they lost the ability to find run-time errors caused by simple type errors. Having come to rely on the type checking and type conversion provided by C with Classes or C++, they lost the ability to quickly find the "silly errors" that creep into C programs through the lack of checking. Further, they failed to take the precautions against such silly errors that good C programmers take as a matter of course. After all, "such errors don't happen in C with Classes." Thus, as the frequency of run-time errors caused by uncaught argument type errors goes down, their seriousness and the time needed to find them goes up. The result was seriously annoyed programmers demanding further tightening of the type system.

The most interesting experiment with "incomplete static checking" was the technique of allowing calls of undeclared functions, but noting the type of the arguments used so that a consistency check could be done when further calls were seen. When Walter Bright many years later independently discovered this trick, he named it "autoprototyping," using the ANSI C term *prototype* for a function declaration. The experience was that autoprototyping caught many errors and initially increased a programmer's confidence in the type system. However, since consistent errors and errors in a function called only once in a compilation were not caught, autoprototyping ultimately destroyed programmer confidence in the type checker and induced a sense of paranoia even worse than I have seen in C or BCPL programmers.

C with Classes introduced the notation `f(void)` for a function `f` that takes no arguments as a contrast to `f()` that in C declares a function that can take any number of arguments of any type without any type check. My users soon convinced me, however, that the `f(void)` notation wasn't very elegant, and that having functions declared `f()` accept arguments wasn't very intuitive. Consequently, the result of the experiment was to have `f()` mean a function `f` that takes no arguments, as any novice would expect. It took support from both Doug McIlroy and Dennis Ritchie for me to build up courage to make this break from C. Only after they used the word abomination about `f(void)` did I dare give `f()` the obvious meaning. However, to this day C's type rules are much laxer than C++'s and any use of `f()` as a function declaration between the two languages is incompatible.

Another early attempt to tighten C with Classes' type rules was to disallow "information destroying" implicit conversions. Like others, I had been badly bitten by implicit `long` to `int` and `int` to `char` conversions. I decided to try to ban all implicit conversions that were not value preserving; that is, to require an explicit conversion operator wherever a larger object was stored into a smaller. The experiment failed miserably. Every C program I looked at contained large numbers of assignments of `ints` to `char` variables. Naturally, since these were working programs, most of these assignments were perfectly safe. That is, either the value was small enough not to become truncated or the truncation was expected or at least harmless in that particular context. There was no willingness in the C with Classes community to make such a break from C. I'm still looking for ways to compensate for these problems.

15.2.4.4 *Why C?*

A common question at C with Classes presentations was, "Why use C? Why didn't you build on, say, Pascal?" One version of my answer can be found in Stroustrup [1986b]:

> C is clearly not the cleanest language ever designed nor the easiest to use so why do so many people use it?
>
> 1. C is *flexible*: It is possible to apply C to most every application area, and to use almost every programming technique with C. The language has no inherent limitations that preclude particular kinds of programs from being written.
> 2. C is *efficient*: The semantics of C are "low level"; that is, the fundamental concepts of C mirror the fundamental concepts of a traditional computer. Consequently, it is relatively easy for a compiler and/or a programmer to efficiently utilize hardware resources for a C program.
> 3. C is *available*: Given a computer, whether the tiniest micro or the largest super-computer, the chance is that there is an acceptable quality C compiler available and that that C compiler supports an acceptably complete and standard C language and library. There are also libraries and support tools available, so that a programmer rarely needs to design a new system from scratch.
> 4. C is *portable*: A C program is not automatically portable from one machine (and operating system) to another nor is such a port necessarily easy to do. It is, however, usually possible, and the level of difficulty is such that porting even major pieces of software with inherent machine dependencies is typically technically and economically feasible.
>
> Compared with these "first order" advantages, the "second order" drawbacks like the curious C declarator syntax and the lack of safety of some language constructs become less important. Designing "a better C" implies compensating for the major problems involved in writing, debugging, and maintaining C programs *without compromising the advantages of C*. C++ preserves all these advantages and compatibility with C at the cost of abandoning claims to perfection and of some compiler and language complexity. However, designing a language "from scratch" does not ensure perfection and the C++ compilers compare favorably in run-time, have better error detection and reporting, and equal the C compilers in code quality.

This formulation is more polished than I could have managed in the early C with Classes days, but it does capture the essence of what I considered important about C, and that I did not want to lose in C with Classes. Pascal was considered a toy language [Kernighan 1981], so it seemed easier and safer to add type checking to C than to add the features considered necessary for systems programming to Pascal. At the time, I had a positive dread of making mistakes of the sort where the designer, out of misguided paternalism or plain ignorance, makes the language unusable for real work in important areas. The ten years that followed clearly showed that choosing C as a base left me in the mainstream of systems programming where I intended to be. The cost in language complexity has been considerable, but manageable.

At the time, I considered Modula-2, Ada, Smalltalk, Mesa, and Clu as alternatives to C and as sources for ideas for C++ [Stroustrup 1984b] so there was no shortage of inspiration. However, only C, Simula, ALGOL 68, and in one case BCPL left noticeable traces in C++ as released in 1985. Simula gave classes, ALGOL 68 operator overloading (Section 15.3.3.3), references (Section 15.3.3.4), and the ability to declare variables anywhere in a block (Section 15.3.3.1), and BCPL gave // comments (Section 15.3.3.1).

There were several reasons for avoiding major departures from C style. I saw the merging of C's strengths as a systems programming language with Simula's strengths for organizing programs as a significant challenge in itself. Adding significant features from other languages could easily lead to a "shopping list" language and destroy the integrity of the resulting language. To quote from Stroustrup [1986b]:

> A programming language serves two related purposes: it provides a vehicle for the programmer to specify actions to be executed and a set of concepts for the programmer to use when thinking about what can be done. The first aspect ideally requires a language that is "close to the machine," so that all important aspects of a machine are handled simply and efficiently in a way that is reasonably obvious to the programmer. The C language was primarily designed with this in mind. The second aspect ideally requires a language that is "close to the problem to be solved" so that the concepts of a solution can be expressed directly and concisely. The facilities added to C to create C++ were primarily designed with this in mind.

Again this formulation is more polished than I could have managed during the early stages of the design of C with Classes, but the general idea was clear. Departures from the known and proven techniques of C and Simula would have to wait for further experience with C with Classes and C++, and further experiments. I firmly believe, and believed then, that language design is not just design from first principles but also an art that requires experience, experiments, and sound engineering tradeoffs. Adding a major feature or concept to a language should not be a leap of faith but a deliberate action based on experience and it should fit into a framework of other features and ideas of how the resulting language can be used. The post-1985 evolution of C++ shows the influence of ideas from Ada, Clu, and ML.

15.2.4.5 *Syntax Problems*

Could I have "fixed" the most annoying deficiencies of the C syntax and semantics at some point before C++ was made generally available? Could I have done so without removing useful features (to C with Classes' users in their environments as opposed to an ideal world) or introducing incompatibilities that were unacceptable to C programmers wanting to migrate to C with Classes? I think not. In some cases, I tried, but I backed out of my changes after complaints from outraged users. The part of the C syntax I disliked most was the declaration syntax. Having both prefix and postfix declarator operators causes a fair amount of confusion. So does allowing the type specifier to be left out (meaning `int` by default).[2]

My eventual rationale for leaving things as they were was that any new syntax would (temporarily at least) add complexity to a known mess. Also, even though the old style is a boon to teachers of trivia and to people wanting to ridicule C, it is not a significant problem for C programmers. In this case, I'm not sure if I did the right thing, though.

---

2 In 1995, the C++ standards committee finally banned "implicit int" in declarations.

The agony to me and other C++ implementers, documenters, and tool builders caused by the perversities of syntax has been significant. Users can, and do of course, insulate themselves from such problems by writing in a small and easily understood subset of the C/C++ declaration syntax. A significant syntactic simplification for the benefit of users was introduced into C++ at the cost of some extra work to implementers and some C compatibility problems. In C, the name of a structure, a "structure tag," must always be preceded by the keyword `struct`. For example

```
struct buffer a; /* 'struct' is necessary in C */
```

In the context of C with Classes, this had annoyed me for some time because it made user-defined types second class citizens syntactically. Given my lack of success with other attempts to clean up the syntax, I was reluctant and only made the change at the time where C with Classes was mutated into C++ at the urging of Tom Cargill. The name of a `struct` or a `class` is now a type name and requires no special syntactic identification:

```
buffer a; // C++
```

The resulting fights over C compatibility lasted for years (see also Section 15.3.4).

15.2.4.6 *Derived Classes*

The derived class concept is C++'s version of Simula's prefixed class notion and thus a sibling of Smalltalk's subclass concept. The names *derived* class and *base* class were chosen because I never could remember what was *sub* and what was *super* and observed that I was not the only one with this particular problem. It was also noted that many people found it counterintuitive that a subclass typically has *more* information than its superclass. In inventing the terms "derived class" and "base class," I departed from my usual principle of not inventing new names where old ones existed. In my defense, I note that I have never observed any confusion about what is base and what is derived among C++ programmers and that the terms are trivially easy to learn even for people without a grounding in mathematics.

The C with Classes concept was provided without any form of run-time support. In particular, the Simula (and C++) concept of a virtual function was missing. The reason for this was that I—with reason, I think—doubted my ability to teach people how to use them and, even more, my ability to convince people that a virtual function is as efficient in time and space as an ordinary function, as typically used. Often people with Simula and Smalltalk experience still don't quite believe that until they have had the C++ implementation explained to them in detail—and many still harbor irrational doubts after that.

Even without virtual functions, derived classes in C with Classes were useful for building new data structures out of old ones and for associating operations with the resulting types. In particular, as explained in Stroustrup [1980] and Stroustrup [1982], they allowed list classes to be defined, and also task classes.

In the absence of virtual functions, a user could use objects of a derived class and treat base classes as implementation details (only). Alternatively, an explicit type field could be introduced in a base class and used together with explicit type casts. The former strategy was used for tasks where the user only sees specific derived task classes and "the system" sees only the task base classes. The latter strategy was used for various application classes where, in effect, a base class was used to implement a variant record for a set of derived classes. Much of the effort in C with Classes and later C++ has been to ensure that programmers needn't write such code. Most important in my thinking at the time, and in my own code, was the combination of base classes, explicit type conversions, and (occasionally) macros to provide generic container classes. Eventually, these techniques matured into C++'s template facility and the techniques for using templates together with base classes to express commonality among instantiated templates (Section 15.6.3).

15.2.4.7 *The Protection Model*

Before starting work on C with Classes, I worked with operating systems. The notions of protection from the Cambridge CAP computer and similar systems—rather than any work in programming languages—inspired the C++ protection mechanisms. The class is the unit of protection and the fundamental rule is that you cannot grant yourself access to a class; only the declarations placed in the class declaration (supposedly by its owner) can grant access. By default, all information is private.

Access is granted by declaring a function in the public part of a class declaration, or by specifying a function or a class as a `friend`. Initially, only classes could be friends, thus granting access to all member functions of the friend class, but later it was found convenient to be able to grant access (friendship) to individual functions. In particular, it was found useful to be able to grant access to global functions. A friendship declaration was seen as a mechanism similar to that of one protection domain granting a read-write capability to another.

Even in the first version of C with Classes, the protection model applied to base classes as well as members. Thus, a class could be either publicly or privately derived from another. The private/public distinction for base classes predates the debate on implementation inheritance vs. interface inheritance by about five years [Snyder 1986; Liskov 1987]. If you want to inherit an implementation only, you use private derivation in C++. Public derivation gives users of the derived class access to the interface provided by the base class. Private derivation leaves the base as an implementation detail; even the public members of the private base class are inaccessible except through the interface explicitly provided for the derived class. To provide "semitransparent scopes" a mechanism was provided to allow individual public names from a private base class to be made public [Stroustrup 1982].

15.2.4.8 *Run-time Guarantees*

The access control mechanisms described above simply prevent unauthorized access. A second kind of guarantee was provided by "special member functions," such as constructors, that were recognized and implicitly invoked by the compiler. The idea was to allow the programmer to establish guarantees, sometimes called "invariants," that other member functions could rely on. Curiously enough, the initial implementation contained a feature that is not provided by C++ but is often requested. In C with Classes, it was possible to define a function that would implicitly be called before every call of every member function (except the constructor) and another that would be implicitly called before every return from every member function. They were called `call` and `return` functions. They were used to provide synchronization for the monitor class in the original task library [Stroustrup 1980b]:

```
class monitor : object {
        /* ... */
        call() { /* grab lock */ }
        return() { /* release lock */ }
};
```

These are similar in intent to the CLOS `:before` and `:after` methods. Call and return functions were removed from the language because nobody (but me) used them and because I seemed to have completely failed to convince people that `call()` and `return()` had important uses. In 1987, Mike Tiemann suggested an alternative solution called "wrappers" [Tiemann 1987], but at the USENIX implementors' workshop in Estes Park, this idea was determined to have too many problems to be accepted into C++.

15.2.4.9 *Features Considered, but not Provided*

In the early days, many features were considered that later appeared in C++ or are still discussed. These included virtual functions, `static` members, templates, and multiple inheritance. However,

> All of these generalizations have their uses, but every "feature" of a language takes time and effort to design, implement, document, and learn. . . . The base class concept is an engineering compromise, like the C class concept [Stroustrup 1982].

I just wish I had explicitly mentioned the need for experience. With that, the case against featurism and for a pragmatic approach would have been complete.

The possibility of automatic garbage collection was considered on several occasions before 1985 and deemed unsuitable for a language already in use for real-time processing and hard-core systems tasks such as device drivers. In those days, garbage collectors were less sophisticated than they are today and the processing power and memory capacity of the average computer were small fractions of what today's systems offer. My personal experience with Simula and reports of other GC-based systems convinced me that GC was unaffordable by me and my colleagues for the kind of applications we were writing. Had C with Classes (or even C++) been defined to require automatic garbage collection, it would have been more elegant, but stillborn. Direct support for concurrency was also considered but rejected in favor of a library-based approach (Section 15.2.2).

15.2.5 Work Environment

C with Classes was designed and implemented by me as a research project in the Computing Science Research Center of Bell Labs. This center provided—and still provides—a possibly unique environment for such work. When I joined I was basically told to "do something interesting," given suitable computer resources, encouraged to talk to interesting and competent people, and given a year before having to formally present my work for evaluation.

There was a cultural bias against "grand projects" requiring many people, against "grand plans" like untested paper designs for others to implement, and against a class distinction between designers and implementers. If you liked such things, Bell Labs and others have many places where you could indulge such preferences. However, in the Computing Science Research Center it was almost a requirement that you—if you were not into theory—(personally) implemented something embodying your ideas and found users that could benefit from what you built. The environment was very supportive for such work and the Labs provided a large pool of people with ideas and problems to challenge and test anything built. Thus, I could write:

> There never was a C++ paper design; design, documentation, and implementation went on simultaneously. Naturally, the C++ front-end is written in C++. There never was a "C++ project" either, or a "C++ design committee". Throughout, C++ evolved, and continues to evolve, to cope with problems encountered by users, and through discussions between the author and his friends and colleagues [Stroustrup 1986b].

Only after C++ was an established language did more conventional organizational structures emerge, and even then I was officially in charge of the reference manual and had the final say over what went into it, until that task was handed over to the ANSI C++ committee in early 1990. On the other hand, after the first few months, I never had the freedom to design just for the sake of designing something beautiful or to make arbitrary changes in the language as it stood at any given time. Whatever I considered a language feature required an implementation to make it real, and any change or extension required the concurrence and usually enthusiasm of key C with Classes and later C++ users.

As there was no guaranteed user population, the language and its implementations could only survive by serving the needs of its users well enough to counteract the organizational pull of established languages and the marketing hype of newer languages.

C with Classes grew through discussions with people in the Computing Science Research Center and early users there and elsewhere in the Labs. Most of C with Classes and later C++ was designed on somebody else's blackboard and the rest on mine. Most such ideas were rejected as being too elaborate, too limited in usefulness, too hard to implement, too hard to teach for use in real projects, not efficient enough in time or space, too incompatible with C, or simply too weird. The few ideas that made it through this filter, invariably involving discussions between at least two people, I then implemented. Typically, the idea mutated through the effort of implementation, testing, and early use by me and one or two others. The resulting version was tried on a larger audience and would often mutate a bit further before finding its way into the "official" version of C with Classes as shipped by me. Usually, a tutorial was written somewhere along the way. Writing a tutorial was considered an essential design tool, because if a feature cannot be explained, simply the burden of supporting it will be too great. This point was never far from my mind because during the early years I was the support organization.

In the early days, Sandy Fraser, my department head at the time, was very influential. For example, I believe he was the one to encourage me to break from the Simula style of class definition where the complete function definition is included, and adopt the style where function definitions are typically elsewhere, thus emphasizing the class declaration's role as an interface. Much of C with Classes was designed to allow simulators to be built that could be used in Sandy Fraser's work in network design. The first real application of C with Classes was such network simulators. Sudhir Agrawal was another early user who influenced the development of C with Classes through his work with network simulations. Jonathan Shopiro provided much feedback of the C with Classes design and implementation based on his simulation of a "dataflow database machine."

For more general discussions on programming language issues, as opposed to looking at applications to determine which problems needed to be solved, I turned to Dennis Ritchie, Steve Johnson, and in particular, Doug McIlroy. Doug McIlroy's influence on the development of both C and C++ cannot be overestimated. I cannot remember a single critical design decision in C++ that I have not discussed at length with Doug. Naturally, we didn't always agree, but I still have a strong reluctance to make a decision that goes against Doug's opinion. He has a knack for being right and an apparently infinite amount of experience and patience.

As the main design work for C with Classes and C++ was done on blackboards, the thinking tended to focus on solutions to "archetypical" problems: Small examples that are considered characteristic for a large class of problems. Thus, a good solution to the small example will provide significant help in writing programs dealing with real problems of that class. Many of these problems have entered the C++ literature and folklore through my use of them as examples in my papers, books, and talks. For C with Classes, the example considered most critical was the `task` class that was the basis of the task library supporting Simula-style simulation. Other key classes were `queue`, `list`, and `histogram` classes. The `queue` and `list` classes were based on the idea borrowed from Simula of providing a link class from which users derived their own classes.

The danger inherent in this approach is to create a language and tools that provide elegant solutions to small selected examples, yet don't scale to building complete systems or large programs. This was counteracted by the simple fact that C with Classes (and later C++) had to pay for itself during its early years. This ensured that C with Classes couldn't evolve into something that was elegant but useless.

15.3 FROM C WITH CLASSES TO C++

During 1982, it became clear to me that C with Classes was a "medium success" and would remain so until it died. I defined a medium success as something so useful that it easily paid for itself and its developer, but not so attractive and useful that it would pay for a support and development organization. Thus, continuing with C with Classes and its C preprocessor implementation would condemn me to support C with Classes' use indefinitely. I was convinced that there were only two ways out of this dilemma:

1. Stop supporting C with Classes, so that the users would have to go elsewhere (freeing me to do something else).
2. Develop a new and better language based on my experience with C with Classes that would serve a large enough set of users to pay for a support and development organization (thus freeing me to do something else). At the time I estimated that 5,000 industrial users was the necessary minimum.

The third alternative, increasing the user population through marketing (hype), never occurred to me. What actually happened was that the explosive growth of C++, as the new language was eventually named, kept me so busy that to this day I haven't managed to get sufficiently detached to do something else of significance.

The success of C with Classes was, I think, a simple consequence of meeting its design aim: C with Classes did help organize a large class of programs significantly better than C, without the loss of run-time efficiency and without requiring enough cultural changes to make its use unfeasible in organizations that were unwilling to undergo major changes. The factors limiting its success were partly the limited set of new facilities offered over C, and partly the preprocessor technology used to implement C with Classes. There simply wasn't enough support in C with Classes for people who were willing to invest significant efforts to reap matching benefits: C with Classes was an important step in the right direction, but only one small step. As a result of this analysis, I began designing a cleaned-up and extended successor to C with Classes and implementing it using traditional compiler technology.

The resulting language was at first still called C with Classes, but after a polite request from management it was given the name C84. The reason for the naming was that people had taken to calling C with Classes "new C," and then C. This last abbreviation led to C being called "plain C," "straight C," and "old C." The name C84 was used only for a few months, partly because it was ugly and institutional, partly because there would still be confusion if people dropped the "84." I asked for ideas for a new name and picked C++ because it was short, had nice interpretations, and wasn't of the form "adjective C." In C, ++ can, depending on context, be read as "next," "successor," or "increment," though it is always pronounced "plus plus." The name C++ and its runner up ++C are fertile sources for jokes and puns—almost all of which were known and appreciated before the name was chosen. The name C++ was suggested by Rick Mascitti. It was first used in Stroustrup [1984b] where it was edited into the final copy in December 1983.

15.3.1 Aims

During the 1982–1984 period, the aims for C++ gradually became more ambitious and more definite. I had come to see C++ as a language separate from C, and libraries and tools had emerged as areas of work. Because of that, because tool developers within Bell Labs were beginning to show interest in C++, and because I had embarked on a completely new implementation that would become the C++ compiler front-end, Cfront, I had to answer key questions:

1. Who will the users be?
2. What kind of systems will they use?
3. How will I get out of the business of providing tools?
4. How should the answers to [1], [2], and [3] affect the language definition?

My answer to [1], "Who will the users be?" was that first my friends within Bell Labs and I would use it, then more widespread use within AT&T would provide more experience, then some universities would pick up the ideas and the tools, and finally AT&T and others would be able to make some money by selling the set of tools that had evolved. At some point, the initial and somewhat experimental implementation done by me would be faded out in favor of more "industrial strength" implementations by AT&T, and others.

This made practical and economic sense; the initial (Cfront) implementation would be tool poor, portable, and cheap because that was what I, my colleagues, and many university users needed and could afford. Later, there would be ample scope for AT&T and others to provide better tools for more specialized environments. Such better tools aimed primarily at industrial users needn't be cheap either, and would thus be able to pay for the support organizations necessary for large scale use of the language. That was my answer to [3], "How will I get out of the business of providing tools?" Basically, the strategy worked. However, just about every detail actually happened in an unforeseen way.

To get an answer to [2], "What kind of systems will they use?" I simply looked around to see what kind of systems the C with Classes users actually did use. They used everything from boxes that were so small that they couldn't run a compiler to mainframes. They used more operating systems than I had heard of. Consequently, I concluded that extreme portability and the ability to do cross compilation were necessities and that I could make no assumption about the size and speed of the machines running generated code. To build a compiler, however, I would have to make assumptions about the kind of system people would develop their programs on. I assumed that one MIPS plus one Mbyte would be available. That assumption I considered a bit risky because most of my prospective users at the time had at most part of a PDP11 or some other relatively low powered and/or time-shared system available.

I did not predict the PC revolution, but by overshooting my performance target for Cfront, I happened to build a compiler that (barely) could run on an IBM PC/AT, thus providing an existence proof that C++ could be an effective language on a PC, thereby spurring commercial software developers to beat it.

The answer to [4], "How does all this affect the language definition?" I concluded, was that no feature must require really sophisticated compiler or run-time support, that available linkers must be used, and that the code generated would have to be efficient (comparable to C), even initially.

15.3.2 Cfront

The Cfront compiler front-end for the C84 language was designed and implemented by me between the spring of 1982 and the summer of 1983. The first user outside the computer science research center, Jim Coplien, received his copy in July of 1983. Jim was in a group that had been doing experimental switching work with C with Classes in Bell Labs in Naperville, Illinois, for some time.

In that same time period I designed C84, drafted the reference manual published January 1, 1984 [Stroustrup 1984a], designed the `complex` number library and implemented it, together with Leonie Rose [Rose 1984], designed and implemented the first `string` class together with Jonathan Shopiro, maintained and ported the C with Classes implementation, and supported the C with Classes users and helped them become C84 users. That was a busy year and a half.

Cfront was (and is) a traditional compiler front-end, performing a complete check of the syntax and semantics of the language, building an internal representation of its input, analyzing and rearranging that representation, and finally producing output suitable for some code generator. The internal representation was (is) a graph with one symbol table per scope. The general strategy is to read a source file one global declaration at a time and produce output only when a complete global declaration has been completely analyzed.

The organization of Cfront is fairly traditional, except maybe for the use of many symbol tables instead of just one. Cfront was originally written in C with Classes (what else?) and soon transcribed into C84 so that the very first working C++ compiler was done in C++. Even the first version of Cfront used classes heavily, but no virtual functions because they were not available at the start of the project.

The most unusual—for its time—aspect of Cfront was that it generated C code. This has caused no end of confusion. Cfront generated C because I needed extreme portability for an initial implementation and I considered C the most portable assembler around. I could easily have generated some internal back-end format or assembler from Cfront, but that was not what my users needed. No assembler or compiler back-end served more than maybe a quarter of my user community and there was no way that I could produce the, say, six back-ends needed to serve just 90 percent of that community. In response to this need, I concluded that using C as a common input format to a large number of code generators was the only reasonable choice. The strategy of building a compiler as a C generator has later become quite popular, so that languages such as Ada, CLOS, Eiffel, Modula-3, and Smalltalk have been implemented that way. I got a high degree of portability at a modest cost in compile-time overhead. Over the years, I have measured this overhead on various systems and found it to be between 25 percent and 100 percent of the "necessary" parts of a compilation.

Please note that the C compiler is used as a code generator only. Any error message from the C compiler reflects an error in the C compiler or in Cfront, but not in the C++ source text. Every syntactic and semantic error is in principle caught by Cfront, the C++ compiler front-end. I stress this because there has been a long history of confusion about what Cfront was/is. It has been called a preprocessor because it generates C, and for people in the C community (and elsewhere) that has been taken as proof that Cfront was a rather simple program—something like a macro preprocessor. People have thus "deduced" (wrongly) that a line-for-line translation from C++ to C is possible, that symbolic debugging at the C++ level is impossible when Cfront is used, that code generated by Cfront must be inferior to code generated by "real compilers," that C++ wasn't a "real language," and so forth. Naturally, I have found such unfounded claims most annoying—especially when they were leveled as criticisms of the C++ language. There are now several C++ compilers that use Cfront together with local code generators without going through a C front end. To the user, the only obvious difference is faster compile times.

Cfront is only a compiler front-end and can never be used for real programming by itself. It needs a driver to run the source file through the C preprocessor, Cpp, then run the output of Cpp through Cfront, and the output from Cfront through a C compiler:

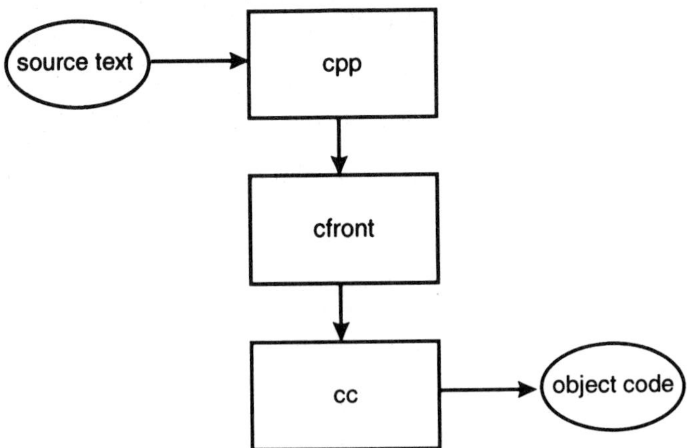

In addition, the driver must ensure that dynamic (run-time) initialization is done. In Cfront 3.0, the driver becomes yet more elaborate as automatic template instantiation (Section 15.6.3) is implemented [McClusky 1992].

As mentioned, I decided to live within the constraints of traditional linkers. However, there was one constraint that I felt was too difficult to live with, yet so silly that I had a chance of fighting it if I had sufficient patience: Most traditional linkers had a very low limit on the number of characters that can be used in external names. A limit of eight characters was common, and six characters and one case only are guaranteed to work as external names in Classical C; ANSI/ISO C accepts that limit also. Given that the name of a member function includes the name of its class and that the type of an overloaded function has to be reflected in the linkage process somehow or other, I had little choice. Consequently, I started (in 1982) lobbying for longer names in linkers. I don't know if my efforts actually had any effect, but these days most linkers do give me the much larger number of characters I need. Cfront uses encodings to implement type safe linkage in a way that makes a limit of 32 characters too low for comfort and even 256 is a bit tight at times (see Section 15.3.3.3). In the interim, systems of hash coding of long identifiers have been used with archaic linkers, but that was never completely satisfactory.

Versions of C++ are often named by Cfront release numbers. Release 1.0 was the language as defined in "*The C++ Programming Language*" [Stroustrup 1986b].

Releases 1.1 (June 1986) and 1.2 (February 1987) were primarily bug fix releases but also added pointers to members and protected members (Section 15.4.1). Release 2.0 was a major clean-up that also introduced multiple inheritance (Section 15.4.2) in June 1989. Release 2.1 (April 1990) was primarily a bug fix release that brought Cfront (almost) into line with the definition in the ARM. (See Ellis & Stroustrup: *The Annotated C++ Reference Manual* [Ellis 1990] (Section 15.6.1).) Release 3.0 (September 1991) added templates (Section 15.6.3) as specified in the ARM. Release 4.0 is expected to add exception handling (Section 15.6.4) as specified in the ARM.

I wrote the first versions of Cfront (1.0, 1.1, 1.2) and maintained them; Steve Dewhurst worked on it with me for a few months before release 1.0 in 1985. Laura Eaves did much of the work on the Cfront parser for releases 1.0, 1.1, 2.1, and 3.0. I also did the lion's share of the programming for releases 1.2 and 2.0, but starting with release 1.2, Stan Lippman also spent most of his time on Cfront. George Logothetis, Judy Ward, Nancy Wilkinson, and Stan Lippman did most of the work for releases 2.1 and 3.0. The work on 2.0 was coordinated by Barbara Moo, and Andrew Koenig organized Cfront testing. Barbara also coordinated releases 1.2, 2.1, and 3.0. Sam Haradhvala from Object Design, Inc., did an initial implementation of templates in 1989 that Stan Lippman extended and completed for release 3.0 in 1991. The initial implementation of exception handling in Cfront was done by Hewlett-Packard in 1992. In addition to these people who have produced code that has found its way into the main version of Cfront, many people have built local C++ compilers from it. Apple, Centerline (formerly Saber), ParcPlace, Sun, HP, and others ship products that contain locally modified versions of Cfront.

15.3.3 Language Feature Details

The major additions to C with Classes introduced to produce C++ were:

1. Virtual functions
2. Function name and operator overloading
3. References
4. Constants (`const`)
5. User-controlled free-store memory control
6. Improved type checking

In addition, the notion of call and return functions (Section 15.2.4.8) was dropped due to lack of use, and many minor details were changed to produce a cleaner language.

15.3.3.1 *Minor Changes*

The most visible minor change was the introduction of BCPL-style comments:

```
int a; /* C-style explicitly terminated comment */
int b; // BCPL-style comment terminated by end-of-line
```

Since both styles of comments are allowed, people can simply use the style they like best. The name "new-function" for constructors had been a source of confusion, so the name "constructor" was introduced.

In C with Classes, a dot was used to express membership of a class as well as selection of a member of a particular object. This had been the cause of some minor confusion and could also be used to construct ambiguous examples. To alleviate this, **::** was introduced to mean membership of class and **.** was retained exclusively for membership of object.

I borrowed the ALGOL 68 notion that a declaration can be introduced wherever it is needed (and not just at the top of some block). Thus, I enabled an "initialize-only" or "single-assignment" style of programming that is less error prone than traditional styles. This style is essential for references and constants that cannot be assigned and is inherently more efficient for types where default initialization is expensive.

15.3.3.2 *Virtual Functions*

The most obvious new feature in C++, and certainly the one that had the greatest impact on the style of programming one could use for the language, was virtual functions. The idea was borrowed from Simula and presented in a form that was intended to make a simple and efficient implementation easy.

The rationale for virtual functions was presented in Stroustrup [1986b] and [1986c]. To emphasize the central role of virtual functions in C++ programming, I will quote it in detail here:

"An abstract data type defines a sort of black box. Once it has been defined, it does not really interact with the rest of the program. There is no way of adapting it to new uses except by modifying its definition. This can lead to severe inflexibility. Consider defining a type shape for use in a graphics system. Assume for the moment that the system has to support circles, triangles, and squares. Assume also that you have some classes:

```
class point{ /* ... */ };
class color{ /* ... */ };
```

You might define a shape like this:

```
enum kind { circle, triangle, square };

class shape {
    point center;
    color col;
    kind k;
    // representation of shape
public:
    point where()        { return center; }
    void move(point to) { center = to; draw(); }
    void draw();
    void rotate(int);
    // more operations
 };
```

The "type field" k is necessary to allow operations such as `draw()` and `rotate()` to determine what kind of shape they are dealing with (in a Pascal-like language, one might use a variant record with tag k). The function `draw()` might be defined like this:

```
void shape::draw()
{
    switch (k) {
    case circle:
        // draw a circle
        break;
    case triangle:
        // draw a triangle
        break;
    case square:
        // draw a square
    }
}
```

This is a mess. Functions such as `draw()` must "know about" all the kinds of shapes there are. Therefore the code for any such function grows each time a new shape is added to the system. If you define a new shape, every operation on a shape must be examined and (possibly) modified. You are not able to add a new shape to a system unless you have access to the source code for every operation. Since adding a new shape involves "touching" the code of every important operation on shapes, it requires great skill and potentially introduces bugs into the code handling other (older) shapes. The choice of representation of particular shapes can get severely cramped by the requirement that (at least some of) their representation must fit into the typically fixed sized framework presented by the definition of the general type shape.

The problem is that there is no distinction between the general properties of any shape (a shape has a color, it can be drawn, and so forth) and the properties of a specific shape (a circle is a shape that has a radius, is drawn by a circle-drawing function, and so forth). Expressing this distinction and taking advantage of it defines object-oriented programming. A language with constructs that allows this distinction to be expressed and used supports object-oriented programming. Other languages don't.

The Simula inheritance mechanism provides a solution. First, specify a class that defines the general properties of all shapes:

```
class shape {
    point center;
    color col;
    // ...
public:
    point where() { return center; }
    void move(point to) { center = to; draw(); }
    virtual void draw();
    virtual void rotate(int);
    // ...
};
```

The functions for which the calling interface can be defined, but where the implementation cannot be defined except for a specific shape, have been marked "virtual" (the Simula and C++ term for "may be redefined later in a class derived from this one"). Given this definition, we can write general functions manipulating shapes:

```
void rotate_all(shape** v, int size, int angle)
// rotate all members of vector "v" of size "size" "angle" degrees
{
    for (int i = 0; i < size; i++) v[i].rotate(angle);
}
```

To define a particular shape, we must say that it is a shape and specify its particular properties (including the virtual functions):

```
class circle : public shape {
    int radius;
public:
    void draw() { /* ... */ };
    void rotate(int) {} // yes, the null function
};
```

In C++, `class` circle is said to be *derived* from class `shape`, and class `shape` is said to be a *base* of class `circle`. An alternative terminology calls `circle` and `shape` subclass and superclass, respectively [Stroustrup 1986c].

For further discussion of virtual functions and object-oriented programming see Section 15.3.7 and Section 15.4.3.

The key implementation idea was that the set of virtual functions in a class defines an array of pointers to functions, so that a call of a virtual function is simply an indirect function call through that array. There is one array per class and one pointer to such an array in each object of a class that has virtual functions.

I don't remember much interest in virtual functions at the time. Probably I didn't explain the concepts involved well, but the main reaction I received from people in my immediate vicinity was one of indifference and skepticism. A common opinion was that virtual functions were simply a kind of crippled pointer to a function and thus redundant. Worse, it was sometimes argued that a well-designed program wouldn't need the extensibility and openness provided by virtual functions, so that proper analysis would show which non-virtual functions could be called directly. Therefore, the argument went, virtual functions were simply a form of inefficiency. Clearly I disagreed, and added virtual functions anyway.

15.3.3.3 *Overloading*

Several people had asked for the ability to overload operators. Operator overloading "looked neat" and I knew from experience with ALGOL 68 how the idea could be made to work. However, I was reluctant to introduce the notion of overloading into C++:

1. Overloading was reputed to be hard to implement so that compilers would grow to monstrous size.
2. Overloading was reputed to be hard to teach and hard to define precisely so that manuals and tutorials would grow to monstrous size.
3. Code written using operator overloading was reputed to be inherently inefficient.
4. Overloading was reputed to make code incomprehensible.

If [3] or [4] were true then C++ would be better off without overloading. If [1] or [2] were true then I didn't have the resources to provide overloading.

However, if all of these conjectures were false, then overloading would solve some real problems for C++ users. There were people who would like to have complex numbers, matrices, and APL-like vectors in C++. There were people who would like range-checked arrays, multi-dimensional arrays, and strings in C++. There were at least two separate applications for which people wanted to overload logical operators such as | (or), & (and), and ^ (exclusive or). The way I saw it, the list was long and would grow with the size and the diversity of the C++ user population. My answer to [4], "overloading makes code obscure," was that several of my friends, whose opinions I valued and whose experience was measured in decades, claimed that their code would become cleaner if they had overloading. So what if one can write obscure code with overloading? It is possible to write obscure code in any language. It matters more how a feature can be used well than how it can be misused.

Next, I convinced myself that overloading wasn't inherently inefficient [Stroustrup 1984c; Ellis 1990]. The details of the overloading mechanism were mostly worked out on my blackboard and those of Stu Feldman, Doug McIlroy, and Jonathan Shopiro.

Thus, having worked out an answer to [3], "code written using overloading is efficient," I needed to concern myself with [1] and [2], the issue of compiler and language complexity. I first observed that use of classes with over-loaded operators, such as complex and string, was quite easy and didn't put a major burden on the programmer. Next I wrote the manual sections to prove that the added complexity wasn't a serious issue; the 42-page manual needed less than a page and a half extra. Finally, I did the first implementation in two hours using only 18 lines of extra code in Cfront, and I felt I had demonstrated that the fears about definition and implementation complexity were somewhat exaggerated.

Naturally, all these issues were not really tackled in this strict sequential order. However, the focus of the work did start with utility issues and slowly drifted to implementation issues. The overloading mechanisms were described in detail in [Stroustrup 1984c] and examples of classes using the mechanisms were written up [Rose 1984; Shopiro 1985].

In retrospect, I underestimated the complexity of the definition and implementation issues and compounded these problems by trying to isolate overloading mechanisms from the rest of the language semantics. The latter was done out of misguided fear of confusing users. In particular, I required that a declaration

```
overload print;
```

should precede declarations of an overloaded function print, such as

```
void print(int);
void print(const char*);
```

I also insisted that ambiguity control should happen in two stages so that resolutions involving built-in operators and conversions would always take precedence over resolutions involving user-defined operations. Maybe the latter was inevitable, given the concern for C compatibility and the chaotic nature of the C conversion rules for built-in types. These conversions do *not* constitute a lattice; for example, implicit conversions are allowed both from `int` to `float` and from `float` to `int`. However, the rules for ambiguity resolution were too complicated, caused surprises, and had to be revised for release 2.0. I still consider these rules too complex, but do not see scope for more than minor adjustments.

Requiring explicit `overload` declarations was plain wrong and the requirement was dropped in release 2.0.

15.3.3.4 *References*

References were introduced primarily to support operator overloading. C passes every function argument by value, and where passing an object by value would be inefficient or inappropriate the user can pass a pointer. This strategy doesn't work where operator overloading is used. In that case, notational convenience is essential so that a user cannot be expected to insert address-of operators if the objects are large.

Problems with debugging ALGOL 68 convinced me that having references that didn't change what object they referred to after initialization, was a good thing. If you wanted to do more complicated pointer manipulation in C++, you could use pointers. Because C++ has both pointers and references, it does not need operations for distinguishing operations on the reference itself from operations on the object referred to (like Simula), or the kind of deductive mechanism employed by ALGOL 68.

It is important that const references can be initialized by non-lvalues and lvalues of types that require conversion. In particular, this is what allows a FORTRAN function to be called with a constant:

```
extern "Fortran" float sqrt(const float&); // '&' means reference
sqrt(2); // call by reference
```

Jonathan Shopiro was deeply involved in the discussions that led to the introduction of references. In addition to the obvious uses of references, such as argument, we considered the ability to use references as return types important. This allowed us to have a very simple index operator for a string class:

```
class String {
    // ...
    char& operator[](int index); // subscript operator
                                 // return a reference
};

void f(String& s)
```

```
{
    char c1 = ...
    s[i] = c1;      // assign to operator[]'s result
    // ...
    char c2 = s[i]; // assign operator[]'s result
}
```

We considered allowing separate functions for left-hand and right-hand side use of a function but considered using references the simpler alternative, even though this implied that we needed to introduce additional "helper classes" to solve some problems where returning a simple reference wasn't enough.

15.3.3.5 *Constants (`const`)*

In operating systems, it is common to have access to some piece of memory controlled directly or indirectly by two bits: one that indicates whether a user can write to it and one that indicates whether a user can read it. This idea seemed to me directly applicable to C++ and I considered allowing every type to be specified `readonly` or `writeonly` [Stroustrup 1981b]. The proposal is focused on specifying interfaces rather than on providing symbolic constants for C. Clearly, a `readonly` value is a symbolic constant, but the scope of the proposal is far greater. Initially, I proposed pointers to `readonly` but not read-only pointers. A brief discussion with Dennis Ritchie evolved the idea into the `readonly/writeonly` mechanism that I implemented and proposed to an internal Bell Labs C standards group chaired by Larry Rosler. There, I had my first experience with standards work. I came away from a meeting with an agreement (that is, a vote) that `readonly` would be introduced into C, yes *C*, not C with Classes or C++) provided it was renamed `const`. Unfortunately, a vote isn't executable so nothing happened to our C compilers. A while later, the ANSI C committee (X3J11) was formed and the `const` proposal resurfaced there and became part of ANSI/ISO C.

However, in the meantime I had experimented further with `const` in C with Classes and found that `const` was a useful alternative to macros for representing constants only if a global `consts` were implicitly local to their compilation unit. Only in that case could the compiler easily deduce that their value really didn't change and allow simple `consts` in constant evaluations and thus avoid allocating space for such constants and use them in constant expressions. C did not adopt this rule. This makes `consts` far less useful in C than in C++ and leaves C dependent on the preprocessor where C++ programmers can use properly typed and scoped `consts`.

15.3.3.6 *Memory Management*

Long before the first C with Classes program was written, I knew that free store (dynamic memory) would be used more heavily in a language with classes than in traditional C programs. This was the reason for the introduction of the `new` and `delete` operators in C with Classes. The `new` operator that both allocates memory from the free store and invokes a constructor to ensure initialization was borrowed from Simula. The `delete` operator was a necessary complement because I did not want C with Classes to depend on a garbage collector. The argument for the new operator can be summarized like this. Would you rather write:

```
X* p = new X(2);
```

or

```
struct X * p = (struct X *) malloc(sizeof(struct X));
if (p == 0) error("memory exhausted");
p->init(2);
```

and in which version are you most likely to make a mistake? The arguments against it, which were voiced quite a lot at the time, were "but we don't really need it," and "but someone will have used `new` as an identifier." Both observations are correct, of course.

Introducing "operator `new`" thus made the use of free store more convenient and less error prone. This increased its use even further so that the C free store allocation routine `malloc()` used to implement new became the most common performance bottleneck in real systems. This was no real surprise either; the only problem was what to do about it. Having real programs spend 50 percent or more of their time in `malloc()` wasn't acceptable.

I found per-class allocators and deallocators very effective. The fundamental idea is that free store memory usage is dominated by the allocation and deallocation of lots of small objects from very few classes. Take over the allocation of those objects in a separate allocator and you can save both time and space for those objects and also reduce the amount of fragmentation of the general free store. The mechanism provided for 1.0, "assignment to `this`," was too low level and error prone and was replaced by a cleaner solution in 2.0 (Section 15.4.1).

Note that static and automatic (stack allocated) objects were always possible and that the most effective memory management techniques relied heavily on such objects. The string class was a typical example; here `String` objects are typically on the stack so that they require no explicit memory management, and the free store they rely on is managed exclusively and invisibly to the user by the `String` member functions.

15.3.3.7 *Type Checking*

The C++ type checking rules were the result of experiments with the C with Classes. All function calls are checked at compile time. The checking of trailing arguments can be suppressed by explicit specification in a function declaration. This is essential to allow C's `printf()`:

```
int printf(const char* ...); // accept any argument after
                             // the initial character string

// ...
printf("date: %s %d 19%d\n",month,day,year); // maybe right
```

Several mechanisms were provided to alleviate the withdrawal symptoms that many C programmers feel when they first experience strict checking. Overriding type checking using the ellipsis was the most drastic and least recommended of those. Function name overloading (Section 15.3.3.3) and default arguments [Stroustrup 1986b] made it possible to give the appearance of a single function taking a variety of argument lists without compromising type safety. The stream I/O system demonstrates that the weak checking wasn't necessary even for I/O (see Section 15.5.3.1).

15.3.4 Relationship to Classic C

With the introduction of a separate name, C++, and the writing of a C++ reference manual [Stroustrup 1984a], compatibility with C became an issue of major importance and a point of controversy.

Also, in late 1983 the branch of Bell Labs that developed and supported UNIX, and produced AT&T's 3B series of computers, became interested in C++ to the point where they were willing to put resources into the development of C++ tools. Such development was necessary for the evolution of C++ from a one-man show to a language that a corporation could base critical projects on. Unfortunately, it also implied that development management needed to consider C++.

The first demand to emerge from development management was for 100 percent compatibility with C. The ideal of C compatibility is quite obvious and reasonable, but the reality of programming isn't that simple. For starters, with which C should C++ be compatible? C dialects abounded, and though ANSI C was emerging, it was still years away from having a stable definition, and its definition allowed many dialects. Naturally, the average user who wanted C compatibility insisted that C++ should be compatible with the local C dialect. This was an important practical problem and a great concern to me and my friends. It seemed far less of a concern to business-oriented managers and salesmen who either didn't quite understand the technical details or would like to use C++ to tie users into their software and/or hardware.

Another side of the compatibility issue was more critical: "In which ways must C++ differ from C to meet its fundamental goals?" and also "In which ways must C++ be compatible with C to meet its fundamental goals?" Both sides of the issue are important, and revisions were made in both directions during the transition from C with Classes to C++, shipped as release 1.0. Slowly and painfully an agreement emerged that there would be no gratuitous incompatibilities between C++ and ANSI C (when it became a standard) [Stroustrup 1986b], but that there was such a thing as an incompatibility that was not gratuitous. Naturally, the concept of "gratuitous incompatibilities" was a topic of much debate and took up a disproportional part of my time and effort. This principle has lately been known as "C++: As close to C as possible but no closer," after the title of a paper by Andrew Koenig and me [Koenig 1989].

Some conclusions about modularity and how a program is composed out of separately compiled parts were explicitly reflected in the original C++ reference manual [Stroustrup 1984a]:

a. Names are private unless they are explicitly declared public.
b. Names are local to their file unless explicitly exported from it.
c. Static type is checked unless explicitly suppressed.
d. A class is a scope (implying that classes nest properly).

Point [a] doesn't affect C compatibility but [b], [c], [d] imply incompatibilities:

1. The name of a non-local C function or object is by default accessible from other compilation units,
2. C functions need not be declared before use and calls are by default not type checked, and
3. C structure names don't nest (even when they are lexically nested).

In addition,

4. C++ has a single name space whereas C had a separate name space for "structure tags" (Section 15.2.4.5).

The "compatibility wars" now seem petty and boring, but some of the underlying issues are still unresolved and we are still struggling with them in the ANSI/ISO committee. I strongly suspect that the reason the compatibility wars were drawn out and curiously inconclusive was that we never quite faced the deeper issues related to the differing goals of C and C++, and saw compatibility as a set of separate issues to be resolved individually.

Typically, the least fundamental issue, [4], "name spaces," took up the most effort, but was eventually resolved [Ellis 1990].

I had to compromise the notion of a class as a scope, [3], and accept the C "solution" before I was allowed to ship release 1.0. One practical problem was that I had never realized that a C struct didn't constitute a scope, so that examples like this:

```
struct outer {
    struct inner {
        int i;
    };
    int j;
};
struct inner a = { 1 };
```

are legal C. When the issue came up towards the end of the compatibility wars I didn't have time to fathom the implications of the C "solution" and it was much easier to agree than to fight the issue. Later, after many technical problems and much discontent from users, nested class scopes were reintroduced into C++ in 1989 [Ellis 1990].

After much hassle, C++'s stronger type checking of function calls was accepted (unmodified). An implicit violation of the static type system is the original example of a C/C++ incompatibility that is not gratuitous. As it happens, the ANSI C committee adopted a slightly weaker version of C++'s rules and notation on this point and declared uses that don't conform to the C++ rules obsolete.

On issue [1], I had to accept the C rule that global names are by default accessible from other compilation units. There simply wasn't any support for the more restrictive C++ rule. This meant that C++, like C, lacks an effective mechanism for expressing modularity above the level of the class and the file. This has led to a series of complaints and the ANSI/ISO committee is now looking into several proposals for mechanisms to avoid name space pollution.[3] However, people like Doug McIlroy, who argued that C programmers would not accept a language where every object and function meant to be accessible from another compilation unit had to be explicitly declared as such, were probably right at the time, and saved me from making a serious mistake. I am now convinced that the original C++ solution wasn't elegant enough anyway.

15.3.5 Tools for Language Design

Theory and tools more advanced than a blackboard have not been given much space in the description of the history of C++. I tried to use YACC (an LALR(1) parser generator) for the grammar work, and was defeated by C's syntax (Section 15.2.4.5). I looked at denotational semantics, but was again defeated by quirks in C. Ravi Sethi had looked into that problem and found that he couldn't express the C semantics that way [Sethi 1980]. The main problem was the irregularity of C and the number of implementation-dependent and undefined aspects of a C implementation. Much later, the ANSI/ISO C++ committee had a stream of formal definition experts explain their techniques and tools, and give their opinion of the extent to which a genuine formal approach to the definition of C++ would help us in the standards effort. My conclusion is that with the current state of the art, and certainly with the state of the art in the early 1980s, a formal definition of a language that is not designed together with a formal definition method is beyond the ability of all but a handful of experts in formal definition.

This confirms my conclusion at the time. However, that left us at the mercy of imprecise and insufficient terminology. Given that, what could I do to compensate? I tried to reason about new features, both on my own and with others, to check my logic. However, I soon developed a healthy

3 In 1994, the C++ standard committee accepted a proposal for a namespace mechanism; see [Stroustrup 1994].

disrespect for arguments (definitely including my own) because I found that it is possible to construct a plausible logical argument for just about any feature. On the other hand, you simply don't get a useful language by accepting every feature that makes life better for someone. There are far too many reasonable features and no language could provide them all and stay coherent. Consequently, wherever possible, I tried to experiment.

My impression was, and is, that many programming languages and tools represent solutions looking for problems, and I was determined that my work should not fall into that category. Thus, I follow the literature on programming language and the debates about programming languages primarily to look for ideas for solutions to problems my colleagues and I have encountered in real applications. Other programming languages constitute a mountain of ideas and inspiration but it has to be mined carefully to avoid featurism and inconsistencies. The main sources for ideas for C++ were Simula, ALGOL 68, and later Clu, Ada, and ML. The key to good design is insight into problems, not the provision of the most advanced features.

15.3.6 The C++ Programming Language (1st edition)

In the fall of 1983 my next door neighbor at work, Al Aho, suggested that I write a book on C++, structured along the lines of Brian Kernighan and Dennis Ritchie's *The C Programming Language* and based on my published papers, internal memoranda, and the C++ reference manual. Completing the book took nine months.

The preface mentions the people who had by then contributed most to C++: Tom Cargill, Jim Coplien, Stu Feldman, Sandy Fraser, Steve Johnson, Brian Kernighan, Bart Locanthi, Doug McIlroy, Dennis Ritchie, Larry Rosler, Jerry Schwarz, and Jon Shopiro. My criteria for adding a person to that list was being able to identify a specific C++ feature that the person had added.

The book's opening line, "C++ is a general purpose programming language designed to make programming more enjoyable for the serious programmer," was deleted twice by reviewers who refused to believe that the purpose of programming language design could be anything but some serious mutterings about productivity, management, and software engineering. However,

> C++ was designed primarily so that the author and his friends would not have to program in assembler, C, or various modern high-level languages. Its main purpose is to make writing good programs easier and more pleasant for the individual programmer.

This was the case, whether those reviewers were willing to believe it or not. The focus of my work is the person, the individual (whether part of a group or not), the programmer. This line of reasoning has been strengthened over the years and is even more prominent in the second edition.

> *The C++ Programming Language* was the definition of C++ and the introduction to C++ for an unknown number of programmers and its presentation techniques and organization (borrowed with acknowledgments if not always sufficient skill from "The C Programming Language") have become the basis for an almost embarrassing number of articles and books. It was written with a fierce determination not to preach any particular programming technique. In the same way as I feared to build limitations into the language out of ignorance and misguided paternalism, I didn't want the book to turn into a "manifesto" for my personal preferences [Stroustrup 1991].

15.3.7 The "whatis?" Paper

Having shipped release 1.0 and sent the camera-ready copy of the book to the printers, I finally found time to reconsider larger issues and to document overall design issues. Just then, Karel Babcisky (the chairman of the Association of Simula Users) phoned from Oslo with an invitation to give a talk on C++ at the 1986 ASU conference in Stockholm. Naturally I wanted to go, but I was worried that presenting C++ at a Simula conference would be seen as a vulgar example of self-advertisement and an attempt to steal users away from Simula. After all, I said, C++ is not Simula so why would Simula users want to hear about it. Karel replied, "Ah, we are not hung up on syntax." This provided me with an opportunity to write not only about what C++ was, but also what it was supposed to be and where it didn't measure up to those ideals. The result was the paper "What is "Object-Oriented Programming?" [Stroustrup 1986], which I presented to the ASU conference in Stockholm.

The significance of this paper is that it is the first exposition of the set of techniques that C++ was aiming to provide support for. All previous presentations, to avoid dishonesty and hype, had been restricted to describe what features were already implemented and in use. The "whatis paper" defined the set of problems I thought a language supporting data abstraction and object-oriented programming ought to solve and gave examples of language features needed.

The result was a reaffirmation of the importance of the "multi-paradigm" nature of C++:

> Object-oriented programming is programming using inheritance. Data abstraction is programming using user-defined types. With few exceptions, object-oriented programming can and ought to be a superset of data abstraction. These techniques need proper support to be effective. Data abstraction primarily needs support in the form of language features and object-oriented programming needs further support from a programming environment. To be general purpose, a language supporting data abstraction or object-oriented programming must enable effective use of traditional hardware.

The importance of static type checking was also strongly emphasized. In other words, C++ follows the Simula rather than the Smalltalk model of inheritance and type checking:

> a Simula or C++ class specifies a fixed interface to a set of objects (of any derived class) whereas a Smalltalk class specifies an initial set of operations for objects (of any subclass). In other words, a Smalltalk class is a minimal specification and the user is free to try operations not specified whereas a C++ class is an exact specification and the user is guaranteed that only operations specified in the class declaration will be accepted by the compiler.

This has deep implications on the way one designs systems and on what language facilities are needed. A dynamically typed language such as Smalltalk simplifies the design and implementation of libraries by postponing type checking to run time. For example (using C++ syntax):

```
stack cs;
cs.push(new Saab900);
cs.pop()->takeoff(); // Oops! Run time error:
                     // a car does not have a takeoff method.
```

This delayed type error detection was considered unacceptable for C++, yet there had to be a way of matching the notational convenience and the standard libraries of a dynamically typed language. The notion of parameterized types was presented as the (future) solution for that problem in C++:

```
stack(plane*) cs;
cs.push(new Saab37b); // ok a Saab37b is a plane
cs.push(new Saab900); // error, type mismatch:
                      // car passed, plane* expected

cs.pop()->takeoff();  // no run-time check needed
cs.pop()->takeoff();  // no run-time check needed
```

The key reason for considering compile-time detection of such problems essential, was the observation that C++ is often used for programs executing where no programmer is present. Fundamentally, the notion of static type checking was seen as the best way to provide the strongest guarantees possible for a program, rather than merely a way of gaining run-time efficiency.

The "whatis" paper lists three aspects in which C++ was deficient:

1. Ada, Clu, and ML support parameterized types. C++ does not; the syntax used here is simply devised as an illustration. Where needed, parameterized classes are "faked" using macros. Parameterized classes would clearly be extremely useful in C++. They could easily be handled by the compiler, but the current C++ programming environment is not sophisticated enough to support them without significant overhead and/or inconvenience. There need not be any run-time overheads compared with a type specified directly.
2. As programs grow, and especially when libraries are used extensively, standards for handling errors (or more generally: "exceptional circumstances") become important. Ada, ALGOL 68, and Clu each support a standard way of handling exceptions. Unfortunately, C++ does not. Where needed, exceptions are "faked" using pointers to functions, "exception objects," "error states," and the C library `signal` and `longjmp` facilities. This is not satisfactory in general and fails even to provide a standard framework for error handling.
3. Given this explanation it seems obvious that it might be useful to have a class B inherit from two base classes A1 and A2. This is called multiple inheritance.

All three facilities were linked to the need to provide better (that is, more general, more flexible) libraries. All are now available in C++. Note that adding multiple inheritance and templates was considered as early as 1982 [Stroustrup 1982].

15.4 C++ RELEASE 2.0

Now (mid 1986), the course for C++ was set for all who cared to see. The key design decisions were made. The direction of the future evolution was for parameterized types, multiple inheritance, and exception handling. Much experimentation and adjustment based on experience was needed, but the glory days were over. C++ had never been silly putty, but there was now no real possibility for radical change. For good and bad, what was done was done. What was left was an incredible amount of solid work. At this point C++ had about 2,000 users worldwide.

This was the point where the plan—as originally conceived by Steve Johnson and me—was for a development and support organization to take over the day-to-day work on the tools (primarily Cfront), thus freeing me to work on the new features and the libraries that were expected to depend on them. This was also the point where I expected first AT&T, and then others, would start to build compilers and other tools to eventually make Cfront redundant.

Actually, they had already started, but the good plan was soon derailed due to management indecisiveness, ineptness, and lack of focus. A project to develop a brand new C++ compiler diverted attention and resources from Cfront maintenance and development. A plan to ship a release 1.3 in early 1988 completely fell through the cracks. The net effect was that we had to wait until June of 1989 for release 2.0, and that even though 2.0 was significantly better than release 1.2 in almost all ways, 2.0 did not provide the language features outlined in the "whatis paper," and consequently a significantly improved and extended library wasn't part of it.

Many of the people who influenced C with Classes and the original C++ continued to help with the evolution in various ways. Phil Brown, Tom Cargill, Jim Coplien, Steve Dewhurst, Keith Gorlen,

Laura Eaves, Bob Kelley, Brian Kernighan, Andy Koenig, Archie Lachner, Stan Lippman, Larry Mayka, Doug McIlroy, Pat Philip, Dave Prosser, Peggy Quinn, Roger Scott, Jerry Schwarz, Jonathan Shopiro, and Kathy Stark were explicitly acknowledged in [Stroustrup 1989b].

Stability of the language definition and its implementation was considered essential. The features of 2.0 were fairly simple modifications of the language based on experience with the 1.* releases. The most important aspect of release 2.0 was that it increased the generality of the individual language features and improved their integration into the language.

15.4.1 Feature Overview

The main features of 2.0 were first presented in Stroustrup [1987c] and summarized in the revised version of that paper [Stroustrup 1989b], which accompanied 2.0 as part of its documentation:

1. multiple inheritance,
2. type-safe linkage,
3. better resolution of overloaded functions,
4. recursive definition of assignment and initialization,
5. better facilities for user-defined memory management,
6. abstract classes,
7. static member functions,
8. `const` member functions,
9. `protected` members (first provided in release 1.2),
10. overloading of operator ->, and
11. pointers to members (first provided in release 1.2).

Most of these extensions and refinements represented experience gained with C++ and couldn't have been added earlier without more foresight than I possessed. Naturally, integrating these features involved significant work, but it was most unfortunate that this was allowed to take priority over the completion of the language as outlined in the "whatis" paper.

Most features enhanced the safety of the language in some way or other. Cfront 2.0 checked the consistency of function types across separate compilation units (type-safe linkage), made the overload resolution rules order independent, and also ensured that more calls were considered ambiguous. The notion of `const` was made more comprehensive, and pointers to members closed a loophole in the type system and provided explicit class-specific memory allocation and deallocation operations to make the error-prone "assignment to `this`" technique redundant.

To some people, the most important "feature" of release 2.0 wasn't a feature at all but a simple space optimization. From the beginning, the code generated by Cfront tended to be pretty good. As late as 1992, Cfront generated the fastest running code in a benchmark used to evaluate C++ compilers on a Sparc. There have been no significant improvements in Cfront's code generation since Release 1.0. However, release 1.* was wasteful because each compilation unit generated its own set of virtual function tables for all the classes used in that unit. This could lead to megabytes of waste. At the time (about 1984), I considered the waste necessary in the absence of linker support, and asked for such linker support. By 1987 that linker support hadn't materialized. Consequently, I rethought the problem and solved it by the simple heuristic of laying down the virtual function table of a class right next to its first non-virtual non-inline function.

15.4.2 Multiple Inheritance

In most people's minds, multiple inheritance, the ability to have two or more direct base classes, is *the* feature of 2.0. I disagreed at the time because I felt that the sum of the improvements to the type system were of far greater practical importance. Also, adding multiple inheritance in 2.0 was a mistake. Multiple inheritance belongs in C++ but is far less important than parameterized types. As it happened, parameterized types in the form of templates only appeared in release 3.0. There were a couple of reasons for choosing to work on multiple inheritance at the time: The design was further advanced and the implementation could be done within Cfront. Another factor was purely irrational. Nobody doubted that I could implement templates efficiently. Multiple inheritance, on the other hand, was widely supposed to be very difficult to implement efficiently. Thus, multiple inheritance seemed more of a challenge, and since I had considered it as early as 1982 and found a simple and efficient implementation technique in 1984, I couldn't resist the challenge. I suspect that this is the only case where fashion affected the sequence of events.

In September of 1984, I presented the C++ operator overloading mechanism at the IFIP WG2.4 conference in Canterbury [Stroustrup 1984c]. There I met Stein Krogdahl from the University of Oslo who was just finishing a proposal for adding multiple inheritance to Simula [Krogdahl 1984]. His ideas became the basis for the implementation of ordinary multiple base classes in C++. He and I later found out that the proposal was almost identical to an idea for providing multiple inheritance in Simula that had been considered by Ole-Johan Dahl in 1966 and rejected because it would have complicated the Simula garbage collector [Dahl 1988].

The original and fundamental reason for considering multiple inheritance was simply to allow two classes to be combined into one in such a way that objects of the resulting class would behave as objects of either base class [Stroustrup 1986c]:

> A fairly standard example of the use of multiple inheritance would be to provide two library classes displayed and task for representing objects under the control of a display manager and co-routines under the control of a scheduler, respectively. A programmer could then create classes such as

```
class my_displayed_task : public displayed, public task {
        // ...
};

class my_task : public task { // not displayed
        // ...
};

class my_displayed : public displayed { // not a task
        // ...
};
```

> Using (only) single inheritance only two of these three choices would be open to the programmer.

The implementation requires little more than remembering the relative offsets of the `task` and `displayed` objects in a `my_displayed_task` object. All the gory implementation details were explained in Stroustrup [1987a]. In addition, the language design must specify how ambiguities are handled and what to do if a class is specified as a base class more than once in a derived class:

Ambiguities are handled at compile time:

```
class A { public: void f(); /* ... */ };
class B { public: void f(); /* ... */ };
class C : public A, public B { /* no f() ... */ };

void g() {
    C* p;
    p->f(); // error: ambiguous
}
```

In this, C++ differs from the object-oriented Lisp dialects that support multiple inheritance.

Basically, I rejected all forms of dynamic resolution beyond the use of virtual functions as unsuitable for a statically typed language under severe efficiency constraints. Maybe, I should at this point have revived the notion of `call` and `return` functions (Section 15.2.4.8) to mimic the CLOS `:before` and `:after` methods. However, people were already worrying about the complexity of the multiple inheritance mechanisms and I am always reluctant to re-open old wounds.

Multiple inheritance in C++ became controversial [Cargill 1991; Carroll 1991; Waldo 1991; Sakkinen 1992] for several reasons. The arguments against it centered around the real and imaginary complexity of the concept, the utility of the concept, and the impact of multiple inheritance on other extensions and tool building. In addition, proponents of multiple inheritance can, and do, argue over exactly what multiple inheritance is supposed to be and how it is best supported in a language. I think, as I did then, that the fundamental flaw in these arguments is that they take multiple inheritance far too seriously. Multiple inheritance doesn't solve all of your problems, but it doesn't need to because it is quite cheap, and sometimes it is very convenient to have. Grady Booch [Booch 1991] expresses a slightly stronger sentiment: "Multiple inheritance is like a parachute, you don't need it very often, but when you do it is essential."

15.4.3 Abstract Classes

The very last feature added to 2.0 before it shipped was abstract classes. Late modification to releases are never popular and late changes to the definition of what will be shipped are even less so. I remember that several members of management thought I had lost contact with the real world when I insisted on this feature.

A common complaint about C++ was (and is) that private data is visible and that when private data is changed then code using that class must be recompiled. Often this complaint is expressed as "abstract types in C++ aren't really abstract." What I hadn't realized was that many people thought that because they *could* put the representation of an object in the private section of a class declaration then they actually *had to* put it there. This is clearly wrong (and that is how I failed to spot the problem for years). If you don't want a representation in a class, thus making the class an interface only, then you simply delay the specification of the representation to some derived class and define only virtual functions. For example, one can define a `set` of `T` pointers like this:

```
class set {
public:
    virtual void insert(T*);
    virtual void remove(T*);

    virtual int is_member(T*);
```

```
        virtual T* first();
        virtual T* next();

        virtual ~set() { }
    };
```

This provides all the information that people need to use a set, except that whoever actually creates a set must know something about how some particular kind of set is represented. For example, given

```
    class slist_set : public set, private slist {
        slink* current_elem;
    public:
        void insert(T*);
        void remove(T*);

        int is_member(T*);

        virtual T* first();
        virtual T* next();

        slist_set() : slist(), current_elem(0) { }
    };
```

we can create `slist_set` objects that can be used as `set`s by users who have never heard of a `slist_set`.

The only problem was that in C++, as defined before 2.0, there was no explicit way of saying: "The `set` class is just an interface: its functions need not be defined, it is an error to create objects of class `set`, and anyone who derives a class from `set` must define the virtual functions specified in `set`." Release 2.0 allowed a class to be declared explicitly *abstract* by declaring one or more of its virtual functions "pure" using the syntax `=0`:

```
    class set {                    // abstract class
    public:
        virtual void insert(T*) = 0; // pure virtual function
        virtual void remove(T*) = 0;

        // ...
    };
```

The `=0` syntax isn't exactly brilliant, but it expresses the desired notion of a pure virtual function in a way that is terse and fits the use of `0` to mean "nothing" or "not there" in C and C++. The alternative, introducing a new keyword, say `pure`, wasn't an option. Given the opposition to abstract classes as a "late and unimportant change," I would never simultaneously have overcome the traditional, strong, widespread, and emotional opposition to new keywords in parts of the C and C++ community.

The importance of the abstract class concept is that it allows a cleaner separation between a user and an implementor than is possible without it. This limits the amount of recompilation necessary after a change and also the amount of information necessary to compile an average piece of code. By decreasing the coupling between a user and an implementor, abstract classes provide an answer to people complaining about long compile times, and also serve library providers who must worry about the impact on users of changes to a library implementation. I had unsuccessfully tried to explain these notions in Stroustrup [1986b]. With an explicit language feature supporting abstract classes, I was much more successful [Stroustrup 1991].

15.5 THE EXPLOSION IN INTEREST AND USE

C++ was designed to serve users. It was not an academic experiment to design the perfect programming language. Nor was it a commercial product meant to enrich its developers. Thus, to fulfill its purpose C++ had to have users—and it had:

C++ Use

Date	*Estimated number of users*	*Date*	*Estimated number of users*
Oct 1979	1	Oct 1986	2,000
Oct 1980	16	Oct 1987	4,000
Oct 1981	38	Oct 1988	15,000
Oct 1982	85	Oct 1989	50,000
Oct 1983	??+2 (no Cpre count)	Oct 1990	150,000
Oct 1984	??+50 (no Cpre count)	Oct 1991	400,000
Oct 1985	500		

In other words, the C++ user population doubled every 7.5 months or so. These are conservative figures. The actual number of C++ users has never been easy to count. First, there are implementations, such as GNU's G++ and Cfront, shipped to universities for which no meaningful records can be kept. Second, many companies, both tools suppliers and end users, treat the number of their users and the kind of work they do like state secrets. However, I always had many friends, colleagues, contacts, and many compiler suppliers who were willing to trust me with figures as long as I used them in a responsible manner. This enabled me to estimate the number of C++ users. These estimates are created by taking the number of users reported to me or estimated based on personal experience, rounding them all down, adding them, and then rounding down again. These number are the estimates made at the time and not adjusted in any way. To support the claim that these figures are conservative, I can mention that Borland, the largest single C++ compiler supplier, publicly stated that it had shipped 500,000 compilers by October of 1991.

Early users had to be gained without the benefit of traditional marketing. Various forms of electronic communication played a crucial role in this. In the early years most distribution and all support was done using e-mail, and relatively early on, newsgroups dedicated to C++ were created (*not* at the initiative of Bell Labs employees) that allowed a wider dissemination of information about the language, techniques, and the current state of tools. These days this is fairly ordinary, but in 1981 it was relatively new. I think that only the spread of Interlisp over the Arpanet provides a contemporary parallel.

Later, more conventional forms of communication and marketing arose. After AT&T released Cfront 1.0, some resellers, notably Glockenspiel in Ireland and their US distributor Oasys (later part of Green Hills), started some minimal advertising in 1986, and when independently developed C++ compilers such as Oregon Software's C++ Compiler (developed by Mike Ball at TauMetric Software in San Diego) and Zortech's C++ Compiler (developed by Walter Bright in Seattle) appeared, 'C++' became a common sight in ads (from about 1988).

15.5.1 Conferences

In 1987 USENIX, the UNIX Users' association, took the initiative to hold the first conference specifically devoted to C++. Thirty papers were presented to 214 people in Santa Fe, New Mexico in November of 1987.

The Santa Fe conference set a good example for future conferences with a mix of papers on applications, programming and teaching techniques, ideas for improvements to the language, libraries, and implementation techniques. Notably for a USENIX conference, there were papers on C++ on the Apple MAC, OS/2, the Connection machine, and for implementing non-UNIX operating systems (for example, CLAM [Call 1987] and Choices [Campbell 1987]). The NIH library [Gorlen 1987] and the Inverviews library [Linton 1987] also made their public debut in Santa Fe. An early version of what became Cfront 2.0 was demonstrated, and I gave the first public presentation of its features. The USENIX C++ conferences continue as the primary technically and academically oriented C++ conference. The proceedings from these conferences are among the best reading about C++ and its use.

In addition to the USENIX C++ conferences, there are now many commercial and semi-commercial conferences devoted to C++, to C including C++, and to Object-Oriented Programming.

15.5.2 Journals and Books

By 1991 there were more than 60 books on C++ available in English alone, and both translations and locally written books available in languages such as Chinese, Danish, French, German, and Japanese. Naturally, the quality varies enormously.

The first journal devoted to C++, *The C++ Report*, from SIGS publications, started publishing in January of 1989, with Rob Murray as its editor. A larger and glossier quarterly, *The C++ Journal*, appeared in the spring of 1991. In addition, there are several newsletters controlled by C++ tools suppliers and many journals such as *Computer Language*, *The Journal of Object-Oriented Programming*, *Dr. Dobbs Journal*, and *The C Users' Journal* run regular columns or features on C++. Andrew Koenig's column in JOOP is particularly consistent in its quality and lack of hype.

Newsgroup and bulletin boards such as comp.lang.c++ on usenet and c.plus.plus on BIX have also produced tens of thousands of messages over the years to the delight and despair of readers. Keeping up with what is written about C++ is currently more than a full time job.

15.5.3 Libraries

The very first real code written in C with Classes was the task library [Stroustrup 1980b], which provided Simula-like concurrency for simulation. The first real programs were simulations of network traffic, circuit board layout, and so forth, using the task library. The task library is still heavily used today. The standard C library was available from C++, without overhead or complication compared with C, from day one. So are all other C libraries. Classical data types, such as character strings, range checked arrays, dynamic arrays, and lists, were among the examples used to design C++ and test its early implementations.

The early work with container classes such as list and array were severely hampered by the lack of support for a way of expressing parameterized types in C with Classes and in C++ up until version 3.0. In the absence of proper language support (later provided in the form of templates (Section 15.6.3), we had to make do with macros. The best that can be said for the C preprocessor's macro facilities is that they allowed us to gain experience with parameterized types and support individual and small group use.

Much of the work on designing classes was done in cooperation with Jonathan Shopiro, who in 1983 produced list and string classes that saw wide use within AT&T and are the basis for the classes currently found in the "Standard Components" library that was developed in Bell labs, and is now sold by USL. The design of these early libraries interacted directly with the design of the language and in particular with the design of the overloading mechanisms.

15.5.3.1 *The Stream I/O Library*

C's `printf` family of functions is an effective and often convenient I/O mechanism. It is not, however, type safe or extensible to user-defined types (classes). Consequently, I started looking for a type safe, terse, extensible, and efficient alternative to the `printf` family. Part of the inspiration came from the last page and a half of the Ada Rationale [Ichbiah 1979], which is an argument that you cannot have a terse and type-safe I/O library without special language features to support it. I took that as a challenge. The result was the stream I/O library that was first implemented in 1984 and presented in [Stroustrup 1985]. Soon after, Dave Presotto re-implemented the stream library without changing the interfaces.

To introduce stream I/O this example was considered:

```
fprintf(stderr,"x = %s\n",x);
```

Because `fprintf()` relies on unchecked arguments that are handled according to the format string at run time, this is not type safe and

> had x been a user-defined type like complex there would have been no way of specifying the output format of x in the convenient way used for types "known to `printf()`" (for example, `%s` and `%d`). The programmer would typically have defined a separate function for printing complex numbers and then written something like this:
>
> ```
> fprintf(stderr,"x = ");
> put_complex(stderr,x);
> fprintf(stderr,"\n");
> ```
>
> This is inelegant. It would have been be a major annoyance in C++ programs that use many user-defined types to represent entities that are interesting/critical to an application.
>
> Type-security and uniform treatment can be achieved by using a single overloaded function name for a set of output functions. For example:
>
> ```
> put(stderr,"x = ");
> put(stderr,x);
> put(stderr,"\n");
> ```
>
> The type of the argument determines which "put function" will be invoked for each argument. However, this is too verbose. The C++ solution, using an output stream for which << has been defined as a "put to" operator, looks like this:
>
> ```
> cerr << "x = " << x << "\n";
> ```
>
> where `cerr` is the standard error output stream (equivalent to the C `stderr`). So, if x is an int with the value 123, this statement would print
>
> ```
> x = 123
> ```
>
> followed by a newline onto the standard error output stream.

This style can be used as long as **x** is of a type for which operator << is defined, and a user can trivially define operator << for a new type. So, if x is of the user-defined type `complex` with the value `(1,2.4)`, the statement above will print

```
x = (1,2.4)
```

on `cerr`.

The stream I/O facility is implemented exclusively using language features available to every C++ programmer. Like C, C++ does not have any I/O facilities built into the language. The stream I/O facility is provided in a library and contains no "extra-linguistic magic."

The idea of providing an output operator rather than a named output function was suggested by Doug McIlroy. This requires operators that return their left-hand operand for use by further operations.

In connection with release 2.0, Jerry Schwarz re-implemented and partially redesigned the streams library to serve a larger class of applications and to be more efficient for file I/O. A significant improvement was the use of Andrew Koenig's idea of manipulators [Stroustrup 1991] to control formatting details such as the precision used for floating point output. Experience with streams was a major reason for the change to the basic type system and to the overloading rules to allow `char` values to be treated as characters rather than small integers the way they are in C. For example:

```
char ch = 'b';
cout << 'a' << ch;
```

would in Release 1.* output a string of digits reflecting the integer values of the characters a and b, whereas Release 2.* outputs ab, as one would expect.

15.5.3.2 *Other Libraries*

There were, and are, many other significant C++ libraries. These will be mentioned only briefly here because even though they were essential to their users, they did not affect the development of C++ significantly. They are, however, most significant to their users, and and the view of most users is that C++ is strongly affected, or even dominated, by a library.

The most significant early libraries were Keith Gorlen's NIH class library that provides a Smalltalk-like set of classes [Gorlen 1990] and Mark Linton's Interviews library that makes use of the X windows system convenient from C++ [Linton 1987]. GNU C++ (G++) comes with a library designed by Doug Lea that is distinguished by heavy use of abstract base classes. Rogue Wave and Dyad supply large sets of libraries primarily aimed at scientific uses. Glockenspiel has for years supplied libraries for various commercial uses. Rational ships a C++ version of "The Booch Components" that was originally designed for and implemented in Ada by Grady Booch. Grady Booch and Mike Vilot designed and implemented the C++ version. The Ada version, 150,000 non- commented source lines compared to the C++ version's 10,000 lines inheritance combined with templates, can be a very powerful mechanism for organizing libraries without loss of performance or clarity.

This is only a very short list of early libraries to indicate the diversity of C++ libraries. Many more libraries exist. In particular, most tools suppliers provide foundation libraries for their users. It seems that the "software components" industry that pundits have promised for years and bemoaned the lack of, has finally come into existence.

15.5.4 Compilers

The Santa Fe conference (Section 15.5.1) marked the announcement of the second wave of C++ implementations. Steve Dewhurst described the architecture of a compiler he and others were building in AT&T's Summit facility, Mike Ball presented some ideas for what became the TauMetric C++ compiler (more often known as the Oregon Software C++ compiler), and Mike Tiemann gave a most animated and interesting presentation of how the GNU C++ he was building would do just about everything and put all other C++ compiler writers out of business. The new AT&T C++ compiler never materialized; GNU C++ version 1.13 was first released in December of 1987; and TauMetric C++ was first shipped in January of 1988.

Until June of 1988, all C++ compiler on PCs were Cfront ports. Then Zortech started shipping their compiler. The appearance of Walter Bright's compiler made C++ "real" for many PC-oriented people for the first time. More conservative people reserved their judgment until the Borland C++ compiler in May of 1990, or even Microsoft's C++ compiler in March 1992. DEC released their first independently developed C++ compiler in February of 1992 and IBM released their first independently developed C++ compiler in May of 1992. In all, there are now more than a dozen independently developed C++ compilers.

In addition to these compilers, Cfront ports seemed to be everywhere. In particular, Sun, HP, Centerline, ParcPlace, Glockenspiel, and Comeau Computing ship Cfront-based products on just about any platform.

15.5.5 Tools and Environments

C++ was designed to be a viable language in a tool-poor environment. This was partly a necessity because of the almost complete lack of resources in the early years and the relative poverty later on. It was also a conscious decision to allow simple implementations and, in particular, simple porting of implementations.

C++ programming environments are now emerging that are a match for the environments habitually supplied with other object-oriented languages. For example, ObjectWorks for C++ from ParcPlace is essentially the best Smalltalk program development environment adapted for C++, and Centerline C++ (formerly Saber C++) is an interpreter-based C++ environment, inspired by the interlisp environment. This gives C++ programmers the option of using the more whizzy, more expensive, and often more productive environments that have previously only been available for other languages and/or as research toys. An environment is a framework in which tools can cooperate. There is now a host of such environments for C++: Most C++ implementations on PCs are compilers embedded in a framework of editors, tools, file systems, standard libraries, and so on. MacApp and the Mac MPW is the Apple Mac version of that and ET++ is a public domain version in the style of the MacApp. Lucid's Energize and HP's Softbench are yet other examples.

15.5.6 Commercial Competition

Commercial competitors were largely ignored and the C++ language was developed according to the original plan, its own internal logic, and the experience of its users. There was (and is) always much discussion among programmers, in the press, at conferences, and on the electronic bulletin boards about which language "is best" and which language will "win" in some sort of competition for users. Personally, I consider much of that debate misguided and uninformed, but that doesn't make the issues less real to a programmer, manager, or professor who has to choose a programming language for his or her next project. For good and bad, people debate programming languages with an almost religious fervor and often consider the choice of a programming language the most important choice of a project or organization.

In the early years, Modula-2 [Wirth 1982] was by many considered a competitor to C++. However, until the commercial release of C++ in 1985, C++ could hardly be considered a competitor to any language, and by then Modula-2 seemed to me to have been largely out-competed by C. Later it was popular to speculate about whether C++ or Objective C [Cox 1986] was to be "*the* Object-Oriented C." Ada [Ichbiah 1979] was often a possible choice of organizations who might use C++. In addition, Smalltalk [Goldberg 1983], and some object-oriented variant of Lisp [Kiczales 1992], would often be considered for applications that did not require hard-core systems work or maximum performance. Lately some people have been comparing C++ with Eiffel [Meyer 1988] and Modula-3 [Nelson 1991] for some uses.

My personal view is different. The main competitor to C++ was C. The reason that C++ is the most widely used object-oriented language today is that it was/is the only one that could consistently match C on C's own turf and that allows a transition path from C to a style of system design and implementation based on a more direct mapping between application level concepts and language concepts (usually called "data abstraction" or "object-oriented programming"). Secondarily, many organizations that consider a new programming language have a tradition for the use of an in-house language (usually a Pascal variant) or FORTRAN. Except for serious scientific computation these languages can be considered roughly equivalent to C when compared with C++.

In the secondary competition between C++ and other newer languages supporting abstraction mechanisms (object-oriented programming languages, languages supporting data abstraction) C++ was, during the early years (1984 to 1989), consistently the underdog as far as marketing was concerned. In particular, AT&T's marketing budget during that period was usually empty and AT&T's total spending on C++ advertising was about $3,000. To this day, most of AT&T's visibility in the C++ arena relies on Bell Labs' traditional policy of encouraging developers and researchers to give talks, write papers, and attend conferences rather than on any deliberate policy to promote C++. Within AT&T, C++ was also a grassroots movement without money or management clout. Naturally, coming from AT&T Bell Labs helps C++, but that help is earned the hard way by surviving in a large-company environment.

In competition, C++'s fundamental strength is its ability to operate in a traditional environment (social and computerwise), its run-time and space efficiency, the flexibility of its class concept, its low price, and its non-proprietary nature. Its weaknesses compared to newer languages are some of the uglier parts inherited from C, its lack of spectacular new features (such as built-in data base support), its lack of spectacular program development environments (only lately have C++ environments of the sort people have taken for granted for Smalltalk and Lisp become available for C++), its lack of standard libraries (only lately have major libraries become widely available for C++ and they are not "standard"),[4] and its lack of salesmen to balance the efforts of richer competitors. With C++'s recent dominance in the market, the last factor has disappeared. Some C++ salesmen will undoubtedly embarrass the C++ community by emulating some of the sleazy tricks and unscrupulous practices that salesmen and admen have used to attempt to derail C++'s progress.

An important factor, both for and against C++, was the willingness of the C++ community to acknowledge C++'s many imperfections. This openness is reassuring to many who have become

---

4 This problem has now been remedied. The standard C++ library provides standard containers, such as list, vector, map, set, and so on. and a library of sorting, searching, and so on. algorithms operating on these containers. These containers and algorithms are all templates. This part of the standard library is based on the work of Alex Stepanov [Stepanov 1994]. In addition, the standard library provides a vector type with associated operations to support numeric calculations based on the work of Ken Budge.

cynics from years of experience with the people and products of the software tools industry, but also infuriating to perfectionists and a fertile source for fair and not-so-fair criticism of C++. On balance, I think that the tradition of throwing rocks at C++, within the C++ community, has been a major advantage. It kept us honest, kept us busy improving the language and its tools, and kept the expectations of C++ users, and would-be users, realistic.

In competition with traditional languages, C++'s inheritance mechanism was a major plus. In competition with languages with inheritance, C++'s static type checking was a major plus. Of the languages mentioned, only Eiffel and Modula-3 combine the two in a way similar to C++. It is widely assumed that Ada will be revised to include inheritance [Tucker 1992].

C++ was designed to be a systems programming language and a language for applications that had a large "systems-like" component. This was the area that my friends and I knew well. The decision not to compromise C++'s strengths in this area to broaden its appeal has been crucial in its success. Only time will tell if this has also compromised its ability to appeal to an even larger audience. I would not consider that a tragedy because I am not among those who think that a single language should be all things to all people and C++ already serves the community it was designed for well. However, I suspect that through the design of libraries C++'s appeal will be very wide.

15.6 STANDARDIZATION

Sometime in 1988, it became clear that C++ would eventually have to be standardized [Stroustrup 1989]. There were now a handful of independent implementations in use or being produced, and clearly an effort had to be made to write a more precise and comprehensive definition of the language and also to gain wide acceptance for that definition. At first, formal standardization wasn't considered an option. Many people involved with C++ considered and still consider standardization before genuine experience has been gained abhorrent. However, making an improved reference manual wasn't something that could be done by one person (me) in private. Input and feedback from the C++ community was needed. Thus I came upon the idea of rewriting the C++ reference manual and circulating its draft among important and insightful members of the C++ community worldwide.

15.6.1 The Annotated Reference Manual

At about the same time, the part of AT&T that sold C++ commercially wanted a new and improved C++ reference manual and gave Margaret Ellis the task of writing it. It seemed only reasonable to combine the efforts and produce a single, externally reviewed reference manual. It also seemed obvious to me that publishing this manual with some additional information would help the acceptance of the new definition and make C++ more widely understood. Thus, *The Annotated C++ Reference Manual* was written "to provide a firm basis for the further evolution of C++ ... (and) to serve as a starting point for the formal standardization of C++" [Ellis 1990].

> The C++ reference manual alone provides a complete definition of C++, but the terse reference manual style leaves many reasonable questions unanswered. Discussions of what is not in the language, *why* certain features are defined as they are, and *how* one might implement some particular feature have no place in a reference manual but are nevertheless of interest to most users. Such discussions are presented as annotations and in the commentary sections.
>
> The commentary also helps the reader appreciate the relationships among different parts of the language and emphasizes points and implications that might have been overlooked in the reference manual itself. Examples and comparisons with C also make this book more approachable than the bare reference manual. [Ellis 1990]

After some minor squabbling with the product people, it was agreed that we'd write the ARM (as *The Annotated C++ Reference Manual* came to be popularly called) describing the whole of C++, that is with templates and exception handling, rather than as a manual for the subset implemented by the most recent AT&T release. This was important because it clearly established the language itself as different from any one implementation of it. This principle had been present from the very beginning, but needs to be often restated because users and implementors seem to have difficulties remembering it.

Of the ARM, I wrote every word of the reference manual proper, except the section on the preprocessor that Margaret Ellis adopted from the C Standard. The annotations were jointly written and partly based on my earlier papers [Stroustrup 1987a, 1987c, 1988a, 1988b].

The reference manual proper of the ARM was reviewed by about a hundred people from two dozen organizations. Most are named in the acknowledgment section of the ARM. In addition, many contributed to the whole of the ARM. The contributions of Brian Kernighan, Andrew Koenig, and Doug McIlroy were specifically noted. The reference manual proper from the ARM was accepted as the basis for the ANSI standardization of C++ in March of 1990. The ARM doesn't attempt to explain the techniques that the language features support. That job was left for the second edition of *The C++ Programming Language* [Stroustrup1991].

15.6.2 Minor Features

The ARM presented a few minor features that were not implemented until 2.1 releases from AT&T and other C++ compiler vendors. The most obvious of these were nested classes. I was strongly encouraged to revert to the original definition of nested class scopes by comments from external reviewers of the reference manual. I also despaired of ever getting the scope rules of C++ coherent while the C rule was in place (Section 15.3.4).

The ARM allowed people to overload prefix and postfix increment (++) independently. The main impetus for that came from people who wanted "smart pointers" that behaved exactly like ordinary pointers except for some added work done "behind the scenes."

15.6.3 Templates

In the original design of C++, parameterized types (templates) were considered but postponed because there wasn't time to do a thorough job of exploring the design and implementation issues. I first presented templates at the 1988 USENIX C++ conference in Denver:

> For many people, the largest single problem using C++ is the lack of an extensive standard library. A major problem in producing such a library is that C++ does not provide a sufficiently general facility for defining "container classes" such as lists, vectors, and associative arrays. [Stroustrup 1988b]

There are two approaches for providing such classes/types: One can either rely on dynamic typing and inheritance, as Smalltalk does, or one can rely on static typing and a facility for arguments of type *type*. The former is very flexible, but carries a high run-time cost, and more importantly, defies attempts to use static type checking to catch interface errors. Therefore, the latter approach was chosen.

A C++ parameterized type is called a class template. A class template specifies how individual classes can be constructed much like the way a class specifies how individual objects can be constructed. A vector class template might be declared like this:

```
template<class T> class vector {
    T* v;
    int sz;
public:
    vector(int);
    T& operator[](int);
    T& elem(int i) { return v[i]; }
    // ...
};
```

The `template <class T>` prefix specifies that a template is being declared and that an argument `T` of type *type* will be used in the declaration. After its introduction, `T` is used exactly like other type names within the scope of the template declaration. Vectors can then be used like this:

```
vector<int> v1(20);
vector<complex> v2(30);

typedef vector<complex> cvec; // make cvec a synonym for
                              // vector<complex>

cvec v3(40);                  // v2 and v3 are of the same type

v1[3] = 7;
v2[3] = v3.elem(4) = complex(7,8);
```

C++ does not require the user to explicitly "instantiate" a template; that is, the user need not specify which versions of a template need to be generated for particular sets of template arguments. The reason is that only when the program is complete can it be known what templates need to be instantiated. Many templates will be defined in libraries and many instantiations will be directly and indirectly caused by users that don't even know of the existence of those templates. It therefore seemed unreasonable to require the user to request instantiations (say, by using something like Ada's 'new' operator).

Avoiding unnecessary space overheads caused by too many instantiations of template functions was considered a first order, that is, language level problem rather than an implementation detail. I considered it unlikely that early (or even late) implementations would be able to look at instantiations of a class for different template arguments and deduce that all or part of the instantiated code could be shared. The solution to this problem was to use the derived class mechanism to ensure code sharing among derived template instances.

The template mechanism is completely a compile and link time mechanism. No part of the template mechanism needs run-time support. This leaves the problem of how to get the classes and functions generated (instantiated) from templates to depend on information known only at run time. The answer was, as ever in C++, to use virtual functions and abstract classes. Abstract classes used in connection with templates also have the effect of providing better information hiding and better separation of programs into independently compiled units.

15.6.4 Exception Handling

Exceptions were considered in the original design of C++, but were postponed because there wasn't time to do a thorough job of exploring the design and implementation issues. Exceptions were considered essential for error handling in programs composed out of separately designed libraries.

The actual design of the C++ exception mechanism stretched from 1984 to 1989. Andrew Koenig was closely involved in the later iterations and is the co-author (with me) of the published papers [Koenig 1989a, 1990, 1990]. I also had meetings at Apple, DEC, Microsoft, IBM, Sun, and other places where I presented draft versions of the design and received valuable input. In particular, I searched out people with actual experience with systems providing exception handling to compensate for my personal inexperience in that area. Throughout the design effort there was an increasing influence of systems designers of all sorts and a decrease of input from the language design community. In retrospect, the greatest influence on the C++ exception handling design was the work on fault-tolerant systems started at the University of Newcastle in England by Brian Randell and his colleagues, and continued in many places since.

The following assumptions were made for the design:

- Exceptions are used primarily for error handling.
- Exception handlers are rare compared to function definitions.
- Exceptions occur infrequently compared to function calls.

These assumptions, together with the requirement that C++ with exceptions should cooperate smoothly with languages without exceptions, such as C and FORTRAN, led to a design with multilevel propagation. The view is that not every function should be a firewall and that the best error-handling strategies are those where only designated major interfaces are concerned with nonlocal error handling issues. By allowing multilevel propagation of exceptions, C++ loses one aspect of static checking. One cannot, simply by looking at a function, determine which exceptions it may throw. C++ compensates by providing a mechanism for specifying a list of exceptions that a function may throw.

I concluded that the ability to define groups of exceptions is essential. For example, a user must be able to catch "any I/O library exception" without knowing exactly which exceptions those are. Many people, including Ted Goldstein and Peter Deutsch, noticed that most such groups were equivalent to class hierarchies. We therefore adopted a scheme inspired by ML where you throw an object and catch it by a handler declared to accepts objects of that type. This scheme naturally provides for type-safe transmission of arbitrary amounts of information from a throw point to a handler. For example:

```
class Matherr { /* ... */ };
class Overflow : public Matherr { /* ... */ };
class Underflow : public Matherr { /* ... */ };
class Zerodivide : public Matherr { /* ... */ };
class Int_add_overflow : public Overflow { /* ... */ };
// ...

try
{
    f();
}
catch (Overflow& over) {
    // handle Overflow or anything derived from Overflow
}
catch (Matherr& math) {
    // handle any Matherr
}
```

Thus `f()` might be written like this

```
void f() throw(Matherr&) // f() can throw Matherr& exceptions
                         // (and only Matherr& exceptions)
{
    // ...
    if (d == 0) throw Zerodivide();
    // ...
    if ( check(x,y) ) throw Int_add_overflow(x,y);
    // ...
}
```

The `Zerodivide` will be caught by the `Matherr&` handler above and `Int_add_overflow` will be caught by the `Overflow&` handler that might access the operand values `x` and `y` passed by `f()` in the object thrown.

The central point in the exception handling design was the management of resources. In particular, if a function grabs a resource, how can the language help the user to ensure that the resource is correctly released upon exit even if an exception occurs? The problem with most solutions is that they are verbose, tedious, potentially expensive and therefore error-prone. However, I noticed that many resources are released in the reverse order of their acquisition. This strongly resembles the behavior of local objects created by constructors and destroyed by destructors. Thus we can handle such resource acquisition and release problems by a suitable use of objects of classes with constructors and destructors. This technique extends to partially constructed objects and thus addresses the otherwise difficult issue of what to do when an error is encountered in a constructor.

During the design, the most contentious issue turned out to be whether the exception handling mechanism should support termination semantics or resumption semantics; that is, whether it should be possible for an exception handler to require execution to resume from the point where the exception was thrown. The main resumption vs. termination debate took place in the ANSI C++ committee. After a discussion that lasted for about a year, the exception handling proposal as presented in the ARM (that is, with termination semantics) was voted into C++ by an overwhelming majority. The key to that consensus were presentations of experience data based on decades of use of systems that supported both resumption and termination semantics by representatives of DEC, Sun, Texas Instruments, IBM, and others. Basically, every use of resumption had represented a failure to keep separate levels of abstraction disjoint.

The C++ exception handling mechanism is explicitly not for handling asynchronous events directly. This view precludes the direct use of exceptions to represent something like hitting a DEL key and the replacement of UNIX signals with exceptions. In such cases, a low-level interrupt routine must somehow do its minimal job and possibly map into something that could trigger an exception at a well-defined point in a program's execution.

As ever, efficiency was a major concern. The C++ exception handling mechanism can be implemented without any run-time overhead to a program that doesn't throw an exception [Stroustrup 1988b]. It is also possible to limit space overhead, but it is hard simultaneously to avoid run-time overhead and code size increases. The first implementations of exception handling as defined in the ARM are just appearing (Spring 1992).

15.6.5 ANSI and ISO

The initiative to formal (ANSI) standardization of C++ was taken by HP in conjunction with AT&T, DEC, and IBM. Larry Rosler from HP was important in this initiative. The proposal for ANSI standardization was written by Dmitry Lenkov [Lenkov 1989]. Dmitry's proposal cites several reasons for immediate standardization of C++:

- C++ is going through a much faster public acceptance than most other languages.
- Delay will lead to dialects.
- Requires a careful and detailed definition providing full semantics for each language feature.
- C++ lacks some important features ... exception handling, aspects of multiple inheritance, features supporting parametric polymorphism, and standard libraries.

The proposal also stressed the need for compatibility with ANSI C. The organizational meeting of the ANSI C++ committee, X3J16, took place in December of 1989 in Washington, D.C. and was attended by about 40 people, including people who took part in the C standardization, people who by now were "old time C++ programmers." Dmitry Lenkov became its chairman and Jonathan Shopiro became its editor.

The committee now has more than 250 members out of which something like 70 turn up at meetings. The aim of the committee was, and is, a draft standard for public review in late 1993 or early 1994 with the hope of an official standard about two years later.[5] This is an ambitious schedule for the standardization of a general-purpose programming language. To compare, the standardization of C took seven years.

Naturally, standardization of C++ isn't just an American concern. From the start, representatives from other countries attended the ANSI C++ meetings; and in Lund, Sweden, in June of 1991 the ISO C++ committee WG21 was convened and the two C++ standards committees decided to hold joint meetings—starting immediately in Lund. Representatives from Canada, Denmark, France, Japan, Sweden, UK, and USA were present. Notably, the vast majority of these national representatives were actually long-time C++ programmers. The C++ committee had a difficult charter:

1. The definition of the language must be precise and comprehensive.
2. C/C++ compatibility had to be addressed.
3. Extensions beyond current C++ practice had to be considered.
4. Libraries had to be considered.

On top of that, the C++ community was *very* diverse and totally unorganized so that the standards committee naturally became an important focal point of that community. In the short run, that is actually the most important role for the committee.

C compatibility was the first major controversial issue we had to face. After some—occasionally heated—debate it was decided that 100 percent C/C++ compatibility wasn't an option. Neither was significantly decreasing C compatibility. C++ was a separate language and not a strict superset of ANSI C and couldn't be changed to be such a superset without breaking the C++ type system and without breaking millions of lines of C++ code. This decision, often referred to as "As close to C, but no closer" after a paper written by Andrew Koenig and me [Koenig 1989a], is the same that has been reached over and over again by individuals and groups considering C++ and the direction of its evolution (Section 15.3.4).

5 We still expect to see a C++ ISO standard in late 1995 to mid-1996.

15.6.6 Rampant Featurism?

A critical issue was—and is—how to handle the constant stream of proposals for language changes and extensions. The focus of that effort is the extensions working group of which I'm the chairman. It is much easier to accept a proposal than to reject it. You win friends this way and people praise the language for having so many "neat features." Unfortunately, a language made as a shopping list of features without coherence will die, so there is no way we could accept even most of the features that would be of genuine help to some section of the C++ community.

So how is the committee doing? We won't really know until the standard appears because there is no way of knowing which, if any, of the backlog of proposals will be accepted. There is some hope of restraint and that accepted features will be properly integrated into the language. Only three new features have been accepted so far: the "mandated" extensions (exception handling and templates), and a proposal for relaxing the requirements for return types for overriding functions.[6]

15.7 RETROSPECTIVE

It is often claimed that hindsight is an exact science. It is not. The claim is based on the false assumptions that we know all relevant facts about what happened in the past, that we know the current state of affairs, and that we have a suitably detached point of view from which to judge the past. Typically none of these conditions hold. This makes a retrospective on something as large, complex, and dynamic as a programming language in large scale use hazardous. Anyway, let me try to stand back and answer some hard questions:

1. Did C++ succeed at what it was designed for?
2. Is C++ a coherent language?
3. What was the biggest mistake?

Naturally, the replies to these questions are related. The basic answers are, 'yes,' 'yes,' and 'not shipping a larger library with release 1.0.'

15.7.1 Did C++ succeed at what it was designed for?

"C++ is a general purpose programming language designed to make programming more enjoyable for the serious programmer" [Stroustrup 1986b]. In this, it clearly succeeded, especially in the more specific aim of letting reasonably educated and experienced programmers write programs at a higher level of abstraction ("as in Simula"), without loss of efficiency compared to C, for applications that were demanding in time, space, inherent complexity, and constraints from the execution environment.

More generally, C++ made object-oriented programming and data abstraction available to the community of software developers that until then had considered such techniques and the languages that supported them such as Smalltalk, Clu, Simula, Ada, OO Lisp dialects, and so on, with disdain and even scorn: "expensive toys unfit for real problems." C++ did three things to overcome this formidable barrier:

6 As I write this, the chance of any significant additions to the C++ language by the standard committee is about zero. Many minor extensions were added, but I think that C++ is now a significantly more powerful, pleasant, and coherent language than it was when the standards process started. The major "new" extensions were run-time type information, namespaces, and the sum of many minor improvements to templates; see [Stroustrup 1994].

1. It produced code with run-time and space characteristics that competed head-on with the perceived leader in that field: C. Anything that matches or beats C must be fast enough. Anything that doesn't can and will out of need or mere prejudice—be ignored.
2. It allowed such code to be integrated into conventional systems and produced on traditional systems. A conventional degree of portability, the ability to coexist with existing code, and the ability to coexist with traditional tools, such as debuggers and editors, was essential.
3. It allowed a gradual transition to these new programming techniques. It takes time to learn new techniques. Companies simply cannot afford to have significant numbers of programmers unproductive while they are learning. Nor can they afford the cost of failed projects caused by programmers poorly trained and inexperienced in the new techniques failing by over enthusiastically misapplying ideas.

In other words, C++ made object-oriented programming and data abstraction cheap and accessible.

In succeeding, C++ didn't just help "itself" and the C++ programmers. It also provided a major impetus to languages that provided different aspects of object-oriented programming and data abstraction. C++ isn't everything to all people and doesn't deliver on every promise ever made about some language or other. It does deliver on its own promises often enough to break down the wall of disbelief that stood in the way of all languages that allowed programmers to work at a higher level of abstraction.

15.7.2 Is C++ a Coherent Language?

C++ was successful in its own terms and is an effective vehicle for systems development, but is it a good language? Does C++ have an ecological niche now that the barriers of ignorance and prejudice against abstraction techniques have been broken?

Basically, I am happy with the language and quite a few users agree. There are many details I'd like to improve if I could, but the fundamental concept of a statically typed language using classes with virtual functions as the inheritance mechanism and facilities for low-level programming is sound.

15.7.2.1 *What Should and Could Have Been Different?*

Given a clean slate, what would be a better language than C++ for the things C++ is meant for? Consider the first order decisions: use of static type checking, clean separation between language and environment, no direct support for concurrency, ability to match the layout of objects and call sequences for languages such as C and FORTRAN, and C compatibility.

First, I considered, and still consider, static type checking essential both as a support for good design and secondarily for delivering acceptable run-time efficiency. Were I to design a new language for what C++ is used for today, I would again follow the Simula model of type checking and inheritance, *not* the Smalltalk or Lisp models. As I have said many times, "Had I wanted an imitation Smalltalk, I would have built a much better imitation. Smalltalk is the best Smalltalk around. If you want Smalltalk, use it" [Stroustrup 1990]. Having both static type checking and dynamic type identification (for example, in the form of virtual function calls) implies some difficult tradeoffs compared to a language with only static or only dynamic type checking. The static type model and the dynamic type model cannot be identical and thus there will be some complexity and inelegance that can be avoided by supporting only one type model. However, I wouldn't want to write programs with only one model.

I also still consider a separation between the environment and the language essential. I do not want to use only one language, only one set of tools, and only one operating system. To offer a choice, separation is necessary. However, once the separation exists one can provide different environments to suit different tastes and different requirements for supportiveness, resource consumption, and portability.

We never have a clean slate. Whatever new we do, we must also make it possible for people to make a transition from old tools and ideas to new. Thus, if C hadn't been there for C++ to be almost compatible with, then I would have chosen to be almost compatible with some other language.

Should a new language support garbage collection directly, say, like Modula-3 does? If so, could C++ have met its goals had it provided garbage collection? Garbage collection is great when you can afford it. Therefore, the option of having garbage collection is clearly desirable. However, garbage collection can be costly in terms of run time, real-time response, and porting effort (exactly how costly is the topic of much confused debate). Therefore, being forced to pay for garbage collection at all times isn't necessarily a blessing. C++ allows *optional* garbage collection [Ellis 1990], and I expect to see many experiments with garbage-collecting C++ implementations in the near future. However, I am convinced (after reviewing the issue many times over the years) that had C++ depended on garbage collection it would have been stillborn.

Should a language have reference semantics for variables (that is, a name is really a pointer to an object allocated elsewhere) like Smalltalk or Clu, or true local variables like C and Pascal? This question relates to several issues, such as coexistence with other languages, compatibility, and garbage collection. Simula dodged the question by having references to class objects (only) and true variables for objects of built-in types (only). Again, I consider it an open issue whether a language could be designed that provided the benefits of both references and true local variables without ugliness. Given a choice between elegance and the benefits of having both references and true local variables, I'll take the two kinds of variables.

15.7.2.2 *What Should Have Been Left Out?*

Even Stroustrup [1980a] voiced concern that C with Classes might have become too large. I think "a smaller language" is number one on any wish list for C++; yet people deluge me, and the standards committee, with extension proposals. The fundamental reason for the size of C++ is that it supports more than one way of writing programs, more than one programming paradigm. From one point of view, C++ is really three languages in one: A C-like language plus an Ada-like language, plus a Simula-like language, plus what it takes to integrate those features into a coherent whole.

Brian Kernighan observes that in C there is usually about one way of solving a given problem, whereas in C++ there are more. I conjecture that there typically is more than one way in C but that people don't see them. In C++, there are typically at least three alternatives and experienced people have quite a hard time not seeing them. There always is a design choice but in most languages the language designer has made the choice for you. For C++ I did not; the choice is yours. This is naturally abhorrent to people who believe that there is exactly one right way of doing things. It can also scare beginners and teachers who feel that a good language is one that you can completely understand in a week. C++ is not such a language. It was designed to provide a tool set for a professional, and complaining that there are too many features is like the "layman" looking into an upholsterer's tool chest and exclaiming that there couldn't possibly be a need for all those little hammers.

15.7.2.3 *What Should Have Been Added?*

As ever, the principle is to add as little as possible. A letter published on behalf of the extensions working group of the C++ standards committee puts it this way:

> First, let us try to dissuade you from proposing an extension to the C++ language. C++ is already too large and complicated for our taste and there are millions of lines of C++ code "out there" that we endeavor not to break. All changes to the language must undergo tremendous consideration. Additions to it are undertaken with great trepidation. Wherever possible we prefer to see programming techniques and library functions used as alternatives to language extensions.
>
> Many communities of programmers want to see their favorite language construct or library class propagated into C++. Unfortunately, adding useful features from diverse communities could turn C++ into a set of incoherent features. C++ is not perfect, but adding features could easily make it worse instead of better [Stroustrup 1992b].

So, given that, what features have caused trouble by their absence and which are under debate so that they might make it into C++ over the next couple of years? The feature I regret not having put in much earlier, when it could be done without formal debate and experimentation was easy, is some form of name space control.[7] C++ follows C in having a single global name space. C++ alleviates the problems that causes with class scopes and overloading mechanisms, but as programs grow, and especially as independent libraries are developed and later used together in a single program, the problem of name space clashes increases. My only defense is that I didn't like the resolution mechanisms I looked at, such as Ada packages and Modula-2 modules, because they had too great an overlap with the C++ class mechanism and, thus, didn't fit.

In the original C++ design, I deliberately didn't include the Simula mechanisms for run-time type identification (`QUA` and `INSPECT`). My experience was that they were almost always misused, so that the benefits from having the mechanism would be outweighed by the disadvantages. Several proposals for providing some form of run-time type identification have arisen over the years and the focus is now on a proposal for dynamic casts, that is, type conversions that are checked at run time by Dmitry Lenkov and me [Stroustrup 1992a]. Like other extension proposals, it is going through extensive discussion and experimentation and is unlikely to be accepted in the form presented in that paper.[8]

15.7.3 What Was The Biggest Mistake?

To my mind there really is only one contender for the title of "worst mistake." Release 1.0 and my first edition [Stroustrup 1986b] should have been delayed until a larger library, including some simple classes such as singly and doubly linked lists, an associative array class, a range checked array class, and a simple string class, could have been included. The absence of those led to everybody reinventing the wheel and to an unnecessary diversity in the most fundamental classes. However, could I have done that? In a sense, I obviously could. The original plan for my book included three library chapters, one on the stream library, one on the container classes, and one on the task library, so I knew roughly what I wanted. Unfortunately, I was too tired and couldn't do container classes without some form of templates.

---

7 A facility for defining and using name spaces was introduced into C++ in 1994; see Stroustrup [1994].

8 After extensive discussion and revision, a mechanism for run-time type information based on this proposal was accepted in 1993; see Stroustrup [1994].

15.7.4 Hopes for the Future

May C++ serve its user community well. For that to happen, the language itself must be stable and well-specified. The C++ standards group and the C++ compiler vendors have a great responsibility here.

In addition to the language itself, we need libraries. Actually, we need a libraries industry to produce, distribute, maintain, and educate people. This is emerging. The challenge is to allow programs to be composed out of libraries from different vendors. This is hard and might need some support from the standards committee in the form of standard classes and mechanisms that ease the use of independently developed libraries.[9]

The language itself, plus the libraries, define the language that a user de facto writes in. However, only through good understanding of the application areas and design techniques will the language and library features be put to good use. Thus there must be an emphasis on teaching people effective design techniques and good programming practices. Many of the techniques we need have still to be developed, and many of the best techniques we do have still compete with plain ignorance and snake oil. I hope for far better textbooks for the C++ language and for programming and design techniques, and especially for textbooks that emphasize the connection between language features, good programming practices, and good design approaches.

Techniques, languages, and libraries must be supported by tools. The days of C++ programming supported by simply a "naked" compiler are almost over, and the best C++ tools and environments are beginning to approach the power and convenience of the best tools and environments for any language. We can do much better. The best has yet to come.

ACKNOWLEDGMENTS

It is clear that given the number of people who have contributed to C++ in some form or other over the last 12 years or so, I must have left most unmentioned. Some have been mentioned in this paper, more can be found in Sectuib 15.1.2c of the ARM, and other acknowledgment sections of my books and papers. Here I'll just mention Doug McIlroy, Brian Kernighan, Andrew Koenig, and Jonathan Shopiro, who have provided constant help, ideas, and encouragement to me, and others, for a decade.

I'd also like to mention the people who have done much of the hard, but usually unnoticed and unacknowledged, work of developing and supporting Cfront through the years when we were always short of resources: Steve Dewhurst, Laura Eaves, Andrew Koenig, Stan Lippman, George Logothetis, Glen McClusky, Judy Ward, Nancy Wilkinson, and Barbara Moo, who managed AT&T Bell Lab's C++ development and support group during the years when the work got done.

Also, thanks to C++ compiler writers, library writers, and so forth, who sent me information about their compilers and tools, most of which went beyond what could be presented in a paper: Mike Ball, Walter Bright, Keith Gorlen, Steve Johnson, Kim Knuttilla, Archie Lachner, Doug Lea, Mark Linton, Aron Insinga, Doug Lea, Dmitri Lenkov, Jerry Schwarz, Michael Tiemann, and Mike Vilot.

Also thanks to people who read drafts of this paper and provided many constructive comments: Dag Bruck, Steve Buroff, Peter Juhl, Brian Kernighan, Andrew Koenig, Stan Lippmann, Barbara Moo, Jerry Schwarz, and Jonathan Shopiro.

Most comments on the various versions of this paper were of the form "This paper is too long ... please add information about X, Y, and Z ... also, be more detailed about A, B, and C." I have tried to follow the first part of that advice, though the constraints of the second part have ensured that this did not become a short paper. Without Brian Kernighan's help this paper would have been much longer.

9 The standard library now provides containers and algorithms serving this need.

REFERENCES

[Babcisky, 1984] Babcisky, Karel. Simula Performance Assessment, *Proceedings of the IFIP WG2.4 conference on System Implementation Languages: Experience and Assessment.* Canterbury, Kent, UK. Sept. 1984.

[Birtwistle, 1979] Birtwistle, Graham, Dahl, Ole-Johan, Myrhaug, Bøjrn, and Nygaard, Kristen. *SIMULA BEGIN*, Studentlitteratur, Lund, Sweden, 1979.

[Booch, 1991] Booch, Grady. *Object-Oriented Design*, Benjamin Cummings, 1991.

[Booch, 1990] Booch, Grady, and Vilot, Michael M. The Design of the C++ Booch Components, *Proceedings of OOPSLA'90.*

[Call, 1987] Call, Lisa A., *et al.* An Open System for Graphical User Interfaces, *Proceedings of the USENIX C++ Conference*, Santa Fe, NM, Nov. 1987.

[Campbell, 1987] Campbell, Roy, *et al. The Design of a Multiprocessor Operating System, Proceedings USENIX C++ Conference*, Santa Fe, NM, Nov. 1987.

[Cargill, 1991] Cargill, Tom A. *The Case Against Multiple Inheritance in C++*, USENIX Computer Systems, Vol. 4, No. 1, 1991.

[Carroll, 1991] Carroll, Martin. *Using Multiple Inheritance to Implement Abstract Data Types*, The C++ Report, Apr. 1991.

[Cristian, 1989] Cristian, Flaviu. Exception Handling, in *Dependability of Resilient Computers*, T. Andersen, Ed., BSP Professional Books, Blackwell Scientific Publications, 1989.

[Cox, 1986] Cox, Brad. *Object-Oriented Programming: An Evolutionary Approach*, Reading, MA: Addison-Wesley, 1986.

[Dahl, 1988] Dahl, Ole-Johan. Personal communication.

[Ellis, 1990] Ellis, Margaret A., and Stroustrup, Bjarne. *The Annotated C++ Reference Manual*, Reading, MA: Addison-Wesley, 1990.

[Goldberg, 1983] Goldberg, Adele, and Robson, David. *Smalltalk-80, The language and its Implementation*, Reading, MA: Addison-Wesley, 1983.

[Goodenough, 1975] Goodenough, John. *Exception Handling: Issues and a Proposed Notation*, CACM, Dec. 1975.

[Gorlen, 1987] Gorlen, Keith E. An Object-Oriented Class Library for C++ Programs, *Proceedings of the USENIX C++ Conference*, Santa Fe, NM, Nov. 1987.

[Gorlen, 1990] Gorlen, Keith E., Orlow, Sanford M., and Plexico, Perry S. *Data Abstraction and Object-Oriented Programming in C++*, West Sussex, England: Wiley, 1990.

[Ichbiah, 1979] Ichbiah, Jean D., *et al. Rationale for the Design of the ADA Programming Language*, SIGPLAN Notices, Vol. 14, No. 6, June 1979, Part B.

[Johnson, 1989] Johnson, Ralph E. *The Importance of Being Abstract*, The C++ Report, Vol. 1, No. 3, Mar. 1989.

[Kernighan, 1981] Kernighan, Brian, and Ritchie, Dennis. *The C Programming Language*, Englewood Cliffs, NJ: Prentice-Hall, 1978.

[Kernighan, 1981] Kernighan, Brian. *Why Pascal is not my Favorite Programming Language*, AT&T Bell Labs Computer Science Technical Report No. 100, July 1981.

[Kernighan, 1988] Kernighan, Brian, and Ritchie, Dennis. *The C Programming Language* (second edition), Englewood Cliffs, NJ: Prentice-Hall, 1988. ISBN 0-13-110362-8.

[Kiczales, 1992] Kiczales, Gregor, des Rivieres, Jim, and Bobrow, Daniel G., *The Art of the Metaobject Protocol*, Cambridge, MA: MIT Press, 1991.

[Koenig,1988] Koenig, Andrew. Associative arrays in C++, *Proceedings of the USENIX Conference*, San Francisco, June 1988.

[Koenig, 1989] Koenig, Andrew, and Stroustrup, Bjarne. *C++: As close to C as possible—but no closer*, The C++ Report, Vol. 1, No.7, July 1989.

[Koenig, 1989b] ———. Exception Handling for C++, *Proceedings of the "C++ at Work" Conference*, Nov. 1989.

[Koenig, 1990] ———. Exception Handling for C++ (revised), *Proceedings of the USENIX C++ Conference*, Apr. 1990. Also, *Journal of Object Oriented Programming*, Vol. 3, No.2, July/Aug. 1990, pp. 16–33.

[Krogdahl, 1984] Krogdahl, Stein. *An Efficient Implementation of Simula Classes with Multiple Prefixing*, Research Report No. 83, June 1984, University of Oslo, Institute of Informatics.

[Lenkov, 1989] Lenkov, Dmitry. *C++ Standardization Proposal*, #X3J11/89-016.

[Linton, 1987] Linton, Mark A., and Calder, Paul R. The Design and Implementation of InterViews, *Proceedings of the USENIX C++ Conference*, Santa Fe, NM, Nov. 1987.

[Liskov, 1987] Liskov, Barbara. Data Abstraction and Hierarchy, *Addendum to Proceedings of OOPSLA'87*, Oct. 1987.

[Meyer, 1988] Meyer, Bertrand. *Object-Oriented Software Construction*, Englewood Cliffs, NJ: Prentice-Hall, 1988.

[McCluskey, 1992] McCluskey, Glen. *An Environment for Template Instantiation*, The C++ Report, Feb. 1992.

[Nelson, 1991] Nelson, G., Ed. *Systems Programming with Modula-3*, Englewood Cliffs, NJ: Prentice-Hall, 1991.

[Rose, 1984] Rose, Leonie V., and Stroustrup, Bjarne. *Complex Arithmetic in C++*, Internal AT&T Bell Labs Technical Memorandum, Jan. 1984; reprinted in AT&T C++ Translator Release Notes, Nov. 1985.

[Sakkinen, 1992] Sakkinen, Markku. *A Critique of the Inheritance Principles of C++*, USENIX Computer Systems, Vol. 5, No. 1, Winter 1992.

[Sethi, 1980] Sethi, Ravi. A case study in specifying the semantics of a programming language, Seventh Annual ACM Symposium on Principles of Programming Languages, Jan. 1980, pp 117–130.

[Shopiro, 1985] Shopiro, Jonathan E. *Strings and lists for C++*, AT&T Bell Labs Internal Technical Memorandum, July 1985.

[Shopiro, 1987] ———. Extending the C++ Task System for Real-Time Control, *Proceedings of the USENIX C++ Conference*, Santa Fe, NM, Nov. 1987.

[Snyder, 1986] Snyder, Alan. Encapsulation and Inheritance in Object-Oriented Programming Languages, *Proceedings of OOPSLA '86*, Sept. 1986.

[Stepanov, 1994] Stepanov, Alexander, and Lee, Meng. *The Standard Template Library*, HP Labs Technical Report HPL-94-34 (R. 1), Aug. 1994.

[Stroustrup, 1978] Stroustrup, Bjarne. *On Unifying Module Interfaces*, ACM Operating Systems Review, Vol. 12, No.1, Jan. 1978, pp 90–98..

[Stroustrup, 1979a] ———. *Communication and Control in Distributed Computer Systems*, Ph.D. thesis, Cambridge University, 1979.

[Stroustrup,1979b] ———. An Inter-Module Communication System for a Distributed Computer System, *Proceedings of the 1st International Conference on Distributed Computing Systems*, Oct. 1979, pp 412–418.

[Stroustrup, 1980a] ———. *Classes: An Abstract Data Type Facility for the C Language*, Bell Laboratories Computer Science Technical Report CSTR-84, Apr. 1980, also *SIGPLAN Notices*, Jan. 1982.

[Stroustrup, 1980b] ———. *A Set of C Classes for Co-routine Style Programming*, Bell Laboratories Computer Science Technical Report CSTR-90, Nov. 1980.

[Stroustrup, 1981a] ———. Long Return: A technique for Improving The Efficiency of Inter-Module Communication, *Software Practice and Experience*, Jan. 1981, pp. 131–143.

[Stroustrup, 1981b] ———. *Extensions of the C Language Type Concept Bell Labs Internal Memorandum*, Jan. 1981.

[Stroustrup, 1982] ———. *Adding Classes to C: An Exercise in Language Evolution*, Bell Laboratories Computer Science internal document, Apr. 1982, *Software Practice & Experience*, Vol. 13, 1983, pp. 139–161.

[Stroustrup, 1984a] ———. *The C++ Reference Manual*, AT&T Bell Labs Computer Science Technical Report No. 108, Jan. 1984. (Written in the summer of 1983). Revised version Nov. 1984.

[Stroustrup, 1984b] ———. *Data Abstraction in C*, Bell Labs Technical Journal, Vol. 63, No. 8, Oct. 1984, pp 1701–1732. (Written in the summer of 1983)

[Stroustrup, 1984c] ———. Operator Overloading in C++, *Proceedings of the IFIP WG2.4 Conference on System Implementation Languages: Experience & Assessment*, Sept. 1984.

[Stroustrup, 1985] ———. An Extensible I/O Facility for C++, *Proceedings of the Summer 1985 USENIX Conference*, June 1985, pp 57–70.

[Stroustrup, 1986a] ———. An Overview of C++, ACM *SIGPLAN Notices*, Special Issue, pp. 7–18.

[Stroustrup, 1986b] Stroustrup, Bjarne, *The C++ Programming Language*, Reading, MA: Addison-Wesley, 1986.

[Stroustrup, 1986c] ———. What is Object-Oriented Programming? *Proceedings of the 14th ASU Conference*, Aug. 1986, pp. 69–84; revised version in *Proceedings of the ECOOP '87*, May 1987, Springer Verlag Lecture Notes in Computer Science, Vol. 276, pp. 51–70; revised version in *IEEE Software Magazine*, May 1988, pp 10–20.

[Stroustrup, 1987a] ———. Multiple Inheritance for C++, *Proceedings of the EUUG Spring Conference*, May 1987; also, *USENIX Computer Systems*, Vol. 2, No. 4, Fall 1989.

[Stroustrup, 1987b] Stroustrup, Bjarne, and Shopiro, Jonathan. A Set of C classes for Co-Routine Style Programming, *Proceedings USENIX C++ Conference*, Santa Fe, Nov. 1987, pp. 417–439.

[Stroustrup, 1987c] Stroustrup, Bjarne. The Evolution of C++: 1985–1987, *Proceedings of the USENIX C++ Conference*, Santa Fe, Nov. 1987, pp. 1–22.

[Stroustrup, 1988a] ———. Type-safe Linkage for C++, *USENIX Computer Systems*, Vol.1, No. 4, Fall 1988.

[Stroustrup, 1988b] ———. Parameterized Types for C++, *Proceedings of the USENIX C++ Conference*, Denver, Oct. 1988, pp. 1–18; also, *USENIX Computer Systems*, Vol. 2, No. 1, Winter 1989.

[Stroustrup, 1989a] ———. Standardizing C++, *The C++ Report*, Vol. 1, No.1, Jan. 1989.

[Stroustrup, 1989b] ———. The Evolution of C++: 1985–1989, *USENIX Computer Systems*, Vol. 2, No. 3, Summer 1989. Revised version of [Stroustrup, 1987c].

[Stroustrup, 1990] ———. On Language Wars, *Hotline on Object-Oriented Technology*, Vol. 1, No. 3, Jan. 1990.

[Stroustrup, 1991] ———. *The C++ Programming Language*, Second edition, Reading, MA: Addison-Wesley, 1991.

[Stroustrup, 1992a] Stroustrup, Bjarne, and Lenkov. Dmitri, Run-time Type Identification for C++, *The C++ Report*, Mar. 1992.

[Stroustrup, 1992b] Stroustrup, Bjarne. How to Write a C++ Language Extension Proposal, *The C++ Report*, May 1992.

[Stroustrup, 1994] ———. *The Design and Evolution of C++*, Reading, MA: Addison-Wesley, 1994.
[Taft, 1992] Taft, S. Tucker. Ada 9X: A Technical Summary, *Communications of the ACM*, Nov. 1992.
[Tiemann, 1987] Tiemann, Michael. Wrappers, *Proceedings of the USENIX C++ Conference*, Santa Fe, Nov. 1987.
[Waldo, 1991] Waldo, Jim. Controversy: The Case for Multiple Inheritance in C++, *USENIX Computer Systems*, Vol. 4, No. 2, Spring 1991.
[Wirth, 1982] Wirth, Niklaus. *Programming in Modula-2*, New York: Springer-Verlag, 1982.

TRANSCRIPT OF PRESENTATION

BJARNE STROUSTRUP: First, I want to thank the Committee for suggesting I should write up the history of C++ and encouraging me to do so. This has led to a large paper, and consequently I'm not going to try to explain what is in that paper. You can read it if you like. Instead, I'll make some comments about why C++ is the way it is, and how it came to be—rather than what it is.

I think it is rather fitting that I am the last speaker in this seminar on languages. C++ is the youngest language presented, and it is also very nice and fitting and a bit of an honor to follow Dennis. I don't know if its surprising or not, but basically I agree with a lot of what he said, including some of his more radical statements. I have written programs in four out of the five little languages that he has presented. The missing one for me is Bliss. My favorite happens to be the ALGOL 68, where I used the ALGOL 68C—but C is by no means bad—and I'll get back to that.

There has been a question going through this Conference: "Was it fun?" It was fun at times. You could see that for most of the speakers here, it wasn't just fun. One day, while I was feeling glum, a friend of mine said, "You know how you recognize the people who are out in front?" I said, "No." (And he said:) "By the arrows in their backs." A lot of the speakers here seemed defensive and maybe a little bit sad. I think I know why—but I don't actually think we have anything to apologize for.

And now, I'll start with what I actually planned to say.

(SLIDE 1) This is a brief overview. I'm sticking to chronological order because that's always easier. This is basically the stages of C++. The pre-history: then a language called "C with Classes" which I designed and which was used at Bell Labs and elsewhere for some time; then C++, as it was originally introduced, and then C++ going through some intermediate stages to its current stage—plus the standardization that is still going on. And if I am not timed out, maybe a little about the future.

(SLIDE 2) I think the most important aspect of a language is its designer's view of what the problem is. What are you trying to do? I very much doubt I would have designed a language just for the fun of designing a language. This may be the wrong place to say so, but maybe not. I think people that

Overview:

1977:	Simula and BCPL
1979:	C with Classes
1984:	C++
1989:	2.0
1989–91:	templates and exceptions
1989–:	standardization
1993–:	looking ahead

SLIDE 1

- A language is someone's response to a set of problems at a given time
- The problems and our understanding of solutions change over time
- A language lives and grows

SLIDE 2

design a language, a general purpose language, if they set out to do so, must be mad. This is a field where the success rate is about zero, and where the amount of trouble over the years descending on a designer is enormous. I had a problem, and I set out to solve it. The solution to a problem, especially when it is successful, leads to different sets of problems. It leads to an evolution of the problem, which leads to an evolution of your understanding of what the problem is, and what the possible solutions are, which again leads to new languages, or new dialects, or to new versions.

By the way, please notice the word "grow." I had not read Fred Brooks' slides when I wrote that. It is one of my favorite words for the way designs, in general, and languages, in particular, evolve.

(SLIDE 3) The problem that I had to face is best explained in terms of a simulator I was writing in Cambridge. I was studying distributed systems, working with the capability architecture of the CAP computer, and trying to find ways of distributing functionality in an operating system and in an operating system kernel; figuring out how machine architecture (which was my old field) could support operating system architectures; studying communication, synchronization, fire walls, that kind of stuff—nothing to do with language. And I was having a hard time. I had a hard time thinking about it; I had a hard time expressing the few thoughts I had about it.

One day in the "grad pad"—that is the place in Cambridge where the Computer Science graduate students and professors tend to have lunch—I was sitting moaning about this and especially bemoaning the fact that I didn't have access to the language, Simula, which I had briefly used in Aarhus a few years before. A guy sitting at the next table, I had no idea who he was at the time—and I still don't know—said, "You want Simula? I paid £10,000 for an implementation of it, and it doesn't run. If you can get it to run, you can have it." I got it, but never found out what the problem was. I guess he fed it something that wasn't Simula source code. [laughter.]

This led to the most pleasant experience in programming that I ever had. The features of Simula were just splendid. The class concept helped me think, helped me to organize my programs. It helped me compose the programs out of the bits and pieces I wrote. I really loved it.

There was a problem, though. When I started to run real examples, I was soaking up the University's mainframe at an astounding rate. I think I could have—in a day or two—soaked up my whole department's monthly budget. So I had to find a solution here. I could get Simula to run faster, but didn't think that was plausible, as the guys who wrote Simula were very smart. I could port Simula to a faster machine, except that we didn't have one. I could port Simula to a less used machine, which we did have, except that I couldn't, since Simula's implementation was proprietary and not portable. I could refrain from using the features of Simula that cost me too much. No, I couldn't, because those features were completely integral to the language—run-time checking, run-time typing, garbage collection, all kinds of good stuff that I could not afford and I, in fact, didn't need. But because of the way the language was put together, I couldn't help using it. Could I call external routines to do the work for me, to speed up critical parts the way that people from a slow language might call a FORTRAN routine? No, I could not; that Simula implementation was a closed system. I could leave Cambridge without a Ph.D., but that seemed an unfortunate thing to have to do. I could try to find somebody who could give me an IBM mainframe for myself. That didn't seem likely either. I could wait for people to invent high performance work stations, but that would have meant waiting for about eight years. Nobody would pay my salary waiting for that, so, instead, I rewrote the simulator in BCPL. That was very, very unpleasant. I lost about half of my hair in the process. [laughter.] My wife still comments on the nightmares I had while debugging that program. BCPL makes C look like a very high level language. But—it ran like the clappers, and it could be ported to a machine that was so poorly supported that the physicists and the astronomers didn't dare follow me. It lacked co-routines, which were absolutely essential for my simulator, so we just put them in—it took hardly

The problem (prehistory):

Simula and BCPL

- program organization
- run-time efficiency
- availability/portability
- inter-operability

SLIDE 3

C with Classes—why C?

the best systems programming language available:

- flexible, efficient, portable
- available, known
- 2nd order flaws not critical

but: improve static type checking

SLIDE 4

any time. For that reason, I can take a slight bit of credit for Martin Richards' addition of co-routines to BCPL. Finally, from BCPL you can easily use code written in other languages—like the CAP operating system written in ALGOL 68; that was important. So, I came away from Cambridge with a Ph.D., and a rather fierce determination never to get myself into that kind of mess again.

(SLIDE 4) So, when I did get myself into that kind of mess again—when I was beginning at Bell Labs in Murray Hill—I backed off and started to build the proper tools for doing this. The proper tool is something that gives me the ability to organize my program, as in Simula, and helps me to design like I would in Simula, but running as fast and with as open a connection to other systems as BCPL. I looked around and chose C.

The reason I chose C was rather simple. Now people might think that it was because it was AT&T's language, or because I had to, or some other such thing. That was not the idea at the time. I considered C the best language available for what I wanted to do. I needed to do some systems programming, I needed access to low-level features, I needed efficiency, flexibility, portability, and, later on when I had users, it was absolutely critical that part of the language was known, so that I wouldn't have to teach people how to write a for-loop.

I was quite aware of a lot of second-order flaws in C. I am among the ones who think that the C declarator syntax is an experiment that failed. The concept is right, but the non-linear notation is awful. However, I didn't think such issues were all that important. The only thing that I felt obliged to do was to improve the static type checking. I had come to appreciate it from Simula and I am not a programmer of the caliber of say, Ken Thompson, who simply doesn't make the kind of mistakes caught by static type checking. I do make those mistakes, so I need the checking.

Here we see a couple of the continuing threads in C++ development. If I don't have to invent something new, I don't. If I feel I must, I do. In this case, static type checking has been improving over the years in C++. It is now becoming possible to write a completely safe program in a well-defined subset of C++. If you don't want to do that, you can break the rules, which is one of the ways you keep the system open.

(SLIDE 5) The other half of C++ is basically the Simula ancestry, the classes. And the answer to "why classes?" is strictly "to help me think, to help me design and organize my programs." The fundamental notion and is that you find your concepts in your application, map them into your language as classes. The view is clearly one of classes as a key design aid as opposed to other views where classes are primarily implementation details. I was also very keen on static type checking. I

C with Classes

- why Classes?
- program organization
- mapping of concepts
- a class is a type - static checking
- (not primarily "re-use")

SLIDE 5

C with Classes

- work & work environment:
- a bit of everything (simulation important)
- emphasis on individual projects
- emphasis on work useful to others
- helpful and encouraging colleagues
- freedom from deadlines, commercialism, fads

SLIDE 6

appreciated the compiler helping me find the bugs in my program sooner rather than later. The explicit static structure helps me read my programs after the event; it helps me trust my code; it helps me reason about the program.

The word "reuse" is one that I have some trouble even understanding. If something can be used and it's general, then it will be used by many. That happens when you have a good concept well represented, well documented, and managed. You're not reusing one of those, you're just using it. The notion that object-oriented programming is for reuse, is to my mind incidental. I am interested in concepts that allow me to reason, think, and express myself clearly, efficiently, etc., and from that comes the good uses. That is the distinction.

(SLIDE 6) In which environment did this kind of work get done, and why is that environment important? A programming language is somebody's solution to a problem. Solutions depend on environments, and what you can do depends on the environment. My working environment included a bit of everything. It is hard to think of a kind of work that is not going on in Bell Labs, and a very large subset of that was done by friends and colleagues that I could talk to.

Users were absolutely essential for the growth of C++. I had solutions; they got refined when people told me they weren't quite good enough. The selection of problems to deal with was very influenced by people who were walking into my office and telling me that I had been a "bonehead" again. The most important work actually was simulation at the time. Bell Labs did not support me because I was writing a programming language; they supported me because I—and people I cooperated with—wrote really nice simulators faster than anybody else around. The first program written in C with Classes was a library; something to support concurrency for simulation of things like network traffic, board layouts in CPU design, things like that. It was very important for me; this was what gave me my funding.

There never was a C++ project—which, on at least three occasions, managers found out when they tried to cancel it. [laughter.] C++, like so many other languages, worked through the early years. There was no sheltered childhood. My environment had a strong emphasis on individual projects. The people in the research center that I'm in are, more or less by choice, anarchists. Since AT&T is a large organization, they have another computer science research center where everybody works in teams, the way the philosophy currently says you have to work. The emphasis on work that was useful to others—and not just sitting around doing things because they were beautiful to you—was strong and very helpful. My colleagues were very helpful, very friendly and encouraging. There was none of that stuff of hoarding good ideas for your next paper. If you had a good idea you barged into somebody's office and argued with them about it a bit. As a matter of fact, large parts of C++ were designed by me deciding that something was a problem, and going into somebody's office and not leaving until we have made progress on a solution—lots of really solid cooperation. And then there is a really nice freedom from deadlines—since there wasn't any project, nobody could tell me when it should finish. They could just judge the progress in what good things my users were saying about it. There was no commercialism, because there was a law saying AT&T couldn't sell software anyway. And there was also a blessed protection from academic and other fads, so that you could actually concentrate on solving problems.

Now, C with Classes was sort of successful; it was a medium success. I had put a lot of emphasis on facilities that would help people get their work done. One of the things that I observed, is that it is much easier to get technical work done than to do anything that requires fundamental changes in the organization, or in your way of thinking as a group—as opposed to individuals. C with Classes was not too successful at that. It allowed you to get medium improvements with medium efforts. It did not allow you to get really large improvements if you were willing to put in a large effort. In some sense, it wasn't a quantum jump—the least jump that would get you to the next stable level. Furthermore, the user community was not, and couldn't become, large enough to support an infrastructure for C with Classes. Remember, this was not a company language, there was policy to for people to use C with Classes, there was no guaranteed user group, there was no guaranteed financing. So I had a choice. I could can the project, and leave my users in a lurch, or I could go on, getting myself into a lot of extra work. Since I didn't feel like leaving my users in a lurch, I developed, from C with Classes, a very similar but more powerful language—and a more consistent language—called C++. There is a third alternative, which has, I think, caused a lot of languages to die at this stage. That is, go commercial, use some advertising, use some hype, and get some more users. That way, you can get them to pay for your mortgage, and get on that way. It did not occur to me. I'm glad.

(SLIDE 7) The design of C++ was guided by some rules of thumb. People really like talking about principles—but that sounds so pretentious. The first rule of the game, is that C++ is a language, and not a complete system. This differs from a lot of modern programming languages and systems, but remember that my users were scattered over more application areas and more hardware platforms than most individuals can imagine—including me. There were users on Cray supercomputers, and there were users programming "gadgets," talking refrigerators, fuel injectors, switching stuff. It was important to disassociate the C++ language from its environment, because most people had an environment and they were pretty happy with it.

What you don't use, you don't pay for. This is a rather strict rule, known as "the zero overhead rule," and that's quite important. Lots of people have known a system written in a bit of C, and a bit of something else. Mostly, they wake up one morning and find that the whole system is in C. I was rather determined that this would not happen to C++; that is, you should not have to choose between the flexibility and the efficiency of C, and whatever else I could offer. If you don't use a C++ feature, you don't ask for it.

C++ must be useful *now*. I'm serving my users. I'm not serving the future, and I'm not in the business of writing academic papers. So C++ has to work on the current machines, not just on the machines that people might get in five years. I did most of my development on a PDP 11/70 and then on a VAX. Those were pretty good machines for the day compared to what the average user had. I wrote some nice simulations using seven hundred tasks (my C++ notion of processes) on the 11/70—which was pretty good for the time, I think. C++ had to address problems now, for users now, with the education level of understanding, and on current machines. Don't try and design the world's best programming language. Nobody will ever agree on what that is anyway.

C++ design rules of thumb (general "principles"):

- C++ is a language, not a complete system
- what you don't use you don't pay for (zero-overhead rule)
- C++ must be useful NOW (current machines, programmers, and problems)
- don't get involved in a sterile quest for perfection

SLIDE 7

C++ design rules of thumb (language "principles"):

- use traditional (dumb) linkers
- no gratuitous incompatibilities with C (source and linkage)
- no implicit violations of the type system
- same support for user-defined and built-in types

SLIDE 8

(SLIDE 8) Some of these principles actually have something to do with programming languages directly, though most do not. I was trying rather hard to put constraints on the solution, rather than saying what the solution was. One rule is that I had to use traditional dumb linkers. Otherwise, I would have spent my whole life porting code and wanting to be portable. To match C's portability led to a lot of decisions, and this was one of them. In fact, we have evidence of one of the early C++ compilers being ported to a new machine architecture—by people that had never written a C++ program before—in four hours. My ideal was a week, and I overshot that target.

No gratuitous incompatibilities with C, neither in source nor in linkage—that was important. We have had some really interesting discussions with the word "gratuitous" here. The areas where incompatibilities are not gratuitous, usually has to do with type safety and the type system. You will find that ANSI C is largely a subset of C++, except for a few cases where it allows type violations that C++ was not willing to live with.

The one technical principle was that the support for built-in type and user-defined types should be the same. I actually over-shot that target a bit, because there is now slightly better support for user-defined types than built-in types.

On the scale you saw before, between dogmatic and pragmatic/empirical emphasis in design, C++ is definitely on the pragmatic and empirical side. I do not think that means unprincipled. When I studied history and philosophy, I definitely preferred somebody like Hume to Decartes or even Kant, even though Kant was clearly smarter. It is just the way I think, and it fits better with my world view. A lot of the work goes into looking at what the language is being used for. What else *could* the language be used for? What is the biggest problem? Fix it. This goes on at many levels, like the little-language level, where you look at individual language features. For example, what's the problem with pointers? Well, too many of them are dangling. What tools do you have for solving them? Well, ALGOL 68 has references. Should we add references to C++? Well it might be a good idea; references support operator overloading also. But what was the problem when I wrote programs in ALGOL 68? Well, 80 percent of my real bugs using ALGOL 68 were problems related to confusion between assignment through a reference and re-assignment of a reference. For that reason, C++ has references, but you cannot reassign a reference after its initialization. People think that's a limitation; I think it protects me from one of my worst sources of bugs.

(SLIDE 9) So what is C++? Well, this slide shows an explanation. Once upon a time, I was asked to give an executive summary to a very exalted being at Bell Labs. Naturally, being a young technical guy, I didn't know what an executive summary was, so I said, "What is it?" "Well," came the answer,

<table>
<tr>
<td>
C++

- is a better C
- supports data abstraction
- supports object-oriented programming
</td>
<td>
How, Why, and Where did C++ use grow:

- no advertising, marketing, support => low price
- encourage self-sufficiency among users
- portability
- powerful/expressive compared with C, Pascal, etc.
- fast, compact, and cheap compared to everything else - worldwide (email, netnews)
- industry and academia
- most important: technology-oriented US industry
</td>
</tr>
<tr>
<td>SLIDE 9</td>
<td>SLIDE 10</td>
</tr>
</table>

"an executive summary is something that fits on half a sheet of paper, using very large print." [laughter.] So, this is the executive summary of C++. It is meant to be a better C, under very strict rules. Anything you can do in C, you can do in C++. Anything reasonable, you can do in exactly the same way. You don't have any extra overhead, and there are some notational conveniences and things to increase safety. But in that sense, it is a better C.

Next, C++ supports data abstraction. I want to be able to organize my program by saying, "Here's my concept, here's my type. The mapping between the two is straightforward and effective." I want to be able to have matrices. I want to be able to have vectors. I want to be able to have switches, lines, whatever exists in the application area. I want to be able to multiply an array with a vector without any problems.

The next level, the object-oriented programming level, is usually for practical reasons associated with the notion of inheritance. I see object-oriented programming as going one step beyond data abstraction, by allowing us to represent hierarchical relationships between concepts. Again, the notion is strictly that if there is some order in your concepts, you may be able to represent that ordering in your classes through inheritance. Not all organizations fit into this, but so what! The hierarchical ones, or rather the lattice-form ones, can be represented directly and they're very useful.

(SLIDE 10) So, why did it work? As someone said, you have to be lucky, and also you have to work hard, and you have to listen a lot. The low price certainly was important. C++ was made available to a lot of users, without anybody trying to make a million from it. This was the result—not so much of a desire to get users—but of a wish to serve existing users well. We had no advertising, no marketing, and offered no support. Therefore, we had to encourage self-sufficiency among the users. We had to have portability. When you go through these concepts a couple of times, iteratively, and in any order you care to, a low price results unless somebody gets greedy.

Users were interested in C++ because compared to C, and Pascal, and such, it was more expressive—you could say more. Usually, you could say more in fewer lines of code and in a clearer way. You could express your concepts more directly—and have them more directly checked—than if you had to go to pointers and bytes and such things. Compared to anything else, C++ was compact, fast, and cheap. That helps! It also was flexible; it fit into more environments with less trouble than just about anything else.

The spread was world-wide from the beginning. Very soon after the development of C with Classes started, people started using it throughout the U.S. and various places in Europe. The feedback I got from those places was very important. A lot of the support and distribution, in the old days, was done

Availability (technical):

Compilers ("more than 1,000,000 sold"):

- AT&T, Oregon (TauMetric), GNU, Zortech (Symantec), Borland, Microsoft, JPI, IBM, DEC, Metaware, Watcom, ...

Environments (dozens):

- ParcPlace, Centerline, HP, Lucid, ...

Libraries (many dozens):

- USL, Interviews, GNU, M++, DBMS interfaces, ...

SLIDE 11

Availability (social):

Conferences

- Usenix, Commercial (SIGS, BU), ECUG, ...

Training/Education (dozens):

- commercial, university, ...

Books (100+)

- introductory, general, design, environment specific, library specific, application specific, ...
  Journals/Bulletin boards/Netnews

SLIDE 12

using e-mail. It was important that both industry and academia were involved, because you get very different views of what the world is, and what the world is supposed to be, and what the problems are from the various angles. Europe and the U.S. are not the same, and they are not the same as Japan and Australia. Academia is not the same as academia, and industry is not the same as industry—if you consider examples from different places. The spread of C++ use was very important for the development of C++. Of course, there was a focus, which was the technology-oriented U.S. industry. It had the kind of problems I understood best, and I think that is why C++ was used there.

(SLIDE 11) This has led to a notion of availability. It is hard to serve your users, if they can't understand what you are doing, or if they can't use it. For that reason, we have encouraged people to go build C++ compilers and tools—"encouraged" simply means talking to people, it doesn't mean government policy or AT&T corporate policy. This fits very well , though. AT&T is the biggest civilian user of software projects in the U.S., so anything that will increase the state-of-art and give better tools, better compilers, better languages, and better ways of designing things, is good for AT&T. Lots of people have joined in this vision.

There was an initial intent to make the C++ language distinct from environments, but of course, some people really want environments—and that's fine—if you're doing the kind of work where you can use an extended environment, you should have one. The only constraint I can see is that code should be able to come from the simplest environment and come into an advanced software development environment. And once you have built something in the software development environment, you have to be able to export it out again. I do not mind my airplanes being built in a large hanger, as long as I do not have to carry the hanger with me when I try to fly. We have similar ideas about libraries; that is, C++ does not demand large run-time libraries—support libraries—you can write programs in C++ using very primitive libraries. That's important if you are trying to program a gadget of sorts. On the other hand, you do not want to write, say, windows code in C++ without support libraries. It is simply too unpleasant, so the libraries are coming. In my opinion, you do not want to write yet another dialog box, and you don't have to.

(SLIDE 12) There is a distinct social aspect to real reusability—people sometimes have really nice language wars over individual features or what language manual is the cleanest. I think that is a very parochial view. It is the totality of what is available to allow you to get the whole job done that's important. And therefore, the social issues matter. USENIX has some conferences. There is a lot of commercialism now, which is sometimes useful. There are users groups. I want to point out that none of these were started by, or supported by, AT&T. There is training and education—lots of it. There are

Standardization:

ANSI X3J16: Dec 1989, ISO SC22-WG21: June 1991

- initiative: IBM, DEC, HP

Why?

- many implementations
- single company control unacceptable
- rule requiring "under standardization"
- forum for debate and dissemination of ideas

SLIDE 13

Standardization:

why not?

- language still evolving
- premature

SLIDE 14

more books than people could possibly dream of, even in their worst nightmares. There are some journals and all kinds of media for exchange. I would like to point out that I sometimes see, on the net, references to the C++ marketing juggernaut, or the AT&T marketing juggernaut. This is highly amusing—especially when this juggernaut is supposed to be running over things like Ada. AT&T once had a marketing budget for C++. It was a total of $3,000 for the first three years of C++'s life. What do you do with $3,000, when you want to market a language? Well, our marketing department's idea was to send a plain white letter to all UNIX system managers, telling them that C++ existed, without explaining what it was. I doubt that had any effect at all. That left us with $2,000. When I heard about it, I got them to give a reception for the first C++ users conference. That was the formal marketing of C++ during the first three or four years.

(SLIDE 13) Next, we are going to standardization. People want a standard. Why? Because there are lots of implementations and because nobody could tolerate single company control. I mean, they may trust me, but would they trust my management? My immediate management they could trust, but AT&T is a very big place. You need something more national and international. Several companies said that they were allowed to use something provided it was under standardization—that is, you didn't have to finish but there had to be a standards group. For that reason, we absolutely had to have it. And I found, for social reasons, that standards groups are very useful for discussion and debate, and for exchange of information. Before that, everything went through my mailbox, which was rather unpleasant—but necessary—when organizations that are not allowed to talk to each other, need to exchange information.

(SLIDE 14) There is a quick "Why not?" I mean, the language is evolving and standardization could easily be very premature. That is just sad if that happens. There have been a few cases where things have been standardized before being implemented. That is sad, and not in the general spirit of C++.

(SLIDE 15) And here comes the last one. I said I might be timed out. Basically, the main challenge is to stay coherent with so many factors, so many people, so many organizations involved. The ultimate purpose of C++ is to allow you to program to a higher level of abstraction, and to organize your programs better. A lot of people do not understand that. A lot of people do not want to understand that, and with a growth rate like C++'s, we can't teach teachers fast enough to get it across. Education is very important. There are also lots of technical challenges that I'll skip, because they are of secondary importance relative to the other. [applause.]

Current Challenges:
Staying coherent
Education
Technical
- Language
- Environments
- Libraries
- Design

SLIDE 15

Thanks

Dennis Ritchie, Kristen Nygaard
Brian Kernighan, Andrew Koenig,
Doug McIlroy, Jonathan Shopiro

SLIDE 16

(SLIDE 16) I really appreciate having worked on the languages designed by Dennis Ritchie and Kristen Nygaard; they are real gentlemen, and that is a very important personal feature. I could mention lots of people, but the four people there are the ones that have given me the most trouble and, therefore, contributed the most to the language. [applause.]

TRANSCRIPT OF QUESTION AND ANSWER SESSION

JEAN ICHBIAH: One of the weakest properties of SIMULA was the confusion between classes used as a unit of knowledge, for example in simulation, and classes used as abstracted data type for which you instantiate objects. Why did you choose to perpetuate this confusion or unification of the two concepts?

STROUSTRUP: I use, and I think of, classes strictly as a type, not as a module or name space. For that reason, I think that C++ has the ability to create types and hierarchies of types, but no further. If you want to partition your system in separate name spaces, if you want to define a group of related classes, which I think is the other aspect of it, you shouldn't use classes. We very often don't use classes. We have a very inferior, in my opinion, concept in terms of the C source file. We are moving towards a separate name space concept in the standards process. But, I think that if there is a confusion, either I have missed it or it is in uses of classes, some of which I will classify as misuses. I'm not 100 percent sure I answered the question.

GUY STEELE (Thinking Machines): The paper notes that the exception handling, in C++, was inspired by ML. But ML uses the word `RAISE` and not `THROW`. I was curious to know whether the words `CATCH` and `THROW` stem from their use in Mac LISP in 1972, and if so—this is the point of the question—by what path?

STROUSTRUP: The exception handling mechanism in C++ was designed, by me, with a fair bit of help by Andy Koenig. It was inspired to a large extent by CLU's mechanism, a little bit by Ada, and some look at what they did in Modula2+—and ML for the use of types. The reason the name is not `RAISE` is that `RAISE` is a standard function in the C library. C reserves half of the names in the universe for its standard library and it doesn't have a name space concept. Basically, we played around with a lot of names for this idea, for saying "help me" or "get me out of here." I knew of the use of `THROW` and `CATCH` in LISP, because somebody had told me, not because I'd used them. I also think I knew whatever names had been used in just about any language with exceptions, and `THROW` and `CATCH` just were the ones I liked best.

ADAM RIFKEN (Cal Tech): How do you feel about new languages being designed with C++ as their base, when C++ itself is still evolving and being standardized?

STROUSTRUP: First of all, I think it is very stupid to fight the inevitable too hard. Second, when people actually are working hard and doing a decent job, which they sometimes do, you should thank them. You should think it is an honor that people are willing to take your work and build on it. There are several dozen extensions of C++, mostly to do with things like concurrency and constraints, and some of them are very nice.

BRIAN MEEK (Kings College, London): There is a school of thought that there should be, not just no gratuitous incompatibilities between C and C++, but no incompatibilities at all. Could you have designed a satisfactory C++ language with that constraint? Have you any general views on incompatibilities between similar languages?

STROUSTRUP: The first answer is no. Much stronger static type checking—in the end approximating total safety, is the ideal. C allows, for historical reasons, some really major unsafety in the function calling mechanism, and in the array concept, and a few other places. Those, I have absolutely no intention of living with. We are now approaching the state where people who want "safe C++" can have it. Don't use casts, don't use arrays—that's it, as far as I remember. Now you can't not use arrays because you need some form of arrays, but we have a standard template that gives you the array concept, that you can use, and that is type safe and checked. Basically, I could not have designed a C++ that would serve the purpose I wanted it to serve, while staying fully compatible with C. But it is much more compatible than you believe. And if you write ANSI C, and if you do it with your strictest compiler options set (so that prototypes are required), you are much closer than you think. In general, I believe in evolution, which implies that you have to move forward, you have to respect where you come from, but sometimes things have to be broken.

MARK DAY (MIT): What was the interaction, if any, between your work and that of Jacob Katz Nelson on enhanced C? Why do you think that C++ made it out of sell Labs, while EC didn't?

STROUSTRUP: There was hardly any interaction. He read my papers, I'm not sure he understood them. I read his papers, I'm not sure I understood them. We had some nice talks, because he is a nice guy. His stuff was deeply macro-based, which I didn't like. Mine wasn't, which he didn't like. I think that I worked a bit harder and had a better language.

Editor's note: the following questions were answered after the conference by the author.

STAVROS MACRAKIS (OSF Research Institute): Why didn't you start with Simula 67 and make it faster & better, rather than start with C and make it better? (Perhaps by eliminating some things?)

STROUSTRUP: First of all, a practical reason: Simula's implementations were proprietary, so that I would either have had to do an implementation from scratch or get involved in negotiations about large sums of money. Neither sounded attractive, and neither would get me closer to my aim of getting real work done on distributed systems design for years.

C had the low-level features necessary for systems work, the raw efficiency, and the ability to interface to other code that Simula lacked. Initially, I could add to that without even touching the internals of a C compiler. To gain the nice features from a Simula dialect, I would have to subtract from a Simula compiler in places very close to the most fundamental aspects of the implementation.

I wasn't even sure that could be done. In retrospect, sticking very close to C has brought a fair bit of frustration, but also the key benefits I was looking for. I don't see another way that would have allowed me to deliver greater benefits to more people.

SCOTT GUTHREY (Schlumberger): The name, and marketing of C++, invite us to regard it as a superset of C. Nevertheless there are many incompatibilities between C and C++. In retrospect, to avoid confusing people, and facilitate clearer design, should C++ have been named "P"?

STROUSTRUP: There aren't that many incompatibilities between C++ and ANSI C. I think ANSI C is close enough to being a subset of C++ for the name to be accurate. Quite a few languages have been designed to be "a better C," and most have been called "D" for obvious reasons. I have not heard of any of those succeeding, but the name was taken. The other "obvious" name "P"—coming from the next letter after C in the sequence BCPL—is too cute, and would have caused confusion with Pascal derivatives.

Finally, I simply like the name "C++." It—correctly I think—emphasizes the evolutionary nature of the change, and leaves the origins of C++ in C for all to see. The other alternative "++C" would have driven producers of indexes, dictionaries, and the like, mad.

If the real question was "Could you have designed a cleaner language if you had broken C compatibility in fundamental ways?" the answer is Yes, I could, but the result would have been of little practical use—and I wouldn't have been here today.

DOUG ROSS (SofTech/MIT): In the context of C++ as OO—Maybe you could ask Bjarne to answer. The point is that call-by-loc hidden yields 00 all along—since 1962.

STROUSTRUP: The basic mechanisms for implementing OO have been available for a very long time—at least since the invention of the subroutine that could be called through a value in memory. However, OO isn't just, and maybe not even primarily, an issue of implementation technique. It is a way of looking at design, a way of structuring programs. The way I see it, Dahl and Nygaard developed a new way of writing programs and designed Simula as a notation for that. We can go back and see that the key techniques for implementing Simula, C++, etc., were available for years before anyone talked about OO, but that doesn't mean that programmers using indirect calls of assembler routines were doing OO. A few did—if I understand some of the early operating system designs correctly—but they didn't get the message to the rest of us, and I suspect most didn't generalize from simple programming tricks to a full-blown design approach the way the Norwegians did.

The key OO breakthrough was in design, in the way of thinking about programming, rather than in programming language implementation techniques. Programmers, in general, need to become more ambitious and more critical about the structure of their code.

S. KELLY-BOOTLE (*UNIX Review*): Can a non-constant member function be called via a temporary un-named object?

STROUSTRUP: Yes, if and only if, the temporary is not constant. For example:

```
class Stan {
public:
    void Kelley ( );
    void Bootle() const;
private:
    // ...
    } ;
```

```
Stan f ( );
const Stan g();

void g()
{
    f()->Kelley(); // ok
    g()->Bootle(); // ok
    g()->Kelley(); // error: non-const function
                   // applied to const object
    g()->Bootle(); // ok
}
```

WENDY MCKNITT (Univ. of Delaware): Thinking of C++ in terms of object-oriented programming, was there a specific reasoning behind the absence of a default base class?

STROUSTRUP: Yes. I think a universal base class encourages sloppy design and programming. In particular, it tempts people to seriously overuse run-time type identification where static type checking is appropriate and leads to superior designs. In addition, the absence makes it trivial to avoid space and time overhead. For many fundamental classes, such as complex numbers and time of day, it is particularly important to avoid space overheard, because space overhead can prevent layout compatibility with languages such as C and FORTRAN.

HERBERT KLAEREN (Univ. of Tubingen): It seems that C++ is to C about the same as LaTex is to Tex. As in that case, it is easy to blow the C++ intents by inappropriate manipulation on the underlying C level. Is there anything that can be done about that?

STROUSTRUP: I strongly believe in making undesirable features redundant rather than outlawing them. Once redundant, you might consider banning them, but why bother. A better approach is style checkers. I actually think that the real problem with "unsafe" and "tricky" features is that many are used in libraries where they are (sometimes) appropriate so that they show up in non-expert users' code using those libraries. This makes it hard to, say, enforce a rule like "never use explicit type conversions" because a reasonable use might occur in an inline library function. I think the right approach in the long run is to provide programmers with good analysis tools, so that they can easily see what they—or their predecessors on a piece of code—have done. Today, few programmers have tools that allow them to simply and effectively examine a program for error-prone constructs and techniques.

I don't think we will succeed before textbooks and foundation libraries set a good example.

ANDY MIKEL (MCAD Computer Center): Why did NEXT consciously choose Objective C over C++ to write NEXTStep?

STROUSTRUP: Did they? The story I heard was that when they first heard of C++, they had already started using Objective C and they asked the PPI salesman to explain C++ to them. Since he didn't make C++ sound attractive, they proceeded with Objective C. By the time they looked at C++ again, they already had a significant amount of code and a design philosophy depending on Objective C's brand of run-time type checking. I have no way of verifying this story (heard about ten years ago), but it is interesting—though not productive—to consider what might have happened if C++ had been commercially available as early as Objective C, or even if I had had a chat with the NEXT guys early on.

JOHN BIGBOTTE: Is "++" in danger of becoming as meaningless as "considered harmfull" ?

STROUSTRUP: Possibly. Any adjective that becomes popular gets overused. I have even seen ++s as an integral part of the ad campaign of a major bank.

RICHARD NANCE (Virginia Tech): Are you familiar with a language called SIM++? If so, how does it relate to C++?

STROUSTRUP: No. Sorry. I have heard the name, but I'm not doing much simulation these days and I don't keep track of all the C++ related simulation language and libraries.

RONALD FISCHER (Consultant): Why do you have two reserved words—`struct` and `class`—for the (semantically) same purpose? Why not simply stick with the word `struct`?

STROUSTRUP: I considered it infeasible to teach the fundamental difference between programming using data structures, and data abstraction without a syntactic "handle" for people to latch on to. I also happen to like the word `class` in this context, and its use is a tribute to Simula.

SCOTT GUTHREY (Schlumberger): C changed very little after it went into use. C++ has changed and continues to change. Which of these language histories is to be preferred?

STROUSTRUP: Ideally, a language springs perfectly formed from its designer's head. In reality, this doesn't happen. C was designed for a relatively well-known problem domain supporting a relatively well-understood set of techniques. Consequently, C was almost adequate from the start and only a few improvements, corrections, and extensions were ever done. Dennis and others decided to live with C—warts and all—and the result has been some frustration, and enormous benefits from its stability.

C++ followed a different path. I think it had to. C++ was attacking a set of problems that was less well understood, and aimed to serve a larger set of techniques directly. I don't think I had any chance of getting C++ as right at the first try as C was. Consequently, I had to use a strategy of implementing and using the ideas I trusted most, getting feedback, then extending the language based on the experience gained. The result has been a much better language than I could have designed initially, but at a loss of stability.

Also, I think that many people underestimate the length of C's "gestation period." ANSI C is notably different from the C first used in 1972. Similarly, people underestimate the stability of the core facilities of C++.

BOB ROSIN (ESPI): What was/is your working relationship with Dennis? What did you learn from him? What do you think he learned from you?

STROUSTRUP: We are colleagues in the same research center, but we are not close collaborators. By the time I arrived, Dennis's interests had drifted from languages (if that ever was a primary interest) into operating systems. I drifted the other way; at least for a while. In the early days of C with Classes, I discussed quite a few language-technical details with Dennis and I think he helped me avoid making some facilities narrow and paternalistic. I think that had effects beyond the features we actually discussed. Importantly, he and the rest of the people in the computer science research center emphasized an approach to work based on the solution of practical problems with moderate means, as opposed to chasing "perfection" without concern for resources and the opinions of the system builders "in the trenches." Dennis can also teach by simple example. In the 16 years I have known him, I have never heard him say an unkind word about any programming language. That absence of fanaticism can be refreshing.

BIOGRAPHY OF BJARNE STROUSTRUP

Bjarne Stroustrup, Cand.Scient. (Mathematics and Computer Science), 1975, University of Aarhus, Denmark; Ph.D. (Computer Science) 1979, Cambridge University, England. Bjarne Stroustrup is the designer and original implementor of C++ and the author of *The C++ Programming Language* (1st edition 1985, 2nd edition 1991) and *The Design and Evolution of C++*. His research interests include distributed systems, operating systems, simulation, design, and programming.

Dr. Stroustrup is the head of Bell Labs' Large-scale Programming Research department and an AT&T Bell Laboratories Fellow. He is actively involved in the ANSI/ISO standardization of C++ as the author of the base document and the chairman of the working group for extensions. Recipient of the 1993 ACM Grace Murray Hopper award, he is also an ACM fellow.

His non-research interests include general history, light literature, and music. He lives in Watchung, New Jersey, with his wife, daughter, and son.

Forum on the History of Computing (April 20, 1993)

Forum Chair: *Robert F. Rosin*

During its deliberations, the HOPL-II Program Committee concluded that, although the work of many computer scientists becomes part of the history of computing, very few computer scientists understand the history of computing or are involved in crafting that history. Assuming that a significant number of skilled computer scientists would attend HOPL-II, the Committee decided to take advantage of this opportunity to sensitize a portion of that community to issues in the history of computing and to entice some of them to become involved.

Therefore, the HOPL-II Program Committee authorized a 1/2-day "Forum on the History of Computing" that was held in conjunction with, and immediately prior to, HOPL-II.

The Forum program had four segments.

- The **opening lecture** introduced attendees to the work and challenges that abound in the history of computing.
- Each of five **overview presentations** discussed briefly one specific activity of which Forum attendees might be, at best, only vaguely aware.
- Four parallel **group discussions** gave attendees information needed to become personally involved in the craft of the history of computing.
- The **concluding panel** was a prelude to HOPL-II itself and addressed issues about computer exhibits. Conference attendees who did not participate in the earlier Forum sessions were welcome to attend.

The complete program, including the names and affiliations of speakers, discussion leaders, and panelists, can be found elsewhere in this book.

The original idea for the Forum grew out of e-mail discussion among HOPL-II Program Committee Members Brent Hailpern, Robert F. Rosin, and Jean E. Sammet. A subset of the Program Committee, consisting of Barbara Ryder, Michael S. Mahoney, Rosin, and Sammet, drafted the proposal for what has become the Forum.

The details of the Forum program were managed by the Forum Committee consisting of Thomas J. Bergin, Michael Marcotty (consultant), Thomas J. Marlowe, Jr. (Seton Hall University), Michael S. Mahoney, and Jean E. Sammet.

Robert F. Rosin, Forum Chair
Enhanced Service Providers, Inc.

ISSUES IN THE HISTORY OF COMPUTING

Michael S. Mahoney

Program in the History of Science
Princeton University
Princeton, New Jersey 08544
e-mail: mike@pucc.princeton.edu

COMPILING THE RECORD

It should be easy to do the history of computing. After all, computing began less than 50 years ago, and we have crowds of eye witnesses, mountains of documents, storerooms of original equipment, and the computer itself to process all the information those sources generate. What's so hard? What are we missing?

Well, the record is not quite as complete as it looks. As the Patent Office discovered during the '80s, much of the art of programming is undocumented, as is much of the software created during the '50s and since. The software itself is becoming inaccessible, as the machines on which it ran disappear through obsolescence. Critical decisions lie buried in corporate records—either literally so, or as trees are in a forest. Many eye witnesses have testified, but few have been cross-examined. Much of the current record exists only on-9line and, even if archived, will consist of needles in huge haystacks. But these are minor matters, to be discussed in the context of broader issues.

The major problem is that we have lots of answers but very few questions, lots of stories but no history, lots of things to do but no sense of how to do them or in what order. Simply put, we don't yet know what the history of computing is really about. A glance at the literature makes that clear. We still know more about the calculating devices that preceded the electronic digital computer—however tenuously related to it—than we do about the machines that shaped the industry. We have hardly begun to determine how the industry got started and how it developed. We still find it easier to talk about hardware than about software, despite the shared sense that much of the history of computing is somehow wrapped up in the famous inversion curve of hardware/software costs from 1960 to 1990. We still cast about for historical precedents and comparisons, unsure of where computing fits into the society that created it and has been shaped by it. That uncertainty is reflected in the literature and activities of the History of Science Society and the Society for the History of Technology, where the computer as the foremost scientific instrument, and computing as the salient technology, of the late twentieth century are all but invisible, not only in themselves but in the perspective they shed on earlier science and technology.

The presentations in the second session today are addressed to the various materials that constitute the primary sources for the history of computing: artifacts, archives and documents, first-person experience both written and oral. The business of HOPL-II itself is to enrich the sources for programming languages. As I noted at the outset, we seem to have no shortage of such materials. Indeed, as someone originally trained as a medievalist, I feel sometimes like a beggar at a banquet. I hardly know where to begin, and my appetite runs ahead of my digestion. It's a real problem, and not only for the consumer. To continue the metaphor, at some point the table can't hold all the dishes, and the pantry begins to overflow.

We have to pick and choose what we keep in store and what we set out. But by what criteria? Conflagration has done a lot of the selecting for medievalists. Historians of computing—indeed of modern science and technology in general—have to establish principles of a less random character.

Once collecting and preserving become selective (I mean consciously selective; they are always unconsciously selective), they anticipate the history they are supposed to generate and, thus, create that history. That is, they are historical activities, reflecting what we think is important about the present through what we preserve of it for the future. What we think is important about the present depends on who we are, where we stand—in the profound sense of the cliché, where we are coming from. Everyone at HOPI-II is doing history simply by being here and ratifying through our presence that the languages we are talking about and what we say about their origin and development are historically significant.

There's an important point here. Let me bring it out by means of something that seems to be of consuming interest to computer people, namely "firsts." Who was first to ... ? What was the first ... ? Now, that can be a tricky question because it can come down to a matter of meaning rather than of order in time. Nothing is entirely new, especially in matters of scientific technology. Innovation is incremental, and what already exists determines to a large extent what can be created. So collecting and recording "firsts" means deciding what makes them first, and that decision can often lead to retrospective judgments, where the first X had always been known as a Y. Let me give an example prompted by a distinguished computer scientist's use of history. I want to return to the topic at the end of this paper, so the example is more detailed than it need be for the present point.

In a review of business data processing in 1962, Grace Hopper, then at Remington Rand UNIVAC Division, sought to place the computer in the mainstream of American industrial development by emphasizing a characteristic sequence of venture—enterprise—mass production—adventure. The model suggested that computing was entering a period of standardization before embarking in daring new directions. The first two stages are tentative and experimental, but

> As the enterprise settles down and becomes practical mass production, the number of models diminishes while the number made of each model increases. This is the process, so familiar to all of us, by which we have developed our refrigerators, our automobiles, and our television sets. Sometimes we forget that in each case the practical production is followed by the new adventure. Sometimes we forget that the Model T Ford was followed by one with a gear shift [Hopper 1962].

That Model T, an icon of American industrialism, deserves a closer look. Shifting-gear transmissions antedated the Model T. But the softness of the steel then available and the difficulty of meshing gears meant the constant risk of stripping them. Concerned above all with reliability and durability, Ford consciously avoided shifting by going back to the planetary transmission, in which the gears remain enmeshed at all times and are brought to bear on the drive shaft in varying combinations by bands actuated by foot pedals. Although the Model A indeed had a gear shift, made reliable by Ford's use of new alloys, it is perhaps more important historically that the planetary transmission had just begun its life. For later, with the foot pedals replaced by a hydraulic torque converter, it served as the heart of the automatic transmissions that came to dominate automotive design in the 1950s. Now, how does one unravel the "firsts" in all this? Would we think to keep a Model T around for the history of automatic transmissions? What then of the first operating system, or the first database? Does the equivalent of a planetary transmission lurk in them too?

DOCUMENTING PRACTICE

In deciding what to keep, it may help to understand that historians look at sources not only for what is new and unusual but also for what is so common as to be taken for granted. In terms of information theory, they are equally interested in the redundancy that assures the integrity of the message. For much of common practice is undocumented, and yet it shapes what is documented. The deep effect of innovation is to change what we take for granted. This is what Thomas S. Kuhn had in mind with the notion of "paradigm shift," the central concept of his immensely influential book, *The Structure of Scientific Revolutions* [Kuhn 1962]. He later replaced "paradigm" with "disciplinary matrix," but the meaning remained the same: in learning to do science, we must learn much more than is in the textbook. In principle, knowing that $F = ma$ is all you need to know to solve problems in classical mechanics. In practice, you need to know a lot more than that. There are tricks to applying $F = ma$ to particular mechanical systems, and you learn how to do it by actually solving problems under the eye of someone who already has the skill. It is that skill, a body of techniques, and the habits of thought that go with them, that constitutes effective knowledge of a subject.

Because all practitioners of a subject share that skill, they do not talk about it. They take it for granted. Yet it informs their thinking at the most basic level, setting the terms in which they think about problems and shaping even the most innovative solutions. Thus it plays a major role in deciding about "firsts." Over time, the body of established practice changes, as new ideas and techniques become common knowledge and older skills become obsolete. Again, one doesn't talk much about it; "everyone knows that!" Yet, it is fragile. It is hard to keep, much harder than machines or programs.

To gain access to undocumented practice, historians are learning to do what engineers often take for granted: to read the products of practice in critical ways. In *The Soul of a New Machine* Tracy Kidder relates how Tom West of Data General bluffed his way into a company that was installing a new VAX and spent the morning pulling boards and examining them.

> Looking into the VAX, West had imagined he saw a diagram of DEC's corporate organization. He felt that VAX was too complicated. He did not like, for instance, the system by which various parts of the machine communicated with each other; for his taste, there was too much protocol involved. He decided that VAX embodied flaws in DEC's corporate organization. The machine expressed that phenomenally successful company's cautious, bureaucratic style. Was this true? West said it didn't matter, it was a useful theory [Kidder 1981, p. 26].

Historically, it is indeed a useful theory. Technology is not a literate enterprise; not because inventors and engineers are illiterate, but because they think in things rather than words.[Ferguson 1979; Wallace 1978] Henry Ford summed it up in his characteristically terse style:

> There is an immense amount to be learned simply by tinkering with things. It is not possible to learn from books how everything is made—and a real mechanic ought to know how nearly everything is made. Machines are to a mechanic what books are to a writer. He gets ideas from them, and if he has any brains he will apply those ideas [Ford 1924, pp. 23–24].

In short, the record of technology lies more in the artifacts than in the written records, and historians have to learn to read the artifacts as critically as they do the records. It is perhaps the best way of meeting Dick Hamming's challenge to "... know what they thought when they did it" [Hamming 1980]. For that, historians need, first and foremost, the artifacts. That is where museums play a central role in historical research. But historians also need help in learning how to read those artifacts. That means getting the people who designed and built them to talk about the knowledge and know-how that seldom gets into words.

As I use the word "artifact" here, I suspect that most of the audience has a machine in mind. But computing has another sort of artifact, one that seems unique until one thinks about it carefully. I mean a program: A high-level language compiler, an operating system, an application. It has been the common lament of management that programs are built by tinkering and that little of their design gets captured in written form, at least in a written form that would make it possible to determine how they work or why they work as they do rather than in other readily imaginable ways. Moreover, what programs do and what the documentation says they do are not always the same thing. Here, in a very real sense, the historian inherits the problems of software maintenance: the farther the program lies from its creators, the more difficult it is to discern its architecture and the design decisions that inform it.

Yet software can be read. In Alan Kay's talk, we'll hear a counterpart to Tom West's reading of the VAX boards:

> Head whirling, I found my desk. On it was a pile of tapes and listings, and a note: "This is the ALGOL for the 1108. It doesn't work. Please make it work." The latest graduate student gets the latest dirty task.
>
> The documentation was incomprehensible. Supposedly, this was the Case-Western Reserve 1107 ALGOL—but it had been doctored to make a language called Simula; the documentation read like Norwegian transliterated into English, which in fact was what it was. There were uses of words like *activity* and *process* that didn't seem to coincide with normal English usage.
>
> Finally, another graduate student and I unrolled the listing 80 feet down the hall and crawled over it yelling discoveries to each other. The weirdest part was the storage allocator, which did not obey a stack discipline as was usual for ALGOL. A few days later, that provided the clue. What Simula was allocating were structures very much like instances of Sketchpad [Kay 1993, p. 71(5)].

In the draft version, Kay added as a gloss to his tale that such explorations of machine code were common among programmers: "Batch processing and debugging facilities were so bad back then that one would avoid running code at any cost. 'Desk-checking' listings was the way of life." Yet, it is not the sort of thing one finds in manuals or textbooks. Gerald M. Weinberg gives an example of how it is done for various versions of FORTRAN in Chapter I of *The Psychology of Computer Programming* [Weinberg 1971], and Brian Kernighan and P.J. Plauger's *Elements of Programming Style* [Kernighan 1974] can be read as a guide to the art of reading programs. But the real trick is to capture the know-how, the tricks of the trade that everyone knew and no one wrote down when "desk-checking" was the norm. We need to think about how best to do that, because for historians without access to the machines on which programs ran or without the resources to have emulators written, desk-checking could again become a way of life. At the very least, it will demand fluency in the languages themselves.

THE IMPORTANCE OF CONTEXT

An emphasis on practice is also an emphasis on context. In focusing on what was new about computing in general and about various aspects of it in particular, one can lose sight of other elements of tradition (in the literal sense of "handing over") and of training that determined what was taken for granted as the basis for innovation. From the outset, computing was what Derek J. DeS. Price, a historian and sociologist of science, termed "big science" [Price 1963]. It relied on government funding, an expanding economy, an advanced industrial base, and a network of scientific and technical institutions. Over the past 40-odd years it has achieved autonomy as a scientific and technical enterprise, but it did so on the basis of older, established institutions, from which the first generations of computer people brought their craft practices, their habits of thought, their paradigms, and their precedents, all of which shaped the new industry and discipline they were creating.

As in many other things, Alan Perlis offered a productive metaphor for thinking about context. At the first HOPL he reflected on the fate of ALGOL 58 in competition with FORTRAN, noting that:

> The acceptance of FORTRAN within SHARE and the accompanying incredible growth in its use, in competition with a better linguistic vehicle, illustrated how factors other than language determine the choice

> of programming languages of users. Programs are not abstractions. They are articles of commerce in a society of users and machines. The choice of programming language is but one parameter governing the vitality of the commerce [Perlis 1981, 1983].

A comment by Kristen Nygaard during discussion led Perlis to expand the point:

> I think that my use of the world 'commerce' has been, at least in that case, misinterpreted. My use of the word 'commerce' was not meant to imply that it was IBM's self-interest which determined that FORTRAN would grow and that ALGOL would wither in the United States. It certainly was the case that IBM, being the dominant computer peddler in the United States, determined to a great extent—that the language FORTRAN would flourish, but IBM has peddled other languages which haven't flourished. FORTRAN flourished because it fitted well into the needs of the customers, and that defined the commerce. SHARE is the commerce. The publication of books on FORTRAN is the commerce. The fact that every computer manufacturer feels that if he makes a machine, FORTRAN must be on it is part of the commerce. In Europe, ALGOL is part of a commerce that is not supported by any single manufacturer, but there is an atmosphere in Europe of participation in ALGOL, dissemination of ALGOL, education in ALGOL, which makes it a commercial activity. That's what I mean by 'commerce'—the interplay and communication of programs and ideas about them. That's what makes commerce, and that's what makes languages survive [Perlis 1981, pp. 164–5].

One can extend Perlis' metaphor ever further, shifting the focus from survival to design. Henry Ford insisted that the Model T embodied a theory of business. He had designed it with a market in mind. The same may be said of any product, including programs. An industrial artifact is designed with a consumer in mind and hence reflects the designers' view of the consumer. The market—another term for "commerce"—is thus, not a limiting condition, an external constraint on the product, but rather a defining condition built into the product. "What does this mean?" can often best be answered by determining for whom it was meant. For both hardware and software, that may not be an easy thing to do. Stated goals may not have coincided with unstated, the people involved may not have agreed, and the computing world has a talent for justifying itself in retrospect.

As Perlis suggested, "commerce" in a general sense extends beyond industry and business to encompass science, technology, and the institutions that support them. The notion emphasizes the role of institutions in directing the technical development of computing and, to some extent, conversely. In *Creating the Computer*, Kenneth Flamm has revealed the patterns of government support that gave the computer and computing their initial shape [Flamm 1988]. The recent historical report by Arthur Norberg and Judy O'Neill on DARPA's Information Processing Techniques Office explores the interplay between defense needs and academic interests in the development of time-sharing, packet-switched networks, interactive computer graphics, and artificial intelligence [Norberg 1992]. What is particularly striking is the mobility of personnel between government offices and university laboratories, making it difficult at times to discern just who is designing what for whom. The study of the NSF's program in computer science, now being completed by William Aspray and colleagues, opens similar insights into the reciprocal influences between programs of research and sources of funding. In *IBM's Early Computers*, Charles Bashe and his coauthors show how commercialization of a cutting-edge technology forced the corporation, until then used to self-reliance in research and development, to open new links with the larger technical community and to play an active role in it, as evidenced by the *IBM Journal of Research and Development*, first published in 1957 [Bashe 1986]. Closer to my own home, the development of computer science at Princeton has been characterized by the easy flow of researchers between the University and Bell Labs, and that same pattern has surely occurred elsewhere.

Taken broadly, then, the notion of "commerce" directs the historian's attention to the determinative role of the marketplace in modern scientific technologies, such as computing. It is one thing to build number-crunchers one-by-one on contract to the government for its laboratories; it is another to develop a product line for a market that must be created and fostered. The explosive growth of computing since the early '50s depended on the ability of the industry to persuade corporations and, later, individuals that they needed computers, or at least could benefit from them. That meant not only designing machines but also, and increasingly, uses for them in the form of computer systems and applications. Henry Ford put Americans on wheels in part by showing them how they could use an automobile. Similarly, the computing industry has had to create uses for the computer. The development of computing as a technology has depended, at least in part, on its success in doing so, and hence, understanding the directions the technology has taken, even in its most scientific form, means finding the market for which it was being designed, or the market it was trying to design.

"Market" here includes people and people's skills. Earlier, I said a program seems "unique until one thinks about it." One may think about a program as essentially the design of a machine through the organization of a system of production. Other people thought about the organization of production and the management of organizations, and in many cases creating a market for computing meant creating a market for the skills of organizing systems of production. In examining the contexts of computing, historians would do well to explore, for example, the close relations between computing and industrial engineering and management. The *Harvard Business Review* introduced its readers to the computer and operations research in back-to-back issues in 1953 [*HBR* 1953a, 1953b], and the two technologies have had a symbiotic relationship ever since. Both had something to sell, both had to create a market for their products and they needed each other to create it. Computers and computing have evolved in a variety of overlapping contexts, shaping those contexts while being shaped by them. The history of computing thus lies in the intersections of the histories of many technologies, to which the historian of computing must remain attuned.

The notion of "computing as commerce" brings out the significance of techniques of reading artifacts, combined with the more usual techniques of textual criticism. To repeat: from the outset, computing has had to sell itself, whether to the government as big machines for scientific computing essential to national defense, to business and industry as systems vital to management, or to universities as scientific and technological disciplines deserving of academic standing and even departmental autonomy. The computing community very quickly learned the skills of advertising and became adept at marketing what it often could not yet produce. The result is that computing has had an air of wishful thinking about it. Much of its literature interweaves performance with promise, what is in practice with what can be in principle. It is a literature filled with announcements of revolutions subsequently (and quietly) canceled owing to unforeseen difficulties. In the case of confessed visionaries like Ted Nelson, the sources carry their own caveat. But in many instances computer marketers and management consultants, not to mention software engineers, were no less visionary, if perhaps less frank about it. What sources claimed or suggested could be done did not always correspond to what in fact could be done at the time. An industry trying to expand its market, engineers and scientists trying to establish new disciplines and attract research and development funding, new organizations seeking professional standing did not talk a lot about failures. The artifacts, both hard and soft, are the firmest basis for separating fact from fiction technically, provided one learns to read them critically. Doing so is essential to understanding the claims made for computers and programs, and why they were believed.

DOING HISTORY

Recognizing the elements of continuity that link computing to its own past, and to the past of the industries and institutions that have fostered it, brings out most clearly the relation of history and current practice. History is built into current practice; the more profound the influence, the less conscious we are of its presence. It is not a matter of learning the "lessons of history" or of exploring "what history can teach us," as if these were alternatives or complements to practice. We are products of our history or, rather, our histories; we do what we do for historical reasons. Bjarne Stroustrup notes in his history of C++,

> We never have a clean slate. Whatever new we do we must also make it possible for people to make a transition from old tools and ideas to new [Stroustrup 1993, p. 294(47)].

History serves its purpose best, not when it suggests what we should be doing, but when it makes clear what we are doing, or at least clarifies what we think we are doing. On matters that count, we invoke precedents, which is to say we invoke history. We should be conscious of doing that, and we should be concerned both that we have the right history and that we have the history right.

Earlier, to make a point about "firsts," I cited Grace Hopper's evocation of the Model T. You may well have felt that my critique focused on a matter of detail that is irrelevant to her main point. Perhaps; but consider the historical basis of that main point. She was taking the automobile industry as a precedent for business data processing and by extension for computing as a whole. It was not the first time she had done so. The precedent she invoked in her famous *Education of a Computer* [Hopper 1952], was also taken from the automotive production line, and it has persisted as a precedent down to the present: look at the cover of *IEEE Software* for June 1984, where the Ford assembly line around 1940 serves as backdrop to Peter Wegner's four-part article on industrial-strength software [Wegner 1984]; then look at the Ford assembly line of the '50s on the jacket of Greg Jones's *Software Engineering* in 1990. These are not isolated examples, nor are they mere window dressing. They reflect a way of thinking about software engineering, and there is history built into it, as there is in the notion of engineering itself; witness Mary Shaw's comparison of software engineering with other engineering disciplines [Shaw 1990]. There were other ways to think about writing programs for computers. If people thought, and even continue to think, predominantly about automobiles or engineering, it is for historical reasons.

In commenting on a draft of this paper, Bob Rosin noted at this point that "automobiles and engineering are (outdated?) paradigms that are largely unfamiliar to younger computer people. Many kids, who grew up hacking on Ataris and PCs and Macs, didn't hack automobiles and rarely studied engineering." The implied objection touches my argument only where I shift from history to criticism of current practice. Historically, at least through the '80s, software engineering has taken shape with reference to the assembly line and to industrial engineering as models. Those models are built into the current enterprise. One only has to read Doug McIlroy's "On Mass-Produced Software Components," presented to the first NATO Software Engineering Conference in 1968, to see where the conceptual roots of object-oriented programming lie [McIlroy 1976]. Ignorance of the automobile and engineering, or at least of their role in the formation of software engineering, will not free a new generation of software developers from the continuing influence of the older models built into the practice they learn and the tools they use. Rather, it means that practitioners will lack critical understanding of the foundations on which they are building.

Moreover, it is not just software engineers who talk about the automobile. How often have we heard one personal computer or another described as the "Model T of computing?" What would it mean to take the claim seriously? What would a personal computer have to achieve to emulate the Model T as a technological achievement and a social and economic force? Would it be useful for historians of computing to take the Model T as a historical precedent? If not, what is a useful historical precedent? Are there perhaps several precedents?

AN AGENDA FOR HISTORY OF COMPUTING

So, maybe the history of computing is not so easy, but what's to be done? Let me conclude by setting out an agenda, for which I claim neither completeness nor objectivity. For one thing, it reflects my own bias toward software rather than hardware.

We need to know more than we do about how the computing industry began. What was the role of the government? How did both older companies and start-ups identify a potential market and how did the market determine their products? What place did research and development occupy in the companies' organization, and how did companies identify and recruit staffs with the requisite skills?

We need to know about the origins and development of programming as an occupation, a profession, a scientific and technological activity. A proper history here might help in separating reality from wishful thinking about the nature of programming and programmers. In particular, it will be necessary for historians of computing to embed their subject into the larger contexts of the history of technology and the history of the professions as a whole. For example, in *The System of Professions*, Andrew Abbott argues that

> It is the history of jurisdictional disputes that is the real, the determining history of the professions. Jurisdictional claims furnish the impetus and the pattern to organization developments.... Professions develop when jurisdictions become vacant, which may happen because they are newly created or because an earlier tenant has left them altogether or lost its firm grip on them [Abbott 1988, pp. 2–3].

That is, the professions as a system represent a form of musical chairs among occupations except that chairs and participants may be added as well as eliminated. Not all occupations are involved. Competition takes place among those that on the basis of abstract knowledge "can redefine [their] problems and tasks, defend them from interlopers, and seize new problems." Although craft occupations control techniques, they do not generally seek to extend their aegis.

One only has to page through the various computing journals of the late '50s and early '60s to see conflicts over jurisdiction reflecting uncertain standing as a profession. Whose machine was it? Soon after the founding of the ACM, it turned its focus from hardware to software, ceding computing machinery to the IRE. Not long thereafter, representatives of business computing complained about the ACM's bias toward scientific computing and computer science. Numerical analysts scoffed at "computerologists," inviting them to get back to the business at hand. One does not have to look hard to find complaints in other quarters that computing was being taken over by academics ignorant of the problems and methods of "real" programming. Similar tensions underlay discussions of a succession of ACM committees charged with setting the curriculum for computer science.

Following from that is the need for histories of the main communities of computing: numerical analysis, data processing, systems programming, computer science, artificial intelligence, graphics, and so on. When and how did the various specialties emerge, and how did each of them establish a separate identity as evidenced, say, by recognition as a SIG by the ACM or the IEEE, or by a distinct place in the computing curriculum? How has the balance of professional power shifted among these communities, and how has the shift been reflected in the technology?

The software crisis proclaimed at the end of the '60s is still with us, despite the accelerated expansion of software engineering in the '70s and '80s. The origins and development of the problem and the response to it provides a rare opportunity to trace the history of a discipline shaping itself. It did not exist in 1969. Throughout the '70s and early '80s, keynote speakers and introductions to books repeatedly asked, "Are we there yet?" without making it entirely clear where "there" was. Today, software engineering has a SIG, its own *Transactions*, its own IEEE publication, an ACM approved curriculum, and a growing presence in undergraduate and graduate programs. One only has to compare

Barry Boehm's famous article of 1972 [Boehm 1973], with reports about DoD software in any issue of *Software Engineering Notes* to doubt that the burgeoning of software engineering reflects its success in meeting the problems of producing reliable software on time, within budget, and to specifications. How, then, has the field grown so markedly in 20 years?

Software takes many forms, and we have begun the history of very few of them, most notably programming languages and artificial intelligence. Still awaiting the historian's attention are operating systems, networks, databases, graphics, and embedded systems, not to mention the wealth and variety of microcomputer programs. This is HOPL-II; we still await HOS-I (operating systems), or any of a host of HOXs. SIGGRAPH undertook a few years ago to determine the milestones of the field, but there has been little or no work since then. In each of these areas, history will have to look well beyond the software itself to the fields that stimulated its development, supplied the substantive methods, and in turn incorporated computing into their own patterns of thinking.

Finally, there remains the elusive character of the "Computer Revolution," first proclaimed by Edmund C. Berkeley, then editor of *Computers and Automation* back in 1962 and subsequently heralded by a long line of writers, both in and out of computing [Berkeley 1962]. Clearly something epochal has happened. Yet, as I pointed out several years ago in an article [Mahoney 1988], it would be hard to demonstrate for the computer, in whatever form, as pervasive an impact on ordinary people's lives as Robert and Helen Lynd were able to document for the automobile, in their famous study of Muncie, Indiana in 1924 [Lynd 1929]. But here I am, back at the automobile again. Maybe I've been spending too much time with computer people.

REFERENCES

[Abbot, 1988] Abbott, Andrew, *The System of Professions: An Essay on the Division of Expert Labor*, Chicago: University of Chicago Press, 1988.

[Bashe, 1986] Bashe, Charles, and Pugh, Emerson, *IBMs Early Computers*, Cambridge, MA: MIT Press, 1986.

[Berkeley, 1962] Berkeley, Edmund C., *The Computer Revolution*, Garden City, NY: Doubleday & Co., 1962.

[Boehm, 1973] Boehm, Barry W., Software and its impact: A quantitative assessment, *Datamation* Vol. 19, May 1973, pp. 48–59.

[Ferguson, 1979] Ferguson, Eugene S., The mind's eye: Nonverbal thought in technology, *Science* Vol. 197, 1979, pp. 827–836.

[Flamm, 1988] Flamm, Kenneth, *Creating the Computer: Government, Industry, and High Technology*, Washington, D.C.: Brookings Institution, 1988.

[Ford, 1924] Ford, Henry, *My Life and Work*, Garden City, NY: Doubleday, 1922.

[Hamming, 1980] Hamming, Richard W., We would know what they thought when they did it, in *N. Metropolis*, J. Howlett, G. C. Rota eds., *A History of Computing in the Twentieth Century: A Collection of Essays*. NY: Academic Press, 1980, pp. 3–9

[HBR, 1953a] Herrmann, Cyril C., and Magee, John F., 'Operations research' for management, *Harvard Business Re iew*, Vol. 31, No. 4, 1953, pp. 100–12.

[HBR, 1953b] First advertisements for IBM and Univac in *Harvard Business Review,* Vol. 31, No. 5–6, 1953.

[Hopper, 1952] Hopper, Grace, The education of a computer, *Proceedings of the Association for Computing Machinery Conference*, Pittsburgh, May 1952; repr. with introduction by David Gries, *Annals of the History of Computing,* Vol. 9, No. 3/4, 1988, pp. 271–281.

[Hopper, 1962] Hopper, Grace, Business data processing—a review, *IFIP*, Vol. 62, pp. 35–39.

[Kay, 1993] Kay, Alan C., The early history of Smalltalk, *SIGPLAN Notices*, Vol. 28, No. 3, March 1993, pp. 69–95.

[Kernighan, 1974] Kernighan, Brian, and Plauger, P.J., *The Elements of Programming Style*, New York: McGraw-Hill, 1974; second ed., 1978

[Kidder, 1981] Kidder, Tracy, *The Soul of a New Machine*, Boston: Little, Brown, and Co., 1981

[Kuhn, 1962] Kuhn, Thomas S., *The Structure of Scientific Revolutions*, Chicago: University of Chicago Press, 1962.

[Lynd, 1929] Lynd, Robert S., and Lynd, Helen Merrell, *Middletown: A Study in American Culture*, New York: Harcourt, Brace & World, 1929; repr. 1956.

[Mahoney, 1988] Mahoney, Michael S., The history of computing in the history of technology, *Annals of the History of Computing*, Vol. 10, 1988, pp. 113–125.

[McIlroy, 1976] McIlroy, M. D., On mass-produced software components, in *Software Engineering: Concepts and Techniques. Proceedings of the NATO Conferences*, Peter Naur, Brian Randall, J. N. Buxton, Eds.,[Garmisch, 1968; Rome, 1969)]. New York: Petrocelli/Charter, 1976, pp. 88–95.

[Norberg, 1992] Norberg, Arthur L., and O'Neill, Judy E., *Promoting technological innovation: The Information Processing Techniques Office of Defense Advanced Research Projects Agency, a report to the Software and Intelligent Systems Technology Office*, DARPA. Minneapolis: The Charles Babbage Institute, 1992.

[Perlis, 1981] Perlis, Alan, The American side of the development of Algol, in *History of Programming Languages*, Richard L. Wexelblat, ed., New York: Academic Press, 1981.

[Price, 1963] Price, Derek J. deSolla, *Little Science, Big Science*. New York: Columbia University Press, 1963.

[Shaw, 1990] Shaw, Mary, Prospects for an engineering discipline of software, *IEEE Software* Vol. 7, No. 6, Nov. 1990, pp. 15–24.

[Stroustrup, 1993] Stroustrup, Bjarne, A history of C++: 1979–1991, *SIGPLAN Notices*, Vol. 28, No. 3, Mar. 1993, pp. 271–97.

[Wallace, 1978] Wallace, Anthony F. C., Thinking About Machinery, in *The Growth of an American Village in the Early Industrial Revolution*, Rockdale, N.Y.: Knopf, 1978), pp. 237ff.

[Wegner, 1984] Wegner, Peter, Capital-intensive software technology, *IEEE Software*, Vol. 1, No. 3, 1984, pp. 7–45.

[Weinberg, 1971] Weinberg, Gerald M., *The Psychology of Computer Programming*, New York: Van Nostrand Reinhold Co., 1971.

ARCHIVES SPECIALIZING IN THE HISTORY OF COMPUTING

Bruce H. Bruemmer

Charles Babbage Institute
103 Walter Library
University of Minnesota
Minneapolis, MN 55455

The following public institutions have a special interest in supporting and documenting the history of computing. A very brief description of each repository's interest in archival materials is noted. For further information, contact the repository directly or refer to one of the guides listed at the end of this section.

Charles Babbage Institute
103 Walter Library
117 Pleasant St. SE
University of Minnesota
Minneapolis, MN 55455
612 624-5050, FAX 612 625-8054
contact: Bruce Bruemmer
(bruce@fs1.itdean.umn.edu)

History of computing largely after 1935. Holds records of individuals, companies (Burroughs and Control Data), professional organizations and individuals. Also, computer literature, film, photographs, and oral history.

Computer Museum
300 Congress Street
Boston, MA 02210
617 426-2800
contact: Oliver Strimpel

Computer manuals, photographs, films, particularly those relating to artifact collection.

Hagley Museum and Library
PO Box 3630
Wilmington, DE 19807
302 658-2400
contact: Michael Nash

Computer industry, particularly around Delaware Valley. Holds Sperry Rand records.

Library of Congress
Manuscripts Division
Washington, DC 20540
202 287-5387

Records of prominent individuals. Holds Hollerith, von Neumann, and Vannevar Bush papers.

National Archives and Records Administration
Office of Records Administration
Washington, DC 20408
202 523-3220
contact: James Moore

Records relating to data processing in the federal government.

Smithsonian Institution. National Air and Space Museum.
Space Science and Exploration Dept.
Washington, DC
202 357-2828
contact: Paul Ceruzzi

Records relating to data processing for aerospace applications.

Smithsonian Institution,
National Museum of American History
Washington, DC 20560
202 357-3270
contact: John Fleckner

Records relating to computing in America. Holds Smithsonian/AFIPS oral history collection, Hopper papers, computer literature collection.

Stanford University Libraries
Department of Special Collections
Stanford, CA 94305
415 723-4602
contact: Henry Lowood

Records relating to science and technology of the Silicon Valley area. Holds records of prominent individuals, businesses, and organizations.

CORPORATIONS WITH ESTABLISHED HISTORICAL PROGRAMS

Many companies have established their own archival and/or museum operations. Individuals holding records relating to these companies may wish to contact their archives or museum.

AT&T Archives
PO Box 4647
Warren, NJ 07059
908 756-1586
contact: Bunny White

Apple Computer, Inc.
Records Management
20525 Mariani Ave.
MS 36R
Cupertino, CA 95014
408 974-1503

Digital Equipment Corp
146 Main St.
MLO 3-4/T83
Maynard, MA 01754
508 952-3559
contact: Craig G. St. Clair

Hewlett-Packard Co.
HP Company Archives
3000 Hanover 20BR
Palo Alto, CA 94304
415 857-8537
contact: Karen Lewis

International Business Machines Corp.
IBM Archives
Rt 100
Bldg. CSB
Somers, NY 10589
914 766-0612
contact: Robert Godfrey

MIT Lincoln Laboratories
Room A082
244 Wood Street
Lexington, MA 02173
617 981-7179
contact:Mary Murphy

MITRE Corporation
Corporate Archives
MS K450 Burlington Road
Bedford, MA 01730
617 721-7854
contact: David Baldwin

Texas Instruments
Corporate Archives, MS 233
PO Box 655474
Dallas, TX 75265
214 995-4458
contact: Ann Westerlin

UNIVERSITY ARCHIVES WITH SIGNIFICANT HOLDINGS

The following university archives have significant archival collections pertaining to the history of computing. Individuals seeking to donate historically valuable records that relate to the programs or research at specific academic institutions should contact the pertinent university or college archivist.

Dartmouth College
Harvard University
Massachusetts Institute of Technology
Stanford University
University of Illinois
University of Pennsylvania

REFERRALS

American Institute of Physics
Center for the History of Physics
335 East 45th St.
New York, NY 10017

212 661-9404

contact: Joan Warnow

Charles Babbage Institute
103 Walter Library
University of Minnesota
Minneapolis, MN 55455

612 624-5050

contact:Bruce Bruemmer
(bruce@fs1.itdean.umn.edu)

Center for the History of Electrical Engineering
IEEE
Rutgers—The State University
39 Union St.
New Brunswick, NJ 08903

908 932-1066

contact: Andrew Goldstein
(agoldstein@zodiac.rutgers.edu)

Society of American Archivists
600 S. Federal
Suite 504
Chicago, IL 60605

312 922-0140
contact: Debra Mills

NATIONAL ARCHIVAL GUIDES

Bruce H. Bruemmer, *Resources of the History of Computing: A Guide to U.S. and Canadian Records*, Minneapolis: Charles Babbage Institute, 1987.

James W. Cortada, Ed., *Archives of Data-Processing History: A Guide to Major U.S. Collections*, New York: Greenwood, 1990.

THE ROLE OF MUSEUMS IN COLLECTING COMPUTERS

Gwen Bell
(with additional editing by Robert F. Rosin)

The Computer Museum
300 Congress Street
Boston MA 02210

SEEING IS BELIEVING

Pictures of a three-dimensional technological object, especially in its original context, are rich in clues about the use of that object. But the object itself, examined closely and from all directions—and in special cases, used or operated—provides an understanding like no other of that object and its technology.

The original and primary purpose of museums of science and technology was for the preservation of artifacts. But many museum artifacts, by their nature, are rare and fragile, so traditionally they have been accessible to only a few professionals and interested people. Students and the public were seldom given the same opportunity, nor was material presented in such a way that they could understand it.

However, in this century, with the widespread movement for universal education, those concepts changed. Museums were reinterpreted as broad-based educational institutions.

MUSEUM CHARTERS

The mission of many museums reflects this historical evolution. Some museums remain only collecting institutions, others were started with the educational theme in mind and have no collections, and some combine these two. The Computer Museum is the third type, combining education and collections. Specifically, its mission is:

1. To educate and inspire all ages and levels of the public, through dynamic exhibitions and programs on the technology, applications, and impact of computers.
2. To preserve and celebrate the history and promote the understanding of computers worldwide.
3. To be an international resource for the history of computing.

COMPUTER COLLECTIONS

Five national museums have computing collections: The Deutches Museum, Munich; The National Museum of Science and Technology, Ottawa; The Science Museum, London; The National Museum of American History of the Smithsonian Institution, Washington; and the National Air and Space Museum, also part of the Smithsonian. By definition, the major focus of their collections is national, although when they build exhibits, they seek examples of significant artifacts from beyond their borders.

Several other museums have smaller computing collections; for example, a computer museum in Bozeman, MT and The Computer Museum of America in Orange County, CA. Other museums have a few computer objects.

Several nonprofit research institutions have computer-related collections and museums that relate to their own history; for example, The Computer Museum at Livermore and the Los Alamos Museum.

Some universities maintain exhibits of locally developed computers such as the Mark I at Harvard, ENIAC at the University of Pennsylvania, components of the ABC at Iowa State University, representative parts of the various Manchester University computers, and parts of TX-2 at the MIT Museum.

A few companies have corporate collections, and some maintain galleries open to the public. These include Cray Research, Digital Equipment Corporation, Fujitsu, IBM, Intel, and Wang Laboratories. IBM has an extensive collection, which they exhibit at the IBM Galleries at various times. Unisys has, for the most part, given its collection to museums and kept very little. Maintaining a corporate collection is governed by the corporation; they have no public contract to preserve their history. Budgets for these collections can be cut instantaneously, and, if no one is around to get the materials at the correct time, they are dumped.

CRITERIA FOR COLLECTING ARTIFACTS

Collecting criteria is fundamentally the same for all institutions. These criteria are not always spelled out, but they represent the practice of many curators. In the larger museums, where computing is only one of the many collections, justification for each addition must be made to an acquisition committee. The rationale is generally to show evidence that the object being acquired is a "first," is a unique artifact, or was the standard of its era. For example, the Smithsonian and the Computer Museum both have exhibits and collections on the UNIVAC I (a first) and the IBM 360 (a standard).

1. **Firsts** are identified as technologically innovative, for example, the first integrated circuit, the first transistorized computer, the first core memory. As the justification becomes finer grained and less clear, questions regarding the acquisitions grow; for example, the first 256K memory chip or the first two-button mouse.
2. **Classics** are the standard devices of any era as evidenced by widespread adoption and use. Examples include the IBM 360, PDP-S, and Apple II. Museums are particularly interested in examples of "classics," as they often want to exhibit a generic example to illustrate social and economic impacts.
3. **Dinosaurs and dead ends** help illustrate the point that technology does not advance in a straight line. Failed technologies often have important lessons for the future that are critical to helping future generations understand technical problems. Reasons for failure include technical, social, and economic problems. Examples include the IBM System 3, 90-column punched cards, the Dvorak keyboard, and 12-bit computers.

   In each case, the precise understanding of why the technology failed, its "story," is critical to any institution making a decision for acquisition. Often curators do not have the time to undertake this research, so it is up to the donor to make a strong case.
4. **Icons** are critical to collect. These are objects that are often not technologically interesting in and of themselves, but they evoke an era or a set of phenomena. Very few artifacts become icons, and when they do, everyone knows it. Examples include Archie Bunker's chair and, for the computer graphics community, "the teapot."
5. **Other kinds of objects** that are collected are:
   - A clone that reflects an important dimension that should not be lost. Although many clones are made, few should probably enter any permanent collection.

- A part of a series which, although unimportant in itself, relates to a collecting area of the institution. For example, all the machines designed by Seymour Cray or all the attempts at parallel structures.
- An object that represents a particular country's development of computing.
- An artifact that has an interesting feature.
- An object that is the best representative that can be acquired under the circumstances.

The Computer Museum also collects items specifically for particular exhibitions and for educational purposes. In the latter case, these are "spares" that can be shared with other institutions or used for teaching.

COLLECTIONS AT THE COMPUTER MUSEUM

The Computer Museum is unique in that it is both nonprofit and international in scope. As outlined in the Museum's application for nonprofit status in 1981 and as carried out in practice, the collections of the Museum are guided by the taxonomy of computing as defined in Bell and Newell, *Computer Structures: Readings and Examples* (1972). The collection focuses on the material technology of computing hardware and associated documentation.

The documents that are collected include manuals, books, photographs, films, videos, CDs, and ephemera such as buttons, models, and advertising materials. These documents lend unity to the artifact collection. Although the same criteria that apply to hardware artifacts also apply to these items, the accessioning process is generally less formal because such items are often less rare, can easily be copied, or suitable substitutes can be found.

Figure 16.1 shows the integration of several of these collections. For the Amdahl 470/6, serial number 10002, the artifact is listed as item X436.84. Additional listings include a photograph, two manuals, and two sets of schematics. Further down the page is an entry for a videotape of a lecture by Gene Amdahl, item VT51.83 which mentions the 470.

THE USE OF THE MUSEUM'S COMPUTER COLLECTIONS

As yet, the Computer Museum collection is not used for serious primary research. In many cases, this is because the inventors are themselves available. For the most part, the photographs are used for illustrations by the trade press and by authors of technical books. The manuals and artifacts are used by researchers investigating "prior art" to establish patent rights.

The Museum staff uses all aspects of the collection in creating exhibits. For example, several artifacts were used to add richness and depth to the recent *Tools and Toys* exhibit.

RESPONSIBILITIES OF COLLECTING

Problems and major costs begin after an item is acquired. Therefore, institutions take extreme care in selection for acquisition. If an entire collection is given to an institution with no strings attached, then, upon review, the institution may acquire some items, dispose of others in a variety of ways, and even "age" a few to see whether they should be acquired.

Once acquired, an object is—and should be—difficult to get rid of. Deaccession has to be a well thought out process. When an object is accepted by a nonprofit institution, the donor rightly can claim

FIGURE 16.1

The Computer Museum—Sample Catalog Page.

Amdahl Computer Corporation

Amdahl 470

Computing Systems Physical Planning Manual #G1004.0.04A (1981) 59[A342]
Cable diagrams and Console Documentation schematics (1974) [A342]
V/5, V6 Computing Systems, Illustrated Parts-Catalog (1980) [AB42]
Computing System Machine Reference Manual #G1014.0-12A (1981) 35[A342]

470/V5-I

Computing System Machine Reference Manual #G1012.0 01A (1979) 26[A342]

470V/6 Computing System 1975 X436.84

s# 10002. Amdahl V/6, No.2, was initially installed at the University of Michigan, Ann Arbor, in 1975. The first system was installed at NASA. At Michigan it was upgraded to a V/6-II, a change in buffer size. In 1979 the system was sold to American Cyanamid in New Jersey, where it remained until August of 1984. Gift of Major Computer, Inc.

Photograph: Dr. Gene Amdahl with a "mock up" of the Amdahl 470V/6 introduced in June 1975. [Amdahl, Gene]
Computing System Machine Reference Manual 470V/6 & 470V/6-II #M1047. 0-01A (1979) 2[A342]
Inside the Amdahl 470V/6-II 5[A342]
System BLCALDS, C-Unit, Buffer schematics [A98]
System BLCALDS Unlabeled schematics [A342]

Amdahl 580

Technical Introduction (1980) 25[A342]
Executive Summary (1980) 8[A342

a tax deduction for the value of that item, and the institution can lose its nonprofit status if it does not keep the item.

WHAT YOU CAN DO TO PRESERVE HISTORIC MATERIALS

- If you see an important artifact, call a collecting institution immediately; don't wait one day.
- If someone says, "I'm throwing this out," and you think it is an important object, get a stay of execution until you can speak with a collecting institution, and try to save it.
- If an individual or a noncollecting corporation insists on keeping what appears to be an important item, make sure that it is clearly identified, arrange for its future donation to an institution, and, in the meantime, see that good care is taken of it.
- If you think an object should be saved, make the case to preserve it as strongly as you can and with as much authority as you can muster.

THE *ANNALS OF THE HISTORY OF COMPUTING* AND OTHER JOURNALS

Bernard A. Galler

EECS Department
The University of Michigan
Ann Arbor. MI 48109-2122

The history of computing is recorded in many places. The *Annals of the History of Computing* is the only journal dedicated to that purpose, and its origins and concerns occupy the bulk of this article. The closing section, including an extensive bibliography, surveys other publications where this history is also recorded.

The *Annals of the History of Computing* was founded in 1978, and a number of lessons have been learned since then about publishing contemporary history. The field of computers and computing is very young and very dynamic. A journal which tries to record its history has unique opportunities, as the creators of the history are still on the scene. On the other hand, there are few disinterested observers around, and "history" can become very personal. Moreover, authors of the papers for the journal are generally not historians.

The *Annals* was founded by the American Federation of Information Processing Societies (AFIPS) when it became clear that the members of AFIPS—societies such as ACM, IEEE, and DPMA—were not actively involved in recording the history of the field. There had been a series of oral interviews sponsored by AFIPS and the Smithsonian, but the pioneers were getting older, and our discipline's early history was potentially slipping away. Moreover, those of us who had been around in the early days weren't going to miss the opportunity to pass on to our successors—who were mainly young people—the excitement of discovery that we had experienced.

We wanted a readable journal that would record the history, a task which would not be easy. Too much detail in the spirit of establishing the record would make the material less readable. Too little detail would make it only a series of anecdotes. Moreover, it was important to encourage the remembrances of the people who lived through those exciting times, along with the historical analyses by those who came after, and who in many cases would be trained as historians to do the analysis professionally. The remembrances of those who lived through periods of decision will help future analysts understand why those decisions were made, even though there may well be conflicting eye-witness accounts! We decided that this journal would welcome all who came to it seriously (or humorously, but with taste!), and would include all the styles and purposes mentioned. There was room in this house for all.

After a couple of years of preparation, we were ready to publish the first few issues, starting in July 1979. It turned out that there were several people who had written serious articles (and in the case of Brian Randell, an excellent bibliography), and who needed a place to publish their work. They furnished the seed material for the *Annals*. Others were encouraged by this work to write about their own experience, and successes and failures. We also encouraged people in other countries and other disciplines to summarize and organize the history of computing in their countries and in their disciplines, such as in graphics and weather prediction. We also sought and received articles on the socioeconomics of the computing field itself, such as an analysis of advertising about computers, to understand the view the public had of computers and computing.

Today, in 1993, with Volume 15 being published, the *Annals* is established as the place to publish history material about computers and computing. We welcome new authors and old authors. To be sure, there are other publications in the history of computing field. There is an excellent series of books published by MIT Press, another series of important reprintings by the Charles Babbage Foundation, a series of proceedings of ACM conferences, and so on. These are complemented by the archival collections of the Charles Babbage Institute, and the Computer Museum. In what follows, however, we discuss some of the issues faced by authors and publishers, primarily through the eyes of the *Annals.*

SCOPE OF INTEREST

The *Annals* originally had a policy of requiring that events being recorded had occurred at least 15 years before the date of publication. The purpose of this is to ensure that the author (and the readers) have some perspective on those events. Thus, although some urged that we publish the history of the personal computer almost as soon as it was invented, it didn't seem wise to do so at the time. It is probably just about the right time now to do that. Hopefully, there are sources of historical material and interested writers who will undertake that task. Of course, if the material is from that long ago, how does an author remember it? It starts with an awareness of the need to record the history of the field. That leads to saving the key ingredients, the important and the nostalgic, from which the past can be reconstituted. We all have old stuff, and that of our friends, on which to draw. It gets easier with practice!

THE FUTURE?

What about predictions of the future? That has always been the province of the science fiction writer, but one could imagine a serious article on the possible directions in which trends of the past might evolve into the future. Or a study of how one might learn from the past to think about the future. If we had tried to predict the present state of our technology, our environment, and our computing community 30 years ago, how far off would we have been, and why? The problem is sometimes that people are hesitant to "stick their necks out." A properly labeled predictive article can stimulate discussion, without much exposure. Who else would have a better prediction?

SUBJECT MATTER

What is relevant to the study of the history of computing? One of the most interesting articles published in the *Annals* covered advertising in the computer field over the years. The role of people relative to the computer, the role of women, and other sociological and political subjects can often be understood better when cartoons, and advertising, and other nonconventional forms of publication are brought together and studied from an historical point of view. The Charles Babbage Institute staff has done several studies of different corporations' business records. What else would be relevant that historians might be overlooking now? It is important to take advantage of the variety of fields of expertise of people in computing, to enlist them in the service of the history of computing! Each brings a different perspective, and each is welcome.

HISTORIOGRAPHY

The writing of history is a subject of interest in its own right. Of course, the *Annals* wasn't created to teach people how to write about history, but we did include a few articles of this kind. They are helpful to both writers and readers, in terms of the pitfalls to watch out for in writing and reading about historical events. We can all learn from those who understand it best.

Some examples of articles in the *Annals* about the writing of history are:

- "Works and Tools," by Peter Drucker, Vol. 4, No. 4, pp. 342–347.
- "The History of Computing in the History of Technology," by Michael S. Mahoney, Vol. 10, No. 2, pp. 113–125.
- "Some Approaches to, and Illustrations of, Programming Languages History," by Jean E. Sammet, Vol. 13, No. 1, pp. 33–50.
- "Guidelines for the Documentation of Segments of the History of Computing," ed. by J.A.N. Lee, Vol. 13, No. 1, pp. 51–62.

WRITING STYLES

Should a journal have a uniform writing style? Does it make articles easier to read? Or do you lose the unique expressiveness that each author brings to the subject? We learned a lesson in the early days of the *Annals*. One author withdrew his article when we tried, perhaps too hard, to help with his English. He was a European who was sure that he knew English better than our editor, and he was not about to let us tell him how to write. Were we wise to try so hard to not let him look foolish? Another (American) author insisted on his particular notation for the subject matter he was writing about. We decided that, in that case, we would not insist on a more standard notation; he was worth it! Over the years, we relaxed more and more in favor of offering help to authors, but trying to preserve their individuality of writing style. This can be a very delicate issue! We would hope that authors would welcome help with their styles, but would keep that unique flavor that only they can bring. It is a cooperative effort all the way through the process.

HISTORICAL STANDARDS

For a conference, such as the first History of Programming Languages Conference (HOPL) in 1979, very strict standards were set, in terms of historical accuracy and completeness. Help was provided to authors by historians and by experts specifically designated for each paper. Should that much support be provided for authors of articles aimed at the *Annals*? It would be very desirable, of course, but quite expensive. A great deal of help and care is provided, to be sure, through the refereeing process, but some reliance has been placed on the section of the journal called "Comments, Queries, and Debate." This is an avenue that is not available to a conference, but can be useful in an on-going journal. Here a reader can take issue with an author, and a dialogue can be established between them, which itself becomes part of the historical record.

One striking example of this occurred with the publication of the article on the ENIAC by Alice and Arthur Burks. We solicited comments from 19 people associated with the ENIAC project, and published their responses in the same issue of the *Annals*, as well as others afterwards. Many of those responses are quite revealing about relationships among the participants, at the time, and now! One person called and threatened to sue the authors and the editor-in-chief if the article was published. Fortunately, while the article was published, there was no lawsuit. Unfortunately, although that person was invited to write his own version of the events for the *Annals*, he never did. But the debate contributed to the history, and it helped elucidate as much as possible of the true history of the ENIAC, whatever that is. The related references (all from the *Annals*) are:

- "ENIAC: First General-Purpose Electronic Computer," Vol. 3, No. 4, pp. 310–399.
- "Mauchly: Unpublished Remarks," ed., Henry S. Tropp, Vol. 4, No. 3, pp. 245–256.

- "Comment on ENIAC Article," by Byron E. Phelps, Vol. 4, No. 3, pp. 284–287.
- "John Mauchly's Early Years," by Kathleen R. Mauchly, Vol. 6, No. 2, pp. 116–138.

AUTHORS AS PARTICIPANTS

This leads to the question as to how disinterested or unbiased a participant can be in writing about an event or an artifact. Clearly each author brings a personal perspective to a writing. That in itself is worth recording, however distorted others might perceive it to be. Actually, that is what historians inevitably have had to deal with, as most of the records they uncover about antiquity were personal recordings in their day. It is only when a number of contemporary writings come to light that we begin to have perspective and understanding of past events. The difference here is that we are watching those different accounts of the same event appear serially in time, instead of unearthing them more or less at the same time. At least we have the opportunity to make them generally available for comment while we are here to continue to question them.

It is interesting to note that the ENIAC controversy continues to this day. The excellent series of television programs on the history of computing that appeared on PBS in 1992 did not mention Atanasoff for some reason, although most historians will agree that he had an important role in the argument about the first general-purpose electronic computer. Arthur and Alice Burks have written to the *Ann Arbor News* (and perhaps other publications) about this, raising the issue as to whether there was some deliberate bias in creating the television series. That might make an interesting study.

REPRINTS?

A question that the editors of the *Annals* wrestled with over the years, was how many articles that had appeared earlier, to include in the journal. A number of principles evolved over time in this regard. First, any article or report that was readily available to the readers should not reappear in the *Annals*, unless there was some special reason to bring it together with some collection of other items. On the other hand, items that were of historical interest and were not readily available were possible candidates, but whenever possible the author would be asked to write a preface putting the original item in perspective, given the hindsight of the present.

Mina Rees was especially helpful in this regard, with several articles about the early days of government support for computing. There was a danger, of course, of too much reliance on reprinted material, which can be deadly for the readers' interest. A general principle was established, at least for the earlier volumes, that no more than 20 percent of the historical material in any one issue would consist of reprinted articles. That seems to have been a reasonable guideline.

ANECDOTES

There is a special place in history for anecdotes. This is the folklore that carries so much of our values, but isn't formal enough or large enough in some sense to be worthy of being written up as an article. It is very important, however, to catch the humor and the stories that come through in the form of anecdotes. The Anecdotes section of the *Annals* has served us well. Hopefully people will continue to contribute this folklore so it can be preserved for our successors.

WHO SHOULD REVIEW HISTORICAL ARTICLES?

When an article is submitted for publication, who should referee it? Other participants? Totally disinterested experts? Historians? Actually, it wouldn't hurt to include all of the above. That is about what is being done for the ACM SIGPLAN HOPL-II conference, in April, 1993. Whether a journal can do that much isn't clear, but as indicated, hopefully the Comments, Queries, and Debate part of the journal can help correct oversights and biases that are not caught and clarified during the refereeing process.

These are some lessons that have been learned. We hope that all of us can continue to contribute to the historical substance of our field, as well as to its recording.

OTHER PUBLICATIONS

We are fortunate that a number of journals quite often publish articles dealing with the history of computing. Of course, the *Annals* is the leading journal in this regard, being dedicated specifically to that purpose. But other journals should be recognized as contributing to the historical record.

There are two particularly valuable resources for locating articles and books on the history of computing, and from which one can glean a great deal of information about journals:

A Bibliographic Guide to the History of Computing, Computers, and the Information Processing Industry, compiled by James W. Cortada, and published by Greenwood Press, Westport, CT, in 1990.

"An Annotated Bibliography on the Origins of Computers," compiled by Brian Randell, *Annals of the History of Computing*, Vol. 1, No. 2, pp. 101–207.

Listed below is a portion of Cortada's bibliography, dealing with periodicals in the field. A scan of the Randell listing, however, reveals several other journals that have rather frequently included historical material on computing:

American Mathematical Monthly
Communications of the Assoc. for Computing Machinery (ACM)
IEEE Computer
IEEE Spectrum
Nature
Science
Scientific American
Technology & Culture

(The portion of the Cortada Bibliographic Guide referred to above is the following.)

PERIODICALS[1]

259 *Abacus* (1982–1988).

This contained numerous articles on the history of computing.

260 Association for Computing Machinery. *Bibliography of Current Computing Literature* (New York: ACM, 1969–1975).

These seven volumes contain thousands of titles on computers, applications, programming, data processing, and other related topics.

---

1 Reproduced with permission of Greenwood Publishing Group, Inc., Westport, CT, from *A Bibliographic Guide to the History of Computing, Computers, and the Information Processing Industry*, compiled by James W. Cortada, Copyright 1990 by James W. Cortada, pp. 41–44. (The numbers in the left margin represent the sequence of the entries in his bibliography.)

261 Association for Computing Machinery. *Comprehensive Bibliography of Computing Literature*. 1966–1967. New York, ACM, 1967–1968.

These two volumes represent a variant of numerous bibliographies published by ACM of current technical publications on data processing.

262 Association for Computing Machinery. *Computing Reviews*. New York: ACM. 1977.

These two volumes are similar in scope to No. 261.

259 Association for Computing Machinery. *Computing Reviews*. Permuted (kwic) Index to Computing Reviews. 1960–1963. (New York: ACM, 1964).

A second volume covering 1964–1965 was published in late 1965.

264 *Association for Computing Machinery Journal* (1954–Present).

This is the main publication of the ACM and often where the first formal explanation of a new technology or programming language appeared.

265 Association for Computing Machinery. *ACM Transactions on Mathematical Software* (1975–Present).

This is a technical journal, reflecting the significant amount of activity present in the area of software development.

268 *Charles Babbage Institute Newsletter* (1979–Present).

This quarterly is a major source of information on historical activities. For details it is the best quick reference. Charles Babbage Institute, 103 Walter Library, University of Minnesota, Minneapolis, Minnesota 55455 (USA).

269 *Computer Journal* (1958–Present).

This British journal is the organ of the British Computer Society and is a technical publication.

278 IEEE Center For the History of Electrical Engineering. Newsletter (1982–Present).

This contains news about IEEE activities, news about research on the history of electricity, computing, and other related fields. It publishes a bibliography and articles on key archival collections.

280 *Mathematical Tables and Other Aids to Computation* (1943–1960).

This was the most important source of articles dealing with computer science in the 1940s and very early 1950s. It served as the primary publication outlet for many technical articles of the period. In total 14 volumes of issues were published.

283 Springer International and American Federation of Information Processing Societies. *Annals of the History of Computing* (1979–Present).

This is the single most important source of material on the history of information processing, particularly on its technology. It also contains book reviews, bibliographies, obituaries, and other useful information. For details write to Springer-Verlag, 44 Hartz Way, Secaucus, N. J. 07094 (USA). [*Annals of the History of Computing is now published by the IEEE Computer Society.*]

284 *Think* (1935–Present).

This is IBM's employee magazine. It contains articles on the company's major activities, operations in various countries, and biographies of key executives. It is published monthly.

285 Williams, M.R. "History of Computation," *CIPS Review* (1980–Present).

This is a two-page column appearing since 1980 on all aspects of the industry's history.

AN EFFECTIVE HISTORY CONFERENCE

Jean E. Sammet

P. O. Box 30038
Bethesda, MD 20824

INTRODUCTION

In order to hold an effective computing history conference it is first necessary to understand why the problems of doing so are different from holding any other type of computing conference. I particularly contrast this with a conference reporting on current work. I will not list problems that are common to all conferences (e.g., getting material done on time, preparing publicity).

Note that, although this information is based primarily on experience with programming language history conferences, the points are general for any history conference dealing with computing. These notes begin with a listing of problems that arise when organizing a computing history conference, offer some suggestions for solutions to these problems, and conclude with a list of examples of previous conferences and conference sessions on the history of computing.

PROBLEMS IN HOLDING A COMPUTING HISTORY CONFERENCE

1. Deciding the scope of the conference
   a. Will it cover specific events (e.g., development of a programming language or an operating system or a computer)?
   b. Will it cover broad themes (e.g., use of computers to do nonnumerical mathematics, personal computers, artificial intelligence)?
   c. What is an appropriate "past" time scale for the subjects covered by the conference (e.g., 5 years, 10 years, 25 years)? (Note that the computer field has moved so quickly that 5 years can be a very long time for some developments!)
   d. Will written papers be required from potential participants, or will (only) talks be sufficient? (In the following questions, the concept of "papers" can generally be replaced by "talks".)
   e. Aside from the time scale, what are the criteria for identifying topics for appropriate papers (e.g., current use, major use at some time, significance, publications)?
   f. Should the papers be all invited, or all submitted, or a combination (i.e., some of each)?
   g. Should the basic flavor be that of a "reunion" of people with a common background for some historical event or activity, or should it be more general and/or higher quality?
   h. Is this conference "one-of-a-kind," or part of a series? Is some type of follow-on conference anticipated, even if not a whole series?
2. Forming a program committee

   All conferences must recruit people with suitable background for the program committee. However, in the case of a history conference it is generally harder to persuade qualified individuals to participate in an activity that may have less value to their professional stature than participating in a conference dealing with more mainstream issues.

The types of individuals who should be considered for inclusion in the program committee are the following: specialists in the subject of the conference, people with formal training in at least the history of science and preferably with some experience in the history of computing, individuals who were direct contributors to the subject of the conference. (Care must be taken with the latter group to tread the fine line between possibly excluding a significant paper because the logical person to write it is on the program committee, or alternatively allowing such a submission but with proper safeguards against a favorable bias from the remainder of the program committee. The sponsoring organization might have specific policies dealing with this issue.)

3. Difficulty in getting people to prepare good papers—whether invited or submitted
   a. Authors tend to be more interested in doing their current work than in resurrecting their past. Academic people may not get much "tenure credit" for such papers, and industrial people have difficulty in getting their manager's approval to spend time on preparing such a paper.
   b. Some senior/older people who are crucial to documenting the history may be physically or mentally unable to make the effort, to prepare a good paper, and/or may lack support (e.g., secretary, access to files).
   c. The basic (and hence old) material needed to prepare good papers may be difficult to find, or nonexistent.
   d. Even after solving problems (a), (b), and (c), the author probably has had no experience with history and may not have any idea how to write a good history paper.
4. Difficulty in getting people to attend

   Most technical individuals—and their managers or granting agencies—do not believe that history can help them in their current work.
5. Difficulty in deciding what type of permanent material to produce for the conference attendees and also for the final general community interested in history. (The result of a computer history conference should itself be a part of the history of computing.)
   a. Written papers may not be sufficient to provide a record of the historical material being covered. Audio/visual records may also be needed.
   b. If papers are issued as a "preprint" conference proceedings, it may be difficult to get the authors to revise/improve their papers for some type of final book.
   c. Cost of audio/visual recording is extremely high.

SOME SUGGESTED SOLUTIONS

1. In deciding the scope, it is desirable to determine either (i) what area of the computing field the organizers want to document or (ii) what audience should be attracted. (These are certainly not mutually exclusive, but it may be necessary to prioritize them in solving other problems.)

   If the answer is (i) then it is just up to the organizers. If the emphasis is to be on the audience (i.e., (ii)), then it is probably true that general themes (rather than specific items) may be more attractive.

   The most appropriate time scale depends on the subjects being covered. For a programming language or an operating system it probably requires 8–10 years to make sure that the specific item is really of value. (For example, consider this time scale as applied to Ada and Unix.) For a more theme-oriented topic, a minimum of 5 years is certainly needed, and the 8–10 year criterion is better.

In selecting invited versus submitted papers, it really depends on whether the scope is on specific topics or on broad themes. If on specific topics, then the organizers are probably better off with people who were direct participants in the activity, and thus need to issue an invitation. (It is of course preferable to invite "key" participants but they may not be available and so it may be necessary/appropriate to invite people who were more junior in the development in order to get some first-hand information.) If the scope is on a broad theme then any qualified person could write a paper, and hence submitted papers are equally appropriate. However, for the reason indicated in (3a), it might be very hard for potential authors to find/take the time to write—and submit for refereeing—a history paper that might be rejected.

2. The best way to persuade someone—particularly a key participant—to write a paper is to persuade him/her that he/she will be able to document—for perpetuity—his/her view of the history involved, by doing such a paper. Such a paper—with its conclusions and advice—might last much longer than the actual technical development being described.

   Unless the underlying historical material is expected to be available to a reasonable extent, there is no point in having a paper written, as it will probably consist primarily of anecdotes rather than detailed historical information/analysis.

   To encourage authors to prepare good papers, try to use all the following techniques:

   - provide questions related to the conference subject to give the author an idea of the type of information to be included in the paper,
   - allow time for (and require) several drafts of the paper,
   - provide program committee intellectual support (e.g., comment on interim drafts),
   - have a consulting historian to make sure that the necessary historical information is being reasonably conveyed and to give guidance to the authors.

3. To improve attendance, it is useful to point out how knowledge of the past might help people do a current job. Solutions to old problems may become obsolete as technology changes, but then may become relevant again with more changes in technology. A good illustration of this is the

   - dedicated use of a computer by a single individual for as much as an hour or two—and associated support software followed by
   - time-sharing with many individuals using a single computer at the same time (because the computer was too expensive to provide dedicated use to a single person) followed by a return to
   - dedicated use of a computer by a single individual for indefinite periods of time (with a personal computer on each individual's desk and available support software).

   Perhaps even a session to discuss this—either in philosophy or with specific examples—can be included in the program.

4. For a permanent record, the ideal is to get papers prepared and issued as preprints, and then revised for a permanent book. However, if this can't be done then it is probably better to get the final papers after the conference. The main disadvantage to this is that the authors will procrastinate because the date is not as firm as when the paper must appear in a conference proceedings to be handed out at the conference.

EXAMPLES OF HISTORICAL CONFERENCES/SESSIONS

The first significant historical conference on computing was the one held in Los Alamos in 1976. The results are in the book edited by Metropolis *et al.* shown in the Reference List. The organizers invited people they deemed appropriate to discuss certain issues, but did little or nothing to ensure the quality of the papers. They used a very short time scale prior to the meeting, and hence, there were people they initially invited who couldn't participate because of prior commitments (myself being one of them).

The first HOPL conference is documented in Wexelblat (editor) shown in the Reference List. That conference used most of the "solutions" described, and they—together with additional experience gained since then—are being applied to HOPL-II.

For a number of years AFIPS held "Pioneer Days," in conjunction with the National Computer Conference. These were generally afternoon sessions focusing on a specific topic (e.g., BASIC, MARK I at Harvard, COBOL, UNIVAC I, FORTRAN). For several years these sessions were tied to key anniversary dates. The organizers invited several people to make presentations. In some cases there were papers or notes available for distribution to the attendees but in many cases there was no documentation provided, and there generally was no permanent record developed.

There was, generally, little or no quality control over the presentations. Because there was great informality about the organization and preparation (relative to a full-fledged conference), the sessions were often fascinating to participate in (as I did for COBOL), or attend (as I did for the others). From the audience viewpoint they often conveyed the flavor of a college reunion!

In addition to the ACM SIGPLAN History of Programming Languages (HOPL) Conference in 1978, there were three history conferences held under general ACM auspices—interactive systems, scientific computing, biomedical computing. In my personal opinion, the quality of the preparation, organization, and written material for those three conferences was poor. Even allowing for my own bias, the HOPL conference is a model but the others are not. The books resulting from these four conferences, as well as the Los Alamos conference mentioned earlier, are shown in the reference list.

REFERENCES

[Blum, 1990] Blum, Bruce I., and Duncan, Karen, Eds., *A History of Medical Informatics*, Reading, MA: ACM Press/Addison-Wesley, 1990.

[Goldberg, 1988] Goldberg, Adele, Ed., *A History of Personal Workstations*, Reading, MA: ACM Press/Addison-Wesley, 1988

[Metropolis, 1980] Metropolis, Howlett, and Rota, *A History of Computing in the Twentieth Century*, New York: Academic Press, 1980.

[Nash, 1990] Nash, Stephen G., Ed., *A History of Scientific Computing*, Reading, Mass., ACM Press/Addison-Wesley Publishing Co., 1990.

[Wexelblat, 1981] Wexelblat, Richard L., Ed., *History of Programming Languages*, New York: ACM Monograph Series/Academic Press, 1981.

UNIVERSITY COURSES

Martin Campbell-Kelly

Dept. of Computer Science
University of Warwick
Coventry CV4 7AL, UK

ABSTRACT

This paper describes the rationales for teaching university courses on the history of computing. The range and scope of typical courses are described in terms of their syllabuses and contents, teaching methods and resources, and coursework and assessment. Finally, the criticism that the history of computing is too "internalist" is discussed.

INTRODUCTION: WHY TEACH THE HISTORY OF COMPUTING?

In this paper I shall mainly address the topic of teaching a history of computing course to computer science undergraduates. Many universities teach courses with a title such as "Computers and Society," but although these courses often include a good deal of elementary historical material, they are not primarily about history. Again, many universities offer courses on the history of technology in which the history of computing could (indeed should) form a component. While I am sure that most computer science undergraduates would benefit from both computers and society courses and history of technology courses, I see these as being complementary to a full-scale course on the history of computing.

The typical history of computing course is taught to a computer science undergraduate in much the same spirit that a history of mathematics course is taught to a mathematics student, a history of physics course to a physics student, or a business history course to a business studies undergraduate. Courses of this type, particularly when taught in the student's final year, can take advantage of two or more years of specialised learning and, therefore, will not in general be accessible to people outside the discipline. Such courses are commonly criticized for being too "internalist"—that is, of interest only to subject specialists and irrelevant to the wider community. I will come back to this point later. For the novice teacher about to start a course on the history of computing, however, there is something to be said for erring on the side of internalism and caution before attempting to launch a deeply historical course. As the distinguished historian Geoffrey Elton advises:

> . . . the professional scholar teaching others will do best if he stays within his professional competence; he may by all means try to enlighten his pupils about humanity at large, but he will be really successful only if he employs the techniques of his craft in the elucidation of the subject matter of his teaching. [Elton 1969, p. 187]

It is all too easy for the professional historian to intimidate the newcomer. I recommend anyone entering the field to read Elton's *The Practice of History* originally published in 1967, but still in print after numerous impressions. Elton's important message is to welcome newcomers to history, and to help them avoid the common pitfalls.

Any lecturer promoting a history of computing course is bound to have to justify its place in an already overcrowded curriculum. This is not a new problem, and not one that is peculiar to computer science. The civil engineer and historian Henry Petroski [1991] recently wrote an inspirational article in the *American Scientist* in which he justified the practice of teaching history in engineering courses. Petroski began by citing the results of a questionnaire completed by Duke University engineering graduates from the 1950s. The graduates were asked (without any prompting) to list the courses that "proved to be most useful in their careers." For these senior engineers, overwhelmingly the most useful course turned out to be a history course they had taken 40 years ago. Petroski surmised that most of the technical courses taken by these students of the 1950s had long been forgotten because they had been taught in "an impersonal manner, providing little, if any, historical or biographical background to the state of the art or its developers." By contrast, the history course had attempted to "make apparent the interrelationships of things and people, of structures and environments, of machines and war, of technology and culture, of engineering and society." The history course enabled the students to integrate their isolated technical studies and to begin to understand the philosophy of engineering.

Petroski's arguments translate very readily to the history of computing. The typical computer science undergraduate of today sees the world through an astonishingly narrow window: the student knows very little about computing before 1980, he or she often has a strong orientation toward the supply-side of computing, is unaware of the economics of computers or software, and is ignorant of the organizations that use them. A good history of computing course can do a great deal to widen this window. If that were all, it would be enough, but the study of the history of computing adds further value. There can be no question that a knowledge of the past can inform the present. As Fred Gruenberger put it so eloquently in the first issue of the *Annals of the History of Computing* in 1979:

> It seems that every single thing we know today about computing had to be learned—and relearned—the same painful and expensive way. It may just be that simple re-reading of history once or twice a year can provide us with insight, and it is insight that we desperately need. [Gruenberger 1979, p. 49]

A course on the history of computing also exposes the student to a new and unfamiliar academic discipline—history. History teaches objectivity; it teaches the use and abuse of evidence; and it teaches the need to question received wisdom. For example, I find that before coming on to my third-year history course, many of my students have absorbed shockingly derisive opinions of FORTRAN and COBOL. But once they have understood the context in which these languages were developed, and something of the economics of innovation and the social construction of technology, they come to realise that there is a good deal more to a programming language than its syntax.

Finally, a history of computing course gives students the opportunity and challenge of producing an extended piece of written work—often for the first time since coming to university.

SYLLABUSES

In order to get a better feel for the content of the history of computing courses currently being taught, last year I made a concerted effort to make contact with people who are currently teaching such courses. Altogether I learned of about a dozen courses world-wide, and I expect there are at least as many again that I do not know about. Several of the organizers of these courses were kind enough to send me copies of their syllabuses, examples of coursework assignments, and specimen examination questions. The discussion that follows is heavily based on these responses, although inevitably there is something of a small-sample problem in drawing broad conclusions from what is clearly still a little-taught subject.

It is clear from the syllabuses I examined that there is a commonly accepted "core" of about 10 topics that appear in virtually all the courses (Table 16.1). Generally, these topics are taught in chronological sequence, though each topic tends to be pursued to its end. And of course, any attempt at a strict chronology breaks down when discussing aspects and applications of computing, such as programming languages or artificial intelligence, that range over a number of decades.

TABLE 16.1

Topics in the History of Computing.

1	Pre-history (e.g., number systems, the development of algorithms, logic and language, calculating instruments, etc.)
2	Babbage's Calculating Engines
3	Hollerith, IBM, and office machinery
4	Mechanical Calculators (e.g., differential analysers, the Harvard Mark I and other relay calculators, etc.)
5	Electronic Calculators (ABC, war-time developments: ENIAC, Colossus)
6	The Stored-Program Concept and EDVAC
7	The Pioneer Phase (e.g., UNIVAC, Whirlwind, early industry)
8	Commercialization (the later computer industry, System/360, giant machines, etc.)
9	Aspects and Applications of Computing (e.g., architecture, programming languages, software engineering, AI, networks, etc.)
10	Personal Computing

In all the courses, the development of the stored-program concept in 1945 is regarded as the central event of the history of computing: it is the pivotal development to which the first half of the course leads, and from which the second half of the course springs. Courses typically spend approximately half the course on pre-1945 events and a half on post-1945, although there are exceptions.

Although the courses have this core material in common, the treatment by individual lecturers varies greatly. Of necessity, each lecturer tailors his or her course to the specific background of the students, and to the lecturer's own technical and historical background, and interests. For example, one course devoted about a quarter of the time to the prehistory of computing, whereas other courses gave it only a token mention. Some lecturers with a strong specialist knowledge—of, say, computer architecture or software—have biased their courses in this direction by including several lectures on topics such as high-speed computing or software engineering. Clearly the criticism of internalism applies most strongly in these cases, but these criticisms are easily answered provided the specific developments are informed by a general background of the history of technology.

A number of courses have attempted to avoid portraying the development of computing as a chain of unstoppable technological progress, by relating developments to such phenomena as World War II, the Cold War, or the Space Race. This has the effect of bringing in the wider context of science and technology policy, as well as making the course more accessible to noncomputer scientists. A much smaller number of courses interpreted the history of computing more as the history of information processing, and avoided discursion into specific technological details. These courses tended to be much richer in business, economic and social history, less supply-side oriented, and did not require heavy technical prerequisites.

Perhaps the emergence of the personal computer shows the most variation in treatment. Several courses eschew the topic entirely—as perhaps being too modern, although the PC is now well within the purview of the "ten-year rule."[2] But it may also be a reflection on the poor state of the secondary

2 Almost since the dawn of interest in the history of computing in the late 1970s there has been an understanding that one should avoid writing history about events more recent than 10 years ago, because there has been insufficient time to develop a proper perspective. Although this is a wise injunction for the most part, one consequence is that almost the only people to write about the history of the personal computer have been journalists stronger on hyperbole than history.

literature; for although there is a vast literature on the development of the personal computer, its quality is generally execrable.

TEACHING METHODS, TEXTBOOKS, AND MATERIALS

All the courses were reading based, with lectures being used to introduce the study topics and to pace students through the course. There were typically 30 hours of lectures on the courses, and there were from as few as a dozen to well over 50 students on the courses. Some courses included seminars giving an opportunity for students to make individual presentations, but this appears to be a vanishing luxury in the face of declining staff-student ratios.

No single textbook covers all the material taught on any course. For the more technologically oriented courses, by far the most popular textbook was Mike Williams's *A History of Computing Technology* [1985b]. This excellent book was originally written as a text to support Williams's history of computing course at Calgary University [Williams 1985a], and covers the prehistory of computing up to System/360. Unfortunately Williams's book is currently out of print and this promises a headache for courses that make heavy use of it. Another popular text is *Computing Before Computers*, edited by William Aspray [1990a], which includes contributed chapters from several pioneers in teaching the history of computing. Unfortunately this text takes events only as far as the invention of the stored-program concept, and so covers only the first half of any course. Another popular book is Herman Goldstine's *The Computer: From Pascal to von Neumann* [1973], which has the merit of being available as an inexpensive paperback but is now showing signs of age. Finally, one should mention Brian Randell's pioneering *Origins of Digital Computers*—first published in 1973, and now in its third edition [Randell 1982]. This book consists of a collection of key papers on the development of computing; although the organization and introduction of the material is exemplary, it is exclusively devoted to computer technology, and is somewhat impenetrable for the average undergraduate.

In the absence of a single textbook, all course organizers have adopted the strategy of supplementing or replacing a textbook with a selection of readings. These fall into three categories: reprints of primary sources (e.g., extracts from von Neumann's *EDVAC Report* [1945]), historical articles (e.g., papers from the *Annals of the History of Computing* or *Technology and Culture*), and chapters from historical monographs. There is an economic problem (not to say a copyright problem) in distributing photocopied handouts to large classes, so that some course organizers have deposited photocopied materials for in-library reading and placed monographs on shelf-reserve.

In fact although the textbook problem is difficult, the wider literature of the history of computing has blossomed remarkably in the last decade, and there are now at least two dozen good monographs on the history of computing. One can mention such highlights as Nancy Stern's *From ENIAC to UNIVAC* [1981], Paul Ceruzzi's *Reckoners* [1983], and the superb histories of IBM's computers [Bashe 1985; Pugh 1991]. The history of programming languages has also been particularly well treated in the impeccably produced proceedings of the first *History of Programming Languages* conference [Wexelblat 1981]; and one must pay tribute to Jean Sammet's pioneering *Programming Languages: History and Fundamentals* which was first published at the remarkably early date of 1969. There are also now several excellent biographies of key figures in the history of computing, such as Austrian's *Herman Hollerith* [1982], Hodges's *Alan Turing* [1983], and Aspray's *von Neumann* [1990b]. In the broader contexts of the information society and policy arenas one can single out James Beniger's *The Control Revolution* [1986], and Kenneth Flamm's *Targeting the Computer* [1987]. One should also mention the contribution of the MIT Press *History of Computing Series*, and the *Charles Babbage Institute Reprint Series for the History of Computing*, now totalling 10 and 16 volumes, respectively. Clearly a well-stocked library is the *sine qua non* of a successful course in the history of computing. The book-review section of the *Annals of the History of Computing* is the best single place for keeping up-to-date on this rapidly growing literature.

Organizers of history of computing courses are evidently conscious of the need to motivate and retain their students, and many have gone to considerable efforts to enliven their courses with visual aids, outside speakers, and other novelties. There is a wealth of visual material in the published literature from which lecturers have prepared slides, and some of the science museums have produced slide sets of their artifacts. Examples of movie films include the 1946 newsreel of the ENIAC, the film of the EDSAC [Cambridge University 1951], the John von Neumann movie [AMA 1966], and promotional films of many first-generation computers. There appears to be no simple way, other than the informal grapevine, of tracking down this material.

A number of course organizers use artifacts or simulations to illustrate early calculating technologies. Relatively easy to find artifacts include abacii, slide rules, mathematical tables, Comptometers and Brunsvigas, punched cards, and wiring boards; computer artifacts include electronic tubes and discrete transistor boards, core memory planes, and recording media. In the absence of artifacts, it is possible to simulate early computers: for example, at Calgary University, Mike Williams enables students to program a 1950s LPG-30 via a simulation program, to avoid wear-and-tear on an actual LPG-30 [Williams 1985a]; and at Warwick and Cambridge Universities, we use an EDSAC simulator that runs on a Macintosh personal computer [Campbell-Kelly 1992].

Where geographically possible, museum visits are an alternative to the ownership of artifacts. For example, at Warwick, we were hosted for a day last year by the London Science Museum, who generously organized a series of demonstrations that tied in with the course. Most notable was a demonstration of Babbage's Difference Engine No. 2 by the engineers who constructed it. The engineers took an obvious pleasure in fielding questions from such knowledgeable and enthusiastic visitors.

COURSEWORK AND ASSESSMENT

The term paper or essay, and end-of-session examination, were the predominant means of assessment on all the courses.

Written work poses difficulties for nonhumanities students, whose writing skills are rusty or nonexistent, and lecturers are sensitive to this problem. One strategy for ramping up writing skills has been to set a relatively undemanding first assessment, such as a 500-word book review or a biographical sketch. A lot of attention was paid to developing students' knowledge of scholarly apparatus and their ability to use library resources. They were taught, formally or informally, how to structure essays and marshal their arguments; how to quote effectively and accurately; to understand the nature of plagiarism; to make proper use of footnotes; and to cite references in a consistent style. Students were generally referred to some such authority as the *Chicago Manual of Style*.

The typical assessment was 2000–3000 words in length, and students were invariably offered a wide range of topics, or even a topic of their own devising. Besides making the grading of dozens of essays less tedious, the wide range of topics gives each student a chance of finding a topic that is personally interesting, and—at least as important—reduces the competition for single copies of library books. Topics ranged from the highly technological through to broadly based business and economic history. Typical assignments were:

1. The Invention and Development of the Positional Number System (Calgary)
2. The History of IBM since the 1940s (UMBC, Maryland)
3. The Controversy over the Invention of the Stored-Program Concept (Warwick)

4. John von Neumann: His Life and Contributions to Computers (several universities)
5. The Evolution of a Programming Language (American University)

The consensus was that students should be required to produce at least one piece of written work. However, for the truly reluctant writer, a programming exercise was sometimes permitted—such as constructing a Turing Machine simulator, or programming a simulated computer. As well as providing training in scholarship, the coursework forces the student to study at least one topic in real depth.

All the courses were additionally assessed by an end-of-session or take-home examination. Questions were similar in spirit to the essay topics, but generally more focused to discourage discursive answers. (Examples: "Describe, and show the importance of, the various steps in the search for memory from the 1940s to the 1980s"—UBC, Maryland; "Describe the main stages leading to the widespread acceptance of high-level programming, and explain why this acceptance took so long to achieve" —Warwick.)

CRITIQUE

Let it be said: Not everyone approves of history of computing courses. For example, Mike Mahoney of Princeton University told me, in a private communication, that he preferred to embed the subject in a larger course on the history of technology. As he rightly observes, "Computing has its own parthenogenic myth of springing full-grown from the heads of Turing and von Neumann, and history would do well to work against it."

As Mahoney intimates, the main criticism of the history of computing is that it is too internalist; that the history of computing is a private history, uninformed by sound methodology, and of little relevance to the wider historical community. The same criticism can, of course, be made of the history of mathematics or the history of physics. In fact, with the honourable exception of Mahoney, I find little evidence that large numbers of historians of technology are rushing to assimilate computing into their courses. So, if the history of computing is to be taught at all, it is likely to be done by enthusiastic academics with a mission to teach the subject: computer scientists with little formal historical training; and a few historians with a modest knowledge of computing.

In fact, I would argue—not least to stimulate debate at this forum—that the history of computing is a special case, and not really like the history of mathematics or physics at all. Computing is the dominant technology of the second half of the twentieth century, which pervades all aspects of economic life. In this, it is much more akin to business history (say). No one who has read Chandler's magisterial *Visible Hand* [1977] can be left thinking that business history is narrow or internalist. At the moment there exists no great synthetic work in the history of computing of comparable stature, although James Beniger's *Control Revolution* [1986] shows clearly the vast canvas on which the history of computing will ultimately be painted.

When it arrives, the great synthetic work on the history of computing will have to draw in full measure from the history of technology, the history of science, business and economic history, and social history. At the present time, the subject is firmly anchored to the history of technology, but increasingly it is drawing on business history (e.g., to explain the development of the computer industry) and the history of science (e.g., to understand the development of algorithms, computability, and artificial intelligence).

Of course, it is a very tall order to expect a teacher of the history of computing to be expert in all these different historical genres. But we should all be aware of them, and as the literature develops we should speedily incorporate it into our courses. For all of us, the development of that literature is a fundamental brake on the development of history of computing courses. For example, at the present time most of us wisely refrain from dabbling in social history. Yet the phenomenon of the computer hacker and the emergence of the personal computer cry out for the attention of the social historian; for the moment we must be patient and give our students the best guidance we can.

ACKNOWLEDGMENTS

I am most grateful to the following who supplied me with information about their courses and/or commented on a draft of this paper: Tim Bergin, Corrado Bonfanti, Colin Burke, Paul Ceruzzi, John Fauvel, Jan Lee, Mike Mahoney, Judy O'Neill, Bob Rosin, Steve Russ, Jean Sammet, James Tomayko, Arthur Norberg, Mike Williams, and Roy Wilson.

REFERENCES

[Aspray, 1990a] Aspray, William F., Ed., *Computing Before Computers*, Ames: Iowa State University Press, 1990.

[Aspray, 1990b] Aspray, William F., *John von Neumann and the Origins of Modern Computing*, Cambridge, Ma: MIT Press, 1990.

[AMA, 1966] American Mathematical Association, *John von Neumann*, 16 mm. film, sound, B/W, 63 min, 1966.

[Bashe, 1985] Bashe, Charles *et al.*, *IBM's Early Computers*, Cambridge, Ma: MIT Press, 1985.

[Beniger, 1986] Beniger, James R., *The Control Revolution: Technological and Economic Origins of the Information Society*, Harvard University Press, 1986.

[Bonfanti, 1993] Bonfanti, Corrado, *A Course on the History of Informatics at the University of Bari (Italy)*, typescript, Jan. 1993.

[Cambridge University, 1951] Cambridge University Computing Laboratory, *The EDSAC Film*, 16 mm. film, sound, colour, 10 min., 1951 and 1976.

[Campbell-Kelly, 1992] Campbell-Kelly, M., *Edsac: A Tutorial Guide to the Warwick University EDSAC Simulator*, University of Warwick, 1992.

[Ceruzzi, 1983] Ceruzzi, Paul E., *Reckoners: The Prehistory of the Digital Computer from Relays to the Stored Porgram Concept*, 1935–45 , West Port, CT: Greenwood Press, 1983.

[Chandler, 1971] Chandler, Alfred D., *The Visible Hand*, Harvard University Press, 1971.

[Elton, 1969] Elton, G. R., *The Practice of History*, Glasgow: Collins-Fontana, 1969. First published 1967, University of Sydney Press.

[Flamm, 1987] Flamm, Kenneth, *Targeting the Computer*, Washington, DC: Brookings Institution, 1987.

[Austrian, 1982] Austrian, G. *Herman Hollerith: Forgotten Giant of Data Processing*, New York: Columbia University Press, 1982.

[Goldstine, 1972] Goldstine, Herman H., *The Computer: From Pascal to von Neumann*, Princeton University Press, 1972.

[Greuenberger, 1979] Greuenberger, F. J., The history of the JONNIAC, *Annals of the History of Computing*, Vol. 1, pp. 49–64, Jul. 1979.

[Hodges, 1983] Hodges, Andrew, *Alan Turing: The Enigma*, London: Burnett Books, 1983.

[Petroski,, 1991] Petroski, Henry, In context, *American Scientist*, Vol. 79, May–June 1991, pp. 202–204.

[Pugh, 1991] Pugh, Emerson W., *IBM's 360 and Early 370 Systems*, Cambridge, MA: MIT Press, 1991.

[Randell, 1982] Randell, Brian, *The Origins of Digital Computers*, 3rd. ed., Berlin and New York: Springer Verlag, 1982.

[Sammet, 1969] Sammet, Jean E., *Programming Languages: History and Fundamentals*, Englewood Cliffs, NJ: Prentice-Hall, 1969.

[Stern, 1981] Stern, Nancy B., *From ENIAC to UNIVAC*, Bedford, MA: Digital Press, 1981.

[von Neumann, 1945] von Neumann, John, First Draft of a Report on the EDVAC, June 1945; reprinted in *Papers of John von Neumann on Computing and Computer Theory*, W. F. Aspray and A. W. Burks, Eds., Charles Babbage Institute Reprint Series for the History of Computing, Vol. 12, Cambridge, MA: MIT Press, 1986.

[Wexelblat, 1981] Wexelblat, Richard L., Ed., *History of Programming Languages*, Academic Press, 1981.

[Williams, 1985a] Williams, Michael R., A course in the history of computation, *Annals of the History of Computing*, Vol. 7, July 1985, pp. 241–244.

[Williams, 1985b] Williams, Michael R., *A History of Computing Technology*, Englewood Cliffs NJ: Prentice-Hall, 1985.

DOCUMENTING PROJECTS WITH HISTORY IN MIND

Michael Marcotty

1581 Witherbee
Troy, Michigan 48084
Tel: 313-646-9812

Three fundamental questions must be addressed when documenting a project with history in mind:

1. How do we know what is going to be an "historically significant" project?
2. What documents need to be retained?
3. How should documents be retained?

The following notes reflect my personal perspective. I look forward to discussing them with Forum attendees and to learning additional insights.

1. How do we know what is going to be an "historically significant" project? Every project is significant, and deserves to be documented from the beginning in that way. Only time will tell whether it has historic significance and even then it will depend on point of view—work group, company, discipline, and so on. In any case, I believe that this is an irrelevant question. I will argue that maintaining documentation, as though the project will be historic, makes good sense from general principles of computer science; it certainly does from the point of view of software engineering. Behind every project should be a database of information about that project. In other words, document every project well for the sake of the project itself. Then, if the documentation is also needed for historical purposes, it will be available.
2. What documents need to be retained?
   a. Probably the most important class of material records the reason why things were done.

      Why was the project undertaken in the first place?

      Why was the particular design chosen? This will include contextual information such as other known similar parallel projects, discussion with others, and other outside influences.

      Why was the particular hardware configuration chosen?

      Why was the particular programming language chosen?
   b. Almost as important as recording the reason why things were done, is to record why other things were NOT done. This means preserving copies of ideas or suggestions that were considered but rejected, along with the reasons for the rejection.
   c. Material that records the expectations of the project's initiators, workers, and expected clientele.
   d. Names of people involved on the project and their responsibilities. This list should include clients, instigators, senior managers, as well as participants. Also recorded should be changes in personnel, in all these areas, over the life of the project. This list is likely to make it easier to ask questions in the future.
   e. Specifications—together with reference material that explains the notation.
   f. Scheduled project milestones, forecasted and achieved. It is also necessary to record "unscheduled events" and the reasons (or at least the rationalizations) why milestones were missed or late.

g. Copies of mandated technical standards, both corporate and external, together with company and project manuals of style for both documentation and programs.
h. All project publications, particularly including early versions.
i. Description of the standard procedures used by the project for the maintenance of the project's database.
j. Description of the processes used for validation and verification of the project's work. Included here are the acceptance tests and a record of their performance.
k. Records of how, and why, the specifications for the project changed during the life of the project, including what changes were made after the first version of the project was released.
i. Major deliverables, together with client and management reactions to them.

3. How should the documents be retained? This will include a discussion of what to retain and what to discard. A discussion of the appropriate media: paper, machine readable, photographic, video recording, will be included.

ISSUES IN THE WRITING OF CONTEMPORARY HISTORY

J.A.N. Lee

Editor-in-Chief, *IEEE Annals of the History of Computing*
Department of Computer Science
Virginia Tech
Blacksburg VA 24061-0106
e-mail: janlee@vtcsl.cs.vt.edu

There are several factors that influence one's interest in, and the potential for writing a paper in, the area of contemporary history. In the beginning is the mere curiosity to learn of one's technological forefathers and their contributions to the present-day science. Such a curiosity may initially be fulfilled by examining the technical literature of the subject, such as may be found in an annotated bibliography, or in the list of a pioneer's publications. However, technical papers, as may be published in the journals of the ACM and the IEEE Computer Society, are the record of the successes of research and development, but they usually contain little of the background or environment that spawned the activity, nor an assessment of the potential impact of the element on future developments. Historical writing then has three responsibilities:

To rediscover and document the environment in which the activity or discovery occurred, and to assess the influence of the environment on the action and its "downstream" impact;

To recover the stories of the false starts, the failed attempts, and the unsuccessful trials that channeled the activity into its successful actions; and

To evaluate the impact of the activity or event in the light of more recent developments.

History that is a mere chronology of events or actions is of little interest or value to the present day scientist or student. The memoirs of pioneers are often little more than a liturgy of their high points, and they are afraid to "toot their horns," or evaluate their impact, when their contributions, viewed in the light of today's technology, appear to be less significant. Although journals such as the *Annals* will accept, and even encourage, pioneers to record their memoirs, these should be looked on only as the starting points for further scholarly work. It is the responsibility of the modern computer historian to put the work of our pioneers in perspective, to apply to history the same scholarly standards as would be expected of technical papers in technical journals.

As a service to the field, a scholarly history provides insights and views of our past that can often be used today. In many ways our technology is an onion to which we add additional layers with each passing (technological) generation. The core can be very simple and straightforward, but we add complications in the name of "ease of use" or "user friendliness" that mask the real nub of an idea. In today's teaching we too often start at an intermediate point of development and ignore the simpler solutions to a problem.

Historical writing provides the pointers back to reveal solutions that were rejected and that may now be applicable in the newer world of (say) massively parallel computation, or expert systems.

The pointers also provide a path to the foundations on which "modern" ideas are built. Educationally, we need to think carefully of where to start on the road of development and to decide consciously whether we can afford to ignore the past, and often the simpler times.

We can visualize the "perceived complexity versus time-since-origination" relationship of a concept as being represented by a parabola. In the beginning, the perceived level of complexity of a concept is high, as the supporting materials are sparse, untried, and often unrecognized. As the idea gains a foothold, new authors provide their interpretations, and the perceived complexity diminishes to the point where the applicability of the concept to the practical world is recognized. The first implementation probably represents the point at which the complexity is lowest. As time progresses, layers of "improvements" are added to the object and its core concepts disappear behind a morass of add-ons and so the complexity increases again, and the visibility of the basic idea fades. It is the responsibility of the historian to provide a map of this developmental cycle, and to provide cross-sections of its structure, in order to allow the student to decide where his or her application can find a useful foothold.

Guidelines, such as those provided to the authors in the HOPL-II Conference, provide an outline of the questions to be answered and the topics to be considered in developing an historical article (see Appendix B). (An edited version of the the HOPL-II author guidelines appeared in *IEEE Annals of the History of Computing* [Vol. 13, No. 1, pp. 51–62].

Forum Closing Panel

Panel Chair: *Robert F. Rosin*

ROBERT F. ROSIN: To those of you who were not with us this afternoon: welcome to the Forum on the History of Computing, which is part of, and prelude to, the ACM SIGPLAN Second History of Programming Languages Conference. This is the concluding event in the forum. It is a panel discussion on "The challenge of public displays about the history of computing." There will be an opportunity to ask questions of the panelists after their presentations. There should be cards available for you on which to write your questions.

I suspect that each of us is a museum visitor, some more frequent than others. I also suspect that each of us has attended at least one museum exhibit that includes artifacts related to the history of computing, perhaps at one of the outstanding institutions represented by our panelists. I'll introduce each panelist prior to his presentation. Each panelist will make a presentation and then afterwards will deal with questions.

David K. Allison is Curator of Information Technology and Society at the Smithsonian Institution's National Museum of American History and acting Associate Director of the Department of History and Science Technology. Dr. Allison studied at Purdue University, Saint Johns College, the University of Bordeaux and Princeton University, where he earned a Ph.D. in History in 1980, specializing in the history of American science. Prior to joining the Smithsonian staff in 1987, he served as historian with the U.S. Department of Energy as Historian of Navy Laboratories. Dr. Allison's responsibilities at the National Museum of American History include overseeing its collection of computers and computer-related artifacts, documents, images, and media. He also serves as liaison between the Smithsonian and the *Annals of the History of Computing*. He was chief curator of the permanent exhibition, "The Information Age: People Information and Technology," which opened in May 1990. This 14,000 square foot display surveys the history of information technology and its relations with American society, from the telegraph to the present. With over 50 computerized displays, it is the most interactive exhibition in the Smithsonian Institution.

DAVID ALLISON: In setting this session up, Bob posed to us several questions related to the challenge of public displays on the history of computing. In my presentation, I am going to go through those questions and provide my answer to them. The other panelist will give a slightly different slant on the subject.

Just by way of introduction, I want to indicate that the largest number of people who find out about the history of computing, probably do so through museum displays. We have had over four million people come to "Information Age" since it opened in 1990. So it is a very important interface with the public.

The first question that we wanted to address was, "What is it that makes exhibits successful?" In all forms of museum display, there needs to be a balance between traditional types of case displays, settings and interactive displays, and computer displays. I will be showing you some slides from "Information Age" in a few minutes to give you some examples from that exhibit to make this point. But the temptation of interactive displays should not blind us to the success of other types of museum presentations.

There are several ways to use interactive exhibits. One important way is a straight narration in a more interactive form. A video display or video selector that allows a visitor to come and choose the video information he or she wants to see, is very valuable. It often gives people an opportunity to see equipment in operation. This can also be done in a menu-driven computer interactive display.

A second technique is allowing exploration of many topics through branching menus. A third form that we don't use as much at the Smithsonian as they do at the Computer Museum, for example, is providing an opportunity to learn some computer skills through interactives. This can involve playing games through interactives, exploring different ways of using software, etc. Unquestionably, when the subject is computers, the use of interactive displays is very attractive.

The second question that Bob posed is, "How are computer exhibits different from other traditional displays?" One of the challenges is the limited effectiveness of computer artifact presentations to convey your messages. This gets more and more true as you come closer to the present. As you look at computer displays, or chips, or plain white boxes that seem not to vary from one generation to another, or one manufacturer to another, the story is not told by the artifacts in the way that it is, for example, with machinery of the 19th century. You need to think about ways to bring out the message of three dimensional objects in new and exciting ways. The technique that we relied on most in the Smithsonian's "Information Age" was to focus on applications. Our visitors, who are coming to a history museum not a computer museum, want to know why computers or other information technologies were important. What difference have they made to history? Answering this question means showing the application of this technology to large scale social, political, and other kinds of problems.

One of the greatest challenges in interactive displays, which Bob pointed out, is the difficulty in keeping the displays up with the technology. For example, in the "Information Age" we use the IBM InfoWindow system, which IBM no longer services, so we understand the problem of keeping up. There is no easy answer to this question. But, there are techniques that you can follow.

A modular planning approach is certainly one good strategy. We use modular planning for the hardware and the software. This means using technology bases that allow you to switch things in and out.

Often, museums are tempted to use special-purpose code, because it can offer the cheapest solution. But when the software engineer or the software developer is gone, so is the knowledge of the application. We try to stay away from that in the "Information Age" and follow industry standards, with standardized software components. That has made it easier to switch and move up through generations. Museums that are always trying to cut costs at the front end usually pay the price in the future.

Most important, is not trying to upgrade everything that you are doing in an exhibition at once. Plan an exhibition so that you know some of the things will remain static for a very long time, including some interactives. Leave another portion of your exhibits for updating, meeting visitor expectations for showing the most modern technology.

Finally, was the question, "Should there be more exhibits about software?" Software is a topic of great interest to this conference. How much should we say about that in the general public museums?

It is important to look at the subject in two ways. On the one hand, you can see software and software development as a subject. On the other, you can see it as a tool for other applications.

Software as a subject, the development of software, the programmer's life, and those kinds of things is of limited interest to the general public. It has a place in our displays, but that place needs to be put in a larger context. We have one exhibition unit that I will show you in our slides, on the subject of software. It's broad in compass. In the Museum of American History that is all that we could afford. On the other hand, software as a tool is a larger subject. Visitors learn about software in relation to its applications in many areas of society.

Another way to do better in displays about software, is through computer interactives. We were struggling for better ways to use them. With the advent of better video animation and simulation, we can bring out more of the dynamics of software in a way that visitors can understand.

Finally, I think a focus on the human side of programmers and how they interact with society around them, is a way that we can bring out more of the software message.

Now, I'll give you a several examples about these points from the "Information Age."

(SLIDE 1) This is the introduction to the very beginning of "Information Age." It shows scenes from today's information society. Here, we also introduce the use of information technology with a bar code scanner. There is an individualized bar code on each brochure that people pick up. We can make a personalized record of their visit as they go through the exhibition. This allows people to interact with information technology and also allows us to keep some statistics on them as they go through the display.

(SLIDE 2) In using information technology in "Information Age" we wanted to use different ways that people learn. This shows some of them. It is a mixture of the artifactual presentation and interactive presentation. The Hollerith machine is in the background. In the foreground we have interactive displays. You can scan your bar code to record what you are doing there. You enter information about yourself and see what your life might have been like in 1890, at the time of the 1890 census, when the Hollerith machine was first used. Our goal was to connect your story as an individual with our story in the exhibition

Over to the right-hand side is a video monitor. It is one of our video selectors where you choose one of four video clips about the displays around you. One of the selections is about social security system processing in the 1930s. It, in turn, relates to the scene in the middle of the floor, where a woman is doing social security processing. So, we use different techniques to bring the story to the public and show both the human side and the technical side.

SLIDE 1

SLIDE 2

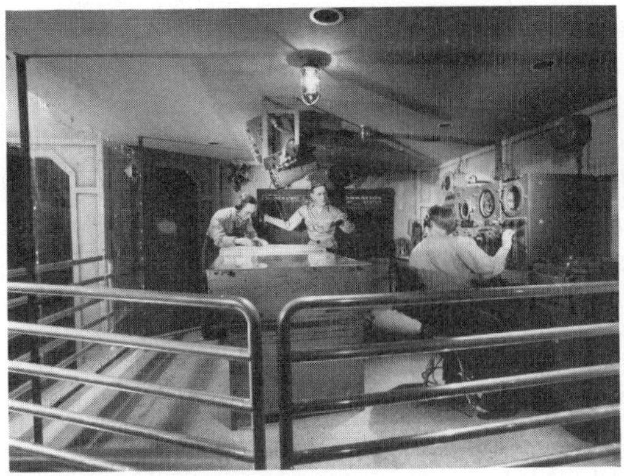

SLIDE 3

SLIDE 4

(SLIDE 3) This scene is on board a combat information center in World War II. It is an example of how we try to use life-size displays. Our general goal was connecting the story of people, information, and technology. Here is a way that we are doing that, with a dramatic presentation.

(SLIDE 4) This is our presentation about software. In the foreground are flowcharts, a bit on Grace Hopper, and Jean Sammet's image of the "Tower of Babel" of early programming languages. In the background we carry the story of software from plug wires up to floppy disks. On the back wall are scenes of programmers at work. We also have examples of coding of various eras. In the middle are some examples of manuals and tools.

This is a brief display, but it shows some of the tools, some of the applications, and some reflections of software development over time. We talked about including interactives at this location, but frankly neither our fiscal budget nor our space budget would allow it.

(SLIDE 5) Here was the scene from the Home Group Computer Club that we used to show the new social environment that led to the creation of early PC technology. In the scene, we have one of the early Apples and an Altair. On the right, we show some of the early developments at IBM, and elsewhere, to illustrate that they were interested in personal computers in the early days, but did not develop viable products.

(SLIDE 6) Finally, this is a scene from our interactive gallery. Unquestionably, one of the reasons people come to computer displays is so they can get their hands on computers and do things. We had

SLIDE 5

SLIDE 6

visitors from all segments of society from the homeless up to CEOs. Many of the school children, in particular, don't have an opportunity to work with computers at home or school and try new things, particularly advanced things. We try to provide a changing array of opportunities to do that in the Smithsonian.

How do you keep something like this updated? It is a lot easier to keep a space like this updated because there is a modular plan. You can replace one computer or you can change an application with very little modification, compared to the static display that you saw earlier.

I hope these illustrations have given you an idea of how we answered the earlier questions in our exhibition, "Information Age! People, Information, and Technology."

ROSIN: Paul E. Ceruzzi is Curator of Aerospace Electronics and Computing at the Smithsonian Institution's National Air and Space Museum. Dr. Ceruzzi earned a B.A. at Yale University in 1970 and a Ph.D. in American Studies at the University of Kansas in 1981. He was a Fulbright scholar at the Institute for the History of Science in Hamburg, Germany and he received a Charles Babbage Institute Research Fellowship in 1979. Before joining the National Air and Space Museum, he taught history of technology at Clemson University. Dr. Ceruzzi's duties include research, writing, exhibits planning, artifact collecting, and public outreach activities concerned with the subject of computing machinery as it applies to the practice of air and space flight. He is the author of several books on the history of computing and related issues, and he served as a consultant on certain computer-related projects, most notably the BBC/PBS Television series, "The Machine that Changed the World," broadcast in this country last year. He also serves as Assistant Editor-in-Chief of the *Annals of the History of Computing*.

PAUL CERUZZI: I'm a curator at the National Air and Space Museum, which is the most popular museum in the world or certainly in the US, some 8,000,000 visitors a year. Sometimes in a good year, that comes out to about 20,000 a day, the size of a small town per day coming through. The particular gallery that I worked on called "Beyond the Limits," which is up on the second floor, doesn't obviously get all twenty thousand, but it does get a very large crowd and certainly, the physical design of the gallery was a very important factor in terms of how to manage an enormous number of people coming through. Never mind the subtle questions of what are you going to tell them about programming languages. I'll get to that in a minute. But just physically getting them in and out without them feeling claustrophobic or getting hurt. There are serious issues that we struggle with. If you have any time left over then you start tackling the content. It is quite a challenge and there is nothing quite like going in there, as I do. I don't know whether I should feel guilty or not, but I do go in there. I take my badge off and I just wander around and look over people's shoulders to see whether or not they are enjoying themselves. Many times they are, not always. Sometimes you have kids say, "Oh this is so boring." But, when they do enjoy it, I feel good and I feel we have accomplished something.

I had prepared some remarks about software and when I got your query, Bob, I kind of restructured it a little bit. I thought I would take some of the issues in somewhat reverse order, here. "Why do so few exhibits focus on software?" I guess that was one of the questions I have been struggling with. I think one of the obvious answers is that we can get philosophical here, which we don't want to get too much. But, by definition, "software is invisible, it is a soap bubble," I guess, is what Allen Perlis said. If you can put your hands on it, it isn't software anymore. A museum by contrast, in this age of DisneyWorld, and Hollywood, and virtual reality, and simulations, and everything else, a museum seems to be the last place on earth where you can see real things. There are fake frontier lands and things like that. There are fake airplanes in a lot of places, but the Air and Space Museum has real artifacts and we never want to lose that. Even though we have a very vigorous program of interactive programs and films, we have an Imax theater which is a huge crowd pleaser, all those things, but they "mediate" between the reality and the visitor. One of the things that is so amazing about the Air and Space Museum is its opening main hall where we have these wonderful icons of the air and space age. The Wright Brothers' airplane, the *Spirit of Saint Louis*, the *Apollo 11* capsule, and there are almost no labels at all. If you can find them, they are very small. You just walk in and you are immediately confronted with the reality of an object. We have been criticized for that, because we don't provide context and we don't provide the political and social dimensions, and all that. Those are valid criticisms. Still, the popularity of that hall really says something. That there is something to be said for just direct experience with the three-dimensional artifact that has a place in history, and we never want to throw that out no matter how much we are conscious of the need to interpret things.

In designing the "Beyond the Limits Gallery," I wrestled with these questions, not only the fact that a computer is not always that interesting to look at, although packaging is a very interesting question. Of course, those of you who are in the computer business know that successful packaging can make a huge difference in the success or failure of a product. And it is no coincidence that Ken Olsen, when he was at Digital Equipment in the early years, took a very active role in the packaging of their minicomputers. In general, the current scene, the packaging, just does not really help you very much. It certainly doesn't give you a sense of what the power is of what is going on inside the computer.

I want to tell a little story because it does fit into the theme of what we are getting at. During the research for this gallery, I had heard about the famous *Mariner 1* hyphen, the missing hyphen in the guidance program that caused the spacecraft carrying *Mariner 1*, which was intended to go to Venus, it caused it to crash into the Atlantic Ocean. Later found out the cause of the crash was a missing hyphen in the program. I tracked down the man who left out the hyphen from the program. He works for TRW in Los Angeles. I wasn't allowed inside the building, but we met in a hotel by the airport. He told me the story. He pulled out his wallet where he had the newspaper clipping from the New York Times that described it. Yes, it really did happen, but no, it didn't get into the exhibit, "Beyond the Limits." I just couldn't figure out a way to explain this without writing a big, long story and you just don't do that in an exhibit. You don't write large reams of text. It did get into the catalog that goes with the exhibit. I assume that some people who visit the exhibit will buy the catalog. But, it just couldn't get in there. I tried and thought about it and have to admit, I failed, even though it is a wonderful story. There is a General in the Air Force, I forget his name now, but I participated in an interview with him a number of years ago where he showed a framed hyphen on his wall because he was involved with the program and I guess he keeps that as a memento.

One of the things that I want to emphasize on getting back to the issue of software, is that for me, personally, it is a distinction, which, as important as it is to you, as important as it is to the organizing of this conference, as a professional historian trained in American studies and history of science and technology, I find that the distinction is somewhat less useful. I use as an analogy the generational model of hardware. It is a wonderful idea for computer engineers to talk about first or second generation; it just confuses the heck out of historians who try to tell the story of the history of computing. Dividing computing into hardware and software, I found, has caused more problems to me than it is worth. I try to avoid that in my writing and in my exhibit work and in anything else I do because, again, I'm mindful of the public who are, and this from Strunk and White, who say, "90 percent of the time people are totally baffled." If that is true of writing, it is even more the case of exhibits. People are confused and they want some guidance. First of all, they are in a big crowded place and they don't have very much time. I try not to complexify things too much. Software is of course very critical to the working of the computer system and there I try to tie it in with the themes that are familiar to museum-goers who remember the classic halls of machinery like steam engines, railroads, and automobiles, and things like that, where you use a set of classic definitions of a machine as something where you channel forces of nature into a particular direction to do a specific thing, whether it be literally through mechanisms, as in a steam locomotive, or through electricity or something. A computer does not fit that definition. The person who is on a production line making DOS clones, for example, doesn't know that the person who buys that computer is going to use it for this or for that. That moment comes when the software is loaded into the machine. But, having said that, again, what is important is what the machine is used for, what does it do? In order to consider that, you have got to consider the whole ensemble of hardware and software. I noticed something else. I have been looking recently into the OEM phenomenon being here in the Boston area, I have been doing a little research about that. I realized that OEM people did something very akin to developing software when they developed specialized pieces of hardware that they would build around something like a PDP8 minicomputer. They put hardware around it and then added customized software. The end result was a special-purpose machine that did some very specific jobs for a specific customer who really didn't know or care what was deep inside it. So again, you see the blurring of distinction. I like that blurring of distinction. The more of that I find, the better. The more that I can convey to the public, the notion of the computer being a way of channeling the forces of nature, what we can do with nature in a specific direction to solve a specific problem, the better, because I think the public can understand that. They can also understand that if you don't use the word, every machine has a software aspect to it. There are rules of how you use things: you don't press this button before you press that button. You don't put your car into reverse when you are going forward at 60 miles an hour, or something like that. Every machine has it. Why make an artificial distinction if it doesn't help you so much.

Well, that has sort of been my philosophy. I also wanted to mention one other thing. Again, coming from a museum of technology where we have this long tradition that Mike Mahoney talked about, of things like Henry Ford's work, I am very fascinated about the way Henry Ford's experience with the mass production techniques for the model T, how he seems to have solved all the problems early in this century. It seemed like he had solved all the problems of human want and need by producing high quality products at low cost in large volume. Then what happened to Ford? The company almost went bankrupt because they could not adapt themselves flexibly to the changing conditions and the personal needs of the marketplace. Now, along comes a computer which, by definition, you can change by just reprogramming it. Of course, there is the sort of bugaboo, because reprogramming it seems to be so simple, but in fact, it isn't. If Professor Brooks speaks about no magic bullet, I think you all know how hard it is really to write programs that zero in like a laser beam on someone's specific problem. But, the point I want to make is that all of this that is so wrapped up in the energies of software development has a long tradition that goes back right into the time of Henry Ford's struggles to keep the Model-T viable, and his competition with General Motors who were introducing annual model changes, and things like that.

I will move on to some specifics about the way we designed the exhibit at the Air and Space Museum. I looked around the museum and looked at the crowds in particular and had long discussions with the designer—we were really sort of partners in all of this. We came up with some rules which are a little bit unorthodox, but I think they withstood the test of time. For me the interactive exhibits, which obviously revealed software as it does something. We kept them very short. Five minutes was about the maximum that we ever had. Three minutes was even better. We tried to have no keyboards, very direct interaction usually with a track ball or a touch screen where in real-time, something that you touched created an instantaneous reaction on the screen. It is no accident that by far the most popular interactive that we have is a flight simulator—one that we have taken from Microsoft but simplified a little bit, removed some of the more difficult things. We have some instructions but nobody reads them. In fact, to the extent that we put any text on the screen at all, I wouldn't say it is a waste because some people read it, but many people don't. Again, you have lots of visitors coming through. They want to get some kind of experience. Now, whether that is a meaningful experience, or not, I'll

SLIDE 1

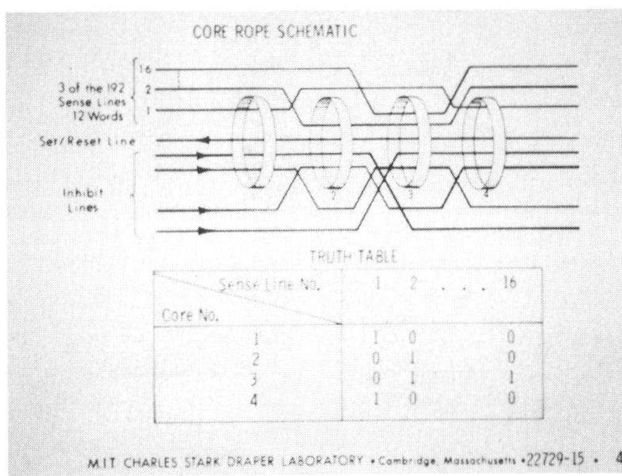

SLIDE 2

defer to some other people about that. But, they do get a sense of what the computer can do. I know that this is not an orthodox way of looking at things, but I insisted on it rather rigidly and I think it has paid off in terms of the popularity of that exhibit. It has held up very well since 1989. It still continues to be popular.

We were compelled to use, in 1989, to go with high-end work stations like Evans and Sutherland for the graphics capabilities. This led to all kinds of maintenance headaches. Especially when companies decided they could, or would, no longer support our application. So, over the years we have been slowly but gradually and inexorably rewriting everything for DOS. In fact, we don't even use Macintoshes if we can avoid it. Just DOS clones that you can buy cheaply and program them. We can program them in-house, and we control all, and we keep the cost down and we are flexible that way. We have had to sacrifice a little bit of the glitz, but for a museum like ours, that is not a problem because we make up for the glitz in some of the other things that we can do.

Let's have the first slide.

(SLIDE 1) I looked for something about software that I actually show in the exhibit. This is a piece of core rope. This is core rope that was prototyped for the way the *Apollo* guidance computer was programmed to go to the moon. They literally wove wire and if a wire went through the core, it was a binary one. If it went around the core, it was a zero.

SLIDE 3

SLIDE 4

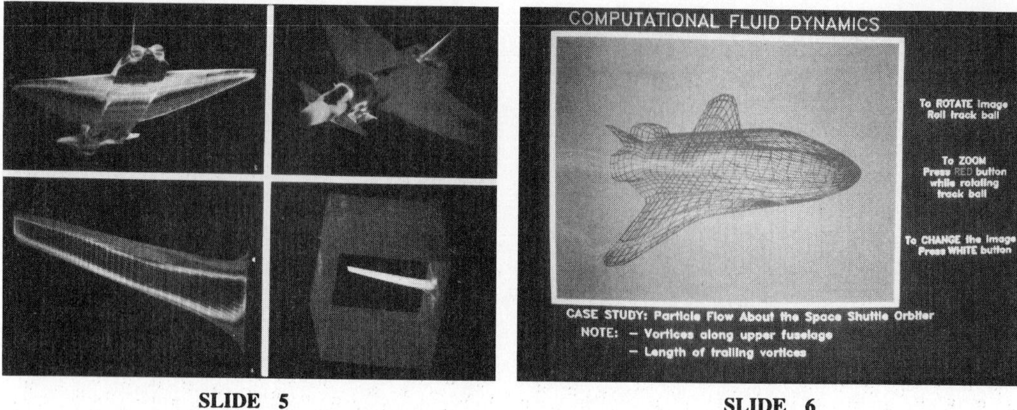

SLIDE 5 **SLIDE 6**

(SLIDE 2) So, I do have one example of an artifact. Here comes the philosophical question. Is it software or is it hardware? It is a hardware realization in the core rope. How many people understand that subtlety, I really can't tell you.

(SLIDES 3 and 4) Which would you rather see? You come to the Smithsonian with your kids or family, do you want to see what is pictured in slide 3 or slide 4?

(SLIDE 3) I have to apologize. This is not yet on public display but it will be. An SR 71 designed by a man named Kelly Johnson who worked with a slide rule, by the way. Tells you what you can do with a slide rule.

What we do try to show is the way the computer, especially computer graphics, has been used in aerospace. I am echoing what David said: we keep drilling the application of computers.

(SLIDE 5) Shuttle reentry. It is popular. We have this on a Silicon Graphics workstation where visitors can manipulate this image. That is one of the very few that we haven't been able to port to a DOS machine yet. But, we probably will soon. Silicon Graphics has been working with us. But again, we have to go to them and ask for their help whenever we want to make changes to this program. We are trying to get as far away from that as we possibly can.

(SLIDE 6) This slide shows another graphics application, in fluid dynamics.

So to sum up, I think the Air and Space Museum is somewhat of a unique place where we have self-selected visitorship of people who already know that they are going to see high technology when they come in. So we don't have that problem to the extent that is a problem for other museums. We have a basic subject that is inherently exciting and we don't have to worry about making it more exciting, namely, air and spacecraft. We have ways of showing the applications. It allows me to think more about some of the philosophical implications. I may not have succeeded at, but at least, I am making a try.

ROSIN: Oliver B. R. Strimpel is Executive Director of the Computer Museum in Boston. He spent his early years in India and Italy before earning degrees in the Sciences in Cambridge University and Sussex University, and a D.Phil. in theoretical astrophysics at Oxford in 1979. He was curator at the Science Museum of London where he helped set up major exhibits including "The Challenge of the Chip," before becoming the curator at The Computer Museum in 1984. Dr. Strimpel was responsible for The Computer Museum's most successful permanent exhibitions, "The Computer and the Image" and "Smart Machines." The more recent "Giant Walk Through Computer," which opened in 1990, was also Dr. Strimpel's idea. His leadership has moved The Computer Museum into the forefront of interactive computer exhibit design, and the museum now exports exhibits to other museums and technology centers around the world.

OLIVER STRIMPEL: David and Paul have said a lot of very interesting things about the challenges of building effective exhibits. I want to cast them in a slightly different way. You have heard a lot about the need to get the context of an exhibit across to people. Museums can communicate with people by letting them experince things first hand. We learn from books, television, other media, talking.

(OVERHEAD SLIDE 1) But in museums you have a chance to *experience* things, whether it is an original artifact, something that is huge, or something that you can do. That is the first challenge of the public display about the history of computing. How do you make it into an experience?

The second challenge of public displays is dealing with an audience composed of a huge array of different ages, knowledge, and interest in the subject.

(OVERHEAD SLIDE 2) Museums like the Smithsonian and ours attract visitors from around the world. We are talking about people with dramatically different cultural backgrounds, as well. The second challenge is: How do you have something for everybody?

The third challenge is something that Mike Mahoney talked about this morning and in a paper he wrote a while ago, which is the issue of how do you get people to think about history from the framework of the time and not by hindsight? Is everything leading inexorably to the present? Basically speaking, we find that our visitors are really looking for evidence to show that history was all leading up to the Apple Macintosh and the 486 PC. So, the big challenge is, how do you get them to think about it a little bit from the point of view from the people who were doing the work at the time?

The final challenge that I want to refer to, is perhaps, the most obvious one, which is of showing original artifacts. That is one of the key ingredients of the museum experience. But, despite the recent nature of this history, these artifacts are sometimes incredibly elusive. As Gwen mentioned earlier, we had a very difficult time finding a UNIVAC I. We wanted to show in our exhibitions machines that come from other countries and, specifically, a lot of pioneering work that was done in England. In fact, our initial plan was to show the Manchester Mark I, but there isn't very much of it left. What there is, is treasured by the University of Manchester. The Smithsonian and The Computer Museum are perhaps best equipped in this country to deal with this challenge because we started collecting

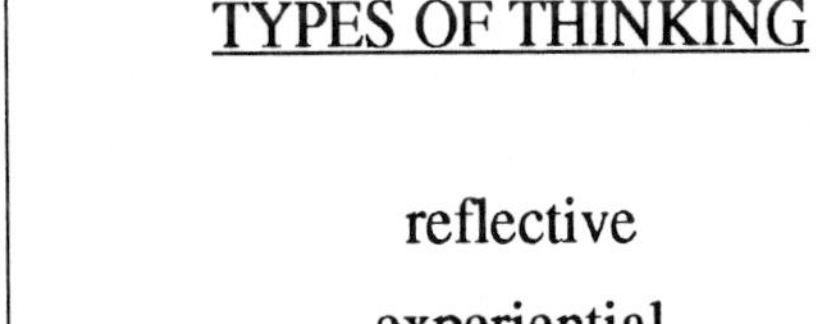

OVERHEAD SLIDE 1

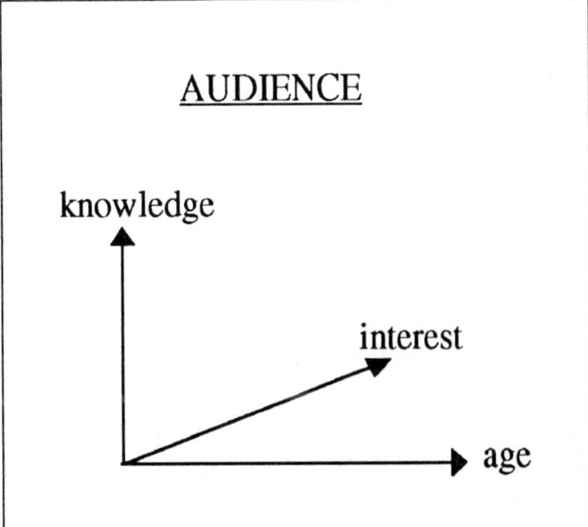

OVERHEAD SLIDE 2

before everyone else. But I don't envy the person who wants to develop a display about the history of computing in another place. The early artifacts are very scarce and those which are on display are not usually available for loan.

How do we meet some of these challenges? One way which hasn't been talked about that much so far is the idea of making something work. One way to get an experience is to see a computer actually doing something resulting in motion. Quite a dramatic virtuoso effort in this direction is just being completed by the Science Museum in London, which recently reconstructed Babbage's Difference Engine #2 at a cost of about half a million dollars. That is on display in London now and has attracted very widespread interest. It is one of the few computing devices whose physical appearance reveals something about its purpose and how it actually functions.

Pegasus is an early machine that the Science Museum has actually managed to get running. It is not on public display. Paul mentioned the PDP-1 which we have running at The Computer Museum, but it is not on display.

(SLIDE 1) One machine that we did have on display at The Computer Museum for a while was a punched card machine. This is none other than Mike Mahoney punching his own card, just in case he can't remember what it was like! That was an exhibit that would make all of us who used punched cards in earnest run a mile from. But it was incredibly attractive with the children of the post-mainframe era. They have never used a punched card machine before. It moved, clicked, you could see the holes in it. It was a hands-on interactive exhibit, one of the most popular in The Computer Museum, believe it or not. A simple working punched card machine.

(SLIDE 2) This slide shows another way to make machines work—a video of them working. This is our Smart Machines theater, which is a collection of historic robots and computer-controlled devices. They are all labeled in front and come from many different places including Stanford, Carnegie Mellon, MIT, and Japan. Those of you who will come to the Museum tomorrow night will get a chance to see all of this. If you can't actually make a robot work, the next best thing is to show a video of it working.

The other way to meet the challenge of giving a diverse public a real experience is to link it to a compelling application. David and Paul have talked a lot about very compelling applications. In Paul's case, the aerospace application is very gripping and really engages the public extremely successfully. The World War II application and robotics and other examples at the National Museum of American History also engage people very effectively.

SLIDE 1 Visitor exploring punch card installation at The Computer Museum in the 1980s. Credit: J. Wayman Williams

SLIDE 2 The Robot Theater in the Robots & Other Smart Machines™ Gallery. Credit: Marjorie Nichols

MILESTONE COMPONENTS

Context-setting "tunnel"

Vignette

Social impact then

Social impact now

Hands-on explanation of the technology

Videos on:
- people: inventors, users
- technologies
- popular culture

OVERHEAD SLIDE 3

Milestone 4: the 1960's
COMPUTING MEANS BUSINESS

tunnel:	Beatles song Images of large office buildings
vignette:	IBM System 360 insurance company application
impact then:	airline reservations
impact now:	mass mailing, junk mail
didn't make it:	PL/I, Dvorak Keyboard, MOBIDIC, 12-bit computers light pen, mini punched cards
pitfalls:	"Tell your own tale" of computer snafus

OVERHEAD SLIDE 4

(OVERHEAD SLIDE 3) We took that approach too at The Computer Museum with our major exhibition of the history of computing called "Milestones of a Revolution," which we opened two years ago. We selected nine milestones from the entire history of computing. Each milestone had several components. I'll go through them to try and explain how they arose. They really arise directly in an attempt to meet the challenges that I mentioned earlier.

First of all, the context-setting tunnel. This is an attempt to acclimatize visitors to each milestone before they came to the vignette depicting the milestone.

Second, we didn't display artifacts on their own sitting on the carpet or in a case. We displayed them in a vignette complete with manikins and ephemera from the time. Then we had two themes in each one which were very explicit attempts to show the social impact of that particular milestone. Social impact then—what impact it had on people at the time; and social impact now—what present-day application emerged from the milestone.

The slide shows "hands-on explanation." The virtues of hands-on interactives have already been extolled, and they are very effective. We have used that technology here to try and give people a better sense either of technology itself, or what the technology was used for.

Lastly, we have interactive video in each milestone. David said they found interactive video very successful in the "Information Age" exhibition. Each video station offers clips of the people, the inventors, the users, the technologies, and popular culture at the time.

(OVERHEAD SLIDE 4) Let me give you an example of a vignette to show how we actually fleshed this out. In the case of the 1960s, we selected the IBM System 360 as the focus of that era. In the tunnel you can hear a Beatles' song as you approach the vignette. You can see images of large office buildings giving the feeling of the growth of big business. The vignette itself is of an IBM 360/30. This is a good example of the challenges of finding artifacts we didn't expect to meet in this particular vignette. We thought that there would be hundreds of IBM 360s around in good working order. In fact, we had one of our Board members from IBM who said, "No problem, I'll just look in the databases at IBM and look at the ones that we service." He looked through three separate databases, each of which had several sets of 360s that were supposed to be in the field. It turned out, in the end, that there was only one System 360 and it was still working—running in 1401 emulation mode. This was in 1990. Our assumption about the easy availability of a System 360 was wrong. We went to this company, which was a market research firm on Wall Street. IBM said to them, "Look, we will replace this for you and you will save in a month of maintenance, the entire cost of the new machine." It was with incredible difficulty that we managed to pry this last 360 out of them, just in time for the exhibit opening.

To help visitors see the machine in context, we simulated an insurance company application. This is not a compelling application, but we were not able to think of very many compelling applications for machines in the '50s and '60s.

The wider social impact of the day that we selected was airline reservation—the SABRE system—which was started at that time. We picked junk mail as a descendent phenomenon that stemmed directly from the kind of business data processing that really gained prominence in the 1960s with the 360. This is shown with a pile of junk mail that lights up behind a partially silvered mirror after the viewer presses a button.

To try and meet the challenge of people's *revisionist* interpretation of technology's forward march to the PCs of today, we showed some technologies that didn't make it: PL/I, Dvorak keyboard, MOBIDIC which was the tractor trailer-sized mobile computer for the military in the 1960s, 12-bit computers that were supplanted by the move to the 8-bit byte standard, the light pen and the mini punched cards from the IBM System 3, which were an attempt to keep the punched card technology going beyond its day. We also have an interactive in which people can see tales of computer errors and write their own stories about the things that have happened to them in which computers have made mistakes. That is surprisingly popular. People all have some horror story to recount.

(OVERHEAD SLIDE 5) The overhead shows the range of videos that we were able to assemble for this period. We try to show the technologies themselves using a humorous touch wherever possible. Life before timesharing is really about the hazards of dealing with punched cards. The main protagonist in one film is carrying large decks of cards which, predictably enough, get shuffled up when he stumbles. It is quite hilarious, as are some of the popular culture examples. The videos help bring it to life and help provide the context.

(OVERHEAD SLIDE 6) For the 5–10 percent of the visitors who really want to know the details, we have a specifications sheet for each of the milestone machines. We also have a comparison in which I am afraid we might be slightly guilty of making the assumption that the IBM 360 was leading

The 1960's VIDEOS

Technologies

- Announcement of the IBM System 360
- Apollo Guidance Computer
- Life before timesharing
- Dartmouth timesharing
- ERMA: automatic banking

People

- T. J. Watson, Jr., on automation
- Union official on automation
- Jerome Weisner, President of MIT, on the thinking machines

Popular Culture

- TV show: Monkees vs. Machine
- Toothpaste commercial
- Digicomp: toy for the computer age

OVERHEAD SLIDE 5

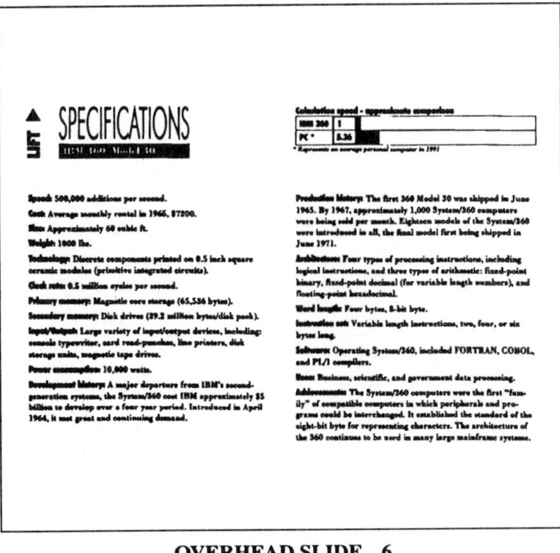

LIFT ▲

SPECIFICATIONS

IBM 360 Model 30

Speed: 500,000 additions per second.

Cost: Average monthly rental in 1965, $7200.

Size: Approximately 60 cubic ft.

Weight: 1000 lbs.

Technology: Discrete components printed on 0.5 inch square ceramic modules (primitive integrated circuits).

Clock rate: 0.5 million cycles per second.

Primary memory: Magnetic core storage (65,536 bytes).

Secondary memory: Disk drives (29.2 million bytes/disk pack).

Input/Output: Large variety of input/output devices, including: console typewriter, card read-punches, line printers, disk storage units, magnetic tape drives.

Power consumption: 10,000 watts.

Development history: A major departure from IBM's second-generation systems, the System/360 cost IBM approximately $5 billion to develop over a four year period. Introduced in April 1964, it met great and continuing demand.

Calculation speed - approximate comparison

IBM 360	1
PC *	5.36

* *Represents an average personal computer in 1991*

Production history: The first 360 Model 30 was shipped in June 1965. By 1967, approximately 1,000 System/360 computers were being sold per month. Eighteen models of the System/360 were introduced in all, the final model first being shipped in June 1971.

Architecture: Four types of processing instructions, including logical instructions, and three types of arithmetic: fixed-point binary, fixed-point decimal (for variable length numbers), and floating-point hexadecimal.

Word length: Four bytes, 8-bit byte.

Instruction set: Variable length instructions, two, four, or six bytes long.

Software: Operating System/360, included FORTRAN, COBOL, and PL/1 compilers.

Uses: Business, scientific, and government data processing.

Achievements: The System/360 computers were the first "family" of compatible computers in which peripherals and programs could be interchanged. It established the standard of the eight-bit byte for representing characters. The architecture of the 360 continues to be used in many large mainframe systems.

OVERHEAD SLIDE 6

SLIDE 3 IBM 360 installation (showing technician installing cabling for a new tape drive) in People and Computers: Milestones of a Revolution™ exhibit. Credit: David Bohl

inexorably toward the PC. But everyone does ask, "How does this machine compare to a PC of today?" The answer is it was about five times as powerful, for a cost of $7,200 a month in 1965.

(SLIDE 3) The slide shows the vignette—the 360 and the manikin putting the false floor cabling underneath. Another challenge of public display, if you approach it this way, is to make sure, if you build a manikin to put it far enough away from the school kids so they don't pull the head of the manikin off. We learned this the hard way.

(SLIDE 4) In a slightly more recent era (1966–1967) the vignette application gets a little bit more compelling. Here we chose brain surgery, which really gets visitors' attention. The computer itself

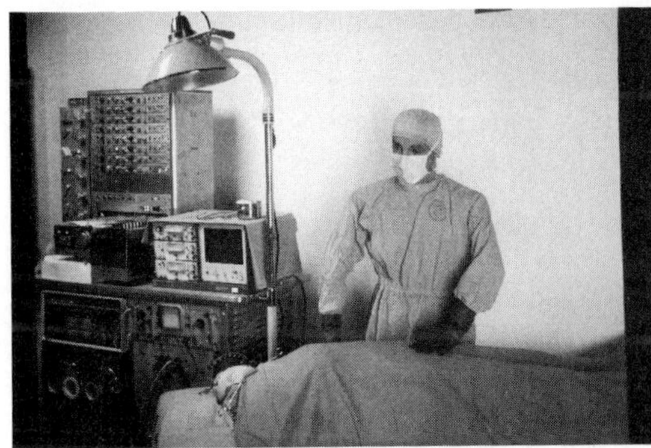

SLIDE 4 Milestone exploring the use of Digital Equipment Corporation PDP-8e mini-computer in surgery (People and Computers). Credit: David Bohl

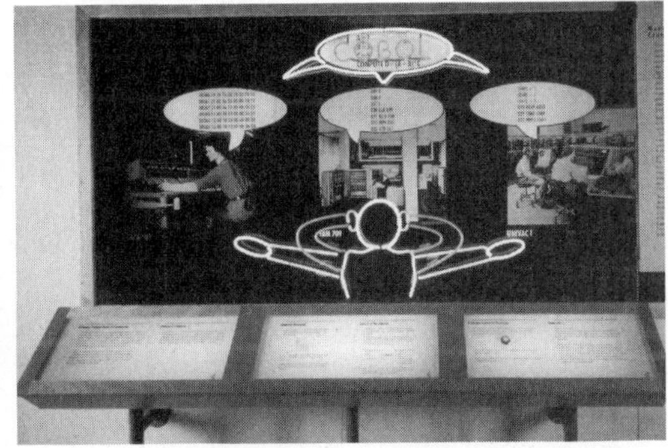

SLIDE 5 COBOL display (People and Computers). Credit: David Bohl

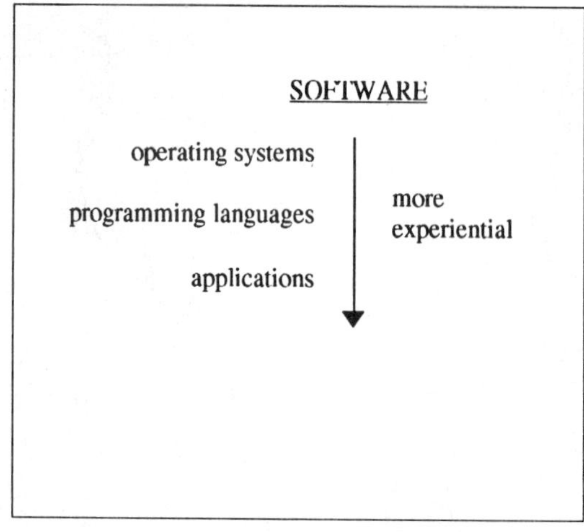

OVERHEAD SLIDE 7

becomes less prominent physically and the application gets more prominent—and that is really one of the main changes that took place with the embedded minicomputer.

(SLIDE 5) I want to talk a little about the challenges of software display. Our exhibits talked a lot about applications. They talked less about programming languages and even less about operating systems and systems software. The Milestones exhibit does have a milestone on the invention of high level programming languages in the late '50s.

(OVERHEAD SLIDE 7) We focused on COBOL. When you press a button you can see how one simple COBOL expression codes for the same thing as that long list of machine-specific text that was assembly code for each of the IBM 709, UNIVAC I, and the RCA 501. The display conveys the purpose of portability and higher level programming languages as simpler means of expression.

(SLIDES 6, 7) We also explain what a programming language is with an interactive station. Visitors write a little program to get this little car to go from the beginning of a maze to the end of the maze by turning right or turning left. You would be surprised how many people actually get an introduction

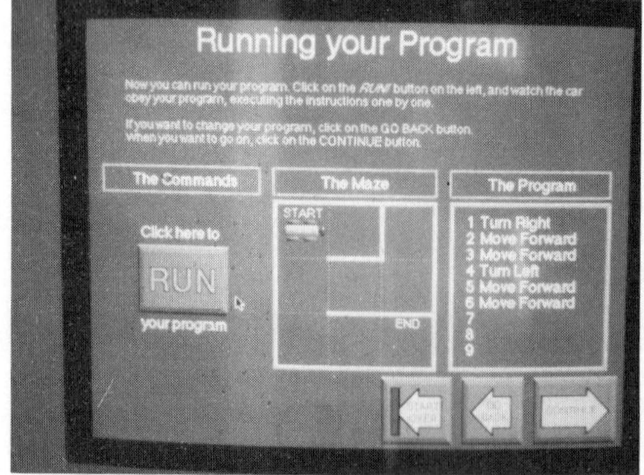

SLIDE 6 Screen shots from interactive computer stations that address running a program and programming languages (People and Computers). Credit: Peter Yamasaki

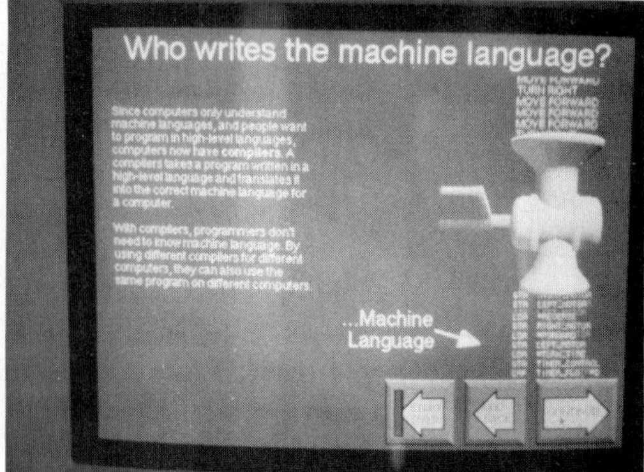

SLIDE 7

SLIDE 8 View inside The Walk-Through Computer.™ Credit: Richard Fowler

SLIDE 9 Visitors inside The Walk-Through Computer.™ Credit: Richard Fowler

to debugging as well as programming when they do this, even though it is a very simple task. At the end of the program the exhibit takes the instructions that they have just written and passes it into an animated meat grinder. Out comes the machine code. This is a way of making an abstract idea—the difference between high-level and low-level langauges—meaningful to the nonspecialist.

(SLIDES 8, 9) The Museum also shows something about operating systems and programming, implicitly through the giant Walk-Through Computer, which is a two-story high model of a desk top computer. In the next slide, you can see inside the computer. The giant processor there is laid out in the foreground of the picture. Projected into the microprocessor is an animation showing what the computer is doing. It is running an application that visitors have used before they enter the large-scale computer, and inside they can actually see how the data gets passed around. So there is an implicit description of some aspects of systems programming and what happens with registers inside the microprocessor.

I am very glad to say that on the occasion of the reception of this conference tomorrow evening, we are opening our first-ever exhibition of programming languages. My thanks to our Conference Program Chair, Jean Sammet, who is also a board member at The Computer Museum, who made this exhibition happen. I look forward to opening it with all of you tomorrow night.

TRANSCRIPT OF QUESTION AND ANSWER SESSION

ROSIN: From **DOUG ROSS (SofTech at MIT)** to David Allison: Please define "cases," and "settings" as types of displays you said to mix.

ALLISON: That is museum jargon. What we mean by cases are artifacts and images brought together for reasons of presenting a specific subject. They were not necessarily together in the time that they were developed. So, you may have a case on software where we bring together a manual from one place, a floppy disk from another, and you would explain them with labels and so on. A "setting" is where the presentation is, as something occurs, which is what you saw with Oliver's display about an office setting which includes a desk, a manikin, and other things to present a scene as it once existed. So those are the two types of displays that are generally mixable.

ROSIN: From **J.A.N. LEE** directed to the entire panel: Isn't one of the major challenges the funding of exhibits?

STRIMPEL: We were very fortunate at The Computer Museum to get major support from the National Endowment for the Humanities. Their only string was that we include humanities themes in the exhibit, which we wanted to do anyway. Martin Campbell-Kelly's pie diagram showed that the history of computing really does fall squarely across a number of different areas which includes humanities areas. One of the questions that we often get is, "Don't you get a lot of pressure from your funders to bias the content of the exhibition?" We are fortunate not to have experienced that. People are very respectful of the need for integrity and objectivity of display in a public institution.

ALLISON: I don't think there is anything to say other than that the problem of funding exhibitions is universal. Almost any exhibition requires outside funding if it is going to be more than a single case. So that is true in exhibits about the Presidents, exhibits about anything. It requires some outside sponsorship, be it a foundation or a corporation, or anything.

ROSIN: From **FRED BROOKS** to Paul Ceruzzi: Explain the context of the missing hyphen. What should the expression have been and what was it?

CERUZZI: I could say go read my book, but I can try to do it in a very brief time. It was not really a hyphen, it was a bar written over the letter "R" which means take the average value of something that was coming over a radio link that was widely fluctuating. The bar was left off, so instead of taking the average value it simply picked off whatever value happened to be coming down at that particular microsecond. That was widely fluctuating, so the rocket started [having problems], and the range safety officer ordered it destroyed. It was literally a bar. Of course, the other interesting thing is that it was not a FORTRAN program but it was in the equations which were then coded correctly by a coder. It wasn't FORTRAN; that has been wrongly reported in the literature. But I straightened it out.

ROSIN: That question was just perfect for this kind of audience. It really highlights something that is reflected in all the other questions that I have received so far. Let me read them to you without asking you to answer them immediately. **HELEN GIGLEY** asked, in response to David Allison's remarks, but I am sure she'd direct this question to all the other speakers as well. "Do you have any ideas how to make such things as software or natural language processes more visible to the general public?" **RALF BAYER** from **Motorola**, asks, "How are the difficulties in presenting software in an exhibit related to the difficulties in presenting literature?" **JOHN GUIDI** asks, "Can you share with us any thoughts or ideas you might have that would present the software construction process? In addition to ideas that might work, what in your opinion should be avoided?"

I am going to turn these questions over to the panel, but I want to put these in the context of a metaquestion. It occurred to me while listening to all of you that the title we used in framing this session, in fact, was very telling. It included a word that many of us in the computing field are very sensitive to, but I think I was ignorant of when I helped write the question. That is the word "public." All of us software folk, I suspect, have felt a certain amount of frustration, no matter when we began in this field and no matter where we are today, in trying to explain to people close to us what it is that we really do. What is software? I have a nephew who was once asked what his father does. His father is an attorney. And at the age of six he said, "My daddy makes A,B,C's." I suspect if anybody asked one of our kids at that age what we did, it might get the same answer, or "My mommy is typist," or something like that. I have never been able to explain to my dear ones really what it is I do when I think I am creating software. I sense that in all of these other questions.

So, in a sense the question we are asking is not, "What can you people do in talking to the public to help them understand what we do," because you have told us pretty well that the public in general doesn't care what we do. The question I would ask all of you, and my apologies to the people who wrote these specific questions, is what do you suggest that we can do to help the public better understand software?

CERUZZI: I wouldn't want to tell you what to do because you do what you do well enough or not well enough, without my advice. I am not really that presumptuous. The only thing I would do is reemphasize what I said earlier, that is, the distinction between software and hardware is probably confusing to the public. That is my personal opinion. Maybe the business that you are in is designing machines that perform work for people that make life better than without it. That is a Dick Rubinstein comment, "Using a computer should be easier than not using a computer."

ROSIN: I have to go back to John Guidi's question which was very particular. He said, "Could you share with us any thoughts or ideas you might have about what would present the software construction process," which in fact is what a lot of us do. Not what the effect of software is, and not what the result is, but the process. This is at the root of all of these questions.

ALLISON: The answer to that particular question, and also an answer to the more general question, can be found in what Oliver said, that the techniques that we use are: simplify, use analogies, make it visual, and make it experiential. We do that over and over again. How can you simplify it? Think of the analogy of moving that program that you showed—which was not really writing a software program, but think of an analogy that somebody does understand. If you can accomplish those things, you can begin to reach out to a public that you can't reach out to otherwise. Also, use techniques in areas that you know they are interested in and reach out through a relationship to a person, rather than to a program, and through a person and the person's need into the program, or something of that sort.

STRIMPEL: The process of constructing a program is something that is hard to make experiential, unless you actually do it. I would like to see the general public and children to have more access to people who do write programs for a living, perhaps sitting with them as apprentices. There is a lot of inexplicit knowledge, as Mike Mahoney said at the beginning of this conference—all kinds of things that are not in the manuals. I am not sure whether a museum display is the right place to actually deal with this topic. On Bob's question of what people like you can do to help explain these topics: I think that sitting on advisory committees and helping us make exhibits that attack the problem from many angles, as Jean has just done with us, is something that is a very tangible contribution. I would urge you all to help us think through the ideas.

ROSIN: Let me go back to Helen's question. "Do you have any ideas on how to make such things as software or natural language processing more visible to the general public?" I think the emphasis there is on the processing of natural language. How can you make something that people cannot see, understandable to them?

ALLISON: You have to figure out an analogy that they can visualize. To actually solve that specific problem would take some brainstorming. Interactive technologies and animation techniques are some of the great tools that are becoming more available and more affordable and can help to make this happen.

STRIMPEL: At The Computer Museum, our best effort in solving that problem was to make "The Walk-Through Computer" work both with the program outside that you use and then see the actual program being executed inside with the instructions being fetched from RAM, taken to the processor, executed, data being pulled from the disk. That was the best way we could think of to make it visible. Still, it is not three-dimensional and not as muscular as one would want but it is a step in the right direction.

ROSIN: I'm going to present Ralf Bayer's question one more time. "How are the difficulties in presenting software in an exhibit related to the difficulties in presenting literature?"

CERUZZI: I'm not sure that we actually present literature in a museum context. Again, I want to emphasize that a museum is a special place because of the fact that it is where you see artifacts and you don't see words or other forms of communications. Of course you do see words, and you do see films and videos and other things like that. If that was your question, it is a very similar problem and I don't have an easy answer to that, nor can I say that experience that other museums have had in trying to present that, have really helped me very much in presenting software.

ALLISON: Probably the best visualization of literature are movies based on novels. I think that a good film that starts off with a very critical problem that software is used to solve would be putting a spacecraft into orbit or something like that. This could follow the process step by step in a dramatically effective movie script. Such a presentation could be a great addition to this field and something that we would be happy to show.

ROSIN: From **RICH MILLER** at **SHC Systemhouse**: Programming is the creation of "a list of instructions." Has that analogy ever worked? Does it go far enough? Oliver, I thought I saw that in several of your slides.

STRIMPEL: Yes, we have tried to show that with the programming of a car station and there is another example in which visitors do a series of instructions that you will see when you see the new exhibition that will be unveiled at The Computer Museum.

ROSIN: There are several suggestions we have now for solving the problem. For Oliver, has there been any user-testing results of kids and adults seeing the Walk-Through Computers? Did they get what you intended?

STRIMPEL: Yes, actually we have done summative evaluation—evaluating something that has been opened. We found that a surprisingly large number of people didn't realize they were inside a computer when they were inside. And once they were inside, we found something like 20–30 percent thought that the processor was the ribbon cable because it was brightly colored and looked interesting. The CPU itself is a drab grey piece of ceramic, albeit with a screen on it. We overlooked some very obvious things. We did find, however, in the history exhibit, "Milestones of a Revolution," that people actually spent quite a lot longer there than we expected. The average Computer Museum visit is about two hours, and people spend about twenty minutes inside the history exhibit.

ALLISON: I think it is something that you don't think about too much if you are not in the museum business. I just want to make explicit—and Oliver referred to this earlier—that the kind of learning that we go after in museum displays is not necessarily conceptual understanding, it is more visual and experiential understanding. So if you ask a visitor, "What did you learn?" often you get a blank expression, because often people don't go to the museum to learn; they say they are going to the museum to *see* or *do*. They later reflect, or use that kind of information in other conceptual learning. But what they take away from the museum may be a set of images, it may be a feeling, it may be something else. That type of learning tends to be undervalued. But it is incredibly important in shaping what people are going to do in their careers and how they feel about things, how they think about things. It is very difficult to measure in a questionnaire something of that sort. But it is an important style of learning that museums are very effective at conveying.

ROSIN: I can't resist the reaction to what Oliver said earlier about "dull grey boxes" and "bright ribbon cables." As a dull grey developer, I often felt that way about marketing people who wore brightly colored ribbons.

CERUZZI: I have had the experience since opening *Beyond the Limits*, of having many adults come up to me and say, "You know I have been working in the aerospace industry for 20 years, and I have been working on these electronic systems, and this is the first time in all my years that somebody has finally recognized what I do and given credit for it. Thank you." They just feel wonderful and it makes me feel great too. They felt undervalued all those years, because they didn't do the sexy stuff like the SR 71 wings or something like that. The message is getting out, but measuring it is kind of hard to do sometimes.

ROSIN: I've got two comments to read and then a final question. In fact they really go along the theme that you were just mentioning Paul, I think. The first is a reaction from Fred Brooks to Helen's question: "Using a WYSIWYG editor makes natural language processing visible and little kids do it. (see Allen Kay's priceless video of the three-year-old teaching MacDraw). And here is another one from Charles Lindsey at Manchester, who says: "One way to show people what software is, is to have a real person who will develop short programs to order in real-time. I did this once. My colleagues thought I was crazy, but it worked. For example, I constructed a working 8-Queens in Pascal."

And that really leads me to the last question, from **ROSS HAMILTON** at the **University Warwick**: "Is the task becoming easier as the children of the post-mainframe era are becoming the parents who bring their families to the museums?"

CERUZZI: It depends on how you define the task. We have children come in, who intuitively seem like they know what to do. I personally feel very strange about whether they are really getting the message that I thought I was trying to convey. That leads me to all kinds of questions about whether I am trying to convey the right message. I am not sure that I can answer that either. It is kind of a tough one.

Let me respond to the other question. This has been very seriously discussed in our museum about having people on the floor doing things, although we didn't mention specifically writing a program. It is a wonderful idea if you can get the money to pay for it. Yes, it is a great idea. I don't know about the others, but there have been many times I have given a tour for a VIP and by the time I'm finished with the tour there is a big crowd of people tagging along listening because they are finding it so fascinating to actually get some live explanation about what all this stuff means that they don't get from the labels. If we could do more of that, we would. But, it costs something.

STRIMPEL: From my perspective, I think that it has become easier to present some of this material to the public. Only a few years ago museums really had virtually no working computers. There was great trepidation: would the keyboards hold up? No one knew how to use a mouse. We were all working on workstations with minicomputers and I remember trying to keep a PDP/70 going to run a graphic display at the museum. It would stay up a few days. The logistical difficulties of keeping interactive exhibits going in museums has decreased dramatically, and as David said they are standardizing everything on PCs. With the convenience of PCs and Macs, we quickly forget the kinds of hassles we have all been through, bending over backwards to get one or two interactives to survive a few days in a museum environment. Things really have changed dramatically in that respect. Whether they are really getting our message is now the challenge as we can move more on to the actual education agenda and get away from the logistical challenges.

ALLISON: To reflect on what Paul said, the task is increasingly changing. When we did "Information Age" one of the big issues was the one of empowerment. There was a real sense of the separation of the haves and have nots in society. With the advent of automatic teller machines, computers at the library and a lot of things, the task is increasingly getting people to open up and be curious enough about computers. As Martin Campbell-Kelly said earlier, they do have a history and there are things beyond just using them that you need to be reflective about. If we were to plan "Information Age" today, I think, instead of trying to make everything as easy as possible, which was one of our goals, there might be something to be said for making it a little bit more difficult—and force people to be somewhat more reflective. So the task continually changes as we move forward in the information age.

ROSIN: We began this afternoon with a talk from Mike Mahoney that set an agenda and put the history of computing in a broader context that some of us were, in fact, quite ignorant of. We had several overview presentations that showed us facets in the work of the history of computing, again, that many of us were ignorant of. These presentations certainly put things in categories that help make it easier for us to understand. Then we had an opportunity to discuss with some experts first hand—up close and personal—how those of us who are not involved might become more involved or might make our contributions more valuable. Then, finally this evening, I got an idea of the relationship between those of us who are professional computing people and those who are professional historians, and the difficulties in relating what we try to do to the general public. Finally, we learned how that public seems to be changing, just as the history of computing represents a changing environment. If we meet again in 15 years, we will see something very different.

What Makes History?

Michael S. Mahoney

Program in History of Science
Princeton University
Consulting Historian, HOPL-II Conference

As you look over the reviewer's and Program Committee's comments on your paper, you may be perplexed by admonitions in one form or another to "make it more historical". After all, you've been talking about the past, you've got the events and people in chronological order, you've related what happened. What more could be needed to make history? The answer is hard to pin down in a series of methodological precepts, as history is ultimately an art acquired by professional practice. But it may help you to understand our specific criticisms if I describe what we're looking for in general terms.

Dick Hamming captured the essence of it in the title of his paper at the International Conference on the History of Computing held in Los Alamos in 1976; "We Would Know What They Thought When They Did It" (N. Metropolis, J. Howlett, G.C. Rota (Eds.)), *A History of Computing in the Twentieth Century: A Collection of Essays* [N.Y.: Academic Press, 1980, pp. 3-90]. He pleaded for a history of computing that pursued the contextual development of ideas, rather than merely listing names, dates, and places of "firsts." Moreover, he exhorted historians to go beyond the documents to "informed speculation" about the results of undocumented practice. What people actually did and what they thought they were doing may well not be accurately reflected in what they wrote and what they said they were thinking. His own experience had taught him that.

Getting beyond the documentation to discover what people were thinking is no easy task, even when the people are still available to ask, or, when they themselves are doing the history. A story, perhaps apocryphal, about Jean Piaget shows why. The psychologist was standing outside one evening with a group of 11 year olds and called their attention to the newly risen moon, pointing out that it was appreciably higher in the sky than it had been at the same time the night before and wondering why that was. The children were also puzzled, though in their case genuinely so. In his practiced way, Piaget led them to discover the relative motions of the earth, moon and sun and thus to arrive at an explanation. A month or two later, the same group was together under similar circumstances, and Piaget again posed his question. "That's easy to explain," said one boy, who proceeded to sketch out the motions that accounted for the phenomenon. "That's remarkable," said Piaget, "How did you know that?" "Oh," the boy replied, "we've always known that!"

Not only children, but people in general, and scientists in particular, quickly forget what it was like not to know now what they now know. That is, once you've solved a problem, especially when the solution involved a new approach, it's difficult to think about the problem in the old way. What was once unknown has become obvious. What once tested the ingenuity of the skilled practitioner is now "an exercise left for the student." The phenomenon affects not only the immediate past, but the distant past as well. When scientists study history, they often use their modern tools to determine what past work was "really about"; for example, the Babylonian mathematicians were "really" writing algorithms. But that is precisely what was not "really" happening. What was really happening was what was possible, indeed imaginable, in the intellectual environment of the time;

what was really happening was what the linguistic and conceptual framework then would allow. The framework of Babylonian mathematics had no place for a metamathematical notion such as algorithm.

These considerations suggest the paradox inherent in the role of pioneers and participants in the history of computing, whether as active members of panels and workshops, as subjects of interviews, or as historians of their own work. On the one hand, they are our main source for knowing "what they thought when they did it," not only for their own efforts, but also that of their colleagues and contemporaries. On the other hand, it is they who reshaped our understanding by their discoveries, solutions, and inventions and who, as a result, may find it harder than most to recall just what they were thinking. Precisely because they helped to create the present, they are prone to identify it with their past work or to translate that work into current terminology.

Doing so defeats the utility, or even the purpose, of their testimony. To the historian, the old way is crucial: it holds the roots of the new way. It does not illuminate history to say, "We were really doing X," where X stands for the current state of the art. Talking that way masks the very changes in conceptual structure that explain the development of X and that history aims at elucidating. It may well be that the roots of modern technique or theory lie in work done thirty or forty years ago. That can only become clear by tracing the growth of the tree determining its branching pattern, and identifying the points at which grafting has occurred. That requires, in turn, that the root be characterized in its own terms. When a pioneer talks about his or her work in the past, it is important for others to listen critically and be ready to say, "Now wait a second, we didn't put the question that way at the time, nor did we know the concept." It is important for the pioneer to develop the same sensitivity to changes in language over time, and which imply changes in conceptualization. Historically, a rose by another name may have a quite different smell.

Having the solution can mask the original problem in several ways. One may forget there was a problem at all, or undervalue the urgency it had, projecting its current insignificance back to a time when it was not trifling at all, but rather a serious concern. One may reconstruct a different problem, overlooking the restructuring of subject brought about by the solution. One may ignore or undervalue alternative solutions that once looked attractive and could very well have taken development in a different direction. Historically, a "right" answer requires just as much explanation as a "wrong" answer, and both answers are equally interesting—and equally important.

Several years ago I asked someone at Bell Labs responsible for maintaining software, what sort of documentation she would most like to have but did not. "I'd like to know why people didn't do things," she said. "In many cases when a problem arises, we look at the program and think we see another, better way of doing things. We spend six months pursuing that alternative only to discover that it won't work, and then we realize why the original team didn't choose it. We'd like to know that before we start." Something quite close to that holds for historians too. They want to know what the choices and possibilities were at a given time, why a particular one was adopted, and why the others were not. Good history, from the historian's point of view, always keeps the options in view at any given time.

Getting the facts right is important, both the technical facts and the chronological facts. But the reasons for those facts are even more important, and the reasons often go well beyond the facts. When people come together on a project or for a meeting—when, indeed, they are creating a new enterprise—they bring with them their past experience and their current concerns, both as individuals and as members of institutions. In both cases, they have interests and commitments that transcend the problem at hand, yet determine its shape and the range of acceptable solutions. It is essential to know, in both the real and the idiomatic sense of the phrase, where they are coming from. In some cases, discretion, propriety of information, or just plain ignorance may preclude a definitive answer. Nonetheless, even when we can't know the answers, it is important to see the questions. They too form part of our understanding. If you cannot answer them now, at least you can alert future historians to them.

What makes history? It's a matter of going back to the sources, of reading them in their own language, and of thinking one's way back into the problems and solutions as they looked then. It involves the imaginative exercise of suspending one's knowledge of how things turned out so as to recreate the possibilities still open at the time. In *The Go-Between*, Leslie Hartley remarked that "The past is a foreign country; they do things differently there." The historian must learn to be an observant tourist, alert to the differences that lie behind what seems familiar.

Call for Papers

The Second ACM SIGPLAN History of Programming Languages Conference (HOPL-II) Boston, Massachusetts, Spring 1993

In 1978, the first History of Programming Languages Conference covered the development and evolution of 13 specific computer programming languages, the people who participated in that work, and the context in which it was undertaken.

Of particular interest was the combined presentation of both technical and administrative factors that influenced the development of these selected languages. That first conference included invited papers on the early giants of our field: ALGOL 60, APL, APT, BASIC, COBOL, FORTRAN, GPSS, JOSS, JOVIAL, LISP, PL/I, SIMULA, and SNOBOL. The original papers were published in *ACM SIGPLAN Notices*, Vol. 13, No. 8, Aug. 1978. A book containing the papers, transcripts of the presentations, and much additional material was published in the ACM Monograph Series by Academic Press with the title *History of Programming Languages*, (Richard L. Wexelblat, Editor, 1981).

TOPICS FOR HOPL-II

During the intervening years, much has happened in this field, and the HOPL-II Conference will address the history of those significant developments. Papers are solicited in the following categories:

- Histories of specific languages—the motivation, context, early development, evolution, people, and technical issues surrounding significant programming languages
- Histories of language features and concepts—the development, introduction, and use of programming language idioms and constructs (e.g., concurrency control, encapsulation)
- Histories of classes of languages— issues underlying sets of languages that are designed around a common paradigm (e.g., functional, object-oriented, logic programming) or an application domain (e.g., civil engineering, graphics, simulation)

As with the first HOPL Conference, HOPL-II is intended to contribute to the historical record. To meet this goal, the Program Committee will work closely with prospective authors to help ensure that the papers are of a high quality.

CRITERIA FOR SELECTION

The Program Committee intends to apply the following criteria to selecting papers; it is necessary, but not sufficient, for the paper to be of historical interest. The word "use" applies to people other than the developer(s). A submission must satisfy both criteria within one category.

Early History of Specific Languages:

1. the language (or a derivative) has had significant influence on the theory or practice of computing
2. preliminary ideas about the language were documented by 1982, and the language was in use or being taught by 1985

Evolution of Languages:

1. the language meets the criteria for "Early History of Specific Languages"
2. there has been significant evolution of the language, as manifested by different versions of the language (e.g., derivatives, dialects, subsets, extensions) or by standards adopted either by different organizations or at different times

Language Features and Concepts:

1. the feature or concept (e.g., concurrency control, encapsulation) has had significant influence on the theory or practice of computing
2. preliminary ideas about the feature or concept were documented by 1982

Classes of Languages:

1. a. for application-oriented languages, a set of languages in a specific application area must be recognizable as significant to people involved in that class of application (e.g., civil engineering, graphics, machine tool control, simulation)

   b. for paradigm-oriented languages, a paradigm defining a class of languages must be clearly regarded as significant (e.g., functional, object-oriented, logic programming)
2. preliminary ideas about a language in this class were documented by 1982, and a language in this class was in use or being taught by 1985

There is much to be learned from "instructive failures." Therefore, prospective authors are also encouraged to document concepts or features that may not have achieved widespread use, but are of historical interest.

Second ACM SIGPLAN History of Programming Languages Conference (HOPL-II)

CONTENT GUIDELINES FOR AUTHORS

Thank you for expressing an interest in participating in the second History of Programming Languages Conference (HOPL-II).

In 1978, the first History of Programming Languages Conference (HOPL-I) discussed the development and evolution of 13 specific computer programming languages, the people who participated in that work, and the context in which it was undertaken. In addition to considering histories of specific languages, HOPL-II will also address the histories of classes of languages, and of language features and constructs. The Call for Papers indicates more clearly the topics to be included in HOPL-II, and also specifies the criteria by which papers will be judged for selection.

The main purpose of these guidelines is to help you develop the appropriate content for your contribution to HOPL-II. The questions herein point to the kind of information that people want to know about the history of some topic in programming languages. A set of questions is included for each of the four major areas to be covered by HOPL-II:

- early history of a specific language
- later evolution of a specific language (usually a language treated in HOPL-I or elsewhere in HOPL-II)
- history of a programming language concept or feature
- history of a class of languages

The sets of questions overlap to some extent, especially for the first two and for the last two categories listed above. This guidelines document includes all four sets of questions, in the hope that having the other sets available may prove useful to you.

Even within a single set, the same question, or very similar questions, may be asked in different contexts. Please draft your paper in light of these different emphases and contexts.

Your paper should try to answer as many as possible of the questions in your topic area; it is understood that you might not be able to address every one of them. Because history can unfold in so many different ways, some of the questions are clearly irrelevant to your particular topic, or to your particular point of view. Or the information requested might be no longer available. But please remember that sometimes a negative comment is as useful as substantive information. Several questions are of the form "How did so-and-so affect whatever?"—it can be important for the historical record to assert that "it didn't."

The question sets suggest the content, not the form, of your paper. (In particular, your paper should not be in question-and-answer format.) The questions are organized into topics and subtopics for your convenience during your research; this structure is not meant as an outline for your paper. (Topics, subtopics, and questions are also numbered and lettered for convenience of reference.) Please feel free to use whatever form and style seems most appropriate and comfortable to you.

The Call for Papers contains the criteria that will be used in the selections of papers. Please be sure to include within your paper a clear indication of how the subject material satisfies the criteria. This information can certainly be provided indirectly as part of the overall text. (For instance, one of the criteria is dates; it suffices to include the dates as part of the historical narrative.)

You might want to examine the proceedings of HOPL-I to see what earlier contributors did. (Of course, each of the papers at that conference dealt with the history of a specific language.) The reference is: *History of Programming Languages*, ed. Richard L. Wexelblat, Academic Press. 1981.

The first History of Programming Languages conference established high technical and editorial standards. We trust that your contribution will help HOPL-II maintain or surpass these standards.

QUESTIONS ON THE EARLY HISTORY OF A LANGUAGE

Background

1. Basic Facts about Project Organization and People
   a. Under what organizational auspices was the language developed (e.g., name of company, department/division in the company, university?) Be as specific as possible about organizational subunits involved.
   b. Were there problems or conflicts within the organization in getting the project started? If so, please indicate what these were and how they were resolved.
   c. What was the source of funding (e.g., research grant, company R&D, company production units, government contract)?
   d. Who were the people on the project and what was their relationship to the speaker (e.g., team members, subordinates)? To the largest extent possible, name all the people involved, including part-timers, and when each person joined the project and what each worked on. Indicate the technical experience and background of each participant.
   e. Was the development done originally as a research project, as a development project, as a committee effort, as a one-person effort with some minor assistance, or ...?
   f. Was there a defined leader to the group? If so, what was his or her exact position and how did he or she get to be the leader? (e.g., appointed "from above," self-starter, volunteer, elected)?
   g. Was there a de facto leader different from the defined leader? If so, who defined this leader, i.e., was it some "higher authority" or the leader of the group, or ... ?
   h. Were there consultants from outside the project that had a formal connection to it? If so, who were they, how and why were they chosen, and how much help were they? Were there informal consultants? If so, please answer the same questions.
   i. Did the participants of the project view themselves primarily as language designers, or implementors, or eventual users? If there were some of each working on the project, indicate the split as much as possible. How did this internal view of the people involved affect the initial planning and organization of the project?
   j. Did the language designers know (or believe) they would also have the responsibility for implementing the first version? Whether the answer is yes or no, how much was the technical language design affected by this?
2. Costs and Schedules
   a. Was there a budget providing a fixed upper limit on the costs? If so, how much money was to be allocated and in what ways? What external or internal factors led to the budget constraints? Was the money allocated formally divided between language design and actual implementation, and if so, indicate in what way?
   b. Was there a fixed deadline for completion and if so, what phases did it apply to?
   c. What is the best estimate for the amount of manpower involved (i.e., in man-years)? How much of what was for language design, for documentation, and for implementation?
   d. What is the best estimate of the costs until the first system was in the hands of the first users? If possible, show as much breakdown on this as possible.
   e. If there were cost and/or schedule constraints, how did that affect the language design and in what ways?

3. Basic Facts about Documentation
   a. In the planning stage, was there consideration of the need for documentation of the work as it progressed? If so, was it for internal communication among project members or external monitoring of the project by others, or both?
   b. What types of documentation were decided upon?
   c. To the largest extent possible, cite both dates and documents for the following (including internal papers which may not have been released outside of the project) by title, date, and author. Recycle wherever possible and appropriate. (In items cl, c4, c9, and c10, indicate the level of formality of the specifications—e.g., English, formal notation—and what kind.)
      - (cl) initial idea
      - (c2) first documentation of initial idea
      - (c3) preliminary specifications
      - (c4) "Final" specifications (i.e., those which were intended to be implemented
      - (c5) "Prototype" running (i.e., as thoroughly debugged as the state of the art permitted, but perhaps not all of the features were included)
      - (c6) "Full" language compiler (or interpreter) was running
      - (c7) Usage on real problems was done by the developers
      - (c8) Usage on real problems was done by people other than the developers
      - (c9) Documentation by formal methods
      - (c1O) Paper(s) in professional journals or conference proceedings
      - (cll) Extension, modification and new versions
4. Languages and Systems Known at the Time
   a. What specific languages were known to you and/or other members of the development group at the time the work started? Which others did any of you learn about as the work progressed? How much did you know about these and in what ways (e.g., as users, from having read unpublished and/or published papers, informal conversations)? (Please try to distinguish between what you as the writer knew and what the other members of the project knew.)
   b. Were these languages considered as formal inputs which you were definitely supposed to consider in your own language development, or did they merely provide background?
   c. How influenced were you by these languages? Put another way, how much did the prior language background of you and other members of the group influence the early language design? Whether the answer is "a lot" or "a little," why did these other languages have that level of influence? (This point may be more easily considered in Section 2 of Rationale of Content of Language.)
   d. Was there a primary source of inspiration for the language and if so, what was it? Was the language modeled after this (or any other predecessor or prototype)?
5. Intended Purposes and Users
   a. For what application area was the language designed, i.e., what types of problems was it supposed to be used for? Be as specific as possible in describing the application area; for example, was "business data processing" or "scientific applications" ever carefully defined? Was the apparent application area of some other language used as a model?
   b. For what types of users was the language intended (e.g., experienced programmers, mathematicians, business people, novice programmers)? Was there any conflict within the group on this? Were compromises made, and if so, were they for technical or nontechnical reasons?

c. What equipment was the language intended to be implemented on? Wherever possible, cite specific machine by manufacturer and number, or alternatively, give the broad descriptions of the time period with examples (e.g., "COBOL was defined to be used on 'large' machines which at that time included UNIVAC I and II, IBM 705.") Was machine independence a significant design goal, albeit within this class of machines? (See also Question (lb) in Rationale of the Content of the Language.)

d. What type of physical environment was envisioned for the use of this machine (e.g., stand-alone system, to be used under control of an operating system, batch or interactive, particular input-output equipment)?

6. Source and Motivation

   a. What (or who) was the real origin of the idea to develop this language?

   b. What was the primary motivation in developing the language (e.g., research, task assigned by management)?

Rationale of the Content of the Language

These questions are intended to stimulate thought about various factors that affect almost any language design effort. Not all the questions are relevant for every language. They are intended to suggest areas that might be addressed in each paper.

1. Environmental Factors

   To what extent was the design of the language influenced by:

   a. Program size: Was it explicitly though that programs written in the language would be large and/or written by more than one programmer? What features were explicitly included (or excluded) for this reason. If this factor wasn't considered, did it turn out to be a mistake?

   b. Program libraries: Were program libraries envisioned as necessary or desirable, and if so, how much provision was made for them?

   c. Portability: How important was the goal of machine independence? What features reflect concern for portability? How well was this goal attained? See also question (1) on Standardization and question (5c) under Background.

   d. User Background and Training: What features catered to the expected background of intended users? In retrospect, what features of the language proved to be difficult for programmers to use correctly, What features fell into disuse and why? How difficult did it prove to train users in the correct and effective use of the language, and was the difficulty a surprise? What changes in the language would have alleviated training problems? Were any proposed features rejected because it was felt users would not be able to use them correctly or appropriately?

   e. Object Code Efficiency: How did requirements for object code size and speed affect the language design? Were programs in the language expected to execute on large or small computers (i.e., was the size of object programs expected to pose a problem)? What design decisions were explicitly motivated by the concern (or lack of concern) for object code efficiency? Did these concerns turn out to be accurate and satisfied by the feature as designed? How was the design of features changed to make it easier to optimize object code?

   f. Object Computer Architecture: To what extent were features in the language dictated by the anticipated object computer, e.g., its work size, presence or lack of floating-point hardware, instruction set peculiarities, availability and use of index registers, etc.?

   g. Compilation Environment: To what extent, if any, did concerns about compilation efficiency affect the design? Were features rejected or included primarily to make it easier to implement compilers for the language or to ensure that the compilers would execute quickly? In retrospect, how correct or incorrect do you feel these decisions were?

h. Programming Ease: To what extent was ease of coding an important consideration and what features in the language reflect the relative importance of this goal? Did maintainability considerations affect any design decisions? Which ones?

i. Execution Environment: To what extent did the language design reflect its anticipated use in a batch as opposed to interactive program development (and use) environment? What features reflect these concerns?

j. Character Set: How much attention was paid to the choice of a character set and what were the reasons for that decision? How much influence did the choice of the character set have on the syntax of the language?

k. Parallel Implementation: Were there implementations being developed at the same time as the later part of the language development? If so, was the language design hampered or influenced by this in any way?

l. Standardization: In addition to (or possibly separate from) the issue of portability, what considerations were given to possible standardization? What types of standardization were considered, and what groups were involved and when?

2. Functions to be Programmed

   a. How did the operations and data types in the language support the writing of particular kinds of algorithms in the language?

   b. What features might have been left out if a slightly different application area had been in mind?

   c. What features were considered essential to express properly the kinds of programs to be written in the language?

   d. What misconceptions about application requirements turned up that necessitated redesign of these application specific language features before the language was actually released?

3. Language Design Principles

   a. What consideration, if any, was given to designing the language so programming errors could be detected at compile time? Was there consideration of problems of debugging? Were debugging facilities deliberately included in the language?

   b. To what extent was the goal of keeping the language simple considered important and what kind of simplicity was considered most important? What did your group mean by simplicity?

   c. What thought was given to make programs more understandable and how did these considerations influence the design? Was there conscious consideration of making programs in the language easy to read versus easy to write? If so, which did you choose and why?

   d. Did you consciously develop the data types first and then the operations, or did you use the opposite order, or did you try to develop both in parallel with appropriate iteration?

   e. To what extent did the design reflect a conscious philosophy of how languages should be designed (or how programs should be developed), and what was this philosophy?

4. Language Definition

   a. What techniques for defining languages were known to you? Did you use these or modify them, or did you develop new ones?

   b. To what extent—if any—was the language itself influenced by the technique used for the definition?

5. Concepts about Other Languages

   a. Were you consciously trying to introduce new concepts and if so, what were they? Do you feel that you succeeded?

   b. If you were not trying to introduce new concepts, what was the justification for introducing this new language? (Such justification might involve technical, political. or economical factors.)

c. To what extent did the design consciously borrow from previous language designs or attempt to correct perceived mistakes in other languages?

6. Influence of Nontechnical Factors

a. How did time and cost constraints (as described in the Background section) influence the technical design?

b. How did the size and structure of the design group affect the technical design?

c. Provide any other information you have pertaining to ways in which the technical language design was influenced or affected by nontechnical factors.

Aposteriori Evaluation

1. Meeting of objectives

a. How well do you think the language met its original objectives?

b. How well do you feel the users seem to think the language met its objectives?

c. As best you can tell, how well do you think the computing community as a whole thinks the objectives were met?

d. How much impact did portability (i.e., machine independence) have on user acceptance?

e. Did the objectives change over time from the original statement of them? If so, when and in what ways? See also question (2d) under Rationale of Content of Language and answer here if appropriate.

2. Contributions of Language

a. What is the biggest contribution (or several of them) made by this language? Was this one of the objectives? Was this contribution a technical or a nontechnical contribution, or both?

b. What do you consider the best points of the language, even if they are not considered to be a contribution to the field (i.e., what are you proudest of about this language regardless of what anybody else thinks)?

c. How many other people or groups decided to implement this language because of its inherent value?

d. Did this language have any effect on the development of later hardware?

e. Did this language spawn any "dialects"? Were they major or minor changes to the language definition? How significant did the dialects themselves become?

f. In what way do you feel the computer field is better (or worse) off for having this language?

g. What fundamental effects on the future of language design resulted from this language development (e.g., theoretical discoveries, new data types, new control structures)?

3. Mistakes or Desired Changes

a. What mistakes do you think were made in the design of the language? Were any of these able to be corrected in a later version of the language? If you feel several mistakes were made, list as many as possible with some indication of the severity of each.

b. Even if not considered mistakes, what changes would you make if you could do it all over again?

c. What have been the biggest changes made to the language (albeit probably by other people) since its early development? Were these changes items considered originally and dropped in the initial development, or were they truly later thoughts?

d. Have changes been suggested but not adopted? If so, be as explicit as possible about what changes were suggested and why they were not adopted.

4. Problems
   a. What were the biggest problems you had during the language design process? Did these affect the end result significantly?
   b. What are the biggest problems the users have had?
   c. What are the biggest problems the implementors have had? Were these deliberate, in the sense that a conscious decision was made to do something in the language design even if it made the implementation more difficult?
   d. What trade-offs did you consciously make during the language design process? What trade-offs did you unconsciously make which you realize only later were actually trade-offs?
   e. What compromises did you have to make to meet other constraints such as time or budget, or user demands or political factors?

Implications for Current and Future Languages

1. Direct Influence
   a. What language developments of today and the foreseeable future are being directly influenced by your language? Regardless of whether your answer is "none" or "many, such as...," please indicate the reasons.
   b. Is there anything in the experience of your language development which should influence current and future languages? If so, what is it? Put another way, in light of your experience, do you have advice for current and future language designers?
   c. Does your language have a long-range future? Regardless of whether your answer is yes or no, please indicate the reasons.
2. Indirect Influence
   a. Are there indirect influences which your language is now having or can be expected to have in the near future? What, and why?

QUESTIONS ON THE EVOLUTION OF A PROGRAMMING LANGUAGE

The principal objective of a contribution in this category is to present the history of a major language subsequent to its original development. In many cases, this entails extending the history of some language whose origins were treated in HOPL-I, or in another paper in HOPL-II. (You will be working with a member of the Program Committee, who will keep you informed of other relevant papers.)

When a programming language is first developed, it is typically the work of an individual or a small, concentrated group. Later development of the language is often the result of an expanded, restaffed group, and perhaps additional individuals or groups outside the original organization. Similarly, while the original work is often focused on language design and implementation for a single environment, later developments are undertaken in a broader arena.

When compared with questions about the early history of a language, these questions reflect this change in context. In particular, these questions are about a set of diverse development activities that surround the language, such as standardization, new implementations, significant publications, language-oriented groups (SIGs and user groups).

These questions are grouped into the same four broad categories that apply to papers on the origins of a language:

- Background
- Rationale

- A posteriori evaluation
- Implications for current and future languages

However, the sub-categories and specific questions are different.

The first question applies broadly to the language itself. It is intended to identify the particular developments and development activities that are the focus of the history paper. In contrast, you should address the remaining questions for each of the activities identified in that initial background section.

You might also have significant information to contribute in response to questions raised about the early history of the language. Please examine the questions provided for authors of "early history" papers.

Where appropriate, your contribution should make reference to related papers from HOPL-I or HOPL-II.

Background

1. Basic Facts about Activities, Organizations and People
   a. What are the categories of developments to be discussed (e.g., standardization, new implementations, significant publications) and what specific activities are reported on?

   (From this point on, each question is intended to apply independently to each development activity identified in question I.l(a).)

   b. What organizations played principal roles in these developments? Identify them as precisely as possible: corporation and division, university and department, agency and office, etc. How were these organizations sponsored and funded?
   c. What, if any, was the nature of the cooperation or competition among these organizations?
   d. Who were the people involved in these developments? How were they related organizationally to each other and to the original developers for this language? Please be as specific as possible regarding names, titles, and dates.
   e. How did the roles of various individuals change during the course of the activity?
2. Costs and Schedules
   a. What was the source and amount of funding for supporting the development? Was it adequate?
   b. What was its schedule, if any?
   c. What was the estimated human effort required to carry it out?
   d. What was the estimated cost for the development?
   e. What were the effects of cost and schedule constraints?
3. Basic Facts about Documentation
   a. What are the significant publications arising from the development? For each provide:
      - a specific reference
      - names of authors (if not part of the reference)
      - intended audience (e.g., user, implementor)
      - format (e.g., manual, general trade book, standards document)
      - availability
4. Languages/Systems Known at the Time
   a. What languages or systems other than the one in question had an effect on the development? In what ways did they affect the development?
   b. How did information about each of these languages or systems become available to the people it influenced?

5. Intended Purposes and Users
   a. What was the intended purpose of the development?
   b. Were the results proprietary, for sale, freely distributed, etc.?
   c. For whom were its results intended? How did this group of people differ from the originally intended set of users for this language?
   d. How did some intended target machine/operating system environment influence the development? How had this operating environment changed since the language was first developed?
6. Motivation
   a. Who was the prime mover for the development?
   b. What was the underlying motivation for the development?

Rationale for the Content of the Development

To the extent that it is appropriate, apply the "early history" questions in each of the following sub-categories to the activity being addressed.

1. Environment Factors
   a. What were the effects on the development of concerns about program size, program libraries, portability, user background, object code efficiency, object computer architecture and speed, compilation environment, programming ease, execution environment, character set, parallel implementation, standardization?
   b. In what ways had the environment changed since the original development of the language?
2. Expected Applications of the Language
   a. How did expected applications influence choice of operations and data types?
   b. What features were essential to meet intended applications?
3. Design Principles Applied to the Development
   a. What, if any, was the underlying, consciously applied design philosophy?
   b. What considerations were made for detecting and correcting errors in the results of the development?
   c. What role did "simplicity" play, and what was meant by "simplicity"?
   d. What role did "understandability" play? Which was given higher priority, ease of reading or ease of writing, and why?
   e. Were certain aspects of language (e.g., data types, operations) considered more fundamental to the development than others? Why?
4. Language Definition
   a. What language definition techniques were used in this development? To what extent was the result of the development influenced by these choices?
5. Concepts of Other Languages
   a. To what extent was the introduction of new language concepts or features a part of this development?
   b. In what ways did concepts from other languages influence this development?
6. Influence of Non-Technical Factors
   a. What was the effect of other, similar developments on this one (e.g., overlapping standardization efforts)?
   b. What was the effect of time and cost constraints on the development?
   c. How did the size and structure of the development group affect results?

A Posteriori Evaluation

1. Meeting of Objectives
   a. How well did the development meet its objectives?
   b. How well did the users of its results feel the development met its objectives?
   c. What was the reaction of the computing community at large?
   d. How did portability of results impact their acceptance?
   e. Did the objectives of the development change over time? If so, when, how, and why?
2. Contributions of the Development
   a. What were the biggest contributions of this development? Were they among the original objectives?
   b. What do you consider its best features? Its worst?
   c. How has this development affected other activities (e.g., development of other languages, dialects, language processors, standards, operating systems, computer hardware)? Which of these have become significant in their own right?
   d. In what way is the computer field better/worse off for this development?
   e. What fundamental effects on programming language methodology have arisen from this development? (e.g., new data types, control structures, techniques for definition, for documentation, and for implementation of languages, application design strategies, theoretical discoveries)
3. Mistakes or Desired Changes
   a. What mistakes were made in the development? Were these mistakes corrected in later developments?
   b. What changes would you now make if you could?
   c. What were the biggest changes made to the development results since they were first released? Had they been considered earlier and then dropped, or were they truly later thoughts?
   d. What significant changes have been suggested but not adopted, and why?
4. Problems
   a. What were the major obstacles in carrying out the development?
   b. What were the major problems encountered by people who used its results: e.g., language users, designers, implementors, those who work on standards?
   c. What trade-offs were made during the development? Which were made consciously and which were recognized after the fact?
   d. What compromises were made to meet other constraints such as time, budget, user demand, and political factors?
   e. Which estimates (time, cost, effort, people) were farthest from reality? Why were they off?
   f. What application-specific features might better have been left out?

Implications for Current and Future Languages

a. Which current and foreseeable developments are being directly or indirectly influenced by this development, and why?
b. Which results, if any, of this development have a long range future? Why?

QUESTIONS ON THE HISTORY OF A LANGUAGE FEATURE OR CONCEPT

The principal objective of a contribution in this category is to record the history of a programming language feature or concept.

This question set has a quite different focus from the set dealing with the development of some particular language. A particular language feature or concept is incorporated in particular languages, so much of the information solicited is comparative. However, to the extent that you were party to the development of particular language(s) embodying this feature, it may be appropriate to be guided by the question set on the history of a single language.

For simplicity, these questions usually refer to a "feature" rather than a "feature or concept."

Basic Background Information

a. Who invented or introduced this feature? What was their background? How did they come to use this background in their development?

b. What are the important publications (e.g., papers, language manuals) about the feature? Please make a special point of identifying as many early publications as possible, including informal and internal documents.

The Nature of this Feature or Concept

a. What are the distinctive characteristics of this feature?

b. What shortcomings of existing languages prompted the discovery and/or the introduction of this feature?

c. What set of expressive or methodological problems did this feature address at the time of its introduction? How was the absence of this feature handled prior to its introduction?

d. How did this feature enhance a programmer's ability to express the solution of a problem?

e. What forces (e.g., theoretical concerns, market demand, error-proneness of alternative forms) supported the introduction and evolution of the feature?

f. What external influences (e.g., changes in technology, new classes of problems, new classes of users) contributed to the need for this feature, or to its introduction and evolution?

g. What other concepts were precursors of this concept? In which language(s) did they exist?

h. In which language(s) was this feature introduced? Who introduced it? How did the people involved with it interact in the process, if more than one person was involved? (Particularly if you were involved with this development, please consult the question set on the history of a programming language for guidance on useful information to include.)

i. What language(s) embody this feature? (Please be as inclusive as you can. However, it may be appropriate to concentrate on a few exemplars in comparisons.) In what ways are these languages similar or different in their incorporation of the feature? How does the feature manifest itself? Give examples.

Evolution

a. How did this feature evolve over time? What has it evolved into in languages currently in use?

b. How did this feature interact with other features in the languages which embody it? How has this interaction influenced the evolution of this or other features? With what other language features is it most or least compatible?

c. What obstacles (institutional, financial, psychological, political, temporal, technological, etc.) were encountered during the introduction and evolution of this feature? How did they affect it? How were they overcome?

d. What is the present incarnation of the feature, if any? In which languages can it be found today?

e. Were there competing or complementary concepts or features that conflicted with this one? If so, what was the nature of this conflict, and how was it resolved?

Evaluation

a. How well did the feature meet (or fail to meet) its expectations and goals? If it failed, why did it fail?

b. How did specific implementations affect its acceptance?

c. How was the feature received by those affected by it (e.g., programmers, problem solvers, managers)?

d. What other concepts or features were influenced by this one?

e. How did this concept contribute to software methodology?

QUESTIONS ON THE HISTORY OF A CLASS OF LANGUAGES

The principal objective of a contribution in this category is to record the history of a class of languages. A class of languages is defined either by the application for which they were intended (e.g., simulation, graphics, machine tool control), or by a language paradigm (e.g., functional, data-flow, object-oriented).

This set of questions has a quite different focus from the set that deals with the development of some particular language. Here the focus is on the distinctive characteristics of a set of languages, and much of the information solicited is comparative. To the extent that you were party to the development of particular language(s) in this class, it may be appropriate to be guided as well by the question set on the history of a single language.

A particular language paradigm or application area often implies particular programming language features, or particular restrictions or extensions of language features. Please consult the question set on language features and concepts for guidance.

Basic Information

a. What language paradigm or application area characterizes this class of languages?

b. Which languages are in this class? (Please be as comprehensive as possible, including early experimental languages.)

c. Did someone (or some group) invent this class of languages, or did it evolve? If invented, by whom? If it evolved, when and by whom was it perceived as being a distinct class? What was the background of these people, and how did they come to be involved in this class of languages?

d. What are the basic publications (e.g., papers, language manuals) about this language class or particular languages within this class? Please make a special point of identifying as many of the early publications as possible, including informal or internal documents.

The Nature of this Class of Languages

a. What are the distinctive attributes of this class of languages? How did these attributes affect the features that the languages' designers included or excluded?

b. What, if any, class of algorithms inspired the emergence of this language class? What application area(s) were these languages intended to address? How were these applications dealt with prior to the introduction of languages in this class?

c. What expectations and goals did the community interested in this class of languages have in mind?

d. Describe the languages comprising the class. (Please discuss as many languages as you can. However, it may be appropriate to concentrate on a few exemplars.) What are the earliest languages in the class? In what ways are they similar? How do they differ? In particular, compare them with respect to

- declarative constructs (types, etc);
- imperative constructs (statements);
- flow of control;
- program modularization constructs;
- concurrency constructs;
- input-output.

In which ways are the languages in the class similar or different with respect to meeting the goals of program maintainability, reliability, readability, portability, run-time efficiency?

Evolution

a. How did this class of languages evolve over time? How did later languages in the class differ from earlier languages? What were the reasons for the changes? In what ways can the later languages be considered superior or inferior to the earlier ones? (A later language could, of course, be superior in some respects and inferior in others: it may be useful to treat the nature of these trade-offs.) To what extent was upward compatibility a constraint?

b. To what extent did the languages in this class reflect external trends in programming language methodology (e.g., extension facilities, support for object-oriented programming, data abstraction, structured programming)?

c. To what extent did the languages in this class reflect external trends or developments in computer hardware and operating systems (e.g., special-purpose hardware, multi-processing, availability of cheap processors and memory)?

Evaluation

a. How well has this class of languages met (or failed to meet) its expectations and goals?

b. Has this class of languages proved to have applications beyond its original focus?

c. In the application area(s) relevant to the class, what are the competing languages (e.g., general purpose languages with special libraries) outside the class? How successful are the languages in the class versus these competing languages?

d. How did the languages in this class influence trends in programming language methodology?

e. How did this class of languages influence trends or developments in computer hardware and operating systems?

f. How has this class of languages influenced languages outside the class (e.g., by the latter incorporating characteristic features without adopting the underlying paradigm)?

C

List of Attendees[1]

Elizabeth Adams	Hood College
Ken R. Adcock	AGC Corporation
Shail Aditya	MIT
David Allison	National Museum of American History
Richard Amick	
William Aspray	IEEE History Center
Stephen Auerbach	Wellington Systems Inc.
Mark Bartelt	Canadian Institute for Theoretical Astrophysics
Joel Bartlett	DEC
Friedrich Bauer	Institue for Informatik
Ralf Bayer	Motorola
Gwen Bell	The Computer Museum
Thomas Bergin	American University
Karen Bernstein	SUNY at Stony Brook
Andrew P. Black	Digital Equipment Corporation
Andre Blavier	Informatique—CDC
George Bosworth	Digitalk Inc.
James Bouhana	Performance International
Frederick Brooks	University of North Carolina
Bruce Bruemmer	Charles Babbage Institute
Peg Cahoon	Digital Equipment Corporation
Martin Campbell-Kelly	University of Warwick
John Carr	University of Pensylvania
Frank Carrano	University of Rhode Island
Mark Carroll	University of Delaware
Paul Ceruzzi	National Air & Space Museum
Cheryl Chang-Yit	University of Delaware
Richard Chapman	Cornell University
Srikrishnan Chitoor	University of Deleware
Boleslaw Ciesielski	Viewlogic Systems Inc.
Bernard Cohen	Harvard University
Jacques Cohen	Brandeis University
Donald Colburn	Crative Solutions, Inc.
Alain Colmerauer	Facult de Sciences de Luminy
Jay Conne	Demystification of Technology Consultant
Philip Conrad	University of Delaware
Edward Council	Timberfield Systems
Paul Cousineau	Worcester Polytech
Carl Covell	Oregon State University
Lawrence Crowl	Oregon State University
Ann Curby	Peritus Software Services
Dorothy W. Curtis	MIT/LCS
Pavel Curtis	Xerox
Chuck D'Antonio	Bates College
Walter C. Daugherity	Texas A&M
Mark Day	MIT Laboratory for Computer Science
Jack Dennis	MIT/LCS
Christine Detig	T.U. Darmstadt
Allyn Dimock	Harvard University
Richard Eckhouse	University of Massachusetts
Sybil Ellery	Apple Computer, Inc.
Arthur Evans	Consultant
Remy Evard	Northeastern University
Michael Feldman	The George University
Stuart Feldman	Bellcore
Ronald Fischer	
Ann Fleury	
John Foderaro	MIT Media Lab
Mark Francillon	Marlboro College
Bob Frankston	
Michael Franz	Institute fur Computersysteme
Chris Fraser	AT&T Bell Laboratories
Bjorn Freeman-Benson	University of Victoria
Natasha Fridman	Northeastern University
Daniel Friedman	Indiana University
Richard Gabriel	Lucid Inc.
Bernard Galler	University of Michigan
Helen M. Gigley	Naval Research Labratory
Joseph Gil	Technion City
David Gladstein	Northeastern University
Adele Goldberg	ParcPlace Systems
Nance Goldstein	(media)
John Goodenough	Carnegie Mellon University
Rick Greer	AT&T Bell Laboratories
Madge Griswold	University of Arizona
Ralph Griswold	University of Arizona
Henry F. Guckes	Continental Insurance
John Guidi	The Jackson Laboratory
Scott Guthery	Schlumberger Laboratory for Computer Science
Brent Hailpern	IBM
Dan Halbert	Digital Equipment Corporation
Michael Halbher	MIT/LCS
Andrew Haley	E.O. Computer
Ross Hamilton	University of Warwick
Per Brinch Hansen	Syracuse University
Charles Hayden	AT&T Bell Labs
Jochen Hayek	

1 Editor's note: the affiliations are shown as those at the time of the Conference.

Stephen Hinton	Dataplex Corporation
Jan Rune Holmevik	University of Trondheim Center for Technology and Society
Christian Horn	FH Furtwangen
Christine Horn	
Corey Huber	Fraser Consulting Incorporated
Randy Hudson	Internetrics
Deborah Hwang	MIT Laboratory for Computer Science
Jean Ichbiah	JDI Technology Inc.
Dave Johnson	
E. Andrew Johnson	Open Software Foundation
Jeremy Jones	Apple Computer Inc.
Peter Juhl	AT&T Bell Labs
Randy Kaplan	Educational Testing Service
Alan Kay	Apple Computer
Benjamin Keller	Virginia Tech. Systems Research Center
Stan Kelly-Bootle	Unix Review
Richard Kelsey	Northeastern University
Gregor Kiczales	Xerox Parc
Kim N. King	Georgia State University
Reinhard Kirchner	University of Kaiserlautern
Bjorn Kirkerud	University of Oslo
Herbert Klaeren	University of Tubingen
Kate Klimukhina	Northeastern University
Robert Knapper	Institute for Defense Analyses
Thomas Knoedler	ACM/SIGPLAN
Andrew Koenig	AT&T Bell Laboratories
Philip Koopman	United Technologies
Joanna Kulik	MIT Laboratory for Computer Science
Richard LeBlanc	Georgia Tech
J.A.N. Lee	Virginia Tech
Karen Lemone	Worcester Polytechnic Institute, Computer Science Department
Michael Lewis	Bard College
Wei Li	Northeastern University
Charles Lindsey	University of Manchester
Barbara Liskov	MIT Laboratory for Computer Science
Joachim Luegger	ZIB Berlin
Joan Lukas	University of Massachusetts
Stavros Macrakis	OSF Research Institute
Peter Mager	Perceptron Technology Corporation
Michael Mahoney	Princeton University
Michael Marcotty	General Motors Research Labs
Thomas Marlowe	Seton Hall University
Stephen Masticola	Rutgers University
Robert F. Mathis	
Michael McClennen	University of Michigan
W.M. McKeeman	Digital
James McKenney	Harvard Business School
Wendy McKnitt	University of Delaware
Brian Meek	Kings College
Andrew Mickel	MCAD Computer Center
Elaine Milito	
James Miller	Digital Equipment Corporation
Richard Miller	SHL Systemhouse
Calvin Mooers	TRAC
Thomas Moog	Data Acquisition for Science and Engineering
Charles Moore	Computer Cowboys
Thomas E. Morgan	Brooklyn Union Gas
Joel Moses	MIT
Steven Muchnick	SunPro & Sun Labs
Richard Nance	Virginia Tech Systems Research Center
Jim Newkirk	
Cindy Norris	University of Delaware
Judy O'Neill	Charles Babbage Institute
Dino Oliva	Northeastern University
Terry Olkin	Oracle Corporation
Nate Osgood	MIT
Kasper Osterbye	Aalborg University
Rajeev Pandey	Oregon State University
John Peters	Practical Computing, Inc.
Lori Pollock	University of Delaware
Allan Price	ACM
Robert Probasco	University of Idaho
Atanas Radenski	Southwest Minnesota State University
Joe Ramey	Texas Instruments
Norman Ramsey	Bellcore
Elizabeth Rather	FORTH, Inc.
Dan Resler	Virginia Commonwealth University
Adam Rifkin	Caltech
Dennis Ritchie	AT&T Bell Laboratories
Robert Rosin	Enhanced Service Providers, Inc.
Douglas Ross	SofTech/MIT
Bernie Rothmel	GBC/ACM
Philippe Roussel	Elsa Software
Barbara Ryder	Rutgers University
Daniel Salomon	University of Manitoba
Jean Sammet	Programming Language Consultant
James Sasaki	University of Maryland Baltimore County
Thomas Schorsch	U.S. Air Force Academy
Joachim Schrod	T.U. Darmstadt
Aaron Seidman	DEC—CRL
Yumiko Sekiya	Northeastern University
Ravi Sethi	AT&T Bell Laboratories
Jean-Marie Szrat	Informatique—CDC
Vincent Sgro	Rutgers University
Andrew Shaw	MIT
Richard Soley	
Ellen Spertus	MIT AI Lab
Raymie Stata	
Paul Steckler	Northeastern University
Guy Steele Jr.	Thinking Machines Corporation
Selden L. Stewart	NIST
Gregory A. Stobbs	Harness, Dickey, and Pierce
Oliver Strimpel	The Computer Museum
Bjarne Stroustrup	AT&T Bell Labs
Greg Sullivan	Northeastern University
Patricia Summers	Virginia Polytechnic
Jeffrey Sutherland	Object Databases
David Tarabar	
Robert Thau	MIT
James Tomayko	Carnegie Mellon University
Prescott Turner	Liant Software Corporation
Mary van Deusen	IBM
Paul van Eykelen	Northeastern University
Mitchell Wand	Northeastern University
Christopher Warack	U.S. Air Force Academy
Peter Wegner	Brown University
Lori Weiss	Apple Computer
Paul Wexelblat	University Massachusetts, Lowell
Richard Wexelblat	Institute for Defense Analyses
William Whitaker	Colonel, USAF
Stephen Wilcoxon	University of Delaware
Michael Williams	University of Calgary
N. Wirth	ETH Zurich

D

Final Conference Program

Conference Staff

Conference chair — J.A.N. Lee
Virginia Polytechnic Institute and State University

Program chair — Jean E. Sammet
Programming Language Consultant

Treasurer — Richard Eckhouse
University of Massachusetts, Boston

Local arrangements — Peter S. Mager
Perception Technology Corporation

Publications — Richard L. Wexelblat
Institute for Defense Analyses

Recordings — Mary van Deusen
IBM

Registration — Karen Lemone
Worcester Polytechnic Institute

Book exhibits *(cancelled)* — James P. Bouhana
Performance International

Publicity — Dan Halbert
Digital Equipment Corporation

Program committee

Jean E. Sammet *(Chair)*
Programming Language Consultant

Michael S. Mahoney* *(Conference historian)*
Princeton University

Robert F. Rosin *(Forum chair)*
Enhanced Service Providers, Inc.

Tim Bergin *(Secretary)*
American University

Jacques Cohen
Brandeis University

Michael Feldman
The George Washington University

Bernard A. Galler*
University of Michigan

Helen M. Gigley
Naval Research Laboratory

Brent Hailpern*
IBM

Randy Hudson
Intermetrics

Barbara Ryder*
Rutgers University

Richard L. Wexelblat
Institute for Defense Analyses

**chair of a Program Review committee*

2

Conference Notes

Conference location

Cambridge Center Marriott
Two Cambridge Center
Cambridge, MA 02142 USA
phone: (617) 494-6600
fax: (617) 494-0036

On-site registration

Tuesday	11:00am - 10:00pm
Wednesday	7:45am - 10:00pm
Thursday	7:45am - 10:00pm
Friday	7:45am - 12:00noon

Local transportation

The Cambridge Center Marriott is a short taxi ride from Boston's Logan Airport. The hotel is adjacent to the Kendall Square subway station, on the MBTA ("T") Red Line. Both Harvard Square and downtown Boston are just two stops away. The airport is also accessible via the T, though you must change trains twice.

Scholarship recipients

These students were awarded scholarships to HOPL-II; they were selected from a very competitive set of applications:

Ross Hamilton
University of Warwick

Jan Rune Holmevik
University of Trondheim

Stephen P. Masticola
Rutgers University

Rajeev Pandey
Oregon State University

Patricia A. Summers
Virginia Polytechnic Institute and State University

Thanks

The National Science Foundation (grant number CCR-9208568) has provided support for the invited speakers as well as four of the student scholarship recipients. SHL Systemhouse Inc. has provided support for one of the student scholarships.

3

Tuesday April 20

Forum on the History of Computing

Forum Chair: Robert F. Rosin
Enhanced Service Providers, Inc.

You must be registered for the Forum to attend its afternoon sessions. The evening panel session is open to both Forum and Main Program registrants.

2:00 - 2:45pm
Salons V-VII

Issues in the history of computing
lecture

Michael S. Mahoney
Princeton University

2:45 - 4:00pm
Salons V-VII

Activities and resources in the history of computing
overview presentations

Documents and archives
Bruce Bruemmer
Charles Babbage Institute

Artifacts and museums
Gwen Bell
The Computer Museum

The *Annals* and other journals
Bernard A. Galler
University of Michigan

Effective conferences
Jean E. Sammet
Programming Language Consultant

University courses
Martin Campbell-Kelly
University of Warwick (UK)

4:00 - 4:30pm
break

4:30 - 5:30pm
locations to be announced

Participating in the history of computing
parallel small group discussions

Preserving and collecting artifacts
Gwen Bell
The Computer Museum

Documenting projects
Michael Marcotty
General Motors Research Laboratories

Writing about the history of computing
Bernard A. Galler
University of Michigan
J.A.N. Lee
Virginia Polytechnic Institute and State University

Teaching about the history of computing
Martin Campbell-Kelly
University of Warwick (UK)

8:00 - 9:30pm
Salons V-VII

this session is open to both Forum and Main Program registrants (badge required)

The challenge of public displays about the history of computing
panel discussion

David Allison
National Museum of American History
The Smithsonian Institution

Paul Ceruzzi
National Air and Space Museum
The Smithsonian Institution

Oliver Strimpel
The Computer Museum

4

5

Wednesday April 21

Main Program

Please note: all conference sessions will start promptly at the listed times.

9:30 - 11:45am
Salon III

Opening session

Introduction and Welcome
John A. N. Lee *(Conference Chair)*
Virginia Polytechnic Institute and State University

Welcoming Remarks
Gwen Bell *(ACM President)*
The Computer Museum

Welcoming Remarks
Stuart Feldman *(SIGPLAN Chair)*
Bellcore

Program Summary and Logistics
Jean E. Sammet *(Program Chair)*
Programming Language Consultant

Keynote address

Language Design as Design
Frederick P. Brooks
University of North Carolina

break

From HOPL to HOPL-II: 15 Years of Programming Language Development
(informal talk)
Jean E. Sammet
Programming Language Consultant

Making History
(informal talk)
Michael S. Mahoney
Princeton University

11:45am - 1:15pm
lunch

Paper sessions: questions and answers

A question and answer session will follow each paper presentation. All questions must be submitted in writing to the collection monitors. Please include your name and affiliation. All questions will be included in the final proceedings, though the speaker may not have time to answer them all.

6

1:15 - 3:05pm
All paper sessions will be in Salon III

Paper session

Chair: Jacques Cohen
Brandeis University

A History of ALGOL 68
C. H. Lindsey
University of Manchester (UK)

Recollections About the Development of Pascal
(invited paper)
N. Wirth
ETH Zurich

Discussant: Andrew B. Mickel
Minneapolis College of Art and Design

3:05 - 3:35pm
break

3:35 - 5:25pm

Paper session

Chair: Michael Feldman
The George Washington University

Monitors and Concurrent Pascal: A Personal History
Per Brinch Hansen
Syracuse University

Ada – The Project
(invited paper)
William A. Whitaker
Colonel USAF, Retired

Discussant: John B. Goodenough
Software Engineering Institute

6:45 - 9:45pm

Conference reception

The Computer Museum
Museum Wharf
Boston, MA

Free buses will provide transportation to and from the Museum. The first buses will be ready for loading on the Broadway side of the hotel at 6:15pm. Buses will shuttle between the hotel and the Museum until the end of the reception.

7

Thursday April 22

Main Program

8:30 - 10:30am

Paper session
Chair: Randy Hudson
Intermetrics

The Evolution of Lisp
Guy L. Steele, Jr.
Thinking Machines Corporation
Richard P. Gabriel
Lucid, Inc.

Discussant: John Foderaro
Franz Inc.

The Birth of Prolog
(invited paper)
Alain Colmerauer
Faculté des Sciences de Luminy
Philippe Roussel
Elsa Software

Discussant: Jacques Cohen
Brandeis University

10:30 - 11:00am
break

11:00am - 12:50pm

Paper session
Chair: Tim Bergin
American University

A History of Discrete Event Simulation Programming Languages
Richard E. Nance
Virginia Polytechnic Institute and State University

The Beginning and Development of FORMAC (FORmula MAnipulation Compiler)
Jean E. Sammet
Programming Language Consultant

Discussant: Joel Moses
MIT

12:50 - 2:05pm
lunch

8

2:05 - 4:00pm

Paper session
Chair: Barbara Ryder
Rutgers University

A History of CLU
Barbara Liskov
Massachusetts Institute of Technology

The Early History of Smalltalk
(invited paper)
Alan C. Kay
Apple Computer

Discussant: Adele Goldberg
ParcPlace Systems

4:00 - 4:30pm
break

4:30 - 6:10pm

Paper session
Chair: Helen M. Gigley
Naval Research Laboratory

History of the Icon Programming Language
Ralph E. Griswold
The University of Arizona
Madge T. Griswold
The University of Arizona

The Evolution of Forth
Elizabeth Rather
FORTH, Inc.
Donald R. Colburn
Creative Solutions, Inc.
Charles H. Moore
Computer Cowboys

7:00pm
Salon IV

Conference banquet
dinner, followed by informal, entertaining stories from language developers

Conference attendees without banquet tickets may attend the story session of the banquet, estimated to start between 7:45 and 8pm.

9

Friday
April 23

Main Program

8:30 - 10:30am

Paper session
Chair: Brent Hailpern
IBM

The Development of the C Language
(invited paper)
Dennis Ritchie
AT&T Bell Laboratories

A History of C++: 1979–1991
Bjarne Stroustrup
AT&T Bell Laboratories

Discussant (both papers):
Stuart Feldman
Bellcore

10:30 - 11:00am
break

11:00am - 1:00pm
Salon III

Panel session
Chair: Michael S. Mahoney
Princeton University

Programming Languages: Does our Present Past Have a Future?
Alain Colmerauer
Alan C. Kay
Dennis Ritchie
William A. Whitaker
N. Wirth

10

Conference book: *History of Programming Languages-II*

Conference registrants will receive copies of the HOPL-II papers in preprint form at the conference. However, a complete record of the conference is planned for publication in 1994. The book, *History of Programming Languages-II*, will contain edited versions of all the papers and much additional new material, including:

- Fred Brooks' keynote address.
- Transcripts of the oral presentations, discussants' remarks, Q&A sessions, the closing panel session, and the stories told at the conference banquet.
- Material from the Forum on the History of Computing, including speakers' handouts, transcripts of presentations, and small-group discussion notes.
- Speaker biographies and photos.
- Photos taken at the conference.
- A comprehensive index.
- Extensive sets of helpful questions for future authors writing about the history of programming languages and other fields.

By filling out a form now, you can ask to be notified as soon as *History of Programming Languages-II* is available. You will also be eligible for a discount. No prepayment is necessary, and you will be under no obligation. In addition, you can now order discounted copies of the 1981 book *History of Programming Languages*, published as the final proceedings of the first HOPL conference, held in 1978.

A form for these orders is included in your preprints; copies of the form are also available at the conference desk.

11

INDEX OF PROPER NAMES

5217